WORLD WAR I

H.P. WILMOTT

WORLD WAR I

DK

LONDON, NEW YORK, MELBOURNE,
MUNICH AND DELHI

Senior Designer Caroline Hill
Designers Joern Kroeger, Mark Stevens,
Colin Goody, Jerry Udall, Mabel Chan,
Alison Gardner, Paul Jackson
Senior Editors Ferdie McDonald, Jane Edmonds
Editorial Contributors Neil Grant,
Margaret Mulvihill
Editors Jane Oliver-Jedrzejak, Janet King,
Elizabeth Wyse, Sam Atkinson, Lee Johnson

For the 2nd edition

Tall Tree
Managing Editor David John
Project Designer Ed Simkins
Project Editor Rob Colson
Picture Researcher Anne-Marie Ehrlich
Special Photography Gary Ombler
Digital maps created by Advanced Illustration,
Encompass Graphics
Project Cartographers Iowerth Watkins,
Rob Stokes
DTP John Goldsmid
Production Wendy Penn
Editorial Direction Andrew Heritage
Art Direction Bryn Walls
Managing Editor Debra Wolter
Managing Art Editor Louise Dick

First published in Great Britain in 2003
This edition published in 2014 by
Dorling Kindersley Limited
80 Strand, London WC2R ORL
A Penguin Random House Company

001—WD163–Feb/14

Copyright © 2014 Dorling Kindersley Limited

A CIP catalogue record for this book is
available from the British Library

ISBN 978-1-4093-5427-7

Colour reproduction by GRB, Italy
Printed and bound by
Hung Hing Offset Printing Co, Ltd, Hong Kong

www.dk.com

A British trench, 1918
Much of a front-line soldier's duty was simply to watch
and wait. These British troops are manning an observation
post in a forward sap at Givenchy.

Jacket Images: *Front:* Getty Images; IWM;
Back: ECPAD France; *Spine:* Hulton Archive/Getty Images

CONTENTS

INTRODUCTION

~

T HE FIRST WORLD WAR HAS a good claim to be the most decisive event of the modern age, changing the world in ways not even the French Revolution could achieve. When war broke out early in August 1914, no one could have predicted just what a cataclysm it would be. After four years of the most costly war in human history, no one could be in any doubt. The political map of the world was transformed, the long period of 19th-century peace was destroyed, and growing confidence in the progressive power of liberal values and modern capitalism eroded. The principal legacy of the First World War was an atmosphere of hatred and resentment, between nations, between classes and between races, whose consequences were to be felt in the bitter political struggles of the 1920s and 1930s, and the eventual slide into a second, even more destructive, war 20 years after the end of the first.

At the start of the war, most of the world was ruled by sprawling dynastic empires. By 1920 most of them were gone. The great European empires – the Habsburg, the Russian and the German – disappeared, to be replaced by modern republics. The Ottoman Empire was defeated and dismembered; a nationalist dictatorship took its place in what is now modern-day Turkey. A necklace of new states emerged from the Baltic to the

Persian Gulf on the basis of national "self-determination". The old Europe of great monarchies, dominated by aristocracy and army, was in decline well before 1914, but the war accelerated and distorted its fall. The Europe of the 1920s is recognizably the Europe of today.

The war brought other changes in the international arena. The USA entered the war late, and began its long ascent to superpower status. The desire to put an end to war once and for all in 1918 bore fruit in the League of Nations, founded in 1920. For all its many weaknesses, the League laid the foundation for international collaboration on issues that have become the key concerns of the post 1945 United Nations. The Russian Revolution of October 1917, which brought communists to power, ushered in the confrontation between capitalism and communism that blighted the international system for 70 years and produced the Cold War of 1945–89.

The war also changed the nature of the modern state. No European state had ever been asked to organize armies in millions. The mobilization of the home front to cope with provisioning the army brought the state to the point where whole economies had to be controlled in the name of the war effort. Everywhere states organized rationing on a national scale, expanded welfare services, encouraged scientific research, collected statistics and engaged in home front propaganda. In the 1920s states kept on many of these responsibilities. The war taught modern states how to police, mobilize and persuade their populations in ways previously unheard of.

The one thing the First World War did not do was to transform the hardware with which war was fought. The war was larger in scale than any before it, but for most of its duration conventional warships, artillery, machine-guns, rifles and horses dominated combat. Aircraft were in their infancy; submarines were used

Mark V tanks in action 1918

From July 1918 Allied forces advanced across France and Belgium, driving the Germans back from their lines of trenches. Tanks played only a small part in the advance.

sparingly, as were tanks, the one major new invention for land warfare. The potential of these new weapons would not be realized until the next war. As a result, much of the war, especially on the Western Front, became a stalemate, as both sides searched desperately for new weapons or ways of fighting which might break through the enemy's lines of trenches and barbed wire.

The terrible cost of the war gave rise to a widespread pessimism, a morbid fear of decline. In the 1920s thousands of angry young men rejected the principles of the older generation that had sent them to the front and hankered for revenge on those they blamed for the disastrous conflict. In Italy and Germany, former veterans Mussolini and Hitler used a thirst for political violence to build up new radical nationalist movements that swept to power, first in Italy in 1922, then Germany in 1933. Rejecting the liberal west, the new dictators saw the war as the harbinger of a new age of empire and war-making.

If the First World War had never happened the world would almost certainly have been spared the horrors of civil war, political terrorism, a second total war and genocide in the 1930s and 1940s. While the outcome of the war laid the foundation of much of the modern world, the uncertainties that went with it created a deeply disturbed Europe, whose darker side opened the way to Stalingrad and Auschwitz.

Richard Overy June 2003

THE ROAD TO WAR
1878–1914

~

ON THE SURFACE, THE YEARS LEADING UP TO THE FIRST WORLD WAR WERE A PERIOD OF PEACE AND PROSPERITY IN EUROPE. WHENEVER THE THREAT OF WAR AROSE, A DIPLOMATIC COMPROMISE WAS FOUND TO AVERT IT. THE GREAT POWERS, HOWEVER, ACTED ON THE ASSUMPTION THAT ONE DAY THERE WOULD BE A WAR. FACTORIES PRODUCED NEW SHIPS, GUNS AND RIFLES, HUGE STANDING ARMIES WERE RAISED AND WAR PLANS WERE PREPARED. YET, WHEN THE SPARK CAME THAT LIT THE POWDER-KEG IN 1914, THE SCALE OF THE CONFLAGRATION WAS GREATER THAN ANY OF THE COMBATANTS HAD IMAGINED.

~

The Krupp steel works, Essen

For 20 years before the First World War Europe armed itself in anticipation of a major conflict. The Krupp works produced Germany's heavy artillery. These naval guns are destined for the ships of Germany's brand new fleet, constructed between 1898 and 1914.

THE CULTIVATION OF HATRED

THE OUTBREAK OF THE FIRST WORLD WAR WAS TRIGGERED BY THE ASSASSINATION
OF THE AUSTRIAN ARCHDUKE FERDINAND AND HIS WIFE BY A SERB NATIONALIST IN
SARAJEVO, THE CAPITAL OF BOSNIA-HERZEGOVINA. THIS ONE EVENT, HOWEVER, WAS NOT
A BASIC CAUSE OF THE WAR. FEW WOULD DISAGREE THAT A COMPLEX INTERPLAY OF
POLITICAL, ECONOMIC AND SOCIAL FACTORS THAT HAD DEVELOPED SINCE THE 1870S
WAS TO BE RESPONSIBLE FOR SHATTERING THE PEACE OF EUROPE IN 1914.

THE FIRST WORLD WAR is commonly seen as a watershed between two distinct periods of history, in many ways marking the end of the 19th century and the beginning of the 20th. It was certainly the first war of the 20th century in terms of its scale and the lethal power of the weaponry involved. At the same time, however, it had very real links with the 19th century, none more obvious than the ideas and beliefs that shaped national and social attitudes and contributed to a climate of mutual hostility between the Great Powers of Europe. The 19th century witnessed the cultivation of that hostility, the 20th century the reaping.

GREAT POWER RELATIONSHIPS

The states of Europe moved to war in 1914 not simply because of immediate political issues and events, but as the result of profound economic and social changes in Europe in the previous four decades. The most significant of these was in the relationship between the Great Powers, where a balance of power had been created that had resulted in instability. Perhaps surprisingly, a balance of power need not produce stability, any more than an imbalance of power need produce war. Given the prevailing circumstances, either may preserve peace or initiate conflict.

For almost 20 years after France's defeat and the creation of a united Germany in the Franco-Prussian War of 1870–71, Bismarck, the German chancellor, sought to ensure peace within Europe by maintaining an imbalance of power. He did so by checking Austria-Hungary and Russia in their dealings with each other – restraining both by holding the power of decision between them – and by ensuring that France remained diplomatically isolated, with no allies, and so unable to challenge German military superiority.

Bismarck's policy, however, barely survived his departure from office in March 1890. The balance created by the existence of two rival alliance systems – the Triple Alliance of Germany, Austria-Hungary and Italy and the Franco-Russian Entente (see map page 15) after 1891 – was one of the major causes of war. One important factor was that the various members of these alliances in 1914 considered themselves obliged to support their ally (or allies); they assumed that failure to do so would result in their being repudiated by the ally, and that the arrangements on which they relied for their security would be destroyed as a consequence.

The end of the Bismarckian diplomatic system was accompanied by further changes that added to the uncertainties of the rival alliance systems. One of these was the uneven spread of industrialization.

THE EFFECTS OF INDUSTRIALIZATION

Britain had taken the lead in embarking on an "industrial revolution", and by the mid-19th century it was known as "the workshop of the world". From the 1830s, however, the other states of northwest Europe had also begun to industrialize, though at different rates. From the 1870s, Germany in particular had increased its production of coal, iron and steel at an incredible pace, to replace Britain as the leading industrial power in Europe by 1913. (It could not, however, challenge the position held by the USA since the end of the 19th century as the world's leading industrial power.) As other states in Europe struggled to keep up with the pace of industrialization in Germany, an imbalance of power developed, with far-reaching implications.

GREAT POWER STATUS

By 1914 there were most definitely two grades of "Great Power" in Europe: Britain, France and Germany; and Austria-Hungary, Italy and Russia.

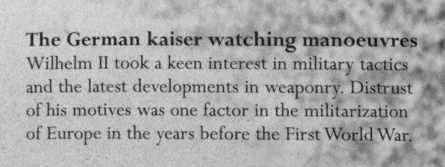

The German kaiser watching manoeuvres
Wilhelm II took a keen interest in military tactics and the latest developments in weaponry. Distrust of his motives was one factor in the militarization of Europe in the years before the First World War.

"Recklessness and weakness will plunge the world into the most horrible war aimed to destroy Germany. For there can no longer be any doubts: England, France and Russia have conspired ... to wage a war of annihilation against us."

KAISER WILHELM II, MEMO SENT ON LEARNING OF RUSSIAN MOBILIZATION ON 30 JULY 1914

Arguably, there were more than two groupings. Britain and Germany were certainly Great Powers of the first rank, on account of their industrial and economic power. France might be included with the other two, but more for historical reasons than any other, because in terms of industrial power and manpower resources it was now overshadowed by Germany, Austria-Hungary and Russia were increasingly hard-pressed to sustain themselves in the first rank, while Italy's status as a Great Power was solely honorary and nothing to do with its power, armed strength or military capability. The Turkish Ottoman Empire, which had for a long time resisted modernization and the benefits of industrial and economic change and was referred to as "the sick man of Europe", was no longer one of this select group of states. An element of instability arose in the wake of Europe's industrialization because France and Russia, both of which had failed to keep up with Germany in terms of economic power, formed an alliance to create a balance between themselves on the one hand and Germany and Austria-Hungary on the other.

THE POWER OF THE STATE

Alongside this redefinition of Great Power status and the balance between Europe's rival alliances were two significant developments. The first was the fact that between the 1870s and 1914 the state effectively defeated all challenges to itself. Separatist and nationalist movements threatened the unity and stability of Austria-Hungary and Germany, and religious-based differences plagued France and, to a lesser extent, the various states of Germany. There was also the political challenge to the state posed by socialist and Marxist ideologies, and the emergence of anarchist and syndicalist splinter-groups. In 1905 a revolution in Russia almost overthrew the tsar and his government; only the loyalty of the imperialist army saved him. By 1907 the revolutionary tendencies within Russian society had been suppressed, although they would resurface again during the First World War. In 1914 it seemed that the state was still the primary focus of allegiance of the vast majority of people throughout Europe.

The second development was the extraordinary growth in state power. By the 1870s the state had acquired unprecedented power over its own population and unparalleled capacity to wage war. The two were related. The Franco-Prussian War of 1870–71 spelt out the need for all states, unless they were prepared to accept German military hegemony, to ensure their security by raising armies through conscription. In doing so, the major European powers acquired the ability to mobilize across hundreds of kilometres of front by raising armies that were no longer numbered in hundreds of thousands, but in millions, of men.

A CLIMATE OF HATE

Mobilization on this scale was only possible because of the willingness of societies to bear the financial burden of the new armies and an equal willingness to allow their young men to be conscripted. This acceptance of the possible sacrifice of men's lives was very much an active one, which developed partly in response to the increasing tendency of governments to view, and refer to, all neighbours as potential enemies. This tendency was accompanied

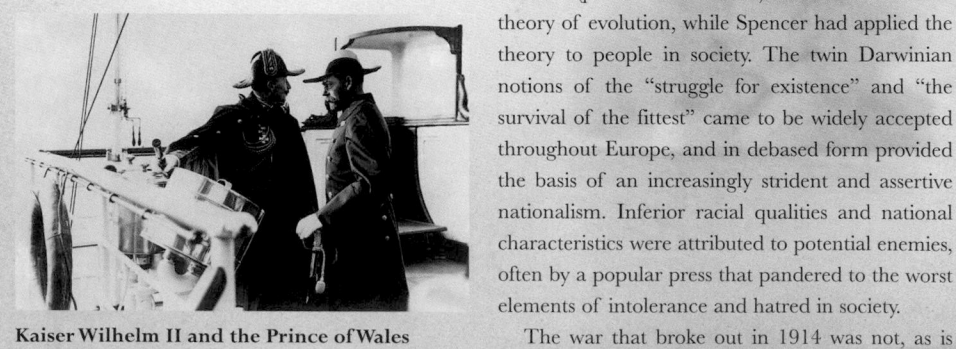

Kaiser Wilhelm II and the Prince of Wales
The Kaiser entertains his cousin, the future King George V of England, on board his yacht in 1907. Both men were grandsons of Queen Victoria, as was Tsar Nicholas II of Russia. Royal family ties proved no insurance against war.

by a general intellectual change that was the legacy of the British naturalist Charles Darwin and the philosopher Herbert Spencer. Darwin, in his epoch-making *On the Origin of Species by Means of Natural Selection* (published in 1859) had described the theory of evolution, while Spencer had applied the theory to people in society. The twin Darwinian notions of the "struggle for existence" and "the survival of the fittest" came to be widely accepted throughout Europe, and in debased form provided the basis of an increasingly strident and assertive nationalism. Inferior racial qualities and national characteristics were attributed to potential enemies, often by a popular press that pandered to the worst elements of intolerance and hatred in society.

The war that broke out in 1914 was not, as is sometimes claimed, the product of a scurrilous press promoting a mixture of nationalism and militarism. However, the fervent nationalism that

Austro-Hungarian dreadnought, SMS *Viribus Unitis*
In the years preceding the First World War all the major European powers built up their navies, even those such as Austria-Hungary that lacked a strong maritime tradition.

greeted the outbreak of war was largely the product of years of demonizing and ridiculing foreigners and the acceptance of ideas of national and racial superiority throughout European societies.

THE EVE OF WAR

Such were the more important general factors at work in shaping the course of events that led to the outbreak of war in Europe in 1914. The instability created by the balance of power within Europe, combined with the sense of apprehension produced by successive crises – notably those in the Balkans in 1908–9 and 1912–13 – were the basic factors that led to the crisis triggered by the assassination of Archduke Ferdinand in June 1914 and the outbreak of war. Compounding these matters, however, were public attitudes, shaped by states that had little difficulty in justifying their actions to their peoples.

The process of industrialization was crucial in that it made possible the raising, organization and arming of unprecedented numbers of fighting men. The armed forces were transformed from those of 1870, most obviously the navies, which underwent fundamental changes in types of warship and their systems of firing and communications. Armies were less obviously affected in that they retained their three

main branches – artillery, infantry and cavalry – and horses were still the main means of moving weapons and supplies. Communications had, however, undergone massive changes since the 1870s, with the refinement of the electric telegraph and the invention of the telephone and the wireless. Meanwhile, in the air a whole new dimension of war had appeared during the Balkan Wars of 1912–13.

The changes that affected armies and navies after 1914 would overshadow those of the previous period. Even so, it is alarming how little the military high commands of the various powers had understood the implications of the changes that had taken place. This would have major repercussions for the way in which they would conduct the war that was about to unfold.

"At first there will be increased slaughter on so terrible a scale as to render it impossible to get troops to push the battle to a decisive issue...Everybody will be entrenched in the next war; the spade will be as indispensable to the soldier as his rifle."

JAN (IVAN) BLOCH, POLISH RAILWAY MAGNATE AND AUTHOR,
FROM *WAR IN THE FUTURE*, 1897

The Years of Plenty

AFTER THE DEFEAT OF NAPOLEON in 1815, 19th-century Europe experienced just six wars between major powers, of which three involved Russia and the Ottoman Empire ('Turkey'). The former sought greater influence in the Balkans and access to the eastern Mediterranean from the Black Sea. The latter ruled over large areas of the Balkans, but was struggling to retain control in the face of increasing nationalism in the region.

After the Russo-Turkish war of 1877–78, the victorious Russians imposed the Treaty of San Stefano on the defeated Turks. The Balkan states of

The Congress of Berlin 1878
The conference marked the highpoint of the career of German chancellor Bismarck. The decisions made there overruled the terms of the Treaty of San Stefano, concluded by Russia and Turkey earlier in the year.

THE CONGRESS OF BERLIN
At the invitation of Austria-Hungary, a congress was convened in Berlin in June 1878, presided over by the German chancellor, Bismarck. All the major European powers – Austria-Hungary, Britain, France, Germany, Italy, Russia and the Ottoman

Serbia, Montenegro and Romania were granted full independence from Turkish control, while a large, new autonomous Bulgarian principality was created. Russian influence in the Balkans was greatly increased as a result, raising alarm bells in the rest of Europe. Austria-Hungary was, in particular, anxious not to encourage nationalism among its own Balkan territories, and considered Russia a rival in the region. The British had already supported the Turks against Russia in the Crimean War of 1853–56, and they were aware that if the Ottoman Empire were to fall to the Russians it would threaten British interests in India, and the vital sea route through the Suez Canal.

The Suez Canal
Though built by the French, the Suez Canal became a symbol of British maritime and imperial power when Britain acquired a controlling interest in the company after occupying Egypt in 1882.

THE ROAD TO WAR
1878 – 1914

In Europe the period leading up to the First World War was an age of industrial and imperial expansion. Local wars were fought in the period, especially in the Balkans, and there were frequent crises that threatened to escalate into war. Yet, despite their rivalries, the Great Powers co-operated to keep the peace. At the same time, however, they made preparations for war on an unprecedented scale.

1878 MARCH
Russo-Turkish war ends in Russian defeat of Ottoman Empire

1878 JUNE
Representatives of European powers gather in Berlin to redraw borders in Balkans, removing some territory from Ottoman Empire

1879 OCTOBER
German Chancellor Bismarck concludes defensive alliance with Austria-Hungary, designed to discourage war between Russia and Austria-Hungary

1882
Triple Alliance formed between Germany, Austria-Hungary and Italy

1885
"Scramble for Africa" starts, in which European powers rush to carve up continent but respect each other's interests, in order to avoid war

1887
Crisis over Bulgaria is resolved without provoking wider conflict

1889
Russia orders French armaments, giving assurance that these will never be used against France. Eiffel Tower completed in Paris

1891
Franco-Russian alliance is concluded to avoid isolation outside Triple Alliance

1895 APRIL
Germany, France and Russia relieve Japan of many gains she had made from China after recent war

1897
Kiel Canal, connecting Baltic with North Sea, opens

1898
British expedition to the Sudan led by Kitchener defeats troops of the Mahdi at Omdurman

1898
First German Naval Bill, signalling attempt to overturn British historical naval supremacy; start of Anglo-German naval race

1899–1902
After suffering serious reverses, British eventually defeat Boer republics, which become part of Union of South Africa

1902 JANUARY
Britain forms alliance with Japan

1904 APRIL
British Entente with France

1905
Russo-Japanese War ends in defeat for Russia at hands of expansionist, rapidly industrializing Japan. Morocco crisis is engineered by Germany, in order to test Anglo-French Entente

1906 FEBRUARY
Britain launches HMS Dreadnought, most powerful battleship in the world, raising stakes in Anglo-German naval arms race

1907
British Entente with Russia

1908 OCTOBER
Bosnian crisis, in which Austria-Hungary unilaterally announces annexation of Bosnia-Herzegovina

1909 MARCH
Russia forced by Germany to endorse Austro-Hungarian annexation of Bosnia-Herzegovina, although powers originally sought to oppose action

1911
Second Morocco crisis settled after Britain shows support for France

1912 OCTOBER
Start of First Balkan War between Serbia, Bulgaria and Greece and Turkey

1913 MAY
Treaty of London makes provision for independent Albania. Ottomans lose most of their European territories

1914 JUNE
Visit of Austrian Archduke Franz Ferdinand and his wife to Sarajevo in Bosnia-Herzegovina

Empire sent their representatives. It was agreed that the fate of Turkish territories in the Balkans should be decided jointly by all the powers, and the Treaty of San Stefano was set aside. Austria-Hungary was allowed to occupy Bosnia-Herzegovina (although not formally to annex it), and Russia gained Bessarabia on its border with Romania, which exchanged its coastline north of the Danube for the Dobruja, the coastal region to the south. Turkey was given back Eastern Rumelia and Macedonia, which the Russians had granted to Bulgaria. The new smaller Bulgaria was autonomous, but still nominally part of the Ottoman Empire. Serbia, Montenegro and Romania had their independence confirmed.

NEW ALLIANCES

The immediate problem that arose from the Congress of Berlin was Russian resentment. Having defeated the Turks, Russia had seen the treaty it had dictated torn up, and it blamed Germany for having sided with Austria-Hungary The latter comprised the Austrian Empire and self-governing Hungary, both ruled by the Habsburg dynasty as a "Dual Monarchy". Germany, which had attempted to mediate between its eastern neighbours at the congress, did now conclude an alliance with Austria-Hungary. The alliance was intended to forestall a clash between the Habsburgs and the rulers of Russia, the Romanovs. It presented Russia with having to face the might of Germany should it attack Austria-Hungary, while at the same time making it clear to Austria-Hungary that Germany would not support any aggression against Russia.

The balance of power came under increasing threat, however. During the 1880s, Russia realized that its freedom of action in the Balkans depended on France maintaining its status as a rival power to Germany. Although Germany professed not to oppose Russian designs on Constantinople, Russia knew that it could never gain control of the Straits (the straits linking the Mediterranean and the Black Sea) without provoking a war with Austria-Hungary, and hence with Germany. In 1882 these two allies formed a Triple Alliance with Italy, which itself had territorial ambitions in the Balkans.

British satirical map of 1877
Russia is depicted as an octopus with designs on the outstretched form of Turkey. Many saw Russian territorial ambitions in the Balkans, the Middle East and Central Asia as the greatest threat to continuing stability in Europe.

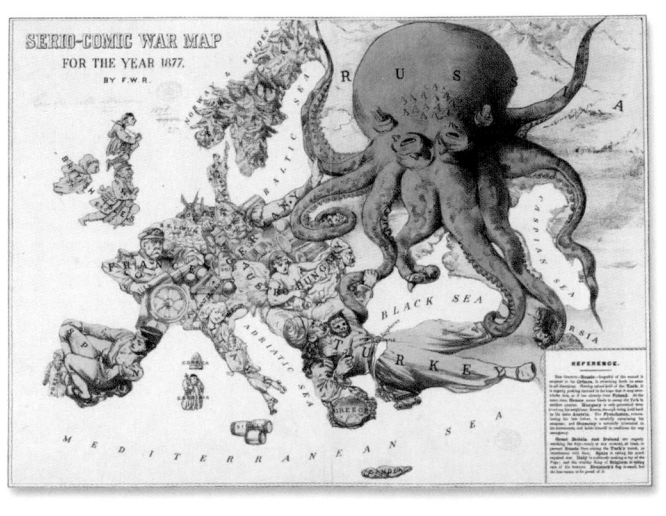

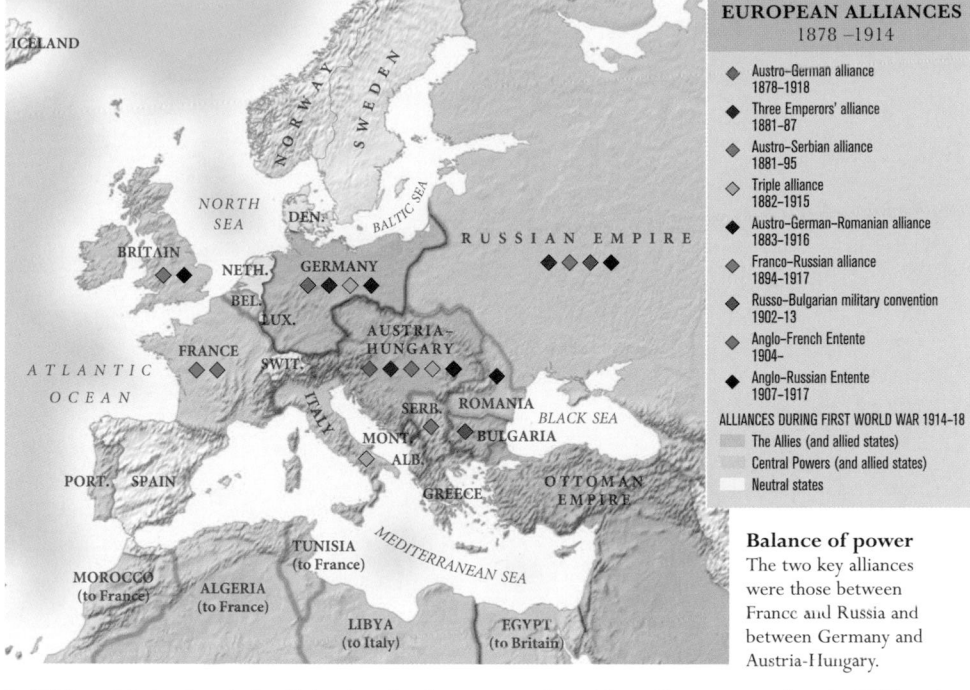

EUROPEAN ALLIANCES
1878–1914

◆ Austro–German alliance
  1878–1918
◆ Three Emperors' alliance
  1881–87
◆ Austro–Serbian alliance
  1881–95
◇ Triple alliance
  1882–1915
◆ Austro–German–Romanian alliance
  1883–1916
◆ Franco–Russian alliance
  1894–1917
◆ Russo–Bulgarian military convention
  1902–13
◆ Anglo–French Entente
  1904–
◆ Anglo–Russian Entente
  1907–1917

ALLIANCES DURING FIRST WORLD WAR 1914–18
 The Allies (and allied states)
 Central Powers (and allied states)
 Neutral states

Balance of power
The two key alliances were those between France and Russia and between Germany and Austria-Hungary.

In 1887 a crisis developed after Bulgaria refused to obey Russian demands that it discourage the people of Eastern Rumelia from revolting against their Turkish rulers and uniting with Bulgaria. This intervention by Russia caused Britain to associate itself with the Triple Alliance in its attempt to maintain the status quo in the Balkans. As a result Russia strengthened its ties with France in an alliance that would play an important role in the events leading to the First World War.

THE FRANCO-RUSSIAN ALLIANCE

Such an alliance seriously disturbed the delicate balance of power in Europe by presenting Germany with a threat on two fronts. A preliminary agreement between Russia and France in 1891 was strengthened by military conventions in 1892 and 1894. The need for secrecy meant that it was not possible for the alliance to be discussed by the French parliament, and it was therefore ratified by an exchange of letters early in 1894, and subsequently confirmed and consolidated in 1899 and 1912. For many years it was a disappointment to both parties. Russia refused to regard it as the means whereby France could recover Alsace and Lorraine, which had been lost to the Germans in 1871, and France felt in no way bound to support tsarist ambitions in the Balkans.

EXPANDING EMPIRES

In the world beyond Europe the Great Powers often came to understandings that cut across the alliances made within Europe. In April 1895 Germany, France and Russia co-operated to relieve the Japanese of gains they had exacted from China after their recent war, and in 1900 the powers jointly suppressed the anti-imperialist Boxer Rebellion, which threatened their interests in China. With almost all the nations of Africa and Asia unable to resist the military technology of the Western powers, imperialism reached its peak around the turn of the century. A number of newcomers – Germany, Italy, Japan and the United States – joined the traditional imperial powers in acquiring overseas possessions.

All the powers exercised restraint with respect to one another's ambitions. Even occasional crises during the "Scramble for Africa", as the powers divided up the continent after 1885, were resolved. No country wanted to risk complications within Europe for the sake of its non-European interests.

Blohm und Voss shipyard, Hamburg 1910
Around the turn of the century, German shipyards began to rival British ones. This steamer is being built for the Hamburg–America Line (HAPAG).

CHANGES IN EUROPE

The Europe of 1914 was very different from that of the mid-19th century, when only Britain and Belgium could be considered industrialized states, in which manufacture and trade were the mainstay of the economy. By 1914 this was true of almost all of northern Europe.

Hand in hand with industrialization went a marked population increase in the region as a whole. This had started in the 18th century, and had been caused by a number of factors, including improved food supplies. Technological developments in agriculture had led to an increase in food production, and improvements in transport systems enabled food to be moved around more easily. Better-nourished people lived longer and had more children who survived into adulthood.

In the second half of the 19th century the populations of European states continued to grow rapidly alongside the rapid spread of industrialization. The exception was France, which, until 1871, was the most

Ford factory 1914
Workers fit a Model-T engine on a Ford assembly line. The methods of production introduced by Ford helped make America the world's leading economic power.

populous state in Europe, apart from Russia. The newly unified Germany took over that position, and increased its population by more than 50 per cent over the next 40 years, while that of France remained static. By 1914, with the exception of Italy, it was the least populous of the powers.

Britain was also overtaken by Germany, and not just in terms of population. For more than 100 years it had been the leading manufacturing nation,

Berlin–Baghdad railway

The railway was instrumental in Germany gaining economic and military influence in the Ottoman Empire. A German consortium won the contract for building the railway in 1888, but it was not completed by 1914.

but, within 40 years of unification in 1871, Germany had taken the lead. (Neither country could, however, compete with America, which had, by 1900, emerged as the greatest manufacturing nation in the world.)

AN IMBALANCE DEVELOPS

The industrialization of Europe after the mid-19th century was very different from the earlier stages of the Industrial Revolution, which had primarily been concerned with iron-working, steam power, textiles and potteries. Chemical industries started to produce a wide range of new substances, from synthetic dyes to powerful new explosives. The year 1889 saw the Eiffel Tower built in Paris; it was also the year when cheap, mass-produced, high-grade steel was used for the first time used in battleship construction. Other developments in the late 19th century included electrification and the internal combustion engine. These new technologies led to profound economic and social changes in the industrializing countries, but eastern and southern Europe were left behind in the process.

A PERIOD OF PEACE

Growing prosperity, advancing living standards and increasingly enlightened social legislation played their part in the easing of internal social tensions in most European states. Vast class differences still remained, but social welfare and parliamentary representation did much to draw the sting of class warfare, though in Russia there remained a social militancy that, for most of this period was not apparent in the rest of Europe.

With increasing literacy and slowly improving social conditions, this was an era of hope. Between 1871 and 1914 much of Europe enjoyed as long a period of peace as any in its history, but paradoxically it was also a period when the states of Europe were preparing themselves for war by maintaining massive armies and filling their arsenals with all the latest weaponry.

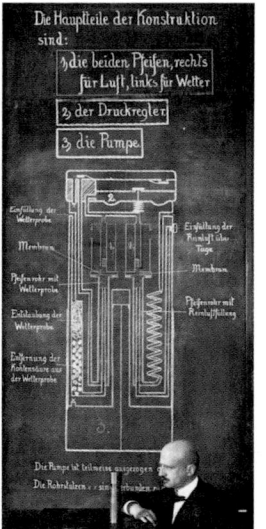

Fritz Haber (1868–1934)

Brilliant scientists such as Haber, Nobel prize winner for chemistry (1918), made great contributions to German industrial growth. Here Haber shows his design for a firedamp whistle to save the lives of coalminers. During the war his method of synthesizing ammonia helped make up for Germany's shortage of nitrates for fertilizer, and he also worked on the gas warfare programme.

Industrialization, the gathering pace of technical change, and the rapid population increase in certain countries were major factors in the militarization of Europe. The invention of the electric telegraph, of the humble typewriter and steel filing cabinet, and later of the telephone, combined with ever-expanding railway networks and police forces, provided European states with unprecedented means of controlling their populations. One of the most obvious uses to which these powers were put was conscription.

INDUSTRIAL GROWTH OF THE GREAT POWERS 1875–1913

EUROPE'S LEADING industrial powers were Britain, which had been the first country to experience an industrial revolution, and Germany, which rapidly made up for lost time following unification in 1871. Both in old, established industries and in, particular, in the new precision and petro-chemical industries Germany had, by 1910, established itself as the leading state in Europe. By 1914 it was the leading trading partner of virtually every other nation in Europe, including Britain, which had become increasingly dependent upon Germany for finished goods.

France, with its limited coal and iron resources, lagged a little way behind Germany and Britain. Austria-Hungary and Russia had been late starters and still had a long way to catch up. In the USA economic growth in the late 19th century was far more spectacular than that in any of the European states, but most of its production was as yet for its vast home market.

POPULATION (millions)

COAL PRODUCTION (millions of tons)

PIG IRON (millions of tons)

RAILWAYS (thousands of km)

1875

1900

1913

KEY

Britain (area 313,571 sq km)   Russia (area 22,397,431 sq km)   Austria-Hungary (area 677,826 sq km)

France (area 536,270 sq km)   Germany (area 540,740 sq km)   United States of America (area 9,670,231 sq km)

THE EVOLUTION OF THE MACHINE-GUN

VARIOUS INVENTORS OVER THE CENTURIES had experimented with rapid-firing guns, but it was not until the third quarter of the 19th century that the first "machine-guns" were developed. The two that enjoyed most success were the Gatling, produced in the USA in 1862, and the French *mitrailleuse*, also developed in the 1860s. Rate of fire was achieved by the the number of barrels. in the Gatling ten and in some *mitrailleuses* as many as 37. Neither was a true machine-gun; both depended on how fast the operator turned the crank handle to fire the next barrel; they did not automatically harness the energy of the gun's recoil to load and fire the next round. This system was developed by the American Hiram Maxim (1840–1916), who acquired the patent for such a gun in 1882 and made the first in 1884. The Maxim gun underwent

extensive trials with all the major European armies in 1887 and in the USA in 1888. The various countries subsequently produced their own national weapons, though machine-guns continued to follow the basic Maxim concept. From the start there were three basic problems: a reliable loading and ejection mechanism, dependable cartridges and overheating (hence need to cool the single barrel). The Hotchkiss, produced in France, worked on slightly different principles, using the gases emitted from each bullet rather than the recoil to reload the gun and dispensing with the water-cooled jacket. Only one nation, Germany, thoroughly integrated machine-guns into its military organization. In 1914 the German armies had about 12,000 machine-guns with between six and twelve guns per regiment. Machine-guns at this point were too large and heavy to be used by individuals: the standard German Maschinengewehr 08 weighed 24.66 kg (58.31 lb), but with water and sledge weighed 32 kg (70.5 lb).

Gravity-feed magazine, refilled directly from box of cartridges

Hand-operated firing crank

Gardner single barrel
The American Gardner, which also came in a twin-barrel version, was used by the British Navy from 1880, installed on fixed mountings on ships.

Tripod mounting

Montigny mitrailleuse
A Belgian invention, this 37-barrel gun was taken up by the French army in 1869. A 25-barrel version, said to be capable of 300 rounds a minute, was used in the Franco-Prussian War.

Magazines – each contained 37 rounds – one for each barrel

Heavy mounting provides stability but makes the gun practically immobile

Machine-gunners in the Balkans Wars
A Bulgarian unit, dug in with a Maxim gun, gives a foretaste of the trench warfare of 1914–18.

Rear ranging sight

Steam generated by heat of barrel drained off, condensed, cooled and reused

Foreward sight

Toggle-lock trigger – fire continues as long as trigger is pressed and held

Water-cooled barrel-jacket to help prevent overheating and jamming

Belt-fed with 250-round fabric belts

Cold water for cooling the barrel fed into jacket through valve

Elevation wheel and lock

.303-in calibre capable of firing up to 600 rounds per minute

Tripod mounting for stability. Collapses for easy transport

British .303-in Maxim Mark 3
This was the standard British medium machine-gun of the prewar era. Adopted by the British Army in 1889, the Maxim was replaced in 1912 by the Vickers. This, however, used the same basic principles of the Maxim as did German, Austrian and Russian machine-guns.

Gravity feed magazine – a variety of magazine capacities were available ranging from 30 to over 100 rounds

Hand-operated firing crank – the rate of fire is increased or decreased by turning faster or slower

Ten rotating barrels enable high rates of fire – up to 1,000 rounds per minute in later models

Locking mechanism to prevent too much movement during firing

Wheeled gun-carriage made moving the heavy gun easier – the wheels could be locked or removed to provide a stable firing platform

US Gatling Gun
The Gatling saw action in the Civil War, but was not officially adopted by the US Army until 1866. It was subsequently used by many European countries, including Britain and Russia.

CONSCRIPTION

Compulsory military service in the late 19th century became "the school of the nation', introducing young men to the responsibilities of citizenship and prevailing patriotic ideals. The German armies owed their victory against the French in 1870–71 to superior organization, the product of the general staff system, and superior numbers – the result of conscription. After 1871 France and most of the other powers followed suit. The result was that, by 1914, Europe was armed on a scale that would have been unthinkable in 1870. In 1914 Germany succeeded in mobilizing an army of 3,500,000 regulars, conscripts and reservists, which enabled it to match Russian numbers.

The exception to the rule was Britain, where the notion of conscription was politically unacceptable. Its small professional army was largely designed for the purpose of subduing uprisings in the empire, for example in the Sudan (1896–98) and in South Africa (1899–1902). The country could rely on its navy for defence.

Maintaining such vast armies obviously inflated military budgets. States found that increased military expenditure could only be justified to elected legislatures by comparing their armed forces with the armies of potential enemies. The constant monitoring of their neighbours' military strength contributed little to the harmony of Europe.

TECHNOLOGY AND THE ARMS RACE

The peace of Europe was rendered ever more fragile by the pace of technological progress. This now necessitated the re-equipment of armies every 18 to 20 years, and of navies once a decade. Industrialization generated an arms race that broke down the existing balance between the powers.

The most important changes resulting from industrialization to be seen in the First World War were in the way armies fought. While railways could transport ever greater numbers of men to the battlefield, changes in weaponry, brought about by developments in metallurgy and chemistry, gave armies far greater firepower. Breech-loader, quick-firing weapons and high-explosive shells combined to bring to the battlefield a heavier volume of accurate, long-range fire that ensured that the defence could break up an attack before the latter could get close enough to represent a threat. The firepower that halted emerged as stronger than the firepower that advanced.

In terms of mobility, larger armies equipped with new weaponry created increasing logistic demands. Supply columns had to double in length. Whereas in 1870 a German corps was supplied by 457 wagons, the number had risen to 1,168 by 1914. In 1870 it was reckoned that an army could operate to ranges of 160 km (100 miles) from its nearest railhead; by 1914 this figure had halved.

A question frequently asked about the First World War is why the effect of such changes was so little appreciated by the generals who had spent decades preparing for war. There was evidence available to suggest that a future conflict might turn into prolonged trench warfare. In the American Civil War (1861–65) the siege of Petersburg had proved an accurate forecast of the trenches of the First World War. The Russo-Turkish War (1877–78) had been the first European war in which "the spade had been more important than the rifle", and more recently the Russo-Japanese War (1904–05)

These wars were, however, far removed in terms of distance and time from the Europe of 1914, where the evidence of the Balkan Wars of 1912–13 suggested that wars could be decided in a matter of weeks. In both conflicts, a heavy concentration of troops and offensive action had led to a speedy outcome before such mundane matters as logistics intervened. Despite the evidence that firepower killed, the belief prevailed that victory would be won as a result of the willingness of infantry to move forwards into fire. The French considered the bayonet an instrument of moral will. The conventional wisdom was still that any war would be short, characterized by offensive action – and won, of course, by the armies.

Fortifications
In the 19th century the powers of continental Europe fortified their strategically important cities and towns. The French town of Verdun (*left*), for example, was ringed by 20 forts and 40 redoubts. In the years leading up to 1914, however, many of these forts were neglected; some were still armed with old iron cannons.

The South African War
Britain's experience in the South African War (1899–1902) was no preparation for the First World War. The Boers' guerrilla tactics were at first very successful against the professional British army. One major change introduced by the British as a result was the khaki uniform.

BRITISH AND GERMAN SEA POWER

For Britain, arguably the most prestigious of the powers, victory would not be won by its armies. In every war it had fought over the previous 250 years it had emerged, if not triumphant, then intact and undefeated as a result of its command of the sea.

The 19th century had seen rapid developments in ship design. Wooden hulls and rows of muzzle-loading cannon had been replaced by ironclad battleships. By 1914 they were sheathed in armour, powered by oil-burning engines that produced speeds in excess of 25 knots, and had massive guns that could fire distances of 20 km (12 miles). Other developments, namely the electric telegraph and then radio, provided admiralties with direct control over even their most distant commands. The second half of the 19th century also saw the development of mines, while the technology that provided the torpedo with reliable depth-keeping qualities – the horizontal rudder and ballast tanks – also made the submarine a practical proposition.

In the Russo-Japanese War of 1904–05, mines claimed three battleships, five cruisers, four destroyers and four other warships. The mine and the torpedo together now made the close blockade of an enemy coastline extremely hazardous. This danger was recognized by the British admiralty, which decided to impose a distant, rather than a close, blockade upon Germany in the event of war.

The growth of Germany's political power, and its increasing industrial pre-eminence, were accompanied by a new assertiveness that did not bode well for the peace of Europe. The first

The siege of Port Arthur, 1904

In the Russo-Japanese War, Port Arthur was shelled by land-based artillery and Japanese warships. The Russian cruiser *Pallada*, seen here in the harbour, was wrecked in December 1904. The Russians surrendered on January 2, 1905.

A new power in the east

Yokohama celebrates Japan's victory over Russia in the war of 1904–05. Japan's defeat of Europe's largest, most populous empire heralded the end of the old world order.

manifestations of this were the German naval laws of 1898 and 1900. These committed Germany to building a fleet powerful enough to threaten Britain's naval supremacy. Germany calculated that problems in various parts of the British Empire, and general hostility to Britain in continental Europe, would oblige the latter to make concessions to Germany's territorial ambitions. Attempts in 1898 and 1901 to negotiate an Anglo-German alliance foundered when Britain refused to give Germany a free hand in Europe. After the conclusion of the South African War in 1902, Britain felt better able to resist German pressure.

THE ANGLO-FRENCH ENTENTE

In an attempt to reduce its problems outside Europe, Britain entered into an alliance with Japan in January 1902 and an entente with France in April 1904. The agreement with France was intended to eliminate a number of imperial issues that had bedevilled Anglo-French relations. In return for Britain's support for French territorial ambitions in Morocco, the French agreed to let Britain have a free hand in its dealings with Egypt.

Germany, convinced that the British and French were still essentially rivals, decided in 1905 to put the new Anglo-French understanding to the test. Choosing a time when Russia was still reeling from the shock of its defeat by Japan, Germany provoked a major crisis when the kaiser, on a visit to Tangier, in Morocco, declared support for the sultan as an independent sovereign.

Britain responded with active diplomatic support for France, and an important consequence of the crisis was that Anglo-French relations were, if anything, strengthened. Britain became ever more convinced that maintaining France as a great power to offset Germany's increasing military strength was essential to Britain's own security.

GROWING OPPOSITION TO GERMANY

Russia's defeat by Japan in 1904–05 cleared the way for the Anglo-Russian Entente of August 1907, aimed at settling the two countries' disputes outside Europe. It also allowed Russia to redirect its attention to the Balkans and its support for the Serbs. In 1908 a *coup d'état* in Turkey by a group known as the Young Turks led the Ottoman Empire to attempt to reassert its sovereignty in Bulgaria (which resisted such interference), and in Bosnia-Herzegovina. The latter had been under Austro-Hungarian administration since the Congress of Berlin in 1878, but Austria-Hungary now announced that it would formally annex it. Neighbouring Serbia felt Bosnia-Herzegovina, with its majority Serb population, should become part of an enlarged Serbia, and Russia was expected to support it in this objective.

At first, Russia considered agreeing to acquiesce in this matter if Austria-Hungary would support its long-held aim of obtaining right of passage for its warships through the Bosphorus and Dardanelles (while the navies of all other powers were denied access to the Black Sea). However, the Austrians pre-empted the conclusion of negotiations and proceeded with the annexation. In March 1909, in the face of a veiled threat of war from Germany, Russia was given no option but to endorse the move.

THE BRITISH NAVY

A T THE OUTBREAK OF WAR the British Navy could match – at least in terms of modern dreadnoughts and battlecruisers – any two of its rivals. It had 22 dreadnoughts and nine battlecruisers, compared with Germany's 15 dreadnoughts and five battlecruisers and America's ten dreadnoughts. In terms of pre-dreadnought battleships, cruisers, destroyers and submarines the British also enjoyed a clear margin of superiority over other navies.

In the two decades prior to 1914, navies underwent fundamental change as submarines, airships and aircraft, and radio came into service. As torpedoes acquired increased range and bigger warheads, the destroyer was developed as the counter to the torpedo-boat. Mines were used extensively and to telling effect during the Russo–Japanese War of 1904–05, so were likely to play an important role in any future conflict. In Britain's plans for a distant blockade of Germany, mines would be laid in the southern part of the North Sea, in the Strait of Dover and around home ports, but British mines proved inferior to Germany's and did little damage.

These developments went hand in hand with another fundamental change: the reduction of Britain's worldwide commitments, and the concentration of the fleet in home waters. An arrangement with France led to a major reduction of British naval forces in the Mediterranean, which, in the 100 years following Nelson's victory at the Nile in 1798, had effectively been a British lake.

Minelaying
During the war Britain called on its vast merchant navy to assist with tasks such as minelaying. Here, mines are attached to nets being laid from a British drifter. This was the kind of mine barrage used to block the Strait of Dover.

HRE2 reconnaissance seaplane
The HRE2 (Hydro Reconnaissance Experimental 2) was one of a series of two-seater aeroplanes built by the Royal Aircraft Factory from 1914. Other versions of the plane were used for reconnaissance work on land.

HMS Dreadnought, launched 1906
The revolutionary 18,110-ton ship with her ten 12-in (330-mm) guns, steam turbines and top speed of 21 knots gave her name to a new class of battleship. Earlier battleships were thereafter dismissively termed "pre-dreadnoughts".

British submarine C3
In 1914 the British Navy had 73 submarines, compared with Germany's 31. In 1918, the elderly C3, packed with high explosive, was used to ram a viaduct at Zeebrugge in a raid designed to trap German U-boats in their bases.

Macedonian revolutionaries 1912 In their struggle to throw off Turkish rule in 1912, the Macedonians were supported by Bulgaria, Greece, Serbia, and Montenegro.

Britain and France took exception to Germany's militant threats, which were repeated in 1911, when French troops occupied Fez in Morocco. This second Moroccan crisis was settled with a minor exchange of colonial territories between France and Germany, but only after Britain supported France. Even as late as 1907 the circle of alliances around Germany had by no means been firm, but following the crises of 1908–09 and 1911, solidarity between the Entente powers – Britain, France, and Russia – was far more robust. In the Balkans, Austria-Hungary's annexation of Bosnia-Herzegovina, designed to forestall Serbian claims on the territory, succeeded in humiliating its neighbour, but failed to curb Serbian nationalism.

ITALIAN ASPIRATIONS

The 1887 treaty that bound Germany, Austria-Hungary, and Italy in alliance had been concluded only after Austria-Hungary conceded that Italy had an equal interest in the Balkans. The least of the powers, and by 1909 little more than a nominal member of the Triple Alliance, Italy emerged from the 1908–09 Bosnian crisis in a familiar situation – with nothing. By 1911, however, it was determined to secure territory. At various times all the powers had endorsed Italy's claims to the Turkish provinces of Tripolitania and Cyrenaica in North Africa, but none supported its declaration of war on Turkey in

1911. The Italians occupied the coastal towns of Tripoli and Benghazi, but the campaign proved more difficult than anticipated, and in 1912 they turned their attention to the Aegean, and occupied Rhodes and the Dodecanese. In the Treaty of Lausanne of October 1912 Turkey conceded its rights over Tripoli and Cyrenaica to Italy.

THE BALKAN WARS

Meanwhile, Turkey was to suffer further territorial losses in the Balkans. In March 1912 Bulgaria and Serbia concluded a pact that provided for the division of Macedonia between them. In May a further pact between Bulgaria and Greece brought

Italian troops in North Africa 1911 The Italians defeated the Turks in 1911–12 and took control of the Libyan coastline, but had great difficulty subduing the local Arab and Berber populations.

into being the Balkan League, which was united in its opposition to Turkish rule in the region. Throughout the summer of 1912 the Great Powers sought to defuse the crisis in the Balkans, but by the time they agreed in October to act in order to maintain the status quo, the First Balkan War had begun, following a declaration of war on Turkey by independent Montenegro. By the time an armistice was concluded on December 3, Turkish armies had suffered a series of defeats and the Bulgarians were within sight of Constantinople.

Complicated negotiations followed, involving the Balkan League, the Great Powers, and Turkey, but after a flareup of Turkish resistance in February and March 1913, peace was eventually concluded on May 30, 1913. The Treaty of London created an independent Albania, an arrangement demanded by Austria-Hungary and Italy as the means of denying Serbia access to the sea. Serbia sought compensation in eastern Macedonia at Bulgarian expense. Bulgaria was also in dispute with Greece over Salonika, and, faced with these difficulties, chose to move against its former allies on June 29, 1913, thus starting the Second Balkan War. With the hitherto quiescent Romania and a vengeful Turkey also taking the field against them, the Bulgarians were defeated within a month. The Treaty of Bucharest of August 13, 1913 established, for the moment, a new set of borders in the Balkans.

STRATIFIED SOCIETIES

FOR ALL THE ECONOMIC SHIFTS and technological advances of the previous 50 years, the Europe that went to war in 1914 was still a network of societies divided starkly along traditional lines. Even in relatively modern Britain, the largest single occupation on the eve of the war was domestic service.

Like Britain and France, Germany had an elected parliament, the Reichstag, with deputies representing the interests of various sections of the male population. But government ministers were not directly accountable to the Reichstag. The German Reich was a federation of states dominated by Prussia. The Prussian king was also the kaiser and Prussian nobles, the Junkers, formed Germany's ruling elite. In Germany, as in Britain and Austria-Hungary, the landowning aristocracies maintained their status as "high society", with a calendar of balls, horse races and country house weekends.

The persistence of the old order was most obvious in autocratic Russia. Answerable only to God, the czar appointed the commanders of the army and the fleet, the ministers and provincial governors. Despite Russia's rapid industrialization, which caused the urban population to double in the 40 years before 1914, well over 80 per cent of the people lived in rural areas. When Revolution came in 1917, it was hardly a surprise that so many chose to support the new order rather than the old.

Porters on the Volga
Although serfdom had been abolished in 1867, there had been little change in the lives of the vast majority of the Russian peasantry. A seemingly unbridgeable gulf still separated them from their former owners.

THE EVE OF WAR

The Balkan Wars had the effect of excluding Turkey from Europe, with the significant exception of Constantinople and the Straits. That this had come about through the actions of the small Balkan states was somewhat surprising. These states had shown themselves able to act in a way that conflicted with the interests of the Great Powers.

For Austria-Hungary, the outcome of these wars was little short of disastrous. Serbia had doubled its territory, and Austria-Hungary had no option but to accept the enlargement of its neighbour. The question of Serbia's strength, and the increase in nationalist feelings in the region, which Austria-Hungary saw as "the south Slav problem", was now pressing. It presented itself at a time when the frequent crises of the

previous ten years had given a momentum to events and a general excitement — increasingly strident, militant nationalism — that had reduced resistance to war. This development, moreover, came at a time when those with the power of decision in Berlin and

Vienna were aware that their countries stood at the peak of their strength relative to their potential enemies. They were well aware that their advantage would decline with the passing of the years. French military reforms and Russian railroad construction programmes would be completed in or about 1916, increasing the military strength and mobility of these countries. In the crises of 1912 and 1913, Germany and Austria-Hungary had held back, despite being aware that it might be in their interest to induce, rather than to postpone, hostilities. In 1914, when faced with another crisis in the Balkans, they were not to show the same restraint.

Fateful visit of June 28, 1914
Archduke Franz Ferdinand, the heir to the Habsburg thrones, and his wife make their way to their car during their visit to Sarajevo, the capital of Bosnia-Herzegovina.

Russian ball 1914
The extravagant lifestyle of the aristocracy shocked foreign visitors to imperial Russia. The war made little difference. Sir Samuel Hoare, British intelligence officer in Petrograd, commented that: "The wealth and the lavish use they made of it dazzled me after the austere conditions of wartime life in England."

Hatred and distrust in the Balkans

As new states were created and new borders drawn in the Balkans, no country could rely on the loyalty of its population. Here Bulgarian troops watch the hanging of suspected Turkish spies during the Balkan Wars of 1912–13.

War is Declared

THE SUCCESSION OF CRISES in the decade before 1914 had left Britain, France and Russia fearful of German military power. Germany, meanwhile, despite its industrial primacy and increasing economic domination of Europe, was conscious that both Russia and France had plans to increase their military strength. Europe was divided into two camps by a system of alliances, with Britain, France and Russia linked by ententes, and Germany and Austria-Hungary part of an alliance with Italy. Neither side, however, was completely secure in their arrangements. France and Russia were aware that their alliance could not survive continued refusal to support each other militarily, and Germany recognized that it could not refuse to stand by Austria-Hungary in its problems with Balkan nationalism for much longer.

The factors that produced the First World War were long in the making, but in the end war broke out as the result of calculations and miscalculations made in the weeks following an incident in Sarajevo, Bosnia-Herzegovina, on June 28, 1914. Archduke Franz Ferdinand, nephew and heir to the Habsburg Emperor Franz Josef, and his wife, the Countess Sofia, were in the city for the summer manoeuvres of the Austro-Hungarian army. Members of "Young Bosnia", a secret society dedicated to liberating Slav lands from Habsburg rule, had laid plans for their assassination.

The first attempt failed, when a bomb thrown at the archduke's car bounced off, injuring two policemen and a number of bystanders. Later that morning, however, the car pulled up where one of the gang, Gavrilo Princip, happened to be standing. Seizing this second chance, he fired his pistol into the open-topped car, killing the archduke and his wife.

The arrest of Gavrilo Princip in Sarajevo
The police hold back members of the public as Princip (second from the right) is led away into custody, following his assassination of Archduke Franz Ferdinand and his wife, the Countess Sofia.

DECLARATIONS OF WAR
June – August 1914

During the diplomatic crisis of July 1914 that followed the assassination of Archduke Franz Ferdinand, there were calls for moderation. However, once Austria-Hungary had rejected Serbia's reply to its ultimatum and declared war on July 28, events began to spiral out of control. Trust evaporated as the Great Powers' decisions were dictated by the fear that their enemies might steal a march by mobilizing before them.

KEY

Moves by Entente powers and their allies	Moves by Central Powers

JUNE 28 — Archduke Franz Ferdinand and his wife assassinated in Sarajevo

JULY 23 — Austro-Hungarian note to Serbia delivered, with demand for reply by July 25

JULY 24 — Austria-Hungary notifies powers of note to Serbia

JULY 25 — Austria-Hungary severs diplomatic relations with Serbia

JULY 25 — Serbian reply to Austro-Hungarian note delivered

JULY 26 — Austria-Hungary orders partial mobilization against Serbia

JULY 26 — Britain seeks agreement for conference to settle Serbian problem: France and Italy indicate acceptance

JULY 27 — Germany indicates refusal to participate at conference

JULY 27 — Russia indicates acceptance of proposed conference

JULY 28 — Austria-Hungary declares war on Serbia

JULY 29 — Germany refuses to confirm adherence to Belgian neutrality

JULY 29 — Britain proposes international mediation to solve crisis; Russia seeks German restraint on Austria-Hungary, Russia orders partial mobilization

JULY 30 — German warning to Russia to halt mobilization. Germany orders mobilization

JULY 31 — German demand that Russia halt mobilization

JULY 31 — Russia orders mobilization. Austria-Hungary orders mobilization in Galicia

AUGUST 1 — Belgium and France order general mobilization

AUGUST 1 — Russia orders general mobilization

AUGUST 2 — Germany declares war on Russia

AUGUST 2 — German violation of Luxembourg; Germany demands right of transit through Belgium

AUGUST 3 — Germany declares war on France; German invasion of Belgium

AUGUST 4 — Germany declares war on Belgium

AUGUST 4 — Belgium severs diplomatic relations with Germany, Britain declares war on Germany

AUGUST 5 — Montenegro declares war on Austria-Hungary

AUGUST 6 — Austria-Hungary declares war on Russia

AUGUST 6 — Serbia declares war on Germany

AUGUST 7 — Landing of first British troops in France

AUGUST 8 — Montenegro declares war on Germany

AUGUST 12 — Britain and France declare war on Austria-Hungary

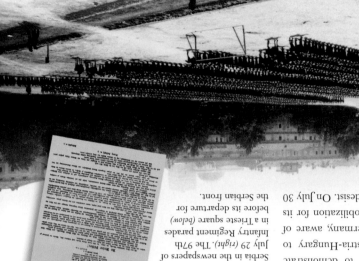

DIPLOMATIC MANOEUVRES

In itself this incident need not have led to war, but Austria-Hungary, acting on a well-founded but unproven suspicion of Serbian complicity in the murder, saw an opportunity to crush Serbia and thereby solve the south Slav problem once and for all. Accordingly, on July 5–6 the Austrian ambassador in Berlin sought an assurance of German support in eliminating Serbia "as a political factor in the Balkans". This assurance was given by the kaiser and the chancellor, the latter with the observation that if war was to come then it was "better now than in one or two years' time when the Entente will be stronger". The German leadership thus surrendered the power of decision to Austria-Hungary, encouraging its ally to start a war with Serbia even at the risk of provoking a larger Europe-wide conflict.

The Habsburg monarchy, however, had no wish to become embroiled in a general war. It simply wanted a victory, a military victory rather than a diplomatic one, in order to demonstrate that it was still a power to be reckoned with. In order to achieve this, Hungarian support for what was primarily an Austrian enterprise had to be secured. In the past, Hungary, wary of Austrian aggrandizement, had opposed an aggressive policy in the Balkans and had used German reluctance to support such a policy as the means of checking Austrian ambitions. The German promise of July 5 thus undercut Hungary's resistance to Austrian policy, and on July 14 Hungary endorsed the Austrian position.

But it was not until July 23 that an ultimatum was delivered to Serbia, couched in such a way that its demands — tantamount to the destruction of Serbia as a state — would prove unacceptable. The Serbian reply of July 25 was consummately conciliatory and diplomatic in tone, as the situation demanded. It accepted all of Austria-Hungary's demands bar two. These would have given the Austro-Hungarian government power to interfere both in an inquiry into the assassination, and in the internal running of Serbian affairs. Serbia suggested the disputed demands could be subjected to arbitration either by a tribunal in The Hague or by the Great Powers. The Serbian reply could not disguise a diplomatic triumph for Austria-Hungary.

Yet, despite this success and the fact that mobilization plans precluded an attack on Serbia before August 12, Austria-Hungary declared war on Serbia on July 28.

From this action all else followed. At first Russia had advised Serbia to comply with Austria-Hungary's demands. Now, however, conscious of the humiliation of 1909 over Austria-Hungary's annexation of Bosnia-Herzegovina, Russia was not prepared to allow Austria-Hungary to destroy Serbia, and thus Russia's prestige and influence in the Balkans. Accordingly, on July 29 Russia ordered a partial mobilization, directed against Austria-Hungary. Given the slowness with which Russia could mobilize, this was a diplomatic rather than a military ploy, designed to demonstrate Russian interest and force Austria-Hungary to back down. But on this day, Germany, aware of the implications of a Russian mobilization for its own war plan, warned Russia to desist. On July 30

The conspirators
Gavrilo Princip (left) with two of his fellow conspirators. Princip was spared the death penalty because he was only 19, but died of tuberculosis in an Austrian prison in 1918.

Austria-Hungary goes to war
The Emperor announces that a state of war exists with Serbia in the newspapers of July 29 *(right)*. The 97th Infantry Regiment parades in a Trieste square *(below)* before its departure for the Serbian front.

Russia, which had never prepared a plan for partial mobilization and faced an all-or-nothing dilemma, ordered general mobilization. Even before they were made aware of this decision, both Germany and Austria-Hungary began their own general mobilization.

GERMAN DEMANDS

On the same day, July 31, Germany presented the French with an ultimatum demanding their neutrality in the present crisis and the surrender of the fortress towns of Toul and Verdun as a guarantee of their intentions. This demand was rejected by France, which ordered a general

> "To try to avoid such a calamity as a European war, I beg you in the name of our old friendship to do what you can to stop your allies from going too far."
>
> TELEGRAM FROM TSAR NICHOLAS II TO HIS COUSIN KAISER WILHELM II, JULY 28, 1914

THE GERMAN ARMIES OF 1914

T HE GERMAN EMPIRE in 1914 consisted of 26 states: four kingdoms, six grand duchies, five duchies, seven principalities, three free cities and the former French provinces of Alsace and Lorraine. It possessed an Imperial Navy but no army. In fact there was no such organization as the German army until after the 1918 armistice. Up until then Germany had four armies, those of the kingdoms of Prussia, Bavaria, Saxony and Württemberg. Before the war these were organized into 217 infantry regiments, of which 166 were Prussian, 24 Bavarian, 17 Saxon and ten Württemberger. The Prussian Guard, the historic bodyguard to the king of Prussia, provided a further 11 regiments. Their activities were co-ordinated by the Greater German General Staff.

The army enjoyed enormous prestige thanks to the kaiser's position as commander-in-chief and his personal enthusiasm for all things military. It was also in many ways independent from control by the civilian government. The general staff's responsibilities covered all military requirements, most obviously the preparation of war plans and mobilization. It possessed powers, for example, to direct railway construction programmes. Six main railway lines stretched across Germany, allowing the rapid transfer of forces between its eastern and western borders. Between 1909 and 1914 the Germans undertook a major construction programme along the borders with Belgium and Luxembourg. Many of the stations there were built with platforms longer than the villages they ostensibly served. Thanks to this planning — and more powerful locomotives and larger rolling stock — Germany was

Readiness for war
Germany's military planning before the war was apparent in the concentration of garrison towns on the borders with France in the west and Russia in the east and in the railways that connected them.

Pre-war manoeuvres
Military manoeuvres attended by the kaiser (far left) were an important annual event in imperial Germany. In the foreground Crown Prince William, wearing a flat-topped uhlan helmet stands stroking his chin.

able to mobilize some four times faster in 1914 than in 1870 – some 11,530 men per line per day compared to 2,580 at the time of the Franco-Prussian War.

In 1912 Germany's armies had a peace-time establishment of some 646,000 officers and men. The law of June 1913 made provision for a much larger army of 870,000 with 669 infantry battalions, 550 cavalry squadrons and 633 artillery batteries. This planned increase was to be implemented over three years. In the event, with the use of first-line reservists, Germany was able to put 1,750,000 officers and men into the field in August 1914. Other reservists totalled 1,800,000 officers and men and, in addition, Germany had some 4,250,000 untrained men of military age, a reflection of the fact that before 1912 Germany had conscripted only 53 per cent of eligible manpower.

German weapons and equipment
The standard rifle was the 7.98-mm Mauser "Gewehr" (1898 model) with a magazine of five rounds. The German infantryman was better prepared for the onset of trench warfare than his French or British counterpart.

LUGER PISTOL

GEWEHR (1898)

AMMUNITION CLIP

SPADE

LOCK KNIFE

PIONEER'S AXE

Identity disc
This was worn round the neck attached to a cotton cord.

Map caption labels:

GERMANY 1914
DIVISIONAL HEADQUARTERS
Prussian
Bavarian
Saxon
Württemberg
Army corps headquarters
Major railway

DENMARK
NETH.
BEL.
LUX.
FRANCE
SWITZ.
AUSTRIA-HUNGARY
RUSSIAN EMPIRE
GERMANY
BALTIC SEA

Flensburg, Kiel, Kiel Canal, Altona, Schwerin, Stettin, Danzig, Königsberg, Insterburg, Allenstein, Deutsch-Eylau, Thorn, Bromberg, Glogau, Posen, Breslau, Dresden, Chemnitz, Erfurt, Leipzig, Halle, Magdeburg, Brandenburg, BERLIN, Hanover, Münster, Kassel, Düsseldorf, Cologne, Liège, Koblenz, Frankfurt, Würzburg, Nuremberg, Landau, Karlsruhe, Strassburg, Metz, Saarbrücken, Trier, Freiburg, Colmar, Basel, Zürich, Munich, Augsburg, Ulm, Stuttgart, Radbon, Danube, Rhine, Weser, Elbe, Oder, Neisse, Vistula, VIENNA, PRAGUE, WARSAW

I CORPS, II CORPS, III CORPS/PRUSSIAN GUARD, IV CORPS, V CORPS, VI CORPS, VII CORPS, VIII CORPS, IX CORPS, X CORPS, XI CORPS, XII CORPS, XIII CORPS, XIV CORPS, XV CORPS, XVI CORPS, XVII CORPS, XVIII CORPS, XIX CORPS, XX CORPS, XXI CORPS, I BAVARIAN CORPS, II BAVARIAN CORPS, III BAVARIAN CORPS

Helmet caption labels:
PRUSSIAN ARTILLERYMAN
PRUSSIAN JÄGER
SAXON CAP
BAVARIAN INFANTRYMAN OF THE RESERVE
WÜRTTEMBERGER INFANTRYMAN

0 miles 50 100
0 km 50 100

of France as an ally through immediate offensive operations. It envisaged the deployment of five armies between Switzerland and the Sambre River on the border with Belgium.

Conceived as a response to an expected German attack through Lorraine and eastern France, the initial French offensive would be on the extreme right in an attempt to secure Mulhouse (Mülhausen) and Colmar in Alsace. Having established the First and Second Armies in Alsace and on the Rhine, the French would then launch a major offensive into Lorraine. The Alsace effort was seen as the first part of an advance down the Rhine valley as far as Koblenz, as well as providing flanking support for the Lorraine offensive. North of Verdun, the French were to deploy three armies, and, depending on German movements, these were to be directed either through the southern Ardennes or into Luxembourg and Belgium.

mobilization on August 1, on which date Germany declared war on Russia and occupied Luxembourg. The German declaration of war on France followed on August 3, the same day that Germany presented an ultimatum to Belgium demanding right of transit through that country. The next day, after learning that its demand that Belgian neutrality be respected had been answered by invasion, Britain declared war on Germany.

Such was the process by which Europe was plunged into war. After July 28, as diplomacy failed, all the powers were carried along by military considerations. Once a country knew or suspected that one of its enemies was mobilizing, it needed to mobilize its own armies, and this had to be done according to a set timetable, dictated by the railway system. The logistics of transporting hundreds of thousands of men and horses to their appointed positions came to be known as "war-by-timetable". The timetables that would dictate the course of the opening weeks of the war were those of the French, the Russians and the Germans.

THE FRENCH WAR PLAN

France's war plan was known as Plan XVII. Its two principal aims were to clear the west bank of the Rhine and to demonstrate to Russia the good faith

Belgian neutrality
This British recruiting poster shows the treaty guaranteeing Belgian neutrality, signed by five nations, including Prussia, in 1837. The British made much of the fact that the Germans, in trying to persuade Britain to keep out of the war, dismissed the treaty as a "scrap of paper".

THE "SCRAP OF PAPER"

ENLIST TO-DAY

The Germans have broken their pledged word and devastated Belgium. Help to keep your country's honour bright by restoring Belgium her liberty.

Germany's view of the war
This patriotic postcard from 1914 shows Germany and its solitary ally, Austria-Hungary, surrounded by enemies bent on their destruction.

On their way to Paris
Germany's vast reserve of men answered the call to arms in 1914 with patriotic fervour.

1914 uniform
The uniform shown is that of an Unteroffizier (a rank between corporal and sergeant) in the Prussian infantry. Infantrymen wore the Pickelhaube (spiked helmet), with a cloth cover to prevent its gleaming in the sun, until the steel helmet was introduced in 1916.

Haversack and water bottle

Boots (1886 model)

Bayonet

Ammunition pouches

Forage cap

Pickelhaube and cover

THE LOST PROVINCES

FRANCE'S WAR PLANS were largely determined by *la revanche* (revenge), a burning desire to reclaim the lost provinces of Alsace and Lorraine. After the lightning Franco-Prussian War of 1870–71, Germany had annexed the province of Alsace and the northern part of the province of Lorraine. In the Middle Ages the region had been part of the Holy Roman Empire, but had been French since the 17th century. Part of it had been confirmed as French by the Treaty of Westphalia (1648), the rest had been annexed by Louis XIV in the second half of the century. After the Franco-Prussian War, Bismarck advised the kaiser to give the people of Alsace and Lorraine as much freedom as possible, so that they kept their local identity and would not resent German rule. But his advice went unheeded and the two provinces were ruled as a conquered territory. Especially galling to the French was the fact that Lorraine's vast iron ore deposits helped build up Germany's flourishing armaments industries.

A constitution granting limited "home rule" in 1911 came too late, and anti-German feeling in the region exploded into public anger in 1913, after a German officer attacked a crippled shoemaker. In the same year Hansi, an Alsatian cartoonist, published *Mon Village*, a collection of scenes from village life, poking fun at the German authorities. In 1914 he was sentenced to one year's imprisonment for libelling public officials.

Events such as these kept the lost provinces in France's national consciousness. Politicians and soldiers alike nursed their "sacred anger". Just as the return of the stork, symbol of Alsace, signalled the return of spring, the war signalled a long-awaited opportunity for French rule to be restored.

Arrival of the stork
In this cartoon by Hansi, Alsatian schoolchildren and their teacher gather to greet the stork. A German policeman goose-steps sulkily up and down on the far side of the square.

French propaganda
A French border guard offers a bouquet to a young Alsatian beauty, who accepts it happily. Sentimental images of this kind appeared as posters and in the French press.

The landscape of Alsace
The French have always had a special fondness for the region's picturesque villages and steep hills cloaked in vineyards.

FRANCE'S LOVE OF THE OFFENSIVE

In the Franco-Prussian War of 1870–71, the French had found themselves fighting against a coalition of German states that collectively had a population equal to that of France. However, the population of the new German Empire grew so fast that, by 1914, it had twice as many men of military age as France. With such a massive inferiority of manpower – and an equally serious industrial inferiority – to try to wage war defensively could result only in defeat. A defensive strategy would only prolong, not win, a war against Germany.

The French army had become a very inward-looking institution. Relations between its commanders and the French government had always been difficult, and the army's prestige had suffered badly after it was found to have unjustly accused a Jewish officer, Alfred Dreyfus, of espionage in 1894, and subsequently imprisoned him. In the face of criticism, the army had sought a return to traditional soldierly virtues and a revival of the Napoleonic legend. The shame of France's defeat in the Franco-Prussian War of 1870–71 came to be seen as the result of the army having been false to its traditions of offensive action, and it became accepted that the offensive suited the French national temperament.

The offensive at least offered France some hope of forestalling German plans and the terms of its alliance with Russia reinforced this way of thinking. The alliance naturally brought with it obligations. France could not consider waging a defensive war and leaving Russia with the burden of offensive operations. Given Germany's overwhelming military superiority, both France and Russia were obliged to undertake offensive operations together or risk defeat and destruction separately.

THE RUSSIAN PLAN

Russia's plan, Plan XIX, was put together in 1910, substantially revised in 1912, and further revised after the outbreak of war. In its original form, Plan XIX envisaged the use of four armies to clear East Prussia, on the assumption that Germany would have few forces in the east. After clearing East Prussia, the Russians would then be free to move directly against Berlin.

By 1912 the conventional wisdom in the Russian army had decided that the armies of Austria-Hungary posed a more immediate threat to Russia than those of Germany. Accordingly, two of the armies earmarked for East Prussia would be redeployed to strengthen forces opposite Galicia. This change left the armies opposite East Prussia short of numbers relative to the length of the front, and even in comparison to whatever limited German force might be left to halt a Russian invasion. In August 1914 a final change assigned two Russian armies to the Silesian front in preparation for an invasion of Germany from the southeast. This was the most distant sector of the front and would take much longer to reach than East Prussia or Galicia.

BRITISH INTENTIONS

Britain was not bound by treaty to support France in a war with Germany, but plans for sending a small expeditionary force to assist the French army had been prepared. Britain's more important task was to impose a blockade on Germany, cutting it off from trade with the outside world. The Strait of Dover would be mined and patrolled. The main fleet, based at Scapa Flow in the Orkney Islands off northern Scotland, would patrol the North Sea, stopping and searching merchant ships for arms or anything that might help Germany's war effort, and confiscating the goods.

GERMANY'S PLAN

Ever since France and Russia signed a treaty of friendship in 1891, the German high command had known that it would probably have to fight a war on two fronts. A plan for dealing with this problem began to take shape as early as the 1890s. Its premise was that France would mobilize much more quickly than Russia, so it was essential to have the vast majority of the German forces ready to deal with France, while a small force in the east stood on the defensive to check any Russian offensive. The German general staff under Alfred von Schlieffen calculated that the Russians would need six weeks to have their armies fully mobilized. It was therefore essential to defeat France in this short space of time. The Schlieffen Plan provided the means of achieving this. The right wing of the German armies would invade France through the neutral Netherlands, Belgium and Luxembourg, then sweep round to trap the French armies, which would be wrongly positioned facing Alsace and Lorraine. The plan was worked out in fine detail, pinpointing exactly where each army should be on any particular day. Refinements and adjustments were made to the plan, especially after Helmuth von Moltke succeeded as chief of staff after Schlieffen's retirement in 1906. Moltke's most significant change was the decision not to send any troops through the Netherlands.

RESPONSIBILITY FOR THE WAR

The First World War is usually regarded as one that arose from a dispute between Russia and Austria-Hungary in the Balkans, but, ironically, it

was not until August 6 – when Russia received an Austro-Hungarian declaration of war sent through the post – that the powers that were the main parties to the Balkans dispute were at war with one another. The decisions that led to a general war in Europe had already been taken between July 25 and July 28.

It is significant that as early as July 26, the Chief of the German General Staff had prepared the ultimatum to Belgium that was to signal the German invasion of France, and which prompted the involvement of Britain. In the Treaty of Versailles of 1919, the victorious Allied powers placed responsibility for the war solely on Germany, which strongly resisted having to make such an admission of guilt. Although Germany had neither planned nor sought war at that precise moment, however, the conflict that erupted in 1914 in Europe can be seen largely as the result of the Germany quest for "mastery in Europe".

Multiply or be defeated
This pre-war booklet urged France to increase its birthrate as Germany's birthrate exceeded it by five to two.

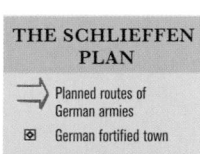

We got here yesterday at 9:30 and after supper set off for the line of forts. Spirits are high, extraordinarily high, as if we were on manoeuvres... No real news. French and Germans just look at each other. I cannot say any more, or my letter wouldn't get to you.

ALEXANDRE JACQUEAU IN A LETTER
TO HIS WIFE FROM VERDUN, AUGUST 6, 1914

THE SCHLIEFFEN PLAN

~

THE PLAN EVOLVED when Alfred von Schlieffen was German Chief of Staff between 1891 and 1906. It was designed as an answer to Germany's dilemma should it find itself at war simultaneously with both France and Russia. The plan envisaged an initial effort in the west in an attempt to defeat France between the outbreak of war and the completion of Russian mobilization.

The original plan
Confronted by French fortifications along the common border, German troops would pass through Luxembourg, the Netherlands and Belgium, then advance through northern France around the rear of the main French armies. Having won a great battle of encirclement, German forces would then be despatched by rail to the east to fight the Russians.

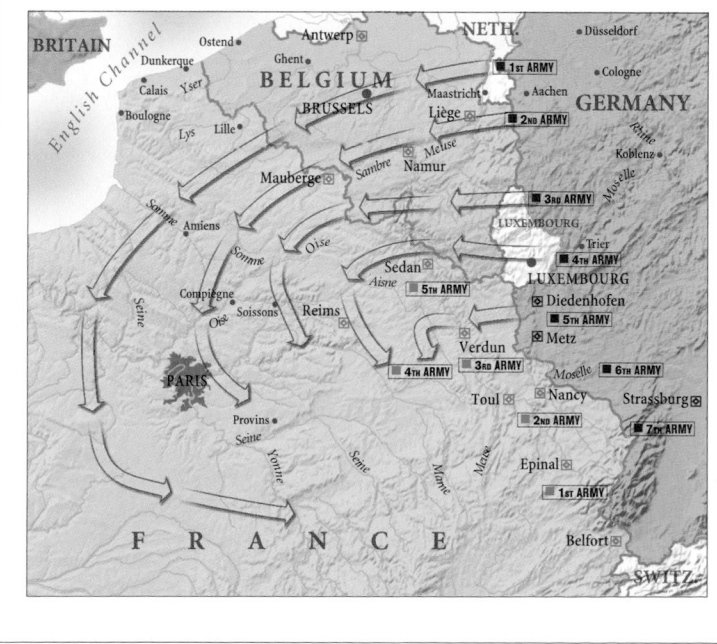

THE SCHLIEFFEN PLAN

→ Planned routes of German armies
⊠ German fortified town
⊡ French fortified town
⊞ Belgian fortified town

THE ARMIES ARE MOBILIZED

Joining up

Volunteers queue to enlist at a London recruiting office in August 1914. Such was the response to the government's appeal for volunteers that 2 million men joined up within a year and Britain did not have to introduce conscription until January 1916.

I N THE FRANTIC FINAL DAYS of July 1914, all of the Continental powers were on the brink of mobilization. First off the mark was Austria-Hungary, which began to mobilize on July 28, bringing chaos to the railways. On July 30, the Tsar of Russia ordered full mobilization, trusting in the "Great Military Programme", which aimed to have all the imperial Russian armies mobilized in 18 days. Fearful that the Russian "steamroller" would reach Berlin before they could defeat the French, on August 1 the Germans began their meticulously planned operation, designed to have 3,500,000 soldiers ready for action within a week. The regular army was swelled by reservists, who hurried to designated depots to be issued with arms and new grey uniforms and taken by precisely scheduled trains to concentration points near the frontiers. Germany's mobilization was the signal for a much less slick operation in France, where

about 3 million men were mobilized. The general staff expected the draft evasion rate to be at least 10 per cent. To their surprise, mobilization was greeted by a surge of patriotic support, with evasion at a little over 1 per cent.

In all the combatant states departing soldiers were cheered on by enthusiastic crowds, confident that their "boys" would be home for Christmas. British men were not liable for military service and Britain sent a force of just 150,000 men, a "contemptibly small army" in the famously mistranslated words of the kaiser. Within a matter of weeks, however, they were joined by half a million voluntary recruits. As mobilization got under way, individual soldiers had their private fears and doubts, but many shared the sentiments expressed by the Austrian writer Stefan Zweig: "As never before, thousands and hundreds of thousands felt what they should have felt in peacetime, that they belonged together."

Algerian tirailleurs leaving for the front
Algerian *tirailleurs* (riflemen), affectionately known as "Turcos", receive a warm send-off at the railway station of Champigny-sur-Marne in August 1914.

Calls to arms
The German order for general mobilization (*right*) was issued on August 1, the French (*above*) later on the same day. The call for volunteers in Britain (*above right*) was launched by Kitchener on August 7, the day after he took office as Secretary of State for War.

Bekanntmachung.

Mobilmachung befohlen.

Erfter Mobilmachungstag, der 2. Auguft.

TO MAINTAIN THE HONOUR AND GLORY
OF THE
BRITISH EMPIRE

A WET SCRAP O' PAPER O' BRITAIN'S BOND

YOUR KING & COUNTRY NEED YOU

ORDRE DE MOBILISATION GÉNÉRALE

ARMÉE DE TERRE ET ARMÉE DE MER

14à18

Opposing views
While the Germans depicted their soldiers as heroes with God on their side (*Gott mit uns*), the British cartoon from *Punch* magazine shows "plucky" little Belgium" standing up to a bullying Germany.

German reservist leaving for the front

"Off to the war; all linked in death we go.
I wish my sweetheart wouldn't blubber so.
What's wrong with me? I'm glad to leave, I feel.
Now mother's crying. You need a heart of steel.
The good old sunset's up there glowing red.
A fortnight's time and maybe I'll be dead."

VERSES FROM ABSCHIED (FAREWELL) BY THE POET ALFRED LICHTENSTEIN, WHO DIED ON THE SOMME ON SEPTEMBER 25, 1914, AGED 25

BRAVO, BELGIUM!

NO THOROUGHFARE

PUNCH, OR THE LONDON CHARIVARI.—AUGUST 12, 1914.

Gott mit uns
1914
HAMBURG

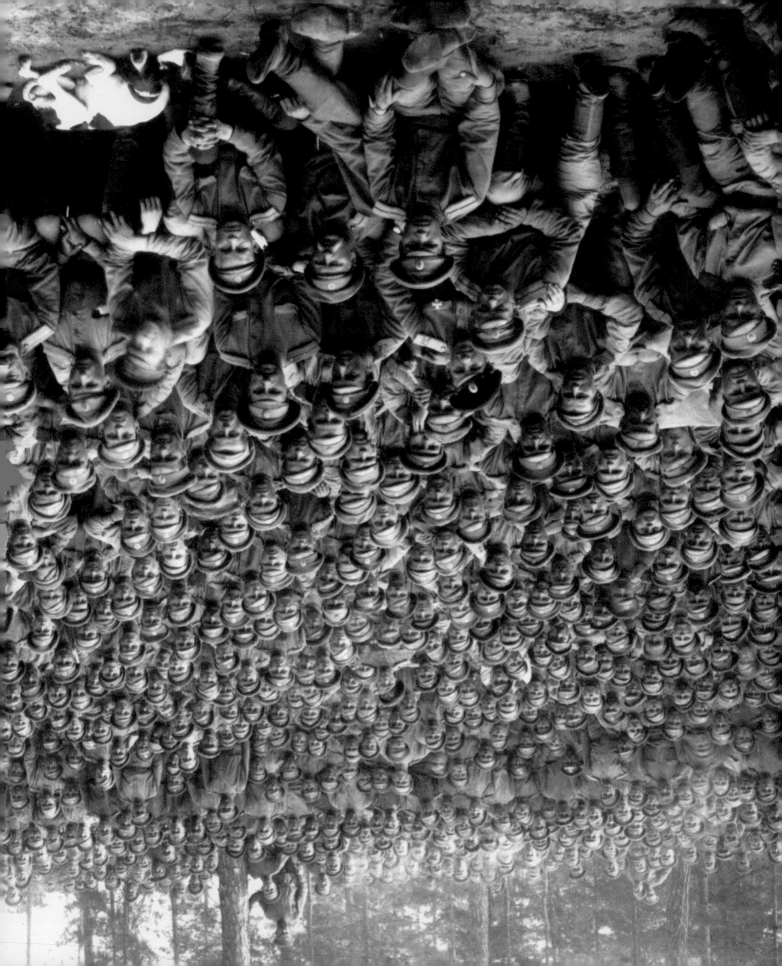

THE OUTBREAK OF WAR
1914

~

EUROPE HAD BEEN PREPARING FOR WAR FOR
MORE THAN 20 YEARS, BUT WHEN IT BROKE OUT IN 1914,
IT SOON BECAME CLEAR THAT THE GREAT POWERS HAD
LITTLE IDEA OF WHAT A GENERAL EUROPEAN
WAR WOULD ENTAIL. AUSTRIA-HUNGARY, GERMANY,
FRANCE AND RUSSIA ALL LAUNCHED OFFENSIVES. NOT
ONE SUCCEEDED IN THE WAY THAT HAD BEEN
ANTICIPATED. EVEN AFTER SUFFERING A CRUSHING
DEFEAT AND LOSING HUNDREDS OF THOUSANDS
OF MEN, ARMIES COULD CALL ON SUFFICIENT
RESERVES TO CONTINUE THE WAR.

~

The Russian steamroller
The sheer numbers of men available to its
armies made Russia appear a possibly invincible
enemy. In the event, manpower alone was not
enough, and by 1917, 1,800,000 Russian soldiers
had been killed and nearly five million wounded.

THE PURSUIT OF ILLUSION

IN 1914 THERE WAS A WIDESPREAD EXPECTATION OF RAPID, COMPREHENSIVE
VICTORY. MOST PEOPLE'S CONFIDENCE WAS BASED ON LITTLE MORE THAN CRUDE
STEREOTYPING OF THE MORAL AND PHYSICAL INFERIORITY OF THE ENEMY.
A CENTURY HAD PASSED SINCE EUROPE HAD SEEN CONFLICT ON SUCH A SCALE,
AND VERY FEW PEOPLE HAD ANY IDEA WHAT A GENERAL WAR MIGHT ENTAIL.

I N AUSTRIA-HUNGARY, the country that had set the whole machinery of hatred in motion by declaring war on Serbia, confidence of victory was naturally high. However, in seeking the destruction of Serbia, the Dual Monarchy had envisaged a swift military victory; what it found it had committed itself to was a war for which it was hopelessly ill-prepared. As Russia mobilized more quickly than anyone had imagined, Austria-Hungary changed its plans: one of its armies, deployed initially on the Serbian front, had to be transported north to counter the Russian threat in Galicia. The two armies entrusted with the invasion of Serbia were unequal to the task. Three times between August and December 1914 the Austria-Hungarians tried to crush their neighbour; three times they were beaten back. It was not until the following autumn, assisted by the Germans and Bulgarians, that they were able to punish Serbia for its impudence in refusing to submit to all of the Austro-Hungarian demands in the wake of the assassination of June 1914.

Austria-Hungary was not alone in its expectation of a short, victorious campaign. France and Germany were equally confident of quick success. Why expectant societies were denied their promised victory in 1914 is a difficult question to answer. One explanation is that armies had simply become too big. They had grown to a size that ensured them against total defeat even if they suffered any number of local reverses. They also enjoyed great powers of recuperation through their reserve strengths. At the end of even the most successful campaign, the offensive faced a reconstituted defence drawn from new drafts. This was certainly the case between 1914 and 1916. Towards the end of the war all the European powers had difficulty making good their losses and, by 1918, none of them were able to do so.

Serbian field artillery
The Serbian armies that drove back the attempted invasions of 1914 were poorly equipped compared to their Austro-Hungarian enemies, but the troops were hardened veterans of the Balkan Wars fighting for the very survival of their nation.

PROBLEMS OF MOBILITY

In August–November 1914 the pursuit of victory was an illusion. None of the great powers was in a position to defeat an enemy of similar status in the course of one, short campaigning season. Thanks to their rail networks, most were able to mobilize across their entire area and they could mobilize in depth.

Explaining the outcome of campaigns in terms of impersonal forces may appear to belittle the

but, once deployed, their armies could not move with the speed and effectiveness of armies of 100 years before. If one considers the Grand Army of Napoleon and the 1805 campaign, the speed and scale of operations were astonishing. The French broke camp at Boulogne on September 2 and with some 210,500 men, crossed the Rhine River on September 26 and the Danube River on October 6. Vienna was occupied on November 13; the Battle of Austerlitz was won on December 2. By 1914 an advance of such a distance in such a short time had become impossible. Attacking armies lacked the mobility to advance and clinch victory. They had no means of paralysing an enemy defence which, operating on home soil, could move larger numbers more quickly over greater distances by rail than an advancing army could move on horseback or on foot. Meanwhile, the defenders had numbers and a strength in depth that ensured against defeat.

> _"There is not much to say about our successes compared with those of the Germans, mainly because German victories have been gained at our expense... The enormous weight of the Russian army is thrown upon us."_
>
> CONRAD VON HÖTZENDORF,
> AUSTRIAN COMMANDER-IN-CHIEF IN A LETTER OF AUGUST 27, 1914

intact rail system and there was also the problem posed by Paris. The forces committed to the invasion through northern France were insufficient either to occupy the French capital or to "mask" it, that is to deploy enough troops to prevent the garrison from moving against an exposed, unguarded German flank. Much of the criticism subsequently directed against Moltke seems unfair; real criticism should be directed instead against the original plan.

FAILINGS AND STRENGTHS OF THE FRENCH

In accounts of the opening engagements of the First World War, the French army often comes in for harsh criticism: it managed to get things wrong in 1870 and appeared to do so again in 1914. That, of course, is grossly unfair. In the matter of the violation of Belgian neutrality, the French were never guilty of the errors committed by the German high command. The French army asked the political authorities if it would be allowed to enter Belgium and was informed that it could not, and the person who asked was dismissed.

The weakness of the French war plan was that it was conceived by the operations section of the staff with scarcely any reference to the intelligence section. The latter had anticipated that the main German effort would be made through Belgium. In so far as this possibility was considered by those in the operations section who drew up the plan, they reckoned that the fortresses of Liège and Namur could withstand a German attack. Since they did not anticipate the German use of reserve formations in the initial assault, they also assumed that any German deployment of forces in Belgium would involve a weakening of forces in the centre and on the German left in Alsace and Lorraine.

First, the Schlieffen plan failed to take account of the political reactions that it would provoke. The German high command justified the violation of Belgium as a "military necessity", a very dubious principle when it results in the loss of trust and goodwill of other neutral states. Second, military plans depend on men for their execution. The Schlieffen Plan set German forces the goal of an advance of some 1,300 km (800 miles), with a series of encounter battles en route, and then fighting – and winning – a battle of encirclement and annihilation in eastern France inside six weeks. How entire armies were to march 32 km (20 miles) a day, brushing aside all resistance as they advanced, every day for six weeks and finally fight and win an enormous battle at the end of a tenuous line of communication defies belief. The advancing armies had no guarantee of being able to capture and use an

achievements of the commanders and troops who have to fight the battles. Even so, an individual general's successes are diminished and his failures may be excused if the outcome of his campaign has been determined largely by other factors. This was especially true of the Schlieffen Plan, with which Germany's chief of staff, Helmuth von Moltke, went to war. Moltke had made changes to the original plan, the most important being his decision not to violate Dutch territory, but to send the German First Army through Belgium rather than through the Netherlands.

IMPOSSIBLE DEMANDS

With or without Moltke's amendments, the German plan was questionable for two reasons – one political and one military.

The BEF
British troops wheel their bicycles through the town of Rouen on their way to counter the German advance through Belgium. The BEF would form the left wing of the Allied line alongside the French Fifth Army. Relations between the two did not always run smoothly, but the British were able to play their part in the Battle of the Marne in September.

BACK FROM THE BRINK

In their offensives against Alsace and Lorraine, the French First and Second Armies met with disastrous defeat in August 1914, suffering some 250,000 casualties, but managed to recover. With the French armies wrongly positioned to meet the German advance through Belgium, the armies in Alsace and Lorraine nonetheless managed to break contact with the enemy and redeploy formations to counter the emerging threat. The French recovery helped stall the German offensive, though in truth the advance was more or less doomed by the time it reached the Marne. With their lines of communication still intact, the French and British were able to counterattack across the Marne in the second week of September and drive the Germans back to the Aisne. From this point both sides tried and failed to turn the enemy's open flank in a series of actions known as the "Race to the Sea". This culminated in the indecisive battle of Ypres in November and the onset of trench warfare.

THE IMPORTANCE OF RUSSIA

There was one other major factor in the French recovery in the first week of September 1914 – the efforts made by Russia to sustain its ally. In the first month of war Russia mounted two offensives, one against East Prussia, the other against Galicia.

Russian forces defeated those of Austria-Hungary but were defeated in turn by those of Germany. This was to be the pattern of operations over the next 30 months: the Russians were able to defeat the armies of Austria-Hungary, but could not compete with the superior organization and equipment that the Germans brought to the battlefield.

In what remained of 1914 both the Austro-Hungarian and Russian armies demonstrated remarkable spirit in extricating themselves from potential disasters. The Russians thwarted two determined German offensives in Poland and fought the Germans to a standstill in front of the city of Lodz, but their losses in these battles,

Road to the Marne
A French unit carries its machine-guns towards the front line. In the background can be seen some of the cars, including the famous "taxis of the Marne", commandeered to ferry fresh troops from Paris to the battlefield.

"Every effort must be made to attack and drive back the enemy. A soldier who can no longer advance must guard the territory already held, no matter what the cost. He must be killed where he stands rather than draw back."

JOSEPH JOFFRE, FROM HIS ORDER OF SEPTEMBER 5, ON THE EVE OF THE BATTLE OF THE MARNE.

plus the exposed position of the city, led the Russians to cede Lodz voluntarily in December. The year closed with both the Austro-Hungarian and Russian empires having lost their best trained and equipped field armies, and both now largely dependent on their allies.

A DIFFERENT BATTLEFIELD

One thing that clearly distinguished the Eastern and Western fronts was the degree of movement. The rail and road systems of northwest Europe were so well developed that it was virtually impossible for either side to gain any significant local advantage of numbers; any threat could easily be countered by the movement of reserves. In the East, however, while Germany had 1.6 km (1 mile) of rail track for every 15 sq km (6 sq miles), Austria-Hungary had 1.6 km (1 mile) for every 50 sq km (20 sq miles) and Russia had just 1.6 km (1 mile) of single track for every 180 sq km (70 sq miles) of its European territories. The scarcity of roads and railways would affect the conduct of the war in the East in many ways, most obviously in the transport of food, raw materials, arms and ammunition. With nearly all the fighting taking place on Russian or Austro-Hungarian soil, local superiority of numbers, sufficient to register local success, could be achieved by both sides. The problem was to sustain an offensive, especially into areas served by an intact rail system of the enemy. In the vastness of the Eastern Front, offensives effectively led nowhere.

The Invasion of Belgium and France

BATTLE OF THE FRONTIERS
AUGUST 1914

While the French launched costly attacks on the lost provinces of Alsace and Lorraine, the German high command methodically put its modified Schlieffen Plan into operation. German progress through Belgium was slowed at first by the resistance of the Liège forts, but by the end of the month the French Fourth and Fifth Armies and the British Expeditionary Force were in full retreat as the German juggernaut swept southwards.

AUGUST 4
German attack on Liège

AUGUST 6
City of Liège surrenders, but troops in forts fight on

AUGUST 7
BEF lands in France

AUGUST 8
French capture Mulhouse in Alsace, but evacuate the city three days later

AUGUST 11
Collapse of French offensive in Alsace

AUGUST 12
Germans bring up heavy siege howitzers to complete destruction of Liège forts

AUGUST 14
Start of disastrous French offensive in Lorraine; they advance to Sarrebourg and Morhange

AUGUST 16
Fall of the last of the Liège forts

AUGUST 20
Surrender of Brussels; withdrawal of Belgian army into Antwerp

AUGUST 20–21
Germans stage counter-offensive in Lorraine

AUGUST 21–22
German 2nd Army crosses the Sambre and bombards Charleroi

AUGUST 22
German attack on Namur

AUGUST 23–24
British defeated in action fought at Mons

AUGUST 24
Start of Anglo-French retreat

AUGUST 25
Maubeuge invested, forced to surrender Sept 8

AUGUST 25
Lille abandoned by the French: occupied by Germans Sept 2–6

AUGUST 25–26
First Belgian sortie from Antwerp; abandoned with realization of Anglo-French reverses at Mons and Namur

AUGUST 26
Action fought at Le Cateau. German occupation of Longwy

AUGUST 28
Montmédy, initially bypassed by Germans, occupied after French abandon it as they withdraw into Verdun. First German attack at Verdun checked

AUGUST 29
Temporary check to German advance in actions fought around Guise and St Quentin

KEY
- Siege of Liège Aug 4–16
- Anglo-French retreat to the Marne Aug 24–Sept 5
- Battle of the Frontiers Aug 7–24

MILITARY OPERATIONS in the West began on August 1 when formations from the German Fourth Army violated and occupied neutral Luxembourg in order to secure the railways needed to complete Germany's mobilization plan. The logic of this act of aggression was not lost on Belgium. When the Germans delivered an ultimatum demanding rights of transit, the Belgian government issued orders for the destruction of bridges and rail installations that the Germans would need and for the concentration of the Belgian army on its eastern borders.

FRENCH REACTIONS

The French high command, although intent on an offensive along the common border with Germany to recover Alsace and Lorraine, had anticipated that the Germans might try to invade France via Belgium. The French Fifth Army was to be raised in the Mézières-Sedan area, covering the border with southern Belgium and with the option of moving to the Longwy area and undertaking an offensive in the direction of Metz. The initial German moves led the French high command to order this army to move into the Belgian Ardennes, and the Fourth Army and part of the Third Army to conform to this movement. What the French had failed to appreciate was that the main German effort was to be made through central Belgium, not through the Ardennes. This error established the course of events in the first month of the war. The French launched their main offensive into Alsace and Lorraine against forces defensively deployed, while the German offensive fell upon the French left flank and the open French left flank (see map page 43).

The initial French attacks into Alsace and Lorraine resulted in the capture of Altkirch, Thann

Belgian resistance

The Belgian army of 117,000 men had no hope of halting the German advance for long, but made use of rivers and canals in holding operations as the troops withdrew to the fortified city of Antwerp.

and, most importantly, Mulhouse (Mülhausen), but the latter was lost on August 10 as battle was joined along the whole of this front. The French managed to take Mulhouse again on August 19, and also fought fierce battles for Morhange and Sarrebourg (August 14–20). In these two battles the French made modest gains, but at inordinate cost, and it was the confidence that flowed from having halted the French attacks that led to the German decision, on August 17, to move from the defensive to the offensive in this area. From August 20, German forces undertook a series of offensives. These were intended to defeat the French forces in this area and allow the German left wing an active role in the planned battle of encirclement and annihilation. It was only with difficulty that the French Second Army, reeling under its losses, retained possession of Nancy and managed to hold the Germans in front of the Verdun-Nancy-Belfort line of fortresses.

THE INVASION OF BELGIUM

By now, however, more significant events were unfolding to the north. While the German First Army completed its mobilization before its advance into the plains of central Belgium, elements of the German First and Second Armies (the Army of the Meuse) were given the task of capturing Liège, which was protected by a ring of 12 forts.

THE SIEGE OF LIÈGE

After crossing the border on August 4, the Germans took Liège itself on the night of August 5/6. As German columns tried to advance through the gaps between the forts, most were halted by stiff Belgian resistance. However, 14 Brigade, approaching from the east, had better fortune, despite losing its general in confused fighting in the dark. Major-General Ludendorff (soon to make his name on the Eastern Front) assumed command and led a

column of 1,500 men into the thinly defended city. On the 8th the Germans began the systematic bombardment of Liège's forts. On the 12th they reinforced their batteries with two mighty 420-mm siege howitzers and on the 16th the last of the forts surrendered. The Germans, having possibly lost just two days through the Belgian defence of Liège, could now begin to move into central Belgium.

THE GERMAN ADVANCE

The German armies swept rapidly west and on August 20 German forces entered Brussels in readiness for a wheel to the southwest into northeast France. Meanwhile batteries from the German Second Army set about the reduction of the fortified towns of Namur and Charleroi. Having learnt much from the siege of the Liège forts, they brought their heavy artillery into action

THE SIEGE OF THE LIÈGE FORTS

~

WHEN THE CITY OF LIÈGE flew white flags at 2:00 pm on August 6, General Leman, in command of the Belgian defence, was in Fort Loncin. He ordered one division to withdraw and join the retreating Belgian army, but refused to surrender. The battle for the city was over, but the 12 forts that ringed Liège remained. Fort Pontisse could direct its guns at the Meuse where German troops were constructing pontoons, while Fort Loncin commanded the roads into the central Belgian plain. The guns in the other forts also kept firing, but, once their observation posts had been knocked out, they had difficulty locating the German batteries. Heavier and heavier guns were brought up to subdue them, culminating in two 420-mm howitzers that went into action on the 12th. The last fort held out until the 16th. Some forts were shelled into submission, others surrendered because of conditions inside. Poor ventilation and sanitation meant that asphyxiating gases from exploding shells combined with the smell of human waste to make the air unbreathable.

Shattered gun cupola
The unreinforced concrete of the Liège forts could not withstand the German heavy guns. Many of the forts' own guns were soon put out of action.

A destroyed gun at Fort Loncin
The ruins of Fort Loncin are preserved as a Belgian national monument. The bodies of the 350 men who died when the fort's magazine exploded lie buried beneath the rubble.

420-mm high-explosive shell

210-mm high-explosive shell

GERMAN 210-MM AND 420-MM HIGH-EXPLOSIVE SHELLS

German siege howitzers
Most of the damage to the Liège forts was inflicted by smaller guns, chiefly 210-mm howitzers. The forts were designed to withstand shells of this calibre back in the 1880s, but modern high-explosive shells could penetrate their defences. The huge 420-mm Mörser, the original "Big Bertha" (right) caused the fall of two of the forts: Pontisse and Loncin.

The Anglo-French retreat
A French column passes a pile of horses lying dead in a field. As the British and French retreated south pursued by the Germans in August 1914, casualties among the horses on both sides were high.

almost immediately. What remained of the Belgian army evaded German encirclement and withdrew behind the ring of fortresses that protected the city of Antwerp.

Despite having failed to prevent the escape of the Belgian army, the German armies had secured very considerable advantages of position and numbers. The French Fifth Army was forced to extend its left flank in an attempt to keep abreast of the German deployment through central Belgium. As the German First and Second Armies

"Where are the prisoners? Where are the captured guns"

HELMUTH VON MOLTKE, EXPRESSING HIS DOUBTS ON THE SUCCESS OF THE SCHLIEFFEN PLAN, SEPTEMBER 1914

approached the Belgian–French frontier, they faced only the overstretched Fifth Army, the British Expeditionary Force (with just five infantry divisions) and a few weak French formations protecting the extreme left flank.

THE BATTLE OF MONS

On August 23–24, eight German corps attacked the British Expeditionary Force, which was attempting to hold a line that stretched for 43 km (27 miles) either side of the Belgian town of Mons. To the west the British had dug in hastily along the Canal de Condé, but around the town itself they occupied an exposed salient. This was where the main attack was launched. At first the German infantry advanced in close order and suffered heavy casualties at the hands of British riflemen and machine-gunners. The Germans then started to direct heavy artillery and machine-gun fire at the British, forcing them to abandon their positions. General French, the commander of the BEF, could have chosen to withdraw into the nearby fortified town of Maubeuge, but did not. The town was besieged by the Germans on the 24th, but its garrison held out until September 8, by which time the main invasion force had moved far to the south.

Heavily outnumbered, the British and French forces in northeast France had no alternative but to cede ground and withdraw to the southwest. The British made another day-long stand at Le Cateau on August 26, but then continued their retreat. On the same day the fortified towns of Longwy and Les Ayvelles were occupied by the German Third Army as the Germans developed their offensive along the whole of the front west of Metz. The Allied front, despite the French intention to stand on the Amiens-Laon-Aisne-Verdun line, was in danger of being turned in exactly the way that the Schlieffen Plan had envisaged.

GERMAN ATROCITIES
~

THE VIOLATION OF BELGIAN NEUTRALITY made the Germans ogres in the eyes of the world's press. Determination to crush popular resistance in Belgium, especially the activities of *franc-tireurs* (civilian snipers), resulted in a number of "atrocities" that the Allies exploited for propaganda purposes. Where resistance was suspected, the Germans burned houses, rounded up civilians and picked out groups of them to be executed. There were well-documented incidents at Dinant, where a large number of civilians, including women and children, were executed, and at Louvain, where the university library with its priceless collection of medieval manuscripts was razed to the ground.

US war bond poster
American propaganda, even four years later in 1918, still recalls the "rape" of neutral Belgium.

REMEMBER BELGIUM
Buy Bonds
Fourth
Liberty
Loan

Belgian woman killed by German shelling
The press in Britain and France published many pictures like this, even though they did not show atrocities as such, in order to whip up anti-German feeling.

PROBLEMS OF SUPPLY

In reality the Schlieffen Plan was incapable of implementation and had begun to break down long before German formations reached the Oise. Staff work could not resolve problems of command and resupply that plagued the German armies as they advanced into northern France. With the French jamming German radio signals, the armies that advanced into France were increasingly without direction from superior authority, while behind them chaos mounted as the German logistic system broke down. Without sufficient specialist troops to clear demolitions and return railways to service at a rate that kept pace with the advancing armies, the nearest available railheads for the various armies were on average some 135 km (85 miles) from the lead formations during the last five days of August. The German Second Army, with support from the First, was able to overcome the resistance of the French Fifth Army around Guise (August 28–29). Although delayed by this action, both German armies continued to advance despite the increasing exhaustion of their troops and horses. That they were able to advance at all was mainly because of captured military supplies and being able to live off the rich countryside. After Mons, the advance involved relatively little fighting, so the troops required less resupply in terms of ammunition.

FALTERING PROGRESS

But the fact remained that the first German horses to die of exhaustion during this campaign died on German soil, and as early as August 11 one German cavalry division had to be withdrawn from operations because of the condition of its mounts. Many German horses were further weakened in the course of the invasion by being fed on green corn. At the same time German troops did themselves no favours by eating unripe fruit picked from the orchards that they passed. Few German infantry formations saw their heavy weapons and supply columns after the German border was crossed, and without motor transport there was no possibility of German formations being supplied much beyond the Aisne. By the time the German forces wheeled inside Paris and came to the Marne in the first week of September, they were spent, and the French high command, after more than two weeks of retreat, was able to consider mounting a counterattack.

German troops waiting to advance

With the French and British armies retreating in front of them, the German troops were faced by very little opposition as they advanced through the French countryside in the brilliant sunshine of August 1914.

The march through Belgium into France
The speed of the German invasion was impressive, not far behind the timetable of the Schlieffen Plan, which allowed six weeks to defeat the French before redeploying Germany's armies to face Russia. In the end, exhaustion and failures of command and supply would bring the invasion to a halt on the Marne.

THE INVASION OF FRANCE
Aug 2–Sept 5, 1914

- German advance (Aug 2–Sept 5)
- German fortified town
- French fortified town
- Belgian fortified town
- Major battle or siege
- German position Sept 5
- French position Sept 5
- Belgian position Sept 5
- British position Sept 5
- German GHQ
- French GHQ
- The Allies (and allied states)
- Central Powers (and allied states)
- Neutral states

German troops entering Brussels
The occupation of the Belgian capital by the German
First Army on August 20, 1914 was unopposed. The
Belgian army had retreated north to Antwerp, allowing
the Germans to pass unimpeded through central Belgium.

The Eastern and Balkan Fronts

AT THE OUTBREAK OF WAR Germany intended to stand on the defensive in East Prussia until victory was won in the West. Both Austria-Hungary and Russia, however, were committed to offensive action. Russia hoped to drive the German forces from East Prussia and the Austro-Hungarians from Galicia in readiness for an advance on Berlin. Austria-Hungary, aware of its long-term military inferiority to Russia, was to attempt a pre-emptive attack in the direction of Warsaw in order to hamper Russia's mobilization. But the first Austro-Hungarian move had to be directed against Serbia – as punishment for the assassinations of June 28. On July 29, before any of the other great powers had entered the war, Austria-Hungary sent gunboats down the Danube to bombard the Serbian capital, Belgrade.

FIRST INVASION OF SERBIA

In the crucial opening days of hostilities, the Austro-Hungarian army, because it also had to counter the Russian threat to Galicia, possessed no appreciable margin of superiority over its Serbian enemy. The latter, aware that the survival of the nation was on the line, concentrated three armies in the north of the country to counter Austrian attacks across the Sava and Drina rivers (see map page 121). When the Serbian high command realized there would be no major offensive across the Sava, it redeployed the First and Second Armies to support the Third Army, which was threatened by the Austro-Hungarian Fifth Army moving across the Drina. The invading army found its left flank, north of the Drina, counterattacked by the First Army, while south of the river its right flank was met by the Second Army. The main battle began on August 17 and, with the flanks of the Austrian army unable to support each other, they were defeated separately on August 19 and then driven from Serbian soil. This first offensive cost the Austro-Hungarians about 40,000 killed and wounded, and provided the Serbs with a useful haul of guns, rifles and ammunition. After a brief Serbian incursion into Bosnia, the Austro-Hungarian Fifth Army again crossed the Drina on the night of September 7-8. In a ten-day battle it secured a number of shallow bridgeheads and the Serbs withdrew to positions in

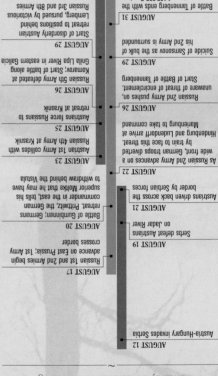

Cossacks advancing through Poland
In 1914 the war on the Eastern Front was far more mobile than in the West. Cavalry was used by both sides for reconnaissance and cavalry skirmishes were common.

SERBIA, GALICIA AND EAST PRUSSIA
AUGUST – SEPTEMBER 1914

On August 12 Austria-Hungary attempted to invade Serbia, but was soon beaten back. The imperial armies enjoyed more success in the opening manoeuvres on the Russian front, but at the end of August suffered a humiliating reverse in eastern Galicia. Russia's fortunes were equally mixed. Victory in the south against the Austro-Hungarians was offset by catastrophic defeat by the Germans at Tannenberg.

AUGUST 12
Austria-Hungary invades Serbia

AUGUST 17
Russian 1st and 2nd Armies begin advance on East Prussia; 1st Army crosses border

AUGUST 19
Serbs defeat Austrians on Jadar River

AUGUST 20
Battle of Gumbinnen; Germans retreat. Prittwitz, the German commander in the east, tells his superior Moltke that he may have to withdraw behind the Vistula

AUGUST 21
Austrians driven back across the border by Serbian forces

AUGUST 22
As Russian 2nd Army advances on a wide front, German troops diverted by train to face this threat. Hindenburg and Ludendorff arrive at Marienburg to take command

AUGUST 23
Austrian 1st Army collides with Russian 4th Army at Krasnik

AUGUST 25
Austrians force Russians to retreat at Krasnik

AUGUST 26
Russian 2nd Army pushes on, unaware of threat of encirclement. Start of Battle of Tannenberg

AUGUST 26
Russian 5th Army defeated at Komarov. Start of battle along Gnila Lipa River in eastern Galicia

AUGUST 29
Suicide of Samsonov as the bulk of his 2nd Army is surrounded

AUGUST 29
Start of disorderly Austrian retreat to positions behind Lemberg, pursued by victorious Russian 3rd and 8th Armies

AUGUST 31
Battle of Tannenberg ends with the capture of 125,000 Russians

SEPTEMBER 3
Lemberg occupied by Russians

SEPTEMBER 7
Germans advance in Masurian Lakes region to clear Russian 1st Army from East Prussia

SEPTEMBER 8
Second Austrian invasion of Serbia

SEPTEMBER 11
Conrad orders Austrian armies in Galicia to fall back behind the San River

SEPTEMBER 13
Germans drive Rennenkampf out of East Prussia, but fail to encircle his forces

SEPTEMBER 17
New German 9th Army sent by rail from East Prussia to reinforce Austrians in the south

SEPTEMBER 17
Austrians halted by Serbian counterattacks, but hold on to small gains on border with Bosnia

SEPTEMBER 24
Russians besiege fortress town of Przemysl and attack passes through the Carpathians, aiming to invade northern Hungary

SEPTEMBER 28
Transfer of German 9th Army complete

KEY
Austrian invasions of Serbia Aug 12-21 & Sept 8-17
Russian campaign in East Prussia Aug 17–Sept 13
Galician battles Aug 23-Sept 28

THE HAZARDS OF RADIO

~

FOLLOWING MARCONI'S EXPERIMENTS in "wireless telegraphy" in the 1890s, the first "radio war" was the Russo-Japanese War of 1904–05. Despite considerable progress made over the following decade, radio was still very much in its infancy in 1914. Equipment was bulky and difficult to transport and the relative slowness of radio transmission meant that all armies were obliged at times to transmit without using code. The Russians were especially negligent in this regard and the Germans often had prior knowledge of their intentions in the early campaigns on the Eastern Front.

Russian radio station
The local inhabitants pose proudly beside a newly erected radio aerial in Russian Poland.

THE EASTERN FRONT

On the Eastern Front, where Russia faced both Germany and Austria-Hungary, events in the northern sector unfolded slightly ahead of those to the south. Reacting immediately to French difficulties as the Germans advanced through Belgium, Russia committed its two best armies against East Prussia (see maps page 49), which was defended by a single German army. The Russian First Army crossed the border on August 17 and cleared the German defensive positions at Gumbinnen on the 20th. The Second Army,

crossing the border on August 20, aimed to establish itself on a line to the rear of the German forces so that the Russians could use their superior numbers and position to encircle and annihilate the enemy.

AUSTRO-HUNGARIAN SUCCESS

In the south the first encounters proved to be collisions rather than planned engagements. The main Austro-Hungarian advance was to be made from Galicia northwards into Russian Poland (see map page 50). The First Army, advancing on Lublin between the Vistula and Bug rivers, met and drove back the Russian Fourth Army around Krasnik on August 23. This success led the Habsburg high command to order the Fourth Army forward with its flank supported by part of the Third Army. The Russian high command reacted by ordering the Fifth Army to move against the Austrian First Army. In so doing, however, the Russian army exposed its left flank to the Austrian Fourth Army and became involved in a losing battle around Komarov.

THE TIDE TURNS

The Austrian high command had failed to appreciate that the main Russian offensive was to be made in the direction of Lemberg (Lvov) in eastern Galicia. Here Austro-Hungarian forces had been thinned to meet commitments in Serbia and to

Serbian artillery position
The Serbian army, hardened in the battles of the Balkan Wars and with the advantage of fighting on home soil, was able to halt all Austrian attempts at invasion in 1914.

front of the Kolubra River. There the front remained until November 5 when two Austro-Hungarian armies renewed the offensive.

support the advance of their forces into southern Poland. Despite their initial successes, lack of co-ordination between the individual Habsburg armies and their overall numerical inferiority now placed them at serious risk of defeat.

GERMAN MOVEMENTS IN THE NORTH

In East Prussia a similar situation developed for much the same reasons. In difficult terrain – thick pine forests and a patchwork of small lakes – that favoured the defence, the Russian First Army failed to follow up its initial successes. This allowed the Germans to withdraw large numbers of troops from the front around Gumbinnen. Making use of East Prussia's efficient rail network, they were then able to redeploy the greater part of their available troops in order to deal with the Russian Second Army advancing from the south.

NEW COMMANDERS

German forces in the East were now under a new command. After the defeat at Gumbinnen on August 20, General von Prittwitz had telephoned the German high command. He appears to have lost his nerve, recommending that the German Eighth Army abandon East Prussia and withdraw to the Vistula. On hearing

Russian prisoners captured at Tannenberg
Pictures of the 125,000 Russians taken at Tannenberg gave an enormous boost to the Germans' faith in the efficiency and fighting qualities of their armies. The mighty Russian "steamroller" was not the threat that had been feared.

this, Moltke, the German commander-in-chief, decided Prittwitz should be dismissed and arranged for him to be replaced by Count Paul von Hindenburg with Erich Ludendorff as his chief of staff. The two men, who had never met before, formed such a successful partnership that they would take over the German high command in 1916. The aristocratic Hindenburg was the figurehead; Ludendorff, who came from humble origins, was the brains.

Hindenburg and Ludendorff reached East Prussia to take over command on August 23. Even before they arrived, a plan, prepared by Colonel Hoffmann, operations officer on Prittwitz's staff, to redeploy German troops to the south to counter the advancing Russian Second Army had already put into action.

THE BATTLE OF TANNENBERG

The Russian Second Army was increasingly disorganized and exhausted as it advanced in the direction of Osterode and Allenstein in its attempt to get behind an enemy that it believed to be still concentrated in the Gumbinnen area. By August 24 formations from I Corps had arrived in the Lautenburg area and on the following day the first clash took place between flanking formations around Soldau. Meanwhile, to the east, the leading elements of the Russian VI Corps had advanced as far as Bischofsburg.

By August 25–26, the situation on both sectors of the front, in East Prussia and southern Poland, curiously were mirror images of one another. In both sectors were armies – Russian in the north and Austrian in the south – advancing in the belief that they faced a defeated enemy and that they would be able to complete successful battles of encirclement, and both unaware of the enemy concentrations that would bring about their defeat.

THE TRAP IS SPRUNG

Dawn on August 26 found the Russian Second Army persisting with its advance in the direction of Allenstein. The army's commander, Alexander Samsonov, was confident that his flanks were in no immediate danger, despite his forces on the left having already run into the enemy around Soldau. On the same day German forces, having marched south from Gumbinnen, routed the Russian VI Corps in front of Bischofsburg, even as other German forces completed their preparations for counter-offensives against the Second Army's centre and left flank. These began on the 27th.

German advance in East Prussia
Throughout the Tannenberg campaign, the Germans had the advantage of fighting on home soil, exploiting their knowledge of the region's forests and lakes. In addition, the intact railway network allowed rapid redeployment of troops.

THE BATTLE OF TANNENBERG
AUGUST 17–31, 1914

Responding to the needs of their French allies, the Russians quickly mounted an invasion of German territory to distract the Germans from their invasion of France. Because the Russians were also engaged on the border with Austria-Hungary in the south, they sent only two armies into East Prussia. Their plan misfired completely as one of the invading armies was surrounded and crushed by the Germans.

The Russian advance
August 17–23
The two Russian armies advanced with a wide gap between them. When the Germans moved against them, they were defeated at Gumbinnen, but then swiftly withdrew to meet the challenge of the Second Army.

The battle switches to the south
August 24–26
Unaware of the troop movements that had brought the bulk of the German Eighth Army south to meet his advance, Samsonov ordered his army forwards. The first encounters took place on August 26. The Russian First Army meanwhile made slow progress, uncertain of the forces that were ranged against it.

The German victory, August 27–31
Outgunned and outmanoeuvred, Russian forces in the centre were defeated in every major engagement. As they attempted to retreat, they found their escape route barred by German I Corps.

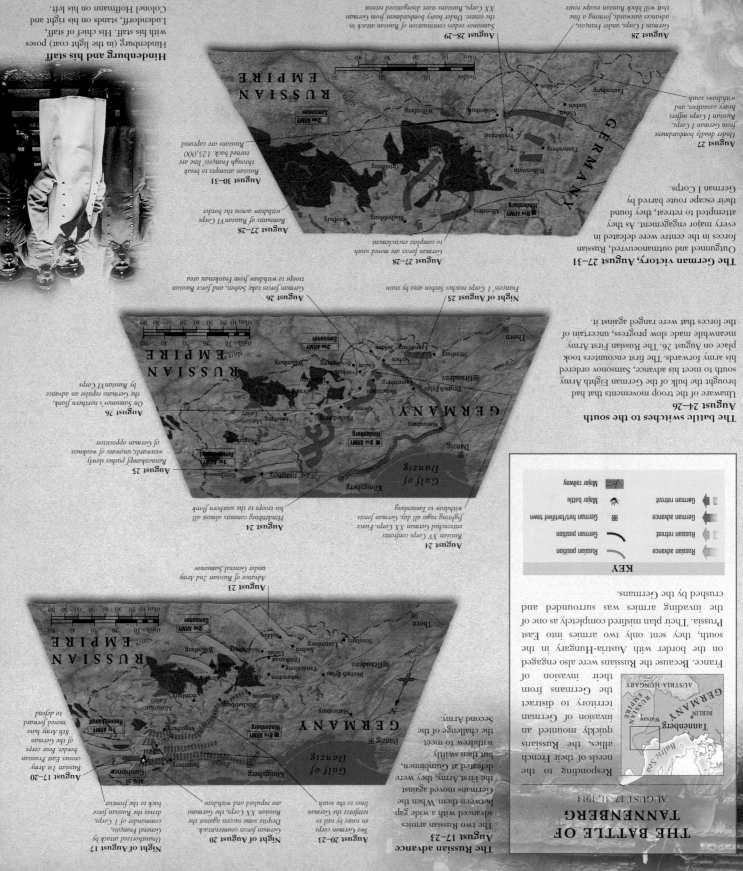

Hindenburg and his staff
Hindenburg (in the light coat) poses with his staff. His chief of staff, Ludendorff, stands on his right and Colonel Hoffmann on his left.

KEY
- Russian advance
- Russian retreat
- German advance
- German retreat
- Russian position
- German position
- German fort/fortified town
- Major battle
- Major railway

Night of August 17
Unauthorized attack by General François, commander of I Corps, drives the Russian force back to the frontier.

August 17–20
Russian 1st Army crosses East Prussian border. 8th Army have moved forward to defend.

Night of August 20
German forces counterattack. Despite some success against the Russian XX Corps, the Germans are repulsed and withdraw lines to the south.

August 20–23
Two German corps en route by rail to reinforce the German lines to the south.

August 23
Advance of Russian 2nd Army under General Samsonov.

August 24
Russian XV Corps confronts entrenched German XX Corps. Fierce fighting rages all day. German forces withdraw to Tannenberg.

August 24
Hindenburg commits almost all his troops to the southern flank.

August 25
Rennenkampf pushes slowly westwards, unaware of weakness of German opposition.

August 26
On Samsonov's northern flank, the Germans repulse an advance by Russian VI Corps.

Night of August 25
François' I Corps reaches Seeben area by train.

August 26
German forces take Seeben, and force Russian troops to withdraw from Frankenau area.

August 27–28
German forces are moved south to complete encirclement.

August 27–28
Remnants of Russian VI Corps withdraw across the border.

August 30–31
Russian attempts to break through François' line are turned back. 125,000 Russians are captured.

August 28–29
Samsonov orders continuation of Russian attack in the centre. Under heavy bombardment from German XX Corps, Russians start disorganized retreat.

August 28
German I Corps, under François, advances eastwards, forming a line that will block Russian escape route.

August 27
Under deadly bombardment from German I Corps, Russian I Corps suffers heavy casualties, and withdraws south.

Russian victory in Galicia

The Austro-Hungarians had the better of the first battles, fought in southern Poland, but they did not realize that the greater Russian threat came from the east. Without sufficient forces to counter it, they were defeated in a series of battles around Lemberg and forced to retreat.

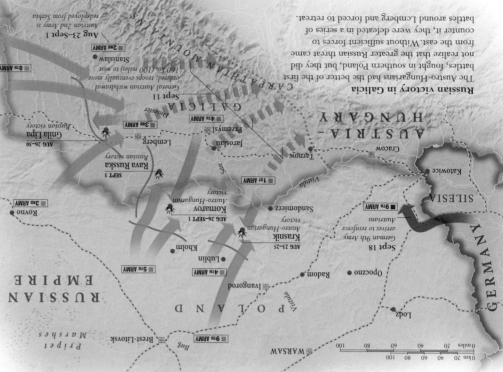

THE GALICIAN FRONT
Aug–Sept 1914

→ German troop movement
→ Austrian retreat (Sept)
→ Russian counterattack
→ Austrian advance (Aug)

The Allies (and allied states)
Central Powers (and allied states)

✳ Major battle
⊠ Fortified city/town
–––– Major railway
······ Austrian line after retreat, Sept 26
⌣ Furthest line of Austrian advance

GERMANY · SILESIA · Katowice · Cracow · AUSTRIA-HUNGARY · Tarnow · Przemysl · Jaroslau · Lemberg · CARPATHIAN MOUNTAINS · GALICIA · Stanislaw · Dniester · San · Vistula
RUSSIAN EMPIRE · POLAND · WARSAW · Radom · Opoczno · Lodz · Ivangorod · Lublin · Kholm · Sandomierz · Brest-Litovsk · Bug · Pripet Marshes · Rovno

2ND ARMY · 3RD ARMY · 4TH ARMY · 1ST ARMY · 9TH ARMY · 8TH ARMY · 5TH ARMY

Aug 23–Sept 1 Austrian 2nd Army is redeployed from Serbia
Sept 11 General Austrian withdrawal ordered; troops eventually move 160 km (100 miles) to west
Gnila Lipa Russian victory AUG 26–30
Rava Ruska Russian victory SEPT 3
Komarov Austro-Hungarian victory AUG 26–SEPT 1
Krasnik Austro-Hungarian victory AUG 23–25
Sept 18 German 9th Army arrives to reinforce Austrians

0 miles 20 40 60 80 100
0 km 20 40 60 80 100

Russian columns

Russian troops advance through Galicia in pursuit of the retreating Austro-Hungarian armies. The Russians had a lot of ground to cover before battle could be rejoined, and lines of supply became seriously overstretched.

The Russian I Corps was crushed around Usdau on the 27th, and on the 28th the Germans moved against the enemy centre around the village of Tannenberg, from which the battle would take its name. Though the Russian forces that had been committed to the advance on Allenstein were pulled back to counter this attack, the battle was already lost. The German advantages of artillery and supply, plus the depth of the previous Russian penetration in the centre, ensured that the Russians could not regain the

safety of Polish territory before the German I Corps secured Willenberg and closed their line of withdrawal. By August 30 three Russian corps had been destroyed and another two had been put to flight.

THE FIRST BATTLE OF THE MASURIAN LAKES

Following the disintegration of the Russian Second Army and the suicide of Samsonov, Hindenburg and Ludendorff switched their attention to

Rennenkampf's First Army. This had been advancing towards the fortified city of Königsberg in the north, while its left flank was making slow progress through the Masurian Lakes region. On hearing the news of Tannenberg, Rennenkampf withdrew to a line between the Masurian Lakes and the Baltic Sea. The regrouped German Eighth Army was ready to go over to the offensive on September 5 and, on the 9th/10th German I Corps struck a damaging blow against the Russian left flank. Aware that his army was in danger of being encircled, Rennenkampf ordered a withdrawal. Distracted by a brief but effective Russian counterattack, the Germans did not pursue fast enough to trap the Russians, but by September 13 had driven them out of East Prussia.

THE FALL OF LEMBERG

In the south, events unfolded very differently. Around Komarov, the Russian Fifth Army persisted until August 31 with an offensive that might have resulted in its being encircled and destroyed. Fortunately for the Russians, the depleted Austrian Third Army, advancing from the Lemberg area, had run into two full-strength Russian armies. Heavily defeated, the Third Army withdrew and the Russians occupied Lemberg on September 3.

The Austro-Hungarian commander-in-chief, Conrad von Hötzendorf, tried to switch the Fourth Army against the open right flank of the advancing Russian Third Army. In its turn, however, the Russian command sought to envelop the Austrian Fourth Army by directing the Third Army northwards. A series of battles were fought in the Lemberg–Rava Ruska sector. The Russian Eighth Army, meanwhile, dealt with a reinforced Austrian Third Army and part of the Austrian Second Army in the area to the south of Lemberg.

THE AUSTRO-HUNGARIAN RETREAT

If the Russians had made more effective use of their Fifth Army, they might have routed either or both the Austrian Third and Fourth Armies. Even so, by

Trenches in Galicia
These well-camouflaged Austro-Hungarian trenches were carefully constructed with earth and brushwood cover and loopholes for the soldiers' rifles, but would prove vulnerable to heavy artillery fire.

Russian trenches
Although campaigns on the Eastern Front in 1914 were extremely mobile, with cavalry advancing to reconnoitre enemy positions, once two armies came face to face, they quickly entrenched in similar fashion to the Western Front.

~ RUMPLER TAUBE ~

THE FRAIL, BIRDLIKE Rumpler Taube ("Dove"), first produced in 1910, was already something of an antique by 1914. Nevertheless, the Germans and Austrians used it as their main reconnaissance plane during the first few months of the war. One even flew over Paris dropping bombs and leaflets. On the Eastern Front, Taubes played an important role in the Tannenberg campaign, providing information on the movements of the Russian armies. In the Galician theatre, it was less effective, its maximum airborne endurance being only four hours. It was also vulnerable to fire from the ground. In 1915 Taubes were relegated to the role of pilot-training.

The engine gave a top speed of only 96 kph (60 mph).

With its pale linen-covered wings, the Taube was hard to spot at heights over 360 m (1,200 ft).

Control in flight was by warping – twisting the wings and tail as in early Wright brothers aircraft, rather than by means of ailerons.

September 11 Russian superiority of numbers and position prevailed along the whole of the Galician front. The Austrians, whose Fourth Army narrowly escaped encirclement, broke off the battle. Thus, at the very time when the Germans, having broken the Russian First Army's left flank on September 10, were clearing East Prussia, the Austrians were beginning a disorderly withdrawal of over 160 km (100 miles) and appealing to their ally for help. In the opening battles on this front they had suffered 350,000 casualties. The Germans responded by reconstituting four of the Eighth Army's corps as the German Ninth Army, which was transported south into the Katowice-Cracow area by the end of the month.

From the Marne to First Ypres

JOSEPH JOFFRE

KNOWN TO HIS TROOPS as "Papa Joffre", Joseph Joffre (1852–1931) led the French army into the First World War. Even before the outbreak of war, he had adopted a doctrine of "attack at all costs". As chief of the general staff from 1911, he had rid the French army of "defensively-minded" commanders and lobbied for increased military spending. Following victory at the Battle of the Marne in September 1914, Joffre was hailed as the saviour of France. An autocratic leader, he had no qualms about withholding information from the French government, which led the Briand administration to attempt to bring him into line towards the end of 1915.

Joffre showed an equally unshakable nerve in victory and adversity. He faced serious setbacks with the repeated failure of the French army to break through in Champagne and Artois in 1915. It was, however, his failure to prepare adequately against the German offensive at Verdun that finally led to his ousting in December 1916. Still very popular, he was promoted to the ceremonial role of Marshal of France.

IN THE COURSE of the German advance to and beyond the Marne, both sides experienced difficulties arising from the transfer of troops. The various armies also had problems co-ordinating movements and operations with their neighbours. Gaps could not always be closed and, whether in advance or retreat, armies struggled to maintain contact with their flanking formations, while on the western end of the line they had to look to their exposed open flanks.

The French had redeployed large numbers of men from their right flank to form the Sixth Army and the Foch Detachment (soon to become the Ninth Army). In spite of this they managed to maintain their positions on the right, opposite Lorraine. Their second major problem was to ensure proper co-ordination between the retreating Fourth and Fifth Armies and between the Fifth Army and the British Expeditionary Force.

One of the Germans' main problems was that its three armies on the right had all had to sacrifice men in the course of their advance. These had been needed to mask Antwerp, hold down central Belgium and besiege the the fortified towns of Givet

French soldiers at the Marne
The battle was fought in open country and the soldiers used hedges, ditches and sunken roads for cover. If there was none, they dug rudimentary trenches and foxholes.

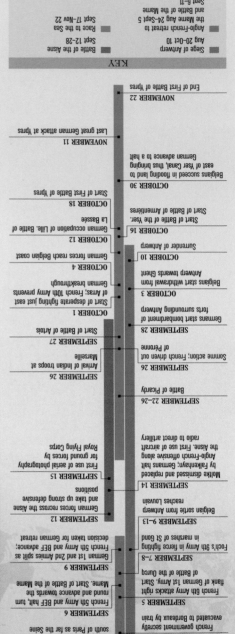

THE MARNE AND THE RACE TO THE SEA

SEPTEMBER – NOVEMBER 1914

At the Battle of the Marne, the French halted their retreat, counterattacked the pursuing Germans and forced them back to the Aisne. The southern half of the front then became fixed and the fighting moved north through Picardy to Flanders in a series of manoeuvres known as the "Race to the Sea". The last major battle of the year in the West was fought at Ypres, after which the Western Front became stabilized from Switzerland to the Sea.

SEPTEMBER 1
Joffre orders armies to fall back south of Paris as far as the Seine

SEPTEMBER 2
French government secretly evacuated to Bordeaux by train

SEPTEMBER 5
French 5th Army and BEF halt, turn round and advance towards the Marne. Start of Battle of the Marne

SEPTEMBER 6
French 6th Army attacks right flank of German 1st Army. Start of Battle of the Ourcq

SEPTEMBER 7–8
German 1st and 2nd Armies split as French 5th Army and BEF advance; decision taken for German retreat

SEPTEMBER 9
Foch's 9th Army in fierce fighting in marshes of St Gond

SEPTEMBER 9–13
Belgian sortie from Antwerp reaches Louvain

SEPTEMBER 12
German forces recross the Aisne and take up strong defensive positions

SEPTEMBER 14
Moltke dismissed and replaced by Falkenhayn; Germans halt Anglo-French offensive along the Aisne. First use of aircraft radio to direct artillery

SEPTEMBER 15
First use of aerial photography for ground forces by Royal Flying Corps

SEPTEMBER 22–26
Battle of Picardy

SEPTEMBER 26
Arrival of Indian troops at Marseille

SEPTEMBER 26
Somme action; French driven out of Péronne

SEPTEMBER 27
Start of Battle of Artois

SEPTEMBER 28
Germans start bombardment of forts surrounding Antwerp

OCTOBER 1
Start of desperate fighting just east of Arras; French 10th Army prevents German breakthrough

OCTOBER 3
Belgians start withdrawal from Antwerp towards Ghent

OCTOBER 4
German forces reach Belgian coast

OCTOBER 10
Surrender of Antwerp

OCTOBER 12
German occupation of Lille. Battle of La Bassée

OCTOBER 16
Start of Battle of the Yser. Start of Battle of Armentières

OCTOBER 18
Start of First Battle of Ypres

OCTOBER 30
Belgians succeed in flooding land to east of Yser Canal, thus bringing German advance to a halt

NOVEMBER 11
Last great German attack at Ypres

NOVEMBER 22
End of First Battle of Ypres

KEY

Siege of Antwerp Aug 20–Oct 10
Battle of the Aisne Sept 12–28
Race to the Sea Sept 17–Nov 22
Anglo-French retreat to the Marne Aug 24–Sept 5 and Battle of the Marne Sept 6–11

The French Army

T HE FRENCH ARMY in 1914 had a peace-time establishment of some 700,000 officers and men. In July 1914 the French army mustered a total of 67 infantry, three colonial infantry and ten cavalry divisions. The standard establishment of a division – with 400 officers and 15,470 men – was two infantry brigades, each with three regiments, a cavalry squadron and a regiment of artillery, plus engineers and support troops. France possessed 173 metropolitan infantry regiments, most with three battalions, one of which was a reserve unit. In addition, in North Africa there were units of XIX Corps,

which was commonly known as l'Armée d'Afrique, while elsewhere in France's empire there was La Coloniale, drawn from regular troops and men from pre-1789 colonies. At the outbreak of war, with first-line reservists, France was able to mobilize about 1,100,000 men. In the course of the war France mobilized a total of between 3.5 and 4 million men.

France, with a relatively small population and low birthrate, raised such numbers only by conscripting 84 per cent of its eligible manpower and, after 1912, extending the period of service to three years. The manpower problem confronting the French army was fundamental, as was the high command's unreasoning adherence to a doctrine of attack.

These were not the only serious problems that it had to face. In the "75" it had the best field gun of any army, but few heavy and medium guns. The standard 1907 St Etienne machine-gun was mechanically unreliable, while the 1893 Lebel rifle was inaccurate. The army's relationship with the government was always difficult, while poor rates of pay meant that in 1914 it lacked its full establishment of officers, warrant officers and NCOs. It has been suggested that about one in ten of its soldiers did not speak French but a local dialect or patois.

Legion d'honneur
France's highest decoration was instituted by Napoleon in 1802.

French artillery
A gun crew demonstrates the loading of a 75-mm field gun, the pride of the French Army and a significant factor in the victory on the Marne in September 1914.

Firearms
The French Lebel was less accurate than the rifles of other armies. Troops at the start of the war were issued with a model dating from 1893. It continued in use throughout the war, but most soldiers preferred the 1915 Berthier.

French uniform of 1914
It seems astonishing today that the French went off to fight the First World War in bright red trousers and dark-blue overcoats. The only concession to camouflage in 1914 was a cover worn over the képi. A less conspicuous blue uniform was introduced in 1915, along with the Adrian steel helmet.

Bayonet
Knapsack
CLASP KNIFE
CANTEEN
FORAGE CAP
Uncovered képi
Képi with cover
8-mm ammunition
ST ETIENNE REVOLVER
The magazine held eight
LEBEL (1893 MODEL)
IDENTITY DISC

BATTLE OF THE MARNE

5–12 SEPTEMBER, 1914

~

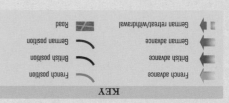

The French are justifiably proud of their victory on the Marne. Their initial offensives against Alsace and Lorraine had been costly failures and the French armies had been wrongly positioned to meet the German invasion. Nevertheless, they were able to redeploy their forces to launch a counterattack against the advancing German armies. The key event in the Battle of the Marne took place just to the east of Paris: the attack launched by the Sixth Army against the right wing of the German First Army led to the creation of a gap between the German First and Second Armies. In heavy fighting further to the east, the French Second, Third and Fourth Armies halted the German Second, Third and Fourth Armies.

and Maubeuge. The Second and Third Armies had each given up a corps while the First Army had had to surrender the equivalent of three corps. Unable to transfer formations from Alsace-Lorraine to the right flank because of the wrecked Belgian railway system, the Germans had neither the manpower nor the time to take or mask Paris. By now there was scarcely any effective control from OHL, the German high command. To make matters worse, the commanders of the three German armies of the right wing – Kluck, Bülow and Hausen – were not noted for their compatibility. This reduced communication between the three armies to a minimum.

A CHANGE OF PLAN

To have attempted to move west of Paris at this point would have left all the advancing German armies west of Sedan over-committed along an extended front. For

this reason Kluck's First Army moved south with the aim of passing to the east of Paris. As the direction of the French Fifth Army's retreat became clear, Kluck shifted the direction of his advance to the southeast. This promised to close

the gap between the First and Second Armies. The Germans still held the initiative and the advantage of numerical superiority. The French attempt to stand on the Somme with the Sixth Army, the BEF and the Fifth Army in the last days of August came to nothing. The Anglo-French retreat continued.

The counter-offensive, September 5–6

Late on September 4, Joffre issued an order to the French armies to stop their retreat on the following day. He also agreed that the French 6th Army should attack the right wing of the German 1st Army just to the east of Paris.

The battlefield

The Battle of the Marne involved a series of engagements stretching from the Ourcq to Verdun. After the general German retreat on September 9, dead men and horses lay scattered over a vast area of northeastern France.

Hit by shrapnel
The transport line of the British 1st Middlesex Regiment comes under fire as it nears the Marne on September 8. The man clutching his head has been badly wounded. The attack left the regiment's water cart riddled with holes.

KEY
French advance
French position
British advance
British position
German advance
German position
German retreat/withdrawal
Road

Sept 5 — French 6th Army encounters Gronau's Reserve Corps. Gronau attacks, defeating leading French divisions

Sept 6 — Gronau withdraws to a strong defensive position west of the Ourcq

Sept 5 — Kluck sends some troops back across the Marne, where he has left only a Reserve Corps, commanded by General von Gronau

Sept 6 — BEF advances northwards

Sept 6 — Kluck's 1st Army advances northwards, but is held back by part of German 1st Army

Sept 6 — Left wing of German 2nd Army forces Foch's 9th Army back south across St Gond marshes

0 mile 10 20 30
0km 10 20 30 40 50

6th ARMY Maunoury — 1st ARMY Kluck — 2nd ARMY Bülow — 2nd ARMY Hausen — 5th ARMY Franchet d'Esperey — 9th ARMY Foch — BEF French — Paris Garrison Galliéni

Oise — Ourcq — Aisne — Vesle — Marne — Petit Morin — Grand Morin — St Gond Marshes — Forest of Reims — Compiègne — Soissons — Juvigny — Fère-en-Tardenois — Château Thierry — Craonne — Reims — Châlons — Epernay — Montmirail — Meaux

FRANCE — GERMANY — BELGIUM — North Sea — PARIS — Marne

THE BATTLE OF THE MARNE

The German First Army, after discounting the possibility of a major French counterattack from the direction of Paris, continued to pursue the BEF and reached the Marne on September 3. On the same day the French abandoned Reims. Joffre, meanwhile, provided himself with a scapegoat for past defeats by dismissing Lanrezac as commander of the Fifth Army and replacing him with Franchet d'Esperey. It was also at about this time that the German high command realized that the First Army was caught between two objectives: it could press forward to complete the encirclement of the French armies east of Paris, but it also had to guard against a counterattack by the Army of Paris.

GALLIENI AND THE PARIS GARRISON

About this time the commander of the Paris garrison, General Joseph Gallieni, in effect assumed a field command. The garrison had recently been strengthened by the arrival of North African troops by train and the despatch of reinforcements from the Alsace-Lorraine sector. The French also became aware of German intentions to pass to the east of Paris. Captured documents, taken from a German corps, outlined the First Army's proposed line of advance from the Oise to the Ourcq. On September 3 the French government left Paris for Bordeaux and Joffre was still insistent on a general retreat as far as the Seine. Gallieni and his staff, however, had now had confirmation of the German change of direction from aerial reconnaissance and glimpsed the possibility of mounting a counter-offensive.

Throughout September 4 Gallieni sought to secure Joffre's agreement to his proposed attack, to which the BEF and the French Fifth Army had to contribute. It was not until late on this day that Joffre authorized the halting the Anglo-French retreat and ordered general offensive operations for September 6, as Gallieni had requested.

THE FRENCH 75-MM FIELD GUN

DEVELOPED IN THE 1890s, the French "75" marked a revolutionary change in the design of field artillery. Its hydraulic recoil mechanism enabled very rapid, accurate fire without the need to re-lay the gun after each shot. The "soixante-quinze" had a crew of nine and a six-horse team to pull the gun, along with its ammunition limber. The gun enjoyed great success at the Marne, both in support of attacking infantry and halting German advances with volleys of shrapnel. However, it lacked the power or high trajectory to be effective against well-made trench systems.

The gun normally fired 6 rounds per minute, but when the need arose, crews could manage up to 20 rounds per minute
Bullet-proof shield · *Recoil mechanism* · *Shoe brake* · *Time fuse* · *Impact fuse* · *SHRAPNEL SHELL* · *HIGH EXPLOSIVE SHELL*

The battle develops September 7–8

Fierce fighting took place in many parts of the region: on the Ourcq, on the Petit Morin and in the Marshes of St Gond. The French did not have the best of all these encounters, but succeeded in enlarging the gap in the German line.

Sept 7 — Kluck orders III and IX Corps north of the Marne to participate in counterattack against French 6th Army
Small detachments of 1st Army left to observe Allied movements
Sept 8 — Surprise attack by French 5th Army across the Petit Morin River forces Bülow to pull back his right flank
03:00 8 Sept — German attack forces Foch to retreat 5 km (3 miles)

The German retreat September 9–12

Although none of the German armies had suffered a serious defeat, the position of the First and Second Armies had allowed the BEF and the French 5th Army to march into the gap between them. Since the German First Army stood in danger of being completely cut off from the other armies, the order was given to retreat to the Aisne.

Sept 9 — BEF crosses Marne, dividing German First and Second Armies
Sept 9 — Bülow orders Second Army to retreat
Sept 12 — German armies cross the Aisne pursued by British and French
Sept 9–12 — French 5th Army able to advance unopposed to the Aisne
Newly formed German 7th Army arrives to fill gap between 1st and 2nd Armies

Captured on the Marne
A column of German prisoners is escorted to captivity after the battle by French cuirassiers in their plumed helmets.

On September 5 the German First Army advanced on the Grand Morin River with four corps spread over 50 km (30 miles) and closed to within 8 km (5 miles) of the BEF and the French Fifth Army.

The other German armies to the east, however, were encountering unanticipated resistance and the German First Army was made aware, by a liaison officer, Colonel Richard Hentsch, that the high command wanted it to retire north of the Marne. As it was, on September 5 and 6 the attack by Manoury's Sixth Army against the right flank of the German First Army just to the east of Paris forced Kluck to change his plans. The German forces facing Manoury amounted to one Reserve Corps commanded by General von Gronau. This put up considerable resistance, even launching a counterattack against the leading French formations before withdrawing to positions to the west of the Ourcq River. Galliéni had to rush reinforcements from the city to support Manoury's army. All available forms of transport were pressed into service, including 600 Renault taxis. These made two trips each, carrying five men at a time, thus transporting 6,000 soldiers to the front. Their contribution to the battle brought them lasting fame as "the taxis of the Marne".

This new development forced Kluck to turn his army westwards. On September 7–8 he redeployed forces from its centre and left flank to support Gronau on the threatened right flank. In doing so, the First Army became separated from the Second Army to the east. It was into the gap thus presented that the BEF and the French Fifth Army

A NEW PHASE OF THE WAR

To the west was an open flank, stretching from Compiègne to the sea and from the Somme to Antwerp. This was an area in which both sides had formations but neither had the upper hand. In the aftermath of the German retreat from the Marne,

advanced on the morning of September 9, and it was among the congested columns in the rear of the First Army that the German decision to conduct a general withdrawal was taken that same day. With communications between the German First and Second Armies, and between the high command and these two formations, all but collapsed, the decision was taken by Hentsch. He ordered the First Army to withdraw to the Soissons area (see map page 55). With the information that a new army was being raised at St Quentin, he drew the approximate line to be reached during this withdrawal phase on a map provided by the First Army's chief of staff. By the 12th the German First Army had retired behind the Aisne, and only the Allies' lack of fresh troops with which to exploit German disarray had prevented the withdrawal from degenerating into a rout.

I spend my day and night in a trench. I have got a hole, partly burrowed out and partly roofed over with branches, just big enough to lie down, it is rather monotonous. I get out for meals but I have to be with my guns day and night as we are in the most forward trench waiting for the attack that never comes, as a matter of fact I think our position is too strong for the Germans' liking, they shell us constantly but we laugh at them from our burrows like rabbits. I couldn't tell you why we are fixed like this but we shall be very glad when we move forward again as this cave life is not to our liking.

CAPTAIN ARTHUR MAITLAND, 2ND BATTALION
ESSEX REGIMENT, IN A LETTER TO HIS PARENTS
FROM THE AISNE, SEPTEMBER 30, 1914

and with manoeuvre impossible in the static conditions east of Reims, the attention of both sides focussed on the Aisne and the open flank.

THE BATTLE OF THE AISNE

Events on the Aisne and to the north unfolded more or less simultaneously, though it was to be the operations on the Aisne that were to become the better known. Here, on the high ground north of the river, the German retreat was halted and fresh troops moved up to close the 30-km (18-mile) gap between the First and Second Armies. At this point Moltke was dismissed as German chief of staff and replaced by the Prussian war minister, Erich von Falkenhayn. The positions the Germans established on the Aisne were easily defended, being sited on a ridge along the north side of the river. This sector of the Western Front came to be known as the Chemin des Dames after the road that had been built along the ridge in the 18th century for the daughters of Louis XV to go for drives in their carriages.

British and French forces, arriving on the Aisne one day behind the First Army, attacked across the river immediately but against an enemy that had established a rudimentary trench system and held major advantages bestowed by choice of ground. The main Allied efforts were made on September 13–14, but to little purpose, and late on the 14th the French and British began to entrench.

French troops awaiting an attack
This staged French photograph of 1914 shows troops entrenched in a commanding position with an aeroplane overhead ready to spot any movement by the enemy. The reality of trench warfare was not quite so neat and tidy.

Blowing up a bridge over the Aisne
As the Germans retreated over the Aisne, they blew up bridges after they had crossed, making it difficult for the British and French to follow. They failed to destroy all the bridges, however, and the Allies were able to cross and mount attacks on the new German positions.

JOHN FRENCH
~

FRENCH HAD BEEN a successful cavalry commander during the South African War of 1899–1902. This led to his being chosen to command the BEF in August 1914. He was, however, to prove inadequate to the task.

French suffered a complete loss of confidence when forced to retreat after his first engagement in August at Mons, and Kitchener, the British Secretary of War, had to make a personal visit in September in order to strengthen his resolve. He was persuaded that the British forces should join the French counter-offensive on the Marne, where victory temporarily boosted his confidence. However, his uncertainty as a leader returned in 1915, manifesting itself in errors of judgement during the Artois-Loos offensive in September and October. His difficulties were compounded by his poor relationship with the French commanders and with his own field officers, and in December 1915 he was replaced by Douglas Haig.

For the remainder of the war, French served as commander of the British home forces, in which role he had responsibility for dealing with the 1916 Easter Rising in Ireland. He was later made Lord Lieutenant of Ireland.

British troops in Flanders
A column of British soldiers advances in single file across a field in Belgium in October 1914. At this stage of the war units were still operating in areas where neither side was aware of the enemy's strength.

THE RACE TO THE SEA

On September 14 the German high command instructed its forces on the Aisne to pin down the Allied troops, while an attempt was made to outflank them by moving troops to the west. Some three days later Joffre issued similar orders to the French. As a result the Battle of the Aisne continued until September 27, when it was allowed to die.

In the meantime, both the French and Germans made unsuccessful attempts to outflank the other, first in the region around Noyon on the 18th and then on the upper Somme on the 23rd/24th. As the battle moved northwards through the fields of

Picardy and Artois towards the Belgian border, both sides continued to try to outflank the enemy, but neither could secure sufficient advantage of position and numbers. In the first days of October the French retained Arras and La Bassée in the face of determined German attacks, but were obliged to cede Lille and Lens before the two sides fought each other to a standstill in this sector (see map page 62).

This sequence of manoeuvres came to be known, rather confusingly, as the "Race to the Sea". Neither side was actually trying to reach the sea before the other, it was just that each failed attempt

The retreat from Antwerp
Cars line up in one of Antwerp's main squares in readiness for the evacuation in the final days of the siege. The decision to evacuate most of the Belgian field army was taken on October 6. Its commander, King Albert, left Antwerp around noon on the 7th.

to sidestep the enemy's forces happened to extend the entrenched front line further to the north and closer to the English Channel.

THE FALL OF ANTWERP

The end of the Battle of the Aisne coincided with the start of German siege operations at Antwerp. After the Germans' triumphal progress through central Belgium in the third week of August, some 70,000 Belgian troops took refuge in Antwerp, the "national redoubt". From there they mounted two sorties and sent saboteurs into German-occupied territories. The second sortie on September 9–13 penetrated as far as Louvain. For more than a month the German forces around Antwerp could do no more than mask the city and contain the garrison's sorties, but at the end of September the situation changed. Beginning on the 28th, with 160

ARMOURED CARS

IN THE MOBILE WARFARE that marked operations in Belgium and northern France in the last stages of the "Race to the Sea", primitive armoured cars could be seen driving along the flat roads of Flanders. The first to use them were the Belgians. The RNAS (Royal Naval Air Service) had a squadron of planes based at Dunkerque that flew reconnaissance sorties over the area. They also had a number of cars, used both for reconnaissance and for going to the rescue of pilots who had been shot down. As such journeys became more hazardous, the cars were provided with improvised armour of boiler plate. Finally it was decided to order customized cars from Rolls-Royce, fully enclosed in armour with a revolving turret. Unfortunately, by the time they arrived in December, the brief period of mobile war was already at an end.

Revolving turret

Machine-gun

The chassis was that of a Rolls-Royce Silver Ghost

THE LAST DAYS OF MOBILE WAR

Meanwhile German cavalry was operating in the No Man's Land between Ypres and Lille and German and Allied forces were working their way northwards from the Somme in their indecisive attempts to outflank each other. They clashed around Arras and Lens on the October 7 and around Hazebrouck and Armentières on the 8th. This meant that there was virtually no room left in which to manoeuvre.

To the north, the Belgian army decided to stand on the Yser. The river was canalized along its last stretch flowing from Dixmude to the sea, and its high embankments commanded the low-lying land to the east, making it a good position to defend. The Belgians would have to face the re-formed German Fourth Army, reinforced by troops freed after the fall of Antwerp. This army, under the command of Duke Albrecht of Württemberg, prepared for a possibly decisive offensive along the coast and from Ypres against the ports of Boulogne and Calais.

the big guns pounded the forts, the field artillery bombarded the trenches that ran between the forts with a mixture of high-explosive and shrapnel shells.

On October 6, when the Belgian defensive line behind the Nete River was forced, the decision was taken to abandon the city. King Albert and the Belgian government left the following day for Ostend. With German forces south of Antwerp trying to cut off the Allied line of retreat, some of the garrison were captured or crossed the border into the Netherlands, where they were interned. The city was finally occupied on October 10.

To the west of Antwerp, Belgian and French forces rejected the possibility of standing on the Terneuzen Canal, which linked Ghent to the sea. Instead they began to concentrate in front of Bruges. The British 7th Division was landed at Zeebrugge on October 6 and advanced as far as Ghent. It then retreated to join the other Allied forces around Ypres.

German forces in Belgium

Infantrymen enjoy the luxury of motorized transport during the fighting in Belgium in 1914. Most of them are wearing *Pickelhauben* (spiked helmets), but cloth camouflage covers to stop them glinting in the sun.

heavy and super-heavy siege guns in the line, the Germans set about the systematic destruction of the city's outlying fortifications.

TOO LITTLE, TOO LATE

Though a small British force of Royal Marines arrived overland in Antwerp on October 4, the morale of a garrison that believed itself to be otherwise abandoned was low. The Belgians' doubts about the strength of Antwerp's fortifications proved well-founded. They were no match for the Germans' super-heavy siege artillery: the formidable Krupp 420-mm "Big Berthas" that had done so much damage at Liège, backed up by highly effective Austrian 305-mm Skoda howitzers. While

Belgian carabineers

The carabineers with their distinctive top have played a major role in the defence of Antwerp. The Belgians used small carts drawn by dogs to carry machine-guns, ammunition and even wounded men.

THE BRITISH ARMY OF 1914

THE BRITISH ARMY of 1914 contained no conscripts – it was a small professional army of 250,000 men. With a history of reliance on the all-powerful navy for the security of the British Isles, there had been no need to maintain a vast standing army like that of Germany, France or Russia. In 1914 Britain sent an expeditionary force of six infantry divisions and one cavalry division, some 150,000 men, to the aid of France. In August four divisions moved up onto the French left flank to face the German armies advancing into France from Belgium. In October, when the British were engaged in fierce fighting at Ypres, they were joined by an Indian corps and some Territorial units. By the end of the year, the BEF had been reduced to half its original strength, with over 30,000 killed and more than 50,000 wounded. A new army was needed; it would be raised from the men who responded to the call for volunteers made in August 1914 by Lord Kitchener, the minister for war.

British Hussars advancing in open country

In 1914 cavalry was used mainly to screen the flanks of infantry formations and for reconnaissance. Here the Eleventh Hussars move north to Flanders in the final stage of the "Race to the Sea."

British uniform and equipment

The British went to war in the khaki they had worn since the South African War (1899–1902). A major innovation in 1916 was the introduction of steel helmets.

ENTRENCHING TOOL

WIRE CUTTERS

CLASP KNIFE

WATER BOTTLE

Bayonet

Knapsack

WEBLEY REVOLVER

LEE ENFIELD .303 RIFLE AND AMMUNITION

Scottish troops marching to the front
In 1914 many Scottish regiments fought in their kilts and glengarry caps. The Germans were astonished at the sight and the German press carried some highly fanciful artistic impressions of the Scots in battle.

Indian troops
The Indian Corps landed at Marseille in September 1914 and saw action at Ypres in October and November. Here men of the 129th Baluchis have improvised a defensive position on the outskirts of the town of Wystschaete, to the south of Ypres.

THE FINAL PHASE OF THE RACE TO THE SEA

The final phase of the "Race to the Sea" is usually reckoned to be synonymous with the First Battle of Ypres. In reality the last Allied and German offensives in Belgium and France before the front stabilized resulted in four battles fought on a 56-km (35-mile) sector from La Bassée to the sea between October 16 and November 11. At the outset there were many gaps in both fronts, but neither side was able to exploit them. The combination of a lack of room in which to manoeuvre, the speed with which reinforcements were moved into this sector, and the fact that neither side possessed any advantage of position and timing that enabled it to dictate events, ensured that these battles ended indecisively.

In part, the course of these final-phase operations was shaped by the occupation of Lille on October 12, which gave the Germans the key industrial centre of northern France even before their main effort opened on the Yser on the 16th. It was in an attempt to retake Lille that the British launched two offensives, also on the 16th. These resulted in battles around La Bassée and Armentières, in which some British formations found themselves opposed by the same German formations they had faced on the Aisne. With no advantage of numbers, artillery or timing on which to base their offensives, the British were held and, in some areas, ultimately thrown back beyond their original start lines.

THE FIRST BATTLE OF YPRES

Even before these British efforts faltered, however, the focus of attention had switched to the north. On October 16 French cavalry and the British V Corps began to move forward from Ypres, only to be confronted on the 18th by three corps of the German Fourth Army. On the same day French armies in the north were ordered to hold rather than attempt to advance. Meanwhile to the south of Ypres the German Sixth Army advanced to recapture recent losses around Armentières. By the 26th the Allied defences around Ypres had been reduced to a salient at no point more than 8 km (5 miles) from the city. French forces had, however, arrived to take over the northern part of the British line.

In the last days of October the crisis of the battle to the north along the Yser was reached. In order to halt a much superior enemy that had fought its way across the Yser and was threatening to breach the Nieuport-Dixmude embankment, the Belgians, having ruled out a further withdrawal, decided on the drastic measure of flooding a large area of low-lying land. They did this by opening the sluice-gates to the sea at high tide. The operation had to be perfectly timed and the first attempts failed. Eventually a large area east of the Yser between Nieuport and Dixmude was successfully flooded, bringing large-scale operations in this area to a halt after October 30.

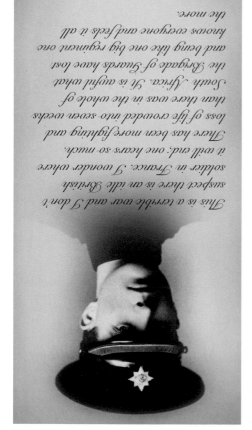

This is a terrible war and I don't suspect there is an idle British soldier in France. I wonder where it will end; one hears so much. There has been more fighting and loss of life crowded into seven weeks than there was in the whole of South Africa. It is awful what the Brigade of Guards have lost and being like one big regiment one knows everyone and feels it all the more.

LIEUTENANT NEVILLE WOODROFFE, 1ST BATTALION IRISH GUARDS, IN A LETTER TO HIS MOTHER. WOODROFFE WAS KILLED IN ACTION AT YPRES ON 16 NOVEMBER

"...of the 1,100 officers and men that came out at the start we have about 80 men left. I believe Yeadon and you have plenty of soldiers at home. Well, we could do with a few here."

CORPORAL GEORGE MATHESON, B COMPANY, 1ST BATTALION, THE QUEEN'S OWN CAMERON HIGHLANDERS, WRITING AFTER THE FIRST BATTLE OF YPRES

After more than a week of heavy but inconclusive fighting along the Ypres salient, on October 30 the Germans began a major attempt to secure the city, their main effort being made by a reinforced Sixth Army between Messines and the Menin Road. The kaiser had optimistically established himself with his field headquarters in Flanders in the expectation of a triumphal entry into Ypres along the Menin Road on October 31.

In the first two days of the offensive, the Germans made – by the standard of later battles for the salient – substantial gains. The British defence was almost reduced to breaking point. On the 31st the village of Gheluvelt on the Menin Road was defended by the remnants of five British battalions, reduced to about 1,000 men, the strength of a single battalion. This tiny force managed to hold off an attack by 13 German battalions for over an hour. Gheluvelt eventually fell, but in the heavily wooded country on either side of the Menin Road German attacks lost their cohesion. The superior fieldcraft and marksmanship of the British defenders gave them a telling advantage over the young, inexperienced German formations.

Last Attempt at a Breakthrough

With French forces stabilizing the line, German attacks around the salient continued for a week as the German high command hesitated between making a final effort at Ypres and switching forces to the East to support the Lodz offensive. A renewed effort, along the entire front between Dixmude and Messines, was ordered for November 10. What

remained of Dixmude was taken, but no gains of any significance were registered elsewhere. On the 11th the Prussian Guard, despite breaking the British line, was cut to pieces in an action that effectively marked the end of the battle. After that the Germans undertook only local offensives in order to improve their tactical position in readiness for the coming winter. The battle is reckoned to have finally ended on the 22nd, two days after the BEF was relieved by the French.

The Stabilized Front

The battles of the final phase of "The Race to the Sea" are significant for three reasons. First, they were the last battles of the opening phase of the war and represented the failure of both sides to turn the other's flank and maintain the momentum of mobile warfare. Second, political considerations now determined that the Allies, having held on to their positions, including a small part of Belgium, at very heavy cost, could not voluntarily withdraw from any part

The Formation of the Western Front

From September to November 1914 the fighting in France moved steadily northwards. Once the Germans had dug in along the Aisne in mid-September, the action switched to the open flank to the northwest. A series of attempts by both sides to turn the enemy's flank brought the action north to Belgium, where the Allied line joined up with that of the Belgian army retreating from Antwerp.

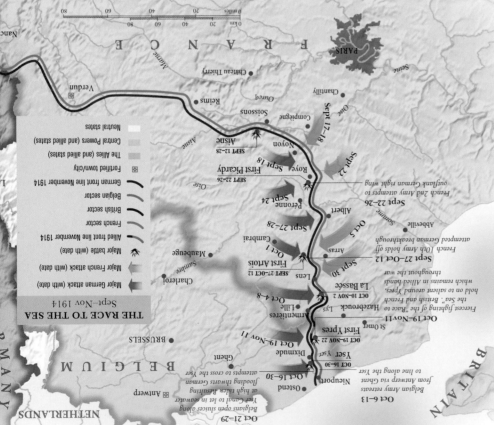

THE RACE TO THE SEA
Sept–Nov 1914

- Major German attack (with date)
- Major French attack (with date)
- Major battle (with date)
- Allied front line November 1914
- French sector
- British sector
- Belgian sector
- German front line November 1914
- Fortified town/city
- The Allies (and allied states)
- Central Powers (and allied states)
- Neutral states

0 km 20 40 60 80
0 miles 20 40 60 80

NETHERLANDS · Antwerp · BRUSSELS · Ghent · BELGIUM · GERMANY · Ostend · Nieuport · Dixmude · Yser · BRITAIN · Lys · Lille · Armentières · Hazebrouck · St Omer · First Ypres · La Bassée · Lens · First Artois · Arras · Cambrai · Albert · Somme · Abbeville · Péronne · Roye · First Picardy · Noyon · Oise · Aisne · Soissons · Compiègne · Chantilly · Ourcq · Reims · Château Thierry · Marne · Seine · PARIS · Verdun · Nancy · FRANCE · Charleroi · Sambre · Maubeuge · Namur

Oct 21–29 · Oct 6–13 · Oct 16–30 · Oct 10–30 · Oct 19–Nov 11 · Oct 19–Nov 22 · Nov 1 · Oct 4–8 · Sept 30 · Oct 1 · Oct 5 · Sept 27–Oct 12 · SEPT 27–Oct 12 · Sept 27–28 · Sept 24 · Sept 22–26 · Sept 22 · SEPT 22–26 · Sept 18 · SEPT 12–28 · Sept 17–18

Belgians open sluices along Yser Canal to let in seawater at high tides. Resulting flooding thwarts German attempts to cross the Yser

Belgian Army retreats from Antwerp via Ghent to line along the Yser

Fiercest fighting of the "Race to the Sea." British and French hold on to salient around Ypres, which remains in Allied hands throughout the war

French 10th Army holds off attempted German breakthrough

French 2nd Army attempts to outflank German right wing

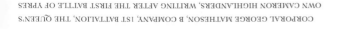

Refugees fleeing Ypres
Scenes like this were common all over western Belgium, as families – their children and a few possessions loaded into carts – fled from the advancing German armies.

of the front. This was despite the limited value of what they held and the fact that the Germans occupied superior positions along virtually the whole of this sector. Third, the final phase of operations witnessed an appalling blood-letting. The German initiative throughout most of this phase was the result of having to hand formations hastily raised from the class of 1914, many of them recruits with just two months' training. The loss of so many of them at Ypres led to the battle being known as the "Massacre of the Innocents".

THE COST OF FIRST YPRES

British, French and German casualties at the First Battle of Ypres totalled 250,000. British losses, which left the battalions sent to France in August with an average of one officer and 30 men of their original establishments (about 1,000 men), prompted the comment that "The high command and staff officers survived: the old army was beyond recall." So, too, were both sides' hopes of a short war and early victory. The Kaiser reluctantly accepted that there was to be no breakthrough along the Belgian coast and a tiny corner of Belgium remained in Allied hands. The salient around Ypres would see many more battles, but would never fall to the Germans.

THE KINDERMORD
~

AT THE OUTBREAK OF WAR, over 35,000 German university and technical college students volunteered enthusiastically for the army. They received just eight weeks training – much of it from elderly officers of the reserve whose military ideas were rooted in the Franco-Prussian War of 1870–71 and who had little idea of the killing power of modern artillery and machine-guns. Instead of being divided up and sent to different units, almost all these volunteers went to make up the numbers in the hastily re-formed German Fourth Army. On October 20 Falkenhayn sent this army to the support the Sixth Army in a desperate attempt to break through in Flanders. The losses sustained as the students and other young men were launched against the Allied lines were more horrific than any experienced by the Germans to date. One of the worst episodes was at Langemarck to the northeast of Ypres on November 10. The slaughter came to be known as the *Kindermord* (the Massacre of the Innocents) and the verdict of those who witnessed it and survived was: "The men were too young and the officers too old."

Youthful enthusiasm
Students in Berlin cheer the declaration of war at the beginning of August. By November many of these young men, and thousands like them from all over Germany, lay dead on the battlefield of Ypres.

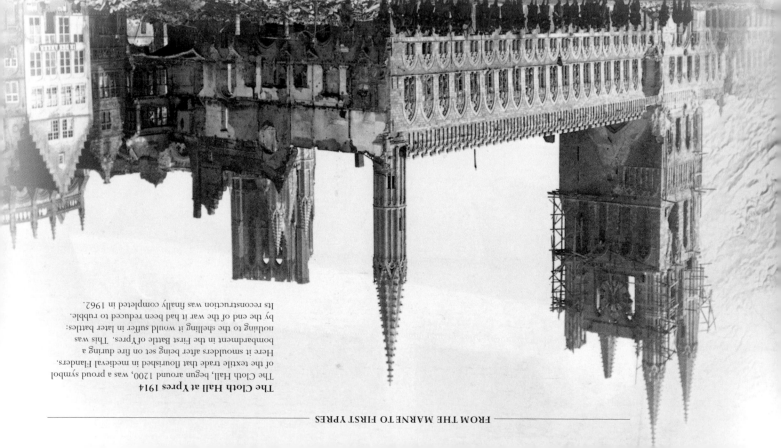

The Cloth Hall at Ypres 1914
The Cloth Hall, begun around 1200, was a proud symbol of the textile trade that flourished in medieval Flanders. Here it smoulders after being set on fire during a bombardment in the First Battle of Ypres. This was nothing to the shelling it would suffer in later battles: by the end of the war it had been reduced to rubble. Its reconstruction was finally completed in 1962.

New Offensives in the East

Austro-Hungarian troops behind the line
An Austro-Hungarian infantry regiment enjoys a moment of respite from the war on the Galician front. In the autumn of 1914 the Russians came perilously close to crushing the Austro-Hungarian armies in this sector.

By October 12 they had almost reached Ivangorod and were about 20 km (12 miles) from Warsaw. Within another five days, however, the Central Powers' intentions had unravelled, the chief reason being that the Russian high command had correctly anticipated the German move. As the German Ninth Army came to the Vistula, two armies were committed to trying to hold German forces in the area above Warsaw, while elements from no fewer than four armies crossed the river below Warsaw in an attempt to strike at the Ninth Army's open left flank. As this threat materialized, the Germans had to abandon their offensive and began to withdraw.

BECAUSE OF THE DIFFICULTIES of the Austro-Hungarian armies in Galicia during early September, the Germans decided on an offensive against Warsaw. This opened on September 29. Ironically, with the defeated Austro-Hungarian armies reaching the safety of the Tarnow-Gorlice position in the first days of October, the immediate crisis facing the Central Powers had passed. Indeed, with the Austro-Hungarian high command having realized that the Russian forces that had advanced across Galicia were mostly unsupported cavalry, its forces went over to the offensive on October 4.

FIRST ADVANCE ON WARSAW

Przemysl, besieged by the Russians on September 24, was relieved by the Austro-Hungarian First Army on October 9, by which time elements of the Ninth German Army had reached the Vistula.

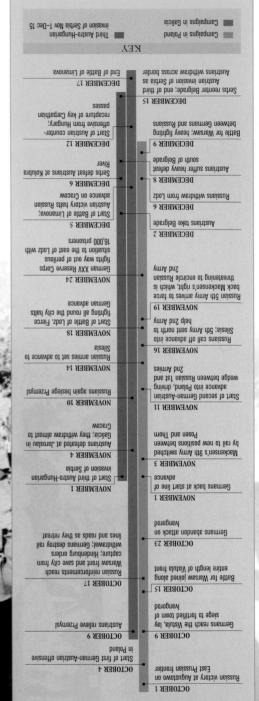

POLAND, GALICIA AND SERBIA
OCTOBER – DECEMBER 1914

In the closing months of 1914, war on the Eastern Front was exceptionally mobile. The Germans launched an offensive on Warsaw, but withdrew, allowing the Russians to advance towards Silesia. The Germans then struck again from the north, but were halted at Lodz. The Austro-Hungarians fell back almost to Cracow, but defeated the Russians in December, when they also made a third unsuccessful attempt to invade Serbia.

KEY
- Campaigns in Poland
- Campaigns in Galicia
- Third Austro-Hungarian invasion of Serbia Nov 1–Dec 15

OCTOBER 1 — Russian victory at Augustowo on East Prussian frontier

OCTOBER 4 — Start of first German-Austrian offensive in Poland

OCTOBER 9 — Germans reach the Vistula, lay siege to fortified town of Ivangorod

OCTOBER 9 — Austrians relieve Przemysl

OCTOBER 15 — Battle for Warsaw joined along entire length of Vistula front

OCTOBER 17 — Russian reinforcements reach Warsaw front and save city from capture; Hindenburg orders withdrawal; Germans destroy rail lines and roads as they retreat

OCTOBER 23 — Germans abandon attack on Ivangorod

NOVEMBER 1 — Germans back at start line of advance

NOVEMBER 1 — Mackensen's 9th Army switched by rail to new positions between Posen and Thorn

NOVEMBER 3 — Start of third Austro-Hungarian invasion of Serbia

NOVEMBER 4 — Austrians defeated at Jaroslau in Galicia; they withdraw almost to Cracow

NOVEMBER 11 — Start of second German-Austrian advance into Poland, driving wedge between Russian 1st and 2nd Armies

NOVEMBER 10 — Russians again besiege Przemysl

NOVEMBER 14 — Russian armies set to advance to Silesia

NOVEMBER 16 — Russians call off advance into Silesia; 5th Army sent north to help 2nd Army

NOVEMBER 18 — Start of Battle of Lodz. Fierce fighting all round the city halts German advance

NOVEMBER 19 — Russian 5th Army arrives to force back Mackensen's right, which is threatening to encircle Russian 2nd Army

NOVEMBER 24 — German XXV Reserve Corps fights way out of perilous situation to the east of Lodz with 16,000 prisoners

DECEMBER 2 — Austrians take Belgrade

DECEMBER 5 — Start of Battle of Limanova; Austrian victory halts Russian advance on Cracow

DECEMBER 6 — Russians withdraw from Lodz

DECEMBER 6 — Serbs defeat Austrians at Kolubra River

DECEMBER 8 — Austrians suffer heavy defeat south of Belgrade

DECEMBER 9 — Battle for Warsaw; heavy fighting between Germans and Russians

DECEMBER 12 — Start of Austrian counter-offensive from Hungary; recapture of key Carpathian passes

DECEMBER 15 — Serbs reenter Belgrade; end of third Austrian invasion of Serbia as Austrians withdraw across border

DECEMBER 17 — End of Battle of Limanova

Russian troops advancing through barbed wire
Trenches and defensive systems did not present enormous obstacles on the Eastern Front at this stage of the war as the front line shifted almost on a daily basis.

J. OSKINE IN *LE CARNET D'UN SOLDAT*

A short while ago when we marched through Galicia and constantly expected to meet the enemy, every soldier was supposed to have not just the regular amount of 120 cartridges, but much more. Sometimes, every one of us had up to 300 cartridges. They weigh almost one pud (16 kg/35 lb). On those long marches, these heavy loads bothered the men. To remedy the situation they threw the cartridges into the ditches where no one picked them up.

Russian infantry receiving a fresh issue of ammunition

crush Russian forces against the upper Vistula.

Central Powers' plan to clear western Poland and German Ninth Army's right flank. Thus evolved the by the promise of German reinforcements, began to thin their forces in Galicia in order to support the same time, the Austro-Hungarian armies, reassured the rear of the Russian armies to the south. At Thorn sector in readiness for an offensive against to move the Ninth Army north into the Posen-mobility provided by their railways, they were able Russian plans. As a result of the superior strategic provided the Germans with the chance to frustrate Russian advance across a devastated western Poland intentions and order of battle. The slowness of the ciphers, by late October were aware of Russian Germans, having broken the Russian signals offensives to failure. Even more seriously, the forces, however, the *Stavka* in effect condemned both

against both enemies. By dividing its available sought to compromise by authorizing offensives against the weaker enemy, but in the event the *Stavka* that the main effort be made in western Galicia.

The Russian Southwest Front command insisted the inferior Austro-Hungarian armies.

German sector of the front or the positions held by high command, was whether to move against the immediate problem faced by the *Stavka*, the Russian them to move against Silesia. However, the gathered in a position and strength that would allow dilemma. For the first time Russian armies were turn, presented the Russian high command with a Russian armies into western Poland. This, in its the Central Powers by bringing no fewer than four German offensive worsened the strategic position of But this relief was short-lived and the failure of the hard-pressed Austro-Hungarian armies in Galicia. that it provided immediate relief to the October 1914 was successful in the sense

The German offensive of September–

RUSSIA POISED TO ADVANCE

attempt in the near future.
intention, merely ensured a renewed invalidated the original German bank of the Vistula. Failure had not renew its attempt to clear the west the Posen-Thorn area in order to transporting the Ninth Army to redeployed their forces by train, advance. The Germans then swiftly order to forestall a general Russian thorough destruction of communications in on its original start line, having conducted a November 1 the German Ninth Army was back of Przemyśl to withstand a second siege. By abandon most of its gains and to leave the garrison To the south the Austrian First Army was obliged to

The siege of Przemyśl
A slow-moving column of ox- and mule-wagons brings supplies to the Russians besieging Przemyśl in Galicia. The town was under siege from September 24 to October 9, then again from November 10 to March 22, 1915.

LODZ AND LIMANOWA

NOVEMBER – DECEMBER 1914

~

It was in the heavy fighting at the end of 1914 that the Eastern Front became fixed. By the end of the year an almost continuous front stretched from East Prussia to the Carpathians in the south. The key battles in this process were Lodz, where the Russians halted a determined German attempt to break through towards Warsaw, and Limanowa, where the Austro-Hungarians drove back the Russians who were threatening to take Cracow.

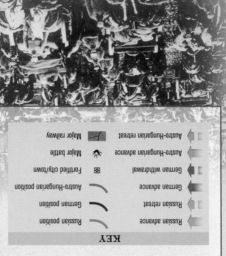

BALTIC SEA
RUSSIAN EMPIRE
GERMANY
AUSTRIA-HUNGARY
BERLIN
Warsaw
Lodz
VIENNA
Limanowa

KEY

Russian position	Russian advance
German position	Russian retreat
Austro-Hungarian position	German advance
Fortified city/town	German withdrawal
Major battle	Austro-Hungarian advance
Major railway	Austro-Hungarian retreat

THE BATTLE OF LODZ

The German offensive opened on November 11 from positions between the Warta and Vistula and immediately broke through a poorly deployed and even more poorly commanded Russian First Army. Within five days, the Germans, with a potentially decisive superiority of numbers, had fought and won a battle at Kutno, split the Second and First Armies and were closing on Lodz.

On November 16, however, the *Stavka* halted the Russian offensive in western Poland and ordered the Fifth Army north to support the Second Army in the defence of Lodz. As a result, on November 18-19 the Germans pressed forward in the belief that all the Russian armies were in retreat and that Lodz would fall. In the event, the Russian Second Army managed to hold the German right flank. The Fifth Army, after a march of some 110 km (70 miles) on appalling roads in just two days, losing half its men in the process, moved to counter the German XXV Corps as it tried to encircle Lodz.

A CONFUSED OUTCOME

Had the Russian First Army moved in support, the German left flank would have been overwhelmed, but a combination of courage and luck, and ineptitude on the part of the Russian First Army's commander, allowed XXV Corps to extricate itself. The Germans fought their way out of a seemingly hopeless position, bringing with them 16,000 prisoners and 64 captured guns. After facing the prospect of disastrous defeat, the Russians had briefly enjoyed the expectation of victory, but in the end the battle could not be counted a victory for either side. In the aftermath, the *Stavka* decided to concentrate on operations against Austria-Hungary in Galicia and the Carpathians.

THE BATTLE OF LIMANOWA

To the south, the battle developed along lines that neither side had anticipated. The Austro-Hungarian high command had assumed that German success would weaken Russian forces in the north and that the Galician front would remain quiet. Both these assumptions proved incorrect. Though the Habsburg Second Army's offensive opened on November 16 and met with early local success, the Russians proved stronger than expected and their Fourth Army yielded little ground. On the right flank, the consequences of having stripped the front had to be paid as the unsupported Russian Third Army, advancing across the San, moved into the Tarnow area by November 20. With the Germans held before Lodz, and unable to provide the support that had been promised, the Austro-Hungarian forces, with their left flank held and right flank crumbling as Russian pressure mounted, faced exactly the same danger as they had nearly three months previously at Lemberg. By November 25, the Russian Fifth Army, having played its part in stopping the German offensive at Lodz, turned south to face the Austrian Second Army, which was forced to withdraw. The situation now facing the Austro-Hungarian forces had become desperate. However, the decision was taken to withdraw most forces to the Cracow area and to move the Fourth Army south of the Vistula in order to take the Russian Third Army in the flank as it approached the ancient Polish capital. Despite the morale-sapping defeats that Habsburg armies had sustained over the

German supply column

The campaigns of late 1914 saw German and Russian troops covering enormous distances as they crossed and recrossed Poland. Road and rail links rapidly deteriorated, causing problems of supply for both sides.

Russian Maxim gun

The Russian machine-gun was similar to the German Maxim, but heavier and more difficult to transport. Here a Maxim is mounted on a motorcycle sidecar for use against aircraft.

Russian prisoners captured in Poland
This group of prisoners being escorted by German reserves during the Polish campaigns of late 1914 reflects the wide range of peoples serving in Russia's armies.

previous three months, the Fourth Army, supported by the German 47th Reserve Division, moved onto the offensive in the last days of November. In fierce battles around around the towns of Lapanow and Limanowa, the Russian Third Army was beaten and forced to retreat to the east, and the threat to Cracow was eliminated. Perhaps even more significantly, the activities of the Russian Eighth Army were halted. This army had advanced to the Carpathians, where it had secured various passes and was preparing for what would have been a barely opposed advance into the plains of Hungary. Its operations were halted in order to concentrate

The German attack on Lodz November 1914
In the north, the German Ninth Army executed a bold manoeuvre, redeploying by train in order to launch an attack between the Russian First and Second Armies. To the south the Russian armies advanced slowly on a wide front, their objectives an invasion of Silesia, an offensive against Cracow and to take the passes through the Carpathians.

Austro-Hungarian recovery December 1914
At the start of December the Russians were confident of taking Cracow and advancing into the Carpathians, but attacks by the Austrian 4th Army on the flank of the Russian 3rd Army south of Cracow proved the turning point in the campaign.

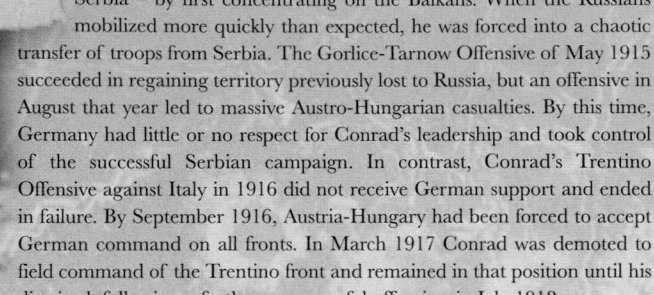

FRANZ CONRAD VON HÖTZENDORF

~

AUSTRO-HUNGARIAN CHIEF OF STAFF from 1906, Conrad von Hötzendorf (1852–1925) had been a close associate of the assassinated Archduke Franz Ferdinand. At the outbreak of war, he attempted to handle his twin objectives – the defence of Galicia and the invasion of Serbia – by first concentrating on the Balkans. When the Russians mobilized more quickly than expected, he was forced into a chaotic transfer of troops from Serbia. The Gorlice-Tarnow Offensive of May 1915 succeeded in regaining territory previously lost to Russia, but an offensive in August that year led to massive Austro-Hungarian casualties. By this time, Germany had little or no respect for Conrad's leadership and took control of the successful Serbian campaign. In contrast, Conrad's Trentino Offensive against Italy in 1916 did not receive German support and ended in failure. By September 1916, Austria-Hungary had been forced to accept German command on all fronts. In March 1917 Conrad was demoted to field command of the Trentino front and remained in that position until his dismissal, following a further unsuccessful offensive, in July 1918.

Russian forces on the upper Vistula. The opportunity that the Russians lost here in November 1914 never presented itself again.

RUSSIAN WEAKNESSES

Thus ended a month in which the Russian and Austro-Hungarian armies had demonstrated remarkable resilience, but from which they, and particularly the Russians, nevertheless emerged as losers. While success on the Eastern Front had eluded the armies of all three empires, the Russian failure was the most acute. Having failed to secure any telling victory when at the peak of their powers in the first weeks of the war, the Russians had subsequently gained no decisive success either in western Galicia or in the Carpathians, and their threat to Silesia had been eliminated. Moreover, their position west of the Vistula was now difficult to defend. This the Russians acknowledged on

Dugout in Galicia
Russian soldiers prepare for a long winter. Campaigning in the Galician sector of the Eastern Front did not stop during the winter of 1914–15. The Russians continued to launch attacks on the passes through the Carpathians.

December 6, when they abandoned Lodz and withdrew to a line closer to Warsaw. The Germans, despite having failed in two major offensives, held a clear strategic advantage at the end of the year.

THE THIRD INVASION OF SERBIA

While the Austro-Hungarians had at least managed to regain some of the ground lost to the Russians in Galicia, they still had embarrassing unfinished business in Serbia. A third offensive got under way in November. The Serbian armies, ably led by the veteran Putnik, fell back across the Kolubra River until they reached good defensive positions. The Austrian armies followed, securing Valjevo, though they made slow progress in increasingly wet and wintry weather. The Serbian army also gave ground in the north, abandoning Belgrade, which was occupied on December 2. On the following day, however, with the front now east of a flooded Kolubra, the Serbian army, having received shipments of French ammunition, mounted its counterattack. Over the next six days they forced the Austro-Hungarian armies to relinquish all their conquests to date and abandon the offensive.

THE COST OF THE CAMPAIGN

With the capital re-occupied by Serbian forces on December 15, the third Austro-Hungarian invasion of Serbia in 1914 was comprehensively defeated. The cost of three offensives had been 227,000 killed, wounded and missing from a total of 450,000 troops committed to the campaigns. Serbian casualties numbered about 170,000 from a total of 400,000. These losses were devastating enough to a small country such as Serbia, but an even greater cost was exacted by the typhus epidemic that ravaged Serbia in the ensuing winter months.

Serbian troops advancing
After a series of well organized retreats, the Serbian army switched to the offensive on December 3. The old king, Peter, appeared in the trenches to urge on the troops.

THE AUSTRO-HUNGARIAN ARMY

IN MILITARY TERMS, Austria-Hungary was the least of the great powers. Its army had the cumbersome title of the *Kaiserliche und königliche Armee* (Imperial and Royal Army) because the Emperor of Austria was also king of autonomous Hungary. In theory the Joint Army, as it was also known, was able to muster 32 infantry and nine cavalry divisions and to put into the field some 1,300,000 officers and men. The real peace-time establishment, however, was about 450,000, and the balance was made up with recalled reservists. In addition, Austria and Hungary each possessed a separate national army, the *Landwehr* and the *Honved* respectively. The reserve (or *Landsturm*) numbered a further million men. With Austria-Hungary calling up only 29 per cent of its eligible manpower for service, the reserve divisions were manned by older conscripts and second-grade conscripts, the latter's period of service being 20 weeks spread over a two-year period.

Austria-Hungary, like Russia, lacked the industrial base needed to wage a protracted war and was not well served in terms of railways and rolling stock for moving formations swiftly between fronts. About one-quarter of all conscripted soldiers were illiterate, and most of the conscripts from the subject nationalities did not understand German or Hungarian. In addition, most of the subject nationalities – Czechs, Slovaks, Poles, Romanians and southern Slavs – had linguistic and cultural links with the empire's various enemies.

Austrian artillery
Despite its lack of a large industrial base, Austria-Hungary did manufacture some good artillery pieces, such as the 305-mm howitzer produced at the Skoda works in Prague.

IDENTITY TAG

COMBAT KNIFE

INFANTRY TUNIC

INFANTRY CAP

Uniform
The blue-grey uniform worn by the Austro-Hungarians at the start of the war dates from 1909. The red stripes on the collar indicate an infantry regiment (in this case a German-speaking one). In 1916 Austria-Hungary adopted a new *feldgrau* uniform similar to that worn by their German allies.

BOOTS

STEYR-MANNLICHER CARBINE (1895 MODEL) AND BAYONET

Firearms
The brand new Steyr factory, completed in 1914, produced the army's 8-mm Mannlicher rifles and carbines, as well as pistols and machine-guns.

STEYR 9-MM AUTOMATIC PISTOL (1912 MODEL)

Cocking lever

Water-filled barrel-jacket to prevent barrel overheating

Muzzle flash hider

Trigger and two-handed grip

Collapsible tripod

Schwarzlose machine-gun
Designed by a German engineer, the Schwarzlose was adopted by the Austro-Hungarian army in 1907. The fact that it had just ten main working parts made it a very reliable gun. Captured Schwarzloses were often used by Russian and Italian troops.

Ammunition box

Belt holds 250 rounds of 8-mm ammunition

THE WIDENING WAR
1914–1916

~

ALTHOUGH THE FIRST WORLD WAR AFFECTED EVERY
PART OF THE WORLD TO SOME EXTENT, IT WAS
ESSENTIALLY A EUROPEAN WAR, CAUSED BY
A BREAKDOWN IN RELATIONS AMONG THE GREAT
EUROPEAN POWERS, THAT SPILT OVER TO OTHER
CONTINENTS. AT THE SAME TIME, AS THE ALLIED
POWERS STRUGGLED TO MATCH THE MANPOWER OF
THEIR ENEMIES, TROOPS RAISED IN DISTANT PARTS
OF THE BRITISH AND FRENCH EMPIRES WERE SENT
TO FIGHT ON THE BATTLEFIELDS OF EUROPE.

~

A long way from home
Algerian troops of the Armée d'Afrique prepare
couscous in a village in northern France in 1914.
At least 150,000 Algerians saw service in France
in the course of the war, along with 39,000
Tunisians and 14,000 Moroccans.

NEW THEATRES OF WAR

WARS HAD BEEN FOUGHT BETWEEN EUROPEANS ON OTHER CONTINENTS BEFORE,

ESPECIALLY IN THE 18TH CENTURY WHEN FRANCE, SPAIN AND BRITAIN COMPETED

FOR COLONIES AND TRADE. BY THE LATE 19TH CENTURY THE SITUATION HAD

BECOME VERY DIFFERENT. COLONIAL CONFLICTS WERE INVARIABLY RESOLVED BY

CONFERENCES AND COMPROMISES. HOWEVER, WHEN FULL-SCALE WAR ERUPTED

IN EUROPE IN 1914, IT IMMEDIATELY SPREAD OUTWARDS TO THE COLONIES.

I T GRADUALLY BECAME CLEAR that the First World War would involve an unprecedented consumption of manpower. Hundreds of thousands of troops were recruited outside Europe, especially from the British and French empires, and they fought in all theatres of the war, including the Western Front – some 80,000 Africans died fighting on the battlefields of Europe.

Staffs may plan strategies, but wars are unpredictable. The expectations of 1914 – that the war would be short and decided in Europe – were totally confounded in a matter of months. The stalemate in the trenches promised a war without foreseeable end, and the entry of other powers – particularly the Ottoman Empire and Italy – extended it to the Middle East and southern Europe. After the Turkish entry into the war in November 1914 the British found themselves involved in three separate, non-European theatres.

GERMANY'S COLONIES

As Germany was late in entering the imperial scramble for "a place in the sun", its colonies tended to be areas of little interest to older competitors. In spite of nervousness about German expansion, the British did not discourage a German takeover of uncolonized territories of Africa – Cameroon, Togo, East Africa and Southwest Africa. Although their total area was huge, they were, for the most part, thinly populated with hardly any resources, industrial development or infrastructure.

The war in Africa was fought predominantly by African, and some Asian, troops, except in Southwest Africa, where the Allies were represented by white South Africans and Rhodesians. Among white colonists, opinion was opposed to war, which they feared would encourage resistance to White rule. The Africans themselves had no say in the matter, and although some African troops were allegedly volunteers, most were, in fact if not officially, conscripts. All the European powers, especially the French, also recruited Africans to fight on the battlefields of Europe.

Germany's African colonies were surrounded by British, French or Belgian possessions and cut off from reinforcement by Allied command of the sea. Inevitably, they were short of supplies, including guns and ammunition (Lettow-Vorbeck's men in East Africa sometimes made their own). Their position appeared hopeless and all had surrendered by the end of 1915 except East Africa, where the last shot of the war was fired

Alpine warfare
Fighting on the Italian front was trench warfare with a difference. Here Austro-Hungarian troops in the Dolomites are dug in at a height of over 3,000 m (10,000 ft).

two weeks after the armistice in Europe. Although campaigns were on a very small scale compared with those in Europe, casualty rates were high, especially among the porters. Many more died from disease and starvation than were killed in battles.

Almost the whole African continent was affected by the war. Oppressive recruitment policies and the general social and economic dislocation caused by war provoked local disturbances in many parts of the continent. However, notwithstanding high rates of desertion, African soldiers in general demonstrated remarkable loyalty and stoicism. Educated Africans generally supported the Allies, hoping – vainly as it turned out – for post-war rewards in the form of civil rights and equal opportunities.

Germany also had a number of tiny bases in the Pacific, important only for their wireless and cable stations, plus the enclave of Tsingtao, seized from China in 1897, which was the only significant German overseas naval base. None lasted long, the islands mostly falling after minimal resistance to Australian and New Zealand forces. Tsingtao required more effort before it fell to the Japanese who, on the basis of their 1911 treaty with Britain, entered the war to further their own long-term strategic aims.

ITALY ENTERS THE WAR

Since unification, Italy had been eager to establish its "Great-Power" status. Despite rapid industrial development in the north, the economy remained primarily agrarian. The division between north and south (where 90 per cent were illiterate) grew wider than ever. Meanwhile, Italy's imperialist dreams led to a disastrous invasion of Abyssinia (Ethiopia) in 1896. Slight consolation for that defeat was gained when Libya was taken from the Turks in 1912.

In 1882 Italy had joined the Central Powers in the Triple Alliance, but the precise terms of the treaty enabled it to declare neutrality in 1914. Italy's chief territorial ambitions were to acquire the Italian-speaking regions within Austria-Hungary – the Trentino, part of the southern Tyrol, Trieste and Istria. These, and more, were promised by Britain and France in the secret Treaty of London, signed on April 26, 1915.

Strategically, Italy was of little significance. It offered few advantages to its new allies apart from forcing the Central Powers to fight on another front. The decision to declare war was taken by a group of ministers backed by the King. Neither the military nor parliament was consulted. Most civilians showed no enthusiasm for the war and the Italian army was seriously under-prepared. Deficiencies in equipment since the Libyan war had not been made good: there were only a hundred or so heavy guns available. General Cadorna, the ruthless chief of staff who enjoyed virtually unlimited authority, had only seven of 25 divisions fully operational.

COUNT LUIGI CADORNA, CHIEF OF THE ITALIAN GENERAL STAFF

"The country was undisciplined and so was the army; we have taken care of the problem by the usual and proper means, the shooting of insubordinates to prevent the sparks from turning into a fire."

"Through the Narrows of the Dardanelles and across the ridges of the Gallipoli Peninsula lie some of the shortest paths to a triumphant peace."

WINSTON CHURCHILL, URGING THE CASE FOR
A RENEWED OFFENSIVE AT GALLIPOLI, SUMMER 1915

Ill-fated British advance into Mesopotamia
British cavalry pass the ruined 6th-century palace of the Persian King Khosrow I at Ctesiphon. In 1915–16 a British force made rapid progress up the Tigris, but after a clash with the Turks at Ctesiphon, turned back to Kut, where it was besieged for almost five months before surrendering.

THE OTTOMAN TURKS

After their defeat in the Balkan Wars (1912–13), the Turks needed a substantial ally. They turned to Germany, which reaped the benefit of its long diplomatic courtship and substantial investments (including the as yet unfinished Berlin–Baghdad Railway). Germany also provided a military mission that undertook to bring the Turkish army up to date and educate a new class of officers.

The Ottoman Empire, historically a land power, had little in the way of a navy. The British had undertaken to rectify this situation, and two dreadnoughts destined for Turkey were being built in British shipyards. On the outbreak of war the British, to Turkish fury, requisitioned them. At that time two German ships, the battlecruiser *Goeben* and the light cruiser *Breslau*, were stationed in the Mediterranean. On August 3 they shelled two French ports in North Africa, then sailed for the Dardanelles, escaping the bemused British fleet, which had expected them to break out west not east. After a short delay, they were admitted to sanctuary off Constantinople. It was Britain's turn to protest, but the Turks claimed the ships were replacements for their lost dreadnoughts. Although the Turkish cabinet was still divided on whether to join in the war, the die was effectively cast. On October 29, the *Goeben* and *Breslau* attacked Russian ports in the Black Sea. Declarations of war duly followed.

TURKISH WAR AIMS

The Turks hoped to restore their authority where it had been lost or superseded, chiefly in the Balkans and North Africa. Their strategy was based on political rather than military considerations and committed them to an impossible number of major enterprises, fighting simultaneously against Britain and Russia with little aid from their allies. Their first and heaviest campaign was fought against their traditional enemy, Russia. In the winter of 1914–15 Enver Pasha, the Turkish minister of war, chose to launch an offensive across their common border in the Caucasus, in spite of the hostility of the terrain.

In North Africa the Italians had taken advantage of Turkish weakness to acquire Tripolitania and Cyrenaica in 1912. Farther east, Egypt was still nominally within the sultan's dominions but it had been administered by the British, ostensibly "advising" the Khedive, ever since their troops crushed a nationalist revolt in 1882. In November 1914 the Khedive proclaimed his loyalty to the sultan, principally because he wished for German favour (and perhaps because he happened to be in Constantinople at the time). To the Germans the

Suez Canal, closed to them by the British, was an attractive strategic target. Egypt therefore became the objective of the second Turkish offensive of the war early in 1915.

PERSIA AND MESOPOTAMIA

In the Middle East the situation was more complicated. Persia was dominated by European powers, but in 1907, after a century of rivalry in the region, Russia and Britain, worried by German expansion, reached an agreement to respect Persian independence. The two powers carefully defined their own spheres of interest, Russian in the north and British in the south. In practice this was little short of annexation: the Anglo-Persian Oil Company's refinery at Abadan became virtually an outpost of the British Empire.

On the outbreak of war the Persian government declared its neutrality, but Britain, wary of the Turks and anxious to protect its oil interests, moved troops to Bahrein (Bahrain) in the Gulf. When Turkey entered the war nearly two months later, they advanced to Shatt al-Arab, the great channel formed by the confluence of the Tigris and Euphrates, which the Turks claimed as their territorial waters. Turkish forces in Mesopotamia were thin and scattered, a factor that encouraged the British in an over-ambitious advance.

THE DARDANELLES CAMPAIGN

Similarly thinly defended was Gallipoli, the Turkish peninsula on the European side of the Dardanelles, one section of the straits that divide Europe from Asia. Allied possession of the straits could lead to the capture of Constantinople and the reopening of the route to the Black Sea and Russia's southern ports. The motive for an attack on the Dardanelles was a request from Russia (January 2, 1915), hard-pressed by the Turks in the Caucasus, for relieving action by their allies. Such an initiative also appealed to the British and French as an alternative to the impasse on the Western Front. One keen supporter was Winston Churchill, at the British admiralty, who had sent ships to bombard the forts at the mouth of the Dardanelles soon after Turkey entered the war. Attempts to force the straits by naval power alone failed and it was decided that an amphibious operation was necessary. Thus was born the disastrous Allied expedition to Gallipoli.

The *Goeben* and *Breslau* at Constantinople
The German battlecruiser Goeben (right) and her escort the Breslau (left) escaped their British pursuers in August 1914 to reach the safety of the Dardanelles. The ships were then renamed and nominally purchased by the Turkish navy.

The Dardanelles Expedition

WHEN IT WAS FIRST MOOTED, the idea of a Dardanelles venture seemed an appropriate way to make use of British sea power. British ships had bombarded the entrance to the straits on November 4, 1914, even before hostilities had officially begun, and on December 13 the submarine *B11* sank the Turkish guardship *Messudieh* at Chanak Kale. These two attacks sacrificed the element of surprise by alerting the Turks to British intentions. The Turks set about strengthening their defences, sowing 344 mines in the straits by March 1915 and siting torpedo tubes at the Narrows. Between February 25 and March 14 the British carried out bombardments and put ashore landing parties to destroy Turkish positions. In spite of this, British and French attempts to sweep the straits failed ignominiously in the face of Turkish artillery.

After these setbacks, London decided that an amphibious assault might be necessary, the navies being given one last chance to force the straits unaided. The attempt was made, with 16 battleships, on March 18. Three were sunk, one beached, and two severely damaged, while the minefields guarding the Narrows were untouched. These failures reflected the essence of the Dardanelles problem: a naval assault could not prevail because Turkish guns could not be silenced until the minefields were cleared, and the minefields could not be cleared until the guns were silenced.

CHANGE OF PLAN

The belated decision was taken to conduct a full-scale amphibious operation to clear the Turkish guns from the landward side. In the absence of proper liaison arrangements between army and navy and with a lack of specialist landing craft, preparations were far from perfect. Nevertheless, by April 21 the newly arrived commander, General Ian Hamilton, had assembled 77 ships at the island of Lemnos and 75,000 men – the ANZAC Corps, the Royal Naval Division, the British 29th Division and one French Colonial division. The time spent in this effort, however, allowed the Turks to reinforce and reorganize their troops under German command. Beaches that could be assaulted were lightly held while strong reserves were deployed locally.

In the trenches at Anzac Cove An Australian sniper aims his home-made periscopic rifle. In Gallipoli's cramped, shallow trenches with the Turkish lines so close, periscopes became essential equipment.

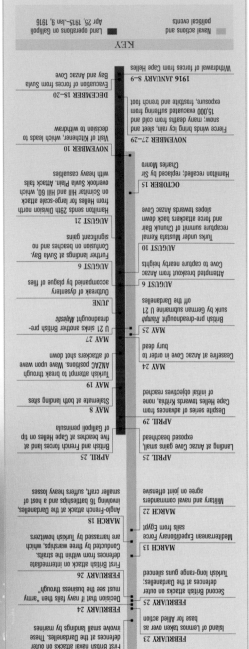

THE GALLIPOLI CAMPAIGN
JANUARY 1915 – JANUARY 1916

Of all the Allied campaigns against the Turks, the most notorious was the the futile Anglo-French expedition to the Gallipoli Peninsula in 1915. At first it was hoped that British and French naval power would find a way through the Dardanelles, but repeated attempts to clear the straits failed. The landings in April failed utterly to reach their objectives and the second phase of operations in August was equally unsuccessful.

1915 JANUARY 15
War Council authorizes naval attack on Dardanelles

FEBRUARY 19
First British naval attacks on outer defences at the Dardanelles. These involve small landings by marines

FEBRUARY 23
Island of Lemnos taken over as base for Allied action

FEBRUARY 24
Decision that if navy fails then "army must see the business through"

FEBRUARY 25
Second British attacks on outer defences at the Dardanelles. Turkish long-range guns silenced

FEBRUARY 26
First British attack on intermediate defences from within the straits. Conducted by three warships, which are harrassed by Turkish howitzers

MARCH 13
Mediterranean Expeditionary Force sails from Egypt

MARCH 18
Anglo-French attack at the Dardanelles, involving 16 battleships and a host of smaller craft, suffers heavy losses

MARCH 22
Military and naval commanders agree on joint offensive

APRIL 25
Landing at Anzac Cove gains small, exposed beachhead

APRIL 25
British and French forces land at five beaches at Cape Helles on tip of Gallipoli peninsula

APRIL 29
Despite series of advances from Cape Helles towards Krithia, none of initial objectives reached

MAY 8
Stalemate at both landing sites

MAY 19
Turkish attempt to break through ANZAC positions. Wave upon wave of attackers shot down

MAY 24
Ceasefire at Anzac Cove in order to bury dead

MAY 25
British pre-dreadnought *Triumph* sunk by German submarine U 21 off the Dardanelles

MAY 27
U 21 sinks another British pre-dreadnought *Majestic*

JUNE
Outbreak of dysentery accompanied by plague of flies

AUGUST 6
Attempted breakout from Anzac Cove to capture nearby heights

AUGUST 6
Further landings at Suvla Bay. Confusion on beaches and no significant gains

AUGUST 10
Turks under Mustafa Kemal recapture summit of Chunuk Bair and force attackers back down slopes towards Anzac Cove

AUGUST 21
Hamilton sends 29th Division north from Helles for large-scale attack on Scimitar Hill and Hill 60, which overlook Suvla Plain. Attack fails with heavy casualties

OCTOBER 15
Hamilton recalled, replaced by Sir Charles Monro

NOVEMBER 10
Visit of Kitchener, which leads to decision to withdraw

NOVEMBER 27-29
Fierce winds bring icy rain, sleet and snow; many deaths from cold and exposure, frostbite and trench foot

DECEMBER 18-20
Evacuation of forces from Suvla Bay and Anzac Cove

1916 JANUARY 8-9
Withdrawal of forces from Cape Helles

KEY
Naval actions and political events
Land operations on Gallipoli Apr 25, 1915–Jan 9, 1916

THE OTTOMAN EMPIRE

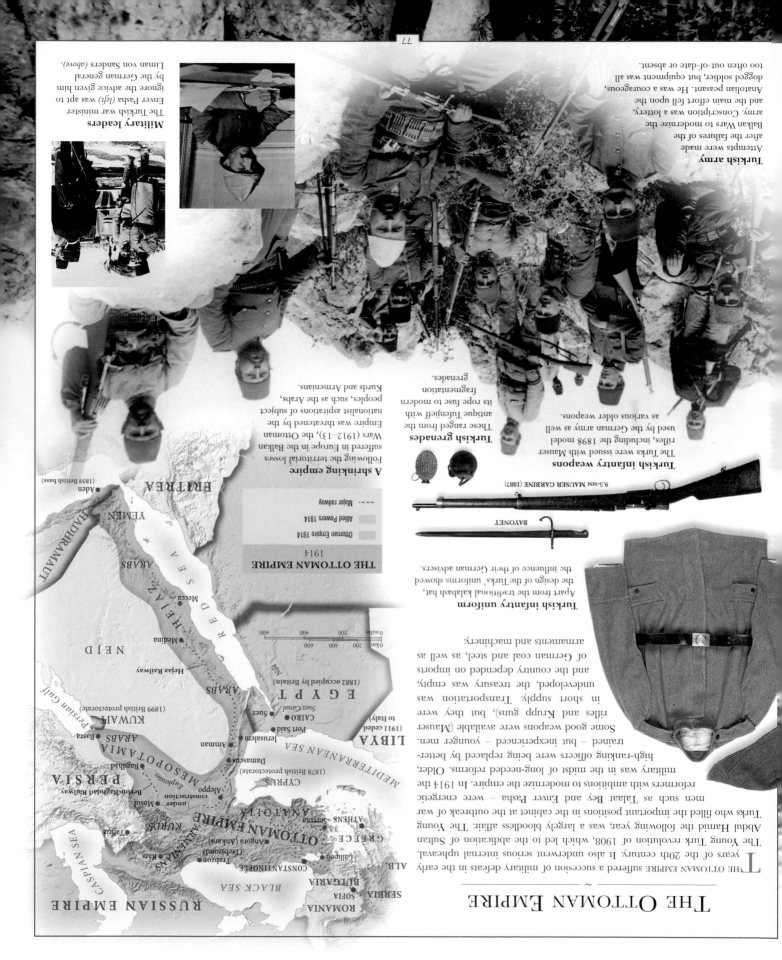

T HE OTTOMAN EMPIRE suffered a succession of military defeats in the early years of the 20th century. It also underwent serious internal upheaval. The Young Turk revolution of 1908, which led to the abdication of Sultan Abdul Hamid the following year, was a largely bloodless affair. The Young Turks who filled the important positions in the cabinet at the outbreak of war men such as Talaat Bey and Enver Pasha – were energetic reformers with ambitions to modernize the empire. In 1914 the military was in the midst of long-needed reforms. Older, high-ranking officers were being replaced by better-trained – but inexperienced – younger men. Some good weapons were available (Mauser rifles and Krupp guns), but they were in short supply. Transportation was underdeveloped, the treasury was empty, and the country depended on imports of German coal and steel, as well as armaments and machinery.

Turkish infantry uniform
Apart from the traditional kalabash hat, the design of the Turks' uniforms showed the influence of their German advisers.

Turkish infantry weapons
The Turks were issued with Mauser rifles, including the 1898 model used by the German army as well as various older weapons.

9.5-MM MAUSER CARBINE (1887)

BAYONET

Turkish grenades
These ranged from the antique Tufenjieff with its rope fuse to modern fragmentation grenades.

A shrinking empire
Following the territorial losses suffered in the Balkan Wars (1912–13), the Ottoman Empire was threatened by the nationalist aspirations of subject peoples, such as the Arabs, Kurds and Armenians.

THE OTTOMAN EMPIRE
1914

	Ottoman Empire 1914
	Allied Powers 1914
- - - -	Major railway

0 km   200   400   600
0 miles   200   400   600

Turkish army
Attempts were made after the failures of the Balkan Wars to modernize the army. Conscription was a lottery, and the main effort fell upon the Anatolian peasant. He was a courageous, dogged soldier, but equipment was all too often out-of-date or absent.

Military leaders
The Turkish war minister Enver Pasha (*left*) was apt to ignore the advice given him by the German general Liman von Sanders (*above*).

RUSSIAN EMPIRE

BLACK SEA

CASPIAN SEA

BULGARIA
SOFIA
ROMANIA
SERBIA
ALB.
GREECE
ATHENS
CONSTANTINOPLE
Gallipoli
Trabzon
(Trebizond)
Kars
Tabriz
Angora
(Ankara)
Smyrna
ANATOLIA
ARMENIANS
KURDS
OTTOMAN EMPIRE
Mosul
Aleppo
Berlin-Baghdad Railway, under construction
Baghdad
PERSIA
MESOPOTAMIA
ARABS
Damascus
Basra
KUWAIT
(1899 British protectorate)
Jerusalem
Amman
Persian Gulf
CYPRUS
(1878 British protectorate)
MEDITERRANEAN SEA
LIBYA
(1911 ceded to Italy)
EGYPT
(1882 occupied by Britain)
Port Said
CAIRO
Suez
Suez Canal
Nile
NEJD
Medina
Hejaz Railway
Mecca
HEJAZ
RED SEA
ARABS
HADHRAMAUT
YEMEN
ERITREA
Aden
(1839 British base)

THE LANDINGS

With the defence dispersed in order to meet the threat of landings in the Gulf of Xeros, on Gallipoli itself or in Asia, the initiative lay in Allied hands (see maps, pages 80–81). The landings of April 25, however, miscarried by narrow but critical margins. The Anzacs were put ashore 1.5 km (1 mile) north of the intended beaches. The resulting confusion delayed an advance on the Sari Bair ridge, giving the leading elements of the Turkish 19th Infantry Division time to occupy it. Checked and then confined to a very shallow beachhead, the Anzac forces were denied permission to evacuate their precarious, cliff-ledge positions.

The British 29th Division, which consisted of regular soldiers, veterans of garrison duty throughout the British Empire, landed around Cape Helles, the tip of the Gallipoli peninsula, at five beaches, Y, X, W, and S. They were transported in rowing boats towed by steam launches, two of them commanded by naval cadets aged just 13. On V Beach, as troops tried to disembark from the steamer *River Clyde* and the smaller boats accompanying her, they were mown down by Turkish machine-gun and rifle fire, suffering over 1,200 casualties. Forces scheduled for

Turkish camp
Turkish troops held in reserve could enjoy the relative comfort of a military camp. Allies not in the line were shipped back to base on the island of Lemnos.

that beach were diverted to W Beach and, by nightfall on the 25th, footholds had been secured on all five beaches; forces from V Beach had advanced almost to Krithia. There, however, they encountered advancing Turkish forces and, having withdrawn to their beachhead, they evacuated Y Beach on the 26th as a result of confusion of orders. To the south, a continuous front was established on that day, but a general offensive along the line on the 28th failed as fresh Turkish forces were fed into the battle. By May 8 the deadlock at Cape Helles was as complete as that on the Western Front.

THE BRITISH DILEMMA

During the summer the Turks tried to drive the Allies back to the shore with a series of very costly attacks. On May 19 suicidal charges were launched along the whole length of the Anzac front. By noon that day the Turks had suffered 10,000 casualties and over 3,000 dead, dying and wounded lay in No Man's Land. As the bodies decayed in the heat, the situation became unbearable. A truce was arranged for May 24 and for nine hours men from both sides dug graves, many exchanging gifts and fragments of conversation. Equally costly attacks and counterattacks continued at Cape Helles.

A precarious toehold
After the landing on April 25 the troops at Anzac Cove dug in wherever they could. Their makeshift scrapes and burrows on the cliffs offered little protection from enemy shelling.

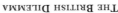

Turkish prisoners
Despite the horrors of the fighting on Gallipoli, the Allied troops respected "Johnny Turk" as a fair and honourable opponent.

throughout the summer with little change in the front line. The Allied forces, living on unsuitable food such as bully beef and biscuits, sharing their crowded trenches with makeshift latrines and millions of flies, were ravaged by dysentery.

THE SECOND PHASE

All the while London grappled with the consequences of failure. The British choice was either to evacuate or to reinforce, but an evacuation, during the short summer nights, was technically impossible. The decision was taken to renew the offensive. A further landing would be made at Suvla Bay, timed to coincide with an offensive from Anzac Cove against the heights of Sari Bair.

The failure of the renewed British offensive in August 1915 has generated much controversy. Apologists for the Gallipoli venture claim that it could have succeeded had the divisions of IX Corps put ashore at Suvla Bay on August 6 pushed forward to secure the Anafarta Ridge – they were barely opposed and should have been able to turn the Turkish defences on Sari Bair. This line of argument has seized on obvious targets: a hopelessly inadequate command system and certain equally inadequate generals. Troops moved to and fro

THE ANZACS

THE AUSTRALIAN AND NEW ZEALAND ARMY CORPS was raised at the beginning of the war. Australia (total population 5 million) sent 322,000 men to fight overseas, New Zealand (1 million) a remarkable 124,000. Anzacs served on the Western Front, in the Middle East and – most notably – in Gallipoli, where their heroic fight in a hopeless cause made a permanent impact, commemorated annually on Anzac Day, April 25.

Australians, with their team spirit and egalitarian scorn for the English class system, received military training at school. The New Zealanders of 1914 mostly sprang from pioneer conditions, reared with guns and spades; moreover, they were culturally committed to the idea of the Empire. The Anzacs came to be regarded as the finest soldiers of the war, and their high casualties reflected their courage and aggression. Australia lost 60,000 men killed, New Zealand 17,000. Yet the survivors of Gallipoli, returning to their Egyptian base, took a more deprecatory view of themselves, and wearily sang:

We are the ragtime army, The A.N.Z.A.C.
We cannot shoot, we won't salute. What bloody use are we?

Before the landings
Troops of the Australian and New Zealand Army Corps (ANZAC) on their way from the Greek island of Lemnos to the landing at Anzac Cove.

across the Suvla Plain, lacking clear orders and maps, or returned to the landing places because they had no water. Hardly any artillery had been landed, so the commanders on shore chose to wait until more arrived. Meanwhile the advance on Sari Bair was being executed with considerable daring and determination. The Anzacs, reinforced by one and a half divisions of British and Gurkha troops, had a clear idea of their objectives, but advancing by night over unfamiliar ground, one of the columns got hopelessly lost. Only small units reached the crest of the ridge at Chunuk Bair and Hill Q, but Turkish reserves, ably directed by Mustafa Kemal, regained the ridge and the moment of opportunity had passed.

ACCEPTING FAILURE

The failure of the August offensive was due to a combination of factors. It was in part the result of IX Corps not having understood its role in a plan that anticipated success elsewhere, in part because the Anzac offensive failed to carry its objectives and in part because of the speed and effectiveness of the

Evacuation of Cape Helles, January 8, 1916
Debris, including unwanted stores and equipment, litters the shoreline at W Beach on Capes Helles. This photograph was taken on the day of the evacuation of British and French troops from the tip of the Gallipoli Peninsula.

reaction of Turkish forces. This last factor is one of particular importance and is often overlooked. Much has been made in British histories of the narrowness of the margin between success and failure, and indeed there were occasions, both in April and August 1915, when victory only narrowly eluded the British. By the same token, the British also came perilously close to comprehensive defeat, most certainly in April. The failure to clear the Sari Bair ridge and the Turkish containment of the beachhead at Suvla spelt the end of British hopes of success at the Dardanelles. Even so, the decision to abandon the expedition was put off for some time. Hamilton was removed from command on October 16 but his successor was in turn removed after having recommended evacuation on the 31st. November, however, saw the onset of winter and, on December 7, the British cabinet authorized an evacuation that was completed, without loss and without any soldiers being left behind, from Anzac Cove and Suvla Bay on December 19–20 and from Cape Helles on January 8–9, 1916.

Recruitment
Young Australians volunteered for the armed services in such numbers that there was no need to introduce conscription.

Comradeship
This photograph of an Australian carrying a wounded friend to the dressing station became an emblem of the spirit of the Anzacs amidst the horrors of Gallipoli.

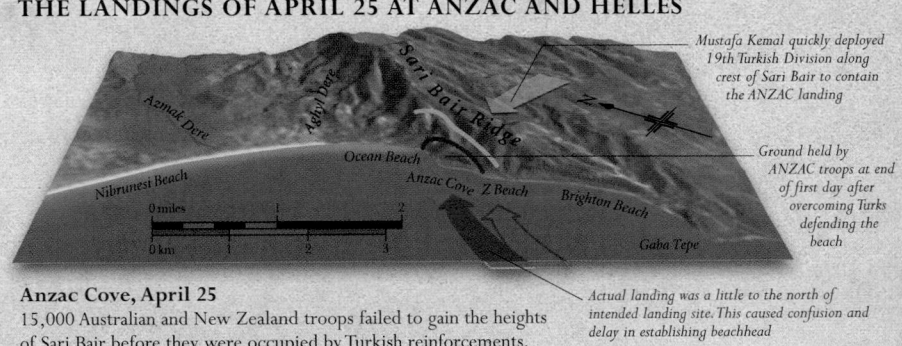

THE GALLIPOLI CAMPAIGN
APRIL 1915 – JANUARY 1916
~

When the Ottoman Empire entered the war in November 1914, the Allies' maritime links with Russia's southern ports on the Black Sea were severed. The British and French determined to to seize the Dardanelles, with the aim of then sailing on to attack the Ottoman capital, Constantinople. It was hoped this might force the Turks out of the war and reopen the sea-route to the Black Sea. After various failed attempts to force the Dardanelles by Anglo-French naval forces, it was decided to land troops on the Gallipoli Peninsula on the European side of the Dardanelles in order to silence the Turkish guns guarding the straits. The two landings of April 25, 1915 both fell far short of their objectives. The troops at Cape Helles and at Anzac Cove were halted by a determined Turkish defence. A renewed offensive came in August with the landing of two fresh divisions at Suvla Bay. Again the offensive was contained by the Turks and, with no prospect of a breakthrough, the Allied troops were evacuated at the end of the year.

KEY

British or Anzac landing/advance	French position
British or Anzac retreat	Turkish position
French landing/advance	Turkish fortified town
Turkish advance	Turkish encampment
Allied objective	Turkish minefield
British or Anzac position	Major battle
	Road

Going through their paces
Australian and British troops exercising at Cape Helles in December 1915, keeping up the illusion for the watching Turks that there was to be no withdrawal from Gallipoli.

Diversionary attack by Royal Naval Division

THE LANDINGS OF APRIL 25 AT ANZAC AND HELLES

Mustafa Kemal quickly deployed 19th Turkish Division along crest of Sari Bair to contain the ANZAC landing

Ground held by ANZAC troops at end of first day after overcoming Turks defending the beach

Anzac Cove, April 25
15,000 Australian and New Zealand troops failed to gain the heights of Sari Bair before they were occupied by Turkish reinforcements.

Actual landing was a little to the north of intended landing site. This caused confusion and delay in establishing beachhead

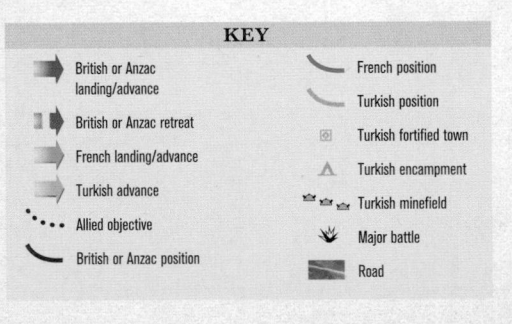

Despite successful unopposed landing, troops here evacuated on April 26 after Turks launch counterattack

Allied warships shell Turkish positions before and during the landings, but their fire is largely ineffective

French landing at Kum Kale

Ground gained by Allies by dusk on first day

The landings at Cape Helles, April 25
Only at V and W beaches did the landings meet serious opposition, the Turks inflicting heavy casualties as the British disembarked.

Disastrous landing of River Clyde; hundreds of disembarking troops mown down by Turkish machine-guns

April 28
A bloody encounter, known as the First Battle of Krithia, results in Allied advance of just a few hundred metres

May 8
Turkish front line

French troops, despite success at Kum Kale, are withdrawn and transferred to the right of British line at Helles

British and French progress at Helles to May 8
Fierce fighting as the British and French struggled towards Krithia resulted in 10,000 Allied casualties in the first three days.

May 6–8
Second Battle of Krithia ends in stalemate, with both the Allies and the Turks securely entrenched

May 8
British and French front line

Anzac Cove
Troops enjoy a period of respite between bouts of Turkish shelling as they walk along the narrow beach at Anzac.

THE EVACUATION
~

THAT THE EVACUATION of Gallipoli was effected without the loss of a single man was a triumph of careful planning. At Suvla and Anzac there were some 83,000 men and 5,000 animals. Troops were taken off night after night, leaving a rearguard of 20,000 to convince the Turks that all was normal. This final group was taken off on the night of December 19/20. Ingenious devices were rigged up to fire the rifles automatically as the trenches were gradually stripped of men. In the end the Turks suspected nothing, nor did they at Helles three weeks later when the procedure was repeated. The Turks attacked on January 7, but were met by such fierce defensive fire that they assumed the Allies planned to maintain the front. That night and the next the remaining troops were evacuated.

Early departures from Suvla Bay
Soldiers being towed away from Suvla on a raft during the days leading up to the final evacuation. This was completed under cover of darkness.

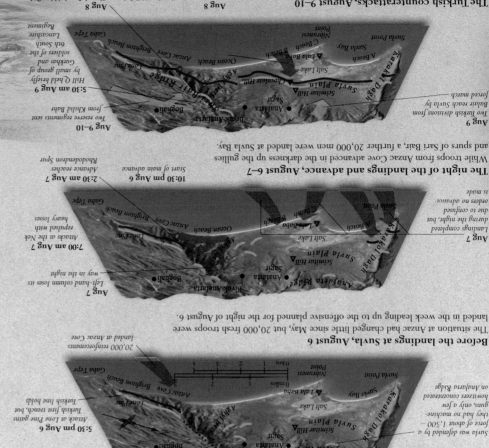

The Turkish counterattacks, August 9–10
Turkish reinforcements swiftly contained the threat at Suvla and drove the Anzacs back from their positions on Sari Bair.

Chunuk Bair held briefly by New Zealand and British troops — Aug 8
Second attack on following day succeeds, but with heavy casualties
Attempt to take Chocolate Hill fails. — Aug 8
5:30 am Aug 9 Hill Q held briefly by small group of Gurkhas and soldiers of the 6th South Lancashire Regiment
Aug 9–10 Two reserve regiments sent from Khilid Bahr
Aug 9 Two Turkish divisions from Bulair reach Suvla by forced march

The night of the landings and advance, August 6–7
While troops from Anzac Cove advanced in the darkness up the gullies and spurs of Sari Bair, a further 20,000 men were landed at Suvla Bay.

10:30 pm Aug 6 Start of main advance
2:30 am Aug 7 Advance reaches Rhododendron Spur
Aug 7 Attacks at the Nek repulsed with heavy losses
7:00 am Aug 7
Aug 7 Left-hand column loses its way in the night
Aug 7 Landings completed during the night, but due to confused orders no advance is made

Before the landings at Suvla, August 6
The situation at Anzac had changed little since May, but 20,000 fresh troops were landed in the week leading up to the offensive planned for the night of August 6.

5:30 pm Aug 6 Attack at Lone Pine gains Turkish first trench, but Turkish line holds
20,000 reinforcements landed at Anzac Cove
Objective of attack from Anzac Cove
Suvla was defended by a force of about 1,500 — they had no machine-guns, only a few howitzers concentrated on Anafarta Ridge

0 km 1 2 3
0 miles 1 2 3

SUVLA BAY AND THE RENEWED OFFENSIVE OF AUGUST 6

The planned landings and routes of advance
The Allies hoped to gain control of the southern half of the peninsula and knock out the guns controlling the Dardanelles in just two or three days.

New minefield laid by Turks on March 8. Four British and French warships struck mines here during naval attack of March 18
Mobile Turkish howitzer batteries active on both sides of the straits
French feint, designed to keep Turkish troops on the Asian side of Dardanelles
First-day objective of Helles landings
Planned direction of advance from Helles
Turkish minefields guarding narrowest parts of the Dardanelles
Most of Turkish 19th Division was concentrated just south of Boghali
Turkish 9th Division was stationed on plateau of Khilid Bahr ready to move to wherever the attack came
ANZAC troops were to cross the peninsula, cutting off Turkish defenders to the south
First-day objective of advance units of ANZAC force
First-day objective of main ANZAC landing force

AEGEAN SEA
DARDANELLES
Cape Helles, W Beach, X Beach, V Beach, S Beach, Sedd el Bahr, Morto Bay, Kum Kale, Y Beach, Krithia, Achi Baba, Maghram, Maidos, Kilid Bahr, Chanak Kale, The Narrows, Boghali
Gaba Tepe, Sari Bair Ridge, Nibrunesi Point, Nibrunesi Beach, Ala Bay, a Point, Salt Lake, Suvla Plain, Biyuk Anafarta, Sagir

0 km 1 2 3 4 5 6
0 miles 1 2 3 4 5

THE STRATEGIC AIMS AND FIRST-DAY OBJECTIVES OF THE LANDINGS

French field kitchen at Gallipoli
The presence of a division of French troops, chiefly North African Zouaves and Senegalese Riflemen, in the Allied landings on Gallipoli is often forgotten. This was increased to two divisions for the renewed offensives in August.

Turkey's War on Many Fronts

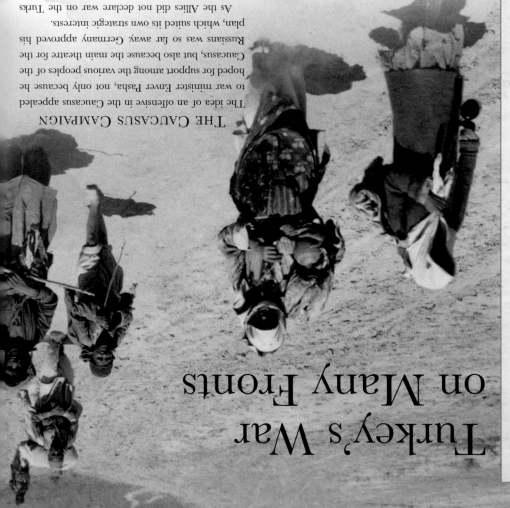

T URKEY'S ENTRY INTO THE WAR dramatically extended the area of fighting. This alarmed the hard-pressed Russians in particular. In the Caucasus, a region conquered by Russia a century earlier, the Russians were worried about the loyalty of their Muslim subject peoples. The Turks were even more concerned by the many Christian Armenian communities on their side of the border.

Turkish prisoners in Ardahan

In the winter of 1914–15 the Turkish Third Army was virtually destroyed and almost all its guns captured. These prisoners were fortunate not to have frozen to death.

THE CAUCASUS CAMPAIGN

The idea of an offensive in the Caucasus appealed to war minister Enver Pasha, not only because he hoped for support among the various peoples of the Caucasus, but also because the main theatre for the Russians was so far away. Germany approved his plan, which suited its own strategic interests.

As the Allies did not declare war on the Turks until November 5, no serious campaigning was anticipated in the Caucasus in the winter of 1914–15. But a Russian advance into eastern Anatolia, checked at Köprüköy, stung Enver Pasha, who took command of the Third Army in person on December 19, into an unwise counter-offensive. The difficulties of campaigning in mid-winter in a region that contained hardly any roads or rail lines (the main means of transport was baggage animals), were seriously underestimated. Enver's plan involved large-scale deployment at an altitude sometimes over 3,000m (9,800ft), in temperatures

CAUCASUS, MESOPOTAMIA AND EGYPT
NOVEMBER 1914 – APRIL 1916

Turkish troops were spread thinly over the Ottoman Empire and Turkish war aims were many and various. The Turks hoped to regain territory lost in recent wars from Russia and Italy and to consolidate their hold over non-Turkish, non-Muslim peoples in their empire. At the same time they needed to oblige their German allies by threatening British interests in the Middle East such as the Suez Canal and Persian oilfields.

1914 NOVEMBER 11
Russian offensive against Köprüköy repulsed by Turks

1914 NOVEMBER 22
Force from India occupies Basra to protect oil pipeline from Persia

DECEMBER 22
Turks launch offensive towards Sarıkamış

DECEMBER 29
Turks stage short occupation of Tabriz in northwest Persia

1915 JANUARY 17
Battle of Sarıkamış ends; Turkish forces, weakened by advancing across mountains in winter, suffer humiliating defeat

Turks assemble troops at Beersheba to cross Sinai and attack Suez Canal

JANUARY 30
Russians recapture Tabriz

FEBRUARY 3–4
Unsuccessful Turkish attacks on Suez Canal

FEBRUARY
Turks initiate policy of deporting Armenians, which is thinly disguised genocide

APRIL 11
British forces led by Sir John Nixon repel Turkish attack on Basra

MAY 19
Russians briefly occupy Van, following Armenian uprising

JUNE 3
British General Townshend takes Amara on Tigris

JULY 25
British occupy Nasiriya on Euphrates

SEPTEMBER 26–28
Battle of Kut al-Amara; British forces defeat Turks

NOVEMBER 22
Start of Battle of Ctesiphon, southeast of Baghdad

NOVEMBER 24
Battle of Ctesiphon ends; British retreat to Kut al-Amara

DECEMBER 7
Turks begin siege of Kut al-Amara

1916 JANUARY 17
Russians force evacuation of Köprüköy, four days after mounting attack

1916 JANUARY 18
British make first of three failed attempts to relieve garrison at Kut al-Amara

FEBRUARY 7
Mus taken by Russian forces

FEBRUARY 11
Russian offensive on Erzurum begins

FEBRUARY 15
Turkish 3rd Army starts to abandon Erzurum, mostly withdrawing towards Erzincan

FEBRUARY 26
Russians take Kermanshah as they advance into western Persia

APRIL 18
Trebizond, abandoned by Turks, is occupied by Russians

APRIL 26
Agreement between British, French and Russians on future partition of Ottoman Empire; British commitments conflict with promises to Arab leaders

APRIL 29
End of siege of Kut al-Amara as British forces surrender to Turks

KEY

Caucasus and Armenia Nov 1914–April 1916	Mesopotamia and Persia Nov 1914–April 1916
Egypt Jan–Feb 1915	

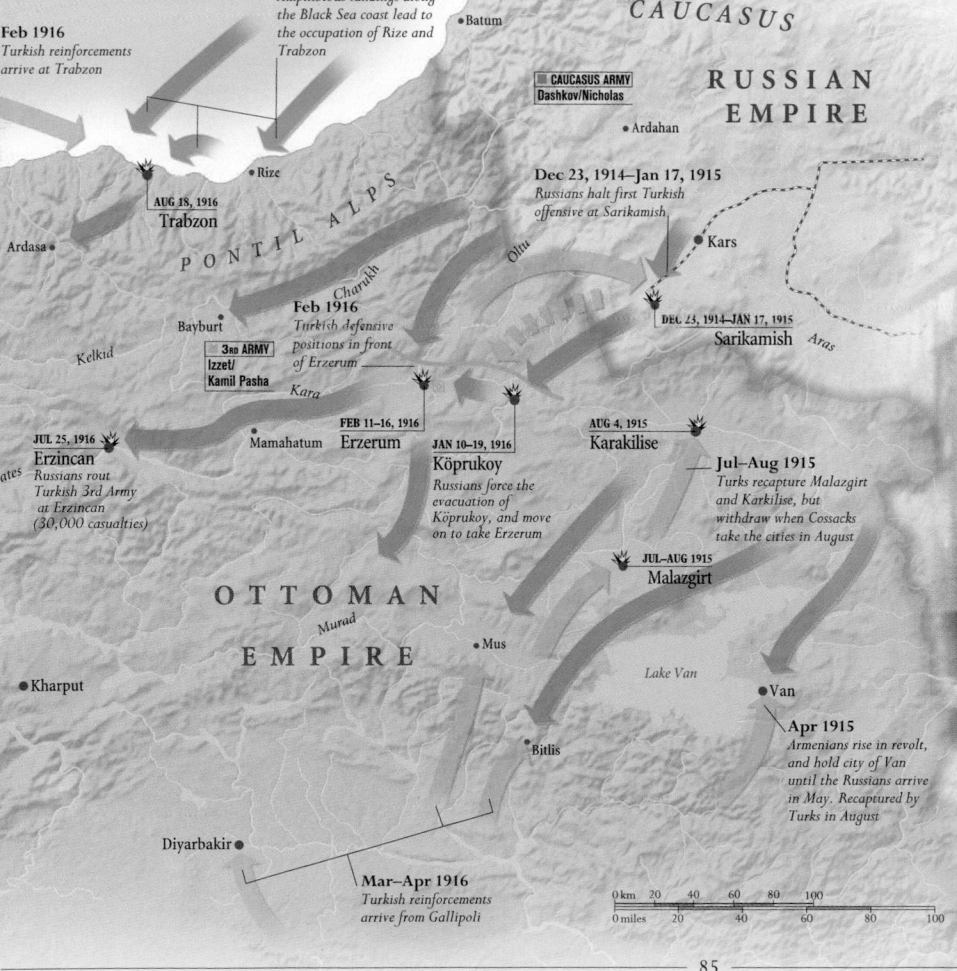

Armenian refugees

The majority of the Armenians killed in 1915 were driven from their homelands into the Syrian Desert. There they either died of starvation or thirst or were killed by Turkish troops or bands of outlaws.

that would freeze an ungloved hand to a rifle barrel on contact. The main objective was the town of Sarikamish, about 45 km (30 miles) south-west of Kars, but by the time the Turks reached it, their X Corps, which spearheaded the attack, had already lost about one-third of its men. Although one Turkish division briefly entered the town, Sarikamish had still not been taken when Russian reinforcements started to arrive by railway from Kars. Enver was reluctant to withdraw and his

Fighting in the Caucasus

The advantage on this front lay with the Russians, but because of commitments on the Eastern Front, they were often unable to exploit their victories. Following the collapse of Russia in 1917 the Turks were able to recover all their lost territory.

troops suffered a disastrous defeat at the hands of the Russian commander, General Mishlaevski. By the time the fighting ended on January 17, the Turkish Third Army had lost up to 90,000 men out of a total of 130,000. According to some estimates, 30,000 Turkish soldiers simply froze to death.

Russia's commitments in other regions prevented the exploitation of this victory until the following winter, when the Russian Army of the Caucasus captured the

Victims of the massacres

Estimates of the Armenians killed range widely: figures as high as 3 million are quoted, but impartial sources suggest a death toll of between 1 million and 1,500,000.

fortress of Erzerum on February 16. Following a series of amphibious operations along the Black Sea coast, Russian forces took the port of Trabzon (Trebizond), disrupting supplies to the re-formed Third Army. Determined resistance by the Turks could not prevent further losses, Bayburt and Erzincan falling in July.

ARMENIAN MASSACRES

As well as fighting the Russians in the Caucasus, the Turks were waging a parallel campaign against their own Armenian subjects. With the rise of Armenian nationalism in the 19th century, relations between the two peoples had deteriorated rapidly. Alleging Armenian support for, and collaboration with, Russian forces, the Turkish authorities began a programme of forced deportation and massacres. The killings continued from April 1915 until 1917. Some groups were murdered in cold blood, others were driven into the desert to die of thirst or starvation. When challenged by the US and other countries, the Turks claimed these horrors were necessary measures of national security; Armenians condemned the policy as nothing short of genocide.

Grand Duke Nicholas in the Caucasus

When he was dismissed as commander-in-chief of the Russian armies in 1915, Nicholas, cousin of Tsar Alexander III, was despatched to take over command of the Army of the Caucasus.

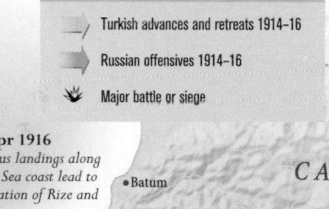

THE CAUCASUS FRONT
1914–1916

↗ Turkish advances and retreats 1914–16

➡ Russian offensives 1914–16

☓ Major battle or siege

BLACK SEA

Mar–Apr 1916
Amphibious landings along the Black Sea coast lead to the occupation of Rize and Trabzon

Feb 1916
Turkish reinforcements arrive at Trabzon

• Batum

CAUCASUS

☐ **CAUCASUS ARMY**
Dashkov/Nicholas

RUSSIAN EMPIRE

• Ardahan

• Rize

AUG 18, 1916
Trabzon

Ardasa •

PONTIC ALPS

Charukh

Dec 23, 1914–Jan 17, 1915
Russians halt first Turkish offensive at Sarikamish

Oltu

• Kars

Feb 1916
Turkish defensive positions in front of Erzerum

Bayburt •

Kelkit

☐ **3RD ARMY**
Izzet/ Kamil Pasha

Kara

DEC 23, 1914–JAN 17, 1915
Sarikamish

Aras

JUL 25, 1916
Erzincan
Russians rout Turkish 3rd Army at Erzincan (30,000 casualties)

Euphrates

Mamahatun •

FEB 11–16, 1916
Erzurum

JAN 10–19, 1916
Köprukoy
Russians force the evacuation of Köprukoy, and move on to take Erzerum

AUG 4, 1915
Karakilise

Jul–Aug 1915
Turks recapture Malazgirt and Karkilise, but withdraw when Cossacks take the cities in August

JUL–AUG 1915
Malazgirt

OTTOMAN EMPIRE

Murad

• Mus

Lake Van

• Van

• Kharput

Apr 1915
Armenians rise in revolt, and hold city of Van until the Russians arrive in May. Recaptured by Turks in August

• Bitlis

Diyarbakir •

Mar–Apr 1916
Turkish reinforcements arrive from Gallipoli

0 km 20 40 60 80 100
0 miles 20 40 60 80 100

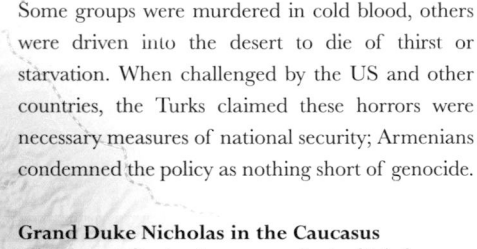

EGYPT AND MESOPOTAMIA

Turkish defeats can be partly explained by the number of campaigns they fought simultaneously. Enver Pasha's ambitious attack in the Caucasus, though the largest, was but one of three offensives they undertook in 1914–15, in addition to fighting elsewhere, notably at Gallipoli, where the Turks won a major victory.

As it became likely that the Turks would side with the Central Powers, Britain took steps to safeguard its interests in the Gulf and in particular the newly important resources of southern Persia that fuelled the new, oil-burning battleships. The Sixth Indian Division was installed in Bahrein (Bahrain) in October and when war was declared, an expeditionary force was sent to the Shatt al-Arab. Within a month it took Basra, the main city of southern Mesopotamia, and advanced to Qurna at the junction of the Tigris and Euphrates.

Persia itself was neutral, but on the outbreak of war the Russians occupied the north and the British parts of the south. The Turks invaded the north and by January 1915 reached Tabriz, before a Russian counterattack drove them back to the border. Minor fighting continued, with Russian cavalry combating Turkish formations and Persian irregulars.

Another Turkish offensive, encouraged by Germany, was aimed at the Suez Canal. The canal was vital to the Allies' communications and its seizure would be a serious setback and an embarrassing blow to the prestige of the British

Scouting over Egypt
A German Rumpler C1 flies over the Pyramids of Giza. The Germans flew bombing raids from Palestine in 1915 in support of the Turkish attack on the Suez Canal.

Empire. The Turks were also keen to regain those parts of North Africa that Italy had wrested from them less than three years earlier.

Egypt was nominally still part of the Ottoman Empire, but the British had exercised political control since the 1880s and the economy was mostly in the hands of Europeans. When the Khedive declared loyalty to his overlord, the Ottoman sultan in Constantinople, the British threw him out and established a "protectorate". They also closed the Suez Canal to their enemies and used Egypt as a staging post for the thousands of imperial troops – Australians, New Zealanders and Indians – making their way to Europe via the canal.

As in the Caucasus, the Turks faced a formidable geographical obstacle. They had to cross the Sinai desert, a hostile landscape without water bar a few wells, depending largely on camels for transport. Moreover, to avoid

detection, the Turks chose the most difficult route.

The task was given to the Fourth Army, based in Damascus and commanded by Ahmad Cemal (Djemal). He was not a soldier by profession, and although he had a gifted German chief of staff, Kress von Kressenstein, the two men did not co-operate well. The Turks had German-made pontoons to cross the canal, and confidently anticipated an Arab revolt in their favour in Egypt. About 50,000 Arab volunteers, including Sinai Bedouin, did join the Fourth Army, but the Egyptian city-dwellers, though they had little love for the British, were not prepared to act on their inclinations, and without their support the Turkish attack had little hope of success.

PROBLEMS OF SUPPLY

The Fourth Army comprised only 19,000 men, which German logistics experts thought was already too many to be supplied across the Sinai (in a study of 1907 the British had calculated that a trans-Sinai dash was only possible for a strike force of two or three thousand). The British had nearly four times as many men in Egypt, though they were widely scattered and of mixed fighting quality.

The objective was well-chosen and the planning was excellent – not a man was lost in the desert – but the Turks still needed the advantage of surprise, an improbable condition. Allied intelligence had suggested a likely invasion from the east and, inevitably, the army was spotted from the air as it advanced across the barren desert. By the time the Turks reached the canal on February 3, the British were ready for them, dug in on the western bank. As the attack was about to start, a sandstorm caused delay and confusion. In a week's fighting, only in

Campaigns in the Middle East
The major offensives in this region – the Turkish attack on the Suez Canal and the British advance into Mesopotamia – were ill conceived. Both broke down as a result of stretched lines of supply and communication.

Transport in Sinai
Camels played an important role in supplying the troops defending Suez and in the later advance into Palestine.

EGYPT AND MESOPOTAMIA 1915–1916	
➤ British offensive	- - - Major railway
▮➤ British retreat	✦ Oil pipeline
— Turkish offensive	▨ Ottoman Empire
▮↗ Turkish retreat	▨ The Allies (and allied states)
✿ Battle or siege	☐ Neutral states

OTTOMAN EMPIRE   **PERSIA**

Aleppo   Mosul

CYPRUS

Homs   Tikrit

Tripoli   Beirut

1915
Turkish troops, attempting to seize the Suez canal, are turned back by British defenders

1916
British build railway across Sinai ready for attack on Palestine

DAMASCUS

SYRIAN DESERT

April 29, 1916
The British surrender Kut

BAGHDAD

**SEPT 26–28, 1915
DEC 5, 1915–APR 29, 1916**
Kut al-Amara

Nov 22–26, 1915
The British advance to Baghdad is turned back at Ctesiphon. The British withdraw to the garrison at Kut al-Amara

NOV 21, 1915
Ctesiphon

JUN 3, 1915
Amara

MESOPOTAMIA

Haifa

Jaffa

JERUSALEM

Gaza

El Arish

Beersheba

May 1915
After the Turks attempt to retake Basra, British troops are reinforced, and move up the Karun valley, forcing a withdrawal to Amara

JUL 24, 1915
Nasiriya

FEB 4, 1915
Ahwaz

MAY 30, 1915
Qurna

Port Said

FEB 3, 1915
Ismailia

CAIRO

Suez Canal
Suez

Petra

Aqaba

ARABIA

Nov 6, 1914
British launch Mesopotamian offensive, taking Basra on Nov 21

NOV 21, 1914
Basra

NOV 21, 1915
Abadan

Fao
Persian Gulf

KUWAIT
(British protectorate)

E G Y P T
SINAI

Nile

0 km   100   200   300
0 miles   100   200   300

two or three places did the Turks manage to erect pontoons across the canal. Their bridging equipment was quickly disabled by Indian troops. Cemal Pasha, who had banked on establishing a bridgehead across the canal immediately and had supplies for only a brief period, broke off the attack in disgust and withdrew under cover of night. The British commander, General John Maxwell, who had planned a purely defensive battle, was not prepared to pursue.

The Turks did not give up the idea of an attack on Egypt and gained a potentially useful ally through the co-operation of the Senussi (Zanussi), an Islamic sect based in Libya but with supporters over a huge region. The Senussi were at first favourable to the British, but their position changed when Italy, which had seized most of the Libyan coastline in 1911–12, entered the war on the Allied side.

The Turkish Fourth Army, however, was in no condition to repeat its march across the Sinai, and although some ambitious schemes were contemplated by the Turks, they achieved little beyond forcing the British to maintain a large garrison in Egypt.

ADVANCE UP THE TIGRIS

In Mesopotamia, General John Nixon, commanding the British and Indian expeditionary force, concluded that its position was vulnerable.

In an attempt to protect his forces around Basra from Turkish attacks, he sent a force of little over a division, under General Townshend, up the Tigris valley to capture the town of Kut al-Amara. Townshend's success in taking Kut at the end of September 1915 inspired a misplaced euphoria that prompted London to authorize him to move directly against Baghdad. Although there were few Turkish forces in the region, it was a foolhardy plan. Townshend's men advanced partly on land and partly by boat up the river. In November, they met a Turkish force at Ctesiphon, 32 km (20 miles) from Baghdad. The battle was indecisive but Townshend, conscious of the fragility of his communications, decided to withdraw to Kut, where his troops dug themselves in within a bend of the Tigris. They were soon encircled by the Turks, who constructed earthworks sufficient to withstand, on the one side, sorties from Kut and, on the other, attacks by a small British relief force. Four attempts were made to relieve Kut. In the last a thousand men died. Shortly afterwards, the annual floods covered the plain, and Kut was cut off beyond hope of relief. Townshend's men were exhausted, under siege for five months with supplies for two, and some Indian soldiers were starving to death rather than eat horsemeat. After the surrender of April 29, 1916, Townshend and his officers were well treated, but the remaining 12,000 British and Indian troops, who were already in poor health, were marched 1,900 km (1,200 miles) to prison labour camps in Anatolia, where more than a third of them died.

Guarding the Suez Canal
ANZAC troops dig gun emplacements in preparation for any renewed Turkish attack on the Suez Canal.

Stripped for action
A party of British signallers manhandles a cablewagon across a Mesopotamian river. Good communications were vital in the desert environment.

The Isonzo Front

ITALY ENTERED the war on May 23, 1915, declaring war only on Austria-Hungary, from which it hoped to gain the territory promised by the Treaty of London, negotiated with the Allies in April. For topographical reasons this was a singularly ambitious task. The border between Austria and Italy, nearly 650 km (400 miles) long, passed through high mountains, which naturally favoured the defence. There were only two areas where the Austro-Hungarian defences might be breached, through the passes to the Trentino to the north, and via the valley of the Isonzo River in the Julian Alps to the east. The Trentino route was ruled out because the passes were in Austrian hands and heavily fortified. The main Italian effort throughout the war was therefore launched across the Isonzo towards Slovenia, Trieste and Istria. This presented huge problems for troop concentration and mobility. The Italian supply lines were always vulnerable to attack from the Trentino, so some forces always had to be diverted in that direction. It also required clearing the vast, windswept Bainsizza plateau to the east, a series of desolate, rocky ridges. The Central Powers were aware of Italy's negotiations with their enemies, and by the time war was declared the Austrians were ready. With only seven divisions in all, they were heavily outnumbered, but were superior in artillery and machine-guns. In initial skirmishes in June, Italian Alpine troops climbed the 2,300-m (7,500-ft) Monte Nero overnight and swept the few defenders from the summit. This early success created unrealistic expectations. The main advance began on June 23 with an artillery barrage that destroyed

Italian gun emplacement 1915

The Italians were very short of artillery, especially heavy artillery, at the beginning of the war. Here a 305-mm howitzer has been installed in the Val Dogna on the Carnic front in order to bombard an Austrian fort.

Trench clubs
Savage hand-to-hand fighting over disputed trenches was a feature of the battles of the Isonzo. Pictured here are two Italian trench clubs and a well-made, flexible Austrian truncheon (centre).

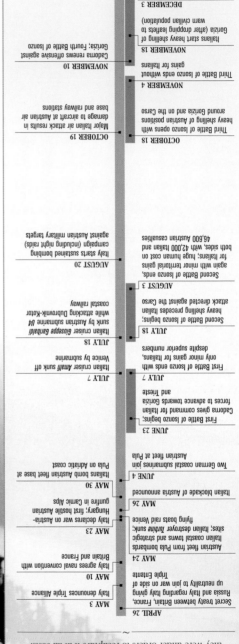

ITALY ENTERS THE WAR
APRIL – DECEMBER 1915

Italy's reason for declaring war was to gain territory, so its armies went on the offensive from the start. The year 1915 was dominated by Italian attempts to break through on the Isonzo River, but there were also naval encounters and bombing raids across the Adriatic. The Austro-Hungarians defended grimly throughout 1915, but whenever they lost territory, even a single hilltop, they were under orders to recapture it at all costs.

APRIL 26
Secret treaty between Britain, France, Russia and Italy regarding Italy giving up neutrality to join war on side of Triple Entente

MAY 3
Italy denounces Triple Alliance

MAY 10
Italy agrees naval convention with Britain and France

MAY 23
Italy declares war on Austria-Hungary; first hostile Austrian gunfire in Carnic Alps

MAY 24
Austrian fleet from Pula bombards Italian coastal towns and strategic sites; Italian destroyer *Turbine* sunk; flying boats raid Venice

MAY 26
Italian blockade of Austria announced

MAY 30
Italians bomb Austrian fleet base at Pula on Adriatic coast

JUNE 4
Two German coastal submarines join Austrian fleet at Pula

JUNE 23
First Battle of Isonzo begins; Cadorna gives command for Italian forces to advance towards Gorizia and Trieste

JULY 7
Italian cruiser *Amalfi* sunk off Venice by submarine

JULY 18
First Battle of Isonzo ends with only minor gains for Italians, despite superior numbers

JULY 18
Italian cruiser *Giuseppe Garibaldi* sunk by Austrian submarine *U4* while attacking Dubrovnik-Kotor coastal railway

JULY 18
Second Battle of Isonzo begins; heavy shelling precedes Italian attack directed against the Carso

AUGUST 3
Second Battle of Isonzo ends, again with minor territorial gains for Italians, with 42,000 Italian and 46,600 Austrian casualties

AUGUST 20
Italy starts sustained bombing campaign (including night raids) against Austrian military targets

OCTOBER 18
Third Battle of Isonzo opens with heavy shelling of Austrian positions around Gorizia and on the Carso

OCTOBER 19
Major Italian air attack results in damage to aircraft at Austrian air base and railway stations

NOVEMBER 4
Third Battle of Isonzo ends without gains for Italians

NOVEMBER 10
Cadorna renews offensive against Gorizia; Fourth Battle of Isonzo

NOVEMBER 18
Italians start heavy shelling of Gorizia (after dropping leaflets to warn civilian population)

DECEMBER 3
Fourth Battle of Isonzo ends, again with minimal Italian gains

KEY

Battles of the Isonzo:
Jun 23–Jul 7, Jul 18–Aug 3, Oct 18–Nov 4, Nov 10–Dec 3

Other events

Italian troops crossing the Isonzo by ferry
The Isonzo front did not simply follow the river. In their initial advance the Italians gained a number of bridgeheads on the east bank, while the Austrians managed to hold on to key defensive positions on the west bank.

High-altitude training
Italian Alpini troops march up a glacier. The Alpini led many of the most daring attacks on the Austro-Hungarian lines as well as arranging the supply of positions high in the mountains.

the monastery of Sveta Gora, a Slovene national treasure, but not many defence posts. Commander-in-chief Cadorna aimed to take Gorizia (whence half the inhabitants had fled) and the bleak Carso plateau, gateway to Trieste. Casualties in the First Battle of the Isonzo (there would be ten more) were heavy – over 30,000 Italians, 20,000 Austrians. A shortage of front-line doctors meant that many Italian wounded were left unattended, and transport problems caused severe shortages of food and water. Some Italian officers forced their men forward at gunpoint, and both sides threw rocks when ammunition ran out (the Italians had no grenades as yet).

On July 7, with Italian advances minimal, Cadorna called a halt to the offensive. Dismissing 27 generals, he blamed the failure on everyone but himself.

The Second Battle of the Isonzo began on July 18, the main objective being Monte San Michele on the edge of the Carso. This time the artillery barrage was heavier and more effective. Every shell bursting in the limestone terrain discharged a hail of rock fragments more deadly than bullets to soldiers without steel helmets. The Italians gained the summit, but were driven off next day in a counter-attack spearheaded by knife-wielding Bosnians. The Italians retook it on July 25, and were again pushed off. The tactics of the Austrian commander Borović were simple: if a position was lost, recapture it immediately.

Fighting on the Carso gradually died away with Trieste still over 30 km (20 miles) distant. A fruitless assault on the upper Isonzo continued, but heroism was unavailing against well-entrenched machine-guns. Cadorna was still convinced he could break through, but he needed two months for recovery and reinforcements – one was the young socialist firebrand Mussolini.

The Third Battle of the Isonzo began on October 18 with a three-day artillery barrage. Gorizia (Görz) was now Cadorna's objective. The Italians reached its suburbs but could not take the town, and the offensive ended at the beginning of November. The Fourth Battle began a week later (November 10) and lasted into December. Italian gains remained insignificant and one regiment mutinied.

The first four battles of the Isonzo
Shots were exchanged all along the front in 1915, but the only serious fighting was on the Isonzo. Estimated Italian casualties were at least 230,000, Austrian about 165,000.

THE ITALIAN FRONT 1915

- Italian advance Jun 1915
- Territory occupied by Italy Jun 1915
- Austrian front line Dec 1915
- Main areas of fighting on the Isonzo River
- Major railway
- The Allies (and allied states)
- Central Powers (and allied states)

AUSTRIA-HUNGARY
CARINTHIA
CARNIC ALPS
JULIAN ALPS
ISTRIA
TYROL
TRENTINO
DOLOMITES
ITALY
A L P S
BAINSIZZA PLATEAU
CARSO (KARST)
Gulf of Venice
Lake Garda

Innsbruck
Linz
Bressanone
Bolzano (Bozen)
Trento (Trent)
Rovereto
Asiago
Arsiero
Feltre
Vittorio Veneto
Udine
Cividale
Tolmein (Tolmin)
Tolmino
Caporetto (Kobarid)
Plezzo
Maggio
Pieve
Fella
Monte Nero
Monte San Michele
Gorizia (Görz)
Montefalcone
Trieste
Treviso
Castelfranco
Montebelluna
Vicenza
Padua
Mestre
Venice
Verona
Verona
Portogruaro

Adige
Piave
Tagliamento
Livenza
Isonzo

2nd ARMY
3rd ARMY
5th ARMY

20 40 60

The war in this theatre was soon concluded with the swift takeover of all the German possessions in the Pacific. The only lengthy operation was the siege of Tsingtao, conducted for the Allies by the Japanese. One potential danger to British interests was the German Far East Squadron, but its commander, Admiral von Spee, chose to sail for the South Atlantic, where his ships were hunted down off the Falkland Islands.

~

SEPTEMBER 2
Japanese land on the Shantung peninsula for attack on Tsingtao

SEPTEMBER 11
Australian force lands at Herbertshöhe in Neu Pommern (New Britain) in the Bismarck Archipelago

SEPTEMBER 22
Arrival of British force at Laoshan Bay to support Japanese attack on Tsingtao

OCTOBER 7
Yap, in the Caroline Islands, occupied by Japanese, who quickly take over the Caroline, Mariana and Marshall Islands

OCTOBER 16
Japanese launch general attack on Tsingtao

NOVEMBER 2
Austrian cruiser *Kaiserin Elizabeth* sunk at Tsingtao

NOVEMBER 7
Surrender of Tsingtao

NOVEMBER 14
Nauru occupied by Australian forces

DECEMBER 1
German squadron succeeds in rounding Cape Horn en route for the Falklands

DECEMBER 14
German armed merchant cruiser *Cormoran* interned at Guam

AUGUST 30
German Samoa occupied by New Zealand forces

SEPTEMBER 7
German squadron under Admiral von Spee cuts British Pacific cable off Fanning Island

SEPTEMBER 17
German New Guinea and surrounding colonies surrender to Australian forces

SEPTEMBER 22
Von Spee attacks Papeete in Tahiti

OCTOBER 16
First New Zealand forces leave for Europe

OCTOBER 17
First Australian forces leave for Europe

NOVEMBER 1
Battle of Coronel in Pacific: von Spee's squadron sinks British ships *Monmouth* and *Good Hope*, with no survivors

NOVEMBER 26–29
Von Spee's ships meet fierce storms off coast of Chile

DECEMBER 8
Battle of Falkland Islands: von Spee's ships caught and destroyed by British squadron; 1,800 men, including von Spee and his two sons, killed

KEY

- ▮ China and the northern Pacific Aug 30–Dec 14
- ▮ Voyage of Spee's squadron Aug 22–Dec 8
- ▮ New Guinea and the South Pacific Sept 11–Oct 17

German Possessions in the East

Japanese battery at the siege of Tsingtao
The Japanese success at Tsingtao was a foregone conclusion. They were able to call on 100 siege guns with 1,200 shells each and also used aircraft to drop bombs.

FROM A BRITISH POINT OF VIEW, the German threat in the Far East was essentially a naval one, specifically the possible depredations the East Asiatic Squadron, commanded by Admiral Graf von Spee and based at Tsingtao, might make on maritime trade and troopships. Although Britain and Japan were allied by treaty, Japan was only obliged to assist Britain in the event of an unprovoked attack on its Far Eastern possessions (chiefly Hong Kong). Other countries with interests in the region – including the USA, Australia, New Zealand and the Netherlands – also feared Japanese expansionism. However, Britain's naval strength in the Pacific was hardly superior to Germany's, and the German ships were more modern. Australia had just five cruisers (one a battlecruiser) and three destroyers, and New Zealand had only begun to train a navy less than a year earlier. In these

A token presence
Japanese soldiers cast curious glances at the South Wales Borderers arriving to join the force besieging Tsingtao.

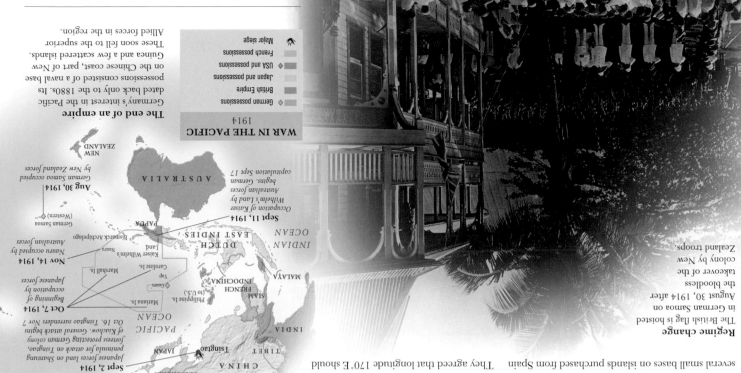

Japan asked Japan for assistance in taking Germany's main overseas naval base, the port of Tsingtao (Qingdao) on the Shantung peninsula. The Japanese operation was supposed to be strictly limited and Chinese neutrality was not to be infringed. On August 23 Japan declared war on Germany.

The Japanese landed forces in Chinese territory – 130 km (80 miles) north of Tsingtao at Lungkow Bay, where they established a supply base, while simultaneously blockading the coast. The main force landed nearer the objective at Laoshan Bay, but still in Chinese territory. The build-up was slow, aggravated by heavy rain, and the main advance only began on September 23. The Japanese had 60,000 men (including one British) and one Indian battalion sent from Tientsin). Meyer-Waldeck, the German commander, having called in every man from out-stations, had fewer than 5,000 men. The heavy guns of the port's fortifications could be trained back to cover the landward approach, but within a month the Germans were running low on ammunition. On November 7 Meyer-Waldeck asked for terms.

MOPPING UP THE ISLANDS

In October the Japanese 1st South Seas Squadron moved into Micronesia, where Germany had several small bases on islands purchased from Spain

Regime change

The British flag is hoisted in German Samoa on August 30, 1914 after the bloodless takeover of the colony by New Zealand troops.

in the 1880s. These islands were valuable to Japan not only for strategic reasons, but also for natural resources such as phosphates.

The German naval squadron had left the area in mid-September, when von Spee sailed for the South Atlantic (see page 176), and within the next month the Japanese mopped up all the German bases in the Caroline and Marshall Islands.

The Australians and New Zealanders were dismayed by this unanticipated Japanese expansion, but they had similar goals of their own. The British invited them to help take over Germany's possessions in the South Pacific but, far from committing them to London's authority as requested, they meant to hold on to them. They agreed that longitude 170° E should

constitute the dividing line between Australia's possessions (to the west) and New Zealand's (to the east).

Escorted by Australian ships, 1,400 New Zealanders landed in Samoa, where they met no resistance. The squadron then covered an Australian invasion of German New Guinea, where the German commanders were a captain in the reserves and a police officer, with few men and no guns. On September 17 they surrendered German New Guinea, the Bismarck Archipelago and the Solomon Islands. Some resistance continued in Papua, from German missionaries and a surveying expedition led by a man named Detzner. He was still at large when the war ended. By the time the Australians and New Zealanders had completed their conquest of the southern islands, the Japanese had taken over the islands of Micronesia to the north.

The taking of Tsingtao

This lithograph shows the novel tactics employed by the Japanese at Tsingtao. They maintained a sharpnel bombardment at night and moved up their trenches in the dark despite the German searchlights.

The end of an empire

Germany's interest in the Pacific dated back only to the 1880s. Its possessions consisted of a naval base on the Chinese coast, part of New Guinea and a few scattered islands. These soon fell to the superior Allied forces in the region.

WAR IN THE PACIFIC 1914

◆ German possessions
◆ British Empire
◆ Japan and possessions
◆ USA and possessions
French possessions
✦ Major siege

Aug 30, 1914
German Samoa occupied by New Zealand forces

German Samoa (Western)

Nov 14, 1914
Nauru occupied by Australian forces

Sept 11, 1914
Occupation of Kaiser Wilhelm's Land by Australian forces begins, German capitulation Sept 17

Oct 7, 1914
Beginning of occupation by Japanese forces

Sept 2, 1914
Japanese forces land on Shantung peninsula for attack on Tsingtao, fortress protecting German colony of Kiachow. General attack begins Oct 16, Tsingtao surrenders Nov 7

NEW ZEALAND

AUSTRALIA

PAPUA

Bismarck Archipelago

Kaiser Wilhelm's Land

Nauru

DUTCH EAST INDIES

INDIAN OCEAN

Marshall Is.

Caroline Is.

Yap

Guam (to U.S.)

Mariana Is.

Philippine Is.

MALAYA

SIAM FRENCH INDOCHINA

INDIA

TIBET

CHINA

Tsingtao

JAPAN

MANCHURIA

PACIFIC OCEAN

RUSSIAN EMPIRE

Alaska

CANADA

War in Africa

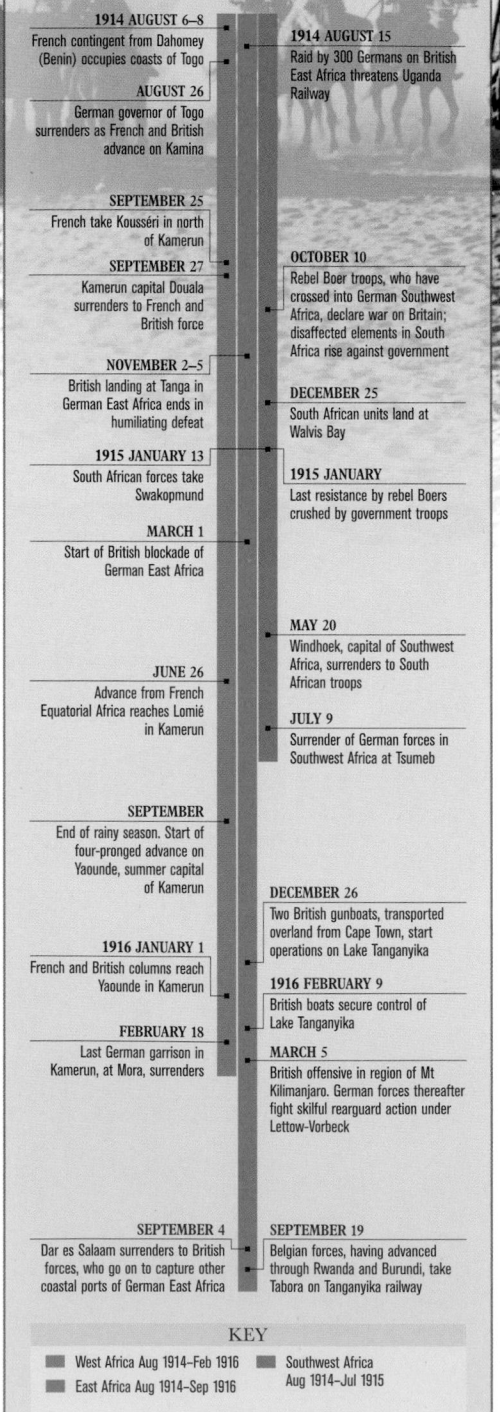

CAMPAIGNS IN AFRICA
AUGUST 1914 – SEPTEMBER 1916

~

Germany had four overseas possessions in Africa: two in East Africa (Togo and Cameroon), German East Africa and German Southwest Africa. None could be resupplied by sea and all were bordered by colonial territories of their enemies. In spite of this, all the German forces in Africa put up strong resistance to invading Allied forces. In East Africa, the campaign led by Lettow-Vorbeck lasted until the end of the war.

~

1914 AUGUST 6–8
French contingent from Dahomey (Benin) occupies coasts of Togo

AUGUST 26
German governor of Togo surrenders as French and British advance on Kamina

SEPTEMBER 25
French take Kousséri in north of Kamerun

SEPTEMBER 27
Kamerun capital Douala surrenders to French and British force

NOVEMBER 2–5
British landing at Tanga in German East Africa ends in humiliating defeat

1915 JANUARY 13
South African forces take Swakopmund

MARCH 1
Start of British blockade of German East Africa

JUNE 26
Advance from French Equatorial Africa reaches Lomié in Kamerun

SEPTEMBER
End of rainy season. Start of four-pronged advance on Yaounde, summer capital of Kamerun

1916 JANUARY 1
French and British columns reach Yaounde in Kamerun

FEBRUARY 18
Last German garrison in Kamerun, at Mora, surrenders

SEPTEMBER 4
Dar es Salaam surrenders to British forces, who go on to capture other coastal ports of German East Africa

1914 AUGUST 15
Raid by 300 Germans on British East Africa threatens Uganda Railway

OCTOBER 10
Rebel Boer troops, who have crossed into German Southwest Africa, declare war on Britain; disaffected elements in South Africa rise against government

DECEMBER 25
South African units land at Walvis Bay

1915 JANUARY
Last resistance by rebel Boers crushed by government troops

MAY 20
Windhoek, capital of Southwest Africa, surrenders to South African troops

JULY 9
Surrender of German forces in Southwest Africa at Tsumeb

DECEMBER 26
Two British gunboats, transported overland from Cape Town, start operations on Lake Tanganyika

1916 FEBRUARY 9
British boats secure control of Lake Tanganyika

MARCH 5
British offensive in region of Mt Kilimanjaro. German forces thereafter fight skilful rearguard action under Lettow-Vorbeck

SEPTEMBER 19
Belgian forces, having advanced through Rwanda and Burundi, take Tabora on Tanganyika railway

KEY

■ West Africa Aug 1914–Feb 1916
■ East Africa Aug 1914–Sep 1916
■ Southwest Africa Aug 1914–Jul 1915

THE NUMBERS ENGAGED IN COMBAT in Africa were small: Lettow-Vorbeck remarked that a company in Africa corresponded to a division in Europe. There was virtually no artillery, the machine-gun being the heaviest and most potent weapon. More men died of disease than in combat, and supply was a bigger problem than fighting. There were very few roads or railways, and in tsetse-ridden areas especially, where pack animals could not be used, all depended on human porters. More Africans were enlisted as porters than soldiers.

Togo, between the British Gold Coast and French Dahomey, contained Germany's most important overseas wireless station at the capital, Kamina. French and British troops fought a brisk campaign and Captain Bryant, in command of the Gold Coast Regiment, took Kamina on August 25. The Germans destroyed the wireless station before surrendering.

The War in Africa
After Germany's defeat, its former African possessions were taken over by Britain, France, Belgium and South Africa under League of Nations mandates.

South African cavalry
The heroes of Southwest Africa, it was said, were the horses; human losses in the campaign were relatively light.

Cameroon (Kamerun) was a different matter, a little-known terrain of great mountains and plateaus, dense jungles and swamps. As elsewhere, the German colony was surrounded by enemies. Its forces in 1915 peaked at about 5,000, including 1,500 Europeans. Allied forces, drawn mainly from West Africa, eventually amounted to nearly 25,000, but poor planning and lack of intelligence hindered

WAR IN AFRICA
1914–1916

■ British Empire
■ French possessions
■ German possessions
■ Belgian possessions
■ Italy and possessions
■ Portugal and possessions
■ Ottoman Empire
✹ Area of conflict

PORTUGAL / SPAIN · ITALY · GREECE · OTTOMAN EMPIRE · PERSIA
MOROCCO · TUNISIA
RIO DE ORO · ALGERIA · LIBYA · EGYPT · ARABIAN PENINSULA
FRENCH WEST AFRICA · FRENCH EQUATORIAL AFRICA · ANGLO-EGYPTIAN SUDAN · ERITREA · ADEN · FR. SOMALILAND · BR. SOMALILAND
PORT. GUINEA · SIERRA LEONE · LIBERIA · GOLD COAST · TOGO · Kamina · RIO MUNI (to Spain) · NIGERIA · Douala · CAMEROON · FRENCH CONGO · BELGIAN CONGO · GERMAN EAST AFRICA · ABYSSINIA · Dar es Salaam · INDIAN OCEAN
ANGOLA · N. RHODESIA
ATLANTIC OCEAN · GERMAN SOUTHWEST AFRICA · Windhoek · S. RHODESIA · BECHUANALAND · UNION OF SOUTH AFRICA · PORTUGUESE EAST AFRICA · MADAGASCAR

Aug 6–8, 1914
French and British forces invade. Germans surrender on Aug 26

Sept 1914
Allies secure capital Douala. A protracted campaign follows. Allies' converging offensives lead to eventual German capitulation, Feb 18, 1916

Aug 1914
German forces withdraw to capital, Windhoek. South African forces capture Windhoek May 20, 1915, and Germans surrender July 9

1914–18
A protracted campaign. German forces extend campaign to Portuguese East Africa

---

— 92 —

their progress. In late August, British troops from Nigeria crossed the border in several places, but were thrown back. The only successful offensive was against the colony's capital and main port, Douala, which fell to French Senegalese troops on September 27.

Tropical rains and skilful defence combined to hold up any significant Allied advance until late in 1915, when they finally pushed into the central region, forcing many Germans to seek refuge in Spanish territory. Even so, the last German stronghold, at Mora in the north, did not surrender until February 1916.

The conquest of Southwest Africa (Namibia), a vast but sparsely inhabited country, was undertaken largely by white South African (and Rhodesian) troops. They numbered about 70,000, but included many Afrikaners, not regular soldiers, who were anti-British, having fought in the Boer (South African) War (1899–1902). About 11,000 rebelled, but a much greater number remained loyal and the "Boer Rebellion" disintegrated by January 1915.

The South Africans invaded from the sea and overland, the main objective being the capital, Windhoek. In one rapid advance 3,000 men traversed 400 km (250 miles) of the Kalahari Desert in two weeks. Following the German abandonment of the south, forces under the command of General Botha, South Africa's prime minister, took Windhoek on May 20, 1915. Facing insuperable odds, the Germans continued to resist in the north until July 9, when they surrendered to Botha.

GERMAN EAST AFRICA

The greatest of the colonial "sideshows" was East Africa. It lasted as long as the war in Europe. The British had many more troops in the region, eventually topping 100,000 men, mainly from Africa and India. They also commanded the sea. The Germans had 15,000 at most, predominantly local African askaris, but they did have a master of bush warfare in General Lettow-Vorbeck.

The British gained control of Lake Victoria and Lake Tanganyika, but an ill-organized expeditionary force landing at the coastal port of Tanga was repulsed. Thereafter, commitments elsewhere meant that no serious effort was made to

Indian troops lying dead at Tanga
The disastrous British landing at Tanga in German East Africa in November 1914 resulted in over 800 casualties.

dislodge the Germans until early 1916, when, the war in Southwest Africa having ended, the South African General Smuts took command. Somewhat out of his depth in the different conditions of East Africa, Smuts was anxious to avoid unnecessary slaughter, especially of his South Africans. Major operations were renewed in the region of Kilimanjaro in 1916, but Smuts was unable to entrap the highly mobile German forces. Lettow-Vorbeck and his troops retreated south, again avoiding encirclement, but lost more men in a fierce battle fought in heavy rain in December. The number of fit men who remained under Lettow-Vorbeck's command was down to 8,400, and food was a major problem.

PAUL VON LETTOW-VORBECK

GENERAL LETTOW-VORBECK (1870–1964) was one of the most remarkable soldiers of the First World War. Appointed military commander of German East Africa in January 1914, he remained undefeated throughout the war by a British army that was ten times the size of his force of Germans and askaris. Lettow-Vorbeck was a master of bush warfare. He knew he could not take on the enemy in a major engagement, and made expert use of mountains, bush and forest to elude his pursuers. His tactics were often very cunning: he positioned his men to lure mounted enemy troops into tsetse-ridden areas, where their horses died. After his victory at Tanga in November 1914 he withdrew inland and launched frequent lightning attacks on the forces sent after him. In late 1917 he led his troops into Portuguese East Africa, from where they continued to make raids against the enemy. Hearing belatedly of the armistice while in Rhodesia, he surrendered on November 25. Fêted as a national hero in Germany, he also won the admiration of his adversaries. After the war, he led the Freikorps that put down the Spartacists in Hamburg.

The key battles of 1917 were fought around Kilwa and Lindi near the coast. German casualties, though much smaller, were relatively more serious. Having moved into Portuguese East Africa, Lettow-Vorbeck's capture of Namakura in July brought vital booty – food, rifles, ammunition and ten machine-guns. He moved north and west, entering Northern Rhodesia in November 1918. On November 12, the last battle of the war was fought between Lettow-Vorbeck's askaris and 750 men of the King's African Rifles. Hearing of the armistice the following day, Lettow-Vorbeck finally surrendered formally on November 25.

Sabotage
The Central Railway, which ran from Dar es Salaam to Lake Tanganyika, was destroyed by the Germans as they retreated south in 1916 pursued by British forces.

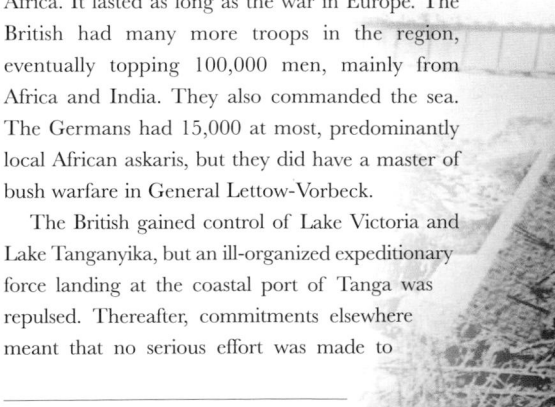

THE BRITISH AND FRENCH EMPIRES AT WAR

LARGE NUMBERS OF NON-EUROPEANS from the British and French empires fought on the battlefields of Europe in 1914–18. The two empires had been created and maintained by British and French troops; now the relationship was reversed with imperial forces helping to sustain the mother countries.

The French army in 1914 consisted administratively of three separate organizations: the Metropolitan Army, l'Armée d'Afrique and La Coloniale (restricted to French overseas citizens and subjects from post-1789 colonies not in North Africa). The colonial armies raised both complete divisions and smaller units for incorporation within the Metropolitan Army. Over 200,000 Algerians, Moroccans and Tunisians served in Europe. From the start of the war Germans found themselves faced by Zouave infantry and spahi cavalrymen from North Africa and Tirailleurs Sénégalais (Senegalese Riflemen) from West Africa. There were also significant contributions from Madagascar and Indo-China.

Britain's declaration of war was binding on all parts of the Empire. The dominions of Australia, Canada and New Zealand associated themselves willingly with Britain's cause, and saw themselves, as overseas British, bound to come to the defence of the mother country. However, on the Western Front both the Canadians and Australians insisted their formations were held in national corps rather than as parts of the British Army. They came to be regarded as imperial shock troops and their contribution to the war was crucial in creating a new independent sense of nationhood. The case of South Africa was somewhat different. With a European male population of military age of 244,000, it raised perhaps three divisions, but the costs of its operations, other than in German Southwest Africa, were borne by Britain. It sent troops to East Africa and maintained an infantry brigade on the Western Front.

India began the war with a long-service professional army of some 241,000 men. The Indian Army fought on the Western Front (in 1914–15) and in the Middle East and East Africa. It was to take until 1917 before the army was re-organized in a way that permitted major expansion. Such was its growth that in November 1918, when 548,311 men served in the Indian Army, India had become the imperial strategic reserve. Had the war continued into 1919, India was to have assumed responsibility for the entire Middle East and Salonika.

The contribution the colonies made to the war was immense, not least in terms of labour, whether for the military or in industry. The war brought ideas of national self-determination to subject peoples. French colonial troops and labour in France enjoyed the privilege of citizenship. However, peace saw a return to pre-war colonial attitudes.

West African troops
Six battalions of Tirailleurs Sénégalais were shipped to France to fight in the opening weeks of the war. In all, 163,000 served on the Western Front. Some 30,000 of them died.

Algerian spahis
In the first months of the war, detachments of spahi cavalry were a common sight on the roads of northern France. Later, like other cavalrymen, they would fight as infantry in the trenches.

SPAHI LEATHER BAG

Spahi uniform
The main items were a short red jacket, Turkish-style trousers, a large cape and a turban wound round a chechia (a small fez).

BOOTS

Soft inner boot

Normal shoe

Zouave club
This hand-carved trench club is decorated with the head of a Zouave, a soldier of the crack North African infantry force founded in 1834.

Laying railway track
Indian labourers worked with the Indian Army in Mesopotamia and other parts of the Middle East. They also worked on the Western Front, as did labourers from China, South Africa, Egypt, the West Indies, Malta, Mauritius, the Seychelles and Fiji.

Annamites in French shell factory
Some 50,000 Annamites (Vietnamese) and 13,000 Chinese from French Indo-China worked in France's munitions factories and in the army's labour corps.

Send-off from Melbourne
The first troopship for Europe sailed on October 17, 1914. Australia, with a population of 2,300,000 males of military age, enlisted 416,809 men.

Join the AIF
Recruiting posters for the AIF (Australian Imperial Force) gave the impression that volunteers would be joining their mates in an exciting adventure on the other side of the world.

Gurkhas in France
In the course of the war, 100,000 Gurkhas enlisted in the Indian Army. Gurkha regiments fought on the Western Front and in Egypt, Gallipoli, Mesopotamia, Palestine and Salonika.

ENLIST NOW

This is Serious!

Join the A·I·F

WAR AND THE RISE OF THE STATE
1915

~

AS IT BECAME APPARENT THAT THE WAR WAS GOING TO LAST FAR LONGER THAN ORIGINALLY ANTICIPATED, THE GOVERNMENTS OF ALL THE BELLIGERENT STATES INCREASED THEIR CONTROL OVER MUNITIONS AND OTHER KEY INDUSTRIES. THEY ALSO, TO VARYING DEGREES, ADOPTED POLICIES AIMED AT LOOKING AFTER THE WELFARE OF THE PEOPLE REQUIRED TO WORK IN THESE INDUSTRIES AND SUPPORT THE WAR EFFORT IN GENERAL. WITH THE INTRODUCTION OF MANY NEW REGULATIONS, THE STATE BEGAN TO INTERVENE IN PEOPLE'S LIVES AS IT HAD NEVER DONE BEFORE.

~

Shell Factory
As the need for munitions became more urgent, the British government took direct control of their production, employing thousands of women in dangerous jobs such as filling shells with explosive.

FACING NEW REALITIES

AT THE END OF 1914 ALL THE COMBATANT NATIONS STILL EXPECTED VICTORY IN
THE NOT TOO DISTANT FUTURE. THE WINTER WOULD OBVIOUSLY LIMIT IMMEDIATE
OPERATIONS, BUT IT WAS GENERALLY BELIEVED THAT THE MOMENTUM OF WAR
WOULD BE REGAINED IN THE SPRING IF THE PRODUCTION OF SUFFICIENT SUPPLIES
OF WEAPONS AND AMMUNITION COULD BE ORGANIZED.

THE DEMAND FOR MUNITIONS had outstripped supply very early in the war: the Prussian War Ministry's stock of artillery shells, for example, had virtually run out after six weeks. It was apparent to many that if the vast material requirements of the war were to be met, governments – which still exercised few bureaucratic controls outside their finance and military departments – would have to undergo fundamental change. They would not only have to assume direct control of industry but would also have to actively promote the welfare of their citizens – a task that was, eventually, to prove impossible for Russia and the Central Powers. Industry could not function, and the armies could not be supplied with manpower and material,

unless the civilian population was kept supplied with adequate food, heating and light. To this end, the British and French governments in particular adopted an interventionist approach as it became apparent that the war was not going to end quickly.

In France, which – like Germany – faced a massive shortage of shells almost immediately, the government took steps to ensure that as many private companies as possible were involved in the manufacture of munitions. Almost 2.5 million men were conscripted during the first weeks of the war but, by the end of 1915, 500,000 had been sent back to work in the factories that were under military jurisdiction. In Britain, where the Defence of the Realm Act (DORA) was introduced in 1914 to give the government powers to direct the

economy and various aspects of public life, little was done initially to ensure an adequate supply of munitions. It was only when the scale of the British army's munitions shortages became apparent, in the spring of 1915, that steps were taken by the government to boost the production of munitions, including the establishment of national factories.

Conscription was not introduced in Britain until May 1916. The success, however, of efforts in 1915 to recruit a mass volunteer army – 2.6 million men by the end of the year – meant that here, as in France, the government had to take an active role in ensuring that industrial and agricultural production continued. Women were encouraged in both countries, and in all the other belligerent states, to undertake the work formerly done by men.

CHOICES FACING GERMANY

Over the winter of 1914–15 the combatants in the war not only had to consider how best to increase their production of munitions; they also had to reconsider their military strategy. Arguably Germany faced greater dilemmas than any other power. In attempting to implement the Schlieffen Plan, it had stood on the defensive in the east while it pursued victory against the French in the west. It had not, however, been able to stay on the defensive in the east once Russia had completed its initial mobilization and prepared to launch offensives into the Carpathians and East Prussia. Germany was now faced with the question of whether it should strengthen its forces in the east, so reducing the likelihood of victory in the west.

Despite the failure of the Schlieffen Plan, Falkenhayn, the German chief of staff, still believed at the beginning of 1915 that victory had to be won in the west. He was unconvinced by the argument being voiced by Hindenburg and Ludendorff – heroes of the German victory over the Russians at Tannenberg in East Prussia in August the previous year – that Germany's interests were now best served by standing on the defensive in the west and taking offensive action in the east. In his view, Russia would always trade space for time and the security of its troops. By ordering the withdrawal of its armies, it could induce the Germans to advance across a country whose sheer size and primitive communications systems, plus the lack of any major objective in front of which the

German cavalry

On the relatively fluid Eastern Front the cavalry was able to play a more significant role than on the Western Front where the trench system signified deadlock.

Russians might be trapped and annihilated, would make victory difficult to achieve. Falkenhayn, however, could not ignore the fact that Hindenburg and Ludendorff had the ear of the kaiser.

Falkenhayn could also not ignore the weakness of Austria-Hungary – a weakness that caused the Germans to view their ally with increasing contempt. The losses of 1914 among the Austrian and Hungarian troops and long-service elements of the Imperial Army had been particularly serious. The halting of the Russian offensive against Silesia and the partial German success at Lodz forestalled

"People out here seem to think that the war is going to be quite short. Why, I don't know; personally I see nothing to prevent it going on forever."

BRITISH CAPTAIN, COLWYN PHILLIPS, WRITING TO HIS MOTHER ON MARCH 12, 1915 FROM THE YPRES SALIENT

any immediate move by Russia against Austria-Hungary. At a time, however, when Austria-Hungary could not confront Russia with any real confidence; it also faced the need to continue the war against Serbia, which in 1914 had driven out, and so humiliated, the Austro-Hungarian armies that had invaded it, Austria-Hungary's problems were to be further increased by the Italian declaration of war in May 1915.

THE PROBLEMS FACING RUSSIA

Russia also faced problems in 1915, problems that were partly caused by an increase in the number of fronts on which it had to fight. Turkey's entry into the war on October 29, 1914 presented Russia with a further front in the Caucasus. This, combined with the losses incurred in the opening months of the war, meant that throughout 1915 Russia could not face Austria-Hungary and Germany with more than an equal number of troops along the 960-km (600-mile) Eastern Front.

The sheer length of this front, stretching from Memel on the Baltic coast to Czernowitz just east of the Carpathians, coupled with insufficient manpower, meant that neither the Austro-Germans nor the Russians were able to concentrate along it in great numbers. Lacking the labour necessary to build complicated trench systems, both sides focused on launching offensives rather than strengthening defensive positions.

From December 1914, the war in the East became comparatively fluid. Initially the Russians pushed back the Austro-Hungarians in the Carpathians, in preparation for an attack on Hungary. Austro-Hungarian and German forces, however, then launched an offensive in May that succeeded in driving the Russians from Galicia by the end of June and from Poland by September.

The Russians were finally able to bring the onslaught to a halt only after they had suffered some two million casualties. The Central Powers had not driven Russia out of the war, but they had exposed many of its army's weaknesses. In addition to huge shortages of basic equipment, weapons and shells – shortages that were to be eased by considerable increases in war production in the summer of 1915 – the Russian army continued to be dogged by the perennial problems of political appointments and appalling administration. There was also a chronic shortage of good-quality junior officers and a lack of proper training at all levels, problems whose seriousness many senior officers failed to appreciate throughout 1915.

Marching to position
Hungarian soldiers march to their positions on the Dniester River, near Lemberg, during the successful Austro-German offensive of May–September 1915, in which the Russians were driven out of Galicia and Poland.

THE WEST ENTRENCHED

It was a very different story on the Western Front, which was viewed by both France and Britain as the most important theatre of operations, where the outcome of the war would in all probability be decided. With most of Belgium and a large area of northern France in German possession, the French – from whom the British took their lead in 1914–15 – were intent on clearing national territory. This meant attempting to undertake offensive action against an enemy which, after November 1914, had the pick of the ground and was able to develop a strong defensive system of trenches.

Trench systems of a rudimentary nature had been constructed in the first months of the war. Then, as it became apparent that there would be no immediate victory for either side, both set about constructing more elaborate systems – generally between 90 and 360 m (100 and 400 yds) apart – the position of which was barely to change for three years. Indeed, the Germans were to add "a tier a year", thus ensuring that their front line could not be broken in a single offensive. What were intended by the Allied strategists to be decisive battles turned into operations in which tens of thousands – sometimes hundreds of thousands – of men were killed for very little gain. In 1915 the Allies launched several campaigns in Champagne and Artois, none of which achieved their objectives.

One of the main reasons for the stalemate that developed on the Western Front was the superiority of defensive firepower – in the form of long-range artillery, accurate rifles and machine-guns. Another was the superiority of strategic mobility over tactical movement: any breach in the front could always be sealed by a defence that was able to move formations by rail to the threatened sector more quickly than an attacker could move on foot or horseback across the battlefield. Adding to the difficulties of the attacking army was the inadequacy of communication systems: effective command and control of operations on the front

...line would only become possible with the miniaturization of the radio. In the First World War most communication was through field telephones whose connecting wires were constantly being destroyed by artillery bombardments.

These military explanations, however, do not in themselves make the three-year deadlock totally understandable. The nations warring on the Western Front were only able to fight on, increasingly determined to fight to the finish to justify the losses already incurred, because the vast majority of troops were prepared to take part in the continuing slaughter.

In his book, *Realities of War*, the British front-line correspondent Phillip Gibbs describes the situation confronting the men in the trenches. They were in "a devil's trap from which there was no escape". This trap encompassed "old tradition, obedience to the laws of war, or to the caste which ruled them, all the moral and spiritual propaganda handed out by pastors, newspapers, generals, staff officers, old men at home, exalted women, female furies, a deep and simple love for England, and Germany...".

On both sides, the societies involved had a social cohesion that meant they simply refused to collapse under the strain of a war that should by rights have destroyed them.

French troops in Artois
Throughout 1915 the French struggled to break through the German lines in Artois. They launched and the British launched major offensives in both the spring and autumn of 1915, but the advances they made were negligible.

"... a thousand complexities of thought and sentiment prevented men, on both sides, from breaking the net of fate in which they were entangled, and revolting against that mutual, unceasing massacre."

BRITISH FRONT-LINE CORRESPONDENT, PHILLIP GIBBS, IN HIS BOOK, *REALITIES OF WAR*

Deadlock in the West

German trench, winter 1914–15
German trenches at this time were very basic compared with those developed later in the war, but the French generally found it impossible to break through them.

O N DECEMBER 10, 1914 the French Tenth Army conducted the first of a series of attacks in Artois, primarily directed against Vimy Ridge. Ten days later, at the opposite end of the bulge in the front line between Flanders and Verdun (see map page 140–41), the Fourth Army attacked along a 32-km (20-mile) front to the east of Reims, in Champagne. Neither operation was a success.

WINTER CAMPAIGNS

In Artois, in atrocious weather and thick mud, a few villages changed hands at the cost of some 8,000 French casualties. In Champagne, exhaustion and the same bad weather led to the offensive being broken off in the first week of January. It was resumed again on February 16, but by the time it came to a halt on March 17, the French had secured the forward German defence lines in just one sector, around "Hill 180". They had done so at the enormous cost of 240,000 casualties.

There was no disguising the extent of the French strategic failure in Artois and Champagne, which largely stemmed from the lack of heavy artillery necessary to destroy the forward German defensive positions. Even in the midst of failure, however, French and British had to prepare for the next phase of operations. It was agreed that the British would take over the French sector in front of Ypres, so freeing the French for offensive action elsewhere. A combined spring offensive would then be mounted in Artois – the British against the German positions on Aubers Ridge and the French against those on Vimy Ridge. There would also be a full-scale French offensive in Champagne.

The plan soon had to be revised as it became clear that the British would not be able to relieve the French at Ypres because of a shortage of troops. This, coupled with the defeats suffered by the French in December and January, meant that the French could not undertake a spring

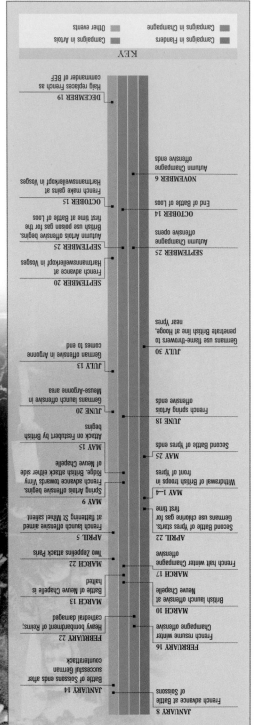

FRANCE AND FLANDERS
~
JANUARY – DECEMBER 1915

Allied winter campaigns in Artois and Champagne met with no success. In April the Germans launched their only major offensive of the year at Ypres in Flanders, and succeeded in almost totally surrounding, but not capturing, the town. In May and June there were further Allied offensives in Artois, and on September 25 major Allied campaigns were launched in both Artois and Champagne. No significant gains were made.

JANUARY 8 — French advance at Battle of Soissons

JANUARY 14 — Battle of Soissons ends after successful German counterattack

FEBRUARY 16 — French resume winter Champagne offensive

FEBRUARY 22 — Heavy bombardment of Reims; cathedral damaged

MARCH 10 — British launch offensive at Neuve Chapelle

MARCH 13 — Battle of Neuve Chapelle is halted

MARCH 17 — French halt winter Champagne offensive

MARCH 22 — Two Zeppelins attack Paris

APRIL 5 — French launch offensive aimed at flattening St Mihiel salient

APRIL 22 — Second Battle of Ypres starts. Germans use chlorine gas for the first time

MAY 1–4 — Withdrawal of British troops in front of Ypres

MAY 9 — Spring Artois offensive begins. French advance towards Vimy Ridge. British attack either side of Neuve Chapelle

MAY 15 — Attack on Festubert by British begins

MAY 25 — Second Battle of Ypres ends

JUNE 18 — French spring Artois offensive ends

JUNE 20 — Germans launch offensive in Meuse-Argonne area

JULY 13 — German offensive in Argonne comes to end

JULY 30 — Germans use flame-throwers to penetrate British line at Hooge, near Ypres

SEPTEMBER 20 — French advance at Hartmannsweilerkopf in Vosges

SEPTEMBER 25 — Autumn Artois offensive begins, British use poison gas for the first time at Battle of Loos

SEPTEMBER 25 — Autumn Champagne offensive opens

OCTOBER 14 — End of Battle of Loos

OCTOBER 15 — French make gains at Hartmannsweilerkopf in Vosges

NOVEMBER 6 — Autumn Champagne offensive ends

DECEMBER 19 — Haig replaces French as commander of BEF

KEY

Campaigns in Flanders	Campaigns in Artois
Campaigns in Champagne	Other events

CHRISTMAS TRUCE OF 1914

FREEZING RAIN DURING November and December 1914 left both sides struggling with flooded trenches and appalling conditions. This led to something of a "live-and-let-live" arrangement along much of the northern sector of the Western Front, especially between the British and German troops. December 24 brought a frost. The ground hardened and the smell of decomposing flesh abated. The Germans placed lighted Christmas trees along their trenches and soldiers on both sides sung Christmas carols to each other in comradely greeting. Next morning a fog lifted to reveal frost-covered trees in brilliant sunlight. All firing stopped and there was shouting between trenches, followed by soldiers moving into No Man's Land. Gifts were exchanged, and both sides took the opportunity to bury their dead.

Allied commanders insisted that such an event should never recur. In subsequent years there were orders to shoot anyone attempting to fraternize with the enemy.

Winners' cup
Several football matches took place between German and British troops during the truce. This beer mug is believed to have been awarded by German troops to a winning English side.

Royal gift
For Christmas 1914, some 427,000 British forces received a brass box containing tobacco, materials and sweets. The scheme, funded by public donation, was the idea of Princess Mary, whose photograph was also enclosed.

Friends for a day
German and British troops met in No Man's Land, shook hands and exchanged gifts of chocolate, tobacco and cigarettes, their hostility temporarily forgotten.

BATTLE OF NEUVE CHAPELLE

The British launched their attack at 7:00 am on March 10 with the immediate objective of taking the village of Aubers less than 1.5 km (1 mile) away. Given artillery and ammunition shortages, plus the certainty of major operations later in the year, the logic behind an unsupported attack at Neuve Chapelle was questionable. It was, however, these same shortages that mainly accounted for whatever success was achieved. Unable to mount a prolonged preliminary bombardment, the artillery opted for a 35-minute hurricane barrage against a very narrow sector, some 3,600 m (4,000 yds) long, in which the British and Indian troops together outnumbered the opposing German forces by 5 to 1.

As a result of careful rehearsals and detailed planning, the British attack achieved total surprise. Neuve Chapelle was secured in the first hour and a breach was created in the German line. What happened next, however, was an illustration of

some of the problems presented by trench warfare. Losses incurred in the assault phase prevented the proper consolidation of gains, and the break-through sector, some 1,800 m (2,000 yds) wide and up to 1,080 m (1,200 yds) deep, was too narrow to provide any real chance of opening and maintaining a breach. The British also failed to feed reserves into the battle quickly enough to prevent the defence from reconstituting the front. This failure was due to inadequate communications and a lack of proper co-ordination at corps level, and provided the German defence with some five hours' respite at a time of maximum vulnerability.

Though the British were able to hold off a German counterattack, the attempt to resume the offensive and drive on to Aubers Ridge was abandoned after three days, on March 13. A total of 7,000 British and 4,200 Indian soldiers had been killed or wounded. The Germans had suffered an equal number of casualties.

PLANS FOR A MAY OFFENSIVE

On March 29, at Chantilly, British and French commanders agreed to revive the plan that had been abandoned during the winter – and launch an

Artois offensive. The British then proposed an attack at the ruined village of Neuve Chapelle in Artois as a demonstration of resolve and to complement the French effort in Champagne.

attack on the Aubers and Vimy ridges in May. What the Allies did not foresee at this stage was the launch in April of the only major German offensive on the Western Front in 1915 – at Ypres.

SECOND BATTLE OF YPRES

On the evening of April 22, the German Fourth Army launched an offensive on the French sector of the Allied positions around the Ypres salient with the aid of a new weapon: poisonous gas. After a short but intense bombardment in which heavy siege artillery was used, two German corps attacked behind clouds of chlorine gas released from 5,730 cylinders. With no protection against the gas, the two French divisions in the line retreated rapidly, leaving an 8-km (5-mile) gap to the left of the Canadian First Division's position. By nightfall the Germans had taken the villages of Langemarck and Pilckem. They did not, however, have sufficient reserves. Consequently, with their infantry wary of following behind their gas too closely, the Germans were unable to exploit what was to prove their best chance of breaking open the Allied front in the West in 1915.

SPRING OFFENSIVES IN ARTOIS

The German effort at Ypres, despite its considerable initial success, failed largely because Falkenhayn's main aim at this time was to cloak the redeployment of forces to the east. To that end, he denied the German Fourth Army the necessary reserves. The Allied Artois offensives in the spring were also to fail, with the French effort falling between an attempt to break open the front and the more modest aim of achieving tactical gains across a restricted sector.

FRENCH ADVANCE TO VIMY RIDGE

The French Tenth Army opened its offensive with a six-day artillery bombardment involving over 1,200 guns. Then, on May 9, troops began to advance towards Vimy Ridge. Those who survived the German machine-gun fire succeeded in advancing over 5 km (3 miles) in just 90 minutes, breaking open the German front and reaching the villages of Vimy and Givenchy. As at Neuve Chapelle, this initial success was due to very detailed planning. But again, as at Neuve Chapelle, French gains, across a 7-km (4-mile) stretch of front, were too narrowly concentrated, and losses too heavy, for effective exploitation to be possible. On the following day the French positions on Vimy Ridge were eliminated by counterattacks.

BRITISH OFFENSIVES

As part of their attempt to take Aubers Ridge, the British launched an attack either side of Neuve Chapelle on May 9. They had only enough shells to maintain a preliminary bombardment for 40 minutes – and few of the shells were high-explosive. Consequently, little damage was inflicted on the German defences, and the British and Indian forces became easy targets for the German machine-guns. They had suffered 11,000 casualties by the time their attack was abandoned the next day.

Between May 15 and 27 the British undertook a second, and very different, offensive at Festubert. This time there was a 60-hour preliminary bombardment to wear down German manpower.

"'The horrible part of it is the slow lingering death of those who are gassed. I saw some hundred poor fellows laid out in the open … slowly drowning with water in their lungs …'"

GENERAL CHARTERIS, WRITING IN HIS DIARY ON APRIL 28, SIX DAYS AFTER THE FIRST GAS ATTACK AT YPRES

Only on the first day of the attack had the Germans had any real chance of strategic success. Subsequently, they had discovered that, though gas could be an effective weapon, there was always the danger of it being blown back by the wind over their own, often unprotected, infantry. However, while the Germans had failed to take Ypres, they had succeeded in taking all the high ground and all but surrounding the town. The British were left holding Ypres but in a position of very considerable military disadvantage.

Collecting the dead
The French did not only suffer huge losses in Artois and Champagne. They also incurred some 65,000 casualties in their unsuccessful attempt in April to eliminate the St Mihiel salient, and between June 20 and July 13 they suffered a further 32,000 casualties in the Argonne sector.

By April 24 the British and Canadians had reconstituted the defence and had improvised protection against gas, but they were unable to prevent the Germans from gaining St Julien and Gravenstafel. In a series of counterattacks that followed, the Allied forces failed to recover any lost ground. They had wholly inadequate artillery support and were completely overwhelmed by concentrated German machine-gun and artillery fire.

ALLIED WITHDRAWAL

From this point the Allies faced an impossible choice at Ypres. If Allied artillery was kept around and to the west of Ypres, it could not properly support the infantry, but if it was moved forward it would be completely dominated by a much superior enemy. Withdrawal was inevitable, though political considerations meant that Ypres and Belgian territory could not be totally abandoned.

The withdrawal began on May 1. The next day, a German gas-supported attack was halted for the first time and, by the 4th, the British Second Army's withdrawal to a new main line of resistance was completed. On this line the Germans attacked the Frezenberg Ridge on May 8–9, and the Bellewaarde Ridge on the 24th and 25th. Mutual exhaustion then ensured that the battle was allowed to die. The Allies had suffered 58,000 casualties, the Germans 38,000.

GAS ATTACKS

THE FIRST USE OF POISON GAS was at Ypres on April 22, 1915. The Germans released chlorine from canisters and relied on the wind to blow gas clouds to the enemy position. After this, both sides began to use different types of gas, including phosgene, an insidious weapon that had had little immediate effect but struck soldiers down 24 hours later. Both gases caused a painful death over a number of days by asphyxiation. The gas that caused the greatest number of casualties was mustard gas. It had the effect of rotting the body both inside and out, so that the skin blistered and the mucous membrane was stripped off the bronchial tubes. The pain was almost unendurable and could last for up to five weeks. It was hard to counteract and victims who survived were left scarred for life.

The first improvised protection used by the Allies at Ypres consisted simply of water- or urine-soaked handkerchiefs and towels. Within three days, cotton pads dipped in bicarbonate of soda had been rushed to the front. Later in 1915 block gauze pads soaked in hyposulphite solution, with an extra flap to cover the eyes and tapes to tie round the head, were used. The British and French went on to develop more elaborate forms of protection. From late 1917 the box respirator, which used charcoal or antidote chemicals to neutralize the gas agents, became standard British issue. The antidotes were only effective for 30 minutes, however, at which point the respirator had to be changed a potentially fatal procedure.

Gas alert

At the first sign of gas, whistles or rattles would be sounded. Soldiers, such as these French troops, would have to find and fit their gas masks as quickly as possible.

German gas shells

Gas shells, first used by both sides in 1916, contained liquid gas, which evaporated on impact. They were a more effective way of delivering gas to enemy lines than relying on the wind.

Primitive protection

Cameronians (Scottish Rifles) in 1915 stand ready for action, wearing early gas masks. These consisted simply of goggles and gauze and provided little protection against chlorine and phosgene.

Gas masks

Early gas protection for British and French troops consisted simply of goggles and a gauze pad. Next came flannel hoods impregnated with phenol, and incorporating mica eye-pieces. Later masks included a rubber-tipped metal tube that was held between the teeth for exhalation. The Germans quickly developed a mask that had a cylindrical screw-fitted filter, still in use in 1917.

FRENCH GAS MASK AND GOGGLES, 1915

EARLY BRITISH "HYPO" GAS HELMET, 1915

Cotton wadding mask

Goggles

GERMAN M1915 GAS MASK, 1917

FRENCH M2 GAS MASK, 1916

Gas alarm rattle

GAS ALARM RATTLE

TRENCH WEAPONRY

~

TRENCHES CREATED A NEW, largely unanticipated, demand from all armies for weapons with which to fight at very short range. The result was the revival of weapons such as fire and grenades. Fire – created by igniting petrol spray with an incendiary bomb – was first used in October 1914, in the Argonne-Meuse sector. A flamethrower was used for the first time on February 26, 1915 against French positions outside Verdun. The first concerted use of flamethrowers was on July 30, 1915. A total of six were employed against the British at Hooge in the Ypres salient, at a point where the trenches were less than 4.5 m (5 yds) apart. Even at such close range, most losses were incurred when the infantry emerged from cover to be attacked by the waiting Germans, rather than by the flames themselves.

In August 1914 only the Germans possessed mortars: a total of 160. During 1915, however, the production and use of many different types of mortar expanded rapidly on both sides. In the first quarter, British factories produced 75 mortars and 8,000 shells; in the last quarter, 524 mortars and 180,000 shells. By July 1916 British infantry divisions had three batteries of light mortars and three of medium mortars, each consisting of four weapons. Single batteries of heavy mortars came later. By 1918 the British had 3,022 mortars on the Western Front.

By spring 1916 the British standard weapon was the light 3-in (7.5-cm) Stokes mortar, which could fire 30 rounds a minute, but initially was employed only to fire smoke rounds. In May 1916 the British introduced a medium mortar, which fired a 132-kg (60-lb) projectile from

GERMAN METAL ROD

BRITISH NAIL CLUB

FRENCH CARVED CLUB

BRITISH SPIKED CLUB

Trench clubs
Some of the weapons used in hand-to-hand fighting in the trenches were almost medieval in appearance. Clubs, many of which were home-made, proved especially useful for night trench raids and patrols.

German 76-mm minenwerfer
The standard German trench mortars were known as *minenwerfers* (bomb-throwers). They came in three sizes, this 76-mm gun being the smallest. By 1917 every German infantry battalion had four of these light mortars. *Minenwerfer* required large teams to move them: six men for the 76-mm, 21 men for the huge 26-cm version.

Shell loaded into barrel end. Barrel rifled to increase range and velocity

Recoil chambers

Elevation gauge

Fired by pull lanyard

Elevation wheel

Detachable wheels for transport. These were removed before firing

HIGH EXPLOSIVE 76-MM *MINENWERFER* SHELL

Base plate for stable firing platform

prepared positions within 140 m (150 yds) of the enemy line. The British heavy mortar, introduced in late 1916, fired a 68-kg (150-lb) projectile to a maximum range of 915 m (1,000 yds). It had to be fired from 7.5 m (25 ft) below the surface, and could gouge out a trench to about the same depth. The German equivalent was a 90-kg (200-lb) version with a range of 550 m (600 yds).

Though used extensively by the Allies during the Russo-Japanese War of 1904–05, the grenade – a hand-thrown bomb detonated by impact or a timed fuse – was only widely issued to German forces in 1914. The British had almost none until spring 1915, and their first Mills Mark II grenades often exploded in the hand of the thrower. It was not until 1916, with the Mark III, that such accidents were reduced to one in 20,000. A total of 75,000,000 grenades were manufactured in Britain, and a discharger cup was devised so they could be fired from a rifle, thus increasing their range. Grenades became so important that orders for their supply were given priority over those for rifle ammunition.

Germans practising the use of flamethrowers
In 1915 flamethrowers came with inflammable liquid sufficient for two minutes' action over a maximum distance of 18 m (20 yards). Most front-line positions, however, were further apart than this, so making it impossible to use the flamethrowers effectively.

FRENCH "HAIRBRUSH" GRENADE, 1915

BRITISH MK III PERCUSSION GRENADE, 1915

Early percussion and improvised grenades
Many early percussion grenades were fitted with streamers, a parachute or a propeller to ensure that they would fall head-first and detonate on hitting the ground. Hand-made grenades, like the French example shown here, had to be ignited before throwing.

FRENCH P2 GRENADE, 1914

AUTUMN OFFENSIVES IN ARTOIS AND CHAMPAGNE

Following the failure at the Dardanelles and Russian defeats in Poland (see pages 76–79 and 116–19), it became essential that a major Anglo-French effort should be launched on the Western Front. The French had originally planned to launch two simultaneous major offensives in July, in Artois and Champagne. In June and July, however, their intentions changed, and it was agreed that the British First Army should make the main effort in Artois, with limited French support, while three French armies undertook the main effort in Champagne.

One of the lessons drawn by the French and British planners from the spring offensives was that additional infantry was required. For the British this meant a lengthening of their front as more divisions arrived in northern France. It was also concluded that the assault sector should be widened in order to break the defence over too great a distance for it to be easily scaled, and heavier and longer bombardment should be employed to neutralize the enemy's defensive positions. Applying these lessons meant that, appalling as the losses in Artois were, far greater losses were to be incurred in the battles that followed over the next 30 months.

SECOND ADVANCE ON VIMY RIDGE

After May 10 the French Tenth Army's effort degenerated into a series of local actions until June 16, when it staged its second major offensive in Artois. The French had learned from their experiences on May 9, and now concentrated more artillery and infantry for the attack. They had also brought up reserves close to the front in order to try to exploit success effectively. But on this occasion the defence was also stronger than it had been on May 9, and the German Sixth Army concentrated artillery fire on No Man's Land once the assault began. Just one of six French corps managed to break the German front. As in May, however, the corps' success in seizing positions on Vimy Ridge was costly and short-lived as, unsupported, its gains were quickly eliminated by German counterattacks. On the 18th, the futility of continuing the battle was recognized by the French high command, and a halt was called. The French had incurred around 100,000 casualties in the five weeks of this offensive; the Germans 60,000.

The ostensible objective was to secure positions just 900 m (1,000 yards) in front of the British defensive line – an objective that was achieved, but at the cost of 16,000 British and Indian casualties.

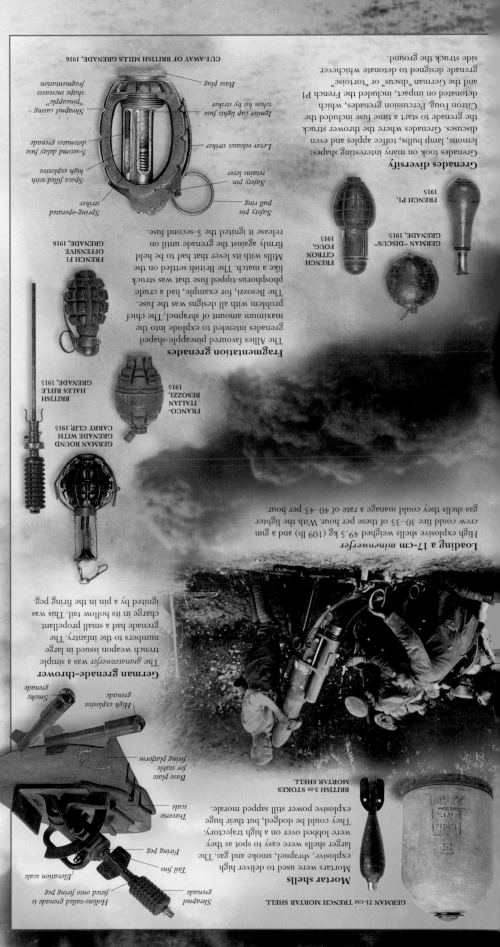

Grenades diversity

Grenades took on many interesting shapes: lemons, lamp bulbs, toffee apples and even discuses. Grenades where the thrower struck the grenade to start a time fuse included the Citron Foug Percussion grenades, which detonated on impact, included the French P1 and the German "discus" or "tortoise" grenade designed to detonate whichever side struck the ground.

FRENCH P1, 1915

GERMAN CITRON FOUG, 1915

GERMAN "DISCUS" GRENADE, 1915

FRENCH P1, 1915

Fragmentation grenades

The Allies favoured pineapple-shaped grenades intended to explode into the maximum amount of shrapnel. The chief problem with all designs was the fuse. The Besozzi, for example, had a crude phosphorus-tipped fuse that was struck like a match. The British settled on the Mills with its lever that had to be held firmly against the grenade until on release it ignited the 5-second fuse.

FRENCH P1 OFFENSIVE GRENADE, 1916

FRANCO-ITALIAN BESOZZI, 1915

BRITISH HALES RIFLE GRENADE, 1915

GERMAN ROUND GRENADE WITH CARRY CLIP 1915

CUT-AWAY OF BRITISH MILLS GRENADE, 1916

Base plug

"pineapple" shape increases fragmentation

Shrapnel casing

Igniter cap lights fuse

token hit by striker

5-second delay fuse detonates grenade

Lever releases striker

Space filled with high explosive

Safety pin retains lever

Safety pin pull ring

Spring-operated striker

German grenade-thrower

The granatenwerfer was a simple trench weapon issued in large numbers to the infantry. The grenade had a small propellant charge in its hollow tail. This was ignited by a pin in the firing peg.

Smoke grenade

High explosive grenade

Base plate for stable firing platform

Traverse scale

Firing peg

Elevation scale

Tail fins

Hollow-tailed grenade is fitted onto firing peg

Shrapnel grenade

Loading a 17-cm minenwerfer

High explosive shells weighed 49.5 kg (109 lb) and a gun crew could fire 30–35 of these per hour. With the lighter gas shells they could manage a rate of 40–45 per hour.

Mortar shells

Mortars were used to deliver high explosive, shrapnel, smoke and gas. The larger shells were easy to spot as they were lobbed over on a high trajectory. They could be dodged, but their huge explosive power still sapped morale.

BRITISH 3-IN STOKES MORTAR SHELL

GERMAN 21-CM TRENCH MORTAR SHELL

With some 35 French divisions assembled in Champagne and six British divisions committed to an attack on Loos in Artois, the Allies possessed a marked advantage over a German defence that had only six divisions in reserve on the whole of the Western Front. In both Artois and Champagne, however, the Germans had the pick of the ground and since the spring offensive they had strengthened their defences. A second, heavily wired, main line of resistance was sited some 2,275 m (2,500 yds) behind the first and, wherever possible, on reverse slopes. The Germans' heavy artillery and ammunition supply was also far superior to that of the British and French combined, and they possessed more and better mortars, grenades and trench-fighting equipment than the Allies.

The reality of the situation in late summer 1915 was that, for all their efforts, the British and French were no better placed to unlock the enemy defence than they had been in the spring. As a result, the offensives that opened on September 25, after a four-day artillery bombardment, conformed to the pattern of those that had gone before: in the opening hours of the assaults both the British and French made considerable but uneven gains. As the defence re-formed itself, however, the attacks degenerated into a series of grim, unco-ordinated local struggles for insignificant features until both sides were exhausted.

BATTLE OF LOOS

In the attack that began on Loos on September 25, among the mines, slag heaps and fortified villages of Artois, the British used poison gas for the first time. They released 150 tons of chlorine from over 5,240 cylinders and a light wind carried it slowly towards the German lines. Over 600 Germans fell victim to the gas, which also drifted back to the British trenches where it caused huge confusion and many casualties, but few deaths.

The British advanced rapidly, at one point covering a distance of more than 3,600 m (4,000 yds). Loos itself was captured in the first hours of the attack, and the German first-line defences over a 6-km (4-mile) front, between Auchy and Lens, collapsed. The German Sixth Army made preparations to evacuate its positions in both the British and French sectors. The British, however, failed to move reserves into the line in sufficient time and strength to exploit the advantage that had been won, enabling the Germans to reconstitute their defence along their second line.

The British attack between Hulluch and Lens on the second day, mounted without artillery support,

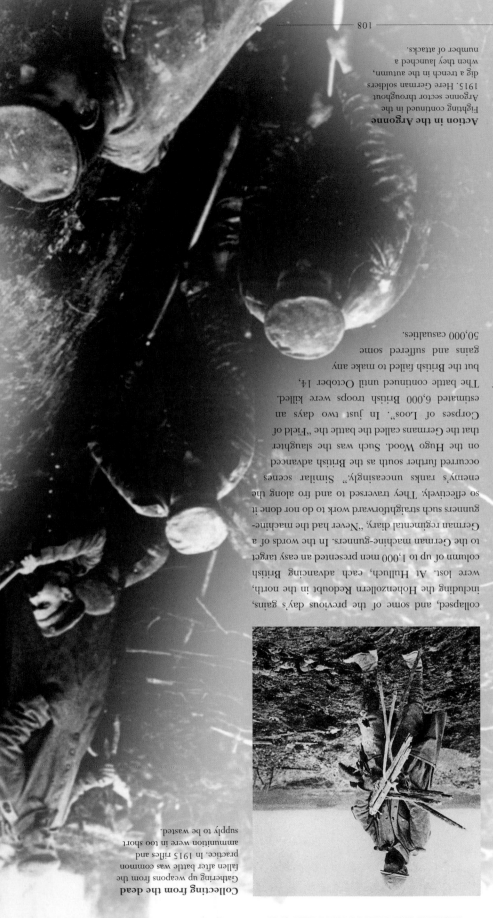

Collecting from the dead
Gathering up weapons from the fallen after battle was common practice. In 1915 rifles and ammunition were in too short supply to be wasted.

collapsed, and some of the previous day's gains, including the Hohenzollern Redoubt in the north, were lost. At Hulluch, each advancing British column of up to 1,000 men presented an easy target to the German machine-gunners. In the words of a German regimental diary, "Never had the machine-gunners such straightforward work to do nor done it so effectively. They traversed to and fro along the enemy's ranks unceasingly." Similar scenes occurred further south as the British advanced on the Hugo Wood. Such was the slaughter that the Germans called the battle "Field of Corpses of Loos". In just two days an estimated 6,000 British troops were killed. The battle continued until October 14, but the British failed to make any gains and suffered some 50,000 casualties.

Action in the Argonne
Fighting continued in the Argonne sector throughout 1915. Here German soldiers dig a trench in the autumn, when they launched a number of attacks.

Loos after the battle
Men of the 15th Scottish Territorial Division were among the troops who captured Loos from the Germans on September 25, the opening day of the attack.

To the south the French incurred some 48,000 casualties in securing Souchez on September 26 and establishing themselves on Vimy Ridge, thus forcing the Germans to move reserves from Loos to this sector. The French retained their positions on Vimy Ridge until the following year, although most of their attention now switched to Champagne. The Germans had suffered some 56,000 casualties in checking the Allied attacks.

Champagne Offensive

In Champagne the French Second Army made significant gains on September 25. It broke open the German front over a distance of some 4 km (6 miles), and advanced up to 3 km (2 miles) in less than an hour. In certain sectors the French advance secured positions behind the German Third Army's second main line of resistance, and gains were consolidated to a depth of about 5 km (3 miles). The Second Army's success was partly the result of the main weight of the assault falling upon the weakest part of the German line. But with the arrival of reserves and fresh artillery after the 26th, the Germans were able to reconstitute their defence, causing the Second Army, despite explicit orders to the contrary, to break off the battle.

There were to be a number of attacks, both in the Champagne region and in Artois, until early November, after which the failure of the Anglo-French autumn campaign was admitted at a cost of some 144,000 casualties (compared to 85,000 German casualties). There was a further, seemingly unimportant, consequence. In order to increase their heavy artillery for the Champagne offensive, the French had stripped their fortresses at Verdun of their artillery, and it was to Verdun that the thoughts of Falkenhayn now turned.

When (the officer's) platoon had run about 20 yards he signalled them to lie down and open covering fire. The din was tremendous. He saw the platoon on the left flopping down too, so he whistled the advance again. Nobody seemed to hear. He jumped up from his shell-hole and waved and signalled 'Forward'. Nobody stirred. He shouted: 'You bloody cowards, are you leaving me to go alone?' His platoon-sergeant, groaning with a broken shoulder, gasped out: 'Not cowards, sir. Willing enough. But they're all f....g dead.' The Pope's Nose machine-gun traversing had caught them as they rose to the whistle.

EXTRACT FROM *GOODBYE TO ALL THAT* BY ROBERT GRAVES, WHO TOOK PART IN THE BATTLE AT THE AGE OF 20

Major offensives on the Western Front
During 1915 the Allies made repeated attempts to break through the German lines in Artois and Champagne. Neither their campaigns, nor that of the Germans at Ypres, were successful, and by the end of the year the Western Front was much as it had been at the beginning.

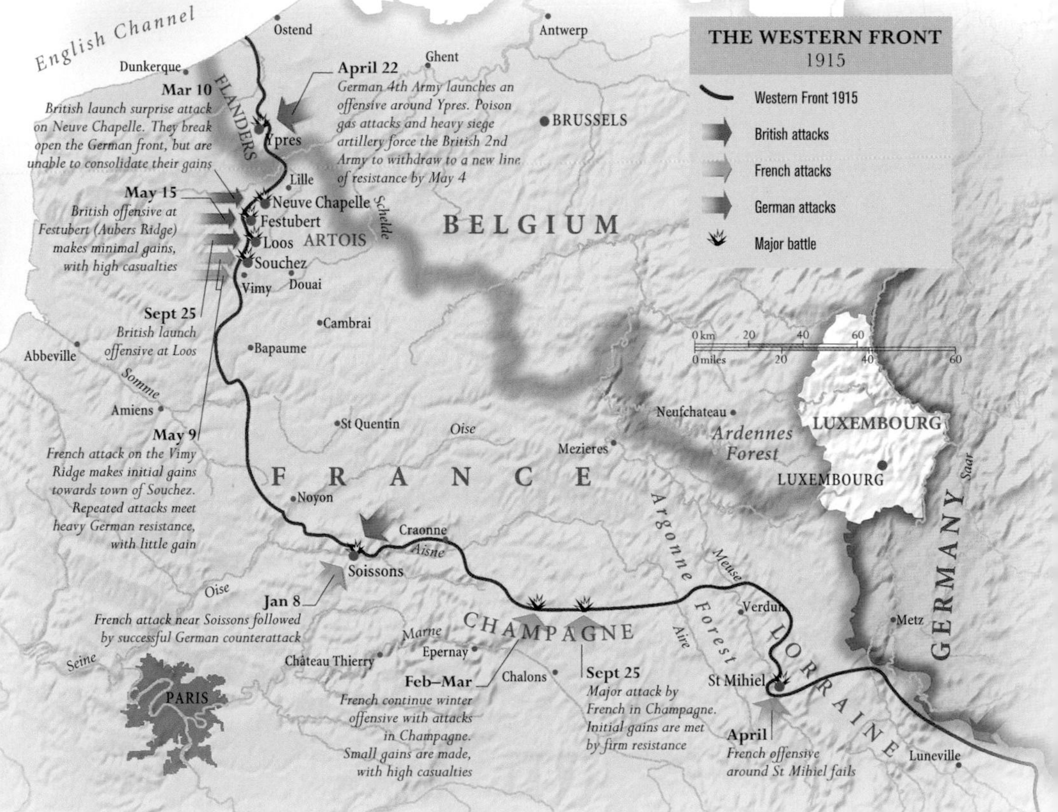

THE WESTERN FRONT
1915
Western Front 1915
British attacks
French attacks
German attacks
Major battle
English Channel
Ostend
Antwerp
Ghent
Dunkerque
BRUSSELS
FLANDERS
Ypres
Lille
Neuve Chapelle
Festubert
Loos
ARTOIS
Souchez
Vimy
Douai
Scheldt
BELGIUM
Mar 10
British launch surprise attack on Neuve Chapelle. They break open the German front, but are unable to consolidate their gains
April 22
German 4th Army launches an offensive around Ypres. Poison gas attacks and heavy siege artillery force the British 2nd Army to withdraw to a new line of resistance by May 4
May 15
British offensive at Festubert (Aubers Ridge) makes minimal gains, with high casualties
Sept 25
British launch offensive at Loos
Cambrai
Bapaume
Abbeville
Somme
Amiens
May 9
French attack on the Vimy Ridge makes initial gains towards town of Souchez. Repeated attacks meet heavy German resistance, with little gain
St Quentin
Oise
Neufchateau
Mezieres
Ardennes Forest
LUXEMBOURG
LUXEMBOURG
0 km 20 40 60
0 miles 20 40 60
FRANCE
Noyon
Craonne
Aisne
Soissons
Jan 8
French attack near Soissons followed by successful German counterattack
Oise
Argonne Forest
Meuse
Aire
Verdun
Metz
GERMANY
Saar
Marne
Epernay
CHAMPAGNE
Château Thierry
Seine
PARIS
Chalons
Feb–Mar
French continue winter offensive with attacks in Champagne. Small gains are made, with high casualties
Sept 25
Major attack by French in Champagne. Initial gains are met by firm resistance
St Mihiel
LORRAINE
April
French offensive around St Mihiel fails
Luneville

TRENCH SYSTEMS ON THE WESTERN FRONT

T HE TRENCHES THAT STRETCHED down the Western Front, from the English Channel to the Swiss border, varied considerably between different armies and over time. The German trenches in 1917–18 were vastly more sophisticated than those of 1914–15.

Dug with miniature picks, shovels and spades, the first trenches were improvised. They were really little more than rifle pits that had been linked together. The assumption that they were only temporary, and that mobile warfare would be resumed in spring 1915, meant that the first trenches were not developed substantially. In fact, throughout the war the French – committed as they were to offensive operations – had a trench system that was the least developed defensively, with only two main lines.

This, however, did not prevent them from protecting their trenches with sandbags and lining them with timber.

In British sectors there were three lines of trenches: the front, support and reserve. The front comprised con-nected fire and command trenches. The fire trenches were continuous but not straight. They consisted of sections known as "firebays", up to 9m (10yds) long, separated from each other by "traverses", which made a crenellated pattern when seen from above. The traverses protected the soldiers in one firebay from the blast of a shell landing in an adjacent bay, and provided shelter from enfilading fire – an attack down the length of the trench. The command trenches consisted of officer command posts, dug-outs for rest, and latrines. Leading to the front were communication trenches, along which telephone cables to battalion and battery headquarters were laid, and fresh reserves and supplies were moved. These were also constructed to minimize blast effect, and had slit trenches for emergency cover.

This forward system, which was protected in No Man's Land by substantial barbed wire entanglements, was some 90m (100yds) in front of what was known as the support line. This held reinforcing troops but had no command line or positions. The reserve line, in which were housed further reinforcements, was generally some 360–540m (400–600yds) behind the support line. Behind the reserve line, and beyond the range of small-arms fire, were the artillery positions. Either within the trench system or independent of it, concrete fortifications might be used to create strongpoints.

The Germans, who were generally more committed to a defensive strategy on the Western Front between spring 1915 and February 1918, gradually developed a three-line system similar to that of the British, but considerably deeper – as much as 5km (3 miles) deep by 1917. With the pick of the ground, the Germans were able to burrow deep into uplands, or use caves such as the Caverne du Dragon below the Chemin des Dames, to house up to 1,000 men. The distance between the front-line systems of the two sides was generally around 90–360m (100–400yds), though in some sectors it could be measured in single figures, and in other sectors it was as much as 900 m (1,000yds). In certain sectors, such as the Vosges mountains, individual strongpoints took the place of trenches.

Communication trench

British soldiers wait in a communication trench on their way to the front. All movement had to be below ground level, out of sight of enemy fire and observation posts. Nevertheless, signallers on both sides were often exposed as they relayed messages using semaphore, or when acting as runners between trenches.

Trench network

The map shows German trenches (in blue) as detected by French intelligence operations. The French trenches to the south, were omitted in case the map fell into German hands.

A RANGE OF PERISCOPES

Keeping watch

A periscope was a useful device for observing the enemy without running the risk of getting shot. It consisted of a tube with two mirrors, one at either end, placed at a 45-degree angle to the sides of the tube so that the image from the upper mirror was reflected in the lower one. More elaborate models provided stereoscopic vision.

Fields of barbed wire

Trenches were usually protected by belts of barbed wire. On the German side the belt was 45–90 m (50–100 ft) deep, and often survived artillery bombardments.

GERMAN BARBED WIRE

BRITISH BARBED WIRE

BRITISH RIFLE WITH CUTTERS

Trench lining

Trench walls were lined with different materials, depending on what was available. Wattle was common in the Argonne and Vosges, but planking and sandbags were widely used elsewhere.

Wire cutters

With No Man's Land a sea of barbed wire, cutters were vital equipment. Although parties were often sent out under cover of darkness to cut the wire in advance of an attack, soldiers frequently became entangled in wire and turned into easy targets for enemy fire. Wire cutters — maybe on the end of a rifle — could save a man's life.

BRITISH FOLDING WIRE CUTTERS

FRENCH WIRE CUTTERS

GERMAN WIRE CUTTERS

German dead in the Meuse sector, April 1915
The French renewed an offensive in the Meuse sector on
April 9, storming the Crête des Éparges. In the action
that followed, some Germans were overwhelmed while
still in their trenches and killed in hand-to-hand fighting.

POLAND, GALICIA AND SERBIA

JANUARY – DECEMBER 1915

On May 2 the Central Powers launched a major offensive in Galicia, between Gorlice and Tarnow, which drove the Russians back out of Galicia within seven weeks. In mid-July they began to advance through northern Poland. The Russians retreated rapidly and by mid-September they had lost their Polish provinces. The following month German, Austro-Hungarian and Bulgarian forces successfully invaded Serbia.

JANUARY 31
German attack at Bolimov on the Vistula front involves first recognized use of gas

JANUARY–MARCH
Attacks by Austrians, supported by Germans, and counterattacks by Russians, in atrocious conditions for control of the passes in the Carpathians

FEBRUARY 7–22
German victory at winter battle of the Masurian Lakes

MARCH 22
Przemysl, with garrison of 120,000, surrenders to Russians

MARCH 26
Successful Russian counterattack in Carpathians takes Lupkow Pass

APRIL 21–30
Preparation for combined German and Austrian offensive in Galicia

MAY 2
Gorlice-Tarnow Offensive begins; German 11th Army spearheads breakthrough on a wide front

MAY 15–23
Germans and Austrians cross the San River

JUNE 3
Przemysl retaken

JUNE 22
Lemberg retaken

JUNE 23–27
Germans and Austrians cross the Dniester

JULY 21–AUGUST 8
Siege of Ivangorod

AUGUST 5
Germans enter Warsaw

AUGUST 7
Russians repulse Germans near Riga

AUGUST 16
Russian army withdrawn to Brest-Osovyets-Kovno line

AUGUST 18
Fall of Kovno

AUGUST 26
Brest-Litovsk falls to Germans

SEPTEMBER 5
Tsar assumes command of Russian army with Alexeyev as his chief-of-staff

SEPTEMBER 3
Grand Duke Nicholas effectively dismissed, appointed Viceroy of Caucasus

SEPTEMBER 25
German advance against Russians comes to a virtual standstill

SEPTEMBER 18
Germans take Vilna (Vilnius)

OCTOBER 7
German and Austrian forces begin to cross Sava and Danube rivers

OCTOBER 9
Germans and Austrians take Belgrade

OCTOBER 11
Bulgarian troops enter Serbia from the east, sealing fate of Serbia

OCTOBER 22
Bulgarians occupy Kumanovo

NOVEMBER 5
Nis falls, giving Germans and their allies rail link with Turkey

NOVEMBER 16
Bulgarians take Prilep and Serbs evacuate Monastir

NOVEMBER 25
Order given for Serbian army to retreat through Albania

DECEMBER 4
German pursuit of retreating Serbians is halted

KEY

- German offensive in the north Jan 31–Feb 22
- Campaigns in Carpathians Jan–Mar
- Combined German-Austrian offensive in Poland May 2–Sept 25
- Campaign in Serbia Oct 7–Dec 4

WHILE ON THE WESTERN FRONT the opposing armies struggled to make any significant advance in 1915, on the Eastern Front the situation was to prove more fluid. The year began, however, with a series of Austro-Hungarian and German offensives that did not achieve a great deal.

THE WINTER CAMPAIGNS

As 1915 opened, the Austro-Hungarians launched an offensive in the Carpathians with the aims of ensuring the relief of the Austrian garrison in the fortress town of Przemysl and forestalling a Russian attack on Hungary. To the north the Germans planned a major offensive that would forestall any renewed Russian attempt to advance further into East Prussia from the Masurian Lakes region by pushing the Russians back beyond the Vistula.

THE CAMPAIGN IN THE CARPATHIANS

In the south, though German forces supported the Austro-Hungarian armies in the Carpathians, the two sides were evenly matched. This, combined with the fact that most of the fighting had to take place in narrow mountain passes where neither side was able to secure any telling tactical advantage, meant that the main battles – on the Dukla, Lupkow and Uzhok passes opposite Przemysl and the Verecke and Wyszkow passes to the east – achieved almost nothing. The cold and snow sometimes claimed whole sub-units overnight, adding to the sense of futility experienced by the troops. In the words of General von Kralowitz, chief of staff of the Austrian X Corps:

> "Every day hundreds froze to death; the wounded who could not drag themselves off were bound to die… there was no combating the apathy and indifference that gripped the men."

Only in March, and in the most southern sector of the front, were the Austro-German forces able to make any gains, driving the Russians to

positions behind the Dniester. This success, however, failed to prevent the Russians from securing the surrender of Przemysl, and its garrison of 120,000 officers and men, on March 22. As winter gave way to spring, the Russians, having recovered the Dukla and Lupkow passes and driven their defenders 48km (30 miles) to the south, made preparations for an invasion of Hungary.

BATTLE OF THE MASURIAN LAKES

Within the German high command there had been many weeks of argument between the "Westerners" and "Easterners" about whether Germany should adopt an offensive strategy in the East. This argument – both the product and cause of a deepening antipathy between Falkenhayn on the one hand and Hindenburg and Ludendorff on the other – was settled in January 1915 with the decision to mount an offensive from East Prussia's Masurian Lakes region into eastern Poland. The somewhat grandiose intention was to force the Russian evacuation of the Vistula salient northwest of Warsaw, and ultimately to cut the Warsaw–Vilna (Vilnius) line of communications. Holding attacks were to be mounted on the Narew River while the German Eighth and Tenth Armies made the main effort on the Gumbinnen–Johannisburg sector, encircling and annihilating the Russian Tenth Army before it could withdraw into the safety offered by Kovno and Grodno. The

Hungarian artillery
Hungarians manning the guns in the northern Carpathians struggled with snow and freezing temperatures during the early months of 1915.

German armies would then develop their offensive to the south. Following a diversionary attack by the German Ninth Army at Bolimov (to the west of Warsaw) on January 31, the Eighth and Tenth Armies opened their offensive on February 7 in blizzard conditions, with the temperature 40° below zero. With no superiority of numbers but perhaps a 9 to 1 advantage in artillery, the Tenth Army immediately broke open the weak right flank of its opposite number. However, though the two German armies trapped and destroyed the bulk of the Russian Tenth Army, it took them so long to do so that they were unable to exploit their success. In the third week of February, the Russian Tenth Army fought itself to destruction in the Augustow Forest (suffering 50,000 casualties), thus buying time for the Stavka to reconstitute the front. In March the Germans voluntarily ceded – and Russian attacks recovered – some of the ground that had changed hands in February.

Meanwhile, across the

Russian prisoners in Augustow
Up to 30,000 Russian troops were taken prisoner by the Germans during the battle in Augustow Forest that destroyed the Russian Tenth Army in February 1915.

Niemen River a surprise Russian offensive resulted in the capture of Memel on the 17th and an assault on Tilsit on the 20th. On the 21st a hastily-improvised German counterattack, supported by warships, resulted in the recapture of Memel, two days before the Austrians in Przemysl capitulated to the Russians. By the end of March the German forces in the Niemen sector had recovered all the ground lost earlier that month: they subsequently captured the Latvian port of Libau (Liepaja) on May 8.

These offensives produced no lasting strategic advantage for either side but were significant in a number of ways, including the first use of gas on the Eastern Front.

Among ruins near the Nida River
During their advance across Poland, Austro-Hungarian troops take up positions among the shattered remains of buildings.

ADVANCE ACROSS POLAND

In the spring of 1915 there was a deepening awareness in Germany of the need to support Austria-Hungary. It was also aware of the need and southern sectors of the Eastern Front.

In the spring of 1915 there was a deepening awareness in Germany of the need to support growing German commitments on the northern and southern sectors of the Eastern Front.

Austria-Hungary and Russia, and a strengthening of the position of Hindenburg and Ludendorff in their dealings with their superiors as a result of the winter campaign represented a significant weakening of both Austria-Hungary and Russia, and a strengthening of the position of Hindenburg and Ludendorff in their dealings with their superiors as a result of the winter campaign. More importantly, the winter campaign represented a significant weakening of both Shells filled with xylyl bromide, a tear-producing chemical agent, were fired by the Germans into Russian positions at Bolimov on January 31, but the intense cold made the chemical freeze, and so it did no harm. More importantly, the winter campaign

GORLICE-TARNOW OFFENSIVE

The Austro-German offensive opened on May 2 between Gorlice and Tarnow. The aim was to break open the Russian Third Army's front and advance eastwards, so trapping major enemy formations against the Carpathians. The Russian army had no more troops at its disposal than the Germans and Austro-Hungarians, and it also suffered from a severe lack of rifles and shells. At a time when 200,000 rifles were needed each month for new recruits, only 70,000 were being manufactured, often making it necessary for soldiers to wait for others to be killed so that they could take possession of their weapons. Further-more, the Germans had over one million shells available to them in the Gorlice-Tarnow sector – far more than the Russians. Over 700,000 German shells were fired in a preliminary four-hour bombardment on the evening of May 1, and within 24 hours the Russians had been driven out of Gorlice.

Advance of the German cavalry
As Russian troops retreated in haste, they sometimes omitted to destroy the bridges over rivers and so failed to delay the onward sweep of the Austro-German forces.

to take some form of offensive action that would cow Italy and Romania, thereby ensuring their increasingly dubious neutrality. In the view of the Austro-Hungarians, an offensive against Serbia was more likely to goad Italy into war than ensure its passivity. Consequently, Falkenhayn planned a major offensive commitment in Galicia, which was to be led by the German commander, Mackensen.

I pushed the clothes back (on one man) and saw a pulp, a mere mass of smashed body from the ribs downwards... The soldier's dull eyes were still looking at me and his lips moved, but no words came. What it cost me to turn away without aiding him, I cannot describe, but we could not waste time and material on hopeless cases, and there were so many others waiting.

The Russian Third Army was unable to resist the advance of the Austro-German forces, which now proceeded rapidly. On May 6, the Austrian Fourth Army captured Tarnow, taking over 30,000 Russian prisoners. On the 8th the German Eleventh Army began to close in on the San River, 130km (80 miles) from its start line. Two days later the Russian Eighth Army began to evacuate its positions along the Carpathians, to avoid being trapped, and by the 11th the whole of the Russian front south of the Vistula was in retreat. Counterattacks between May 15 and 22 checked the Austro-German forces around Opatow, but in the second half of May they were able to establish themselves east of the San.

After a brief period of reorganization, the Austro-German forces resumed the offensive on June 12, and by the 17th had broken through the fronts of the Russian Third and Eighth Armies.

Collecting weapons
Austro-Hungarian infantry collect weapons from a captured Russian trench. The Russians were very short of rifles and they could ill afford to lose them to the enemy.

Offensives in Galicia and Poland
The Russians could do little to resist the advance by the Austro-Hungarians and Germans that began on May 2 between Gorlice and Tarnow, and by the end of June they had lost Galicia. The relentless onslaught of the Central Powers was resumed on July 13 when they turned their attentions to northern Poland. By mid-September the Russians had also been driven out of Poland.

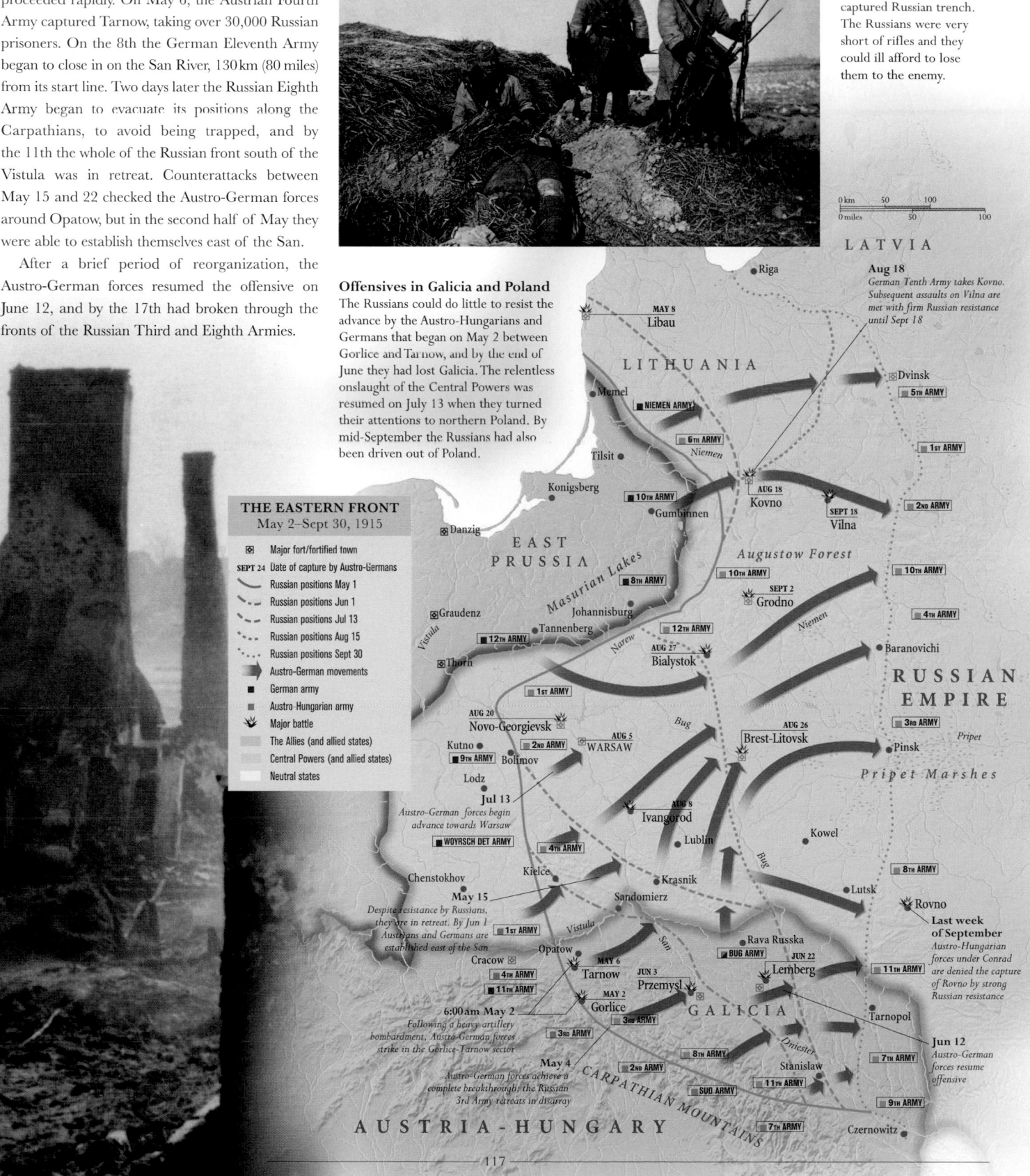

THE EASTERN FRONT
May 2–Sept 30, 1915

- ⊠ Major fort/fortified town
- SEPT 24 Date of capture by Austro-Germans
- —— Russian positions May 1
- – – Russian positions Jun 1
- –·– Russian positions Jul 13
- ···· Russian positions Aug 15
- ···· Russian positions Sept 30
- ➤ Austro-German movements
- ■ German army
- ■ Austro-Hungarian army
- ✹ Major battle
- The Allies (and allied states)
- Central Powers (and allied states)
- Neutral states

Aug 18
German Tenth Army takes Kovno. Subsequent assaults on Vilna are met with firm Russian resistance until Sept 18

Jul 13
Austro-German forces begin advance towards Warsaw

May 15
Despite resistance by Russians, they are in retreat. By Jun 1 Austrians and Germans are established east of the San

6:00am May 2
Following a heavy artillery bombardment, Austro-German forces strike in the Gorlice-Tarnow sector

May 4
Austro-German forces achieve a complete breakthrough; the Russian 3rd Army retreats in disarray

Last week of September
Austro-Hungarian forces under Conrad are denied the capture of Rovno by strong Russian resistance

Jun 12
Austro-German forces resume offensive

LATVIA

Riga

Libau · MAY 8

LITHUANIA

Memel · NIEMEN ARMY · 6TH ARMY · Niemen

Tilsit

Dvinsk · 5TH ARMY · Aug 18

1ST ARMY

2ND ARMY · SEPT 18 · Vilna

Kovno · AUG 18

Konigsberg

Gumbinnen · 10TH ARMY

EAST PRUSSIA

Danzig

Masurian Lakes · 8TH ARMY

Augustow Forest · 10TH ARMY · SEPT 2 · Grodno

10TH ARMY

4TH ARMY

Graudenz

Johannisburg

Tannenberg · 12TH ARMY · Narew · AUG 27 · Bialystok

Baranovichi

RUSSIAN EMPIRE

Thorn · 12TH ARMY

1ST ARMY

Novo-Georgievsk · AUG 20 · Bug · Brest-Litovsk · AUG 26

3RD ARMY · Pinsk · Pripet

Kutno · 2ND ARMY · AUG 5 · WARSAW

9TH ARMY · Bolimov

Lodz · Jul 13

Pripet Marshes

Ivangorod · AUG 8

Kowel

8TH ARMY

Lublin

WOYRSCH DET ARMY

4TH ARMY

Lutsk

Chenstokhov

Kielce

Krasnik

Rovno ✹

Sandomierz

Vistula

Opatow · May 15

Cracow · May 6 · Tarnow · MAY 2 · Gorlice · 3RD ARMY

4TH ARMY · 11TH ARMY

San · Przemysl · JUN 3

Rava Russka · BUG ARMY

Lemberg · JUN 22

11TH ARMY

Tarnopol

GALICIA

2ND ARMY · May 4

8TH ARMY · Dniester · Stanislaw · 11TH ARMY

7TH ARMY · 9TH ARMY

SUD. ARMY

CARPATHIAN MOUNTAINS · 7TH ARMY · Czernowitz

AUSTRIA-HUNGARY

0 km 50 100
0 miles 50 100

Frozen in time
Two Russian soldiers, caught in barbed wire and turned into easy targets for the Austro-German forces. The Russians suffered around 1,000,000 casualties during the Austro-German advance through Poland.

The Russians were in no state to put up a strong resistance, having incurred 412,000 casualties in May alone and lacking 500,000 rifles by mid-June. On the 17th they accepted the loss of Galicia, and on the 20th, with Austrian forces closing in on Lemberg – the most important of the east Galician cities – they gave orders for its evacuation. The city was captured on the 22nd. In just seven weeks the Austro-German offensive had pushed the Russian armies back to the start lines from which they had begun the war in Galicia.

ADVANCE ON WARSAW AND BREST-LITOVSK

Having transformed the position in the south, Falkenhayn and Conrad now agreed to continue the offensive with an advance on Brest-Litovsk. With the Russian forces now facing Galicia, the renewed offensive would necessarily involve frontal attacks and was unlikely to secure Brest ahead of a Russian withdrawal from central Poland. This, however, did not present a problem to Falkenhayn, whose basic aim was to conquer Poland and eliminate any immediate or direct threat to the Central Powers. Concerned to release formations for operations elsewhere, he was not prepared to accept Hindenburg and Ludendorff's plan to attempt to cripple Russia through an offensive that began on the Baltic coast and made its main effort in the Kovno-Vilna sector. The

advance into northern Poland began on July 13. The Russians proved unable to resist it, and on August 5, Warsaw – which had been under Russian control since 1815 – fell to the Germans. The Germans drove on, leaving a force to surround and besiege the fortress of Novo-Georgievsk. The garrison of 90,000 men. The garrison surrendered on the 20th. Further south Ivangorod was besieged from July 21 and captured on August 8, and Brest-Litovsk was secured on the 26th and Bialystok on the 27th. An understrength German Tenth Army took Kovno on August 18.

At this point Falkenhayn inconsistently sanctioned an assault on Vilna. The German armies pushed back the Russian flank to the north of the city but failed to inflict more than a local defeat on a well-conducted defence. The city was voluntarily ceded by the Russians on September 18 as part of a deliberate Russian retreat. Russian forces then successfully defended Molodechno, retook Smorgon and inflicted a local defeat on the Germans around Logishin. Knowing that any further Austro-German success would be hard won, Falkenhayn closed down offensive operations in the east on September 25.

As a result of the fighting for possession of Poland, 750,000 Russian soldiers had been sent to prisoner-of-war camps, where conditions were generally appalling. Civilians had also suffered

Refugees during the Russian retreat
Forced to leave their homes, refugees not only suffered considerably themselves but added to the difficulties of the retreating Russian troops by blocking the roads.

AUGUST VON MACKENSEN
~

AUGUST VON MACKENSEN (1849–1944) was one of the most impressive German field commanders of the First World War, renowned for operations requiring speed and surprise. After contributing as a corps commander to the German victory at Tannenberg in August 1914, he joined the Ninth Army in Poland and as its commander led it in the capture of Lodz in December.

In May 1915 Mackensen, as commander of the Eleventh Army, spearheaded the successful Gorlice-Tarnow offensive in Galicia. Promoted to field marshal, he further displayed his mastery of breakthrough tactics in the German summer advance through Poland. In September and in the autumn of 1916 he led the multi-national Danube Army during the successful Romanian Campaign. He spent the remainder of the war overseeing the occupying forces in Romania.

"Men who had fought in several wars and many bloody battles told me that no horrors of a field of battle can be compared to the awful spectacle of the ceaseless exodus of a population..."

RUSSIAN GENERAL GOURKO DESCRIBING THE REFUGEES
WHO FLED DURING THE RUSSIAN RETREAT IN POLAND

considerably. The Russian government had ordered the complete evacuation of the country, and to this end whole communities were driven from their villages. Deprived of any regular means of livelihood, many were to die from starvation or succumb to epidemics.

RUSSIAN LOSSES IN POLAND

Russia had lost some of its richest and most heavily industrialized provinces and its threat to the Central Powers was broken. Despite, however, losses on a scale that would have finished any other army, the Russians withdrew from Poland in surprisingly good order and remained aggressive even in defeat. The capture of Vilna alone cost the German Tenth Army 50,000 casualties. Furthermore, in the last week of September, as Austro-Hungarian forces sought to secure a victory in the south, the Russians inflicted a very sharp and severe defeat on them in front of Rovno. The Habsburg armies may have incurred as many as 300,000 casualties before German forces stabilized the situation by recapturing Lutsk.

Destroyed bridge over the San at Przemysl
On June 3, after heavy fighting, Austro-German forces retook the fortress town of Przemysl, which the Austrians had lost to the Russians in March.

THE CONQUEST OF SERBIA

In the first months of 1915, the Austro-Hungarians had been concerned that their involvement in a another offensive against Serbia would encourage Italy to declare war. It was only after the Italian declaration of war in May, followed by the defeat of the Russians in Galicia and Poland, that the Austro-Hungarians and Germans felt ready to consider the elimination of Serbia from the war. They did so, but from very different perspectives. For Austria-Hungary, a Balkans campaign represented no more than the opportunity to deal with Serbia, but for Germany it was also a means of re-establishing overland communications with Turkey and securing the support of Bulgaria.

A SECONDARY ROLE FOR AUSTRIA-HUNGARY

Austria-Hungary was painfully aware of its need for German support: the three offensives it had launched against Serbia in 1914 had all failed, with the loss of 227,000 men. Germany, however, was not prepared to play a supporting role, recognizing that it would have to take the lead in so important a task as the conquest of Serbia. In the event, Austria-Hungary's defeat at Rovno during the campaign in

Poland in September 1915 rendered it unable to play anything but a secondary role.

In fact, by the time the German Eleventh Army took up its positions below Belgrade in order to lead Austro-German forces across the Save and Danube rivers, the success of the campaign was assured. In the autumn of 1915 Serbia was considerably weaker than in the previous year, partly because of the heaviness of its 1914 losses and partly because of the typhus epidemic that was still affecting the country. Added to this was the fact that during the summer of 1915 the Germans had drawn Bulgaria to their side, its bitter rivalry with Serbia being critical in making it decide to conclude an alliance on September 6. Aware of Bulgaria's intentions to invade their country, the Serbs had no alternative but to disperse their depleted formations along extended front lines. In doing so they found themselves facing an enemy that possessed overwhelming advantages of position, timing and numbers. The Serbs had only around 200,000 troops to face over 300,000 under the overall command of Mackensen. They were also desperately short of artillery and ammunition.

Compounding Serbia's difficulties was the failure of Allied attempts to provide effective aid. After a long delay, an Anglo-French force finally began to arrive in Salonika on October 5. It was planned that this force would advance through Macedonia and provide direct support for the Serbian army. As events were to prove, however, it represented little more than strategy by gesture.

Advancing Bulgarians

Two Bulgarian armies invaded Serbia from the east on October 11. Here Bulgarian infantry can be seen advancing towards Serbian lines on the opposite hillside.

THE ADVANCE ON BELGRADE

The Austro-German forces launched their attack on October 6. They captured Belgrade on the 9th, but made only very limited gains during the first ten days because of the strength of Serbian resistance and the problems experienced in moving heavy equipment over the rivers. The state of the Serbian army, however, meant that whatever success it commanded in these opening days was transitory. It was subjected to an ongoing attack that would have ensured defeat even without the Bulgarian invasion of the 11th. The Bulgarians advanced to Kumanovo, through which the vital north-south railway ran, and captured it on the 22nd. This ensured that no relief force would arrive from Salonika, while the Serbian army could not attempt to withdraw through Macedonia.

RETREAT THROUGH THE MOUNTAINS

With the German Eleventh Army outflanking or reducing successive Serb positions in the Morava valley, the Serbian army was forced into the mountains. The Germans were unwilling to contemplate either an attempt to encircle the Serbs to the west or a move southward that might lead to a commitment against Greece. Consequently, reasoning that the remnants of the Serbian army were unlikely to survive a winter retreat through the mountains of Albania, they withdrew five divisions.

The German calculation proved to be more or less correct. By mid-November the Serbian army, with King Peter and the government, had withdrawn to Kosovo. Defeated at Gnjilane on November 22, the army was forced on the 25th to order its formations to withdraw to Albania. So began a terrible 160-km (100-mile) march by some 200,000 Serbian troops and civilians through the mountains. In the course of three weeks, thousands died from cold, hunger and disease, or at the hands of Bulgarian troops and Albanian tribesmen.

As, during December, Austro-Hungarian forces moved to occupy Montenegro, some 150,000 Serbian troops survived the mountains to reach the Albanian coast. In January 1916 they were evacuated by Allied ships from Durazzo and Valona to Corfu, where many more were to die from hunger.

Final invasion of Serbia

Austro-German forces under the overall command of Mackensen took Belgrade within four days of crossing the Serbian border in the north. They then pressed on southwards as, on October 11, the Bulgarians invaded from the east. The Serbian army was overwhelmed and finally forced to retreat to Albania.

Serbian retreat over the Drina

In the winter of 1915 the Serbian headquarters staff were among those who retreated through the Albanian mountains. With them was Radomir Putnik, celebrated military leader of the Serbs, who had to be carried in a sedan chair because of ill health.

THE SERBIAN CAMPAIGN
Oct 6–Nov 23, 1915

- Serbian positions Oct 6
- Austro–German offensives Oct 6–Nov 23
- Bulgarian offensives Oct 6–Nov 23
- Anglo–French relief force from Oct 3
- Serbian retreat from Nov 25
- Town captured by Central Powers, with date
- Major railway
- The Allies (and allied states)
- Central Powers (and allied states)
- Neutral states

0 km 20 40 60 80 100
0 miles 20 40 60 80 100

Map labels:

Danube
AUSTRIA-HUNGARY

Oct 7 Austro-German forces begin to cross Sava and Danube rivers

BELGRADE
Oct 9
Sava
Shabatz
Valjevo
Drina
BOSNIA
3RD ARMY
1ST ARMY
11TH ARMY
Orsova
Vidin
ROMANIA
Morava
SERBIA
TIMOK ARMY
1ST ARMY

Oct 11 Bulgarian forces begin their attack

Nish
2ND ARMY
SOFIA
BULGARIA
KOSOVO
Pristina
Oct 22
Prizren
Gnjilane
Kumanova
2ND ARMY
MACEDONIAN ARMY
Skopje
MONTENEGRO

Nov 25 Serbians begin an epic retreat through the mountains

ALBANIA
Scutari
Tirana
Durazzo
Berat

Jan 1916 Allied warships evacuate Serbian forces to Corfu

Valona
Lake Ohrid
Monastir
Gornichevo
Lake Ostrovo
Kastoria
MACEDONIA
Strumitsa
Lake Doiran
Doiran

Oct 3 Advance elements of Anglo-French force reach Salonika. French column pushes north, establishing position in Doiran area. Under increasing Bulgarian pressure, Doiran position is abandoned on Dec 3

Konitsa
Salonika
GREECE
CORFU

The Home Front

AT THE OUTSET OF THE WAR, the talk was of weeks, or possibly months, of combat. None of the countries involved was prepared for a conflict that would last for years and devour an unprecedented mass not just of human beings, weapons and ammunition, but also of food, coal, clothes, boots, medicine, soap, tents, spades, wire, transport vehicles and horses. To wage such a war, governments had to direct, and in some cases assume direct control of, particular key industries. It also had to sustain the workforce in these industries.

INTERVENTIONIST APPROACH IN FRANCE

At the outbreak of war, all classes in France combined in patriotic unity. The government of "Sacred Union" – President Poincaré's description of the coalition formed on August 26 – embraced a uniquely wide political spectrum and was granted exceptional powers over economic affairs and national security. Arrest without trial and very strict censorship were introduced and, in December,

Cutting back on alcohol consumption

All the powers involved in the war introduced measures to reduce alcohol consumption. In France, bar opening hours were restricted and resources were diverted from the production of wine and pastis to that of foodstuffs.

Like the other combatants, France had not foreseen the importance of shell-guzzling heavy guns, and within a matter of weeks it was facing a shell shortage. Its ammunitions industry was producing about 100,000 shells per week, but the actual requirement was more like 700,000. In addition to this shell shortfall, the French war

politicians were forbidden to visit the front (though this was later permitted under certain conditions).

French women making rifle barrels
Once the shortage of armaments became clear in the early months of the war, existing factories were adapted for the production of munitions, and women were drawn into working in them.

THE HOME FRONT
AUGUST 1914–NOVEMBER 1918

From the beginning of the war, governments in all the belligerent states introduced measures to increase their control over industrial production and the welfare of the population. How far-reaching and effective these measures were varied from country to country. France and Britain adopted a more interventionist approach than the others, with the result that their populations suffered privation rather than starvation.

KEY
- Events in France and Britain
- Events in Germany and Austria-Hungary
- Events in Russia

1914 JULY 30 — Austro-Hungarian War Production Law is put into effect

1914 AUGUST 8 — Defence of the Realm Act (DORA) passed in Britain

SEPTEMBER 8 — Germany's Department of War Raw Materials (KRA) is set up

1915 JANUARY — British women are employed as munitions workers

1915 APRIL — Ration cards introduced for "war bread" in Vienna and other Austro-Hungarian towns

MAY — "Shell scandal" in Britain results in new Ministry of Munitions; in France, further action taken to boost military production

JULY 1 — Formation of Central War Industries Committee to coordinate war production

JULY–AUGUST — "Great Retreat" from Poland triggers economic and political turmoil in Russia

1916 JANUARY 1 — German coal industry placed under state control

1916 MAY 1 — British summer time introduced as "daylight saving" measure

MAY 25 — Universal conscription introduced in Britain

JULY 12 — Riots in Austria-Hungary force down government-fixed price of bread and flour

AUGUST 29 — Under the Hindenburg Programme, Germany is organized as a war economy

OCTOBER — Famine, distress and political unrest in Russian cities; wave of strikes in Petrograd

DECEMBER 7 — New War Cabinet organizes Britain for total war

1917 JANUARY — "Turnip winter" in Germany after failure of potato harvest

MARCH 8 — "February Revolution" leads to tsar's abdication and creation of liberal Provisional Government

1917 MARCH 28 — Formation of Women's Auxiliary Army Corps in Britain

MAY 24 — Strikes in Vienna's war production factories

MAY–JUNE — Strikes and unrest among French civilians at same time as mutinies in army

AUGUST — Food riots in German towns

NOVEMBER 6–7 — "October Revolution": Bolsheviks take over Provisional Government

NOVEMBER — Vienna is close to starvation as war production doubles

1918 JANUARY — 1,500,000 German workers strike; widespread food riots in Austria-Hungary

1918 JANUARY 1 — Food rationing for individuals introduced in Britain

JUNE — "Spanish flu" reaches Britain after spreading from Middle East

10 JUNE — Representation of the People Act gives vote to some British women

JULY — French government takes control of key war production industries

NOVEMBER — Revolutionary strikes erupt all over Germany

economy was challenged by the effect of German occupation, which included about two-thirds of France's iron and steel capacity, and 40 per cent of its coal mines. The government recalled thousands of conscripts to return to the industrial war effort and the number of workers in the French armaments industries rose from just 50,000 in 1914 to 1.7 million by 1918. One-third were women, who were increasingly taking over men's jobs in a wide range of occupations in heavy and light industry and transport, and doing clerical work.

THE FRENCH WAR ECONOMY

In the first months of the war, France's economy was totally disorganized – with a resulting sharp rise in unemployment. The industrial crisis was largely overcome during 1915, but at the cost of increasing national debt. The revival of the working-class movement from 1916 brought further disruption, and in May–June 1917, coinciding with the mutinies among the troops, over 70 industries were hit by strikes in Paris and St Etienne, the chief armaments centre.

Nevertheless, the majority of workers adhered to the patriotic ideal, and most French people backed Clemenceau, who in November 1917 became, at the age of 76, both prime minister and war minister. With a war cabinet of only five members, he was a virtual dictator, suppressing all criticism and prosecuting any public figure who expressed defeatist attitudes.

The middle classes were generally hardest hit economically, at least in relative terms. Salaries were frozen while the cost of living more than doubled. It was matched by wage rises among munitions workers, though not by the smaller rises in other industries. Soldiers' families received subsistence payments of 1.25 francs per day plus 50 sous for each child. Together with the rise in food prices (though there was no serious food shortage in France), the payments made many peasant households better off. Peasant families, however, suffered relatively higher casualties than those of urban workers.

GOVERNMENT CONTROL IN BRITAIN

Within days of the outbreak of war, the British government was empowered by the Defence of the Realm Act (DORA) to direct the economy and public life. It lost no time in taking control of the railways, buying up all the raw sugar, regulating prices, guaranteeing banks, printing more paper money, doubling income tax and raising customs duties. The long arm of DORA even reached out to

Ploughing up London's Richmond Park
War-time shortages encouraged resourcefulness on the home front. In the country, pasture was converted to arable land. In towns and cities, recreational parks served as vegetable gardens.

THE ESCALATING COST OF WAR

DURING THE WAR public expenditure increased on an enormous scale. The first war-time budgets were considerably higher that any peace-time budget, and continued to rise throughout the war. In Britain expenditure increased by almost 500 per cent between 1914 and 1917, followed by a dip in 1918. In Germany it increased by just over 500 per cent up to 1917, in France by 560 per cent up to 1918, and in Russia by 315 per cent up to 1916. It is hard to determine exactly how much of this rise represented an increase in military expenditure together with other expenditure related directly to the war effort, such as spending on transport and the bureaucracy required to implement various controls. Among the reasons for the huge increase in spending was a rapid rise in inflation and the requirement to pay interest on an ever-increasing national debt. No country was able to finance the war from taxation. All had to rely on borrowing from other countries and from their own population, who were encouraged to support the war effort by buying government war bonds.

SHORTAGES AND RATIONING
~

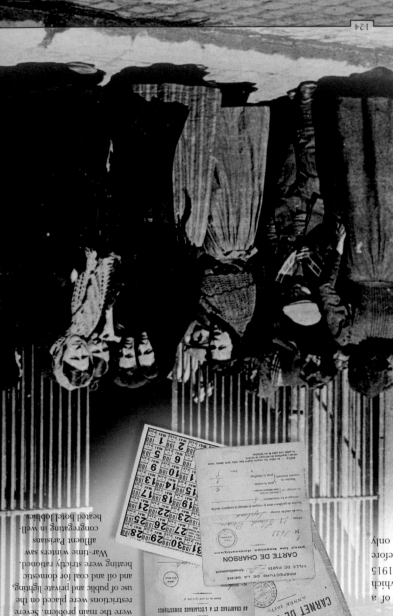

Waiting in line
Armed with baskets, French women put in their waiting hours. Long queues for government-controlled rations of essential foods and commodities became an everyday sight in the towns and cities of the home fronts.

T HE AGE-OLD CONNECTION between food and military success was expressed by Napoleon's dictum: "An army marches on its stomach". The First World War, however, saw a new situation, in which civilian populations far from any battlefield became vulnerable to war-induced famine and disease.

Food was a matter of life and death in war-time Russia's northern cities, where by 1917 there were endless queues for minimal, unregulated supplies of the most basic provisions. The bread queues of Petrograd, where people gathered for hours every day – and sometimes every night – acted as unofficial information centres and became hotbeds of revolution. Queuing also became part of life in war-time France, where government rationing of coal, oil and some foods began in 1918.

In Britain, the war meant privation rather than starvation. By the end of 1916, government controls meant that food retailers were only allowed half of their usual stocks, which they rationed on a household basis. Gradually, state controls over the distribution of food were tightened. Early in 1918, by which stage intensified submarine warfare was seriously affecting food imports, rationing for individuals was introduced, principally of sugar, tea, margarine, bacon, cheese and butter and then, from April, of meat.

On the outbreak of war, German civilians trusted the state's promise of a short war. They were not prepared for the effects of the Allied blockade, which began to bite within months, particularly in Hamburg and Berlin. In 1915 Berliners were the first Germans to be issued with bread ration cards. Before long, meat, dairy products, potatoes, sugar, cereals and soap were only obtainable through ration cards. As meat grew scarce, people resorted to such dubious delicacies as pickled walrus and boiled crow. The black market flourished, and everywhere there were queues. The winter of 1916–17 was known as the "turnip winter" because, after a disastrous potato harvest, turnips and beets became staples.

A similar situation of acute shortages, poorly administered, ever-shrinking rations, "ersatz" substitution foods and rampant profiteering was enacted in the towns and cities of Austria-Hungary. Riots and, eventually, revolts were triggered by the food crisis, which began when supplies of grain and oil were drastically affected by the Russian advance through Galicia in 1914. To add to the tension between war workers and war bosses, the political gap between Austria and Hungary widened as, by 1917, Hungarian grain was feeding the army while civilians in the western, Austrian half of the empire were starving.

French ration cards
In France there was rationing of foodstuffs such as bread and sugar, but in fact fuel shortages were the main problem. Severe restrictions were placed on the use of public and private lighting, and oil and coal for domestic heating were strictly rationed. War-time winters saw affluent Parisians congregating in well-heated hotel lobbies.

encompass Britain's horses, 165,000 of which were requisitioned for army service within the first months of the war. However, little was done in the early months to increase the supply of shells.

In the spring of 1915 Britain experienced a "shell scandal". Newspapers took the line of General French, who blamed the failure to break through on the Western Front on a shortage of shrapnel and high-explosive shells. The government was stung into action, and created a new Ministry of Munitions under the future prime minister Lloyd George, who set about co-ordinating, controlling, and boosting production in all of the country's armaments industries. In addition to the established armament firms, there were now national factories, specializing in the mass production of rifles, shells, small arms ammunition, powder and explosives. This was dangerous work, often done by women who became known as the "munitionettes".

Trusting in the overwhelming superiority of its navy, Britain was the only major European power without conscription. Indeed, at the outset, there was so much patriotic enthusiasm in Britain that the army could barely cope with the number of volunteers. Despite the huge losses on the Western Front, there were enough volunteers until May 1916, when conscription was introduced.

In the previous year it had become apparent that relying on volunteers was having an adverse effect on the production of munitions. The National Registration Act had been introduced with the aim of establishing what proportion of men of military age were still eligible for service and what proportion were employed in work vital to the war effort. These men, who were employed on the railways and in mining and agriculture, as well as in munitions, were not to be enlisted in the army.

To improve workers' efficiency, there was a campaign against the consumption of alcohol that included such measures as watering down beer and reducing pub opening times. Working hours were extended, with "summer time" – by which all the clocks in Britain were put forward by an hour – being introduced in May 1916. At the same time, the new Ministry of Food supervised agriculture and, eventually, introduced rationing.

Many war-time initiatives were to develop into permanent institutions. Britain's Medical Research Council, for example, began as a war-time medical committee. During the war the citizens of both Britain and France not only learnt to live with a plethora of new regulations – curfews, rations, passports and the like. They also came to expect greater government involvement with their welfare.

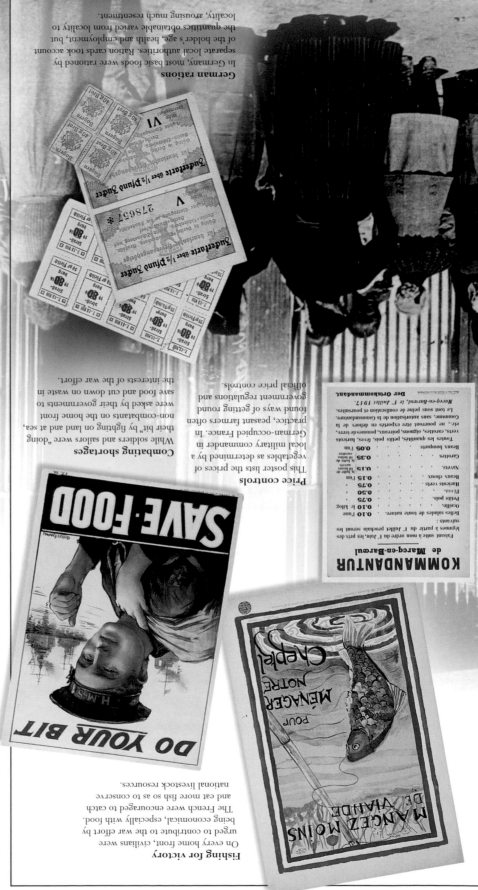

Fishing for victory
On every home front, civilians were urged to contribute to the war effort by being economical, especially with food. The French were encouraged to catch and eat more fish so as to conserve national livestock resources.

Price controls
This poster lists the prices of vegetables as determined by a local military commander in German-occupied France. In practice, peasant farmers often found ways of getting round government regulations and official price controls.

Combating shortages
While soldiers and sailors were "doing their bit" by fighting on land and at sea, non-combatants on the home front were asked by their governments to save food and cut down on waste in the interests of the war effort.

German rations
In Germany, most basic foods were rationed by separate local authorities. Ration cards took account of the holder's age, health and employment, but the quantities obtainable varied from locality to locality, arousing much resentment.

DEPRIVATION IN RUSSIA

Counting, like all the other belligerent states, on a short campaign, the Russian War Ministry had made no long-term plans. It also failed to appreciate the importance of industry to the war effort. Existing stocks of weapons and ammunition only lasted for the first few weeks of the war, and instead of responding to calls of alarm from generals at the front, the tsarist government dismissed them. By the spring of 1915 the shortages were so bad that whole battalions of the Russian army were being trained without rifles, while in battle some Russian troops depended for weapons on those taken from the dead and wounded.

The munitions crisis eased after the summer of 1915, when a new, tsar-approved War Industries Committee began to co-ordinate the supply of materials and orders to the big armaments factories. Between January and April 1915 the whole army had received only 2,000,000 shells, although the stated requirement of the *Stavka* (Supreme Command) was 3,500,000 per month. By the autumn of 1916 production had risen to 4,500,000 shells per month. The production of rifles had also increased, from around 70,000 per month in 1915 to 111,000 per month, but this was still well short of the estimated monthly requirement for 200,000.

While the supply of munitions improved, the soldiers continued to be deprived of the most basic requirements. On the occasion of one inspection by

the tsar, a single company was kitted out by dint of raiding several regiments' resources, leaving the unseen men in the trenches without boots, knapsacks, trousers and hats. In the absence of any competent government action, Russia's war effort was supported by volunteers. In towns and cities patriotic clubs and committees organized the collection and distribution of the food, linen and medicine donated by the public, and women volunteered themselves as nurses to the ever-increasing number of casualties. From June 1915, under the leadership of liberal aristocrat Prince Lvov, a movement based on the Russian empire's network of local councils, the Zemstvo Union, took on the job of supplying and supporting the army. Its volunteers led the way in setting up field canteens and medical units at the front, evacuating the wounded, helping refugees and providing relief to soldiers' families. Meanwhile, civilians starved. This was partly because of problems with the production of food, particularly after the loss of Poland in 1915. More significant, however, was the inability of the Russian railway system to ensure the proper distribution of food or, indeed, anything else.

SHORTAGES IN GERMANY

In common with all the other governments of the belligerent states, Germany was so beguiled by the short-war fallacy that it had no plans for a continuing war. It was certainly not prepared for

Patriotism and profit
This 1916 poster invites Russians to help the motherland in her hour of need, and make themselves a good profit, by buying government war bonds at 5.5 per cent interest. The extra finance was needed to boost production in the war industries.

Working as painters
Once the men had been called up, the young, the old and the female were called upon to fill the labour gap. Here, watched by their foreman, French women paint and label railway carriages.

CONSCIENTIOUS OBJECTORS

ONCE THE WAR BEGAN, a great tide of patriotism rolled over any pacifist inclinations of Christians, feminists, anarchists and socialists all over Europe. As the only major combatant state without a conscripted army, Britain was also the only country where open opposition to the war on religious or political grounds continued to be an option, but it was a distinctly uncomfortable option. As the death toll on the Western Front mounted, and the national war effort intensified, pacifist dissidents were increasingly vulnerable to popular rage.

The various strands of the pacifist movement united in opposition to conscription, which came for unmarried men early in 1916, and then, in May, for all men. Conscription represented a sharp break with Britain's tradition of voluntary military service and, in framing the new Military Service Acts, the government was mindful of this tradition. The Conscription Acts allowed for the exemption of non-religious "conscientious objectors" as well as members of Britain's historic peace churches, notably the Society of Friends (Quakers).

In theory, the Military Service Acts were generous – and far ahead of the times – but in practice many "conchies" were treated as criminals. For many of the elderly worthies who made up the local tribunals, which were set up to hear claims for exemption, conscientious objectors were unprincipled "shirkers" who only wanted to save their own skins. Across Britain, there was wide variation in the fairness and efficiency of the tribunals, and great confusion over the difference between "absolutists" and "alternativists". One in ten of the 16,500 men who applied for exemption were "absolutist" pacifists like Stephen Hobhouse, a Quaker who, rather than agree to serve with the Friends' Ambulance Unit as a condition of exemption, was sent to prison, where his brutal treatment caused an outcry. The majority of the conscientious objectors were "alternativists", who agreed to non-combatant military service and spent the rest of the war working in hospitals, farms and kitchens.

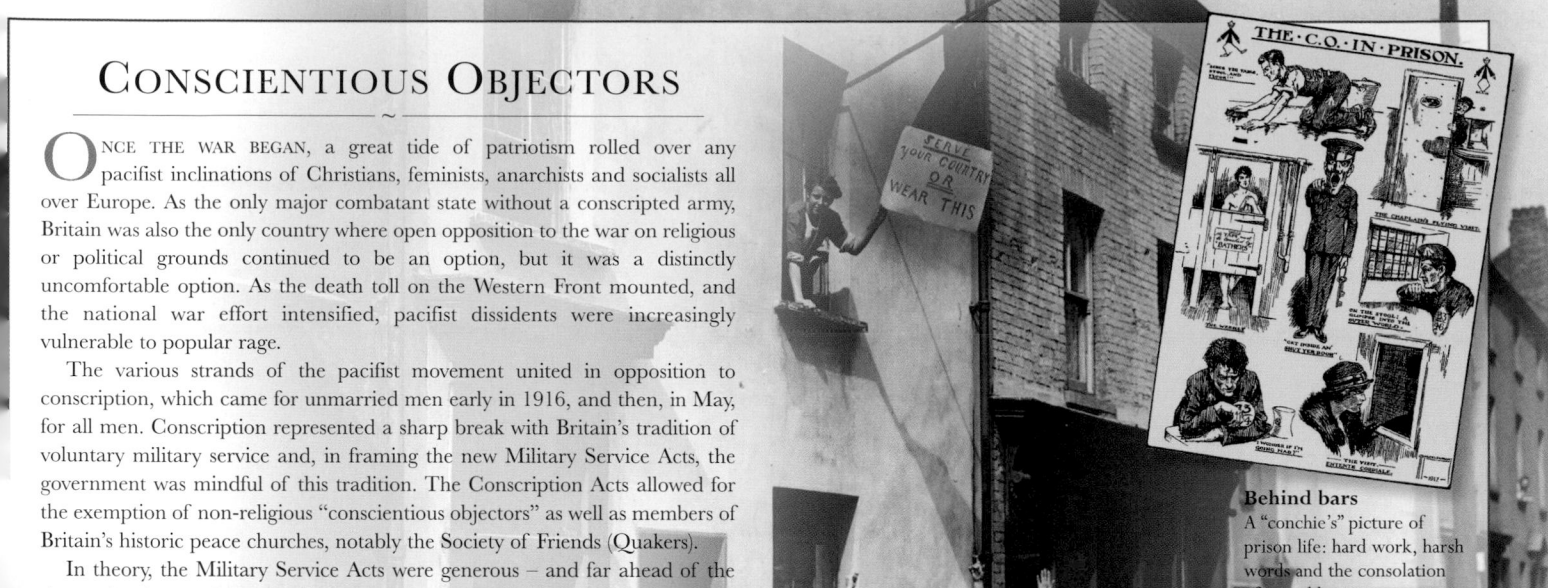

Behind bars
A "conchie's" picture of prison life: hard work, harsh words and the consolation of a weekly visit.

White feather campaign
In Britain, female vigilantes handed out white feathers to able-bodied, young men not in uniform as tokens of their supposed cowardice.

the Allied blockade, which cut off Germany from its overseas sources of food and essential raw materials. Within a few days, however, the Minister of War had set up a War Materials Department (KRA) which set about collecting supplies and distributing them among businesses producing for the war effort. Without this, and the skill of German scientists in devising substitutes for unobtainable materials, it is doubtful whether Germany would have been able to stay in the war.

The KRA system was reasonably effective until 1916, when the massive requirements of the battles at Verdun and on the Somme revealed the need to increase production. In place of the partnership between the government on the one hand, and industry and the army on the other, a

Using new skills in aeroplane production
A young woman, using woodworking and joinery skills, puts the finishing touches to an aeroplane propeller blade at a factory in Ipswich, eastern England. Before the war, few women had acquired such skills.

WOMEN IN INDUSTRY AND ON THE LAND

W ARS HAVE ALWAYS INVOLVED women as carers and casualties and victims, but the first "total" war called for the participation of more women than ever before in many more ways. In Britain, where there was already a strong movement for female democratic rights, suffragette leader Emmeline Pankhurst demanded women's "right to serve", and do no more than "nurse soldiers or knit socks". Women's willingness – and war-time requirements – facilitated the entry of thousands of "munitionettes" into the war industries.

Unlike the suffragettes, so many of whom were "ladies" and highly educated, most of "Tommy's sisters" in the war production factories were ordinary, unskilled working women. Before turning their hands to the operation of machine lathes, and the manufacture of everything military – from guns and gas masks, to shells and aeroplane propellers – many of them had worked as domestic servants.

The war was also a stimulus to the opening up of new employment opportunities in France. Women were drawn into the revamped French factories first by private employers and later by the state. By 1918 more than a million French women were working in national defence, armaments and aeronautics. In Austria-Hungary, too, where by 1916 42.5 per cent of workers in heavy industry were female – as compared with 17.5 per cent in 1913 – the war had the effect of diverting women from traditional female jobs into "skilled men's work".

By 1915 women in Germany were working at everything from chemicals, electrical equipment,

Women in agriculture

Over 113,000 women took up agricultural work in Britain during the war. Initially, many were part-time volunteers. The Women's Land Army was formed in 1917 in response to the need for a full-time, paid workforce. Thousands of women joined up, but ex-soldiers and German prisoners of war continued to be of vital importance to agricultural production.

and metalwork to precision instruments and leather goods, and by 1918 they formed 55 per cent of the industrial workforce. Although the pressure on them to volunteer for industrial war work was higher than in Britain and France, their health and safety conditions were much worse. In France, for example, young mothers were not permitted to do munitions work, but this was not the case in Germany where 60-hour weeks were not uncommon for women of all ages.

The war drained millions of men from the land. On small family farms, women and grandfathers and children coped as they have always coped in times of crisis, and shouldered the extra burden themselves. In France the drop in food production was compounded by German occupation, and was so serious that by 1917 the government had released 300,000 soldiers from the army to work on the land. Forced labour was the German government's solution to the land crisis, and by 1918 100,000 Belgians and 600,000 Poles were at work on German farms and factories.

In Britain, women were asked to take the place of the men who had been diverted from agriculture. The first official, government-sponsored organization was the Women's Forage Corps, founded in 1915, and this was followed by the Women's Forestry Corps and the Women's Land Army.

NATIONAL SERVICE
WOMENS LAND ARMY

GOD SPEED THE PLOUGH AND THE WOMAN WHO DRIVES IT

Munitions workers

Munitions meant more than guns and shells, the term being applied to everything required by the war machine, from gas masks to propellers. These women are making aircraft components.

Fodder-makers

Summer 1918, a team of British women, members of the Forage Corps, operate a monster hay-baling machine driven by a steam engine. It was the job of the Women's Forage Corps to provide food for the thousands of horses on which the army depended.

virtual military dictatorship over the entire economy – the Hindenburg Programme – was established. A War Office was set up with responsibility for labour, weapons, munitions, raw materials, and food supplies for the armed services. Because of the continuing Allied blockade, Germany's war production could not match that of its enemies, even though the munitions workers worked longer hours while surviving on much less food.

The food-related crimes of speculation, hoarding and adulteration were rife on the German home front, and the worst affected civilians were the urban poor. German city-dwellers got used to spending much of their waking lives in queues. Women would get up in the middle of the night, and take their knitting and sewing to the shops, hoping to be among the first at the scene of a morning food delivery. People who waited in line, only to find that supplies had run out, and who were then forced to join yet another queue, were said to be dancing a "polonaise".

Bread became so scarce in the German capital that an escaping British prisoner-of-war was recaptured when his sandwich, made of white bread and obtained in a parcel from home, gave him away. Although Berlin was far from any front line, life there was utterly changed by the war. Theatres, museums and street markets were closed, and there were cuts in public transport, electricity and street lighting. As early as 1915 Berlin had lost its copper roofs and wrought iron railings, and coal carts were pulled by old horses, donkeys and even circus elephants.

Waiting for the soup
The huge city of Berlin was particularly vulnerable to the effects of the Allied blockade. By 1916 thousands of Berliners depended on the soup doled out from kitchens set up by the German Women's National Service.

MILITARIZATION IN AUSTRIA-HUNGARY

The 51.3 million people in the Austro-Hungarian Empire were the subjects of Franz Josef I, who was titled the emperor of Austria and the king of Hungary. While the Austrian half of the empire was largely industrialized, with factories capable of producing armaments and heavy machinery, the Hungarian half had a predominantly agrarian economy. They shared an imperial currency and a customs union, but each half had considerable control over its own national armies and resources. In 1914 Austria-Hungary had the theoretical advantage of a war production law, which allowed for the "militarization" of life on the home front. Thus, the railways were strictly for army or army-related use, and men under 50 who were not deemed fit enough for combat duty were still liable for work in the war production factories. A pre-war law banning night work by women was lifted,

as was the traditional ban on Sunday working, and the wages of war workers were kept to a government-controlled minimum.

A poor harvest in 1914, combined with the destruction of so much farmland on the Eastern Front and the impact of the Allied blockade, meant that Austria's industrial war workers were soon beginning to experience the effects of food shortages. Increasing tension between workers and their military bosses was matched by the tension between Austria and Hungary. The war disrupted the symbiotic relationship between Austria's factories and Hungary's farms, and the imperial government lacked the authority and power to impose or enforce a centralized food policy. As a result, urban Austria slowly starved while rural Hungary had a surplus. An embittered Viennese writer described the war as an operetta for which Berlin supplied the libretto and Budapest the music, which was an elegant way of expressing Austria's increasing deference to German militarism and dependence on Hungarian grain.

Composed of 15 nations, the Habsburg empire did not command the undivided loyalty of its subjects. In fact, the multi-national character of Austria-Hungary was a factor in the young Adolf Hitler's decision to enlist as a German rather than an Austrian soldier. The loyalty of the starving populations of the cities of central Europe was further strained by the unchecked behaviour of "profiteers", ruthless entrepreneurs who took conspicuous advantage of hard times on the home front. Theatregoers in Budapest, for example, were disturbed by the war-enriched sounds of the home front devouring black market salami and gherkins.

A woman's touch
In French war production, women were concentrated in the chemical, wood and transport sectors, where they generally performed handling tasks and specialized in operating all sorts of machine tools, from lathes to welders.

Dangerous work
As precautions against the risks of explosion and TNT poisoning, British munitions workers were equipped with overalls, caps and gloves. Even so, female shell-fillers were nicknamed "canaries" because the powder turned their skin bright yellow.

THE IMPACT OF THE WAR ON WOMEN

WOMEN'S ROLES EXPANDED during the First World War, moving beyond the traditionally sanctioned realm of Kinder, Kirche, Küche ("children, church and kitchen") in all of the combatant states. Although the war-time press made much of the obvious novelty of females driving omnibuses and ambulances, and wearing overalls and trousers for their jobs in heavy industry, there were no less significant changes in spheres such as medicine, where women were already established.

Florence Nightingale was never as close to the action as the front-line nurses of the First World War. Mairi Chisholm and her colleague Elsie Knocker (later the Baroness de T'Serclaes) joined a "flying column" and ran a wound-dressing post from a cellar on the Western Front: "We started the day by being heavily shelled – shrapnel just bursting their heads off". The Scottish Women's Hospitals (SWH) was founded by Scottish surgeon Elsie Inglis, who died in Russia in 1917 and whose very first enquiries at the War Office were met with: "Go home and sit still".

Scottish Women's Hospitals ran 14 fully equipped hospitals on every Allied front except those controlled by the British army, which was supported by the VADs (below). Led by Mabel Stobart, the SWH unit in Serbia stayed with the Serbian army throughout the "Great Retreat", a march of epic heroism and hardship over the mountains of Albania and Montenegro. One of the British women, Flora Sandes, joined the Serbian infantry and having survived combat, and a serious wound, ended the war as a commissioned officer.

Flora Sandes' career as a soldier was unusual, but there were other unusual women. The Russian army's all-female Battalion of Death was organized by Maria Bochkareva, who had worked as a factory foreman before the war. After making a direct appeal to the Tsar, she was allowed to become a soldier and spent two years in the trenches. In 1917, when she had achieved the rank of sergeant, she formed her Women's Battalion of Death in the hope of raising the morale of her fellow soldiers, and shaming them into a victorious drive against the enemy. The commander-in-chief on the southern sector of the front, General Brusilov, supported Bochkareva's initiative because he believed that Russia's war effort would gain from greater participation by patriotic volunteers of both sexes. Bochkareva's women shaved their heads and wore regular army uniforms and before they left for the front, they assembled in Moscow to be blessed by the Russian Church.

The effect of the war on "white collar" women was less spectacular, but more enduring. In France alone, the state bureaucracy mushroomed as a result of the war effort, increasing by 25 per cent in just four years. An army of women typed the letters and lists, and answered the telephones of war-time government agencies and offices. The rise of office jobs was just one of the changes that were well underway in industrialized countries before 1914, but which the war accelerated and made more obvious. After 1918, prosperous British households suffered from "servant problems", and fewer young women were prepared to work as maids.

Voluntary Aid Detachments

Britain's Voluntary Aid Detachments pre-dated the war and included men and women. But as the army claimed more and more men, most of the volunteer support workers were female.

A moving hospital
A British nurse tends to her patients while they are being transported by ambulance train from the front to hospital. Of all the war-time women's organizations, the British women's medical services were undoubtedly among the most professional.

Coping alone

By removing millions of men from their families, the war had a huge impact on the role of women. For thousands of mothers, the war years were a testing balancing act between duties of home-making in a time of exceptional privation and the demands of war work.

Transport workers

As the men of Berlin left for the front, women donned uniforms and began to run the city. As well as driving horse-drawn buses and mail-wagons, they operated the city's trams. This war-time substitution crew, which includes a boy, was photographed in 1917. After 1918, few of these women would continue in their war jobs. Nevertheless, important precedents had been set for women's work.

Brevet de Marraine

A French government certificate acknowledges the holder as a "marraine". The marraines (literally, godmothers) were women who sponsored individual soldiers in the French Army by writing letters to them. The idea behind the scheme was that these concerned yet cheerful penpals would keep up morale at the front and assure the soldiers in the trenches that their efforts and sufferings were appreciated by those at home.

EDITH CAVELL

EDITH CAVELL (1865–1915), the daughter of a Norfolk clergyman, was the matron of a nursing school in Brussels, which became a Red Cross hospital for the care of wounded men from both sides of the Western Front. She became involved in an underground movement that helped more than 200 English, French and Belgian soldier-prisoners to escape from German-occupied Belgium into neutral Holland. Along with the Belgian resistance organizer, Philippe Baucq, Nurse Cavell was arrested by the local German authorities and condemned to death. Her execution by firing squad on October 12, 1915 caused a wave of revulsion and fierce anti-German propaganda in Britain and the USA. Her own last reported words were: "I realize that patriotism is not enough. I must have no hatred or bitterness towards anyone".

BATTLES OF ATTRITION
1916

~

FOLLOWING THEIR FAILURE TO BREAK THE STALEMATE ON THE WESTERN FRONT IN 1915, BRITAIN AND FRANCE PLANNED A MAJOR OFFENSIVE ON THE SOMME IN THE SUMMER OF 1916. BEFORE THIS COULD TAKE PLACE, HOWEVER, THE GERMANS LAUNCHED THEIR OWN MAJOR OFFENSIVE IN FEBRUARY AT VERDUN. BOTH OFFENSIVES WERE TO BECOME GREAT BATTLES OF ATTRITION, COSTING THE LIVES OF HUNDREDS OF THOUSANDS OF MEN FOR LITTLE GAIN. THE ALLIES ONLY MET WITH SUCCESS ON THE EASTERN FRONT, DURING THE BRUSILOV OFFENSIVE, AND EVEN THIS WAS SHORT-LIVED.

~

French and British troops in a trench
On the Western Front, from Flanders to the Somme, British and French soldiers met as they took over sections of the front line from each other. The position of this line was to change very little during 1916.

STALEMATE AND SLAUGHTER

THE ALLIES ENTERED 1916 WITH A CERTAIN OPTIMISM. BRITAIN NOW HAD

38 DIVISIONS ON THE WESTERN FRONT, AND RUSSIA COULD AT LAST MATCH THE

NUMBER OF GERMAN AND AUSTRO-HUNGARIAN DIVISIONS ON THE EASTERN FRONT.

BRITAIN AND FRANCE WERE ALSO CONVINCED THAT THE FAILURES OF 1915 COULD BE

ATTRIBUTED TO SPECIAL FACTORS THAT WOULD NOT BE REPEATED IN THE FUTURE.

IN REALITY, THE ALLIES had many reasons to be concerned. They had widening commitments at Salonika and in the Middle East, plus the continuing campaigns in Cameroon and East Africa to pursue. Much more serious, however, was the weakening of Russia as a result of its territorial and manpower losses during 1915. Russia had never been able to conscript more than a relatively small part of its available manpower, and by the end of 1915 it was clear that it would exhaust its supply of trained soldiers within a year. For Russia, victory in 1916 was essential.

MISREADING THE LESSONS OF 1915

Beneath Allied confidence in late 1915 was a failure to realize the exact nature of the problems associated with offensive action. In the course of the year German wire defences on the Western Front had been considerably thickened, and it had become apparent that high explosive was the only means of cutting through the fields of barbed wire. Prolonged bombardment, however, not only resulted in the loss of surprise, but also overlooked the fact that the defence was continually evolving and increasing in strength.

By the end of 1915 the German defence on the Western Front was still far removed from the system that was to be in place by 1917, but the defensive positions being prepared for front-line troops were elaborate and formidable. Moreover, by the end of 1915 the British remained badly under-equipped in terms of heavy artillery, and they had only remedied their shortage of shells by sacrificing quality. The Russians had overcome the worst of their equipment shortages so that virtually every soldier at the front now had a rifle. However, even more than the British, they had insufficient supplies of all types of artillery. On top of these deficiencies was the fact that British and Russian planning for a breakthrough was rudimentary.

Both Britain and France were aware of Russia's increasing weakness and their own in-effectiveness in diverting German attention away from the Eastern Front. Consequently, at and after the Chantilly conference (December 5–8, 1915), they drew up a plan of campaign based on unity of action. The British high command favoured an attack in Flanders supported by an amphibious landing behind the German flank, but the French insisted on an attack on the Somme. Ostensibly this was because the terrain there was better than in Flanders. The real reason, however, was simply that it was on the Somme that the British and French armies met. Without any major railway close to the

Somme landscape
From the last week of June 1916 a series of relentless bombardments, in which miilions of shells were fired, produced a landscape of total desolation.

"A shell-hole strewn with bully-tins, broken weapons, fragments of uniform, and dud shells, with one or two dead bodies on its edge... this was the never-changing scene that surrounded each one of all these hundreds of thousands of men."

GERMAN WRITER ERNST JÜNGER DESCRIBING THE
SOMME BATTLEFIELD IN HIS NOVEL, *STORM OF STEEL*

Somme in which the British would play their full part. It was agreed that the Russians would mount an offensive in mid-June 1916 while the Italians would attack in August at the same time as the British and French began their offensive on the Somme. There was, however, disagreement between the British and French over who should be responsible for the preliminary attacks that would divert German attention from the scene of the main effort. The French high command insisted that the British stage these attacks while the British high command, aware of the limitations of the new divisions coming into the line, resisted the demand. German attention was diverted from the Somme nonetheless, though in a way that neither the British nor the French anticipated.

FALKENHAYN'S PLAN

By the end of 1915 there appeared to be no immediate demands upon Germany's resources and attention from secondary theatres of war. Aware that in 1916 the French would renew their offensive efforts and the new armies of Britain would enter the field in strength, Falkenhayn reasoned that it was time once again to take the initiative in the West. He believed that Britain was the cornerstone of the alliance opposing Germany. Recognizing, however, that it was not possible to strike directly and fatally at Britain, he concluded that Germany should strike indirectly in 1916 by attacking France. He argued that if the French people could be made to understand clearly that "in a military sense they have nothing more to hope for, (the) breaking point would be reached, and England's best sword knocked from her hand". The means to be employed was not to break the French front *en masse*, but to bleed France to death by attacking an objective "for the retention of which the French would be compelled to throw in every man they have". The objective he selected was Verdun.

front, an attack on the Somme lacked any real strategic purpose, while the openness of the terrain and the naturally strong defensive position of the Germans in the sector meant there was no tactical rationale. In fact, the French high command, recognizing that the breaking of the German front in a single battle was very unlikely, sought a battle of attrition on the

" A short time ago death was the cruel stranger, the visitor with the feared footsteps ... today it is the mad dog in the house ... One eats, one drinks beside the dead, one sleeps in the midst of the dying, one laughs and one sings in the company of corpses ..."

THE BATTLE OF VERDUN

Falkenhayn's plan for the Verdun offensive has been criticized for its ghoulishness, although his intentions were really not very different from those of British and French commanders on the Western Front at this time. The plan was, however, flawed by one fundamental ambiguity. To draw the French into a killing zone where the artillery could do its work, German forces had to mount their effort against an objective worth defending. If, however, it was worth defending, for the Germans it was worth taking. Falkenhayn could not reveal what his real intention was to the formations committed to the offensive, and he hesitated between prosecuting the battle as planned and setting out to take Verdun, which would have defeated his own purpose. In fact, the losses suffered by the Germans were to be almost as high as those of the French: between February 21, when the first attack was launched, and the end of March, the Germans suffered over 81,600 casualties while the French suffered 89,000. By the end of the year a German advance of just a few kilometres had resulted in almost a million casualties.

THE ITALIAN AND EASTERN FRONTS

Early in the year Conrad von Hötzendorf, chief of staff of the Austro-Hungarian army, sought German agreement to an expedition against Italy, reasoning that eliminating Italy from the war, or inflicting a major defeat on it, would free Habsburg forces for the Eastern Front. Conrad requested that the Germans provide four divisions for the assault and take over part of the Austro-Hungarian line in

Caring for the wounded
Gordon Highlanders transport a wounded comrade along the Albert-Bapaume road in July 1916 – just one of the 630,000 Allied casualties incurred during the Battle of the Somme.

Galicia in order to release divisions for the attack. However, such was the poor state of relations between Conrad and Falkenhayn that the request was not even acknowledged. Conrad went ahead and withdrew six divisions from Galicia without informing Berlin in an attempt to carry out the offensive against the Italians in April. At the same time Falkenhayn, in preparing for the Verdun offensive, stripped the southern sector of 90 per cent of its German forces. In fact, bad weather in the Trentino was to delay Conrad's attack until May with what proved to be disastrous implications for the Austro-Hungarians on the Eastern Front.

During the summer of 1915 the Russians had been defeated in Galicia and pushed out of Poland, suffering two million casualties in the process. They had also seen the removal of their commander-in-chief, Grand Duke Nicholas. They had, however, made what was in many ways an impressive recovery in September. The fact that on September 1 Tsar Nicholas II assumed personal command of the army, despite his lack of military knowledge, was coincidental.

In agreeing to tie its summer 1916 effort to that of the British and French, the Russians had insisted that all the Allies should undertake relieving offensive action if one was subjected to German attack. They wished to ensure that there would be no repetition of the events of 1915 when the British and French had been singularly ineffective in diverting German attention during the Central Powers' summer offensive. The German attack at Verdun and the subsequent French request for assistance was not something they had anticipated.

French involvement at the Somme

Although they did not play as great a role as originally planned in the Battle of the Somme, the French met with more success than the British during the initial advance.

THE BRUSILOV OFFENSIVE

The Russian attempt to come to the aid of France initially resulted in failure north of the Pripet River, where they launched an attack on Vilna (Vilnius) in March. Only around Lake Naroch did they achieve any success, but even their few gains were eliminated by German counterattacks in April. However, Brusilov, commander of the Southwest Front, then proposed an offensive that was to inflict a devastating defeat on the Austro-Hungarian army. Launched on June 4, the offensive succeeded partly by achieving total surprise. Within eight days the Austro-Hungarian front south of the Pripet had given way and the Russians had taken 250,000 prisoners. The result was a collapse in morale and ultimately the integration of German and Austro-Hungarian forces under German command.

THE SOMME

Meanwhile, the offensive on Verdun was having a major impact on British and French plans for the Somme campaign. As the French commitment at Verdun deepened, so their planned role on the Somme diminished. In June, when the Germans renewed their Verdun offensive, the British brought forward the date of the Somme offensive. On July 1 over 100,000 Allied troops began a battle that was to last until November 18. By that date the Allies had failed to take a single town of any size and had incurred 630,000 casualties. The Germans, too, had suffered terrible losses. Falkenhayn, before being removed from command in August 1916, had insisted that "not a foot's breadth of ground must be voluntarily abandoned". In fighting to defend every foot of ground at the Somme, the Germans incurred over 660,000 casualties.

Lying as he fell
The remains of a German soldier, killed in a British assault on Beaumont-Hamel, in November 1916. Trench rats grew fat on a diet of human flesh.

Battle of Verdun

VERDUN WAS A FORTIFIED CITY surrounded by a ring of forts that were held by skeleton garrisons and had almost no heavy artillery. These had been dispatched to the Champagne battlefields in 1915 by a French high command that saw no need to maintain strong defensive positions around Verdun. It did not believe the Germans would attack Verdun, even as Falkenhayn made his very thorough preparations at the beginning of 1916 to launch an offensive in the sector in front of the city that would "bleed France white".

In a huge feat of organization, the Germans moved some 1,400 guns up to a 5-km (3-mile) front east of the Meuse River, ready for an assault by their Fifth Army on February 12, 1916. In the event, a ferocious blizzard forced a postponement and gave the French the opportunity to make some much-needed improvements to their defences.

The German Fifth Army possessed a clear advantage over the opposing French Second Army. On the 5-km (3-mile) front, between the Meuse and Orne, where its main effort was to be made, it had mustered nine divisions compared to the two available to the French. As well as this advantage in manpower, the Germans had a 4 to 1 advantage in artillery and had secured clear superiority in the air. The Germans also had a telling logistical advantage. The Fifth Army was served by no fewer than a dozen rail lines, of which ten were broad gauge, and had secured bridges over the Meuse. Three rail lines met at Verdun, but the southern route had been severed by the German capture of St Mihiel in 1914, while the main route to Paris could be closed by German artillery fire. This left the French with the totally inadequate combination of one narrow gauge rail line and one road, both from Bar-le-Duc, along which to transport men and supplies. They also had no ready means of transferring forces from one bank of the Meuse to the other except through Verdun itself.

ADVANCE TO FORT DOUAUMONT

The German offensive finally began on February 21 with a shot from a Krupp 380-mm (15-in) naval gun that hit the cathedral in Verdun almost 32km (20 miles) away. After a massive nine-hour artillery

The moment of death

This image – thought to be a still from a German film about the Battle of Verdun – captures a French soldier being thrown backwards by the force of a bullet. He was just one of over 500,000 French casualties of the battle.

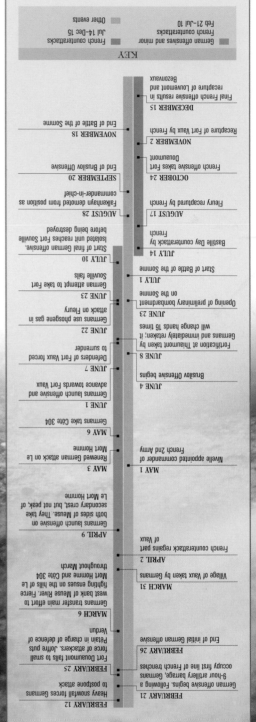

VERDUN
FEBRUARY 21 – DECEMBER 18, 1916

The huge offensive mounted by the Germans northeast of Verdun on February 21 initially resulted in limited gains. The Germans then came to a temporary halt at the end of February, and although they launched several new attacks over the following months, they failed to capture Verdun. On October 24 the French launched a counterattack and that drove the Germans back to within 8km (5 miles) of their original line.

KEY

- German offensives and minor French counterattacks — Feb 21–Jul 10
- French counterattacks — Jul 14–Dec 15
- Other events

FEBRUARY 21 — German offensive begins. Following a heavy snowfall forces Germans to postpone attack

FEBRUARY 25 — Fort Douaumont falls to small force of attackers. Joffre puts Pétain in charge of defence of Verdun

FEBRUARY 26 — End of initial German offensive

MARCH 6 — Germans transfer main effort to west bank of Meuse River. Fierce fighting ensues on the hills of Le Mort Homme and Côte 304 throughout March

MARCH 31 — Village of Vaux taken by Germans

APRIL 2 — French counterattack regains part of Vaux

APRIL 9 — Germans launch offensive on both sides of Meuse. They take secondary crest, but not peak, of Le Mort Homme

MAY 1 — Nivelle appointed commander of French 2nd Army

MAY 3 — Renewed German attack on Le Mort Homme

MAY 6 — Germans take Côte 304

JUNE 1 — Germans launch offensive and advance towards Fort Vaux

JUNE 4

JUNE 7 — Defenders of Fort Vaux forced to surrender

JUNE 8 — Brusilov Offensive begins

JUNE 22 — Germans use phosgene gas in attack on Fleury

JUNE 23 — German attempt to take Fort Souville fails

JUNE 23 — Opening of preliminary bombardment on the Somme

JULY 1 — Start of Battle of the Somme

JULY 10 — Start of final German offensive. Isolated unit reaches Fort Souville before being destroyed

JULY 14 — Bastille Day counterattack by French

AUGUST 17 — Fleury recaptured by French

AUGUST 28 — Falkenhayn demoted from position as commander-in-chief

SEPTEMBER 20 — End of Brusilov Offensive

OCTOBER 24 — French offensive takes Fort Douaumont

NOVEMBER 2 — Recapture of Fort Vaux by French

NOVEMBER 18 — End of Battle of the Somme

DECEMBER 15 — Final French offensive results in recapture of Louvemont and Bezonvaux

bombardment, which buried many French soldiers alive in their trenches, at 4:00pm three German corps – a total of 140,000 men – began to move forward. By the end of the day one of the corps had occupied the Bois d'Haumont, but the other two had run into greater resistance than anticipated. The French troops fought tenaciously, making local counterattacks in the face of a continuing artillery attack. They could not, however, hold back the German advance for more than an hour or two, and on the 25th the Germans reached Douaumont, the greatest of the forts surrounding Verdun.

Many of Douaumont's guns had been removed the previous year and 500 infantrymen had been withdrawn. As a German regiment advanced towards it, the majority of the six regular and 57 Territorial gunners now manning the fort were inside, listening to a lecture. Just one gun was in action as the Germans overcame the few defenders in the surrounding trenches, and a lone sergeant climbed into the fort. The sergeant managed to find and lock up both the gunners and the men who had

been listening to the lecture, and he was shortly joined by two German officers, one of whom now took command of the fort. Douaumont had been lost without a shot being fired in its defence.

FRENCH RESISTANCE
The loss of Douaumont was a disaster for the French and could well have led to their deciding to withdraw from Verdun to a more defensible line. Instead Pétain, the much-respected general who was appointed on the night of the 25th to organize Verdun's defence, set about keeping the city out of German hands. The French army poured men, artillery and aircraft into the area as a spring thaw set in, turning the area into a quagmire and adding to the misery of the soldiers on both sides. The German Expressionist painter Franz Marc was to write on March 3: "For days I have seen nothing but the most terrrible things that can be painted from a human mind". The next day he was dead, one of over 400,000 casualties to be suffered by the Germans in the Verdun sector.

By the end of February the French had secured at least a rough equality in the air and in the number of heavy guns in the area. Pétain – a steadying and inspiring influence – ordered the re-arming of the forts around Verdun, and the extension of trenches and field positions so that infantry and forts might better support one another. Nonetheless, for the next two months the French situation on the heights of the Meuse remained desperate.

In Germany the fall of Douaumont was regarded as a victory that foreshadowed the fall of Verdun itself. In reality Germany's best chances of victory had gone by the 25th. Had the attack not been delayed for nine days, the Fifth Army would have fallen upon a wholly unprepared defence. In any event, a full-scale infantry assault on the first day might well have carried the French position. It had been a mistake to restrict the attack to the east bank of the Meuse, which meant that the German forces, even on the 22nd and 23rd, were subject to heavy enfilading fire from French artillery that was concentrated on the hills across the river.

LA VOIE SACRÉE

THE ROAD BETWEEN Bar-le-Duc and Verdun played such a vital role in the battle that it was subsequently christened the Voie Sacrée or Sacred Way. Along its 72km (45 miles), day and night, there were normally 3,500 trucks on the move, ferrying men, ammunition and supplies to the beleaguered city. During the initial crisis of February 21 to March 6 it delivered 23,000 tons of ammunition, 2,500 tons of other material and 190,000 men. One truck passed every 14 seconds, submitting the road surface to considerable wear and tear. Over the course of ten months, 8,500 men from 16 labour battalions worked to keep the road in a good state of repair and open.

The special unit responsible for controlling traffic and servicing the vehicles numbered 300 officers and 8,500 men; there were 30 breakdown trucks always on the road and repair crews stationed beside it. A broken-down vehicle was immediately moved to the roadside so as not to interrupt the flow of precious supplies. Automobile repair shops at Bar-le-Duc and Troyes worked ceaselessly, as did the hydraulic presses turning out solid rubber tyres.

Alongside the road ran a narrow-gauge single-track railway, Le Meusien. This was able to move about 1,800 tons of supplies per day. It carried the bulk of the food for the army in Verdun – some 16,600 officers and 420,000 men, not to mention 136,000 horses and mules – and brought back many of the wounded from the front.

Mending the road
Members of 16 labour battalions worked on resurfacing the road, breaking and shaping the stone which they first had to quarry.

Joining the queue
French infantry line up for transport to the front along the Voie Sacrée. The road was narrow in February, but it would soon be doubled in width under Pétain's orders.

ACTION ON THE WEST BANK

On March 6 the Germans began an attempt to clear the west bank and secure Le Mort Homme and Côte 304. Fighting for possession of these two hills continued through March. It also continued on the east bank around the ruins of the village of Vaux, which in one month changed hands 13 times.

On April 9 the Germans launched an offensive on both sides of the river, across a 32-km (20-mile) front. They took the secondary crest of Le Mort Homme on the first day, but they subsequently failed in their attempt to take the summit. Four days later all operations on the west bank ground to a halt in the relentless rain. Fighting, however, continued on the east bank around Forts Douaumont and Vaux, throughout April.

The German Fifth Army had lost some 120,000 men by the end of April. However, on May 3 it renewed its effort on the west bank of the Meuse no weaker in manpower and artillery than it had been at the start of the campaign ten weeks previously. Pétain had maintained forward defensive positions on the west bank of the Meuse to hold on to the main crest of Le Mort Homme and the neighbouring Côte 304. The French, however, could not withstand the renewed German advance. By May 6 the Germans had gained control of Côte 304 and by the end of the month they had cleared Le Mort Homme of all French troops.

The French, now under Nivelle, launched a series of attacks on the east bank, one of which reached, but failed to retake, Fort Douaumont on May 22–23. It was not until June 1 that the Germans could undertake a renewed offensive on the east bank and advance towards Fort Vaux, where they met with particularly strong resistance.

BATTLE OF VERDUN

FEBRUARY 21 – DECEMBER 18, 1916

The battle in front of Verdun was the longest single battle of the First World War. It was the only major German offensive undertaken on the Western Front between November 1914 and March 1918, and brought France perilously close to disastrous defeat at various times between February and July 1916. The German attacks on the east bank of the Meuse in February resulted in the capture of Fort Douaumont and forced the French to abandon the Wöevre Plain, but they failed to secure any major tactical advantage for the Germans. In March and April they captured the main French positions on the west bank before becoming embroiled in further attacks and counterattacks on the east bank in which, after July, neither side was able to secure the advantage. This situation changed in October when the French began a series of attacks that resulted in the recapture of Fort Douaumont and the end of the battle.

KEY	
French front line	Fort/fortified site
German front line	Road
German advance	Railway
French advance	

Raynal, leader of the defence of Fort Vaux
When Major Raynal – shown here flanked by his second-in-command and a German officer – was finally forced to surrender Fort Vaux, the Germans treated him as a hero.

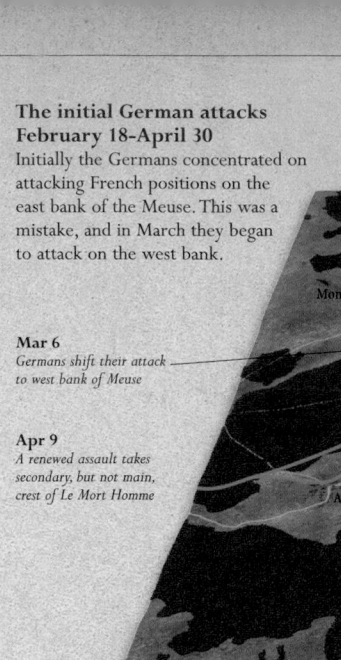

The initial German attacks February 18–April 30
Initially the Germans concentrated on attacking French positions on the east bank of the Meuse. This was a mistake, and in March they began to attack on the west bank.

Mar 6
Germans shift their attack to west bank of Meuse

Apr 9
A renewed assault takes secondary, but not main, crest of Le Mort Homme

Montfaucon

Avocour

Parois

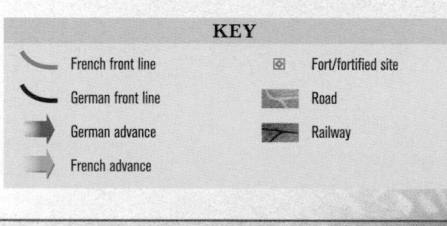

French front-line trench
Many French trenches at Verdun were very basic. Soldiers would sometimes shelter from the rain in holes they had dug in the side of the trench, though they then ran the risk of being buried alive by the mud thrown up by the explosion of a shell nearby.

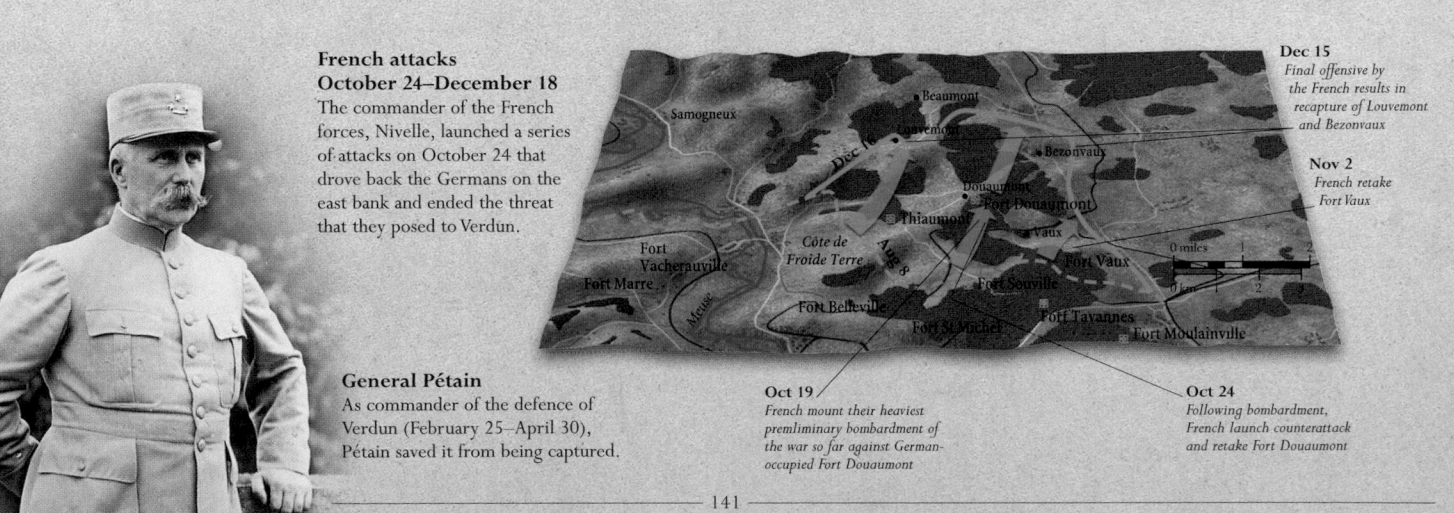

Feb 21–Mar 6
Germans make major error during first phase of their offensive by not attacking on the west bank

Feb 21
German offensive begins. A 9-hour artillery bombardment pulverizes French defences

Feb 21
Bois d'Haumont captured by end of day, but elsewhere Germans meet with greater resistance than anticipated

Feb 24
French trench lines north of Verdun breached

Feb 25
Germans seize Fort Douaumont without a shot being fired in its defence

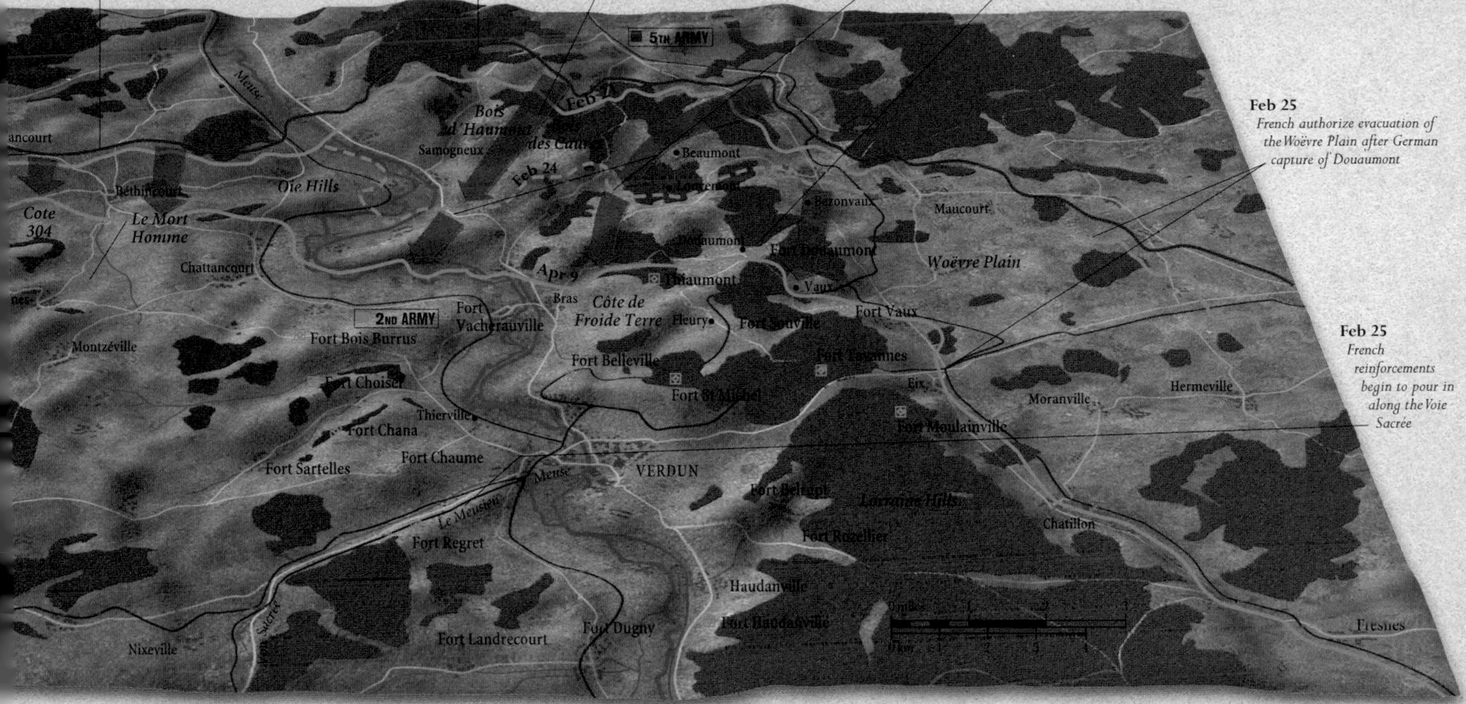

Feb 25
French authorize evacuation of the Woëvre Plain after German capture of Douaumont

Feb 25
French reinforcements begin to pour in along the Voie Sacrée

Attrition on the east bank
May 1–August 8
With the German capture of the main French positions on the west bank, the Germans made one final attempt to defeat the French on the east bank before the Somme offensive began.

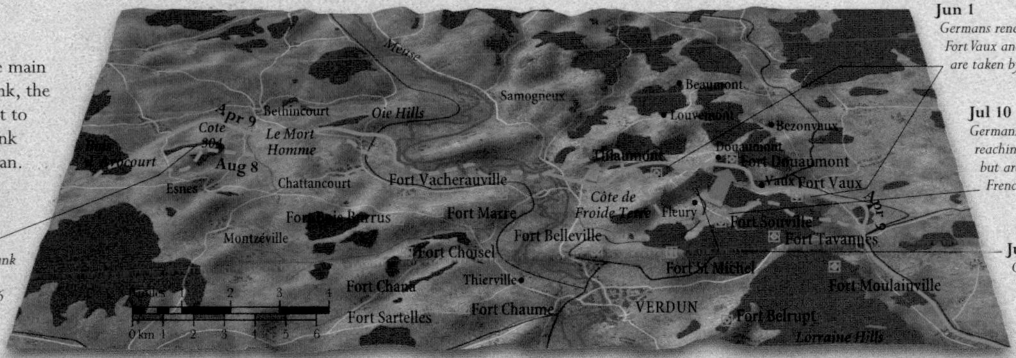

May 3
Germans renew offensive on west bank of Meuse, taking Côte 304 on May 6

Jun 1
Germans renew attack. Fort Vaux and Thiaumont are taken by Jun 9

Jul 10
Germans succeed in reaching Fort Souville, but are turned back by French counterattacks

Jun 23
Germans reach ridge line that commands Verdun and Meuse bridges, and Côte de Froide Terre

French attacks
October 24–December 18
The commander of the French forces, Nivelle, launched a series of attacks on October 24 that drove back the Germans on the east bank and ended the threat that they posed to Verdun.

Dec 15
Final offensive by the French results in recapture of Louvemont and Bezonvaux

Nov 2
French retake Fort Vaux

General Pétain
As commander of the defence of Verdun (February 25–April 30), Pétain saved it from being captured.

Oct 19
French mount their heaviest premliminary bombardment of the war so far against German-occupied Fort Douaumont

Oct 24
Following bombardment, French launch counterattack and retake Fort Douaumont

DEFENCE OF FORT VAUX

The German bombardment of Fort Vaux began on June 1, at one point firing shells at the rate of 1,500 to 2,000 an hour. Inside were 600 troops, many of them injured, under the command of Major Raynal. Just before dawn on the 2nd, the barrage suddenly stopped and two German battalions moved forward. By mid-afternoon they had overwhelmed the defenders and occupied a large part of the superstructure. Raynal was determined to resist, and he and his men withdrew to the underground corridors where a grim battle was fought in the darkness with grenades and machine-guns. On June 4 the Germans used flamethrowers in an attempt to drive out the French with asphyxiating black smoke. With all radio contact severed, at midday Raynal sent out his last message by carrier pigeon:

"We are still holding our position, but are being attacked by gases and smoke of very deadly character. We are in need of immediate relief. Put us into communication with Souville again at once for visual signalling. We get no answer from there to our calls. This is our last pigeon!"

The following day the first French relief force arrived. Like the four that followed, it suffered terrible casualties in the course of trying, but failing, to relieve the garrison. The men in the fort were now suffering from lack of water and in their desperation they were licking the moisture on the walls or drinking their own urine. On June 7 Raynal decided that there was no alternative but to surrender. Remarkably, in their brave defence of the fort, the French garrison had suffered a hundred casualties; the Germans had suffered over 2,740.

On June 8 the German Fifth Army reached the fortification at Thiaumont, within 5km (3 miles) of Verdun. In almost getting to Pétain's designated last line of resistance in front of the city, the Germans had inflicted appalling losses on the French, stretching their defence to breaking point. The French were now confronted by the very real prospect of losing Verdun and, with it, many of their guns. They were, however, determined to hold on to the city no matter what the cost. In the words of Pétain, writing to Joffre on June 11: "Verdun is menaced and Verdun must not fall. The capture of the city would constitute for the Germans an inestimable success which would greatly raise their morale and correspondingly lower our own."

In the second week of June, when the defences around Thiaumont consisted mostly of gaps, there was a pause in the fighting. On June 4 the Russian Brusilov Offensive had been launched (see pages 148–50) and had quickly overwhelmed the opposing Austro-Hungarian forces along a 450-km (300-mile) front. Falkenhayn was now forced to suspend operations at Verdun in order to attend to the needs of the Eastern Front.

Trench near Douaumont
The heroic French counterattacks at Verdun gave rise to the slogan "on les aura" ("we'll get 'em"), used here on a war-bond poster. But while the French succeeded in recapturing the Verdun forts and occupying German trenches, they did so at a terrible cost. Almost 650,000 men lost their lives in the ten-month long battle.

2ᵉ EMPRUNT de LA DÉFENSE NATIONALE Souscrivez

On les aura !

> "What a bloodbath, what horrid images, what a slaughter. I just cannot find the words to express my feelings. Hell cannot be this dreadful."
>
> ALBERT JOUBAIRE, FRENCH SOLDIER AT VERDUN

GERMAN OFFENSIVE ON FORT SOUVILLE

The Germans renewed their offensive at Fleury on June 22, their objective to take Fort Souville, which overlooked Verdun itself and all the bridges over the Meuse. Like the advance of February 21–25, this latest advance raised the question for the French high command of whether it should evacuate the east bank. While, however, this may have been conceivable in February, it was totally out of the question in June. Too much had been invested in holding Verdun, and too much artillery was in place on the east bank, for the French to accept defeat and reorganize their defences on the west bank.

Surprised by the German use of phosgene gas near Fort Souville on the evening of June 22, the French lost Fleury the following day. However, an immediate counterattack brought the German advance in this critical sector to a halt. A further German offensive planned for early July was then delayed for two days by torrential rain that turned the battlefield into a morass of mud. The attack was finally launched at midnight on the 10th, with the French artillery being engulfed by gas until well after the German infantry had begun to advance. The Germans succeeded in reaching Souville and made further gains in the next two days, but these were eliminated by a French counterattack on the 14th.

The fact that the tide of battle had been brought to Souville a second time was a reflection of German failure to make the decisive breakthrough. A German victory at Verdun no longer appeared to be a real possibility. This did not mean, however, that the battle was allowed to die. The summer passed with a series of local attacks and counterattacks, the Anglo-French Somme offensive launched on July 1 denying the German Fifth Army the reserves needed for a resumption of large-scale operations. Indeed, repeatedly subjected to French artillery fire, the Germans would have relinquished many of their gains if shattered villages such as Fleury had not now acquired an exaggerated significance. After Falkenhayn's dismissal on August 28, the German leadership sought to limit commitments at Verdun as pressure from the French intensified.

The success of French offensives in the last three months of the battle stemmed largely from the employment of the creeping barrage, a tactical innovation developed by Nivelle, in which artillery fire moved forward in stages, just ahead of the advancing infantry. In a rapid attack on October 24 the French recaptured Fort Douaumont in the process of recovering ground that the German Fifth Army had taken four months to capture. On November 2 Fort Vaux was retaken. The final French attack on December 15 resulted in the recapture of Louvemont and Bezonvaux, lost in the first days of the original German attack. Both sides then allowed the battle to die.

The resilience of the French at Verdun was as remarkable as it had been unanticipated by Falkenhayn when planning his offensive on the city. It strengthened French morale, but it also came at the cost of an estimated 542,000 French casualties, of whom about half were killed. Also unanticipated by Falkenhayn was the number of German casualties. The Germans lost almost as many men as the French – 434,000 – in the course of achieving an advance of just 8 km (5 miles) or less along a 32-km (20-mile) front during ten months of fighting.

Railway gun

Both sides used railway guns at Verdun. The French brought up two massive 40-cm (16-in) Modele 15 howitzers to pound the defences of Fort Douaumont before finally recapturing it on October 24.

NIEUPORT 17

~

INTRODUCED IN MARCH 1916, the Nieuport 17 played a major role in France winning back control of the skies over Verdun from the Germans. An improved version of the Nieuport 11, the "*bébé*", the first fighter to compete successfully against the formidable German Fokker Eindecker, the larger Nieuport 17 was soon nicknamed the "*superbébé*". With a ceiling of 5,300 m (17,388 ft), it could easily outclimb its chief rival, the Fokker E.III. Armed with a single Vickers machine-gun, it was flown by many French aces, including Charles Nungesser, ten of whose 43 victories were scored over Verdun. The Nieuport was the first plane ever to be equipped with air-to-air rockets. On May 22 five out of six German balloons in the Verdun sector were shot down in flames by French airmen.

The synchronized Vickers .303 machine-gun fired through the propeller. Early versions had a Lewis gun fitted on the top wing

The 9-cylinder, 110-hp rotary engine gave a top speed of 177 kph (110 mph)

The struts were often fitted with Le Prieur rockets, used for shooting down observation balloons

OBSERVATION AND COMMUNICATION

BEFORE 1914 THE BELIEF IN THE PRIMACY OF OFFENSIVE action largely negated the need for strategic reconnaissance, while cavalry was expected to provide adequate tactical reconnaissance. In the war's opening weeks, however, aircraft successfully conducted strategic reconnaissance at Tannenberg and the Marne, and cavalry failed to provide adequate tactical reconnaissance.

Trench systems – with an area behind the enemy system to which access was impossible except from the air – changed requirements. At the strategic level proper reconnaissance could only be conducted by aircraft and cameras. The wireless was needed for the rapid transmission of reports. The British had designed and tested an airborne wireless before August 1914, but they only put it into general service in 1915. During the Artois offensive in May, they employed aircraft that spotted targets and reported to the artillery by morse transmissions. Morse keys were, however, difficult to use while flying, and in February 1916 airborne wireless telephony – the transmission of voice messages – was tested for the first time. Instead of aerials, the first sets had a trailing wire that had to be reeled

in as necessity dictated. A reliable transmitter became available in sufficient numbers to equip formations in early 1917, but the British kept the majority of aircraft with wireless telephony around London for home defence. Just two squadrons on the Western Front were similarly equipped, and these were not given an offensive role in case a set was captured and copied. The range of these sets was about 160 km (100 miles), rising to 290 km (180 miles) in 1918.

At the tactical level, observation had a crucial role to play in directing artillery fire, and could be conducted from balloons linked by telephone cable to command posts on the ground. The first balloons for tactical reconnaissance were produced by the Germans and the French, and the latter supplied one to the British army in May 1915. At this stage responsibility for airships and balloons was vested solely in the Royal Navy. By 1916 the Royal Flying Corps had assumed responsibility for balloons on the Western Front, though their two-man crews were drawn exclusively from the artillery. Ultimately the British were to have a balloon company for each of their five armies on the Western Front.

Message shells
Shells were used to send written messages up the line.

Case
Message holder
Cap

Telephone communication
The field telephone enabled artillery forward observation officers to relay the results of shelling back to the gunners, so that they could adjust their aim accordingly.

Bird's-eye view
A soldier on a ladder inside this fake tree, peered through a peep-hole and passed down information on enemy positions to a colleague, who transmitted it to the artillery battery.

Wireless communication
Wireless sets that received and transmitted morse messages were used by troops once they had moved beyond the reach of field telephone cables.

Portable field telephone
A portable telephone was carried in a leather shoulder bag. In addition to a telephone handset for verbal communication, it had a key for transmitting morse when the line became too noisy for speech to be heard clearly.

Nonetheless, French avoidance of defeat at Verdun was very dearly bought. Many French divisions moving up to Verdun saw themselves as lambs being driven to the slaughter. As they approached they heard the constant roar of the great guns, reminding them, in the words of one soldier, of "a gigantic forge that ceased neither day nor night". All around was a sea of mud in which stood a few solitary tree stumps – all that remained of the once extensive forests. The so-called communications trenches that began up to 3 km (2 miles) from the front line were often little more than ditches surrounded by water-filled shell craters into which heavily-burdened soldiers might fall and drown. Invariably hanging above this desolate scene was a pall of smoke and the stench of rotting corpses. Few could go through such an experience without being psychologically scarred for life.

Unlike the Germans, who fed reinforcements to the divisions that were in place, the French rotated divisions in the line. As a result, four-fifths of the French army saw service in the war's longest, and one of its most horrific, battles.

ACTION ON VIMY RIDGE

While the French were pouring virtually all their forces into the Verdun sector, the British were active on Vimy Ridge in Artois. In the autumn of 1915 the French had given up their struggle to recapture the ridge from the Germans. Instead they had spent the winter months tunnelling deep underground, creating a system of galleries and saps. However, as the British were to discover on their arrival in March, the Germans had dug deeper and more extensively. A battle began for control of the mine shafts, in which the tunnellers of both sides attempted to blow up sections of the line above. By mid-May, eight British and five French tunnelling companies had begun to get the upper hand, but on May 21 the Germans launched a surprise offensive which began with an intensive bombardment of the British front line. Those who survived were half buried in earth and unable to prevent the Germans moving forward to construct a new line.

On the 23rd the Germans began to bombard the British lines again. Although this time the British were ready to launch their own offensive, they lost many men to accurate German shelling. By late May the British had suffered almost 2,500 casualties while the Germans had suffered over 1,340. With the British high command refusing to divert any artillery from the Somme to Vimy Ridge, there was no likelihood of the Germans being driven off the ridge in the immediate future.

Pigeon post
Often the only means of communication, pigeons were widely used to carry messages from the front to headquarters. During the German siege of Fort Vaux near Verdun, the French defenders relied on pigeons to carry their requests for help.

Star shells
Magnesium flares, known as star shells, were fired into the air to send pre-arranged signals, often using different colours. Some shells had parachutes that slowed their descent. Star shells were also used to illuminate No Man's Land and reveal enemy activity.

BRITISH PARACHUTE FLARE PISTOL

GERMAN FLARE PISTOL

Star shells

Parachute flare cartridge

Dog messengers
Dogs were used by both sides to carry messages between trenches, in tubes attached to their collars. They were trained to leap barbed wire, and their speed and agility made them difficult targets for snipers.

Observation from a great height
Balloons anchored to the ground were an ideal way of observing enemy activities, but the operator had little chance of survival if a gas-filled balloon was set alight by enemy fire.

Russia Fights Back

Putting on a brave face
This picture of Russian front-line troops gives no hint of the equipment shortages that had bedevilled the army since the outbreak of war, nor of the spirit of defeatism that was spreading among the troops in early 1916.

I N THE SPRING OF 1916 the Russian armies had twice as many men as the Germans and Austro-Hungarians in both the northern and central sectors of the Eastern Front but only about the same number in the south. It was therefore predictable that the Russians, when asked by the French to mount an attack that would divert German attention from Verdun, should choose to do so north of the Pripet River and advance towards Vilna (Vilnius). The Lithuanian town contained an important railhead and was at the centre of a major road network, which meant it was well worth recapturing from the Germans.

VILNA AND LAKE NAROCH

The Russian offensive opened on March 18. However, there was a notable lack of co-ordination between army groups and between artillery and infantry. There was also little knowledge of enemy positions because of a lack of reconnaissance, forcing much of the artillery to fire blind: one of the corps commander, as "Pleshkirov's *son et lumière*". Despite the length of front, the attacks were very narrowly directed, with the result that the attacking forces were mown down by flanking fire. The Russian troops who managed to reach the German trenches found themselves shelled by German artillery who had received two week's warning of what was to come as a result of the only too common lack of Russian security. Only in one sector, around Lake Naroch, where the Russians attacked on the 21st across the ice and through thick fog, did they achieve any success. However, the few small gains made were eliminated by German counterattacks in April.

Perhaps the only surprising aspect of this action was that the Germans were obliged to move three divisions to the threatened sectors and sustained 20,000 casualties. The Russian armies lost some 110,000 men, including 12,000 fatalities from frostbite. According to the Russians' own figures, 300,000 Russian troops, with artillery support on a scale greater than that available even to the Central Powers in 1914 and 1915, had been routed by 50,000 Germans. The debacle left the Russian armies in this sector badly demoralized.

THE EASTERN FRONT
MARCH 18, 1916 – JANUARY 1917

With the aim of reducing German pressure on the French at Verdun, the Russians launched an offensive in March north of the Pripet River. This achieved little. Far more successful was the Brusilov Offensive south of the Pripet in June, though by September it had petered out. The Romanians invaded Austria-Hungary in August, thus provoking a campaign of conquest by the Central Powers that ended with the defeat of Romania.

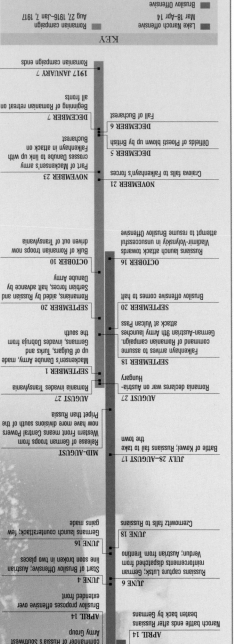

KEY
- Romanian campaign — Aug 27, 1916–Jan 7, 1917
- Lake Naroch offensive — Mar 18–Apr 14
- Brusilov Offensive — Jun 4–Sept 20

1916 MARCH 18 — Russian offensive from positions east of Vilna begins; limited gains at cost of heavy casualties

1916 APRIL 4 — Brusilov takes up position as commander of Russia's Southwest Army Group

APRIL 14 — Brusilov proposes offensive over extended front

APRIL 14 — Naroch battle ends after Russians beaten back by Germans

JUNE 4 — Start of Brusilov Offensive; Austrian line soon broken in two places

JUNE 6 — Russians capture Lutsk; German reinforcements dispatched from Verdun; Austrian from Trentino

JUNE 16 — Germans launch counterattack; few gains made

JUNE 18 — Czernowitz falls to Russians

JULY 28–AUGUST 17 — Battle of Kowel; Russians fail to take the town

MID-AUGUST — Release of German troops from Western Front means Central Powers now have more divisions south of the Pripet than Russia

AUGUST 27 — Romania invades Transylvania

AUGUST 27 — Romania declares war on Austria-Hungary

SEPTEMBER 1 — Mackensen's Danube Army, made up of Bulgars, Turks and Germans, invades Dobruja from the south

SEPTEMBER 18 — Falkenhayn arrives to assume command of Romanian campaign

SEPTEMBER 20 — Romanians, aided by Russian and Serbian forces, halt advance by Danube Army

SEPTEMBER 20 — Brusilov offensive comes to halt

OCTOBER 10 — Bulk of Romanian troops now driven out of Transylvania

OCTOBER 16 — Russians launch attack towards Vladimir-Volynsky in unsuccessful attempt to resume Brusilov Offensive

NOVEMBER 21

NOVEMBER 23 — Craiova falls to Falkenhayn's forces

DECEMBER 5 — Part of Mackensen's army crosses Danube to link up with Falkenhayn in attack on Bucharest

DECEMBER 6 — Oilfields of Ploesti blown up by British

DECEMBER 6 — Fall of Bucharest

DECEMBER 7 — Beginning of Romanian retreat on all fronts

1917 JANUARY 7 — Romanian campaign ends

THE RUSSIAN ARMY

~

I N 1914 THE RUSSIAN army had around 1.3 million men, with a reserve of about 4 million. In theory there were an additional 22 million men of combat age, but almost half were exempt from conscription. There was a belief in Europe that the Russian army would have a steamroller effect, but this failed to materialize. In 1914 alone, Russia lost the equivalent of its first-line strength, and in its disastrous retreat from Poland in 1915 it lost a further 3 million. As a result, successive call-ups merely covered losses rather than increasing numbers. There was also a shortage of trained officers, the majority of whom were killed in 1914–15. In 1916 an infantry regiment of 3,000 troops had only 12 officers.

The Russians had not anticipated a protracted war and suffered from material shortages throughout 1915. The production of 70,000 rifles a month fell fell far short of requirements – under-estimated at 200,000 a month – and unarmed reinforcements were a common sight in 1915. The need to import 2,300,000 rifles also gave rise to logistical problems caused by having ten different rifles in service.

By the summer of 1916 the army was better equipped and organized, but by the autumn Russia's mounting economic problems were impinging on troops, who were consequently becoming increasingly poorly fed and clothed. Even more ominous was the fact that Russia stood at the end of its manpower resources. After March 1917 the available reserves would not cover normal losses.

HELMET BADGE

Russian cavalry
The main weapons of the cavalry were the lance and the sabre. They also carried a rifle over the shoulder.

КТО ПОДПИШЕТСЯ НА

Bebout
A knife such as this, with a carved handle and sheath, was carried by a gunner, to be used in close fighting instead of a bayonet.

PAPAKHA

EPAULETTES

Hand grenade
A pre-war design, this stick grenade had an effective time fuse that was activated as the handle was released.

Russian uniform
Khaki was adopted by the Russians as the colour for their uniforms as early as 1907. The winter hat, the papakha, carries the oval cockade in the Romanov colours.

COAT

Moisin-Nagant rifle
Like all Russian rifles, this 7.62-mm (0.3-in) rifle was used with its bayonet fixed. Rifle production reached 111,000 a month in 1916, but demand still outstripped supply.

Revolver
This Moisin-Nagant revolver would have been carried by machine-gunners and artillery men.

THE BRUSILOV OFFENSIVE

Following the Naroch debacle, the new commander of the Russian Southwest Front, Brusilov, made a radical proposal. It was clear that lengthy preparations and prolonged bombardments sacrificed the element of surprise and enabled the defender to ensure adequate reserves were in position to counter any breakthrough. Furthermore, relative shortages of guns and shells enforced concentration on frontages that were very narrow, adding to the ease with which breaches could be sealed. Brusilov recommended that the armies under his command should launch a general offensive, with each army attacking along 48-km (30-mile) frontages after a brief bombardment, thus tying down enemy reserves and preventing effective counterattack. By paying very careful attention to artillery fire plans, ensuring close co-ordination between artillery and infantry, sapping to within 100m (110yds) of enemy positions and constructing defensive shelters for reserves, Brusilov sought to minimize weaknesses. His formula represented a radical departure from anything seen previously on the Eastern Front.

AUSTRO-HUNGARIAN DEBACLE

Brusilov's proposals were not well received within the Russian high command. However, the defeats of the Italians in the Trentino in May (see pages 232-33) led to appeals for a Russian diversionary offensive, and with only the four armies of the Southwest Front able to take action immediately, Brusilov was authorized to begin operations on June 4.

The Brusilov Offensive spelt disaster for the four Austro-Hungarian armies along the 450-km (300-mile) front that stretched from the Pripet to Czernowitz. Thinly spread over an extended front, they had invested far too much confidence in the strong defensive positions they had prepared, and, critically, they had not expected attack. In many sectors they had dug trenches up to 8m (20ft) deep – sometimes five lines of them – and with sufficient supplies of food and water, the troops had made themselves comparatively comfortable.

Austro-Hungarian prisoners

The Austro-Hungarian forces in Galicia were completely unprepared for the offensive launched by Brusilov on June 4, and by June 10 over 193,000 of them had been taken prisoner by the Russians.

Advance in the south

The Brusilov Offensive, launched on June 4 along a 450-km (300-mile) front, was initially very successful in taking the Austro-Hungarians completely by surprise. There were major breakthroughs near Lutsk and Czernowitz, but the offensive began to falter in July.

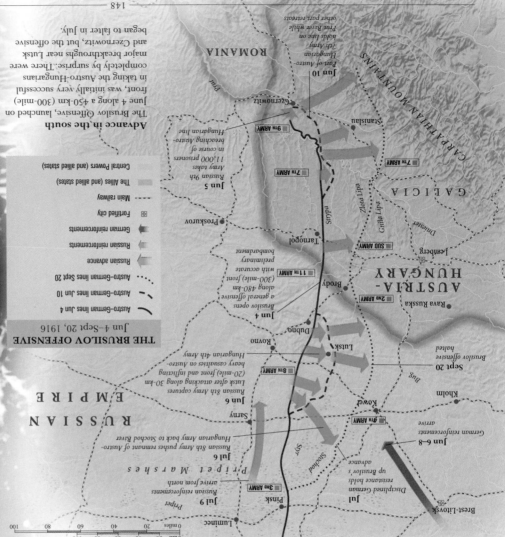

THE BRUSILOV OFFENSIVE
Jun 4–Sept 20, 1916

- ◟ Austro-German lines Jun 4
- ◟ Austro-German lines Jun 10
- ⋯ Austro-German lines Sept 20
- ⟹ Russian advance
- ⟹ Russian reinforcements
- ⟹ German reinforcements
- ◉ Fortified city
- --- Main railway
-   The Allies (and allied states)
-   Central Powers (and allied states)

Jun 4 Brusilov opens a general offensive along 480-km (300-mile) front with accurate preliminary bombardment

Jun 5 Russian 9th Army takes 11,000 prisoners in course of breaching Austro-Hungarian line

Jun 6 Russian 8th Army captures Lutsk after attacking along 30-km (20-mile) front and inflicting heavy casualties on Austro-Hungarian 4th Army

Jun 6-8 German reinforcements arrive

Jun 9 Russian reinforcements arrive from north

Jun 10 Part of Austro-Hungarian 7th Army holds line on Prut River while other part retreats

Jul Disciplined German resistance holds up Brusilov's advance

Jul 6 Russian 8th Army pushes remnant of Austro-Hungarian Army back to Stochod River

Sept 20 Brusilov offensive halted

ROMANIA
RUSSIAN EMPIRE
AUSTRIA-HUNGARY
GALICIA
CARPATHIAN MOUNTAINS
Pripet Marshes

Czernowitz, Stanislau, Lemberg, Brody, Rava Russka, Dubno, Rovno, Lutsk, Kovel, Kholm, Brest-Litovsk, Pinsk, Sarny, Luninec, Proskurov, Tarnopol

Prut, Zlota Lipa, Gnila Lipa, Dniester, Strypa, Styr, Stochod, Bug, Pripet

9TH ARMY, 7TH ARMY, SÜD ARMY, 11TH ARMY, 2ND ARMY, 8TH ARMY, 3RD ARMY, 9TH ARMY

0 km 20 40 60 80 100
0 miles 20 40 60 80 100

Russian field hospital
Although the Russians met with great success in the initial stages of the Brusilov Offensive, they continued to suffer enormous casualties. By the end of July they had incurred 450,000 and their reserves had fallen from 400,000 to 100,000 men.

ALEXEI BRUSILOV
~

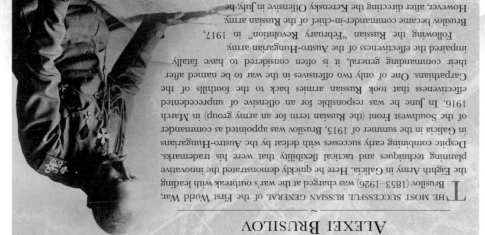

T HE MOST SUCCESSFUL RUSSIAN GENERAL of the First World War, Brusilov (1853–1926) was charged at the war's outbreak with leading the Eighth Army in Galicia. Here he quickly demonstrated the innovative planning techniques and tactical flexibility that were his trademarks. Despite combining early successes with defeat by the Austro-Hungarians in Galicia in the summer of 1915, Brusilov was appointed as commander of the Southwest Front (the Russian term for an army group) in March 1916. In June he was responsible for an offensive of unprecedented effectiveness that took Russian armies back to the foothills of the Carpathians. One of only two offensives in the war to be named after their commanding general, it is often considered to have fatally impaired the effectiveness of the Austro-Hungarian army.

Following the Russian "February Revolution" in 1917, Brusilov became commander-in-chief of the Russian army. However, after directing the Kerensky Offensive in July, he was replaced by Kornilov. He was not involved in the initial stages of the Russian Civil War, but in 1920 he led the Red Army into Poland.

The Russian bombardment on June 4 took the Austro-Hungarians completely by surprise. The Russian forces advancing behind it found that many enemy forces had become trapped in their deep shelters and had no alternative but to surrender.

Immediately south of the Pripet Marshes, the Russian Eighth Army under Kaledin advanced along a 30-km (20-mile) front towards the town of Lutsk, which it took on June 6 after overwhelming the Austro-Hungarian Fourth Army. By June 10 the Fourth Army had lost 60,000 men, and despite being helped by marshy terrain that channelled Russian attacks, it only just managed to hold positions. Relief was to come only on June 16, when four German divisions withdrawn from Verdun and four Austro-Hungarian divisions withdrawn from the Trentino went into action. Initially these divisions made only slight gains while suffering heavy losses.

Further south, breakthroughs on a smaller scale were made by the Russian Eleventh and Seventh armies. In the far south the Austro-Hungarian Seventh Army initially stood its ground behind the Dniester River, using all its reserves to withstand an attack by the Russian Ninth Army under Lechitsky. It was, however, forced to retreat when the Russians broke through defences north of the river on June 7.

By mid-June the Seventh Army had been almost completely destroyed, losing over 100,000 men. As one part after being split in two by the Russians, retreated westwards, the other attempted to hold positions along the Prut River west of Czernowitz, before withdrawing southwestwards to the Bukovina region.

By the end of the month the Russians had advanced over 96 km (60 miles) in sections of the front south of the Pripet, and had taken 350,000 prisoners and more than 700 guns. They were ready to press on towards the Carpathian foothills.

By the end of July the Southwest Front's offensive was faltering. The advantage of surprise was inevitably dissipating itself and the Russians were beginning to become exhausted. Lacking reinforcements, Brusilov now concentrated on taking action to protect his northern flank, which was exposed to German forces that separated his armies from the Russian army group in the central sector. On July 28 he launched an assault north of the Pripet Marshes in an unsuccessful attempt to capture the important railway junction of Kowel.

INCREASED GERMAN INVOLVEMENT

The German offensive at Verdun had come to a halt by the end of June, and with the attack on the Somme in July revealing the Allied hand, the Germans were free to move good-quality formations to Galicia. By mid-August, the release of 18 divisions from the Western Front brought the number of German divisions south of the Pripet to 24, which meant that the Central Powers had 72 divisions in comparison with Brusilov's 61. Perhaps more importantly, the German high command had insisted on a number of

changes to give itself virtually total control of the Austro-Hungarian armies at both the operational and administrative levels. By insisting on German appointments to command and staff positions, and by integrating German and Austro-Hungarian formations ultimately to company level, Berlin ensured that Vienna lost its freedom of action everywhere except on the Italian Front. Austria-Hungary might have resented the German connection and after 1916 hope to conclude a peace that would leave the Empire intact, but after the Brusilov Offensive its separate existence was little more than a fiction. With the entry of Romania into the war on August 27, the Germans extended the command arrangements they had imposed upon Austria-Hungary to both Bulgaria and Turkey.

Romania's entry into the war extended Russia's commitments over another 400km (250 miles) of

Russians standing over Austro-Hungarian dead
Although the Brusilov Offensive came to an end in September, sporadic fighting continued in the Carpathians through October, adding to the estimated total of 1.5 million casualties suffered by the two sides.

front and were later deemed by the Russian military to have cost them the chance of securing Kowel. In reality, had such a chance existed then it was in June rather than in August and September. Although the last actions of the main Brusilov Offensive south of the Pripet did not take place until September, Brusilov's real effort was over after July.

EFFECTS OF THE OFFENSIVE

The Brusilov Offensive is seen as evidence of what Russian armies could achieve when well commanded and led. However, it ultimately involved very heavy Russian losses – almost a million men, half of them prisoners – for what were strictly limited gains. Both at the time and after the offensive ended, its costs caused domestic anguish. The various towns that were captured and military successes that were registered generated no popular enthusiasm, merely the knowledge that what had been gained would be lost.

> "In the mountains, bad, quite inadequate shelter, icy cold, rain and mist. An excruciating life."
>
> FROM THE DIARY OF AUSTRIAN GUNNER
> (AND PHILOSOPHER) LUDWIG WITTGENSTEIN, JULY 15, 1916

RUSSIA IN TURMOIL

D URING THE SUMMER OF 1915, as the Russian army was driven back eastwards across Poland, hundreds of thousands of refugees, their homes and farms destroyed, headed for the cities and towns. Along with disease, misery and panic, there were widespread rumours of treachery, which focused on the Tsarina Alexandra, a German princess by birth.

The catastrophe exposed the incompetence of Russia's autocratic government, but Tsar Nicholas II had neither the will nor the wit to change. Instead of liberalizing his regime by appointing efficient, experienced ministers, and securing the support of the duma (Russia's parliament), the zemstvos (municipal councils) and the industrialists' War Industries Committee, Nicholas decided to rule like a true autocrat and take personal command of the Russian army. In his absence, power passed to the tsarina, who was herself under the demonic influence of the faith-healer Rasputin.

While Nicholas was away at the front, Alexandra and Rasputin began to exercise a disastrous influence over government appointments. From September 1915 to February 1917 Russia had four prime ministers, five ministers of the interior, three foreign ministers, three war ministers, three ministers of transport and four ministers of agriculture. "I am here, don't laugh at silly old wifey," wrote Alexandra to her husband, "but she has trousers on unseen."

The Russian bourgeoisie was in despair. The Zemstvo Union – based on a network

of local councils – had become virtually a state within a state, but could do little to alleviate the ever-worsening situation. The scarcity of food and fuel, rampant inflation, the collapse of the transport system and the rapidly rising crime rate were combining to create an explosive, revolutionary situation.

At the outset of the war many liberal-minded Russians had hoped that a successful military campaign would unite the Russian people and forestall the need for radical reform of the state. However, they now came to the conclusion that radical reform was a pre-condition for military success. In December 1916 Rasputin was murdered by group of young nobles hoping to save the honour of Russia and the imperial family. But they were too late. Russia was already on the brink of a revolution that would consign the Romanov dynasty to history.

Recruiting troops at Bogorodsk, near Moscow

Heavy Russian losses throughout 1914–16 meant that there was a constant need to call up more men just to maintain numbers. A shortage of weapons in the first two years meant that many soldiers were not even equipped with rifles. The supply of munitions, however, began to improve as the political situation deteriorated.

Promoting war bonds

In common with other governments, the Russians raised extra funds by encouraging citizens to invest in war bonds. This poster promises a return of 5.5 per cent, but investors never saw this money.

"War victims need your help"

Russian citizens were exhorted to rally round and support those wounded in the war, who could expect little help from the autocratic, inefficient government.

Rasputin surrounded by court admirers

Rasputin's hypnotic powers, which apparently relieved the suffering of the haemophiliac Crown Prince Alexis, gave him a powerful emotional hold over the tsarina.

THE ROMANIAN CAMPAIGN

At the beginning of 1916 Romania was still neutral and was seeking to exploit the opportunity provided by the war to advance its territorial ambitions – directed particularly against Austria-Hungary over Transylvania, but also against Russia over Bessarabia. It was, however, aware of the risks involved in pursuing such a policy if it failed to intervene on the winning side before the war's end. By 1916, following the conquest of Serbia, and the entry of Bulgaria into the war, the Central Powers had secured for themselves a potentially overwhelming advantage in the Balkans. But in the course of the year, Allied inducements, initial Russian success in the Brusilov Offensive, and the growing signs of Austria-Hungary's disintegration, prompted Romania to declare war on the Central Powers on August 27.

Allied support – in the form of an offensive from Salonika in Macedonia and a Russian move against Bukovina – provided the basis of a Romanian plan of campaign to stand on the defence against Bulgaria while striking through the Carpathian mountains against Austria-Hungary. However, by the time Romania had shown its hand, the Brusilov Offensive was faltering and Austria-Hungary and Germany had forces available with which to meet a new commitment in the Balkans. On top of this was the fact that, with the Salonika front quiescent, the Bulgarian army was able to spend the

German troops enter Bucharest, December 6
A Romanian attack on the Danube Army as it advanced towards Bucharest was defeated following the intervention of the Austro-German Ninth Army.

summer of 1916 preparing for the expected Romanian intervention in the autumn. This meant that the imbalance of forces, in terms of both numbers and quality, was very clearly against Romania when it entered the war. The nature of the terrain added to the disadvantages it faced, as did the inadequacy of the Romanian rail system, which made it impossible to move rapidly between the two fronts facing Transylvania.

Burning oil near Constanza
As the Romanian armies retreated, British agents played a major role in destroying oil dumps and wells in order to keep them out of the hands of the Central Powers.

THE INITIAL OFFENSIVE

The initial Romanian offensive into Austria-Hungary, launched on August 27, met with little opposition and succeeded in advancing some 80km (50 miles) into Transylvania before being halted. On September 1, however, a combined army of Bulgarians, Turks and Germans invaded the region of Dobruja and advanced almost to Constanza before being repulsed by the Romanians with the support of Russian and Serbian formations. Then, as the Romanians began to send more troops to meet this threat, the Austro-German Ninth Army opened its counter-offensive on September 18 at the Vulcan Pass. The main effort unfolded in the centre over the next 16 days, and by October 10 the Romanians had been

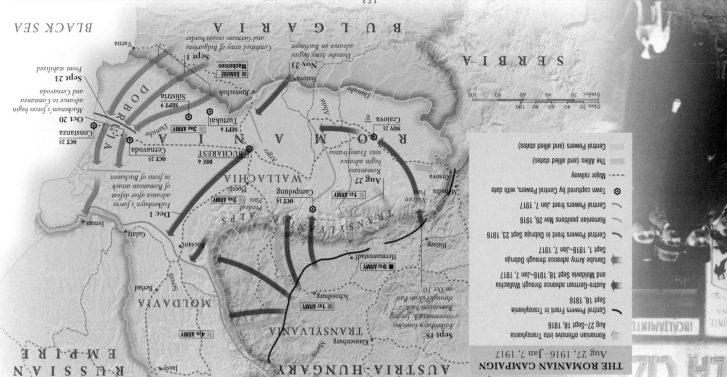

THE ROMANIAN CAMPAIGN
Aug 27, 1916 – Jan 7, 1917

- Romanian offensive into Transylvania Aug 27–Sept 18, 1916
- Central Powers Front in Transylvania Sept 18, 1916
- Austro-German advance through Wallachia and Moldavia Sept 18, 1916–Jan 7, 1917
- Danube Army advance through Dobruja Sept 1, 1916–Jan 7, 1917
- Central Powers front in Dobruja Sept 23, 1916
- Romanian positions Nov 26, 1916
- Central Powers front Jan 7, 1917
- Town captured by Central Powers, with date
- Major railway
- The Allies (and allied states)
- Central Powers (and allied states)

forced to evacuate Hungarian territory. Within another two weeks the Austro-German Ninth Army had secured the critically important Predeal Pass. But shortly after, as the Russians extended their front southwards in support of the Romanians, the onset of winter brought the closing down of major operations in Moldavia.

THE ADVANCE OF THE CENTRAL POWERS

The Germans redirected their attention to Wallachia and the Dobruja and made advances in both areas. Craiova fell on November 21, and two days later the Danube Army, formed from units of each of the Central Powers, crossed the lower Danube around Sistova (Svishtov) and began to advance on Bucharest. Its consequent separation from the German Ninth Army provided a desperate Romanian army, which faced certain defeat if it remained on the defensive, with a final opportunity to counterattack and perhaps buy the time needed to allow more Russian reinforcements to arrive. The initial Romanian drive pinned down the left flank of the Danube Army. But as the Ninth Army moved to the

latter's support, the Romanian offensive collapsed and Bucharest fell on December 6.

The subsequent Central Powers' pursuit of the retreating Romanian armies was slowed by the poor state of the roads, but by the new year southern Moldavia and the whole of Wallachia and the Dobruja had been cleared of Allied forces. The Central Powers had gained control of Romania's oil- and grain-producing regions and Russia had been left with a widening commitment in its vulnerable southern regions. The situation in this

the Romanians had been defeated by stronger forces.

The Central Powers' invasion of Romania

The Romanian invasion of Transylvania, launched on August 27, was halted after an 80-km (50-mile) advance. An Austro-German offensive then drove the Romanians out of Hungary by October 10, while the Danube Army advanced northwards through the Dobruja. By December

sector was to remain more or less unchanged until December 7, 1917 when Romania, left to its own resources after the Bolshevik Revolution in Russia, concluded an armistice with the Central Powers.

High-level discussions

Mackensen (left), commander of the Danube Army, confers with Archduke Friedrich (centre), commander of the Austro-Hungarian First Army, during the Romanian campaign. Mackensen remained in command of the army of occupation in Romania until the end of the war.

LIFE AT THE FRONT

T HE AMOUNT OF TIME A MAN spent in the front-line trenches varied over the course of the war, but the most usual period of duty was between four and six days. At any one time, only a minority of soldiers were in "active" sections of the line – firing or being fired at. The rest were battling against hunger, sleeplessness and the miseries arising from the weather and their cramped, damp and unsanitary living conditions.

The quality of dugouts varied. While German reserves were relatively comfortable in deep bunkers, the French hunkered down in notoriously wretched trenches. Sleep in the trenches was a snatched luxury and clean water was in short supply. Most dugouts had a brazier for heat and for warming food; for toilets there were buckets, or the nearest shell-hole.

After heavy rain, trenches became mucky, stinking cesspits: breeding grounds for disease and the agonizing condition known as "trench foot". Another common complaint was "trench fever", spread by lice – another great scourge of the trenches. Soldiers could visit delousing stations behind the lines for baths and clean clothes, but within a few hours they would be "lousy" again. Rats, grown huge on the corpses of the dead, also played a part in the trench nightmare. Killing them was one way of relieving the boredom of life in the line.

Food was a major cause of complaint. Officially, each soldier was supplied with daily rations of about 4,000 calories, but in practice the rations carried up the lines at night were, at best, irregular and monotonous, at worst irregular and barely edible. British troops despised the tins of corned beef, or "bully", their usual fare, though German soldiers developed quite a taste for it. Maconochie's, a mixture of meat and root vegetables, was highly prized by the British.

Trench life became a world apart, with its own code of behaviour. "Mucking in" was the British term for looking out and looking after one another. Soldiers didn't always appreciate their official "rest" periods, which too often meant clearing roads, digging defences or shifting ammunition, as well as the tedium of drills and parades.

Front line rations

Rations generally came in tins so tin openers were vital equipment. The French issued their men with hard mint sweets and biscuits. Raisins, tobacco and chocolate were usually shared by the soldiers.

SWEETS

BÉTISES de CAMBRAI

AFCHAIN SEUL INVENTEUR

BÉTISES de CAMBRAI

NON! MAIS ÇGUITZ MOI! ÇA

BISCUIT TIN

Biscuits Pelin

A BAGNOLET (Seine)
PRÈS PARIS

TIN OPENER

Field kitchen

If they were lucky, soldiers would receive hot food from a field kitchen, though meals usually had to be carried on foot up to the front and were, at best, lukewarm on arrival. A shortage of cooking vats meant flavours becoming intermingled, with tea tasting of vegetables.

Mess Kit

Every French soldier was issued with a mess kit (in a design unchanged since 1855), consisting of a cup, spoon and fork (but no knife), and containers for his vital alcohol and chocolate rations.

Alcohol ration

Chocolate ration, not to be eaten until the order is given

Home comforts

German propaganda photographs showed soldiers at the front enjoying a comfortable life in their dug-outs. Packs of cards were issued that used images of the Kaiser, the Crown Prince and Graf Zeppelin, among other prominent Germans.

Anything for a laugh . . .

Humour was used to cheer up French troops (*top left*). The Germans used it to show an over-jolly image of the war. It even appeared on postcards (*right*) sent by soldiers loath to describe the true horror of their experiences.

Trench art

Life on quiet sectors of the front could be rather dull. To help pass the time some soldiers fashioned objects from spent cartridge and shell cases.

MODEL PLANE

LIGHTER

LETTER OPENER

ROLLING PAPERS

Getting comfortable

Soldiers of the Border Regiment, notoriously self-sufficient, rest in hollowed-out shelters in the side of a captured German trench in Thiepval Wood, August 1916.

Wash time

There was little chance to wash properly at the front, with water in short supply. Despite attempts to repel them, lice infested the clothes of almost every soldier and proved impossible to exterminate.

INSECT REPELLENT

Destruction on the Somme, 1916
German soldiers search through the wreckage of a Red Cross vehicle hit by a shell. Members of the medical services were frequently victims of shell fire.

Battle of the Somme

A cheerful front
Members of the Worcestershire Regiment put on a brave face for the camera on their way to the front on June 28. This was the type of image that was welcomed by British politicians, anxious to show the war in a good light.

AT THE CHANTILLY CONFERENCE in December 1915, the Allies agreed to mount a major offensive on the Western Front in the following year. Joffre, the commander of the French Army, wanted the assault to be launched on the Somme River, a quiet front up to this time. Haig, the new commander of the BEF, preferred the idea of a further offensive in Flanders, but ultimately agreed to Joffre's choice of battlefield. The offensive was to begin in August and would be led by the French with 39 divisions. A total of 25 to 30 British divisions would be committed to the battle.

This planned division of responsibility for the Somme campaign was to change after the launch of the German offensive on Verdun in February. As more and

Shell blast
Artillery bombardments were used to try and break the Germans' resistance and destroy their barbed wire. But even the million shells with which the Allies pounded the Germans in the week prior to the attack of July 1 did not have the desired effect.

more French troops were sent to Verdun, fewer were available for the Somme, and it became clear that the British would have to bear the brunt of the fighting. By May, the situation at Verdun was so desperate that Joffre called on Haig to bring forward the date of the attack. A date of June 29 was agreed, in the event postponed until July 1.

Under Haig's original plan, two divisions of the British Third Amy under Allenby were to draw away German reserves at Gommecourt to the north, while the Fourth Army under Rawlinson plus the French divisions under Foch broke through the German trenches on a 30-km (20-mile) front. These attacking forces would then turn northwards, driving back the German flank and creating a gap for the British cavalry. Initially, Haig considered that if no breakthrough took place swiftly, the attack should be stopped. He had, however, changed his mind on this particular point by the time the attack began.

German casualties
A direct hit from a shell could kill a dozen men in an instant. Often, bodies would lie unburied or, if buried, would be disinterred by subsequent action. Soldiers sometimes had to live alongside such corpses for weeks on end.

THE ROLE OF ARTILLERY

Rawlinson did not agree with aspects of Haig's plan. He doubted that a single major effort would be decisive and argued for a series of smaller, related attacks to secure positions of tactical advantage from which a battle of attrition could be launched. Although Rawlinson's formula was rejected, he shared with Haig and the French General Nivelle, an artillery expert, the belief that a massive artillery barrage over several days had the ability to inflict enormous damage on defenders.

Haig certainly had a massive supply of shells, which he assumed would be sufficient for his heavy guns and howitzers, posted less than 60m (197 ft) apart over about 24km (15 miles), to destroy the German defence, and for the field artillery to destroy the barbed wire. This would compensate for the inexperience of a large proportion of the British forces. The battle would, essentially, be won at the outset by the artillery, giving infantry the role of marching in and mopping up afterwards.

These assumptions were, in fact, incorrect in 1916. Haig did not have the weight of guns and shells required to overwhelm the defence over a front that was extended to protect the advancing troops, in the centre, from enemy flanking fire. Besides a large number of dud shells, there were also technical deficiencies. The shells of 1916 burst on impact with the ground. Used against barbed-wire entanglements, they tended merely to throw the wire about, rather than create large gaps through which the infantry could advance unchecked.

British planning discounted past evidence that no bombardment, however massive, could create the opening for a breakthrough. It also ignored the hard-learned lesson that the attacking infantry should advance as fast as possible and employ fire- and-movement tactics, with each group periodically dropping to the ground, making use of any available shelter, to provide covering fire for others. Instead, the British troops were to advance in lines, almost shoulder to shoulder, at a steady pace.

PRELIMINARY BOMBARDMENT

A small number of the British troops had served in Flanders or Gallipoli, but the vast majority were inexperienced volunteers who knew little of trench warfare. They were confident of making a dramatic breakthrough – and their optimism was increased by the massive artillery bombardment that began on June 24 and continued for over a week.

Haig's strategic purpose was increasingly unclear. The small town of Bapaume, 16km (10 miles) behind the German front, was his immediate objective, but first the Pozières ridge, between the Ancre and Serre rivers, had to be taken. Since the Germans held the advantage of high ground along the entire front and had considerably strengthened their defences as Allied intentions became evident, even this modest objective was optimistic. The French objective was the town of Péronne.

Field guns in batteries 900 m (1,000 yds) behind the front, together with heavy siege guns a further 1.5 km (1 mile) or so behind, bombarded a 24-km (15-mile) front, firing over 1,500,000 shells in seven days. Although most of the German troops on the Somme were battle-hardened units who had been in position for many months, a bombardment of such relentless ferocity was beyond their experience. In the words of Lieutenant Stefan Westmann, a German medical officer:

"Day and night, the shells came upon us. Our dugouts crumbled. They would fall on top of us and we'd have to dig ourselves and our comrades out. Sometimes we'd find them suffocated or smashed to pulp. Soldiers in the bunkers became hysterical – they wanted to run out, and fights developed to keep them in the comparative safety of our deep bunkers. Even the rats became hysterical and came into our flimsy shelters to seek refuge from this terrific artillery fire."

The Allied attack was supposed to begin on June 29, but was postponed for two days owing to heavy rain and the discovery by raiding parties that the bombardment had been less effective than hoped. Assurances then came from above that the wire was cut, but there was more than one soldier equipped with binoculars who could see for himself that, despite the pounding it had received, long stretches of the wire were still intact.

OVER THE TOP

It was a perfect summer's morning when on July 1, at 6:25, the final Allied bombardment began. Continuing for over an hour at a firing rate of 3,500 shells a minute, the noise was so intense that it could be heard as far away as England. When the guns stopped, the air was split by massive eruptions as the British exploded mines they had laid under the German defences. The awesome demonstration of destructive power heartened the attacking troops.

After the bombardment came a brief interval of silence before whistles blew to send the men up the scaling ladders. Once over the top, they formed lines holding their rifles in front of them, and began to walk towards No Man's Land. All advantage of surprise had been sacrificed; it was broad daylight, visibility was perfect, and there was little cover – conditions, in short, that heavily favoured the defenders. The advancing infantry could have been protected by a "creeping barrage", laid down by the field guns and moving just ahead of them. This tactic, however, was a new one that required exact

timing between the artillery and infantry, and was still in the process of being developed. It was to be used effectively at Verdun in October, but in July all that could be achieved was the bombardment of each enemy line at a pre-arranged time. In fact, afraid of hitting their own men, the gunners advanced the barrage beyond each line of German trenches long before the infantry reached it.

Ahead of the troops lay the German barbed wire, which in many places had gaps that were so few or so small that they created bottlenecks. They reduced the slow advance to a virtual standstill, as the Germans began to appear from their 9-m (30-ft) dugouts, hauling their machine-guns into place in a drill they had rehearsed many times.

KILLING FIELDS

From a distance the ragged lines of slowly advancing soldiers looked like clockwork dolls, and equally vulnerable, as individuals began to stagger and fall under the withering machine-gun fire before they had fired a shot themselves. As the first line of men disintegrated, the next line came under fire. The German artillery was in action too, and shrapnel vied with machine-gun bullets in clearing

Helping the wounded

Although soldiers in offensive action were ordered not to break the line to give assistance to those who had fallen, many later risked their own lives to try and get the wounded back to safety. The Allies suffered 630,000 casualties on the Somme; the Germans even more.

...for the first short distance there seemed to be no casualties, but soon it became apparent that men were going down rather thicker that one realized... My officer called across to me and said, 'You stick to me, and I'll stick to you.' I said 'Right,' but immediately lost sight of him. I don't know what happened to him. At that point, to my great surprise, a hare ran along in front of me, its eyes bulging with fear, but I don't think it was half as frightened as I was.

TROOPER R. J. MASON OF THE 10TH HUSSARS DESCRIBING THE ADVANCE ACROSS NO MAN'S LAND

the ground of marching men. Whole battalions were reduced to a hundred or so men. Following orders, the lines continued to advance, further impeded by the bodies of the dead and wounded. More bodies, grotesquely posed, were tangled in the uncut wire. Elsewhere those firing the machine-guns concentrated on the gaps. The Germans were outnumbered and fighting for their lives, but eventually many of them tired of the easy slaughter and refrained from firing on wounded men attempting to drag themselves back to their own line. In a few places the British did manage to capture a German trench, but as no reinforcements reached them they were soon forced out again.

Behind the British lines the field dressing stations were overwhelmed. The wounded who seemed unlikely to survive were placed on one side and treated last, if at all. As the day ended, many of the bodies strewn about the battlefield appeared to come to life, as wounded men emerged from shell holes and depressions and struggled to to get back to their lines under cover of darkness.

A total of 13 British divisions went into action on July 1. By the end of the day, they had suffered over 57,000 casualties, a third of them killed – the highest total of any day in the history of the British army. The only progress they had made was in the southern sector, where the German-held villages of

Mametz and Montauban were captured. Haig's objective, Bapaume, was not reached on July 1 – nor in the five months of attacks that followed.

The five French divisions – all that could be spared – were mostly south of the Somme. They had heavier guns in support and gained some element of surprise by delaying their attack to the last moment. They encountered less opposition and

were more successful, taking 3,000 prisoners and forcing the evacuation of the Germans' second line during the night. But their objective, the town of Péronne, remained safely in German hands.

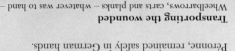

Transporting the wounded
Wheelbarrows, carts and planks – whatever was to hand – were used to carry the wounded back to the field dressing stations on the first day of the Somme offensive.

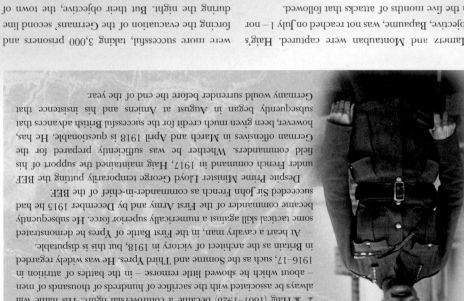

DOUGLAS HAIG
~

As COMMANDER-IN-CHIEF of the BEF from 1915 to 1918, Douglas Haig (1861–1928) became a controversial figure. His name will always be associated with the sacrifice of hundreds of thousands of men – about which he showed little remorse – in the battles of attrition in 1916–17, such as the Somme and Third Ypres. He was widely regarded in Britain as the architect of victory in 1918, but this is disputable.

At heart a cavalry man, in the First Battle of Ypres he demonstrated some tactical skill against a numerically superior force. He subsequently became commander of the First Army and by December 1915 he had succeeded Sir John French as commander-in-chief of the BEF.

Despite Prime Minister Lloyd George temporarily putting the BEF under French command in 1917, Haig maintained the support of his field commanders. Whether he was sufficiently prepared for the German offensives in March and April 1918 is questionable. He has, however, been given much credit for the successful British advances that subsequently began in August at Amiens and his insistence that Germany would surrender before the end of the year.

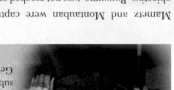

BATTLE OF THE SOMME
JULY 1–NOVEMBER 18, 1916
~

As a result of the German offensive on Verdun, the Battle of the Somme was fought largely by British troops with French support. The British planned to break through the German lines between Serre and Maricourt, and advance to Bapaume. The French objective was Péronne. In fact, neither Bapaume nor Péronne were to be captured in the five-month long battle. On the first day – when the British army suffered higher casualties than on any other day in its history – six German divisions withstood an attack by 13 British and five French divisions. Very limited progress was made in the southern sector; none was made in the north. Over the next two weeks the Allied troops inched forward to capture the German second line around Bazentin-le-Petit. The battle then went through a period of local encounters until a second attempt at a major advance was launched on September 15 with the aid of a new weapon – the tank. However, after some initial success at Flers, the battle again turned into one of attrition before dying out on November 18.

KEY

French advance	British advance
French front line	Road
British front line	Railway

German troops with captured weapons

German machine-gunners valued the British Lewis machine-guns that were somewhat lighter than the models, such as the Maxim, with which they were issued.

On July 6–7 the British captured La Boiselle and Contalmaison, which the Germans regained hours later. A British attack on Mametz Wood was repulsed; it was taken a week later. After ten days of fighting, the Germans had been pushed back on average only one or two kilometres. At Verdun meanwhile, the failure of the last German attacks in June and July, combined with the demands of the Somme and the Eastern Front, had compelled Falkenhayn to go over to the defensive.

Wrecked German trench

When Allied troops managed to capture a German trench, they were amazed at how deep and strong it was. The Germans had spent many months improving their defences.

FOLLOW-UP ATTACKS

As a result of the failure on the part of the Allies to achieve the planned breakthrough on July 1, the Battle of the Somme became in effect one of attrition, with numerous limited offensives directed at specific villages, ridges or woods. Combat was ferocious, and a Somme battlefield in the wake of the fighting was, in the words of Christopher Nevinson, the British war artist, a hellish environment of "…shrieks, pus, gangrene and the disembowelled". The smell was indescribable.

The British, having repelled a German attempt to retake Montauban on July 2, renewed the offensive next day, but failed to take Ovillers, less than 1.5 km (1 mile) from the front. The French in the south again made better progress, breaking through the German second line of defences and taking many prisoners. Casualties were heavy; units of the Foreign Legion lost one-third of their men.

German Maxim MG 08/15

This lighter version of the 1908 Maxim — 19 kg (43lb) when filled with water — was designed to be carried quickly into battle. It normally had a crew of three, but could be operated by a single gunner.

Pistol grip

Spiked bipod

Crank handle

Butt

Backsight

Water jacket

Flash hider

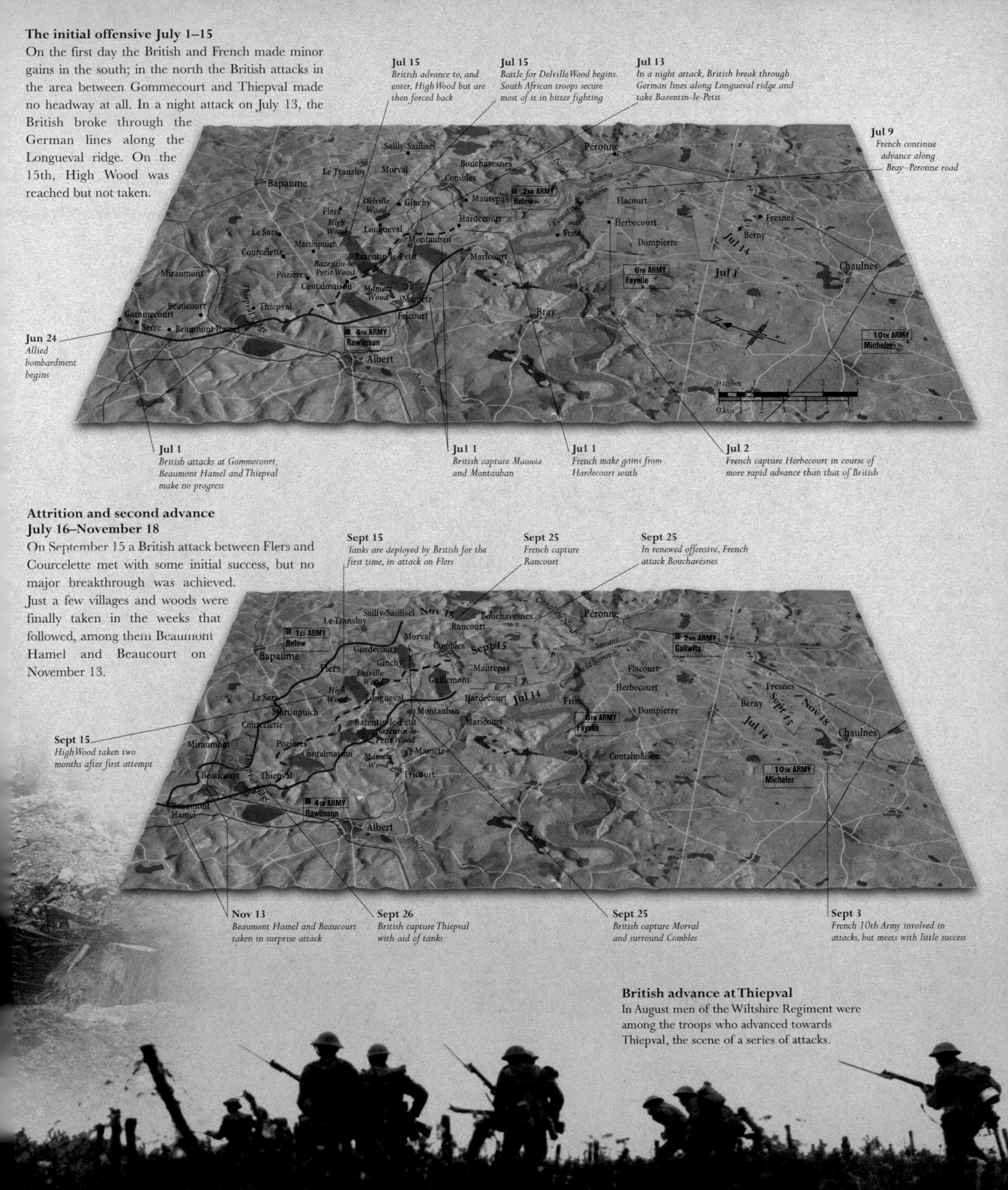

The initial offensive July 1–15

On the first day the British and French made minor gains in the south; in the north the British attacks in the area between Gommecourt and Thiepval made no headway at all. In a night attack on July 13, the British broke through the German lines along the Longueval ridge. On the 15th, High Wood was reached but not taken.

Jul 15
British advance to, and enter, High Wood but are then forced back

Jul 15
Battle for Delville Wood begins. South African troops secure most of it in bitter fighting

Jul 13
In a night attack, British break through German lines along Longueval ridge and take Bazentin-le-Petit

Jul 9
French continue advance along Bray–Peronne road

Jun 24
Allied bombardment begins

Jul 1
British attacks at Gommecourt, Beaumont Hamel and Thiepval make no progress

Jul 1
British capture Mametz and Montauban

Jul 1
French make gains from Hardecourt south

Jul 2
French capture Herbecourt in course of more rapid advance than that of British

Attrition and second advance July 16–November 18

On September 15 a British attack between Flers and Courcelette met with some initial success, but no major breakthrough was achieved. Just a few villages and woods were finally taken in the weeks that followed, among them Beaumont Hamel and Beaucourt on November 13.

Sept 15
Tanks are deployed by British for the first time, in attack on Flers

Sept 25
French capture Rancourt

Sept 25
In renewed offensive, French attack Bouchavesnes

Sept 15
High Wood taken two months after first attempt

Nov 13
Beaumont Hamel and Beaucourt taken in surprise attack

Sept 26
British capture Thiepval with aid of tanks

Sept 25
British capture Morval and surround Combles

Sept 3
French 10th Army involved in attacks, but meets with little success

British advance at Thiepval

In August men of the Wiltshire Regiment were among the troops who advanced towards Thiepval, the scene of a series of attacks.

THE DEVELOPMENT OF THE TANK

ODDLY IT WAS THE BRITISH NAVY that first realized the need for some kind of cross-country armoured vehicle. In the early months of the war armoured cars (see page 59) had been used by the Royal Naval Air Service based in Dunkerque. Once the front became fixed in November 1914, they were of little further use since they could not cross trenches or barbed wire. A number of men turned their minds to possible solutions to this problem. The War Office was sceptical, but Winston Churchill, First Lord of the Admiralty, took a keen interest and, in February 1915, established a Landships Committee. Many designs were considered, one specifically for bridging trenches, one for cutting wire, another to carry troops across No Man's Land. One school of thought favoured vehicles on huge wheels, another the caterpillar track used on tractors. In the end it was the caterpillar track that prevailed.

The design that was given the go-ahead was the creation of Walter Wilson and William Tritton, working at Fosters engineering works at Lincoln. When tested on February 2, 1916, government officials and army top brass were (with the exception of Kitchener) impressed and an order was placed for 100 machines. In essence this was the design that the British army would use for the rest of the war and thus the prototype came to be known as "Mother". It gave birth to the Mark 1, which saw action at the Somme later in the year. This came in two versions: the "male", armed with two naval 6-pounders in sponsons (half-turrets projecting from the sides of the tank) and four machine-guns, and the "female", with seven machine-guns. The reason for the "female" version was a fear that male tanks might be swamped by masses of enemy infantry. Production of the Mark 1 began at Fosters and at the larger plant of the Metropolitan Carriage Co, Birmingham. To preserve the weapon's secrecy the name "tank" was coined because, without its guns, it looked like a vehicle for carrying water.

An unimpressive trial
On June 30, 1915 the Navy gave a demonstration of this American Killen-Strait tractor fitted with wire-cutters at the front. It was clearly not the answer to the deadlock in the trenches.

Little Willie
This prototype, produced by Tritton and Wilson in September, 1915, looked quite like the tanks of the future. Its trench-crossing abilities, however, were very limited and nobody gave it any serious consideration. It survives as a museum exhibit.

Disinformation
The army was determined that the first appearance of tanks on the Western Front should take the Germans by complete surprise. Accordingly the tanks' bodies (without sponsons or guns), when they were loaded on trains for transport from the factory, were labelled "to Petrograd" in case they were spotted by spies.

BRITISH NIGHT ATTACK

In a surprise night attack on July 13, the British broke through the German lines across a 5.5-km (3.5-mile) sector along the Longueval ridge, taking Bazentin-le-Petit, west of Delville Wood. For a moment, penetration to a depth of around 900 m (1,000 yds) renewed hope of breaking through the entire German front, and brought Haig's beloved cavalry briefly into action. But poor communications, among other difficulties, allowed the Germans to restore their defences.

On July 15, British forces reached High Wood, but could not capture it. On the same day, to the east, the battle for Delville Wood began – the moment of truth for the South African Brigade that had been ordered to capture it. The fighting was marked by ruthless hand-to-hand combat as well as pulverizing bombardments that reduced the wood to shreds within two days. The South Africans had been told to hold the wood at all costs. A week later the 4th Regiment of the South African Infantry Brigade consisted of just 42 men.

Meanwhile, on July 19, Australians and New Zealanders from the Gallipoli campaign carried out a diversionary attack on Fromelles, far to the north, to prevent German reinforcements reaching the battlefield. The German defences appeared formidable, and since no reinforcements were moving southward, the main reason for the attack no longer existed. The Australian General Elliott, advised by a British staff officer that "a holocaust" was in prospect, questioned the need for the operation, but was told that it would be bad for morale to cancel it. The first Australian casualties were victims of their own supporting fire. The guns did not, however, disable the German machine-gun emplacements, and the result was as predicted. Total casualties were about 1,700 dead (plus 400 British), 4,000 wounded, and 500 captured.

The intense local battles of attrition that were typical of the Somme campaign were everywhere, resulting in tens of thousands of casualties on both sides. In an attempt (not the first) to capture Guillemont on August 8, one battalion lost half of its officers and one-sixth of its men.

In late July Haig learned that the British government was becoming restive at the casualties, but he thought another six weeks of "steady offensive pressure" would break the Germans. The weather continued fine: "not the weather for killing people," noted Harold Macmillan, a future British prime minister. But as autumn came it brought heavy rain and, with it, murderous mud.

THE ENGINEERS

WILLIAM TRITTON

WALTER WILSON

THE TWO MEN given credit for designing and building the first tank are William Tritton, managing director of the Fosters factory in Lincoln, and Lieutenant Walter Wilson of the Royal Naval Reserve. In peacetime Wilson, a genius in matters of gearing, had been an engineer working on cars and lorries. The two men had both worked on a number of experimental designs before coming up with one that would be used in battle. Tritton, for example, had produced a giant trench-crossing vehicle with huge wheels, shown in the picture above behind its inventor. He and Wilson worked together on the Lincoln No. 1 machine (later known as "Little Willie"). It ran on American-made Bullock "Creeping Grip" tracks. In a trial these proved completely inadequate, so Tritton devised stronger, more reliable ones. However, "Little Willie" was superseded by a tank conceived principally by Wilson – a "quasi-rhomboidal" vehicle, on which the tracks ran all the way round the hull – the Mark I.

Big Willie or "Mother"

Big Willie, the prototype of the first British tank, Mark I, succeeded at its trials in January and February 1916 in crossing a 3-m (10-ft) trench and riding over a vertical obstacle 1.4 m (4 ft 6 in) high. This performance so outstripped that of any previous prototype that it was given the job. Its wheeled tail, for steering and balance, was dispensed with in later models.

Mechanized warfare

Nobody knew quite what to expect of the new tanks when 50 of them were despatched to battlefield of the Somme in 1916. The general hope was that they would knock out machine-guns, crush barbed wire and serve as a shield for infantry advancing across No Man's Land.

The first tanks to go into battle were fitted with a roof of wood and wire to protect them from the full blast of grenades and shells.

The guns fitted in the sponsons were naval 6-pounders with their barrels cut down. When a tank went into battle it carried 324 rounds for each gun.

Mark I tank

The tank used at the Somme was manned by a crew of eight: an officer and the driver sitting up front, a gunner and his mate in each sponson and two gearsmen who worked the gears on the drive shafts to the the sprocketed wheels that turned the caterpillar tracks. The tank was powered by a 105 hp Daimler engine originally designed to drive tractors.

DAIMLER MARK IV TANK ENGINE

Loopholes for tank commander and driver

"The mud makes it all but impassable, and now sunk in it up to the knees, I have the momentary terror of never being able to pull myself out."

The Allied front line inched forward. At the beginning of September, it had advanced between 1.5 and 5km (1 and 3.5 miles) since July 1. The French had gone a little farther, but they were tied to the pace of the British advance. Ginchy (where the Irish secured a victory), Delville Wood and Guillemont were all finally taken before September 15, when the main British offensive was renewed.

A NEW WEAPON

Tactics had improved since July. The "creeping barrage" was now more effective at subduing enemy trenches, if not artillery. More important, on September 15 a new weapon appeared: the tank. This would eventually prove to be the antidote to the stalemate of trench warfare. In 1916 only 50 were available – not enough to be effective – and they were used in the wrong way, operating individually in support of infantry. But, like Hannibal's elephants, they had a dramatic

psychological effect. The Germans initially felt quite powerless against what they saw as "monsters" that crawled along the top of trenches, enfilading them with continuous machine-gun fire.

In fact, about one-third of the tanks broke down, and many others were destroyed by artillery fire. Nevertheless, those that kept going long enough succeeded in driving the Germans out of the village of Flers, and they were largely responsible for the British advance on September 15 of about 1,800 m (2,000 yds) on an 8-km (5-mile) front between Flers and Courcelette. This included High Wood, finally taken two months after the first attempt.

The British registered another advance ten days later, taking Combles on the 25th. On the following day, Thiepval – besieged since July 1 – was captured with the aid of 13 tanks. At Gueudecourt, they took 500 prisoners for only five men lost. The tanks and the support of spotter aircraft, with

however, demanded 1,000 of them.

Conservative officers remained sceptical of the tank, and the German high command was not sufficiently convinced by what it has seen to press forward with developing their own tank. Haig,

At the end of the month came heavy rain. The downpour rapidly demonstrated, once again, a

Stuck in the mud
Torrential rain in November 1916 turned the battlefield into a quagmire. Supplies of ammunition were badly delayed as roads became virtually impassable to man or beast.

major disadvantage of bombardments by heavy artillery: they cut up the ground over which the infantry hoped to advance, and, once soaked by rain, it turned into mud. The consequence was described by the official historian of the South African Brigade, John Buchan:

"'There were now two No Man's Lands – one between the front lines, and one between the old enemy front and the front we had won. The second was the bigger problem, for across it must be brought the supplies of a great army. Every road became a watercourse, and in the hollows the mud was as deep as a man's thighs….Off the roads the ground was one vast bog, dugouts crumbled in, communication trenches ceased to be."

Behind the British front lay 9km (6 miles) of "sponge, varied by mud torrents". Artillery could not be shifted, and men died as a result of the sheer effort of carrying a message across the glutinous mud. A wounded man hesitated before seeking shelter in a shell hole, fearing that do so might mean being sucked down to his death.

POLICY OF FORWARD DEFENCE

The relative ease of the final British advances indicated German exhaustion. Falkenhayn's strategy of "forward defence", insisting that all lost ground be immediately recovered, regardless of inferior numbers and limited reserves, largely explained the bitterness of the August fighting.

Despite the conditions, October saw a series of British attacks of the kind that deservedly gave generalship in the First World War a bad name. Rawlinson, complaining that the bad weather "has given the Boche a breather", hoped to "be aggressive" all winter. But, after the capture of Beaumont-Hamel and Beaucourt, snow on November 17/18 brought the Somme campaign to an end, and Bapaume was still in German hands.

German casualties were even higher than those of the Allies: about 660,000 compared with 630,000. By the end of August, when Hindenburg and Ludendorff took over, a rethink was clearly needed. In future the front line would be held lightly, and non-vital defences would be surrendered, thus restoring tactical flexibility to the defence.

Meanwhile, the Allies agreed to resume the attack on the Somme in the spring. Joffre, who resigned on December 12, added a rider: France had sufficient manpower for only one more major effort. It was clear, therefore, that in the following year the main burden of responsibility on the Western Front would pass from France to Britain.

MARK I TANK ADVANCES

Just before Zero Hour we heard this damned racket, and I remember saying, 'What the hell is this?' Then these tanks appeared, one on our front and one a bit away from us. We were all absolutely flabbergasted. We didn't know what to think. We didn't know what to think. It was an amazing sight… They came up right in front of us and swung round and went straight for the German line. The barbed-wire entanglements had been pretty well smashed by our artillery but the tanks just rolled over what remained of them. They smashed them all to pieces. They scared the guts out of the Germans. They bolted like rabbits.

BRITISH CORPORAL EDWARD GALE ON THE ARRIVAL OF TANKS AT THE SOMME

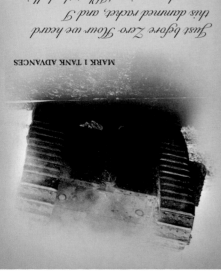

THE ARTILLERY OF TRENCH WARFARE

T HE FIRST WORLD WAR BEGAN as a war of movement and very quickly became a siege war, a fact that did much to determine how artillery developed. Initially, great faith was placed in field artillery, generally in the 75 to 85-mm (3 to 3.3-in) range, but the development of trench systems spelt the need for bigger guns and howitzers (which had short barrels and fired heavier shells on a high trajectory). Their volume of fire over protracted periods was deemed critical to infantry success, with saturation of the enemy defence system being considered far more important than the achievement of surprise.

In many ways the French offensives of spring and autumn 1915 reflect the transition from one system of warfare to the other. In the Artois offensive in May the French employed some 300 heavy guns. Just a few months later, in the Champagne offensive – for which three railway lines were built in order to get artillery and ammunition into position – they employed 2,000 guns in support of 11 corps against two German corps with 600 guns. The intensity of the French bombardment ensured the destruction of three German infantry regiments before rain transformed the battlefield into a sea of mud.

The battle in Champagne lasted 15 days and at heavy cost to the attacking French forces, but the lesson derived from it was that an even greater concentration of firepower was needed. In 1915 the British at Loos had only 12 guns per km (19 guns per mile) of front, and heavy guns were limited to 96 rounds a day – that is, one shell every 15 minutes. At Messines in 1917 they had 756 heavy guns and 1,510 field guns on a 13.5-km (8.5-mile) front.

As well as an increase in the number of heavy weapons, there were three major developments in artillery over the course of the war. First, various medium guns and howitzers were developed. Initially the maximum size was determined by what a horse team could draw, but in the final stages of the war, horses were replaced by tractors. Second, mobile artillery was developed in the form of the tank. This was a response to the fact that the shattering of defensive positions by artillery firepower made it virtually impossible for the artillery to move across the battlefield in order to repeat the process against the next enemy line. Third, a new kind of artillery – the rail gun – was developed when it became apparent just how expensive medium and heavy guns were in terms of manpower, their crews of up to 28 men invariably being subjected to intense counter-battery fire. Some rail guns, such as the British 9.2-in (234-mm) gun, and the American 14-in (356-mm) gun were standard weapons mounted on flatcars. However, the most famous model – the Paris Gun with which the Germans bombarded Paris in 1918 – was purpose-built.

60-pounders at the Somme

The 60-pounder was Britain's largest field-gun, pulled by a team of heavy horses. Noted for its accuracy, it had a range of 9,400 m (10,300 yds).

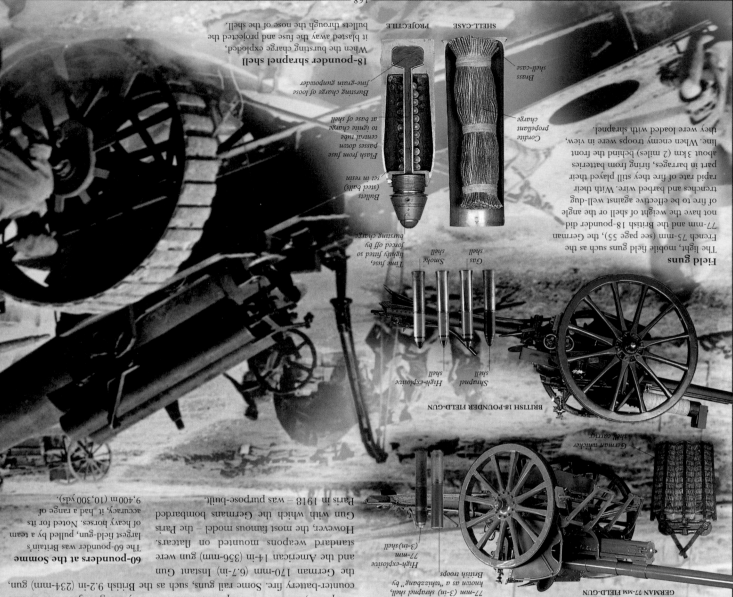

Field guns

The light, mobile field guns such as the French 75-mm (see page 55), the German 77-mm and the British 18-pounder did not have the weight of shell or the angle of fire to be effective against well-dug trenches and barbed wire. With their rapid rate of fire they still played their part in barrages, firing from batteries about 3 km (2 miles) behind the front line. When enemy troops were in view, they were loaded with shrapnel.

GERMAN 77-MM FIELD-GUN

77-mm (3-in) shrapnel shell, known as a "whizzbang" by British troops

High-explosive 77-mm (3-in) shell

German wicker shell carrier

BRITISH 18-POUNDER FIELD-GUN

High-explosive shell

Shrapnel shell

Gas shell

Smoke shell

Time fuse, tightly fitted so forced off by bursting charge

18-pounder shrapnel shell
When the bursting charge exploded, it blasted away the fuse and projected the bullets through the nose of the shell.

Bursting charge of loose fine-grain gunpowder

Flash from fuse passes down central tube to ignite charge at base of shell

Bullets (steel balls) set in resin

SHELL-CASE

Brass shell-case

Cordite propellant charge

PROJECTILE

German 305-mm howitzer
A gun crew prepares a well-concealed howitzer for firing. The gun had to be fired from a solid platform and its massive shells weighed 390-kg (858 lb). The Austro-Hungarians also had a 305-mm howitzer, made by Skoda.

Decorated dud
Many shells, especially in the first year of the war, did not explode. This British shell was fired in Flanders. The Germans in the opposing trenches painted it with a patriotic design and "Greetings from Flanders".

FRENCH
ARTILLERY
THEODOLITE

RANGE
CALCULATOR

FRENCH
ARTILLERY
OFFICER'S
BINOCULARS

Range-finding
Officers were well trained in the science of artillery and had many aids to calculate the required trajectory of fire. In the heat of a battle, however, communication with observation posts might be cut and batteries would often accidentally shell their own men.

DIAL SIGHT OF BRITISH
18-POUNDER FIELD-GUN

BRITISH 4.5-IN HOWITZER

4.5-in (114-mm)
high-explosive shell

British howitzers
At the start of the war, heavy howitzers were thought of as siege weapons, while lighter more mobile guns were intended for use on targets such as railway stations or bridges. Trench warfare brought them to the battlefield, sited in hollows and woods behind the lines. Once in place they were very difficult to move. The 9.2-in howitzer weighed 15 tons and it took 36 hours to dismantle it ready for transportation.

BRITISH 9.2-IN HOWITZER

BRITISH 6.5-IN HOWITZER

ramrod

EVENTS
BEYOND THE
BATTLEFIELD
1914–1918

~

IN THE ABSENCE OF CLEAR VICTORY ON LAND, THE
FIRST WORLD WAR WAS DECIDED BY SEA POWER.
IT WAS A SIEGE WAR, BUT ONE UNLIKE ANY OTHER
IN HISTORY – A SIEGE NOT OF CITIES BUT OF
CENTRAL EUROPE. SEA POWER WAS THE MEANS BY
WHICH BRITAIN, FRANCE AND THE USA, ABLE
TO DRAW ON RESERVES OF MANPOWER AND
INDUSTRIAL AND FINANCIAL RESOURCES FROM
THE OUTSIDE WORLD, WERE ABLE TO WAGE
AND ULTIMATELY WIN THE WAR OF EXHAUSTION
AGAINST THE CENTRAL POWERS.

~

Hunting for U-boats
One of the chief tasks of the British Navy was to seek
out and destroy the U-boats that threatened to drive
Britain from the war. The means of detecting U-boats
underwater was the hydrophone. One is seen here being
lowered from the deck of the Scottish trawler *Thrive*.

THE WIDER PERSPECTIVE

AS THE LAND WAR WAS FOUGHT OUT ON THE BATTLEFIELDS OF EUROPE, DECISIVE

EVENTS THAT ALLOWED THE COMBATANTS TO KEEP THEIR ARMIES IN THE FIELD WERE

TAKING PLACE IN THE WAR AT SEA. THESE AFFECTED RELATIONS WITH NEUTRAL STATES,

ESPECIALLY THE USA. IT WAS THE GERMAN DECISION TO RESUME UNRESTRICTED

SUBMARINE WAR IN 1917 THAT LED TO THE ENTRY OF THE USA INTO THE WAR.

IN THE COURSE of four centuries since 1500 Europe had established primacy over every continent in the world, but by the end of the 19th century it had passed the peak of its power. Two significant non-European powers – the USA and Japan – had emerged. It was the dealings of Europe in 1916–17 with one of these powers that would change forever the relationship of Europe with the outside world.

THE POWER OF THE USA

As early as 1890 the United States had emerged as the greatest manufacturing state in the world; by 1900 it produced more than Britain and Germany combined. Anglo-French attempts to involve the United States in the war on the side of the Allies was evidence of European awareness of the reality of American power. But America's declared policy was one of neutrality and President Wilson's government offered more than once to broker a peace settlement. In 1915, and again in 1916, American missions to various European capitals were politely received, but on December 12, 1916 the German chancellor, Bethmann-Hollweg, stated Germany's willingness to seek a negotiated end to the war and invited the United States to act as mediator between the belligerent powers. Such an unprecedented action – an initiative that would have established a non-European state as arbiter of Europe's disputes – was indicative of the seriousness of the situation in which Germany found itself at this stage of the war. What had prompted this invitation to the United States to act as mediator was the situation in the war at sea.

THE NAVAL WAR

The course of the war at sea in 1914–18 was largely determined by Germany's decision, taken around 1900, to build a fleet to rival the British navy. The policy was pursued with no regard to Germany's geographical position and its strategic inferiority to its potential enemy. Britain's ports commanded the North Sea and the English Channel, the only routes available to German ships if they wished to reach the open ocean. Britain responded to this challenge to its supremacy by joining in the naval arms race, and the German navy, the *Hochseeflotte* (High Sea Fleet), was never able to catch up and threaten British numerical superiority.

In 1906 Britain launched the *Dreadnought* – faster, more heavily armoured, and with more powerful guns than any battleship that had gone before. This was followed by the battlecruiser, faster still but less heavily armoured. The naval arms race intensified as all the powers, including France, Russia and even Austria-Hungary, decided that they needed dreadnoughts too. In the years 1906–14 Britain built a total of 32 modern dreadnoughts and battlecruisers;

The might of the British Navy
The *Queen Elizabeth*, launched in 1915, was the first of a new class of dreadnought armed with eight 15-in guns. These firde 870-kg (1,920-lb) shell a distance of 25 km (16 miles).

Allied merchant shipping and conducting fleet operations. The German navy wanted to fight, but the high command dared not risk the fleet in a classical sea battle. It aimed to weaken the British navy by means of mines and torpedoes until battle could be joined in circumstances where Germany held a significant advantage. Britain's naval strategy was similarly cautious. The decision, taken before the war, to impose a distant blockade on Germany, basing the Grand Fleet at Scapa Flow, ensured that the war at sea would remain a stand-off.

THE BATTLE OF JUTLAND

Both sides provoked skirmishes in the North Sea, designed to try to lure parts of the opposing fleet into battle with larger formations. One such encounter led to the inconclusive Battle of Jutland in 1916. This, the first and only time in the war the two fleets clashed, brought home to Germany the lesson that tactical victories in the North Sea were never going to improve its strategic situation. After the failure to inflict any lasting damage on the British fleet, the German high command was won round to the idea of an unrestricted submarine campaign against shipping. The third period of the naval war, after February 1917, witnessed a German offensive against shipping that initially proved very successful before being contained during and after the second half of 1917.

UNRESTRICTED SUBMARINE WARFARE

The great majority of the sinkings by German U-boats in the course of the war were conducted according to Prize Regulations. The submarine would stop the merchantman (its prize), allow the crew to take to the lifeboats, then finally sink the ship, normally by gunfire. In an "unrestricted" campaign, submarine commanders ignored these rules and would torpedo targets without warning.

Germany built 23. Many of the German ships were superior to their British counterparts, but the High Sea Fleet's numerical inferiority condemned it to spend the war acting as a coastal defence force.

THE PHASES OF THE NAVAL WAR

The war at sea can be conveniently divided into three main parts. The opening phase lasted until December 1914, by which time the Central Powers' shipping had been driven from the high seas and the threat presented by German warships outside European waters had been largely eliminated. After April 1915 there were no warships at all at large to challenge Allied naval supremacy.

The second period, between January 1915 and February 1917, was one in which, as the noose of economic blockade tightened on the Central Powers, Germany hesitated between waging a campaign against

"All of us, from the commander-in-chief down to the latest recruit, shared the same opinion about the attitude of the English fleet. We were convinced that it would seek out and attack our fleet the minute it showed itself and wherever it was. This could be accepted as certain from all the lessons of English naval history."

GERMAN ADMIRAL REINHARD SCHEER, WRITING IN HIS WAR MEMOIRS, 1920

In 1915 a number of ships had been torpedoed in this way, including the liner *Lusitania*, in which 128 American passengers had been drowned.

For Germany, 1916 had brought failure at Verdun, an increasingly serious defensive obligation on the Somme and the disastrous weakening of Austria-Hungary by the Brusilov Offensive. When the German approach to the United States to negotiate a peace came to nothing, there seemed no possibility of Germany defeating its enemies other than by means of a campaign against shipping. This, it was hoped, would drive Britain from the ranks of its enemies. Otherwise Germany faced defeat in a war of attrition and exhaustion.

"It is much more important to destroy a railroad station, a bakery, a war plant, or to machine-gun a supply column, moving trains, or any other behind-the-lines objective, than to strafe or bomb a trench. The results are immeasurably greater in breaking morale...in spreading terror and panic."

GIULIO DROUHET, ITALIAN GENERAL AND
ENTHUSIASTIC ADVOCATE OF STRATEGIC BOMBING

A new kind of warfare

Germany's principal fighting force at sea proved to be not its magnificent dreadnoughts and battlecruisers, but its U-boats as they waged a war on merchant shipping.

war on shipping conducted by submarines armed with torpedoes – a weapons system that had not existed 20 years previously.

THE POTENTIAL OF THE AEROPLANE

Another new weapon, which had been developed even more recently, was the aeroplane. Unlike the submarine, however, the aeroplane did not realize its full potential during the course of the war. When the war broke out, little over a decade had passed since the first powered flight, by the Wright brothers, of a heavier-than-air machine.

The first operational aircraft of the war were, typically, powered by engines of 100 hp or less, capable of a maximum speed of about 130 kph (80 mph) at sea level. They were unarmed, and most would have been incapable of carrying anything heavier than a rifle. Their role was exclusively reconnaissance, yet within four years almost every aspect of aerial warfare as waged in the 20th century had been developed.

extraordinary developments: direct American involvement in the affairs of Europe and a full-scale

role in the war. As a result, 1917 would see two the Americans could start to play a significant Britain of food and raw materials before enough British, Allied and neutral shipping to starve

The Germans gambled that they could sink as a result of the British blockade.

trade with Germany had dwindled almost to nothing States and Britain and France. Meanwhile American economic and historical links between the United *Lusitania* and other ships had reinforced the political, actions. American indignation at the sinking of the been challenged by previous German submarine freedom of its citizens to travel. These rights had as a neutral state: the freedom to trade and the had grown increasingly assertive in claiming its rights certainty of American hostility. The United States The problem with such a course of action was the

The potential of air warfare was not unforeseen. It had inspired visions of universal destruction by aerial bombardment, such as H.G. Wells's *The War in the Air* (1908), in which civilization is destroyed by the bombs of airships. Germany had great faith in the power of its airships to undermine the morale of its enemies. One of its first actions in 1914 was to send Zeppelins flying over London and a number of British ports. As bombers, however, they proved too vulnerable, and Germany, like the other powers, turned instead to building huge long-distance aircraft that could bomb industrial targets and civilian populations deep inside enemy territory. By the end of the war the future development of aerial warfare was clear. Heavy bombers would deliver ever larger payloads, while fast, lightweight fighters armed with machine-guns would do battle for control of the skies.

The shape of things to come

Air power played a limited role in the war, but by 1918 it was possible to imagine how future wars would be fought. These giant British Handley Page aircraft were the forerunners of the heavy bombers of the Second World War.

Opening Moves at Sea

THE WAR AT SEA
~
AUGUST 1914 – MARCH 1916

The naval war was remarkable for the caution displayed by both sides. The British navy, after clearing the high seas of enemy shipping, concentrated on a distant blockade of Germany. At first the Germans aimed to weaken the superior British navy by means of mines and torpedoes, but then turned their attention to commercial shipping, deploying their U-boat force in an attempt to cripple British trade.

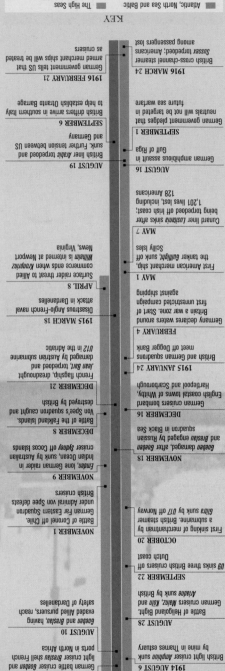

1914 AUGUST 3
German battle cruiser *Goeben* and light cruiser *Breslau* shell French ports in North Africa

AUGUST 6
British light cruiser *Amphion* sunk by mine in Thames estuary

AUGUST 10
Goeben and *Breslau*, having evaded Allied pursuers, reach safety of Dardanelles

AUGUST 28
Battle of Heligoland Bight. German cruisers *Mainz*, *Köln* and *Ariadne* sunk by British

SEPTEMBER 22
U9 sinks three British cruisers off Dutch coast

OCTOBER 20
First sinking of merchantman by a submarine, British steamer *Glitra* sunk by *U17* off Norway

NOVEMBER 1
Battle of Coronel off Chile. German Far Eastern Squadron under Admiral von Spee defeats British cruisers

NOVEMBER 9
Emden, lone German raider in Indian Ocean, sunk by Australian cruiser *Sydney* off Cocos Islands

DECEMBER 8
Battle of the Falkland Islands. Von Spee's squadron caught and destroyed by British

DECEMBER 16
German cruisers bombard English coastal towns of Whitby, Hartlepool and Scarborough

DECEMBER 21
French flagship, dreadnought *Jean Bart*, torpedoed and damaged by Austrian submarine *U12* in the Adriatic

1915 JANUARY 24
British and German squadrons meet off Dogger Bank

FEBRUARY 4
Germany declares waters around Britain a war zone. Start of first unrestricted campaign against shipping

1915 MARCH 18
Disastrous Anglo-French naval attack in Dardanelles

APRIL 8
Surface raider threat to Allied commerce ends when *Kronprinz Wilhelm* is interned at Newport News, Virginia

MAY 1
First American merchant ship, the tanker *Gulflight*, sunk off Scilly Isles

MAY 7
Cunard liner *Lusitania* sinks after being torpedoed off Irish coast; 1,201 lives lost, including 128 Americans

AUGUST 16
German amphibious assault in Gulf of Riga

AUGUST 19
British liner *Arabic* torpedoed and sunk. Further tension between US and Germany

SEPTEMBER 1
German government pledges that neutrals will not be targeted in future sea warfare

SEPTEMBER 6
British ships arrive in southern Italy to help establish Otranto Barrage

1916 FEBRUARY 21
German government tells US that armed merchant ships will be treated as cruisers

1916 MARCH 24
British cross-channel steamer *Sussex* torpedoed; Americans among passengers lost

KEY
Atlantic, North Sea and Baltic — The High Seas
Mediterranean and Black Sea — Aug 1914–Apr 1915

I N THE OPENING PHASE OF HOSTILITIES the British navy set about clearing the seas of enemy trade and carrying the war to enemy home waters and overseas possessions. Britain's geographical position astride Germany's lines of communication with the outside world ensured that German oceanic trade declined rapidly. In the first six months of the war the Allies detained, sank or captured 383 German and Austro-Hungarian steamers. Another 788 ships sought safety in neutral ports. Overall, Germany and Austria-Hungary were deprived of the use of 61 per cent of their merchant fleets.

RAIDERS ON THE HIGH SEAS

German ships that were either at sea when war broke out or sailed soon after included one battlecruiser and 14 cruisers and armed merchant cruisers. These posed a threat to Allied shipping and so were pursued, not always successfully. Two of the ships, the battlecruiser *Goeben* and the light cruiser *Breslau*, first bombarded two French North African ports, then evaded superior British forces before escaping into the Dardanelles. The arrival of the two ships at Constantinople on August 10, 1914 set the seal on the secret treaty concluded by Germany and Turkey on August 2.

Germany's Far Eastern Squadron, commanded by Admiral Graf Maximilian von Spee, found itself in the Caroline Islands at the start of the war. After Japan entered the war, the squadron could not hope to survive in the northern Pacific, so attempted to return home as a formation, except for the light cruiser *Emden*, which was despatched for a short but eventful career as a commerce-raider in the Indian Ocean. She was eventually destroyed by the Australian cruiser *Sydney* in November. That same month another successful German raider, the light cruiser *Karlsruhe*, which operated off the coast of Brazil, was destroyed in an accidental explosion.

The Far Eastern Squadron also met with some success. On November 1 it met and destroyed a hastily assembled force of three British cruisers and a converted merchantman off Coronel in Chile. However, within hours of this defeat, two British

battlecruisers were sent from home waters to form the nucleus of a new squadron in the South Atlantic. Arriving at Port Stanley one day before von Spee's squadron, the British force sank all but one of the German cruisers off the Falklands on December 8. The *Dresden* escaped to lead a furtive existence until trapped and scuttled at Mas a Fuera in the Juan Fernandez Islands off Chile in March 1915. With the *Königsberg* remaining in the Rufiji delta in East Africa where she had taken shelter, and the *Kronprinz Wilhelm*, last of the armed merchant cruisers, putting into Newport News, Virginia, in April 1915, the raider threat to Allied commerce effectively came to an end. Five cruisers and three auxiliaries had accounted for 47 Allied ships.

BLOCKADE AND THE NORTH SEA

The Falklands action was the second time that German cruisers had been defeated by the superior firepower of British battlecruisers. The first was in the action fought off Heligoland in August 1914. At the outbreak of war, Britain had immediately imposed a blockade on Germany's fleet and merchant shipping. This was enforced by the fleet which patrolled the waters between Scotland and Norway and another small force guarding the Strait of Dover. The blockade also involved the mining of German waters plus the use of submarines for reconnaissance and attacks on enemy units. The Germans, in their turn, mined British waters, sent out submarines and conducted defensive patrols with light forces in the Heligoland Bight.

HELIGOLAND BIGHT

The first sea battle of the war resulted from two British destroyer flotillas attempting to surprise and overwhelm a German torpedo-boat patrol in the Heligoland Bight on August 28. The would-be attackers found that their intended prey was supported by superior forces.

In the event only the timely and somewhat fortuitous intervention of Admiral Beatty's First Battlecruiser Squadron saved the British from serious embarrassment. An ill-planned affair on the British side, the Heligoland Bight action, with three German light cruisers and one torpedo-boat sunk, was nevertheless a clear victory. It was quickly offset, however, by the sinking by German submarines of a light cruiser off the Firth of Forth on September 6 and of three armoured cruisers off the Dutch coast on the 22nd. One more British light cruiser was sunk in the North Sea in October, in which month the dreadnought *Audacious* was lost off the north coast of Ireland in a minefield laid by the *Berlin*, a liner converted into a mine-layer. These German successes had the effect of forcing the British to pull back their patrols from the northern North Sea to the Scotland–Iceland gap. In spite of this, the blockade remained intact and the Germans suffered similar losses. In 1914 no fewer than ten German cruisers were lost in the North Sea and the Baltic.

REINHARD SCHEER

A TORPEDO EXPERT and champion of submarine warfare, Reinhard Scheer (1863–1928) was a Vice-Admiral in command of Germany's Second Battle Squadron at the start of the First World War. In December 1914 he took command of the Third Battle Squadron, which comprised Germany's newest dreadnoughts. When Admiral Hugo von Pohl fell gravely ill in January 1916, Scheer succeeded him as commander-in-chief of the High Sea Fleet. Scheer envisaged a more active role for the German navy, in which U-boats would work together with the surface fleet. He could claim a tactical victory in the Battle of Jutland, in 1916, with more British vessels sunk and the German ships managing to slip away undetected. After this the kaiser expressly forbade any further forays of this kind and Scheer had to acknowledge that he could not risk sending his surface fleet into the North Sea. He pressed instead for a return to unrestricted submarine warfare, a move that was eventually to bring the United States into the war.

Shortly before the end of the war Scheer planned a dramatic final assault on the British Grand Fleet but this was thwarted by the Kiel mutiny in November 1918, and he was dismissed soon afterwards. Following the armistice he was retired from the navy. He published his account of the war at sea in 1920.

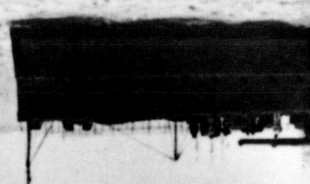

Double German threat
The German dreadnought *Ostfriesland* and Zeppelin *L31* take part in a pre-war exercise in the North Sea. Zeppelins were intended to play a key role in naval reconnaissance, as were airships in the British navy, but often proved ineffective as a result of strong winds or poor visibility.

Naval blockade

The first 18 months of the war at sea were relatively uneventful. The British laid mines, sent out patrols and intercepted neutral shipping, while the Germans centred their efforts for the most part on submarine activity. The North Sea saw only minor naval engagements until the two fleets met at the Battle of Jutland in 1916.

Women preparing mines at Dover
An important part of the British blockade was creating an effective barrier to stop German vessels, in particular U-boats, passing through the Strait of Dover. These women are preparing the mines that will be attached to net barriers.

4-in quick-firing Mark IV naval gun
This gun was fired by the British destroyer *Lance* in the action off the Dutch coast that sank the German minelayer *Königin Luise* on August 5, 1914. The semi-automatic Mark IV was capable of 15–20 rounds a minute.

Map labels

GREENLAND

ARCTIC OCEAN

Reykjavik
ICELAND

ATLANTIC OCEAN

Faroe Islands

1915–1918

1915–1918

Shetland Islands

Orkney Islands

NORWAY
Bergen
CHRISTIANIA
Stavanger

Scapa Flow
Cromarty
NORTH SEA
SWEDEN

Rosyth
Edinburgh

SKAGERRAK

MAY 31–JUN 1, 1916
Jutland

JAN 24, 1915
Dogger Bank

AUG 28, 1914
Heligoland Bight

DENMARK
COPENHAGEN

IRELAND
DUBLIN

Hartlepool
Whitby
Scarborough
Hull

GREAT BRITAIN

Bremerhaven
The Jade
Borkum
Emden
Wilhelmshaven
Bremen
Hamburg
Kiel
Cuxhaven

Great Yarmouth

Queenstown

IRISH SEA

Lowestoft
Harwich
Sheerness
LONDON Chatham
Weymouth
Portsmouth
Dover
Calais
NETH.
AMSTERDAM
Zeebrugge
BRUSSELS
BEL.

BERLIN

May 7, 1915
Sinking of Lusitania

1914

ENGLISH CHANNEL
Brest

GERMANY

PARIS
FRANCE

AUSTRIA-HUNGARY

0 km 100 200 300 400 500
0 miles 100 200 300 400 500

BLOCKADE OF GERMANY
1914–1916

- Western Front 1916
- British naval base
- German naval base
- British naval blockade
- British mine barrage of 1914–15
- Explosive net mines laid during 1916
- Significant naval battle
- British port bombarded by Germans
- Main area of U-boat activity 1915

EVENTS IN THE NORTH SEA

Before the war little thought had been given to the possibility of using submarines in an all-out campaign against enemy merchant shipping. In August 1914 Germany had only 28 U-boats in service. At first their main roles were mine-laying and using torpedoes against British warships, but in the first five months of war they did little to reduce British fleet strength. On October 20, 1914, however, *U17*, acting in accordance with

The stricken *Blücher* at Dogger Bank
German sailors cling to the hull of the German armoured cruiser as it capsizes in the action at Dogger Bank on January 24, 1915. Some 260 survivors were picked up by British ships.

international law, stopped, searched and then sank the British steamer *Glitra* off Norway.

In November the British blockade, plus the glimpse of the possibilities presented by the sinking of the *Glitra*, converted the German naval staff to the idea of waging an unrestricted submarine campaign against shipping. There were doubts as to whether the 29 U-boats available for operations at the end of 1914 could achieve anything significant. At the same time the civilian leadership hesitated to embark on a course of action that might add to the list of Germany's enemies. But with Germany

confronted by the prospect of protracted war on two fronts, caution, born of fear of alienating neutral states, was undermined by events.

In December 1914 German units bombarded Hartlepool, Scarborough and Whitby and only narrowly missed being intercepted by British battlecruisers. In January 1915, however, a German cruiser squadron conducting a reconnaissance off Dogger Bank was intercepted. Though on the British side the subsequent action was poorly conducted, the dramatic picture of the *Blücher* sinking gave the confident impression of British victory. The German naval high command was very conscious that its three battlecruisers had been lucky to escape and for the remainder of 1915 made no attempt to challenge British supremacy in the North Sea. On February 4, 1915 Germany announced that the waters around the British Isles constituted a war zone in which shipping was liable to be sunk without warning after February 18.

THE FIRST GERMAN U-BOAT CAMPAIGN

The first ten weeks of the campaign did not suggest that this was the answer to Germany's strategic problems. Between February 18 and April 30, 1915 U-boats accounted for just 39 merchantmen of 105,000 tons, mostly by gunfire or scuttling. In May the monthly total of British, Allied and neutral shipping sunk reached 120,000 tons, but a quarter of the figure represented the liner *Lusitania* on which 1,201 people, including 128 Americans, died (see page 197).

In spite of American protests, submarine operations continued and were responsible for 149,000 of the 185,000 tons of shipping sunk in August 1915. This was the peak of German achievement before 1917 and it was the first month in which losses exceeded new construction. On August 19 *U24* sank the liner *Arabic* off Iceland with the loss of 40 lives, three of them American. Subsequent American protests led to U-boats being ordered to spare passenger ships, to sink by gunfire rather than torpedo, and not to operate west of the British Isles. The German navy announced the end of its submarine campaign on September 18. This was a largely cosmetic gesture: U-boat activity was simply redirected to the Mediterranean and away from American shipping routes.

In 1915 U-boats sank 748,000 tons of shipping, and the German navy was now convinced that an unrestricted submarine campaign could drive Britain from the war. The U-Boats' success won over the military leadership, but the civilian

A COASTAL RAID

~

ON DECEMBER 16, 1914, hoping to lure the British Grand Fleet, or part of it, within range of their submarines and minefields, the Germans despatched four fast, modern battlecruisers and a heavy cruiser, accompanied by a number of smaller ships, to bombard ports on England's east coast. The raid had a secondary motive – to boost morale after the destruction of Graf von Spee's squadron at the Battle of the Falkland Islands eight days earlier. Soon after dawn the cruisers loomed out of the mist to fire over 2,000 shells at Scarborough, Whitby and Hartlepool. About 40 people were killed and hundreds injured – the first British civilian casualties of enemy action since the 17th century. Many buildings were damaged or destroyed, among them Whitby Abbey and West Hartlepool gasworks. A Whitby schoolgirl recalled running for shelter with "the deafening noise in our ears, the echo ringing even when the actual firing stopped for a moment". A "mantle of heavy smoke, yellow, unreal", hung over the town. The Admiralty's Room 40, where German wireless traffic was read, gave warning of the raid, but in drizzle and fog Admiral Beatty's squadron failed to engage, although a couple of British destroyers came briefly under fire. The raid was said to have stimulated British recruitment, and in the press the Germans became "the baby killers of Scarborough".

The shelling of Whitby Abbey
The Abbey Church on the cliffs above the port of Whitby was already a ruin when it was shelled, but pictures like this still made good anti-German propaganda.

government continued to oppose the idea. A restricted campaign in British home waters was authorized for April 1, 1916, but, even before it began, the torpedoing of the cross-channel ferry *Sussex* on March 24 spelt its end. On April 18 the United States threatened to sever diplomatic relations unless Germany curbed the activities of its submarines. The German government issued an order that U-boats conform to Prize Regulations,

stopping and warning ships before sinking them. As a result, on April 25 the High Sea Fleet recalled its submarines. The opening rounds of the campaign against shipping had ended in Britain's favour, but it was a hollow victory. British countermeasures had failed to curb mounting losses of merchant shipping and, between August 1914 and May 1916, Germany had lost only 34 U-boats. In addition, 100 new U-boats had been ordered in 1915.

German contact mines
At the outbreak of war, German mines were far more effective than British ones. The Germans set about minelaying as early as August 5, 1914, when the *Königin Luise* laid a field off the east coast of England.

Germany's Search for a Strategy

THE BATTLE OF JUTLAND

I N SPRING 1916, WITH GERMANY'S ARMIES UNABLE to secure victory and the submarine offensive stalled, the battle fleet had to begin to justify the resources lavished on it over the previous decade. The new fleet commander, Scheer, began to adopt a more aggressive policy. The German battlecruisers under Hipper put to sea briefly on March 26, 1916 in response to an attempted British bombing raid on Zeppelin sheds in Belgium. This was followed by a sortie to bombard the ports of Great Yarmouth and Lowestoft on the east coast of England on April 25. On both occasions British forces, deployed as a result of timely intelligence, narrowly missed intercepting the German ships. It was again on the basis of intelligence warnings that the British were able to sail on May 30 in anticipation of an enemy move even before German warships had reached the open sea. On this occasion the Battlecruiser Squadron under Admiral Beatty was followed by the full might of the Grand Fleet under Admiral Jellicoe.

Both sides sent their battlecruiser forces forward on exploratory sweeps with their main fleets in a covering role up to 110km (70 miles) astern. The German aim was to trap and overwhelm part of the British forces before the Grand Fleet could intervene in full strength. The smaller ships screening the battlecruisers made contact shortly after 2:00pm on May 31. This led to "The Run to the South" as Hipper sought to draw Beatty's force south on to the guns of Scheer's battleships. In the process, Hipper's ships managed to sink two of the British battlecruisers even before Beatty's force encountered the German battleships. Then the British began "The Run to the North" in an attempt to lead the High Sea Fleet into contact with Jellicoe's main battle force.

In poor light, for the only time in the war British and German battle fleets engaged each other in the course of two brief actions. In both, the High Sea Fleet found itself confronted by the entire strength of the Grand Fleet deployed

Boy hero of Jutland
Mortally wounded, with his ship ablaze around him, 16-year-old Jack Cornwall remained at his post manning a gun on the cruiser *Chester*. He was posthumously awarded the Victoria Cross.

THE WAR AT SEA

~

APRIL 1916– NOVEMBER 1918

The Battle of Jutland, fought between the British and German fleets on May 31–June 1, 1916 had no clear victor. Nevertheless, it was one of the most significant battles in naval history. Never again did the German fleet challenge the superior British fleet. Instead, the German high command decided on a strategy of unrestricted submarine war in an attempt to starve Britain from the war. This led to the entry of the US into the war and ultimately to Germany's defeat.

KEY

- ▮ Atlantic, North Sea and Baltic
- ▮ Mediterranean and Black Sea

1916 APRIL 25
German bombardment of Great Yarmouth and Lowestoft

1916 MAY 31–JUNE 1
Battle of Jutland, only major naval engagement between British and German fleets

JUNE

JULY 10–AUGUST 20
Most destructive single cruise by German submarine: *U35* accounts for 54 ships of 90,000 tons

1917 JANUARY 31
Germany notifies US and other neutrals that it will resume unrestricted submarine warfare

1917 FEBRUARY 1
German resumption of unrestricted submarine warfare

FEBRUARY 10
First use of convoy for British coal shipments to France

APRIL
High point of German submarine success: 833,408 tons of Allied and neutral shipping sunk in just one month

APRIL 17
Arrival of two Japanese destroyer flotillas in Mediterranean

MAY 10
First Allied use of convoy to escort shipping in Atlantic

MAY 15–16
Night raid on Otranto Barrage by three Austrian cruisers

AUGUST 13
First outward-bound convoy of merchantmen sails from Britain

AUGUST 21
Sopwith Pup launched from light cruiser *Yarmouth* shoots down the Zeppelin *L23* in North Sea

DECEMBER 7
Squadron of US battleships arrives at Scapa Flow

NOVEMBER 21
Hospital ship *Britannic* sunk by mine in eastern Mediterranean. At 47,000 tons, it was the largest ship ever to have been sunk by mine

1918 JANUARY 14
German destroyers bombard Great Yarmouth on east coast of England

1918 JANUARY 20
Naval action at entrance to Dardanelles; German cruiser *Breslau* and British monitor *Raglan* sunk; *Goeben* damaged

FEBRUARY 1
Mutiny in Austrian navy at Cattaro

APRIL 23
Attacks on Ostend and Zeebrugge, intended to block German submarine bases, are only partly successful

JUNE 10
Italian torpedo boat sinks Austro-Hungarian dreadnought *Szent István*

OCTOBER 2
Allied force, including British, French, Italian, Australian and US ships attack Durazzo in Adriatic

NOVEMBER 11
Armistice: German Navy agrees to surrender major warships and all submarines to Allies

NOVEMBER 12
Allied fleet sails through Dardanelles to Constantinople

NOVEMBER 3–4
Outbreak of mutiny within High Sea Fleet at Kiel

NOVEMBER 21
Arrival of nine German battleships and 51 other ships in Firth of Forth

British battlecruisers going into action
The British battlecruisers *Lion*, and Admiral Beatty's flagship, *Princess Royal* and *Queen Mary* at Jutland. This was the last picture taken of the *Queen Mary* before she sank on the evening of May 31, ripped apart by a huge explosion.

The might of the Royal Navy
The 4th Battle Squadron of the Grand Fleet, including the dreadnoughts *Iron Duke*, *Royal Oak*, *Superb* and *Canada*, steams across the North Sea. At Jutland the British had 28 dreadnoughts in the line compared to Germany's 16.

across its path, and the ships at the head of the German line were subjected to severe punishment. In both actions, however, the German line extricated itself from potential disaster by reversing course, and in neither case was this manoeuvre seen by or reported to Jellicoe. As night fell, Scheer, intent on avoiding a resumption of battle the following morning, set course for Horn's Reef off the Danish coast. Jellicoe, no less determined to avoid the lottery of a night action, steered a course that would ensure contact if the enemy

made for the Ems or Heligoland. Thus during the night, Scheer's formation passed astern of Jellicoe's battleships. By dawn the Germans had cleared the battle zone. With no prospect of resuming the battle, the British fleet turned for home.

REACTIONS TO THE BATTLE

This bare record of events at Jutland gives no inkling of the controversy that followed the battle. Both sides were guilty of errors, and with national and personal reputations at stake, the outcome and detail of the battle were fiercely disputed. The British had suffered heavier losses: 14 ships sunk, including three battlecruisers, the *Queen Mary*, *Indefatigable* and *Invincible*, to the Germans' 11. Such statistics provided a basis for German claims to victory, but, whereas 32 British capital ships were ready for sea on June 2, the High Sea Fleet was unable to proceed to sea until August. Crucially, the battle left Germany's strategic position unchanged.

The eight months that followed Jutland were a twilight period in the war at sea. The one real battle fought in these months was within the German high command. The navy argued that, with the U-boat service having doubled in size since 1914, an unrestricted submarine campaign should be able to sink 600,000 tons a month. This, it calculated, would destroy 39 per cent of Britain's shipping within five months. It would also frighten off neutral shipping and so drive Britain from the war.

At first the politicians and generals questioned the accuracy of the navy's figures, fearing the reaction of the neutral states, in particular the Americans, to an unrestricted campaign against shipping. As the war entered its third year, however, the privations caused by the British blockade began to erode the policy of caution that seemed to offer no prospect of victory. At a conference held on August 30, 1916 Chancellor Bethmann left the final decision on the navy's demands to the army. This coincided with the dismissal of Falkenhayn from his position as commander-in-chief, so the decision had to be deferred. The new military leadership was prepared to sanction only the resumption of a

restricted campaign after October 6. All U-Boats were instructed to follow Prize Regulations: before sinking any merchantman, they had to stop and warn their quarry, then allow the crew to escape.

Victory souvenir
This silk scarf leaves no doubt that Jutland was a British victory, which in effect it was. The German fleet never again ventured out to fight in the North Sea.

Souvenir OF THE VICTORY OF JUTLAND

MAY 31st 1916.

There was a terrific explosion aboard the ship, the magazines went. I saw the guns go up in the air just like matchsticks – 12-inch guns they were – bodies and everything. She was beginning to settle down. Within half a minute the ship turned right over and she was gone. I was 180 foot up and I was thrown well clear of the ship otherwise I would have been sucked under. I was practically unconscious, turning over really. At last I came on top of the water. When I came up there was another fellow named Jimmy Green and we got a piece of wood. He was on one end and I was on the other end. A couple of minutes afterwards some shells came over and Jim was minus his head so I was left on my lonesome.

SIGNALLER C. FALMER, INDEFATIGABLE

In a period of just four months 516 merchantmen of 1,388,000 tons were sunk, and only eight U-boats were lost. To compound Allied problems, losses in the Mediterranean in the second half of 1916 were so heavy that shipping had to be diverted around the Cape. Meanwhile, a disastrous American harvest was forcing Britain to look to Australia for grain supplies in 1917. This would lead to a further reduction of available cargo space. Moreover, by the end of 1916, losses threatened to halt the vital British coal trade with France and Italy.

With only half the available U-boats committed to the attack on shipping, the implications of German success at sea were not lost on the Army's new leaders, Hindenburg and Ludendorff. They were ultimately won over by the argument that Germany had to achieve victory in 1917 rather than endure a fourth winter at war and that Britain would be defeated before the US could intervene on the battlefields of Europe. It was decided to unleash the U-boats on February 1 – the neutral states were not notified of the German intention until January 31. The resumption of unrestricted submarine warfare was

Coming up for air
A U-boat crew takes advantage of fine weather and a calm sea to come up on deck for a shower.

probably the most important single decision made in the course of the whole war. It all but guaranteed that the world's greatest industrial power would soon join the ranks of Germany's enemies.

UNRESTRICTED SUBMARINE WARFARE

Between February and June 1917 the German navy accounted for some 3,844,000 tons of shipping and achieved a rate of sinking that it had claimed would result in Britain's defeat in the summer of 1917. The effectiveness of the German campaign in its

initial stages has been attributed to its unrestricted character, the fact that U-boats were free to sink any ship without warning or regard for lives lost. In fact, the increase in merchantmen sunk after February 1917 was the result of the number of active submarines rather than the nature of their operations. By February 1917 U-boat strength had risen to 152, of which 111 were operational. The Germans were able to keep 50 at sea and 24 on station in their area of operations at any one time.

Another factor in the U-boats' success was the route they now followed when sailing to intercept shipping. During 1916 most U-boat sailings had been via northern Scotland, but operations in the Strait of Dover had revealed the ineffectiveness of British patrols and minefields there. On January 17, 1917, therefore, U-boats were ordered to sail through the Strait, thereby gaining immediate access to the heavy concentrations of shipping in the English Channel and the southwest approaches. This saved six days on passage, a major consideration for boats limited to a 25-day operational cycle, allowing the Germans to deploy many more U-boats for much longer periods.

THE SURVIVAL OF BRITISH TRADE

Britain's ability to survive the German onslaught has been generally attributed to the convoy system. This was initiated in February 1917 for the French coal trade and first used for oceanic trade in May. Over the 21 months of the German unrestricted campaign convoys did indeed reduce shipping losses and ensure Britain's survival. However, during the first five months of the campaign, when Britain came close to defeat, convoys saved no more than 80 ships – the difference between convoy losses and losses that might have been expected had these ships sailed independently.

> "Our armies might advance a mile a day and slay the Hun in thousands, but the real crux lies in whether we blockade the enemy to his knees or whether he does the same to us."
>
> ADMIRAL SIR DAVID BEATTY, JANUARY 1917

Sinking of the *Parkgate* by *U35*
The British freighter was sunk according to Prize Regulations. The Germans ordered the crew of the *Parkgate* into the ship's lifeboats and took the ship's documents from the captain. The ship was then sunk by gunfire.

THE U-BOAT THREAT

IN THE FIRST WORLD WAR, U-boats spent little of their time beneath the waves. Diving was a complicated manoeuvre generally reserved for firing a torpedo or for making an escape. To avoid burning up their air supply, submerged submarines ran on electric motors, powered by a series of huge rechargeable batteries, rather than the diesel engines used on the surface. This slowed them down and they could only dive for limited periods.

In 1914, the German navy was equipped with two basic types of submarine: small, coastal *UB1* class craft and longer-range "overseas" patrol boats of the *U5* and *U19* classes, known as the *Mittel-U* type. The former were capable of a top speed of just 7.5 knots and had two 450-mm (17-in) torpedo tubes and a crew of 14. The latter had a surface speed of 14 knots (8 knots when submerged) and they carried four torpedo tubes, one 51-mm (2-in) gun and a crew of 28. Wartime development resulted in the addition of the minelayer as a third category of submarine.

In the torpedo room
Torpedo tubes were situated at either end of the U-boat. The crew had to work in incredibly cramped, hot conditions. Casualty rates for the service ran at 40 per cent, but there was never any shortage of volunteers.

The improvement in the fleet was such that by the end of the war German coastal submarines were built to roughly the same specification as the patrol submarines of 1914. In the later stages of the war, patrol vessels were able to reach North American waters.

Torpedoes brought about some of the most notorious Allied shipping losses of the war, including the sinking of the Cunard liner *Lusitania* in 1915. However, they were expensive and against merchantmen the most practical method was sinking by gunfire or boarding the ship and placing charges to scuttle it. In response, the British used Q ships, well-armed ships disguised as merchantmen, to lure U-boats into making an attack. Following the resumption of unrestricted submarine warfare in 1917, the U-boats came close to breaking the Allies, but Britain was able to call on enough shipping, despite its increasing losses.

Propaganda poster
This German poster, dating from 1917, declares "The U-boats are out!"

Loading torpedoes onto a U-boat
Although the most feared weapon in a U-boat's armoury, torpedoes were likely to fail with targets beyond 800 m (900 yds). Single hits might sink a cruiser, but rarely succeeded with a shallow-draught merchantman.

Submarine gun
A rapid-fire, high-velocity 10.5-cm (4.1-in) gun was mounted on the deck of all U-boats in the 560- and 900-ton classes. This one is from *U98*, which in the last year of the war sank three merchant ships.

The control room was abaft the crew's space, shut off by bulkheads forward and aft ... A WC stood in one corner of the control room. It was screened by a curtain and, after seeing this arrangement, I understood why the officer I relieved had recommended the use of opium before all trips which were to last more than twelve hours.

JOHANNES SPIESS, WATCH OFFICER, *U9*, QUOTED IN *SUBMARINE BOATS*, R. CROMPTON-HALL

The key to British survival into autumn 1917 was neutral shipping. With the start of the unrestricted campaign, neutral shipping mainly confined itself to harbour in the hope that American pressure would force the Germans to moderate their new aggressive policy. Neutral sailings to and from British ports in February and March fell to 37 per cent of the January 1917 level. By July, however, neutral sailings had recovered to four-fifths of the January level. The neutrals obviously needed to continue to trade and Britain and the United States subjected them to intense political and economic pressure, while offering lucrative financial inducements to do so. These measures saw Britain through the critical months of 1917, but its long-term survival was ensured only by a comprehensive convoy system.

In the first 27 months of war, in which time no single month saw British losses exceed 150,000 tons, the Admiralty consistently refused to sanction the general introduction of convoys. It did so on the grounds that there were not enough warships to provide escorts and that the sheer numbers of

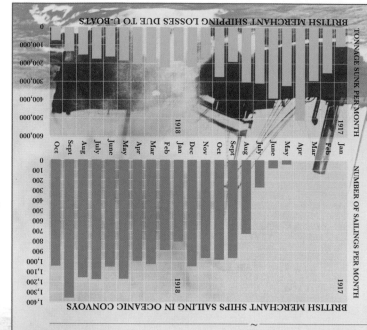

CONVOYS AND REDUCED SHIPPING LOSSES

BY THE END OF 1917 a total of 26,404 ships had sailed in convoys at a cost of 147 of their number. As a result the volume of British imports in 1917 increased from 1916 levels despite an 8 per cent loss of shipping capacity. The basic system that was to curb the U-boat threat was in place by November 1917 but it accounted for only half of all shipping movements. By October 1918 convoys accounted for 90 per cent of all sailings. In the course of 1918 U-boats sank a total of just 134 escorted merchantmen.

BRITISH MERCHANT SHIPPING LOSSES DUE TO U-BOATS

TONNAGE SUNK PER MONTH

0 — 100,000 — 200,000 — 300,000 — 400,000 — 500,000 — 600,000

1917 — 1918

Jan Feb Mar Apr May June July Aug Sept Oct Nov Dec Jan Feb Mar Apr May June July Aug Sept Oct

NUMBER OF SAILINGS PER MONTH

0 — 100 — 200 — 300 — 400 — 500 — 600 — 700 — 800 — 900 — 1,000 — 1,100 — 1,200 — 1,300 — 1,400

1917 — 1918

BRITISH MERCHANT SHIPS SAILING IN OCEANIC CONVOYS

An ideal convoy
A well-protected convoy sails with an escort of dazzle-painted warships and an RNAS (Royal Naval Air Service) airship. In the course of 1918 only two merchantmen were sunk by U-boats when their convoy had both sea and air escorts.

sailings to and from British ports, and the congestion caused by holding ships in harbour, rendered convoys impossible. In spite of these arguments, rising losses forced the Admiralty to accept the principle of sailing merchantmen under warship protection on three routes even before April 1917. A convoy system was introduced on the route to and from the Hook of Holland in July 1916 and on the Scandinavian route in January 1917. On February 10, at French insistence, the Admiralty also began sailing convoys of colliers to France at night.

Only three ships were lost in the first year of the Dutch "Beef Run", and losses on the French coal routes were reduced to just five out of a total of 2,583 sailings by escorted colliers in March and April 1917. The Admiralty nevertheless refused to consider the introduction of oceanic convoys even as losses rose alarmingly after February 1917. Prime minister Lloyd George was to claim that it was his intervention in April 1917 that forced the Admiralty to accept convoys; the Admiralty claimed that by then it had already come round to the idea.

CONVOYS PROVE THEIR WORTH

The first oceanic convoy of 17 merchantmen sailed from Gibraltar on May 10. It arrived in British waters without loss two days earlier than ships sailing independently might have been expected to do. On May 24 a convoy sailed from Hampton Roads, Virginia and arrived in Britain on June 10, just one straggler having been lost. In June four convoys arrived in British waters and July saw the start of regular convoy sailings from North America. In August regular convoys were instituted on the homeward South American and Gibraltar routes. Nonetheless the convoy system had its failings. Because homeward convoys were dispersed in the Channel and Irish Sea, unnecessary losses were incurred in home waters. In the first three months of oceanic convoys no attempt was made to escort outward shipping, and here losses continued on the scale of previous months. Losses of unescorted shipping also continued to be heavy.

Camouflaged convoy
The dazzle painting of individual merchant ships may have enhanced the success of the convoy system introduced in 1917.

CAMOUFLAGING SHIPS

THE FIRST SUGGESTIONS FOR SHIP CAMOUFLAGE centred, naturally enough, on hiding the vessel in question against the backdrop of sea, sky and horizon. It was discovered that this technique could deceive conventional craft. Unfortunately a U-boat's periscope was still able to pick out a camouflaged ship as a silhouette. Then the new idea of dazzle-painting was proposed: not to hide the ship, but to create an optical illusion that made it very difficult to read its course accurately. By late 1917 the dazzle painting of the entire British merchant fleet, and some warships, was under way.

Dazzle patterns
Artists at London's Royal Academy, led by Norman Wilkinson, who had first proposed the idea, created the dazzle designs. Dummy bridges and painted anchors were sometimes used, in addition to colour blocks.

A dazzle-painted ship
The Underwing, a British Q ship, here typifies the use of angled black and white stripes to create a distorted perception.

Dropping depth charges
It is estimated that a total of 29 German U-boats were lost to depth charges, most of them in 1918. Here the British torpedo boat destroyer Tempest prepares to drop depth charges in the North Sea.

The years 1917 and 1918 saw successive reductions in U-boat production from the peak levels of 1916. As a result, Germany entered 1918 with no more U-boats than in June 1917. In the course of 1918 Germany lost 69 U-boats. This was offset by the commissioning of 80 new boats, but the return per boat per month continued to decline. Moreover, after March 1918 new British minefields and patrols in the Strait of Dover forced U-boats to sail around the north of Scotland to and from their operational areas. While the number of U-boats at sea remained more or less the same as in 1917, this was achieved only by shortening periods of rest and refitting. Right up to the end of the war, the U-boats continued to inflict damage on Allied shipping, but the U-boat offensive never again came close to its goal of forcing Britain out of the war.

Better reconnaissance and more effective use of mines and depth charges claimed 46 U-boats against the 42 commissioned between August 1917 and January 1918. In this six-month period both the number of U-boats at sea and sinkings per boat per month declined by 27 per cent. The German navy, however, still believed it was sinking merchantmen at a rate that would bring about Britain's defeat. In reality, less shipping was sunk in 1918 than in the first four months of the unrestricted campaign. The decline of the rate of sinkings through 1918 was primarily the result of the convoy system.

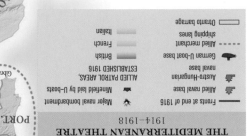

THE MEDITERRANEAN THEATRE 1914–1918

Fronts at end of 1916	Major naval bombardment
	Minefield laid by U-boats
ALLIED PATROL AREAS, ESTABLISHED 1916	Allied naval base
	Austro-Hungarian naval base
	German U-boat base
British	
French	
Italian	
Allied merchant shipping lanes	
Otranto barrage	

THE MEDITERRANEAN

Geography and superior numbers ensured that the Allies exercised command of the Mediterranean, although this never extended to the Dardanelles and the Adriatic. It was from these areas that the challenges to Allied naval power emerged. The challenge from the Adriatic proved the greater, once Germany had chosen to make its main U-boat effort in the Mediterranean. In a sea that witnessed some 350 daily sailings of merchantmen, many carrying British, Dutch and French imports from the Far East, Germany's decision largely determined the course of the Mediterranean campaign.

Initially, the British and French had attempted a close blockade in the Adriatic but had been forced to withdraw their larger ships to Malta and Bizerta. After a brief flurry of raids and counter-raids following Italy's declaration of war on Austria-Hungary in 1915, the Adriatic became quieter, largely because of the vulnerability of large warships to submarine attack. The Allies then attempted to prevent U-boats sailing from the Adriatic to the Mediterranean by assembling a fleet of small fishing boats, mainly British drifters, to patrol the Straits of Otranto.

In the event the Straits were too deep to be mined and netted effectively and too wide to be patrolled properly. The Otranto barrage was described as "a large sieve through which

U-boats could pass with impunity". The barrage itself invited raids. On the night of May 14–15, 1917 three Austrian cruisers sailed through the barrage. They approached the drifters one by one, ordering the crews to abandon ship, then opening fire. Of the 47 drifters on duty, 14 were sunk and three seriously damaged. Not all such sorties succeeded. When the Austro-Hungarian navy sent a force to raid the barrage in June 1918, its four dreadnoughts also put to sea. One of these, the *Szent István*, was torpedoed by an Italian motorboat on June 10.

The ease with which U-boats operated in this theatre was the result of the political infighting and lack of co-operation between the Allies. In 1916 the Mediterranean was divided into 18 separate Allied commands. Their patrols, which by 1916 involved 140 destroyers and sloops and some 200 armed trawlers, were so ineffective that in 1915 and 1916 only three U-boats were sunk, two by unknown causes. In August 1916 one boat, the *U35*,

Naval war in the Mediterranean

War in this theatre centred on the U-boats operating out of the Adriatic and the Dardanelles. The Allies tried, with very little success, to counter this threat by means of patrols and a barrage across the Straits of Otranto.

Austro-Hungarian dreadnoughts at Pola

Pola, today the port of Pula in Croatia, was the main Austro-Hungarian naval base in the Adriatic. It was frequently the target of Italian raids by air and sea, although these inflicted only limited damage.

accounted for two-thirds of worldwide Allied losses for that month in a single three-week cruise in which she did not fire a single torpedo. Losses reached a peak in April 1917, when there were 28 U-boats in the Mediterranean, with ten at sea on any one day. Not a single U-boat was sunk, while the Allies lost 94 ships. At worst, the voyage from Gibraltar to the Suez Canal could take a month.

As elsewhere, the counter to the U-boat in this theatre was the convoy system, first introduced by the Italian navy in spring 1917. Despite usually having no escort other than a single armed merchant cruiser, these Italian convoys immediately cut losses, as did the British introduction of convoys between Alexandria and Malta in May 1917. The first through convoy from Britain to Suez was run in October and the first homeward convoy in November. Shipping losses fell steadily between June 1917 and October 1918 when Germany recalled its U-boats as a result of the collapse of its allies. The war in the Mediterranean ended with the Allied navies supporting military operations and occupying various ports to enforce armistice terms. On November 13, 1918 an Allied fleet sailed through the Dardanelles and anchored at Constantinople.

Drifters of the Otranto barrage at Taranto
Most of the drifters were British, each armed with a 6-pound gun and depth charges. They were supported by small Italian motor launches. In the course of the war only two U-boats were ever caught in the drifters' nets.

War in the Air

Knight of the air
A French pilot demonstrates the perils of flying in the First World War as he lets go of the controls to man the Lewis gun mounted on the upper wing of his aircraft.

The first time I ever encountered a German plane in the air both the pilot, Harvey-Kelly, and myself were completely unarmed ... The German observer did not appear to be shooting at us ... We waved a hand to the enemy and proceeded with our task. The enemy did likewise. At the time this did not appear to me to be in any way ridiculous ... But afterwards just for safety's sake I always carried a carbine with me in the air.

WILLIAM SHOLTO DOUGLAS ON HIS EARLY EXPERIENCES
OF AERIAL RECONNAISSANCE IN FRANCE

AERIAL WARFARE
1914–1918

Although air power had only a minimal influence on the outcome of the war, the years 1914–18 were crucial in the development of the aircraft from a flimsy means of reconnaissance into a powerful weapon. By 1918, with fighters armed with machine-guns flying in huge squadrons and giant bombers capable of dropping 1,000-kg (2,200-lb) bombs, it was clear that the aeroplane would play a key role in any future war.

By THE OUTBREAK OF WAR, all combatants had an air force of some sort. In spite of their particular interest in airships, the Germans had about 250 aircraft. Their organizational set-up and aircrew training were generally superior to that of the Allies. The Austrian air force was tiny by comparison, though the bird-like Taube ("Dove"), the chief German reconnaissance aircraft in the early months of the war, was of Austrian origin.

The French were outnumbered in aircraft by the Germans by about 3 to 2 and their command structure was less efficient, but in other, qualitative respects they were superior. Moreover, they had the largest manufacturing base, and were able to increase production quickly when war began. That was fortunate for Britain, which lagged behind both the French and Germans. The Royal Flying Corps was created in 1912, two years after the French equivalent, and deployed only about 60 aircraft at the front in August 1914. For the first year or two the British were heavily dependent on French engines and aircraft frames. However, Britain had the greater industrial base, and by the end of the war its aviation industry led the world.

The Russians had more aeroplanes than the British, and produced the giant four-engined Sikorsky Ilya Mourometz, the world's first heavy bomber, in early 1915. But the confusing variety of Russian types made maintenance of their aircraft difficult. The same problem affected the French but they were quicker to realize the importance of standardization. Despite inept organization, Italy (the first nation to carry out aerial bombing – against the Turks in North Africa in 1911) produced some fine aviators and at least one outstanding designer, Gianni Caproni, whose bombers played a significant role in the campaigns on the Isonzo. His monstrous, three-engined, triplane bomber, the Ca 42, appeared in early 1918.

1914 AUGUST 20 — German Zeppelins fly over London and British ports

1914 AUGUST 30 — Paris bombed by German Taube

SEPTEMBER 3 — French aerial reconnaissance spots crucial gap between German armies advancing to Marne

SEPTEMBER 5 — Russian gunfire brings down Zeppelin at Lemberg; British planes begin night patrols over London

SEPTEMBER 16 — First attack by sea-based aircraft: Japanese Farman bombs German warship at Tsingtao

SEPTEMBER 22 — First British air raid on Germany; Zeppelin sheds at Dusseldorf and Cologne bombed by four Tabloids

DECEMBER 9 — Warsaw bombed by Germans

1915 JANUARY 19 — Beginning of Zeppelin campaign against Great Britain: Great Yarmouth bombed

1915 FEBRUARY — Frenchman Roland Garros uses fixed, forward-firing machine gun, with deflectors to protect propeller

MAY 31 — First Zeppelin raid on London; 28 dead and 60 injured

JUNE 7 — Zeppelin destroyed in flight by hand-launched bomb near Ghent

AUGUST 1 — Start of "Fokker Scourge": German Fokker monoplanes dominate skies over Western Front

1916 FEBRUARY 18 — Heavy bombing raid by Italian Caproni's in retaliation for earlier Austrian raid on Milan

1916 JULY 1 — Anglo-French air supremacy on the Somme: 201 French and 185 British aircraft pitted against 129 German planes

OCTOBER 28 — Oswald Boelke, whose superior tactics returned aerial dominance to Germans, killed in action

1917 APRIL — "Bloody April", in which British airscrews suffer 50 per cent casualties in one month

1917 JUNE 13 — "Diamond formation" Gotha bombers target London causing 158 deaths and 425 wounded: worst civilian casualties of war

OCTOBER 8 — German Airforce (Luftstreitkräfte) established (previous groups amalgamated)

1918 MARCH 21 — Major German air offensive, to support Ludendorff offensive in northern France, but subsequently British regain air superiority

1918 APRIL 1 — British RFC (Royal Flying Corps) and RNAS (Royal Naval Air Service) unite to form RAF

APRIL 21 — Manfred von Richthofen, the "Red Baron", shot down and killed

MAY 13 — British form force for strategic bombing raids

AUGUST 8 — Amiens: British planes drop 1,563 bombs and fire 122,150 rounds in support of ground offensive

SEPTEMBER 12 — 1,476 Allied aircraft support American attack at St Mihiel

KEY
Western Front ■ Other events ■

AERIAL RECONNAISSANCE

Reconnaissance in all its aspects, including artillery-spotting, was the most valuable task performed by aircraft throughout the the war. Army high commands failed, however, to anticipate that successful tactics would breed counter-tactics. Since reconnaissance proved so effective, the enemy naturally took steps to prevent it, while protecting its own reconnaissance operations. Nor did it take long to realize that if you can see the enemy, you can hit him, and so surveillance expanded into attack. The fighter, the bomber and the ground-attack aircraft were inevitable developments.

In spite of the pre-war predominance of monoplanes, the majority of aircraft throughout the war were biplanes, which were structurally more robust. Reconnaissance aircraft were generally two-seaters, and the observer was often senior to the pilot. Speed was unimportant and the main danger in the early months, apart from occasional ground fire, was engine failure. In the skies, opposing pilots allegedly exchanged salutes. They soon turned less friendly, taking shots at each other with rifles or revolvers, but there always remained among air crews respect and admiration for their opponents.

Mobile aerial reconnaissance rapidly proved its worth. As early as August 1914 British planes gave notice of the German outflanking movement at Mons, and German Taubes warned of the Russian advance at Tannenberg, enabling the outnumbered Germans to strengthen their forces at the vital point

to gain a sensational victory. Airborne French observers noted the gap between the advancing German First and Second armies on the Marne (September 3, 1914), prompting the successful Allied counterattack. The usefulness of aerial reconnaissance to the artillery, especially in correcting the gunners' range, was proved at the outset of trench warfare, on the Aisne in mid-September. The potential of reconnaissance aircraft increased as their role came to be better appreciated by army commanders, and they were fitted with two-way radios and effective automatic cameras, instead of relying on the observer's verbal reports and scribbled notes. By 1915 the need to deny reconnaissance and artillery-spotting to the enemy had expanded the role of air forces. No longer "above the battle", aircraft became participants. The first fighters were existing aircraft armed with a machine-gun. But to attack enemy aircraft and observation balloons required different qualities, in particular speed and manoeuvrability, and the superior power-to-weight ratio of French rotary engines gave them the initial advantage.

Aerial camera
Aerial photography, though still fairly crude, was widely used. By 1918 some French reconnaissance units were developing as many as 10,000 plates a night.

Lens

Cable release

Back plate for exposing film

AN EFFECTIVE FIGHTER

Another requirement was a fixed, forward-firing machine-gun that did not hit the propeller. Various solutions were tried. With a pusher-type aircraft, the engine and propeller were mounted behind, but this entailed some loss in performance. A French designer, Raymond Saulnier, devised an interrupter gear that enabled a pilot to fire through the propeller. This was adopted by the famous aviator Roland Garros with added metal plates to deflect bullets striking the propeller blades. When Garros was shot down and his plane captured intact, the mechanism was passed to the Fokker workshops, where an improved gearing system was devised that gave the Germans marked superiority.

FOKKER EINDECKER E III

~

DUTCH-BORN ENGINEER Anthony Fokker (1890–1939) produced about 40 types of aircraft for Germany during the war. He was adept at organizing production, most innovations originating with his design staff. The most striking of these was the interrupter gearing system that allowed a pilot to fire a machine-gun through the propeller. Fokker benefited from the capture of a French Morane with a crude device of this kind. Fitted to a Fokker Eindecker (monoplane), Fokker's improved interrupter achieved a pronounced superiority over Allied fighters and initiated the so-called "Fokker scourge" of 1915.

The Eindecker was an old pre-war machine that used wing-warping, governed by wires to control aircraft roll

The synchronized Spandau machine-gun fired through the propeller

Eindecker engine
The only surviving Eindecker is this one at the Science Museum, London. The photograph below is of a model.

The 9-cylinder, 120-hp rotary engine gave a top speed of 137kph (85mph)

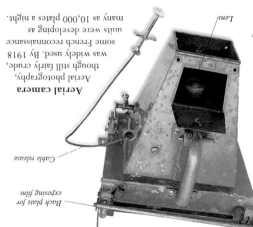

Bristol BE2A
Strong, stable and easy to fly, the Bristol BE2 was the most reliable of the reconnaissance planes brought over to France by the British Royal Flying Corps at the outbreak of war.

GEORGES GUYNEMER

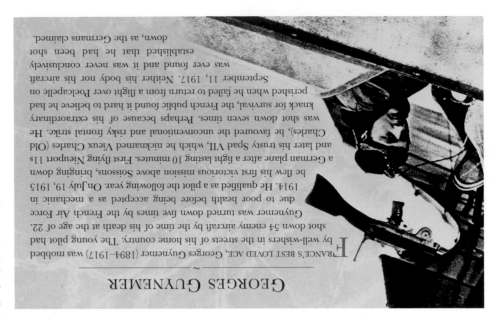

FRANCE'S BEST LOVED ACE, Georges Guynemer (1894–1917) was mobbed by well-wishers in the streets of his home country. The young pilot had shot down 54 enemy aircraft by the time of his death at the age of 22. Guynemer was turned down five times by the French Air Force due to poor health before being accepted as a mechanic in 1914. He qualified as a pilot the following year. On July 19, 1915 he flew his first victorious mission above Soissons, bringing down a German plane after a fight lasting 10 minutes. First flying Nieuport 11s and later his trusty Spad VII, which he nicknamed Vieux Charles (Old Charles), he favoured the unconventional and risky frontal strike. He was shot down seven times. Perhaps because of his extraordinary knack for survival, the French public found it hard to believe he had perished when he failed to return from a flight over Poelcapelle on September 11, 1917. Neither his body nor his aircraft was ever found and it was never conclusively established that he had been shot down, as the Germans claimed.

The so-called "Fokker Scourge" was partly neutralized by the adoption of formation flying (disliked by individualistic French pilots), by the creation of elite units like *Les Cigognes* ("The Storks"), and by adopting one type of aircraft, rather than a miscellany for individual squadrons. It was finally overcome by better fighters – the British FE2 series, best of the pusher type, the new generation of Nieuports and later the tough and speedy Spad VII with its synchronized Vickers gun, which totally outclassed the Fokker Eindecker.

Tactics were developed largely on the wing by gifted pilots. Solo fighters soon learned the advantage of attacking from above and behind, preferably out of the sun. When operating in pairs, one approached from the side and opened fire early to distract attention from the other diving on the enemy from the rear. Some manoeuvres were associated with particular pilots, such as Max Immelmann. The "Immelmann Loop" required the attacking pilot to dive past the enemy, pull up into a near-vertical climb, turn sharply and dive a second time – not a tactic for the faint-hearted.

Immelmann's fellow-ace, Oswald Boelcke was even more influential. He was an early advocate of the 14-aircraft Jasta (short for Jagdstaffel, "hunter squadron"), commanding one of the first, which became operational in autumn 1916. Among his protégés was Manfred von Richthofen, most durable of German aces.

The brave and skilful fighter pilot rapidly became a cultural hero, a "knight of the air", perfect for national propaganda. His daring aerial exploits offered a welcome contrast to the anonymous industrial massacres going on below in the smoke and mud of Verdun and the Somme.

Aircrew were absurdly overworked, required to fly several patrols each day, for weeks and months. Allied pilots were pitched into the battle scandalously under-trained and inexperienced: 80 per cent of British casualties had flown less than 20 missions. The Germans were more careful, until heavy losses forced the sacrifice of standards. They were also better disciplined. By 1917, the day of the lonely hunter, such as Georges Guynemer, Albert Ball or Werner Voss, was over. Manfred von Richthofen, the most successful pilot of the war, was essentially an outstanding squadron leader.

CONTROL OF THE SKIES

The German Albatros biplanes regained fighter superiority for the Germans in late 1916 and retained it beyond "Bloody April" (1917), when British pilots' life expectancy dropped to 11 days. The Allies were able to win back control of the skies later in 1917, partly – and significantly – because German production was falling behind. French and British aircraft production in 1917 was double the German figure. To an extent the Germans compensated with their Jagdgeschwader or "Flying Circus" formations, made up of several Jastas and backed by extensive ground support and transport to move them quickly to where they were needed.

Several hundred US flyers had enlisted with the Allies at an early stage, but American impact on the air war was less than anticipated. In April 1917 the future USAAF, then a division of the Signal Corps, consisted of about 1,000 men and 250 aircraft, none fit for European combat. The US squadrons active on the Western Front in 1917–18 generally flew French aircraft.

Ironically, what was probably the best fighter of the war, the steel-framed 200-kph (125-mph) Fokker DVII, appeared when the battle was already lost and the Germans, bereft of vital materials, were hugely outnumbered by the Allies' SE5As, Sopwith Camels and Spads.

Manfred von Richthofen, the "Red Baron" Richthofen stands in front of his trademark red Fokker triplane. He was credited with the destruction of a record 80 Allied aircraft between September 1916 and April 1918, when he was shot down over enemy lines.

FIGHTER PLANES

ADVANCES IN AIRCRAFT DESIGN were rapid: the fighters of 1918 were quite different from those of 1915. Air superiority changed sides often in the course of the war. The German Fokker Eindekker (*see page 189*) was superseded by French Nieuports and Spad VIIs over Verdun in 1916. Then the Albatros D series, with their in-line Mercedes and Daimler engines and twin machine-guns, regained fighter superiority for the Germans towards the end of 1916.

By 1917 the British aircraft industry was finally getting into its stride. The Royal Aircraft Factory's SE5 and SE5A were equipped with the outstanding Hispano-Suiza V8 engine, which also powered the French Spad XIII. The Sopwith Camel – in total 'kills' the most successful fighter

of the war – was operational from June 1917. The Sopwith Triplane (1916) proved marvellously manoeuvrable, but it was made for the RNAS (Royal Naval Air Service), not the RFC (Royal Flying Corps), and production was relatively small. The Germans reproduced its virtues in the Fokker Dr I triplane (late summer 1917), Richthofen's favourite. Right up to the end of the war both sides continued to come up with improved designs. In the end, however, superior performance was not enough; the advantage passed to the side with the greater industrial resources and greater number of planes.

Spad XIII
The sturdy single-seater with its twin synchronized Vickers guns was popular with all Allied pilots. It could reach a speed of 222 kph (138 mph) at 2,400m (6,500ft).

French pilot's kit
A pilot's clothing and equipment usually reflected his individual style. Essential elements were goggles and a fur-lined leather jacket, helmet and gloves to combat the intense cold.

FLYING HELMET

GOGGLES

ALTIMETER

Fokker Dr I
The triplane (1917) had a rapid rate of climb and was very manoeuvrable, but its top speed was only 165 kph (103 mph). Structural failures led to relatively few being built.

SE5A
This fast, reliable British plane could reach 221 kph (137.5 mph) at sea level. It had a nose-mounted Vickers plus a wing-mounted Lewis gun.

Sopwith Camel
The Camel's idiosyncrasies, notably a viciously sharp right-hand turn, which could cause a spin, were an advantage in the hands of experienced pilots.

Main armament was synchronized Vickers machine-gun fired through propeller

130hp Clerget rotary engine gave maximum speed at sea level of 190 kph (118 mph)

Lewis gun used on Allied fighters
The Lewis gun was quickly adapted for use on fighters, either fixed above the upper wing of a biplane or mounted in the rear of a two-seater.

Fore sight

Aircraft Lewis gun had no cooling system

Magazine held 97 rounds with a counter indicating cartridges remaining

Back sight

Spade grip

Albatros DIII
This powerful biplane, armed with twin Spandau machine-guns, served from January 1917 until the armistice. Its maximum speed at sea level was 175 kph (109 mph).

Anti-aircraft guns
All kinds of gun, from machine-guns to field artillery, were pressed into service to shoot at aircraft. Here British troops rush to man a gun in the Vimy Ridge sector of the Western Front.

STRATEGIC DEVELOPMENTS

Although fighters became the dominant planes of the war, the only important roles for aircraft foreseen in 1914 were reconnaissance and bombing. Strategic bombing never became really effective in 1914–18, but its future potential became obvious.

The ineffectiveness of early bombers made the Germans' faith in Zeppelins understandable. For safety's sake they flew at night and maintained radio silence, which made navigation exceptionally difficult and bombing highly inaccurate. Secrecy was essential and, in spite of searchlights, they were frequently heard before they were seen. They carried out raids on Paris and other French cities, and – the most prestigious target – on London. However, they were becoming increasingly vulnerable and were withdrawn from a combat role after five were shot down over England in September 1916.

Specialized ground-attack aircraft were a late development. The Germans employed specialized two-seater aircraft in large formations called *Schlastas* (*Schlachtstaffeln*, "Battle flights"). They had a devastating effect at Cambrai (November 1917) and in the first German offensive of 1918, dropping bombs, strafing the enemy with machine-gun fire and at the same time providing information on the progress of the advance.

By 1918 air power was beginning to play an important role in action. The size of units was massively increased. The French, for example, operated a division of 700 mixed aircraft. With the development of ground attack, troop movements were seriously inhibited. The Germans often despatched 30-aircraft raids against targets behind enemy lines. The war was decided by events on the ground, but in 1918 events on the ground were dramatically affected by activities in the air.

In proportion to the numbers engaged, casualty rates were high. The rate among 22,000 British pilots was over 50 per cent, and German and French rates were similar. More pilots were lost through accidents than in action. Fewer might have died if parachutes had been issued. They were provided for balloon observers but were considered impractical in aircraft, at first because they were too heavy. The Germans introduced them towards the end of the war, but the RFC command feared that parachutes would encourage aircrew to abandon their aircraft unnecessarily. The sight of an unharmed pilot jumping to his death rather than burn in his flaming aircraft was not easily forgotten.

ZEPPELINS – RIGID AIRSHIPS

ALL PARTICIPANTS HAD AIRSHIPS – essentially powered balloons – of some kind. They were normally used for surveillance and naval duties. The Germans' rigid-frame Zeppelins were the best and were considered ideal for long-range bombing. They could climb quickly to an altitude beyond most fighters and their range and bomb-carrying capacity were far greater than any aeroplane. But they were vulnerable to ground fire, totally dependent on weather conditions and, as fighters improved and tracer was introduced, the hazards of flying in a slow-moving target under a vast bag of inflammable gas became unpleasantly obvious. However, there was no doubting the endurance of Zeppelins. On a (failed) mission to carry supplies to the German forces in East Africa in 1917, the L59 flew over 6,400km (4,000 miles) in 95 hours.

Three-engined rear gondola

Metal frame covered with outer fabric

Hydrogen-filled gas cells

Forward gondola with engine and controls

Machine-gun

HEAVY BOMBERS

~

THE FIRST BOMBERS WERE ADAPTATIONS of the heavier, two-seater, reconnaissance planes such as the Austrian Aviatik and the French Voisin, and the first bombs were artillery shells tossed hopefully out of the open cockpit. None of the early bombers were capable of delivering a significant bomb load and, although great progress was made during the next four years, the bomber remained a minor weapon, more valuable for its psychological impact than for the destruction it caused. The Royal Naval Air Service, operating from Belgian bases, mounted bombing raids on the Zeppelin base at Friedrichshafen as early as October–November 1914. The targets being large and inflammable, even 9-kg (20-lb) bombs were successful. By 1915 genuine bombers (all biplanes) were operational in Russia (Sikorskis), Italy (Capronis, the earliest and among the best bombers of the war) and Germany (twin-engined Gothas). The first British bomber, the Handley-Page O/100, first flew in December 1915. Bombing, however, remained a fringe operation until 1917. These included the R (Riesenflugzeug) planes, in particular the Zeppelin-Staaken series, which had two pilots sharing the cockpit, each holding a marine-type wheel (as used in airships), and engine pods containing compartments for in-flight mechanics. Strategic bombing of industrial targets was adopted in 1918 by the new Royal Air Force and advocated in France by Pétain. By that time bombers such as the Handley-Page O/400 could carry a bombload of around 900kg (2,000lb). Targets were industrial sites and railway stations

Air Marshal Trenchard told his pilots they need not be too careful of civilian lives, though in practice he concentrated on tactical rather than strategic bombing.

Handley Page O/400
With a span of 30.5 m (100ft), the O/400's wings folded for storage. Powered by two 360hp Rolls Royce Eagle V-12 engines, it had a top speed of 156kph (97 mph).

Caproni Ca 3
Gabriele D'Annunzio, poet, patriot and right-wing man of action, sets off in a giant Caproni bomber to attack the Austro-Hungarian lines on the Isonzo front.

Zeppelin-Staaken RVI
This giant bomber had a range of eight hours and was used for night raids over London. It could carry a payload of 2,000 kg (4,400lb).

British bombs
The two small bombs shown are a 9-kg (20-lb) Martin Hale high-explosive bomb (above) and a carcass incendiary bomb (below). The latter, usually dropped in large numbers, had perforated casing to allow the flames to spread.

Bomb damage
Territorials search the rubble of a London house bombed by a zeppelin. Over 500 British civilians were killed in zeppelin raids in the course of the war and a further 1,000 died in raids by aircraft.

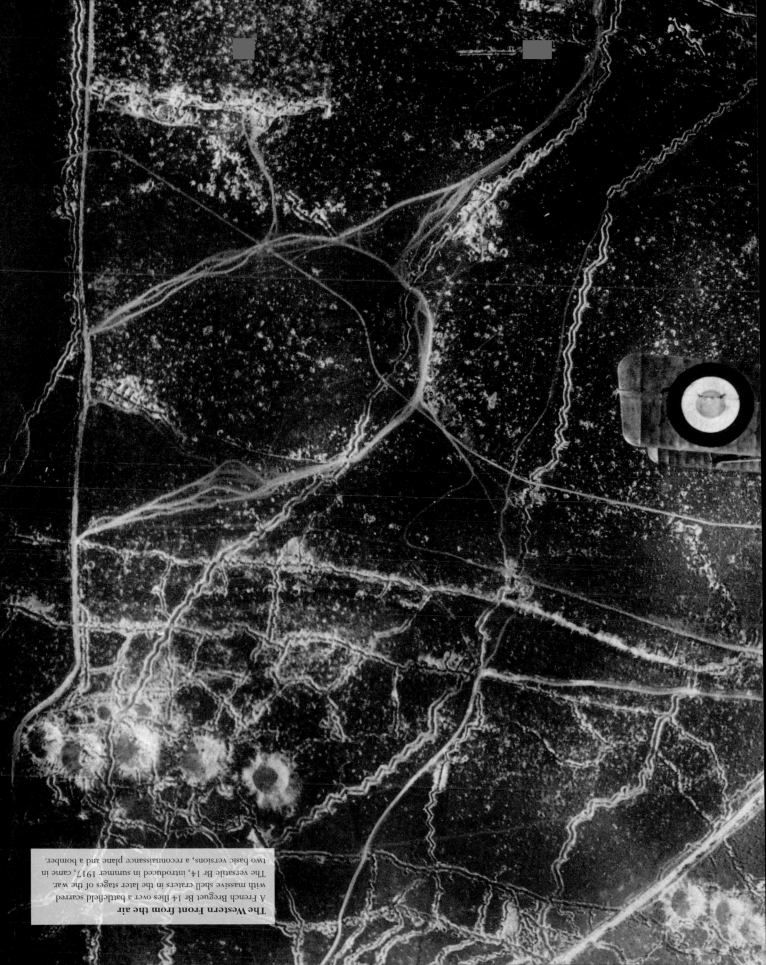

The Western Front from the air

A French Breguet Br 14 flies over a battlefield scarred with massive shell craters in the later stages of the war. The versatile Br 14, introduced in summer 1917, came in two basic versions, a reconnaissance plane and a bomber.

The USA and the War

THE ALMOST UNIVERSAL reaction of Americans to the outbreak of war in Europe was a determination to stay well out of it. Proclaiming US neutrality, President Wilson said that Americans should be impartial "in word and thought," as well as action, a characteristically high-minded but – in view of the strong cultural affinities with Britain and France – improbable aspiration.

Strict neutrality was impossible, and policies that were even-handed in principle turned out to favour the Allies in practice. At first loans to either side were barred, but this worked to the advantage of the Allies because they held substantial assets in the USA which they liquidated to buy goods. Then, when their credit was exhausted, the no-loans policy was abandoned for the sake of US export trade. Huge credits were extended, but loans to the Allies by 1917 were 75 times greater than loans to the Central Powers. An open-trade policy also favoured the Allies, as German ships could not cross the Atlantic.

The peace ticket
In the US presidential election of 1916 Wilson ran for re-election on a manifesto based on peace and prosperity.

In maintaining their blockade of Germany, the British published certain restrictions on trade. The confiscation of goods bound for a neutral port if likely to reach the enemy was not strictly within international law, but it had been practised by the USA in the Civil War. The British also extended the authorized ban on goods linked with war-making to all goods, including food. Ruthless enforcement brought protests from Washington – and soothing replies, plus compensation, from London.

More serious problems arose when Germany began a submarine blockade in February 1915. The Germans declared waters around Britain a war zone in which ships would be attacked on sight. One or two US ships were attacked in the following months and a few Americans killed, for which Germany promptly apologized. But the sinking of the *Lusitania*, with 128 Americans among the drowned, provoked a furious reaction.

Impartial spectators
President Wilson throws the ceremonial pitch to open the 1916 baseball season. For 32 months Wilson managed to keep the USA out of the conflict that had engulfed Europe.

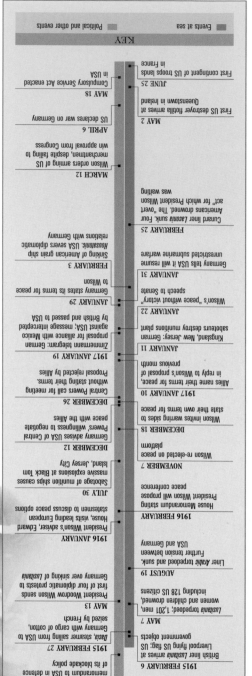

EVENTS IN THE USA
~
AUGUST 1914–JUNE 1917

However much the USA wished to stay out of the war, the declaration of neutrality and the observation of it proved to be two different things. Insistence on the right to trade and the right of free transit for neutral states inevitably brought the USA into conflict with Germany. After Germany's resumption of unrestricted submarine warfare in 1917, President Wilson was able to persuade Congress that the USA would have to enter the war.

1914 AUGUST 4 – USA declares its neutrality

1914 DECEMBER 29 – British government sends memorandum to USA in defence of its blockade policy

1915 FEBRUARY 6 – British liner *Lusitania* arrives at Liverpool flying US flag; US government objects

1915 FEBRUARY 27 – *Dacia*, steamer sailing from USA to Germany with cargo of cotton, seized by French

MAY 7 – *Lusitania* torpedoed; 1,201 men, women and children drowned, including 128 US citizens

MAY 13 – President Woodrow Wilson sends first of four diplomatic protests to Germany over sinking of *Lusitania*

AUGUST 19 – Liner *Arabic* torpedoed and sunk. Further tension between USA and Germany

1916 JANUARY – President Wilson's adviser, Edward House, visits leading European statesmen to discuss peace options

JULY 30 – Sabotage of munition ships causes massive explosions at Black Tom Island, Jersey City

NOVEMBER 7 – Wilson re-elected on peace platform

DECEMBER 12 – Germany advises USA of Central Powers' willingness to negotiate peace with the Allies

DECEMBER 18 – Wilson invites warring sides to state their own terms for peace

1917 JANUARY 10 – Allies name their terms for peace, in reply to Wilson's proposal of previous month

1917 JANUARY 19 – Central Powers call for meeting without stating their terms. Proposal rejected by Allies

JANUARY 11 – Kingsland, New Jersey: German saboteurs destroy munitions plant

JANUARY 22 – Wilson's "peace without victory" speech to Senate

JANUARY 29 – Germany states its terms for peace to Wilson

FEBRUARY 3 – Sinking of American grain ship *Housatonic*. USA severs diplomatic relations with Germany

Zimmermann telegram: German proposal for alliance with Mexico against USA; message intercepted by British and passed to USA

FEBRUARY 25 – Cunard liner *Laconia* sunk. Four Americans drowned. The "overt act" for which President Wilson was waiting

Germany tells USA it will resume unrestricted submarine warfare

MARCH 12 – Wilson orders arming of US merchantmen, despite failing to win approval from Congress

APRIL 6 – US declares war on Germany

MAY 18 – Compulsory Service Act enacted in USA

MAY 2 – First US destroyer flotilla arrives at Queenstown in Ireland

JUNE 25 – First contingent of US troops lands in France

KEY
Events at sea | Political and other events

THE SINKING OF THE LUSITANIA

~

BOUND FROM NEW YORK TO LIVERPOOL, with 1,962 passengers and crew, the *Lusitania* was off southern Ireland on May 7, 1915. In spite of warnings (apparently unreceived) of submarine activity, Captain Turner was not following recommended tactics – full speed on a zig-zag course – but maintaining a straight course at reduced speed 20 km (12 miles) offshore. At 2:00 pm the liner was hit by a torpedo, fired without warning by the German submarine *U20*. The *Lusitania* sank in 18 minutes. Of the 1,201 passengers drowned 128 were US citizens, among them public figures who included the millionaire Alfred Vanderbilt. The Germans contended that the *Lusitania* was an armed merchant cruiser (a legitimate target), and carried Canadian troops and munitions. She was not armed, carried no troops, and the only munitions were 5,000 cases of cartridges, and probably some explosive fuses.

The *Lusitania* in New York harbour
When she was launched in 1907, the Cunard liner was, at 31,550 tons, the largest ship in the world. She was also one of the most luxurious and a great favourite on the transatlantic passenger route. Her turbine engines gave a speed of 25 knots, easily fast enough to outrun a U-boat.

Life saver
This relic of the *Lusitania*, a lifebelt fitted with canvas breeches in which to place the legs, is preserved at the Imperial War Museum, London.

Heroic survivors
Two exhausted crew members from the *Lusitania* pose for the local Irish press after spending hours trying to help passengers to safety.

Grim memento
Germany issued an official apology for the sinking, but the German press was exultant: "With joyful pride we contemplate this latest deed of our navy." When a commemorative medal was struck, the British seized on this as a propaganda weapon, reproducing it in large numbers as an illustration of the enemy's baseness.

Burying the dead
Some of the victims of the sinking are buried in a mass grave outside Queenstown (Cobh).

The sinking of the *Lusitania* in May 1915 seemed to have been a planned operation, not the result of an unauthorized decision by a U-boat commander (as the Germans explained it), since veiled warnings had been published in New York advising Americans against sailing in the delineated war zone. Moreover, there had been no warning. The Hague Convention of 1907 required a warship before attacking a merchant vessel to give warning, then, if she were suspected of carrying contraband, to carry out an inspection, and finally to make provision for saving crew and passengers.

The outrage helped to swing US opinion further against Germany, and in the long run towards participation in the war. Two more American citizens died when the British liner *Arabic* was torpedoed in the Atlantic on August 19. In reply to a fresh wave of protests, the German ambassador in Washington gave a somewhat vague undertaking that unrestricted submarine warfare would henceforth be suspended.

American pilot of the Escadrille Lafayette

Long before the US entered the war American volunteers were serving in Europe – fighting in the Foreign Legion, driving ambulances, or flying with the Escadrille Lafayette, the American air squadron with its Indian chief emblem.

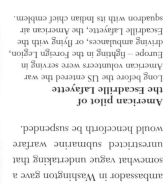

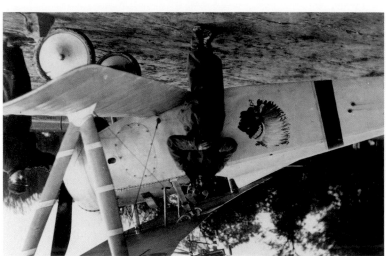

The debate between American interventionists and isolationists intensified during 1916. The interventionists, led by former president Theodore Roosevelt, were growing stronger, but in spite of anti-German feeling, many Americans remained strongly anti-war: Midwestern farmers, who had never even seen the sea, cared little for the problems of Europe. Irish Americans' anti-British feelings were strengthened by the Easter Rising of 1916, and people of German, Austrian and Hungarian origin were naturally sympathetic to the Central Powers. Above all there was a strong peace lobby. Andrew Carnegie funded his Foundation for International Peace with $10 million.

The president appearing before Congress

Wilson asked Congress for a declaration of war on Germany on April 2, 1917. Four days later he received an overwhelming vote of support for the war: 373 to 50 in the House of Representatives and 82 to 6 in the Senate.

Wilson had to face an acute moral dilemma. He was convinced that war was not only evil in itself but unreliable in its results. He was equally certain that in this war the Allies were in the right, and the Germans, to whose society and traditions he was by nature hostile, were in the wrong. Hence, after all his efforts to secure peace had failed, he was able to justify the war as the one way to "make the world safe for democracy". More practically, a German victory would be a disaster. Not only was the USA's traditional isolation dependent on Britain's command of the seas, but if the Allies were defeated their vast debts would never be repaid (the Germans later insisted this was the US motive for war).

Wilson won the presidential election of 1916 on the slogan, "He kept us out of war". Four months later, on April 2, 1917, he appeared before Congress to seek a declaration of war, determined to uphold American values by "force, force to the uttermost, force without stint or limit".

AMERICAN INDUSTRY

~

LIKE OTHER COUNTRIES, the USA faced a daunting task in converting to a war economy. This was aggravated by the size of the country and by traditions unsympathetic to federal controls. In 1914 the USA was the world's largest manufacturing state, and the stimulus of war provided incentives for investment and employment. In 1914–16 Britain, France and Russia depended heavily on US manufactures, food and credit. While some industries suffered as a result of the war, others, such as steel, shipbuilding and chemicals (in the absence of German competition), flourished. Agriculture, after a long recession, enjoyed vast increases in demand and hence prices – wheat rose from 70 cents a bushel in 1913 to $2.20 in 1917. The federal government's attitude towards free competition went into reverse. It took over communications and railways, controlled production and distribution of food and fuel, regulated labour and prices and (from February 1918) foreign trade. The war stimulated industrial changes already underway, such as standardization and assembly-line production. It also brought social change, for example the movement of Southern black workers to Northern cities.

Civic pride
New York's skyline was the wonder of the modern world, with new skyscrapers, such as the City Municipal Building (1913), springing up each year.

John D. Rockefeller
The war brought prosperity to the country. In 1916 it was announced that Rockefeller, founder of Standard Oil, had become the world's first billionaire.

American oil wealth
Between 1859, when oil production started, and 1920, the USA was responsible for over 60 per cent of the world's petroleum production. Many prolific new fields were opened during the First World War.

American confidence
This poster advertises a film of an air trip to Panama. The USA prided itself on its modernity in contrast to Europe.

Shipbuilding fever
Before the war, shipbuilding was not a major industry in the USA, but shipyards and their workers joined in the war effort with patriotic enthusiasm and competitions were staged between shipyards. The Mare Island shipyard set itself a challenge – to build a destroyer in 17 days. The ship, the Ward, fired the first shot of the Pacific War on December 7, 1941.

GEO. F. CROSBY Present
M.B DUDLEY

PANAMA AND THE CANAL FROM AN AEROPLANE
...IN SIX PARTS

THE FEATURE FILM SENSATION OF THE CENTURY

SHE'S SOME BABY
Keel Laid May 15th, DAYS 14 OLD Will Be Launched JUNE 1st. TO-DAY

The call to fight for Uncle Sam
When the USA declared war on Germany there was an initial flood of volunteers, but it was soon realized that conscription would be necessary. On May 18, 1917 the Selective Service Act was passed, allowing for a "selective draft". Eventually 11 million men were registered for military service and 4 million were actually called up.

Election slogans notwithstanding, Wilson had intimated during the election that US intervention might in the end be unavoidable. Many Americans agreed that the Allies were fighting a just war. Theodore Roosevelt wrote that if the Allies should seek US assistance it would be because they could fight no longer, "not because they regard us as having set a spiritual example to them by sitting idle, uttering cheap platitudes, and picking up their trade, while they have poured out their blood like water in support of the ideals in which, with all their hearts and souls, they believe."

GERMAN PROVOCATION

The Germans knew that the resumption of unrestricted submarine warfare would bring the US into the war. A German attempt to strengthen its position in such an event rendered the cause of neutrality a further blow when the Zimmermann telegram came to light in January 1917. This was sent by Zimmermann, a German foreign office minister, to the German ambassadors in Washington and Mexico City. It outlined a scheme to persuade Mexico to enter the war against the USA in return for German subsidies and a promise of the return of its lost territories in the American Southwest. It was intercepted and decoded by British Naval Intelligence, but by the time it was published in the press, Berlin had already announced the resumption of unrestricted submarine warfare on January 31. Eight US ships were sunk in February and March.

Although the Germans' main fear was the potential of US industrial production, it took time

to convert to a war economy and the Americans depended heavily on the European Allies for munitions and equipment throughout the war – no US aircraft made it to Europe before the armistice. But the Allies' most pressing need was for more troops, especially when collapsing Russian

WOODROW WILSON

~

Son of a Presbyterian minister, Wilson (1856–1924) had a brilliant academic career as a professor of history and politics, becoming president of Princeton in 1902. After serving as governor of New Jersey from 1910, he won the 1912 presidential election against the divided Republicans with 42 per cent of the vote. He secured a programme of progressive legislation, while pursuing mediation abroad. Instinctively opposed to war, he finally accepted US participation so as to promote American democratic and liberal values. To his dismay, the Senate refused to ratify the Versailles treaty. In October 1919 he suffered a disabling stroke.

resistance allowed the Germans to reinforce the Western Front with troops from the East. Despite efforts to achieve "preparedness" for war during 1916, the USA was no better prepared in 1917 than Britain in 1914: the regular army numbered only

145,000. Once it had been decided to raise a large, independent army, conscription was introduced and 32 training camps set up. Initially, equipment was scarce and training rudimentary: six months' drill and rifle practice. However, it was obvious that the army would not be ready until 1918 (only 176,665 soldiers reached France by the end of the year). The US Navy was in slightly better shape, with six destroyers despatched immediately to Queenstown (Cobh) and 12 more operational within weeks, helping to patrol the waters around Britain.

The USA never became one of the "Allies", remaining an "Associated Power", and its military leaders, including General Pershing, the stiff-necked commander, were determined to keep the AEF (American Expeditionary Forces) under US command, so that "they could never be anything but an instrument of US policy". A handful of US troops – the first ever to appear in Europe on active service – arrived in England on June 7, 1917 on their way to set up Pershing's headquarters in France. Landing on the French coast at dawn at a supposedly secret destination, they were greeted by cheering crowds.

Over there
US troops disembark in France in 1917. In some respects the Americans were well equipped — in motor transport, for example — but the tanks, guns and aeroplanes with which they fought were usually French.

7

DISILLUSION, MUTINY, AND REVOLUTION
1917

~

ALLIED HOPES THAT VICTORY MIGHT BE WON
IN 1917 COLLAPSED WITH THE FAILURE OF A MAJOR
FRENCH SPRING OFFENSIVE ON THE AISNE. MUTINY
IN A DEMORALIZED FRENCH ARMY SOON FOLLOWED.
THE BRITISH THEN LAUNCHED A CAMPAIGN IN
FLANDERS WHICH MANY VIEWED AS SO FUTILE THAT IT
CONTRIBUTED TO GROWING DISENCHANTMENT
WITH THE WAR IN BRITAIN AND FRANCE. SUCH
DISENCHANTMENT WAS EVEN GREATER IN RUSSIA
WHERE IT CULMINATED IN THE "OCTOBER
REVOLUTION" AND RUSSIA'S EXIT FROM THE WAR.

~

Australians at Château Wood, near Ypres
In October 1917 the Australians were involved in what, even at the time, was considered to be the most futile part of the Third Battle of Ypres: the struggle in the mud to capture the ruined village of Passchendaele.

FALSE HOPES

IN 1916, DESPITE SUFFERING HUGE CASUALTIES FOR LITTLE GAIN, THE ALLIES WERE CONVINCED AT THE END OF THE YEAR – AS THEY HAD BEEN AT THE END OF 1915 – THAT VICTORY WAS WITHIN REACH. AT THE CHANTILLY CONFERENCE IN NOVEMBER, THE FRENCH PROPOSED, AND THE BRITISH ACCEPTED, A PROGRAMME THAT WAS ALMOST IDENTICAL TO THE ONE THEY HAD ADOPTED THE YEAR BEFORE.

THE BRITISH AND FRENCH high commands believed that the Allies were now in a stronger position than a year earlier, and that the enemy was weaker. It was true that, despite the losses on the Somme, the British had more troops on the Western Front at the end of 1916 than at the beginning of the year. Both France and Russia, however, had serious problems with regard to manpower.

The French had only sufficient troops for one more offensive. France at this time had about 2,900,000 men on the Western Front, a total of some 110 infantry and seven cavalry divisions. But heavy losses in three successive years, plus the low birth rate in the decades before 1914, meant that the country had more or less exhausted its manpower reserves. Moreover, after its ordeal at Verdun, the morale of the army was uncertain.

The situation in Russia was even worse. In theory, Russia had a reserve of about 27,000,000 men of military age. However, a large number of exemptions, which included, most crucially, the whole of the Muslim population, meant that in reality this total was actually some 15 to 16 million.

Russia had already suffered perhaps as many as 7 million casualties, and by the end of 1916 it had an army of about 6,500,000 men – a total of about 150 infantry and 40 cavalry divisions. Just how serious Russia's lack of manpower was can be gauged from the fact that in the summer of 1916, the tsarist regime tried to impose conscription upon the Muslim population. Predictably, the result was widespread disturbances, which ironically but inevitably, had to be suppressed by the army.

By the end of 1916 the Russian military leadership knew that available reserves could soon not cover regular losses of some 200,000 men per month. Although Russian forces were as well supplied with weapons as at any time since September 1914, the Russian army was at the end of its strength. This situation could not be redeemed by success on the Italian, Salonika, Mesopotamia and Sinai fronts – not that success seemed very likely in any of these other theatres.

In the event, the shortage of manpower would not determine what happened on the battlefield in 1917 as much as other matters, the first of which was a change of personnel in the British government and in the French high command.

French artillery practice
The offensive planned by Nivelle for the spring of 1917 relied on the effective deployment of artillery to achieve immediate success in breaking through the German lines.

> *"The headlong pace of the advance was nowhere long maintained... The attack gained at most points, then slowed down, unable to follow the barrage which, progressing at the rate of a hundred yards in three minutes, was in many cases soon out of sight."*

GENERAL E. L. SPEARS, A BRITISH LIAISON OFFICER, DESCRIBING THE FRENCH ADVANCE ON THE FIRST DAY OF THE APRIL OFFENSIVE ON THE AISNE

A CHANGE OF COMMAND

On December 7, 1916 the British prime minister, Asquith, was ousted by Lloyd George, who was less than impressed by chief of staff Robertson and commander-in-chief Haig, and the way in which operations had been conducted in 1916. At this time, however, Lloyd George saw himself in office rather than in power, and hesitated to move directly against Robertson and Haig or to attempt to direct policy. Strategic policy had, in any case, been more or less settled by the decision at the end of 1915 to abandon the Gallipoli venture and by the defeats in

the Balkans. The military high command, rather than the civil authorities, was now considered to be very much in charge of strategic policy.

In France, on December 12, Joffre was dismissed as commander of the French army. Throughout 1916 both the government and the National Assembly had become increasingly disenchanted with him, initially because of the situation at Verdun, and subsequently because of the failure on the Somme. But Joffre was not replaced by Foch or Pétain, as might have been expected, but by Nivelle, the French commander in the final successful stage

of the Verdun campaign. Nivelle was certain that the tactics he had employed at Verdun would guarantee success over a wider front – namely, a massive bombardment of the German defensive positions, followed by a creeping barrage and a ferocious infantry attack. He envisaged a series of short assaults that could be halted if success was not immediate – not that he expected anything but total victory for his proposed offensive on the Aisne. This was to be carried out by the French, while supporting operations were conducted by the British and French between Arras and the Oise.

ENDORSEMENT OF NIVELLE'S PROPOSALS

Nivelle's proposals were immediately endorsed by the British and French governments. Not only did they seem to offer the prospect of a victory without huge attritional cost, at a time when civilian morale was perceptibly beginning to falter, but they were also presented by a very unusual commander – suave, bilingual and highly articulate. The contrast with Haig, Joffre and Pétain could not have been more marked, and was certainly enough to ensure the support of Lloyd George. The British prime minister arranged for a conference to be held at Calais at the end of February 1917, ostensibly in order to resolve problems of transportation and lines of supply affecting the British and French armies, but in fact organized to place the British armies in France under Nivelle's direct command. The plan miscarried, and Lloyd George was forced to backtrack in the face of furious opposition from Robertson and Haig. In one respect, however, he and Nivelle were successful: the Nivelle proposal for the main effort on the Aisne and a secondary operation around Arras received approval, and the British armies were placed under the general direction of Nivelle. The problem was that this was to be about the sum of Nivelle's success.

GERMAN PREPARATIONS

The events of 1917 were also shaped by Germany's plans. At the strategic level, the new German military leaders – Ludendorff and Hindenburg – spent the autumn of 1916 considering Germany's military options. The most obvious point to take into account was that, on the Somme, the battle was now being fought on ground that marginally favoured the British and French; the Germans' marked tactical advantage in July 1916 had very largely disappeared. Thus, in the first weeks of 1917 the Germans began to make arrangements for the withdrawal of forces on the Western Front in March to what became known as the Hindenburg Line. In fact, the first defensive positions had been prepared as early as September 1916 but, by February 1917, a comprehensive defensive line from Neuville Vitasse, near Arras, to Cerny, east of Soissons,

had been prepared in depth. The forward defensive positions were up to 2,300 m (2,500 yds) deep, while the triple defensive lines extended over 7,300 m (8,000 yds). On the Aisne and Chemin des Dames, German arrangements were not on the scale of those of the Hindenburg Line. They were, however, sufficiently strong to ensure that Nivelle's formula was doomed to failure. The German positions could not be broken with a single blow.

Russian revolutionaries in March
Among the actions of mutinous troops in Petrograd was the seizure of a Rolls Royce used by the imperial family. The mutiny helped to persuade the tsar to abdicate.

As spring arrived, doubts about Nivelle and his proposed offensive became widespread throughout the French military hierarchy, and there were fears that it would end disastrously. By this time, however, it was too late to halt proceedings that, in any case, Nivelle had promised he would end if the predicted victory did not happen straight away. He assured all doubters that his tactics would not just gain territory but would win the war – so raising expectations to a level where they could not be fulfilled. The result was to be a catastrophe that would further decrease what was left of the morale of the French troops and provoke the first serious mutiny of the war.

EVENTS AFTER NIVELLE'S FAILURE

Following the failure of the French offensive on the Aisne, the British took control of strategic policy on the Western Front. Haig was still devoted to the idea of an offensive that would win control of the Belgian coast, and to this end he launched a series of attacks in Flanders between June and November that would culminate in one of the most futile battles of the war: Passchendaele. Fought in particularly appalling conditions, and resulting in over 250,000 Allied casualties, it was regarded by Haig's contemporaries as the most notable example of his pointless sacrifice of men's lives.

As soldiers were dying in the mud around Passchendaele, the war on the Eastern Front was coming to an end. A revolution in March had forced the tsar to abdicate and had established a Provisional Government that was determined to maintain Russia's participation in the war despite mounting opposition. Following further Russian defeats, the Bolsheviks seized power on November 7 with a promise to take Russia out of the war.

The kaiser in Riga after victory over Russia
The capture of Riga by the Germans in September 1917 signalled the end of the war on the Eastern Front and promised the arrival of more German troops in the West.

"Do not trust the promises of the Bolsheviks! Their promise of an immediate peace is a lie! Their promise to provide bread is a fraud! Their promise to distribute the land is a fairy tale for children!"

RUSSIAN PRIME MINISTER KERENSKY IN A DECLARATION MADE FOLLOWING THE LOSS OF RIGA IN SEPTEMBER, 1917

Further Attrition on the Western Front

T HE COLDEST WINTER of the century ended any possibility of an early offensive. As the British completed their preparations to launch a spring offensive at Arras, the Germans – between March 15 and April 5 – withdrew to the Hindenburg Line. Hindenburg and Ludendorff had decided on this withdrawal as a means of shortening the line by 40 km (25 miles), so reducing the number of troops needed to defend it. During the withdrawal, the Germans systematically destroyed all the roads, railways, bridges and buildings in their way, thus presenting the Allies with a devastated wasteland to cross before coming up against a purpose-built defensive position of intimidating strength.

THE BATTLE OF ARRAS

The main British effort at Arras was to be made by 20 divisions of the Third Army under Allenby. It was to be supported to the north by nine divisions, including the Canadian Corps, of the First Army, and to the south by seven divisions, including the I ANZAC Corps, of the Fifth Army.

BRITISH AND CANADIAN SUCCESSES

After a five-day preliminary bombardment, the offensive opened, in sleet and snow, on Easter Monday, April 9. At first both the British and Canadians were successful. On its right flank the Third Army captured Neuville Vitasse, while in the centre it pushed forward over a distance of between 3 and 5 km (2 and 3 miles) and captured a German gun park. On its left flank, the Allies broke through the German defences to secure Fampoux, their final-phase objective, in an advance of 5.5 km (3.5 miles), the greatest single advance registered in one day on the Western Front since November 1914.

The Canadians advanced rapidly towards Vimy Ridge. During the morning of April 9 the 1st and

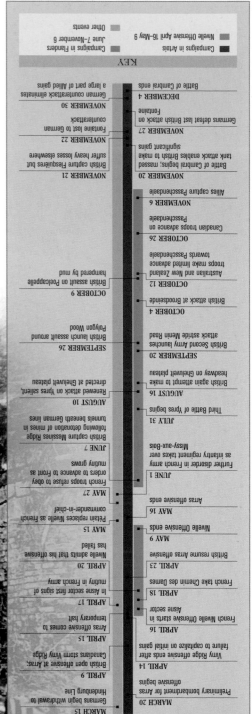

The rubble of Caulaincourt Château
During their withdrawal to the Hindenburg Line, the Germans practised a "scorched earth" policy and destroyed a number of impressive buildings. Here British soldiers are confronted by the evidence of this policy.

FRANCE AND FLANDERS
~
MARCH – DECEMBER 1917

Shortly after the Germans withdrew to their new Hindenburg Line defences, Nivelle launched a disastrous offensive that was to help provoke mutiny in the French army. Later in the year the British became embroiled in another terrible battle of attrition around Ypres. The only bright points for the Allies were the innovative tactics seen at Vimy Ridge, Messines and in the tank attack at Cambrai, which were not exploited.

~

MARCH 15 — Germans begin withdrawal to Hindenburg Line

MARCH 20 — Preliminary bombardment for Arras offensive begins

APRIL 9 — British open offensive at Arras; Canadians storm Vimy Ridge

APRIL 14 — Vimy Ridge offensive ends after failure to capitalize on initial gains

APRIL 15 — Arras offensive comes to temporary halt

APRIL 16 — French Nivelle Offensive starts in Aisne sector

APRIL 17 — In Aisne sector first signs of mutiny in French army

APRIL 18 — French take Chemin des Dames

APRIL 20 — Nivelle admits that his offensive has failed

APRIL 23 — British resume Arras offensive

MAY 9 — Nivelle Offensive ends

MAY 15 — Pétain replaces Nivelle as French commander-in-chief

MAY 16 — Arras offensive ends

MAY 27 — French troops refuse to obey orders to advance to front as mutiny grows

JUNE 1 — Further disorder in French army as infantry regiment takes over Missy-aux-Bois

JUNE 7 — British capture Messines Ridge following detonation of mines in tunnels beneath German lines

JULY 31 — Third Battle of Ypres begins

AUGUST 10 — Renewed attack on Ypres salient, directed at Gheluvelt plateau

AUGUST 16 — British again attempt to make headway on Gheluvelt plateau

SEPTEMBER 20 — British Second Army launches attack astride Menin Road

SEPTEMBER 26 — British launch assault around Polygon Wood

OCTOBER 4 — British attack at Broodseinde

OCTOBER 9 — British assault on Poelcappelle hampered by mud

OCTOBER 12 — Australian and New Zealand troops make limited advance towards Passchendaele

OCTOBER 26 — Canadian troops advance on Passchendaele

NOVEMBER 6 — Allies capture Passchendaele

NOVEMBER 20 — Battle of Cambrai begins; massed tank attack enables British to make significant gains

NOVEMBER 21 — British capture Flesquières but suffer heavy losses elsewhere

NOVEMBER 22 — Fontaine lost to German counterattack

NOVEMBER 27 — Germans defeat last British attack on Fontaine

NOVEMBER 30 — German counterattack eliminates a large part of Allied gains

DECEMBER 4 — Battle of Cambrai ends

KEY

- Campaigns in Artois
- Campaigns in Flanders — June 7–November 6
- Nivelle Offensive April 16–May 9
- Other events

THE CANADIANS

A T THE OUTBREAK OF WAR the Canadian government pledged formations for the British imperial cause. Between August 1914 and January 1917 five Canadian divisions were raised, though the last was used only for British home defence. Throughout 1916 numbers stayed at around 300,000, and Canada experienced increasing difficulty in maintaining its formations. Conscription came into force on October 13, 1917, but with very mixed results: there was widespread rioting in Quebec in March 1918 as a result of the arrest of a French Canadian who had refused to be conscripted. Ultimately some 628,000 Canadians enlisted, mostly voluntarily, of whom 365,000 – including 46,000 conscripts – served overseas. The total number of casualties was around 210,000.

The Canadian effort on the Western Front, where the Canadian 1st Division arrived in February 1915, is always associated with the offensive on Vimy Ridge in April 1917 and more generally with the Third Battle of Ypres (Passchendaele). At Vimy Ridge, in an episode etched into the Canadian national psyche, all four divisions of the Canadian Corps, working together for the first time, stormed a position thought impregnable and took it virtually in a morning. Canadian troops were at Ypres in April 1915 and Amiens in August 1918, but perhaps their greatest achievement was during the Hundred Days – between late August and October 1918 – when they breached the defences of the German Hindenburg Line. Their actions compounded a formidable reputation for professionalism, steadfastness and reliability; theirs was a full contribution to Allied victory.

Progress after the first day

All the Allied forces lost momentum after the first day. Last-minute plans had been made for the Fifth Army's operations to include a massed armour attack. The tanks, however, were not ready for offensive operations on April 10, and when the next day just four crossed the start line, they did so late and behind the infantry they were supposed to lead and protect. The offensive was a complete failure, and at Bullecourt the Australians lost more troops than on any other day of the war.

The taking of Vimy Ridge, coming after the many failures to capture it in previous years, was a major accomplishment. It was one of the greatest single day's achievements in the history of the Western Front and rightly became an important part of the Canadian military legend. The Canadians, however, were to suffer over 11,000 casualties in less than one week during their attempt to build on their success of the first day.

Vimy Ridge, in the late afternoon. 4th Division secured Hill 145, the highest point on Folie Farm, was checked. On its left, however, the main objective. The 3rd Division, after taking La 2nd Divisions secured Thélus and Farbus, some 3,660 m (4,000 yds) from their start line and the

Canadians firing a captured German 105-mm howitzer
Men of the Canadian Field Artillery turn a German gun on its former owners. When the Canadian Corps stormed Vimy Ridge in April 1917, they captured some 4,000 prisoners and large amounts of equipment, including over 50 artillery pieces.

Canadian artillery supply column
A Canadian artillery unit uses mules to transport ammunition along a relatively good road. During the Third Battle of Ypres, both supplies and mules were often swallowed up by bottomless mud.

Uniform and equipment

The Canadian "pattern service dress" was based on the British khaki uniform of 1902. The standard Canadian rifle, the Ross Mark III, was heavier than the British Lee Enfield. It was fitted with an unusual short, wide bayonet.

PENKNIFE

ROSS BAYONET

INFANTRY CAP

THE NIVELLE OFFENSIVE

On April 16, after a number of delays because of bad weather, Nivelle launched his long-planned offensive along a 40-km (25-mile) front on the Aisne River after a two-week preliminary bombardment. For the main attack, east of Soissons, Nivelle had mustered two armies – the Fifth and Sixth – with some 3,810 guns, plus 128 tanks which were used by the French for the first time. He also had a third army in reserve and a fourth earmarked for a support and deception role east of Reims.

Nivelle's plan was for 20 French divisions to carry out a rapid assault behind a creeping barrage and capture the heights above the Aisne before breaking through the German lines on the Chemin des Dames road. Despite the failure of the French artillery to cut the German wire or to carry out an effective creeping barrage, the French made some impressive initial gains. On April 16 the Fifth Army penetrated up to 5 km (3 miles) and took the area around Fort Condé. From the start, however, the French effort was plagued by problems and it soon began to go disastrously wrong.

On the first two days, French artillery support was minimal, and the French tanks – which were better suited to break-out rather than breakthrough battles across open ground – were shot to pieces

the Germans had brought up reinforcements and reconstituted their defence. The British – after the capture of 112 guns and over 7,000 prisoners in two days at what was regarded as the comparatively modest cost of around 8,220 casualties – were beginning to feel more confident. This confidence, however, soon disappeared when their attempt to move forward on April 11 resulted in major losses.

As snow blizzards intensified and it became clear that the British troops were suffering from the intense cold as well as fatigue, the offensive was maintained only to distract attention from preparations for the French offensive effort in Champagne. It was halted on April 15.

On April 11 the Third Army secured Monchy Le Preux, but its attempts to move its artillery across the muddy battlefield, and send reserves and cavalry through the breaches that had been made in the German defensive line on April 9, foundered. There were the same basic problems that had plagued all previous offensives: those of command, movement and co-ordination.

Adding to the problems that now beset the British offensive was the recovery of the German defence. On April 9 the Germans had too many formations in forward defensive positions and held reserve formations too far from the battle zone to be able to counterattack quickly. By April 11, however,

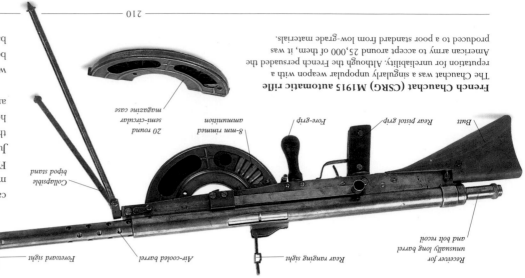

French Chauchat (CSRG) M1915 automatic rifle
The Chauchat was a singularly unpopular weapon with a reputation for unreliability. Although the French persuaded the American army to accept around 25,000 of them, it was produced to a poor standard from low-grade materials.

20 round semi-circular magazine case

8-mm rimmed ammunition

Fore-grip

Rear pistol grip

Butt

Collapsible bipod stand

Foresward sight

Air-cooled barrel

Rear ranging sight

Receiver for unusually long barrel and bolt recoil

THE END OF THE OFFENSIVE

A shortage of ammunition imposed a halt on French operations on April 20, the day after the French president, Poincaré, had tried to halt the offensive. Nivelle's ambitions were now reduced to securing the Chemin des Dames, which had been reached on the third day. On April 23 Poincaré banned all further offensive operations, in effect spelling the end of both Nivelle as commander of the French armies on the Western Front and of his offensive. What he had promised – a major breakthrough in 24 hours – had not materialized. Instead of achieving an overall advance of 9 km (6 miles), they had made a general advance of just 500 m (600 yds). In the first ten days the number of casualties had reached almost six figures, instead of Nivelle's estimate of 15,000, and French medical support had all but collapsed.

By the time the last attacks in this offensive ended on May 9, the French had suffered 187,000 casualties. The Germans, despite their success in withstanding the offensive, had fared little better, suffering 167,000 casualties. The contrast between the promises of success and the offensive's failure amid heavy casualties proved particularly corrosive to the morale of the French army.

French infantry advances along Aisne front
Nivelle's Chemin des Dames offensive, launched amid such high hopes but against an enemy forewarned of French intentions, would push the French army beyond breaking point and ruin Nivelle's reputation and career.

before they could have any impact. Furthermore, the French air force was unable to contest German superiority in the air, with obvious repercussions in such matters as artillery spotting. The Germans, who had advance notice of what the French were intending after acquiring detailed operational plans in routine raids, had strengthened their defences so that they were four lines deep in places. The artillery was sited beyond the range of French fire, which meant that it was able to shred the French infantry after it had secured the first defensive line during the first two days of the offensive.

TYPES OF BARRAGE

~

IN THE FIRST MONTHS OF THE WAR, artillery bombardments generally began with concentrated fire upon enemy defensive positions, followed by fire directed at other targets in the rear once the infantry assault began. In effect, this simplistic arrangement meant that infantry attacks were unsupported by direct fire. The development of trench systems spelt the need for heavier bombardments in order to ensure the destruction of defensive positions, and this meant larger guns and howitzers, and mortars with heavier shells. The loss of surprise was accepted as the price to be paid for what was hoped would be the neutralization of the enemy defensive positions. The hurricane barrage – a short, intense bombardment – was an anomaly in that it was used by the British in 1915 simply because they lacked the number of guns and shells for a protracted bombardment. In March 1918 the Germans used a hurricane barrage that was notable for its employment of gas. If an area could be saturated for more than 30 minutes, then defending troops would have to change their respirator filters, with obvious results.

The creeping barrage was different, involving as it did fire moving ahead of the infantry at a set rate, thus ensuring the suppression of the defence until the attacking infantry was all but upon the enemy positions. Employed in October 1916 to real effect during the Battle of Verdun, it was refined with a rate of advance set at 45 m (50 yds) a minute. Its success depended upon careful timing on the part of both guns and infantry, and upon the ability of the latter to move across No Man's Land at a rate that ensured it stayed close behind, and under the protection of, the curtain of fire. The fundamental weakness of the arrangement was that inadequate means of communication meant that the infantry were unable to summon fire on new positions or call a halt to bombardments. Inevitably, there were many casualties from friendly fire. It has been estimated that the French army's dead from its own artillery reached six figures over the course of the war.

French 270-mm howitzer
Once the war became a static affair, both sides sought to breach their opponents' defences with ever larger guns – larger even than the old French 270-mm howitzer. In fact, it was better co-ordination between infantry and artillery that would prove to be the key to success.

MUTINY IN THE FRENCH ARMY

The French infantry had been promised certain victory, not another pointless attritional battle. Coming after Verdun, failure on the Aisne temporarily broke the will of the French to launch another offensive. The number of desertions had increased significantly since the beginning of 1917, and in April – as the failure of the Nivelle Offensive caused disillusionment and anger within the army – there were the first signs of mutiny.

Faced with the need to restore order, the French authorities turned to Petain, appointing him as chief of staff on April 29, and then as Nivelle's replacement in the position of commander-in-chief on May 15. Petain had a reputation within the army for being more economical with men's lives than other generals, and having empathy with his troops, but ironically, the worst of the troubles that were to afflict the French army took place after this date. Up to 30,000 soldiers had abandoned the front along the Chemin des Dames when, on May 27, troops in four towns refused to obey officers' orders to advance to the front and seized some buildings. Two days later, several hundred troops already at the front refused to move into front-line trenches. On June 1 a French infantry regiment took over the town of Missy-aux-Bois, and for a week there was chaos.

Signs of unrest were normally short-lived and focused upon two matters – the seemingly pointless offensives and the often appalling conditions in which the soldiers were expected to live, whether in or out of the line. Contrary to the impression conveyed by the word "mutiny", only on one occasion was there a refusal to take part in combat. In fact, 44 divisions were wholly unaffected, and of the 68 that were affected, 17 had just single incidents. Amongst the remainder, there was a total as an increasing number of French soldiers refused to return to the trenches. Generally, however, such incidents were rare.

THE WESTERN FRONT
Jan–May, 1917

Western Front Jan 1917
German withdrawal to Hindenburg Line
British Arras offensive
French Nivelle Offensive
--- Major railway
Hindenburg Line Mar 15–Apr 5
Hindenburg Line Apr 5

Spring offensives

Following the withdrawal of the Germans to the Hindenburg Line, the British Arras offensive took place along a 20-km (13-mile) front either side of the city where the German positions had not changed. After some initial success, the offensive achieved little. The French Nivelle Offensive, which began a week later, was a disastrous failure within a few days.

French troops at Fleury

French infantry move up to the line in the Verdun sector. During the mutiny most troops were prepared to defend the line against German attack, but they refused to take part in any further futile offensives.

In some regiments in the French Army, the poor injured officers said, "Well, you promised us that once we'd attacked we'd be relieved, and yet we stay here in the lines. It is always us that are killed."... And we, as cavalrymen, were on the front line, so we knew when there was bad feeling among the soldiers. This was not in all the regiments, but in those that had attacked too often, or where there were heavy casualties, they were somewhat discouraged. They refused to obey their officers. I saw poor officers walking here and there sadly and men not saluting them.

PRIVATE ROBERT POUSTIS, FRENCH CAVALRYMAN, ON THE MUTINY AMONG THE INFANTRY

MUTINY AND DESERTION

FOR MOST OF THE WAR, indiscipline was not a serious problem in any of the armies on the Western Front. On the whole, the morale of the British, French and German armies did not crack, because the soldiers were committed to their governments' war aims and respected their officers. Major though they were, the French mutinies lasted for little more than two months, and German troops only rose up against their commanders during the last stages of the conflict. Between 1914 and 1918 some 3,080 British soldiers were sentenced to death by court martial, mainly for desertion. Instead of being shot, most were shipped off to British colonies. Far from being "cowards", a high proportion of the 307 men who were not reprieved were victims of "shell shock".

The incidence of desertion is hard to assess, partly because no army could admit to dwindling numbers. It is clear that away from the Western Front it became a major problem in the later years of the war. In 1916, for example, Czechs and Ruthenes deserted *en masse* in the Austro-Hungarian armies resisting the Russian Brusilov Offensive, and in the course of 1917 tens of thousands of Russians deserted. By December 1917 at least 300,000 of Turkey's poorly treated soldiers had also deserted. These deserters roamed the countryside, living off the land and turning into robber bands.

Court martial in session
Although military justice could be draconian, only 27 French soldiers were executed after the mutiny of 1917. Others were imprisoned or sentenced to forced labour.

Poor living conditions
The living conditions of the common French soldier were improved as part of Pétain's campaign to rebuild the army's morale. An end to costly offensives and greater emphasis on defence in depth were also promised.

Don't strike
A poster calls on French workers not to strike. There was much industrial unrest in France during the mutiny, and Pétain saw it as a malaise that affected the army.

of 250 incidents in 152 regiments, mostly infantry. Not one officer was murdered and there was only a single incident of a general being manhandled. In the vast majority of cases, French units refused to involve themselves in costly, hopeless offensives but declared a willingness to man the line.

PÉTAIN'S RESPONSE

Pétain responded by ordering mass arrests. It appears that 3,335 soldiers were court-martialled and 449 were condemned to death. Of these, 27 were actually shot; the remainder were imprisoned. A total of about 24,000 soldiers were punished at unit level. Unrest rumbled on until October, but the crisis had passed by mid-June after it became clear that Pétain also intended not just to punish but to change tactics and improve conditions. From now on there would be limited attacks, in which the infantry operated in small groups rather than *en masse*, and there would be greater emphasis on defence in depth, with the front-line trenches only thinly held and troops in the rear line being relieved by reserves on a more regular basis. Troops would have seven days' leave every four months, and more trains would be run to take them on leave. Rest areas would be improved through the provision of more beds, and food would be much improved through the regular delivery of fresh vegetables and the establishment of regimental co-operatives offering extra, cheap provisions. There would not, however, be any increase in pay.

Pétain personally visited 90 divisions to explain these improvements. He also brought a temporary halt to all offensives. He would not feel ready to launch another until August, when an attack at Verdun would drive the Germans back to the positions they had occupied before their advance in February 1916. Thus in June the immediate burden of the Allied cause fell upon Britain.

TUNNEL WARFARE

DIGGING TUNNELS TOWARDS AND UNDER the enemy's trenches (sapping), and then detonating one or more mines to create a breach in the enemy's defences, became an increasingly important tactic in trench warfare from the end of 1914. The Germans were the first to try it when they tunnelled towards a small section of the Western Front in Belgium in December and used ten small mines – each weighing between 23 and 137 kg (50 and 300 lbs) – to blow up an entire Indian brigade. It was only then that both the French and the BEF began to consider establishing their own effective tunnelling forces. Without them their men in the trenches would live in fear of being blown to pieces by an unseen foe – and no similar threat could be turned on the Germans.

In 1914 the French army had some *sapeurs-mineurs* with training but only archaic equipment, while the BEF had no mining specialists at all. At the end of the year the British created brigade mining sections, made up of men with no experience, tools

FRENCH SAPPER'S ELECTRIC TORCH

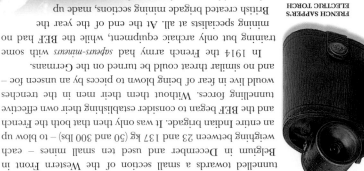

or listening equipment, to work out where the German tunnels were. From February 1915 these men were joined by special tunnelling companies made up largely of coal miners.

British breathing apparatus

It was often essential for miners to use special apparatus to help them breathe in an environment where foul air or potentially fatal fumes could build up rapidly. The bags on this equipment contained compressed oxygen, which was released through the air tubes. Straps held the mouthpiece in place.

Regulator

Gas tank

tubes

Skull cap

Underground activity

It took a year for miners to dig the network of tunnels under Messines Ridge in what was the most successful, and spectacular, use of mines in the war. The explosion on June 7, 1917 was heard in London, 210 km (130 miles) away, 10,000 German soldiers disappeared off the face of the earth.

British detonator

The detonator sent a small electric charge to a primary explosive charge which discharged the high-explosive mine. The high explosives favoured by the British were amotal (TNT and ammonium nitrate) and ammonal (TNT, ammonium nitrate and powdered aluminium).

Throughout 1915 the Germans dominated the underground war. However, in 1916 the British and French tunnellers began to pose a serious threat, and by early 1917 they had gained the ascendancy. Great improvements had been made in their equipment: they now had sophisticated listening devices, such as the geophone; silent air and water pumps; and ammonal explosive charges in place of the more volatile gunpowder and guncotton.

Whatever the men's experience of working underground, it could not prepare them for the terror of being in a tunnelling party under No Man's Land. Each side would be listening out for the other, ready to blow a "camouflet" – a small charge that could entomb the enemy's miners without damaging one's own tunnel. Sometimes the two sides dug into each other's tunnels, resulting in bitter hand-to-hand fighting in which shovels and picks were employed as weapons. Other hazards included gas that could asphyxiate or ignite, shortage of oxygen, and having to work up to 12 hours at a time in 30 cm (1 ft) or more of water in bitterly cold conditions.

German explosive

Westfalit was the standard explosive in German mines. Sixty tons were detonated in one mine at Vauquois in the Argonne on May 14, 1916.

> "… the noise of the guns deadened all sound from the mine, except that we could hear, even above this crescendo, the screams of the imprisoned Germans in the crater."
>
> BRITISH OFFICER ANTHONY EDEN ON THE EFFECTS OF A MINE EXPLOSION ON THE MESSINES RIDGE

determine strategic policy for the remainder of the year. Haig's initial reaction was to assume the defensive, but Russia's disarray, the danger of the Central Powers concentrating their attention on Italy, and the risk that a German attack on the Western Front might expose French weakness, finally made him decide on offensive action. He had long sought an offensive in Flanders, and in spring 1917 he received support for this from an Admiralty convinced that the war at sea would be lost if the U-boats were not denied the use of Belgian ports. Consequently, as a first step to gaining control of the Belgian coast, Haig gave the go-ahead for a long-planned attack designed to clear the Messines Ridge, at the southern end of the Ypres salient.

MESSINES RIDGE OFFENSIVE

The 76-m (250-ft) high Messines Ridge, with its German trenches and fortifications, dominated British positions to the south of Ypres. In the early hours of June 7 there were a number of enormous explosions – so loud they could be heard in southeast England – when 19 of the 21 mines placed in tunnels 15 to 30 m (50 to 100 ft) below the German lines on the ridge were detonated. The tunnels, one of which was 610 m (2,000 ft) long, had been dug by British, Canadian and Australian tunnellers over a 12-month period.

Arras town hall in ruins, May 1917
Although initial progress in the British offensive at Arras was promising, the battle degenerated into yet another one of attrition. The British lost more than 150,000 men, but the Germans also suffered some 100,000 casualties.

RESUMPTION OF THE ARRAS OFFENSIVE

On April 23, to support French operations on the Chemin des Dames, the British resumed their offensive at Arras, on the Scarpe River. By the last week of April it was clear that the French offensive had failed, that Nivelle's days were numbered, and that the offensive capacity of the French armies had been impaired. Yet Haig was determined that the offensive should continue and ignored protests from Allenby about heavy casualties for very little gain. The offensive was only finally called off in late May, the British and French high commands agreeing on a series of limited offensives over the following months. On June 2, however, Haig learned that the unrest within the French army made the offensive scheduled for the 10th at Malmaison impossible.

The French army's difficulties in spring 1917 left the British to

Germans detonating mines
The detonation of mines had to be synchronized with some precision. Blow the mine too early and the enemy could reoccupy the ground, too late and you risked friendly troops being caught in the blast.

Australians at work below Messines Ridge
Members of the 1st Australian Tunnelling Company were among the tunnellers who excavated under the ridge and packed 21 chambers with 600 tons of explosive. Many Australian tunnellers had acquired their expertise while working in gold-mines.

The effect was devastating. About 10,000 German soldiers were killed or buried alive. A British artillery barrage – involving over 2,250 guns – added to the terror. Many of the Germans were too stunned by the explosions to resist the British Second Army. Around 7,500 were taken prisoner. By 7:00 am Messines itself had been captured; by 3:00 pm the whole ridge had been taken and Allied troops were moving down the eastern slopes. They quickly dug in and on the following day withstood all attempts by the Germans to counterattack. By June 11 the Germans had begun an orderly withdrawal and were establishing a new front line further east, convinced that there would be follow-up attacks and that they might have to give up ground north of the Lys. Haig, however, did not have the necessary forces in place to build on the success at Messines. Instead, he made preparations for a major offensive at Ypres later in the summer.

THE THIRD BATTLE OF YPRES

The British, with support from the French, began their major assault on the Ypres salient on July 31. In the weeks after the capture of Messines Ridge, the German Fourth Army had concentrated on strengthening its positions, and it now had three defensive lines, each some 1,800 m (2,000 yds) deep. It planned to hold the first line lightly, with reserve formations in the third. The artillery was positioned behind Gheluvelt where, on a reverse slope, it could enjoy considerable immunity from British gunfire. As early as the 27th the British had succeeded in occupying a number of German forward positions that had been evacuated during preliminary bombardments. The main attack on the 31st, however, met with mixed success. The two flanking armies, the French First Army in the north and the British Second Army in the south, registered major gains. In fact, as on the Somme in 1916, the French achieved considerably more success than the attacks they were supposed to support – the attacks of the Fifth Army. The Fifth Army generally secured the first German line and in some places broke through it, but on the right it made very little progress. Furthermore, most of the 22 tanks committed to the attack became stuck in the heavily cratered ground. It was not until the British high command had considered the results of this first day's fighting that it began to realize the importance of the Gheluvelt position to the German defence. By this point, however, the rains that were to turn the battlefield into a swamp had begun.

After a three-day struggle the British secured control of the first German line, more than had been achieved by any other offensive on the salient, though far less than the progress envisaged by Haig. When, however, the main attack was resumed on August 10 – this time directed specifically against the Gheluvelt position – the German defensive measures proved to be extremely effective. Their losses were held to a minimum by the organization of a counter-barrage to isolate attacking units and the launching of counterattacks by local reserves. A renewed British offensive on the 16th was no more successful than that of the 10th. On the 22nd a series of attacks yielded such disappointing results, with over 3,000 men lost for the gain of just 800 m (880 yds) on the Menin Road, that Haig had to accept that the offensive was not going to break the front. Instead, all that could be aimed for was the gradual wearing down of German defences.

THE SECOND PHASE

Other First World War battles lasted longer and claimed more casualties than the Third Battle of Ypres. But it was this battle, and in particular, the phase that focused on capturing the small village of Passchendaele, that gained particular notoriety in Britain. Not only was the battle fought in appalling conditions, but even by the standards of the First World War, it was particularly futile. No amount of

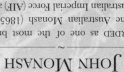

JOHN MONASH

GENERALLY REGARDED as one of the most brilliant generals on the Western Front, the Australian Monash (1865–1931) was only commissioned to join the Australian Imperial Force (AIF) after the outbreak of the war – previously he had served in the reserves. He insisted on doing everything possible to protect the lives of his men and developed new tactics such as the joint advance of tanks and infantry in order to achieve this.

Having commanded an infantry brigade sent to Egypt in 1915 as part of the ANZAC (Australian–New Zealand Army Corps) force, Monash later served at Gallipoli. Towards the end of 1916, he was transferred to France to lead the Third Division, which went on to serve with distinction at Messines and Passchendaele. Taking over from William Birdwood, in May 1918, as commander of the Australian army on the Western Front, Monash demonstrated remarkable leadership. This was apparent in his counterattacks during the German push of 1918, notably at the battle of Hamel in July and in the Australian advance of August 8, 1918, described as the "black day of the German army". He also led Australian forces in the capture of Mont St Quentin in September and the autumn offensive on the Hindenburg Line.

Irish troops at Messines
Irish troops survey the unrecognizable ruins of the village of Wytschaete. The village was captured by men of the 16th Irish Division and the 36th Ulster Division on the first day of the Battle of Messines.

The Australians

THE GALLIPOLI CAMPAIGN of 1915 produced an upsurge of recruitment in Australia, but meant that I ANZAC Corps (the 1st and 2nd Australian Divisions and the New Zealand Infantry Division) did not arrive in France until March–April 1916. II Corps, consisting of the 4th and 5th Divisions, arrived in France in June; the 3rd Division was raised after the arrival of its constituent units in Britain in July 1916. Australian horse units did not proceed to France, but remained in the Middle East where they fought in the Sinai and Palestine.

In action the Australians quickly acquired a reputation as the elite in the British imperial army, and also for insubordination, bloody-mindedness and "resolute lack of military etiquette". No doubt the latter was partly a reaction against the class distinctions they found in British civil and military life. For their part, the Australians came to resent their use at the cutting edge of the British effort. I Australian Corps, formed in November 1917, sustained 25,588 casualties between August 8 and October 5, 1918 and, after a series of incidents tantamount to a refusal to undertake offensive operations, the formation was withdrawn from operations. Unable to replace losses, which meant that divisions were some 3,000 men under strength by the end of 1917, the Australians were obliged to break up three battalions in May 1918 and eight in September, when in effect two divisions were reduced to reserve status.

The increasing manpower problems of Australian formations after July 1916 provoked the bitterly divisive conscription issue within Australia. Referenda that would have resulted in the national application of conscription were defeated on October 28, 1916 and December 20, 1917. Nonetheless, with some 2,300,000 men of military age, Australia enlisted 416,809 men and despatched some 322,000 troops overseas in the course of the war: the Australian Imperial Force had a strength of some 200,000 men in February 1918. Australian casualties totalled some 280,000 with almost 60,000 killed.

Calling up more volunteers
Throughout the war there was a vigorous campaign in Australia to attract volunteers. Of the large number who responded, the great majority served as front-line troops.

Australian soldier with a wounded German
Australian troops were invariably among the wounded themselves. They suffered a higher proportion of casualties than any other nationality in the war.

Band of the 5th Australian infantry brigade
The brigade entered Bapaume in March 1917 during the Allied advance across territory abandoned by the Germans as they withdrew to the Hindenburg Line.

rationalization on the part of Haig and his apologists could ever disguise this fact. Haig resolutely ignored the warning made on August 16 by Gough, commander of the Fifth Army, that "tactical success was not possible under these conditions" and that it was now time for the attack to be abandoned. He preferred to believe that the morale of the Germans was steadily deteriorating and would finally be broken by the prolonged pounding of their lines.

Towards the end of August, Plumer, commander of the Second Army, was put in charge of operations in place of Gough. Haig still hoped for a breakthrough, but he accepted Plumer's very deliberate formula – four set-piece attacks, conducted with an overwhelming preponderance of firepower and for very limited objectives, with some six days between each attack.

ASTRIDE THE MENIN ROAD

Plumer's first two attacks were very similar: both were on very narrow frontages by formations attacking after artillery bombardments more severe than any before. Plumer, by limiting objectives to less than 1.5km (1 mile), sought to shatter an enemy defence now concentrated forward after the loss of its first line, and to destroy German counterattacks by forcing them to come within the range of the British artillery. In both operations, along a 13-km (8-mile) front astride the Menin Road on September 20, and an 8-km (5-mile) front around Polygon Wood on the 26th, forward German positions were pulverized and immediate counter-attacks broken. However, while most objectives were secured, the average gain on both days only amounted to around 900 m (1,000 yds). Moreover, on the Menin Road, Australian and British forces incurred some 22,000 casualties and at Polygon Wood about 17,000 casualties. German losses were about the same as those incurred by the Allies.

Haig continued to be hopeful that the German line could be broken, and a further attack was planned for October 4, in which corps of the Fifth Army were to attack Broodseinde Ridge. The attack, carried out with no preliminary bombardment but with simultaneous artillery and infantry assaults, inflicted some 26,000 German casualties on what was the first of the "Black Days" recorded by Ludendorff. British losses, however, were scarcely fewer. They were also unable to exploit their initial gains of just 640 m (700 yds), which despite being so limited were paraded as a great victory. Preparations were made for yet further major attacks.

DEATH IN THE MUD

At this time the rains returned to Flanders. In August, daily rain, combined with the smashing of the local drainage system by British operations, had created a marsh. This had drained itself during the abnormally dry September, when dust clouds were a regular sight, but as the rains began to fall in October the dust turned into liquid mud.

Despite this, and despite a considerable rise in desertion and sickness that was evidence of a decline in morale among British troops, Haig was determined to proceed with attacks due to be launched on October 9 and 12. Thus began what was without doubt the worst and most futile part of the Third Battle of Ypres.

The attack of October 9 at Poelcapelle made virtually no gains while the mud smothered both men and guns. New Zealand troops suffered particularly badly. Even the habitual optimism of Haig's staff wilted in the aftermath of this day. On the 12th, in the first of the two "Battles of Passchendaele", Australian and New Zealand troops were sacrificed in an advance of just 90 m (100 yds) towards the village. An attack on the 26th, the first involving Canadians, did scarcely any better; another on the 30th, with the Germans deliberately thinning their front, came to within 450 m (500 yds) of the village. The final attack was conducted on November 6 at a time when the Italian disaster at Caporetto (see page 235) and the Allied creation of a war council pointed to the curbing of Haig's freedom of action. Canadian and Australian troops were among those who succeeded in taking the ruins of Passchendaele. The following day Haig's chief of staff visited the salient for the first time.

Sheltering in holes in the mud
These Canadian machine-gunners were among the men who had to endure the miseries of fighting in the mud at Ypres. While holes in the mud might provide shelter, they could also become death-traps in which men drowned.

Scene near Zonnebeke in September
In the vicinity of Polygon Wood, dead Germans lie at the entrance to a dug-out that has been destroyed by British artillery. This area was at the centre of a British attack in September, when losses on both sides were high.

THIRD BATTLE OF YPRES

JULY 31 – NOVEMBER 6, 1917

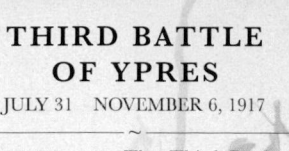

The Third Battle of Ypres was to become notorious for the particularly appalling conditions in which it was fought. In the first main offensive, launched on July 31, some small gains were made over three days before heavy rain brought operations to a halt. The offensive was renewed on August 10, and again on the 16th, but little progress was made. Accepting that there would be no immediate breakthrough, the British then decided on a series of set-piece attacks – to begin on September 20 – in which prolonged pounding would gradually wear down the Germans. The battle culminated in a terrible struggle in the mud to capture the village of Passchendaele – finally accomplished on November 6.

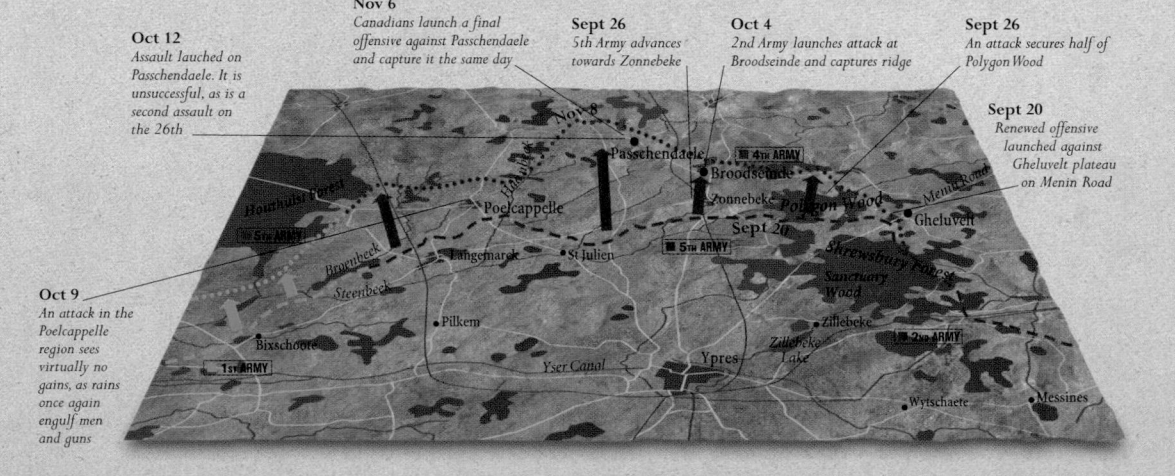

British troops at Langemarck
Langemarck was captured on August 16. According to the original battle-plan, the date should have been August 2 or 3.

KEY

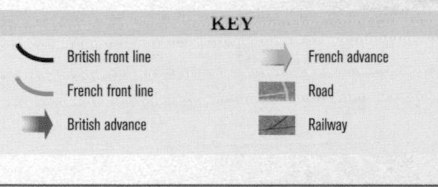

- British front line
- French front line
- British advance
- French advance
- Road
- Railway

The first offensives
July 31–August 22

The French 1st Army and British 2nd Army met with more immediate success than the army they were supporting – the British Fifth. However, after three days, control of the German first line had been secured.

3:50 am July 31
Offensive launched. Gains are made on Bixschoote, Pilkem and St Julien ridges to north of Ypres

Aug 16
Langemarck is taken in renewed offensive, but there is little progress on the right

Aug 10
Following a halt in the fighting, British launch offensive against Langemarck-Gheluvelt line

Aug 22
The British Fifth Army is halted on the Menin Road

The build-up to Passchendaele
September 20–November 6

The first of a series of set-piece attacks against the Germans was launched on September 20 on the Menin Road. Further attacks then followed, at intervals of five or six days, on Polygon Wood, Broodseinde Ridge and Poelcappelle, before the attempt to take Passchendaele began on October 12.

Oct 12
Assault lauched on Passchendaele. It is unsuccessful, as is a second assault on the 26th

Nov 6
Canadians launch a final offensive against Passchendaele and capture it the same day

Sept 26
5th Army advances towards Zonnebeke

Oct 4
2nd Army launches attack at Broodseinde and captures ridge

Sept 26
An attack secures half of Polygon Wood

Sept 20
Renewed offensive launched against Gheluvelt plateau on Menin Road

Oct 9
An attack in the Poelcappelle region sees virtually no gains, as rains once again engulf men and guns

Official casualty figures for the Third Battle of Ypres suggest that the British suffered 245,000, the French 8,000, and the Germans 260,000. However, most of the 380,000 casualties suffered by the British in the second half of 1917 were incurred at Ypres. A particularly appalling statistic is that in the final stages of the battle, up to one in four British dead may have drowned in the mud.

> *We were never hit, by the grace of God, for the deep mud was our salvation, that mud which we cursed and in which we stuck and staggered, slipped and slid, tugging our boots out of it each time we made a fresh step. Jerry's shells showered us with filth, they disturbed the riddled and broken corpses, they re-shredded the putrid flesh into scraps. It was easy to go "missing"... if you got hit, the chances were you slipped into some yawning shell-hole full of greyly opaque water concealing unmentionable things and you drowned there.*
>
> GUNNER LIEUTENANT R.G. DIXON, 14TH BATTERY,
> ROYAL GARRISON ARTILLERY

THE BATTLE OF CAMBRAI

The failure to make any real gains at Ypres put pressure on the British generals to produce a victory, any victory, on the Western Front in the autumn of 1917. In June, August and again in early September, the Tank Corps had proposed that it should lead a limited offensive over ground of its own choice. However, the fighting in Flanders meant that it was October before the proposed offensive was approved. The need to distract German attention from the Italian front provided an additional motive for launching an attack in front of Cambrai, a major rail centre, where the German defences on the Western Front were at their strongest.

The Tank Corps calculated that the depth and nature of the German trench system in this sector pointed to it being relatively lightly manned by an enemy that would not be expecting an attack. The element of surprise would be enhanced by the lack of preliminary artillery bombardment and the first use of tanks *en masse*.

The majority of tanks would be used in groups of three and would carry fascines (large bundles of brushwood) to drop into trenches and provide crossing points. Once each of the Germans' three main trench positions had been crossed, the tanks and accompanying infantry would clear the trenches. Cavalry would be held in reserve for the exploitation of any breach that might be made. Vague plans were devised for the crossing of the Sensée and driving northward in order to roll up the German first line.

INITIAL SUCCESS

After slowly reaching their start lines, at 6:20 am on the morning of November 20, 381 fighting tanks began to advance towards a 9-km (6-mile) stretch of the German first line.

Under a cloak of secrecy, the British Third Army assembled a total of 474 tanks, 1,003 guns and mortars and six of its 19 infantry divisions in a sector held by seven under-strength divisions of the German Second Army. Only on the eve of the British attack was security compromised and then not seriously: the Germans were not convinced by the information they received of the impending attack. In any case, the information came too late for them to act upon it effectively.

British troops at work in the Flanders mud
Men of the 2nd Monmouthshire Regiment repair a plank road near Hooge during the Third Battle of Ypres. In the background an injured man is carried away on a stretcher.

MEDICAL SERVICES AT THE FRONT

FOR THE MEDICAL PROFESSION, the First World War was an intensive learning experience – a huge laboratory and clinical trial – which directly involved thousands more medical staff than any previous war. Far fewer soldiers fell to "invisible enemies" such as typhoid than in the past. Yet despite medical advances, one in three casualties died in the First World War, compared to one in seven in the Second.

In their battle against germs and infections, the British army's "khaki doctors" drew on recent experience in the South African War of 1899–1902 and rose to the challenges of trench warfare. "Trench foot" was treated by purifying water with chlorine, fumigating clothes and ensuring regular bathing during rotations out of line. Injections averted tetanus and, for gas gangrene infections, there was "Dakin's solution", an antiseptic fluid developed by a British chemist and a French-American surgeon.

Wounds from shellfire were often fatal unless treated immediately, but once soldiers on the Western Front reached a field hospital they had a good chance of survival. Casualties were carried to regimental first aid posts, and then advanced dressing stations behind the front line. From there, they went by road to casualty clearing stations, then by rail to the stationary base hospitals. British troops with seriously disabling "blighty wounds" were evacuated to the UK, although fewer soldiers were evacuated after 1916. By 1917 casualty clearing stations had been developed into proper field hospitals, where American surgery teams played a key role.

The huge casualties and duration of hostilities forced governments and aid organizations to co-ordinate a vast range of medical services. Thousands of buildings were requisitioned. Army doctors worked with administrators, surgeons and specialists, and nursing became a major field of war work.

Wounded soldiers waiting for transport
Many men on both sides dreamed of a serious, but not fatal, wound that would get them sent home for treatment in a hospital far away from the front line.

Vital tools
The tools for treating injuries did not include antibiotics, which meant that even minor wounds could result in limbs being amputated.

AMPUTATION TOOLS

MEDICAL ORDERLY'S POUCH

MORPHINE AMPOULES

STERILIZING EQUIPMENT

Dressing station
The condition of wounded men was checked on arrival at a dressing station. It would often take some time to then move the men on to the casualty clearing station, out of range of enemy artillery.

Front-line treatment
American stretcher-bearers apply a field dressing before taking the casualty to a regimental aid post.

Horse-drawn ambulances
Critically injured men had to endure a slow and bumpy ride when taken by ambulance to the casualty clearing stations.

THE TANK: NEW DEVELOPMENTS

~

THE NATURE OF TRENCH WARFARE required both a main battle tank to breach the enemy's defences, and a light tank capable of exploiting a breakthrough. The British improved their Mark I battle tank, leading to the Mark IV and then the Mark V. The Mark V was slightly longer with better trench-crossing capability and was the first main battle tank with a single driver.

The French heavy tanks were of limited use. Of the 132 Schneiders committed on April 16, 1917, 57 were destroyed and many others damaged beyond repair; of the 16 St Chamond tanks used in May 1917, 15 ditched as a result of limited trench-crossing capabilities. The German A7V was equally unsuccessful with only 15 built. The Germans preferred captured Mark IVs.

The French decided to concentrate on their Renault FT 17 light tank, building over 4,000 by the end of the war. Its performance was unremarkable, but its single gun in a rotating turret was pioneering. The British light tank, the Medium A or Whippet, was unusual in having engine and fuel tanks at the front, and its turret with three fixed machine-guns in the rear.

All early tanks had problems that limited their effectiveness. The main battle tanks lacked the speed and range to penetrate deeply, while light tanks could not negotiate heavily-cratered ground or survive enemy fire. Both had limited visibility and lacked the radios necessary to communicate with one another or supporting arms. Heat and lack of ventilation left the crews exhausted.

British Mark IV tank
The tank that fought at Cambrai in 1917 was not very different from the Mark I of 1916, but it did have a better radiator, a silencer and tracks with better grip. It dispensed with the rear wheels.

pistol grip

Renault FT 17 Tank
The most successful French tank of the war, the Renault also served with the American forces. Here a Renault operates with US infantry during the summer of 1918.

Preparing for battle
These British Mark IV tanks awaiting rail transport to the front to take part in the Cambrai attack are equipped with fascines. These large wooden bundles were dropped into an enemy trench, enabling the tank to get across.

Whippet or Medium A
With a twin 45 bhp engine, the Whippet was capable of a speed of 13.4 kph (8.3 mph), positively sprinting when compared to the slow pace of other First World War tanks.

German failure
Germany's only war-time tank was the A7V Sturmpanzerwagen. With a 57-mm (2.2-in) main armament, six machine-guns and a crew of 18, it was slow, unstable and not capable of crossing heavily cratered or rough ground. "Wotan", shown here, took part in the German spring 1918 offensive.

village over the next two days failed. The tanks were able to fight their way into Fontaine, but they were at a disadvantage in the narrow streets, where the Germans found they could be halted by throwing bundles of grenades underneath them. On the 23rd the British took Bourlon Wood, with heavy losses. They failed, however, to take Bourlon village, and their positions in the wood soon became untenable. By the 26th the British had few tanks available and the German reinforcement of the Cambrai sector was all but complete. On the 27th the Germans defeated the last British attack on Fontaine and decided to undertake the entire operations. They intended to eliminate the British salient by striking directly into the original British positions on the right.

GERMAN COUNTERATTACK

On November 30 the German attack ripped open the 29th Infantry Division's line around Gouzeaucourt. A British collapse was only averted by German confusion following initial success, and the timely intervention of a few British tanks. The battle ended on the right of the 4th, with an ordered withdrawal by the British. On reaching their new line they still retained the area around Flesquières. They had, however, ceded their other gains and had even lost fresh ground to the south.

Both sides had suffered about 45,000 casualties. The outcome of the battle — particularly disappointing for the British after the success of the first day — was partly due to the unreliability of the tanks and the lack of adequate reserves to consolidate the gains that had been made.

the German front. The tanks terrified the Germans, who were powerless to stop them smashing through the barbed wire in front of their trenches. By the end of just one day, the Third Army had penetrated 8 km (5 miles), destroying the equivalent of two German divisions and capturing 120 guns and 7,500 prisoners. There was jubilation back in Britain, where church bells rang for the first time since 1914 and the newspapers proclaimed the greatest British victory of the war.

Although successful, the operation had been marred by the failure to capture Flesquières in the centre, less than halfway between the starting point and Cambrai. One infantry division had not adopted tank corps procedures, leaving armour and infantry exposed to needless losses. The village was captured on the 21st, but that same day the British suffered heavy losses in securing Anneux, Cantaing and Fontaine, and they failed to capitalize on a temporary 5-km (3.5-mile) breach in the German line around Fontaine. Tank losses were also heavy; by November 23 only 92 would still be operational.

GERMAN RESISTANCE

British losses on the 21st were partly due to the arrival of a fresh German division from the Eastern Front. German counterattacks at Noyelles and Nine Wood marked the beginning of the British struggle to retain their gains. On the 22nd the Germans took Fontaine, and British attempts to recapture the

Ditched Mark IV tank at Cambrai
British troops survey a tank that failed to cross a German trench 1 km (half a mile) west of Ribecourt on November 20. Such sights were common at Cambrai.

Head protection
Tank crews used many purpose-built and adapted items of head gear to protect them-selves from the splinters of hot metal created by bullets hitting the tank.

LEATHER TANK CREW HELMET
Chain mail visor
Slatted eye-protectors
Riveted leather helmet

ADAPTED BRITISH HELMET
Chain mail eye guard

Anti-tank rifle
The Germans developed this new weapon to try to neutralize the tank. Known as the "elephant gun", it fired single 13.3-mm rounds that penetrated armour up to 30 mm (1.18 in) thick.
Spiked bipod support
Front sight

British troops in Belgium, 1917
Almost all the British troops in Belgium in 1917 were in the Ypres salient, where from July they fought in what became known as the Battle of Passchendaele. Rain and mud helped to turn the battlefield into what many saw as a "living hell".

Russia and the Eastern Front

REVOLUTION AND THE WAR IN RUSSIA
MARCH – DECEMBER 1917

1917 saw the efforts of succeeding Russian governments to maintain the war effort finally unravel. The Provisional Government that took power in the wake of the "February Revolution" remained committed to the war. However, the failure of the Kerensky Offensive and the increasing disintegration of the Russian army allowed the Bolsheviks under Lenin to seize power and sue for an armistice with Germany.

BY THE END OF 1916 it was clear that the tsar's days as an autocratic ruler were numbered. Nicholas II had proved an incompetent commander and continued to exclude representatives of the Duma (parliament) from real power. At the same time, the mass of the people were suffering from the consequences of a poorly managed war economy, and city-dwellers in particular were increasingly desperate for change at the top. In the first eight weeks of 1917, Petrograd saw strikes, lock-outs and queues for inadequate supplies of flour.

THE FEBRUARY REVOLUTION

On March 8 (February 23 by the old Russian calendar) a march by women in honour of International Women's Day grew into a mass demonstration against the continuation of war and Russia's autocratic government. Petrograd's military commander tried to use the army to restore order but the troops sided with the protestors, and anti-tsarist revolutionaries took over the railway stations, telephones and artillery supplies.

This "February Revolution" united the workers', peasants' and soldiers' deputies of the Petrograd Soviet (council) with the politicians of the Duma, who elected a Provisional (provisional) Government in that it was to precede the adoption of a democratic constitution and election). On March 14 (March 1 by the old Russian calendar), the Petrograd Soviet called on every military unit to elect a soviet of its own. On the following day the Provisional Government issued an eight-point programme calling for the appointment of elected officials in local government and the replacement of the imperial state police by a people's militia. That same day, Nicholas II was compelled to abdicate.

The Provisional Government was immediately recognized by the Allies, concerned to keep Russia in the war. It remained committed to the war, believing that a compromise peace could not be obtained.

International Women's Day demonstration
Carrying a banner that reads "Comrades, Women and Soldiers, support our demands", women march in the demonstration that triggered the "February Revolution". The tsar abdicated, but Russia stayed in the war.

Lenin addresses a crowd
The driving force of the Bolshevik Party, Lenin was helped by the Germans to return home from exile.

KEY
- Events in Russia Mar 8 – Dec 15
- Main offensives on the Eastern Front Jun 29–Sept 5

Timeline

- **MARCH 8** — March in Petrograd on International Women's Day grows into mass demonstration; start of "February Revolution"
- **MARCH 12** — Troops mutiny and join demonstrations in Petrograd
- **MARCH 14** — Provisional Government proclaimed, with liberal Prince Lvov as prime minister
- **MARCH 15** — Tsar Nicholas II abdicates
- **MARCH 22** — Provisional Government recognized by several foreign nations, including Great Britain, France, Italy and USA
- **APRIL 16** — Lenin returns from exile in Switzerland, his safe rail passage organized by Germans
- **MAY 16** — Kerensky becomes war minister
- **MAY 19** — Provisional Government issues declaration stating its intention not to seek separate peace for Russia
- **JUNE 21** — Kerensky reviews new Women's "Death Battalion" in Petrograd
- **JUNE 29** — Kerensky Offensive begins with two-day preliminary bombardment
- **JULY 16** — "July Days" uprising, backed by Bolsheviks, begins in Petrograd
- **JULY 19** — Germans advance 15 km (10 miles) on first day of counterattack
- **JULY 19** — "July Days" uprising put down; Lenin flees to Finland
- **JULY 21** — Kerensky becomes prime minister
- **AUGUST 1** — General Kornilov replaces Brusilov as commander-in-chief
- **AUGUST 3** — Austro-Hungarian forces reach Czernowitz
- **AUGUST 6** — Mackensen's Danube Army begins successful counter-offensive in Moldavia
- **SEPTEMBER 1** — German Riga offensive begins
- **SEPTEMBER 5** — Fall of Riga
- **SEPTEMBER 8** — Kerensky dismisses Kornilov, who then marches on Petrograd
- **SEPTEMBER 14** — Kerensky proclaims socialist republic. Kornilov surrenders in suburbs of Petrograd
- **OCTOBER 8** — Kerensky gives moderate socialists a majority in new coalition government
- **NOVEMBER 5** — Kerensky attempts to arrest Bolshevik leaders, sparking off
- **NOVEMBER 6/7** — Kerensky flees Petrograd. Bolshevik coup sees Lenin heading government and Trotsky as foreign minister — the planned "October Revolution"
- **NOVEMBER 26** — Bolshevik government requests armistice
- **DECEMBER 15** — Armistice signed between Russia and Germany

THE EASTER RISING

THE IMPACT OF THE WAR on civilians caused unrest on the home fronts of the combatant states. Outside imperial Russia, however, this did not develop into armed insurrection before 1918. The one exception was Ireland where, in April 1916, a group of radical nationalists staged an uprising against British rule and proclaimed an independent Irish republic.

They seized key buildings in Dublin on April 24, and in the six-day battle that followed the city centre was extensively damaged. This "Easter Rising" was crushed by around 8,000 British troops stationed in Ireland. The nationalists numbered no more than 3,000 men and women, and initially they did not receive much public support. However, the execution of 15 of their leaders increased sympathy for their cause. (Eamon de Valera, later premier and president of the Republic of Ireland, escaped execution as, technically, he was an American citizen.) In all but the northeast of the country, support grew for

British forces in Dublin, 1916
During the six days of fighting to suppress the rising, 116 British soldiers were killed.

independence, as opposed to the more limited "home rule" promised by a 1914 Act of Parliament but shelved for the duration of the war.

Despite this growth in nationalism, thousands of Irishmen enlisted in the British Army, their contribution has only recently been acknowledged. After the execution of the rising's leaders, one Irish soldier commented: "These men will go down in history as heroes and martyrs and I will go down – if I go down at all – as a bloody British officer".

Easter Rising aftermath
British troops patrol outside the battle-scarred General Post Office building on Sackville Street after its recapture on April 28. This had served as the rebels' Dublin headquarters.

German rifle shipped to the Irish
The 20,000 German-supplied rifles that the Irish nationalist Roger Casement attempted to ship to the rebels were captured, as was Casement himself.

Government. Translated into the slogan "Land, Peace and Bread", the Bolsheviks' anti-war stance won great support among the Russian soldiers, mostly peasants who only wanted to stay alive and get home to benefit from the Provisional Government's promised land reforms.

Vladimir Lenin. With regard to the war, Lenin believed that the defeat of Russia would facilitate a further, more radical revolution. After the February Revolution, some Bolsheviks, including Stalin, had returned from exile in Siberia to Petrograd and Moscow. The Germans could see some benefit in Lenin also returning to Russia, and through intermediaries they made an offer that allowed him to cross German territory in a "sealed" train. A single-carriage train carried Lenin and 31 of his comrades back to Russia via Frankfurt, Berlin and Stockholm, and on April 16 he arrived at the Finland Station in Petrograd.

Since February, soviets of workers, soldiers and sailors had sprung up all over Russia, and the Bolshevik Party had grown into a mass movement. Many of the activists were stunned when Lenin scarcely acknowledged the achievements of the February Revolution, instead proclaiming his uncompromising "April Theses" against the "imperialist" war and the "capitalist" Provisional

with enemy forces occupying considerable areas of imperial Russia's territory. Moreover, the Russian army began 1917 better equipped than at any stage since September 1914. Russia's new leaders hoped that war weariness would be balanced by a new spirit of democratic patriotism.

BOLSHEVIK ACTIVITY

The eagerness of the Provisional Government to stay in the war was not shared by the Bolshevik Party (later known as the Communist Party), whose leader was the Zurich-based exile

And now the people take their revenge. There are fires everywhere in Petrograd, in all prisons, all police headquarters. If they set fire to the Palace of Justice it is because in the eyes of the people it was a fortress for the police, in the same way as the Bastille was the symbol of tyranny for the people of Tsars.

MARYLIE MARKOVICH ON EVENTS
IN PETROGRAD, FEBRUARY 1917

THE KERENSKY OFFENSIVE

It was against this background that the Provisional Government pressed ahead with plans to launch an offensive in July – the Kerensky Offensive. Alexander Kerensky, who had made his mark in the pre-war Duma as a moderate socialist, was appointed war minister in the Provisional Government of Prince Lvov on May 16. He then set about planning a "revolutionary offensive" with the aim of recapturing Lemberg (Lvov). The main effort, by the Seventh Army to the north of the Dniester River, was to be supported by the Eleventh Army in an attack directed

"War until Victory"
The Provisional Government believed that the war should continue in defence of Russia – a policy promoted in this poster.

against Zloczow (Zolochiv). Over a front of some 64 km (40 miles), the Russians concentrated 370 heavy, 158 medium and over 800 light guns. Unfortunately, this unprecedented number of guns meant that the tactics used in the Brusilov Offensive of 1916 – taking the opposition by surprise by attacking after a light bombardment – were rejected in favour of saturation bombardment.

From the outset, two major problems threatened to turn the offensive into a disaster. First, in revolutionary Russia no plan of campaign could remain secret. By the end of May the Germans had detailed knowledge of the plan, giving them time to prepare defensive positions in depth. Second, Russian preparations were woefully inadequate. Co-operation between artillery and infantry was minimal, reserves were kept too far from the front, the rear areas were congested with unused cavalry divisions, and commanders, staffs and formations changed constantly. There were also increasingly deep divisions within the army that rendered it, according to one onlooker, a debating society rather than a military organization.

The "Women's Death Battalion", July 1917
The Russian Orthodox patriarch blesses a women's battalion in Moscow before it departs for the front. The battalion was formed by Maria Bochkareva at a time when large numbers of men were deserting the Russian army.

OPENING STAGES OF THE OFFENSIVE

A two-day preliminary bombardment was followed, on July 1, by infantry attacks. The Germans withdrew to their second defensive line and the attacking Russians were generally cut to pieces. In a few places they succeeded in breaking into the third German line, and there was fierce fighting around Bresany (Bereshany) and Lysonia, the two strongest German positions. The Russians, however, were exhausted and were subsequently overwhelmed.

The Eleventh Army was able to register some gains against the Austro-Hungarians. South of the Dniester, an ill-prepared Austro-Hungarian Third Army was defeated and obliged to withdraw 50 km (30 miles) to Lomnica, the Russian Eighth Army securing Halicz (Galich) on July 12. But these counted for little alongside the failure elsewhere; by July 6 the main Russian effort had ended.

HUTIER TACTICS
~

OSKAR VON HUTIER WAS A CORPS COMMANDER on the Eastern Front from April 1915 and became commander of the Eighth Army in front of Riga in 1917. In September 1917 this army routed the Russian Twelfth Army in a matter of hours – a result of Russian demoralization and weakness, and the German employment of tactics that bore the name of the army commander. The Hutier, or Infiltration, Tactics, involved the use of infantry companies, with high firepower provided by light machine-guns, flamethrowers and mortars, moving behind short but overwhelming artillery barrages. Their aim was to get into enemy rear areas, specifically the artillery positions. Gas and smoke shells were to be used to engulf the main points of enemy resistance, which were to be bypassed and left to a follow-up infantry attack to eliminate.

After Riga, the Hutier format was employed in October 1917 at Caporetto and in the counterattack at Cambrai on the Western Front, where Hutier was given command of the Eighteenth Army. This formation was to register major gains in the March 1918 offensive and modest initial gains in June 1918; thereafter it was forced onto the defensive. Hutier Tactics were distilled in *Der Angriff im Stellungskriege* (Attack in static warfare), published in 1918, setting out the idea that infantry should determine the pace of advance and stressing the importance of surprise and use of the *Feuerwalze* (creeping barrage).

Russian trench during German gas attack
"Hutier Tactics" involved bypassing major enemy strongpoints, which were to be dealt with by later waves of troops. Smoke and gas shells were used to suppress these positions during the initial assault.

Oskar von Hutier
Von Hutier's innovative tactics were first used during the Riga offensive at the beginning of September 1917. They proved so successful that they were replicated at Caporetto in Italy and again in the German offensives on the Western Front in the spring of 1918.

GERMAN COUNTER-OFFENSIVE
The problems that beset the attack now combined with the arrival of eight German divisions in Galicia. With these forces the Germans launched a counter-offensive on July 19. Tarnopol (Ternopil) was taken on July 26 and Czernowitz on August 3. General Kornilov – appointed as commander-in-chief in place of Brusilov on August 1 – attempted to reconstitute the Russian defence with the aid of draconian discipline that resulted in thousands of summary executions. The Russian army was, however, on the brink of disintegration.

THE RIGA OFFENSIVE
On September 1 Hutier's German Eighth Army attacked Kornilov's Twelfth Army around Riga, on the Baltic. The German plan was to cross the Dvina above the port and advance to the north and east – thus threatening Petrograd – while turning west to eliminate the Riga salient. After a brief bombardment, in which gas and smoke shells were fired at Russian positions on the north bank, three German divisions crossed the river on pontoon bridges.

The Kaiser's retinue in German-occupied Riga
The Riga Offensive effectively ended the war between Germany and Russia, although the Germans subsequently pursued the Russian Twelfth Army along the Dvina River.

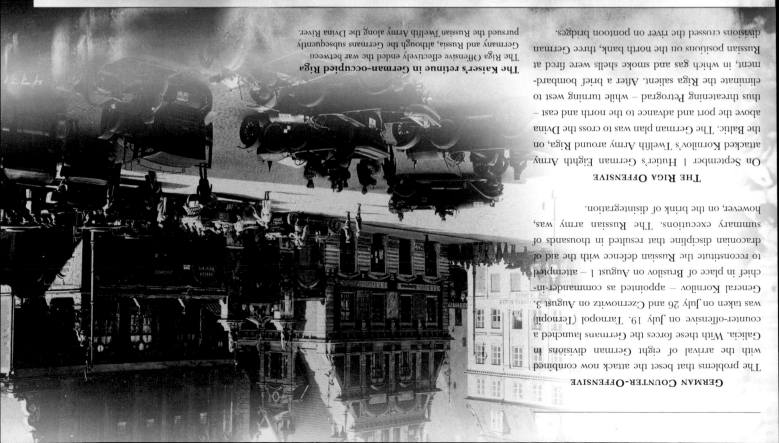

They turned west to capture Riga, which the Russians evacuated on the 2nd as they began a rapid retreat. The Germans occupied the port on the 5th and for the next three weeks pursued the remnants of the Russian army along the Drina. They abandoned their plans to advance on Petrograd as it became clear that the Russian Provisional Government – led by Kerensky as prime minister since July 20 – was on the brink of collapse.

THE OCTOBER REVOLUTION

The Provisional Government had maintained the imperial government's fiscal and taxation policies and both inflation and the amount of money in circulation doubled between March (February) and November (October). As real wages fell and food shortages continued, the Provisional Government had lost the good will of workers in the cities. In the "July Days" uprising of July 16–19, armed workers, sailors and soldiers had tried, and failed, to seize power in Petrograd. Lenin had been forced into hiding, eventually taking refuge in Finland.

Architect of the Red Army
Leon Trotsky was the Commissar for War during the Russian Civil War that followed the October Revolution. He proved an inspired military organizer and played a key role in securing victory for the Bolsheviks over the forces of the opposing "Whites".

On September 8 the Provisional Government dismissed Kornilov, who marched on Petrograd with the aim of establishing a law-and-order dictatorship. He reached the suburbs five days later, but armed workers blocked his way. Alexeev, the

Demonstration in front of the Winter Palace
Economic hardships, war-weariness and lack of confidence in the government only served to increase popular demonstrations in Petrograd and elsewhere.

Bolshevik propaganda poster
The army, bourgeoisie, clergy and landowners were all opposed to the Bolshevik-led "October Revolution". In this poster they are caricatured proclaiming, "Down with the soviet".

new commander-in-chief, persuaded him to surrender on September 14, but governmental authority was hopelessly compromised.

In early October, Lenin slipped back into Petrograd, convinced the time was ripe for a Bolshevik coup. Kerensky knew of the threat posed by the Bolsheviks but could not take decisive measures against them as they were in control of the crucial Military-Revolutionary Committee of the Petrograd Soviet. Led by Leon Trotsky, this now served as a committee for the overthrow of the Provisional Government. On the evening of November 6/7 (October 24/25), it put its plans into effect, and by November 8 a Bolshevik-controlled government had been set up. In the words of Lenin:

"The task for which the people have been struggling has been assured – the immediate offer of a democratic peace, the abolition of the landed property of the landlords, worker control over production, and the creation of a Soviet Government."

Lenin was the leader of the new government and Trotsky was in charge of foreign affairs.

ARMISTICE WITH GERMANY

On November 26 the Bolshevik government asked for an armistice, and within days negotiations had begun at Brest-Litovsk. They were concluded on December 15, 1917; peace talks began a week later. Russia ceased to be a military factor in the war, allowing the German high command to draw upon some 80 divisions in the east as reinforcements for the Western Front. For the next three years, however, Russia was to be devastated by the civil war – between the "Reds" (Bolsheviks) and the "Whites" (anti-Bolsheviks) – which cost more lives than all the Eastern Front battles.

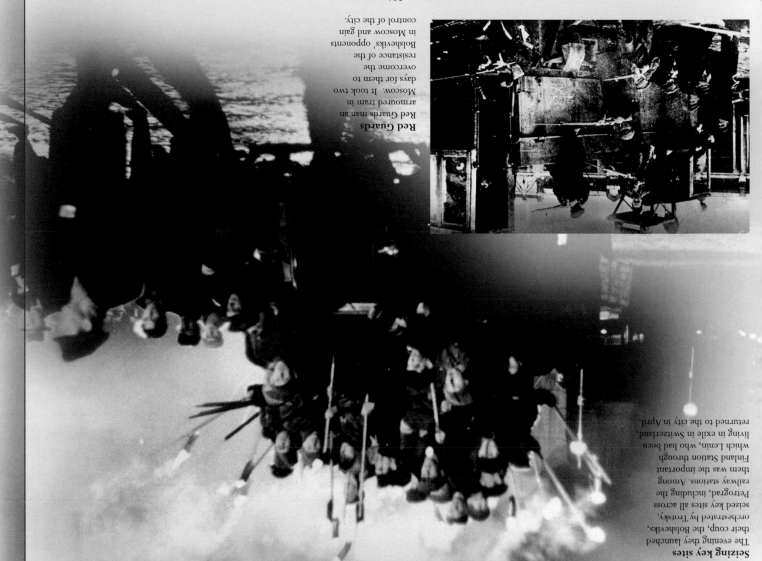

THE BOLSHEVIK COUP

O N THE EVENING OF November 6/7, the Military-Revolutionary Committee's forces picked key government buildings in Petrograd, and took control of the telegraph offices and railway stations. They also set up roadblocks on the bridges and around the Winter Palace, where the Provisional Government was in session. None of these actions was resisted, and the streets of Petrograd remained calm. That same night, Lenin joined the other Bolshevik leaders at the Smolny Convent, once a girls' school and now the headquarters of the Petrograd Soviet. On the following day, the revolutionary forces surrounded the Winter Palace, where the politicians of the Provisional Government were waiting, in vain, to be rescued. Very early next morning, the palace fell to the Bolsheviks but, contrary to later accounts, it was never "stormed". From the cruiser *Aurora*, which was moored on the Neva River across from the Winter Palace, Bolshevik sailors fired one blank salvo, and Kerensky was able to slip out of the building by a side entrance and leave the city by car. It was not a coincidence that a Congress of Soviets from all over Russia was due to open on the very next day. Packed with Bolshevik delegates from the provinces, it enabled the leaders of the October Revolution to neutralize opposition from other socialists and radicals, and to clinch the transfer of power from the Provisional Government to the Bolshevik-controlled Soviet of People's Commissars.

Seizing key sites
The evening they launched their coup, the Bolsheviks, orchestrated by Trotsky, seized key sites all across Petrograd, including the railway stations. Among them was the important Finland Station through which Lenin, who had been living in exile in Switzerland, returned to the city in April.

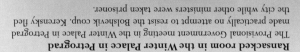

Ransacked room in the Winter Palace in Petrograd
The Provisional Government meeting in the Winter Palace in Petrograd made practically no attempt to resist the Bolshevik coup. Kerensky fled the city while other ministers were taken prisoner.

Red Guards
Red Guards man an armoured tram in Moscow. It took two days for them to overcome the resistance of the Bolsheviks' opponents in Moscow and gain control of the city.

The Italian Front

DURING THE FIRST 19 months of their involvement in the First World War, the Italians launched a series of offensives on the Isonzo and took part in operations in northern Albania and at Salonika. Only once in this period, in the spring of 1916, did Austria-Hungary initiate an offensive against Italy. The offensive was intended to raise morale among both troops and civilians. Deprived, however, of any support from Falkenhayn – who was concentrating on making preparations for the German offensive at Verdun in February – it soon became clear that his hopes for a quick, decisive victory would not be realized.

THE TRENTINO OFFENSIVE

The Austro-Hungarian attack was staged by the Third and Eleventh Armies. Sometimes called the "Asiago Offensive", it opened on May 15 in the Trentino, in a sector stretching through the mountains from west of Rovereto to west of Borgo. Up to now this had been the quiet sector, where the resident Italian First Army was known as "the convalescent corps" on account of the importance attached to it by the Italian high command. Conrad's intention was to cut through the left flank of the First Army and advance towards Venice, thus cutting off the Italian forces on the Isonzo.

The Austro-Hungarians had gathered together 2,000 guns, and were able to open their offensive with a punishing barrage. The Italians, knowing that the attack was coming, resisted it heroically and fought in defence of one position after another, but they were slowly driven back. At the same time, the Austro-Hungarian forces were greatly hampered by the difficult, mountainous – sometimes snow-swept – terrain. Within five days their supply lines were being stretched to their limit and their artillery was no longer able to give them the support they so greatly needed.

War in the mountains
With all but a small section of the Italian frontier with Austria-Hungary in the mountains, specialist *Alpini* mountain troops were at a premium.

Austrian mountain gun
Artillery used on the mountainous Italian Front had to be more portable than usual.

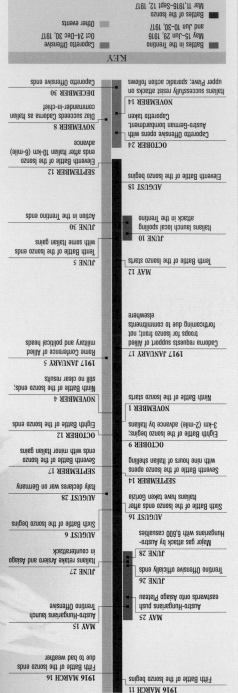

BEYOND THE ISONZO
MARCH 1916 – DECEMBER 1917

By mid-March 1916 Italy's five Isonzo offensives, fought in some of the most extreme conditions of the entire war, had made limited progress against the Austro-Hungarians. But the Austro-Hungarian Trentino Offensive in May, followed by more assaults on the Isonzo front, undermined the Italian army's morale. It was rapidly pushed back 95 km (60 miles) by the Austro-German Caporetto Offensive in October 1917.

1916 MARCH 11 — Fifth Battle of the Isonzo begins

1916 MARCH 16 — Fifth Battle of the Isonzo ends due to bad weather

MAY 15 — Austro-Hungarians launch Trentino Offensive

MAY 25 — Austro-Hungarians push eastwards onto Asiago Plateau

JUNE 26 — Trentino Offensive officially ends

JUNE 27 — Italians retake Arsiero and Asiago in counterattack

JUNE 28 — Major gas attack by Austro-Hungarians with 6,600 casualties

AUGUST 6 — Sixth Battle of the Isonzo begins

AUGUST 16 — Sixth Battle of the Isonzo ends after Italians have taken Gorizia

AUGUST 28 — Italy declares war on Germany

SEPTEMBER 14 — Seventh Battle of the Isonzo opens with nine hours of Italian shelling

SEPTEMBER 17 — Seventh Battle of the Isonzo ends with minor Italian gains

OCTOBER 9 — Eighth Battle of the Isonzo begins; 3-km (2-mile) advance by Italians

OCTOBER 12 — Eighth Battle of the Isonzo ends

NOVEMBER 1 — Ninth Battle of the Isonzo starts

NOVEMBER 4 — Ninth Battle of the Isonzo ends; still no clear results

1917 JANUARY 5 — Rome Conference of Allied military and political heads

1917 JANUARY 17 — Cadorna requests support of Allied troops for Isonzo front, not forthcoming due to commitments elsewhere

MAY 12 — Tenth Battle of the Isonzo starts

JUNE 5 — Tenth Battle of the Isonzo ends with some Italian gains

JUNE 10 — Italians launch local spoiling attack in the Trentino

JUNE 30 — Action in the Trentino ends

AUGUST 18 — Eleventh Battle of the Isonzo begins

SEPTEMBER 12 — Eleventh Battle of the Isonzo ends after Italian 10-km (6-mile) advance

OCTOBER 24 — Caporetto Offensive opens with Austro-German bombardment. Caporetto taken

NOVEMBER 8 — Diaz succeeds Cadorna as Italian commander-in-chief

NOVEMBER 14 — Italians successfully resist attacks on upper Piave; sporadic action follows

DECEMBER 30 — Caporetto Offensive ends

KEY

Battles in the Trentino	May 15–Jun 29, 1916 and Jun 10–30, 1917
Caporetto Offensive	Oct 24–Dec 30, 1917
Battles of the Isonzo	Mar 11, 1916–Sept 12, 1917
Other events	

ITALIAN WITHDRAWAL AND COUNTERATTACK

On the 20th, when the Italians' appeals to Russia for assistance assumed a certain desperation, they took the decision to withdraw across most of the front. Though this withdrawal was completed by the 24th, the most threatening phase of the Trentino Offensive unfolded on the 25th, when Austro-Hungarian forces pushed forward towards Posina, while to the east they began the task of clearing the Asiago Plateau. By the 30th the Italians had withdrawn from both Asiago and Arsiero, and the Austro-Hungarians had established themselves within 6 km (4 miles) of the Sugana and in the rear of Italian positions around Borgo. They were not able to advance any further, however, the arrival of Italian Fifth Army reinforcements in effect spelling the end of the offensive. Though the Austro-Hungarians mounted further attacks in June, after the 12th their main effort was halted in readiness for the transfer of forces to Galicia where the Russian Brusilov Offensive (see pages 148–50) had been launched on June 4. The offensive officially ended on the 26th and the Italians reoccupied Arsiero and Asiago on the following day.

Nowhere had the Austro-Hungarian forces succeeded in advancing more than 19 km (12 miles), and while their losses were far lower than those of the Italians – 80,000 compared with 147,000 – they never posed any real threat of a breakthrough. The campaign had also worsened Austro-Hungarian relations with Falkenhayn, who had been angered by Conrad's disregard for his view that the Central Powers should concentrate on the Western Front and stay on the defensive against the Italians.

MOUNTAIN TRANSPORT

WAR IN THE ALPS created supply problems unlike those faced in any other theatre. Unable to outflank the Austro-Hungarians in the traditional manner, Italian troops climbed higher and higher up the mountains in an attempt to dominate the enemy positions. The Austro-Hungarians replied in kind, with the result that tens of thousands of soldiers found themselves spending whole winters at heights of over 3,000 m (10,000 ft). All needed to be supplied with ammunition, food and fuel for cooking and heating. The Italians erected *teleferiche*, overhead cableways, that were driven by oil or electric motors. The largest were up to 8 km (5 miles) long and rose by as much as 1,500 m (5,000 ft) between the starting-point and the destination. Smaller ones could be dismantled and re erected where required some of these were driven by manpower. Even in the most isolated positions guns would be hauled up and the wounded evacuated on swinging cradles.

Fresh rations
Food and ammunition were the most important supplies to be delivered. In 1917 there were 530 motor-driven *teleferiche* supplying the Italian army.

Mountain artillery
In the mountains any peak or ridgeline was a potential gun emplacement, but moving even one gun into position required technical expertise and muscle.

BATTLES OF THE ISONZO

Between Italy's entry into the war and the Trentino Offensive, Italian forces had undertaken five offensives across the Isonzo. The fifth, from March 11 to 16, had barely carried the Italians beyond the enemy outpost line. Following the failure of the Trentino Offensive, however, the Italians were able, in the Sixth Battle of the Isonzo, to take the fortified town of Gorizia (Görz) on August 9, and then to clear part of the Carso (Karst). The Austro-Hungarian defence had been weakened by the diversion of forces to Galicia, but the Fifth Army continued to hold Tolmino, so ensuring that the northern sector remained closed to the Italian Second Army. The losses of the Austro-Hungarians were limited to the south, where they were pushed back to the their original last line of resistance.

The Italian Third Army's performance in a series of actions on the Isonzo after August – in the Seventh, Eighth and Ninth battles of Isonzo – was doggedly determined, but there was no escaping the fact that the new Habsburg defences in the Carso threatened to make 1917 as exhausting as 1916 had been. Furthermore, by the end of the year, the Italian state and army, which had no strong national and military traditions to draw on, had been severely weakened by its efforts.

ALLIED PLANS FOR 1917

Over the winter of 1916–1917 the Allies agreed to synchronize their offensive efforts in the spring, launching an Italian offensive at the same time as the Arras and Aisne offensives. This, however, was made impossible for the Italians by the lateness of the spring. In the following weeks, as spring gave way to summer, Italy was the first of the Allies to feel the effects of Russia's February Revolution. The arrival on the Isonzo of Austro-Hungarian forces that had been transferred from the Eastern Front convinced the Italian high command of the need to retain the initiative for the remainder of 1917. Accordingly, it decided to launch two offensives south of Tolmino, with the main effort being made by the Third Army on the Carso. In fact, in both offensives – the Tenth and Eleventh Battles of the Isonzo – it was the Second Army, to the north of Gorizia (Görz), that made the major gains.

In the tenth battle, launched on May 12, the Second Army secured most of the mountains that barred the way to the Bainsizza Plateau. The Third Army, however, lost some of its gains in the area around Kostanjevica on the Carso to an Austro-Hungarian counterattack in the first days of June.

ACTION IN THE TRENTINO

On June 30 the Italians launched a local offensive in the Trentino. This was intended to eliminate the positions won by Austro-Hungarian forces in 1916, from which they could threaten Venice and the areas to the rear of the Italian armies on the Isonzo. The pattern of the Isonzo offensives, however, repeated itself, with a series of hard-fought and costly battles for individual peaks bringing few Italian gains. Furthermore, most of the gains were quickly eliminated by a major Austro-Hungarian effort, which inflicted significant morale-sapping losses on the Italians.

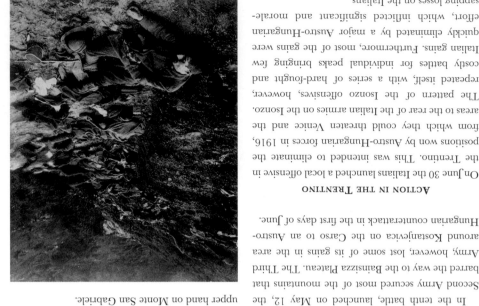

ELEVENTH BATTLE OF THE ISONZO

In the Eleventh Battle of the Isonzo, the Italian Third Army broke through the Austro-Hungarian front on August 21, and then cleared most of the Bainsizza Plateau. To the south, the Second Army failed to make any immediate major gains but broke two of the strongest enemy positions on the front. On August 21 the Italians cleared Monte Santo and on September 4 they succeeded in gaining the upper hand on Monte San Gabriele.

Such success cost the Italian army 155,000 casualties and exhausted it. The battle, however, convinced the Austro-Hungarians, reduced to their last defensive positions, that they could not face a twelfth battle of the Isonzo. Consequently, they sought the assistance of the Germans. Their request came at a time when Berlin, with some six divisions available for operations away from the Western Front, was contemplating a campaign in Moldavia to drive Romania from the war once and for all. Deciding, instead, to make a virtue of necessity, the German high command insisted upon command of an operation in which the Austro-Hungarian army was to play the supporting role.

THE CAPORETTO OFFENSIVE

Gathering some 15 divisions in the Fourteenth Army, the Germans planned to strike in the Tolmino area, where their ally had retained a bridgehead over the Isonzo, and to force an Italian withdrawal to the Tagliamento by threatening

A desperate defence

On the second day of the Caporetto offensive, Italian troops tried, unsuccessfully, to stem the Austro-German advance at Cividale to buy time to allow the Italian Third Army to retreat. The odds were overwhelming and these Italian troops paid the ultimate price.

Austro-Hungarian river crossing
The pursuit of the Italians following the breakthrough at Caporetto was delayed by supply problems. Here Austro-Hungarian troops transport supplies across the Tagliamento on a bridge that has been only partially repaired.

Collapse at Caporetto

In the weeks leading up to the Caporetto Offensive, the deployment of Italian troops in defensive positions was an inadequate response to the massing of German as well as Austro-Hungarian forces on the Isonzo front. The Italians were pushed back to the Piave before being able to stand their ground in mid-November. French and British divisions arrived in December to help strengthen front-line positions against future attacks.

the rear of the Italian Second and Third Armies. Some of the German staff thought that greater success might be possible and that a simultaneous effort should be made in the Trentino. However, the Central Powers lacked sufficient forces to make this second effort, and the armies committed to the offensive lacked the cavalry and motor transport to exploit success to the full.

What neither the German nor the Austro-Hungarian staffs could know was how far the battles on the Isonzo had completed the demoralization of the Italian army. Its awareness of failure and the futility of its sacrifices, of the little regard in which it was held by friend and foe alike, the example of the Russian revolution and the seething discontent within Italian society, had sapped the will of the Italian army. It was an army in which the treatment of the rank and file was at best abysmal and in which relations between regimental officers and staff were usually worse. Consequently, despite receiving detailed plans from deserting enemy officers and some six weeks' notice, the Italians did very little to strengthen defences in the Tolmino sector. The deployment of the Italian armies, with

the bulk of Second and Third Armies beyond the Isonzo, invited a defeat that was to be turned into a debacle by the refusal of many formations to fight.

AN AUSTRO-GERMAN ROUT

After a two-day delay caused by bad weather, the offensive began, on October 24, with a four-hour bombardment. A large number of gas shells was fired as it was known that the Italians had only primitive protection against gas. Two Italian corps were then annihilated as the Germans advanced 19 km (12 miles) from Tolmino and Plezzo, crossing the Isonzo and taking the town of Caporetto. Within three days the Italian Second Army abandoned all its mountain positions. On the 25th

the Italians fought to hold Cividale to allow the Third Army time to withdraw to the Tagliamento. Cividale fell on the 27th, Gorizia (Görz) on the 28th, and Udine – headquarters of Cadorna – on the 29th. Because of movement and supply problems, the Austro-Hungarian forces did not start to push back the Italians from the Tagliamento until November 2. It took another five days to cross the Livenza. Two divisions in the Trentino then joined the offensive, securing Asiago on the 9th, but the pace of the Austro-German offensive was slackening because of lengthening supply lines and a lack of reserves. The fall of Belluno on the 10th was among the last of the Italian losses.

On the 14th the Italians repulsed a series of attacks on the upper Piave. For the moment, and behind a river that in 1916 Cadorna had selected as the army's last line of resistance in the event of an emergency, the Italian army was safe and had the time to recover its 96-km (60-mile) retreat. It had lost about 10,000 killed, 30,000 wounded and 295,000 prisoners, and at one stage had not been able to account for more than 400,000 troops. Its recovery was to be slow.

Italian prisoners in Udine
On the eve of Caporetto the morale of the Italian army was very low. The Italians taken prisoner at Udine on October 29 were among almost 295,000 who surrendered to Austro-German forces during the offensive.

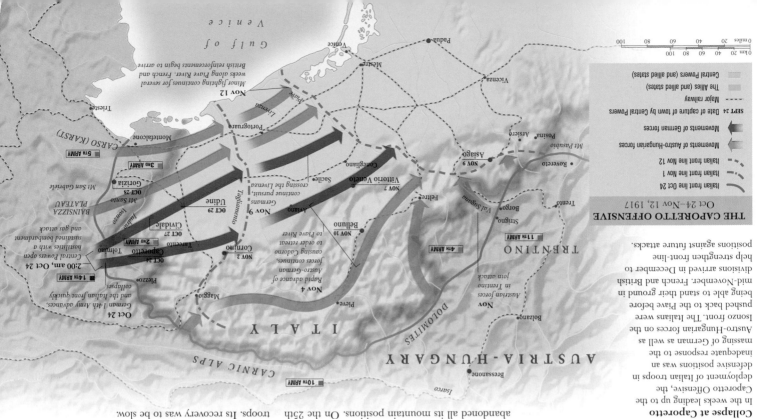

THE CAPORETTO OFFENSIVE
Oct 24–Nov 12, 1917

Legend:
- Italian front line Oct 24
- Italian front line Nov 1
- Italian front line Nov 12
- Movements of Austro-Hungarian forces
- Movements of German forces
- SEPT 24 Date of capture of town by Central Powers
- Major railway
- The Allies (and allied states)
- Central Powers (and allied states)

Map labels: Gulf of Venice; Venice; Padua; Mestre; Vicenza; Trieste; CARSO (KARST); 5TH ARMY; 3RD ARMY; Gorizia; Montefalcone; Mt San Gabriele; BAINSIZZA PLATEAU; Mt Santo; OCT 28; Udine OCT 29; Cividale OCT 27; 2ND ARMY; Tarcento; Caporetto OCT 24; Tolmino; Plezzo; 14TH ARMY 2:00 a.m., Oct 24; Cormino; Sacile; Conegliano; Vittorio Veneto; Portogruaro; Piave; Livenza; Tagliamento; Aviano; Belluno; Feltre; Pieve; Maggio; DOLOMITES; CARNIC ALPS; ITALY; AUSTRIA-HUNGARY; TRENTINO; Asiago NOV 9; Arsiero; Posina; Mt Pasubio; Rovereto; Trento; Borgo; Strigno; Val Sugana; 11TH ARMY; 4TH ARMY; Bolzano; Bressanone; Isarco; 10TH ARMY.

Map annotations:
- Nov 12 — Minor fighting continues for several weeks along Piave River. French and British reinforcements begin to arrive.
- 2:00 a.m., Oct 24 — Central Powers open hostilities with a sustained bombardment and gas attack.
- Oct 24 — German 14th Army advances, and the Italian front line collapses quickly.
- Nov 9 — Germans continue pursuit, crossing the Livenza.
- Nov 4 — Rapid advance of Austro-German forces continues, causing Cadorna to order retreat to Piave River.
- Nov — Austrian forces in Trentino join attack.

Scale: 0 20 40 60 80 100 miles; 0 20 40 60 80 100 km

The Middle East

MESOPOTAMIA AND PALESTINE

JANUARY 9 – DECEMBER 11, 1917

After the disappointments of 1916, the British needed results. Kut and Baghdad fell to Maude early in the year. In Palestine, however, Murray's failures at Gaza led to his replacement by Allenby, who reinvigorated British efforts. In July the Arabs seized Aqaba, resulting in enhanced British support for the Arab Revolt. In October Allenby succeeded in driving the Turks out of Gaza and Beersheba, to seize Jerusalem in December.

AFTER THE SURRENDER of the British forces under General Townshend in Kut in April 1916, imperial prestige seemed to demand Britain's prompt recapture of the town. This did not, however, accord with the ideas of William Robertson, chief of the imperial general staff, who favoured a defensive posture. He was reluctant to commit more troops, and he considered that the purpose of the British presence was essentially to protect the Persian oil fields and guard the Shatt al-Arab waterway, not to embark on further conquest.

Robertson's appointee as the commander in Mesopotamia, General Maude, proved to have more ambitious aims. Having spent most of 1916 in preparation, building up supplies and raising morale, in December Maude began to extend his front farther up the Tigris, where he was supported by the naval guns of eight new gunboats plus a number of armed river steamers.

Advancing across the Sinai
British troops march to El Arish in February 1917 during preparations for the First Battle of Gaza.

Beersheba
Turkish cavalry pass through this key town on their way to southern Palestine in April 1917.

JANUARY 9 — British capture Rafah

JANUARY 24 — Feisal, leader of Arab Revolt, captures Al Wejh, with help from Royal Navy

FEBRUARY 25 — British take Kut

MARCH 11 — Baghdad taken by British after withdrawal of Turks the previous night

MARCH 26 — First British attempt to take Gaza fails due to premature order to withdraw

APRIL 17 — Second British assault on Gaza begins; Turks, backed by German units, force British to retreat with heavy casualties

APRIL 24 — British take Samarra

JUNE 27 — General Edmund Allenby replaces Archibald Murray as leader of British forces in Palestine

JULY 6 — Fall of Aqaba to Lawrence and Arab forces

JULY 10 — Lawrence meets Allenby at Cairo and gains subsidy for Arabs

SEPTEMBER 16 — Lawrence leads attack on Hejaz railway in Arabia

SEPTEMBER 29 — British capture Ramadi on Euphrates

OCTOBER 31 — Beginning of third British bombardment of Gaza provides diversion that helps them take Beersheba

NOVEMBER 1 — Main assault on Gaza starts

NOVEMBER 5 — British take Tikrit

NOVEMBER 6–7 — Turks forced to evacuate Gaza; Gaza-Beersheba line is broken

NOVEMBER 14 — British capture Junction Station on Jerusalem railway

NOVEMBER 16 — Turks retreat from Jaffa on road to Jerusalem

DECEMBER 7–8 — British break through Turkish defences on the Jaffa–Jerusalem road

DECEMBER 9 — British capture Jerusalem, thus achieving Lloyd George's aim of taking the city by Christmas

DECEMBER 11 — Allenby officially enters Jerusalem

KEY

- Allied campaign in Mesopotamia Feb 25-Nov 5
- Allied campaign in Egypt and Palestine Jan 9-Dec 11
- Other events

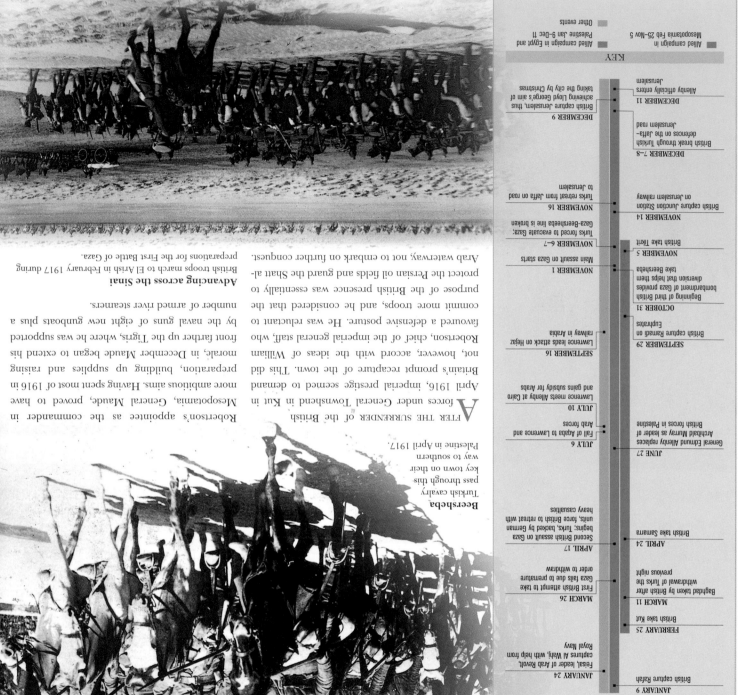

ADVANCE THROUGH MESOPOTAMIA

The Turkish Sixth Army, commanded by Halil Pasha, who had accepted Townshend's surrender, was heavily outnumbered – ultimately by as much as four to one – and had severe logistical problems. As well as lacking equipment, weapons and essential draft animals, the Turks suffered from a shortage of food and clothing. Maude's advance was very cautious, but he did not want to provoke an order from London to bring operations to a halt. Although the British and Indian troops had better supplies than the Turks, but they did not find conditions comfortable and many fell victim to disease. Maude himself was to die of cholera before the end of 1917.

By mid-February 1917 the Turks around Kut were in a vulnerable position, and the town fell on February 25. Maude was then authorized to advance on Baghdad, and his forces reached the city two weeks later. It fell without resistance on March 11, the Turks – outnumbered and outflanked – having withdrawn the previous night. The British continued to advance, taking Samarra in April and Ramadi and Tikrit in the autumn. The demands of the Palestine campaign, however, increasingly inhibited operations in Mesopotamia.

THE ARAB REVOLT

The main, and eventually decisive, British effort against the Ottoman Empire in the Middle East came in Palestine. Here they were aided by the Arab Revolt against the Turks, proclaimed by Sherif Hussein Ibn Ali of Mecca – later king of the Hejaz (Al Hijaz) – in June 1916. The British had been encouraging Hussein to revolt for some time, and had supplied him with rifles.

The revolt was timed to coincide with the advance across the Sinai peninsula of Archibald Murray's Egyptian Expeditionary Force (EEF). Substantial British forces had been kept in Egypt since the Turkish attack on Suez. Owing, however, to demands from elsewhere, Murray had recently had to give up one division, and his remaining forces, which included the ANZAC Mounted Division, lacked adequate supplies of artillery and munitions. Initial progress was slow, though chiefly

because the troops were building roads, a railway and a vital water pipeline as they went. On December 20, 1916, the EEF took El Arish, clearing the Sinai peninsula of all Turkish forces.

Meanwhile, attempts were being made to revive the Arab Revolt, which had languished after the surrender to Hussein of the Turkish governor of the Hejaz in September. In October a British fact-finding mission arrived from Cairo. Its members included a young officer who had already made a reputation in military intelligence: T. E. Lawrence. A speaker of Arabic, and with some knowledge of Turkish and Arab customs, Lawrence had already written a memo on the Arab Revolt in which he

accurately forecast the future strategy of disrupting the Hejaz railway. He believed that the most promising leader – with whom he would form a close relationship – was Hussein's third son, Feisal, who was currently trying to hold together a band of largely untrained tribesmen based inland from the port of Yenbo (Yanbu).

Desert artillery
Although primarily used on the North West Frontier in India, the British 10-pounder mountain gun saw extensive service in the Mesopotamia and Palestine campaigns.

"It was never easy for us to keep our movements secret, as we lived by preaching to the local people, and the unconvinced would tell the Turks."

T. E. LAWRENCE ON CROSSING THE DESERT WITH ARABS WHO WERE IN REVOLT AGAINST THE TURKS IN JUNE 1917

The retaking of Kut
In March 1917 Allied troops retook Kut, scene of the humiliating surrender of General Charles Townshend's British force in April 1916.

Having become Feisal's official British adviser in November, Lawrence assisted Feisal in his defence of Yenbo against a Turkish attack. The Turks succeeded in breaking up Feisal's forces and in December they drove him back to the port. Faced, however, by the presence of five British warships a short distance offshore, the Turks withdrew.

CAPTURE OF AL WAJH

The failure of the Turks to capture Yenbo persuaded more tribesmen to join Feisal's forces and revived the Arab Revolt. With encouragement from Lawrence, Feisal captured the port of Al Wajh from the Turks in January 1917. The port then served as a base for attacks on Turkish positions throughout northern Arabia, forcing the Turks to mount a defensive campaign. In July Feisal captured Aqaba, on the northeastern tip of the Red Sea. This was to become his main base as later in the year he moved northwards into Palestine, where he recruited more followers and launched raids on the Turkish railway.

THE CAMPAIGN IN PALESTINE

Southern Palestine has a natural southern boundary – the hills between Gaza, near the coast, and Beersheba, 40 km (25 miles) inland. For Murray's EEF (five divisions plus other units), advancing along the coast in March 1917, Gaza became the objective. The town was surrounded by gardens and fields interlaced with cactus barriers, presenting formidable natural defenceworks as well as shelter for machine-guns. But the most crucial problem facing the EEF, as so often in desert warfare, was water. Only one day's supplies could be carried, and it was therefore essential to capture Gaza, where supplies were plentiful, within a day. If it were not captured before nightfall, total withdrawal would be necessary.

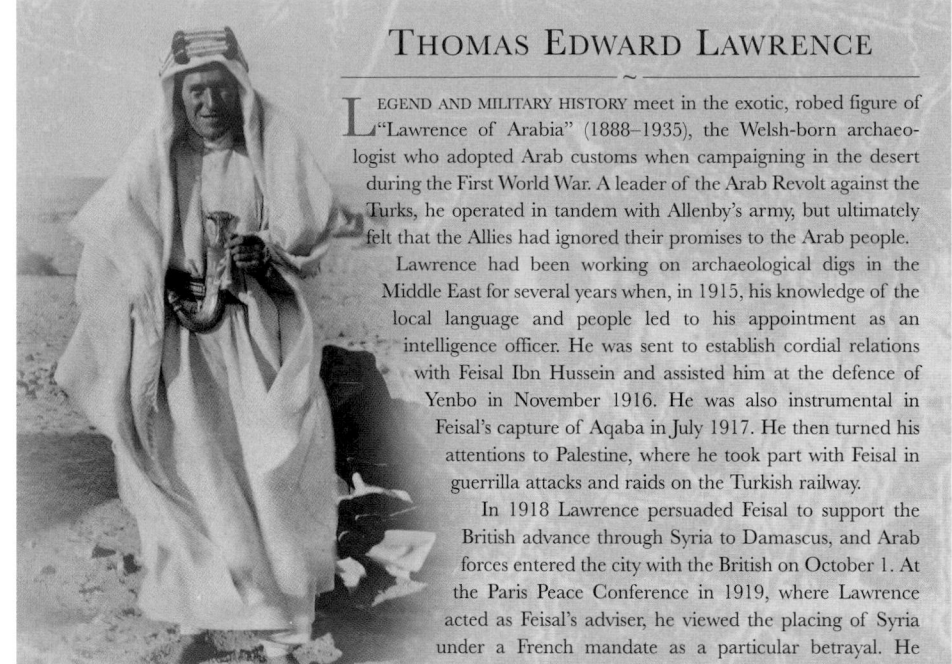

THOMAS EDWARD LAWRENCE

~

LEGEND AND MILITARY HISTORY meet in the exotic, robed figure of "Lawrence of Arabia" (1888–1935), the Welsh-born archaeologist who adopted Arab customs when campaigning in the desert during the First World War. A leader of the Arab Revolt against the Turks, he operated in tandem with Allenby's army, but ultimately felt that the Allies had ignored their promises to the Arab people.

Lawrence had been working on archaeological digs in the Middle East for several years when, in 1915, his knowledge of the local language and people led to his appointment as an intelligence officer. He was sent to establish cordial relations with Feisal Ibn Hussein and assisted him at the defence of Yenbo in November 1916. He was also instrumental in Feisal's capture of Aqaba in July 1917. He then turned his attentions to Palestine, where he took part with Feisal in guerrilla attacks and raids on the Turkish railway.

In 1918 Lawrence persuaded Feisal to support the British advance through Syria to Damascus, and Arab forces entered the city with the British on October 1. At the Paris Peace Conference in 1919, where Lawrence acted as Feisal's adviser, he viewed the placing of Syria under a French mandate as a particular betrayal. He subsequently wrote a number of accounts of his wartime experiences. *The Seven Pillars of Wisdom* is the most famous.

Martini-Henry
This 1870s-vintage British rifle was typical of the outdated firearms supplied as part of the support for the Arab Revolt.

Arab flintlock pistol
Although antique and largely worn for show, it is possible that weapons such as this did see service.

Sea fog delayed the start on March 26, but by dusk British troops were within the town. The defending Turkish troops were taken by surprise, and the German commander decided that he had no alternative but to surrender. At this point, however, the British commanders based some distance away received reports of approaching Turkish relief and – to the astonishment of the local commanders – gave the order to withdraw.

The second battle of Gaza started on April 17. The situation was now entirely different. The advantage of surprise had been lost, the Turks defending Gaza had been reinforced (though still outnumbered), and they had added a labyrinth of trenches to the cactus hedges. Murray was given a few battered tanks and some gas shells (both proved virtually useless) but not the two extra divisions that he believed necessary. Water supplies were still inadequate. Murray ordered the new British attack without adequate reconnaissance, and after two days the Turkish defences were undented, British casualties were heavy (over 6,000), and a "temporary" cessation of fighting was ordered. The failure heralded considerable changes.

Arab irregulars enter Yenbo
In December 1916 Arab troops under the command of Feisal were forced to withdraw to Yenbo by the Turks. They subsequently engaged in guerrilla warfare.

COPING WITH THE DESERT

F OR THE ALLIED FORCES CAMPAIGNING in the Near and Middle Eastern areas of the Ottoman Empire, the natural environment presented an extra, deadly enemy. To cope with the searing heat, soldiers were issued with sun helmets and spine pads (to protect their backs from the sun), but clean water was always in short supply. Water was crucial to the survival, as well as the success, of armies in the desert. To keep going for just one day, the Allied troops in Syria and Palestine required some 1,800,000 litres (400,000 gallons) of water. It was needed for animals – horses and mules – as well as men because many desert "roads" were not negotiable by motorized vehicles. Extreme heat and poor sanitation meant that the Allied forces were dogged by a host of infectious diseases. Dysentery was the biggest killer, but whole regiments were also afflicted by malaria, yellow fever and typhoid. Until their rations were supplemented to include Vitamin C, Indian troops were also vulnerable to scurvy. In the last six months of 1916, more than 11,000 Indian soldiers succumbed to this "disease of deficiency".

In the desert, the conscript soldiers of the Turkish army also suffered, with seven times as many men dying of disease – dysentery, malaria, typhoid and syphilis – as died of wounds during the war. During the entire war the Turkish army employed no more than 2,500 doctors to treat its soldiers. Technically, there was no overall shortage of food in the Ottoman Empire, but getting it to the armies in the field was a problem. Sea transport was impossible because of the British blockade, and the limited, overburdened railway system could not cope. At one stage, Turkish troops in Palestine were surviving on rations of 350 grams (12.5 oz) of bread a day. They were badly equipped, and so often without footwear that to this day the war is referred to in Syria as "the barefoot war".

Surgeon's instrument set
Issued by the Indian Army, this instrument set contains forceps, clamps, scalpels and saws to deal with the effects of wounds. Disease, however, generally posed a greater threat than combat to the soldiers who fought in the desert.

Water
This engraved silver bottle was used to carry the most precious commodity in the Mesopotamian campaign: water.

Camel ambulance
Australian medical orderlies prepare to load a casualty on to a cacolet on a camel's back at Rafa. The camel's swaying motion must have been excruciating for a soldier suffering anything but the most minor of wounds.

THE ARRIVAL OF ALLENBY

In late June Murray was replaced by Allenby. A South African War veteran, Allenby gave the appearance of being a conventional, old-fashioned cavalry officer. But he also had an inclination towards the unorthodox and was tolerant of unconventional warriors, as his relations with Lawrence and the Arabs were to demonstrate. With the British prime minister Lloyd George now asking for Jerusalem as "a Christmas present", Allenby received the reinforcements that Murray had been denied. There were still, however, problems with transport – dependent on mules – and water.

Allenby decided on Beersheba as the objective. An element of surprise was necessary if it was to be taken before the Turks could destroy the wells, and to this end efforts were made to convince the Turks that, while diversionary action might be expected at Beersheba, the main attack would be on Gaza. Having heard from Lawrence about the achievements of the Arabs, Allenby requested that they should cut the railway at Der'a (Dar'a) at the beginning of November to coincide with his intended attack. This was a risky operation involving a 560-km (350-mile) ride through the desert and then settled territory, making surprise problematic. In fact, there may have been a traitor in the group, for the Turks gained advance warning. The raid failed, although Lawrence's band did succeed in cutting the line farther south.

Meanwhile, the Turks set about improving their defences prior to the arrival of the Turkish-German Yilderim ("Thunderbolt") Force under the command of Falkenhayn. Based on two Turkish divisions, but with largely German officers, the force had been intended for action in Mesopotamia before the success of the British in Palestine.

The Sakultuan Pass

While Allenby pressed on towards Jerusalem, Allied forces also advanced through Mesopotamia. On December 3 and 4 they occupied the Sakultuan Pass, a main Turkish supply route across the Jabal Hamrin, northeast of Baghdad.

CAPTURE OF BEERSHEBA AND GAZA

Allenby's campaign to take Beersheba began with an intensive bombardment of Gaza to reinforce the notion that the main blow would fall there, while troops moved east towards Beersheba under cover of night. On October 31 Allenby launched an attack with 40,000 men and over 100 guns on a front about 5 km (3 miles) wide. The infantry advanced, cutting their way through barbed wire while under Turkish artillery fire. Meanwhile, after a hazardous night-time ride of nearly 50 km (30 miles), the ANZAC division attacked from the north and east where the Turks had not laid barbed wire. Sheer speed across the ground kept their casualties down and, when faced with concentrated rifle and machine-gun fire, they dismounted and fought their way forward on foot. They then galloped through two lines of trenches and into Beersheba, creating havoc among the defenders and taking 1,400 prisoners while suffering fewer than 200 casualties themselves.

The seizure of Beersheba forced the Turks to begin moving forces from Gaza in order to reseal the front. As they did so, the Allied forces launched their main assault on Gaza on November 1; by the night of November 6/7 the Turks were in retreat. The Gaza-Beersheba line was now broken, and the way to Jerusalem lay open for the Allies.

Turkish military band in Damascus
The Turkish army was driven back through Palestine and Mesopotamia during 1917, but despite shortages of food, clothes and weapons, it continued to be a reliable fighting force which was not easily defeated. It was to stay in control of Damascus until October 1918.

ADVANCE TO JERUSALEM

With Lawrence and the Arabs forming a detached flanking force on the right, in the desert, Allenby's forces advanced across the plain beyond Gaza, covering 80 km (50 miles) in 17 days and taking some 10,000 prisoners. Allenby then had to decide whether to pause and consolidate, or make a dash for "Jerusalem by Christmas". He decided on the latter and resumed the advance on November 18, despite the arrival of the winter rains, which for the moment created greater difficulties than the Turks. The camels in particular suffered.

On November 27 Falkenhayn, whose Yilderim force had only begun to arrive in late October, launched a counterattack against a weak point in the Allied forces – a comparatively small cavalry force guarding British supply lines. The Turks made some impression, but their efforts soon petered out as Allenby called upon his reserves.

The Allied advance continued along the Jaffa-Jerusalem road during a pause in the rains that allowed the supporting artillery to move up. Although rain and mist soon returned, an attack on the night of

Allenby enters Jerusalem

Allenby made his official entry into the city through the Jaffa Gate on December 11. The Turks, for whom the loss of the city was a terrible blow to morale, had begun to retreat towards Nablus and Jericho on the night of the 8th/9th.

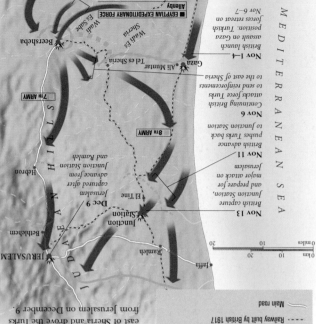

December 7/8 on the outskirts of Jerusalem, took the Turks by surprise. The EEF broke through their defences, pushing them back 7 km (4 miles) before pausing to wait for more troops to arrive from Bethlehem. Both sides were under orders to spare Jerusalem from fighting, and on the morning of December 9, Allenby's troops discovered that the Turks just to the north of the city had taken advantage of the lull in the fighting to withdraw during the night. Four centuries of Ottoman rule over the city had ended, and Lloyd George had his Christmas present.

CAMPAIGNS IN PALESTINE
Oct 31–Dec 9, 1917

Turkish defensive positions Oct 31	
Turkish positions Nov 13	
Turkish positions Dec 7	
Turkish outposts	
Allied offensives	
Railway	·····
Railway built by British 1917	- - - -
Main road	

Major battle

Allied advance from Gaza

After launching a surprise attack on Beersheba on October 31 and then capturing Gaza at their third attempt, EEF forces advanced northwards both up the coast and east of Sheria and drove the Turks from Jerusalem on December 9.

THE CAUCASUS FRONT

Throughout 1917 the Turks had focused on the Mesopotamian and Palestine fronts, and paid little attention to the Caucasus front. Following the "February Revolution" the Russian army in the region had not been able to contemplate anything other than defensive action, and after the "October Revolution" the Russians had withdrawn altogether. This had left the way open for a revival of nationalist Armenian activity, and in the following months an estimated 50,000 non-Armenians were killed. In September the Armenians, Azerbaijani and Georgians established the joint republic of Transcaucasia, but there were deep divisions between the three nationalities, resulting in a very confused situation at the end of the year. It would not be difficult for the Turks to gain control again in spring 1918.

Gurkha Lewis gunner

The Gurkhas had a reputation for being particularly determined fighters. It was one they lived up to in the fierce encounters that took place between Allied and Turkish troops in both Palestine and Mesopotamia.

Map labels

EGYPT

PALESTINE

MEDITERRANEAN SEA

JUDAEAN HILLS

7TH ARMY

8TH ARMY

EGYPTIAN EXPEDITIONARY FORCE
Allenby

N

Rafah

Beersheba

Gaza

Ali Muntar   Tel es Sheria

Wadi es Saba

Wadi es Sheria

El Tine

Junction Station

Jaffa

Ramleh

Hebron

Bethlehem

JERUSALEM

0 km   10   20
0 miles   10   20

Oct 31 *Allenby launches a surprise attack on Beersheba. Australian Cavalry Division captures town by nightfall.*

Nov 1 *British launch assault on Gaza position. Turkish forces retreat on Nov 6–7.*

Nov 6 *Continuing British attacks force Turks to send reinforcements to the east of Sheria.*

Nov 11 *British advance pushes Turks back to Junction Station.*

Nov 13 *British capture Junction Station, and prepare for major attack on Jerusalem.*

Dec 9 *Jerusalem captured after advance from Junction Station and Ramleh.*

WAR POETS AND NOVELISTS

FOR MANY OF THE YOUNG MEN who donned uniforms in 1914, the war was a noble adventure, a chance to emulate the chivalrous knights of old. The brutal reality of the conflict – more hellish than any previously imagined hell – transformed this early idealism into an intense disenchantment, which found expression in a body of powerful literature.

The Western Front was especially conducive to poetry. Soldier-poets found themselves, as never before, in the very thick, or stalemate, of battle. In poems jotted down on the backs of envelopes and letters, they immortalized the tribulations of their comrades and the desolate landscape of corpses, churned mud, gaping shell-holes, barbed wire, splintered trees and smashed buildings.

Writing home from his first tour of duty on the Somme, 24-year-old Wilfred Owen wrote of "everything unnatural, broken, blasted, the distortion of the dead, whose unburiable bodies sit outside the dug-outs all day, all night, the most execrable sights on earth". His poems, not published until after his death, raged against the human cost of the war. Yet after being invalided home, he chose to return to the front line and was killed a week before the signing of the Armistice.

Another casualty was Isaac Rosenberg. A frail and diminutive young man, he enlisted partly in the hope that his army separation allowance would benefit his mother, and was killed on a night patrol at the beginning of April 1918.

However, not all of writers were anti-war. While poets such as Owen and Sassoon were deeply critical of the war machine, and heedless politicians and generals, they did not consider the war itself to be futile. They would not have taken issue with the last verse of *In Flanders Fields*, in which the dead call upon the living to "take up our quarrel with the foe".

First published anonymously in 1915, *In Flanders Fields* was written by John McCrae, a Canadian doctor tending to Allied soldiers near Ypres. It remains one of the most famous and popular poems of the war.

Like other English soldier-poets, notably Siegfried Sassoon and Robert Graves, Owen and Rosenberg expressed the gulf of understanding between the brotherhood of "those who were there" and civilians at home. A similar theme – intense suffering alleviated by comradeship – runs through *Le Feu (Under Fire)*, the war novel written by French writer Henri Barbusse, which contains many harrowing passages. In some cases, the bond of shared suffering was so strong it extended to the "enemy" on the other side of No Man's Land. This attitude pervades *All Quiet on the Western Front (Im Westen nichts Neues)*, a novel written by twice-wounded German veteran Erich Maria Remarque. First published in 1929, Remarque's pacifist message led to his work being publicly burned by the Nazis, and cost him his German citizenship. Elsewhere, *All Quiet on the Western Front* was a huge success, contributing to a retrospective perception of the war as a tragic catastrophe.

In Flanders fields the poppies blow
Between the crosses, row on row,
That mark our place; and in the sky
The larks, still bravely singing, fly
Scarce heard amid the guns below.

We are the Dead. Short days ago
We lived, felt dawn, saw sunset glow,
Loved and were loved, and now we lie
In Flanders fields.

Take up our quarrel with the foe:
To you from failing hands we throw
The torch; be yours to hold it high.
If ye break faith with us who die
We shall not sleep, though poppies grow
In Flanders fields.

EXTRACT FROM *IN FLANDERS FIELDS* BY JOHN McCRAE, FIRST PUBLISHED IN 1915

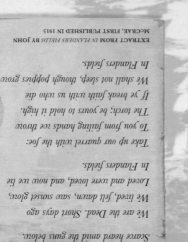

Pressed poppy The poppy became a powerful image of the soldiers' sacrifice.

A self-portrait by Rosenberg Isaac Rosenberg grew up in the poor Jewish communities in London's East End in the early years of the 20th century. His poor health, and particularly his weak chest, was ill-suited to the cold and wet conditions of trench life.

APOLLINAIRE

BORN WILHELM DE KOSTROWITZKY in 1880, Guillaume Apollinaire was the most influential avant-garde poet in early 20th-century France. A close friend of Picasso and a champion of Cubism, he wrote classical, lyrical poems and also bold, provocative, modernist works. In many of these he sculpted his words into graphic images on the page. After receiving a commission in the infantry in 1915, he was badly gassed, and then, in March 1916, suffered a serious shrapnel wound to the head that put him out of action for the rest of the war. He died in the influenza epidemic as it swept through Europe in November 1918.

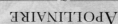

The darkness crumbles away –
It is the same old druid Time as ever,
Only a live thing leaps my hand –
A queer sardonic rat –
As I pull the parapet's poppy to stick behind my ear.
Droll rat, they would shoot you if they knew
Your cosmopolitan sympathies.
Now you have touched this English hand
You will do the same to a German –
Soon, no doubt, if it be your pleasure
To cross the sleeping green between.

EXTRACT FROM *BREAK OF DAY IN THE TRENCHES* BY ISAAC ROSENBERG, WRITTEN JUNE 1916

Erich Maria Remarque

Remarque's novel *All Quiet on the Western Front* depicted the horrors of the war from the point of view of the ordinary German soldier and remains probably the most famous novel about the war.

EXTRACT FROM *ALL QUIET ON THE WESTERN FRONT* BY ERICH REMARQUE, PUBLISHED 1929

... just like Kat.

Comrade, I did not want to kill you ... You rifles and this uniform you could be my brother of this uniform you could be my brother you be my enemy? If we threw away these same fear of death, and the same dying and the same agony – Forgive me, comrade; how could just as anxious as ours, and that we have the are poor devils like us, that your mothers are stabbed ... Forgive me, comrade. We always see it too late. Why do they never tell us that you appropriate response. It was that abstraction I that lived in my mind and called forth its were only an idea to me before, an abstraction

Le Feu

Henri Barbusse's novel, describing the experiences of a group of French soldiers with stark realism, was published in Paris in 1916.

EXTRACT FROM *LE FEU*

Ribs are scattered over the ground like the bars of old broken cages along with bits of blackened leather and battered drinking mugs and mess tins ...

Sometimes from elongated humps in the ground – for all the unburied dead end up by becoming part of the soil – a scrap of cloth pokes out to indicate that here some human being was destroyed.

EXTRACT FROM *RENDEZVOUS WITH DEATH* BY ALAN SEEGER, WRITTEN 1916

God knows 'twere better to be deep Pillowed in silk and scented down, Where love throbs out in blissful sleep, Pulse nigh to pulse, and breath to breath, Where hushed awakenings are dear ...

But I've a rendezvous with Death At midnight in some flaming town, When Spring trips north again this year, And I to my pledged word am true, I shall not fail that rendezvous.

Scene of desolation

The impression made on young, idealistic and articulate men by the horror and suffering that characterized the Western Front produced a body of powerful literature and poetry protesting at the loss of a generation.

Siegfried Sassoon

Before the war Sassoon was something of an idle country dilettante, but the war transformed him and he wrote emotionally about the realities of the conflict. Unlike many of his contemporaries, he survived the war to write several volumes of memoirs.

Alan Seeger

When war broke out, Alan Seeger, although a US citizen, quickly volunteered for the French Foreign Legion. Seeger was killed on the Somme on July 4, 1916 and the statue in Paris commemorating the American volunteers is modelled on him.

Wilfred Owen

Not a pacifist, Owen was a courageous officer, liked and respected by his men. He won the Military Cross in October 1918.

EXTRACT FROM WILFRED OWEN'S POEM, *DULCE ET DECORUM EST*, DRAFTED IN OCTOBER 1917

Bent double, like old beggars under sacks, Knock-kneed, coughing like hags, we cursed through sludge, Till on the haunting flares we turned our backs And towards our distant rest began to trudge. Men marched asleep. Many had lost their boots But limped on, blood-shot. All went lame; all blind; Drunk with fatigue; deaf even to the hoots Of tired, outstripped Five-Nines that dropped behind.

Gas! Gas! Quick, boys! – An ecstasy of fumbling, Fitting the clumsy helmets just in time; But someone still was yelling out and stumbling And flound'ring like a man in fire or lime ... Dim, through the misty panes and thick green light, As under a green sea, I saw him drowning. In all my dreams, before my helpless sight, He plunges at me, guttering, choking, drowning.

THE LAST GREAT BATTLES
1918

WITH THE ARRIVAL OF LARGE NUMBERS OF AMERICAN TROOPS IMMINENT, THE GERMANS KNEW AT THE BEGINNING OF 1918 THAT THEY HAD TO SECURE VICTORY AGAINST THE BRITISH AND FRENCH IN THE SPRING. IN MARCH THEY LAUNCHED A SERIES OF FIVE OFFENSIVES ON THE WESTERN FRONT, BUT ALTHOUGH SOME MAJOR ADVANCES WERE MADE, THERE WAS NO DECISIVE BREAKTHROUGH. BY JULY THE ALLIES WERE READY TO COUNTERATTACK. MEANWHILE, GERMANY'S ALLIES WERE STRUGGLING TO AVOID A COLLAPSE ON OTHER FRONTS.

~

American soldiers in action

"Doughboys", as the American soldiers were known, head out on a trench raid carrying hand grenades in canvas bags. The arrival of the Americans spelt the end of German hopes for victory in the war.

A RACE AGAINST TIME

AT THE END OF 1917, PEACE APPEARED TO BE FARTHER AWAY THAN AT ANY TIME
SINCE JUNE 1914. THE BRITISH ARMIES ON THE WESTERN FRONT WERE EXHAUSTED
AND THE FRENCH ARMIES HAD STILL NOT FULLY RECOVERED FROM THE EFFECTS OF
THE SPRING NIVELLE OFFENSIVE. FACING THEM WERE GERMAN ARMIES THAT WOULD
SHORTLY ENJOY THE ADVANTAGE OF SUPERIORITY OF NUMBERS AND HOLD THE
INITIATIVE FOR THE FIRST TIME SINCE THE OPENING WEEKS OF THE WAR.

FOLLOWING THE SIGNING of the armistice with Russia in December 1917, Germany had regained the position it had secured for itself in the period before the war – that of the strongest single power in Europe, with such advantages of size, position, population and industrial capacity that it could not be defeated by the other European powers. The entry of the United States into the war had, however, changed the balance of power. The question in the minds of all the combatants at the end of the year was whether Germany would be able to defeat Britain and France before the Americans could arrive in time to tip the scales decisively against it.

GERMAN STRATEGY FOR 1918

On November 11, 1917 Ludendorff and selected chiefs of staff met at Mons to determine German military strategy for 1918 – or, more accurately, to determine when and against which enemy to mount an attack in the spring. Without the means to conduct a general offensive on the Western Front, the German high command took the decision to mount a series of massive, closely-phased attacks that would either break the Allies' front conclusively or break their will to resist. Either way, the result would be a defeat that no number of American troops arriving in Europe could reverse.

The Germans also decided to focus on the strongest of their enemies, Britain, and to launch the initial attack on the Arras–St Quentin sector against the British Third and Fifth Armies. They calculated that a British defeat in northern France, where the British armies lacked space in which to manoeuvre and could be divided from the French armies, would seriously affect the French. On the other hand, victory over the French, in sectors of the Western Front where there was space for them to retreat without grave strategic risk, would not

necessarily affect British capacity to pursue the war. It is true that Germany's best chance of securing victory probably did lie in defeating Britain. But the vulnerability of the British armies on the Western Front was greatest in the north – where the ability of the armies to manoeuvre was more limited than in Picardy and where the Channel ports might be secured. In any event, an assault on the Arras-St Quentin sector required an advance to the southwest if the British armies were to be divided from the French, but to the northwest if the British armies were to be rolled up from the south. An offensive against the British armies in Picardy would also involve a German advance across the Somme battlefield and the area left devastated by the Germans themselves in the course of their withdrawal to the Hindenburg Line in 1917.

Despite the obvious problems, the German high command believed it had little choice in the matter. Ludendorff would have preferred to strike at the northern British armies, but it was vital to take the state of the ground into consideration. Having seen the difficulties created by the mud at Ypres in 1917, the Germans concluded that a March offensive was possible over the ground of Picardy, whereas the ground in Flanders would not be sufficiently dry before April. With time at a premium, the Germans committed themselves to a battle across the most devastated part of the front against an enemy they considered tactically less skilled and less able to respond effectively to events than the French.

FLAWS IN THE GERMANS' PLANS

The Germans planned to have a thin fighting line, into which reserves would be fed under the direction of the formations leading the attack. The fighting line itself would be firepower-heavy, and include artillery withdrawn from parent units in order to give direct support to the infantry. Special

"storm battalions" would be trained to operate in small groups that could exploit gaps and bypass resistance to break through the enemy rear positions after the initial assault. The assault would employ a detailed fire plan that had been used to great effect against the Russians at Riga in September 1917.

The preparations of the Germans for the offensive were impressive but not flawless. The assault was primarily dependent upon manpower and had no means other than men for the break-out phase that would follow any breakthrough. This was because Germany had been unable to maintain large cavalry forces on the Western Front and had failed to provide itself with light tank formations. It was also the case that unless the initial offensive in Ludendorff's planned series resulted in a decisive victory, the Germans would be forced to occupy conquered ground with fewer troops than were available beforehand. Each successive attack would inevitably worsen the Germans' problems. If the

Allied forces were able to weather the initial assault, they would be able to reconstitute the line with the growing numbers of American troops.

In preparing for the 1918 offensive Ludendorff stated a willingness to accept the loss of a million men as the price of victory. Leaving aside all moral considerations, such a price was beyond German means in 1918. The "storm battalions" could only be raised by combing line units for their best officers and men. The price of this concentration of quality

German infantry staging an attack
This photograph was probably taken during training, but it gives a vivid impression of the assault faced by the British Fifth Army in the first of the German spring offensives.

"Reinforcements were brought up from somewhere but it was hopeless. The Fifth Army was well whacked, with a German division facing one battalion of our lads. Hopelessly outnumbered."

BRITISH LANCE-CORPORAL SHARPE DESCRIBING THE IMMEDIATE EFFECTS OF THE FIRST GERMAN OFFENSIVE, LAUNCHED ON MARCH 21, 1918

Australian victims of a gas attack, May 1918
Gas played a significant role in the Germans' preliminary bombardments in 1918, often being employed against the Allied forces' second line of resistance.

American troops landing at Le Havre, July 1918
The American troops, whose numbers began to swell rapidly from May, were much admired by the other Allied forces for their physique and initial enthusiasm for battle.

in elite formations was the degrading of the combat performance of all other divisions. This meant that the greater part of German losses would be sustained by the elite formations — the battalions least able to absorb losses — while the task of defence would be left to forces of lower quality. The only way of hiding this weakness was to retain the initiative — but this would involve continuous offensive action, which was beyond German means.

RELATIONS BETWEEN BRITAIN AND FRANCE

In preparing for the spring offensive, Ludendorff made the assumption that the German armies would be able to defeat the British without French intervention. This was not an unnatural assumption to make given how the war had been fought to date. In November 1917, however, an organization was created that would ensure the effective co-ordination of Anglo-French efforts after March 1918. The Passchendaele offensive in October had cost Haig whatever confidence his prime minister, Lloyd George, had ever had in him. Unable to dismiss his senior field commander, the premier sought ways of curbing Haig's freedom of action, one of which was the creation of a supreme war council. The council would have executive powers, so reducing Haig to a position of inferiority vis-à-vis its chairman, Foch.

The proposal that Foch should be chairman made the council wholly unacceptable to Haig and his faithful defender, Robertson, the Chief of the Imperial General Staff who, in February, was replaced by the francophile Wilson. In March 1918 Haig sought to avoid Foch's council by a bilateral personal arrangement with Pétain, under which the two national commanders undertook to support each other should the need arise.

ERICH MARIA REMARQUE DESCRIBING, IN HIS NOVEL, *ALL QUIET ON THE WESTERN FRONT*,
THE SITUATION THAT CONFRONTED THE GERMAN FORCES IN THE AUTUMN OF 1918

"Our lines are falling back. There are too many fresh English and American regiments over there. There's too much corned beef and white wheat bread. Too many new guns. Too many aeroplanes."

ON THE BRINK OF DEFEAT

The arguments over the role of Foch and the nebulous arrangements in which Haig placed his trust would have mattered little if the British had not become in urgent need of French support in March. Haig was to be converted to the principle of co-ordination of effort as a result of defeats in March that arose at least in part from mistaken British assumptions. The most significant of these was the failure to anticipate the nature of the German offensive. To the British high command, used to measuring its advances in terms of yards per month, it seemed impossible that the Germans would break the line and so achieve what had been beyond the Allies for more than three years. At the end of 1917 the British had adopted the defensive tactics employed so effectively by the Germans, and had then assumed that the Germans would be no more successful than the Allies in restoring mobility to the battlefield. Compounding this error was the fact that the part of the British line on which Ludendorff proposed to unleash his armies was the weakest. The British Fifth Army was the worst commanded and administered of the four British armies on the Western Front, but it had the longest and least prepared sector to defend, and only 11 battalions in the front line compared to the Third Army's 21. Furthermore, up to five days before the German offensive began, Haig's headquarters insisted that it would not be subjected to attack.

As February gave way to March, and as the significance of all other fronts lessened, the British armies on the Western Front stood on the edge of their greatest defeat of the war in the first of the German spring offensives: the Michael Offensive. Whether or not the defeat would be fatal to the Allied cause would only become apparent as each offensive planned by Ludendorff failed to achieve a conclusive breakthrough before the arrival of significant numbers of American troops. By July the Allies would be ready to launch the first of many counter-offensives against the Germans.

Treaties and Civil War

Following the signing of an armistice by Russia and Germany on December 15, 1917, formal peace negotiations between the two countries began at Brest-Litovsk on the 22nd. Trotsky, the Bolshevik commissar for foreign affairs, put forward proposals based on no indemnities, no annexation, and self-determination for subject peoples. Negotiations were long and angry, and in February, when Trotsky rejected the punishing German demands, the Germans renewed the fighting. Lenin, almost alone, recognized that a "breathing spell" was vital for the revolution, and he eventually forced his opinion through the Soviet Central Committee by threatening resignation. The treaty was duly signed on March 3, 1918.

THE TREATY OF BREST-LITOVSK

The terms of the treaty were harsh, stripping Russia of large swathes of its former empire, and leaving Poland and the Baltic states and, in effect Finland and the Ukraine, in German hands. In reality, these lands were already outside Bolshevik control. The Central Powers had agreed to recognize an independent Ukraine on January 9, 1918, signing a peace treaty with the new state a month later. Their

troops had thereby been able to advance deep into Ukraine, putting further pressure on Russia to sign the treaty. The Bolsheviks also agreed to pay financial "compensation" for war losses.

The Turks gained some territory and the promise of control of Baku and its oilfields.

Armistice and treaty lines
Between December 1917 and March 1918 the Russian Empire lost control of a large area to the east of the armistice line. As a result of the treaty, it lost 32 per cent of its arable land and 69 per cent of its industry.

Germans standing by dead countrymen
German troops were killed in February 1918 by Bolshevik forces when, with treaty talks in deadlock, they began to advance through Latvia towards Petrograd.

TREATY OF BREST-LITOVSK
March 3, 1918

BALTIC SEA · BLACK SEA

RUSSIAN EMPIRE · GER. · AUSTRIA-HUNGARY · BULGARIA · SERBIA · ROMANIA · UKRAINE

MOSCOW · Petrograd · Novgorod · Pskov · Riga · Tallinn · Minsk · Smolensk · Kursk · Pinsk · Kiev · Warsaw · Brest-Litovsk · Danzig · Odessa · Sebastopol · Rostov · Yekaterinoslav · Czernowitz

Don · Dnieper · Dniester · Bug · Pripet · Vistula

0 km 200 400
0 miles 200 400

— Armistice line Dec 15, 1917
— Line set by Treaty of Brest-Litovsk Mar 3 1918

An armistice between Russia and Germany led to nearly three months of negotiations before treaty terms were agreed. The Bolsheviks fought for control of Russia, but lost large swathes of territory in the west, including the Ukraine. By the end of 1918 White Russians, supporters of the tsar, were on the ascendant. In May 1918 Romania agreed a treaty with the Central Powers that greatly advantaged Germany.

1917 DECEMBER 9
Armistice signed by Romania and Central Powers

1917 DECEMBER 15
28-day armistice signed by Russia and Germany

DECEMBER 22
Brest-Litovsk peace talks start

DECEMBER 22
First major battle of Russian Civil War begins in Rostov, following its capture by Red Guards

DECEMBER 26
Bolsheviks temporarily break off negotiations because of German demands

1918 JANUARY 9
Kornilov and Alexev issue White Volunteer Army manifesto, outlining policy of resistance against Reds and Germans

JANUARY 24
Lenin's policy of seeking immediate peace rejected in favour of Trotsky's "no war, no peace"

FEBRUARY 6
Germany gives ultimatum to Romania regarding peace talks

FEBRUARY 10
Trotsky quits Brest-Litovsk talks for fourth time

FEBRUARY 14
Red Army formed

FEBRUARY 18
Germany resumes war with Russia

FEBRUARY 23
German negotiators arrive in Bucharest; peace terms for Romania become harsher

FEBRUARY 24
Russian Soviets accept German terms

FEBRUARY 27
Germany issues ultimatum to Romania insisting its peace terms are accepted

MARCH 3
Treaty of Brest-Litovsk signed

MARCH 5
Romania and Central Powers sign preliminary peace at Buftea

APRIL 13
Kornilov killed and is succeeded by Denikin as leader of White Volunteer Army in southern Russia

MAY 7
Treaty of Bucharest signed by Romania and Central Powers

MAY 14
Czech Tsarist POWs seize town out of Chelyabinsk

MAY 24
British squadron lands at Murmansk

JUNE 29
Czech forces capture Vladivostok, having taken a number of towns along the Trans-Siberian Railway

JULY 31
Allied forces take Archangelsk in northern Russia

AUGUST 3
British and Japanese land at Vladivostok

AUGUST 30
Assassination attempt on Lenin marks beginning of "Red Terror"

OCTOBER 1
Ironside arrives in Archangelsk to take up his role as new Allied commander-in-chief

NOVEMBER 18
Kolchak installed as supreme leader of Whites

NOVEMBER 26
Allied troops land at Odessa in southern Russia

DECEMBER 25
White forces seize Perm; French land at Sebastopol

KEY

Treaty of Brest-Litovsk Dec 15, 1917–Mar 3, 1918 negotiations	Treaty of Bucharest Dec 9, 1917–May 7, 1918 negotiations
Russian Civil War Dec 22, 1917–Dec 31, 1918	

Austria-Hungary gained nothing, while minor concessions in Ruthenia, eastern Galicia and Bukovina were granted to the Ukraine, thus permanently alienating the Poles from the "peace".

THE TREATY OF BUCHAREST

The collapse of the Russian armies in late 1917 had prompted Romania to sign an armistice with Germany on December 9. Treaty negotiations were complicated by the territorial demands of the other Central Powers, and the Treaty of Bucharest, signed on May 7, 1918, awarded some territory to Austria-Hungary and Bulgaria. Romania was made economically servile, with its agricultural surpluses and oil resources placed at Germany's disposal.

Occupying territories and enforcing these treaty provisions was to prove costly to the Germans who, despite keeping about 40 divisions in the east, were still unable to exploit the resources fully. Neither treaty lasted long, the Allies annulling them, as promised, when victory was achieved.

CIVIL WAR IN RUSSIA

One effect of Brest Litovsk was to end the coalition government of the Bolsheviks and the Social Revolutionaries, who voted against the treaty. An assassination attempt by the Social Revolutionaries against Lenin on August 30 marked the beginning of the "Red Terror". The Bolsheviks moved their government to Moscow and adopted the title "Russian Communist Party (Bolshevik)".

By May, when the Treaty of Bucharest was signed, Russia was in chaos, embroiled in a civil war in which the Bolsheviks had to fight many different enemies, some of whom were as willing to fight each other as the Bolsheviks. They ranged from socialists who supported the February Revolution, but not the Bolsheviks' October Revolution, to former tsarist generals. Considerable numbers of these counter-revolutionaries ("White Russians") gathered in Siberia, under the leadership of Admiral Kolchak, who made his headquarters at Omsk. They had support from the Allies and also from an unexpectedly influential group, the Czech Legion. During the war some 30,000 deserters from the Austro-Hungarian army had fought for tsarist Russia. They now transferred their allegiance to White Russia. As a trained force, they were more than a match for the Bolsheviks who, by the end of July, had lost most of Siberia and the Urals, with the Czechs controlling the Trans-Siberian Railway.

ALLIED INVOLVEMENT

In the summer, the counter-revolution received further support when Allied forces landed in the north and later at Vladivostok. Their motives were confused and, in spite of the view of both Wilson and Lloyd George that the government of Russia was the business of the Russians, the Allies soon became involved with the White Russian forces. By the end of 1918 a largely British force, supplemented by Latvians, Finns, Estonians, and even Australians and Italians, held substantial territory in the north. Vladivostok was occupied by US and Japanese forces (the latter seeking territorial gains); the French were in Odessa and Sebastopol, and Allied troops were co-operating in the east with Kolchak.

At the end of 1917, the Don Cossacks in the south had rebelled. In 1918 a number of tsarist generals, including Kornilov, Denikin and Wrangel, led further risings in the south. The counter-revolutionary movement encouraged the separatist tendencies of the peoples recently liberated from tsarist rule, who were also encouraged by the Allies' espousal of the principle of self-determination. In Finland, civil war between communists and their opponents erupted, and revolt in the Ukraine was only prevented by the German presence.

With White Russian forces advancing from all sides, by the end of 1918 the Bolsheviks' situation looked hopeless.

Workers unite
A 1917 poster calls on workers to unite with the Red Army to fight the tsar's forces in Petrograd.

Faced with the need to consolidate their control in Russia, the new leadership agreed to an armistice with the Central Powers, but balked at the peace terms offered.

Czech Legion
Czech soldiers were on their way through Siberia to Vladivostok when fighting broke out between them and the Bolsheviks. They seized part of the Trans-Siberian Railway and controlled it through the use of heavily armoured trains.

The German Spring Offensives

"Michael", the first of the offensives planned by Ludendorff for 1918, broke the British Fifth Army on the Somme, but was only a partial success because it then failed to take Arras. This set a pattern for the next two offensives, both of which met with initial success but subsequently failed to achieve their main objective. By the time of the last two offensives, in June and July, there were obvious signs of German exhaustion.

T HE WITHDRAWAL OF RUSSIA from the war enabled Germany to send troops from the Eastern Front to the Western Front, giving them a slight superiority in numbers. It was essential to take advantage of this before the Americans entered the line in significant numbers, and Ludendorff set about planning successive attacks that would drive a wedge between the British and French armies and destroy the British. The first of the attacks was codenamed Michael, after Germany's patron saint.

THE MICHAEL OFFENSIVE

The Michael Offensive – also known as the *Kaiserschlacht* (Kaiser's battle) – was directed by the German Second, Seventeenth and Eighteenth Armies against the British Third and Fifth Armies on the Somme (see map page 254). In the initial assault, launched on March 21, the Germans were supported by 6,473 guns – almost half the number of German guns on the Western Front – plus more than 3,500 mortars and 730 aircraft. To meet this powerful force, the British, who were stretched out along a 95-km (60-mile) front, had just 2,500 guns, 1,400 mortars and 579 aircraft.

When the men in the British Fifth Army were woken by the Germans' preliminary bombardment in the early hours of the morning, they immediately felt that it was more intense than any they had experienced before. It was, in the words of Gough, the Fifth Army commander, "a bombardment so sustained and steady that it at once gave me the impression of some crushing, smashing power". Before midday the Fifth Army was in retreat, over-whelmed by the German artillery and then what appeared to be inexhaustible

German infantry preparing to attack
Soldiers cross the Aisne-Oise Canal in preparation for an attack on the first morning of the Michael Offensive. The offensive was spearheaded by "stormtroopers", specially trained infantry whose role was to advance rapidly through any gaps that had been created in the enemy line.

A stormtrooper's equipment
The shock troops of the 1918 offensives already resembled the German stormtroopers of the Second World War. Armed with lightweight submachine-guns and stick grenades, some even wore a *Totenkopf* (Death's Head) badge.

STICK GRENADE

DEATH'S HEAD BADGE

MP 18/1 SUBMACHINE-GUN

32-round "snail" drum magazine

Air-cooled barrel

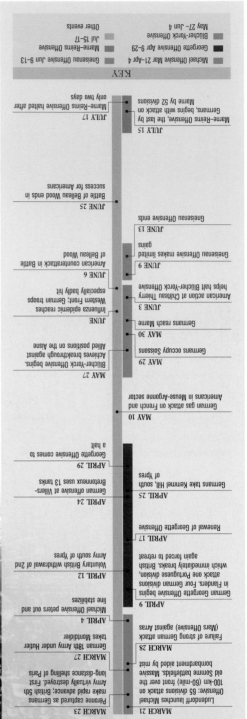

KEY

- Michael Offensive Mar 21–Apr 4
- Georgette Offensive Apr 9–29
- Blücher-York Offensive May 27–Jun 4
- Gneisenau Offensive Jun 9–13
- Marne-Reims Offensive Jul 15–17
- Other events

MARCH 21 — Ludendorff launches Michael Offensive: 65 divisions attack on 100-km (60-mile) front over the old Somme battlefields. Massive bombardment aided by mist

MARCH 23 — Péronne captured as Germans make rapid advance; British 5th Army virtually destroyed. First long-distance shelling of Paris

MARCH 27 — German 18th Army under Hutier takes Montdidier

MARCH 28 — Failure of strong German attack (Mars Offensive) against Arras

APRIL 4 — Michael Offensive peters out and line stabilizes

APRIL 9 — German Georgette Offensive begins in Flanders. Four German divisions attack one Portuguese division, which immediately breaks; British again forced to retreat

APRIL 12 — Voluntary British withdrawal of 2nd Army south of Ypres

APRIL 17 — Renewal of Georgette Offensive

APRIL 24 — German offensive at Villers-Bretonneux uses 13 tanks

APRIL 25 — Germans take Kemmel Hill, south of Ypres

APRIL 29 — Georgette Offensive comes to a halt

MAY 10 — German gas attack on French and Americans in Meuse-Argonne sector

MAY 27 — Blücher-York Offensive begins; Achieves breakthrough against Allied positions on the Aisne

MAY 29 — Germans occupy Soissons

MAY 30 — Germans reach Marne

JUNE — Influenza epidemic reaches Western Front; German troops especially badly hit

JUNE 3 — American action at Château Thierry helps halt Blücher-York Offensive

JUNE 6 — American counterattack in Battle of Belleau Wood

JUNE 9 — Gneisenau Offensive makes limited gains

JUNE 13 — Gneisenau Offensive ends

JUNE 25 — Battle of Belleau Wood ends in success for Americans

JULY 15 — Marne-Reims Offensive, the last by Germans, begins with attack on Marne by 52 divisions

JULY 17 — Marne-Reims Offensive halted after only two days

numbers of advancing German troops. On the first day alone German forces took about 25,500 hectares (98.5 square miles) of British-held territory, which was about the total amount of German-held territory reconquered by the British during the whole of the 140 days of the Somme offensive in 1916. Over the next two days, they reached the line of the Somme between Péronne and St Simon. Without in-depth defensive positions, the British Fifth Army was literally ripped to pieces. At the end of the third day, for example, the XIX Corps could only muster 50 men from the eight battalions that had held the original forward positions astride the upper Somme and St Quentin Canal on March 21.

The Germans continued to advance across the old Somme battlefield, taking Albert, on the Ancre, on March 26 and Montdidier on the 27th. In doing so they briefly divided the British and French armies. The French had already made divisions available to help the British Fifth Army. Faced, however, with the need to maintain formations in order to cover routes to the south, they concluded that they could not make more divisions available to support their ally.

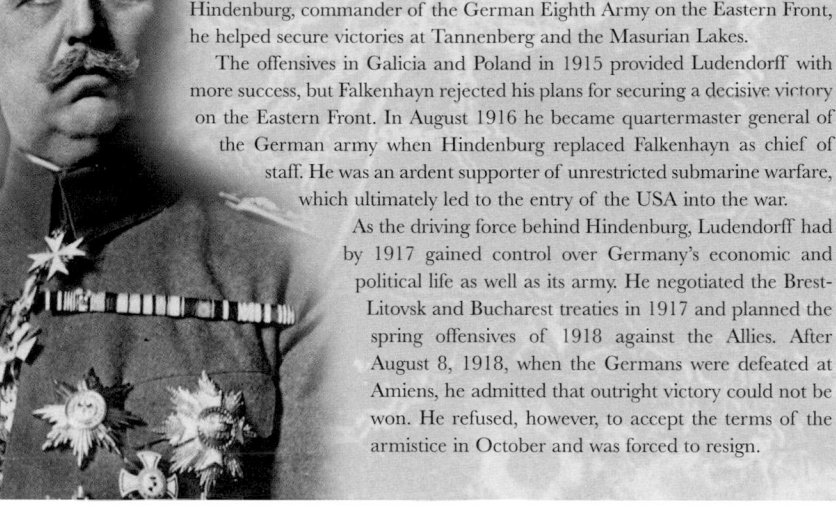

ERICH LUDENDORFF
~

I N AUGUST 1914 ERICH LUDENDORFF (1865–1937) demonstrated his dynamic leadership skills at Liège. Subsequently serving as chief of staff to Hindenburg, commander of the German Eighth Army on the Eastern Front, he helped secure victories at Tannenberg and the Masurian Lakes.

The offensives in Galicia and Poland in 1915 provided Ludendorff with more success, but Falkenhayn rejected his plans for securing a decisive victory on the Eastern Front. In August 1916 he became quartermaster general of the German army when Hindenburg replaced Falkenhayn as chief of staff. He was an ardent supporter of unrestricted submarine warfare, which ultimately led to the entry of the USA into the war.

As the driving force behind Hindenburg, Ludendorff had by 1917 gained control over Germany's economic and political life as well as its army. He negotiated the Brest-Litovsk and Bucharest treaties in 1917 and planned the spring offensives of 1918 against the Allies. After August 8, 1918, when the Germans were defeated at Amiens, he admitted that outright victory could not be won. He refused, however, to accept the terms of the armistice in October and was forced to resign.

GERMAN HALT AT ARRAS

In the first few days of Michael, many British troops had felt that defeat was not far away. But impressive as the initial success of Michael had been, not everything had gone the Germans' way. The German forces involved in the advance to Montdidier were now exhausted and their success had been in the sector where it had not been anticipated. The Germans had planned for their main success to be around Arras, from where they were to advance against the British armies to the north. The forces on the upper Somme had been intended to have only a covering role, and when it became clear that they needed the support of fresh formations, the German high command was unable to provide them. Checked in front of Arras on March 28, the Germans allowed Michael to run down even as their Fourth and Sixth Armies were reinforced in readiness for the next offensive, Georgette. This was to be directed against the British First and Second Armies along the Lys in Flanders.

British gun in action
British troops attempted to withstand the German advance during the Michael Offensive, but they were soon overwhelmed. The Germans reached the British gun-line on the first day, capturing 383 guns from the Fifth Army and 150 from the Third.

Refugees from Armentières
The Germans entered Armentières on April 10. It had been occupied by them once before, in 1914, but it had quickly been recaptured by the British. The Georgette Offensive reduced the town to ruins.

THE WESTERN FRONT
Mar 21–Jun 4, 1918

German front line Mar 21

German front line Jun 4

German offensive

Tank battle

Mar 21
Michael Offensive opens. Within days British 5th Army is destroyed although 3rd Army is able to hold its main positions

Apr 9
Georgette Offensive opens. Germans enjoy an unopposed 5-km (3-mile) advance on the first morning

May 27
Blücher–York Offensive opens. Germans advance to a maximum depth of 65 km (40 miles) within 5 days

BELGIUM

FRANCE

FLANDERS

English Channel

Nieuport
Dunkerque
Calais
Ypres
2ND ARMY Plumer
Kemmel 1915
Hazebrouck
Lille
Armentières
Neuve Chapelle
Béthune
1ST ARMY Horne
Souchez
Arras
Bapaume
Albert
Péronne
Cambrai
2ND ARMY Marwitz
3RD ARMY Byng
17TH ARMY O. von Below
6TH ARMY Quast
BELGIAN King Albert
Schelde
Lys
APR 24 Villers Bretonneux
Somme
St Quentin
18TH ARMY Hutier
Vervins
La Fère
7TH ARMY Böhn
Montdidier
5TH ARMY Gough
Noyon
Laon
Aisne
Craonne
Soissons
Compiègne
Oise
1ST ARMY F. von Below
6TH ARMY Duchène
5TH ARMY Micheler
Reims
Rethel
Vesle
Château Thierry
Épernay
Chantilly
Meaux
PARIS

0km 10 20 30 40 50
0miles 10 20 30 40 50

Things were so sudden, so hopelessly unexpected, and those who should have given warning had none themselves. Even in our just position, people would come weeping to us to know if they should go or stay, and we couldn't tell them. They looked to us for help and we couldn't give them it, they looked to us to stay the attack while they collected their few belongings and we couldn't do it.

BRITISH MAJOR "JOHN" LYNE DESCRIBING THE EFFECT OF THE GEORGETTE OFFENSIVE ON THE LOCAL POPULATION IN THE VICINITY OF ARMENTIÈRES

THE GEORGETTE OFFENSIVE

Georgette opened on April 9, and – with nine German divisions initially directed against four comparatively inexperienced Portuguese brigades – it resulted in immediate and major German gains. An advance of 6 km (4 miles) brought the German Sixth Army to the Lys River on the first day, Neuve Chapelle, Messines and Armentières were then captured in quick succession. But despite gains that by April 17 had forced the British to abandon the Passchendaele ridge and to withdraw almost into Ypres itself, the German Sixth Army had failed to achieve major, still less decisive, strategic success. It had broken open the front between Béthune and Armentières in the first two days, but had then failed to secure the crucial road junction at Hazebrouck before British, Australian and French divisions could arrive from the south.

The Germans continued to attack, capturing Kemmel Hill on the 25th and the neighbouring Scherpenberg Hill – from French forces – on the 29th. More significantly, however, they failed in their attempt to revive the offensive in front of Amiens when, on April 24, the first tank battle of the war was fought in Villers Bretonneux. The Germans succeeded in capturing the village, but it was retaken in a night attack on April 24/25 and the battle then died. On April 29 the Georgette attack as a whole was abandoned.

THE IMPORTANCE OF FRENCH SUPPORT

The fact that the British had survived both Michael and Georgette had much to do with the support they had received from the French. As British troops had reeled before the two onslaughts, the French had fed divisions into the path of the Germans.

German offensives

With the aim of defeating the British before the French, the first German offensive in 1918 was launched on the Somme. It resulted in the capture of Montdidier, but not Arras as planned, so failing, like the four offensives that followed, to win the war.

taking over British sectors in order to free British divisions, and allowing six badly depleted British divisions to move into quiet sectors of the French line. It was a terrible irony that as a result of this policy, British divisions were sent to the Chemin des Dames and the Aisne, sectors to which the Germans turned their attention following their failure to defeat the British on the Somme and Lys.

BLÜCHER-YORCK OFFENSIVE

If the German plan of campaign for spring 1918 was to succeed, individual offensives had to be halted early enough for assault forces and reserves to be redeployed even as Allied reserves were being committed to threatened sectors. There was also a

Propaganda poster
Although the German offensives in March and April had not quite gone according to plan, they had inflicted great damage on the Allies – as this German poster proudly proclaimed.

Der erste Monat deutsche Westoffensive!
127000 Gefangene
1600 Geschütze ca 200 Tanks
Viele 1000 Maschinen- gewehre
Ungeheure Mengen an Munition u. zahlreiche Flugzeuge
Geländegewinn 4100 Qkilometer

need for each offensive to follow hard on the heels of its predecessor in order to exploit advantages of numbers and timing. These conditions were not met with Michael and Georgette. Michael was initially so successful that the German high command persisted with it, so delaying the start of Georgette, while the employment of 46 divisions in Flanders during the Georgette offensive meant a delay of one

A casualty at Hazebrouck
The British successfully resisted the German advance on Hazebrouck. They were helped by the fact that German troops, deprived of alcohol by the Allied blockade, had found huge depots of wine and spirits and had got drunk.

month in moving formations into position for the third offensive: Blücher-Yorck. Yet this offensive, launched on May 27, was perhaps the most successful of the German efforts in 1918.

REASONS FOR SUCCESS

On the first day of Blücher-Yorck, divisions from the German Seventh Army achieved advances of 19 km (12 miles) and in one sector there was an advance of 65 km (40 miles) within five days. There were a number of reasons for this success. The First and Seventh Armies had gathered some 41 divisions and 3,719 guns for the attack, with the result that the initial bombardment was to represent the peak of German artillery achievement in 1918. Adding to the effectiveness of the bombardment was the French failure to prepare in-depth defences in the 40-km (25-mile) sector of attack, on the eastern Chemin des Dames. This failure was compounded by the refusal of the commander of the French Sixth Army, Duchêne, to conduct an in-depth defensive battle. He preferred to man front-line defensive positions in strength, and Pétain chose not to over-rule him.

As a result of the need to release troops to the reserve, the over-extended French Sixth Army had lengthened its front to 88 km (55 miles) until, by late May, its front-line divisions were holding sectors of some 7,300 m (8,000 yds). Compounding this weakness was the fact that four British divisions savaged in the earlier fighting were in the line, a result of the policy of moving exhausted formations into quiet sectors in order to release French reserves. Three of the divisions were in the sector immediately west of Reims, directly in the path of the main German effort.

Pétain had originally suspected that the main German attack in 1918 would fall on this sector, but after March 21 it had been concluded that this was now unlikely to happen. It was not until the final two days before Blücher-Yorck that German intentions became clear, by which time it was too late to remedy Allied defensive shortcomings. With the greater part of Allied infantry and artillery massed in forward positions and thus exposed to the full force of the initial German bombardment, four Allied divisions were destroyed and another four ruined within hours of the start of the Blücher-Yorck Offensive on May 27. By mid-morning the Germans had crossed the Aisne. The piecemeal commitment of reserves by Duchêne on May 27 and 28 only ensured that they were lost.

REVISION OF THE GERMAN PLAN

At this point the Germans abandoned their initial intention – to force the commitment of Allied reserves in this sector preparatory to a renewed effort north of the Somme. Instead, they decided to

FERDINAND FOCH

THE UNDENIABLE CONTRIBUTION to French wartime tactics by Ferdinand Foch (1851–1929) began well before the First World War at the Ecole de Guerre, where his influential lectures stressed the importance of offensive thinking.

Commander of the elite XX Corps from 1913, Foch launched successful counterattacks to protect Nancy and at the first battle of Marne in 1914. Although he had not yet had the chance to show his true offensive spirit, these defensive victories led to his appointment as leader of the French Northern Army Group on the Western Front. However, after two failed offensives at Arras in 1915 and his involvement in the first battle of the Somme, the value of which he had been sceptical about, Foch was sidelined in December 1916.

When Pétain took over from Nivelle as commander-in-chief in May 1917, Foch became chief of staff and really made his mark in the battles of 1918. Serving as Allied Supreme Commander on the Western Front from April that year, his armies the German offensives and recovered most of occupied France and part of Belgium before the end of the war.

expand Blücher-Yorck and drive on to Paris, so provoking the decisive battle. That same day Fère-en-Tardenois was captured and the Ourcq crossed.

On May 29 the Germans took Soissons and pressed on to the Marne, where they entered Château Thierry, just 90 km (56 miles) from Paris. They had taken some 65,000 prisoners and 800 guns, but by this time their advance was slowing down. On May 31 the Allies brought the German drive on Reims to a halt, and after minor actions over the next three days, the German Seventh Army cancelled plans to renew the offensive.

THE PEAK OF GERMAN SUCCESS

The Michael, Georgette and Blücher-Yorck offensives represented the peak of German success in 1918. Georgette very literally left the British armies in northern France and Belgium with no further room for

Prisoners at Laon
These French prisoners were among the 55,000 captured by the Germans between May 27 and June 4. At the end of the three spring offensives, over 355,00 Allied troops were either prisoners or missing.

withdrawal. Indeed, the situation in which the British armies found themselves on the Lys provoked Haig to issue a proclamation on April 11 which included the words: "With our backs to the wall and believing in the justice of our cause, each one of us must fight to the end." Against this, however, was the fact that while the German drive that secured Montdidier had separated the British and French armies, it had done so only briefly. It thus represented a failure for the German high command which had intended the separation to be permanent, laying the ground for the German defeat of first the British and then the French.

The disintegration of the British Fifth Army within three days of being attacked in the Michael Offensive had helped to convert Haig to the merits of a single French commander-in-chief who would ensure that the British received French support. Consequently, at the Doullens conference on March 26, the British and French military had decided that their separate efforts should be co-ordinated by Foch, the French chief of staff since 1917. This decision was to be of considerable benefit to the Allied effort in the future.

Also of great significance for the future was the fact that the Michael, Georgette and Blücher-Yorck offensives had exacted a toll that the German army could not afford. While, for example, the Michael attack cost the British 178,000 casualties and the French 77,000, it cost the Germans 239,000 casualties, of whom some 81,200 were from the Seventeenth Army opposite Arras. The Georgette Offensive cost the Allies around 118,00 casualties compared with German losses of 95,000. German casualties were high – during Michael some 11,000 a day – even if they were not as high as those of the

THE PARIS GUN

FROM AUGUST 29, 1914, the Germans made 30 air raids on Paris. On March 8, 1918 they dropped more than 90 bombs on the city, causing 200,000 people to flee. Consequently, Parisians were already living in some fear when, on March 23, the Germans began the first of four long-range bombardments using a weapon that they called "Wilhelm's Gun" in honour of the kaiser. Made by boring out a 38.1-cm (15-in) naval gun and inserting an inner tube, 30 m (98 ft) long and 21 cm (8.27 in) wide, the gun had a life expectancy of only 60 rounds because the powder charge was so powerful. The gun was fired at an elevation of 50° and, with a muzzle velocity of some 1,645 m (5,400 ft) per second, the 120-kg (264-lb) shell rose to a height of 38 km (24 miles). The maximum range was about 132 km (82 miles).

The first bombardment, which lasted until May 1, was from three emplacements at Crépy, near Laon; the last (August 5–9) was from the Bois de Corbie, further to the west. The Germans claimed to have fired a total of 367 shells in all, though the Parisians recorded only 320 hits on the city. With a light shell travelling a vast distance through unpredictable atmospheric conditions, what was hit was a matter of chance. The most destructive shell was one that hit a church on March 29, killing 88 people and wounding another 68. The gun was so inaccurate that it could only be used against a target the size of a city.

The Paris Gun in action
The Paris Gun did not stop the city and the government from functioning. It did, however, kill 256 and injure 620, and it increased fear among a population already subjected to air raids at night.

Bomb damage in Paris
Shortly before the first bombardment by the Paris Gun, the city was subjected to an air raid in which a number of buildings, including the War Ministry, pictured here, were destroyed.

Allies. Furthermore, they were suffered by the divisions who could least afford them – those that contained the highly trained stormtroopers.

German forces now held an extended front with lines of communication reaching back across a wasteland. (During the retreat of the Fifth Army, 248 bridges had been destroyed, and 300 locomotives and 20,000 burnt-out rail wagons abandoned.) Even more ominously for the Germans, Allied losses were being covered by the arrival of American forces. During May the number of American troops in France rose from 430,000 to 650,000 – and this was just the beginning of American deployment in strength.

INVOLVEMENT OF THE AMERICANS

The fact that the spring offensives had so far been conducted against little more than one-sixth of the total number of Allied divisions on the Western Front meant that Allied reserves could now be

A German casualty near the Aisne
The Germans had no difficulty in advancing across the Aisne on the first morning of the Blücher-Yorck offensive. However, as in the previous two spring offensives, they suffered high casualties.

"There has grown a wonderful mutual admiration and understanding between our boys and the Yanks. I'm sure the Yanks are going to prove excellent fighting troops."

AUSTRALIAN LIEUTENANT EDWIN TRUNDLE WRITING TO HIS WIFE IN JUNE

effectively redeployed. By the first days of June 1918 Allied forces were arriving on the Marne, and the French Fifth and Tenth Armies were taking over the Sixth Army's flank positions. American troops were also arriving to aid the Allied effort.

Pershing, commander of the American forces in France, had been determined that his forces should fight as one army rather than be divided up between the armies of the Allies. He had, however, been prepared to listen to the pleas of the British and French commanders for American support before it was too late. On May 28–29 the US Ist Infantry Division, in the first wartime attack of the American Expeditionary Force, had retaken the village of Cantigny and held it against German counterattacks. More significantly, on June 3 the US 3rd Infantry Division was involved in action to the east of Château Thierry, where they blew up a bridge to prevent the Germans crossing the Marne. They also held the line on the Paris–Metz road.

Three days later, the US 2nd Infantry Division became engaged in the Battle of Belleau Wood, northwest of Château Thierry. It was to last for three weeks and cost the lives of 5,000 Americans, but it resulted in a victory that for the Germans was an ominous sign of things to come. The Americans were inexperienced but enthusiastic, and seeing them buoyed the spirits of the Allied troops.

American troops in Château Thierry
The Germans captured Château Thierry on May 30 and stayed in control of the town until forced to abandon it by an Allied advance on July 21. On both occasions, American troops were involved in the fighting that took place either nearby or within the town itself.

THE GNEISENAU OFFENSIVE

The German high command should, perhaps, have sought an armistice at the end of the Blücher-Yorck Offensive. If German armies at full strength could not win with their first attack, then successive offensives, conducted with declining strength, would not bring Germany victory. Whether Germany's enemies would have been prepared to concede an armistice is, of course, another matter. As it was, even before Blücher-York had run its course, the German high command prepared for their next offensive – Gneisenau. It was to be launched against the Montdidier–Noyon bulge with the aim of clearing Blücher-York's right flank and perhaps opening the road to Paris. The defences in this sector were not well-prepared, but fortunately for the French Third Army, the haste with which the Germans attempted to redeploy formations meant that Gneisenau was the least organized of their spring attacks.

Forewarned of German intentions, the French were able to gather reserves and artillery for the counterattack. This did not, however, prevent three divisions of the French Third Army being destroyed in the opening hours of the German Eighteenth Army's attack on June 9. After an orderly withdrawal of its remaining forces, the French Third Army – with support from the Tenth – launched a counterattack on the 11th. This partially forestalled the German attack on June 12, with the result that the German advance was limited to a maximum depth of approximately 9 km (6 miles) across a 30-km (20-mile) front.

THE MARNE–REIMS OFFENSIVE

The failure of Gneisenau led the German high command to begin preparations for a fifth offensive, despite very obvious signs of German exhaustion. Each of the German offensives was marked by widespread looting and drunkenness, and in June 1918 measures were introduced to curb the rising tide of desertions and, more seriously, the outbreak of an influenza epidemic. All armies were affected, but the Central Powers, weakened by blockade, were less able to resist than their enemies.

The German plan was to attack either side of Reims and across the Marne, so pinning down Allied reserves before launching a greater offensive in Flanders. The offensive had, however, been widely discussed throughout Europe in June, which meant that when it opened on July 15 it faced an alert defence prepared in depth in strong natural positions. Reserves concentrated against the exposed flank of the German Marne salient added to the Germans' difficulties.

Out-thought and out-fought both strategically and tactically, the Germans made only the most modest of gains outside the sector to the east of Château Thierry, where the French Fifth and Sixth Armies met. Even in this sector the German advance was grinding to a halt by the evening of the 16th. As the French fed fresh troops into position in the forested Mont des Reims, the German high command conceded failure.

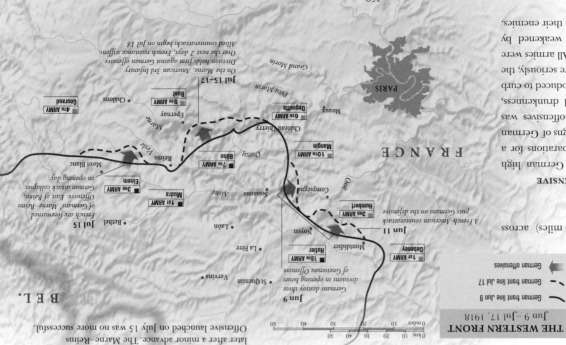

THE WESTERN FRONT
Jun 9 – Jul 17, 1918

German front line Jun 9
German front line Jul 17
German offensives

miles 0 10 20 30 40 50
km 0 10 20 30 40 50

Jun 9
Germans destroy three divisions in opening hours of Gneisenau Offensive

Jun 11
A French-American counterattack puts Germans on the defensive

Jul 15
French are forewarned of Germans' Marne–Reims Offensive. East of Reims, German attack collapses on opening day

Jul 15-17
On the Marne, American 3rd Infantry Division holds firm against German offensive. Over the next 2 days, French resistance stiffens. Allied counterattacks begin on Jul 18

FRANCE
PARIS
BEL.

Rethel · Laon · La Fère · Vervins · St Quentin · Noyon · Montdidier · Compiègne · Soissons · Reims · Châlons · Épernay · Château Thierry · Meaux

Aisne · Oise · Ourcq · Vesle · Marne · Petit Morin · Grand Morin · Mont Blanc

1ST ARMY Debeney
18TH ARMY Hutier
3RD ARMY Humbert
1ST ARMY Mudra
7TH ARMY Boehn
3RD ARMY Einem
10TH ARMY Mangin
6TH ARMY Degoutte
5TH ARMY Buat
4TH ARMY Gouraud

German offensives in June and July

Launched against the Montdidier–Noyon bulge on June 9, the Gneisenau Offensive destroyed three French divisions before grinding to a halt just four days later after a minor advance. The Marne–Reims Offensive launched on July 15 was no more successful.

Black Americans constructing trenches

Some 200,000 Black American troops were sent to France, where many worked as labourers. Black soldiers and officers were segregated in the US standing army and they continued to be segregated during the war, although the French were more inclined to treat them as equals.

THE WAR IN ART

A MONG THE MILLIONS OF SOLDIERS who served in the First World War were thousands of artists. They included the German artist, Franz Marc, who died at Verdun in 1916, and the Italian Futurist, Umberto Boccioni, who died in a cavalry exercise. The British army even had an officer training unit, the Artists' Rifles, which attracted architects, surveyors and draughtsmen as well as sculptors and painters. One way or another, artists in uniform found ways of being useful, and expressing their war experiences. The English artist Stanley Spencer even painted signs for the sergeants' and the "men's" toilets.

From a fear that they might reveal strategy and new technology to the enemy, British soldiers were forbidden to draw while they were in the trenches. Even so, many of them evaded the regulations, concealing their sketchbooks. In 1916 the British government began to appreciate the propaganda value of authentic, "eyewitness" images, and around 100 artists were eventually licensed to record their impressions of the war. Other nations, on both sides, made arrangements similar to these.

French trench newspaper
Many artists drew cartoons to illustrate the morale-boosting trench newspapers produced by both sides on the Western Front.

Despite their official status, war artists were often obstructed by on-the-spot military commanders, irritated by the tendency of artists to "sit down and look at a place for a long time". Nor did their work always present the image of war the government desired. After Passchendaele, British war artists were banned from depicting the dead of either side.

Even once the fighting was over, the war was not necessarily finished for the artist, whose experiences might take several years to emerge, as with Otto Dix's powerful cycle of etchings, *War* (1924). After serving as a medical orderly, Max Beckmann had a nervous breakdown. In 1916 he began painting *Resurrection*, in which wounded soldiers emerge from the dark night of war into a frail and uncertain daylight. Stanley Spencer also chose this theme as the climactic scene in a series painted for the Burghclere memorial chapel in England. The dead soldiers come back to life, but there is neither joy nor sorrow on their faces.

War artist at work
War artists, such as Australian James Quinn, would record their visual impressions in the field, using them later as the basis for their final work.

Sir Stanley Spencer:
Travoys Arriving with Wounded at a Dressing Station at Smol, Macedonia
Stanley Spencer's experience of the effects of war, first as a hospital orderly in Britain, and then as a soldier in Macedonia, led him to portray in his paintings the acts of compassion shown by one human being to another. In this painting, the stretcher-bearers reach out to try and protect their wounded charges, as men and beasts gather round the lighted window of the dressing station in a scene reminiscent of the Nativity.

John Nash:
Over the Top
John Nash saw action in France before being appointed as a war artist in 1918. This painting depicts his worst experience as a soldier in an action he described as "pure murder". In December 1917 his company was ordered to carry out a diversionary attack in daylight in the snow, making them an easy target for German machine-gunners.

Wartime sketchbook
This watercolour portrait is from the sketchbook of Alexandre Zinoviev, a Russian, later a well-known stage designer, who joined the French Foreign Legion in 1914.

Otto Dix:
Setting Sun (Ypern) 1918
Otto Dix enlisted in 1914 from a desire to experience humans in their "unleashed state". This painting shows the violence of war engulfing even the natural world, with the setting sun exploding like a bomb above cowering soldiers.

Egon Schiele:
Russian Officer
The Austrian Expressionist Egon Schiele was refused a post as an official war artist, but this did not stop him painting portraits of the Russian prisoners in his charge. His admiration for their stoicism in captivity is evident. He later admitted to feeling more in sympathy with the enemy countries, where he considered there to be "more thinking people", than in his own country, which was suffocating in the stultifying atmosphere of the decaying Habsburg monarchy.

Fernand Léger:
Soldier Smoking a Pipe
The French artist Léger served as an engineer, and his visual appreciation of the durable materials of war machinery is shown in the mechanical construction of this soldier. Other paintings by Léger, however, portray the terrible damage inflicted by war on human flesh.

Beginning of the Allied Advance

COUNTER-OFFENSIVES ON THE WESTERN FRONT

JULY 18 – OCTOBER 3, 1918

The German armies were exhausted by the time their offensive on the Marne ground to a halt on July 17. They were in no state to repel a series of Allied counterattacks that began with a French-American campaign to recapture the Marne salient. This did not mean, however, that the Allies were able to push back the German forces with ease. Almost everywhere, the Germans fought hard to retain their positions.

BETWEEN JULY 18 AND NOVEMBER 11, 1918 the Allied armies conducted a series of offensives, each with limited aims, which eliminated the Germans' spring gains, took the war into territories that for years had lain well behind the front lines, and broke the German will to resist. In these four months the Allies out-fought, at both the strategic and tactical level, the Germans on ground they had held since September 1914. The key to the success of the Allies was their ability to mount a series of closely-phased offensives, each with marked local numerical superiority and for limited objectives. Taken together, they imposed an ultimately intolerable pressure on the Germans.

In fact, an Allied counterattack had taken place before July 18. On July 4, the Australian corps had mounted a small operation at Hamel, near Amiens, with the support of American infantry companies. Aiding the attack were 60 new Mark V tanks plus aircraft that parachuted supplies to forward units. The Allied forces advanced across a 3,500-m (6,000-yd) front, and in a 90-minute attack they took Hamel. They also captured over 1,500 prisoners, two field guns and 171 machine-guns, for the loss of fewer than 1,000 casualties.

ATTACK ON THE MARNE SALIENT

On July 18 three French armies – with five American divisions – opened a campaign to recapture the Marne salient from the Germans. The inclusion of 225 Renault light tanks aided the Allies' initial attack on the vulnerable Soissons-Château Thierry road, where the Germans had failed to prepare their defensive positions properly. By marching late to their start-lines, the Allied forces took the Germans by surprise and by July 20 they had reached the Marne itself. They crossed the

German prisoners near Amiens
On August 8 the British and French launched an attack to the east of Amiens, in the Somme sector, against six German divisions that were outnumbered 6 to 1. The British alone took 13,000 prisoners on the first day.

KEY

■ Action in Champagne-Marne sector Jul 18–Aug 20	■ Action in Flanders Aug 18–Oct 3
■ Action in Meuse-Argonne sector Sept 12–29	■ Action in Somme sector Aug 8–Oct 3
■ Other events	

JULY 18 — Allied counter-offensive begins with French advance to clear Marne salient

AUGUST 1 — French forces occupy Soissons

AUGUST 3 — Germans complete withdrawal from Marne salient

AUGUST 6 — Franco-American force reaches Vesle River, thus straightening out Soissons–Reims salient

AUGUST 8 — Launch of British offensive, with French in support, at Amiens, (the "black day of the German army")

AUGUST 10 — French forces occupy Montdidier

AUGUST 18 — Start of French offensive that results in capture of Aisne Heights on 20th

AUGUST 18 — British offensive in Flanders begins

AUGUST 21 — British renew offensive on Somme

AUGUST 22 — British forces capture Albert

AUGUST 27 — French forces occupy Roye

AUGUST 28 — Canadians smash through Hindenburg Line to reach Wotan position on 30th

AUGUST 29 — New Zealand forces occupy Bapaume

AUGUST 30 — Austro-Hungarian intention to sue for peace communicated to Germany

SEPTEMBER 2 — Australian forces occupy Péronne; Canadian forces break through Wotan position

SEPTEMBER 5 — German General Headquarters moved from Avesnes to Spa

SEPTEMBER 6 — Germans complete withdrawal from Lys salient

SEPTEMBER 12 — Launch of offensive on St Mihiel salient by Americans with some French support

SEPTEMBER 15 — Start of Austro-Hungarian peace initiative and Allied offensive at Salonika

SEPTEMBER 16 — Elimination of St Mihiel offensive salient completed in first victory by independent American army

SEPTEMBER 26 — American and French forces begin Argonne offensive

SEPTEMBER 27 — Start of British offensive between Lens and Épehy

SEPTEMBER 28 — British, Belgians and French launch offensive: Fourth Battle of Ypres

SEPTEMBER 29 — British offensive opens with Battle of St Quentin Canal

SEPTEMBER 29 — Ludendorff calls for immediate armistice

river the following day. After this, however, progress was slow, partly because the land was so broken up. Fère-en-Tardenois was taken on July 27 and Soissons on August 1. On the 2nd/3rd the German Seventh and Ninth Armies completed a general withdrawal from the Marne salient. By August 4, when the offensive came to an end, the Allies had taken some 25,000 German prisoners in the course of advancing 50 km (30 miles).

OFFENSIVE AT AMIENS
On August 8 the British Fourth Army mounted an attack in front of Amiens with 456 tanks. In just one day the German front was broken over 24 km (15 miles) of its length to a maximum depth of 4 km (7 miles). Six weak German divisions were destroyed, with the British taking 13,000 prisoners

and 400 guns. To the south the French First Army slowly advanced 5 km (3 miles) over a similar frontage before grinding to a halt.

The results achieved by the Fourth Army were little different from those registered on the first day at Cambrai in 1917. But in front of Amiens the

Wounded German prisoner
In many of the battles fought from July onwards, the German soldiers were not only outnumbered but had far less support from tanks and aircraft than the Allied troops. The toll of German prisoners steadily mounted.

German defeat was marked by a collapse of formations which led Ludendorff to describe this as "the black day of the German army". Nonetheless, the German high command was able to respond quickly and effectively to this defeat. By midday on the second day, nine German divisions had been fed into the line. The British, with 145 tanks, advanced just 5 km (3 miles). On the third day of the offensive, when just 67 tanks remained in service, the only gains made were in the centre and to a depth of about 1.5 km (1 mile), at which point the British offensive was brought to an end.

PHOTOGRAPHY AND FILM

PHOTOGRAPHS WERE USED in training and propaganda, but photography in battle areas was severely restricted, and newspapers did not illustrate the actuality of trench warfare. Film, however, played an ever-increasing part in the effort to mobilize public support for the war effort. Newsreels, such as the French *Annales de la Guerre* and the official British record of the Somme in 1916, provided images of the front that were heavily censored or even staged. Cinema was immensely popular, and after 1916 films, commercial or state-funded, comedy or melodrama, took the lead in projecting the war as a contest between Good and Evil. Most commercial films were escapist, but others spread a moral message. Charlie Chaplin, in the outstanding *Shoulder Arms* (1918), was hugely popular, not least among Allied troops. Some films, such as D.W. Griffith's *Hearts of the World* (1918), encouraged an hysterical hatred of the enemy that complicated the task of the Versailles peacemakers. In Germany, a consortium of film companies, Universum Film AG (UFA), was set up as a state enterprise to make films under military control. Cinemas drew in the cold and hungry in 1917–18 as they received priority in coal and electricity supplies.

Hearts of the World
D.W. Griffith (wearing a bow-tie) during the shooting of *Hearts of the World* in France. His film attempted to bring the experience of battle and the reality of war into the movie theatre.

BOX OF SLIDES

FRENCH STEREOSCOPIC CAMERA

GLASS SLIDE WITH DOUBLE IMAGE

Stereoscopic camera
The war coincided with the arrival of affordable, easy-to-use cameras, thanks largely to Kodak. Particularly fashionable at the time was the stereoscopic camera, designed to mimic human vision. A special viewer was needed to appreciate the stereoscopic effect.

Attention now switched to the south where, on August 10, the French Third Army had occupied Montdidier, which had been abandoned as German forces withdrew from their most forward positions. This French effort continued, primarily around Lassigny, until the 16th. It was followed by an offensive by the Tenth Army on the 18th that resulted in the capture of the Aisne Heights on the 20th and the taking of some 8,000 prisoners in front of Noyon. As a result of what Ludendorff described as "another black day" of "heavy and irreplaceable losses", the French now threatened the German lines along the north bank of the Vesle.

BATTLE OF BAPAUME

Following diversionary attacks on the Lys, the British Third Army, with almost 200 tanks, attacked on August 21 along a 16-km (10-mile) sector between Albert and Arras. In the Battle of Bapaume that followed, Albert was retaken on the 22nd. The following day the British Fourth Army came to the support of the Third Army, and Bapaume was taken on the 29th. The battle came to an end on the 31st.

On the 26th the British First Army launched an offensive on the Arras-Cambrai road. With the weight of the offensive switched between different sectors,

Australian formations were able to push across the Somme at Péronne on August 30 and secure the town on September 2. On the same day the Canadians, supported by two British divisions and 59 tanks, breached the German line, between Drocourt and Quéant, on an 8-km (5-mile) front.

With this latter success the British broke open the Hindenburg Line at one of its strongest points. In so doing, they not only carried the tide of battle into areas that had been under enemy control since August 1914 but made it impossible for the Germans to continue holding positions to the north. On August 31 German formations began to evacuate their positions on the Lys and around Kemmel Hill, so reducing the front line by 80 km (50 miles). Despite this reduction, the Germans were in no better position in September

Welcoming the Americans
A French poster welcomes the arrival of American troops. From the moment the United States declared war on Germany, in April 1917, the French looked forward to American troops joining them on the front line.

than in August to resist attack. The German armies had incurred 228,000 casualties and received only 130,000 replacements in the period between Amiens and Quéant. Consequently, in August, 21 German divisions were broken up and the Army Group Rupprecht's reserve was reduced from 36 to just nine divisions. In comparison, the Allies were in a position to clear the St Mihiel salient and move against the Hindenburg Line, to which the Germans had withdrawn in the spring of 1917.

ST MIHIEL OFFENSIVE

On August 30 the American First Army – activated on August 10 – was assigned the sector south of St Mihiel. With the aim of freeing the Paris-Verdun-Nancy railways, the Americans launched an attack on St Mihiel on September 12. One French corps was in the line and the French provided half of the gunners, but this was effectively the first action of an independent American army on the Western Front. Its objective was achieved with little difficulty, the Germans having started to evacuate their positions before the attack began. In the first two days of the offensive, the Americans took some 8,000 prisoners and a huge total of 443 guns.

Allied attacks in Flanders and France
From July 18 the Allies slowly pushed back the Germans all along the front line. The Germans reduced the length of the line in Flanders at the end of August in an attempt to halt the advance, but to no avail. They were more successful in the south, where they held up a French-US advance in the Argonne.

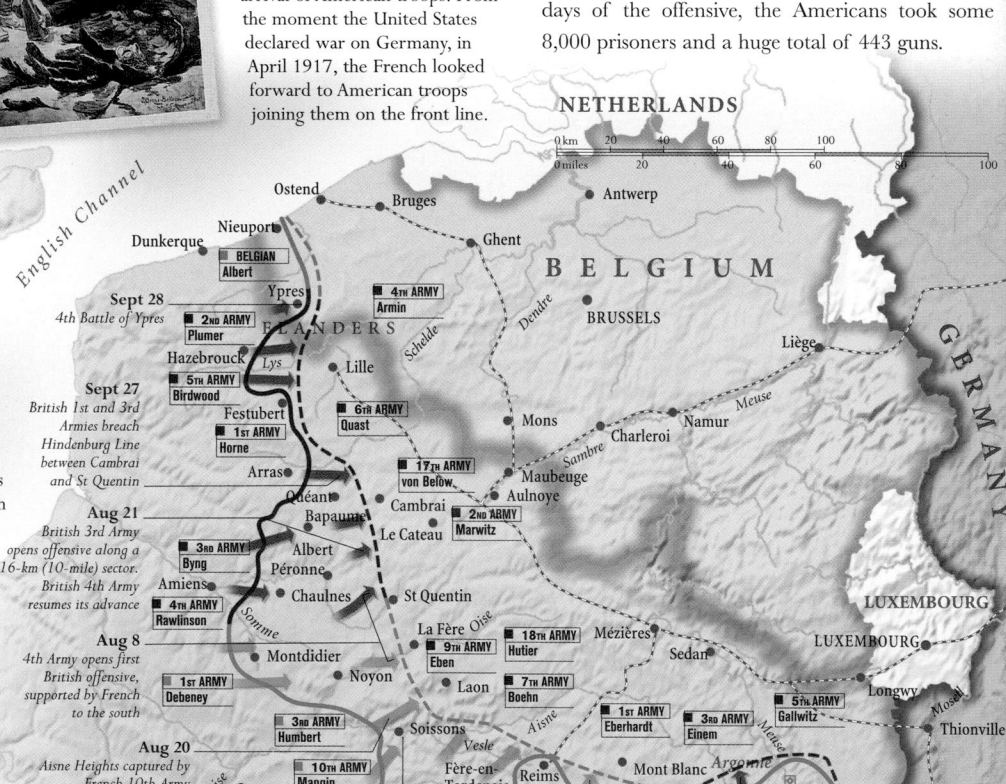

THE WESTERN FRONT
Jul 18–Oct 3, 1918

ALLIED FRONT LINE JUL 18:	ALLIED ATTACKS:
Belgian sector	➤ British offensives
British sector	➤ French offensives
French sector	➤ American offensives
American sector	The Allies (and allied states)
ALLIED FRONT LINE SEPT 25:	Central Powers (and allied states)
Belgian sector	Neutral states
British sector	⊠ Fortified town
French sector	--- Major railway
American sector	

Sept 28
4th Battle of Ypres

Sept 27
British 1st and 3rd Armies breach Hindenburg Line between Cambrai and St Quentin

Aug 21
British 3rd Army opens offensive along a 16-km (10-mile) sector. British 4th Army resumes its advance

Aug 8
4th Army opens first British offensive, supported by French to the south

Aug 20
Aisne Heights captured by French 10th Army

Jul 18
French launch counterattack to clear Marne salient

Aug 1
Soissons taken

Sept 26
Argonne offensive opens. Slow progress is made over difficult country by French and US forces

Sept 12
Americans begin attack on the St Mihiel salient. It is cleared by Sept 16

NETHERLANDS
BELGIUM
GERMANY
LUXEMBOURG
FRANCE
FLANDERS
English Channel
PARIS

BELGIAN Albert
4TH ARMY Armin
2ND ARMY Plumer
5TH ARMY Birdwood
6TH ARMY Quast
1ST ARMY Horne
17TH ARMY von Below
2ND ARMY Marwitz
3RD ARMY Byng
4TH ARMY Rawlinson
1ST ARMY Debeney
3RD ARMY Humbert
10TH ARMY Mangin
5TH ARMY Berthelot
9TH ARMY Eben
18TH ARMY Hutier
7TH ARMY Boehn
1ST ARMY Eberhardt
3RD ARMY Einem
5TH ARMY Gallwitz
4TH ARMY Gouraud
1ST ARMY Pershing
19TH ARMY Bothmer

Ostend, Bruges, Antwerp, Nieuport, Ghent, Dunkerque, Ypres, BRUSSELS, Liège, Hazebrouck, Lille, Mons, Namur, Charleroi, Festubert, Maubeuge, Aulnoye, Arras, Cambrai, Le Cateau, Quéant, Bapaume, Albert, Péronne, St Quentin, Amiens, Chaulnes, La Fère, Montdidier, Noyon, Laon, Mézières, Sedan, LUXEMBOURG, Longwy, Thionville, Soissons, Reims, Mont Blanc, Verdun, Metz, Chantilly, Fère-en-Tardenois, Château Thierry, St Menhould, Chalons, Bar le Duc, St Mihiel, Troyon, Nancy, Seine, Oise, Somme, Aisne, Vesle, Marne, Meuse, Moselle, Scheldt, Dendre, Sambre, Lys, Argonne Forest

THE SUSTAINED PSYCHOLOGICAL and physical stress of soldiering in the trenches led to a new kind of war damage known as "shell shock". In dealing with victims of shell shock, army commanders and medical officers tended to be unsympathetic, partly because the condition ranged from frayed nerves to complete mental collapse. After 1918 there was a public debate in Britain about shell shock, and in 1922 a War Office Committee of Enquiry published its report on the phenomenon of shell shock, which was now termed "war neurosis". Although the report made it clear that loss of nerve or mental control would not be tolerated as an escape route by soldiers, it did acknowledge shell-shock victims as genuine casualties of 20th-century warfare. To prevent war neurosis, it recommended shorter tours of front-line duty, and more attention to the health and welfare of soldiers. It also recommended psychotherapy for the treatment of shell shock, which gave a boost to Sigmund Freud's revolutionary theories about repression and defence mechanisms.

Shell-shocked soldier
Faced with men displaying paralysis, muscular contractions and loss of sight that had no apparent physical basis, the military authorities saw cowards, "malingerers" and men who has simply failed to "get a grip".

Under fire
Men who deserted after repeatedly coming under fire may well have been suffering from shell shock.

ARGONNE OFFENSIVE

The American high command had wished to follow the clearing of the St Mihiel salient with an advance on Metz, aimed at severing the Strasbourg–Lille rail link. However, even before the St Mihiel offensive, it had been forced to accept a commitment in the Argonne as the price of ensuring its own distinctive national contribution to the common cause. Haig had drawn up a plan under which the Allies were to conduct complementary, converging offensives – the British from the Le Cateau area and the Americans against the Sedan–Mézières sector. Many American commanders at the time, and many American historians since, have portrayed this plan as the means of denying the Americans "the victory that would have won the war". The reality was that the war was not going to be won by

American troops in action
Many of the guns used by the Americans were supplied by the French, but here they are firing a US-made 356-mm (14-in) railway gun.

Australians near St Quentin
The 5th Australian Division were among the troops who breached the Hindenburg Line between Cambrai and St Quentin on September 27. The infantry were supported by a Mark V tank battalion.

Salonika. On the 19th the British offensive in northern Palestine had begun and within three days it had destroyed the Turkish Seventh and Eighth Armies. On the 29th, as German positions on the Hindenburg Line crumbled, Bulgaria concluded an armistice.

REQUEST FOR AN ARMISTICE

In July, members of the German high command had urged a general withdrawal to the positions held before the Michael Offensive. This had been resisted in the belief that Germany could not abandon the gains of the previous four months without compromising its political and strategic position. Following the Allied attack at Amiens in August, the German high command, fearing that it faced an immediate collapse on the Western Front, had demanded that an armistice should be sought. This demand had been set aside with the slackening of Allied pressure. However, German losses of 230,000 men in September, coupled with a series of defeats towards the end of the month, destroyed any confidence that the German armies could still retain a coherent defensive position in the west. On September 28 Ludendorff suffered a seizure and collapsed, and on the 29th the German military authorities demanded that an approach for an armistice be made immediately.

a single victory, or the capture of a single town and railway, and that if German lateral communications were to be severed then both Luxembourg and Metz would have to be taken. But leaving aside these facts, whether the Americans could have taken Metz, the most strongly fortified city in Europe, is doubtful.

What cannot be doubted, however, is that the commitment of American forces to an offensive in the Argonne was both unnecessary and un-fortunate. It was unnecessary because the British were to break the Hindenburg Line and could have done so without any supporting offensive. It was unfortunate because American formations were thus committed to an offensive on September 26 that was poorly organized and quickly descended into chaos as a result of the over-concentration of forces and the inadequacy of staff and transport arrangements. Fought over very difficult country and in almost continuous rain, the Argonne offensive took the form of a series of slow, bitterly-contested advances. The French Fourth and US First Armies had advanced to the outskirts of Sedan by November 11, but by this time the focus of events had shifted elsewhere.

CAMBRAI AND YPRES

The main focus of fighting on the Western Front in September was in front of Cambrai. Here, on September 27, the British First and Third Armies crossed the Canal du Nord and, with the Australians and US 2nd Corps in the line, breached the Hindenburg Line between Cambrai and St Quentin. The offensive was halted on October 5.

To the north, in a two-day action on September 28 and 29 known as the Fourth Battle of Ypres, the Belgians secured Dixmude and the British Second Army took Messines and its ridge, so threatening the German positions on the Belgian coast. On the second of these days, as Allied forces reached the outskirts of Cambrai, the various elements of German defeat came together. On September 15 Austria-Hungary had in effect sought a separate peace, while the Allies opened their offensive at

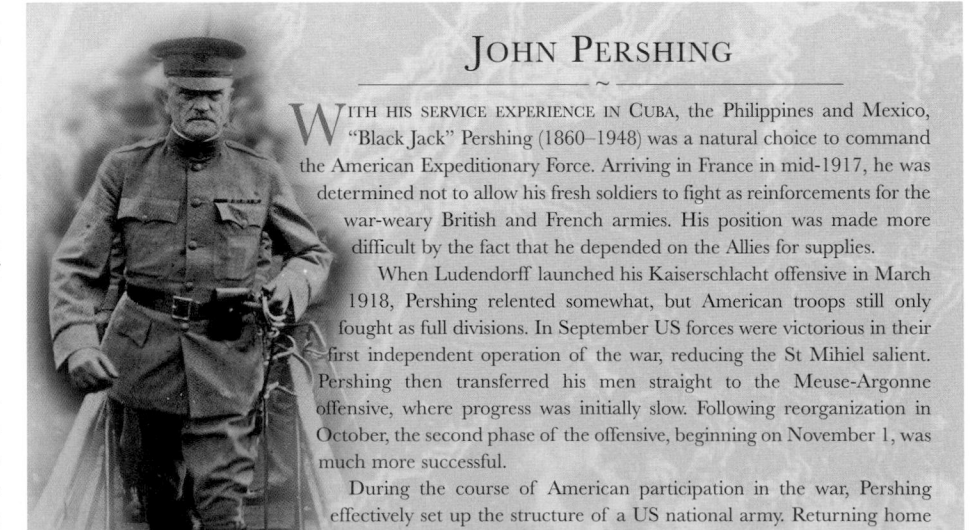

JOHN PERSHING
~

WITH HIS SERVICE EXPERIENCE IN CUBA, the Philippines and Mexico, "Black Jack" Pershing (1860–1948) was a natural choice to command the American Expeditionary Force. Arriving in France in mid-1917, he was determined not to allow his fresh soldiers to fight as reinforcements for the war-weary British and French armies. His position was made more difficult by the fact that he depended on the Allies for supplies.

When Ludendorff launched his Kaiserschlacht offensive in March 1918, Pershing relented somewhat, but American troops still only fought as full divisions. In September US forces were victorious in their first independent operation of the war, reducing the St Mihiel salient. Pershing then transferred his men straight to the Meuse-Argonne offensive, where progress was initially slow. Following reorganization in October, the second phase of the offensive, beginning on November 1, was much more successful.

During the course of American participation in the war, Pershing effectively set up the structure of a US national army. Returning home in 1919, he was awarded the unique rank of "General of the Armies".

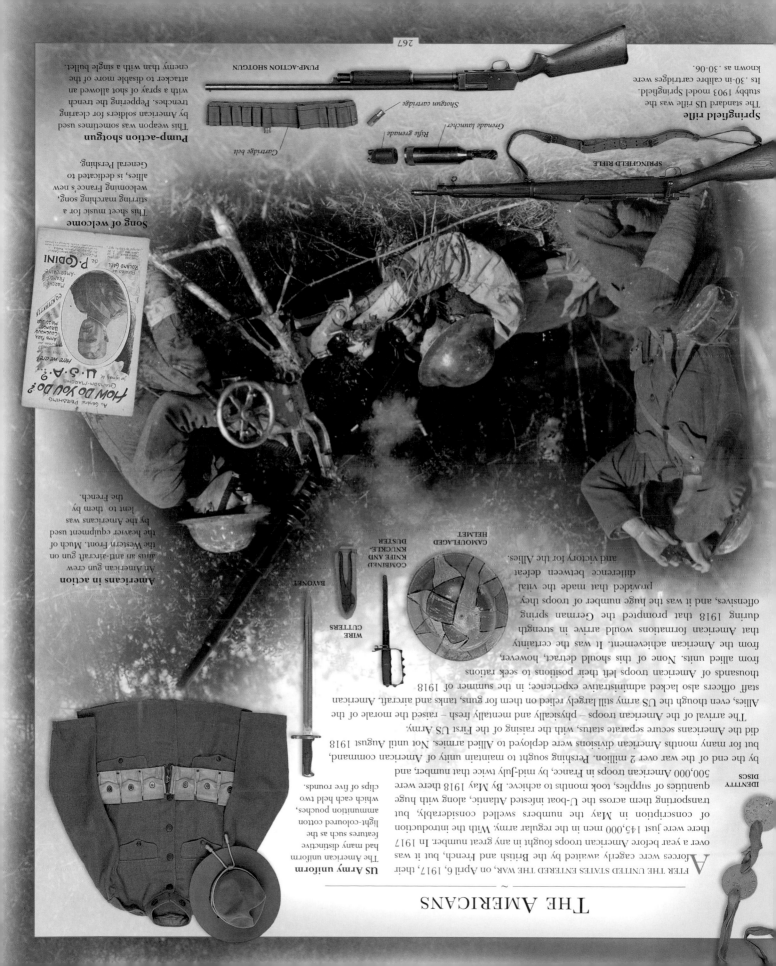

THE AMERICANS

AFTER THE UNITED STATES ENTERED THE WAR, on April 6, 1917, their forces were eagerly awaited by the British and French, but it was over a year before American troops fought in any great number. In 1917 there were just 145,000 men in the regular army. With the introduction of conscription in May the numbers swelled considerably, but transporting them across the U-boat infested Atlantic, along with huge quantities of supplies, took months to achieve. By May 1918 there were 500,000 American troops in France, by mid-July twice that number, and by the end of the war over 2 million. Pershing sought to maintain unity of American command, but for many months American divisions were deployed to Allied armies. Not until August 1918 did the Americans secure separate status, with the raising of the First US Army.

The arrival of the American troops – physically and mentally fresh – raised the morale of the Allies, even though the US army still largely relied on them for guns, tanks and aircraft. American staff officers also lacked administrative experience; in the summer of 1918 thousands of American troops left their positions to seek rations from allied units. None of this should detract, however, from the American achievement. It was the certainty that American formations would arrive in strength during 1918 that prompted the German spring offensives, and it was the huge number of troops they provided that made the vital difference between defeat and victory for the Allies.

US Army uniform
The American uniform had many distinctive features such as the light-coloured cotton ammunition pouches, which each held two clips of five rounds.

Americans in action
An American gun crew aims an anti-aircraft gun on the Western front. Much of the heavier equipment used by the Americans was lent to them by the French.

Song of welcome
This sheet music for a stirring marching song, welcoming France's new allies, is dedicated to General Pershing.

Pump-action shotgun
This weapon was sometimes used by American soldiers for clearing trenches. Peppering the trench with a spray of shot allowed an attacker to disable more of the enemy than with a single bullet.

Springfield rifle
The standard US rifle was the stubby 1903 model Springfield. Its .30-in calibre cartridges were known as .30-06.

PUMP-ACTION SHOTGUN

Shotgun cartridge

Cartridge belt

Rifle grenade

Grenade launcher

SPRINGFIELD RIFLE

BAYONET

WIRE CUTTERS

COMBINED KNIFE AND KNUCKLE-DUSTER

CAMOUFLAGED HELMET

IDENTITY DISCS

German prisoners after Amiens, August 1918
By the end of the Allied offensive launched at Amiens on
August 8, the Germans had lost 18,000 killed and wounded
and 30,000 had been taken prisoner. Never before in the
war had German troops surrendered in such numbers.

The Collapse of Germany's Allies

GERMANY'S ALLIES were unable to summon up the same strength in terms of manpower and firepower as their much larger and more heavily industrialized senior partner. They did, however, serve a useful function, which was to draw British and French forces away from the main theatre of war – the Western Front.

DEFEAT OF BULGARIA

The campaign against Bulgaria had this effect. Between the end of 1915 and mid-1918 Salonika, in northern Greece, was referred to by the Germans as their "largest internment camp" because of the huge number of Allied troops stationed there.

For the Central Powers, especially Germany, an offensive against Salonika would have been a massive undertaking at the end of a long and inadequate line of communication, and any success would only have aggravated the conflicting territorial ambitions of Austria-Hungary, Bulgaria and Turkey in the region. For the Allies, on the other hand, there was a need to recover Serbia and to carry the war to Germany's partners. However, although there were 600,000 Allied troops in Salonika by mid-1917, priority was given to the Western Front and to the Middle East.

The Allies were also racked by national and personal differences and hampered by the ambiguous position of Greece towards their cause, but in 1917 certain of their problems eased. Growing and relentless Allied pressure on Greece bore fruit in June with the abdication of the pro-German king and the inauguration of the Venizelos administration. Greece declared war against the Central Powers on June 29, and Greek troops were added to the Allied forces.

In France, the new administration of Georges Clemenceau chose to recall Sarrail – a commander who had managed to alienate virtually all his subordinates. His replacement was Guillaumat, whose arrival in December ushered in a period of intense Allied activity, including the improvement of lines of communication and a slow recovery of morale. Careful plans were prepared for limited offensives, but the series of Allied crises on the Western Front meant that these had to be shelved and Guillaumat was in turn recalled, to be replaced by Franchet d'Esperey in June 1918.

Moment of recoil
British troops fire a 2.75-in gun in the mountains above Salonika, as part of the September offensive that led to the defeat of Bulgaria and the liberation of Serbia.

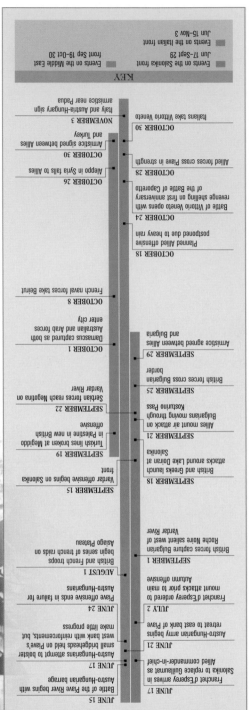

ITALY, SALONIKA AND THE MIDDLE EAST
JUNE 15 – NOVEMBER 11, 1918

Apart from a failed offensive by the Austro-Hungarians on the Piave in June, the initiative rested with the Allies. In mid-September they launched offensives in Salonika and Palestine, and in October they fought their way across the Piave in a reversal of the action there in June. In all three regions they met with only limited resistance from opponents who had largely lost the resources, the energy and the conviction to fight.

KEY
- Events on the Salonika front: Jun 17–Sept 30
- Events on the Middle East front: Sep 19–Oct 30
- Events on the Italian front: Jun 15–Nov 3

JUNE 15 — Battle of the Piave River begins with Austro-Hungarian barrage

JUNE 17 — Franchet d'Esperey arrives in Salonika to replace Guillaumat as Allied commander-in-chief

JUNE 17 — Austro-Hungarians attempt to bolster small bridgeheads held on Piave's west bank with reinforcements, but make little progress

JUNE 21 — Austro-Hungarian army begins retreat to east bank of Piave

JUNE 24 — Piave offensive ends in failure for Austro-Hungarians

JULY 2 — Franchet d'Esperey ordered to mount attacks prior to main Autumn offensive

AUGUST 1 — British and French troops begin series of trench raids on Asiago Plateau

SEPTEMBER 1 — British forces capture Bulgarian Roche Noire salient west of Vardar River

SEPTEMBER 15 — Vardar offensive begins on Salonika front

SEPTEMBER 18 — British and Greeks launch attacks around Lake Doiran at Salonika

SEPTEMBER 19 — Turkish lines broken at Megiddo in Palestine in new British offensive

SEPTEMBER 21 — Allies mount attack on Bulgarians moving through Kostumino Pass

SEPTEMBER 22 — Serbian forces reach Negotina on Vardar River

SEPTEMBER 25 — British forces cross Bulgarian border

SEPTEMBER 29 — Armistice agreed between Allies and Bulgaria

OCTOBER 1 — Damascus captured as both Australian and Arab forces enter city

OCTOBER 8 — French naval forces take Beirut

OCTOBER 18 — Planned Allied offensive postponed due to heavy rain

OCTOBER 24 — Battle of Vittorio Veneto opens with revenge shelling on first anniversary of the Battle of Caporetto

OCTOBER 26 — Aleppo in Syria falls to Allies

OCTOBER 28 — Allied forces cross Piave in strength

OCTOBER 30 — Armistice signed between Allies and Turkey

OCTOBER 30 — Italians take Vittorio Veneto

NOVEMBER 3 — Italy and Austria-Hungary sign armistice near Padua

THE VARDAR OFFENSIVE

By mid-1918 the Allies held the advantage on the Salonika front. The new commander, fortified by the belief of his Serbian forces that the Bulgarians could be broken by a surprise attack through the mountains, sought official endorsement for a general offensive. Meanwhile, the French undertook the difficult task of secretly moving heavy artillery into the mountains, while the British undertook a local offensive in the Vardar valley to distract Bulgarian attention from what was happening to the west.

Final approval for an offensive was given on September 10, and the action opened with a heavy artillery bombardment on the night of September 14. At 5:30 am next morning, French, Serbian and Italian forces launched their assault. Within two days they had penetrated 10 km (6 miles) across a 30-km (19-mile) front; a day later the leading formations were 30 km (19 miles) beyond their start lines. With virtually no fresh forces to reconstitute the front, and Allied forces threatening to break into the Vardar valley, the Central Powers had reached crisis point. On the 18th and 19th, however, crack Bulgarian troops did manage to repulse British and Greek attacks around Lake Doiran, although the town of Doiran was taken by Greek forces.

With their defence to the west breaking, the Bulgarians proposed that their forces should disengage around Doiran in order to counterattack the Allied forces advancing in the Cherna valley. However, as incredulous Bulgarian soldiers obeyed orders to break contact around Doiran and move through the Kosturino Pass, they were subjected to

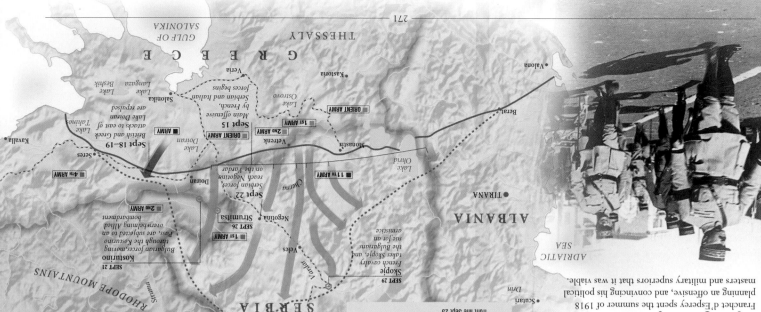

Inspecting the troops in Salonika
Franchet d'Esperey spent the summer of 1918 planning an offensive, and convincing his political masters and military superiors that it was viable.

overwhelming Allied air attack. Their cohesion crumbled, and so too did Bulgarian morale. By September 22 Serbian forces had reached Negotina on the Vardar, and three days later, as French colonial forces moved through the mountains on Skopje, British formations crossed the Bulgarian border. On September 28, Bulgaria, swept by anti-

war riots and the proclamation of soviets in various cities, requested an armistice, and agreed to Allied terms the next day, with the armistice effective on September 30, 1918.

A British force continued eastwards through Thrace, seizing the bridgeheads over the Maritsa, in readiness for an offensive against Constantinople.

Advance in Salonika
Following the launch of the Allied offensive on September 15, the Serb forces in the centre made rapid progress into Serbia. In the west the Bulgarians collapsed, but they put up stronger opposition on the Vardar before being overwhelmed in the Kosturino Pass.

THE VARDAR OFFENSIVE
Sept 15–29, 1918

ALLIED ATTACKS:
- Serbian
- French
- British

- The Allies
- Central Powers (and allied states)
- Central Powers (and allied states)
- British

◎ Town captured by Allies, with date
--- Major railway
--- Allies front line Sept 14
--- Central Powers front line Sept 29

Map labels: GREECE · THESSALY · GULF OF SALONIKA · Veria · Kastoria · Langaza Beshik · Lake Langaza · Lake Beshik · Salonika · Lake Ostrovo · Lake Doiran · Kavalla · Seres · Doiran · Strumitsa · Negotina · Cherna · Vardar · Veles · Vodar · Skopje · Drin · Scutari · Lake Ohrid · Monastir · Veternik · Berat · Valona · TIRANA · ALBANIA · ADRIATIC SEA · SERBIA · BULGARIA · RHODOPE MOUNTAINS · Struma · 2ND ARMY · 4TH ARMY · 1ST ARMY · 11TH ARMY · ORIENT ARMY · 1ST ARMY · 2ND ARMY

SEPT 21 Kosturino – Bulgarian forces moving through the Kosturino Pass, are subjected to an overwhelming Allied bombardment

SEPT 26 – Serbian forces reach Negotina on the Vardar

Sept 22 – Serbian forces reach Negotina

Sept 29 Skopje – French cavalry takes Skopje, and the Bulgarians sue for an armistice

Sept 15 – Main offensive by French, Serbian and Italian forces begins

Sept 18–19 – British and Greek attacks to east of Lake Doiran are repulsed

0 miles 20 40 60 80 100
0 km 20 40 60 80 100

Turkish cavalry
Turkey was threatened by the Allied action against Bulgaria, which was quite close to its European border.

This was made unnecessary by the Turkish acceptance of an armistice on October 30. French and Serbian forces, meanwhile, advanced to the north, reaching the Danube on October 19 and liberating Belgrade on November 1. With the signing of the Austro-Hungarian armistice on November 3, 1918, the Balkans campaign was over.

OPERATIONS IN THE MIDDLE EAST

After the British capture of Baghdad and Jerusalem in 1917, enforced inactivity characterized the situation in Mesopotamia and Palestine for much of 1918. Turkey, encouraged by the collapse of Russia, pursued extravagant territorial ambitions in Persia and Turkic Central Asia, while allowing its position in Arabia to all but collapse.

During 1918, Turkish forces in Mesopotamia were weakened by epidemics, desertions and a lack of reinforcements, which reduced the number of troops in the Kirkuk–Mosul area to about 20,000 by October 1918. The British, despite having 550,000 troops in Mesopotamia, were constrained by fears that German forces would advance through Persia and Afghanistan, and failed to make any significant moves until late October, when they finally launched a campaign that led to a Turkish surrender and the British occupation of Mosul.

PALESTINE AND SYRIA

Meanwhile, the Turkish Fourth, Seventh and Eighth armies holding the line in Palestine totalled around 32,000 infantry and 3,500 cavalry, but lacked overall strategy or mobility (despite the Seventh army being under the command of the future Turkish leader, Mustafa Kemal). They gathered no effective intelligence, and their line of communication from Damascus was in a state of collapse. They could only await defeat.

The intention of the British Egyptian Expeditionary Force under General Allenby to clear Turkish forces from Syria was, however, initially thwarted by the need to transfer five divisions to the Western Front in response to the German offensive of March 1918. In return, it gained Indian cavalry from France, and further Indian units were brought in from India and Mesopotamia. Training up these troops, however, and turning them into an effective fighting force took most of the summer.

The British had a number of advantages over the Turkish forces in Palestine. Apart from their numerical superiority (they had 57,000 infantry and 12,000 cavalry) and air supremacy, they also had a strategy. Part of Allenby's build-up to his main offensive in September was a series of decoy operations to the east of the Jordan that led the Turkish command to expect their railway supply line through Deraa to be the focus of any British attack. Instead, Allenby left that task to the Arabs, and made detailed preparations for an offensive from positions on the coastal plain, aiming to trap Turkish forces in the Judean Hills, and leave a route to Damascus clear. He secretly amassed troops on this coastal sector, moving cavalry divisions westwards under cover of darkness, and using the RAF to keep Turkish reconnaissance planes away. By the opening of the offensive, Allenby had 35,000 infantry, 400 guns and 9,000 cavalry lined up on the coastal plain, facing an unsuspecting Turkish force of only 8,000 infantry and 130 guns.

THE BATTLE OF MEGIDDO

Defeat for the Turkish forces began to unfold at 4:30 am on September 19, 1918, and took only three days. In the coastal sector, the initial bombardment overcame the two corps of the Turkish Eighth Army, and by 7:30 am Indian and Australian cavalry had broken through the Turkish lines and headed northwards to block a Turkish retreat. The Turks were pursued by British infantry into the hills, where they engaged in fierce rear-guard actions. Meanwhile, the lead

Action and inaction in Mesopotamia
One of 3,000 Turkish soldiers taken prisoner near Kirkuk on April 29, 1918, after which British forces withdrew south to Kifri for five months of inactivity.

Lawrence of Arabia
T.E. Lawrence standing surrounded by members of his bodyguard. He fulfilled an important role in liaising between British forces and sympathetic Arab leaders, and organizing action by Arab irregulars against the Turks.

The hill was about 2,500 feet high, very steep, and it was the heat of the day. There was very heavy machine-gun fire and some shelling. We captured a village en route and had to bomb the Turks out of a few houses. The hill was so steep and the men so done about three-quarters of the way up. If the Turks had counterattacked we should have had a bad time. I was so done myself that if a Turk had come for me, I think I should have been too tired to shoot.

BRITISH LIEUTENANT-COLONEL H.J.H. DAVSON ON THE ACTION DURING THE BATTLE OF MEGIDDO

the first to enter Damascus on October 1.

dispute over whether Australian or Arab forces were tying to withdraw to Damascus. Their involvement had great political significance, as indicated by the destroyed columns of the Turkish Fourth Army lines of communication. During the offensive they attacked the railway around Deraa, cutting Turkish Before Allenby's offensive, Arab guerrilla forces of the Turks in northern Palestine was considerable. The military contribution of the Arabs to the defeat

THE ARAB CONTRIBUTION

a post-war romantic view of the Arab Revolt.

speed of the Turkish collapse, and overshadowed by been subsequently obscured by the totality and command and supply in the First World War, has described as the most comprehensive disruption of Jordan. The air campaign, which has been RAF and Arab irregulars operating east of the became the target of a double attack – from the lines of communication and withdrawal, which Jordan and established themselves astride Turkish 20th. The British had now secured the upper Majamie, Jenin and Beyt Shean by the end of the morning of the attack, and Afula, Nazareth, by exhaustion. Megiddo was in their control on the to Beisan in 34 hours at the cost of just 26 horses killed cavalry division advanced 110 km (70 miles)

Advance through Palestine

Allied forces launched a surprise cavalry-led attack in the West, supported by action in the centre, and the destruction of Turkish communication lines in the northeast by Arab irregular forces.

MEDITERRANEAN SEA

BATTLE OF MEGIDDO
Sept 19–23, 1918

→ Turkish front line Sept 18
→ Turkish front line Sept 21
SEPT 19 Date town captured
----- Railway
Allied offensives
Turkish retreat

Acre
SEPT 23

Haifa
SEPT 20

Nazareth
SEPT 20

Afula
SEPT 20

Majamie
SEPT 20

Beyt Shean
SEPT 20

Megiddo
SEPT 19

Samakh

Safed•

Sea of Galilee

Jordan

7th ARMY
Mustafa Kemal
Jenin

8th ARMY
Djevad Pasha
Tulkharm
SEPT 19

El Tire

Nablus
SEPT 19

Sept 19
Allied attack launched at 4:30 am. Within 3 hours Turkish line broken and Megiddo area taken by cavalry

Sept 20

Ramleh•

•Jaffa

4th ARMY
Djemal Küçük

Cavalry corps crosses the Jordan, blocking the retreat of the 7th and 8th Armies
Sept 21

Deraa

Sept 18
Arab raids disable the main Turkish supply route

Hejaz railway
(main Turkish supply route)

to Damascus —

Sept 22
Turkish 4th Army is ordered to retreat. Harried by Arab irregulars, the disintegrating army is pinned down along Hejaz railway. Survivors surrender near Damascus, which falls to Allenby on Oct 2.

PALESTINE

JUDEAN HILLS

AMMAN –

JERUSALEM
•Jericho

Ramallah•

EGYPTIAN EXPEDITIONARY FORCE
Allenby

Dead Sea

0 km 10 20 30 40 50
0 miles 10 20 30 40 50

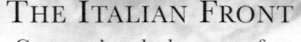

Austrian prisoners
Some Austrian soldiers at Montello failed to escape the Italian counterattack of June 18.

THE ITALIAN FRONT

Following Germany's redeployment of troops from Italy to the Western Front for its spring offensive, 53 Austro-Hungarian divisions faced 59 divisions under Italian command in the mountains east of Lake Garda and across the Piave River. While both Austria-Hungary and Italy might have preferred to await the outcome of the conflict between their senior partners on the Western Front, those partners were looking for complementary action on the Italian Front. Consequently, both Austria-Hungary and Italy planned offensives, although once the Italians realized the enemy was preparing to attack, they decided to stand on the defensive.

The Austro-Hungarian offensive was beset by difficulties. There was not enough food to feed the troops, some of whom were reaching starvation point. The army was short of horses, and there was a lack of spare parts for their locomotives and motor vehicles. There was also the question of what form the offensive should take. A concerted attack from the Trentino would have been the best plan, but it brought the risk of weakening the front by redeploying troops to just one sector. There were also the issues of how to exploit any advantage that might be gained by such an offensive and who should be called on to command it.

In the end, a compromise was reached: a simultaneous two-pronged attack by separate army groups – one in the mountains, and the other along the Piave. The plan was for the Eleventh Army to break through Italian lines and move towards Verona and Castelfranco, joining up with the Sixth and the Isonzo Armies, once they had crossed the Piave. Such an offensive, involving simultaneous attacks that were not mutually supporting, was bound to result in failure.

THE PIAVE OFFENSIVE

The Austro-Hungarian Eleventh Army opened its main offensive in the mountains on June 15 (following diversionary attacks to the west). Although some initial gains were made, these had been eliminated by the end of the first day, and late on the 16th the battle in this sector petered out.

In the Piave valley itself, things at first went a bit better for the Austro-Hungarians. The Sixth Army at Montello, and the Isonzo Army at the lower end of the river, made gains of 5 km (3 miles) on June 15, helped by smoke and fog. By the 16th they had five isolated bridgeheads over the Piave. By the 18th they had established a 19-km (12-mile) front across the river, but it was clear that success would be elusive for the Austro-Hungarians. Already, demands were being made on their reserves, the Piave River was in flood, and Italian aeroplanes were attacking their lines of communication.

The Austro-Hungarian high command hesitated to abandon its offensive, just as the Italian high command had hesitated in the first three days to mount counterattacks. On the 18th, however, the Italians committed themselves in the Montello sector. The Austro-Hungarians ordered a withdrawal behind the Piave, and an orderly evacuation took place on the nights of 21st/22nd and 22nd/23rd. The Italians, taken by surprise by the withdrawals, did not immediately attempt to pursue the Austro-Hungarian armies, although at the beginning of July troops were moved up to face the Austro-Hungarians across the river.

Aftermath of the fighting
The town of Nervasa was caught up in both the Austro-Hungarian attack and in the Italian counterattack in June 1918.

THE ITALIAN ARMY

IN 1915, ITALY WAS ABLE to put 900,000 officers and men into the field – organized into 35 infantry, four cavalry and 12 militia divisions, plus one elite light infantry division (the *Bersaglieri*) and 52 mountain battalions (the *Alpini*). The army's obvious weaknesses included lack of artillery and low levels of literacy among its infantry. However, in the course of the Isonzo offensives (1915–17) the army proved its toughness while fighting over some of the worst terrain in Europe, and its tenacity in the face of repeated failure. The autocratic chief of staff, Luigi di Cadorna, made impossible demands of his troops, and casualties in the course of the war amounted to 2,200,000, including 650,000 killed.

Much changed after the disaster of Caporetto in November 1917, during which the Italian army could not at one stage account for more than 400,000 officers and men. The final prisoner count was 270,000. Eleven British and French divisions moved into northern Italy to help stabilize the front. Cadorna was dismissed and replaced by Armando Diaz, while widespread reforms were introduced to rebuild the army. These included improvements in the pay, rations and leave arrangements

of ordinary soldiers, who also received free life insurance policies. The army managed to raise 25 new divisions by February 1918, and Italian industry replaced the 3,500 guns lost at Caporetto by mid-1918 .

Understandably, the new high command was content to remain on the defensive for a time, and it was not until the last weeks of the war that it authorized a major offensive. New tactics involved concentration on firepower rather than manpower, and defence in depth, based on strongpoints and counterattacks. In these, the assault battalions of the *Arditi* (Daring Ones), an elite founded in 1917, played an important role. They became the heroes of an adoring populace who, anxious to avoid defeat by a detested enemy, united behind the war effort.

IDENTITY TAGS

Bersaglieri hat
The Bersaglieri were an elite regiment of sharpshooters. Their usual form of transport was the bicycle.

Helmet, based on French Adrian helmet

HEAVY HELMET

Alpine fighters
Men of the *Alpini* were expected to be able to fight at high altitudes. The special corps had been founded in 1872, specifically to protect the mountainous northern borders of the new Kingdom of Italy. This inhospitable terrain called for special skills and demanded extraordinary powers of endurance. The First World War was the first time they had been called on to perform this duty.

FOLDING SHOVEL

Arditi badge

Italian uniform and weapons
Most Italian uniforms were grey-green in colour. Shown here is the superior quality tunic of the Arditi, who were also issued with a warm roll-neck sweater for mountain warfare. The standard rifle of the Italian army was the 6.5-mm Carcano (1891 model). The Carcano carbine had a retractable bayonet that folded back along the barrel when not in use.

BERETTA AUTOMATIC PISTOL

ARDITI UNIFORM

CARCANO CARBINE WITH FIXED BAYONET

Gun hole
An Italian patrol occupies a shallow gun hole with a Fiat-Revelli Model 1914 machine-gun, at Fossalta on the Piave River in June 1918.

the imminent defeat and collapse of the Empire.

BUILD-UP TO A FURTHER OFFENSIVE

During the summer of 1918, as victories over the Germans on the Western Front multiplied, widening differences emerged between Italy and its allies, who demanded that it capitalize on its victory over the Austro-Hungarians and launch an offensive across the Piave River. The Italian high command balked, citing, with good reason, the problems the enemy had encountered in crossing the river in its offensive in June, and the shortages faced by the Italian army. It was painfully aware that war had exhausted Italy's resources and had opened dangerous political and social divisions. It reasoned that Italy had strength left for only one offensive and that, given the likelihood of the war continuing into 1919, such action would be best deferred until the following year.

In September, however, the Allies broke out from their positions around Salonika and, as Bulgaria fell

The Italians had halted a major enemy offensive, with disastrous results for Austria-Hungary. In the wake of the failure, an increasing number of its Slav soldiers began to "vote with their feet", foreseeing

by the wayside, so Austria-Hungary began to fall apart. On October 6, two days after the German request for an armistice, the state of Yugoslavia was proclaimed by a provisional government that met in Zagreb, and on the 14th, a Czech provisional government was formed. On the 16th the Habsburg emperor put out a proclamation declaring Austria a federal empire. The Italian high command, fearing that unless Austro-Hungarian forces were driven back, Italy might lose territory in any peace settlement, felt forced to launch an offensive.

MONTE GRAPPA AND VITTORIO VENETO

The Italians planned a double attack: by the Fourth Army on Monte Grappa to the west, and by the Eighth Army on the Piave to the east. The aim was for the two armies to encircle and isolate the Austro-Hungarian Sixth Army. Three other armies – the Sixth, Tenth and Twelfth – which included British, French and American divisions, would support them. In the event, it was the supporting armies that broke through the enemy positions after the attacks by the Fourth and Eighth armies miscarried.

The British divisions of the Tenth Army established themselves across the Piave on the night

Allied advance in northeast Italy

The combined forces of Italian, British and French divisions succeeded in overcoming stiff initial resistance from Austro-Hungarian troops. Once through the enemy lines, the Allied forces advanced rapidly.

THE VITTORIO VENETO OFFENSIVE
Oct 24–Nov 4, 1918

The Allies (and allied states)
Central Powers (and allied states)
NOV 1 Date of capture of town

Austro-Hungarian front line Oct 24
Armistice line Nov 4
Major railway
Italian offensives

of October 23/24 in advance of the main offensive, which began at dawn. The Eighth Army was able to secure shallow bridgeheads over a swollen Piave on the 26th. But it was the success of the Tenth and Twelfth Armies in securing the east bank of the Piave that enabled the Italians to cross the river on October 28 and take Vittorio Veneto on the 30th.

Meanwhile, a series of attacks carried out by the Italian Fourth Army on Monte Grappa failed to make any impression on a resolute Austro-Hungarian defence. On the 29th, Italian operations were halted in this sector as attention focused else-where. British and French divisions of the Sixth Army co-operated to break the Asiago position, thus ensuring the capture of Trento on November 3, just ahead of the arrival of lead elements of the Italian First Army. The main thrust of the offensive now began to unfold across the Venetian plain.

ITALIAN VICTORY

The Austro-Hungarians had fought tenaciously, but following the Allied crossing of the Piave, they were an army with days of existence left to it, fighting for a state that no longer existed. By November 1 the Italians had secured Sacile, and from this point the pace of the Allied advance quickened. Udine was secured on the 2nd, and the old battlefields on the Isonzo and at Caporetto on the 3rd. On the same day, Trieste was occupied by naval forces, and an armistice, effective the next day, was concluded.

The final battle of the Austro-Hungarian army cost it 30,000 dead and wounded and some 430,000 prisoners. At a price of some 38,000 casualties, Italy had secured the victory it needed to justify its territorial claims, and its right to be considered as a worthy partner of the Allies in their negotiations at the Paris Peace Conference in 1919.

Italian forces in Udine
The commander of the Savoy Cavalry (centre) leads the first patrol into the Piazza Contarena in the town of Udine on November 3 – the day after the Italians had succeeded in capturing it in their final advance.

Italian medical post on Monte Grappa
The mountainous terrain presented the problem of how to transport equipment and supplies, and how to bring back the wounded. Networks of cables were installed by both sides to provide lift systems.

Turkish prisoners

For many Turks, conscripted reluctantly into an army that was often unable to feed and equip them properly for the terrain in which they were expected to fight, being taken prisoner was not necessarily an unwelcome option. By 1918, the army was down to 200,000 men.

THE CAUSES OF COLLAPSE

By late summer 1918 all three of Germany's allies had faced similar circumstances – dire hardship among their citizens, which a disastrous harvest and the onset of winter would only worsen, and a string of German military defeats that dashed any hopes of territorial gains. These, combined with factors specific to each of the countries, led to their collapse in the autumn of 1918.

THE COLLAPSE OF BULGARIA

Bulgaria had been the last of the Central Powers to enter the war and was the first to break ranks, with its separate armistice agreement made with the Allies on September 29, 1918. It would probably have preferred the war to end much sooner. By December 1915 it had gained all the Serb territory it had sought and, by December 1916, it had defeated Romania. Thereafter, the war had seemed pointless to many Bulgarians, and the social costs disproportionate. Even in 1914 living costs were high, and urban wages low. By July 1918 prices had inflated by 750 per cent. This had an impact on the morale of soldiers, who returned home on leave to find conditions even worse than in the army.

Meanwhile, Bulgaria's motives for joining the war in 1915 had become largely irrelevant. They included resentment of the Russians for their support of Serbia in the Balkan Wars, and a distrust of the Allies, whom Bulgaria (correctly) suspected of having promised Constantinople to Russia in the event of victory over Turkey. The defeats inflicted on Russia, however, reduced the threat that it posed. Bulgaria's desire for peace grew as it became apparent that it would receive little reward for its continued support of Germany. This was confirmed during the peace negotiations with Russia and Romania in Brest-Litovsk and Bucharest, when Bulgaria was not even awarded territories it had been forced to relinquish to Romania in 1913. Northern Dobruja was effectively placed under German military and economic occupation. The Bulgarian prime minister, Vasil Radoslavov, commented that his country had been treated more like a defeated enemy than as a victorious ally.

After 1916 Germany and Austria-Hungary had made increasing demands on Bulgarian agricultural resources, while Bulgarians in some regions starved. With the 1918 harvest threatening to be disastrous, and the resignation of the prime minister on June 20, Bulgaria had reached the end of the road.

THE COLLAPSE OF AUSTRIA-HUNGARY

Food shortages and the rising tide of socialism led to political unrest in Austria-Hungary. There was also a growing feeling among its ethnic minority groups – which included Bosnians, Czechs, Croats, Italians, Poles, Serbs, Slovaks, Slovenes and Romanians – that an allied victory would bring freedom from Austrian and Hungarian domination. The Czechs, Slovaks, Yugoslavs and Poles, in particular, were inspired by the promise made by the American President, Woodrow Wilson, in his Fourteen Points, of "the opportunity for autonomous development" for the nations of Austria-Hungary. The Habsburg Empire was disintegrating even as it signed an armistice on November 3, 1918.

GERMAN DOMINATION

One further factor was perhaps shared by all three of Germany's allies – a growing fear of, and resentment towards, Germany on account of its economic, industrial and financial strength, and its crass insensitivity toward its partners. By 1918, many people in Austria-Hungary and Bulgaria, in particular, wished for an end to the war as the means of escaping German domination.

THE COLLAPSE OF TURKEY

The First World War was in so many ways a war of exhaustion, and each year saw Turkey lose ground. A poor and relatively underdeveloped country such as Turkey, although rural Turkey was largely self-sufficient, flour still had to be imported by sea to feed Constantinople and Trebizond. Military demands for manpower and draught animals reduced Turkey's agricultural output, and an economic blockade prevented supply ships from reaching Constantinople. Food shortages and the collapse of public health and sanitation programmes were producing 50 per cent infant mortality rates. Typhus, malaria and smallpox were widespread.

Russian territorial gains meant a flight of civilians to other provinces hopelessly ill-placed to support them. In 1918 there was a scramble the other way, when Russian armies abandoned their conquests, but with no harvest, famine and death were the inevitable results.

By 1918 the army was estimated to be at little more than one-sixth of its full strength. Estimates put the number of military casualties at over 1,500,000. Mass desertion seems to have been crucial in the saving of military lives and provided a further reason for signing an armistice with the British at Mudros on October 30.

FAMINE IN THE EMPIRE

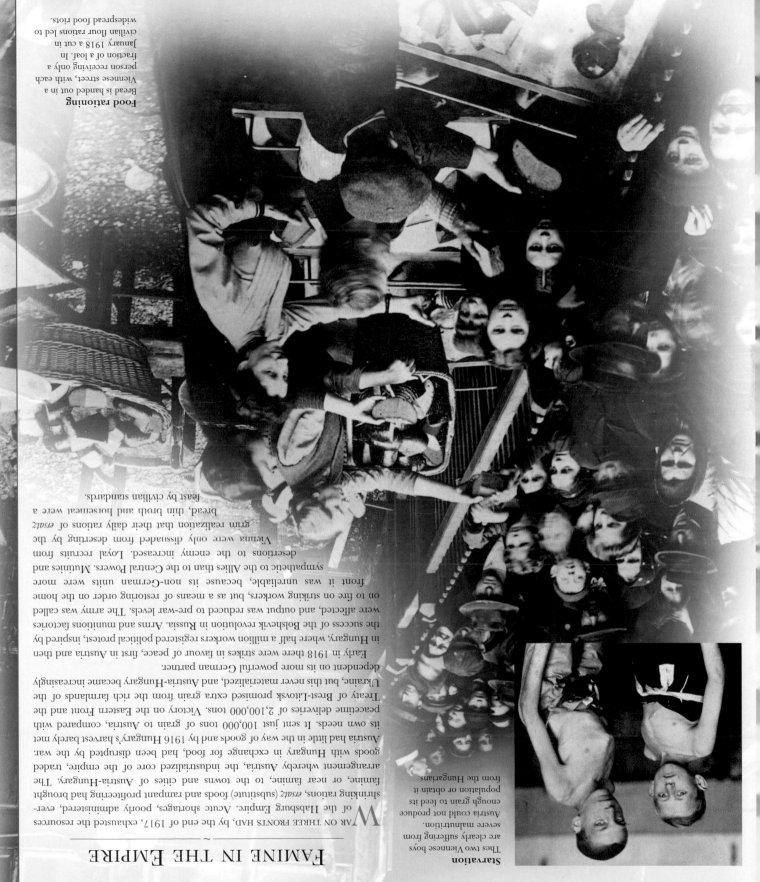

Food rationing
Bread is handed out in a Viennese street, with each person receiving only a fraction of a loaf. In January 1918 a cut in civilian flour rations led to widespread food riots.

Starvation
These two Viennese boys are clearly suffering from severe malnutrition. Austria could not produce enough grain to feed its population or obtain it from the Hungarians.

WAR ON THREE FRONTS HAD, by the end of 1917, exhausted the resources of the Habsburg Empire. Acute shortages, poorly administered, ever-shrinking rations, *ersatz* (substitute) foods and rampant profiteering had brought famine, or near famine, to the towns and cities of Austria-Hungary. The arrangement whereby Austria, the industrialized core of the empire, traded goods with Hungary in exchange for food, had been disrupted by the war. Austria had little in the way of goods and by 1916 Hungary's harvest barely met its own needs. It sent just 100,000 tons of grain to Austria, compared with peacetime deliveries of 2,100,000 tons. Victory on the Eastern Front and the Treaty of Brest-Litovsk promised extra grain from the rich farmlands of the Ukraine, but this never materialized, and Austria-Hungary became increasingly dependent on its more powerful German partner.

Early in 1918 there were strikes in favour of peace, first in Austria and then in Hungary, where half a million workers registered political protest, inspired by the success of the Bolshevik revolution in Russia. Arms and munitions factories were affected, and output was reduced to pre-war levels. The army was called on to fire on striking workers, but as a means of restoring order on the home front it was unreliable, because its non-German units were more sympathetic to the Allies than to the Central Powers. Mutinies and desertions to the enemy increased. Loyal recruits from Vienna were only dissuaded from deserting by the grim realization that their daily rations of *ersatz* bread, thin broth and horsemeat were a feast by civilian standards.

American troops with German wounded
German prisoners receive attention at an American field dressing station during the St Mihiel offensive of September 12, 1918. The Americans successfully cleared the St Mihiel salient in 36 hours, taking 8,000 prisoners.

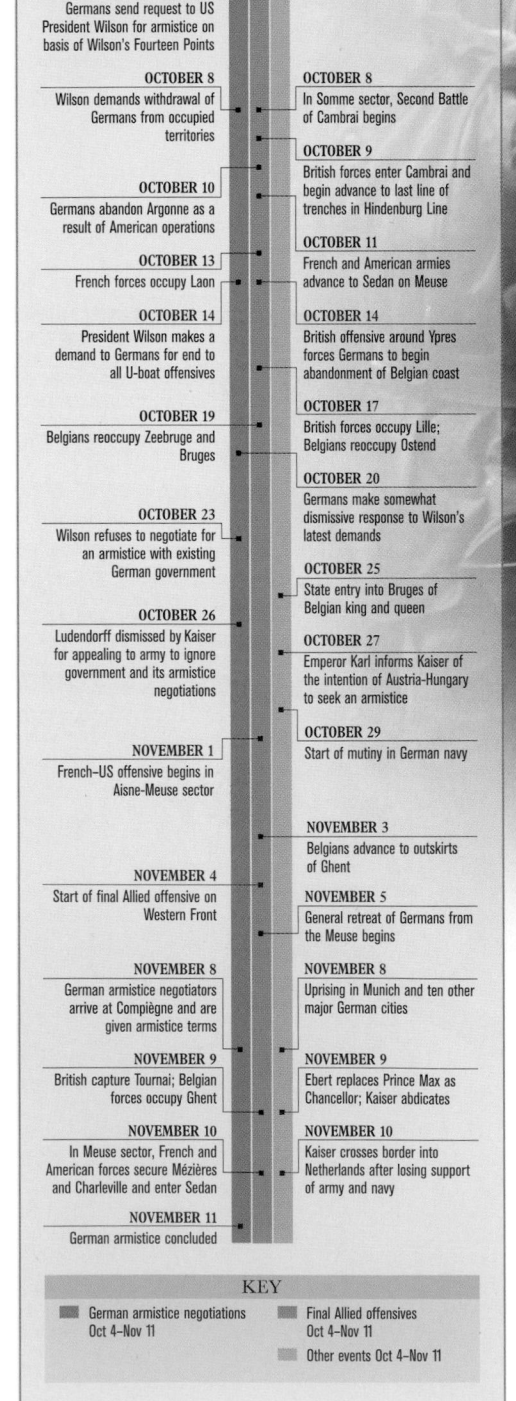

THE WESTERN FRONT
OCTOBER 4 – NOVEMBER 11, 1918

Bitter fighting continued after the Germans had made a formal request to US President Wilson for an armistice to be negotiated on the basis of his Fourteen Points. While Wilson made, and the Germans resisted, a number of demands, the Allies launched another series of offensives, forcing the Germans into a general retreat. German army discipline had been broken by the time the Armistice was signed on November 11.

~

OCTOBER 4
Germans send request to US President Wilson for armistice on basis of Wilson's Fourteen Points

OCTOBER 8
Wilson demands withdrawal of Germans from occupied territories

OCTOBER 8
In Somme sector, Second Battle of Cambrai begins

OCTOBER 9
British forces enter Cambrai and begin advance to last line of trenches in Hindenburg Line

OCTOBER 10
Germans abandon Argonne as a result of American operations

OCTOBER 11
French and American armies advance to Sedan on Meuse

OCTOBER 13
French forces occupy Laon

OCTOBER 14
President Wilson makes a demand to Germans for end to all U-boat offensives

OCTOBER 14
British offensive around Ypres forces Germans to begin abandonment of Belgian coast

OCTOBER 17
British forces occupy Lille; Belgians reoccupy Ostend

OCTOBER 19
Belgians reoccupy Zeebruge and Bruges

OCTOBER 20
Germans make somewhat dismissive response to Wilson's latest demands

OCTOBER 23
Wilson refuses to negotiate for an armistice with existing German government

OCTOBER 25
State entry into Bruges of Belgian king and queen

OCTOBER 26
Ludendorff dismissed by Kaiser for appealing to army to ignore government and its armistice negotiations

OCTOBER 27
Emperor Karl informs Kaiser of the intention of Austria-Hungary to seek an armistice

OCTOBER 29
Start of mutiny in German navy

NOVEMBER 1
French–US offensive begins in Aisne-Meuse sector

NOVEMBER 3
Belgians advance to outskirts of Ghent

NOVEMBER 4
Start of final Allied offensive on Western Front

NOVEMBER 5
General retreat of Germans from the Meuse begins

NOVEMBER 8
German armistice negotiators arrive at Compiègne and are given armistice terms

NOVEMBER 8
Uprising in Munich and ten other major German cities

NOVEMBER 9
British capture Tournai; Belgian forces occupy Ghent

NOVEMBER 9
Ebert replaces Prince Max as Chancellor; Kaiser abdicates

NOVEMBER 10
In Meuse sector, French and American forces secure Mézières and Charleville and enter Sedan

NOVEMBER 10
Kaiser crosses border into Netherlands after losing support of army and navy

NOVEMBER 11
German armistice concluded

KEY
■ German armistice negotiations Oct 4–Nov 11
■ Final Allied offensives Oct 4–Nov 11
■ Other events Oct 4–Nov 11

The German Search for an Armistice

British troops in Lille
Lille was captured on October 17 without a single shot being fired after an offensive, launched on the 14th, forced the Germans to begin abandoning the Belgian coast.

FOLLOWING THE RECOGNITION by the German military authorities of the need for an armistice, a request for armistice discussions was sent via the Swiss to US President Wilson on October 4. In the weeks that followed, two sets of events moved in tandem: the events on the battlefield and the political events that were to flow from the request for an armistice – a request that had been made in order to avoid a military defeat that had yet to become comprehensive. Throughout this time the Allies sustained pressure on the German armies on the Western Front, inflicting losses that, coming on top of those of August and September, finally brought home to Germany's political and military leaderships the hopelessness of their country's position.

FURTHER ALLIED OFFENSIVES
In October, the Allies maintained the pattern of their earlier operations with successive offensives. On October 5 they broke through the last main positions on the Hindenburg Line, enabling them to carry war into areas that had not seen fighting since 1914. The British Third and Fourth Armies, after

taking some 8,000 prisoners on October 8 alone, mounted an offensive that resulted in the recapture of Cambrai on the 9th and Le Cateau on the 10th. The extent of the German army's administrative disorder and the improvised nature of its defensive measures can be gauged by the fact that at Méricourt, Prémont and Sérain, the Germans lost 4,000 prisoners drawn from no fewer than 15 different divisions. By the 13th, German forces were engaged in a general retreat across a front between St Quentin and the Argonne. On the 14th the British offensive around Courtrai forced the Germans to begin to abandon the Belgian coast and Lille. As a result, King Albert returned to Ostend on the 17th, and two days later Belgian troops entered Zeebrugge and Bruges.

A DECLINE IN PRESSURE

From this point, pressure on the Germans slackened as Allied supply problems mounted. But as early as the 20th, British forces established themselves on the Scheldt, east of Lille, between Pecq and Lienfer and three days later, on the 23rd, the British Third and Fourth Armies mounted offensives between the Scheldt and Sambre. By this time German forces had abandoned their positions on the Aisne and were involved in a general withdrawal from all their positions west of the Meuse opposite the French and American armies. On November 1, with the French Fourth and US First and Second Armies resuming their offensives either side of Verdun, the Battle of the Sambre opened in Belgium. It was to end on the 11th with Belgian forces entering Ghent and British forces entering Mons. That same day, the Germans agreed to accept the armistice terms that had been presented to them. The Americans, after an advance of 40 km (25 miles) since November 1, were on the heights overlooking Sedan, and the French were outside Mézières.

In the last three months of hostilities, the Allied armies captured some 363,000 prisoners and 6,400 guns, evidence that the cohesion and discipline of German armies was breaking down. The Allied forces, particularly the British, had inevitably suffered checks, and losses that were serious and ever less acceptable as victory came in sight. The checks, however, were temporary and tactical and at least partly caused by the very small number of tanks available for offensive operations. In any event, they were very quickly overturned by Allied success at the strategic level. There was no rupture of the German front in these weeks, just a persistent erosion of position and strength that the German forces could not prevent, still less reverse.

THE GERMAN HOME FRONT

The revelation of national military helplessness had come as a devastating shock to Germany's political leadership and civilian population in the first week

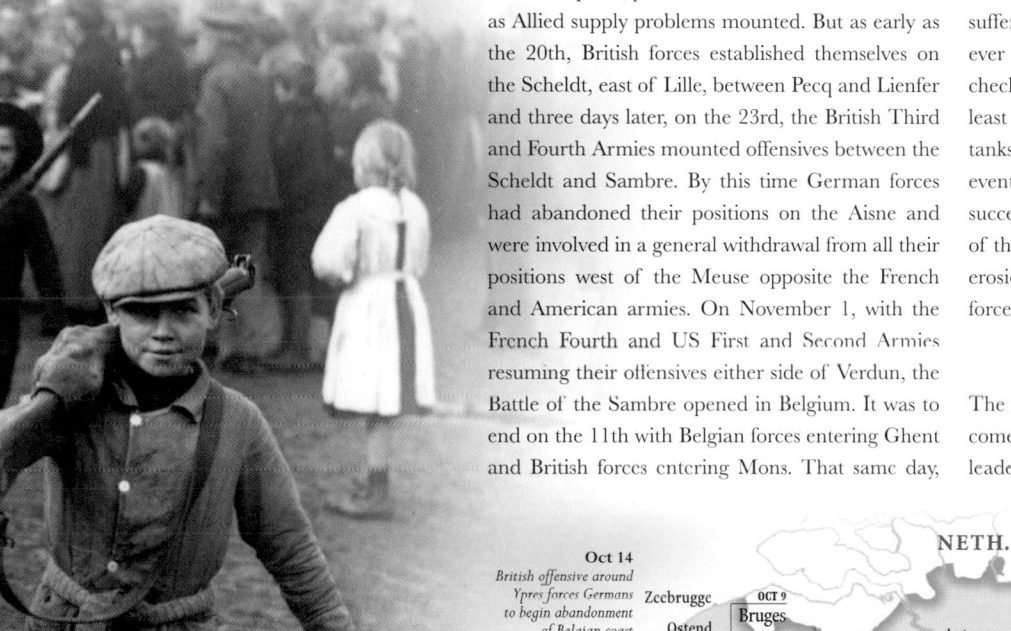

Allied advances in the final months
On October 4 the Americans renewed their offensive in the Argonne. On their left, the French advanced to the Aisne and crossed it on November 1, by which date the Americans had begun to race up the Meuse valley to Sedan. To the north, the British and Belgians advanced over the Ypres Ridge and through Flanders,

THE WESTERN FRONT
Oct 4–Nov 11, 1918

ALLIED FRONT LINE SEPT 25:
- Belgian sector
- British sector
- French sector
- American sector

ALLIED FRONT LINE NOV 11:
- Belgian sector
- British sector
- French sector
- American sector
- Allied offensives
- The Allies (and allied states)
- Central Powers (and allied states)
- Neutral
- Fortified town
- Major railway

Oct 14
British offensive around Ypres forces Germans to begin abandonment of Belgian coast

Oct 23
British and Belgian forces begin advance through Belgium

Oct 14
British advance at Cambrai and Le Cateau sends Germans into retreat

Oct 11
French and US armies advance to outskirts of Sedan

American troops advancing
Beginning with the first all-American minor action in June, American troops played an increasingly significant role in driving back the Germans. By the end of September their active participation had convinced the German high command of the need for an armistice.

of October. Until August the German civilian population had shown remarkably few signs of unrest, despite the hardships caused by the war. But from early autumn the problem of ensuring national solidarity had grown. During the spring offensives, trainloads of prisoners and German wounded had arrived on German railways, but the autumn fighting brought only more wounded. In August there was a further cut of food rations that were already barely adequate to sustain existence, while the worldwide influenza epidemic worsened throughout the summer. In the autumn the epidemic reached its peak in Germany, with 3,000 deaths occurring in October in the capital alone. (German civilian deaths from influenza were to number about 400,000 in 1918.)

On September 30 Chancellor Hertling was replaced by Prince Max of Baden, a cousin of the kaiser known for his liberal views. This could not, however, prevent the growth of unrest. On November 3, after warships of the High Sea Fleet were ordered to sea for one last climactic battle, crews at Kiel and Wilhelmshaven mutinied. Both cities were in revolutionary hands by the 7th, when Bavaria was declared an independent republic.

WILSON'S FOURTEEN POINTS

The request for armistice discussions that was sent to President Wilson on October 4 stated a German willingness to negotiate on the basis of Wilson's Fourteen Points. The president had first presented the points to the American Congress in January 1918 as the foundation for a lasting peace, and had subsequently elaborated on them in a speech delivered in New York on September 27. In general, they embraced the principle of national self-determination. They called for the restoration of the Belgian state, the liberation of all French territory, and the return to France of Alsace and Lorraine. Elsewhere in Europe, Wilson envisaged an end to the Habsburg and Ottoman empires, and the creation of new national states in central and eastern Europe. These were to include an independent Poland with full access to the Baltic Sea.

Wilson, in his Fourteen Points, also urged the nations of western Europe to welcome Russia "into the society of free nations under institutions of her own choosing". Most importantly from the German point of view, he called for open diplomatic negotiations, the removal of economic barriers to trade, and "mutual guarantees of political independence and territorial integrity" to all states. Wilson recognized that the British and French should play the leading role in drawing up the terms of an armistice. However, he succeeded in using his position to make a series of demands of Germany: the withdrawal of German forces from all occupied territories (October 8), an end to the U-boat offensive (October 14), and a recognition that peace could not be concluded with the existing German imperial and military authorities (October 23). He thus forced upon the German high command a piecemeal surrender that could not be reversed, and inextricably linked the armistice and peace treaty with the Fourteen Points.

Communication by telephone
Although wirelesses were beginning to appear on the battlefield in 1918, their use was by no means universal and there was still a heavy reliance on field telephones.

GERMANY IN 1918

S INCE THE SEVERE WINTER OF 1916–17 there had been a marked deterioration in the living conditions of Germany's civilian population. Those with insufficient funds to purchase food on the thriving black market had gone hungry; according to some estimates over 700,000 Germans died from malnutrition-related disease in the years 1914–18. People living in towns and cities suffered most. In an attempt to eke out the meagre supplies of food, government scientists offered *ersatz* concoctions such as "meat" made of vegetable flour, barley and mushrooms. In a register of licensed *ersatz* goods set up by the government in 1918, over 11,000 had been listed by the end of the war.

Shortages of coal and soap meant that German civilians were not only hungry but cold, dirty and vulnerable to disease. At every turn, the complete failure of the authorities – state, military and local – to manage the war economy and keep up civilian morale was clearly visible.

While the Bolshevik Revolution in Russia of November 1917 enabled the German army to shift resources to the Western Front, it also gave a new, revolutionary dimension to civilian unrest. January 1918 saw a strike of more than 500,000 workers in Berlin and of about 1,000,000 in Germany as a whole, and the protests increasingly involved soldiers and sailors. By the end of August 1918, desertion from the German army had begun in earnest and was linked to the plundering of army food stocks and other stores.

By November there were 10,000 "Soldiers' Councils", whose members were to be seen in all large German cities and towns, distributing flour, cocoa and tea to the civilian populations.

Starvation

Malnutrition left children and adults alike vulnerable to infectious diseases such as tuberculosis, influenza and pneumonia.

Ersatz products

Substitutes used for coffee included dandelion roots and barley, Raspberry-leaf tea was also sold. Cotton was in short supply, so material was made from paper reinforced by woven fibres.

Their efficiency contrasted unfavourably with the failures of the government, and helped to increase its unpopularity.

ERSATZ COFFEE

ERSATZ SOAP

ERSATZ TEA

ERSATZ CLOTH

Food riots

Soldiers guard the remains of a looted butcher's shop in Invalidenstrasse, Berlin. The chemist's shop and bookshop either side of it were left untouched by the starving rioters, who were clearly only interested in food.

Soup Kitchens

Children are given food from a field kitchen set up to feed returning soldiers. By 1917 nearly a third of the population of Hamburg was surviving on "beggar's soup", doled out from such makeshift canteens.

285

> "On November 9 Germany, lacking any firm hand, bereft of all will, robbed of her princes, collapsed like a house of cards."
>
> GENERAL ERICH LUDENDORFF

Wilson's third demand, for a change of regime, caused Hindenburg and Ludendorff to call upon the army to ignore the government and its negotiations. For this act of insubordination, Ludendorff was forced to resign by the kaiser. Acceptance of the third demand was given on October 29 in a note that assured Wilson of the German government's credibility – although this was then undermined by the mutiny among the crews of the High Sea Fleet at Wilhelmshaven and Kiel. Meanwhile, Chancellor Prince Max was unconscious for 36 hours after taking a sleeping draught to alleviate the symptoms of influenza.

ARMISTICE NEGOTIATIONS

On November 5 Wilson informed the German government that negotiations could proceed on the basis of the Fourteen Points, and advised that an armistice would have to be secured from Foch. This was duly done, and at 2:30 am on the 7th the French radioed instructions for a German delegation to present itself at 8:00 pm that day. The delegation was taken by rail to Rethondes where, on the morning of the 8th, it was forced to ask formally for terms. Without access to radio and denied right of transit for 24 hours, the German delegation was unable to communicate the terms to German headquarters until the 10th.

On the previous day Prince Max had resigned as chancellor and had been replaced by the socialist

Ebert. The kaiser had been persuaded to abdicate. After authorizing acceptance of the armistice terms on the 10th, he took refuge in the technically neutral Netherlands, while his family remained in Berlin. Although the German high command judged the armistice terms to be punitive, it knew it had no alternative but to accept, and was authorized to sign by Prince Max (although no longer the chancellor) and by Hindenburg. When the German and Allied delegations met at 2:05 am on the 11th, the Germans were able to secure some minor concessions. This included a reduction in the amount of weapons and military equipment they had to surrender – on the grounds that they would need a certain military capability with which to maintain public order. With that the German delegation had to be content. The armistice, effective from 11:00 am, was signed at 5:10 am. The war, in effect, was finally over.

Armistice train
The armistice was drawn up and signed in a railway carriage *(above)* in a siding in the Forest of Compiègne, in northern France. The Allies were represented by Admiral Wemyss and Marshal Foch *(left)*. The German delegation, led by Erzberger, was given almost no room for negotiation and little opportunity to confer with the German government on the terms being offered.

ARMISTICE TERMS

The terms the Germans had signed amounted to total defeat. They were not only committed to evacuating all their troops from Belgium, France, Luxembourg and Alsace-Lorraine within 15 days, but also to withdrawing troops within Germany as far back as 40 km (25 miles) east of the Rhine, leaving all installations intact. The treaties of Brest-Litovsk and Bucharest, agreed between the Central Powers and the Russians and Romanians earlier in the year, were annulled and the Germans were ordered to make a start to the evacuations of the territories they had occupied in eastern Europe. They were also to allow the Allies right of access to Polish territories through Danzig on the Baltic Sea. German troops were also to cease fighting in East Africa (an order that took two days to reach them) and to evacuate the region.

Germany was to surrender almost all its artillery, machine-guns, mortars and aircraft, as well as 5,000 locomotives, 150,000 railway trucks, and 5,000 motorized trucks (along with sufficient spare parts for maintenance purposes). In addition, the Allies reserved the right to requisition further equipment and supplies from Germany, where necessary, with the cost to be borne by the German government.

SPANISH FLU
~

AFTER FOUR YEARS OF WAR, which saw massive movements of people between and across continents, the world was ripe for a pandemic. It took the form of a virulent strain of influenza that became known as "Spanish flu", possibly because, as a non-combatant state, the Spanish government saw no reason to suppress the news that the country was in the grip of an unusually severe kind of flu. It affected many non-combatant as well as combatant states.

The Spanish flu came in three waves, the first of which occurred in the spring of 1918, and began either in the USA or in American army camps in France. This first wave aroused little attention because it was a comparatively mild illness. Then, in August, a second, more virulent, wave struck at the same time in several localities thousands of miles apart: Freetown, the capital of Sierra Leone; Brest, the French port of disembarkation for American troops; and Boston in the USA. This highly infectious flu turned rapidly into pneumonia, against which medicine had no defence. It spread like wildfire among American soldiers at home and abroad. In all, 62,000 American service personnel died of the flu – more than were killed in battle.

The third wave, which happened in the spring of 1919, ravaged the war-strained, malnourished civilian populations of Europe. Despite frantic efforts to control and treat it, between 21 million and 25 million people died. Then, as mysteriously as it had arrived, the Spanish flu disappeared.

Repelling the germs
Mint throat lozenges – promoted here in an advertisement – were just one of the many anti-flu medicines available. All of them, however, proved to be totally ineffectual.

Caring for flu victims in the USA
Some of the American soldiers struck down by flu were nursed in large canvas tents in Lawrence, Massachusetts. Fresh air was thought to be beneficial.

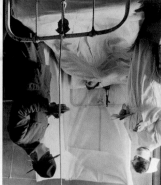

Protective measures
Attempts were made to protect medical staff from infection by the use of gauze face masks, but many nurses and doctors contracted flu and died.

The German airforce was to be assembled at one location and immobilized, and the naval fleet was to be interned and disarmed – a process that duly took place and involved a total of 114 German submarines being escorted into Harwich harbour in England between November 19 and 27.

All Allied prisoners of war were to be handed over by the Germans, and Allied nationals in occupied territories were to be repatriated. The Allies did not, however, state that they would reciprocate this arrangement. The Allied blockade of German ports, which was causing severe food shortages and hardship among German civilians and soldiers, was to continue, although the Allies agreed to "contemplate the provisioning of Germany... as shall be found necessary".

POLITICAL CHANGE
As Ebert took over as chancellor on November 10, the radical socialists Karl Liebknecht and Rosa Luxemburg held a rally at which they proposed a Russian-style soviet republic. To wrong-foot the radicals, Ebert's followers declared Germany a socialist republic, and named the provisional government the Council of Peoples' Commissars.

A period of political unrest followed, during which Liebknecht and his communist followers, known as Spartacists, staged an uprising on January 6, 1919 and seized control of key government buildings. Their revolution was violently suppressed within a week by the right-wing *Freikorps* – private armies formed by senior German army officers.

Exile for the Kaiser
When it became clear that the kaiser no longer commanded the support of the army or navy, he left his headquarters in Belgium and crossed the border into the Netherlands. His abdication was announced by Prince Max on November 9, although the kaiser did not actually sign an official proclamation until November 28.

Going home
Alsatians cross a bridge at Kehl, just east of Strasbourg, on their way back home in November 1918.

might be treated as an equal partner by the Allies at the Paris Peace Conference were dashed as the Germans were forced to wait on the sidelines until early April before being summoned to Paris to be dictated the terms of peace.

EUROPE AFTER THE ARMISTICE

What followed in the days, weeks and months after the signing of the armistice was very far from peace. While the institution of a republic in Germany was of huge significance, affecting as it did the most powerful single nation within Europe, events also occurred elsewhere – particularly in central and eastern Europe – that reflected profound political, economic and social changes. There was a vast movement of people during and after the German evacuation of Belgium, Alsace-Lorraine and Luxembourg in the west, and of Poland and the Ukraine in the east. The French occupied Strasbourg on November 25, and on December 9 the Allied armies moved into Germany, crossing the Rhine three days later. Meanwhile, Europe was gripped by an influenza epidemic that was to affect 100 million people worldwide.

In Eastern Europe, Poland, proclaimed as a state on October 7, 1918 and formally constituted in the week after the armistice, held a general election in January 1919. Not included in this election was an area in Galicia, around Lemberg, where there were clashes between Polish and Ukrainian forces in November 1918. In January 1919 Bolshevik forces occupied Vilna, an action that foreshadowed war between Poland and Russia.

In the south, where a French army stood on the Danube for the first time in over 100 years, a kingdom of the Serbs, Croats and Slovenes was proclaimed on October 29 in Zagreb. It was formally established in the Serb city of Belgrade three days later, the new country was beset by border disputes with Italy, Romania and Bulgaria. Its main difficulties were, however, more basic: the land was ravaged by war and destruction and the peasantry by disease and starvation.

Elsewhere, countries such as Czechoslovakia, came into existence. Independence was declared from Austria by the Czechs on October 29, 1918, and from Hungary by Slovakia two days later. By January 1919, the integrated army of the newly united state had driven Polish forces from the disputed area of Teschen in Moravia.

All these developments were part of the legacy of what was, perhaps, the greatest single change within Europe as a result of the war: the collapse of the Habsburg Empire and the reconstitution of its territories on the basis of national self-determination. It was a change without parallel in Europe since 1453, when Constantinople had fallen to the Ottoman Turks. In the last days of the war, as Austria-Hungary collapsed, some 500,000 of its troops surrendered. Others abandoned their positions to march home across countries in chaos.

Surrender of the fleet
The German fleet, led by British warships, steams up the Firth of Forth on November 21. It was subsequently interned at Scapa Flow in the Orkney Islands, Scotland.

The election of an assembly to draw up a new German constitution went ahead on January 19, and included women voters for the first time. Parties that supported democracy received 75 per cent of the votes, and the elected assembly met in Weimar on February 6. The German provisional government, of which Ebert was now president, was, however, given little credit by the Allies for its overthrow of the old, autocratic order. Any hopes that a democratic and demilitarized Germany

~ ARMISTICE ~

ON 11 NOVEMBER AT 11 AM the guns on the Western Front at last fell silent. Within hours, church bells were pealing again in Britain, where it seemed that the entire population had come out into the streets to celebrate "Victory Day". Factories closed, pubs stayed open, and the flags of the Allied nations were unfurled under the dull November sky. In France, too, flags fluttered and huge crowds sang the "Marseillaise," but the celebrations were more muted than those of the Americans and the British, perhaps because the French people had suffered the highest proportion of deaths of any combatant nation, as well as the trauma of German occupation.

In Germany, news of the armistice was of minor significance, compared with reports of the kaiser's abdication and cities falling under revolutionary control. Among the German people, shielded from the events at the Western Front until the very last minute, there was bewilderment, and denial. They felt that because the armistice had been signed while their army still occupied parts of Belgium and France, they had not lost the war, but had been betrayed by their leaders. If the Allies had mounted victory parades in Berlin and Munich, the reality of defeat might have sunk in sooner. Instead, the terms of the armistice allowed German soldiers to march home, and be hailed as victors by the new German Chancellor, Friedrich Ebert. With the armistice began the myth of the "stab in the back", of which Adolf Hitler was to be the eventual beneficiary.

Thanksgiving menu
The Thanksgiving dinner given for American military personnel in London on November 28, 1918 was an especially momentous event.

Thanksgiving Day
Eagle Hut, London
November 28th 1918

Cheering Australians
News of the armistice was received with joy and relief around the world. Crowds gathered to celebrate in Martin Place in central Sydney.

French victory postcard
The significance of the eleventh of the eleventh hour of the eleventh day of the eleventh month would never be forgotten.

German capitulation
The headlines on the front page of this French newspaper of November 11 announce the abdication of the kaiser and revolution in Germany, and look forward to the signing of the Armistice later in the day.

Celebrations
Among the crowds who celebrated on the streets of London were an American sailor, a Red Cross nurse and British soldiers, united in their enthusiasm for the peace.

Hailing "Victory Day"
In England, as in the other Allied states, the celebration of victory lasted for just a few hours before people began to remember the reality of what had occurred over the previous four years.

6

A NEW
WORLD
ORDER
1919–1923

~

THE PARIS PEACE CONFERENCE WAS
CONVENED AMID HIGH HOPES OF A EUROPE IN
WHICH OLD RIVALRIES AND RESENTMENTS WOULD BE
HEALED, BUT WHILE THE MAP OF EUROPE WAS
RADICALLY ALTERED BY THE TREATIES, MANY OF THE
UNDERLYING CAUSES OF THE WAR WERE NOT
ADDRESSED. THE HARDSHIP EXPERIENCED BY THE
PEOPLE OF CENTRAL AND EASTERN EUROPE, AND THE
EXAMPLE OF THE RUSSIAN REVOLUTION, LED TO
A PERIOD OF POLITICAL UPHEAVAL IN WHICH
EXTREMIST LEADERS GAINED POPULAR SUPPORT.

~

Wounded Red Army soldiers in 1919
Soldiers of the Red Army fought to consolidate the
hold of the Bolsheviks over Russia. They experienced
many setbacks, before eventually winning the war
against the counter-revolutionary forces.

THE PEACE THAT FAILED

THERE WERE HOPES THAT A POST-WAR EUROPE COULD BE FOUNDED ON
THE PRINCIPLES OF NATIONAL SELF-DETERMINATION AND DEMOCRACY, AND
THAT FUTURE INTERNATIONAL CONFLICTS COULD BE SOLVED PEACEABLY
BY A LEAGUE OF NATIONS – ASPIRATIONS THAT HAD BEEN EXPRESSED BY
THE AMERICAN PRESIDENT WOODROW WILSON IN HIS "FOURTEEN POINTS".

WHEN PRESIDENT WILSON arrived in London in December 1918, on his way to Paris for the peace conference, he was greeted by many as though he were a divine messenger, bringing light to the Old World from the New. His proposals for a lasting peace, set out at the beginning of the year as his "Fourteen Points" (see page 284) and further elaborated in later speeches, had been the basis on which the German leadership had requested an armistice. He could thus be credited with playing a substantial role in bringing the war to its conclusion.

The Paris Peace Conference opened in January 1919 and was attended by representatives from 32 nations. A large number of commissions were set up to deal with different aspects of the settlement, which included separate treaties with each of the Central Powers, and a covenant establishing the League of Nations. The conference was unusual in not involving negotiations between opposing sides. The victors alone decided the terms, which the vanquished were then forced to accept. The main decisions were taken by the French prime minister, Clemenceau, the British prime minister Lloyd George, and the American president, Wilson. The Italian prime minister, Orlando, was somewhat sidelined, and the head of the Japanese delegation, Saionji, stood aside from the discussions when Japanese interests were not involved.

JUSTICE OR REVENGE?

There was strong public feeling in both Britain and France that Germany should make substantial financial reparations to compensate the Allies for the cost of the war. Lloyd George, a Liberal, was more moderate in his views, but his government depended on Conservative votes and he was thus a prisoner of vengeful public opinion. The Germans objected strongly to the demand for reparations, and to being made to a sign a "war guilt" clause. They had agreed to armistice talks on the basis of the principles embodied in the Fourteen Points, and they profoundly resented the way in which, in their view, the terms of both the Armistice and treaty contravened these principles. The Allies pointed out that the requirement for compensation had been included in a note Wilson sent to the Germans on November 5. Furthermore, they were, in effect, demanding no more than the Germans had exacted from the Russians and the Romanians in the treaties of 1918. In the event, agreement could not be reached on the amount of reparations to be paid by Germany, and the matter had to be left open.

The treaty stripped Germany of its overseas possessions in Africa, China and the Pacific, and imposed the added humiliation of the reduction of the German army to 100,000 officers and men, and the navy to nothing more than a coastal defence force; Germany was denied an air force.

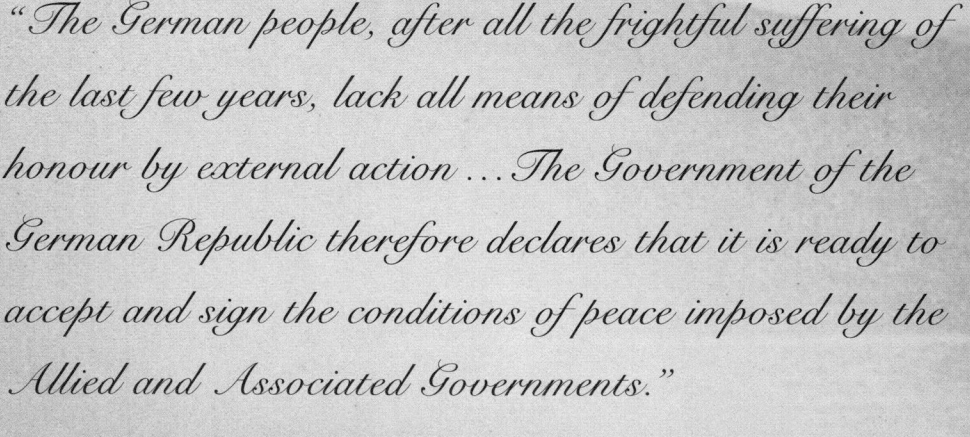

"The German people, after all the frightful suffering of the last few years, lack all means of defending their honour by external action … The Government of the German Republic therefore declares that it is ready to accept and sign the conditions of peace imposed by the Allied and Associated Governments."

EXTRACT FROM THE STATEMENT ISSUED BY THE GERMAN GOVERNMENT
IN WHICH IT AGREED TO SIGN THE VERSAILLES TREATY

THE FUTURE SECURITY OF FRANCE

In a speech made in February 1918 Wilson had expounded the principle that territorial settlements should be made in the interest of the populations concerned, and not on the basis of claims by rival states. Set against this, however, was the Allies' concern for the long-term security of Belgium and France in the face of Germany's potential economic might. The return of Alsace-Lorraine (annexed by Germany in 1871) had been established by Wilson as the eighth of his Fourteen Points and was thus easily agreed upon. French demands for German territory in the Rhineland, indeed the division of Germany itself, were, though, seen by Wilson and Lloyd George as likely to ensure future conflict. A compromise was agreed in April that provided for a military occupation of the Rhineland by the Allies extending 50km (30 miles) to the east, lasting for 15 years, and for its permanent demilitarization. The Saarland would be under French control in order to provide compensation for the German wrecking of the coalfields of northern France, its ultimate fate to be decided by plebiscite.

These arrangements were incorporated into the Treaty of Versailles, which, despite misgivings by Wilson and Lloyd George about certain of its provisions, was presented to Count Brockdorff-Rantzau on May 7, 1919. After minor amendments it was reluctantly signed by the German delegation in the Hall of Mirrors on June 28. The treaty was subsequently ratified by the governments of all parties except the United States, whose Senate had no enthusiasm for becoming further involved in international affairs through the League of Nations. An Anglo-American guarantee to France, offered in return for the modification of French demands on the Rhineland, was thereby lost, and Clemenceau, widely blamed for having failed France in these matters, was defeated in the 1920 election.

Scuppered at Scapa Flow
The commander of the German fleet, anticipating that the Versailles Treaty would require him to hand over his ships, despatched an order on June 21, 1919 for the fleet to be sunk. A total of 74 ships were sent to the bottom.

"You may strip Germany of her colonies, reduce her armaments to a mere police force and her navy to that of a fifth-rate power; all the same, in the end if she feels she has been unjustly treated in the peace of 1919 she will find means of exacting retribution from her conquerors."

LLOYD GEORGE, THE TRUTH ABOUT THE PEACE TREATIES, 1938

THE CREATION OF STATES

The principle of national self-determination had been accepted, in some cases reluctantly, by all parties, but putting it into practice was not straightforward. The collapse of the empires of Austria-Hungary, Russia and Turkey left the whole of Eastern Europe virtually a blank slate. New nation states were created, and old ones enlarged (or shrunk), according to boundaries agreed by a series of commissions at the peace conference, but the integrity of the process was called into question by an evident bias against the Central Powers, and by the Allies' desire to create relatively strong states bordering on Bolshevik Russia. These matters were dealt with in individual treaties with Austria (Treaty of Saint-Germain), Hungary (Treaty of Trianon) and Bulgaria (Treaty of Neuilly).

Finland and the Baltic states were granted their independence, and Poland, which had ceased to exist in the late 18th century, was reconstructed. Territory of the former Habsburg Empire was divided between seven states, of which Austria was, ironically, the smallest. Although borders were dictated, as far as practicable, by ethnic groups, there were exceptions. Czechoslovakia and Romania gained territories in which many people were Magyar-speaking, and others (as in Sudetenland) that were largely German-speaking. Among the gains Italy acquired as reward for its war efforts were German-speaking areas in the Tyrol.

THE BREAK-UP OF THE OTTOMAN EMPIRE

The defeat of the Turks resulted in the disappearance of the Ottoman Empire. In August 1920, the last and in some ways the most difficult of the peace treaties was signed at Sèvres, although it was almost immediately overtaken by events and was almost never ratified.

The harsh treatment of Turkey in the Treaty of Sèvres was apparently designed to terminate its independence. The sultan surrendered all territory already lost by the empire and gave up any claim to territories outside the boundaries of Turkey. Britain and France had already staked out territories for themselves in the Middle East, which they held under the legal form of a mandate from the League of Nations (a form of government also adopted for the former German colonies). Turkey handed over eastern Thrace, including Gallipoli, to the Greeks, who also occupied Smyrna (Izmir). An independent Armenia was projected, and provision was made for a self-governing Kurdish state that would incorporate parts of Anatolia and Mesopotamia (Iraq).

ITALIAN RESENTMENT

It was not only Germany and its allies that considered themselves ill-treated by the peace settlement. Ever since its unification, Italy had exhibited, as Bismarck observed, a giant appetite for territory without possessing the requisite teeth. Italy's allies considered its contribution to the war effort small, which was true in terms of its effect, but ignored its high casualty rate. Italy's rewards from the peace settlement fell short of the claims it had made in the Treaty of London when it entered the war in 1915, which included, among other things, the Dalmatian coast. The Italians resented the secret wartime diplomacy of Britain and France, notably the Sykes–Picot Agreement of 1916, in which the British and French had divided up the Middle East to their mutual benefit. They also objected to the creation of the Slav state that was to become Yugoslavia, inhabited by many of the people Italy had been fighting.

The rejection of Italy's demand for Fiume on the Adriatic coast caused particular bitterness. The Italian delegation withdrew briefly from the peace talks, and in September 1919 the poet D'Annunzio seized it for Italy. His proto-fascist regime lasted a year before the Italian government suppressed it. In spite of this episode, and the widespread social unrest that appeared to threaten revolution in 1919–20, there was little real support for parties of the far right at this time, although over the next two years parliamentary democracy in Italy collapsed.

Under the terms of the Treaty of Sèvres, Turkey effectively ceased to be an independent state. Control of the straits between the Black Sea and the Mediterranean was given to an international commission. The army was reduced to a token force. Trade and financial affairs were to be controlled by a commission representing Britain, France and Italy, with each country being awarded a "sphere of influence" within Turkey.

Destruction of weapons
Under the terms of the Treaty of Versailles, Germany was forced to disarm. This included the destruction of its tanks – even this British model, captured during the war.

The peacemakers
The British prime minister, Lloyd George, the French prime minister, Clemenceau, and the American President, Wilson, arrive at Versailles in 1919.

Aftermath of the War

Hungarian Red Army troops The disillusionment of defeat, and sympathy for Bolshevik Russia fuelled the revolution in Hungary, where Béla Kun was supported by a Hungarian Red Army.

T HE PRINCIPLE OF NATIONAL self-determination, espoused by the peacemakers, ensured the liquidation of what remained of the ancient, multi-ethnic Habsburg Empire – the Dual Monarchy of Austria-Hungary. As well as the Versailles Treaty, separate treaties were made with Austria at Saint-Germain-en-Laye and with Hungary at Trianon. Austria was reduced to a state of only 6.5 million people, over a third of whom lived in Vienna. Except for the loss of the South Tyrol to Italy, the borders roughly outlined the German-speaking area, and the chief Austrian complaint was that union (*Anschluss*) with Germany was forbidden, in breach of the principle of national self-determination. There were doubts over whether a truncated Austrian state was economically viable, and the state was further weakened by tensions between the citizens of Vienna (who were primarily socialist in sympathy) and the agrarian population (who were primarily Catholic and conservative).

In Hungary there was acute indignation at the loss of more than 70 per cent of its pre-war area and nearly 65 per cent of its population. Just days before the war ended Hungary had declared its independence from Austria and instituted a democratic regime under Count Károlyi, in the hope of being treated as one of the newly independent nations, rather than as an enemy. The disillusionment provoked by the peace process led to Károlyi's resignation, the setting up of a short-lived communist republic led by Béla Kun, and a brief Romanian occupation of Budapest. Not until the reactionary regime of Admiral Horthy established itself was the Treaty of Trianon ratified.

SOUTH SLAVS, CZECHS AND SLOVAKS

Serbia, now part of the Kingdom of Serbs, Croats and Slovenes (renamed Yugoslavia in 1929), was represented at the peace conference, but the new kingdom was not officially recognized until May 1919, mainly because of objections by Italy, whose territorial ambitions it thwarted. The new nation's economic weakness, revolutionary ideas among workers and intellectuals, and hostility towards the Serbs among the other ethnic groups (especially the Croatians) created political problems. These were aggravated by religious differences – the Serbs being Greek Orthodox, the Croats and Slovenes Roman Catholic – and social tensions. The Serbian army and police established a reasonable degree of stability by 1920 under Nikola Pasic, but it seemed that the disintegration of the kingdom could only be prevented by a strong authoritarian regime.

In 1914 most Czechs and Slovaks had been sympathetic towards Russia. Thousands were interned or shot for disloyalty to Austria-Hungary.

PEACE TALKS AND CONFLICT
1919 – 1923

~

The peace negotiations of 1919, which involved individual peace treaties being made with each of the defeated countries, did not take place in a world devoid of conflict. Several countries in Europe experienced short-lived periods of violent political upheaval, while the Bolsheviks battled with the White Russians for control of Russia. The Turks meanwhile proved that they would not submit to European domination.

~

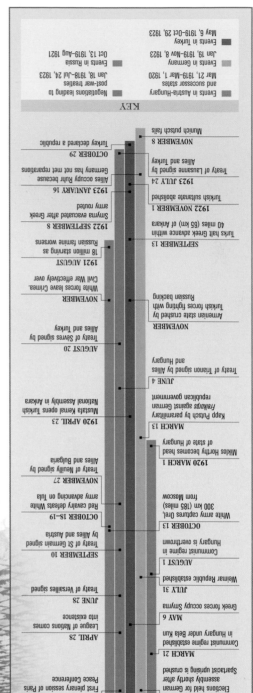

KEY

Events in Austria-Hungary and successor states Mar 1, 1919–Mar 1, 1920	Negotiations leading to post-war treaties Jan 18, 1918–Jul 24, 1923
Events in Russia Oct 13, 1919–Aug 1921	Events in Germany Jan 19, 1919–Nov 8, 1923
	Events in Turkey May 6, 1919–Oct 29, 1923

1919 JANUARY 18 – First plenary session of Paris Peace Conference

1919 JANUARY 19 – Elections held for German assembly shortly after Spartacist uprising is crushed

MARCH 21 – Communist regime established in Hungary under Béla Kun

APRIL 28 – League of Nations comes into existence

MAY 6 – Greek forces occupy Smyrna

JUNE 28 – Treaty of Versailles signed

JULY 31 – Weimar Republic established

AUGUST 1 – Communist regime in Hungary is overthrown

SEPTEMBER 10 – Treaty of St Germain signed by Allies and Austria

OCTOBER 13 – White army captures Orel, 300 km (185 miles) from Moscow

OCTOBER 18-19 – Red cavalry defeats White army advancing on Tula

NOVEMBER 27 – Treaty of Neuilly signed by Allies and Bulgaria

1920 MARCH 1 – Miklós Horthy becomes head of state of Hungary

MARCH 13 – Kapp Putsch by paramilitary *Freikorps* against German republican government

1920 APRIL 23 – Mustafa Kemal opens Turkish National Assembly in Ankara

JUNE 4 – Treaty of Trianon signed by Allies and Hungary

NOVEMBER – Armenian state crushed by Turkish forces fighting with Russian backing

AUGUST 20 – Treaty of Sèvres signed by Allies and Turkey

NOVEMBER – White forces leave Crimea. Civil War effectively over

1921 AUGUST – 18 million starving as Russian famine worsens

SEPTEMBER 13 – Turks halt Greek advance within 40 miles (65 km) of Ankara

1922 SEPTEMBER 8 – Smyrna evacuated after Greek army routed

1922 NOVEMBER 1 – Turkish sultanate abolished

1923 JANUARY 16 – Allies occupy Ruhr because Germany has not met reparations

1923 JULY 24 – Treaty of Lausanne signed by Allies and Turkey

OCTOBER 29 – Turkey declared a republic

NOVEMBER 8 – Munich putsch fails

TERMS OF THE PEACE SETTLEMENT

T REATIES WERE DRAWN UP at the Paris Peace Conference with each of the Central Powers. All were modelled on the Treaty of Versailles.

VERSAILLES (JUN 28, 1919) – WITH GERMANY

Alsace-Lorraine ceded to France and northern Schleswig to Denmark; large area in east ceded to Poland, including a "corridor" giving Poles access to Baltic; plebiscites in disputed regions, including the Saar (under temporary international control); Rhineland demilitarized; Danzig made a free city; international access guaranteed to Kiel Canal and stretches of Danube, Elbe, Niemen, Oder and Rhine; reparations to be made, although amount unspecified; all colonies ceded to Allies or League of Nations; army and navy reduced; air force banned. A covenant established the League of Nations.

SAINT-GERMAIN (SEPT 10, 1919) – WITH AUSTRIA

Recognized independence of Czechoslovakia, Poland, Hungary and Yugoslavia; all states to protect ethnic minorities; Trentino, South Tyrol, Trieste and Istria ceded to Italy, eastern Galicia to Poland, unification with Germany forbidden without League of Nations approval; armed forces circumscribed, the need for reparations acknowledged, although amount unspecified.

NEUILLY (NOV 27, 1919) – WITH BULGARIA

Independent Yugoslavia recognized; Aegean coast ceded to Greece; armed forces reduced; amount of reparations agreed (uniquely among the peace treaties); most of which was subsequently paid on time and without serious problems.

TRIANON (JUN 4, 1920) – WITH HUNGARY

Slovakia, Bratislava and part of Ruthenia ceded to Czechoslovakia; Croatia and Slovenia and part of Banat to Yugoslavia; Transylvania and most of Banat to Romania; Burgenland to Austria, Fiume to Italy; armed forces limited, reparations imposed.

SÈVRES (AUG 20, 1920) – WITH TURKEY

Ottoman Empire abolished; all non-Turkish territories removed; independence of the Hejaz, Yemen and Armenia recognized; Syria made a French mandate of the League of Nations; Mesopotamia and Palestine made British mandates; Dodecanese islands and Rhodes ceded to Italy, other Aegean islands and the region of Smyrna in Anatolia, pending a plebiscite, to Greece; the Dardanelles and the Bosphorus straits internationalized. The treaty was rejected by nationalists and was never ratified, although the mandates in the Middle East remained in force.

LAUSANNE (JUL 24, 1923) – WITH TURKEY

This treaty superseded that of Sèvres (never ratified). Eastern Thrace, Smyrna, and control of the straits returned to Turkey; an exchange of populations with Greece agreed and implemented.

Protest in Berlin
Friedrich Naumann, leader of the German Democratic Party, expresses the outrage felt by many Germans at the harsh peace terms Germany was forced to accept.

A welcome fit for heroes
Front-line German soldiers returning to Berlin were greeted with much rejoicing. Having been largely kept in ignorance of the circumstances surrounding the armistice, many Germans did not realize that they would be expected to pay the price of defeat.

Masaryk, Beneš and others lobbied in Allied capitals for Czecho-Slovak independence, and by September 1918 all the Allied nations had affirmed support for an independent state. An interim Czecho-Slovak government was set up in Paris in October shortly before Austria's surrender, which led to a declaration of independence in Prague. An interim constitution established a democratic republic, with Masaryk as president. The hostility of the substantial German minority in the Sudetenland led to violence, and some Hungarians were forced out of former Hungarian territory in 1920 Under the constitution of 1920 Czechoslovakia became the most stable and prosperous of the new states – and the only one in which democracy survived until 1939.

POLAND REBORN

Poland was reconstituted from the lands of the three imperial powers that had partitioned it among themselves between 1772 and 1795 – Austria, Prussia and Russia. The Bolsheviks had renounced Russian claims on Poland at Brest-Litovsk, but angered the Poles by ceding Polish territory to Austria and to the short-lived republic of the Ukraine. The Allies accepted a united, independent Poland in June 1918, and the Poles themselves drove the Germans out of Poznan.

The circumstances of the newly restored state, a democratic republic with Pilsudski as head of state, was unenviable. The peace terms left intractable territorial problems that were not resolved by plebiscites, with Danzig becoming a free city under League of Nations protection. Frontier quarrels provoked armed conflict with the Germans, Czechs and Ukrainians, arbitrated by the Council of the League, and war with Bolshevik Russia, which ended in March 1921.

These territorial disputes set back the immense task of the reconstruction of Poland. As a result of war, the country's industry was at a virtual standstill, communications were disordered, and the civil service non-existent. Polish agriculture was laid waste by famine and disease. New laws limiting land holdings were largely ignored by the nobility, who held on to their vast estates with the support of elements of the urban middle class, fearful of communist influence among workers and peasants.

The collapse of the Russian empire in 1918 gave Estonia, Latvia and Lithuania a chance to declare their independence, although they subsequently came into conflict with the Bolsheviks. During the early 1920s they made peace with Russia and were granted international recognition, although Lithuania lost its capital, Vilna (Vilnius), to the Poles.

> *What honest man can sign such a capitulation? Would not the hand wither that put itself into such bonds? This treaty will make a corpse not just of Germany but of the right to self-determination, of faith in treaties. It will be the beginning of a general process of barbarization.*
>
> CHANCELLOR SCHEIDEMANN ON THE TERMS PRESENTED TO THE GERMAN DELEGATION AT VERSAILLES ON MAY 8, 1919

GERMANY AFTER VERSAILLES

The Treaty of Versailles was presented to a German delegation led by Count Brockdorff-Rantzau on May 7, 1919. The Germans responded with an outcry of protest at the harsh terms that were being dictated to them. In the days that followed notes were exchanged but there was no face-to-face discussion. On June 16 the Allies threatened to renew hostilities if the Germans did not sign within a week. Seven days later they agreed that they would sign. The official ceremony took place in the Hall of Mirrors at Versailles on June 28. Germany at the time of the ceremony was under a provisional government, while an elected National Assembly met in Weimar to work out a new, democratic constitution for the country. This was finalized in July 1919, and the Weimar Republic was born. Parliament was to consist of two houses, the more important of which was the Reichstag, to which ministers were responsible, and whose members were elected by univeral suffrage. The president, who was to be directly elected, would normally have only a ceremonial role, but in an

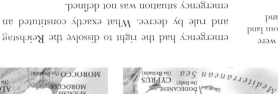

Spartacists on the march
Germany's provisional government faced many challenges including, in January 1919, a short-lived revolution in Berlin by the Spartacists, who made the mistake of thinking the country was ripe for communist revolution.

The remapping of Europe
From the Baltic to the Aegean, European borders were redrawn. Seven new nation states were created from land once ruled over by Austria-Hungary and Russia, and France regained Alsace-Lorraine from Germany.

emergency had the right to dissolve the Reichstag and rule by decree. What exactly constituted an emergency situation was not defined.

POLITICAL AND ECONOMIC DIFFICULTIES

The Weimar Republic was dominated by problems connected with the Versailles Treaty, especially the payment of reparations and the reduction of the army. The generals blamed the politicians rather than themselves for defeat, and in the so-called Kapp Putsch of March 1920 the *Freikorps* – a voluntary paramilitary group formed from demobbed soldiers – attempted to overthrow the republican government. The coup failed thanks to a general strike in Berlin, but the campaign of political terrorism pursued by the *Freikorps* was to continue for the next three years.

Negotiations with the Allies over reparations were dogged by the wide divergence between Allied demands and Germany's estimate of its ability to pay. Both sides were divided within themselves, with Britain favouring more tolerant treatment of Germany than did France. The sum to be paid was eventually fixed by the Reparations Commission in 1921 at the equivalent of £6,600,000,000 ($28 billion), to be paid over 12 years.

POST-WAR EUROPE State borders in 1923

PRE-WAR EUROPE State borders in 1914

Cartloads of money
German inflation in the early 1920s led to scenes such as this, in which money to pay employees' wages had to be wheeled from the bank in laundry baskets.

On the German side, the Right argued for obstruction and non-compliance, the Centre and Centre-Left for a more willing attitude, in the hope of negotiating future reductions. The moderates were weakened in June 1922 when their leader, the extremely able foreign minister, Walter Rathenau, a Jew, became the most notable victim of a series of assassinations by rightists. Ironically, two months earlier he had concluded, as a concession to the hard-liners, the Treaty of Rapallo for economic collaboration with the Soviet Union, which included a secret clause permitting Germany to manufacture armaments in Russia, in defiance of the Versailles Treaty.

With Rathenau removed, the obstructionists gained the ascendancy and, in response to Germany's failure to make reparations on schedule, French and Belgian troops occupied the industrial region of the Ruhr in January 1923. Their intention was to divert the output of the mines to France. The miners went on strike, with the backing of the German government, which was then faced with the problem of how to prevent the miners and their families from starving.

A thorny welcome in the Ruhr
A cartoon by Erich Schilling in the satirical journal *Simplicissimus* draws attention to the fact that the French occupation of the Ruhr was not going smoothly, thanks to the non-cooperation of the miners.

Die Belegung des Ruhrgebietes

RAMPANT INFLATION

Germany had largely paid for the war, not by taxation, but simply by printing money, and this policy was adopted again, with the mint's presses stretched to the limit. The result was a total collapse of the currency, which within eight months, at 4,200 billion marks to the dollar, was not worth the paper it was printed on.

Naturally, wages and salaries failed to keep pace, while pensions and investments became almost worthless. People survived by selling possessions and bartering for food and necessities (although some benefited from speculation). Worst affected were the middle classes, normally a conservative element, who were radicalized by this bitter experience. The Republican government was discredited, the country in chaos. Separatism became a powerful force once more, and extremist parties of both right and left gained power in several states.

Gustav Stresemann, once an extreme nationalist, admirer of the kaiser, supporter of the military, and in 1923 leader of a right-wing party in the Reichstag, took the lead in persuading the Germans of the futility of passive resistance in the Ruhr. In his brief period as chancellor of a national coalition from August 13 to November 23 he managed to stabilize the currency. Indeed, the situation was sufficiently improved to undermine popular support for Adolf Hitler's Munich putsch on November 9.

The destabilization of Germany was not in the interest of the rest of Europe and there were international moves to help resolve the country's economic problems. Under the Dawes Plan of April 1924 arrangements were agreed for Germany's payment of reparations, made possible by a substantial initial international loan.

Stresemann served as Foreign Minister from late 1924 until his early death in 1929, and was involved in negotiating the Locarno Pact of 1925 – a set of agreements guaranteeing peace in Europe. It led to Germany's acceptance into the League of Nations in 1926, to improved relations with its neighbours, and, in 1930, to the evacuation of Allied troops from the Rhineland, five years ahead of schedule.

REVOLUTIONS IN EUROPE

THE RUSSIAN BOLSHEVIKS confidently anticipated the spread of communism throughout Europe in the wake of their own revolution, but although leftist uprisings broke out in Germany and elsewhere, the looked-for international revolution never occurred.

In Germany, the Spartacists, a group of radical socialists led by Karl Liebknecht and Rosa Luxemburg, founded the German Communist Party. In January 1919 they instigated an uprising in Berlin against the socialist-led provisional government, but it was violently suppressed within a week. Liebknecht and Luxemburg were shot by the right-wing *Freikorps*. Risings in Hamburg, the Ruhr and other areas were also suppressed.

On November 8, 1918 the Wittelsbach dynasty in Bavaria was overthrown in a coup led by Kurt Eisner – a socialist. He declared a republic, but his party failed in the elections of January 1919, and in February he was assassinated. The communists responded by taking control of Munich and instituting a "Red Terror". The local *Freikorps* recaptured Munich in May and imposed their own "White Terror".

In March 1919 the Hungarian president, Count Károlyi, resigned and handed power to a communist regime led by Béla Kun, a Russian Jew and Soviet agent. His promise to enlist Soviet assistance to regain land confiscated from Hungary by the Allies gained widespread support. His Red Army forces attacked the Czechs, but were forced to withdraw by the Allies. His increasingly dictatorial rule eroded popular support, and an invasion and advance to Budapest by the Romanian army caused him to flee in August. After the restoration of the monarchy by the Hungarian parliament, Miklós Horthy was elected regent in March 1920. He encouraged a purge of revolutionaries and Jews.

Rosa Luxemburg
Luxemburg, a Pole, studied in Switzerland, where she gained a doctorate. She was imprisoned for her revolutionary activities in Warsaw in 1905 and for her opposition to the war in Germany.

Béla Kun
A founder of the Hungarian Communist Party, Kun allied himself with the Russian Soviet government and, in his short period in power in 1919, used ruthless methods in his drive to rid Hungary of its capitalist system and establish a soviet state.

Lenin sweeps the world clean
The aim of the Bolsheviks in the early days of their revolution was not just to transform Russia into a communist state, but to rid the rest of the world of its ruling monarchs, capitalists and clerics. The dream was not realized, however, as the proletariat of the defeated states tended to favour nationalism over socialism.

Тов. ЛЕНИН ОЧИЩАЕТ ЗЕМЛЮ ОТ НЕЧИСТИ.

Revolutionary cheer
Crowds in Budapest, Hungary, on March 21, 1919 celebrate the new soviet regime, which the next day seized all private property and took control of banking and trade.

THE RUSSIAN CIVIL WAR

This brutal and destructive war cost an estimated 13 million lives, many of which were lost as a result of famine caused by the extensive disruption to food supplies that reduced production to one-seventh of 1914 levels. At the end of 1918 the Bolsheviks had been in danger of losing control of Russia. That they eventually won the civil war was partly thanks to the strength and unity of their leadership, but also to the divisions among their enemies.

The counter-revolutionary leaders of 1918 had included socialists and others opposed to the Bolsheviks, none of whom had any experience of military leadership. They were gradually pushed aside by the generals – members of the old, aristocratic, ruling class. Although the moderate socialists badly needed the military ability of the tsarist generals, and the generals

White Army gunners

Wrangel's White Russian Army in the Crimea in 1920 included survivors of Denikin's army, which had been decimated by the Bolsheviks earlier in the year. Wrangel himself was forced to withdraw in November in the face of the overwhelming strength of the Red Army.

The Red Army advance into Poland
A detachment of Red Army cavalry enters Soldau, north-west of Warsaw, in its advance into Poland. Only splits within the Red Army leadership and the clever strategy of Piłsudski saved the Polish capital from invasion.

needed the popular support that the socialists commanded, the inevitable antagonism between them was ruinous to the counter-revolutionary cause. Most of the Russian people were peasants, on whom all parties relied for food and transport. They were far from natural allies of the Bolsheviks, but they came to see the Bolsheviks as representing "the people" against the reactionary White Russian generals.

Other factors contributed to the Bolshevik victory. They held a strong position in the centre of the country, and they were able to sustain the morale and discipline of their supporters at a time of near-total social breakdown. Trotsky's outstanding organization and leadership of the Red Army produced, from almost nothing, a force that was superior to any of the ill-assorted counter-revolutionaries could raise. As for the intervention of the Allies in support of the White army, this may well have worked in the Bolsheviks' favour. While the number of Allied troops sent to Russia was too small to affect the result of the war, it was large enough for the Bolsheviks to be able to brand their White opponents as lackeys of the imperialists.

VICTORY IN THE NORTH, EAST AND SOUTH

For much of 1919 the survival of the Bolshevik regime hung in the balance, but by the end of the year, it had won victories on all fronts. In the north, the withdrawal of Allied forces in the autumn left the Whites weakened and demoralized. In the east, Kolchak's White forces had seemed set to continue their successes of the previous year, but they had been gravely weakened by a split with the moderate socialists in late 1918, which lost them popular support and resulted in the Czech soldiers fighting alongside them losing interest. Kolchak's successes at the beginning of 1919 proved misleading. Confronted by the full force of the Red Army on the Volga, his men were soon in rapid retreat back across Siberia. Omsk was lost in November, and in February 1920 Kolchak was captured and shot. By the end of the year communist rule was restored in Siberia, barring an eastern strip where Japanese forces remained in occupation until November 1922.

The greatest threat came from the forces of Denikin in the south. Advancing steadily from the region of the Caucasus, he conquered a huge swathe of territory north of the Black Sea, and by October he was less than 320 km (200 miles) from Moscow. There, he was brought to a halt when confronted for the first time by the Red Army in strength. He retreated to the northern Caucasus, where his army was destroyed early in 1920. Meanwhile, Yudenich had launched an attack from Estonia. In October, at the time when Denikin was threatening Moscow, Yudenich's forces were in the suburbs of the former capital, Petrograd. His defeat, however, coincided with that of Denikin, and within a few days the communists' near-disaster had turned into near-total victory. The only White Russian force remaining was that commanded by Wrangel in the Crimea.

WAR WITH POLAND

At this point another player entered the stage. Russia had not been represented at Versailles in 1919 and it was therefore difficult to fix its border with the newly recreated Poland. The proposed Curzon Line (similar to the current border) had not satisfied the Poles, and with Russia in disarray the opportunity to advance it eastwards was tempting. The Poles did not want to support the campaign of the counter-revolutionaries, who could be assumed to be more antagonistic than the Bolsheviks to an independent Poland, so they waited until the Red Army had largely ended the counter-revolutionary threat before invading the Ukraine in April 1920.

In less than two weeks the Poles were in Kiev, but the defeat of the White Russians had released more Red Army troops, and over the next three months the Poles were driven back to the walls of Warsaw The threat of a Soviet presence deep in Europe prompted the swift despatch of a French military mission under Weygand, but it was the strategic grasp of Pilsudski in his counter-attack against the Soviet lines of communication, and the exhaustion of the Bolshevik forces, that saved the Polish capital. It was the Red Army's turn to retreat. The matter was concluded at the Treaty of Riga in March 1921, when the Russo-Polish border was drawn along a line more generous to the Poles than the Curzon Line, although short of the boundary they aspired to. Ukraine, granted nominal independence in 1918, came once more under Russian domination as a part of the new Soviet Union.

The final campaign, undertaken by the Red Army after the armistice with the Poles, was their defeat in the Crimea of Wrangel's forces, who put up considerable resistance. By November 1920, however, the Bolsheviks had triumphed in the west, although Central Asia was not secured until 1923.

THE MIDDLE EAST

Even in the thick of war the British and French had discussed how to divide up the Ottoman Empire. Under the secret Sykes–Picot agreement of May 1916 France was to receive a substantial portion – not only present-day Lebanon and Syria, but areas of southern Turkey and northern Iraq. Britain was to have southern Mesopotamia and the ports of Haifa and Acre; Palestine was to be placed under international rule. An Arab state or confederation was mooted for the centre of the region – divided into French and British spheres of influence.

Polish troops off to war
Soldiers of the newly re-formed state of Poland march into action against the Bolsheviks in a drive to expand their country's eastern territory.

Revolutionaries
The role played by the peoples of the Caucasus Red Army in 1920 in the defeat of the White Russian forces is celebrated on this poster.

MUSTAFA KEMAL (ATATÜRK)

GIVEN THE NAME KEMAL ("Perfect") while at school, Mustafa Kemal Pasha (1881–1938) was an intuitive wartime leader. Although strongly opposed to Turkey siding with Germany, once war was declared in October 1914 he did more than any other general to defend his country against Russian, British and French invasions. Kemal's first command was at Gallipoli in 1915, where he correctly predicted the Allied forces' landing places in both April and August, held the strategically important Sari Bair Ridge and provided the inspired leadership that enabled the Turks to hold back the Allies. Promoted to general, he then served in the Caucasus, before being transferred to Syria as commander of the Seventh Army. With Allenby's final offensive in Palestine in August 1918, Kemal retreated to the Turkish border rather than surrender, and held this position until the armistice.

After the war Kemal organized nationalist resistance to the Greek invasion, and negotiated improved terms for Turkey in the Treaty of Lausanne. He became the first president of the Turkish Republic in 1924, later taking the name Atatürk ("Father of the Turks").

The Arabs, however, had expected to be awarded much more, following pledges made by the British in letters sent to the Sharif of Mecca in 1915–16, as an inducement for his support against the Turks. Balfour, in November 1917 had compounded the confusion, by writing to Lord Rothschild of his sympathy for the idea of establishing a Jewish national home in Palestine.

By the end of the war, however, Lloyd George had concluded that Britain's much greater involvement in fighting in the region entitled it to more territory than had been agreed by Sykes and Picot. Further negotiations took place, and although the British allowed the French to remain in control of Lebanon and Syria, they insisted on control of the oil-rich region of northern Mesopotamia (Iraq). Feisal became king of Syria, but was driven out by the French after attempting to expand his kingdom, and in 1921 was installed as king of Iraq by the British. The British also controlled Palestine, which dashed the hopes of those who had looked for an Arab Palestinian state within a federated Syria.

Following an agreement made at San Remo in April 1920, all these territories were governed under the legal form of a mandate from the League of Nations. Although this arrangement assumed that the counties would eventually become independent, it did little to appease Arab nationalist leaders, who had looked for more immediate rewards for their help in vanquishing the Turks.

TURKEY

The Treaty of Sèvres of 1919 allowed for a nominally independent Turkish government under the sultan, but for large "spheres of influence" in Anatolia for the British, French, Italians and Greeks. Events moved so swiftly in the region, however, that by the time the treaty was signed in August 1920, it was largely redundant.

In May 1919 the Greeks had occupied the port of Smyrna (Izmir), in an area of Turkey that was home to a large Greek population. The Allies, who had provided military protection for the Greeks, watched from their warships as Turkish residents were massacred. This incursion by the Greeks stirred up nationalist feelings already fermenting among the Turks. The successful general Mustafa Kemal, sent on a mission by the sultan to the east of the country, instead met resistance leaders at Amasia in June 1919, where they signed a protocol stating their determination to oppose both the Allies and the sultan. During the summer Kemal presided over meetings of resistance groups and decided that Ankara, in the middle of Anatolia, should be the

focus of the nationalist movement. On April 23, 1920 a Grand National Assembly declared its right to represent the nation, with Kemal as its president.

Greek refugees in Smyrna

As Turkish troops closed in on Smyrna (Izmir) in September 1922, many of the Greeks who lived there, anticipating the massacre that was to take place, waited desperately on the quayside for ships to take them to safety. In the fighting that ensued the old town was almost completely destroyed by fire.

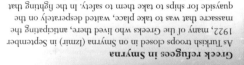

GRECO-TURKISH WAR

On June 20, 1920 the Greeks sent forces beyond the confines of Smyrna into the hinterland and, despite various setbacks, by August 1921 were threatening Ankara. In a three-week battle on the Sakarya River, Turkish forces, under Kemal's command, forced the Greeks to regroup east of Eskişehir. The following year the Greek army was routed, and in September 1922 the Turks retook Smyrna (Izmir), where they, in turn, massacred civilians. The Greeks, in the Treaty of Sèvres, had also been

Turkish celebrations

Turks surround a huge Turkish flag, made to celebrate the retaking of Smyrna (Izmir). Animosity between the Greeks and Turks in the surrounding region was intensified by the war, and led to the relocation of around 1.5 million people.

awarded control of eastern Thrace – Turkey's foothold in Europe. Kemal pressed on to reclaim this area, reached the Dardanelles and entered into a stand-off with a small British force protecting the neutral zone on the eastern shore. The British prime minister, Lloyd George issued an ultimatum for the immediate withdrawal of Turkish forces, but the British commander deliberately omitted to pass it on. While diplomats discussed a possible resolution of the crisis, British and Turkish troops confronted each other over the barbed wire. Kemal, confident of being awarded his objective in any subsequent peace conference was, in fact, unwilling to attack. Lloyd George backed off, and shortly afterwards, having lost the Conservative support he relied on in Parliament, resigned as prime minister.

TREATY OF LAUSANNE

The Treaty of Sèvres was replaced by the Treaty of Lausanne, signed on July 24, 1923. In recognizing the boundaries of the modern Turkish state, it met almost all Turkey's demands. The losers under the new treaty were the minority populations in the region. Animosity between Greek and Turkish communities led to a "population swap" involving around 1.5 million Christian Greeks and Muslim Turks. The Kurds, under the Treaty of Sèvres, had been granted some degree of autonomy. All that was now forgotten. The Armenians, hundreds of thousands of whom had died in 1915–16 as a result of forced relocation by the Turks, had been granted an independent state under the first treaty. This had, however, been crushed by Kemal's forces in January 1921, with the Turks gaining further land from a supportive Russian Bolshevik government.

Kemal terminated the sultanate and converted the Ottoman Empire into the Turkish republic in October 1923. He became its first president – a post he held until his death in 1938.

THE MIDDLE EAST
State borders in 1914

RUSSIAN EMPIRE
Caspian Sea
Black Sea
ROMANIA
BULGARIA
GREECE
OTTOMAN EMPIRE
PERSIA
CYPRUS (to Britain)
DODECANESE (to Italy)
Mediterranean Sea
EGYPT (British protectorate)
KUWAIT (British protectorate)
NEJD
LIBYA (to Italy)
Red Sea
ANGLO-EGYPTIAN SUDAN
FRENCH EQUATORIAL AFRICA
ERITREA
ABYSSINIA
ADEN (British protectorate)

THE MIDDLE EAST
State borders in 1923

U.S.S.R.
Caspian Sea
Black Sea
ROMANIA
BULGARIA
TURKEY
GREECE
SYRIA (French mandate)
IRAQ (British mandate)
CYPRUS (to Britain)
DODECANESE (to Italy)
Mediterranean Sea
PERSIA
PALESTINE (British mandate)
TRANSJORDAN (British mandate)
KUWAIT (British protectorate)
NEJD (1932: Saudi Arabia)
ASIR
LIBYA (to Italy)
EGYPT (British protectorate)
Red Sea
ANGLO-EGYPTIAN SUDAN (condominium)
ERITREA
YEMEN
FRENCH EQUATORIAL AFRICA
ABYSSINIA
ADEN (British protectorate)

Lines in the sand

The map of the Middle East was almost completely redrawn following the dissolution of the Ottoman Empire. Britain and France divided much of it in between them, controlling "mandates" that gave them access to countries' raw materials (such as oil), while they guided them towards independence.

THE LEGACY OF THE WAR

The turmoil let loose in August 1914 did not end with the peace settlement, but only after two disturbed and threatening decades had culminated in a second world war – a legacy of the political extremism the first had helped to create. To prescient statesmen this was already apparent in 1919: "We shall have to fight another war all over again in 25 years," said Lloyd George at Versailles.

The unnecessary war of 1914–18 was, regardless of long-term effects, one of the greatest tragedies Europe had experienced since the Black Death. In human terms it was almost as destructive and cruel: maybe as many as 10 million men dead ("the lost generation"), and countless millions permanently damaged in body or soul, or emotionally destroyed by the decimation of families.

CULTURAL CHANGE

Cultural damage is less easily expressed in figures. Pre-1914 European culture, whatever its faults, was relatively liberal, tolerant, progressive, and confident that society – even human nature – could be improved. The mechanized abattoir of the trenches shattered these ideals. In the immediate aftermath of the war, many survivors and the bereaved wanted to put it from their minds, and the 1920s became a period in which people focused on trying to enjoy themselves. Ten years later, however, attitudes were changing. People began to visit the battlefields, with 15,000 people signing the visitors' book at the Menin Gate in August 1928, and towns such as Ypres becoming tourist centres.

Books on the war began to sell in huge numbers, led by Erich Maria Remarque's famous novel *All Quiet on the Western Front*. Published in 1929, it had

Reburying the dead

After the war there was the massive task of disinterring the corpses of the fallen and reburying them in dedicated war cemeteries, where the ranks of white crosses stand like soldiers on endless parade.

From a broad historical viewpoint the war could be seen to have brought some social benefits. Like most wars, it stimulated overdue changes, including the loosening of the stranglehold exerted by the class system. No one could suggest, though, that this made it worth fighting. The sacrifice of the cream of European youth left enduring scars. But for the war, and the failure of governments to prevent the disasters that followed, the names of Stalin, Mussolini and Hitler might now be unknown.

sold 4 million copies by 1931. Books, plays and films, whose influence on the popular conception of the war was more powerful than the events themselves, universally pictured it as a vast, horrible and pointless disaster, distressing those who clung to the idea that their sons and husbands had not died in vain. The political extremists of the 1930s promoted a different idea of the soldier, as agent of progress rather than exploited victim, but few even of their own people were truly convinced.

France and Britain went to war again in 1939 with the utmost unwillingness. The even greater slaughter of the Second World War, with the mass murder of civilians on an unimaginable scale, suppressed memories of the First, which passed swiftly from contemporary consciousness into faded history. It seemed, by comparison, a minor affair.

Attitudes changed again as a new generation grew up and the second war lost its immediacy. Something of the cynical wit, black humour and nihilistic politics of the 1920s was reflected in the culture of the 1960s, and people began to regard the First and Second World Wars as part of the same catastrophic conflict.

THE CONTINUING IMPACT

The First World War still engages contemporary writers, and its impact is keenly felt, not least by visitors to the vast cemeteries that are strung out across the main battlegrounds. Not all of the visitors have been directly affected by the war – some are the great-grandchildren of those who fought – but strong emotions sometimes break through the banal phrases in the visitor's books as people struggle to express their feelings on being confronted by the evidence of such slaughter. The sounding of the Last Post every evening at the Menin Gate cannot fail to haunt the listener – whether it inspires thoughts of military glory or of the futility of death in battle.

Temporary grave
This wooden cross was placed over the battlefield grave of a Frenchman, later reburied in an official war cemetery.

WAR LOSSES
~

Estimates of the number of men killed in fighting during the First World War range from around 8.5 million to 10 million, with over 20 million wounded. These figures may well be under-estimates. The war was also directly responsible for a large number of civilian deaths – including around 2 million in both Russia and Turkey, 275,000 in Bulgaria, 500,000 in Romania and 600,000 in Serbia.

Allied Powers	Number mobilized	Military dead	Military wounded	Civilian dead
RUSSIA	12,000,000	1,800,000	4,950,000	2,000,000
FRANCE	8,660,000	1,390,000	4,330,000	40,000
BRITISH EMPIRE	8,780,000	900,000	2,090,000	1,000
ITALY	5,900,000	460,000	960,000	unknown
UNITED STATES	4,350,000	50,000	230,000	none
OTHERS	2,320,000	405,000	320,000	1,260,000

Central Powers	Number mobilized	Military dead	Military wounded	Civilian dead
GERMANY	13,400,000	2,040,000	5,690,000	700,000
AUSTRIA-HUNGARY	7,800,000	1,020,000	1,940,000	unknown
TURKEY	1,000,000	240,000	1,270,000	2,000,000
BULGARIA	1,200,000	80,000	150,000	275,000

Visiting a battlefield in France
A party of tourists visits the battlefield at Viel Armand after the war. This was the site of savage fighting between the Germans and the French in the Vosges mountains between 1915 and 1918.

IN MEMORIAM

~

WORLD WAR I BATTLEFIELD SITES SEEM TO CAPTURE THE IMAGINATION MORE THAN THOSE OF ANY OTHER CONFLICT. THIS IS PARTLY EXPLAINED BY THE NATURE OF THE CONFLICT. FOR LONG PERIODS DURING THE WAR, BATTLEFIELDS WERE STATIC, AND THE LASTING LEGACIES OF THE GREAT BATTLES ARE MARKED IN THE EARTH WHERE THEY WERE FOUGHT. MOST BODIES WERE NOT REPATRIATED, AND WORLD WAR I CEMETERIES AND MEMORIAL ARCHITECTURE CAN BE FOUND RIGHT ACROSS THE WORLD. WHEN EXPLORING WAR SITES IT IS IMPORTANT TO BE GRACIOUS AND RESPECTFUL TO LOCALS, OBEY THE FUNDAMENTAL COUNTRY CODES, AND NEVER PICK UP WHAT APPEARS TO BE ORDNANCE – PEOPLE ARE KILLED EVERY YEAR TAKING UNEXPLODED ORDNANCE AS TROPHIES.

~

American cemetery
Arlington National Cemetery in Arlington, Virginia, was established during the American Civil War (1861–65). Veterans and casualties from all wars in which the United States has been involved are interred here.

THE WESTERN FRONT
~

The Western Front is the most extensive region for World War I pilgrimage and tourism. Although a subsequent global war rolled over both France and Belgium, and urbanization has destroyed many war sites, Western Europe still holds a rich variety of Great War monuments and semi-preserved battlefields. The remains of tens of thousands of war dead lie in cemeteries that are well tended even after the passage of nearly 100 years, and the mood at some of the great monuments, such as Verdun or the Tyne Cot Cemetery, is extremely affecting.

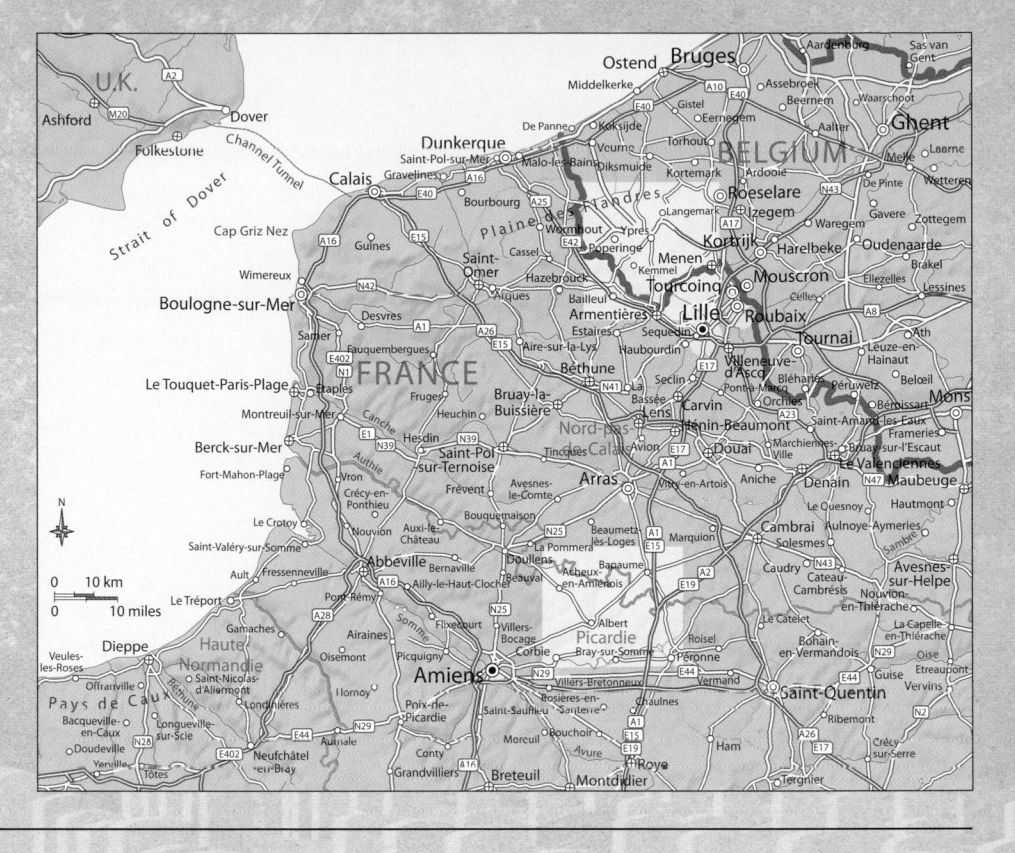

The battlefields

The battlefields on the Western Front extended from the sand dunes of the Belgian coast in the north to the Swiss border 700km (450 miles) further south. Some of the worst fighting took place around Ypres in Belgium and the River Somme in Northern France (shaded right).

BELGIUM
~

LANGEMARK GERMAN WAR CEMETERY

LOCATION: Near Langemark, Belgium

FEATURES: Cemetery and commemorative statuary; memorial annex to German students

VISITOR INFORMATION: North of Langemark village, 6km (3.7 miles) northeast of Ieper (Ypres), exit in direction of Houthulst. Open access

An official German War Graves Commission site, the Langemark cemetery contains more than 40,000 burials, accumulated between 1915 and the 1930s. The cemetery was officially designated German Military Cemetery 123 in 1930, and was inaugurated two years later. Of the soldiers buried in the cemetery, 24,917 lie in mass graves. The German Students' Memorial annex lists the names of 3,000 students killed in the battle of Langemark in 1914. A sculpture of mourning soldiers by Emil Krieger is a visual landmark in the cemetery.

VLADSLO GERMAN WAR CEMETERY

LOCATION: Near Diksmuide, Belgium

FEATURES: Cemetery and commemorative statuary

VISITOR INFORMATION: 3km (1.8 miles) northeast of Vladslo, signposted from N363 from Beerst. Open access

This haunting German cemetery is the resting place for 25,644 soldiers, most of whom were moved here from other locations in the 1950s (the site was used as a combat cemetery from 1914). Although there are original headstones, most of the names were later inscribed on flat granite slabs, each bearing 20 names (giving name, rank, and date of death). Notable features of the cemetery include *The Grieving Parents*, a pair of statues made by the German sculptor Käthe Kollwitz in memory of her son.

The Grieving Parents

This statue is one of a pair at Vladslo carved by German sculptor Käthe Kollwitz following the death of her youngest son Peter on the battlefield in October 1914. It was finally installed in 1932.

SAINT JULIEN MEMORIAL

LOCATION: Near Ieper, Belgium

FEATURES: War memorial

VISITOR INFORMATION: 7km (4.3 miles) northeast of Ieper, off the N313 towards Roulers. Open access

The Saint Julien Memorial is a granite memorial designed by the Anglo-Canadian architect Frederick Chapman Clemesha. It stands 11m (36ft) high. Known as "The Brooding Soldier", its summit is the head and shoulders of a Canadian infantryman, his head bowed in mourning. The memorial remembers the Canadian dead of 22–24 April 1915, when 2,000 Canadian troops were killed around Saint Julien in the Second Battle of Ypres. Many of the dead were killed by the first German use of poison gas (chlorine) on the Western Front, as the memorial inscription attests: "This column marks the battlefield where 18,000 Canadians on the British left withstood the first German gas attacks of the 22nd–24th of April 1915. 2,000 fell and here lie buried."

FLANDERS FIELD AMERICAN CEMETERY AND MEMORIAL

Flanders Fields

A restored trench in Flanders Fields, the poppy-strewn battlegrounds immortalized in Canadian doctor and poet John McCrae's famous poem "In Flanders Fields".

LOCATION: Near Waregem, Belgium

FEATURES: American Battle Monuments Commission cemetery and memorial

VISITOR INFORMATION: Southeast of Waregem, along the Lille–Gent autoroute E-17. Staff escort for grave identification; memorial chapel. Open daily 9am–3pm except 25 December and 1 January.

F ar smaller than many of the war cemeteries in Belgium, the Flanders Field cemetery commemorates the American contribution to the war on the Western Front. (It is the only American Battle Monuments Commission cemetery in Belgium.) In total it contains 386 burials, with the headstones arranged around the central chapel. Many of the casualties interred here came from the US 91st Division, killed in fighting around this location in October and November 1918. The chapel itself includes 43 names on the Walls of the Missing.

YPRES SALIENT BATTLEFIELD

LOCATION: In and around Ieper, Belgium

FEATURES: Numerous cemeteries, museums and battlefield sites

VISITOR INFORMATION: Ieper Tourism Office (Dienst Toerisme), Grote Markt 34, 8900 Ieper. Tel: +32 (0)57 239 220. Fax: +32 (0)57 239 275. Email: toerisme@ieper.be

A fter the Somme, the area around the Ypres Salient, centred on the modern town of Ieper, is the most popular destination for battlefield visitors. Within the town itself are the Menin Gate and St George's Memorial Church, both moving memorials to those lost around Ypres, and also the In Flanders Field Museum. Outside the town there are also a great number of sites of interest. There are more than 140 military cemeteries and military burial grounds – British cemeteries alone contain 40,000 unidentified graves. These cemeteries are tended by the British, Belgian, French, and Italian war graves commissions, and make for haunting visits. There are also several worthwhile museums around Ieper, including the Sanctuary Wood Museum Hill 62, the Hooge Crater Museum, the Memorial Museum Passchendaele (at Zonnebeke), and the Messines Historical Museum (Mesen). Another destination

1. Langemark German War Cemetery
2. Saint-Julien Memorial
3. Passchendaele New British Cemetery
4. Crest Farm Memorial
5. Tyne Cot Cemetery
6. Sanctuary Wood Cemetery
7. Passendale Memorial 1917 Museum
8. 85th Battalion Memorial
9. British 7th Division Memorial
10. In Flanders Field Museum
11. St George's Memorial Church
12. Menin Gate
13. Wytschaete Military Cemetery
14. New Zealand Memorial Park
15. Messines Ridge Military Cemetery
16. Island of Ireland Peace Park

is the town of Poperinge, about 13km (8 miles) to the west of Ieper. Poperinge was a major centre for British troops heading to the front, and today includes the Talbot House museum in a building that was a club house for British Army troops during the war. Although much of the Ypres Salient has been developed, the area is certainly well worth a visit.

THE "ODE OF REMEMBRANCE"

They shall not grow old, as we that are left grow old:
Age shall not weary them, nor the years condemn.
At the going down of the sun and in the morning,
We will remember them.

EXTRACT FROM THE "ODE OF REMEMBRANCE", IN LAURENCE BINYON'S 1914 POEM "FOR THE FALLEN". THE FINAL PHRASE, "WE WILL REMEMBER THEM", IS SOMETIMES REPEATED IN RESPONSE BY THOSE LISTENING.

On British and Commonwealth war memorials, and in the ceremonies that often surround them, one short passage of words has become more famous than any other. In 1914 the poet Laurence Binyon wrote "For the Fallen", a poem reflecting on the mounting death toll on the Western Front that was published in *The Times*. One verse in particular stuck in the public consciousness: now known as the "Ode of Remembrance", this passage is recited in thousands of UK, Australian, Canadian, and New Zealand remembrance ceremonies every year, particularly on Remembrance Sunday and ANZAC Day.

SANCTUARY WOOD CEMETERY AND MUSEUM HILL 62

LOCATION: Near Ieper, Belgium

FEATURES: Commonwealth War Graves Commission (CWGC) cemetery; museum; preserved trenches

VISITOR INFORMATION: 5km (3 miles) east of Ieper town, off the N8. Address: Canadalaan 26, 8902 Zillebeke. Tel: +32 (0)57 466 373. Disabled access to cemetery. Museum open daily 10am–7pm

In 1914, Sanctuary Wood acted as a protective barrier between British and Commonwealth troops and the frontline. During 1915–16, however, it too was swamped with heavy fighting, principally between Canadian and German forces, and three Allied cemeteries were established in the area at this time. The remains of one provided the foundations for the present cemetery, designed by Sir Edwin Lutyens. During the 1920s and 1930s, the cemetery expanded with additions from the wider Western Front; today it contains 1,989 burials (spread over five plots), of which only 637 are identified.

Within a short distance of the cemetery is the Sanctuary Wood Museum Hill 62, a privately run institution; outside the museum is an extensive series of preserved trench lines, all open to walk through. Another feature of the Sanctuary Wood area is the Canadian Memorial at Hill 62, which remembers the thousands of Canadians killed in futile battles to retake Hill 62 in June 1916.

Gate to the frontline
Menin Gate, originally just a gap in the town of Ieper's ancient fortifications, is now the site of a much-visited memorial to the fallen.

IN FLANDERS FIELD MUSEUM

LOCATION: Ieper, Belgium

FEATURES: Museum and archive centre; library of more than 5,000 books

VISITOR INFORMATION: Address: Lakenhallen Grote Markt 34, B8900 Ieper. Tel: +32 (0)57 239 220. Website: inflandersfields.be. Opening hours: 1 April–15 November, open daily 10am–6pm; 16 November–31 March, open Tuesday–Sunday 10am–5pm

The In Flanders Field Museum, located in the Cloth Hall on the Market Square in the centre of Ieper, houses major collections of World War I artefacts and documents. The exhibitions cover the human experience of war around Ypres, and also explore how war affected the town itself. The museum offers engaging interactive audio-visual exhibits, and receives about 200,000 visitors a year. The impressive documentation centre includes extensive original trench maps, a photographic library and postcard collection, and various contemporary newspapers. Access to the centre is free, although some collections are viewable only by appointment.

ST GEORGE'S MEMORIAL CHURCH

LOCATION: Ieper, Belgium

FEATURES: Church built as a memorial to British and Commonwealth dead of Ypres

VISITOR INFORMATION: Address: Elverdingsestraat 1, 8900 Ieper. Tel: +32 (0)57 215 685. Fax: +32 (0)57 215 927. Open daily 9:30am–dusk (4pm winter)

The foundation stone of St George's Church was laid in 1927 by Field Marshal Lord Plummer. The building finally opened for services two years later, and is still an active place of worship and remembrance today. The church was built primarily to remember the British and Commonwealth dead of Ypres, and its stained glass, wall plaques, banners, and kneelers reflect individual British regimental histories. It is now the memorial church for all those who died in battle in Flanders during both world wars.

MENIN GATE

LOCATION: Ieper, Belgium

FEATURES: War memorial and listing of dead

VISITOR INFORMATION: On the Meensestraat, Ieper (Open access). For CWGC information, visit www.cwgc.org

The inspiring Menin Gate memorial, one of the most visited on the Western Front, was designed by Reginald Blomfield and unveiled in 1927. It marks the point at which most British soldiers marched out of the town to the battlefields of the Ypres Salient. The memorial's towering Hall of Memory has the names of 54,896 British and Commonwealth troops inscribed upon stone panels fixed to its walls. These list the men killed in the Ypres Salient before 16 August 1917.

PASSCHENDAELE BATTLEFIELD

LOCATION: Various locations in and around Zonnebeke and Passendale, Belgium

FEATURES: Several CWGC cemeteries, including Tyne Cot; memorial features in Passchendaele Church; battlefield markers and memorials; Passendale Memorial 1917 Museum

VISITOR INFORMATION: Sites accessible from the N303 running south through Passendale and the N332 running through Zonnebeke

Few battlefield areas evoke the tragedy of the Ypres Salient more than Passchendaele (the modern village is known as Passendale). The area is littered with memorials to individual battles, including the Canadian memorial at Crest Farm, the 85th (Nova Scotia Highlanders) Battalion Memorial, and the memorials to French soldiers and the British 7th Division, both at Broodseinde. Cemeteries in the area include the Passchendaele New British Cemetery, containing 2,101 British and Commonwealth burials, and the awe-inspiring Tyne Cot just southwest of Passendale. In Zonnebeke is the vivid Passendale Memorial 1917 Museum, which contains a fascinating display of artefacts ranging from barbed wire to Maxim guns.

TYNE COT CEMETERY

LOCATION: Southwest of Passendale, Belgium

FEATURES: Major CWGC cemetery; Memorial to the Missing monument; three German blockhouses

VISITOR INFORMATION: Signposted off the N332 after passing east through Zonnebeke. For more information, visit www.cwgc.org. Open access

Tyne Cot contains a total of 11,953 burials, mostly British and Commonwealth troops but including four Germans. The majority of the dead come from the Third Battle of Ypres. The Tyne Cot name comes, possibly, from the Northumberland Fusiliers, who felt that a barn on the ridgeline had the appearance of their homes back in Britain. Seemingly endless ranks of gravestones create a powerful impression, especially as 8,366 burials are of unidentified men. Landmarks of the cemetery include the Cross of Sacrifice monument and the curved Memorial to the Missing, which displays nearly 35,000 names of those with no known grave.

Cross of Sacrifice

Located in Tyne Cot Cemetery, this monument was built on top of a German pill-box. Tyne Cot is the largest cemetery of Commonwealth war dead in the world.

ROYAL MUSEUM OF THE ARMED FORCES AND OF MILITARY HISTORY

LOCATION: Brussels, Belgium

FEATURES: Major 1914–18 exhibition; large documentation centre

VISITOR INFORMATION: Address: Jubelpark 3, 1000 Brussels. Tel: +32 (0)2737 7833. Email: infocom@klm-mra.be. Website: www.klm-mra.be. Open Tuesday–Sunday 9am–12pm and 1pm–4:45pm

This museum houses collections relating to the entirety of Belgian military history, not just to World War I. It does have a substantial collection of World War I artefacts, documents and memorabilia in a permanent 1914–18 exhibition, however. The displays include firearms, artillery pieces, uniforms, armoured vehicles, and even a Fokker triplane. The museum also has a well-stocked shop and a cafeteria.

MESSINES BATTLEFIELD AND MEMORIALS

LOCATION: Around Messines (Mesen), Belgium

FEATURES: Several CWGC cemeteries and memorials; craters from Allied mining; Messines Church; New Zealand Memorial Park

VISITOR INFORMATION: Sites can be accessed at various points from the N365, mainly between Wytschaete and Messines

The successful Allied offensive to take the Messines Ridge has left many legacies for the battlefield investigator. The St Eloi, Peckham Farm, Spanbroekmolen, Kruistraat, and St Yvon craters bear testimony to some of the 19 enormous mines detonated beneath the German lines. A board in the village of Wytschaete gives directions to some of the craters, and the village also contains more than 1,000 burials at the Wytschaete Military Cemetery. A much smaller cemetery near Spanbroekmolen is the Lone Tree Cemetery, which has 88 burials, mainly soldiers of the Royal Irish Rifles. On the N365 between Wytschaete and Messines is a memorial to the London Scottish. In Mesen itself, which was completely destroyed in the battle, there is the rebuilt church where Adolf Hitler reputedly received treatment for combat injuries in 1914, the New Zealand Memorial Park, and the Messines Ridge Military Cemetery. To the south of Messines is the modern Island of Ireland Peace Park, opened in 1998 to remember soldiers of Ireland killed during World War I.

FRANCE

CANADIAN NATIONAL VIMY MEMORIAL PARK

LOCATION: Near Arras, northern France

FEATURES: Monument; trench lines and preserved trenches; cratered landscape; Canadian cemetery; Grange Tunnel

VISITOR INFORMATION: Between Lens and Arras, take Neuville-St-Vaast exit from A26 autoroute; follow D49. Address: 62580 Vimy. Tel: +33 321 487229. Fax: +33 321 583834. Open access. Free guided tours available April–November

Site of the epic battle between Canadian and German troops in 1917, the Canadian National Vimy Memorial Park is dominated by the incredible Vimy monument, carved from a single piece of stone and unveiled in 1936. Many parts of the Memorial Park grounds undulate from the contouring effects of shellfire, and both German and Allied trenches have been preserved for public access. The underground Grange Tunnel is poignantly impressive, and is explored in the company of a Canadian guide. There are two Canadian cemeteries in the area: Canadian Cemetery No. 2 and Givenchy Road Canadian Cemetery.

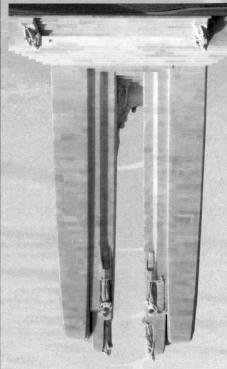

The Vimy monument
Designed by American sculptor Walter Seymour Allward, the imposing Canadian National Vimy Memorial took 16 years to create.

ARRAS AND VIMY RIDGE BATTLEFIELD

LOCATION: Around Arras, Pas-de-Calais

FEATURES: Numerous cemeteries and memorials (Allied and German)

VISITOR INFORMATION: From west (Calais) follow A26 autoroute, following the signs to Arras

The Arras battlefield area has an enormous amount to interest, and space here only allows us to note some important features. One of the most popular destinations within the area is Vimy Ridge, but there is much elsewhere. Cemetery sites include the Zivy Crater Cemetery, the Lichfield Crater Cemetery, the La Targette French and British cemeteries, the Cabaret Rouge British Cemetery, and the forbidding, huge Neuville-Saint-Vaast German War Cemetery. Memorials to the dead of specific battalions, regiments, and divisions dot the region, including those to the 9th Scottish Division, the Seaforth Highlands, and the 4th and 7th Royal Tank Corps. A visitor who is armed with a good battlefield guide will be able to walk around many of the critical locations of the battle.

NEUVILLE-SAINT-VAAST GERMAN WAR CEMETERY

LOCATION: Near Arras, France

FEATURES: Largest German cemetery in France

VISITOR INFORMATION: Just south of Neuville-Saint-Vaast on D937 toward Arras. Open access

Established by the French in 1919 to hold German war dead, this German War Graves Commission cemetery, also known as La Maison Blanche, is the largest in France and contains a breathtaking 44,533 burials. Its power is in its simplicity – the cemetery consists of nothing but a sea of metal crosses, laid during the 1970s to replace the earlier wooden versions, with four soldiers sharing each grave. There is also a mass grave that contains the remains of more than 8,000 soldiers. Visitors to the cemetery frequently attest to a heavy mood of loss hanging over the site.

Trench raids
Restored trenches at Vimy Ridge. Small-scale, night-time "trench raids", aimed at causing havoc and confusion, were used extensively by Canadian forces on this battlefield.

NOTRE DAME DE LORETTE

LOCATION: Ablain-Saint-Nazaire, near Arras, France

FEATURES: Basilica (containing ossuary) and cemetery; French National Memorial; museum

VISITOR INFORMATION: Off D937 north of Arras. Open daily 8am–7pm depending on the month (longer opening hours during summer)

Religious buildings have occupied this ridge to the northwest of Arras since the 18th century, but the cornerstones of the basilica and ossuary that currently occupy the site were laid in 1921. The ossuary – a building where bones of the dead are kept – contains the remains of some 23,000 unidentified soldiers from both world wars and French conflicts in Algeria and Indochina, and the basilica, adorned with colourful mosaics, is a suitable venue for reflection. The cemetery outside covers 13 hectares (32 acres) and contains 45,000 burials, with the bulk of these from World War I. Behind the cemetery is a military museum that is well worth a visit.

Hallowed ground
The Notre Dame de Lorette cemetery lies on a high, strategically important site that saw some of the bloodiest battles of the Western Front.

ÉTAPLES MILITARY CEMETERY

LOCATION: North of Étaples, France

FEATURES: CWGC cemetery

VISITOR INFORMATION: On the Boulogne road between Boulogne and Étaples. Open access

The huge number of British military camps and hospitals in the Étaples area yielded a large cemetery, which today includes 10,733 British and Commonwealth burials from World War I and is overseen by the CWGC. There are 11,479 burials in the cemetery, which stayed in practical use until May 1940.

Étaples Military Cemetery
The area surrounding the site of Étaples Military Cemetery contained many Allied hospitals and reinforcement camps during the war.

CAMBRAI BATTLEFIELDS

LOCATION: Around Cambrai, northern France

FEATURES: Louveral Military Cemetery; Cambrai Memorial to the Missing; numerous other cemeteries and memorials

VISITOR INFORMATION: Cambrai town located on N43 southeast of Arras

The Cambrai area was the scene of bitter fighting, particularly in the last two years of the war, and the area is replete with military memories. The major site for war burials in the area is the Louveral Military Cemetery. This also features the Memorial to the Missing, which lists the names of more than 7,000 British soldiers with no known grave. Other cemeteries within easy driving distance of Louveral include the Five Points Cemetery near Ytres, the Rocquigny-Equancourt Road British Cemetery, and the Ribecourt Road Cemetery near Trescault. Between Trescault and Havrincourt there is also a German bunker by the side of the D15. At the village of Flesquieres you will find recovered British tank D51, dug up in 1998.

FRICOURT GERMAN WAR CEMETERY

LOCATION: Near Fricourt, the Somme

FEATURES: German War Graves Commission cemetery

VISITOR INFORMATION: East side of the D147 road from Fricourt to Contalmaison. Open access

Although not the largest German war cemetery in the Somme area – that "honour" goes to Vermandovillers, with its 26,000 burials – the Fricourt cemetery is a place of intense mood and sadness. It contains 17,027 German soldiers, about 10,000 of whom were killed during the Somme battles in 1916. (The burials date from 1914 to 1918.) Only 5,057 of the burials have individual graves, while nearly 12,000 are contained in four mass graves.

AISNE-MARNE AMERICAN CEMETERY AND MEMORIAL

LOCATION: Near Chateau-Thierry, France

FEATURES: Cemetery and memorial

VISITOR INFORMATION: Follow cemetery signs from Chateau-Thierry. Open daily 9am–5pm

This American Battle Monuments Commission site contains the graves of 2,289 American war dead, mostly killed in the fighting around the Marne Valley in 1918. It is located at the foot of the infamous Belleau Wood, where the US Marine Corps gained distinction. The cemetery is overlooked by the Memorial Chapel, decorated with military motifs and insignia inside and inscribed with the names of 1,060 missing.

TIME WILL NOT DIM THE GLORY OF THEIR DEEDS

A wing and a prayer
This eagle stands on the east face of the Chateau-Thierry Monument in the Aisne-Marne Cemetery. The monument commemorates US soldiers who died in battle in France.

SOMME BATTLEFIELD

LOCATION: The Somme, France

FEATURES: Cemeteries; battlefield walks; museums; memorials

VISITOR INFORMATION: For travel directions and guidance, visit official website at www.somme-battlefields.com/en/index.aspx

As the site of one of the greatest and most costly battles in human history, the Somme region is naturally a magnet for military tourism and has an almost overwhelming variety of features to absorb. It is highly recommended that a visit to the Somme is accompanied by an extensive modern guide book, or is directed by one of the many military tour companies operating in the area. One way of tackling the area is the officially recommended "Tour of Remembrance", which takes in such locations as Albert (including the Somme 1916 Trench Museum and the CWGC-maintained Albert Communal Cemetery), Beaumont-Hamel, Thiepval, Ovillers-la-Boiselle (site of the Lochnagar Crater), Longueval (including the New Zealand Memorial and Pipers' Memorial), and Peronne. All these places have vivid histories and much of interest, including cemeteries, military relics, museums, and memorials, and the Somme countryside still yields much in the way of munitions and artefacts (remember not to touch any munitions you might find). The best way to get around the battlefield privately is by car, as many of the sites are easily accessible from the A29 or A1.

1. Beaumont-Hamel Newfoundland Memorial Park
2. Thiepval Memorial to the Missing
3. Authuille Military Cemetery
4. Ovillers Military Cemetery
5. New Zealand Memorial
6. Delville Wood South African Memorial and Museum
7. Pipers' Memorial
8. Lochnagar Crater
9. Somme 1916 Trench Museum
10. Fricourt German War Cemetery
11. Dantzig Alley British Cemetery
12. Albert Communal Cemetery
13. Point 110 Old and New Cemeteries

BEAUMONT-HAMEL NEWFOUNDLAND MEMORIAL PARK

LOCATION: Near Albert, the Somme

FEATURES: Memorial park with trench lines and battle-scarred landscape; memorial statuary and cemetery

VISITOR INFORMATION: Drive 10.5km (6.5 miles) north of Albert. For official guide to the park, visit the Veteran Affairs Canada website at www.vac-acc.gc.ca. Open access

This memorial park covers 34 hectares (84 acres) and commemorates the terrible sacrifice made over this area by the Newfoundland forces and others during the Battle of the Somme. The ground is visibly scarred by shellfire and trenches, and it features the enormous crater made by the so-called "Hawthorn mine" at the opening of the Somme Offensive. Several trench lines are preserved to give an impression of the Somme battle experience. There are three cemeteries within the park containing both Newfoundland and British burials. The park also contains many monuments, the most famous being the "Caribou Monument". A visitor centre gives historical context and information.

THIEPVAL MEMORIAL TO THE MISSING

Location: Thiepval, the Somme

Features: Largest British war memorial in the world

Visitor information: 3.2km (2 miles) from Beaumont-Hamel, 8km (5 miles) from Albert, on the D73. Open daily 10am–6pm.

This huge memorial was designed by Sir Edwin Lutyens and opened by the Prince of Wales in 1932. Inscribed on its surfaces are the names of 73,357 Allied soldiers who died in the Somme area between 1916 and 1918, but who found no grave. A ceremony is held here on 1 July every year.

MUSÉE DE L'ARMÉE

Location: Paris, France

Features: Major World War I exhibition

Visitor information: Located in Les Invalides. Open daily, except for the first Monday of every month, and 1 January, 1 May, 1 November, and 25 December. For further details, visit www.invalides.org

The Musée de l'Armée is one of the world's largest military museums, with more than 500,000 artefacts from every period of French military history. Its World War I exhibits are particularly impressive, especially in terms of uniforms and weaponry. The collections of small arms and artillery pieces are worth a detailed visit.

BOMB AND AMMUNITION DISPOSAL

Unexploded munitions from World War I remain a challenge along the line of the old Western Front even today. The problem is acute: more than 600 bomb disposal experts have been killed in France since 1946 dealing with such munitions, and the writer Nicholas Saunders notes that "In 1991, a total of 36 French farmers were killed when their machinery hit unexploded shells." The muddied ground of the Western Front, plus the poor quality of some munitions, meant that many artillery shells fired during the war simply buried their way into the ground, there to lie undisturbed but still explosively active and increasingly unstable with the passing years. In Ypres alone, 250 tonnes of explosives are found and detonated every year.

Thiepval Memorial to the Missing

The cemetery at the foot of this memorial contains 300 French and 300 British graves, representing comradeship between the two nations on the battlefields of the Somme.

THE ITALIAN AND BALKAN FRONTS

A|lthough many of the Italian and Balkan World War I sites do not have the notoriety of those on the Western Front, they still contain much to see. Some of the high-altitude locations along the Isonzo Front are arguably the most spectacular of all the battlefield sites, with ghostly positions clinging to the mountainsides. There are also epic reminders of Italy's sacrifice, such as the Sacrario Militare di Redipuglia: the huge historical park there has many days' worth of sites for investigation. In the Balkans there is, of course, the Gallipoli peninsula;

MEUSE-ARGONNE AMERICAN CEMETERY AND MEMORIAL

LOCATION: Romagne-sous-Montfaucon, France

FEATURES: Cemetery and memorial

VISITOR INFORMATION: 42km (26 miles) northwest of Verdun. Open daily 9am–5pm, except 25 December and 1 January

T|he Meuse-Argonne Cemetery and Memorial is the largest American military burial site in Europe, with a total of 14,246 servicemen buried over 52 hectares (130 acres). The ranks of beautifully ordered headstones are sobering to witness, and the Memorial Chapel contains the inscribed names of 954 missing, with rosettes indicating those bodies subsequently discovered and identified. Staff members at the Visitor Centre can provide guidance on finding your way through the graves.

DOUAUMONT OSSUARY AND VERDUN MEMORIAL

LOCATION: Douaumont, France

FEATURES: Ossuary; audio-visual show; shop

VISITOR INFORMATION: Off the N3 or D964 running through Verdun. Open daily, except from 1 January–February school holidays. For full details, visit www.verdun-douaumont.com/en/index.html

T|he Douaumont Ossuary is arguably one of the most powerful memorials on the Western Front. Building work on a provisional ossuary began in 1920, to provide a location for the hundreds of thousands of bones scattered throughout the Verdun battlefield site. The permanent ossuary was built from 1920, and from 1927 it began to receive the transfer of bones. The ossuary cloister contains the bones of 130,000 unidentified soldiers, arranged according to the area of the Verdun battlefield in which they were found.

Douaumont Ossuary This 46m (150ft) tower contains a bell that sounds at official ceremonies and a "lantern of death" that shines on the battlefield.

ITALY

SACRARIO MILITARE DI REDIPUGLIA

LOCATION: Monte Sei Busi, Italy

FEATURES: Italian war memorial and shrine

VISITOR INFORMATION: Signposted from Redipuglia fogliano in Gorizia. Open daily, dawn to dusk

O|pened in 1938, the Sacrario Militare di Redipuglia is an impressive military shrine in the north of Italy, set on the slopes of Monte Sei Busi. It is a majestic monument expressed on a grand scale, and in total it holds the remains of 100,000 Italian soldiers killed during World War I – the 22 steps to the top of the shrine alone contain the remains of 40,000 soldiers. The shrine also contains the tombs of five generals and of the Duke of Aosta, the commander of the Third Army. The site includes a chapel for paying respects, and a museum containing a poignant collection of artefacts from the Italian front.

ITALY/SLOVENIA

ISONZO FRONT BATTLEFIELDS

LOCATION: Along the Slovenian/Italian border

FEATURES: Battle sites; museums; fortresses; tunnel sections; cemeteries; memorials

VISITOR INFORMATION: Guided tours available for the whole Isonzo Front

I|n terms of battlefield tourism, the Isonzo Front is often overlooked in preference for battlefields in France and Belgium, but it is just as rich in heritage and places of interest. The challenges for touring the Isonzo Front are the distances involved and the arduous terrain. A typical route might run from Kranjska Gora in the north down to Duino in the south, although there are many other options. There are constant highlights to such a trip. The Soca Valley contains numerous mountainous positions in the rockfaces, and the journey along the Vrsic road pass takes you along the road built by Russian prisoners in 1916. There is also the Kluze fortress with its military tunnels nearby, and you can walk along former trench lines at Kobarid (Caporetto), where there is also an excellent museum devoted to the battles along the Isonzo Front. Combined with many other places of military significance, plus spectacular Alpine scenery, the trip can be memorable.

THE DARDANELLES EXPEDITION
~

GALLIPOLI BATTLEFIELD

LOCATION: Gallipoli peninsula, Turkey

FEATURES: Extensive historical park; numerous monuments, cemeteries, museums

VISITOR INFORMATION: Easy travel access by road and public transport from Istanbul

Outside the Western Front, the Gallipoli peninsula is one of the most rewarding sites for military history tourists and researchers. The battlefields now form part of the Gallipoli Peninsula Historical National Park, some 33,000 hectares (81,500 acres) in size. There are 31 CWGC cemeteries in Gallipoli, most of which are easily accessible, and numerous memorials. All are worth looking at, but must-see examples include the V-Beach Cemetery, Helles Memorial, and Redoubt Cemetery in Helles; the Beach Cemetery, No. 2 Outpost Cemetery, Courtney's and Steel's Post Cemetery, Chunuk Bair Cemetery and Memorial, 4th Battalion Parade Ground Cemetery, and the particularly moving Lone Pine Cemetery and Memorial, all in Anzac; and the Green Hill Cemetery and Azmac Cemetery in Suvla. There is also the Çanakkale Martyrs Memorial, the principal memorial to the Turkish dead of Gallipoli.

THE EASTERN FRONT
~

The political history of Eastern Europe has meant that many of its war sites have been scoured from the Earth, but careful research can yield some surprising discoveries.

ROMANIA
~

MAUSOLEUM OF MARASESTI

LOCATION: Vrancea County, Romania

FEATURES: Mausoleum

VISITOR INFORMATION: Between Focsani and Adjud. Open daily 9am–5pm

Built between 1923 and 1938, the Mausoleum for the Heroes from the National Unity War, to give it its full title, is an imposing monument to the Romanians killed around Marasesti in 1916. Impressive sculpture and sheer scale gives the mausoleum (which stands some 30m tall) genuine gravitas, as do the remains of 6,000 Romanian soldiers contained within the crypts. The mausoleum also includes the sarcophagus of General Eremia Grigorescu, who died in 1919, and a rotunda containing the flags of the Romanian units who fought at Marasesti. The main edifice is topped by the "Dome of Glory"; a great bas-relief on the dome depicts scenes from the battle at Marasesti.

THE MIDDLE EAST
~

The Middle East still has some World War I monuments and cemeteries dotted around the region, but ongoing conflict has made many of them inaccessible to the modern traveller.

ISRAEL
~

RAMLEH CWGC CEMETERY

LOCATION: Near Ramla, Israel

FEATURES: CWGC cemetery

VISITOR INFORMATION: Ramla signposted from road number 1 from Tel Aviv. Open daily 6am–2pm

The Ramleh Cemetery contains 3,300 Commonwealth burials from World War I, plus nearly 1,200 burials from World War II and a number of other burials of non-Commonwealth and non-combat personnel. The cemetery itself was established in December 1917, accompanying the field hospitals set up in the area, although some of the graves there were moved into Ramleh from other cemeteries in Palestine/Israel. There is also a memorial to Commonwealth, German, and Turkish servicemen buried elsewhere in Israel but in cemeteries that are no longer maintained; the memorial was built in 1961.

Turkish memorial
Gallipoli is dotted with memorials to all those who fought in the region. This bas-relief commemorating Turkish soldiers is located in a public park.

OTHER IMPORTANT CEMETERIES, MEMORIALS, AND MUSEUMS

World War I was a global conflict, and even outside those countries on whose ground battles were fought, there are many poignant reminders of the sacrifices made. Places as far flung as the United States, India, and Ireland all have memorials or cemeteries, while in countries such as the UK the extent of the losses is memorialized in almost every village, town, and city. Memorials are almost as ubiquitous in Canada, New Zealand, and Australia, and most of the countries that took part in World War I also have relevant museums and archive centres.

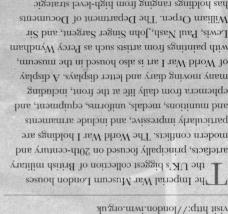

IMPERIAL WAR MUSEUM guns

The two 381mm (15in) guns mounted outside the Imperial War Museum London were both constructed during World War I, but neither saw action until 1920.

UNITED KINGDOM

IMPERIAL WAR MUSEUM LONDON

LOCATION: London, England

FEATURES: Major World War I collections

VISITOR INFORMATION: Situated on Lambeth Road, London, SE1 6HZ. Open daily 10am–6pm, except 24, 25, and 26 December. For information, visit http://london.iwm.org.uk

The Imperial War Museum London houses the UK's biggest collection of British military artefacts, principally focused on 20th-century and modern conflicts. The World War I holdings are particularly impressive, and include armaments and munitions, medals, uniforms, equipment, and ephemera from daily life at the front, including many moving diary and letter displays. A display of World War I art is also housed in the museum, with paintings from artists such as Percy Wyndham Lewis, Paul Nash, John Singer Sargent, and Sir William Orpen. The Department of Documents has holdings ranging from high-level strategic documents through to the personal writings of common soldiers. The museum also features an extensive library and photo archive.

THE CENOTAPH

LOCATION: London, England

FEATURES: National monument

VISITOR INFORMATION: Open access. National Service of Remembrance held on Remembrance Sunday (nearest Sunday to 11 November)

Designed by Sir Edwin Lutyens, the Cenotaph is a simple but imposing memorial made from Portland stone – it was initially constructed from wood and plaster in the first year after the Armistice, but this was replaced with stone for its unveiling in 1920. Each year the Cenotaph is the focus for the National Service of Remembrance on Remembrance Sunday. The basic format of the service – which includes a minute's silence at 11am – was laid down in 1921. Although the Cenotaph was built for the dead of World War I, it is dedicated to all of Britain's war dead.

The Cenotaph

Uniformed British service members always salute Britain's most famous war memorial as they pass it.

BROOKWOOD MILITARY CEMETERY

LOCATION: Brookwood, Surrey, England

FEATURES: Largest CWGC cemetery in the UK; American Military Cemetery and Memorial

VISITOR INFORMATION: On A3142 from the village of Pirbright, or take the train from Waterloo Station, London, to Brookwood. Open access

The Brookwood Cemetery predates World War I, but land for war burials was granted in 1917. A large number of the burials in this military cemetery date from World War II, but there are 1,601 burials from the previous conflict. The Brookwood (United Kingdom) 1914–18 Memorial also commemorates, according to the CWGC, "more than 200 Commonwealth casualties who died in the United Kingdom during the First World War but for whom no graves could be found". In the grounds of Brookwood, the World War I American Military Cemetery has 468 graves and commemorates 563 American servicemen with no known grave.

UNKNOWN WARRIOR – WESTMINSTER ABBEY

LOCATION: Westminster Abbey, London, England

FEATURES: Commemorative grave of the Unknown Soldier

VISITOR INFORMATION: The abbey is subject to various opening times, and remains an active place of worship. For details, visit www.westminster-abbey.org

T The Tomb of the Unknown Warrior holds the remains of an unidentified British soldier. He was exhumed from the Western Front along with several others and chosen by Brigadier-General J. L. Wyatt as the individual to represent all those British soldiers who had no known place of death or who couldn't be identified. The body was buried with full military ceremony and royal attendance on 11 November 1920; 1.25 million people viewed the tomb in the following week.

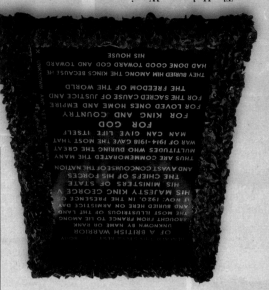

The Unknown Warrior

The idea of a memorial to an unidentified soldier was conceived in 1916 by David Railton, an army chaplain serving on the Western Front.

SCOTTISH NATIONAL WAR MEMORIAL

LOCATION: Edinburgh, Scotland

FEATURES: War memorial; Rolls of Honour

VISITOR INFORMATION: Memorial part of Edinburgh Castle, set on Castlehill, Edinburgh. Tel: +44 (0)131 225 9846. Website: www.edinburghcastle.gov.uk. Opening hours: 1 April–30 September, 9:30am–6pm; 1 October–31 March, 9:30am–5pm

T The Scottish National War Memorial was built to remember the 150,000 Scottish servicemen who died in World War I. It was a conversion of the North Barracks of Edinburgh Castle, and its architect was Robert Lorimer, who had to run the gauntlet of much public opposition to his plans (many were opposed to the idea of making modifications to the castle). The shrine was finally opened in 1927 by the Prince of Wales. Its Rolls of Honour also contain the names of World War II dead.

AUSTRALIA

ANZAC WAR MEMORIAL

LOCATION: Sydney, Australia

FEATURES: War memorial

VISITOR INFORMATION: Set in Hyde Park, Sydney. Open daily 9am–5pm

D Designed by C. Bruce Dellit, the ANZAC War Memorial is Sydney's principal war monument. It is made of granite in an art deco style, with statuary and bas-reliefs created by the artist Rayner Hoff. The eye is drawn to the buttresses on the outside of the building, each topped by a mournful figure, while the bas-reliefs depict scenes from Australian campaigns at Gallipoli and the Western Front. Ceremonies are held at the memorial on Remembrance Sunday and ANZAC Day.

AUSTRALIAN WAR MEMORIAL

LOCATION: Canberra, Australia

FEATURES: Memorial; Remembrance Park; museum; Sculpture Garden; Research Centre

VISITOR INFORMATION: 30 minutes' walk from Canberra city centre, on Treloar Crescent (top of ANZAC Parade). Website: www.awm.gov.au/visit/index.asp. Open daily 9am–5pm (Research Centre closed Sundays and Saturday mornings)

T The Australian War Memorial is Australia's national monument to its war dead. Built in the aftermath of World War I, it serves to commemorate Australian service personnel killed in all conflicts. The main parts of the memorial are the Commemorative Area (which includes the Hall of Memory), ANZAC Parade, and Sculpture Garden, while the ANZAC Hall is a recently added exhibition space.

ANZAC War Memorial bas-relief
This relief over the eastern portal of the ANZAC War Memorial depicts Australian troops on the Eastern Front. A relief over the western portal shows the Western Front.

SHRINE OF REMEMBRANCE

LOCATION: Melbourne, Australia

FEATURES: Memorial shrine; visitors' centre; guided tours; computerized war records displays

VISITOR INFORMATION: On St Kilda Road, Melbourne. Open daily 10am–5pm

T The Shrine of Remembrance is one of Australia's great memorials, built to remember Victoria's war dead of 1914–18. Inspired by the mausoleum to Mausolus, King of Caria, at Halicarnassus in Turkey, the shrine is of unusual size and splendour, and was opened in November 1934. The sanctuary contains the Stone of Remembrance inscribed with the words "Greater Love Hath No Man", a shaft of sunlight (or artificial light) falling on the word "Love," at 11am on 11 November. More than 120 ceremonies are held at the shrine during the year.

NEW ZEALAND

AUCKLAND WAR MEMORIAL MUSEUM

LOCATION: Auckland, New Zealand

FEATURES: Military collections; Halls of Memory; cenotaph biographical database; Armoury Information Centre

VISITOR INFORMATION: Open daily 10am–5pm, except Christmas Day and ANZAC Day morning (25 April). For directions and further information, visit www.aucklandmuseum.com

The Auckland War Memorial Museum, more generally referred to as the Auckland Museum, has its origins in the 1850s and houses extensive general collections related to all of New Zealand's history, not just military history. The modern museum, however, was built in memory of Auckland Province's many war dead from World War I (it was opened in 1929). The War Memorial Galleries and Armoury Information Centre present extensive collections and research facilities relating to World War I, and there are frequent events, lectures, and exhibitions, particularly around commemorative days. The cenotaph database provides computerized bibliographic records of 35,000 New Zealanders who have lost their lives in wars since the late 19th century. The Halls of Memory provide places of reflection, as does a cenotaph in the grounds.

The Response

Canada's National War Memorial, which commemorates the 60,000 Canadians lost in the Great War, is also known as "The Response".

CANADA

NATIONAL WAR MEMORIAL

LOCATION: Ottawa, Ontario, Canada

FEATURES: Cenotaph and memorial statuary

VISITOR INFORMATION: Confederation Square, at the corner of Elgin Street on Confederation Boulevard. Open access

Much like the Cenotaph in London, the National War Memorial in Canada was built for the dead of World War I, but came to represent all of Canada's war fatalities. The combination of a sombre granite arch and dynamic statuary is arresting — 22 bronze figures, representing Canada's armed forces, proceed through the arch, the procession including a cavalry horse and an artillery piece. In front of the Memorial is the Tomb of the Unknown Soldier, containing the remains of a World War I soldier buried at the site in 2000.

COMMONWEALTH WAR GRAVES COMMISSION

As the death toll expanded with every passing month, the British authorities were alerted to the organizational problem of how to maintain burial arrangements, death records, and cemeteries. Their response was the formation of the Imperial War Graves Commission in 1917 – the Commonwealth War Graves Commission (CWGC) title was adopted in 1960. Today the CWGC has responsibility for remembering 1.7 million fallen soldiers worldwide. It is jointly funded by the governments of the UK, Canada, Australia, New Zealand, South Africa, and India.

NATIONAL WAR MEMORIAL (NEWFOUNDLAND)

LOCATION: St. John's, Newfoundland

FEATURES: Memorial monument

VISITOR INFORMATION: Between Water Street and Duckworth Street. Open access

The National War Memorial (Newfoundland) was opened on 1 July 1924 by none other than Field Marshal Douglas Haig, and was the fruit of efforts by the Great War Veterans' Association and the Newfoundland Patriotic Association to commemorate the dead of World War I. It features five statues by English sculptors F.V. Blundstone and Gilbert Bayes. At the summit of the monument is a spirited woman holding a flaming torch and a sword, representing Newfoundland's loyalty to the British Empire. On either side of this are a soldier and a sailor, representing the Royal Newfoundland Regiment and Royal Naval Reserve respectively. The final statues depict a fisherman and a lumberman, recognizing the efforts of the Merchant Marine and the Forestry Corps.

CANADIAN WAR MUSEUM

LOCATION: Ottawa, Ontario

FEATURES: National war museum; research centre; restaurant; theatre; memorial features

VISITOR INFORMATION: Address: 1 Vimy Place, Ottawa. Tel: +1 (819) 776 7000 or +1 1 800 555 5621. Website: www.civilization.ca. Opening hours: 1 May– 13 October, 9am–6pm; 14 October–30 April, 9am–5pm

The Canadian War Museum's primary focus on World War I is in its Gallery 2 permanent exhibition, which explores Canada's military history between 1885 and 1931. The exhibits bring to life battlefields such as Ypres and Passchendaele with reconstructed landscapes and trenches, while numerous artefacts focus on the personal experience of those on the front line. The World War I focus is also felt in other parts of the building, such as the Regeneration Hall, which contains a plaster model of Walter Allward's sculpture *Hope* (a figure from the Vimy Memorial), and the Memorial Hall, which features the headstone of the Unknown Soldier.

ĨRELAND

IRISH NATIONAL WAR MEMORIAL GARDENS

LOCATION: Dublin, Ireland

FEATURES: Memorial gardens

VISITOR INFORMATION: Address: South Circular Road, Islandbridge, Dublin 8. Tel: +353 1 661 3111. Open Monday–Friday 8am–dusk.

The Irish National War Memorial Gardens were built to remember the 49,400 Irish soldiers who died during the Great War. The gardens were another of Sir Edwin Lutyens's masterpieces. They went through some times of neglect in the 1960s and 1970s, but have recently been restored and improved maintenance procedures are now in place. The park itself covers 8 hectares (20 acres) and includes two book rooms, in which are kept Rolls of Honour with the names of 50,000 Irish dead. The site also features the Ginchy Cross, a wooden monument built by soldiers of the Irish 16th Division and originally erected on the Somme.

Irish National War Memorial Gardens
During this site's construction in the 1930s, use of machinery was deliberately limited so that the project would generate more employment.

ĨNDIA

INDIA GATE

LOCATION: Delhi, India

FEATURES: War memorial

VISITOR INFORMATION: Located on Rajpath, Delhi. Open access

Another memorial design by Sir Edwin Lutyens, the India Gate was built between 1921 and 1931 in remembrance of all Indian soldiers who had died in the Afghan Wars and in World War I. Originally called the All India War Memorial, the monument is an impressive 42m (137ft) tall and consists of an arch on which the names of more than 70,000 soldiers are inscribed. Lit up at night, it bears more than a passing resemblance to the Arc de Triomphe in Paris. Beneath the arch is the Amar Jawan Jyoti (The Flame of the Immortal Warrior) and also the Tomb of the Unknown Soldier. The cenotaph is surrounded by four flaming torches that are kept constantly lit.

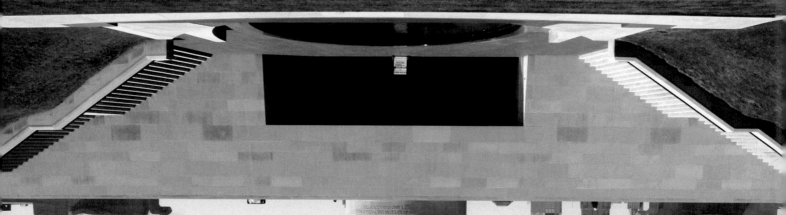

UNITED STATES

LIBERTY MEMORIAL

LOCATION: Kansas City, Missouri, United States

FEATURES: National World War I War Memorial of the United States; National World War I Museum

VISITOR INFORMATION: Located in Penn Valley Park, Kansas, off the I-35. Tel: +1 (816) 784 1918. Website: www.libertymemorialmuseum.org Open Tuesday–Sunday 10am–5pm

This powerful, towering monument was opened on 11 November 1926, and stands today as the National World War I War Memorial of the United States. It was designed by Harold Van Buren Magonigle, who won a design competition set up by the American Institute of Architects, and dedicated by US President Calvin Coolidge. An accompanying museum was dramatically redeveloped and opened in 2006. The museum has fascinating displays of artefacts and documents, and is one of the finest centres of World War I research in the United States. The site's centrepiece is the 66m (217ft) Memorial Tower, which features four figures representing courage, honour, sacrifice, and patriotism. At night, a jet of steam illuminated by orange light emanates from the tower, giving the appearance of a burning pyre. The Great Frieze wall depicts the transition from war to peace, while another memorial wall features bronze busts of the five Allied leaders.

Liberty Memorial sphinxes

The two carved stone sphinxes that stand guard on either side of the Liberty Memorial's central tower are named "Memory" and "Future".

ARLINGTON NATIONAL CEMETERY

LOCATION: Arlington, Virginia, United States

FEATURES: US national military cemetery

VISITOR INFORMATION: On Virginia side of Potomac River, across the Memorial Bridge from Washington, D.C. Opening hours: 1 April–30 September, 8am–7pm; 1 October–31 March, 8am–5pm

The foundations of the Arlington National Cemetery date back to the Civil War, and the cemetery has taken many of the bodies of America's military dead ever since. It covers 253 hectares (624 acres) and contains more than 300,000 burials, including large numbers of those killed in World War I. One moving feature built in the aftermath of the Great War was the Tomb of the Unknowns, the first of the unidentified soldiers being interred there in 1921. Numerous World War I memorials also grace the cemetery, including the Argonne Cross Memorial, the Canadian Cross of Sacrifice, and the simple World War One Memorial.

Arlington graves

Designated an official military cemetery in 1864, Arlington National Cemetery now conducts an average of 28 funerals a day.

GLOSSARY

ABBREVIATIONS

BEF
The British Expeditionary Force.

OHL
Oberste Heeresleitung, the German military high command.

Stavka
Shtab glavnogo verkhovnogo komandovaniya, the Russian supreme military headquarters.

MILITARY ORGANIZATION

GENERAL TERMS:

unit
The basis of military organization. For administrative purposes, "unit" usually meant a battalion, but a unit's size depended on circumstances. For tactical purposes in battle it could be much smaller.

formation
A number of units joined to form a single organization. The term was applied specifically when a military command had under its authority units of all the different "arms" – infantry, artillery and cavalry – as, for example, in a division.

establishment
The formally approved size, composition and equipment of a military unit or formation.

SPECIFIC TERMS:

Although there was a fundamental similarity in the way the armies of different countries were organized, there were differences in terminology. As the war progressed, changes were made to the organization, and in countries where manpower was a problem, the number of men at each level was reduced.

battalion
The standard organizational unit for infantry (about 1,000 men). The battalion was further broken down into companies, platoons and specialist sections such as machine-gun, mortar, pioneer and trench artillery sections. The equivalent unit for cavalry was the regiment, and for artillery the battery.

battery
Unit of organization for artillery, normally consisting of six guns (France four, Russia eight). Three batteries constituted a group (named a brigade in the British army), and two or three groups a regiment.

regiment
Military formation for continental infantry comprising three battalions (3,000 men); in the Russian army it comprised four battalions (4,000). For British infantry, the formation equivalent size was the brigade. A cavalry regiment was a basic unit of between 500 and 1,000 men, which was further broken down into squadrons.

brigade
A military formation under one command. In continental armies it consisted of two infantry regiments (6,000 – 8,000 men); in the British army, four infantry battalions (4,000 men). This level of formation was generally either reduced or discarded during the course of the war.

division
The smallest body of men fully organized for the conduct of war, complete with infantry, artillery, cavalry and other specialist troops, as well as the necessary administrative services (17,000 – 20,000 men at full strength). The infantry strength of a continental army division was normally two infantry brigades (12 battalions). British army divisions included three infantry brigades (12 battalions). The size and composition of a division changed during the course of the war.

corps
Military formation, usually consisting of two division (around 40,000 men).

army
Highest military grouping, found necessary only in time of war. Its size varied considerably, from three to six corps.

TYPES OF WARSHIP

dreadnought
Type of battleship, powered by turbines, with standardized heavy armament. It was named after HMS *Dreadnought* (authorized by the British government in 1905 and launched in 1906).

pre-dreadnought
Term applied to all battleships with mixed heavy and medium main armament. A few such warships were built after the launch of the superior HMS *Dreadnought* 1906, but only because they were so advanced in planning that cancellation was not a realistic possibility.

battlecruiser
Term that came to be applied to the class of warship that was initiated with the *Invincible* class (1905). It had a standardized heavy armament, but less armour and a higher speed than a dreadnought. Originally conceived of as fast battleships, battlecruisers were better suited to guarding sea routes and acting as an advance guard or scouting force than to fighting in line of battle.

cruiser
There were three types of cruiser: the armoured cruiser, the protected cruiser and the light cruiser. When *Invincible* class battlecruisers first appeared in 1905 they were termed armoured cruisers. The older armoured cruisers, hopelessly outclassed in terms of firepower, speed and armour, were reduced to secondary duties. The British nonetheless had some at the Battle of Jutland.
The protected cruiser had some measure of armour, but was not intended to operate against powerful enemy formations. By 1914 it was being superseded by the light cruiser, which was fast enough to play a reconnaissance role, and had sufficient armament to deal with enemy destroyers.

destroyer
A class of fast, lightly armoured warship. It was developed in the 1890s to combat the torpedo boat, but took on many other functions. During the First World War it was armed with torpedoes and anti-submarine equipment.

WEAPONRY

carbine
Short rifle usually carried by cavalry.

howitzer
Short-barreled, high-angle artillery piece, normally a heavy or medium gun used for destroying fortifications, buildings and trench systems of high-trajectory, high-explosive shells.

limber
Simple trailer, consisting of two wheels, an axle and a pole, attached to the rear of a gun carriage for transporting ammunition.

mines
Explosives laid in tunnels excavated under enemy positions. Also explosive devices floating on or just below the surface of the sea.

mortar
High-angle, short-ranged artillery piece. Primarily a trench weapon, not a field piece.

shrapnel shell
A projectile containing a number of small bullets that exploded before impact.

tracer bullet
A small arms or machine-gun bullet with illuminant to allow sighting and correction of fire.

MILITARY TERMINOLOGY

bridgehead
Position occupied on the far side of a river, with communication ensured by either a captured or built bridge.

communications trench
The means of access between successive lines of trenches and forward defensive positions.

creeping barrage
A form of artillery bombardment intended to creep ahead of advancing infantry and thereby prevent the enemy re-occupying forward fire positions. It was first employed during the First World War, in 1916.

cuirassiers
Type of cavalry that wore a metal breast and back plate (a cuirass).

defence-in-depth
A concept that emerged in 1916 when the Germans abandoned the practice of defending from forward positions, at the point of first contact and within range of enemy artillery, in favour of defending from successive positions that stretched back 8–10 km (5–6 miles). This was too great a distance to be overcome in any single attack. As German defensive capacity increased, so did losses for both sides, as the real battlefield moved from No Man's Land into the defensive labyrinth. Neither the British nor the French, committed as they were to offensive operations, really adopted the principle of defence-in-depth.

enfilade
To fire from the flank of an enemy formation along its length. Enfilading fire caused heavy losses among advancing troops.

hurricane bombardment
Name given to intense bombardment of very short duration, minutes rather than hours or days. First employed in 1915.

mask
To position a force in order to prevent enemy movement, such as when a city is controlled from the outside by a force that intends not to take it but to neutralize it and prevent sorties from within by enemy formations.

sap
A deep, narrow trench used to approach or undermine an enemy position; the act of digging such a trench.

sapper
Term used for an engineer.

screen
A small force protecting a larger force.

scuttle
To deliberately sink a ship to prevent its surrender or capture.

turn the enemy's flank
To pass around the enemy's unsecured flank and take up a position behind or alongside it. Rather than a frontal attack, this was the recommended manoeuvre for surrounding and crushing an enemy formation.

uhlan
A lancer – a cavalryman armed with a lance.

INDEX

ACKNOWLEDGEMENTS

The publisher would like to thank the following for the their kind permission to reproduce the photographs:

ABBREVIATIONS KEY:

a = above, b = bottom, c = centre, l = left, r = right, t = top

Bundesarchiv: Bundesarchiv, Koblenz

Firepower: courtesy of Firepower, The Royal Artillery Museum, Royal Artillery Historiacal Trust

Hulton: Getty Images/Hulton Archive

TAA: the**art**archive, London

Ullstein: Ullstein Bild, Berlin

Verney: Collection Jean-Pierre Verney, Paris

front endpaper TAA

1 t Verney; b IWM

2–3 Hulton

4–5 Hulton

6–7 TAA

8–9 AKG

10–11 Imperial War Museum

12 bl Bundesarchiv

12–13 Heeresgeschichtlichen Museum, Vienna

14 t Hulton; b AKG

15 b TAA

16 t Ullstein; bl AKG; br Hulton

17 t Ullstein; b AKG

18 t and tl DK/Firepower; cr Hulton; bl DK; br DK/Firepower

19 tr TAA; b Deutsches Historisches Museum, Berlin

20 t Hulton; b Novosti

21 tr, cl, cr and b Imperial War Museum

22 t Hulton; b Roger Viollet

23 t and cr Endeavour Group; b TAA

24–25 Roger Viollet

26 Imperial War Museum

27 t and cr Imperial War Museum; b Heeresgeschichtlichen Museum, Vienna

28 TL Verney; tc Firepower; all other images Verney

28–29 b Bundesarchiv

29 tl Verney; tr Imperial War Museum; c Deutsches Historisches Museum, Berlin; br TAA

30 tr TAA; cl Verney; cr Robert Harding Picture Library

31 tl Verney; tr Roger Viollet

32 bl TAA

32–33 Roger Viollet

33 tr Hulton; tl AKG; tc, cl and cr TAA; br DK

34–35 Endeavour Group Uk/States Archives of Film, Photography and Documents, St Petersburg

36–37 Heeresgeschichtlichen Museum, Vienna

38 b Roger Viollet

38–39 Roger Viollet

40 TAA

41 background image TAA; bl John Foley; bc Imperial War Museum; br TAA

42 t Verney; bc TAA

43 b Robert Hunt Picture Library/Imperial War Museum

44–45 TAA

46–47 t TAA

47 tr Hulton; b Novosti

48 t Hulton; b Ullstein

49 t Ullstein; br Imperial War Museum

50 t Imperial War Museum; b Hulton

51 tr Corbis; c Roger Viollet

52 b TAA; t Roger Viollet

53 background image Roger Viollet; other images Verney

54 t Imperial War Museum; b TAA

55 tc and tr Firepower; b Robert Hunt Picture Library

56–57 b Hulton

57 t Hulton; b TAA

58–59 t Imperial War Museum; b Robert Hunt Picture Library

59 t, c and b IWM

60 tr Imperial War Museum; t and tl Verney; cl Firepower; c Verney; bl Imperial War Museum

60-61 background image Verney

61 bl Verney; tr and br Imperial War Museum

62 bl Robert Hunt Picture Library

63 t TAA; b Ullstein

64 Oesterreichisches Institut für Zeitgeschichte, Vienna

65 t TAA; c Imperial War Museum; b Novosti

66 t Robert Hunt Picture Library; b Bundesarchiv

67 t Imperial War Museum

68 tl Museo Storico della Guerra, Rovereto; c Weltkriegbucherie Stuttgart; b Robert Hunt Picture Library

69 background image Imperial War Museum; other images Verney

70–71 Roger Viollet

72–73 Oesterreichisches Institut für Zeitgeschichte, Vienna

74–75 Robert Hunt Picture Library/Imperial War Museum

75 b Hulton

76 TAA

77 tl Verney; cl Firepower; cr Verney; cb Imperial War Museum; bl and bc Roger Viollet; br Robert Hunt Picture Library

78 t, bl and br TAA

79 tr and tl TAA; cr Australian War Memorial; b TAA

80 t and br TAA

81 br TAA

82-83 TAA

84 t TAA; b Roger Viollet

85 br Novosti

86 t IMM; br Robert Hunt Picture Library

87 t Robert Hunt Picture Library; b Imperial War Museum

88-89 t Hulton

88 bl TAA; c Verney

89 b Hulton

90 t and b Imperial War Museum

91 t Imperial War Museum; bl Bildarchiv

92 t Robert Hunt Picture Library

93 t and c Robert Hunt Picture Library; b TAA

94 background image Roger Viollet; tl and bl Verney; br Roger Viollet

95 br Robert Hunt Picture Library; tl Imperial War Museum; tr Hulton; c TAA; bl Roger Viollet

96–97 TAA

98–99 TAA

100 t Oesterreichisches Institut für Zeitgeschichte, Vienna

100–101 Roger Viollet

102 TAA

103 bl Imperial War Museum; cr Firepower; br TAA

104 Roger Viollet

105 background image and tr Verney; bl Imperial War Museum; br TAA

106 al Verney; tc Imperial War Museum; tr Firepower

106–107 background image TAA

106 br Verney

107 tl and tr Verney; c TAA; cr and b Verney

108 t Verney

108–109 Robert Hunt Picture Library

109 t TAA

110 bl Verney

110–111 background image TAA

111 t, tl, cl, cr Imperial War Museum; bl Verney; br Corbis

112–113 Roger Viollet

114–115 Robert Hunt Picture Library

115 Oesterreichisches Institut fur Zeitgeschichte, Vienna

116 t Imperial War Museum

116–117 b Heeresgeschichtlichen Museums, Vienna

117 t Imperial War Museum

118 tl AKG; b Heeresgeschichtlichen Museums, Vienna

118–119 Imperial War Museum

119 b Heeresgeschichtlichen Museums, Vienna

120 l TAA

120–121 b TAA

122 t Verney; b Roger Viollet

123 t Hulton; b Roger Viollet

124 t Verney

124–125 b Roger Viollet

125 tl Verney; tr Imperial War Museum; cl and br Verney

126 t TAA; b Verney

127 t Hulton; tr Imperial War Museum; b TAA

128 background image and cl Imperial War Museum; b TAA

129 tl TAA; tr Hulton; bl Verney

130 background image and c IWM; br TAA

130–131 background image AKG

131 tl TAA; tr Verney; br Hulton

132–133 Corbis

134–135 TAA

136 l Imperial War Museum

136–137 TAA

137 tr TAA

138 Hulton

139 background image and cr TAA

140 bl and br Roger Viollet

141 bl Roger Viollet

142 tl Roger Viollet; tr TAA

142–143 b Roger Viollet

143 bl Austin Brown

144 bl Imperial War Museum; bc Firepower; c Verney; br IWM

144145 TAA

145 t Robert Hunt Picture Library; tc Verney; bc Firepower; bl TAA; br Imperial War Museum

146–147 Novosti

147 tl, cl Imperial War Museum; tr TAA; cr, bl and br Verney; b Firepower

148 t Novosti

148–149 b Novosti

149 tr IWM

150 Bildarchiv fur Preussischer Kulturbesitz

151 tr Roger Viollet; cl TAA; b Novosti; br TAA

152 t Robert Hunt Picture Library; b Imperial War Museum

153 t Imperial War Museum

154 t and bl Verney

154–155 TAA

155 tl TAA; tlc Verney; tc, tr and ctr TAA; cl, cr and bc Verney; bl and br TAA

156–157 Hulton

158 t and b TAA

159 Robert Hunt Picture Library

160 TAA

161 t IWM; b TAA

162 t and cr Imperial War Museum; bl Verney;

162–163 TAA

164 t and cl Tank Museum; b Imperial War Museum

164–165 background image Imperial War Museum

165 tl and tc Tank Museum; tr Imperial War Museum; bl and br Tank Museum

166-167 b TAA

167 t Imperial War Museum

168 tl Firepower and DK/Imperial War Museum; cl and b Firepower

168–169 background image Imperial War Museum

169 tl Imperial War Museum; tr Verney; cl and bl Firepower; cr and br DK/Imperial War Museum

170–171 Imperial War Museum

172–173 TAA

174–175 Imperial War Museum

175 Imperial War Museum

176–177 TAA

177 br TAA

178 t and c Imperial War Museum

178–179 b Imperial War Museum

179 t Imperial War Museum; b Roger Viollet

180 b Imperial War Museum

180–181 t TAA

181 b Imperial War Museum; br TAA

182 t Imperial War Museum; b Bundesarchiv

183 tr, background image and bl TAA; br Imperial War Museum

184 t Imperial War Museum; b TAA

185 t TAA; b and cb Imperial War Museum; cr TAA

186 t Heeresgeschichtlichen Museum, Vienna

186–187 Imperial War Museum

188 Verney

189 tl DK/IWM; tr Verney; cr Science and Society Picture Library; b Quadrant

190 t Corbis; b Verney

191 background image and tr Imperial War Museum; cl and cr Verney; bl DK/Imperial War Museum; bra TAA; br Philip Jarret

192 t Imperial War Museum; b TAA

193 tr, cr Imperial War Museum; c Museo Storico della Guerra, Rovereto; cl DK/Imperial War Museum; b TAA

194–195 Verney

196 t and b Corbis

197 background image Roger Viollet; cr Imperial War Museum; bl Verney; bc and br Hulton

198 t Hulton; b TRH Pictures

199 background image, tl, tr and c Hulton

200 tl Hulton; tc TAA; tr Culver Pictures

200–201 Roger Viollet

202–203 TAA

204–205 Roger Viollet

206 b Novosti

206–207 Ullstein

208–209 Robert Hunt Picture Library/IWM

209 tr Verney; bl and br TAA

210 b Verney

210–211 Roger Viollet

211 Roger Viollet

212 Roger Viollet

213 t TAA; tl and b Verney

214 background image Imperial War Museum; tl and tr Verney; bl DK/Imperial War Museum/Andy Crawford; br Verney

215 tl Corbis; bl TAA; br Imperial War Museum

216 t and b TAA

217 background image, tr and cl TAA

218 t Imperial War Museum; b TAA

219 t TAA

220 t Imperial War Museum

220–221 Imperial War Museum

221 tr Roger Viollet; cl and cr Verney; bc Roger Viollet

222 tl Tank Museum; tr Verney; bl Ullstein

223 tl DK/IWM; tr Imperial War Museum

222–223 c Firepower; cl Imperial War Museum; b Tank Museum

224–225 Hulton

226 t Novosti

226–227 b Hulton

227 tr and tc Imperial War Museum; c DK

228 t Novosti; b TAA

229 t Bildarchiv für Preussischer Kulturbesitz; c Robert Hunt Picture Library; b Novosti

230 tl Hulton; tr TAA; b TA

231 t, c and bl Novosti

232 t Museo Storico della Guerra, Rovereto; b Firepower

233 t Museo Storico della Guerra, Rovereto; c Robert Hunt Picture Library

234 t Heeresgeschichtlichen Museum, Vienna; b Ullstein

235 t Heeresgeschichtlichen Museum, Vienna

236 t and b Robert Hunt Picture Library

237 t Firepower; b Robert Hunt Picture Library

238 t IWM; c Verney; cr and b Imperial War Museum

239 tl Firepower; tr Imperial War Museum; b Australian War Memorial

240 t Ullstein; b Robert Hunt Picture Library

241 t Robert Hunt Picture Library; b TAA

242 tc and cl Imperial War Museum; b Bridgeman Art Library

242–243 background image TAA

243 tl and tr TAA; b Verney

244–245 Imperial War Museum

246–247 TAA

248 BL TAA

248–249 Imperial War Museum

250 Bildarchiv für Preussischer Kulturbesitz

251 t TAA; b Corbis

252 Ullstein

252 bl Firepower; br Verney

253 t Hulton; b TAA

254–255 t TAA

255 bl Deutsches Historisches Museum, Berlin; br Imperial War Museum

256 t Imperial War Museum; B Deutsches Historisches Museum, Berlin

257 t Roger Viollet; cl Imperial War Museum; br Roger Viollet

258 t ECPA

259 t Imperial War Museum

260 tl Verney; b Imperial War Museum

260–261 t Australian War Memorial

261 tl Bridgeman Art Library © ADAGP, Paris and DACS, London 2003; tr Albertina, Vienna; c Städtisches Galerie, Albstadt © DACS 2003; bl Imperial War Museum; br Verney

262 Imperial War Museum

263 t TAA; bl Verney; br Roger Viollet

264 Verney

265 tl and tr TAA; b Imperial War Museum

266 t TAA; b Verney

267 background image and other images Verney

268–269 Imperial War Museum

270 Robert Hunt Picture Library

271 t Robert Hunt Picture Library; bl Roger Viollet

272 b TAA

272–273 t Imperial War Museum

274 t Museo Storico della Guerra, Rovereto; b Robert Hunt Picture Library

275 background image Museo Storico della Guerra, Rovereto; br Museo Storico della Guerra, Rovereto; other images Verney

276–277 t Museo Storico della Guerra, Rovereto

277 b Robert Hunt Picture Library

278 Imperial War Museum

279 tl Imperial War Museum; c Hulton

280–281 Corbis

282–283 TAA

284 t and b Verney

285 tr Ullstein; cl and cr Imperial War Museum; b Ullstein

286 t TAA; c Imperial War Museum

287 t Imperial War Museum; c Advertising Archives; bl Culver; br Hulton

288 t TAA/Imperial War Museum; b Roger Viollet

289 background image John Frost Newspapers; c TAA; cr and bl Verney; bc TAA; br Verney

290–291 Endeavour Group

292–293 TAA

294–295 Hulton

295 Hulton

296 t Ullstein

297 t Bildarchiv für Preussischer Kulturbesitz; b Hulton

298 b Bildarchiv für Preussischer Kulturbesitz

299 b Bildarchiv für Preussischer Kulturbesitz

300 t Bildarchiv für Preussischer Kulturbesitz; b Ullstein

301 tr Corbis; cl AKG; bl and br David King Collection

302 t and b Roger Viollet

303 tr Corbis; b Roger Viollet

304 b Private collection

304–305 t Roger Viollet

305 b Hulton

306–307 Roger Viollet

307 tr Verney

308–309 Roger Viollet

310 Marcia Crayton/Dreamstime.com

312 Krisk Van campenhout/Dreamstime.com

313 Craig Mcwilliams/Dreamstime.com

314 Pyewackett/Dreamstime.com

315 tr Sally A. Morgan; Ecoscene/Corbis

316 t, b Pir6mon

317 David Crowther/istockphoto

318 Michael St. Maur Sheil/Corbis

319 Adam Woolfitt/Corbis

320 Ahmet DALKILIÇLA/istockphoto

321 tl, Nik Wheeler/Corbis; b, Hulton-Deutsch Collection/Corbis

322 t, Jason Ruck; bl Angelo Hornak/Corbis

323 David P. Lewis/istockphoto

324 The Irish Image Collection/Corbis

325 Trevor Goodwin/Dreamstime.com

DK PHOTOGRAPHY:
Peter Chadwick, Andy Crawford, Geoff Dann; Anthony Haughey

CREDITS FOR QUOTATIONS
Every effort has been made to gain permission from the relevant copyright holders to reproduce the extracts that appear in this book. The following have kindly given permission for extracts to be quoted in the book:

109 Extract from *Goodbye to All That* by Robert Graves. Used by permission of Carcanet Press Limited.

114; 150; 205 Extracts from *The First World War* by John Keegan published by Hutchinson. Used with permission of the Random House Group Limited.

135 Extract from *Storm of Steel* by Ernst Jünger, published by Penguin Books.

160; 212 Extracts from *Forgotten Voices of The Great War* by Max Arthur published by Ebury. Used by permission of the Random House Group Limited.

233 Extract from *War and the Future: Italy, France and Britain at War* by H. G. Wells. Used by permission of A. P. Watt Ltd on behalf of The Literary Executors of the Estate of H. G. Wells.

237 Extract from *Revolt in the Desert* by T. E. Lawrence, published by Wordsworth Editions Ltd.

242 Extract from *Break of Day in the Trenches* by Isaac Rosenberg, taken from The Complete Works of Isaac Rosenberg (1979), edited by Ian Parsons.

243 Extract from *Dulce et Decorum Est* by Wilfred Owen, taken from Complete Poems and Fragments of Wilfred Owen (1983), edited by John Galsworthy.

243 Extract from *Le Feu (Under Fire)* by Henri Barbusse, published by Penguin Books.

247; 254; 258 Extracts from *The Imperial War Museum Book of 1918* by Malcolm Brown, published by Macmillan, London, UK.

DK WOULD LIKE TO THANK:
Jean-Pierre Verney for all his help and advice. Les Smith and his staff at Firepower, the Royal Artillery Museum, Elizabeth Bowers and her staff at the Imperial War Museum. Tom Coulson at Encompass Graphics. Alex Reay and Phil Crowcroft at Advanced Illustration.

THE AUTHOR WOULD LIKE TO THANK:
Everybody at DK's History and Cartography department who worked on this book. He would also like to thank the following for their professional help and guidance in the making of the book: Tony Clayton, Michael Coles, Spencer Johnson, Terry Lilley, Adam Lynde, Gordon Angus Macinley, John Andreas Olsen, William O'Neil, Jack Sweetman, Tohmatsu Haruo, John Votaw and Steven Weingartner. He is also grateful for the invaluable support of his professional colleagues, Tim Bean, Patrick Burke, Nigel de Lee, Christopher Duffy and Paul Harris. Special thanks are also due to librarians Jennie Wraight, Iain MacKenzie, Andrew Orgill, Ken Franklin and John Pearce, for providing access to their libraries, collections and personal knowledge.

HOWLING NEAR HEAVEN

Marcia B. Siegel

HOWLING

NEAR

HEAVEN

Twyla Tharp and the
Reinvention of Modern Dance

METHUEN

Copyright © 2006 by Marcia B. Siegel. All rights reserved. The right of
Marcia B. Siegel to be identified as the author of this work has been asserted
in accordance with the Copyright, Designs and Patents Act, 1988

First published in Great Britain by Methuen in 2006
Methuen Publishing Ltd, 11–12 Buckingham Gate, London SW1E 6LB

www.methuen.co.uk

Design by Kathryn Parise

A CIP catalogue record for this book is available from the British Library

ISBN 10: 0-413-76570-9
ISBN 13: 978-0-413-76570-3

Printed in the United States of America

10 9 8 7 6 5 4 3 2 1

For Rose and Sara
and all the others who made Tharp dance

CONTENTS

HOWLING NEAR HEAVEN

I

Leotard Days

1965–1966

J udson Memorial Church, in the geographical center of Greenwich Village, stands like an exotic souvenir today on the southern edge of Washington Square Park, among the modern monoliths of New York University. Its Italian Renaissance–style ochre brickwork, ten-story campanile, and tile roofs link it to its neighbor across the park, Washington Square Arch—both were designed by the distinguished American architect Stanford White. The church has seventeen stained-glass windows by John La Farge and a bas relief altarpiece by Augustus St. Gaudens. It was declared a New York City landmark in 1966. The sanctuary has recently been restored to its turn-of-the-century beaux-arts splendor, a high, airy space of imposing beige marble Corinthian pillars; soaring vaults inset with vibrant arched and circular stained-glass windows; a paneled mansard ceiling; and a color scheme of beige, aqua, and cream to complement the marble wall panels.

Revisiting this beautiful house of light, it's hard to recall the way it looked when it was filled with rebellious performance events decades ago. In fact, at the end of the 1990s Judson's Baptist congregation agonized about whether to restore this grand space at all. According to senior minister Peter Laarman, Judson Church has always been more about ephemera than about preservation. Founded in 1890, the church was dedicated to serving the needs of the city. From immigrant job training programs and health centers to teenage sports, civil rights, antiwar protests, and gay-pride marches, the church has taken a leading role in New York's progressive dynamic. The showcasing of avant-garde dance events only extended its mission.

Beaux-arts architecture represented a form of cultural imperialism to the reformers of the 1960s. Over a period of time the walls, ceiling, and columns were painted a political dirt brown, though the altar and stained-glass windows remained. Regular Sunday services never ceased, but by 1966 the pews had been removed from the sanctuary to accommodate art happenings and Judson Dance Theater experiments. Judson Poets Theater held forth in the choir loft, next to the boxy old pipe organ with its pillars, carved wreaths, and trumpeting angels. Protest rallies shook the building and militants gathered outside to begin marches and demonstrations. For dance performances, the audience trudged up a set of creaky wooden stairs to the sanctuary. You came in under the choir loft, through a kind of low cavern, which was usually littered with a random assortment of thrift-shop chairs, props, piano, and equipment. Sometimes this "lobby" area was curtained off from the performance space.

On October 29, 1966, for the first of three concerts by Twyla Tharp and Company, chairs for the audience of about one hundred had been placed on three sides, facing away from the altar. Three pieces were on the program: *Re-Moves (in four sections and two introductions)*, *Twelve Foot Change*, and a revival of Tharp's first work, *Tank Dive*, given only the year before in a small theater within the Hunter College art department. *Twelve Foot Change* was subsequently called *Yancey Dance*, after the music by jazz pianist Jimmy Yancey. *Re-Moves* was forty-five minutes long and had big ambitions.

Not that there was anything tentative about what Tharp had already done. Just out of college, she had danced for a season with Paul Taylor, then quit to find her own way. To earn money, she'd appeared for a summer at the Alaskan Pavilion of the New York World's Fair, dancing a "sort of furry hootchy-kootchy" in a bearskin rug. Following the approved modern dance practice of throwing out all that preceded one's own discoveries, Tharp's first two serious concerts encapsulated her idea of the basics, nonchalantly disguised in improper elements. After the eight-minute *Tank Dive*, which constituted the entire event at Hunter, she produced a second, slightly longer concert in the same small space. She made a twenty-minute film-dance, *Stride*, which was not intended for a live audience. The same filmmaker, Robert Barry, had also documented *Tank Dive*, just as if it were a dance classic in need of preservation.

With hindsight, one could say she'd laid out all her major credentials in her first year: the talent, ego, and determination to make an individual style, the embrace of popular culture, the fascination with film as a medium for both experimentation and preservation, and the pragmatic exploitation of whatever resources were available in order to create what she deemed worthy. At once a rebel and a puritan, Tharp embraced the avant-garde as an opportunity to experiment with ideas, not as an aesthetic or political statement. She had come from a deeply eccentric family; nonsense was perfectly all right with her. The oldest of four children, she had an ambitious mother who pushed her into improving studies from preschool age: piano, violin, viola, elocution, painting, German and French, baton twirling, and of course, dance lessons. She learned early how to schedule her time so as to get the most out of it, knocking off her school homework in the car as her mother drove her from their home near San Bernardino to classes in Los Angeles. On weekends she worked in the food concession of her mother's drive-in movie. Too busy taking lessons to have a teenage social life, she learned how to be an overachiever, a discriminating workaholic.

Nowadays, Tharp downplays her relationship to Paul Taylor, but her brief presence in his company came at an important time. Taylor in the early '60s was at a crossroads in his career. He'd started out with a dual citizenship in the commonwealth of modern dance, as a member of the Martha Graham Company and a dancer with Merce Cunningham. Taylor began doing his own choreography around 1958. He'd given a few notorious, dadaistic concerts and assembled the core of a company. *Aureole* (1962) scandalized the modern dance community at the American Dance Festival, not for its outrageousness but for its conservatism. A "white ballet" with formal, musical choreography to Handel, it affronted the expressionistic sensibilities that prevailed at the time. The next year he reverted to the bizarre and dissociated. *Scudorama* was just about finished when Tharp came into the company, and as a junior member she was given things to do that she considered beneath her. At one point she executed a slow, deranged somersault across the back of the stage, and at another she made an entrance under a beach towel, perched on the head of Dan Wagoner.

She says Taylor interested her as a dancer but not as a choreographer. After appearing in three other new works, *Party Mix, Junction,* and *Red Room*, she voiced her disapproval so loudly that he gave her what became a permanent leave of absence, advising her to go try doing her own work and see how easy it was. Taylor succeeded in molding his experimental impulses into a repertory and a company that were conventional enough to survive. Tharp faced a similar transition five years after her own initial borderline works.

In staging a concert at Judson Church, Tharp was treading on the turf of the avant-garde dance community, but the concert was anomalous, both in Tharp's career and in the annals of Judson Dance. Tharp was quite aware of the symbolic significance of performing at Judson. After the concert was over, she says, "we had passed through the vale and come out whole . . . we had situated ourselves in the vanguard of the investigation into how dance could relate to and deal with our lives." Tharp was, and always would be, an independent. A tireless inventer of movement, she would try anything, but she wasn't drawn into the waves of communal dissatisfaction that flooded the dance world of the '60s. Her connection to Judson and to the avant-garde was her partner, Robert Huot, a visual artist and filmmaker. Huot had performed at Judson two years earlier in *War*, a collaborative performance piece with his friend, the artist Robert Morris. He designed the costumes and sets for all Tharp's dances from *Tank Dive* until they broke up in 1971.

Tharp's Judson program, on the surface, could have been any one of the avant-garde custard pies that were being pushed into the face of traditional dance at the time. Each of the three works presented a collage of incompatible elements. Unrelated things happened simultaneously. The audience was left to make its own sense of what it saw—or didn't see. The costumes for *Twelve Foot Change/Yancey Dance* consisted of long, hooded sweatshirts over leotards, with dark glasses and bare legs. *Twelve Foot Change* and *Tank Dive* lasted less than ten minutes each.

In *Tank Dive* Tharp, wearing heeled sandals and a leotard cut very low in back, spun a yo-yo out of her fist, bounced it once, and reeled it back. Stepping into a pair of three-foot planklike clogs, she slowly folded her body forward into an upside-down L, then straightened from her flat-back position into a forward lean. She stepped backwards out of the flippers and went up some steps onto a tiny stage. She stood for a long time in relevé, as perfectly posed as a ballerina, her legs turned out and spaced in a wide second position, her arms reaching out and up from her sides. She descended into a plié, rose again and held another relevé, in profile to the audience, absolutely motionless for another forty-four counts, the duration of a recording of Petula Clark's "Downtown."*

---

*In the Hunter performances, after Huot and Christopher Constance had sprinted into a collision, she returned for a series of violent somersaults and a sudden reiteration of her X-relevé pose. She recounts the scenario differently in her autobiography. It's unclear how much she edited the piece for Judson. By then even she had forgotten its original date—the program lists its premiere as 1964, a year before the real date, April 29, 1965.

For *Re-Moves* the leotards had low scoop necks and three-quarter sleeves, a dancerly effect undermined by the one white tennis shoe and one white glove that the dancers wore, and by the stiff white headdresses that curved up from a squared-off back, which framed their necks and dipped into a triangle bisecting their foreheads. Sara Rudner walked inside of a large hoop, and Margaret Jenkins imitated the rhythms of a bouncing ball. At some point Tharp reached into a bag and took out eggs, which she dropped, one by one, on the floor. Rudner rigged a rope ladder from the balcony and climbed down it with very precise steps and a concave torso. Descending, she uncoiled smoothly until she achieved a stretched-out shape on the floor. Later on, she tap-danced, unaccompanied, in a strictly laid out rectangular pattern that wove in and out of the audience's sight lines from under the curtained-off balcony.

In an annotated chronology, Tharp describes *Re-Moves* as "a trio in which visibility is determined by the sets: section one, in the open; section two, half-hidden; section three, one-third visible; section four, entirely hidden." An eight-foot-high plywood box was placed in the space for *Re-Moves*, leaving about ten feet of working space between the box and the surrounding audience. During part three of the work, the dancers circled the box with precise formations and step patterns. As they disappeared from view, the audience could hear their repetitive stepping on the other side of the box. In a revival of the piece a couple of years later, Tharp added a fourth section, where the dancers went inside the box and rehearsed whatever new thing they were working on, heard but unseen by the audience.

Tharp's terse description of *Re-Moves*, probably written at the end of the 1970s, focuses on the formal structure of the piece and eliminates all its sensual, visual, and aesthetic effects. In a time when it wasn't fashionable to use music, she kept quiet about Jimmy Yancey. The statement reveals the compositional preoccupations that never abated during Tharp's multifaceted work of the next decades. Her noncommittal, anti-interpretive '60s prose suited the posture of neutrality demanded by the avant-garde, as well as her personal reticence and her conviction that the audience too had a job to do in discovering what the dance meant. If playing up to the audience was considered manipulative by the downtown dancers, Tharp positively ignored the audience, wrapping herself and her cohorts in a performing style that was taken as disdainful, belligerent, noncommunicative, and indifferent by some critics for years to come.

At the same time, she was cultivating whatever critics she could win

over. She invited them to rehearsals, courted their attention. Don McDonagh and his friend Clive Barnes were early supporters. Barnes, only recently
appointed as dance critic of *The New York Times*, found himself sitting in a
corner chair at Judson. Tharp admits now that she had deliberately placed
him there so that at the beginning of *Re-Moves* he would be in a crucial spot.
As Tharp describes the moment, "I came out, pushed a stop watch, paced
out around the space, fell onto Clive Barnes's shoulders and fell towards the
floor—I turned, probably in passé, rolled down his left arm, extended my
arm, brushed his knee, and then brushed by all the ankles in that row."

Tharp understood that at that moment the avant-garde was the only place
to align herself. Unknown to the participants, of course, 1966 was a significant moment in the life of downtown dance and the counterculture, a peak,
perhaps, in the long curve of creative dissent that had begun a decade before with the Beats and John Cage and the abstract expressionists. Compared to the political and social paroxysms that soon engulfed the artists,
1965–66 seems a moment of idyllic innocence. Experimental theater, dance,
art, and music had so thoroughly interacted and dissolved into each other
that the term *performance* began to seem more appropriate than any genre-
specific label.

After the flamboyant high jinks of the Fluxus group, the Happenings,
and a dozen other freewheeling responses to the aesthetic rigidity of the
'50s, incongruity had become not only acceptable but desirable. Definitions
of who could make art had temporarily expanded. Dances were made by
painters and performed by lay persons with no previous dance training.
Everyday objects, which weren't supposed to belong on a dance stage except as props in a narrative, became a creative challenge. If a flower did appear in a performer's hand, the last thing you'd expect was that the
performer would smell it. More likely, the flower would be painted blue in
the course of the performance, or inserted into some orifice of the body or
the building. The everyday was treated like a treasure and treasures were
trashed. Events occurred irrationally and out of sequence. The audience was
subjected to shocks and tedium in equal doses.

The downtown artists created performance spaces in churches and studios, and also in gymnasiums, parks, anywhere but conventional stages.
Dancing didn't belong on a stage anyway, they thought. Proscenium stages
automatically coerce the audience into set ways of seeing. They predeter-

minc the dancers' focus, groupings, floor patterns, and they separate the performers from the spectators, to affect both parties' experience of the dance. Dancers wanted to be more human, less remote and awe inspiring than the precious beings found in opera house performances.

Dancing didn't belong in a dance performance either, if the experimenters were to head off the responses and effects that traditional dancing evoked. During the 1960s American modern dance had begun a decline, greatly accelerated by Merce Cunningham and the downtown performers. The founders, Martha Graham, Doris Humphrey, Hanya Holm, and their colleagues, had done their pioneering work in the 1930s and '40s. They had established schools and styles. As the founders aged, their innovative fires cooled. Their work began to look familiar, even formulaic. The passions that had ignited their rebellion against ballet simmered down into a more sensible, rational theater practice. By the end of the '50s, modern dance had become as conventionalized in its own ways as ballet. Bodies were highly trained in specialized individual techniques, and choreographic action was patterned and theatrical. Modern dance's subject matter was often quite contemporary, but it tended to be abstract in a literary sense, asking the audience to see physical activity as a metaphor for psychological interplay.

Leadership was passing to less innovative followers like José Limón, Valerie Bettis, Mary Anthony, Alvin Ailey, and Pearl Lang. They enunciated a credo of humanism with statements like this: "The contemporary artist can do no less than to dedicate the power of his spirit and the flame of his art to bring light to the dark places." (Limón) Young artists in the 1960s didn't aspire to carry flames or light up the dark. Nor were they receptive to the words of authority. The two great theorizers of modern dance composition, Louis Horst and Doris Humphrey, disappeared from college curriculums. Young dancers embarking on choreographic careers sneered at Humphrey's book *The Art of Making Dances*, and didn't see how her advice could inform them. "Dance form is logical," she wrote, "but it is all in the realm of feeling, sensitivity and imagination." Humphrey's point of view, with its underlying idealism, its confidence in the choreographer's right and ability to impose her vision on her dance, struck dissenters as dictatorial. Dance technique and the expressive urges that had given rise to choreography from Isadora Duncan through five decades of modern dance were played out, they thought. Played out and arbitrary and decadent.

According to Ronald Sukenick, one of the chroniclers of the postwar-to-postmodern avant-garde, postmodernism was concerned with dissolving the boundaries between art and life. "If nothing else is clear about Postmodernism, it is glaringly obvious that it is impelled by a passion for reengagement with common experience, including the experience of the citizen in process of helping to create his environment through the imagination." Judson Dance Theater was only one of many loose coalitions of artists that pursued these new directions. The Judson dancers, along with painters, musicians, filmmakers, and writers, wanted to explore what else could be done in the intersection of life and art besides codified theater work. Three years of workshops in dance composition, inspired by John Cage and given by Robert Dunn, had brought together dancers, musicians, and artists for a systematic investigation of alternative artmaking processes. When they decided to show their work to the public, Judson Church opened its doors. Forms and conventions were being shattered; new forms were on the way.

The realignment of life and art was to be effected through a large array of compositional and presentational strategies. Abolishing the proscenium frame and de-emphasizing all established forms of dance training were only the most obvious ones. John Cage's statement that anything can be art was often misinterpreted as a license to throw art itself away. In reality, it simply lifted the power to make art off the exclusive shoulders of the artists. Together with Cage's other Zen-inspired writings, his potent remark became a question about the nature of art and an invitation to find new answers:

Anything can be art if you *think* it's art. This mandated some degree of thought or perceptual activity on the audience's part.

Anything can be art if the processes of art are applied. Countless dances were made by subjecting ordinary activities to structuring in time and space, to ordering, layering, distortion, and triggers outside the dancers' control. Activities were reduced or expanded, elaborated, upended, and juxtaposed with unrelated activities. All these conventional effects could be further removed from an individual artist's conscious control by the systematic use of chance procedures—defining and arranging a given set of elements by random selection, like throwing dice.

Anything can be art if the performer thinks it is. People experimented with the experience of performing, explored whether *any* movement being done before a spectator could be called natural. They induced altered states of consciousness, practiced diffused and inward styles of focusing. They rehearsed material, then intentionally performed it in a different space or with different music, lighting, costumes. They subjected everyday movement to

other classic devices for reconfiguring the familiar so as to give it strange-
ness: exaggeration, interruption, incongruous fit, metacommentary, and un-
derstatement. Even dancing could be art renewed, provided it was thrust
out of its accustomed locations, effects, conventions, and attitudes.

Paradoxically, this work was almost never the simple, spontaneous, and
uncrafted event that it seemed. When movement looked free, it was often
governed by rules or restricted by sets, costumes, or props designed to prevent total spontaneity. When movement was improvised, it had to stay
within a preset range of choices and decisions. The events of the early
dance avant-garde relied on a delicate balance between control and abandon, discipline and anarchy. The successful reform of dance aesthetics
would depend on performers with mind, imagination, and a gift for
collaboration—a sensitivity to the whole event, a responsiveness to their
fellow performers, and a highly developed ability to relinquish their ego demands for the sake of the work.

Only a few months before Tharp's Judson concert, Yvonne Rainer, the
recognized goddess of downtown dance, had stunned the Judson audience
with *Parts of Some Sextets*, a concert of "simple, undistinctive activities made
momentous through their inaccessibility." Rainer published her reflections
on this work in *TDR*, the journal of progressive theater that was still being
published at Tulane University but was soon to move to Greenwich Village
and New York University. *Parts of Some Sextets* was probably the biggest and
best known of the avant-garde dance works of the '60s. Rainer described the
challenge of the piece: ". . . how to move in the spaces between theatrical
bloat with its burden of dramatic psychological 'meaning'—and—the imagery and atmospheric effects of the non-dramatic, non-verbal theatre (i.e.
dancing and some 'happenings')—and—theatre of spectator participation
and/or assault."

Rainer spelled out a whole list of now-unacceptable resources: "NO to
spectacle no to virtuosity no to transformations and magic and make-
believe no to the glamour and transcendency of the star image no to the
heroic no to the antiheroic no to trash imagery no to involvement of performer or spectator no to style no to camp no to seduction of spectator by
the wiles of the performer no to eccentricity no to moving or being moved."
This extraordinary statement became, oddly, both a denial and a revelation.
Seeming to rule out the whole spectrum of dance possibilities, it nevertheless opened up enough new thoughts to inspire the next generation. By the
time it became the manifesto of what was to be called postmodern dance,

Rainer had already violated some of its precepts and moved into filmmaking.

After the last of Robert Dunn's classes, in 1964, the population of Judson Dance held together for a while. Concerts were given at the church by members of the original workshops and by newcomers like Tharp, Meredith Monk, and Kenneth King, all of whom were in college during the workshop years. Rainer gathered her closest Judson associates and formed the improvisational group Grand Union. People gave independent concerts at Judson and elsewhere, digging into the particular aspects of the new liberation that interested them. People returned to their original specialties—painting, plastic arts, dance—with new perspectives. Gradually "postmodernism" emerged from anarchy. Structure and objectivity got more serious. Tharp had these from the beginning. A loner by instinct, she avoided existing centers of the avant-garde, but she shared the utopian impulse toward community, and built a succession of dance communities around her own ideas.

Twyla Tharp went along with the everyday. Uneasily. She wanted to dance and make dances. She continued going to the most exacting classes she could find, mainly at Merce Cunningham's studio, but in her choreography she suppressed the inordinate amount of technical training she had put her body through since childhood. As demanded by the NO imperative, she stipulated walking, hopping, rolling on the floor. But the apparent pedestrianism of the movements was tightened down with rigorous instructions. Everything was meticulously counted, detailed, and spaced. In *Re-Moves*, when Rudner came off the rope ladder, she had to walk backwards on her toes, making a figure eight through the room, avoiding whatever audience members were seated in her path, and eventually fold herself down into the same position on the floor that she'd taken at the end of her descent. She walked around the perimeter of the space, toe to heel, inside the hoop, while Tharp and Jenkins went down to the floor and rose in alternation. They took their timing from Rudner, who years later recalled their anxiety because she performed it much more slowly than in rehearsal.

Sara Rudner had danced most of her life but obliged her family by getting a degree in Russian literature from Barnard before allowing herself to imagine a dancing career. Tharp herself, an art history major, had graduated from the same college only a year before Rudner, having stolen as much time as possible from her academic studies to enroll in the full catalogue of dance classes the New York City studios had to offer. Rudner learned of Tharp's first concerts from her friend Margaret Jenkins.

Jenkins, after intensive training as a conventional modern dancer at the Juilliard School and UCLA, had found her ideal in Cunningham and Cage. When Tharp spotted her in Cunningham's technique class and enlisted her for the second Hunter College concert in 1965, Jenkins was dancing in the independent concerts of Cunningham company member Gus Solomons Jr. Tharp was an unknown in the firmament, but, according to Jenkins, "she was kind of a formidable physical presence in class and I had a lot of respect for how she worked."

She was formidable enough to attract reviewers, and both *The New York Times* and *Dance Magazine* reported on the second Hunter concerts, December 1, 2, and 3, 1965. The two works on the program were a continuation of the concerns outlined in *Tank Dive. Cede Blue Lake*, whose title came from a newspaper headline about the government's return of some land to a disfranchised Indian tribe, was called "a silent ritual" by *Dance Magazine*'s Marcia Marks.

In addition to classroom steps repeated and slightly varied, there were props engineered to evoke unlikely movement. Huot had built a slide from the balcony of the little theater to the stage, and Tharp and Jenkins made one of their several entrances that way. Jenkins remembers being wound in elastic or masking tape, and other performers unwinding it to reveal her costume. "I had to walk down backwards on the stairs, with elastic wrapped around my body. Or something that bound me. And I got to the bottom of the stairs and there was a very simple sequence to unwind the bindings. And then I had to go into a kind of deep parallel plié, go down to the floor on my back. I remember doing this backward somersault and I remember it because it was not easy for me." Marcia Marks also noted differences between the two performances. The winding tape, when pulled off Jenkins's body, left a white spiral on the first evening, a black one on the second. Someone dragged a cloth on the floor with her foot—people remembered it later as a paintbrush. At the second concert, the person just dragged a foot.

Bob Huot returned for the second time to his earlier performance piece, *War*. In *Tank Dive*, he had abstracted the gladiatorial duet to a single crouch and shoulder impact with fellow painter Christopher Constance. They looked like football players scrimmaging. For *Cede Blue Lake*, he and Constance, again costumed in heavily padded chest protectors and fencing masks, went at each other so vigorously in rehearsal that Constance was knocked out. Huot remembers performing alone because his partner had several stitches in his forehead. Barnes, reporting in the *Times*, said, "a man . . . indulged in some mock fantasy duel with himself while two girls gravely circled the main dance area."

Unprocessed, another almost-forgotten piece on the same program as *Cede Blue Lake*, had a cellophane or plastic canopy by Huot billowing over it. Marks thought Tharp was suggesting that the ballet, yoga, and athletic movements of the concert, common events in everyday experience, could be looked at in a new way through her "processing" of them.

Margy Jenkins continued dancing in Gus Solomons's performances until about 1967. Dancers, even those attached to major companies, didn't have full-time dance jobs. Choreographers would accumulate regular colleagues around them, who rehearsed when a concert was in prospect and looked for other opportunities. Jenkins says, "There certainly wasn't anything like being paid for what you did and everyone was very respectful of the fact that I would go up to CCNY in the morning from seven to eleven to model for art classes and then I'd rush to take class from Merce and then I'd go to rehearsal with Gus and then I'd work as a waitress and then I'd go work with Twyla. . . . That's what everybody did." Jenkins had taken over a $38.98-a-month apartment on Broome Street vacated by Solomons, and Rudner was her next-door neighbor. During a particularly impoverished period they put ballet barres near their windows and gave each other class across the airshaft between their apartments.

Rudner had been dancing with Paul Sanasardo, a choreographer in the Martha Graham/Anna Sokolow tradition. "It was very dramatic stories," Rudner says of Sanasardo's work. "We would be dressed in slips. We were sisters, and tossing our hair about, and doing things. I didn't have enough background to do that . . . I didn't understand what I was doing." Rudner had a clerical job and had considered giving up dancing more than once. Margy Jenkins suggested Tharp take a look at her in a recital when she needed another dancer for *Re-Moves*, and Tharp made up her mind immediately. She told Rudner to come to rehearsal and they tried out some things. Rudner's longing for dance that represented her own experience *and* challenged her finely developed dance intelligence found an answer in Twyla Tharp. "Thank *God* I'm walking!" she thought, when she got in the studio with Tharp.

Jenkins loved the extremes represented by Tharp's work and that of Solomons. She thought, "I've been trained for fifteen years and I'm walking around with a stopwatch. With Gus it was much more physically rigorous and with Twyla it was much more intellectually, conceptually rigorous." She too was fascinated with Tharp's imposition of paradoxical agendas—exactitude and release: "That I would spend my whole day trying to perfect where my leg was in relationship to my hip and get that kind of clarity that Merce has always demanded, and that I would then spend my evenings bound. I just loved the irony of it . . . being so bound and so restricted and kind of precise in ways that I had never ever had to do in any other kind of dancing. . . . And then the dropping of the egg for me—it was a fuck-you, but it felt like everything that was completely contained in our bodies and wrapped, contained within the egg, was just completely let go. But then the body could never let it go."

Tharp had the services of other friends for *Cede Blue Lake, Stride,* and *Tank Dive,* including Paul Taylor dancers Sharon Kinney and Renée Kimball, Graham dancer Jeanne Nuchtern, and downtown newcomers, Juilliard-trained Marcia Lerner and Art Bauman. But Jenkins and Rudner formed the first Tharp company. After they'd rehearsed for eight months preparing the Judson concert, she gave them each one hundred dollars. They were stunned.

Before all of these dancers, Tharp's first collaborator was Robert Huot, whom she lived with (and later married) at 104 Franklin Street. Huot was deep into the post-Beat art scene by the time he met Tharp. A follower and then denier of abstract expressionism, Huot was one of the artists included in the first important exhibition of minimal art, at the Hudson River Museum in October 1964, curated by his boss, E. C. Goossen, who chaired the Art Department at Hunter College. Besides providing Tharp with an entrée to the art world and its presenters, Huot influenced her thinking at this crucial time. A teenage habitué of Birdland and progressive jazz, Huot took her to clubs in the Village and shared his records of early jazz greats like Jelly Roll Morton. A sports fan, he took her to games and some of his costume designs for her were influenced by sports uniforms. He thought it might be possible to create a new barre exercise that would expand the dancer's movement range, and she incorporated some athletic movement in her first pieces, including a baseball slide in the last part of *Tank Dive.* Tharp was a socially recessive personality, but she quickly absorbed his jockish confidence.

2

Dance Activities

1967–1969

After the Judson concert, Tharp engineered a European tour. Typically, she was thinking big even though her resources were miniscule. She had two fine dancers in addition to herself, and an embryonic repertory—*Re-Moves* and *Tank Dive* seemed solid enough, and she started making new pieces. Jenkins and Rudner were delighted with the opportunity, and all of their parents helped pay their expenses. They hand carried their costumes and props, and, like thousands of young Americans backpacking around the world in those days, they stayed in whatever modest accommodations they encountered.

The infant company didn't have any professional management or office staff, but Tharp leveraged some crucial connections to put together the three-week round of galleries and studio spaces in Cologne, Stuttgart, The Hague, Amsterdam, Paris, and London. Bob Huot had exhibited his work in Germany and Switzerland, and he prepared the ground for Tharp with his dealer in Stuttgart. Robin Howard, the English impresario and patron of Martha Graham, had spotted Tharp's potential at the Judson concert. Despite his more conservative tastes, he thought she should be seen in the U.K. He arranged performances in Queen Alexandra's House at the Royal College of Music, and put up the little troupe in an apartment he owned during their stay in London. The Paris engagement was arranged by Bénédicte Pesle, an important European promoter of Merce Cunningham and a number of other avant-garde dancers. Pesle had also attended Tharp's Judson concert.

On February 15, 1967, tagged onto the end of a longer notice about the plans of Martha Graham's company, came an announcement in *The New York Times* that Tharp was embarking on a tour and would open the next day in Cologne. She may have been a minnow compared to the mighty Graham, but the *Times* headlined them as equals: "2 Dance Companies Will Visit Europe."

Bob Huot's influence pervaded the tour. In Germany and Holland his work as a minimalist was well-known, and his following of avant-garde art-goers probably constituted most of Tharp's audience. Huot had designed the sets and costumes for the repertory, and he had also helped conceptualize the dances. *One Two Three*, the first of two pieces Tharp made for the tour, was accompanied by football signals: "Ready, set! or hut two, hut three!" according to the sports-minded Huot. Tharp later described this as a "classical trio with long repetitive introduction built of fouettés en dehors and en dedans." Rudner remembered endless turns into arabesque, meticulously counted in odd-numbered sets, and a solo where she ran in circles and changed to movement in place without warning.

One Two Three represented Tharp's first overt linkage to Balanchine. When one dancer was doing her solo, one of the others would make "a crossover behind a scrim or curtain that was raised just high enough to see our sneakered feet," according to Rudner. Perhaps only a voracious art historian would have been aware of the startling way George Balanchine had carried out one of his first jobs in the West. He had joined Serge Diaghilev's Ballets Russes at the end of 1924 and two seasons later was assigned to do the entr'acte for Bronislava Nijinska's avant-garde *Romeo and Juliet*, designed by the surrealists Max Ernst and Joan Miró. The classic story was told within a modern-day ballet rehearsal, and the lovers eloped in an airplane at the end. Balanchine's contribution was to raise the act curtain just high enough for the audience to see the dancers' feet moving behind it, preparing for their next appearance. Tharp's 1967 dance antedated the revival of interest in Diaghilev by several years, and she has no recollection of this incident today, but if she wasn't quoting Balanchine deliberately, the coincidence was uncanny.

After two years of acting like a Judson dancer, Tharp was frustrated with denying or disguising what she wanted to do most of all, which was dancing. *Jam*, a "melodramatic trio," was later characterized by Rudner as "a total rage." Highway warning beacons flashed on one side of the space and glared from the other side with a relentless white beam, providing appropriate shock value. During the thirteen-minute piece, the dancers picked the lights up and aimed them around at one another. Merce Cunningham's *Winterbranch*, choreographed three years earlier, might have inspired this dramatic design. For that dance Robert Rauschenberg had created notorious effects with spotlights, alternately aimed into the eyes of the audience and turned off so that the stage went dark, while the dancers kept on doing the choreography.

In *Jam*, Tharp and Rudner performed intense, disjointed moves, while Jenkins had a more lyrical part. They all wore heavy, clear plastic jumpsuits over leotards. Says Rudner: ". . . when you took a step, [the costume] made this awful noise. And so while we were throwing a fit . . . it would be rattling and crunching and cracking." Tharp had choreographed the piece to James Brown's music, but it was danced in a crumpling-plastic silence. Rudner thought the title came from the jam they were in, longing to dance but having to somehow endorse the avant-gardist prohibition against dancing.

Jam had a New York preview on a concert at Columbia's Minor Latham Playhouse, part of the Barnard College Dance Uptown series. Tharp insisted that it be given the opening spot on the program, over the misgivings of the dance department. After an advance viewing, the faculty had tried to put the piece at the end, according to Rudner, "because they felt it would ruin your palate for the rest of the dances. At which point Twyla wanted to be the first on the program. Whatever she wanted. And she got what she wanted."

Tharp was acquiring a reputation for contrariness and ego. She certainly had a big sense of self, and a disconcerting but useful propensity to make last-minute changes. With an imagination unimpeded by the rules, she could improvise brilliant solutions to unanticipated roadblocks. In Paris, she discovered that the performing space at the American Center was smaller than the audience space, so she reversed the locations. She seated the audience on the stage and reserved the rest of the room for the dancers. In London, the audience's chairs were placed in a rectangle and the dancers moved around them. Some spectators, including one critic, refused to swivel around to follow the movement behind them, but John Percival got into the spirit of the event. Percival, who wrote for two important venues, *The Times* (London) and the periodical *Dance and Dancers*, was an early Tharp supporter. Like Robin Howard, he had great confidence in Tharp although he didn't really know why. Something about the London concert grabbed him. "I must say I found the evening rather fun. Which probably proves something rather odd about me, but I can't help it. I tried to be high-minded like other

people, but happiness kept breaking in. Could it be that she really *was* dancing after all?"

At the end of the tour, Margy Jenkins left the company. Jenkins had always been more attuned to Merce Cunningham than to Tharp, and her
silent hopes of getting into his company had received an unexpected boost.
The Cullberg Ballet of Stockholm had requested *Summerspace* for its repertory.
The 1958 work, with its pointillist costumes and backdrop by Rauschenberg,
was one of Cunningham's most harmonious dances. It had been set on the
New York City Ballet in the spring of 1966. This would be a rare occasion,
the first revival of a Cunningham dance in Europe and only the second time
he allowed his choreography to be performed outside of his own company.
He wondered if Jenkins would go to Sweden and teach it. Cunningham
didn't make any further commitment to Jenkins, but she felt the offer established a closer tie between them. In any case, she saw the opportunity as an
honor and an important personal challenge. She accepted the job.

Jenkins also felt, perhaps wrongly, she thinks now, that Tharp was moving away from her, toward developing Rudner's special abilities rather than
her own. After a post-tour vacation in Majorca with Rudner, she went on to
Stockholm. No one remembers now whether Jenkins purposely delayed
telling Tharp she wouldn't return after the Cullberg job or whether she herself didn't decide the break would be final until they parted company in
London. Tharp was hurt. The company had no immediate prospects, but
she had assumed Jenkins would continue working with her indefinitely.
Jenkins's departure was the first the company sustained, and as in many subsequent breakups, the warm relationship between Tharp and the defector
frosted over immediately.

The process of dancer turnover is a painful one for every company director and choreographer. Dancers grow and need to find their own identities; they want diversified experiences; they get injured doing one style and
feel they have to try another, or they need long therapeutic layoffs. They
leave, and especially in small, marginal groups, they leave a hole. Every role
in the repertory, every distinctive body in the studio, is essential. There are
few understudies, and when a dancer is gone, the company feels the loss
deeply. Knowing of the Stockholm possibility, Jenkins tried to ease the
transition by scouting a new dancer before leaving New York.

Theresa Dickinson, another highly intelligent dancer with an eclectic
background, got her B.A. from Radcliffe/Harvard. Her family disapproved of
dancing as a career. She had danced all her life but "I had given it up a few

times because smart people go to college and don't become dancers. The pressure was very intense from my family," who had "a puritanism about the intellect." Like Tharp and Rudner she was small and dark haired and quick. She had studied ballet as a child with Leon Fokine in Washington, but her teenage trajectory toward American Ballet Theater was cut short when her family moved to Philadelphia and she couldn't find any ballet teachers she liked. At Harvard she gravitated to the extracurricular theater group, where exciting new work was being done. There she became devoted to Robert Cohan of the Martha Graham company, who was teaching movement for actors. Having satisfied her family by graduating, she went off on her own for a year in Europe, then landed in New York, where she quickly shifted from Graham classes to Cunningham. She became friends with Margy Jenkins, who urged her to see Tharp's Judson concert.

Dickinson knew Tharp casually from Cunningham classes. The scene after the Judson concert is imprinted on her mind. "Twyla's sitting there smoking furiously and looking very uptight because the show has just finished and I'm the first person backstage afterwards, and she's kind of hunched over with the cigarette going in and out of her mouth real fast. And I said, Oh I loved the show and do you want any other dancers, can I dance with you? And she said, Yes. And that was the end of the conversation." Dickinson started rehearsing soon after that.

Tharp got what she wanted out of the tour: international recognition from critics, and the inevitable cachet conferred by foreign appearances. The audiences were small but influential—artists and patrons who would spread Tharp's name among the culturati. With opportunities to perform out of town as well as an occasional New York concert booking, she settled down to a period of exploration. Two tall women joined the company, blond and beautiful Margery Tupling, a Connecticut College graduate; and Carol Laudenslager (now Carolyn Lord), a ballet dancer and graduate of the University of Chicago. Tharp still relied on Bob Huot's contribution of costume and set designs, but she grew increasingly confident about her dance focus. Serious viewers got past their initial impression of her as an offbeat character, an individualist with promise, and started taking notice of her special gifts for movement and choreography.

Jill Johnston, the dance critic of the *Village Voice*, went to a concert in the gym at Wagner College in Staten Island (9 February, 1968), and devoted a

thoughtful and admiring column to Tharp. In her literary pose of the innocent but receptive dancegoer, Johnston claimed she didn't know anything
much about Tharp, but "this girl is no drooping daisy." She appreciated the
movement most of all, and gave a detailed description of the program. Although she could see Tharp probing various choreographic approaches, "I'm
more impressed by the extraordinary range of movement and her performing
assets: Cool confident commanding aggressive relaxed and a bit of a hostile
'damned what you think, I know that I'm good' sort of thing."

Johnston's interests were already veering away from dance and, after
what she describes as a kind of breakdown, she had committed herself to
personal journalism. The 1968 column is apparently the only time she reviewed Tharp. She left the *Voice* a year later and was succeeded by Deborah
Jowitt. But Johnston wasn't the only follower of downtown dance to skim
over Tharp. When the evolved Judson dance became canonized as "postmodern dance," with Sally Banes's 1980 survey, *Terpsichore in Sneakers*, Tharp
wasn't even included. It might have been her dance emphasis that distanced
her from the post-Judson avant-gardists. Her poorly hidden ambition didn't
endear her to the determinedly dirt-poor avant-garde either.

But she couldn't be ignored. She was asked to appear on several shared
concerts during the late '60s. She was still doing pieces that defied conventional definitions, and she thought of everything as a potential for extending dance. At C. W. Post College on Long Island in 1967 she did *Forevermore*,
which she later described as a "three and a half minute spectacular for
soloist, trio, and two marching snare drummers." In a balcony above the
main performing space, Tupling, wearing a long black dress, walked in a circle, fell to the floor and rose again, rolled and unrolled her long blond hair,
in a calm but somehow glamourous sequence. Meanwhile, Tharp, Rudner,
and Dickinson, wearing leotards with sequins, ran and jumped in increasingly larger circles on the gym floor below. The drummers simply entered,
crossed the space, and left, producing a sound that got louder and then re-
ceded. The dance may have struck the audience as repetitious, or pure
Dada, but Rudner described it as "highly controlled and choreographed.
Very formal, very beautiful, very simple, very direct."

There were other eccentric gestures, but they became fewer, and were
always justified in relationship to the surrounding movement ideas. *Disperse*,
a twenty-one-minute dance from 1967, explored the idea of compression.
Each of the five sections used a successively smaller amount of space and
time. There was no music but the dancers called out numbers seemingly at

random. Blackouts signaled the start of each new section, and one reviewer thought Tharp was using "light and absence of it as a metrical accompaniment." The movement began with twisted turns and stops on relevé, each dancer using a slightly different speed and personal accent, and became more and more detailed as the dancers worked more tightly together. When the group had squeezed into a corner, Tharp brought out a red-painted wooden chair and smashed it. Later she said she was working on the idea of infinity: even when the space and time seemed used up, there would always theoretically be more possibilities. Breaking the chair, she said, represented "a little chaos in this pristine, artificially controlled world. Only the form of the chair was altered: its matter retained all its energy."

Discovering that Sullins College, where they were to perform in 1970, had a student body of girls and a faculty dominated by men, Tharp choreographed a solo for Graciela Figueroa, who was to dance it once topless and once bottomless. The series of solos into which this was inserted had an unpronounceable title taken from a newspaper misprint, *PYMFFYPPMFYPNM YPF.* The school threatened to cancel the performance, so when the time for the offending solo arrived, the dancers froze and Tharp clapped the appropriate counts. At intermission, Tharp announced that the piece would be repeated in its entirety, giving the fainthearted an opportunity to leave. No one left. She was trying out ideas of "duality," such as how the same movement would look with changes of clothing; perhaps nudity seemed a logical phase of the experiment. But even more daring and demanding, the movement itself had built-in contrasts. Rudner remembered a section in which the legs and arms were choreographed separately, at different speeds, and then performed together, in what they called the "slip phrase."

Like the rest of the avant-garde, Tharp had discovered that simple movement could go only so far in creating viable performances. Steve Paxton, Yvonne Rainer, and Simone Forti had exhausted pure pedestrianism in the first years of Judson. Having opened the audience's eyes to the diversity and even complexity of commonplace movement, they began to reattach theatrical elements: props and costumes, sublimated stories, references to animal behavior. The other downtown dancers adopted a wide range of devices for structuring ordinary, nontechnical movement in order to give the audience some thread of logic to follow. There were games, like Trisha Brown's *Falling Duets,* where one performer would start to fall without warning and another had to catch him or her before the first person hit the ground. There were tasks—performers had to build something or carry something, or, in one of the more elaborate plots, Ann Halprin's *Processions*, pick up objects that were strewn in their path and continue slowly across a predefined space as they coped with these encumbrances. Trisha Brown made dances where people had to maneuver through difficult environments. Deborah Hay made quasi–folk dances out of walking steps. Meredith Monk began to create childlike representations of historical characters.

All these strategies made for fascinating, often theatrical, experiences, but they conscientiously excluded the movement vocabularies of ballet and modern dance. During the '60s Tharp was almost alone in developing her work from a dance foundation. But she was in sync with the avant-garde in discarding conventional ways of constructing and presenting dance. She preferred nonproscenium spaces. She disliked thinking any one movement was more interesting than any other; she didn't work for rising and falling curves of excitement, dramatic climaxes, picturesque stage effects. If there was to be any thrill involved, it should come from the extraordinary range of challenges she threw at the dancers and the audience. What she was looking for was ways to move. The body plastique and externalized emotional states that had served the modern dancers didn't interest her, but ballet's rigor did. So did the expertise of athletes. Outside of a few French ballet terms, she talked about movement in everyday language, but she did not want people in her company to look like they had walked in off the street.

Tharp never organized her movement into a formal technique, and the concept of company class didn't exist for her dancers. They all took a daily class somewhere else. During the late '60s Tharp and several of the company members were going to the ballet teachers Richard Thomas and Barbara Fallis, who were noted for giving hard and intellectually provocative combinations. Working with her own dancers, Tharp was didactic, conceptual, smart. But also intuitive and exceptionally physical.

She would begin each day working in the studio by herself, trying out movement ideas to music. By the time the dancers arrived, she would have a set of notes, often accompanied by diagrams, drawings, and charts, and for the next several hours they would develop these ideas. She would teach a turn, for instance, and then the dancers would manipulate the movement— repeat it, do it in different directions or on opposite sides of the body, change the rhythm, do the segments of it in scrambled order, or throw the whole thing into retrograde. She drew on compositional techniques of music, film editing, and an acute instinct for pushing the physical envelope. All her dancers knew that more was being demanded of them than they had ever experienced. Jenkins thought "it was incredibly invigorating, and very very challenging to use the mind in that way." Dickinson was "very attracted to Twyla's almost mystical interest in math, in rational proportions and fractionalizing things. . . . I was extremely excited by that relationship, between the intellectual reason for dancing and the physical reason for dancing."

Tharp was making movement so highly developed that the dancers had to stretch to process it. Some were adept at picking up her train of thought as the ideas poured out of her body; others had to take the movement apart more meticulously in order to learn it. Theresa Dickinson and Carol Laudenslager, who were less kinesthetically quick than Rudner or Tupling, did master Tharp's complexities in their own ways. Dickinson remembers rushing into Merce Cunningham's advanced class with Laudenslager, late one afternoon after Tharp's rehearsal. Cunningham was teaching an exercise, and both of them did it immediately, twice as fast. Another time, after being invited to a rehearsal, dancers from the Cunningham company marveled at the speed of Tharp's dancers. "They said that we were working at a level that they didn't think they could do," says Dickinson.

An obsessive student and consumer of information, Tharp was creating material so fast that she had to develop some mental storage banks to allow her to change things without backtracking or interrupting the flow of collective invention. In college she had made use of the shorthand lessons her mother had pressed on her, by taking notes in class, then carefully transcribing them at night so that she would retain all the professors' words. She thought of choreographing as problem solving; she approached rehearsing and even performing as lessons to be learned. Early in the 1970s, when video recording equipment hit the market, Tharp acquired a primitive Panasonic and began taping rehearsals. This didn't necessarily save any time for her—when she was choreographing she would spend her evenings reviewing the day's output and extracting the useful material. But it did mean that nothing got lost.

When Tharp was picked by producer Charles Reinhart to do a split week at the Billy Rose Theater in February of 1969, with Yvonne Rainer, Meredith Monk, and Don Redlich, she had clearly arrived in another league. The Billy Rose concerts were part of a prestigious series of modern dance companies under the aegis of Richard Barr and Edward Albee's Theater 1969, and Tharp, Rainer, Redlich, and Monk represented the most important directions Reinhart thought new dance was taking. This was the first Broadway engagement for all four groups. Tharp made the cover of *Dance Maga-zine*, eccentrically bent into a right angle for *Tank Dive*, to publicize the Billy Rose series, and the younger generation scowled at photographer Jack Mitchell in a tense, historic family portrait for *The New York Times*, with Martha Graham at the center, and Merce Cunningham, José Limón, and Er-ick Hawkins completing the picture.

But downtown, according to Theresa Dickinson, "There was a little bit of contempt for those of us who counted and wore leg warmers. . . . We were not supposed to take ballet classes or count, anymore. That was out. Judson dancers wore regular clothes, dirty and tattered. . . . It was part of their ethos to not do these hyper-tight little tricky moves. That was exactly what they were legislating against. So in that sense we felt very isolated. I still see us as being in between cycles." *The New York Times* assigned its junior dance critic to the Tharp evening at the Billy Rose instead of Clive Barnes, and Anna Kissel-goff seemed caught on the edge between Tharp's "cool detached style" and "the high level of energy [that] left anything but a cool impression."

The Billy Rose season was immediately followed by a series called "Works for an Open Space," *Generation and Group Activities*, at the Brooklyn Academy Opera House. One of the important assets Theresa Dickinson had brought to the young company was her partner, Lewis Lloyd, then an administrator at the Cunningham Dance Foundation. Lloyd set up the ma-chinery for the foundation to accept funds for Tharp, since she had no ap-paratus of her own for doing that, and he acted as an unofficial manager for a couple of years. In the fall of 1969 he became general manager at the Brooklyn Academy of Music, where a very active dance program was get-ting under way under a former modern dancer, Harvey Lichtenstein. Lloyd may have been instrumental in booking Tharp into the Opera House. As she had in Paris, Tharp dislodged the audience from its usual viewing seats. This time she made room for spectators right on the large stage with the dancers. This novel arrangement attracted attention in itself, but it also al-lowed the dances to be seen from two sides, in closeup, without the inter-vention of the proscenium and orchestra pit.

These two engagements established Tharp as a major player and a cho-reographer of repertory. Despite her assertions that repertory didn't interest her, she had by 1969 made five important dances in addition to *Re-Moves*: *Disperse; Generation; Excess, Idle, Surplus; After "Suite," and Group Activities*. These were unapologetically dance pieces, exhausting and stark except for Huot's fine costumes. There was enough consistency among them for the audience to see Tharp's emerging movement style: highly flexible, exacting, objective, and unpredictable, with an inner-focused sensuality.

Generation was five solo dances performed together. At certain moments in the choreography the dancers had to coordinate their timing, but mainly they concentrated on their own movement rather than on interacting. Tharp thought of it as the first dance where she "dealt with movement as any kind of working material." She played Beethoven records—the *Apassionata Sonata* and the thirty-two Variations, Op. 191—while choreographing some of the solos, but the dance was always performed in silence. Tharp played music incessantly and almost indiscriminately, often basing her phrases or other structures on what she heard, then discarding the musical prompt. When Anna Kisselgoff saw *Generation* at the Billy Rose, she noted the "centered balletic movements."

Tharp was making *Generation* when Carol Laudenslager entered the company; she and other dancers later realized that Tharp had specifically been looking for someone with ballet training, and probably Laudenslager's solo was intended as a contrast with those of Rudner, Dickinson, Tupling, and Tharp. As Laudenslager/Lord remembers it now, she had a lot of ballet movements, speeded up and without the conventional orientation to a single front. "It wasn't really close enough to ballet to feel familiar in that sense," Lord says. "It felt foreign on me because it was a little freer and thrown around than I had been used to." She had trouble getting the "feel for the flow of the fall or the throw or the drop of the weight," but after months of rehearsal, she was comfortable enough to do a short improvised section at the end of the solo.

Huot designed sleeveless jumpsuits for the piece, in a different tone and texture of silver fabric for each dancer. They rehearsed it from the spring, after returning from the European tour, until its scheduled premiere in February of 1968. Bob Huot had secured them an engagement at his alma mater, Wagner College on Staten Island. *Generation* was laid out for the Wagner gym. The concert included a severe reconfiguration of that large open space, *One Way*, in which the dancers crossed and recrossed the floor with repeated preset stepping patterns, keeping within lanes like swimmers or sprinters, while Tharp zigzagged around and through them. The costumes were blue velvet tunics with long, Pierrot-esque sleeves.

After Wagner College there was another rehearsal period, leading to a performance at Notre Dame University in the spring. The new piece was *Excess, Idle, Surplus*, a "Quintet in three sections: 'Excess' being five 7-minute solos performed simultaneously; 'Idle,' a lyric stream lit by the projected beam of Hollis Frampton's 16 mm film 'Information' running overhead; 'Surplus,' an isorhythmic re-structuring of the movement in 'Excess'." Tharp may have been building on the ideas in *Generation,* or she may have actually folded the basics of *Generation* into the later piece. The movement for the first section involved traveling and then holding still for diminishing numbers of seconds. Tharp remembered it as "very very dancey and very complex movement."

In Part II the decor was by avant-gardist Hollis Frampton, a friend of Bob Huot, who made what film historian Gerald Mast called "logical exercises." The dancers remembered his film as a bright white beam coming from above. Jennifer Tipton, who had lit all of Tharp's work since *Tank Dive,* was credited with the lighting design, a cloud of smoke drifting across the space and into Frampton's projection. Lacking a smoke machine, the Notre Dame stagehands were instructed to exhale their cigars and cigarettes in the direction of the dance space. The dancers, individually twisting and turning, moved slowly together in a clump, down a diagonal through the smoky space. Morton Feldman's music accompanied this middle section. In the last section a tape of the dancers' voices during a rehearsal was the only accompaniment.

The dancers liked *After "Suite"* best of all the works of this period. A tribute to Merce Cunningham's *Suite for Five,* the piece once again brought out the attributes of the dancers in individually choreographed solos. Its main distinction was its spatial construction, ". . . performed in three adjacent squares. As each section of the work is completed, it is immediately repeated in an adjacent square as a variant of itself." The dance's overall form was to be an "arrangement of many situations—never completely developed at one time, constantly interrupting one another thus providing for repetition • variation • development." Tharp arrived at rehearsals with fiendish counted patterns, different for all the dancers. Rudner felt like an overloaded computer, processing all this "neurological information." There were flowing silk flesh-color pajamas by Huot, and no score except a metronome. At the Brooklyn Academy performances, Sharon Kinney, Tharp's old friend from her Paul Taylor company days, sat at a table and called out counts when a dancer asked for her place.

As choreographing for *Group Activities* began in the fall of 1968, Carol Laudenslager was becoming increasingly uncomfortable with Tharp's demands. She felt too inexperienced to keep up with the other dancers in learning the work, and Tharp let her know she would have liked a higher energy level from the newcomer. When she took Laudenslager out of *Generation* and replaced her with Rose Marie Wright, Laudenslager thought it was time to leave.

Wright was the ideal dancer for Tharp's needs at that point, and she soon proved invaluable in ways no one had anticipated. Gifted with impeccable technique and a willingness to try anything, she possessed an indelible memory for movement as well. She soon became the company's informal archivist, mental notator, and coach, a reference source for anything the rest of them had forgotten. Already a seasoned performer at twenty, Wright had been a teenaged member of the Pennsylvania Ballet, but she became stalled on the way to solo roles because of her height, six feet in flat shoes. Tharp spied her in Richard Thomas's class. She thought Wright would be too professional to bother with an obscure modern company that spent most of its time in unpaid rehearsals, so with Thomas's collusion she staged a fake audition and got Wright to attend. Wright found her way to the designated Harlem gym and saw immediately that this was serious dancing. She prayed that she would be accepted, and Tharp in turn could hardly restrain herself. She and Dickinson ran into the dressing room and made Wright an offer before she had time to get into her street clothes.

Two other new dancers arrived around the same time, Sheila Raj, a tiny Indo-English powerhouse, and Graciela Figueroa, a solidly built Uruguayan with folk-dance training. The roster stood at seven, and Tharp felt expansive. *Group Activities* started as a quintet but for the Brooklyn Academy performances she doubled the forces, adding a couple of extras. She herself didn't dance in the piece in Brooklyn; she was going through a period of sitting in the audience, finding out what her dances looked like to different eyes. For the expanded version of *Group Activities* she assigned each of the original five dancers an "analog" to whom the originator was to teach her part. The dance was made up of quite individual parts anyway, and this procedure spared Tharp from having to teach the whole thing herself. The device of doubling, apart from its practical advantages, became an effective choreographic tool in many later dances.

In its quintet-version premiere at the Philadelphia Theater of Living Arts, *Group Activities* impressed the critics, along with *Disperse* and *Excess, Idle, Surplus,* as "enigmatic but forceful," "organized spontaneity." But once doubled and released from the proscenium focus, at BAM, *Group Activities* became even more disconcerting. Tharp described a "Double quintet in which each group occupies a gridded area 20' × 40'. In order that one group will be an accurate duplication of the other, a metronome runs through the work's 40 minutes." From this tart description one might imagine two neat ensembles working companionably side by side, but Tharp refused to map out the dance so that it would be conventionally visible.

With the dancers facing different directions and moving individually but simultaneously, *Group Activities* didn't look amplified or inflated in any known stage sense. The twin groups intermeshed so that they became untrackable. The dance looked wayward, willful, scattered, but somehow fascinating. Cunningham too had abandoned strict frontality in his stage arrangements, but he left most of the other organizing rules of his game to be determined by chance operations, so his dance was in a way more consistent. Tharp's dance was contradictory and that gave it an extra edge. You couldn't dismiss someone who would choreograph an exacting structural scheme while at the same time exploding the stage's most trusted visual code.

Tharp liked the comment of Arlene Croce best of all the favorable reviews that followed the concert: "Watching a piece like *Group Activities*, one has the feeling of having emerged on the other side of some barrier to perception . . . brilliantly irrational to the eye. I know only two other choreographers who give the same effect, and they're Mr. B. and Merce."

These years generated a tremendous exhilaration in the dancers. It wasn't so much the successful performances or the increasing respect they were earning from the press, but the work in the studio with Tharp, weeks and months on end, exploring, exerting, exceeding themselves, that acted like a marathon runner's endorphin high. "We weren't thinking about getting famous, we weren't thinking about getting paid . . . we were just doing the work," says Wright. Dickinson had an "extreme moment of Nirvana" one day, working with Rudner on a piece she no longer remembers the name of. "Just the two of us, this endless kind of getting it right, counting it again, going over it again, making these little junctures in the pattern of the rhythms." And Tharp speaks almost blissfully about the fellowship that held the company together. "We knew one another's abilities and sensibilities so well that each of us became an extension of the others, moving as a genuine team of spirit as well as body." Rudner thought "The things we worked on were so inspiring for dancers . . . they weren't only dances. They were prayers. They were ways of investigating your own self."

3

The End of Amazonia

1969–1971

The avant-garde was spreading out. After finding alternatives to prosce-nium spaces in gyms and churches, they invaded outdoor plazas, col-lege campuses, parks, forests, fields, and swimming pools. The definition of dance opened up to make room for pretty much anything that moved with a purpose, but technique was still taboo. When one looks back on the late '60s and early '70s, it seems like a period of wonderful, eye-opening enter-tainments and games—motorcycles paraded in formation, people slunk across lawns like tigers, peculiar behaviors were enacted in skyscraper win-dows. Many prechoreographed dances got transposed into unorthodox spaces, and many spaces suggested their own nondance movement. Trisha Brown made the most dazzling synthesis of movement and environment, in *Man Walking Down the Side of a Building*, *Walking on the Wall*, *Floor of the Forest*, *Planes*, and *Roof Piece* from the early '70s. But however effectively they stretched the perceptions of the audience, not even Brown's environmental pieces represented an expansion of technical dancing. She returned to the stage and to a self-invented dance vocabulary in the mid-1970s.

As the avant-garde was becoming less anarchistic, more serious and crafts-manlike, the modern dance was receding. Established at Connecticut College in 1948 as a successor to the pioneering Bennington School of Dance, the American Dance Festival and its School of Dance now represented a modern old guard, caught between the paroxysms of the counterculture and the perceived regressiveness of ballet. Two of the pillars of modern dance pedagogy had died, Doris Humphrey in 1958 and Louis Horst in 1964, but their teachings lingered on under the guidance of others. Martha Graham and José Limón controlled the school's faculty and dominated ADF performances. Merce Cunningham, Alwin Nikolais, and other mature dissenting choreographers made only rare appearances, and the younger revolutionaries hadn't been able to get a foot in the door. The festival and school were experiencing lower enrollments and smaller audiences. When Charles Reinhart took over the directorship in 1969, he acknowledged the shifting scene with a big overhaul.

Reinhart felt a clean sweep was necessary, and the committee of festival overseers gave him their blessing to try. All the staples of technique and composition that had served the School of Dance since its inception were swept away, though many of the basic offerings were later reinstated. José Limón reluctantly took the summer off from both school and festival, and his teaching disciples left the scene too. Martha Graham was represented by only two technique teachers, June Lewis and Richard Kuch, and the Graham and Limón choreography classes virtually disappeared, along with the compositional "forms" courses developed in the 1930s by Louis Horst. For the first time, ballet and jazz technique appeared, and an array of avant-garde–related courses took the place of the traditional curriculum for dance educators and musicians. Paul Taylor and Alvin Ailey, the youngest of the major modern dancers, held on to their presence, but the Festival wore a drastically different look. Ailey contributed the only important new stage work of the summer, *Masekela Langage*, while Taylor showed a work in progress as his only premiere. The other performances included works by outsiders Talley Beatty, James Clouser, James Cunningham, Yvonne Rainer, and Tharp.

Charles Reinhart had known Tharp since her association with Paul Taylor—he had been representing Taylor as a manager and producer since the early '60s. He recognized in Tharp's earliest work a rapprochement between classicism and the avant-garde, and as planning began for the 1969 American Dance Festival, he proposed Tharp for the festival's prestigious Doris Humphrey Choreographic Fellowship. The jury drew the line at this, and no award was made that year. Nevertheless he found a $10,000 commission, part of a larger grant from the National Endowment for the Arts, that brought the Tharps, as well as dancers from the companies of Rainer, Taylor, and Ailey, to teach on the campus for two weeks prior to their performance. This boon allowed Tharp's dancers to go on "salary"—thirty dollars a week, for twenty weeks, long enough to qualify them for fourteen dollars a week in unemployment compensation. After rehearsals in New York, Tharp and the company arrived on the campus in New London, to work with thirty-three students from the Festival who were to complete the expansive and beautiful piece *Medley*.

Following her emergence into the public eye at the Billy Rose and BAM, Tharp had sustained the first serious attack of a malady from which she never entirely recovered: the horror of stagnation. Having made four years' worth of successful dances, she began to feel pinned down by them. She writes in her autobiography that she feared "we would find we couldn't live up to our reputation; we would get too many proscenium opportunities and become caught in our repertory, chewing the gum long after the flavor was gone; we would lose our creativity, which maybe came only with being outside the system. . . . I sensed we were spinning our wheels." To combat her own sense of impending boredom—it doesn't seem to have affected the dancers—she developed a choreographic scheme for Connecticut that would not only showcase the company but deploy a small army of performers across a vast empty field.

Medley began and ended without fanfare, or even punctuation. The dance was in progress as the audience arrived to sit on the grass in front of the college art museum, and it finished long after the spectators had left to attend Rainer's gymnasium piece, *Connecticut Composite*, on the other side of the campus. Tharp later said she wanted to blur the distinctions between art and life. This was still a mantra of the avant-garde, but Tharp gave it a unique interpretation. *Medley*'s casual beginning and ending made it seem that the dance had been there all along, waiting for the audience to arrive and turn it into a performance. The work unfolded in a series of set-pieces meant to integrate performing into the open-field setting, to bring students into a relationship with the members of the company, to incorporate the audience's movements into the choreography, and, in a final series of long adagio solos, to present each company dancer's special qualities.

In some notes written while she was working on the piece, Tharp wondered how to bring out what was natural to a dancer, how to provide technical challenges to each dancer's personal preferences. To what extent did the choreographer's instructions enhance or interfere with the dancer's own presence? And if each dancer's choreographic material encouraged her to be herself—or her ideal self—then how would this group of individuals be able to relate to each other when dancing together, and how could you be sure they'd all be equally appreciated by the audience? She considered "natural" movement potentialities: improvisation, everyday gesture or action, technique done in the nude. She made the movement for one section by having the dancers "learn" their own movements from videotapes of themselves as they casually prepared for rehearsal in the studio. Each of the six dancers then became captain of a team of students, who learned the learned naturalism.

Influenced by Merce Cunningham's techniques of chance and indeterminacy, Tharp considered building in moments when the dancers would have to make split-second decisions, inevitably revealing their reactions and adaptations as "a dramatic situation." But everything would need to be formalized at some point or else the audience would become bored. She needed to "do away with the pretension that a 'new' piece is anything other than a continuation of all the work . . . a progression, development, standstill or denial."

Medley turned out to be a mind-bending experience for those who saw it—not only original but sensually pleasing. Tharp's exacting compositional structure seemed released in the huge open-field space, so that the piece looked more free-form than it actually was. After the preliminaries, including a pointe solo danced by Rose Marie Wright on a square of plywood set down in the grass, there were several mass effects. A group of students imitated Theresa Dickinson, who picked up the audience's actions as they arrived. Sheila Raj's "gnat" solo gave her the fastest movement possible, and a group of thirty students backed her up with "staccato chunks" of the variation. Tharp dubbed this the "movement machine." The most stunning effect came from a witty, contrary, typically Tharpian manipulation of movement. All six company dancers and thirty-three students spread out over the whole field. They were given a phrase that probably took less than a minute to perform, but each person used his or her slowest personal timing— Theresa Dickinson could draw it out to as long as forty-five minutes. The audience was confronted with a field of virtual statues, imperceptibly changing their positions. If you focused on one individual, the person would be moving too slowly to catch the change; only by looking away, then back, would any shift be apparent. The choreographed phrase simply disappeared, and the image emerged, satisfying and provocative.

Besides the planned indeterminacy in the piece, there were things Tharp couldn't control, and she felt it went wrong at the end. She had timed the entire piece so that the final Adagio solos would start precisely at sunset and end in darkness. This would have provided another perceptual revelation for the audience, the eye-opening effect of discovering how much one can continue to see in a gradually diminishing light. Not only did the audience leave for Rainer's scheduled performance but the dancers were attacked by mosquitoes and Tharp finally moved the remaining solos indoors. The dance finished in Windham House, a dormitory, where the postperformance party was going on. As Reinhart remembers it, he came upon Sara Rudner in a closet when he was looking for the men's room. Actually, Rudner was dancing for a few rapt onlookers in one of the dorm's public spaces, perhaps a dining room that had been cleared out for summer use as a studio. Tharp spent the rest of the evening in her room with a filched bottle of gin, inexplicably depressed and lonely for Bob Huot, who had stayed in New York. She hadn't danced in *Medley*. It wasn't the first time she'd chosen to watch her work from the audience, but this was the biggest thing she'd done and she felt she'd made herself superfluous.

Medley was a milestone in Tharp's career—not only because it succeeded so well as a dance integrated into a unique natural setting. It satisfied her appetite for gigantism, and she went on to imagine other large-scale projects, at least two of which were soon realized. But in spite of this success, environmental work wasn't really where she wanted to go. She spent the next two years exploring the conceptual questions that had come up while making *Medley*, never hesitating to put her research before the public in innovative formats both on and off the stage.

Tharp loved structure and she loved the working process. She could be in the studio six hours a day with the dancers, trying out phrases, then go home and write pages of new combinations. For example, her notes during the spring of 1969 could be simple:

> small relevés + head scratching sequence
> Balanchine 4th
> . . . back walk + slide bkwds
> sit on bottom
> dead kipp
> finger
> Look out for
> dance sequences
> that exist
> only for their
> complexity

Or minutely detailed:

Arrange 55 torso mvts 116 mvts of the legs for 30 people over 90 secs. Put moves into groups of 10 torso mvts/20 leg mvt. Leg mvts will be basically in place, but when they travel time must be allowed for dancer to return to place. Each set of 10TM/20LM (and leftover 5/26) will be distributed over 15 secs

Her tremendous capacity for invention was humanized by her unconde-scending inclusiveness. She thought football players and tap dancers moved beautifully. She liked to give vernacular names to things the dancers were learning; sections of *Medley*, for instance, were called "Street Moves," "Lay-outs (put-downs)" and "Audience pick-ups." She seldom visualized in terms of a technical dance vocabulary. She may have chosen the most exacting dance techniques for herself—ballet and Cunningham—but she respected whatever her dancers brought with them, as long as they could move with fluency from fundamental movement instructions. Not only the company dancers in *Medley* but students, audience members, and passersby could have their movements incorporated, subject to the utmost physical refining. For Tharp, the axiomatic pedestrianism of the avant-garde was not an end in it-self but a beginning of dancemaking. She thought in order to make dancing recognizable, it should be like "a near relative, not a distant European cousin," and that mirroring the daily movements of themselves or the audi-ence was the first step toward this recognition. "As dancers we had to first be mundane, before we could buy into the heavenly."

At the end of the summer, *Medley* was performed again in New York's Central Park, with an even bigger complement of extras. Contending with the usual occupants of the Great Lawn—Frisbee players, joggers, bikers, mounted policemen, ball games, and strolling civilians—gave the dancers a more realistic chance to test their art-is-life proposition. This time, Tharp's desired effect of having the piece end in gradually diminishing light was ac-complished, with an added flutter of alarm for some viewers, as darkness swallowed up the faraway dancers. *The New York Times*'s Anna Kisselgoff called the Adagio "a masterly coup . . . an impression of richness in sparseness."

As Tharp started the next big project, her working and living situations be-gan to change. Within half a year, four of the six dancers withdrew from the company. Sheila Raj and Graciela Figueroa were both having visa problems which would force them to leave the country by early 1970. Margery Tupling married and moved away. Theresa Dickinson, who had been with Tharp since

1966, was drifting away too. Dickinson relished the way Tharp combined rigorous dancing with pedestrianism. She was excited by the challenges Tharp constantly threw at the dancers' bodies and minds. But she felt "a mounting density of movement and images that was more pressured than I enjoyed." She saw Tharp's ambition as pulling the company toward theatrical dancing and respectability. "Twyla wanted to be famous and important. . . . She thought it was terribly important to be successful young, so that she wouldn't struggle for a long time in obscurity and then feel obligated to repeat a success when it happened." Dickinson reflects that the dancers themselves were changing. "We had acquired a certain amount of centrifugal force as a group . . . we were gaining power as dancers and as people, both because time had passed and because the work we were doing was so thrilling to us. . . . I think *Medley* gave us tastes of who we could be in other ways."

Dickinson was happy with parts of *Medley*, "the lovely long areas" of slowness and the "expansive, sort of running waltz material that was just beautiful beyond belief." But she dreaded going back to the confinement of long hours in the studio. Attracted to the more free-floating, hippie lifestyle, Dickinson wanted to leave New York. Her marriage to Lewis Lloyd was breaking up, and at the end of the summer, after *Medley* in Central Park, she took off for San Francisco.

Meanwhile, Bob Huot had received a grant from the National Endowment for the Arts. After some hesitation, he decided to keep it when friends convinced him that turning it back in protest over the Vietnam War would be a mistake. In September of 1969 he used it, together with a loan from Tharp's parents, for a down payment on a 215-acre farm in New Berlin, New York, a four-hour drive from New York City. Huot thinks Tharp didn't really want to move to the farm, but she agreed when he asked if she liked the big old house and its rolling fields. For the winter term he managed to compress his full-time teaching job at Hunter College into a three-day week, and after they moved upstate in January, he began commuting. He kept the loft on the fifth floor of 104 Franklin Street, where he and Tharp had been living and working. Putting her art-as-life concept to the ultimate test, Tharp hatched a spectacularly unrealistic scheme to relocate to New Berlin.

Before *Medley*'s second performance, she had started work on a new open-space piece, *Dancing in the Streets of London and Paris, Continued in Stockholm and Sometimes Madrid*, to be performed in Hartford, Connecticut, at the

Wadsworth Atheneum, a bastion of avant-garde arts in New England. Tharp's extravagant title seems to be a reference to another icon of modernism, the Blaise Cendrars/Sonia Delaunay *affiche*, *La Prose du Transsibérien et de la petite Jehanne de France*. Published in 1913 as the First Simultaneous Book, the seven-foot-long poem with color-swatch design describes a railway trip across Russia and its resonances. A cornerstone of collage aesthetics, the simultanist credo of Cendrars and Guillaume Apollinaire "requires that our minds entertain concurrently and without synthesis two or more contradictory propositions." Historian Stephen Kern calls Cendrars's verse "verbal montages [that] unite what is distant as if they were quick-cut camera directions," a collapsing of time and space made possible by modern engineering: "Now I've made all the trains run after me/Basel-Timbuktu/I've also played the horses at Auteuil and at Longchamps/Paris–New York/Now I've made all the trains run alongside my life/Madrid–Stockholm." Tharp had a similarly panoramic and contemporary project in mind.

None of the dancers remembers exactly how she got this opportunity, but the main connection was probably one of Bob Huot's admirers, Henry Geldzahler, who had become curator of twentieth-century art at the Metropolitan Museum of Art in New York. Geldzahler encouraged not only minimalists like Huot but experimental art, performance, and mixed media. He had appeared in happenings by Claes Oldenburg, narrated Jean Tinguely's "The Construction of Boston," and, as a friend and supporter of the Judson dancers, had also checked out Tharp's downtown concerts. At the end of 1969 he organized the Met's show of New York Painting and Sculpture 1940–1970, which was called "the last of the great '60s art spectaculars" by Calvin Tomkins, the chronicler of downtown art of the period. Around the same time, Geldzahler commissioned *Dancing in the Streets*, to be performed at the Met in January 1970. (Tharp says she talked him into it.) It's possible he made the contact for the first performance with James Elliott, director of the Wadsworth Atheneum, who was continuing the museum's avant-garde mission.

In Hartford, Tharp and the dancers took over the five galleries, and the auditorium passages, stairwells, elevators, and mop closets, according to one observer, for a variety of activities designed never to be seen intact because they would be going on simultaneously. Tharp thought of this polymorphic presentation as a dance analog to the pictures hanging in the separate galleries of a museum. Three cameras from Hartford's Channel 24 videoed the action like a news pickup, so the audience and the dancers could track it on monitors posted around the building. This in itself was a violation of the idea that a theatrical performance should occur in a sequestered space for the consumption of one privileged audience. Today, of course, lobby monitors are posted in major theaters for latecomers, and multiple cameras can broadcast live performances across the country. But this was unheard-of in 1969. Tharp gives several other reasons for using live television in the museum piece. For the big space of the Atheneum, she was acutely conscious of how few dancers she had, even with the addition of nine extra women. Video images would amplify the piece. The closed-circuit monitors would also reassure the crowd and encourage them to move around from one space to another.

Tharp felt that video gave credence to ordinary movement. "People are more accustomed to looking at movement on television and in film than they are [to] using their eyes on the street," she says. The frame of the TV screen rendered movement user-friendly, was her theory. She was still working out ways to make dancing more like life, or more acceptable as a life activity. A few days after the *Medley* performance at Connecticut College she was in Hartford "walking around the museum surreptitiously dropping moves, hiding them." She was acutely aware of the differences between conventional performance with its mandatory high audience visibility, and "invisible" dance, where the choreography would either be deliberately hidden (like the rehearsal inside the box in *Re-Moves*) or so minimal that the dancers would just seem to be casually moving around in sight of the audience. She mused about the psychic distance created when dancers were on a stage, and considered the intimacy that could occur when a dancer came upon a few people in a small space, "quietly watching a monitor or talking. Do a small something for them."

Tharp isn't fond of teaching but she's a dedicated explainer. She can be owlishly didactic—one of her dancers saw her as a nerd in disguise—and also lucid, erudite, ironic, funny, and occasionally profound in her attempts to disclose her methods to the audience. Confident that being "factual" about her choreographic designs would explain everything, she invited critics and friends to see studio previews of dances, where she gave rapid-fire expositions of the creative process that became legendary. Variants of this format appeared in lecture-demonstrations and in postperformance sessions, with the dancers present to answer questions and demonstrate. For the Atheneum, she distributed an eighteen-by-twenty-eight inch program sheet covered on both sides with hand-printed notes, observations, snapshots, company credits, and helpful hints for the audience. Embedded in the wordy text, she had thoughtfully laid out the elements of the choreography and set a timetable for the ninety-minute event.

According to the plan, the five company members, Rudner, Raj, Figueroa, Wright, and Tharp, plus four extra dancers, would work in the galleries and related spaces for two half-hour segments, while five more recruits performed excerpts from the repertory twice on the small Avery Stage in the basement. There would be a fifteen-minute intermission during which the company was to determine how they would restructure the same material for the second part. The audience got two five-minute opportunities to participate. They could dance the Audience Phrase, based on simple steps— walk, run, chassé—laid out in an Arthur Murray-type diagram on the floor. And in another gallery, Sara Rudner would be taking requests for anything the audience wanted to see her do. Rudner was hoping she'd be challenged to make up a modern version of *The Dying Swan* or the pas de deux from *Don Quixote*, but instead the requests were rather mundane: "jump off the window and land on your tocs, and crawl across the floor on your ear."

Planned activities for the company included The Drift, a long, heavy phrase that was passed among the dancers and performed nonstop throughout the piece. The Traveling Phrase, which took them from one space to another, was "very dancey and steppy" according to Rose Marie Wright. Cluster Breakers, another set of choreographed moves, were used for infiltrating and separating the audience when it gathered together too tightly. In The Talky, Tharp and Rudner had a conversation while Rudner worked out choreographic problems that Tharp had given her. Wright had a specific dance for moving the audience away from a spot where she was going to perform. Her solo, the Wall dance, was a problem of leverage and balance, with her whole foot in contact with the floor on pointe, then on demipointe, and finally for her whole body affixed to a wall. Raj had fifty quiet moves, called The Parlor Phrase, to do in areas with low audience density. Fascinated with the rigor and precision, and the absolute objectivity, of gold medalists in Russian Olympic skating, Tharp made a phrase that would demand maximum exertion and no inflection.

Tharp had been making one minute of movement per day, which she put together for her own twenty-minute "diary" solo. After the Met performance, *Dance Magazine* critic Jack Anderson described it as "a spectacular solo study in energy flow and dynamic shifts, in which somnambulistic staggers followed staccato jabs; fierce lunges gave way to casual slides and dainty skips."

Besides the performance at the Metropolitan Museum of Art in New York two months after Hartford (22 January 1970), versions of *Dancing in the Streets* appeared in benefit performances that winter at the New York Public

Library for the Performing Arts Dance Collection in Lincoln Center; and at
the Worcester Art Museum, preceded by a tryout showing in a lobby of the
MIT administration building in Cambridge. While patrons at the public
performances were prepared for something unconventional, partygoers at
the benefits were taken aback by these casual young women in dirty jeans,
rushing around and rolling on the floor near the skirts of their evening
gowns. For each incarnation of the piece, which was never intended to be
finished, the dancer population changed and material was added, eliminated, or adjusted to fit the space. For one of Tharp's favorite additions, the
Drop-Bys, "we'd just walk by somebody and do . . . this little spurt of movement with the hope that we would be undiscovered and be gone before
they caught us." At the library, Tharp and Figueroa put on their boots (it
was snowing outside) and did their duet on Lincoln Center Plaza. Most dramatic of the site-specific segments was the dance on the Grand Staircase of
the Metropolitan. Chains of dancers passed each other doing complex patterns of going up and down stipulated numbers of steps. Tharp created a
new solo for Wright to do at the Met, weaving down among the chains.

By the time she made *Dancing in the Streets*, critic Don McDonagh thought
Tharp had developed a distinctive style of "aristocratic movement with a
vernacular phrasing." But despite the amount of precisely choreographed
material, what people remember most vividly about the work is how "everyday" and unassuming it looked. In Hartford, one girl "chewed gum and did a
sort of Swedish drill in the lobby." The Minutes specified that each dancer
perform exactly the actions and words she'd been doing during two predetermined one-minute periods of a given day. During The Home Phrase,
they read from a fairy-tale book and traded parts of their clothing. Counts
were shouted from one room to the other, and in Hartford, "At the count of
42, the troupe, who had by this time all assembled in the Austin Gallery for
calisthenics, collapsed on the floor and started applauding themselves."

The audience and the performers were to remain separate entities, even
when the dancers adopted pedestrian movement or entered the audience's
physical space. Although they were often packed tightly together and almost indistinguishable from one another, a certain reserve would always be
maintained. Rosalind Newman, who joined the expanded company for the
piece when it was done at the Metropolitan, remembers finding herself
dancing face-to-face with one of her teachers, the modern dancer–choreographer William Bales. "I couldn't pass him and he wouldn't move and he
kept saying, 'We did this stuff before. We did this stuff years ago. She can't

tell us. . . .'" Newman's instructions, and her embarrassment, prevented her from answering him.

Newman was recruited for the piece by Graciela Figueroa. Tharp had given each of the company dancers the responsibility of signing up new people they thought were interesting—people who would be willing to come to unpaid rehearsals—to augment the New York version of the work. The company then acted as teachers and leaders of what would become different groups in the performance. Newman thought this was in part a strategy to shield the dancers from Tharp's peremptory manner. By this time many people had experienced problems with what several of them called Tharp's communications skills. Interposing the company as teachers and coaches not only broke in the new people faster, it took some of her boiling intensity out of the rehearsal process.

Tharp's gruff and tough demeanor was a way of showing fondness—she trusted close associates not to take offense. In choreographing and rehearsing, her goals were the proper execution of the steps, precision and accuracy in the ensemble work. "She'd tell us if it was working or not, or if we needed to do something here or there or phrase differently," says Rose Marie Wright. According to Rudner, "Twyla didn't come up to you and say, 'God, that was great.' She would not say anything. . . . When she watched . . . a rehearsal or a section, you could never tell what emotion she was feeling." Rudner attributed Tharp's reticence to a certain puritanism, the aftereffects of her Quaker background. The company at that time considered itself a "democratic dictatorship," according to Wright. They understood that Tharp was choreographing for their individual talents, and even giving them choreographic tasks to work out on their own, but she was a little bit more equal than the rest of them. "She encouraged me through giving me work to do," Rudner says. "Not by saying, 'Oh, you're really good at this' and 'This is wonderful for you, dear.' She'd say, 'Do this!'" Wright perceived her the same way: "Twyla, when she *loves* you, she makes dances for you. She gives you things to do, she gives you work. That's her way of showing love."

The unusual responsibilities taken on by the dancers and administrators in the early days gave the company a close-knit solidarity. The team formations in *Medley* and *Dancing in the Streets* were a palpable demonstration of the real bonding among the dancers. They felt they had a fundamental part in making the work, and they shared the company's success as well as hardships. Newman remembers some resentment and misunderstanding because Tharp insisted on nonstop rehearsals though she couldn't pay the dancers. "She really did care, that dancers should be getting paid, and yet somehow people didn't see that." The core dancers shared not only their work but sometimes their apartments and their miniscule resources. Says Tharp: "We shared adversities, welcomed sacrifices, created community much like a religious society. We were a bunch of broads doing God's work. The pleasure of those days of extraordinary and total equality is my ideal still." Tupling confirms this: "I always felt when I was looking at her that she was on the edge of a new frontier, and we were all working for that and had faith in her vision, even though we didn't know what her vision was." But the long-standing financial dilemma became more and more vexing as the devoted first cadre of dancers began to leave.

For the Worcester and Library benefits, Tharp supplemented the dancers' practice clothes with costumes borrowed from choreographer-designer James Waring. She was always scouting for rehearsal space she could afford, free if possible. *Dancing in the Streets* was developed in makeshift circumstances: a studio in Great Jones Street that belonged to Waring and Kermit Love, a forgotten mezzanine with a concrete floor that Tharp discovered in the City Center building, and the Metropolitan itself, after hours. The Met was undergoing renovation at the time, and in an attempt to disguise the dust of the construction work, Bob Huot came up with the idea of sprinkling an aluminum powder on the floor, so that when a dancer fell or rolled on it, she would be transformed into a "silver creature." Unfortunately, the paint turned out to be ordinary gray, and it was delivered too late to be taken back to Canal Street for exchange. He used it anyway, creating a ghostly effect.

Word had spread in advance somehow that the Metropolitan performance was going to be a big event in New York's cultural life. Tharp had no money for professional publicists or advertising campaigns, so she and the dancers mimeographed, mailed, and hand-delivered announcements to dancing schools, critics, universities, Bob Huot's contact list, and everyone else they knew. In addition to whatever the Met did to publicize the event, Merce Cunningham made his mailing list available to the company, and Lewis Lloyd let them use office facilities that the Cunningham company occupied at Brooklyn Academy. As a result, an unexpectedly large crowd arrived at the museum.

Tharp's timing and mapping of the simultaneous events, carefully rehearsed in the Met's deserted galleries, were demolished when the closed-circuit television failed to materialize. The crowd became disoriented. Anxious spectators milled around, and the dancers lost track of each other. Roz Newman remarks:

Twyla never figured out how to use crowd control. Or how to get the crowd to go from one spot to the next, or how we would even recognize who was one of us and who was one of the crowd during the piece. So . . . we were going, wait, where's Sheila? Wow, I see a little purple shirt, is that her? Are we supposed to start yet? Where is so and so? People would be trying to get from one room to the next to tell the next people to start their next thing or move, and there was no way they could get there on time. So that the timing got totally screwed up. Nobody knew where anybody was. We were just sort of wandering—I mean, things happened, you saw things. But it was totally not the piece that she had planned.

Tharp played Pied Piper, leading stragglers from one room to another, barking over her shoulder, "I know they can't see, so what?" At one point she had a long solo that she had never rehearsed with the company, and Newman remembers the dancers hesitating at the edge, not knowing where they should be or when to enter. She danced up to them and yelled, "Get the fuck back!"

Anna Kisselgoff of *The Times* was among the confused and frustrated members of the audience. All very well, Kisselgoff thought, for experimenters to try out new spaces. After all, that tradition went back to Isadora Duncan. But "It is nonetheless disappointing to see a previously disciplined and original talent . . . lose control of the performing situation . . . Her once-brilliant movement patterns appear less than interesting and smothered by an unpredictable participant public whose presence—if not obstructive—seems beside the point." Jack Anderson admitted that he found the trudging from room to room "wearisome" although he was intrigued by the relationship of the dancers to the architecture. Not everyone was put off by the discomforts of the situation. The work's unpredictability, its good nature and wit, and the evident fact that the dancers were often as unprepared for what happened as the viewers, made for a conviviality seldom found at an avant-garde event. Indeterminacy worked. Art met life in a cheerful, jostling accommodation, if not exactly adhering to the scenario Tharp had in mind.

The dancers found it satisfying despite its mishaps. Roz Newman remembers Sheila Raj's series of what seemed like a hundred phrases, with subtle dynamic shifts that capitalized on Raj's special abilities. They were like "unraveling a cloth of beautiful dancing." After Newman and some of the other extra dancers had learned these phrases, Tharp said they could spread out anywhere they wanted in the museum at the end of the piece, and do as many of the phrases as they wanted, in any order. "It was just like a mountain of material, it was like your whole life," Newman says. "Or maybe it was an encyclopedia of everything she's done since. . . . So I just remember doing my phrase and changing the order, and how that to me was *the* most amazing part."

By the start of 1970 Tharp was recognized as a major figure in the world of experimental dance, as choreographer, dancer, and developer of a distinctive company style. Important presenters and administrators like Reinhart and Geldzahler followed her work and opened up possibilities for it to be seen. She had been appreciatively reviewed by *The New York Times* and had received significant critical attention in the United States and England. In New York, where a new generation of writers was developing alongside the dance avant-garde, a strong and receptive press tracked her moves, notably Deborah Jowitt of *The Village Voice* and independent writers Arlene Croce, Tobi Tobias, Don McDonagh, and Laura Shapiro, soon to join *The New Yorker, New York* magazine, *The New York Times*, and *Newsweek* respectively. The journal *Dance Scope* featured a long profile by Tobias, a fellow Barnard alumna, and Croce's influential *Ballet Review* published the first of several Tharp-centered pieces, her minutely detailed notes for *Group Activities*. She had acquired an audience eager to see anything new she made, and she had received significant help in the form of grants and commissions.

Nevertheless, sometime in winter of 1969–70, without telling the dancers (consisting by then of Sara Rudner and Rose Marie Wright), she turned over the company records to the New York Public Library's Dance Research Collection. "I had every intention of quitting," Tharp says. She recalls being "very angry" at this point, but the gesture may have been disingenuous. Tharp had already shown she was capable of extreme actions on behalf of the company; a sign that she was closing it down might bluff potential donors into writing checks. Despite the performance opportunities being offered to the company, she still couldn't pay the dancers on any regular basis. She saw herself as scrambling to maintain an impossible compromise: although the company worked full-time all the time, it operated like a part-time avocation, with the dancers doing temp work and baby-sitting to support themselves.

Tharp was also very much under the influence of Bob Huot's "political declamations about war and taxes and let's not support this capitalistic society, et cetera, et cetera." Living on the farm and giving up the company seemed like a feasible alternative to struggling with the high cost of living in the city. She embraced Huot's pioneering ideas; they would grow their own food, restore the dilapidated house, and live a healthy life in the country. Agrarian communities had been constructing alternatives to American mainstream culture for a century, and in its benign aspects, the counterculture of the 1960s was an offshoot of this utopianism. Tharp's hometown of San Bernardino had served for a few years in the 1850s as a communal settlement for Mormons crossing California to their capital in Utah. And as recently as 1946, pacifist Quakers had established Tuolomne Farms in northern California, to carry on their businesses, farms, and schools in seclusion from what they considered the increasing militarism of American life. In California alone, historian Robert V. Hine identifies utopian cells devoted to dissident religions, sexual liberation, pacifism, health, mysticism, rural escapism, and social reform at the height of the counterculture.

For Tharp no gesture was too radical in pursuit of an ideal. She had taken on a strong secular moralism and independence from her Quaker grandparents, and nothing about her immediate family had been remotely conforming. Periodically she would be seized with the desire to go back to the land, to live in the idyllic simplicity she recalled from her earliest years in Indiana. Contemplating the inventiveness of nature inspired her to "go back in and do better." Now she persuaded herself that she could construct a good working life in withdrawal from the urban hustle. Dance for her was a kind of monasticism anyway; not so much a deliberate renunciation of other attractions as a single-minded immersion in the life of the studio. Huot adopted the rural lifestyle and was still running the farm thirty years later, but if Tharp ever thought about giving up dancing entirely, the vision lasted about six weeks. After a winter's retreat, she started dancing again and, almost casually, began inviting dancers up to the farm to work with her.

Nothing provoked Tharp's latent romanticism like the idea of New Berlin. She had her own dancing space, a big room at the top of the house that she and Huot fitted out with a new floor. She could work there as many hours a day as the household chores allowed; she didn't have to answer the telephone. Deep in domesticity, surrounded by nature, and pregnant by June, she saw herself as part of a huge process of biogenesis. "I made more dance that summer than I ever had before or since," she comments in her autobiography. In rhapsodic pages devoted to the early days on the farm, she describes grocery shopping, sheets drying on the line, making dandelion wine, raising and butchering cattle. Somehow, dancing merged with all of this in her imagination.

When the dancers arrived, first Wright, then Rudner and several others over the next months, they were less enthusiastic about the improvised living quarters, the severe weather, the housekeeping and gardening and paint stripping that were part of the package. Nor did they like leaving their families and social lives in New York City for unspecified periods of time. Besides that, they all sensed the displeasure of Bob Huot, who felt his home and his new work life were being invaded by these women. If this was utopia, it was a bit different from the fellowship of poverty they had shared in New York. But they still believed, with their leader, that what they were doing produced good in the world. "We were like people who went out and dug coal, and brought it up and made heat," Rudner told writer Laura Shapiro. "We were going into that studio and being laborers."

Isabel Garcia-Lorca had wanted to dance all her life. Her intellectual European family (she is the niece of the famous playwright) disapproved of dancing although they didn't stigmatize the other performing arts. By the time she was seventeen she was resigned to giving up her dream—she was too old, she thought, to begin training seriously. To satisfy her family, she got a liberal arts degree at Barnard. After graduation she was holding down an aimless job at the information desk of the Metropolitan Museum of Art when a friend invited her to Tharp's performance there. Garcia-Lorca was bowled over. "I thought it was fabulous," she says. "Plus, I thought, Well, I could do this. I could be one of those extras."

She made contact with Tharp first by phone, to invite her to participate in a benefit concert for Bobby Seale and the Black Panthers that was being arranged in St. Paul's Chapel at Columbia by Garcia-Lorca's boyfriend. Among the other artists were comedian Dick Gregory and rock-and-roll musician Country Joe. Tharp accepted. It was another opportunity to experiment. She laid out a space the size of a jail cell and put the dancers inside it: herself, Wright, Rudner, Raj, and Figueroa. According to Wright, she made several phrases, "some of them went on the ground, some of them were big, some were little and fast. . . . .And all five of us could put them together however we wanted to, but we were in this space all together, and of course *she* chose the big one. And it was supposed to make a statement about how to keep yourself mentally and physically together if you're in jail."

Garcia-Lorca says she doesn't remember much of the concert because she had decided to speak to Tharp afterwards. She nervously asked if there was any chance someone twenty-two years old, without any dance training, could still be a dancer. They had a long talk, during which Tharp discerned that Garcia-Lorca was highly intelligent and no dilettante, besides being unaffected, beautiful, and a natural mover. With intensive work it might be possible, she said. Garcia-Lorca would have to quit her job though, and come up to the farm where Tharp would work with her for two trial weeks. Garcia-Lorca agreed at once. The two weeks passed and Tharp didn't say anything. Garcia-Lorca went down to the city and got some more clothes.

From the spring of 1970 to the spring of 1971 the company flowed in and out of New Berlin. Breaking up the periods of intensive work were several important teaching residencies. For Amherst College in August Tharp made two country pieces, a "sowing of the seeds" piece and a forty-five-minute solo for Wright called *Rose's Cross Country.* Tharp's notes for this ambulatory variation include balletic steps that Wright excelled at, plus things like: "little drops enlarging, pick branch chew, slip fall, brush-off, twiddle hands s pattern, hand rhythms on leg maint s turning to back, 2 back falls." Then: "fouettés wiggle wiggle." Every day, Wright would dance this piece between buildings on the campus, trying to disregard the bewildered reactions of onlookers.

Following Amherst the company worked for two weeks with children's groups in three inner-city Boston neighborhoods: East Boston, Dorchester, and Hyde Park, leading up to Summerthing performances in three parks. Tharp didn't really know anything about juvenile dancers, but in New Berlin she invited two of the neighbor's children to come and learn some games the dancers were making up. According to Boston critic Jane Goldberg, during the workshop the Boston youths were quickly enlisted as teachers for newer arrivals.

The residencies, like the farm, served primarily as laboratory time for Tharp. She was making movement incessantly, trying it on dancers, putting it together different ways. She might not have had specific choreographic goals in mind, but the movement chunks would start to cohere and evolve, and eventually a dance would be made. Amherst saw the first performances of two unique works that have evolved over the years but have remained identified with her throughout her career, *The Fugue* and *The One Hundreds.*

Making up phrases was a discipline for Tharp, a task she set herself every day, like warming up or doing a barre. They poured out of her. During the spring before Amherst she taught Wright ten phrases a day, while also making movement for *The Fugue.* She was pondering contexts big enough to contain this flood of invention. Perhaps prompted by a dream of Margery Tupling's she had recorded in 1968, she was thinking about 150 combinations of eleven counts, maybe with three-second pauses in between. All 150 could be done by two soloists simultaneously, side by side, with the option of skipping the pause sometimes, or getting out of sequence by forgetting. Then five people would each do thirty of the phrases, without pauses, followed by 150 children doing one phrase each, simultaneously. Edited down by one-third, this colossal event became *The One Hundreds*, which Tharp subsequently put under the heading of "trying to get the world to dance so that they'd understand us." Tharp and Wright danced the first, marathon section; the five sets of twenty were done by Rudner, Garcia-Lorca, Douglas Dunn, and two apprentices who had been working at the farm, Elizabeth Fain and Sybille Hayn. The hundred civilians were rounded up and rehearsed when the dancers got to Amherst.

More densely structured but no less mind-boggling was *The Fugue*, a series of variations for three women. Tharp compared it to a man's game, like chess. Men had "the time and the interest to examine a process," a luxury she didn't think was ordinarily granted to women. *The Fugue* demonstrated that a dance can be abstract and compelling at the same time. Without musical accompaniment, three women (Tharp, Rudner, and Wright) danced a series of variations on an initial phrase. The rhythms ranged from rapid-fire tattoos to edgy suspensions and hair-trigger canons. With little upper-body elaboration, like tap dancers, they stomped out the intricate counterpoint patterns with a businesslike yet comradely efficiency.

The Fugue's original phrase is done twenty times, with the dancers in different spatial relationships to each other and to the audience. The phrase revolves in different directions, moves upstage and downstage. It retrogrades and inverts in sequence. It's done in double time and with different meters. Over the years it has acquired built-in ornaments and stylistic additives. It's a demonstration of invention and counterpoint, deliberately acknowledging Bach. Severe yet playful, *The Fugue* was seen by some of its early critics as a militant feminist statement. Since its first all-women version it has been danced by all-men and by mixed-gender casts.

In performance *The Fugue* and *The One Hundreds* represent contrasting ways to reconcile the art/life dichotomy. The movement for *The Fugue* cranks up everyday walks, turns, stamps, and slaps to acute levels of timing and structural virtuosity that only highly sensitive dancers can manage. In *The One Hundreds*, ordinary people get to approach a small task: mastering one nontechnical phrase that requires them to give extended, dancerly concentration to problems of coordination, timing, placement, and exact repeatability.

Tharp started work on *The Fugue* with Wright and Garcia-Lorca; she didn't intend to be in the piece herself. When Rudner returned to the farm from a trip to Europe with her then partner Douglas Dunn, who was touring with Merce Cunningham's company, Tharp decided *The Fugue* would be too demanding for Garcia-Lorca and finished making it for herself and Rudner with Wright. Skeletal and intricate, *The Fugue* was performed in an atmosphere of almost religious concentration. At Amherst it was done every day at three o'clock in a small meeting-house building. Tharp liked the sound of their sneakers on the floor and made a tape recording of it. At the end of the residency, when they performed it outside, she used the tape as accompaniment. For this performance, people turned on their car headlights as darkness settled over the field.

Tharp took advantage of every opportunity to perform. She usually gave titles to the phrase clusters in progress, so they could be shown in some kind of coherence even before they had totally evolved into dances. She used old dances as training material for newly arrived dancers, and in November of 1970 she showed ten minutes' worth of old and new work at Judson Church, where the downtown dance world was celebrating the publication of Don McDonagh's *The Rise and Fall and Rise of Modern Dance.* This was the first book on the Cunningham/Judson dance revolution, and Tharp was the subject of a whole chapter. All the major figures were performing, including Trisha Brown and Yvonne Rainer, but it was Meredith Monk who turned the occasion into a scandal. Monk had at first refused to take part; she thought the book had serious flaws. At the last minute she appeared. Dressed in white with her hair in braids all over her head, she played the Jews' harp and chanted a litany of McDonagh's offenses. The audience cheered. But Tharp was furious; she liked McDonagh and thought Monk's gesture was disrespectful.

For the Judson appearance Tharp rounded up some extra dancers, and either during the one-week rehearsal period or right after the concert, she held an audition. The people selected would go up to work with her at the farm. Two of her top choices had just arrived in New York to feast on the array of dance there. Kenneth Rinker danced with Tharp in the McDonagh tribute, but he was studying with Merce Cunningham and decided it wasn't the right time for him to take off. It wasn't until a year later that he joined the company, becoming its first male dancer. Dana Reitz had just graduated from the University of Michigan. She heard about the audition from Rudner at the Cunningham studio. When she saw Wright and Rudner dancing "fast and furious," she was stunned. This would be a great learning experience, she thought. She quit her job as a nanny on Staten Island and, with the rest of the group, drove up to the farm on Thanksgiving Day, as Tharp insisted they do.

This time, the dancers lived in a small house down the road. One person would stay at the big house with Tharp when Huot was away. They cooked huge meals for themselves after the long days of rehearsing, but the life was still hard. Reitz remembers that the attic studio was cold, and that her mind and muscles were stretching all the time to keep up with what Tharp demanded. There was no regular class, but after each person did her own warm-up routine in the morning, either Rudner or Wright would lead a ballet barre. Then they would spend hours learning phrases and working on them. Tharp was in the middle stages of her pregnancy, and she would demonstrate her ideas for a videotape, expecting the dancers to refer to it when she needed to rest. Reitz found this very difficult, but she was amazed at Wright's ability to pick up and translate any movement from tape, and then, as Tharp was demonstrating and inventing, "[Wright] could reverse it and invert it and retrograde . . . then remember that version, and remember the retrograde version."

When Tharp and six dancers went off to Oberlin College for three weeks in January, she had prepared a quantity of material called *The History of Up and Down*. It included the Exercise Book, which she thought of as a training manual for Isabel Garcia-Lorca, the member with the least dance technique. One set of exercises could serve for the beginning students at Oberlin and one would suit the intermediates. With Wright, Rudner, and the other dancers as teachers and captains, the company worked with students every morning and rehearsed alone in the afternoons.

The Oberlin residency was organized by Brenda Way, a graduate of the college who had just been hired to teach dance and create an interarts program. She had met Tharp in New York shortly after *Dancing in the Streets* and was immediately impressed by her intellect and the way she worked. For the free-form winter term, Way raised the money to bring in Tharp and company. The dance program at Oberlin, as in most American colleges at the time, had been struggling to gain status as an art discipline, and had finally worked its way out of the Athletics Department and into Theater Arts. Tharp thought this was a bad idea, says Brenda Way. "She thought I had made a terrible mistake . . . we should have stayed in the Athletics because that's where the money was." As if to prove her point, Tharp commandeered all the resources she could, and made two versions of the prepared material, one for the open space of the field house and one for the theater, with the same material rearranged by chance and minutely keyed to a computerized light plot. *The History of Up and Down* was a kind of choreographic nexus: at least three entities wove together, exchanged information, and separated out again. Besides the Exercise Book, which the beginning and intermediate students performed along with the company in the field house showing, the movement came from the draft material Tharp called the Willie Smith series.

In New Berlin, with the cumbersome but workable videotape recorder she had acquired after the Amherst and Boston residencies, she aimed the camera on her increasingly pregnant self as she did her daily improvisation sessions. She was making up phrases as usual, and factoring the changing condition of her body into her creative investigations. For background music she happened to have on hand some records of stride pianist Willie "the Lion" Smith. At the Oberlin field house, in her seventh month, she performed the Willie Smith material as a solo. Brenda Way says that as a feminist during the Oberlin residency she was enthusiastic about the novel idea of a pregnant woman dancing. She remembers Tharp as a "solid round middle, and these legs flying all around. The strongest image I have of the whole residency is of Twyla dancing."

After the solo she led the students in a snake-dance version of the basic phrases. Accompanying this was another record from her stash in the attic, featuring the jazz pianist Jelly Roll Morton and his Red Hot Peppers. While the intermediate students did their Exercise Book, the company dancers went through the Willie Smith material. Spaced out over half the gym floor in practice mode, they did slow lunges and reaches with sudden arm gestures and fast head rolls, gradually building up the intensity into flinging turns and jittering step trills. Combined and reworked, these segments made up the dance called *Eight Jelly Rolls.* Willie Smith's music reemerged ten years later to accompany the suave ensemble piece *Baker's Dozen.*

Tharp was dancing and thinking even more expansively after her son Jesse Huot was born, on 10 March 1971. She thought pushing herself to move bigger and broader would be an efficient way to get back in shape. And she had taken on what was going to be the biggest of her nonproscenium pieces yet. Charles Reinhart had offered her a commission to do an environmental New York City work, and she decided nothing less than a dance that encompassed all of Manhattan Island would be appropriate. She wanted to put the dancers on a barge, dancing broadly enough so that people in apartments bordering the rivers could see their performance. When she encountered snags in implementing this scheme, she settled for three spaces, two in lower Manhattan and one uptown, all of them free and highly visible. The dance would surround a single day, 28 May, beginning in Fort Tryon Park at sunrise, continuing in Battery Park at lunchtime, and concluding in the evening at City Hall. Tharp, Rudner, and Wright performed the basic dance material for all three sections. The first was set to the Baroque music of Giuseppi Torelli, and *Torelli* became the umbrella title for the three sections, "Sunrise," "Midday March," and "Evening Raga."

Part One was, according to Wright, "a very exhausting little piece," where the phrases were first demonstrated in silence and then put together at the dancers' discretion, to Torelli's music. Wright remembers a "leg phrase, an arm phrase, a floor phrase and a fast little phrase." Hardly anyone showed up at Fort Tryon Park—not surprising at 6:30 A.M. No sooner had they finished the dance when a large group of spectators appeared, having first gone to the wrong place. The dancers repeated everything for this audience. At Battery Park, Tharp had enlisted a marching band from a Brooklyn high school to play Sousa in formations that intersected with the dance. Fourteen extra dancers rehearsed gratis for three weeks at Wagner College to augment the marches.

City Hall proved the biggest challenge. The city's official welcoming site, Tharp reasoned, was Gracie Mansion, the mayor's residence, but she couldn't persuade anyone to let her use it, so she accepted the elegant, Federal-period City Hall as second choice. She intended to have each dancer accompanied by her own musician playing Indian ragas in the rotunda, and a mechanical player-piano cranking out rags in another space, with the audience and dancers going between them. To interviewers for *Ballet Review* she gave a fanciful explanation of the connection between rags and ragas: the dance consisted of "fairly elaborate improvisations along the lines of things that are done in Indian palaces."

But there was trouble about Kermit Love's costumes—white pants with halter tops in a silky, quasi-Indian fabric, pink with gold embroidery—which were delivered at the last minute. These were the first real costumes made for the company since Huot's last designs, *Group Activities* and *After "Suite."* Tharp felt self-conscious about her body less than three months after giving birth. Rudner and Wright thought the costumes were too fancy and simply refused to wear them. So Tharp told the audience they'd decided the floor was too dirty to risk spoiling them. They performed, as they had for the past two years, in ordinary clothes.

In addition to the costume snafu, city officials wouldn't let the player-piano into the building—in these days of anti-establishment protests, City Hall could be a target for a slightly mad artist with a hidden bomb. The performance went ahead with the Indian musicians seated to one side of the City Council Chamber and the dancers punching a little tape recorder to play their piano-roll selections. All the movement was improvised.

In the months between Oberlin and *Torelli* Tharp's concentration was severely tried. Dancers came and went. There were difficult visits from parents after Jesse was born. Huot and Tharp's father had a couple of arguments, which Tharp suspected were a contributing cause of her father's death from a heart attack later that spring. Huot wasn't taking on as much of the responsibility for the baby's care as she had expected, and she regarded nursing and diapering as barely tolerable distractions. The stress of her double life increased, as she juggled the baby, the farm, the tensions with Huot, and her burgeoning career.

She and Huot were no longer on the same page artistically. At the start of their relationship they had shared searching discussions about the meaning and purpose of art, and Huot's already-established minimalism buttressed her initial goal of stripping away everything to get down to core dance values. Like him, she was unconventional, she didn't crave material comforts, let alone luxuries, and she had a highly developed conscience, a determination to live by her own ethics. But these affinities held them together for only so long. Huot wanted a wife whose main occupation was the traditional family he thought they were starting. Tharp knew another child would put an impossible strain on her career. She had given her marriage a heroic try but it was clear her heart was in her creative work.

At the same time as she was making the motions of closing down the company, Paul Epstein, an attorney and founder of the pro-bono Volunteer Lawyers for the Arts, had initiated the process of incorporating Tharp Dance as a nonprofit organization. After Oberlin Tharp let all the dancers go, but almost immediately following Jesse's birth, Wright, Rudner, Garcia-Lorca, Reitz, and two other dancers reappeared to start rehearsals. She tried commuting in to New York with Huot and Jesse, but the periods when she stayed in the loft grew longer and longer. During the summer she and the baby moved into 104 Franklin Street full-time. Essentially her marriage was over, although she didn't complete her divorce from Huot until 1974.

4

The Entertainer
1971–1973

At the farm Tharp had sampled utopia and discovered its limits. Now she embarked on another principled experiment, one that would be equally hard to sustain. She intended to find a path between remaining aloof from the culture of dance production and becoming enmeshed in it. To separate from Bob Huot and take up her life in New York again was only an initial move toward what she wanted, which was nothing less than creative independence *and* material success.

To Huot, the farm symbolized a rejection of the art world's career-building machinery. "I realized early on that I was going to have to be my own patron," he says, and by the end of the '60s he felt he no longer needed to cultivate moneymaking contacts or public visibility. In fact, one of his last projects, a series of sand paintings in homage to the Oglala Sioux, wasn't seen by anyone and couldn't be put on the market. In about 1971 he obtained the keys to the Paula Cooper Gallery, where he had exhibited in previous years. After closing time, he would go in with his sand and dry pigments, and create "these rather beautiful things" on the floor. Next morning, before the staff arrived, he'd return and sweep away the night's work. The only trace of it would be a small card he tacked to the baseboard of the room he'd worked in. "I think I was probably *the* most minimal minimalist," he says. Tharp was unwilling to take conceptual art to such an extreme.

Dancing in the Streets played hide-and-seek with the audience, but the dancing, after all, was what she most wanted them to see.

In the 1970s America experienced a period of unprecedented interest in the arts. Not only had the big funding structures been established on the national, state, and municipal levels, the tax laws made it attractive for individuals and businesses to channel significant dollars to art work and performance. The media reflected this healthy cultural activity with generous coverage and programming. Dance was routinely being mentioned alongside the other arts for the first time. Companies and schools that had never before developed strong institutional means for survival now became more stable. A broader, more knowledgeable public was being cultivated through touring performances and special shows on TV. The obvious course for any artist was to establish oneself as a nonprofit business and enter the subsidized world. In the case of a choreographer with a company to pay, studio space to rent, creative collaborators and managers to be enlisted, productions to be designed and built, this transition was mandatory.

Tharp made the necessary gesture. She had taken the first steps to qualify the company for public funding, and early in 1971 she met a young lawyer who wanted to help. William Peter Kosmas was starting an independent law practice after working for the firm of Greenbaum, Wolff and Ernst. He wasn't a dance fan, but through an associate who dated a dancer, he learned that Tharp might need a manager. He had seen the *Fugue* and the *One Hundreds* at the 1970 Delacorte dance festival in Central Park, and he was interested.

Between 1962 and 1980 the Delacorte Theater, an outdoor thrust stage built for Joseph Papp and the New York Shakespeare Festival, became an end-of-the-summer showcase for New York dance. Offering free tickets and a chance to see several different attractions in one evening, the series was extremely popular with the faithful, and lured new audiences as well. In 1970 Tharp and a group that included Rudner, Wright, Garcia-Lorca, Douglas Dunn, and two women they'd picked up in one of their Boston-area residencies appeared on a marathon evening with five other downtown choreographers. Tharp had asked for the closing spot. The Tharps wore their usual noncostumes, and the intricate *Fugue*, followed by the *Hundreds*, added up to an hour of uncompromising choreography. It was almost midnight before the company plus 104 extras delivered their eleven-second punch line. What remained of the audience broke out in cheers, hisses, boos, and loud arguments. Bill Kosmas didn't understand the controversy but he was intrigued with "this determined little figure . . . in sloppy sweatwear" who could provoke such a strong reaction.

She arrived at his office sometime in January or February of 1971. Pregnant with Jesse and probably dressed in her usual dumpy working attire, she made an incongruous entrance, lugging shopping bags full of canceled checks, bills, and company business that had never been properly recorded. The dapper Kosmas, who was wearing one of his handmade Italian suits, whisked "this beleaguered little person" past the disbelieving eyes of his office mates. They talked things over and he thought he could help her, although he refused to deal with her jumbled bookkeeping. "I was intrigued by someone who would make such demands and requests," he says, "and I thought it betrayed either great despair or a great sense of humor or chutzpah, or all of it." He doesn't remember a formal arrangement between them, but at the end of the meeting she said, "You'll do."

Company members and outside observers agree that it was Kosmas who turned the company around by convincing Tharp she needed to make her work more personable. He saw no point in forcing the audience to work so hard to see it. At first Kosmas regarded Tharp as a kind of savage, a strange young woman who was "sort of ashamed for not knowing how to walk around properly or what it meant to walk around properly." He thought a certain antimaterialistic primitivism had rubbed off on her from Bob Huot: "You don't wear nice clothes because that's decadent." The dancers' downscale style, on and offstage, was only partly attributable to their poverty-level income, Kosmas thought. They treated costuming "as though it were some sort of moral or ethical issue as opposed to what's most effective onstage. . . . I didn't think it was a question of good and bad, I thought it was a question of what would convey best what they were doing."

Whether prompted by Kosmas or not, after the birth of Jesse, Tharp was indeed evaluating her ragamuffin image along with everything else in her shifting life. Dana Reitz, who was rehearsing at the farm in the spring, watched Tharp building up a resolve "that she was going to become a famous choreographer. She sort of looked at everything and she said, I have to go for this. . . . She noticed that we were a mess and that she was a mess too. She made us clean up our clothes." The fastidious Reitz was dismayed. "I had worked so hard to get the look of the Twyla company, which was very disheveled." Tharp put Garcia-Lorca in charge of buying proper clothes for the dancers, no easy task in New Berlin. It was all part of the new plan. Says Reitz: "I think she just decided, no, she was not gonna be the housewife, in the country, with some dancers some of the time. She was gonna have to do this seriously."

The company had received another prestigious invitation, to appear in Paris at the International Festival of the Dance in November 1971, and in September they were booked at the Delacorte again. For the Central Park performance, Tharp scheduled a repeat of *The Fugue* and the New York premiere of *Eight Jelly Rolls*. Kermit Love made striking new costumes for *The Fugue*, which had been given before in motley clothes. The dancers wore black tailored jackets nipped in at the waist with three-quarter sleeves, and black pants in different lengths—short shorts for Tharp, knickers for Rudner, and calf-length gaucho pants for Wright. The miked stage floor amplified the shifting rhythms of their high suede boots. The *Jelly Rolls* were danced in the unused white pants from *Torelli* and brightly colored undershirts dressed up with little cutout holes near the neckline. Two Oberlin students joined the cast as apprentices. Kosmas insisted all six dancers get really good haircuts at Vidal Sassoon's salon—and let the public know about it. Professionally styled hair, even more than dressy costumes, signified Tharp's transit into a new sphere. She programmed the two pieces so that the austere and demanding *Fugue* would be followed by the affable *Eight Jelly Rolls*.

A series of videotaped records makes it possible to trace the development of *Eight Jelly Rolls* from its first performance in the field house of Oberlin College to its polished, possibly final form on a London Weekend Television broadcast three years later. These records, and other documentation of Tharp's early choreography, confirm how absolutely sui generis her dance was. It didn't look like the full-bodied, sculptural yearnings of modern dance, or the antitechnical perambulations of the avant-garde. It resisted both the musical theater and the dancehall, where jazz music normally accompanied dancing. It certainly wasn't proper and virtuosic like ballet, though it employed the ballet's vocabulary and strong, adaptable bodies.

In some notes for a lecture she gave at Oberlin, Tharp explained that she had not intended *Eight Jelly Rolls* as a stage work; it had been transplanted to the theater because a basketball game preempted the field house. Naturally, she could not present the dance on the stage the same way as she had in the open space, she said. So she had worked out a very elaborate way of coordinating the dance phrases, which she reconfigured by randomizing them on a computer and appending them to a "score" or lighting plot. Each of the eighty-six lighting instruments was correlated with "specific fractions of the dance materials." So when a certain instrument was in use, the dancers could do the corresponding phrase. This took long hours to put together and rehearse, and Tharp and lighting designer Lee Herman simplified their chart-making for the latter parts of the dance. What resulted was a fragmented, half-invisible performance. The audience accompanied it with derisive clapping. Brenda Way described "an excruciatingly specific time score that was connected to the light plot. And that of course was enormously exciting for us and completely irritating for the audience because there was no through-line. So all the artsy people thought it was fantastic, and the general audience thought, why did you bring this person?"

Eight months later, when *Eight Jelly Rolls* appeared on a stage for the second time, there would be no such experimental challenges. Tharp says she noted the places where she got laughs at Oberlin and cut out all the "technical problems" except ones that "were so fiendishly difficult that even the audience could delight in their perversity."

In form, the first four *Jelly Rolls* remained fairly constant throughout the dance's later evolution. At Oberlin Tharp incorporated the intermediate students to make a large ensemble, but in the company version three or four dancers backed up the core trio. Although the dance has no narrative, it does have a theatrical build. It begins with Wright dancing solo, then introduces Rudner and Tharp, completing the core trio. Rudner solos, the other members of the group enter and Tharp solos against them, there are small solos for the members of the group, a solo for Wright against the group, and a finale with everyone dancing their individual phrases simultaneously. The company thus emerges in a smoothly expanding sequence, and all the dancers complement each other in formal ways. Considering that Tharp hadn't really made a dance in the shape of a dance before, and that she hadn't abandoned her usual method of putting together phrases in no preconceived order, *Eight Jelly Rolls* is a gem of choreographic form.

But it was the movement, and the performers who created it, that captivated the audiences at the Delacorte. *Eight Jelly Rolls* is always referred to as a jazz piece, and the Jelly Roll Morton selections are authentic Dixieland, with a steady beat pumping behind successive instrumental solos and unifying choruses. Recorded around 1927, the music—grave, declarative, sometimes raunchy—comes directly out of the New Orleans funeral processions and saloons where jazz got started. At a time when the use of popular music of any kind was considered slumming on the concert dance stage, the *Jelly Rolls* astounded Tharp's Delacorte audience.

Tharp's relationship to music that carried so much cultural resonance was poorly understood. Although she quoted the Charleston, Suzy Q, shimmy, camel walk, Shorty George, and a dozen other steps, she put them through a process of metamorphosis and folded them imperceptibly into her own fusion style. For the 1974 broadcast of the dance on London Weekend Television, she explained how she applied techniques of inversion, retrograde, sudden changes of timing and direction, miniaturization and expansion, to render her sources almost unrecognizable. She further disguised them by eliminating the stops and starts between them, so that there were no obvious transitions or special emphases. Her dancers had become superb performers of this lightning-fast, multiplexed information. To her pre-*Jelly Rolls* audiences this loosely placed movement had often seemed untrackable or out of control. But when Tharp finally acknowledged the music, referring to and riffing on a regular beat, the whole enterprise gained coherence. The rhythmic variety, surprise, and humor that had been implicit moved out front. What had seemed intimidatingly cerebral in *The Fugue* and *The One Hundreds* now looked casual enough that anyone could do it.

Within this more accessible choreographic context, the core dancers projected as distinct personalities. Rudner was smooth and sensuous, and quickwitted. For the third Jelly Roll, she had a limited amount of material that she could put together however she wished in performance, so the solo was different every time. But whatever movements she was doing, Rudner always looked natural, composed. Rudner felt the *Jelly Rolls* was a watershed for the dancers because it brought all the improvisational possibilities into play. In a 1995 interview, she pointed out that Tharp disliked the casual connotations of the term improvisation: "I think she felt that it meant that we were making it up as we went along. When, in fact, they were like jazz improvisations. We had very specific material—just as you do with a song." For Rudner's solo, "Twyla said, 'Oh, everybody make a series of positions.' . . . So I put my arm here, I put my leg down there. And then she took me and she connected those positions, and we made an order out of them, which was the order that I had made them in. . . . [T]hat took up maybe one-eighth of the song. And the rest of the song was new combinations of time, space, and rhythm of that material . . . however I wanted them." Rudner remembered her duet with Wright in Number Two "had sections of intense unison and then . . . see how many of these arm gestures you can fit in before someone stamps their foot."

Wright, rebounding from her years as a ballet dancer, concerned herself with doing the movement, not with showing it to the audience. She says the transition from open spaces to stage performance was hard for her: "I hated that separation of audience and performer. And that's when I started questioning what I was doing separated from the audience. What I was doing up there, and they're in the dark. I always was about the process." Tharp thought of her as tough but trusting. "You don't mess around with a lady that big," she told the 1974 TV audience.

For her own solo, Tharp imported the experiments with weight and balance she'd made in the attic at New Berlin during her pregnancy. The first of several brilliant comic roles she played in her own work, the solo became a modern-dance analog of Charlie Chaplin's famous drunk scene in the 1916 two-reeler *One A.M.* Chaplin staggered and maneuvered through the clutter of what was presumably his own house, unable to recognize any of the objects or figure out how they worked. Constantly misjudging or making the wrong connections, he thought up shrewd but bizarre solutions, and finally went to sleep in the bathtub. Tharp performed her solo locked into a state of half-consciousness. On the 1974 video, she doesn't seem to know where she is or what her immediate surroundings might mean. The other dancers are doing their own somnambulistic slow dance behind her, a "drill" phrase of over one hundred counts, in which precise unison frays into individual interpretations of left and right. Tharp, in front of them, senses their momentum but can't figure out which one of them she should synchronize with. Weaving, skidding, lurching, flopping forwards or sideways and jerking upright again, she falls, has trouble assembling her limbs to get up. She dimly hears the music; its most emphatic notes jar her like a noise in the night, but she can't hang on to the thread of its rhythm. She staggers toward the wings, rockets back on a series of unpredictable cadences from the band, and finally collapses on her face.

Tharp, Rudner, and Wright danced with a certain inner focus at that time, which became part of the company's performing style. It was similar to the neutral performing attitude adopted by all avant-gardists. Besides that, the Tharp dancers had a lot of internal information and choices to pull together. They showed their concentration, but they also had rehearsed so long that the movement felt comfortable; they could be themselves. Rudner and Garcia-Lorca projected a fashion model's self-awareness; Wright seemed to want to shut out the audience and dance for herself alone; Tharp could look obstinate, challenging, and, in the Drunk solo, befuddled. Detachment, even alienation, might have served as a protective device for all the countercultural dancers, Tharp included, but for her, objectivity was a classical value as well. As the film historian Gerald Mast points out, one can't identify too closely with the audience one wants to reform: "The greatest film comedians are antisocial, but in this antagonism they reveal a higher morality."

Through some alchemy that clicked into operation with the *Jelly Rolls*, choreographic tropes that Tharp had used so often before to diversify the dance action now also facilitated personal interplay. Game structures, individual variations, unison, and the digression from unison, all reappear in the *Jelly Rolls*, but here they read as the activity of a slightly dopey bunch of people who find themselves together in a dance. As soon as they realize they're all doing the same thing, one of them veers off on her own. For Number Six, thinking of the way musicians in a Dixieland band step out and take solos, Tharp made little variations for each dancer apart from the ensemble. To make sure the audience won't be distracted, the backup group make their moves as small as possible. In the next section, Wright seems to noodle around languidly, and the group, behind her, captures and holds her shape in a series of "dots," or poses that they've learned by precisely imitating her performance on a videotape. Tharp may have borrowed the "dots" from Fred Astaire, whose backup chorus in the title number of *Top Hat* copied and held his first few moves. Even here, the Tharps make the transitions between the dots in their own ways. The last Jelly Roll is a companionable ensemble of solos, where the dancers have a pool of material they can draw from and structure on the spot.

On the London tape, the dance completed its transformation into stageworthiness with the addition of new and androgynous costumes by Kermit Love: black pants with backless tops made to look like tuxedo shirt-fronts, and patent-leather pumps. Kenneth Rinker, Tom Rawe, and Nina Wiener had joined Tharp, Wright, Rudner, and Garcia-Lorca in the company, and Tharp had made individual solos for all of them in the last sections.

With the 1971 Delacorte performance Tharp could no longer be written off as a brainy malcontent who disregarded the audience. In *The Fugue* and the *Jelly Rolls* she emerged as a choreographic giant who could command at least two different styles. Many of her most provocative gestures, like the box in *Re-Moves* and the nudity in *PYMFFYPPMFYNM YPF*, had been earnestly offered for the audience's own good, to open their eyes to more possibilities, and the *Jelly Rolls* were no different. She had simply decided to be entertaining. She wasn't a newcomer to jazz either, she just hadn't played it in performance. As more than one critic observed, *Eight Jelly Rolls* wasn't a drastic departure from what Tharp had been doing all along, but it did seem, in that single September performance, that she was releasing something she'd been holding back for a long time. At last she was fully acknowledging the music, the dance, and the audience, as necessary and equal components of her work.

Clive Barnes, who always seemed baffled by Tharp but wanted to believe, lost interest in *The Fugue* after the first few minutes, and he mistook the sound of the dancers' feet for a percussion accompaniment. But Barnes could see the *Jelly Rolls* was something different, "far more approachable," even though he overinterpreted it as "an essay in abstract jazz dance and urban despair." Critics for the mass press hated having to take Tharp seriously, and *Cue* magazine's Greer Johnson dismissed the Delacorte segment as "two gawky, interminable essays by the humorless (or deadpan?) Twyla Tharp Company."

Arlene Croce's admiring analysis appeared in the winter issue of *Ballet Review*. Tharp suited Croce's taste for nerveless brilliance: "Twyla Tharp's subject is not your life or hers, and in that sense she is a classical artist. She doesn't present herself as a force for change or as a vehicle for new ideas, and her aggressiveness is not the least bit hostile in its attitude toward the audience. She is radically different and radically new, but, whatever else you may think of it, after about a minute her kind of dancing doesn't even look strange. You find you can take more and more of it."

Tharp didn't appear in New York City again for a year, but the buzz circulated around the country as the company toured. The 1971–72 season was momentous for her. With the *Jelly Roll* material essentially shaped and put before the public, she began to process the personal crises she'd gone through—the birth of her son, the end of her marriage, and the death of her father—as she prepared *The Bix Pieces*. She had received her first significant funding, grants from the National Endowment for the Arts and the New York State Council on the Arts, and the first of two John Simon Guggenheim fellowships for choreography. *Harper's Bazaar* named her one of the hundred outstanding women in America. In April 1972 she won a prestigious Brandeis University Creative Arts Citation for younger artists— Merce Cunningham got the Medal of Achievement for his lifetime work. At the award ceremony at the Whitney Museum, Tharp gave her thousand-dollar prize, in two equal checks, to Sara Rudner and Rose Marie Wright. Later on she said, "You can't get to feeling safe and secure, or else you'll never get on with your work. I needed to pass on that money, and the dancers deserve it more than I do." She certainly wasn't taking her success for granted; she bit into it like a juicy plum.

Although *The Bix Pieces* became her second big hit, it started inauspiciously. The producers of the Paris International Festival had booked Tharp and former Cunningham dancer Viola Farber for two weeks on the 1971 program, partly on the advice of Bénédicte Pesle. Perhaps because both choreographers were reputedly avant-garde, they were assigned the Théâtre de la Cité Universitaire, a "less bourgeois" venue than the more centrally located and familiar Théâtre du Champs-Elysées, where the Batsheva Dance Company of Israel was to appear later on. Still operating on her antitheatrical instincts, Tharp wanted to perform in an open space, or a theater *and* an open space, as she told an interviewer, maybe hoping to fulfill her thwarted two-space plan for *Torelli*. She was given a huge gallery at the Cité Universitaire, while Farber appeared in a small theater with a company from Sunda, West Java, that was doing traditional Indonesian dance. All three groups shared the evening. Tharp was programmed last, and the audience balked at having to move to a new space for a performance that didn't begin until nine o'clock. What Tharp had in store was hardly designed to appease them.

Preparations didn't go well. The hall was too big and the floor was too slippery. Bill Kosmas hadn't arranged the season and this was his first tour with a dance company. While he anxiously argued with the sponsors about lighting and sound arrangements, Tharp watched rehearsals hunched at one end of the space with a towel over her head. The floor was scrubbed and doused with Coca Cola to eliminate excessive wax, and the dancers had to rubberize the bottoms of their shoes for safety. Nevertheless, someone fell at every performance. Tharp refused to dance *The One Hundreds* and Rudner had to step in for her. Normally the two initiators would perform side by side, relying on their kinesthetic radar to keep together, but Rudner only knew eighty of the phrases, so for security she and Wright faced each other. Though the *Bix* had been rehearsed in jazz shoes, Tharp decided on low heels for the women at the last minute, compounding the dangers of the slippery floor. "It completely destroyed the movement," Wright says. "We cried." The seats were arranged in sparse rows at each end of the long, narrow space. To compensate for the anticipated visibility problems, Tharp hit on the idea of stationing the dancers in separate spotlit areas for *Torelli* and inviting the audience to walk around them like sculptures. This didn't endear her to the unadventurous Parisians either.

The press was generally hostile to the whole Cité Universitaire program. Some liked Farber for her obvious technical authority and her connection to Cunningham, whom they dared not disrespect. The Indonesians had a certain exotic appeal. But Tharp offended nearly everyone, provoking the French critics to outdo each other with derisive remarks. *Le Figaro* announced that there was nothing but pretension in the company's humorless, unprofessional, and unspectacular performance. This was mild. "Poor Torelli!" mourned Jean-Pierre Barbe in *L'Aurore*. "How could they massacre such beautiful music! The dancers . . . with shocking vulgarity and heaviness, devote themselves to a sort of acrobatic jerk. . . ." He resented having to "endure this hairy and untidy outburst" and took the dancers in the spotlights to be a Happening, whose only advantage was that it allowed him to slip away through the ambulatory audience.

But there were proponents, principally Claude Sarraute of *Le Monde*, who appreciated Tharp's choreographic invention, the subtlety of the dancers' rhythm and their articulate bodies. The game-playing aspect of her work reminded him of the early days of abstract painting. John Percival came over from London and praised both Tharp and Farber, especially Tharp, for their originality. After the Festival was over, Kosmas waged a bitter fight with the sponsors, who accused Tharp of artistic fraud and refused to pay her fee until threats of a lawsuit forced them to ante up most of it. Tharp later acknowledged that the arrangements for the appearance had been unrealistic—the location too far out to attract a big enough audience to cover the sponsors' expenses in making the space workable. Her tour contracts after that became microscopically detailed.

For some reason, none of the French critics mentioned *The Bix Pieces* by name, which originally was *True Confessions*, or *Les Vraies Confessions*. The *Bix* contained Tharp's true confession—perhaps her first formal acknowledgment of what she was doing—a spoken script that accompanied part of the dance. Historically the *Bix* surfaces as a more important work than the *Jelly Rolls*, with the script to give it intellectual validation and an ongoing material existence. The two dances have chronological and stylistic connections, and they both were preserved and aired in professionally produced telecasts soon after their initial performances. Musically contemporaneous, they made a pair, one black jazz, one white. It could be argued that the *Jelly Rolls* is a more coherent and, for Tharp, a riskier work, a suite of dances in a unified choreographic and musical style, while *The Bix Pieces* mixes musical sources, dance ideas, and verbal narration. It's a collage, a lecture-demonstration in the form of a theater dance. Conceptually layered and inclusive, the *Bix* reveals Tharp's thinking more openly, if theatrically, than almost any of her other works.

As recorded for television's *Camera Three* in 1973, Tharp begins the dance in a follow spot, twirling a baton, a reference to her own overeducated childhood. Her solo distills a cluster of Americana references she would have absorbed as a cute, precocious little girl who spent a large part of her life in dancing school and at the movies. Her hair cut short with bangs screening off her gaze, Tharp wore another of Kermit Love's tuxedo-front tops, with short shorts in gray satin, sheer black hose and little low-heeled pumps that flattered her shapely legs. All the *Bix* costumes exposed the dancers' backs and shoulders, slyly drawing attention to their bodies. In most of Tharp's work from this point on, sex appeal seethes below the surface, subliminally heating up the cool performing atmosphere being cultivated.

Tharp was fantastic at playing two theatrical games at once. In her baton solo, she diluted the wiles of the music hall performer with the impassivity of the avant-garde trickster. To the legendary jazz musician Bix Beiderbecke playing his piano piece "In a Mist," she steps from foot to foot, keeping her body moving in slow shrugs, twists, and head turns. Without missing a beat, she catches a second baton thrown to her from off-camera, and briefly twirls two-handed. She drops one baton, glances at it, then catches another and another, trundling ahead like some gallant but maladroit comedian of the low stage. At one point, the offstage prop person goes amok and batons fly at her so fast she ends up with a fistful, which she drops. Finally she throws the last one down and leaves.

Like *Eight Jelly Rolls*, *The Bix Pieces* introduces each member of the company against the accumulating group, in four more bouncy recordings featuring Beiderbecke playing cornet, with Paul Whiteman's 1920s dance band and vocalist Bing Crosby. Tharp and Rudner begin a playful, girlish duet that slides in and out of a fox-trot. Tharp retrieves the drum-majorette struts and swaggers she hinted at in her solo. Rudner kicks, shakes her shoulders, and skips, with the innocent awareness of a Lolita. Wright is more purposeful, with spiky hand gestures and head jerks, as Rudner and Tharp do a sort of droopy chorus line around her. Garcia-Lorca's solo is the slowest of all, with luxurious leg gestures and tiny wiggles, against the trio's doodling.

When Kenneth Rinker appears, with Rudner, he uses less torso articulation but a lot of legs and arms. Wright and Garcia-Lorca join them soon to complete the ensemble. The dancers have appeared in the order in which they joined the company, a practice Tharp maintained in company listings and program credits until 1991.

Having gotten the introductions out of the way and pretty much dispensed with Bix Beiderbecke, Tharp now gets to the heart of *The Bix Pieces*, the extraordinary text called "Why They Were Made." The *Camera Three* video cuts to Marian Hailey, dressed in flowing white blouse with a bow at the neck, satin breeches, and black stockings and pumps, a modern adaptation, perhaps, of an eighteenth-century dancing master's costume. Hailey, a professional actress, was one of several narrators for *The Bix Pieces* over the years. Garcia-Lorca wasn't in this part of the dance, and she delivered the text frequently until she left the company in 1974. Tharp herself stood in for an indisposed Hermione Gingold at a performance in Brooklyn in 1977. The text was deadly serious, even sentimental, and Hailey's polished, technical way of delivering it warded off the laughter that Tharp's audiences were always ready to let loose during this period.

"I hated to tap-dance when I was a kid," she says on behalf of Tharp, who at first is tapping off-camera. The script goes on to a recital of Tharp's early classes, then comes to an abrupt stop with her father. "My father died this Spring and this dance was to commemorate the time when he was young." Tharp imagines the life of the '20s as relaxed, innocent, "concerned with style," like Beiderbecke's music. For Tharp, style is a way of evoking the past and all its associations. But her deeper point is that regardless of style, the real content of art doesn't change from one era to the next. "It seems to me that art is a question of emphasis. That aesthetics and ethics are the same. That inventiveness resides first in choice and then in synthesis—in bringing it all together. That this action is repeated over and over again, the resolutions being somehow marvelously altered each time." This credo still underlies her choreography three decades later.

Tharp/Hailey describes the main components of her dance: lyricism translated as a flowing, nonpercussive rhythm; the illusion of fluidity that results from compressing many small pieces of movement into a very short duration; the amalgamation of seemingly different stylistic ideas; improvisation as a process where the performer makes choices among very well-known materials; and finally the certainty that art has a long, unfolding life: "Can anything be new, original, private?"

After Tharp's baton-and-tap vignette, the company members arrive again—Rudner, Wright, and Rinker—while Hailey continues the lecture. Rudner solos to illustrate the idea of lyricism. Wright plunges into seventeen punchy numbered moves that Hailey commands her to assemble into a swift but nonlinear web, the edges rounded off by the speed of the transitions. Wright and Rinker demonstrate a sequence of steps that have balletic names but that can be executed classically by Wright and with modern looseness by Rinker. To eyes now accustomed to the conflation of ballet and modern movement, Wright and Rinker don't seem that stylistically divergent. But even when Tharp used classically trained dancers—Wright was the first—they were never cookie-cutter paragons anyway. Wright had enough individuality and Rinker had enough technique so that they already embodied the fusion Tharp perfected during the next decade.

After this lesson, Hailey/Tharp reveals that all the movement for the *Bix* was choreographed to the Op. 76 Haydn string quartets. According to Wright, the whole dance was built on four phrases. Performed to the initial Beiderbecke/Whiteman songs, they take on the gloss and lightness Tharp felt would evoke her father's generation. During the step demonstration with Hailey, the music switches to Haydn's Adagio Rondo on a folk theme, known during the pre-Hitler era as the German national anthem ("*Deutschland über Alles*"). The quartet begins another set of variations on the phrases, sometimes pairing off and later working together. There were instructions for each variation, but throughout, the dancers were supposed to stick to the original phrase material even when they were pushing each other around or lifting one another.

For example, Wright would start a phrase and Rinker had to respond with a different one. Then they'd trade roles and continue with a new set. It's unlikely that the audience could identify the original phrases. Even if they appear intact at any point—perhaps Rudner's phrase is number one, Wright's is number two and so on—the dancers borrow pieces of each other's movement from the outset, and Tharp has done her compositional play with the shape, timing, size, and placement of the core movements. Rudner's little two-handed digging gesture across the body flowers into Wright's sudden full-body evocation of a Greek nymph. During the ballet-modern litany, when Wright does a grand battement, Rinker throws an arm high instead of a leg.

A brief coda for Wright, Rudner, Rinker, and Garcia-Lorca uses the material again, this time to a chorus of "Abide with Me" arranged for brass by

Thelonius Monk. Staying in a tight cluster, they begin a phrase, then turn and gesture percussively toward the center. After an instant's hold, they pivot out, unfurl another phrase, lock together, spin out. In the short space of the music, they generate extreme and unpredictable changes of speed, emphasizing the stops and starts, in pointed contrast to the fluidity of all the earlier dancing in the piece. "Can anything be new? original? private?"

The company toured New York State, the Midwest and Los Angeles early in 1972. By the time *The Bix Pieces* came to New York, in September at the Delacorte Theater, Tharp had made another jazz piece, almost offhandedly. *The Raggedy Dances* to Scott Joplin and other composers was quite elusive. It was still unfinished when Tharp decided to show it, unannounced, as a "sampler" after the *Bix* at the Delacorte. It had its official premiere a month later on an evening Tharp shared with the Erick Hawkins company, part of a big modern dance series at the ANTA theater. Then she began to cut the dance, eventually dropping two-thirds of its twenty-four minutes, and took herself out of the cast. After a few years on the road, the reduction became known as the *Rags Suite*.

The slouchy, rhythmic Tharp style was now established, although each new jazz piece differed slightly from the others. *Eight Jelly Rolls* had delivered the shock of Tharp as musical and fun, and *The Bix Pieces* drew the audience's attention to individual dancers and then to Tharp's spoken manifesto. *The Raggedy Dances* seems more settled. Not only the dancing style but the look of the stage began to seem characteristic of Tharp and no one else. Once again she used separate, even wildly unrelated musical selections, but *The Raggedy Dances* seemed continuous. People entered while other people were finishing a section, did contradictory riffs, then left, seemingly ignoring the music's entrance and exit signals. There was one section of more or less conventional unison movement—the big finale—but instead of lining up symmetrically and facing the audience for it, the five dancers moved in a flock, using only one side of the stage. In fact, the dancers frequently didn't orient themselves to the audience at all, but worked facing their partners. Soloists often seemed self-absorbed, inwardly focused.

The idea of simultaneous but uncoordinated activities had pervaded Merce Cunningham's dance for decades, and Tharp took to it. The more dancing she could produce, the better she liked it. With Cunningham, the audience could make its own choices among the different activities going on at the same time, pick out particular individuals to follow. But Cunningham's theatrical randomness was intentional and largely unedited. Tharp always operated with some internal organization in hand. The dancers shared a limited amount of choreographic material, seldom falling into unison but resounding off one another in canons and other displaced timing. They were working with a musical impulse even when they worked in silence or when they'd learned the movement to different music. Tharp's stage could look busy, highly energized, but there was some principle at work keeping it together. It felt harmonious even when it looked crazy. William Whitener, who later became a Tharp dancer, has commented on the relation between her dance and New York street life: "It's the amount of traffic on the stage. The way people maneuver through space with large groups of dancers on the stage. I mean it's of course all choreographed, but so are the streets of New York in their way."

Simultaneity also assured that each dancer would be seen in his or her own right. During the early '70s, when Tharp was making the transition to outright theatricality, she worked at the problem of how to help the audience sort out the people on the stage—without assigning permanent rankings to the members of the company. In *The Bix Pieces* she speaks of affording the soloist some consideration as against the chorus, and to her formalist mind this usually translated into counterpoint. Working with six or seven dancers, or a corps of twenty, she didn't resort to the usual balletic tactics of positioning clumps of people to frame or mimic the important dancers in front.

The "dots" section of the *Jelly Rolls* was one solution—as the backup group captured and held Rose Marie Wright's movement in a series of poses. In *The Bix Pieces* and the *Rags*, solo dancers and backups are usually doing contrasting but equally interesting movement. Their floor patterns set them apart from one another. With the soloist stationary, one or more other dancers will circle around her or drift back and forth. Sometimes they're linked rhythmically or choreographically, but sometimes their movement is quite different. During Wright's solo in the first part of the *Bix*, Tharp and Rudner scurry around like windup dolls, strut like drum majorettes, chase each other with little skipping steps, show off with slow extensions and stretches. During Garcia-Lorca's sexy solo, Tharp, Rudner, and Wright periodically lounge and slide against each other.

Another important contrapuntal device was the crossover. Tharp used it early in the *Jelly Rolls*, in her fast, shadowboxing appearances with Rudner.

The background crossover was well developed in Paul Taylor's work. In fact, Tharp had been a resentful participant in at least two of them (*Scudorama* and *Junction*) during her short career with Taylor—both required anonymous, crablike acrobatics across the floor. Later, Taylor arranged crossovers to open up suppressed layers of psychological or cultural meaning, as in the war scenes silhouetted behind the swinging Lindy Hoppers in *Company B*. Tharp used the device as a choreographic tool to provide contrast, to showcase the small units of the company, and frequently to add comic possibilities.

The *Rags* started out with an ambling, companionable duet for Rose Marie Wright and Ken Rinker, and proliferated into syncopations and good-natured gamesmanship that carried through as three other dancers appeared. Rudner, Garcia-Lorca, and Nina Wiener comprised the rest of the company at that time, but the casting shifted constantly during its two-year run as a complete piece. Tharp created a strange solo for herself in a two-piece purple bathing suit, featuring the slow rotations and body-part isolations of a stripper. The title of the music, Scott Joplin's "The Entertainer," was ironically applied to the solo. According to critic Deborah Jowitt, "She dances for a long time, looking with every passing minute smaller, lonelier, tireder. A stripper seen through the wrong end of a telescope . . ." Garcia-Lorca soon learned the solo from Tharp, and without much prompting she understood "that it was somebody doing something that she didn't really want to do, but knew that she was good at. And got some satisfaction from feeling a connection with the person watching her. But ultimately felt very alone." Tharp was certainly aware of the conflicting agendas inherent in a stripper's performance, and indeed in any dancing for the public. She no doubt experienced ambivalence about it herself, and years later, when she was approaching forty, she did a similar but more aggressive dance within a longer solo called *1903*, to Randy Newman's insidious, voyeuristic "Suzanne."

As she had in *The Bix Pieces*, Tharp once again pointed out the relationship between the popular and the classical idiom, this time capping the *Rags* with a duet to Mozart's variations on "*Ah, vous dirai-je, Maman,*" better known as "Twinkle, Twinkle, Little Star." Nothing about the five-minute sequence, made on Wright and Rudner, violated ragtime's easygoing reciprocity and intuitive rhythms, which had been seen in the rest of the dance, but somehow the classical purity of Mozart invoked swifter footwork and unmistakable counterpoint. The Mozart duet was made as a birthday present for Bill Kosmas; Rudner and Wright performed it for him at a party in the studio. Tharp's personal references weren't meant to be identified by the audience, but the initial tone of cordiality and casualness, the playful cross-purposes of the later sections, plus Tharp's mordant "Entertainer," gave the work texture.

The Delacorte and ANTA performances brought more enthusiastic reviews. Clive Barnes loved *The Bix Pieces*, and after *The Raggedy Dances'* official premiere he remarked: "her work has a mixture of sloe-eyed innocence and intense professionalism that I find totally endearing." Ellen W. Jacobs, soon to become a successful dance publicist, surveyed the entire ANTA Marathon in the alternative paper *Changes*. Jacobs found the six-week, twenty-one-company season disappointingly mainstream except for Tharp. Noting that the project hadn't attracted the general public as hoped, Jacobs asked, "Are modern dancers eternally doomed to dance for family and friends?"

Jacobs, one of the many young writers Tharp inspired to eloquent prose, noted the deceptively spontaneous look of the company in *The Raggedy Dances*. She went on to probe Tharp's "Entertainer," so different in tone from the nonchalance of the rest of the piece. "Where a strip teaser's movements are expansive and outward, hers are stingy and minimal—though definite. I shudder, yet my eyes are glued. . . . Aggressive in her privacy, she is seductive only in the questions her performance provokes. If anything the work is anti-sensual. Who is she performing for?"

Entertaining had become a necessary part of Tharp's drive for success, despite her mixed personal feelings about it. After *Eight Jelly Rolls*, the company took its first bows ever, instead of simply vanishing at the end of the performance, and critics recorded the event. Anticipating a tumultuous reaction to *The Bix Pieces*, she had prepared the *Raggedy* preview as an encore. From the inception of Tharp's jazz cycle, the audience, on its own, began to acknowledge individual sections of a dance. This broke all the rules. You were supposed to take in a modern dance silently and respectfully until the end, even if it was made in suite form. A live performance videotaped in Minneapolis in 1972, a month after *the Raggedy Dances* premiere, records frequent appreciative laughter and applause.

Perhaps more important for Tharp than the added critical validation was the fact that Robert Joffrey attended the Delacorte performance in September 1972. His second company, the Joffrey II, was performing a piece that night by its director, Jonathan Watts, but, prompted by his partner, Gerald Arpino, and others, he was also checking out the up-and-coming Tharp. Since the 1960s the extraordinary Robert Joffrey had been building a small ballet company, and he was in the process of acquiring for it the most extensive repertory of twentieth-century revivals in the history of American ballet. In addition to restoring landmark works from Diaghilev's Ballets Russes, the English choreographer Frederick Ashton, and the Americans George Balanchine, Jerome Robbins, and Agnes de Mille, he mounted a few choice nineteenth-century items and programmed new works by himself and his resident choreographer Arpino, plus outsiders. Still, commissioning a new ballet from the unpredictable Tharp was a stretch of even his imagination.

Along with its devotion to archival preservation, the Joffrey Ballet cultivated an image of lively contemporaneity. Like Tharp, Robert Joffrey understood what he needed to do to survive, and he never presented the popular works any less respectfully than the classics. Though he started as a ballet purist, he fostered Arpino's glitzy eclecticism and brought back modernist experiments from the past, like Léonide Massine's *Parade*, which was revived in New York during the same 1973 winter season as Tharp's *Deuce Coupe*. *Parade* might be seen as a forerunner of *Deuce Coupe*, with its clashing elements, modern dress, low-culture milieu, and quasi-popular Erik Satie score. Robert Joffrey and Tharp approached contemporary dance fusion from opposite directions: Joffrey spreading out and diversifying a technical focus that had started with a solid ballet base, and Tharp infusing modern dance with the strength, mobility, and charisma of classicism.

The Joffrey repertory already included several jazz ballets, and modern dancers Alvin Ailey and Anna Sokolow contributed to early Joffrey seasons. But it was Robert Joffrey himself, an infrequent choreographer, who ignited a new wave of popularity with *Astarte* in 1967. A year before that, the company had taken up residence at New York City Center and had incorporated three ballets with special resonance for the troubled American conscience: Sokolow's 1955 drama of urban alienation, *Rooms*; Jerome Robbins's 1959 ballet in silence "about relationships," *Moves*; and the 1932 antiwar masterpiece *The Green Table*, by the German expressionist Kurt Jooss. *Astarte* tapped into the introspective sensibility underlying those older works, with a visual flamboyance borrowed from hippiedom and the peace movement, which were thriving on the West Coast as Robert Joffrey began developing the piece during a summer residency.

To a commissioned score by assembled-for-the-occasion rock band Crome Syrcus, an Everyman rose from his seat in the orchestra and strode, hypnotized, to the stage, where a woman enticed him from inside a psychedelic web of strobe lights and peacock designs. Four projectors threw a voyeuristic film of their own distorted images onto their actions. He stripped to his briefs and they made love with a cool eroticism. Then all the theatrical contrivances cleared away, and he walked out into 56th Street through the back door of the stage. Titillating but tasteful, *Astarte* was the first big mixed-media ballet, and it earned the Joffrey an eager new audience and a tidal wave of publicity. Arpino followed it up with several numbers featuring spectacular dancing and trendy trimmings. *Trinity* (1970) dignified a defiant virtuosity with ceremony—the dancers solemnly placed candles on the stage and left them burning as they exited to a pounding musical heartbeat. By 1972 *Trinity* had become the company's signature work.

Tharp had to come up with something to equal this. She says she studied the Joffrey repertory and audience during the fall season to assess the best way to make her mark. Without exploiting psychology, politics, or virtuosic display, she created something spectacular and immediate, something that transformed the dancers and made the ballet stage seem newly invented. *Deuce Coupe* was so successful that several performances were added to the season. And like a real American product, it had a built-in obsolescence; after only two years it had to be retooled before it could be performed again.

Robert Joffrey had already thought of the rock and harmony group the Beach Boys for a ballet, and Tharp welcomed the idea, although she'd considered the Beatles. The budget precluded having either group appear live. She used fourteen of the Beach Boys' recorded songs. Tharp by now had a lot of experience with putting together existing music, and she had no qualms about bending the Beach Boys to her purposes. Composer David Horowitz wrote four piano variations on "Cuddle Up," which she used as a kind of throughline for the dance, calling it "Matrix." The rest of the songs were subtly edited to make a coherent score on tape.

Deuce Coupe was probably the first ballet accompanied by pop records. The Joffrey's previous scores had included modern composers (Paul Creston, Lou Harrison, David Diamond), contemporary symphonic works with a jazz influence (Morton Gould), third-stream jazz (Kenyon Hopkins, Teo Macero), and the made-to-order rock of *Astarte* and *Trinity*. All of these had acceptably artistic dimensions. It was exactly the familiarity of the Beach Boys, their *not* being art, that was such an asset to *Deuce Coupe*. In his remarkable book about rock 'n' roll, *Mystery Train,* the critic Greil Marcus notes the lack of condescension in certain American pop artists, who have "hoped, no matter how secretly, that their work would lift America to heaven, or drive a stake through its heart." Marcus was launching a discussion about Randy Newman and the Beach Boys, but he might well have been describing Tharp.

Deuce Coupe became a phenomenal hit, but it had a stressful incubation, right up to its premiere at Chicago's Auditorium Theater on 8 February 1973. From the start of her discussions with Robert Joffrey, Tharp stipulated that her own company would dance in the work. This would be another first, for even in the legendary 1959 two-company encounter between Martha Graham and George Balanchine, *Episodes,* the modern dancers appeared in Graham's dance, the ballet dancers in Balanchine's, with a token crossover dancer in each piece (Sallie Wilson in Graham's dance and Paul Taylor in Balanchine's). *Deuce Coupe* was to be a fully integrated production, and this caused anxiety on both sides.

Tharp's dancers were in awe of the Joffreys' technical abilities. She broached the idea of the project to them before she took it on. Garcia-Lorca says: "I was not a strong technical dancer, which of course I knew better than anyone else. And being with these ballet dancers was a little daunting. A little scary." Rinker felt intimidated too, even though Tharp had already steered him into taking ballet class. He says: "I'm not a ballet dancer and never was and never wanted to be, but I tried to do it like I was." The prospect of being seen in the City Center Joffrey context was irresistible to the Tharp dancers, though, and Tharp worked out most of the movement on them in her usual way before Joffrey rehearsals began.

Beatriz Rodriguez was among the Joffrey dancers who welcomed the project enthusiastically. She had just come up from the Joffrey II and "I was just open to anything that came along! And it was a wonderful experience with her." But there was intense resistance from others. The more militant company members resented Tharp's jazz orientation and the "white" jazz of the Beach Boys. Besides that, she was an unknown, a funky downtown apparition in mismatching clothes, nothing like the star presences who'd come to them before. Once she began work, they felt confused and threatened. Richard Colton had recently joined the main company after two years in Joffrey II. He was understudying several roles in *Deuce Coupe* so he attended most of the rehearsals. He thought one source of the antagonism was Tharp's openness. She wasn't asking the dancers to imitate, to reproduce movement exactly, as they strove to do in their encyclopedic repertory of revivals. "Steps were being thrown out and you as a dancer were taking them and shedding a kind of new light on them. She was excited about mistakes or what things happened, and she was bringing a new breath and life, and a kind of spontaneity. . . . It was a company based on counting. There were no counts. It was just this great music."

People were grumbling in the dressing rooms: what *was* this? Tharp assigned Rose Marie Wright to lower the anxiety level. "I became Twyla's liaison between the dancers and the ballet. Because the Joffrey Ballet people really rebelled against this movement. I mean we went in there and they didn't know what to make of us. . . . There were dancers that Twyla wanted in the piece, and they didn't want to be in it. And I'm the one that said, Look, this is really a glissade, this is really an arabesque. . . . I was very excited because she was doing really interesting things with the ballet vocabulary. And it was really challenging to do and I was helping."

The project was hard on Tharp too. Added to her innate ambition and her struggles to realize this biggest project of her career, the Joffrey's plans for the winter season aroused her competitiveness. Preceding *Deuce Coupe*'s City Center premiere by two weeks, there was to be a new ballet by Eliot Feld, to a symphonic-jazz score by Morton Gould. Feld, just a year younger than Tharp, was considered the rising young ballet choreographer of the time. He had as eclectic a background as Tharp, including performances with modern dancers Pearl Lang, Sophie Maslow and Donald McKayle. Like Tharp and company, he developed a close relationship with Richard Thomas, the guru of classically minded but unconventional young dancers. Feld had created the role of Baby John in Jerome Robbins's *West Side Story* on Broadway, but his first choreographies, as a member of American Ballet Theater, were classical, innovative, and very successful. In 1969, with strong support from Clive Barnes, Feld had started his own company at Brooklyn Academy of Music. Tharp too was eyeing this newly created dance venue, and she felt let down when Lewis Lloyd left Cunningham to work at BAM and shifted his concentration to Feld's new enterprise.

As Tharp and Feld rehearsed at the Joffrey in the fall of 1972, Tharp suspected—probably wrongly—that her rival was getting more rehearsal time, better dancers, and a bigger production budget than she. When money problems seemed about to curtail *Deuce Coupe* plans, Robert Joffrey supported her, and two Joffrey board members raised the money she needed. Feld's *Jive* turned out to be "a 1950's ballet in sneakers" according to Clive Barnes, one of the few reviewers who were lukewarm about *Deuce Coupe*. "It isn't half the ballet *Jive* is," he wrote in his first notice. A few months later, Barnes reaffirmed his opinion that Tharp's "choreographic squiggling" wore off quickly even if it had some initial appeal. Nevertheless, Feld's work disappeared quickly while *Deuce Coupe* became a landmark.

No one anticipated this outcome during *Deuce Coupe*'s pockmarked journey to the stage. The day came when Tharp stopped rehearsal and announced that anyone who didn't want to be in the piece could leave; she wouldn't hold it against them. At least half the dancers walked out. Rebecca Wright was a leading ballerina in the company at the time. She had just been cast as Titania in Frederick Ashton's *The Dream*, but Tharp had passed over her for *Deuce Coupe*. When she heard about the mass exodus, she went to Robert Joffrey and told him she wanted to do Tharp's work. "I said, I think I can do that work really well, and I think she's in—I was so arrogant!—she's kind of in trouble, maybe I can help her out. Privately I was thinking I am going to *overwhelm*. I am going to be her saviour." As soon as she walked into the studio, Wright realized her mistake. "Oh my God, what am I doing here? I don't understand this stuff. . . . Syncopation I get, reversal I get, but putting this all together and watching Rose, watching Sara, watching these people do this work, rapidly!" Wright decided to stay with it, even practicing at home, until she could master the material. She became one of the three dancers who opened the ballet.

Deuce Coupe had a didactic subtext that reflected the actual circumstances of two vastly different dance companies working together. Though they came from opposing traditions, the two camps had a lot in common and were going to find a way of working together. Individuals would learn to accommodate to each other and submit to form. Structurally, the dance followed an exquisite Tharpian logic. Movement material came from the ballet lexicon, demonstrated throughout the piece by a soloist, Erika Goodman, who symbolized tradition and remained fixated on her own steps while the rest of the large cast surged around her. Additional phrase material was drawn from popular culture, rock 'n' roll, and Tharp's distinctive vocabulary, then shaped and mixed until it finally coalesced into a large, formal group section near the end.

The piece opened quietly on Goodman's first long sequence of steps, with Rebecca Wright and William Whitener behind her, doing a pas de deux to the first version of the Matrix, a romantic piano solo. The duet, confined to an upstage corner, began with small adjustments and port de bras, and expanded into leaps, a high lift, and a supported arabesque. Glenn White, Henry Berg, and Starr Danias appeared, and suddenly the Beach Boys' "Little Deuce Coupe" burst out as the rest of the dancers, led by Rodriguez, trouped in one by one across the footlights. The young writer Robb Baker later described this moment in *Dance Magazine*: ". . . out comes Beatriz Rodriguez, leading on a whole line of slinky/sleazy Joffrey/Tharp movement-makers. And the audience *knows* at once. Understands the juxtaposition. Whistles and cheers. By damn, it *is* the Beach Boys!" As the line advanced, one character cracked his knuckles, one shuffled forward with wrists dangling from outstretched arms and her head thrown back, one sauntered, one gazed into the audience. Movements repeated, and it became evident that they were all performing the same phrase, but in their own ways. On opening night in Chicago, the audience broke into yells of pleasure and recognition as this began to unfold. The dancers couldn't conceal their astonishment. Apprehension about the project vanished in that instant. The next day, defectors were clamoring to get back into the ballet.

The heart of *Deuce Coupe* consisted of "character" dances, where the accompanying songs inspired the movement. Dancers surfed across the stage in their socks to "Catch a Wave," hunkered down with caveman sluggishness to "Alley Oop." Rudner did an unforgettable sexy solo to "Got to Know the Woman." Tharp trotted around like a frisky calf begging to be roped and captured by "Long Tall Texan" Rose Marie Wright. There was a furious and funny mock battle-chase between Tharp and Gary Chryst that ended in an elaborate high-five truce. Several other individual dancers got a chance to stand out, sparked by Tharp's own tough, wry performing among them. Impersonating kids on the loose, leading the California life that Tharp had missed out on, they celebrated pals and play, reckless excitement, cars, sunshine, and pot. The audience adored them.

After the long, feisty string of variations, the exuberance subsided. "Don't Go Near the Water" and "Mama Says" introduced serious matters. The individuality, overload, and confusion must be disciplined and calmed down. Romantic love—"Wouldn't It Be Nice?" and "Cuddle Up"—brought the high spirits under control. Again a phrase, resembling the one introduced by Wright and Whitener at the beginning of the ballet, was passed among a group of dancers. This time they all stood facing the audience and politely waited while one or two at a time did a piece of the phrase. Tharp danced a brief solo version of Goodman's phrase. Then the whole group streamed across as they had in the first song, but this time they were doing the Matrix phrase, a fusion of ballet steps and expansive transitional movements. At a musical climax, the ensemble collected into a pose, with a girl held high in the air by several men as other dancers gazed up at her. Tharp had wanted this freeze to be lit in an explosive, blinding flash, but Jennifer Tipton couldn't manage it. She created a silhouette instead. The image evoked a news photographer's flashbulb event, like some tragic student demonstration in 1968.

Then the girl was slowly lowered to the floor and the others drifted away, leaving Goodman to go on with her lexicon. Like the eruption of "Little Deuce Coupe" at the beginning of the ballet, this denouement signaled a change and a continuation—perhaps the end of adolescence, an embarkation into a future of responsibility and order. Richard Colton felt at this point that the group was maturing. "If someone would run and go to the side, there'd be someone there for them. . . . There was this sense of being able to know yourself and your movement but also to . . . have this wonderful awareness of this community around you." According to Ken Rinker, by the end of the tempestuous rehearsal period, "it felt like we were all dancing together in the same manner." Tharp endeared herself to the dancers and reinforced the bonding process by gathering the cast in a circle before the opening night performance. She spoke to them while they all held hands. According to Christine Uchida, "She was one of us, we were all together. . . . She dropped that soon after that, which I always missed. But that was a really nice thing. And I think it really brought everyone together."

Tharp added one more brilliant stroke to the ballet—no one can remember whether it was in place for the Chicago performances. For a couple of years, an increasingly flamboyant display of graffiti had been appearing around New York, most prominently on the outsides of subway cars. By 1972 hot disputes foamed around these designs. Were they expressions of defiance against the Establishment? Wanton vandalism against public property? Or a refreshing antidote to the grim daily commute? This was the age of resistance and threats, claims to entitlement, and an exhausted fury at the waning debacle in Vietnam. It was also the age of Pop Art, junk sculpture, found objects, and musique concrète. Art was coming out of the cloister and into a more public arena. Even nonpolitical work offended some people. The city put Sanitation Department crews to work scrubbing the paint off the trains; next morning new decorations would appear. In fact, the graffiti contained few threats or profanity. Journalists eventually found the perpetrators, who turned out to be youths from Spanish Harlem, writing and embellishing their own noms de plume.

Tharp says she had a sudden inspiration for the *Deuce Coupe* decor while riding the subway one day: "An ongoing upstage mural by adolescent boys." What better way to equal the Joffrey's spectacular production values without imitating them, to project a timely image without resorting to Miliskin or candles. An assistant in Bill Kosmas's office spoke Spanish, and she located the United Graffiti Artists, an agency newly formed to market what the artists had been giving away to the city for free. The Joffrey Ballet hired Rick II, Coco 144, SJK 171, Stay-Hi 149, Rican 619, and Charmin 65 for each performance of *Deuce Coupe*. The street artists entered during one of the first mass dance numbers and began spray-painting their designs on three huge paper panels. As they covered the space, the paper rolled up to give them more. When they left, before Tharp's Matrix solo, the paper continued rolling out, so that once again the background was blank at the end of the ballet.

The bold, colorful graffiti made a lively setting for the dance and deepened its meaning. Tharp thought of the designs as a form of teenage identity advertisements, matching the Beach Boys' milieu. The writers in their jeans and big hair reinforced the central conflict of the ballet by contrasting street art with the rarefied behavior of studio-bred dancers. They could all occupy the same stage, Tharp was insisting. But the graffiti also gave the work a political edge. Just two years before, Tom Wolfe's famous piece "Radical Chic" had captured a certain naive desire on the part of wealthy and artistic types to support liberal causes that might be more dangerous than they seemed. Like Tharp, who thought of *Deuce Coupe* as a commercial proposition—"I never lost sight of the fact that Bob Joffrey was hiring me to make successful art," she wrote—the graffiti writers were hoping to come in out of the tunnels and get a piece of the money. *New York* magazine, ever alert for a new blip on the culture scope, ran a cover story on graffiti three weeks after the *Deuce Coupe* premiere, complete with a hokey competition for the finest subway decoration and a five-page story by Richard Goldstein on the whole phenomenon. The magazine's music critic, Alan Rich, thought *Deuce Coupe* a great addition to the Joffrey's roster of pop ballets.

Tharp had rejuvenated an old idea with "the marvelously zany, insinuating, made-up quality of the ensemble, the flickering, rock-steady wit of it all, and, as that final little genius-ridden touch, the setting of the action in front of those inspired graffiti artists puttering and sputtering away at the backdrop."

Tharp certainly was not preoccupied with world or national politics, savvy as she was about style, nor was she aiming to improve life for the disadvantaged in Spanish Harlem. But employing these semi outlaws from the margins did have a feeling of rescue. The hippie lifestyle too had a certain exotic appeal for the audience, though in real life Tharp had now made a definitive turn away from impoverished bohemia. As a ballet *Deuce Coupe* made a soft but provocative and financially rewarding statement. It was hardly abrasive or threatening, like Anna Sokolow's *Rooms*, which offended so many people that it was pulled from the repertory. *Deuce Coupe*'s message of rapprochement and fun was one the Joffrey audience could embrace. If graffiti writing was politically provocative at all, given its origins in East Harlem and its association in people's minds to radical groups like the Young Lords, the artists of *Deuce Coupe*, like Tharp, had crossed over into a more pragmatic and materialistic world.

5

Local to Express
1973–1975

Deuce Coupe's great success intensified the pace and expanded the reach of Tharp's career. She had more opportunities than ever, and she wanted to accept them all. By the time an altered and more stable company was functioning, in the spring of 1977, she had made new works for two ballet companies; reconfigured *Deuce Coupe* for the Joffrey dancers alone; and choreographed *After All*, to the Albinoni Adagio for Strings and Organ, for ice dancer John Curry. She had worked for months on an abortive TV project at WGBH in Boston, completed professional videos of three major dances, and taped the extant repertory for documentary purposes. The Tharp company toured with the Joffrey and on their own during this period. They went to Europe three times and had productive out-of-town residencies as well as their first invited seasons at the American Dance Festival, Jacob's Pillow, and Brooklyn Academy of Music. Most of the Tharp dancers who had created *Deuce Coupe* left, and important new members arrived: Tom Rawe, Jennifer Way, Shelley Washington, and the first of several defectors from the Joffrey Ballet.

Tharp choreographed steadily for her own dancers, but only one company work from this period, *Sue's Leg*, endured over the years in its original form. Everything else, about ten pieces, was soon scrapped, reworked, or folded into another production. Deeply parsimonious, Tharp hated to

throw anything away. She had long made a practice of recycling choreographic material she hadn't quite used up. After 1973 she was taking more
chances in more exposed places; there were more loose ends and delayed
consummations. She made the first of several new models of *Deuce Coupe*, for
the Joffrey dancers alone, early in 1975. Each of the later versions, with different numbers of dancers redistributed among the roles, retained some of
the original material arranged in new sequences.

"I got on the Twyla Tharp train at a time when it was changing from local to express," says Ken Rinker. ". . . the wheels turning faster and the train
getting grander and the stops being spiffier." Rinker had joined Tharp at the
inception of *The Bix Pieces*. When she approached him earlier, he had his eye
on Merce Cunningham's company and was seriously taking classes there.
Rinker had studied modern dance while getting a degree in English at the
University of Maryland, and when he arrived in New York in 1970 he'd already had considerable experience, dancing in the company of Ethel Butler
and doing his own choreography. The only thing he remembers about his
first brush with Tharp—as an extra in the 1970 Judson Church McDonagh
book party and benefit—was being nervous because Cunningham was in the
audience. Rinker eventually realized that he would never be bold enough to
ask the imposing but noncommittal Cunningham for a place in his company.
Just at that moment, the summer of 1971, Tharp's invitation came, and he
accepted.

Rinker taught dance twice a week at the Brooklyn Ethical Culture school
to supplement his hundred-dollar-a-week income from Tharp. Apprehensive at first about switching from Cunningham's work to Tharp's, which was
so different, he found his bearings when he realized it was all right to dance
to the music of *The Bix Pieces*. "Twyla was never the type to come out and say,
We're doing a new dance and you're going to do a solo and it's gonna be a
trio and I'm gonna use you, you, and you. No. We just sort of all got behind
her and danced, and then the next day it was either the same thing or it
wasn't the same thing. Or you were doing that and she was doing this, and
then suddenly you were doing it with this music: Oh well, we'll try it with
this music. . . ." Tharp could make tremendous demands on dancers but at
the same time ignite and incorporate their individual contributions. Her
challenge—not all the dancers who loved her work were up to it—was for
them to accept her extreme resourcefulness in making up steps and then
continue working the steps in their own ways. "The more I trusted myself in
making decisions," Rinker says, "the more I felt like I was becoming like Sara

and Rose. Where they were doing Twyla's work obviously, but had a differ-ent point of view. . . . Twyla was very good about letting people go."

Initially Rinker felt like a pickup dancer. Tharp didn't make any long-term commitment to him outright. When the company finished the Paris engagement, he ran into Tharp and Kosmas at the airport. He told her he was going back to New York after a visit to Berlin, and "She said, 'I really like you.' And I remember there was a pause, like there was supposed to be another part to this sentence and it didn't come. . . . It was her saying I'd like you to keep dancing with the company. . . . I'd just *assumed* that I was going to be dancing with the company." After this encounter Rinker felt he had been admitted to the inner circle.

Tharp was chronically ambivalent about maintaining a permanent com-pany of her own. What she really wanted was a group that would work around the clock without expecting a salary. Not that she begrudged paying them when money was available. But she saw herself being drawn into the seemingly unbreakable loop that bound the whole American dance busi-ness. Touring would pay the dancers but interfere with making new chore-ography. Touring meant keeping a repertory of old pieces that presenters could sell to their audiences and that the company could put up in new the-aters with little rehearsal. Performing on the road and maintaining the repertory while at home ate up the hours and held creativity at bay. Tharp thought this was self-defeating and maybe even immoral. Ken Rinker shared her concern about "getting stale, and not forging ahead. . . . How do we do rep and not be a repertory company?" In some ideal world, a major dance company would have a theater and working space at its disposal, and be given subsidies so it could survive without debilitating months on the road. This never really happened in America, not even during the "Dance Boom" of the 1970s and '80s.

Twyla Tharp kept trying to circumvent the system she found corrosive and demeaning. One way of getting the bodies she needed was to offer young dancers the chance to work with her as a learning experience. She tried this in various ways over the years—first with the group that went to New Berlin in 1970. She experimented with adding the two Oberlin stu-dents as apprentices in 1970–71. At the beginning of 1972, facing a tough schedule of tours to Upstate New York, the Midwest, and Los Angeles, she signed on almost twenty young dancers as a "farm club." Sometimes these schemes would yield a regular company member, but they were usually ad hoc arrangements, financed by specific engagements or grants. She never worked out a long-term way to keep some of the company in New York making new work with her while the rest trudged around the touring circuits to earn the company's living.

After *Deuce Coupe*, Tharp capitalized on her growing prestige and personal charisma to charge high fees for company appearances, for the use of her dances by other companies, and for freelance choreographing jobs. She was offered commissions; some were prestigious and even creatively interesting, like the ice-dance number she made for John Curry. These jobs earned income she could use for her company, but they also took her away while she worked on them. A certain pecking order had developed naturally within the company, with Rudner and Wright as trusted lieutenants and advisors. Everyone shared teaching responsibilities. On tour, one dancer would be assigned to keep track of the costumes, another made out the rehearsal schedule. There were group meetings where new members were evaluated and future plans discussed. But when Tharp was called away on independent jobs, the dancers missed her bonding presence.

Immediately after *Deuce Coupe* Robert Joffrey wanted another ballet, for his company alone. In the *Deuce Coupe* deal, Tharp had successfully traded weeks of contract work for getting her dancers on a payroll, and she often used this per-project strategy later on. But *Deuce Coupe* took a lot out of the Tharp dancers. Rather than dance in every piece as they did on their own programs, they had to wait through a whole evening to do their parts in that one ballet. Away from home on a tour that summer to the West Coast, there were whole empty days between *Deuce Coupe* performances. Tharp injured her foot and took herself out of the ballet despite her great success with the audience. Sitting out front and seeing her work alongside the Joffrey's repertory, which she felt was unworthy of *Deuce Coupe,* she wondered if the audience could really tell the difference between it and an Arpino pop number. She was also inspecting the Joffrey dancers with her next project in mind. A classical ballet, on pointe, seemed to her the logical follow-up, and she wasn't sure the Joffreys had the skills. This was hedging against her own uncertainty. Now that she had the chance to realize a great ambition, perhaps it was she who wouldn't measure up.

As Time Goes By premiered in New York on 24 October 1973, and it had almost as big a success as *Deuce Coupe*. It stayed in the Joffrey repertory for years, and brought several young dancers into prominence. Tharp made the choreography quickly but there were problems that taxed her in a different way from *Deuce Coupe*. Now she was all alone inside the Joffrey machinery, without any of her own dancers to appreciate her choreographic extravagance. For the first time she was experiencing the inner dynamics of a major ballet company—the rivalries among dancers, and among choreographers, all vying for the audience's favor; the gossip and rumors; the scrutiny of a national press. Robert Joffrey was making his first ballet in years, a heavy, romantic work to songs of Richard Wagner, and she suspected he was economizing on her production in order to finance his own. *Deuce Coupe* was still a box-office draw—about six performances were scheduled that fall—but Ashton's *The Dream*, a favorite among balletomanes, was coming into New York after a Joffrey debut on tour during the summer, and the repertory was laced with Arpino's classical and pop confections. Ballets were jockeying for placement even after the season started. There were discussions about an all-Tharp evening, with *Deuce Coupe*, *As Time Goes By*, and the Tharp company doing *The Bix Pieces*, but the Joffrey hadn't yet given such recognition to an outsider's work. Perhaps in deference to the resident choreographer, Arpino, the idea was allowed to evaporate.

As Time Goes By was set to the last two movements of Haydn's Symphony No. 45, *The Farewell*. Tharp began choreographing with a sextet, an intricate, fast, and spatially tight combination of individual phrases and partner work. Haydn's minuet set up what Tharp hoped would be a classical tone. Early in rehearsals, the dancers started to get uneasy. William Whitener and Pamela Nearhoof were ready to do anything she had in mind, but the other four weren't so trusting. Burton Taylor, perhaps the Joffrey's most finished classical male dancer, asked one day whether this was supposed to be a classical ballet. "Define classical," was Tharp's response, and she talked for a while about the aesthetics of art. To her mind, classicism didn't mean something frozen forever in one mold. She regarded Balanchine's *Agon* as a classical ballet for the twentieth century, and now she was going to explore classicism her own way.

But the dancers had more than aesthetic reservations—the Joffrey Ballet, after all, based its credibility on being able to reproduce any style of historic or contemporary classicism. But Tharp was pushing their classical technique to extremes. When one man considered taking jazz classes to prepare for her rehearsals, she pointed out that she wasn't asking them to throw away their classical technique but to extend it. For some of the older dancers, her off-center turns, transitionless changes, and fast adaptations meant overriding long-ingrained, safe body habits. The complicated spacing, daredevil partnering, and agile switches from individual to ensemble movement constituted a mental challenge that proved daunting too.

Eileen Brady remained but Burton Taylor, Paul Sutherland, and Denise Jackson withdrew, and there were weeks of uncertainty about this core casting. Beatriz Rodriguez and Joseph (Adix) Carman, recently elevated from the Joffrey II, were enthusiastic recruits for the sextet, but none of Tharp's prospects for the third man's part made it to the opening. There were injuries, doubts about the skewed movement Tharp was making, and besides, she thought, some of them were saving themselves for their featured roles in *The Dream*. Henry Berg, who'd assisted her on *Deuce Coupe* and whom she'd already named as regisseur for the Haydn ballet, danced in the first cast. Tharp slyly subtitled this section "Ten Make Six," a reference to the departed Jackson, Sutherland, Taylor, and Russell Sulzbach.

After the sextet, the ballet opened out into a large ensemble—she envisioned twenty-four dancers but ended with seventeen. What Tharp had in mind for the ballet was a series of subtle contrasts: harmony and dissonance; big, loose effects versus compressed, precise ones; unexpectedly quick versus unexpectedly slow movement. In the Farewell Symphony, Joseph Haydn is said to have been hinting to his patron, Prince Miklós József Esterhazy, that it was time to return to Vienna after the royal party's long stay in their summer quarters. During the fourth-movement adagio, the musicians blew out their candles and exited section by section, until only two violinists were left to play the final notes. Tharp thought it would be too obvious to duplicate this scenario, so she set the fourth movement with a commotion of exits and entrances, called "The Four Finales." Different subgroupings of the big ensemble played out each return of Haydn's presto theme in different ways. Each group retained dancers and movement elements from the previous sections. During the adagio after the fourth finale, a soloist, Larry Grenier, kept on dancing as the others gradually dispersed.

She had originally thought of the adagio as a trio, but she was so impressed with Grenier's particular qualities that she decided to feature him instead. And this meant rethinking the concept of the whole ballet. Grenier, accompanied by the disappearing group and the two traces of the trio, Ann Marie de Angelo and Christine Uchida, would suggest not finality but continuity, with his serene, looping, legato phrase. Haydn's reduction to the minimum would be represented at the beginning of the ballet instead, in a version of the phrase material condensed to less than a minute and danced with spiky intensity by Beatriz Rodriguez.

The duration of Rodriguez's solo was proportionate to that of the sextet that followed, which in turn foretold the timing of the four finales. The ballet had other inner workings that most audiences couldn't have detected. As each dancer crossed the stage and departed in the adagio, an element of Grenier's movement went too, but there would still be something left for him to do at the end of the ballet; in fact, the curtain went down as he was still moving. During the finales, Tharp built in moments when, within stipulated time slots and directions in space, the dancers could adopt any movement they liked from the material they'd learned. Says Richard Colton: "We knew exactly the direction but we would have to sculpt the movement to move in that direction, that was our job. But we'd have that freedom. And then she knew everyone would be picking movement that they would burst out with . . . and if they feel good doing it, they usually look good doing it." After the dancers' choices were made in rehearsal, the section was set and always performed the same.

In the intricately woven sextet, Tharp began exploring partner work. Without extending anything beyond a few measures, she made forays into the vocabulary of classical lifts and supports that required unusual trust and timing between the dancers. A woman launched into a low skid that would have ended on the floor if a man hadn't been there to stop her. You'd notice a woman high in a man's arms, then suddenly she'd be airborne for a second and end in another man's arms. No one stayed with the same partner, and in fact, by the end of the movement women were steadying other women on pointe and a man was caught in a lift by another man. Tharp simply disregarded the balletic prescription for stalwart males and passive females. Whenever she was quizzed about accepting Ken Rinker as the first man in her company, she replied that she was interested in using whatever skills dancers could add to her work—she'd just been waiting for one who was good enough. But she was aware that the audience has preconceptions. In *As Time Goes By* she deconstructed ballet's gender bias by refusing to differentiate the ensemble into separate male and female groups. Even more important, she chose Rodriguez and Grenier for the opening and closing solos because they could work against gender typing. They represented opposite ends of a spectrum, William Whitener thought, illustrating Tharp's concept of "the more feminine side to masculinity and the masculine side to femininity, and how it flipped in the ballet. Bea did very strong dancing and Larry was lyrical."

As Time Goes By constantly shuttles the audience between the satisfaction of beautiful form and the tension of form disrupted. If the dance looks chaotic or fuzzy, a moment later it locks into perfect balance. Its brevity alone was disorienting. Since Tharp didn't use the whole symphony, there were only about twelve minutes of music, prefaced by Rodriguez's forty-five seconds in silence. Yet in this short duration Tharp had shown the technical workings of a ballet company, the big and small units of the ensemble. She had focused attention on dancers who hadn't been singled out before. And she'd offered the chance for reflection and laughter.

With the exception of *The New York Times*, the reviews were appreciative. Tharp had tried to cultivate Clive Barnes, not very subtly, by inviting him out for drinks after a performance at Jacob's Pillow the previous summer. But he sent Anna Kisselgoff for the opening night review and then wrote a patronizing Sunday piece himself. Kisselgoff delivered the dubious compliment that Tharp had retreated from her recent audience-friendly pop phase to the "austere and highly interesting pure-movement style" of her prejazz days. Kisselgoff liked *As Time Goes By* but labeled it less accessible and entertaining than Tharp's recent hits. Barnes backed off his initial enthusiasm for *Deuce Coupe;* his pleasure in it, he said, "decline[s] markedly." And as for the Haydn, he liked it less each of the four times he saw it. Under the title "Ballets That Must Be Seen—Once" Barnes labeled *As Time Goes By* a "gorgeous putdown" of Haydn and classicism in general, comparing it to "the special cuteness of a moustache painted on the Mona Lisa." Like the stodgier Joffrey dancers, Barnes apparently resented Tharp's intrusion into classical music and, even worse, classical ballet. Rather than welcoming her efforts to revitalize ballet, he dismissed her as a serious classical contender:

> Miss Tharp creates for the moment. She would choose a Kleenex, with its registered trademark, rather than a lace handkerchief with its possibility of well-laundered permanence. Normally I would object to this. Yet I can see that ballets such as "Deuce Coupe" and "As Time Goes By" give a lot of surprised pleasure to people. People who never understood how much ballet could be like your friendly neighborhood discotheque.
>
> This kind of ballet is not so much to be savored as to be gulped. In the frenzied gasp of recognition you are expected to comprehend that all of classic ballet is nothing but a cute shuffle and a shamble. And totally unfrightening.

ᛦ *Re-Moves* in rehearsal at Judson Church, 1966. Sara Rudner.

(PHOTO: Robert Barry)

ᛦ *Jam.*

(PHOTO: Robert Barry)

🖎 *Disperse.*
Sara Rudner, Margery
Tupling, Twyla Tharp,
Theresa Dickinson.
(PHOTO: Robert Barry)

🖎 *Dancing in the
Streets* at Wadsworth
Atheneum, 1969.
Rose Marie Wright,
Twyla Tharp, Sheila
Raj, Graciela Figueroa
and audience.
(PHOTO: James
Elliott/Wadsworth
Athenuem)

The Fugue. Rose Marie Wright, Twyla Tharp, Sara Rudner. (PHOTO: Tom Rawe)

The Fugue. Tom Rawe, Raymond Kurshals, John Carrafa. (PHOTO: Nathaniel Tileston)

🙰 *Eight Jelly Rolls.* Sara Rudner, Rose Marie Wright.

(PHOTO: Tony Russell, courtesy of London Weekend Television.© REX Features Ltd)

🙰 *The Bix Pieces.* Sara Rudner, Twyla Tharp. (PHOTO: Tom Rawe)

᷾ *Deuce Coupe.* Twyla Tharp. (PHOTO: © Migdoll 1973)

᷾ *Half the One Hundreds* rehearsal at Brooklyn Academy, 1977. Twyla Tharp and civilians.
(PHOTO: Nathaniel Tileston)

෪෨ *Sue's Leg.* Twyla Tharp.

෪෨ *Push Comes to Shove.*
Mikhail Baryshnikov.

&c; *Push Comes to Shove*. Mikhail Baryshnikov, Marianna Tcherkassky and corps de ballet.
(PHOTO: © Martha Swope)

&c; *Country Dances*. Tom Rawe, Shelley Washington, Christine Uchida, Jennifer Way.
(PHOTO: © Lois Greenfield 1977)

ॐ *Baker's Dozen*. Raymond Kurshals, Sara Rudner. (PHOTO: © Martha Swope)

ॐ *Baker's Dozen*. William Whitener, Christine Uchida. (PHOTO: © Martha Swope)

Later on, when the Joffrey Ballet showed it on tour, *The San Francisco Chronicle*'s Robert Commanday, much more susceptible to the overt romanticism of Arpino, thought *As Time Goes By* was "more to be censured than pitied." Calling Tharp's take on Haydn "vandalism," he called various parts of the dance "deliberately dissonant," "confusing to the eye," and "cheap and offensive."

But the new ballet had many powerful admirers. It prompted Arlene Croce, who had just become the dance critic of *The New Yorker*, to proclaim Tharp "the Nijinska of our time." Croce appreciated what Barnes did not about Tharp's work: "It seems to seek out first principles and turn them over with curiosity, finding new excitement in what lies on the other side of orthodoxy." Deborah Jowitt of *The Village Voice* was delighted to see Tharp retrieving "a whole range of dynamics that have slipped away from Western dance." She called Tharp the reigning queen of the new virtuosity.

During the same Joffrey season that saw the premiere of *As Time Goes By* and the reprise of *Deuce Coupe*, Tharp gained more visibility when the videotape of *The Bix Pieces* was broadcast on *Camera Three* one Sunday morning in October. For the next several months the Tharp company had a full schedule of touring and a date at New York's Town Hall. *Eight Jelly Rolls*, *The Rags*, and *The Bix Pieces*, with the women's *Fugue*, had become the standard repertory. A residency at the Walker Art Center in Minneapolis in January provided a chance to work on something new, *In the Beginnings*, in anticipation of the WGBH video. But no other new work was completed until the summer, when the *Bach Duet* for Wright and Rinker premiered during an American University–Wolf Trap residency in Washington. It was planned as the finale of the video.

Immediately after the two months of teaching at AU, the company went to Boston to do the filming. Titled *All About Eggs*, the video was to gather several big strands of Tharpian interests. She wrote rambling notes while working on it, exploring illusion, reality, and belief, and thinking about how to ask questions, how to deal with one's mistakes. Perhaps she was obsessing about her divorce from Bob Huot, which was finalized after much unpleasantness over the custody and care of Jesse, in November of 1974. It seemed life presented an overwhelming and inescapable assortment of dualities: "end begin, right wrong, perfect imperfect, yes no, red blue, today tomorrow—each part of the pair existent only in its promise of the other. Lifeless in itself and death to the other." And in another place: "This piece is an epistemological survey. Some things are known by association. Some things are known through physical perception. Some things must be taken on faith . . ."

While working on *In the Beginnings* she'd talked to Mike Steele of the *Minneapolis Tribune* with her usual bravado. "Staring success in the face is like staring down on death. To keep your integrity in the face of rankest commerce takes real mettle." About to film the repertory at the Annenberg School of Communications in Philadelphia, she figured she'd then have a working asset, like a Motherwell painting. She'd sell the Annenberg tapes as rehearsal aids to other companies that were willing to pay well to acquire her repertory. She thought she could beat the system, she told another interviewer later that spring. The company was popular enough to support itself decently, "but that means traveling about thirty weeks in a year and means forfeiting our standards and we are not prepared to do that. So it really amounts to going back to where we were in the beginning and not supporting ourselves by this work." She hoped television and videotape, being more tangible and mass-accessible commodities, would buy her way out of the loop.

The symbolism of eggs gave Tharp a way to ventilate these concerns in dance. She thought of the egg as idea, as creativity. But there might be no way to interrupt the chicken-egg cycle. How could you tell where tradition gave way to innovation, where inspiration lapsed into history? As she took her own wary steps toward fame, she was thinking about the dancer's fantasies, and she wondered which came first, the chorus or the star. She had always been committed to the individuality of each member of the ensemble; was the Cinderella spotlight creating false divisions within the dance company?

She liked the visceral associations between eggs and the female reproductive system, even if the consequences could be troublesome. Jesse, her very own chick, was supposed to appear on film somewhere in the video. In one of the three *Egg Stories* from *In the Beginnings* that were to open *All About Eggs*, Wright, wearing a white bandeau and briefs, does a series of gestures reminiscent of her Big Bang solo in *The Bix Pieces*. A fast-changing slide show runs on three screens behind her, like the unpredictable images on a slot machine: body parts, fruit, fried eggs, snapshots, a Renaissance painting, a bottle of pills for menstrual cramps. In a dry, stagy voice-over Tharp reads her own text about a sudden adolescent distaste for her mother's breakfast menu. She'd smashed eggs on the floor after a 1966 abortion, in *Re-Moves*, and one of her first critic-fans, John Percival, had titled his review in *Dance and Dancers* "Eggs Don't Bounce." Marian Hailey, who narrated the seven *Egg Stories* in Minneapolis, first broke raw eggs, then dropped hard-boiled ones, noting, "Some assumptions can be made; others can't."

Inspired as always with what new dancers could do, Tharp created a five-part fugue for Tom Rawe. TV technology would make it possible for him to partner himself. Rawe, who had joined the company the spring after the premiere of *Deuce Coupe*, spent most of the summer learning the choreography. "It involved a linear sequence continued throughout the piece with restated themes splitting off at points, with first a duet, then a trio, et cetera, until there was a short moment of five voices dancing at the same time," Rawe remembers. "Each point of a split was initiated by the same movement, which messed with my physical memory," and eventually he had to graph it on paper, but, "It was fun to do, and I think that it established me as a hard worker." The fugue was shot in Chromakey, the predigital process that allowed an unrelated background to be applied behind the central image. In the unfinished tape, which still exists, Rawe seems to be hatching out new versions of himself as he dances along in no-space.

At the end of the second and last day of shooting in Boston, an exhausted Wright and Rinker taped the *Bach Duet*. It was choreographed to the soprano-alto duet from the Cantata No. 78, *Jesu, der du meine Seele*. Wright recalls almost marking the dance in the very tight space of the TV studio. She and Rinker performed the piece again later on, but by 1980 it had disappeared, and Tharp made a different Bach work for dancers Whitener and Uchida, *Duet from the Third Suite*.

The Minneapolis critics were impressed with *In the Beginnings*. Mike Steele thought Tharp was "taking dance into a larger context of social space. She's dealing with fantasies, American mythology, with collective perception. She's using popular modes—even the music is full of patriotic and pop ditties—to penetrate that part of us that believes in popular dreams. She seems interested now in why she creates dances. As she probes deeper, disassembling and looking under the clichés, even banalities, of culture she's finding a poetry beneath. She's discovering fundamentals." Peter Altman saw her introspection beneath the entertainment, sunlight mingled with shadows.

For most of the year, Tharp had prepared not only the dance material for the WGBH adventure but the text, artwork, and film she wanted to incorporate. She expected to have a chance to work creatively with the television medium as well as with dance. This enterprise grew from so much self-examination that its sprawling, unruly elements got out of control. The production team at GBH hadn't anticipated a project of such complexity. The taping was a disaster and the video was never completed.

Tom Rawe and his wife, Jennifer Way, first encountered Tharp during the company's marathon one-day residency at Ohio State University in 1972. They were dazzled by the whole event—taking class, learning *The One Hundreds* and parts of *The Fugue*, and, during the concert that evening, absorbing the group's prodigious dancing. They became groupies, following the company to Antioch College and Minneapolis, and later driving all the way to New York in a yellow Volkswagen bus to see *Deuce Coupe* during its first season. Rawe had been playing the trumpet and dancing since his high school years as a student at the Interlochen Arts Academy in Michigan. His parents hoped he'd pursue a conventional career, but after earning a bachelor of science degree at Clarkson College of Technology, he returned to his first love, dance. Jennifer Way's mother taught dance in her hometown of Waverly, Ohio, and by junior high school was ferrying her daughter to study with ballet teachers in Columbus. Way enrolled in the Ohio State Dance Department after high school.

Rawe joined Tharp first. Having finished his M.F.A. in dance at OSU, he was driving a cab in New York in the spring of 1973. He heard about an audition at 104 Franklin Street and, with misgivings, decided to try out. He was one of three men Tharp provisionally accepted. For two weeks, Rawe was to work on getting the movement into his body: "She wanted to find out if I was able to get better. Was able to tolerate that work process." Rawe appreciated the fact that "I didn't have to show her my stuff in ten seconds, I could just work on the material." He thought the endless repetition in Tharp's rehearsal process brought about a feeling of such security that by the time the dancers got to perform anything, "it seemed improvisational, because it was like putting on an old pair of shoes. . . . We loved it. In the rehearsal studio it was good. It was a lot of work but that was good." Like others before him, Rawe didn't know when his trial period had ended. After rehearsing for the whole summer, he got up the nerve to ask whether he'd been taken into the company. He stayed for eleven years.

Way took classes during Tharp's American University residencies of 1973 and '74. The first summer she was earning the final credits toward her Ohio State bachelors degree. The next year dancers were leaving the company and Way filled in, teaching a ballet and a tap class. She wasn't sure Tharp had a clear idea who she was until the following fall in New York. Way was working in a health food restaurant and taking classes with Viola Farber when she went to a Tharp audition. After separate men's and women's tryouts, the dancers were paired up together. Way says, "I think it was only then, when I started dancing with this guy, that she saw something in me that she thought would work for the company. . . . I think she really liked the way I handled myself or handled him." She joined the company in early 1975.

Throughout the Tharp company history, dancers bonded intimately with Tharp and each other. They had chosen Tharp and stayed with her work because they felt it was stimulating and challenging beyond any other dancing available to them. Aside from injury or exhaustion, only extreme circumstances prompted them to leave. As happens in most modern dance companies, those with choreographic ambitions saw time rushing ahead and felt they had to break away in order to gain some different experiences and try their own creative ideas.

Sara Rudner became restless, partly for this reason, and left in 1974 after a difficult period of indecision. She and Rose Marie Wright had been not just long-term principal dancers; they had contributed as much as Tharp herself to the developing Tharp style, and to the strength and flexibility of a company that essentially had no formal organization. Rudner went on to a formidable career as a teacher and choreographer, but her imprint on Tharp's work was indelible. She returned, after a guest appearance in 1977, to create another series of extraordinary roles between 1978 and 1985. Since then she has remained a devoted friend, guest artist, and coach.

Nina Wiener, who had moved into the company after touring with the 1972 Farm Club, also had independent ideas. She didn't seem to fit in as well with the comradely spirit of the company, and there may have been some subtle element of competition between her and Tharp. Wiener was a gifted dancer but she sometimes held back. She could look merely correct when the others were putting their personal imprint on the material. At the request of Tharp and the company, Wiener left in June of 1974, and a short time later she formed her own dance group.

Tharp's unquenchable choreographic ambition kept pushing up the technical ante, and there were always dancers who felt pressured by this.

Powerfully attracted by something in Tharp's sensibility, they would find, down the line, that she had moved past what they'd initially embraced or even what they were prepared to execute. Isabel Garcia-Lorca's position was the most poignant of all. Twenty-five years after leaving the company, she wept when she talked about it. Admittedly without technical training, she'd been drawn to Tharp during the "people dance" phase. When Tharp brought her to New Berlin she'd worked hard to keep up with the others and learn the movement Tharp created especially for her abilities. Her long, elegant line and enigmatic composure were a great asset to the jazz pieces and *Deuce Coupe.* "When she was performing, it was like la créme de la créme," says Ken Rinker. "It made you look. You'd work with her, you watched her, you looked at her and you wanted to see more."

But increasingly Tharp craved a technical depth that only classical training could satisfy. She was grounding her choreographic invention in the ballet vocabulary rather than the "natural" locomotion and gesture of everyday life. The '60s avant-garde had rejected technique on principle and demanded dancers who looked like ordinary people. This programmatic pedestrianism was essential to their goal of clearing away excess and automatism. For laypersons like Garcia-Lorca, a window opened into a long-desired world of dancing and performing.

But choreography could develop only so far in the absence of technique. Judson anarchy quickly succumbed to simple organizing principles—games, worklike tasks, minimalist repetition. Tharp incorporated these along with anything that facilitated her innate sense of structure. But she quickly outgrew the overtly pedestrian inclusiveness with which she'd first assembled the company, and although she continued to look for individual qualities in dancers, she needed them to bring more technical skills into the studio. Garcia-Lorca saw the train speeding on. She was taking two ballet classes a day in New York, but when the company began working on *Deuce Coupe* she recognized a logical trend in Tharp's thinking. "It just makes sense," she says now, "that she would want to explore that vocabulary. . . . I just didn't have the technique. I mean fine, I was talented. . . . But the fact is, technically I couldn't keep up."

During the early part of 1974 Tharp, Rudner, Wright, and Rinker held discussions about whether to keep Tom Rawe, what to do about Wiener and Garcia-Lorca, and how to deal with a growing friction between Tharp and Bill Kosmas. Garcia-Lorca's fate was sealed, as she knew it would be. Her last performances took place at the Round House in London, in May, and after teaching a ballroom dance class with Rinker during the summer residency at American University, she left. She remembers a fateful meeting when Tharp seemed unable to tell her the painful truth. Garcia-Lorca bailed her out: "I made it easy for her. I said, I understand. I know what direction you're going, and I know I can't do it. So I know I have to go. She said, Right. That's it." It was the end of Garcia-Lorca's dance career. When she considered dancing for anyone else, she saw that other downtown choreographers hadn't yet taken on technical challenges, but she was underqualified for those with a conventionally demanding technique, like Cunningham. In any case, there was no other company that offered half the fascination of the work she'd been doing with Tharp.

Kosmas and Tharp conducted prolonged negotiations for the company's 1974 London season. Ten days of performances were booked for the Round House, an unconventional space formerly used as a railway turnaround. A thrust stage was built to afford some theatrical credence to the three jazz pieces, which were interspersed on two different programs with *The Fugue* and *The One Hundreds*. It was a risky venture—the company's fee wasn't guaranteed—and the advance publicity was carefully planned. Tharp spent a week in London in March, and an interview she gave to Peter Williams resulted in a four-page spread in the May edition of *Dance and Dancers*. The company arrived in London a month ahead of the season for workshops and open rehearsals. They had also arranged to make a one-hour video for London Weekend Television, and Tharp and Kosmas, looking to stimulate ticket sales at the Round House, hammered out a deal to have the completed video broadcast just before the season.

Both the video and the season were very successful. *The Financial Times's* Clement Crisp wrote two glowing reviews. *Dance and Dancers* sent Percival and two other critics, publishing nearly five pages of commentary with photos in July. Tharp's choreography disarmed Peter Williams, who, even after his interview with her, dreaded "encounters with American lady dance pioneers. It's all that dedication and intensity that worries us. . . ." Williams was greatly relieved to find Tharp putting forth no "portentous meaning, no hidden depths, but just what dance is all about and what American dance in particular is all about." Percival remarked that although many of his colleagues missed the point, the packed and cheering audiences got it. He expanded on Arlene Croce's Nijinska analogy, which he thought might have put off the English critics, for whom the Russian choreographer was a kind of totem: "Tharp now, like Nijinska in the '20s, produces ballets with a flippant, amusing surface concealing the meticulously worked structure; she has the same perfectionist approach to dancing . . . and like Nijinska she is a true innovator, therefore ahead of general taste."

The other major British dance periodical, *Dancing Times*, after printing a condensed version of Arlene Croce's *Eight Jelly Rolls* review in its May issue, offered its own rave. Mary Clarke chided those of her colleagues who thought Tharp needed taking down a peg or two. Clarke had had "one of my happiest evenings in the theater for years. The performance was totally exhilarating and I came out feeling that Isadora's dream had come true—I had seen America dancing." She disagreed with the critics who persisted in seeing Tharp's work as a put-on. "They are doing things which would be quite impossible for the classically trained dancer." Peter J. Rosenwald reported to the American magazine *Dance News* that the season had been an "unqualified success . . . If classicism in dance is about pointe shoes then Tharp's work fails by this definition, but in the broader context of authoritativeness and traditional values her ballets are some of the most profoundly classical being produced today."

This set of reviews clearly established the critical battle lines from which Tharp's reputation would be assessed for the rest of her career. The British dance scene was still centered around its prestigious ballet tradition. Its strong ties to the Diaghilev era, including Nijinska, and even further back to the Russian Imperial school through revivals of nineteenth-century classics, were a matter of national valor as well as aesthetic pride. Modern dance, on the other hand, maintained a faint presence within the field of British dance education, as a practice somewhere between recreation and physical culture, but with scant visibility on the professional dance stage. Some English critics, Clive Barnes included, went reflexively on the defensive whenever they saw Tharp venturing onto classical ground. Critics from the mainstream press—in America they were often not dance specialists—followed the conservative line about Tharp. Her jazz dances were great fun but anything that looked serious raised their suspicions.

But the "verbiage" some critics objected to in *The Bix Pieces*, and in the London Weekend Television production, was intentional, reflecting Tharp's determination to be understood as an artist and craftsman beneath her entertainer's persona. By this time she had mastered the lecture-demonstration format, developed by modern dancers early in the twentieth century to familiarize audiences with their innovative work. Tharp blossomed in this environment. She could slide into an offhand mode with an audience of dancegoers or critics. Casual, irreverent, self-deprecating, she would speed through the intricate construction of her dances in a chatty singsong, interrupting herself to get up and demonstrate a phrase or two. These monologues took the sting out of her most austere works and gave credibility to the popular ones. *Twyla Tharp and "Eight Jelly Rolls"* introduced the English public to this brainy character with a collage of shots from the London lecture-demonstrations and rehearsals. Then it launched into a performance of the dance itself. The 1927 Jelly Roll Morton numbers were played by a band of English musicians under Max Harris, who had arranged and rehearsed every nuance.

In the documentary-demonstration part of the video, Tharp introduced the dancers—they too were smart, serious, and devoted to the work. Despite the obvious informality of her working process, Tharp came across as a perfectionist, articulate, unpretentious, interested in the history of her own dance as it fitted into dance history. By linking together images where she rehearses the company in the studio, presents them informally in dance examples to the theater audience, and describes the Jelly Rolls in some detail, the documentary captures the choreographer in different guises. After one chorus of the fifth Jelly Roll (the Drunk) running under the opening credits, the documentary leads off with Rudner musing:

> With Twyla it was the intelligence of it, the physical challenge and the great intelligence of it. I didn't know what I was going to be doing the next moment. All of those [other] situations, it was obvious to me what I was going to be doing the rest of my life. Sort of like run run run *arabesque*. And run run run *jump*. And this was different. This kept on changing. And it changed from being—the pieces we do now are nothing like the pieces we did then. But they're all rooted in the same integrity and intelligence and the desire to work and find out what dancing is and what we wanted to do.

A portion of the Drunk gets shown in a clip from a lecture-demonstration. By the time it occurs in the full performance, the viewer can savor not only Tharp's comic solo but the carefully rehearsed, disintegrating precision of the ensemble behind her.

Tharp came down with the flu on arrival in London and couldn't work, so the dancers spent several days going over the dance with director Derek

Bailey. The finished tape, made in consultation with Tharp when she recovered, defies the conventions of dance on film at the time. TV and tape cassettes were about to give dance wider public exposure than it had ever enjoyed, and by the end of the decade most misgivings about the camera had evaporated. But in 1974, dancers were still skittish about how they would look on the screen; critics and scholars still balked if the camera took any liberties with the choreography. From her years working at her mother's drive-in movie, Tharp had no qualms about the effects of the camera, and she was well aware of the difference between straight-on documentation of a dance and showcasing it for the screen. Already experienced with recording her work, she was eager to explore television further. She'd learned from the Camera Three *Bix Pieces*, produced by Merrill Brockway, and she probably picked up some more tricks from Bailey to add to her cache of expectations for *All About Eggs*, which was to founder in Boston a few months later. Along with *Eight Jelly Rolls* Derek Bailey taped *The Fugue* quite conventionally with the original cast, but only excerpts of this tape were included on the *Jelly Rolls* video, and neither tape was ever broadcast in the United States.

Twyla Tharp and "Eight Jelly Rolls" recorded not only the choreography but the seven-member company (Tharp, Rudner, Wright, Rawe, Rinker, Wiener, and Garcia-Lorca) at the peak of its form. Bailey filmed each section with a different stylistic treatment, avoiding the potential monotony of a single-perspective shoot. Number One, basically a solo for Wright, features the dancer against a white space. The camera frequently closes in on her legs and torso, emphasizing her size by peeking beyond her to Tharp and Rudner crossing in the background. In real life almost a foot shorter than Wright, they look even smaller because of the video camera's tendency to make objects exaggeratedly small as they get farther from the wide-angle lens. Bailey adds his own game of editing to Rudner and Wright's high jinks in Number Two. The screen periodically splits into two halves, keeping both figures in the frame as they separate from each other. The dancers pop in and out across an invisible dividing line, and sometimes there are two sets of them. At the end of the number they fade to white instead of exiting. Rudner is shot from above as she dances in a spotlight in Number Three. Her shadow on the floor shares the circle of light with her, and later a second shot of her upper body is superimposed on the long shot, lingering romantically on her arms and shoulders, and her expressive face.

Bailey's most controversial tactic occurs first in Number Four, when a giant film of the musicians fills the backdrop. This dance is the Tharp-Wright-

Rudner trio doing their three simultaneous solos. Busy already, and dwarfed by the Brobdingnagian musicians, the choreography gets reshaped further by sudden disappearances and reentries of the dancers. Rudner and Wright carry Tharp off after the unison final chorus, as the other dancers make their confused false entrance. The camera shoots Number Five, Tharp's Drunk solo, from all around, so that the viewer becomes as disoriented as she is. We see her falling and trying to balance, but we also see the group from her capsizing perspective, as they march inexorably and sometimes silently in the background, the foreground, and above her. For the individual solos in Number Six, we always see the soloist in harmony with all or part of the group. In Number Seven, the group fades to a doubled exposure behind Wright. This allows us to see exactly how they're copying the "Dots" poses from Wright as she lounges along. Toward the end, the group doubles again, reinforcing the choreographic idea of mechanical replication.

For the finale, the dancers do their nostalgic social dance steps, as giant black-and-white archival films of '20s dancers in night clubs and variety shows flicker behind them. Derek Bailey and the London team, with some help from Tharp, found the archival footage in their own library. Once the historical connection is made, the old films disappear and the dance finishes against a white space. The dancers exit, leaving Tharp to make a floppy bow.

The arrangements for the long and diverse London engagement put additional stress on Tharp's relationship with Kosmas. Bill Kosmas was the second man who exerted a crucial influence on Tharp's personal and professional life. The extent of their intimacy is hard to determine. Tharp is cagey about it in her own book—she admits to pursuing him with increasingly frustrating results. The dancers didn't know just what their relationship was; many people close to the company assumed they were not only lovers but were living together. Whatever their emotional attachments, she depended on his advice and managerial help during this period when her fortunes were changing dramatically. Kosmas contributed to her first public acclaim by insisting, from his first contact with her in 1971, that the company adopt a respectable, accessible image. At a time when downtown dancers, including Rudner and Wright, still clung to the moral authority of "poor theater," Kosmas saw straight down a more populist path to success. It wasn't until the end of the 1970s that countercultural stalwarts like Trisha

Brown, David Gordon, and Brenda Way's Oberlin Dance Collective decided to slick up their costumes and capitalize on their high-profile connections. By then, Tharp had been out of the pedestrian-dance business for a decade.

Tharp was receptive to Kosmas's ideas of conventional art presenting. They reflected her own middle-class instincts. She had, after all, grown up in an early version of a trophy house, a sprawling place her father built for the big family, where eight-year-old Twyla had her own wing. Her parents were successful businesspersons, proud of the advantages they could give their children. Twyla's mother, Lecile, provided her oldest with so many extracurricular lessons she became a driven professional instead of a cultivated young lady. On the other hand, her parents weren't aristocrats who could take their possessions casually. Lacking a built-in sense of entitlement, Tharp worked too hard for what she thought she deserved, and then doubted whether she had truly earned the rewards.

Kosmas, brought up in the professional world, thought the dancers shouldn't have to do menial work like renovating the Franklin Street loft. Rehearsing many sweaty hours a day was unusual, but Tharp, as director of the company, should have a more privileged status than the rank and file. He probably disapproved of her living and working in the same place. He lived on Riverside Drive, and by 1974 she had also moved to the Upper West Side. She could have afforded a beautiful loft in pregentrification Soho or Greenwich Village, but instead she got an apartment high over Central Park. Eventually she came to expect to be driven in hired cars and put up in elegant hotel suites out of town. As soon as Kosmas started negotiating her contracts, they became detailed and overcautious. Working eight hours a day with her own dancers in the studio was different from trying to fit her extreme rehearsal needs into the schedule of a ballet company where many choreographers were competing for the dancers' time, or a television shoot where the crew had little experience with the needs of dancers. Presenters had to suffer through the combination of his lawyerly caution and her gigantic imagination.

Kosmas not only dressed up the company's onstage and offstage appearance, he introduced Tharp to people outside the dance world who became collaborators, like Kermit Love, Jeff Moss, and Marian Hailey. He understood the importance of social contacts and thought "showing up for an event or being nice to people or going out for dinner" was part of Tharp's responsibility. But this was never her strong suit. She could be rude to patrons or drink too much and behave badly at postperformance parties. She didn't have the patience for obligatory socializing, Kosmas thought later. He wanted to protect and help her, of course, but he also had a personal stake in her social skills. She made him look bad, he thought, when she mishandled situations that he'd set up for her benefit.

Ironically, the more he facilitated her visibility, the more she was attracted to situations he disapproved of. She began a workshop at the request of theater director Andre Gregory. With Sharon Kinney as teaching assistant, she gave dance classes for the actors of his Manhattan Project and prepared material for them to show at a Tharp company performance at New York's Town Hall in April 1975. Gregory may have introduced Tharp to Richard Avedon, and she and the company were featured in two pages of his glamour photographs in the June 1975 *Vogue*. Along with people like opera director Sara Caldwell and painter Helen Frankenthaler, Tharp was one of that month's "People Are Talking About . . ." personalities, dubbed by an anonymous writer "the most decisive young American dance power today. What Jerome Robbins was to the 'fifties . . ." The actors' project petered out, but Tharp and Avedon remained close friends. Perhaps Kosmas thought Tharp was headed for the wrong kind of stardom; perhaps the trajectory he'd started her on was zooming beyond his grasp. He began to feel that she was somehow compromising the quality of her work, and he "backed off and became less interested."

The professionalization that Kosmas set in motion meant that the company became less intimate and informal, at the same time that Tharp was having to acknowledge a responsibility as their boss. Even without the pressures of a high-profile career, modern dance companies inevitably undergo a gradual shift in the relationship between choreographer and dancers over time. Major figures like Martha Graham, Paul Taylor, Alvin Ailey, and Merce Cunningham all experienced the phenomenon. Every choreographer finds his or her own solution to the gap that opens with age and managing a successful business. Starting out as dancers themselves who've gathered friends around them to begin their group explorations, they all see new and younger members replace the original dancers. As their ideas mature and their opportunities expand, they dance less, yet the young dancers can do more. Their choreography becomes less a reflection of themselves than an idealization. Tharp continued to dance onstage well into her fifties, but her company was evolving fast. In a 1975 lecture-demonstration, responding to an audience question about why she chose the music she did, she reflected back to working on the *Jelly Rolls*. She felt a kinship with Jelly

Roll Morton and his Red Hot Peppers of the 1927 recordings: "I was out on a farm working [in New Berlin] and nobody knew anything about it, and here were these black guys that nobody had ever heard of in their time and they went through whatever they went through and they worked because they loved to work. . . . I responded to that feel about it." Now she was no longer unknown, and she and the dancers were working for a little more than the love of it.

Kosmas wanted to gain some distance, and since he was still conducting his law practice, he couldn't carry the role of full-time manager anyway. He saw himself as an executive producer, paving the way for Tharp's projects but keeping out of the day-to-day business of the company. Late in 1974 he and Tharp hired Rhoda Grauer, an enthusiastic young Vassar graduate who'd been working in the administration of the Spoleto Festival in Italy. Grauer had returned to New York to try her wings as a theater director; she didn't know much about dance but she'd been impressed with *The Bix Pieces* on *Camera Three*. Tharp met her at a party, and after a long talk she asked Grauer to come and work half-time for the same salary she'd made at Spoleto. Grauer was affable, practical, and the perfect administrator for Tharp at the time. In her years at Spoleto she'd worked with artists, dancers, big stars of the theater and music worlds. Famous prima donnas didn't intimidate her. She quickly decided that Tharp was unusual, that "She processed information in a way that is different from the way other people processed information. She thought differently. She was wired differently." Grauer wanted to devote herself to Tharp. "I thought, this girl is endless. . . . My life will be getting her whatever she needs to do what she has to do."

Grauer put the company on a fifty-two-week salary, unprecedented in modern dance, inventing how to do it without excessive touring. She raised money, worked out contracts and bookings, and traveled with the company for important dates. She remembers making a deal with Harvey Lichtenstein, the director of Brooklyn Academy of Music, for the company's first big season at the BAM Opera House in 1976. Lichtenstein was apprehensive about the size of the audience, so Grauer agreed to a small fee and a large percentage of the box office profits. The season was a smash hit and the company made $90,000. It was Kosmas, a Minneapolis native, who established the initial contact with Suzanne Weil, director of programming at the Walker Art Center, for the first Minnesota residency, but Grauer implemented the more elaborate one that followed a year later. Everyone remembers the 1975 Twin Cities residency with pleasure. With cosponsorship from the Walker Art Center and the National Endowment for the Arts (both Weil and Grauer later became director of the NEA dance program), the month-long residency was to culminate in two performances, but the project was much more ambitious and community oriented.

Weil, Tharp, and Grauer drove around the Twin Cities to find a working space, and Tharp decided on the decrepit St. Paul Civic Center. This 1906 building housed a fine though half-abandoned theater and several other spaces, including a school for boxing. It was slated to be demolished and replaced by a more modern building. Tharp liked the offbeat reputation of the place, and disregarded the prickly politics of working in St. Paul while being sponsored by a major Minneapolis institution. Sue Weil arranged housing for the dancers, Jesse, Grauer, and stage manager Pennie Curry, welcoming them with baskets of groceries and pots of crocuses to ease them into the severe Minnesota winter. Grauer saw Weil as an ideal sponsor, who smoothed the way for the dancers and facilitated Tharp's most farfetched ideas.

As soon as the company arrived at the end of January, they set up a schedule of free, open classes and rehearsals every day, working in the king-sized, seventy-by-forty-foot Veterans Hall above the Civic Center Theater. They gave themselves class and rehearsed in the mornings, then invited the community in. The dancers thrived on this contact with the public. In addition to the open rehearsals and classes, they had sessions with local choreographers and public school teachers, they gave their own lecture-demonstration, and the day after the performances they appeared at a public evaluation session. They acquired a contingent of regular attendees who'd greet them on the street and talk about the day's work. Tharp was convinced that this kind of exposure to the working process was bound to enrich the experience of the future audience.

Initially there wasn't enough repertory for the final performances. Tharp had carried out her plan to mothball her old dances after making the Annenberg and London videotapes. Except for an early June repertory performance at the Henry Street Playhouse in New York, only *The Bach Duet* had been shown since London. In the fall, with the three dancers who remained, Wright, Rinker, and Rawe, Tharp had choreographed a new piece for the Walker, but there wasn't much else to fill in the programs. She came up with an elegant solution. During the daily two-hour open rehearsals over the month in St. Paul, she would create a new piece—she proposed to make a minute of movement a day. To fill in the rest of the program, they'd perform the other new dance twice. Sue Weil thought it was a great idea, and began advertising. Tickets for the performances went for a top price of six dollars.

Working on new choreography in public could be embarrassing and nerve-wracking, but the dancers were game for it. By the end of the residency, only eight minutes of new dance had been finished. Undaunted, Tharp staged *The Double Cross* to a series of radically different musical selections, with live readings of her meditations on performance and illusion, and *The Bach Duet* as a finale. Rose Marie Wright danced on pointe to the "Parade of the Wooden Soldiers," Rinker and Rawe did somersaults and pushups, and, according to Allen Robertson, who'd watched it being made, "The result is like a spinning trip down a radio dial band. A variety of contrasting choices, all of them usable but easily disposed of, are rapidly sketched in, glanced at and tossed away. . . . Given an overabundance of possibilities to choose from nobody knows where to go."

At the same time she'd been preparing for the residency, Tharp had reconfigured *Deuce Coupe*, which the Joffrey Ballet premiered as *Deuce Coupe II* in Chicago, 1 February, and in New York on the 26th, just after the end of the Minnesota residency. In addition to schedule pressures, Tharp was unhappy over the departure of Sara Rudner and her deadlocked relationship with Kosmas. *The Double Cross* as such disappeared quickly; Tharp filtered the movement material into her Chuck Berry piece, *Ocean's Motion*, which was coming up for a premiere at the Spoleto Festival in June. But *Sue's Leg* was a triumph. Easygoing almost to the point of negligence, it showed few signs of the difficult working situation that led up to Minneapolis. Tharp had found some choice old Fats Waller records, and she says she began making material for Wright, Rawe, and Rinker as a way of deflecting her gloom. In her autobiography Tharp asserts that the dance's final section, "In the Gloamin'," reflected "four desperate people clinging to one another for dear life," and there may have been other personal resonances or even a story. The title was a tribute to Suzanne Weil and a hint that the dance was intended as one "leg" of a three-part theater work that never materialized.

For the first time Tharp commissioned costumer Santo Loquasto—it's possible she used her 1974–75 Guggenheim Fellowship to hire him. Loquasto, who was a newcomer to dance, looked at a rehearsal and loved the dancers' idiosyncratic practice clothes. He decided to duplicate them, in elegant fabrics and tasteful shades of beige and brown. For the St. Paul performances, and again a few weeks later at Wesleyan University, the dance was repeated after *The Double Cross*, only this time in the original working attire. These costumes, so wonderfully suited to the dancers and to their movement, drew attention to the importance Tharp had always placed on what her dancers wore. Showing the costumes doubled, and redoubled when *Sue's Leg* ran twice in the St. Paul and Wesleyan performances, emphasized the idea that they were precisely *not* the clothes worn in the studio, but a theatricalized representation. They were neither the stark, black-and-white studio gear in which Karinska dressed Balanchine's modern ballets nor the fussy, skin-with-adornments of Willa Kim's many Eliot Feld productions. Throughout her career, Tharp used costumes as close to everyday clothes as possible, translated for the stage. Loquasto's layered jerseys and ankle warmers set a style for casual fashions in the world at large.

The *Sue's Leg* costume doubling itself echoed *The Bix Pieces*, where Kermit Love's little gray dresses, shorts, and pajamas for the Beiderbecke songs were replicated, for the lecture-demonstration and Haydn sections, in silky white fabrics. For the final quartet, "Abide with Me," Isabel Garcia-Lorca retained her gray costume. The white costumes were supposed to be the ghosts of the songs costumes, says Wright, and the final quartet "really is a recapitulation of everything that you've seen before, including the costumes. . . . So it's all, whatever the words are in the lecture-demonstration, it's all new again but it's also what has come before."

Sue's Leg, the last of Tharp's chamber-sized jazz pieces, had a close relationship to *The Bix Pieces*. Rose Marie Wright felt that the last Waller song, "In the Gloamin'," resembled the Haydn quartet section of the *Bix*. In both those pieces, four dancers worked closely together, entangling and freeing themselves in a continuous knot of movement. The difference for the dancers was that in the *Bix*, they had to make spontaneous choices from movement material that had been predetermined and rehearsed. Since all four of them were making choices that were unforeseen by the others, the whole dance became an improvisation. In *Sue's Leg*, the process of how they would work with each other was set, but the specific movement was not. "The material was much more mushy and nebulous," Wright thought.

Sue's Leg may be the last important piece in what's still considered—and lamented—as the definitive Twyla Tharp style. After only four years, the offhand performing attitudes and the loose, jazzy movement that seemed easy enough for anyone to do were verging on decadence, but her choreographic plan was still quite open and relaxed. After this her choreography became structurally tighter and clearer, more rooted in ballet technique, and more presentational. There wouldn't be so much breathing room. The dancers loved performing *Sue's Leg*—Tom Rawe called it a give-back piece.

Their performance was chosen to initiate the PBS *Dance in America* series, in a video directed by Merrill Brockway. Since the dance is less than half an hour long, it was supposed to be paired with a work by Eliot Feld. When this fell through, the producers prefaced Tharp's dance with a remarkable half-hour documentary on popular dancing, scripted by Arlene Croce. Uncannily related clips from *Sue's Leg* were spliced into the archival footage of square dancing, social dancing, tap dancing, chorus lines, marathons, burlesque, and ballroom. The documentary provided a context for Tharp's '30s nostalgia, but it may also have implanted the idea that her dance was simply a compendium of those old styles. Tharp reportedly was unhappy with the coupling, and Ken Rinker observed, "In my wildest imagination . . . I *never* related [*Sue's Leg*] to social dancing." Tharp certainly didn't elicit the dancers' recollections of popular steps, as she did in the last part of *Eight Jelly Rolls*, although the few minutes of archival footage on the London Weekend Television *Jelly Rolls* might have inspired the *Dance in America* treatment.

With its inner construction concealed under its goofy noodling-around behavior, and—in the video—overlaid by the historicizing documentary footage, *Sue's Leg* seems ultracasual, even thrown-away. Unlike the '30s performers on the documentary, the dancers aren't engaging in courtships, and if they're conscious of having an audience, they try hard not to play up to it. They seem to be pals or siblings, so intimate that they can trust each other completely, upstage each other without incurring offense, and fall in with foolhardy stunts and mischief. They may not have specific antecedents in Tharp's own four-sibling family, but they do play consistent roles. Wright is the benign big sister, tolerantly watching her two brothers act up. Rinker and Rawe are enough alike to be twins, but Rinker seems introverted, willful, while Rawe enjoys his own awkwardness. Tharp is at once the coy little sister and ringleader.

Most of the movement of the dance grows out of a walk that modulates from strolling to shambling to strutting, propelled by Fats Waller's bouncy theater organ and swing band. With their arms free, shoulders loose, torsos responsive to the possibility of twisting, they embellish the musical beat with understated shuffling and foot rotations. At times they break into overt tap dancing, but when Rawe goes into the shim-sham, accompanied by a tap soundtrack and an upbeat instrumental, he soon gets out of sync and proceeds with his own variation unfazed. Tharp has two solos, one very knowing, one naive. In the first, to "I Can't Give You Anything but Love," she peeps out from under her low-cut bangs and balances steady as a rock on half-toe, shimmying her shoulders, and twitching isolated parts of her body at the audience. Later, to Waller's clownish singing of "Ain't Misbehavin'," she could be doing the same movements, but as a professionally cute little girl. She alternates tiny, close-in attention-getting moves with huge assemblé turns and fast chaînés, inserting sudden scissors-jumps and drops to the floor.

All four dancers are featured in *Sue's Leg*, but they're equally memorable when they work in combination. Rawe and Rinker shadow each other in slightly-off unisons and canons. They circle around Wright and eventually engage in a shoving match with her. Later the three are gathered close together but looking away nonchalantly as one topples over against another. They seem to team up against Tharp as the outsider at moments, but they copy her as she shows an intricate step. They all link arms and bounce up and down together. In the windup, they begin scrambling over each other's backs, hoisting one another up, and suddenly they line up, taking a perfect preparation and joining hands for a bow. The music changes and they regroup for a fast chorus of "I've Got My Fingers Crossed," a sort of choreographed encore. They modulate from playful bouncing on two feet to tight step-turns and suddenly a replay of the hoisting and scrambling sequence. There's the lineup, the preparation, and finally they all bow while still holding hands.

6

The Big Leagues
1975–1978

The company's engagement at the 1975 Spoleto Festival in Italy probably originated through Rhoda Grauer's connections, and it was Grauer
who booked the performances for the opera house, the Teatro Nuovo, instead of a smaller theater. This proved to be a miscalculation. The repertory,
consisting of *Ocean's Motion*, *Sue's Leg*, *Bach Duet*, and a reduced version of *The
One Hundreds*, eluded the high-culture European audience. But the engagement proved momentous anyway.

Tharp's career had been headed for an intersection with that of the extraordinary Russian dancer Mikhail Baryshnikov for several months. He had
defected from the Soviet Union only a year earlier. A phenomenon as a performer, a tremendous virtuoso and box office attraction, he had become a
regular guest artist at American Ballet Theater. By the time he met Tharp in
Spoleto he had danced eleven roles in the West, most of them classical, but
he was looking for new choreographic challenges. He was collaborating
with Charles France on a picture book, *Baryshnikov at Work*, and France, a
close friend of Arlene Croce, was a devoted Tharp fan who steered everyone he knew to see her work. American Ballet Theater codirector Oliver
Smith, always scouting for new choreographic talent for the company, had
his eye on Tharp. Early in 1975 her work was visible in New York both at

the Joffrey Ballet and at Town Hall in May, where her company did several small items and the New York premiere of *Sue's Leg*.

When Smith brought his codirector, Lucia Chase, and Baryshnikov to a performance of *Deuce Coupe II*, Baryshnikov was fascinated with the way Tharp made the dancers look: "sort of men and women on stage being in a way very whole and very themselves and very grounded and without playing a character, being the people of the streets." According to Tharp, Chase and Smith offered her a commission soon after the *Sue's Leg* debut. Tharp guessed that Baryshnikov had proposed the idea, and she scandalized the directors by naming a $10,000 fee.

In June Baryshnikov was appearing at the Spoleto Festival with Carla Fracci in a quasi–Martha Graham creation about Medea by John Butler. On the Tharp company's program the customary *Half the One Hundreds* mob scene, with a cast including Spoleto artistic director Gian-Carlo Menotti, was dubbed *The 49 Amici* for the occasion. Tharp decided to dance the introductory *Fifties* as a solo, she said, so that the dancers would have time to change costumes, but she wasn't naive. She knew Baryshnikov would be in the audience and she intended to win him over decisively, with her dancing. Seated in the Director's box with Grauer and Clive Barnes, Baryshnikov saw "how refined and delicate and impossibly difficult her vocabulary is." Later Barnes remembered that "they were both obviously amazed and astounded at each other. For Mr. Baryshnikov this was clearly a new world, and for Miss Tharp this was clearly a new dancer." After Spoleto, the deal with ABT was a fait accompli.

The artistic and personal relationship between Tharp and Baryshnikov that began at Spoleto stretched her fraying bond with Bill Kosmas to the breaking point. He resigned a few months later, before the premiere of the ballet that propelled her into superstardom, *Push Comes to Shove*.

Tharp began working in the studio with Baryshnikov after they returned from Spoleto, on what became the opening sections of the ballet. For hours they looked at films of black tap dancers and soft-shoe entertainers. "She was trying to explain to me where the movement comes from, it's not just like she invented it," he says. Tharp used the Bach Partita in D Minor for their initial improvising, and Baryshnikov thought she wanted to translate "the ease and grace of a flatfooted dancer . . . into a kind of virtuoso element." As in *Sue's Leg*, Tharp wasn't going to quote her vernacular sources so much as impose their temperament onto a different set of circumstances.

The ballet opened with a slouchy, sexy Baryshnikov, in another elegant Santo Loquasto practice outfit, just noodling to three minutes of ragtime. This Tharpian image was familiar enough by then, and the sight of the Russian prodigy goofing across the forestage, slinkily joined by ballerinas Marianna Tcherkassky and Martine Van Hamel, was both a shock and a delight to the audience. But when the rag and the prologue ended, the curtain went up on the real transformation. In rehearsals, by the time Van Hamel and Tcherkassky joined the work, Tharp had switched from the Bach Partita to Haydn's Symphony No. 82. Its subtitle, "The Bear," supplied an apt Russian reference, and it provided a spirited musical base for her revelation of the star, dancing classical steps in an unimaginably relaxed way.

The first movement belonged to Baryshnikov even though the women each entered and danced briefly. At first glance his solo seemed merely a string of alternating ballet steps and pedestrian movements, taken at maximum speed. He launched into ballet flash—multiple pirouettes, leaps, fancy leg designs and foot changes—interrupting this offhand virtuosity to rake his fingers through his hair or sink into one hip as if waiting for a bus. But in a sense, the street gestures are the least surprising thing about what he did. It's as if Tharp planted them there in order to establish an antithesis to the ballet steps, but what's in between is most interesting. Some part of each step is done in proper form, but the dancer's preparation, attack, and alignment reshapes it. Starting a pivot turn, he visibly initiates from his pelvis and throws his whole upper body and head back against the direction of the turn. He flings his arms across his body to change to a new stance, then finishes with exquisitely calm gallantry. He takes exaggerated preparations, or goes from one feat to another with no preparation at all. He whips from a set of hunched-over spins into a punch. He anatomizes a gesture by jerking through it one body segment at a time, what would be called "popping" twenty years later by hip-hoppers. When the music rears up and growls, he pitches forward into an upside-down arabesque, then springs upright.

With phenomenal control, he can uncork sudden speed or a sudden complete stop, accelerate or slow down in the middle of a phrase. He assumes the ballet body attitude: pulled-up torso, noble head, spread-out chest and arms, pointed legs and feet, assured address to the audience. The next moment he lets go of all this placement and relaxes into a comfortable, everyday slump. After a cascade of deranged beats, jetés en tournant, brisés, and combinations packed with steps, he ends with six pirouettes that decelerate into a perfect fourth position. You have the sense that he's thinking his way through the dance, choosing what to do, how to be. Everything is musical and everything draws attention to the classical dancer that he is, even when he's turning himself inside out.

Baryshnikov's appetite for new experiences, and his adaptability to them, made *Push Comes to Shove* possible. His personality and his role within the company became one theme of the many-layered ballet. *Push* was neither Tharp's first pointe ballet nor her first entry in the classical arena, but American Ballet Theater was this country's foremost traditional ballet ensemble. Since its founding in the 1930s ABT had maintained a contemporary wing, but its ongoing repertory of important classics asserted its connection to the great Russian/French heritage. The '70s were both an exhilarating and a demoralizing time for the company. By 1975 its roster was top-heavy with international stars. Besides creating a modern vehicle for Baryshnikov, Tharp set out to depict a company in which he and other celebrated guest artists dominated not only *Giselle, Coppélia, La Sylphide*, but contemporary works as well. Their every appearance enriched the box office, but when they were the main attraction, the other dancers faded into the background.

Playing on the double entendre of Baryshnikov as generic guest star and Misha as interloper and role model, Tharp developed a kind of fairy tale. Having lured the audience in with his name and gratified them with his pyrotechnics, she redirected the limelight to the rest of the company. Baryshnikov was known for his modesty during bows, the way he stepped back and let his ballerina accept the audience's ovation. In *Push*, he defers to his female partners in the first movement, leaves altogether for the two middle movements, and submits in the end to a rambunctious effusion of attention-grabbing stunts from everyone else. With this premise, *Push* became an insider ballet, in the tradition of Antony Tudor's *Gala Performance*, choreographed in 1938, and Jerome Robbins's 1956 *The Concert*.

During the preliminary rehearsals, as Baryshnikov was absorbing Tharp's casual style, she was quizzing him about ballet steps. Although she'd taken ballet class for years, she didn't know the refinements, and she needed a lot of information. According to Baryshnikov, "She was trying to understand how the girls go on pointe and what propels them around, and figure out classical coordination, where is croisé, what's éffacé, why it's écarté . . . and what's the difference between the first arabesque where it's flat and the fourth arabesque . . ." For the second movement of *Push*, she introduced a double corps de ballet, two groups of eight girls in identical short filmy dresses, one group in pale blue, the other in beige; led by Tcherkassky and a new soloist, Kristine Elliott. Recalling Robbins's famous Mistake Waltz in *The Concert*, they behaved almost properly but with misalignments and "wrong notes" that enlivened the static, secondary role traditionally prescribed for the corps.

Dance critic Laura Shapiro, writing in *The Boston Globe* shortly after *Push*'s premiere but without having seen it yet, remarked on Tharp's perennial choreographic "veneer of chaos." Shapiro felt that even when the audience couldn't see Tharp's underlying craft, it would always sense the form holding together her seemingly undefined activity and be reassured. The corps in *Push* initiates a long descent into this deceptive messiness. Tharp's vocabulary here consists of heeled-over ballet steps, multidirectional group poses, and port de bras exercises gone haywire. The two semichoruses alternate at first, working out Haydn's simple theme with several different floor patterns and subdivisions. The groups converge and appear to be trying to resolve all these designs into one, but it takes a lot of scrambled interweavings before they agree on four lines perpendicular to the footlights. Even this order is temporary, and they continue to rearrange it. When their movement finally unifies, they face different directions. As this brilliantly engineered machinery slips through its paces, the dancers disclose the boredom, competitiveness, and mishaps they usually conceal. A girl from one side somehow shows up in the other corps' territory and casually fades back into her correct place. Off to the side, the two lead sylphs claw at each other spitefully. Individuals saunter off when it appears they're not needed. At the end, only a few women are left to bow with their leader.

Egalitarian yet deeply respectful of rank and power, Tharp wanted every sector of Ballet Theater's population to be noticed. She told interviewer Jane Perlez that she didn't understand "alphabet dancing." That is, company rosters that listed all dancers equally. "Some dancers should be in the chorus—that's their level," she said, without intending any condescension, so she was making "trios and quartets which are very difficult and small featured parts for a dancer who can hold a small responsibility and excel at it."

Susan Jones was a member of the Ballet Theater corps when Tharp started rehearsals for the second movement, which was to be her showcase for the translated coryphées. "We were a bit afraid of working with her," Jones says. The usual dire preconceptions about Tharp had percolated through the company, but they were forgotten immediately. Tharp had worked out the corps movement and taught it to Jennifer Way, who came along as her assistant and demonstrator. Jones remembers: "From the very first day you had to be totally impressed with her, not just her pace but the homework . . . and her calculations of how long it would take for us to go across the room doing these complicated combinations, changing fronts and at a rapid pace, [it] was just unbelievable to all of us. It really blew us away." Jones noticed that Tharp had an uncanny ability not only to make up steps and groupings but to visualize how these would coordinate spatially and musically, before she taught them to the dancers.

Jones was given a tiny featured part, and a year later, after the untimely death of ballet mistress Fiorella Keane, took over the job of overseeing *Push* and most of Tharp's subsequent ABT repertory. She never lost her admiration for Tharp's work. "She crafted [that second movement] like the most highly crafted Petipa or Balanchine ballet. . . . It's like the bar is raised from the first minute of the rehearsal. . . . You rise to the occasion and you get in that zone and you work at the same pace that she does." Jones cherished her inside knowledge of the corps movement, subtle choreographic detail that she knew the audience probably wouldn't be able to discern. When she set *Push* on Britain's Royal Ballet several years later, Jones shared "secrets" with Monica Mason, then the Royal's ballet mistress, like the movement phrase that travels in a snakelike canon through the ranks of the corps. "You feel the effect of that wave getting bigger and bigger on the stage but you don't really see how it happens."

Not only did *Push* call attention to the hierarchy of dancers in ballet companies, specifically ABT, the piece had a shadow plot. Similar to the way Balanchine skimmed what he wanted from the classics, Tharp garnered the dance component from one or more actual story ballets in the repertory. She then reassembled these elements and reinvested them in a new tale of threat, dissension, and harmony restored. After focusing on Baryshnikov and his two female partners, and reinterpreting the corps, the "plot" moved on to a skewed pas de deux by Van Hamel and Clark Tippett, surrounded by male and female courtier types. As in some nineteenth-century party scene, the nobles—the men dressed like Baryshnikov and the women in long, somewhat dowdy dresses and turbans—enter in small groups, admiring and

bowing to Tippett and Van Hamel, who grandly ignore them. Haydn's minuet serves as a processional, keeping all the nobles streaming across the
stage behind the principal couple or posing in gracious attendance.

As the movement progresses, Van Hamel and Tippett's regal duet becomes contentious. Their timing goes slightly off; she hogs the spotlight
and he contrives ways to be seen, burrowing under her arm, making extra
gestures. Unnoticed by the principals, the nobles vie for the audience's attention with gratuitous bows and upstaging tactics. Tippett circulates
among the courtiers while his partner waits for him temperamentally. Van
Hamel is courted by three other men, who throw her bodily into Tippett's
arms when he returns.

Tharp always resisted clichéd beginnings and endings; she loved movement that went on after the music finished, exits that didn't coincide with
musical conclusions. Baryshnikov's second appearance, alone in the spotlight after the rag, deferred belatedly to his star status. At the end of the first
movement, the women of the corps have already entered before the audience has stopped applauding his solo. As the music begins again, he leaves
with a tremendous barrel turn into the wings. This is the first of three transitional interludes between movements. As the corps is petering out in the
second movement, Tcherkassky brings Baryshnikov on for a flirtatious moment. In silence, they speed through a series of mistimed changes and lifts,
then race off, to the audience's amusement. After the third movement, Van
Hamel and her three courtiers saunter near the wings, passing a derby
among them.

This hat, the only prop in the ballet, symbolically adds to the theme of
competition and attainment. Baryshnikov is wearing it when he first appears. His two female partners snatch it, put it on, pass it between them
slyly, like teenagers with a basketball hero's jacket. In the fourth movement,
the derby becomes a desired trophy for everyone in the corps, and is tossed
from one dancer to another. The hat doubles before the end of the ballet as
the competitive activity takes over; Baryshnikov loses the symbol of his superior rank. When the dance was revived in the '80s Tharp made choreographic changes too, so that Baryshnikov, then ABT's artistic director,
actually stepped back as the whole company acquired hats of their own. On
closing night of the winter 1976 ABT season, with *Push* a certified hit,
Tharp's fans orchestrated a surprise exclamation of derbies and deluged the
stage with them.

The fourth movement begins with Baryshnikov leading two sylphs on for a bow. From there on, the ensemble and the principals dance in ever-mixing patterns, until the big finale, where they never quite get symmetrically organized. The corps women skitter on half-toe clutching their foreheads and making other desperate gestures. Even amid this planned breakdown, Tharp had encouraged the dancers to choose which choreographed phrases to do. But they finally assemble with Baryshnikov in the center on Haydn's volley of cadences, as if for a series of family snapshots.

The dancers knew *Push Comes to Shove* was funny, but none of them anticipated the ecstatic response that greeted the ballet's premiere, at the Uris Theater on 7 January 1976. Ovations are common on opening nights, but this was special. Tharp was brought onstage by Baryshnikov during the endless bows, and managed to grin while receiving bouquets and applause from the dancers. Friends said they had never seen her happier. Afterward, Gelsey Kirkland walked out shaking her head and saying "I'm never going to dance again. How could I be so stupid?" Kirkland, who had left New York City Ballet to dance with Baryshnikov at Ballet Theater, began learning the part that later went to Tcherkassky but withdrew after a few rehearsals, perhaps considering Tharp's movement too eccentric. *Hamlet Connotations*, the new John Neumeier ballet she and Baryshnikov performed that season with Erik Bruhn and Marcia Haydee, was dubbed "simplistically Oedipal" by *Time* magazine, and it quickly disappeared.

Although some critics still refused to take Tharp's comedy seriously, most of the press was delighted with *Push*. Clive Barnes unequivocally endorsed it. "It has charm, vivacity, humor, kinetic understanding . . . Miss Tharp has not merely done it again . . . she has done it better than ever before." Croce thought it was "a real work of art and an entrancing good time in the theatre," but almost too subtly balanced between real invention and spoof. The comic aspects of *Push* were so successful that they took over the ballet in many people's eyes. Pundit Roger Copeland objected to the "slapstick." The humor in *Push* was "facile and unadventurous" compared to *The Bix Pieces*, he thought, "not the result of delicately modulated sensibilities, but rather of a broad and rather obvious parody."

But Dale Harris saw the audience's spontaneous reception of the ballet—and of Tharp—differently. Unlike the "rites of personality worship" that cluttered the ABT repertory, *Push* made the audience understand "that [Tharp's] share in the evening's success was the determinative one, and, by extension, that first-class choreography is a rare and precious commodity." Hardly had the curtain come down when George Gelles of *The Washington*

Star declared Tharp "the hottest ticket in American dance today." Gelles thought that what some viewers saw as "jokey and facile" was in fact "parody of the highest sort . . . a combination of homage and criticism in one." ABT's own historian, Charles Payne, called it "a hit of such proportions as is apt to occur only once in a decade, and [it] went on to become the triumph of Ballet Theatre's 1977 European tour." Still, the company thought of *Push* as a comic vehicle for Baryshnikov, who "adjusted his classic technique unerringly to the grotesqueries" of Tharp's far-out ballet.

Despite the huge success of *Push Comes to Shove*, Tharp didn't make another company ballet for ABT until 1984, when Baryshnikov had become its director. Tharp's former associates can't account for this except to point out that she was working on other things—chiefly some big media projects and her own expanding company. But there were probably less visible issues.

Tharp was already notorious for charging high fees and insisting on other contractual perks that distressed the money-conscious ABT management. The company was committed to the star system at that time, an expensive practice that nevertheless yielded big box office and high prestige. Its paradigm had been set in the 1940s and '50s by Markova, Alonso, Bruhn, Youskevitch, Fracci, Lander, Serrano, and later by the defecting Russians Nureyev, Makarova, and Baryshnikov. From its inception, ABT set out to be the American company that would carry on the Russian ballet tradition— along with producing English and American works. Under Lucia Chase and Oliver Smith it had mounted full-length productions of *Swan Lake, Giselle,* and *Raymonda*, with *Sleeping Beauty* scheduled to go up in the summer season of 1976. Charles Payne relates in his company history that by the beginning of the '70s ABT had come to think of itself as a company with a repertory of standard works, vehicles for the great international stars, much like the Metropolitan Opera. Roving bands of dancers, singers, and conductors needed minimal rehearsal time to step into the schedule. Jet travel facilitated the process. As a touring company, without a permanent theater in New York or anywhere else, ABT achieved an alternative stability with its revolving supply of headliners, but its own principal dancers were constantly struggling to compete with visiting celebrities. Morale was dropping. Dale Harris took note of American ballerina Cynthia Gregory's resignation midseason (it turned out to be temporary) due to management's "lack of artistic encouragement." This state of affairs, of course, was the sub-text situation of *Push Comes to Shove.*

Baryshnikov in real life set out to reform the system during his tenure as artistic director of ABT (1980–89). He cut back the star system and further repaired morale by cultivating the in-house dancers, polishing up the indif-ferent technique of the ensemble, and summoning avant-garde choreogra-phers to enliven the repertory. Ironically, when he left, the company was better able to produce the classics than ever before.

Despite shifts of economics and taste, ballet culture continues to privi-lege the classics and their top interpreters. Tharp herself partook of this mystique in her adoration of classical dancers. There was no point in taking on commissions unless she could begin her journey to the technical strato-sphere from the tallest launching pad. "I cannot think seriously about a dancer who lacks technical control," she told Alan Kriegsman of *The Wash-ington Post.* "But there are technically expert dancers who are terrified of dancing. . . . There must be a real passion to do it. And also a certain lust for adventure, the audacity to throw away any of that technique, to get beyond it." From the first Joffrey rebellions to French and English resistance years later, there were dancers who found Tharp's deconstructed classicism dis-orienting. Martine Van Hamel admits to needing time to master her unusual coordinations and timing. "You had to repeat it so it became natural. It had to get into my muscle memory." Her shruggy, comedic role in *Push* wasn't likely to add any luster to her ballerina's tiara either. Within ABT, a dancer of Van Hamel's stature did have the power to opt out, and by the time *Push Comes to Shove* was filmed in 1984 she had ceded her part to Susan Jaffe.

For Tharp there was one immediate follow-up to *Push.* ABT's annual fund-raising gala was scheduled for the New York State Theater in July af-ter the *Push* premiere, and the management naturally wanted to showcase its prize acquisition, Baryshnikov. The ballet gala, a ritualized enactment of the ballet mystique, features invited stars and home talent in glamourous ex-tracts from the repertory. Baryshnikov declined to trot out the expected pas de deux from *Don Quixote* or *Le Corsaire* for the 1976 extravaganza. Instead he asked Tharp to make something new. The two were just starting to work on a television project and she decided to double up assignments. The ABT commission would give her more time to work on the material for the TV taping. Besides, she couldn't resist the opportunity to choreograph—and dance—in the home of the New York City Ballet, what she called "Balanchine's stage." *Once More, Frank* turned out to be a notable failure—another possible reason ABT's management cooled to Tharp. It also touched off some of her greatest successes.

Eventually she got terrific mileage out of a dozen or so Sinatra songs that she selected from the durable crooner's recordings of the '60s, with their romantic Nelson Riddle arrangements. *Nine Sinatra Songs* (1982) was a Tharp company favorite for years; some considered it her all-time best dance. *Sinatra Suite* made its way into the ABT repertory, and it was danced by Baryshnikov and Elaine Kudo on the same commercial video that featured *Push*. In 1984 the Tharp company performed the *Nine* at the White House for President Reagan, and, as part of Reagan's 1985 inaugural events, Baryshnikov and Kudo danced the *Suite* with Sinatra singing in person.

For the 1976 ABT gala Tharp used "Something Stupid," "That's Life," and "One for My Baby." Dressed by Santo Loquasto in identical white jazz shoes, short-shorts and rugby shirts, with their small, compact, and superbly trained bodies, she and Baryshnikov looked like twins. *Once More, Frank* was never performed on a stage again, but twenty-six photographs by Martha Swope, published in *Baryshnikov at Work*, give some idea of what it looked like. Tharp took the idea of the pas de deux seriously. She made lifts, jumps, and parallel dancing for the two of them, but as in *Push* the classical ideas were either interpreted casually or gunned to extremes. He hefts her to his shoulder, where she puts on an anxious grin but points her feet in a kind of swan-dive assemblé. They slump against one another, spring up into circular jumps. In one photo, she seems to be pleading with him, like Giselle, while he edges away. In another, he seems to have just tumbled onto his back and is rolling with his legs in the air.

The gala audience had no taste for this, and the performance was loudly booed. Baryshnikov had to pull her on for their bow, and she ran from the theater in tears. He thinks now it was a "nice little piece," but the audience wasn't ready for it. They had expected to see a prince and instead they got two tomboys having fun. Baryshnikov found it interesting "to experience Twyla constantly changing from the authoritative figure the choreographer must be to the co-dancer whose psychological level was very much the same as mine." Charles France considered the idea too sophisticated: Tharp had miscalculated the degree of style-mixing the audience would tolerate, especially when she herself was dancing alongside the great danseur noble of the era.

But the gala was almost incidental to Tharp's real project. *Once More, Frank* was conceived to illustrate the dancemaking process as it related to television. David Loxton, director of the Experimental Television Lab at New York's public TV outlet WNET/Channel 13, had some funds to try new things, and he had offered Tharp his facilities. This suited her very well, because, having made primitive records of her work for years, she was eager to learn what professional television could do. She contributed a $100,000 grant for company development that she'd received at the end of 1975 from the Andrew W. Mellon Foundation. Loxton brought on board a young television director, Don Mischer, who welcomed the chance to work with a rule-breaker.

The project that became *Making Television Dance* was being documented in black and white by independent filmmaker Joel Gold, and his footage became a key element in the finished video. When Tharp and Baryshnikov were rehearsing the Sinatra, Gold captured their relationship superbly. (The unfortunate gala performance that was the ostensible end product didn't appear in the video.) Baryshnikov leans against a mirror, beaming and gasping with admiration as Tharp demonstrates a phrase to "That's Life." They practice lifts, trying tricky things. At one point she's nosediving over his shoulder, aiming for his outstretched leg. Laughing, she crawls down. On the next try, something goes wrong; he grabs her waist but she tumbles onto her head, to his dismay. He remembers that he just couldn't hold on to her when she giggled and let go. Tharp was fond of saying she didn't like to be lifted, it made her sick—but that was all the more reason to try it, and here she had the classiest escort in the business. Baryshnikov says she wasn't the easiest person to partner. "She was very spontaneous, of course, and trying too much to help the partner. And that's always wrong."

The edited sequence ends with "One for My Baby," shot entirely in sensuous close-up. Tharp explains in voice-over that the duet was intended to be very private, intimate, to be seen by a single viewer at home. You don't see the arms and legs because "I didn't make anything for the arms and legs. It was made for the void between us." She'd been thinking about close-ups two years earlier, as part of a multimedia production scheme for *Sue's Leg*. Six screens were to flank the stage, with previously filmed close-ups of the movement projected during the dance. Given the available resources and the capability of television at the time, the scheme proved unworkable, fortunately for *Sue's Leg*.

Don Mischer recalls that from the outset Tharp brushed aside the prevailing dictum that dance must be televised in a consistent full-stage shot with all the bodies visible at all times. They argued about it. One of her initial ideas was to "create dance with imagery that was not full-bodied dancers. She thought we could shoot close-ups of eyes or knees or fingers. Or elbows, and manipulate these images with video and create dance that way." The "One for My Baby" sequence was probably the best they could do with this idea, but she had plenty of others; some worked and some didn't. In a black-and-white shot early in the video, Tharp quizzes Mischer about the gadgetry in the control room. She wanted to use things television people took for granted, like the color-bar test pattern and the numbers that ran on top of the picture, counting seconds. She didn't care about the conventions of television, or televised dance; she wanted to see what the two media could do together. Loxton thought their trial-and-error process would be as interesting as the work, even when the idea failed, and midstream he brought in Joel Gold to record it.

Making Television Dance, still one of the most imaginative dance videos ever made, turned out to be a sort of anthology. There were three main segments with an epilogue, surrounded by Gold's black-and-white footage of the process—rehearsals, preparation, messed-up attempts, and commentary by Tharp, the dancers, and the crew. In addition to the Sinatra sequence, she choreographed "etudes" for the particular qualities or skills of four Tharp dancers, using video editing to underscore her compositional themes. Each etude was filmed in a different space, from the prehistoric Great Jones Street loft to Franklin Street to the ABT studios uptown. The square TV screen suggested an American square dance, which she turned into a group variation for herself—laboriously overdubbed eight times—and a company work that became *Country Dances*.

By the summer of 1976, Tharp's company had begun its evolution into the perfectly blended ensemble of modern and ballet dancers that created her work for the next decade. For *Making Television Dance* she was temporarily down to a quartet again. Ken Rinker didn't like the stop-and-go pacing of film and video work, so he declined the television project. Rose Marie Wright was taking some time off to care for a knee injury. At that point the first key players in the company's subsequent adventures, Shelley Washington and Christine Uchida, had arrived on the scene.

Washington was a student at the Juilliard School in 1973, apprenticing with the José Limón company, when she took Tharp's summer classes at

American University. The students had to learn one hundred numbered positions, do them on the right or left side, in slow motion, in retrograde, and be able to put them together in any order to make a dance phrase. Washington was dazzled. She was good at it too. Tharp even called her onstage from the audience to demonstrate the positions while the company conducted a lecture-demonstration. "All of a sudden, it was like every variable on your body and your brain," Washington said years later. She knew immediately that Tharp dance was what she wanted to do, but the company didn't have an opening until two years later, when she was dancing with Martha Graham. Washington auditioned for the dancers—Tharp wasn't present—and they invited her to work with them. It was a very big deal to leave a job in modern dance's most prestigious company for a small, ill-paid troupe that didn't even have separate dressing rooms for men and women. But, says Washington, "Something about the way Twyla worked in 1973, when I was seventeen years old or whatever, just . . . got me. I just had to do it."

Uchida, feeling stalled in the Joffrey Ballet, had left to try dancing in musicals. She'd loved working with Tharp and the company in *Deuce Coupe* and *As Time Goes By*, and she'd already let Tharp know she was interested in joining them. Tharp did call her but at a bad time, just before Uchida was about to leave on tour with a show that subsequently flopped on Broadway. Finally in the spring of 1975 Uchida heard Tharp was having auditions and decided to go. She got lost looking for Franklin Street and arrived late. But Tharp signed her up immediately, and she started learning Isabel Garcia-Lorca's part in *Eight Jelly Rolls*.

The etudes for *Making Television Dance* were ingenious one-to-two-minute miniatures, layered, Tharpian fashion, to display not only the dancers but the way choreography works, and the way television can both enhance and complexify dance. For "Speed" Tharp introduces Shelley Washington as a dancer with charm, warmth, and the physical courage of a big jumper. Washington spirals up into the air and down to the floor. In what Don Mischer calls "freezes with moves away," the camera captures the dancer at the peak of a jump or a turn, holding the dramatic moment over as she continues in real time, and then slowly fading out the still image. This is an almost uncanny adaptation of Tharp's old "dots" device, where the backup chorus arrested Wright's moves in *Eight Jelly Rolls*.

Tharp celebrates Tom Rawe's work ethic and endurance, his determination to analyze and conquer movement material, in "Repetition." Rawe jogs into some easy turns with his upper torso stretching and folding loosely; he runs in place with his hands flapping; he does pushups with handclaps. Much of the time he's accompanied by a shadow of himself, so he seems to be doing twice the work. Rhoda Grauer remembers that Tharp visualized Rawe "skipping rope, and then his body jumps out of his body, and then [he'd] keep skipping rope, and this other body that jumps out of his body goes over and does pushups, and then another body jumps out of that body. And Don going, it's not possible. Can't be done." But Tharp insisted until Mischer found a way to do it.

For "Focus" Jennifer Way performs the same phrase twice, simultaneously, as filmed by two cameras. She duets with herself and with the cameras, pulling the movement in close to the body and releasing it as one camera pulls back, and adjusting her space the opposite way for the other camera, which starts at a distance and zooms in. Before the shoot, Tharp and Way meet on the sidewalk near Columbus Circle, to go over the solo. Tharp is going to stand in for Way in rehearsal, and Way has to remind her how the sequence goes.

"Retrograde," says Tharp, is something only a mother could love. She then launches into one of her rapid-fire explanations as Chris Uchida gives a pristine demonstration of another doubled phrase. It's almost impossible to follow the words, the sequence, and the manipulation, but the gist of it is that in midphrase one Uchida starts dancing it backwards, while the other Uchida is filmed in reverse. Tharp wants to show the difference between mechanical and live retrograde. "Television can come closer to a conceptual rendition of movement in space than is actually possible," she remarks. "It's right—but it's wrong."

Tharp loved double images. Perhaps, as a child with twin brothers, she had realized early the advantages of pairing. In choreographic practice, the viewer would learn more, and enjoy more, by seeing two ideas side by side rather than one after the other. Ever since the days of Rudner and Wright, she'd deliberately put dancers of different styles and temperaments together within the same choreography. Wright and Rinker's demonstration of steps in *The Bix Pieces*, the duo that performed the first part of the *One Hundreds*, even the man-woman/ballet-modern symbiosis of *Once More, Frank*, all asked the audience to see contrasts within a finely tuned unit. Television was an ideal medium for this witty didacticism.

Although most of *Making Television Dance* was conjured up in the privacy of a studio, *Country Dances* needed a live audience. Conceptually, this brought a natural climax to the video process that began with one person dancing with herself in television no-space and ended in a stark coda where the outline of a dancer sinks and merges into a flat-line horizon. The circumstances of a proscenium theater wouldn't give the television crews enough freedom to do their work, so they booked a sound stage and set it up in arena style, for an all-day rehearsal and showing. Mimeographed notices were posted all over the city to summon the audience. It was Mischer who realized that after the first take the audience would be exhausted, and they came up with the slightly devious idea of scheduling two showings, both free. They'd set up in the morning and then tape a runthrough, which would serve as a dress rehearsal for the dancers and the crew. There'd be a dinner break, during which Tharp and Mischer could review the tapes and make adjustments. A second performance would be the actual take. Neither audience knew that this was the scheme. Both showings were booked solid a week in advance.

Tharp found a real bluegrass band, Snuffy Jenkins, Pappy Sherrill, and the Hired Hands, to play for *Country Dances*. On the video, she goes to South Carolina to hear them and select tunes for the dance, relaxing into a theatrical down-home accent as she banters with the boys. In New York the final rehearsals and performances began at 9:00 A.M. on a hot Sunday in August. In the backstage documentation, Gold's grainy, improvised black-and-white footage communicates the stress and exhaustion of this last phase of shooting. At the studio entrance Tharp is stopped by the guards and moans that she has no ID, someone will have to vouch for her. Santo Loquasto fusses with the costumes. The crew announces that the linoleum floor is bubbling; they decide to go with it, in hopes it will stretch out under the dancers' feet.

The careful schedule crumbled but the audience was patient. The first shift waited outside for half an hour, then listened to the band while the crew finished a mandatory break. Mischer warmed up the audience, encouraging them to respond with enthusiasm—stomp their feet if they liked. Tharp introduced the dancers, and a larger ballet began, as the videographer moved around the dancers, followed by a helper attending to his equipment, followed by Joel Gold and several assistants moving cable out of the way. Two cameras offstage filmed the whole thing. On the video, as Tharp is making her way out after the wrap, a man pokes his head out of the crowd, and says, "I don't like television but I like you a lot."

Country Dances set Rawe, Way, Uchida, and Washington romping to four numbers by the Hired Hands. The music seems to propel them into sketchy square-dancing steps and patterns—swing your partner, grand right and left, do-si-do. Way and Washington face each other in profile at the beginning. As the camera moves in, their faces become a frame, an open curtain, and they enter through it in an overdubbed shot. Woven among the quartet's swings and twirls and hopping there are ballet steps, lifts, including the racing dive Tharp did in *Once More, Frank,* and some lazy chumminess left over from *Sue's Leg.* The camera reads all this in edited long shots and close-up. When the music switches to an easy waltz, Rawe partners Uchida and Washington in turn, and the camera comes in to savor their odd, upside-down grapplings. The last number is fast and jittery; the dancers skid into slapstick. Washington lifts Uchida, and on the last split second, Way up-ends Rawe and they all gesture into a goofy final pose.

Mischer used his freezes with moving away, and something he calls "video lag, where an arm would sweep through the picture and there would be fifteen other arms just a split second behind it sweeping through." At one point Rawe starts a slow series of chaîné turns around Way and Washington. They pick up his step and are suddenly transformed into a fifty-woman Virginia reel. Mischer notes how labor intensive these effects were at the time. For the chorus line reel, and to trace the trajectory of some swooping lifts later on, the tape had to be stopped a few frames into the dancers' movement, recorded and fixed on the master tape, stopped again a few frames later, and so on. Mischer says it could take a whole evening to edit a single phrase. Today it would all be done digitally, in no time.

The live-audience segment ended with a short but intense solo for Tharp. Using some of the material she had sketched in her eight-part opening solo, she throws foot-slaps, jumps, ballet steps, and seductive shimmies into a casual stroll. After sixteen fast hopping fouettés with her extended leg gradually sweeping from front through side to back, and a few more wiggles and jerks, she glares, takes a giant step toward the camera, and disappears.

Making Television Dance didn't go on the air until October of 1977, but in the meantime Tharp turned *Country Dances* into a stage work. She first took it on tour with her company, to Edinburgh and Berlin in September of 1976. A month later it began a long transition where it slid between two companies, changed titles, and emerged with the addition of a showpiece for Wright and five men called *Cacklin' Hen.* Tharp had renewed her relationship with Robert Joffrey, and *Country Dances* became the first part of a longer piece, *Happily Ever After,* which premiered at the end of the Joffrey Ballet's fall City Center season. Her company was part of the initial package, dancing the quartet followed by her solo. A second quartet of Joffrey dancers did a slimmed-down version of the first, and the piece closed with *Cacklin' Hen*. This configuration occurred only once, on opening night. For the remaining three performances, the Joffrey presence diminished as Tharp withdrew their quartet section. She gave her own solo to Ann Marie De Angelo, the strongest technician Joffrey had. When the Joffrey took the dance on its winter tour, the Tharp company was gone; the quartets were gone; De Angelo's solo and the final sextet, led by Jan Hanniford, were all that remained; and the piece was renamed *Cacklin' Hen*.

The folksy-Americana mode was unusual for Tharp, although she was a great fan of country music and often used Hank Williams and Earl Scruggs recordings in the studio. The Bicentennial commemorations of 1976 fostered a certain amount of hayseed-chic, and *Country Dances* fit this sensibility. Robert Joffrey was planning to observe the Bicentennial by reviving George Balanchine's *Square Dance* with its original onstage caller, and by taking *Rodeo* into the repertory. Agnes de Mille's beloved classic would be a coup for Joffrey, appropriate for his young dancers, and doubly appealing to the audience because the choreographer was making a gallant recovery from a serious stroke. Bea Rodriguez danced the Cowgirl. The great success of this Western early in the season may have undercut Tharp's barn dances. Analyzing *Happily Ever After* in *The New Yorker*, Arlene Croce thought Tharp's initial quartet revealed a new dynamic amplitude that "makes an across-the-board difference: in momentum, which is now released to its fullest sway; in the legibility of the group dances; in the consistency of 'characterization' in the solos."

Tharp and Robert Joffrey must have hoped her dance would prove as durable as the remodeled *Deuce Coupe*, but the Joffrey Ballet was sliding into one of its periodic administrative abysses. Faced with serious financial trouble, Robert Joffrey canceled the spring New York season, so the final *Cacklin' Hen* wasn't seen in New York until the fall of 1977. *Country Dances*, with *Cacklin' Hen*, served as a repertory piece for Tharp's company until the fall of 1979. But she had little time to focus on it after it did its main job in the television project.

Besides keeping her own company in shape for touring—after BAM (May 1976), there were dates in Minneapolis, Europe, Florida, and Delaware—she made an exquisite piece for Olympic figure-skating champion John Curry. *After All* premiered at Madison Square Garden in November as part of Curry's Superskates show. Tharp never learned to skate when she was growing up. This wasn't the fault of the Southern California climate—she didn't learn to swim either, or drive—but her overscheduled childhood didn't leave room for recreational sports. Curry had wanted to dance before he became a skater, and he was an innovative boundary crosser himself. Dissatisfied with the rigidly defined figure-skating world, Curry started a company of ice-dancers and invited real choreographers to make ballets for it, beginning with Tharp.

She didn't think his challenge was unusual. "I've always wanted to have—it's sort of a fantasy—the 'glide factor' possibility," she told dance writer Amanda Smith. On the ice, where gravity didn't impede the dancer's locomotion, she could develop a new range of rhythms. With the piece she made, to the familiar Adagio from Albinoni's Concerto for Trumpet, Smith felt, "the dimensions of figure skating expanded so dramatically that . . . the seven-minute solo signaled a new era. . . ." Mary Grace Butler, a skater who served as a production assistant for Superskates, remembered *After All* as "dance, real dance, on ice skates, with theatrical lighting, in front of fifteen or twenty thousand people who usually saw spins and twirls. . . . I remember the hush of all those people holding their breath as John performed, and the explosive applause when it was over."

The country music pieces, the ice dancing, postproduction work on the video, and the busy company schedule of 1976–77 all proceeded alongside the biggest project Tharp had yet undertaken, her first Hollywood movie. The Czech film director Milos Forman had seen her work at ABT and invited her to set the dances for *Hair*. It took her a while to accept. "I wasn't sure that I wanted to be involved with a director, that I wanted to have to be put at the mercy of the project," she says now. She saw the opportunity as a turning point, not only in her career but in the life of her dance company. Commercial work offered financial rewards unheard of in the nonprofit dance world—Tom Rawe and Jennifer Way were able to make a down payment on a house in Brooklyn from their earnings on the movie. Tharp worried the dancers might be tempted to desert her after they tasted relative affluence. Finally she accepted Forman's offer. With Ken Rinker as her assistant, she was at work long before shooting began in New York, in October 1977.

The musical *Hair*, ten years old when Forman translated it to the screen, could claim several distinctions. One of the first successful rock shows, it started in a downtown workshop production directed by Gerald Freedman at the New York Shakespeare Festival. With successive renovations, it made its way to Broadway under Tom O'Horgan's direction, ran for 1,700 performances, then spawned innumerable regional and international productions and a best-selling record album. The show's nearly nonexistent plot uncorked a pageant of countercultural defiance—bad language, uninhibited sex, and antiwar outrage. Twenty-eight songs by Galt MacDermot, Gerome Ragni, and James Rado marked the era's turbulent politics and equally turbulent liberation. By the time the movie was made, the nation had climbed out of Vietnam and absorbed the best of the hippie lifestyles. *Hair* the movie made the '60s seem a colorful memory, much the way the music and dance of *Deuce Coupe* had romanticized other aspects of the period. Reviewing *Hair* after its release in March of 1979, *Newsweek*'s Jack Kroll commented that it "treats the 'American Tribal Love-Rock Musical' exactly as it should be treated—as a myth of our popular consciousness."

With ballet and television under her belt, movies were the logical next challenge for Tharp, but her fears about relinquishing control over the product proved well-founded. So far she'd been fortunate to have sympathetic collaborators who understood her intentions and contributed to their fulfillment: the dancers especially, and Bob Huot, Bill Kosmas, Jennifer Tipton, Santo Loquasto, Rhoda Grauer. Professionals in other fields often learned as much from her as she learned from them. Don Mischer finally appreciated her radical ideas about TV dance: "She made me realize how much editing can affect what you walk away with. . . . I've learned a lot about questioning the rules and trying to do things even if everybody around me says, that won't work." On *Hair*, with Milos Forman making the ultimate decisions, the dancing would be an integral but subordinate element. The dancers felt that initially Forman undervalued them. "Milos didn't know anything about dance really, and Twyla educated him," Ken Rinker says. "Twyla made him give us some respect, not that he wasn't going to. He's not a nasty person or anything like that, it's just that dance for some people is like a costume. No, we really do work at this. We rehearse, we study, we know what we're doing, we have point of view, we can articulate it. She brought him to that point."

Making *Hair* was difficult for the dancers. Much of the movie took place outside, and the weather didn't always cooperate. Just as they were about to shoot the be-in on the Sheep Meadow it snowed. The crew was preparing to melt the snow with airplane engines and supply the dancers with ice cubes to suck so their breath wouldn't vaporize, but Forman managed to get the work suspended until green returned to the trees. During one period, the company was touring on weekends and returning to New York for all-night shoots during the week. On the set, there were interminable waits while the crew set up or reshot other scenes. All the dancers complained about the problem of keeping their muscles warmed up; they never knew when they would be summoned to perform. Some figured out how to stay in what Tom Rawe calls "a slight state of readiness," and then be prepared for retakes. On the day they finished the scene in the Sheep Meadow, a group of dancers, still in scruffy costume and makeup, went off to the upscale Café des Artistes for lunch with Tharp. They had a celebratory meal and many drinks—none of them had any money but the restaurant trusted Tharp to come back later and pay the bill. When they finally rumbled back to Central Park they found the crew desperately searching for them to shoot one more scene—which didn't make it into the film.

A great deal of the dancing was deleted during the editing, and Tharp never got over her sense of work wasted. Both she and Milos Forman were trying for a sort of through-danced scenario, but they approached that goal from opposite poles. He wanted to splice dance into the narrative. She wanted everything in the film to dance. Seven extended sequences involve the principal actors, Tharp's company, about forty additional dancers, and hundreds of choreographed extras. The dancers, together with horses, puppets, singing groups and soloists, are woven into the escapades of the hippie tribe. Tharp was already accomplished at making dancers look like ordinary people, and she gave the nondancing actors movement to do that blended them in with the dancers and singers. There was only one extended dance number made for a stage, and except for a few cryptic remnants, it was cut. But she did think in terms of self-contained dances throughout, and in the event, her choreographic coherence was sacrificed.

Conceptually, Forman adopted the hippie point of view: life, as they saw it, was a celebration, a deliberate disconnect from society. Transfigured by drugs, the runaways become performers, producers of illusion. Horses can dance. People can levitate. War can be stopped. The hippies do extravagant and risky things; the camera hallucinates even more flamboyantly, juggles time, fractures the landscape. Once released, the movie was very successful, and today it looks thoroughly permeated with dance. Years of MTV and high-tech editing have conditioned our eyes to negotiate its extreme jumps in continuity and sequence. Even Tharp might have approved the restless, sometimes surreal way the camera conveys the sensibility of *Hair* if she'd had a hand in it. In fact, three years later she used the technique of splicing to intercut two entirely different groups of characters, in one of her great stage works, *The Catherine Wheel*.

Milos Forman kept most of *Hair*'s original music; Michael Weller wrote a new screenplay that clarified the characters, gave momentum to the action, and instituted several spectacular setpieces. The movie's plot concerns a little family of hippies led by Berger (Treat Williams). Claude, a white-bread draftee from Oklahoma (John Savage), meets them on his way through New York en route to boot camp. The hippies induct Claude into a new way of life before he gets to the army, and in a macabre coda, Berger's most daring prank turns fatal. Having half-converted Sheila, Claude's debutante ladylove (Beverly D'Angelo), the hippies cross the country in a stolen car to visit him at the army base. Berger impersonates a soldier, gets into camp, and takes Claude's place for the night while Claude goes to meet Sheila and the hippies. It turns out to be the night Claude's unit is shipped overseas. In the last scene, the hippies visit Berger's grave at a military cemetery. Tharp went on location with the actors to the National Guard base in Barstow, California, where she staged the exercises for John Savage and 1,500 trainees. She did all the slogging and heavy drill herself, of course.

The film streaks through an increasingly bizarre progression of escapades and celebrations, and then pitches forward to its ironic denouement. It starts in the stark absolutism of an Oklahoma dawn, as Claude's father drives him to the bus stop. But the edges of reality grow ragged as soon as the draftee gets to Central Park. He rebuffs the hippies' first advances and they dismiss him as a square. But he quickly wins their respect by catching a runaway horse with tricks they've only seen done by fancy rodeo riders. They introduce Claude to marijuana, and the next morning it doesn't seem at all strange when Berger spots the face of the girl Claude noticed riding in the park the day before, right there on the page of a discarded newspaper. Or that the article tells them where to find her.

Just as hippie belief in magic can make amazing coincidences happen, film magic constructs the mythic journey that ends in the death of the antihero. A kind of cinematic counterpoint continually sets the hippies' freewheeling lifestyle against the conventions and enforcement of the uptight world. The hippies seem to beat the system with their brash disregard of the proprieties, and they persuade at least three characters to abandon the straight life, but in the end it's the charismatic, eternally confident Berger who gets destroyed.

Most of *Hair* was shot on location in Central Park. The huge spaces of the park—the Sheep Meadow, the band shell, the stone staircase near Bethesda Fountain—were a total contrast to the studio confines of *Making Television Dance*. For Tharp, the park had its own resonance, dating back to the New York rehearsals and performances of *Medley* in 1969. Intermittently throughout her life, Tharp looked back on her early childhood at her grandparents' farm in Indiana—and translated her nostalgia into dance. The prospect of a pastoral work-life persuaded her to decamp for New Berlin with Bob Huot in the '60s. Much later she spoke seriously—though not for long—about running off to live in the country with a lover as famous and sophisticated as she was.

Improbable as these schemes were, the utopian idea of free, natural living has informed a surprising amount of her choreography. Before *Medley* there had been the outdoor experiments during the idyll at New Berlin, with Rudner, Wright, and the volunteers working their way toward a style. There had been Wright mingling with the campus population in *Rose's Cross Country*. And on stage, the surfer allusions of *Deuce Coupe*, the whomping rusticity of *Country Dances*, and, as late as 1996, the sprightly Quaker exaltations of *Sweet Fields*. After quitting New Berlin and Huot's determined stance as an antiestablishmentarian, Tharp moved quickly away from the poverty and invisibility of the counterculture. Her later choreographic reflections on it preserved its romantic aspects but stepped around its liabilities. Democracy and inclusiveness were all very well but not when it came to implementing her choreographic ambitions.

Hair looked back to that festive era where life was a dress-up party and anyone could be a dancer. In an early version of the screenplay Tharp circled every reference to action with a green marker, intending to stage movement wherever she could. She choreographed gestures throughout the movie, basic training exercises, Frisbee games, and a massive peace rally. Her tactics ranged from full-out dancing to ingeniously scaled-down steps for the actors with limited dance ability. When dance scenes called for more than her nine company members, she would set their parts first, then distribute the additional dancers into their groupings. There were excellent dancers among the extras (Chris Komar from the Cunningham company, Christian Holder and Cameron Basedon from the Joffrey, modern dancers Marta Renzi, Mark Morris, and Deborah Zalkind, for example) but it was more efficient to work out the choreography on her inner circle.

The numbers are expansive, almost flung into space. In Claude's first view of Central Park as a perennial be-in ("Aquarius"), at the Sheep Meadow free-for-all where he takes his first LSD trip, and during the peace demonstration on the Mall in Washington, D.C., Tharpian looseness and spontaneity seems pushed to its highest level of abandon. Dressed in ragamuffin finery, the dancers race across lawns, skip in formation down a hillside, do flips and jetés, charge up and down a flight of steps like Bill Robinson. In spasms of self-absorption, they spin meditatively and practice tai chi. On the Sheep Meadow, Tharp gets tossed in the air by a group of men dancers.

But outdoorsy casualness isn't the only kind of dancing in *Hair*. When the hippies crash Sheila's coming-out party in Short Hills, New Jersey, Berger climbs on the dinner table and breaks up the banquet with the orgiastic "I Got Life." There's a heavily edited fight in the jail after Sheila's father has the intruders arrested ("Hair"). The disorderly gatherings and punchy jail fights are countered by a crowd of downtown businesspeople Claude sees when he heads for the army induction center. As he walks along the street singing "Where Do I Go," the corporate troops move in perfect formation, heading uptown, then downtown, then kneeling, then dispersing into all directions.

After this vision of the straight world's conformity, Claude reports for his army physical. The procession of naked draftees has a strange effect on the uniformed board of five black and three white inspectors. Grim and official, they display no reaction to the assorted bodies that come before them, but a raunchy montage reveals their subconscious thoughts. "White boys are delicious," sings a trio of miniskirted black women in the park, followed by three white women with a taste for black boys. The song cuts back to the army board, now rocking with pleasure. For the black officers' share of this homoerotic fantasy ("White boys are delicious"), the shot cuts to their legs, dancing in unison under the table. Since the officers' upper bodies didn't appear in the frame, Tharp was able to use five of her own dancers, male and female, for the routine. The dancers thought the idea was original with Tharp, but editing tricks weren't new to the movies. Before she started choreographing *Hair*, Tharp had studied a collection of movie musicals. Among them must have been the popular *Bye Bye Birdie*, choreographed by Gower Champion on Broadway and by Onna White for the 1963 film version. This movie, about a rock star's tumultuous guest appearance in a small town, has an almost fetishistic interest in feet. In one scene, kids are talking on the phone ("Goin' Steady"), and their legs, seen from the waist down, turn in and out in unison.

Hair reaches its phantasmagoric, psychedelic heights in the scene at the Sheep Meadow ("Electric Blues"), where Claude and the hippies kneel as if at a Communion rail, to receive cubes of LSD from a dealer with a painted face and dollar signs on his hat. Crowds of fun seekers swarm through competing singing groups, processions of giant puppets, chanting Hare Krishnas, and antiwar orators, and it all blurs into Claude's acid trip. He marries Sheila in a giant church (it was actually an immense film studio in Queens), lit by hundreds of candles, with white-clad ballet dancers in attendance. Tharp, once again taking advantage of high-budget technical opportunities, arranged the dancers on moving platforms and rigged them for flight. Rose Marie Wright, as the Virgin Mary, walks on air while appearing to sing in an otherworldly soprano. Tharp, in the front of the church, spins out of her clothes and into a pseudo-Indian robe, then seems suspended in midair like a Hindu deity as she intones the marriage vows. Sheila immediately sprouts a pregnant belly and joins the dancers, who are laughing and undulating like spaced-out devidasis in front of flaming incense burners. Eventually the madness melts back into the sirens and Hare Krishnas in Central Park, a reality only slightly less demented.

As shooting progressed, Tharp pressed Milos Forman for more dance, and he sometimes placated her by shooting scenes straight through with a second camera. The dancers realized this was going on, and many continue to believe that the outtakes still exist somewhere, preserving all the choreography that was cut from the film. The outtakes never surfaced, but Tharp did stage three of the deleted dances during her 1979 BAM season, just weeks before the movie's world premiere.

7

Hodge Podge Rummage
1976–1979

Immediately after the huge success of *Push Comes to Shove,* Tharp started to experience the downside of fame as well as the dividends. Everywhere the
Tharp company toured that season, tickets were sold out, extra performances
were added, and hopeful crowds lined up at box offices for last-minute cance-
lations. She and the company were featured in mass magazines (*People, Time,
MS, US, Vogue, Rolling Stone*) as well as brainy ones (*Atlantic, The Nation*), often
pictured adopting Richard Avedon's cheeky poses. *The New York Times* commented on Tharp's wedge haircut, along with those of Pia Lindstrom,
Dorothy Hamill, and other notables. Media and entertainment personalities
signed up to be in the cast whenever she put on *The One Hundreds.* She received
her first honorary doctorate, from California Institute of the Arts, in 1978.

But only a month after *Push* premiered, when the company returned to
Lisner Auditorium in Washington, critic Noel Gillespie announced that "the
most inflated reputation in United States dance today is that of Twyla
Tharp." Critics outside the orbit of her longtime supporters doubted that
anyone could possibly be that popular and also that good. Some experienced
Tharp-watchers began complaining she was repeating herself. "Tharp has
created one good work [*The Bix Pieces*] and proceeded to rewrite it ad nau-
seam," said Gillespie. Even some of her most loyal critics thought they saw
slippage. Alan Kriegsman of *The Washington Post* had scathing words for *Mak-*

ing Television Dance, calling it "one of the most disjointed, hectic, jumbled items ever to cross the screen, parading under the banner of creative innovation." Kriegsman blamed this on Tharp's "erratic sense of form" and said the show reflected "the same sort of indiscriminate frenzy that has characterized Tharp's choreography of late." *New York* magazine parodied her, alongside prominent politicians and athletes, in an alphabetical sendup of the year's municipal "Power Failures." Music critic Alan Rich wrote the jingle:

> Wiggle, waggle, twist that fanny—
> Twirling Twyla's not too canny.
> See one dance, you've seen them all.
> Modernism casts its pall.

Tharp's relationship to the company was changing too. In the spring of 1975, around the time of the *Deuce Coupe II* premiere, she indicated to *The New York Times* writer John Rockwell that she was feeling overloaded. She thought of her company as a workshop, she said, that facilitated "discoveries and advances . . . Artists must be allowed to wallow around in their own confusions, and that can lead to other, more finished things." Her working process had always been exploratory, but until the Joffrey ballets it had been her own company that brought the experiments to completion. Now, as the company handled the dual role of touring machine and laboratory, she started to work out ways to maximize its productivity, and her own.

She'd never flinched at delegating responsibilities to the dancers. When new members were taken into the company, they learned the existing repertory from videotape, and their colleagues often ran rehearsals. They talked to the media on tour, since Tharp usually didn't go along. She passed on invitations for extra jobs to them, both to increase their earning power and to make more efficient use of her own time. During residencies they did the teaching and often presided over lecture-demonstrations. For instance, during a multipart "residency" linked to the 1977 Brooklyn Academy spring season, there were master classes at Long Island University and a workshop for the basketball team at Brooklyn Polytechnic Institute. Tom Rawe gave classes to the team and organized a demonstration for an audience of eighty-five students and faculty members.

The tours were intense. Federal, state, and local funding for the arts was reaching its peak, and although Tharp was wary of the tradeoffs implicit in the nonprofit world, her company, along with the other major modern

dance groups, became prominent on national touring circuits and subscrip-
tion seasons. In 1977, with *Hair* set to begin shooting in October, the company went straight from its Brooklyn Academy season (12–22 May) to
Minneapolis for two weeks, then on to summer festivals at Ravinia, Jacob's
Pillow, Connecticut College/American Dance Festival, and Artpark in New
York State. Between the end of September and the beginning of November
they played Washington, D.C.; Boston; Wilmington, North Carolina; Detroit; Poughkeepsie; and Nashville. During the winter hiatus of *Hair*, in January and February 1978, they traveled to the Caribbean, Princeton,
Philadelphia, and the West Coast, for eight engagements.

In May of '77, as she was preparing the movie and working on a television
special with singer-songwriter Paul Simon, Tharp announced her withdrawal from dancing, "for now." She told *The Minneapolis Star and Tribune*: "I
can't carry on this kind of schedule and also perform." This put presenters in
a tricky position. Modern dance companies ordinarily took the name of
their founder-choreographers, and now Tharp was highly marketable. Sponsors used her picture and her name in bold type, but they had to downplay
the inconvenient fact that the company would appear without her. There
were, inevitably, disappointed ticket holders. In Nashville, at least one newspaper preview claimed she would perform, and the sponsors then had to in-
sert an elaborate disavowal into their advertisements. Comparing Tharp to
Beethoven, the revised ad urged the public to view her as a great composer,
whose creativity was implemented by her company rather than being dependent on her performing personality. "Informed dance fans know that to
see her choreography is to see the woman and when you visit the Opry
House on November third you'll see the greatness of Twyla Tharp. . . ."

Perhaps because she was preoccupied with bigger projects and the company was touring so extensively, she began filling out programs with short
subjects—excerpts from older pieces, spinoffs from commercial projects,
fragments or studies for longer works—that could be shuffled around to suit
the company's immediate needs. During the period 1976–79 the company
toured with three staple dances, *Eight Jelly Rolls*, *Sue's Leg*, and *The Fugue*. To
these major works were added *Country Dances* and *Cacklin' Hen*, sometimes in
their spliced-together form and sometimes as separate items; four small
pieces: the *Bach Duet*, *Rags Suite*, *Half the One Hundreds*, and a seven-minute remnant from the Paul Simon special; and, for a season or two, *Ocean's Motion*.

Tharp's musical methods made it fairly easy to lift sections out of longer
dances. She had always foraged freely in the musical repertory, and either

by brilliant synthesizing or intuitive good luck she could put together isolated pieces by the same composer (Jelly Roll Morton in *Eight Jelly Rolls*, Fats
Waller in *Sue's Leg*), or by disparate composers (Beiderbecke and Mozart in
The Bix Pieces, Joseph Lamb's "Bohemia Rag" and Haydn's 82nd in *Push Comes to
Shove*). In fact, her finished works are so musically persuasive that hardly
anyone has noted how seldom she's used a single piece of music for a whole
dance. With the exception of a few symphonic ballets and commissioned
scores later in her career, she has applied the cut-and-paste method ever
since early days. In her own mind she devised logical sequences, and sometimes even quasi-narratives, for her choices, but submitting to a composer's
throughline was another matter.

She never felt attached to her dances after she considered them finished;
repertory was an expedient at best. She would work on a dance—most often whittling it down—until it reached her idea of perfection and she had
learned what she could from it. She made large cuts in *The Raggedy Dances*,
for instance, and reduced the cast from five to two within three years of its
premiere. As the *Rags Suite*—the Mozart section sandwiched between two
rags—it served for years, often performed by Way and Rawe. The practice
of extracting self-contained numbers meant she didn't have to revive whole
dances; it might even be an improvement. She'd keep the best parts and
didn't need to bother anybody with the rest. As she once wrote: "the best
poems are sent by night letter—21 words counting signature and address."
This reductionist practice reached a peak on tour in fall 1976, with *From
Hither and Yon*, described as a compilation of excerpts from thirteen repertory
pieces since 1965, and its subsequent, further-refined version, *The Hodge
Podge*. Television was even better at collating the smallest recognizable tokens from the repertory, and in 1982 she glossed twenty-two items in the
hour-long PBS anthology called the "Scrapbook Tape."

At a time when the standard dance concert lasted about two and a half
hours, her programming began to look skimpy. One writer complained that
a 1977 performance at Lisner Auditorium took only two hours *including* two
intermissions. By the early 2000s she could program three miniature pieces
and one longer work, with an intermission, for a performance in a major
venue that lasted one and a half hours. She felt she was giving the audience
a lot for its money.

The dancers made the best of the touring. They stayed in decent hotels and
flew between dates instead of taking uncomfortable buses. They enjoyed interacting with the public in master classes and other events. Surprise castings and

bonuses kept the limited repertory from becoming routine. At the American Dance Festival in 1978, the *Bach Duet* was done twice, with two casts (Colton and Uchida, Wright and Kurshals), and *The Fugue* could sustain different combinations of men and women. Besides, the work itself was an ongoing challenge. "For me," says Raymond Kurshals, "it was such a treat to get out there and to do the work. . . . It was different every time." Even on tour, they kept working on the material in the studio. Anthony Ferro, who joined the company during *Hair*, felt a great sense of responsibility to the work, especially because Tharp was entrusting the dancers to present it on the road without her.

When the company had expanded to about twelve dancers, Tharp divided it into two units, the red and blue teams. She had conceived the ingenious scheme of sending one team on the road to earn money while the other team stayed in New York, where she could work with them on new material. This innovation addressed Tharp's chronic fear that the business of touring would undermine her creativity. She could keep on choreographing and preserve a personal schedule flexible enough to accept freelance projects. The dancers enjoyed the extra performing opportunities they got in the small ensembles, but the plan had stressful aspects.

The touring works had to be double-cast, which usually meant one person would be learning a part choreographed on someone else at a different time in the company's history. Given how closely identified Tharp's dances always were with the dancers who created them, a few rivalries took root and were stifled. Interpretations could change, but not too much. Technical problems arose when the original dancer's strengths were different from those of his or her replacement. Often one team would be rehearsed and ready to go on the road when Tharp would decide she needed a particular dancer for the ongoing work in New York. This necessitated frantic last-minute shifting or reworking. For the rehearsal directors, Way and Rawe in the latter years of the plan, the tours could mean nonstop rehearsing, performing, and teaching. Then, when both teams reassembled for performances in New York or another big city, there were hard decisions about which cast would perform. Not all the dancers disliked the team concept. Christine Uchida, who shared Tharp's role in *Sue's Leg* with Shelley Washington, enjoyed seeing the alternate versions.

It was in the creative process that these changes most affected the dancers. By the time he left in 1977, Ken Rinker perceived a subtle shift in Tharp's choreographing process. At one time, he thought, the movement had been simple but the treatment was complex; now the movement grew more complex and the treatment simpler. Rinker thought Tharp was using more balletic movement as she worked with ballet dancers, and that during her own company's reduced rehearsal time there was less problem-solving for the dancers to do. *Ocean's Motion,* which she made in 1975 before the company went to the Spoleto Festival, may have been the closest Tharp came to a potboiler in those days. Set to the music of rock-'n'-roller Chuck Berry, the dance used material recycled from *The Double Cross.* It didn't offer the dancers enough challenges, Rinker thought. She dropped it quickly, calling it "glib and facile." Five years later, she doubled the five-member cast and simply put one set opposite the other. They danced two whole songs in mirror image.

Tom Rawe and Jennifer Way discussed the evolving company with Mike Steele of *The Minneapolis Tribune* in the spring of 1977. While Rawe had spent his first year learning the repertory and performing only one section of the *Jelly Rolls,* rehearsing like that was now a luxury. New dancers had to have a strong technical background and be able to learn fast. According to Way, "Twyla has to concentrate harder now because she's doing so much more. Her new works are getting more and more complicated, but they're also more set. Dancers still get a lot of freedom, which is one of the great things about working for her, but she knows exactly what she wants now." Rawe added: "It's all more condensed. Where four phrases might have gone over a long period of time before, they will be done in thirty seconds now. There's more material in each dance."

For the company's first extended New York season, ten performances at Brooklyn Academy in March of 1976, Tharp offered a new "suite" dance, *Give and Take.* She used three seemingly incompatible modes of music: a prelude and fugue by the eighteenth-century composer Gregor Werner; four American marching band numbers; and the popular song "Willow, Weep for Me," in a recording by the great jazz pianist Art Tatum. Offsetting this apparent incongruity, the dance had several simultaneous throughlines. By manipulating the same movement material for solos and groups, Tharp laid out a company style that could hold its own against the most diverse accompaniments; and via that stylistic consistency she suggested there might be some relationships in the musical selections as well.

Trendy themes were invoked by the use of patriotic marches like "The Stars and Stripes Forever," which suited the American Bicentennial. Tharp cited George Balanchine's ballet *Stars and Stripes* with Sousa's music, and inserted a few movement quotations like the wedge-shaped formations adopted by Balanchine's perky ballerinas and cadets. She made explicit ref- erence to Balanchine in a printed collage of words and graphics inserted in the program. The company announced it had invited the master to the opening and Balanchine did make a rare appearance. How he reacted to Tharp's tribute is not recorded.

As the six dancers assembled and dispersed, attended to the music or ig- nored it, *Give and Take* illustrated the tension between regimentation and freedom, conformity and individualism. Possibly these qualities needed their polar opposites to exist at all. The pulled-in, pulled-up strut of the drum majorette was countered by the far-flung, free-wheeling arms of the sports fan. The dance projected a familiar Tharpian casualness, but it was all neatly structured—the accidents choreographed in, the falling and getting caught in the nick of time, the "mistake" lineups where someone is facing the wrong way or moving on the wrong beat, the slightly ragged unisons. The dancers scuffled their way into the formality of the wedge patterns and ambled out of them.

Solos for Tharp, Wright, and Shelley Washington drew attention to each woman as a special component in the company's identity. Tharp opened the piece, introducing the movement vocabulary and the contrast- ing attitudes of rigor and nonchalance. Several times during Werner's Pre- lude she dropped whatever she was doing and started again after a cooling-off aside. Rose Marie Wright remembers that in the studio, while Tharp was making the dance, she was deluged with phone calls regarding her other projects and company business. She finally translated her annoy- ance into a thematic element. Interruptions punctuated her solo and the trio that followed for Way, Washington, and Wright. The group marches for the women, Rinker, and Rawe (originally there were four marches, but she soon eliminated one of them), and the solo for Wright that ended the dance, were full of unexpected stops and starts.

Without fanfare, in the midst of "American Patrol," Tharp brought Shel- ley Washington into the foreground. *Making Television Dance* had not yet been broadcast and these were Washington's first performances for the company's home audience. Her brief solo showcased a unique and accom- plished contributor. According to Washington, Tharp had given her "every- thing that I couldn't do. Well, it turned out I had more this than that, more everything." The group faded away as she stepped out and crossed the stage with fast changes of arms and legs, and her star power was instantly per- ceived. The audience applauded her as she danced back to her returning companions, and on opening night Washington gave a nod of acknowledgment, right in time to the music.

Tharp's other generous gesture in *Give and Take* was Rose Marie Wright's final solo. Wright had been dancing in every company piece for years and had been Tharp's creative collaborator as well as keeper of the repertory. She felt miffed when the huge success of *Push Comes to Shove* seemed to fall exclusively on Tharp and the ballet dancers without a nod to the choreographer's longtime dancer-partners. Tharp may have gotten wind of Wright's feelings, and she dedicated the Brooklyn Academy season to her. After the marches in *Give and Take*, everyone left and the imperturbable, elegant Wright went through another reshuffling of the thematic material, to Tatum's rhythmically eccentric piano playing, demonstrating how she could make Tharp's stylistic contradictions seem perfectly logical. She ended on a long relevé in fourth position, then dropped the pose and walked off. After the Brooklyn performances Arlene Croce proclaimed Wright the season's dance heroine. "She has an unassertive style," Croce wrote, "but a clearly defined and exceptionally spacious one, and she warms you with her air of patient good sense." When Wright came on for a solo bow opening night, Tharp loped out from the other side of the stage with six dozen long-stemmed roses, a bouquet almost as big as she was, and nearly collided with the astonished Wright as she presented them.

Give and Take was set for the company's May performances in Minneapolis. Wright injured her knee in New York just before the trip. With the help of doctors and physiotherapists, she got through that run, then took a leave over the summer. She helped in the studio while Tharp finished *Once More, Frank* and made the men's movement for *Cacklin' Hen*.

Although *Give and Take* was the season premiere at BAM, it proved a lesser attraction than the repertory pieces. Croce thought: "As an audience piece, it's a courageous work for Twyla Tharp to have made at this moment—Twyla the toast of New York—because it's so unaccommodating. Not that it's unfriendly or anti-entertainment, but it just doesn't give away any secrets. It's anti-success." The other dances, *The Fugue, Eight Jelly Rolls, Sue's Leg,* the *Bach Duet,* and the *Rags Suite,* already had important reputations but they'd never been shown in such concentrated array for a big New York audience. So in a sense, the Brooklyn season consolidated Tharp's personal success by showcasing her own extraordinary dancers and the work they had made together.

◌◌◌

When the company returned to BAM in May of 1977, Tharp had only one new dance to offer, *Mud*, but she surrounded it with repertory works and festive events. Celebrities made guest appearances, dances were imported to the stage from the screen, and one-time-only gift packages were unwrapped for the audience. Paul Simon accompanied the medley Tharp drew from their forthcoming television collaboration. Before that show aired all the dances were dropped, but the *Simon Medley* on stage turned out to be fairly inconsequential. Tharp invited the press to rehearsals of *Half the One Hundreds*, enabling writers to spot participating luminaries like Estelle Parsons, Hermione Gingold, Milos Forman, Bobby Short, and City Councilman Robert Steingut, who would scarcely be visible among the throngs onstage.

For *The Hodge Podge*, Tharp strung together tiny excerpts from dances dating back to the '60s. In a way, the whole season was a kind of anthology, dominated by guest appearances and special happenings. It aroused great excitement but didn't encourage the audience to deepen its appreciation for specific dances. Arlene Croce thought things in *The Hodge Podge*, like smashing a chair (*Disperse*, 1967) and walking inside a large hoop (*Re-Moves*, 1966), were extraneous to the serious dance work Tharp had made even in the early days. Croce pointed out the uncompromising inwardness of lost dances like *Generation* and *Group Activities*, a quality she saw in evidence during the season only in *The Fugue* and *Cacklin' Hen*. Croce saw Tharp going overboard in her attempt to accommodate the BAM audience. "[R]eviving those antics today in the form of a montage tells us more about the taste of an era than it does about the emergence of Twyla Tharp," she wrote.

Far more momentous than the visiting movie stars and politicos was the return of Sara Rudner, dancing in *The Bix Pieces* and doing cameos from her early roles in *The Hodge Podge*. When Rudner left in 1974 she had already started choreographing on her own, and she wanted to try an independent career. She established a small group of dancers and gave concerts, as well as teaching and setting her dances for other companies. Her work was well received but the slow developmental process that she loved took a lot of energy and enterprise to sustain. She learned she had no taste for undertaking major touring or permanent payrolls, and this gave her a renewed admiration for Tharp. She agreed to come in for the final scenes in *Hair*—the rally at the Lincoln Memorial—when another dancer was injured. Rudner realized how much she loved dancing Tharp's work, and agreed to rejoin the company as a quasi–guest artist, with enough scheduling leeway to continue her own creative work. She moved to the bottom of the company's chronological roster and stayed until 1984.

Ken Rinker too was trying out an independent career, choreographing for his own group of dancers. He danced in the 1977 BAM season but then left permanently. As Tharp's first male dancer, Rinker had ignited what became a major energy source for her. Years later, the choreographer Rachel Lampert wrote in appreciation: ". . . when I first saw Ken dancing it was almost a shock. The precision and exquisite nuances the women could bring to the movement was perfect. Men dancers just didn't have that kind of finesse. . . . When Twyla added Ken to the company I think it changed how men danced from that time forward." And Richard Colton remembers Rinker in *The Bix Pieces*, the first time he saw Tharp's work: "I don't think I'd ever seen a male dancer move like that before." Perhaps no choreographer, then or later, equaled Tharp in creating male dancing roles that were both demanding and personal. After Rinker, she explored the potential of individuals as different as Larry Grenier in *As Time Goes By*, Tom Rawe in *Sue's Leg*, Mikhail Baryshnikov in *Push Comes to Shove*, and decades of others. With Rinker's departure, two important new men, Richard Colton and Raymond Kurshals, arrived in the company. A short time later, William Whitener joined them.

Colton's infatuation with ballet began at the age of seven, when he saw the spectacular Moiseyev Russian folk dance troupe at Madison Square Garden. Besides his strong, sturdy body, he had two big advantages from the start: supportive parents and a home just outside Manhattan, in Little Neck, Queens. Throughout his childhood and teenage years he studied with major Russian teachers, first at the Ballet Theater school, then at the Joffrey. While still in the High School of Performing Arts, Colton encountered the crossover artist James Waring. A great mentor-teacher and pioneer in the choreographic fusion of classical ballet and popular culture, Waring epitomized the aesthetics of camp in the mid-'60s, and he opened up the downtown dance world for Colton, who appeared at Judson Church in Waring's *Winter Circus* (1968).

Colton's commitment to Tharp developed gradually. He was named an understudy in *Deuce Coupe* as a young dancer in the Joffrey Ballet. He learned several parts but never went on in the original version of the Beach Boys ballet. Tharp saw his extraordinary technical ability and cast him for the Four

Finales in *As Time Goes By*, then later worked out much of the men's movement for *Cacklin' Hen* on him. That one-on-one session made a big impression on Colton. Tharp's choreographic detail, her unusual working out of the phrase, her "physical molding" of the body shapes rather than fitting shapes to an existing balletic norm, all reminded him of James Waring's compositional process. He felt his personal contribution to her choreography was as important as what he was learning from her. When he heard Ken Rinker was leaving the company, Colton wrote a note to Tharp from his vacation in New Mexico, asking her to save him a place. His colleagues at the Joffrey thought he was making a big mistake, but he stayed with Tharp until 1989.

Raymond Kurshals also entered the company via *Cacklin' Hen*. He was on layoff from Merce Cunningham's company in the summer of 1976, but he had succumbed to Tharp's dynamism years before. Kurshals had led a checkered young life in Honolulu and San Francisco—he says he attended half a dozen high schools and did some hanging out on the streets of Berkeley during the hippie years. As a floundering teenager he had a sudden revelation that dance was what he should be doing. By luck, he found his way to the Shawl-Anderson school, where the teachers provided a solid grounding in modern, ballet, and jazz techniques. He feels now that dance saved him from life on the street. "Dance literally gave me the discipline and the focus to change my life," he says.

When the Tharps came to Ohio State for their one-day residency in 1971, Kurshals was dancing with Ruth Currier in a small José Limón–influenced company affiliated with the university's dance department. He'd begun a friendship there with Rawe, Way, and Sharon Kinney. They maintained their connections over the years; Kurshals was best man at Rawe and Way's wedding and stayed with them when he arrived in New York in 1973. With Merce Cunningham (1975–76), Kurshals danced in the repertory and one new piece, *Squaregame*, but the Cage/Cunningham musical aesthetic didn't satisfy him. When Tom Rawe brought him into Tharp's rehearsals for *Cacklin' Hen*, he reconnected. She offered him a place in the company if he should decide to leave Cunningham, which he did soon afterward. His status not yet established, Kurshals wasn't allowed to perform *Cacklin' Hen* for the Joffrey season, but he danced it later in the Tharp repertory.

Tharp had a longstanding practice of pre-rehearsing—actors call it workshopping a piece. She made movement on herself each day before the dancers came in to work. But she began to need more bodies and she grabbed them whenever she could. In fact, even though the company was evolving into a more or less conventional organism, it was hard to separate "work" periods from what conventional workers call overtime. When the company went on a salaried basis, rehearsals still could extend into long hours. If the company was on tour, before the invention of the red and blue teams, she'd gather the best outside people available to develop new choreography. Sometimes the work attained a performable shape; sometimes it was warehoused until needed for a later project.

The workshopping process also allowed Tharp to try out new dancers before making a long-term commitment to them. With her extraordinary sense of inclusiveness, she could imagine her choreography beautifully realized by dancers as diverse as star ballerinas and Martha Graham neophytes. Many dancers lusted after her work, but not all of them could handle its demands, even some she thought were technically and temperamentally suitable. The company was entering a decade of relative stability, but it always had an outer ring of more-or-less temporary players. Dancers from other companies tried out and left: Joseph Lennon from Cunningham, Larry Grenier and Robert Blankshine from the Joffrey. People came in and stayed a year or two: Kimmary Williams, France Mayotte. Friends like Sharon Kinney and Gary Chryst lent their services in emergencies.

Tharp might have been directly charting this gift for diversity in the dance called *Mud*. Subtitled Speed, Air, Fire, Water and Earth, *Mud* was a wonderful dance about synthesis. Serious and comic, dense but concise, the choreography showed what the dancers could do together and as individuals. Once again Tharp was commenting on dance style, mainly ballet. With movement ranging from awkward to elegant, she showed what ballet is capable of encompassing, and how it can adapt. In the hodgepodge of the 1977 BAM season, *Mud* looked more like patchwork than it was.

Described in Tharp's official annals as "a dance in five movements for Adidas and pointe shoes," *Mud* began with the extreme contrasts promised by the footwear. The vernacular component was introduced by sneaker-shod Raymond Kurshals and Jennifer Way, who streaked across the space with a two-minute display of gender-linked ballet steps, attacked in fast, rough spurts. A trio of women in pointe shoes and white dresses were waiting to begin as they ran off. Tharp emphasized the women's dissimilarity by giving them basic classical steps, port de bras, and canonic patterns that, in any ballet company, would demand exact uniformity. Originally the cast was to comprise Rose Marie Wright, once a teenaged ballerina, who hadn't danced on pointe in over a decade; ballet-trained newcomer Kimmary Williams; and Robert Blankshine, a phenomenal Joffrey dancer who quickly found Tharp's complexities beyond him. Before the premiere, Christine Uchida replaced him in the trio.

Tharp arranged the trio's academic vocabulary into prim, in-place groupings, like a classroom demonstration, and the music was Mozart. But the dancers' bodies were oddly skewed at times, and their groupings veered off instead of interlocking. The audience laughed from their first moves, perhaps in stunned reaction to the clash with Way and Kurshals, or perhaps reading Tharp's witty comment as a sendup. Because of the discrepancy in the sizes and the off-key classical deportment of the trio, Wright was taken as a klutzy misfit, unable to keep in step with the others. Choreographed head motions made it seem all three were checking each other for cues. They were allowed some freedom in their timing, so one woman would finish a phrase a little ahead of the others and lapse into a waiting pose. The audience took all this for accidental ineptitude instead of a relaxed canon. Tharp's purpose was to show a unanimity among diverse dancers, not an imposed but simulated uniformity.

In an unpublished essay on *Mud*, Allen Robertson points out the extremes of rhythmic interpretation between ". . . Wright, [with] that uncanny ability of hers to be askew from the metronome rhythm of the music," and ". . . Uchida, so dead center on the beat that if she glides off of it the viewer is almost forced to swear that the metronome must have shifted tempo too." He thought Williams's neutrality left a hole where the "middle voice" should have been. Tharp's original intention of putting a man on pointe might have filled the gap with another dissonance.

New dancers kept appearing right up to the end of the dance, but each section contained holdovers from a previous section, so it seemed to develop organically despite its stylistic contradictions. Washington (now on pointe) and Kurshals were joined by Uchida and Richard Colton for the Fire quartet, a fast commotion of upside-down lifts, wheelbarrow promenades and fast switches in silence. With its topsy-turvy partnering, its ballet progressions begun, thwarted, and inserted when apparently abandoned, the quartet had echoes of the sextet in *As Time Goes By*. At the end of it Colton threw Washington over Kurshals's shoulder and walked away casually. Kurshals took her off while Uchida waited on pointe for him to come back and carry her away too.

A Mozart andante accompanied Colton's beautiful solo, Water. Colton has commented that the choreography "incorporates even the staccato movements into one long harmonious dance which emphasizes the long line of Mozart's music." The movement was balletic, as if Tharp had started with Colton's Joffrey Ballet persona, and then, applying twists, vigorous flings, and directional shifts to his attitude turns, jumps, pirouettes, and luxurious opening arms, she transformed him into her own adaptable, surprising, but no less virtuosic dancer. He was joined by Washington, minus the pointe shoes but wearing a feminine, off-the-shoulder dress and a Billie Holiday flower in her hair. After a short duet, they strolled off together. Allen Robertson saw their encounter as a fulfillment of Colton's "pensive yearnings . . . the most open and extended instance of emotionalism that Tharp has ever let flow."

To extinguish any possible indulgence, the final quartet was a precise rush of oppositions. Tom Rawe appeared for the first time, with Way, Wright, and Kurshals, in a stream of disagreements about positions and spacings. This section was also choreographed to Mozart, but was performed in silence. Colton described the way the dancers' muscles became imprinted with the music during this process: "The Mozart still served the movement in performance . . . in the manner that a clear container holds water." Finally the four dancers clicked into arabesque together. As if nothing more than this one move was needed to demonstrate the classical ideal, they melted into a twisted lunge and fell over in a pile.

Twyla Tharp Dance, like other modern dance companies, often arranged a day or two of local activities around its touring dates. These short stays gave the dancers a respite from traveling and brought them to the community in an informal way through master classes, lecture-demonstrations, and other activities. Every few years, Tharp was able to put together a longer residency—Amherst, Oberlin, and American University had set the precedent—and the two summers at Osgood Hill in North Andover, Massachusetts, were outstanding from her point of view as well as that of the company. Osgood Hill was built in 1886 by North Andover's Stevens/Osgood textile mill family, and was acquired in the 1950s as a conference center by Boston University. Initiated by Gerald Gross, a vice president of BU who loved Tharp's dance, the residency was designed to clear time and eliminate distractions so that she could make new work. For four weeks in 1978 and again in 1980, the entire company lived full-time at the old Victorian mansion surrounded by 150 acres of wooded parkland.

Tharp had a strong following in Boston. The company had appeared the previous fall at the 1,100-seat Hancock Hall, and all three performances were sold out hours after the box office opened, a hot-ticket record. When the Osgood Hill plan was announced, Boston dancers were ecstatic. The first year's scheme involved some intricate fund-raising and a rather large tradeoff in the form of teaching. Every day company members would drive the forty miles into Boston to give classes at BU's Sargent Gym for about twenty-five local dancers and dance teachers. A second group of twenty stayed at Osgood Hill. Some of the funding came from the National Endowment for the Arts, and the Massachusetts Council on the Arts and Humanities provided seven scholarships to dancers who auditioned for one of the two venues. A fifth week of performances and lecture-demonstrations in Boston culminated in a gala benefit performance of *The Bach Duet, Sue's Leg,* and *Half the One Hundreds.* Except for their classes and a one-day excursion to Osgood Hill, the in-town group didn't have any interaction with Tharp and the company.

Some of the Boston participants complained after the workshop was over that the project hadn't met their expectations. They got the ear of dance critic Debra Cash, whose account of the whole residency, "The Selling of Twyla Tharp," was featured in *The Real Paper* and touched off a controversy. Tharp was installed at Osgood Hill to choreograph; it was unreasonable to expect she'd involve herself in the Boston dance community as well. But BU hadn't made it clear, Cash thought, that Tharp wasn't going to be available. Angry letters appeared, but other participants felt the workshop more than fulfilled their dreams. Judith Cohen and Ramelle Adams, young Boston dancers, were both impressed with the repertory classes, where they learned phrases from *The Fugue* with associated structural manipulations, like reversal and retrograde. Cohen says, "I had never experienced anything like that and it was very intimidating. And it was very cerebral." Cohen felt it was a privilege to work with Tharp's "wonderful teachers. And to be exposed on that level, that very intimate level, to her repertory." According to Adams, "it gave a real insight into her work, and I've always really loved her work."

The schedule at Osgood Hill was demanding but there was time for play too. Tharp roused everyone early in the morning for a pre-breakfast run through the woods followed by a set of exercises she'd developed. Perhaps inspired by the basic-training sequences she'd been filming for *Hair,* this "boot camp" routine was more strenuous than any studio warmup although it wasn't exactly calisthenics. The dancers complained about it and started scheming to be excused. After ballet class, taught by Colton or Whitener, the rest of the day was given to rehearsals out on the lawn, and, for the students, repertory class. Once again *The Fugue* served as a teaching instrument. One of the scholarship students, Jeff Friedman, recalls "learning the twenty-count base phrase, so you absolutely do it forward, to the right, and then we would learn all of the different operations, and they would allow us to solve those problems for ourselves. . . . And that was definitely part of the purpose, to start to flex those muscles of kinesthetic intelligence." Friedman also remembers sessions devoted to learning repertory from videotapes. This had become so common a company practice that they'd discovered little tricks like turning the monitor toward a mirror to correct the video's reversed image. Tharp worked with these students, and with company members, on new material she was making.

Visitors arrived constantly, not only the dancers' families but professional writers, artists, and theater folk, who were curious about what was going on. The dancers remember killer volleyball games, relaxing in the pool, trips to local ice-cream stands and vegetable farms, and riotous evening charades. The dancers slept in the big house, while Tharp had her own quarters in a small building nearby, a former plant shed, with a big room on the ground floor and a loft above. There were no meals to cook, no laundry or housekeeping to do, and best of all from Tharp's point of view, no office interruptions. Touring, especially in the small red and blue groups, brought the dancers together, and the Osgood Hill experience bonded them even closer as a company. Tharp moved a little further away, psychologically as well as physically. She didn't always eat with the group, and she probably didn't take a regular part in the social hilarity. She stayed in her own cottage and listened to the Bach B Minor Mass late into the night.

The residency in 1978 folded some new members into the company. After months of missed connections, William Whitener had arrived. Whitener achieved outstanding success in the Joffrey Ballet's repertory of Tharp and Arpino works, as well as dancing Tudor, Ashton, Jooss, Balanchine, and the leads in *Petrouchka* and Flemming Flindt's *The Lesson*. He felt it was time to settle down with one choreographer. Whitener had been attracted to Tharp ever since *Deuce Coupe*. "First and foremost," he explains, "was the enjoyment that I received from working with her in the studio. I loved listening to her talk about dance. And was fascinated by her mind. I found the style challenging and unique. And felt that . . . she was in the process of redefining the male classical dancer." He wanted to be engaged in her creative process. "Her loft down there on Franklin was like a laboratory," he says now. "And I was ready." After talking with Robert Joffrey and affirming his decision, he danced his final performances at the end of 1977. At that point, *Hair* was in its postponed shooting stages. While Tharp was finishing the movie, Whitener joined the cast of Bob Fosse's *Dancin'* for a few months, but finally their schedules synched up.

John Carrafa was the other scholarship student at Osgood Hill the first year. Jeff Friedman accurately perceived the residency as a kind of tryout period for them, and he felt a certain competition and anticipation about the possibility of being taken into the company. Eventually it was Carrafa who was chosen. Friedman had protected himself from disappointment by applying to architecture school, and he later realized, as Tharp developed the partnering and character work she started at Osgood Hill, that she was going in a different direction from what had attracted him. Carrafa, who had recently come to Boston from Maine, had been accepted as a member of Concert Dance Company, a Boston-based group that did modern dance repertory. At the end of the Osgood Hill residency he remained with Tharp instead of taking up the job in Boston.

Katie Glasner had a protracted transition into the company—she calls it a "ghosting affiliation"—that went on for nearly two years. She'd been spotted by the ballet teacher Jonathan Watts during her freshman year at the University of Wisconsin–Milwaukee. Watts told her she was wasting her time in college and should go to New York to dance. She fixed her ambitions on Tharp after seeing a videotape of *Sue's Leg* in the Dance Department's library. Glasner flew to New York to audition for the 1977 Tharp summer workshop at City Center. She went on tour with the company, dancing in *Eight Jelly Rolls*, but both she and Tharp thought she was too inexperienced to become a permanent member at that time. Tharp hired her for the expanded choruses in *Hair* and brought her to Osgood Hill in '78 as a kind of apprentice.

Before the end of the residency Glasner fell into a hole while running in the woods and sprained her ankle badly. Once that healed she had just began working her way into the repertory when an unexpected surgery felled her again. The day she got home from the hospital in early June 1979, she learned that she was expected to be rehearsed and ready to go with the company to the Avignon festival in mid-July. Glasner met the challenge. "I was very drawn to this woman's dancemaking and then the kinesthetic power that it had," Glasner says now. "I wanted to move this way. I needed to move this way."

Among other things, the 1978 Osgood Hill residency saw the beginnings of a major work. By the time *Baker's Dozen* premiered eight months later, the company had expanded again, to include John Malashock and Mary Ann Kellogg. *Baker's Dozen* can be seen as completing and exemplifying the process of synthesis that had started with *Give and Take*. From this period until the company was dissolved in 1988, Twyla Tharp Dance represented the most successful fusion of ballet and modern dancers in the history of independent American dance companies. Without giving up her more visible exploits in films, TV, and freelance choreography during those years, Tharp made an astonishing number of original and challenging dances for the company, including *Short Stories*, *The Catherine Wheel*, *Nine Sinatra Songs*, *Fait Accompli*, and *In the Upper Room*.

Tharp has given many explanations for the genesis of *Baker's Dozen*. Years later she reflected on it as one of several "rebound" dances, responses to failed love affairs or tragic events in her life. *Baker's Dozen* followed the breakup of a doomed two-year romance, and she says she was beginning to suspect she "needed loss to create art." But this romantic construct greatly oversimplifies the inherent contradictions of her personality. Both sensual and puritanical, she craved love and stability but refused to let her own accomplishments attain a fixed identity. She fought for complete control of her artistic product but couldn't have realized the work without sympathetic collaborators. Beginning with Bob Huot, Tharp's sexual partners usually shared her professional life and contributed to it in important ways. The relationships didn't last, but she collected new reserves of creative energy from them. As one of her dancers from this period remarks, ". . . she quite often needs a new palette. And new dancers. For creativity to spark her."

Dancing in the studio was what kept her going; it made her happy and drew the dancers to her. Perhaps *Baker's Dozen* was a sublimation of the ideal family she'd never had in real life. Tharp had always buried her feelings superbly in form and abstraction. Some of her most heartfelt dances were perceived as formal, stylistic essays. *Give and Take* and *Mud* didn't stay in the repertory long enough for their subtle undercurrents to be appreciated. In these, and in *Baker's Dozen*, Tharp was offering the dancers a challenge and an opportunity. For her that meant offering them love.

Introducing *Baker's Dozen* on the videotape *Confessions of a Cornermaker*, made for the shortlived CBS Cable TV network in 1981, Tharp seemed to be rebounding as well from her disappointment with *Hair*. "I had been exposed to waste on a massive scale. No one's intention, but a project as large as a Hollywood picture seems destined to deny any fair correlation between investment and return. Therefore when I started to work on a new piece for my company, I was thinking a lot about economy. Nothing should be squandered or disregarded. As in Nature all things would be recycled and would accrue. A good cook wastes nothing. But this is not to be confused with stinginess. And so I named the piece *Baker's Dozen* in reference to a fair and generous measure." She unearthed the videotapes she'd made during her pregnancy, improvising to the records of Willie "The Lion" Smith. She wanted to project some of this footage as part of the new dance, and the "fair and generous measure," translated to the stage, meant that the audience was to get twelve dancers and a bonus—Twyla on tape with a baby, Jesse, in the oven. As the production went into technical rehearsals, difficulties arose with projecting the old video. When it was blown up to stage size it looked too blurry, and just before the premiere she scrapped it, along with the expensive set she'd had built to replicate the attic at New Berlin.

Baker's Dozen took shape in Tharp's imagination as a theatrical piece. The dancers were to enter in silhouette behind a scrim, and the videotape would appear between dance numbers accompanied by the sound of baby Jesse crying. Tharp even had a scenario of sorts. The harmonious work of the family (the dancers) kept being disrupted by the demands of this offstage infant. At one point Tharp, who was planning to be in the piece, "is trying to go on dancing with this kid crying and she finally exits to go take care of the kid." All the theatrical trappings, including Tharp's own participation, were discarded during a painful dress rehearsal at the urging of Santo Loquasto and Jennifer Tipton, her trusted collaborators. Loquasto says Tharp sometimes visualized more than the audience could keep up with. "Because of her own perceptions being lightning fast, the mortals can't keep up—Twyla, there's too much to look at." Cleansed of everything but the dancing, *Baker's Dozen* turned out to be perfect.

She had choreographed her own part on Shelley Washington, and she began rehearsing it. In the exquisitely calibrated universe of *Baker's Dozen*, Tharp provided herself with an amicable tribe of siblings, flexible companions who could be her life partners. Not since *Sue's Leg* had she actually danced on an equal basis with the rest of the company. Even in dances where she appeared to be one of the gang, like *Eight Jelly Rolls*, her irrepressible comic sense came to the foreground. Sara Rudner, who took over her role in *Baker's Dozen*, remembered her being "this one extraordinary comic, free spirit, messing everything up . . . like the kid who is so exuberant and everything has to revolve around her." Rudner thinks Tharp was wise to drop out. The dance needed precision timing and performing; it was a puzzle that the dancers needed the utmost skill to put together, and Tharp at that point was still in choreographing mode. "She didn't really know [the dance]," Rudner says.

Tharp has described *Baker's Dozen* as resembling a game of jacks, where you pick up an increasing number of pieces with one hand while your other hand bounces a little ball. This analogy captures the playfulness and dexterity of a dance that in fact is structured with geometric elegance. The dancers are introduced one couple at a time. They then group together in trios, quartets, sextets, and finally as an ensemble, out of which each member emerges for a small solo. Santo Loquasto dressed them in creamy white, the men in pants and collarless shirts, the women in slim, draped skirts with skimpy tops, over velour leggings. They all wore white jazz shoes, and all the clothes flowed beautifully with the movement. The costumes suggested the pre–World War I era of Vernon and Irene Castle, who popularized a more dignified social dancing than the risqué rompings of the turkey trot and the bunny hug.

Tharp took her primary cue from Willie "The Lion" Smith, a leading exponent of Harlem jazz piano, whose career stretched across the first half of the twentieth century. For the premiere at Brooklyn Academy, 15 February 1979, and as often as possible on tour, the music was played live by Dick Hyman. Smith's music was more embellished and orchestral, less predictable than the barefaced rhythms of ragtime or the regular beat of stride piano. Willie Smith may never have accompanied silent movies, but his compositions suggest the melodramatic, rapidly shifting moods those early musical improvisers had to establish. The four numbers Tharp chose for her dance, "Echoes of Spring," "Tango à la Caprice," "Concentrating," and "Relaxin'," flow almost untrackably through rippling arpeggios, trills, shifts of melody and key, hesitations, suspensions, and drastic tempo changes.

The dance too is a stream of invention and surprise, but the numerical sorting out of the dancers prevents the whole thing from becoming lost in continual novelty. You know the equation will fulfill itself even if you can't predict how. The dance begins and ends with couples in completely different configurations. First they enter one at a time in a strolling rhythm with a slight hitch step or skip. Each pair takes a different approach to partnering conventions, hinting at social dances, ballet dances, or children's games, and they each overturn the conventions in the same breath. When all six couples have come and gone, one or two dancers start to sprint on, as if they're too revved up to let the dance subside for even a moment; they're pulled back from behind the scene.

The tango section begins with large emphatic gestures and accents, slides to the floor, screwball lifts, long and short phrases with sudden halts. The trios comprise two men partnering one woman and two women with one man. This setup was used by Balanchine in *Agon*, one of the few ballets Tharp has publicly admired. Again she finds unlimited ways to play with the groupings, flipping from extravagant approaches and luxurious back-bending embraces to sudden releases and interruptions. The trios become quartets, with tight partner switching. The music goes into a softer varia-tion of the tango theme, and the dance structure slides into the beginning of a long retrograde. The first quartet returns, then the remaining sets of four, and they in turn peel back to their original trios.

A new musical number begins, a chirpy, rippling theme, and the dancers fall into studied nonchalance, drooping and sliding against their partners, nudging and hauling each other about. For the first time a compact group of six crosses the stage, then another. The section ends in a series of escalating surprises. One sextet slowly unfolds into a unison pose, then, on an explo-sion of music, they all rip into a scrambling chase and vanish. Richard Colton is left alone looking bewildered. (Gary Chryst took the part in the *Cornermaker* video when Colton was injured.) He starts the solo section by shrugging off a woman who jumps onto his back, then another who topples into his arms from the wings.

As the fractional units have been accumulating and dissolving, the idea of ensemble grows stronger. When the group rises to its maximum organiza-tional strength, in the unison sextets and finally a smart lineup that sweeps across the stage, Tharp counterpoints a solo for each person. Some are ab-breviated; others are quite extended—Colton's riff on the romantic vignette he had in *Mud*, microexpositions of ballet technique for Whitener and Uchida, a stream of asymmetrical jumps for Washington. Only the part Tharp intended for herself has no special solo. At last the whole group threads casually in and out of a lineup to find their original partners, and like a movie going in reverse, they skip backwards couple by couple, and leave. When five pairs have gone off, it's Rudner, the Tharp-surrogate figure, who returns for the last, partnerless man (Raymond Kurshals) and leads him off by the hand. Shortly before the opening, when she was still in the piece, Tharp told Robert J. Pierce of the *Soho Weekly News*: ". . . theoretically the last passage is myself packing up that youngster and just walking off with him."

8

Family Business
1979–1981

Tharp has compared *Baker's Dozen* to Edward Hicks's well-known painting *The Peaceable Kingdom*, "a place where each dancer comfortably and naturally fits." She's also referred to the dance as "a society whose conventions are clear," a place where even a member who strays will be welcomed back into the fold. At the same time as she was envisioning this idyllic community, she began exploring the flip side of familial accord, a much less benign thematic territory. Osgood Hill in 1978 saw the first moves that led to *When We Were Very Young* and *The Catherine Wheel*. She had decided to confront the question of narrative, and some of the visitors to the 1978 workshop were prospective composers or script writers. Richard Colton remembers the balletomane and satirist Edward Gorey appearing and working with Tharp on what never got past being a skit: "Chris Uchida ran a Chinese laundry and I forget whether she hid me—there was some kidnapped boy, and I remember being in one of those rolling things, and the wheel fell out of it."

For a while there were only fragments. At the end of the residency the company gave performances in Boston, including a lecture-demonstration. After Tharp and Tom Rawe each took the dancers through a set of the dreaded daily calisthenics, there was a showing of material made during the residency, "a series of small allegorical studies" according to Christine Temin of *The Boston Globe*. The characters included two Evildoers (Rudner and Rawe); two housemaids, representing Chaos (Shelley Washington did something reminiscent of Tharp's drunk dance in *Eight Jelly Rolls*) and Order (Chris Uchida); Innocence (Jennifer Way with a pretend jump rope) and Authority (Rose Marie Wright in a long skirt). There was a seedy Greek chorus that, Temin observed, "do not further the plot, but are very good for getting rid of dead bodies," and a street scene with stomping punks played by some of the workshop students.

Tharp and the company had been listening all summer to the recently released album of The Band's farewell concert, *The Last Waltz*, and for a press showing at Osgood Hill, they did some of the new material using the song "The Shape I'm In." Without relinquishing the popular music idiom that had helped make her work look so contemporary and attracted such excited audiences, she was moving past the generalized types she had evolved—the kids in the schoolyard, the blasé sophisticates, the laid-back square dancers and hippies. Now she wanted to project more specific characterizations and action.

Baker's Dozen made its appearance the following winter during another packed season at Brooklyn Academy, along with four pieces from the repertory (*Country Dances, Eight Jelly Rolls, Sue's Leg*, and the men's *Fugue*) and three other new works. Tharp danced a powerful, introspective solo to three songs by Randy Newman, *1903*, a dance she referred to as "a study in genteel cynicism." She used movement from *The One Hundreds*, reinterpreted with a personal inflection that suggested she shared some of the hunger and disillusion in Newman's "Sail Away," "Suzanne," and "Dayton, Ohio—1903."

With the release of the movie *Hair* scheduled for two weeks after the BAM season, she laid claim to three dances from her edited-out choreography. In *Electric Blues*, she began as a playmate being tossed around by Rawe, Kurshals, Colton, and Ferro, and then metamorphosed into the hippie-deity who would preside over the film's hallucinogenic wedding scene. A big allegory, *3-5-0-0*, with Rose Marie Wright as a "macabre figure of death masquerading as a bride" and Tom Rawe stripping the valuables from the corpses of soldiers, was more than slightly redolent of Kurt Jooss's 1932 antiwar ballet *The Green Table*. In *What a Piece of Work Is Man*, Rawe danced with a drill team from the Army's Pershing Rifles Company. For the BAM performances of *3-5-0-0*, the company was expanded to include Deborah Zalkind, Richard Caceres, Kristin Draudt, and Mark Morris. An extraordinary dancer with a linebacker's physique, Morris auditioned more than once to join the company but Tharp hadn't figured out how to use big men.

A year and a half later Morris produced his first concert in New York and began his own history.

The fourth BAM premiere was the narrative work that had been in development since Osgood Hill, *Chapters and Verses*. It was introduced with a program note: "Three sections extracted from a larger piece, these dances are thought of as chapters published in advance of the completed novel." The dancers called it *Captured Nurses*. Though the five numbers bore some movement relationships, the work had the musical eclecticism and discontinuous throughline of Tharp's other "suite" pieces. As in some of her subsequent narratives, the characters fought with each other constantly but reconciled in an apotheosis of brotherhood. After a circusy opening, with the dancers leaping and grandstanding to a rousing march by Edwin Franko Goldman, the piece spun from one raucous episode to another, and then unwound into an almost monotonous disco sequence. Even when it looked most improvised, *Chapters and Verses* was choreographed on a musical beat. In the group sections canonic and counterpointed phrases piled on top of each other, but the musical high points emerged at the peak of the lifts and the emphatic phrase endings.

After the opener, "The Hard Circus," each part incorporated new Tharpisms. "Scenes from the Boy's Education" began with a condensed version of the Osgood Hill calisthenic workout. Tom Rawe bullied and harangued Kurshals, Ferro, Whitener, and France Mayotte, and they complained loudly as they labored through fast stretches, twists, bends, and sit-ups. Dancers didn't actually speak onstage at that time, let alone yell and scream. For Tharp, speech was going to be a component of drama. Though the dialogue in *Chapters and Verses* looked spontaneous, the dancers had memorized and rehearsed their lines along with the movement. Around the same time, she was getting them to work on hysterical laughter and oversized facial expressions, which made their way into *The Catherine Wheel*.

Without a pause the exercisers were joined by the rest of the company in a rowdy session of pushing, shoving, and belligerent vocalizing, set to Clarence "Frogman" Henry's "Ain't Got No Home," recorded by The Band. A real car, possibly a golf cart, drove onto the stage and as many of them climbed onto it as could fit. The rest followed it off. Cars, as an icon of youth culture, had been appropriated by Tharp as early as *Deuce Coupe*, and the arrival of a working model onstage caused a tremor of identification in the audience. She used the same device later in both her Broadway shows, *Singin' in the Rain* and *Movin' Out*.

She invoked another icon, along with fond memories of "The Nursery," with recordings of the theme song from the television kiddie show the *Mickey Mouse Club*. A small group marched in and out, leaving William Whitener behind to dance a solo. Wearing an abstracted expression, he glided through a string of balletic poses and extended transitions, most of the time keeping his legs in parallel position rather than turned out. In contrast to the aggressive physicality of the group, he seemed almost puppet-like. The effect was odd and sweet at the same time.

The fighting resumed in "Street from the Night Before," to disco music by John Simon, concert-music producer for the *Last Waltz* album, whom Tharp had enlisted to create the collage score. Richard Colton thinks the musical idea behind *Chapters and Verses* was to re-create the variegated energy of The Band's historic concert. For the last section Simon came up with a pounding, hypnotic number with a female singer doing gospel riffs on the theme of "Us Together," and a meter that shifted from four counts to three unexpectedly through the twelve minutes of the dance. Individual disco dancers swirled in and out seemingly at random while Sara Rudner maintained a calm ongoing presence. Gradually her centeredness seemed to smooth out the punchy hostilities everyone had exhibited before, and their movements became springy, even spongy, with bursts of quick accents. The tempo speeded up after a long time, and the dancers drew closer together. Packs of them were still moving when the dance ended.

Most of the critics were noncommittal about *Chapters and Verses*. It was, after all, offered as a work in progress, and on the BAM season it was overshadowed by *Baker's Dozen*, which everyone recognized as a major work. But two significant critical voices came out on opposite sides of the discussion about it. Anna Kisselgoff, who had succeeded Clive Barnes as chief dance critic of *The New York Times*, questioned Tharp's political credibility in a Sunday overview of the season. Kisselgoff had always admired Tharp's pure-dance works, and in *Baker's Dozen* she welcomed "the combined complexity of structure and ease of choreographic inevitability that mark Miss Tharp at her most creative and innovative." But she read "social commentary" into all the other new pieces and the musical pegs that held them together. *Hair* was mere "cosmetics" and *Chapters and Verses*, though sharper in tone, ultimately had a "soft center." Kisselgoff's colleague at the *Times*, Jack Anderson, had already noted Tharp's neutral stance toward provocative subjects. Perhaps she was "declining to sermonize" so she wouldn't offend anyone, he thought.

But Kisselgoff expected Tharp to dissect the social situations she portrayed; instead she was mythologizing them. Like a latter-day Agnes de Mille, Tharp was creating a "benign view of popular culture."

Nancy Goldner, then the dance critic of *The Nation* and five years younger than Kisselgoff, was no less appreciative of Tharp's compositional distinction, and she too saw *Baker's Dozen* as "obviously the great dance of this collection." But for her, the messier *Chapters and Verses* rang true, and she embraced the postures of adolescence warmly. Goldner loved the dance's boisterous humor, the awkward physicality, and "the marvelous excess of its content and form . . . Never have I seen anarchy so fully embodied or the bêtes noires of American life so wholeheartedly endorsed or sympathetically examined." In the *Christian Science Monitor*, where Goldner was a regular contributor, she noted the emblematic car and the transistor radio that Sara Rudner clutched in her hand. But for Goldner these tokens of materialism added poignancy to the picture of kids trying to communicate: "In connecting teen-agerism with commercialism, and then celebrating both with such brio, Tharp has pulled off a coup de théâtre as well as a true comment on our times."

Tharp was gradually getting out of dancing as she neared forty, and it wasn't easy for her. Few people noticed that after *Sue's Leg* she'd either left herself out of new work entirely or made a singular role for herself within the dance: the yogic priestess in *Hair*, the soloist in *Country Dances* and *Give and Take*. After rescinding her plan to dance in *Baker's Dozen*, she made star appearances when necessary, covered for company members in emergencies, and confined new roles to more or less overt reflections on her immediate personal concerns. Following her role as the mother figure in *When We Were Very Young* she choreographed again for herself only three more times: *Fait Accompli* (1983), a work of merciless difficulty, in which she confronted her own aging and disengagement from dancing; *Men's Piece* (1991), a menopausal reflection on sexuality and role-playing; and *Cutting Up*, for the celebrity tour she made with Mikhail Baryshnikov in 1992–93.

When We Were Very Young was a natural successor to the narrative investigations she'd been pursuing. Now she not only wanted to tell a story but to dramatize her own conflicts, about age, motherhood, and responsibility, in a more objective frame. She was looking for something literary, and she set her sights high. Through mutual contacts she was bold enough to approach

writers like Harold Brodkey, John Updike, and John Irving for projects she
was contemplating during this period. She had begun building the movement material for *When We Were Very Young* and even drafted a couple of
scripts herself, when her agent at the Lantz office put her in touch with another of his clients, playwright Thomas Babe. A regular in Joseph Papp's unofficial stable of writers at the Public Theater, Babe hadn't worked with
dancers before, but he hit it off with Tharp. He saw right away that the
dancers were doing something more elemental than the literal treatment
Tharp had written. He told John Rockwell of the *Times*, "The characters [in
her scripts] were defined by facts, not feelings, but the dancing was *full* of
feelings. . . . It was primitive, it was muscular, it was passionate. So, we
started over." Babe, who had a poet's fondness for whimsy, found the A. A.
Milne lament on childhood insecurity, "Disobedience," with its story about
three-year-old James James Morrison Morrison, who warned his mother not
to leave home without him.

Nine revisions later, they had a sort of composite memoir on the theme
of growing up. The poem pointed the way to an exploration of role reversal,
generational overlap, and some slippery questions of individuality, fidelity,
and guilt. To Tharp "it seemed to make growing up the ultimate and cardi-
nal sin." For practical reasons Tharp discarded the idea of giving the dancers
dialogue to speak, and Babe wrote the script as a conversation between a father and daughter. In performance he took the father's role, opposite a child
actress, Gayle Meyers. His own daughter was nearly the same age as Jesse
Huot, and the final script was an impressionistic meditation on both his and
Tharp's parental anxieties and defenses. The narrators traded roles so that
the identities of mother, grandmother, parent, and child wrapped around
one another.

Onstage the work was almost as diffuse as the text. The dancers shifted
through time periods, characters, and situations with only tenuous reference to the spoken narrative, which often dominated the audience's attention. Santo Loquasto had devised a set made of large cardboard packing
boxes; the dancers shoved them around to create settings for different
scenes. Tharp had made two discrete cadres of dancers. For the four main
characters—a son and daughter (Raymond Kurshals and Katie Glasner), a
brother/husband (Tom Rawe), and the perpetually dissatisfied mother/child,
Jane—she developed an exaggerated acting style that carried over into the
next and more successful version of the tortured tale, *The Catherine Wheel*.
Then there was an anonymous ensemble that supplied additional characters

to the wispy plot. Whitener's Mickey Mouse solo and the disco dance from *Chapters and Verses* were incorporated in abbreviated form, as were the company calisthenics. There was a Little Match Girl (Washington), a juggler (Carrafa), a thirty-ninth birthday ruefully observed, a twenty-six piece orchestra, and the lines from "Disobedience," chanted in march cadence by dancers crossing the stage like squads of recruits. The noise and fractured activity rose to a crescendo as Jane/Tharp discarded the clothing and symbolic objects she'd accumulated during the journey and casually dropped off the edge of the stage into the orchestra pit. "I could hear the intake of breath in the audience, the eight times we did it," Babe reflected later. "You got us, you moved us, the audience said; you left us, and we care." This response confirmed what Tharp had always wanted for her work.

Arlene Croce, though she deemed the dance a failure, acknowledged that Tharp had reached the audience, "a genuine, pleasure-seeking Broadway crowd [which] behaved as if being up to its eyes in murk were perfectly normal" and granted its "hearty approval" at the end. The following fall Tharp explained to Susan Reimer-Torn of *The International Herald Tribune*: "I do want my work to be in the mainstream of people's lives. Great composers, like Brahms, for example, have always picked up on the social dances and music around. . . . When my dancers do the impossible developed from the possible, it gives people something to connect to."

When We Were Very Young was the centerpiece of a big gamble for Tharp, her first advance onto Broadway. Having won acclaim with her concert dances and television work, she now embarked on a new phase in her lifelong campaign to attract bigger and broader audiences. Instead of returning to Brooklyn Academy where she could count on a loyal following and some subsidy, she booked the Winter Garden Theater through her own foundation for three early-spring weeks of old and new repertory. Ticket sales were excellent even though the season coincided with a subway strike. The Tharp company, now numbering fifteen dancers, was in peak form. In addition to *Baker's Dozen*, *Eight Jelly Rolls*, *The Fugue*, and *Ocean's Motion*, the repertory included a revised version of *Deuce Coupe* and another new work, *Brahms' Paganini*.

Set to Book I and II of the Variations on a Theme of Paganini (the same theme that later inspired Rachmaninoff), the Brahms began with a Tharpian tour de force, a twelve-minute solo that pushed its alternating dancers, Richard Colton and William Whitener, to extreme limits of technique, endurance, and performing ingenuity. Following the solo, she set one of her

minutely engineered quartets, with Jennifer Way as a recurring outsider figure. In form the dance was odd looking. Way's solitary figure was like a distant echo of the first solo, but she was elusive against the quartet's frenetic
changes and soaring, perilous lifts.

Nancy Goldner thought the quartet was "about the strenuousness of
partnering. It dwells on rough edges, near misses, and harsh bodily impact.
Canon structure usually produces buoyancy. Here it produces a jagged,
bumpy ride." But Deborah Jowitt saw the movement as a double-edged
metaphor: "Ironically, it is through cooperativeness and considerateness and
skill, which have to figure in any dance this difficult, that this work creates
an illusion of debating, fighting, yielding, winning, and turning to enter a
new competition." Tharp told an interviewer at the time that she was finally
dealing with passion, a subject that had always embarrassed her. "I acknowledge the difficulty of getting through—your life. That's what it's all about as
you get older. The man's variation is a heroic undertaking. . . . And the
quartet shows the underside of romance, a lot of unlovely stuff."

Tharp had choreographed different parts of the solo on Colton,
Whitener, and John Carrafa, whenever one of them was in town between
tours with the red or blue team. For Colton, these choreographing sessions
were among the most stimulating moments of his career. Tharp's foot was in
a cast at the time from an injury, and she trusted the dancers to follow her
suggestions since she couldn't demonstrate. Colton also taught the solo to
Mikhail Baryshnikov, in anticipation of a special appearance on opening
night. Baryshnikov was up to the technical demands, but he'd been shooting a movie and didn't have the stamina to get through it just then, so
Colton danced the premiere.

The solo was a breathtaking stream of invention. Characteristically,
Tharp packed so much into it that the casual viewer, dazzled by the performance itself, could take in only the rudiments of her composition. A tape of
William Whitener in performance reveals just how much she was able to say
about dancing without resorting to mime or literalism. While Whitener
does a repertory of fairly conventional steps—pirouettes in various positions, high open jumps and small hops and staggers, tight spins, wide balances, and skids—his upper body is equally active and consistently
unpredictable. You have the sense that you've never seen these steps before,
and that perhaps you'll never see them again, because whenever they repeat,
the whole body is shaped, phrased, and focused differently. He goes from
relaxed to precise energies, and as he becomes more exhausted this range

widens, to include a drooping or dangling of weight and flung motions of the whole arm or leg. The gestures seldom look placed or stopped. With typical articulateness, a Tharpian dancer of that period could make small initiating moves with shoulders, chest, neck, head, even the whole upper torso. Instead of being held and proper, the body could twist against itself, spiral around to the back, make small adjustments. Whitener and Colton's movement never halted between the fourteen musical variations, effectively stifling any applause until the end.

Later Whitener told Texas critic Josie Neal that the solo "encompasses just about everything I know about dancing and endurance and theatrics and performance. That's the most satisfying role I've ever danced." Colton says he didn't feel competitive with Whitener in the role because each of them danced it in his own way, and the critics saw this too. Colton felt that Whitener represented the Paganini, or classical, side of the music while he himself danced the more romantic Brahmsian aspects. Critic Deborah Jowitt contrasted the two interpretations: "Whitener is a superb dancer. A trace of sharp, almost foxy intensity keeps him from being unbearably elegant. . . . But if I hadn't seen Colton perform it, I don't think I would have seen quite as much in it. Colton is capable of changing the nature of a gesture in the middle of it, of beginning to let a particular quality take over one part of his body while something else is still going on in another part. Perhaps because he is a small man, he has taught himself to expand immensely in space, to prolong a gesture with almost voluptuous lyricism, even to jump slowly."

Tharp disliked double casting a new piece. She wanted the dancers to make the steps their own, "to breathe and behave," in Colton's words, before setting the choreography and transferring it to a second cast. It's a common rehearsal practice for alternates to shadow the first dancers from the sidelines, but Tharp found this distracting during the creative process. She didn't like teaching old roles either, and she had no reservations about entrusting this task to the dancers and the videotapes. Tharp did envision two dancers sharing a role choreographically. In fact, she utilized doubling so often and in so many ways that it could be called a major aspect of the way she looked at the ensemble.

Her younger twin brothers, who had made up their own private language, provided early lessons in the behavior of bonded siblings. She had noted her "fascination with duplication" as a choreographic ploy back in 1969, in her program notes for *Dancing in the Streets*. The same year, she put together the overlapping double-quintet version of *Group Activities* for the stage of the Brooklyn Academy Opera House. Her analytical mind found endless structural possibilities in this simple idea. She loved setting two dancers, or two groups of dancers, against each other doing the same things. This device could act as a formal element of design, like the two female anchors in *In the Upper Room*. It could impose a formal rigor on a dance that might be perceived as just another youthful romp (*Ocean's Motion*), or teach the audience to take note of the dancers' differences, like having two dancers demonstrate the one hundred phrases side by side in *The One Hundreds*. To create a nonstop frame around the long last section of *Known by Heart* she made a marathon shuffle for a team of male dancers, perhaps in fond remembrance of the two-of-a-kind soft-shoe numbers she'd cut her teeth on in the old Gene Kelly movies. When she wanted to poke a little fun at ballet's vanities, she split the corps into two gangs of feckless ladies (*Push Comes to Shove*).

Tharp even carried the notion of duplication into costuming. The device could be didactic. The gray costumes turned white in *The Bix Pieces* to signify that the ghosts of history are always with us. The white-to-black-to-white outfits in the 1995 ballet *How Near Heaven* imposed a shadow of death on the community. It could be a charming trick. In *Sue's Leg* the four dancers' dressy versions of their own practice clothes made a witty comment on the porous borderline between studio and stage, with another layer of reflexivity added when the dance was repeated on a single program in the original work clothes.

Tharp was well aware of the drama inherent in competitive twinning, and she fully exploited the other compositional tools that called for exact imitation: canon, mirroring, and repetition. *Uncle Edgar Dyed His Hair Red*, one of the smaller offerings of 1981, was built entirely on the idea of six women dancing in pairs. Wearing black tank suits and sneakers, the side-by-side couples began in unison and proceeded to a full panoply of duet manipulations. There were trompe l'oeil sections where pairs swept through the space and left with different partners. Behind an upstage scrim, couples passed by in silhouette, sometimes mirroring other couples in the foreground. The movement was unforgiving, with bodies skewed into slow twisting falls, or arms and legs levering in monolithic motions reminiscent of the women's aquatic exertions to "Don't Go Near the Water" in *Deuce Coupe*. Tharp told an audience at a preview showing of *Uncle Edgar* that she was thinking up "new ways to torture the female form." When it premiered in New York in the fall of 1981 Anna Kisselgoff thought it was one of the season's best. She appreciated the dance's exploration of "formal movement problems—not coating them with attitudes or social comment."

As a producing experiment, the 1980 Winter Garden confirmed to Tharp that she could escape what she considered the confines of assured dance venues and take her work to a less specialized audience. Self-producing, with contributions from independent backers and promoters, she exited the BAM reservation and traded the college touring circuit for legitimate theater situations whenever possible. She opted out of Brooklyn Academy's prestigious and handsomely funded annual Next Wave series. That would have required her to accept commissioning money for new choreography with inevitable strings attached, and besides, she disdained being just one among a cluster of performing groups marketed together as each year's new thing.

In 1981 she formed a relationship with rock promoter Bill Graham. She booked the company into Graham's Warfield Theater in San Francisco, antagonizing the biggest Bay Area dance presenter. The Committee for Arts and Lectures at the University of California, which administered Zellerbach Auditorium on the Berkeley campus, insisted on securing an exclusive on the company's appearance. This would have prevented them from going into any other theater within thirty miles. Tharp considered Zellerbach a suburban enclave. "Brooklyn, like Berkeley, represents something slightly outside the center of things," she told *The San Francisco Chronicle*. "A campus is not a city." She withdrew from the Zellerbach series, incurring a small scandal and threats that she'd never be booked there again. Tharp was also uncomfortable with the guidelines imposed under National Endowment for the Arts sponsorship, and she wasn't reluctant to share her displeasure with the press. "We get the same fee whether we're dancing for a 300-seat house or a 4,000-seat house. We can fill a theater like the Music Hall in Detroit. We should charge our Endowment fee while somebody else is taking all the box office? It was getting to the point where I couldn't afford the Endowment."

Tharp's activities during the early 1980s were so prolific that the business became increasingly complicated. The Twyla Tharp Dance Foundation handled the company business, booked tours, and raised money for projects. Twyla Tharp Enterprises was the corporate entity under which Tharp negotiated her independent work—movies, choreographing commissions, and other outside assignments. Tharp would receive a separate fee for doing a movie or video, but she would try to get the dancers hired on the project wherever feasible. A small administrative staff worked with the foundation's board of directors to facilitate her work. For years, the two company units toured relentlessly and worked with her, while she took on extracurricular jobs, projecting her protean selves out into the world as choreographer, filmmaker, television director, theater director, and super-energized celebrity.

Going into theaters where dance hadn't established a beachhead was one way of getting the work out to more people, but film and television were even better. In the first half of the 1980s Tharp worked on four Hollywood movies and four in-house videos. She contributed incidental dances to Milos Forman's *Ragtime* and Woody Allen's *Zelig* (for which she didn't take a credit). These were essentially period pieces—turn-of-the-century waltzes, chorus lines, and popular dances for *Ragtime*, and a pseudo-Charleston called the Chameleon among other trifles for *Zelig*.

Forman called on her again to do *Amadeus*, and this was more substantial. Tharp choreographed the dances and staged the operas for Peter Shaffer's fantasy on the life of Mozart as told by his rival Salieri. *Amadeus* was shot in Prague over a period of months. The music was recorded in London under Neville Marriner's direction, but Tharp needed people who could move credibly as well as lip-synch the singing. For the comic operas she ignored protocol and enlisted members of Prague's popular-theater company; she considered them more flexible than the classical singers at the National Theater. After checking out the local ballet dancers, she arranged for her own company to come over and appear in two of the big opera scenes.

She delegated Shelley Freydont to research the culture of the late-eighteenth-century Viennese court. Freydont had concentrated in ballet and art history when she was getting a masters degree; she'd taught undergraduates in California and danced with Louis Falco in New York before joining the Tharp company following a 1979 audition. Freydont was able to decipher the old dance notations, and with the help of period dance specialist Elizabeth Aldrich she reconstructed examples of the galop, schottische, ländler, and other dances for herself. Then Freydont would fly to Prague, where Tharp was directing the opera scenes. She'd demonstrate some of the possibilities she'd found, and after Tharp made her choices Freydont would go back to New York and teach the material to the company. When the dancers arrived in Prague, Tharp staged the material for the camera. Freydont also set some of the social-dance scenes that ended up in the background of the movie. She says she had such a great time working on the set that she didn't mind being listed only as one of the Tharp company dancers.

Tharp also choreographed for Taylor Hackford's film *White Nights*, the thriller about a dancer who accidentally finds himself back in the Soviet Union after defecting, and is then used as a political pawn. Mikhail Baryshnikov starred, with Gregory Hines as a disappointed American tap dancer who's emigrated in the opposite direction. Hines is assigned to befriend Baryshnikov and persuade him to stay in Russia. For the scene where they face each other down in the studio, Tharp made one of her fusion dances. Each man tries to outdance the other in a tap-ballet competition and they end up in mutual admiration. She started choreographing the scene where Baryshnikov returns to the empty Maryinsky Theater and dances his farewell, but Baryshnikov felt he needed something more personal, more Russian, to express the Mussorgsky music, so he took over making the dance and she offered her advice. Hines choreographed his own tap solos.

Each of the four videos of this period demonstrates a different solution to one of Tharp's ongoing dilemmas: how to preserve her repertory so that she wouldn't have to keep maintaining it in performance. *Confessions of a Cornermaker* (taped in late summer 1980 and first aired in October 1981) was a camera-adapted documentation of three important dances, *Short Stories*, Uchida and Whitener's duet from the Bach *Third Suite* (both choreographed in 1980), and *Baker's Dozen*. Like the London Weekend Television *Eight Jelly Rolls* and *The Fugue*, *Cornermaker* not only preserves prime examples of Tharp's choreography, it showcases the extraordinary Tharp company dancers at their peak. Tharp doesn't dance in this video, but she appears in it as mastermind. Wearing a fisherman's sweater and jeans, she's filmed on a blustery beach, introducing the dances with provocatively quotable commentary she scripted with Allan Robertson. At the end, she confesses that working with the human body's "passion and precision" seems as close as she can come to "nature's righteousness." Then the camera pans past her to look at the ocean for a full minute before going to black.

The *Cornermaker* project, first broadcast on 13 October 1981, was conceived as a first dance offering by the new CBS Cable Television network. For that brief moment, the arts seemed a workable premise for television, and CBS Cable was launched with great optimism. Merrill Brockway joined the venture as executive producer of arts programming. He thinks he was offered the job partly because he could bring stars like Tharp and Balanchine to the table. Although he had directed many shows at *Dance in America*, Brockway wanted Tharp to do her own directing for the CBS Cable show. As usual, she was incredibly demanding—she worked with the cameraman for a week before the shoot in Nashville—and as usual she defied the rules.

Both *Baker's Dozen* and the *Bach Duet* were filmed in a completely white space. The no-space white background had become a trademark of Richard Avedon's fashion photography. With the "horizon" line erased, the dancers appeared suspended in some utopian void. She edited the Bach dance freely but discreetly, and did the whole first half of *Baker's Dozen* in one long take, using the screen as a proscenium frame for the dancers' frequent entrances and exits. For *Short Stories*, a much darker dance about destructive relationships, she used a black background, lighting that smoldered like a half-extinguished blaze, and camera closeups that zeroed in voyeuristically on the dancers' bad behavior.

Tharp got paid $50,000 for the *Cornermaker* work, and the company negotiated a deal for half the net profits on future uses of the show. CBS Cable featured Tharp in a full-page ad announcing the network and its roster of forthcoming attractions: "When you want an original, go to a master!" But the new venture started to lose money right away, and within a year after it went on the air it announced it was folding due to insufficient advertising revenues. It reportedly lost $30 million. The government was starting to pull back on arts funding but hopes for television as a cultural medium didn't die immediately. Five public television stations announced an alliance to produce the *Great Performances* series, and this coalition contributed funding for Tharp's 1983 video remake of *The Catherine Wheel*.

For ARTS cable, another commercial television venture at the time, Tharp put together the *Tharp Scrapbook*, clips from her extensive video archives, with a voice-over about the way the dances were developed and related. Besides generous examples of dancing, the compilation included interactions with interviewers and celebrities. Tharp plays straight man to Dick Cavett, who's trying to learn one of the *One Hundreds* in a 1979 PBS episode. There's a bit of an ice-dancing solo she made for John Curry, and a segment from the Gene Kelly special *Dance Is a Man's Sport Too*. This curiosity was another compare-and-contrast duet, for New York City Ballet star Peter Martins and Pittsburgh Steelers linebacker Lynn Swann, joined briefly by Tharp. It had aired on the ABC *Omnibus* series 15 June 1980. According to Don Mischer, who cocreated the segment with her, they marked out yardlines on a black floor to simulate a football field, and Tharp gave the men jumping and throwing movements that each would do in his own way.

In 1984 the whole American Ballet Theater cast went up to Toronto, for reasons of economy, to film *Push Comes to Shove, The Little Ballet,* and *Sinatra Suite,* under the codirection of Tharp and Mischer. It first aired on PBS in October of 1984, and this time Tharp was nowhere to be seen or heard, except as the choreographic force behind it. The video was intended to showcase Baryshnikov, both as star of the three ballets and as a genial host who presented a kind of ballet primer with helpful illustrations by the other dancers. It was issued as a videocassette and stayed on the market for years. *Baryshnikov by Tharp* won an Emmy and was later retitled *Baryshnikov Dances Sinatra.*

Reflecting on the 1980 Winter Garden season, Arlene Croce didn't think the Broadway challenge brought out anything in Tharp that her fans hadn't already seen. Perhaps, having taken the craft of choreography as far as she could go in *Brahms' Paganini,* observed Croce, Tharp was trying to develop "a fresh area of expertise," but in *When We Were Very Young* "she gets nearly everything wrong, and when she's right—for Broadway—she's terrible." Notwithstanding this brickbat from one of her staunchest admirers, Tharp wasn't about to give up on conquering the commercial theater. It took twenty years and several expeditions into "Broadway" territory until she succeeded fully with *Movin' Out.*

After the Winter Garden (24 March–12 April) and some tour dates, the company returned to Osgood Hill, undaunted by the critical failure of *When We Were Very Young.* Thomas Babe was there too, with his daughter, to work on a new project, for which, he said later in an affectionate program essay, Tharp had only a vague idea. John Philip Sousa was to be the hero of a new tale with a cryptic title, *Gat Dickers.* Babe and Tharp worked together on a script for a few weeks, trying it out day by day on the company. No one remembers anything about it except some bathroom episodes and scatological sound effects, and to the dancers' relief it was dropped.

Osgood Hill was the sole base of operations for the 1980 workshop; there were performances in Boston before it began. With forty students in North Andover, classes and rehearsals took place in a tent on the grounds of the mansion and overflowed into the Grange Hall in town. At a final lecture-demonstration Tharp tallied the number of sprained ankles and hours worked—the company rehearsed for 163 hours during the month, she said. An interviewer for the *Boston Herald-American* asked her how she liked Osgood Hill's baronial arrangements. It was nice, she told him. "Her voice was neutral, like that of an oilman admiring a profitless patch of daffodils. 'The best thing about all this is that it's paid rehearsal time.'"

Despite the derailed Babe project, she emerged from the residency with several new dances. She set the Third Orchestral Suite of Bach for the full company, but edited it down to Uchida and Whitener's duet when it got a poor critical reception in Paris. From two retired earlier dances she extracted material she couldn't bear to give up. *Assorted Quartets* comprised the "Fanfare," "Clap," and "Manners" quartets from *When We Were Very Young* and the final quartet from *Mud*, which had already migrated into *Chapters and Verses*. Danced to silence and varying selections of music, *Assorted Quartets* became a serviceable addition to the touring repertory for the next several years. The dancers worked hard to bring off the seemingly reckless partnering of these fast, brief sketches, and they called them *Sordid Quartets*. *Short Stories* and *Uncle Edgar* also joined the repertory for the next intensive touring cycle. Before *The Catherine Wheel* made its debut in the fall of 1981 the company had done another season at the Warfield in San Francisco, toured the West Coast and the Midwest, and made two trips to Europe, appearing in Belgium, Paris, Milan, London, and Holland. When John Curry presented Tharp with the Dance Magazine Award in the spring of 1981, she called the dancers to the platform to share the applause with her.

Tharp now took the biggest financial and creative risk of her career. The first Winter Garden season had recouped its expenses and made a small profit for the company. Buoyed by this outcome she headed back to Broadway. The company booked into the Winter Garden again for four weeks, with the full-length *Catherine Wheel* as the centerpiece, plus two programs of old and new works including the first New York performances of *Short Stories, Uncle Edgar,* and another new version of *Deuce Coupe*. Although this plan resembled previous concert seasons, when Tharp thought "Broadway," she thought "commercial theater," and she intended *The Catherine Wheel* as a legitimate show, a hit of course. For several reasons, this didn't happen. The cost of the production itself was high, with its elaborate scenery and costumes by Santo Loquasto. She commissioned the music from David Byrne, the brainy young leader of the Talking Heads band. With the month's associated back- and front-of-the-house costs, she had to do capacity business in order to recoup her expenses.

In 1981 the Broadway musical was shifting away from the traditional book show with interpolated music-dance numbers. Jerome Robbins, Michael Bennett, and Bob Fosse had brought dance forward as an integral conveyor of plot, and with shows like *Black and Blue, Follies*, and *Jerome Robbins' Broadway*, the plot became nearly nonexistent. *The Catherine Wheel* should have fitted into this fluid picture, but as a product of the dance field rather than show business, it was judged as choreography, not as theater. Probably its closest analogue at the time was Stephen Sondheim and Hal Prince's *Sweeney Todd*, which was winding up a highly successful two-year run. Like *The Catherine Wheel*, the experimental *Sweeney* was a macabre epic about corruption and violence. It too had cumbersome, mechanistic scenery, extravagant characters who engaged in bizarre behavior, and a contemporary score that didn't easily fall into the popular idiom of musical comedy. Sondheim's monstrous hero is redeemed at the end when he finds out his grisly rampage has been a mistake, and he breaks down in remorse. Tharp's characters never did acquire a human dimension; redemption was only possible when they lost their personas entirely and became dancing angels in the *Golden Section*.

The Catherine Wheel foundered under its densely layered symbolism and over-the-top presentation. Tharp admitted that "My company has never done anything as complicated as this." Everything about it was shouted through a megaphone. Tharp piled her own contradictory dance resources into the piece. Instead of finding a way to reconcile her recent narrative preoccupations with her genius for pure dance composition, she kept them severely cordoned off in distinct sections of the piece. She restored the family from *When We Were Very Young* almost intact, replacing herself with Jennifer Way in the mother's role. Now the autobiographical implications resided, much less obviously, in a new character, the leader of the chorus, played by Sara Rudner. Once again, Tharp says, she had planned to dance this role but gave it up so she could work on the piece from the outside. Rawe, Glasner, and Kurshals returned as the father and children. Two of the allegorical sketches from the 1978 Osgood Hill workshop, Chaos and Order, matured into Shelley Washington's Maid and Christine Uchida's Pet, and John Carrafa's Juggler in *When We Were Very Young* became a Poet.

Instead of being awkward, unfocused, and lovable like their predecessors, the *Catherine Wheel* family were mean and grasping cartoonish exaggerations. They danced in a simplistic, almost slapstick mode. Hardly models of domestic harmony to begin with, they soon begin bickering over a pineapple given to them by Rudner. Tharp saw this object as not only the traditional domestic welcoming gift that turns into forbidden fruit, but as a symbol of escalating ambition for material possessions, and a destructive device that looks like a hand grenade or a bomb. As the family grows increasingly greedy they pummel and abuse each other. The mother teaches the children to tap-dance so that they can become street beggars. The father chases the Pet, gropes her and mounts her from behind. The Maid shrieks and mugs hysterically. When the Poet arrives, he fondles the pineapple in awe. He's momentarily attracted to the Pet, but later attacks the fruit in an orgiastic binge.

Throughout this frenzy, Rudner and a cadre of anonymous figures surge in the background, unseen by the family, commenting on their actions and perhaps accepting punishment for them, like a Greek chorus. Santo Loquasto's scenery and Jennifer Tipton's lighting situated all this in a harsh and threatening environment—a forest of twenty-four metallic poles planted on the stage, and a network of sinister machinelike objects that hung overhead and sometimes descended with clanking noises—and the family's action was echoed on back curtains by doppelgängers, in a life-size, even more exaggerated shadowplay.

As the perversion and aggression mount nearly out of control, the parents try to bury the hatchet with a duet of social dances in period styles—waltz, bunny hug, jitterbug, twist—but the contentious children keep pushing between them. By this time the pineapple, grown as big as a person, has been torn to bits, swept up by the chorus, and stuffed in a trash bag. Rudner tries to dispose of it by shoving it into the most menacing of the overhead machines, but is almost impaled herself.

Finally, three-quarters of the way through the seventy-five-minute piece, the madness exhausts itself. The machines and the poles fly out, the light turns warm, and the two groups are united. Transformed into a splendid ensemble in fancy gold sportswear, they end the work with fifteen minutes of the fastest, most airborne, and closely coordinated dancing this company of virtuosos had ever done. *The Golden Section* went into the repertory two years later as a self-contained piece.

David Byrne's music—twenty-two short numbers in different styles—was a propulsive mix of recorded electronic, instrumental, and vocal performance. For the musical material, Tharp didn't give Byrne more than a general idea where she was going with the piece, nor did she specify counts for each number. Byrne figured that "If I made music that was rhythmically multilayered and busy, then the dancers would link to beats anyway, though not necessarily the most obvious ones." He would bring his musical ideas into rehearsal and adjust as needed, so the score grew organically, the music and dance influencing each other as they went along. Byrne was interested in West African music at the time, especially the ways in which rhythm can both reflect and reinforce community. One of his mentors was the ethnomusicologist John Miller Chernoff, author of the groundbreaking study *African Rhythm and African Sensibility*, and Chernoff supplied basic rhythms for some of the tracks. Byrne did the main lyrics (only seven of the numbers had words), a spacey commentary on life slipping "through the cracks."

The musical and dance numbers had different titles. The company produced a big fold-out program, with construction plans for Loquasto's scenery on the back, to crosslist how the dance numbers corresponded to the music. This probably created another source of confusion for the audience because both sets of titles were evocative in oblique ways. For instance, "The Leader Repents," a dance for Rudner and four men of the chorus, was accompanied by Byrne's "Big Business." "Think you've had enough/Stop talking, help us get ready," he sang. For each number the program meticulously identified the dancers, the musicians, and the eclectic instrumentation, which included guitars, Western and African drums, synthesizers, calliope, gongs, flutes, and homemade percussion. For "Cloud Chamber"/"The Poet's Decline" Tharp played the water pot.

Byrne, like Tharp, had a reputation for stretching his own boundaries, and both of them had developed specialized ensembles to perform their work. But they were both big creative egos, and though they found *The Catherine Wheel* a good working collaboration, the performance was imprinted with their divergent temperaments. The collaboration generated pre-performance buzz in both the dance and pop music columns. *The Catherine Wheel* was the first score she commissioned from a rock composer, and Byrne was working with theater dance for the first time too. She already knew what a drawing card pop music could be for the audience. Hooking up with contemporary composers could also bring her visibility outside the dance field. In the next few years she commissioned three prominent avant-gardists (Glenn Branca, David Van Tieghem, and Philip Glass), with predictably attention-getting results.

The *Catherine Wheel* score was released soon after the season. It was chosen as one of 1981's ten best recordings by both *The New York Times* and the *Soho Weekly News*. At the time it struck listeners as loud and abrasive; two decades into the age of multicultural techno-fusion, it seems intriguing and almost lyrical. David Byrne says: "I was hugely proud of being involved in the piece. It was like nothing else out there," and he was pleased when *The Golden Section* was spun off as a touring piece. Byrne and Tharp had been inseparable during the creation of the dance, but they quarreled bitterly over ownership of the score, and they severed their relationship. A complicated disposition of the rights was worked out, allowing Tharp to use the music while Byrne retained ownership. She had foreseen that commissioned dance music might have a life of its own, and indeed, all three of her next new scores came out as audio recordings.

The *Catherine Wheel* reviews were mixed. Anna Kisselgoff seemed disturbed the morning after by the "message she has so purposefully muddled" and the atmosphere of "youth culture," though the golden denouement of the piece was "Tharp at her best." Following up with a Sunday piece, Kisselgoff was even more critical. Tharp undermined her formal brilliance with "lapses in seriousness that greater choreographers would not. Most of Miss Tharp's immaturity takes the form of platitudes she expresses as social commentary." The more positive weekly critics didn't get into print until late in the season. Arlene Croce called *The Catherine Wheel* "a major event in our theatre," but even she saw the first part of the piece as murky, overloaded with alternative references. *The Golden Section* saved not only the characters but the whole piece:

> Tharp's abrupt alchemy substituting harmony for chaos is almost painful in its honesty. It's as if she were substituting art for life, knowing that no solution to the palpable terrors she has invoked is possible. Art, less than a solution yet more than a consolation, offers terms she can settle for; it's the great alternative to the dilemma of life, the only other reality that isn't death. "The Golden Section" is the classical "white" ballet, with all its implications of redemption intact.

Afterward Tharp claimed that *The Catherine Wheel*'s twelve scheduled performances weren't enough; one more week would have allowed it to build a solid audience and recover her outlay. But a revival of *Camelot* was already booked into the theater and she could neither extend her run nor move the cumbersome *Catherine Wheel* elsewhere. The production's size and complexity made it unfit for touring. When the Winter Garden season closed, the piece was essentially gone and Tharp was left with a $200,000 deficit. She and some board members underwrote a loan to cover it and she didn't get out of debt for several years.

Tharp was disappointed by the reaction to *The Catherine Wheel*. She'd counted on it to be a Broadway success; she'd even invested some of her own money in it. Not only had she lost out on the economic gamble, she felt she hadn't molded her ideas into a suitable package. The critics all saw the dichotomy between what Kisselgoff called the "Bumstead" narrative and the cathartic idealism of *The Golden Section*. It was a problem of conflicting aesthetics— expression versus abstraction, hot versus cool. Tharp felt she simply hadn't made her thesis clear. With her usual tenacity, she made two further stabs at the problem in addition to salvaging *The Golden Section* for the repertory. After drastically revising the dance for video, she staged a condensed version in 1984 during the company's Brooklyn Academy season.

Even those critics who scratched for a path through the underbrush of meaning interpreted *The Catherine Wheel* in terms of the Guignol story and its golden antithesis. According to Janice Berman Alexander in *Newsday*, *The Golden Section* "sets forth the idea that once you abandon that archaic family structure, life can take place." Linda Winer of the *Daily News* wrote: "[It] begins as a grim epic of sensory overload and family torment. Then, without clear explanation, everybody gets happy and unbinds in a golden abstraction of just about every hurtling impossibility on the Tharp physical highwire."

Most of the critics, pro and con, skimmed over the masked chorus and their leader. But Sara Rudner's character, more than anything else, embodied the notion of purity being eroded, destroyed, and finally reclaimed. As a dancing figure she glowed and suffered while the family acted out the perversion, greed, and misogyny her gift of the pineapple had ignited in them, and she disappeared when the others ascended to the exalted plane. To Tharp, clarifying this figure would fix what was wrong with the dance. She enlisted Rhoda Grauer to produce and fundraise, made a coproduction deal with the BBC, and enthusiastically began rethinking the dance for video.

Tharp had done considerable research into the fourth-century martyr Catherine of Alexandria. The religious zealot was executed amid purported miraculous events, for refusing to marry. According to an elaborate scenario Tharp constructed, Catherine was both flawed and admirable, "a woman of extraordinary spirit and adventure whose sole desire is to seek the truth in all things and thus, control the world." Tharp's story line, like a Hindu epic, describes how Catherine steals the symbolic pineapple in her desire for power, thus disrupting the world's balance and bringing about destruction. The family, inheritors of this war and chaos, bicker among themselves for the pineapple. Their increasingly horrid behavior thwarts Catherine's efforts to restore order. She steals the remnants of the symbolic pineapple from them, tries to restore it to its place of origin, but is unable to reassemble its pieces. Finally, she renounces her own ambition and acknowledges her guilt. The overlapping cycles of suffering come together and a great release of energy allows everyone to be free.

As a character in search of superhuman perfection, Catherine might have resembled any rigorously trained dancer, but on-camera in the preface to the video, Tharp admitted that no mere mortal could have achieved such heights. To represent this "anti-physicality" she used a computer-generated animation. On-screen the Computer Catherine looked like a bundle of lines assembled into human form—perhaps an early version of what we now know as motion capture. This animated figure became one aspect of the creation/destruction myth that Tharp had tried to combine in Rudner's part onstage. So when the family misdeeds became intolerable for Rudner and the ensemble, the Computer Catherine would appear and teach Rudner an idealized movement sequence to calm their ravings. According to Tharp, Rudner's character in the original dance "was too complex to work theatrically, because she was both her own undermining and her own inspiration. Now the Catherine figure, the computer, teaches Sara the theme that she uses to make something from. It's not that she simultaneously has to invent and take apart."

Despite this effort to clarify, on tape the story line wasn't any more lucid than it had been in the stage version. By the time she videoed *The Catherine Wheel*, Tharp was quite experienced in television technology. She plotted every shot ahead of time on a storyboard, so that she only needed a single camera for each take. But she'd then have to move the setup for the next take. She incorporated as much of Santo Loquasto's scenery as she could, then tried for even more complicated effects with it. Having used most of the twelve-day shooting schedule on these time-consuming arrangements, she filmed the whole *Golden Section* on the last day, with insufficient lights. During the editing she added other new elements—interpolated fireworks, a flashback through the family history in retrograde, shots of Rudner striding across a hilltop toward an ancient castle, a tricky final ascent for Rudner before *The Golden Section,* and a slow-motion final leap into the stratosphere for Uchida.

The video premiered at the end of January 1983 on the BBC's *Arena,* and two months later on PBS's *Great Performances.* There were some good reviews, but the video was even less coherent than the dance had been on the stage, and in videocassette release it failed to achieve the commercial success Tharp was hoping for.

At this point she was becoming more and more pessimistic about maintaining a dance company. The Winter Garden season in 1981 had been a downer for her, not only because of the dubious fate of *The Catherine Wheel.* Before the season Rose Marie Wright had conclusively retired from dancing. With some reluctance Wright accepted the role of rehearsal director and Katie Glasner learned her roles, but she was a great loss to the company. The long season on Broadway brought financial burdens and injuries. Tharp wasn't happy about stagehands she didn't feel were conscientious enough. One night during a performance, a street woman got past the front door and wandered onto the stage. For several anxious minutes no one knew what to do. Whoever was supposed to be manning the act curtain wasn't at his post to bring it in. While the music continued playing, the dancers weren't sure if the woman was dangerous or not. Tharp went on stage prepared to wrestle the intruder into the orchestra pit, but the curtain finally went down. The woman slipped away and was caught by the police outside the theater. At another performance before this unnerving event, the show had to be stopped because of a small fire. Tharp was so disgusted she left town before the end of the season. A month later she was vowing not to make any more stage dances until *The Catherine Wheel* was safely on tape.

Television had long seemed a solution to the problem of repertory. Soon after the release of *Confessions of a Cornermaker,* she told a writer for *The Wall Street Journal:* "It's quite clear that the future of dance economics is in the recorded medium." If she could commit the dances to tape, she could reach the public in a controlled way, and use the dancers to make new work. *The Catherine Wheel's* escalating chaos, the glamour and sensual provocations of the dancing and the music, may even have invited the deranged woman onto the stage, she thought. She longed for a way to make her own working life replicate the fable, she wanted the responsibilities smaller and the thinking time quieter.

In June of 1982 Harvey Lichtenstein made a generous offer that seemed to answer her prayers. The company had been rehearsing in some unused spaces at Brooklyn Academy for some time, with its administrative offices housed at BAM as well. Now, through a new BAM agency, the Local Development Corporation, Lichtenstein proposed that Tharp take over the former Strand Theater, a city-owned building two blocks from the Academy. The company would renovate the building for studios, offices, and a television production center, and perform as usual in theaters, principally the BAM Opera House. When the scheme was announced, Tharp Dance Foundation manager Steve Dennin estimated that the foundation would have to raise $4 million for the work, but in the long term, the opportunity would give the company permanent rehearsal space and allow Tharp to realize her dream of opening a school.

Within a year, the scheme had collapsed. Besides the financial commitment, Tharp had strong objections to locating the company in downtown Brooklyn. It was a long commute from the Upper West Side of Manhattan, where she lived, and the seedy Brooklyn neighborhood made her nervous. Lichtenstein had seen BAM as the anchor for a revitalization of the area ever since he took over the Academy, but in the 1980s the process seemed stalled. BAM was surrounded by blocks of parking lots and demolished or deteriorating buildings. Tough and street-smart as Tharp was, she couldn't face subjecting herself and the dancers to that environment every day.

9

Romance and the
Opposite
1982–1983

Despite the mishaps at the Winter Garden and the divided press for *The Catherine Wheel*, the season was a success with the audience. The old repertory drew former admirers and attracted new fans. As for new works, each one was a surprise. With her horror of repeating herself and her unquenchable imagination, Tharp seemed to reconceptualize the choreographic act every time. Naturally, there were certain useful tropes she returned to—the flying, tumbling episodes of partnering and partner switching, the mirroring and canonic imitations, the pedestrian gestures and attitudes, the retrogrades of everything from step combinations to entire dramatic encounters. By now the dancers shared a movement vocabulary and an easygoing, articulate, and fearless approach to dancing, but the look of each dance was always different. The hooty synthesizer music and the formal pairings of the tank-suited women in *Uncle Edgar* was a far cry from the urban romances of *Short Stories*, set to rock songs by Supertramp and Bruce Springsteen. Both *The Golden Section* and *Baker's Dozen* may have pictured utopian harmony, but the ensemble of one dance could hardly be mistaken for the other. *The Bix Pieces* taught lessons about the interrelationship of art forms; *Deuce Coupe* taught the same lesson for a generation that spoke in another idiom.

When she deliberately recycled material, she gave it new surroundings. For 1981 *Deuce Coupe* returned in a new, fourth version, with ABT star Cynthia Gregory in the ballerina role and a new "composite" ballet-modern role for the effervescent longtime Eliot Feld dancer Christine Sarry. The street graffiti writers were back, and a supplementary ensemble of seven young ballet dancers surrounded Gregory. Anna Kisselgoff called it "an abstraction of her original pop ballet," and many people thought it the best *Deuce Coupe* since the first model. *The Catherine Wheel* looked unique even though it had evolved out of several previous works. All of its predecessors had disappeared except for the seedlings in *Assorted Quartets*, and few spectators noticed those connections.

Tharp insisted that repertory was a dead issue for her once she had learned everything she could from a dance. Then she was done with the piece and didn't need to see it anymore, even if this was the point at which it could serve the repertory most effectively. As the company prepared for performances in Frankfurt and at Vienna's Theater an der Wien early in 1982, she didn't see the need to check on how the dances played with European audiences. Sometimes she gave in to sponsor demand and made an appearance when the company was touring to some especially important venue, but she begrudged the time she had to spend to do it. She had Rose Marie Wright to oversee the repertory and the administrative staff to do the office work, but: "My priority has always got to be to ignore them and to make dances . . . in a way that is challenging to me creatively and that makes sense to an audience."

The company continued touring intensively. They did two international trips and seven months on the road in 1982; three trips abroad in 1983 plus several other dates and a summer residency; four months of tours, two of summer festivals, and a trip to Germany in 1984. All this activity began to have a synergistic effect. With the New York and international press coverage drumming up interest, the company was avidly anticipated and widely covered. They developed a faithful constituency across the country, which in turn stimulated interest whenever they had a New York season. Many new works were shown on the road, so that they would be well broken in and cleaned up before premiering in New York.

Tharp submitted to telephone interviews with eager local journalists during these years, but frequently the dancers were delegated to deal with the press. Along with the extra responsibilities of residencies—teaching master classes, running lecture-demonstrations, giving their own company class—most of them now became spokespersons. Self-possessed, thoughtful and lively personalities, they could reflect on the work they were doing. Wright, Way, Rawe, and Washington had years of experience dancing and teaching Tharp's work to draw on. Colton was especially insightful about the choreographic process. Linda Shelton, who was company manager during the '80s, usually worked with local sponsors to identify who should be interviewed. It might be the newest dancer in the company, someone who'd grown up or gone to school locally, or someone with a featured role in a new dance. These interviews and feature stories brought the dancers special attention and of course made the performances even more appealing.

The mounting success didn't make Tharp happy. Committing to the BAM/Strand Theater project might have solved some of her chronic discontents, with a permanent home for the company and a laboratory for her creative work. But putting down roots in Brooklyn would have tied her firmly to the long-term life of the company and committed her to the school she knew she needed but couldn't take the time to establish. Though Tharp didn't like to teach, there were excellent teachers in the company. As long as they could wedge master classes and short-term workshops into their residencies, they could still perform, but a school would have drawn them off the stage or required former Tharp dancers to sign on as a regular faculty. She had never codified a technique to be taught on a predictable basis. Any established classroom technique would be doomed to obsolescence because Tharp was always moving on in her technical demands. As she saw it, with a home base the company would have to get bigger, the budget would get bigger, and she would have to do more to hold it all together, not less.

Once she gave up the Strand opportunity, touring was the surest way for the company to earn its livelihood. While she was preparing to rescue *The Catherine Wheel* from its imperfections, the company was winning rapturous audiences and great reviews across the U.S. and Canada, Germany, Austria, Israel, and Japan, their visibility bolstered by the release of the videos and films they'd made. The period between the fall of 1981 and the spring of 1983 saw the premieres of *Confessions of a Cornermaker* (13 October 1981), *Ragtime* (18 November 1981), and the *Scrapbook* tape (25 October 1982). In New York, waiting for the dancers to return to the studio, Tharp carried on her extracurricular activities. She collaborated and appeared with Andre Gregory in *Bone Songs*, a misbegotten off-off-Broadway play. By mid-1983, she was planning the movie *Amadeus* and she'd reestablished her relationship with American Ballet Theater, where Mikhail Baryshnikov was now artistic director. During this period Tharp also made two of her most unusual dances for the company: *Bad Smells*, which nearly everyone found repellant, and *Nine Sinatra Songs*, which became its signature piece.

Tharp was better at capturing the events of a relationship than she was at showing how a story unfolded. As early as *Chapters and Verses*, Richard Colton noticed she was creating a "world of vignettes . . . little pieces that didn't yet have any kind of narrative flow but were evocative. . . . It was character without building a story." These vignettes often had to do with the past, Colton thought, but they weren't an indulgence in nostalgia. Tharp made more than one "Dance of the Ages," stringing together successive period dances like a movie montage, to show the passage of time. In *Short Stories*, she illustrated how the same group of people could behave differently toward one another at different times. Dispensing with narrative connections, she simply looked from different angles, the way one turns a stone over to view its facets.

Short Stories never attained the iconic status of some other Tharp dances. Like *Nine Sinatra Songs* it was a portrait of moods rather than a continuous story. Both works used social dancing as a baseline for human interaction as well as physical display. All the dancers in *Short Stories* were dressed in pants or shorts and polo shirts, but viewers usually thought of the first group as teenagers and the second as twenty-somethings. The three couples in Part I (Supertramp's "Lover Boy") are show-offs, riding the music and amplifying their slow-dancing with flamboyant circular flings, dips, lifts, head tosses and backbends. When Shelley Washington openly flirts with the other men, her partner, William Whitener, pulls her in possessively. This doesn't restrain her, though, and her extroverted behavior infects the others (Katie Glasner and Raymond Kurshals, Mary Ann Kellogg and John Carrafa on the *Cornermaker* tape). Their circular dance moves bring them into eye contact with each other and they begin switching partners. The switches seem casual, but there are competitive tensions, threatening glares, momentary failures to synchronize, more switches. What started as playfulness builds to hostility.

After a standoff, the song ends and begins again. Kellogg is alone, moving inwardly, as if to distance herself from the others, who are now dancing with open aggressiveness, still exchanging partners. Carrafa tries to bring Kellogg back from her reverie, and they dance together intimately, erotically, for a short time. Then, for no apparent reason, he backs away from her. She goes limp and the men slide her from one to another. Soaring, dramatic lifts and intimate holds have escalated into brutality. When they're done with her they leave her on the floor. The dancing continues, pausing only momentarily as one person or another glances down at Kellogg.

In Part II, the two couples (Sara Rudner and John Malashock, Jennifer Way and Tom Rawe in the video) seem older, more serious. They too switch partners, fight, go back together, dance passionately, but everything is more intense and more personal. (The music is Springsteen's apocalyptic "Jungle Land.") The couples seem committed to each other, spouses or roommates. Their duets seem like domestic love scenes. They jog in squabbling, and after dalliances, fights, and reconciliations, they leave, in choreographed retrograde, the same way they came.

What's remarkable about *Short Stories*, apart from the extraordinary dancing, is that the drama going on between all these people arises out of the way they're dancing in Part I, or the way they're arguing while they enter in Part II. The characters were temperamentally disagreeable, and the dance acquired a downbeat reputation. Anna Kisselgoff called it unpleasant, derivative of Jerome Robbins. Tharp used "clichéd youth culture as a pretext for delving into relationships." Tharp herself may have done it no favor with her over-the-top introduction on the *Cornermaker* tape: "Its people are out of sync with themselves. Their love seems incestuous and somehow devious. Intimacy is a threat and their only recourse is to split, whether literally, as in the first of the *Short Stories*, or more subtly, simply to withdraw, as in the second."

But the dance also was handicapped by underexposure. Less than thirty minutes long, it seemed pedestrian at first viewing, not heavily choreographed, too much like other Tharpian takes on young people and social dancing. Tharp often wanted to disguise her craft and evoke the audience's emotional response by making movement just a little more artful than everyday behavior. Stealthily she could close the distance between "verbs that we all know and recognize" like walking, running, pushing and shoving, and the abstract vocabulary of ballet. Perhaps *Short Stories* was too deceptive in this way for its own survival.

Its truncated career also illustrates the way Tharp handled repertory as an expedient. Before its stage premiere, in Ghent, Belgium, in the fall of 1980, she had already translated it to videotape for *Confessions of a Cornermaker*. Its first U.S. performances were given on the West Coast in March of

1981, and when it appeared in New York during the 1981 Winter Garden season, it was overshadowed by *The Catherine Wheel* and further upstaged by the *Cornermaker* tape, which was broadcast before that season came to an end. *Short Stories* served in the touring repertory for about three years, but when only part of the company was on the road Part I was omitted and the pocket-size Part II was performed alone. By the time the company appeared in New York again (Brooklyn Academy, early in 1984), *Short Stories* was gone.

Nine Sinatra Songs carried a working premise similar to that of *Short Stories*: the rhythms and attitudes of social dance evoked real-life behaviors and temperaments. Sometime after she had made the *Sinatra*, Tharp said it was meant to show the stages in a relationship. It didn't need any thematic rationale, though, and achieved its success as nothing more than a glamorous suite of romantic dances. Tharp had been working with Frank Sinatra recordings for several years, and she reused all three songs she'd choreographed for her disastrous duet with Baryshnikov, *Once More, Frank*. Now she had a magnificent company of dancers, and instead of setting out to overturn convention, she mounted a full-scale ballroom dance extravaganza, with the men in tuxedos and the women in Oscar de la Renta cocktail dresses, and a mirror ball revolving above the stage.

In comparison with the choreographed intricacies of *Assorted Quartets*, *Uncle Edgar*, and *The Golden Section*, or the steamy revelations of *Short Stories*, *Nine Sinatra Songs* was stunningly straightforward. The company was now big enough to yield seven couples. Tharp chose recordings from Sinatra's glossy Nelson Riddle period and gave each couple one number. Midway through the dance and again at the end, they assembled to the effusive "My Way," recorded at different times. But there was no partner switching and no group work at all. Each pair danced its own variation and focused on its own partnership. Overall, the dance achieved its continuity through Tharp's sequencing of the numbers. As always, she brought out the strengths of the individual dancers. She worked out the early material on Sara Rudner, Keith Young, John Carrafa, and then the other members of the blue team, Shelley Washington, Mary Ann Kellogg, and John Malashock. When the red team returned from tour, she assigned the rest of the roles and they began developing the partnering and the personas that went with each duet. The dancers felt it took over a year for the dance to find its feet. Premiered on the West Coast in late 1982, it didn't reach New York until the Brooklyn Academy season of January–February 1984. Early reviewers felt Tharp was working below par, and some may have been put off by the piece's uncharacteristic romanticism.

Amy Spencer, who'd had extensive ballet training and worked with downtown choreographers, particularly Rudner, had joined the company in 1981, after *The Catherine Wheel* was choreographed. At that time Tharp was expanding the company's red-and-blue capability, and Spencer learned the repertory. She remembers the *Sinatra* as one of the first roles Tharp choreographed on her. She saw that the dancers had a big responsibility in bringing it off, perhaps because the material was less intricately structured than some of the other works: "[*Sinatra*] had to have inner life . . . another layer to it, to make it more than just some flip ballroom piece. And I think it took everybody a while to get a handle on it." Performing the piece over time also gave the dancers a sense of "how the narrative ran in the audience mind." This "narrative" was more like an expressive throughline that carried over from one duet to the next. Tharp made some small adjustments and one major change to improve the flow of the action. As the dance was performed by successive casts, in Tharp's company and others, it gradually grew tighter, jokier, and more flashy, but the creators of the roles were never equaled. Unfortunately, their performance wasn't professionally filmed.

The piece opened on a bare stage, dark except for the revolving mirror ball, and the audience often screamed with the first bars of the music. Shelley Washington and Keith Young, the original lead-off couple, appeared as Sinatra began "Softly as I Leave." Their dance seemed to float on waves of expectation, dipping and rising in a single line from beginning to end. Toward the end of the song, the moves became more pressured, the mood more ecstatic. As they left, Mary Ann Kellogg entered with Gary Chryst. (John Malashock, on whom this dance was created, was on a leave of absence at the time of the first performances.) "Strangers in the Night" was a pseudo-tango, packed with close embraces, averted eye contact, and tight supported turns. There were intricate, over-and-under lifts, and changes of positions with crossed hands. These tricky moves expanded into some upside-down lifts and other oddities near the end.

Rudner and Carrafa's "One for My Baby" ignored the singer's morose tale of rejection, except for his slow, relaxed tempo. Like two affectionate drunks, they slid and climbed over each other, clasping together almost by reflex and groping for whatever limb was nearest when they drifted out of contact. Nearly unfocused, they seemed drawn together by instinct, and determined to keep manipulating each other as if that were the only way to

Brahms' Paganini.
William Whitener.
(PHOTO: © Martha Swope)

Brahms' Pagnini.
Richard Colton.
(PHOTO: © Martha Swope)

ॐ *When We Were Very Young.* Tom Rawe, Twyla Tharp, Raymond Kurshals, Katie Glasner.
(PHOTO: © Martha Swope)

ॐ *The Catherine Wheel.* John Carrafa, Christine Uchida.
(PHOTO: © Paul B. Goode)

꩜ *The Golden Section.* Stephanie Foster, William Whitener, Cheryl Jones. (PHOTO: © Monroe Warshaw)

꩜ *Short Stories.* William Whitener, Raymond Kurshals, Shelley Washington. (PHOTO: © Martha Swope)

Nine Sinatra Songs.
Jennifer Way, William
Whitener, Richard
Colton, Barbara Hoon.
(PHOTO: © Martha Swope)

Bad Smells. (PHOTO: © Paul B. Goode)

🖎 *Fait Accompli.* Keith Young, Sara Rudner.
(PHOTO: © Tom Caravaglia)

🖎 *Bach Partita.* Robert La Fosse, Cynthia Harvey, Cynthia Gregory, Fernando Bujones, Martine Van Hamel, Clark Tippett. (PHOTO: © Martha Swope)

🖎 *In the Upper Room.* Jamie Bishton, Cynthia Anderson, Daniel Sanchez, Isabella Padovani, Kathleen Moore, Kevin O'Day. (PHOTO: Marty Sohl)

🕮 *Octet.* Allison Brown, Kevin O'Day. (PHOTO: © Martha Swope)

🕮 *Men's Piece.* Twyla Tharp, Kevin O'Day. (PHOTO: © Martha Swope)

🕮 *Demeter and Persephone.* Christine Dakin, Terese Capucilli. (PHOTO: © Tom Brazil)

∜ *Noir a. k. a. Bartok.* John Selya, Stacy Caddell. (PHOTO: © Tom Brazil)

∜ *How Near Heaven.* Kathleen Moore, Susan Jaffe.
(PHOTO: © Jack Vartoogian/FrontRow Photos 1995)

∜ *Known By Heart.* Ethan Stiefel, Susan Jaffe.
(PHOTO: © Tom Brazil)

🔊 *Sweet Fields.* (PHOTO: © Jack Vartoogian/FrontRowPhotos 1997)

🔊 *Surfer at the River Styx.* John Selya with Elizabeth Parkinson, Benjamin Bowman.
(PHOTO: © Tom Brazil)

🔊 *Variations on a Theme by Haydn.*
(PHOTO: © Tom Brazil)

keep from passing out. This duet was probably the last of Tharp's low-key, befuddled comedy dances.

After the three-couple "My Way" Christine Uchida and Richard Colton were a sweet, almost demure duo in "I'm Not Afraid." Tharp felt this number didn't provide enough contrast, and when Uchida left the company she re-did the section for Colton and Barbara Hoon as fumbling kewpie-doll characters, to Sinatra's "Somethin' Stupid." This dance was almost a burlesque of the complicated linkages and extravagant yearnings of the other couples. Then the goofiness gave way to a sedate but intimate duet ("All the Way") for Amy Spencer and Raymond Kurshals. At moments the woman took the lead, but despite their physical contrasts—Spencer was tall and refined, Kurshals strong and rugged—they conveyed a partnership of equals. Their turns and lifts were closer together, less outwardly demonstrative, and their moves leisurely enough for them to unfold into supported attitudes and arabesques. The tempo turned upbeat again for "Forget Domani," a quick, frivolous step dance for Jennifer Way and William Whitener. Tossing the skirt of her shocking pink dress with deep ruffles on the hem and neckline, she flirted and led him on. Both of them bobbed up and down with small steps and syncopated skips.

The last duet before the ensemble finale was Tom Rawe and Shelley Freydont's "That's Life," which Tharp called an apache but which had almost no dance steps in it. Rawe was the antihero whose shopworn but sexy girlfriend likes to be treated rough. These types descended from a long line of movie toughs—James Cagney and Shanghai Lil, the hoofer and the striptease girl in Balanchine's *On Your Toes*, and endless reworkings by Astaire, Kelly, and others. Rawe played him lanky and hardnosed. Deadpan, Freydont submitted to all his abuse and finally flounced away, only to change her mind and dive into his arms just as he was putting on his jacket to leave. She thought of it as a French nightclub dance. In the final "My Way" number, all the couples returned for a ballroom scene that gradually opened up and out, until the lifts were rising and cresting in overlapping waves, and then subsiding as the couples ambled away and the music died down.

Tharp said she'd been inspired by films she'd seen of Vernon and Irene Castle when she was researching the period dances for *Ragtime*, but *Nine Sinatra Songs* owes only an initial spark to the stylishly decorous Castles. It draws on the sweeping, sophisticated escapades of Fred Astaire and Ginger Rogers, the lovelorn yearnings of Gene Kelly, and the annals of physical comedy from silent movies to Lucille Ball and Betty Hutton. What was innovative about the dance was the volumes of new lifts and partnering possibilities. Tharp's ice-dancing experience let her try some skimming, swooping mechanics on dry land. Using the momentum of turning, running, or two-stepping, the couples created a lexicon of lifts and falls. The men could sling a partner to the floor and up again into locomotion or twist her into a behind-the-back or over-the shoulder revolution, while she unfolded her legs or changed the shape of her whole torso. One partner could act as a fulcrum to wheel the other at arm's length or link into a set of spins. They could lean or fall or even jump with their full weight, into each other's arms or against each other's bodies. Their trust and sensuality was what saved the dance initially from its own excesses. After one break-in performance in Los Angeles, Burt Supree of *The Village Voice* remarked on "the careful, faithful interdependency that permeates *Nine Sinatra Songs* and creates its atmosphere."

Riding the creative high of working with David Byrne on the new score for *The Catherine Wheel*, Tharp had remarked to the *New York Times* music critic Robert Palmer that she didn't intend to use previously recorded music for a dance again: "Older music has all its connotations in place; everyone knows what they think about it." But the cost of commissioning new music was significant. Within months she was choreographing to Sinatra. The question of live music versus recordings had troubled modern dancers throughout their history. Only Martha Graham in her later years had the resources to commission composers and hire orchestras on a regular basis. Until at least 1950, the modern dance was notable for its small scale musical ingenuity, and its aesthetic was very much influenced by the experimental composers it attracted: Henry Cowell, Harry Partch, Dane Rudhyar, Lou Harrison, and others. In the early days Louis Horst composed chamber scores for piano and one or two other instruments. When tape recorders and synthesizers arrived, choreographer Alwin Nikolais was the first to make his own electronic scores. But existing music on tape, often overamplified in an effort to simulate acoustic sound, became the standard modern dance accompaniment. One thing that distinguished Mark Morris as a major player from the outset was his resistance to this alternative.

Tharp was just as constrained by her financial resources as other choreographers. A musical sophisticate, she started her career with a sparing use of the classical material that inspired her in the studio and provided so many structural ideas. For the first ten years, silence or seemingly offhand quotations accompanied her dances. Recorded Haydn or Mozart were slipped in bashfully next to archival jazz; recorded Bach was permitted because it was supposed to be used in a video (*All About Eggs*). She didn't fully employ classical music on stage until she had an orchestra to play it, for *As Time Goes By*. Then came recorded excerpts, collages, and pastiches, and it wasn't until the *Brahms' Paganini* that she used a complete classical work on tape.

The jazz and rock artists and arrangements that established her reputation were so inimitable no one would have wanted live substitutes, and their prior credibility took her halfway to success. When she could afford live musicians, she had the material transcribed: the Willie Smith numbers played by Dick Hyman for *Baker's Dozen*, the English jazz band on the *Eight Jelly Rolls* video. If she had to perform to tape, the original Beach Boys or Chuck Berry were fine with the audience; these records were part of their lives. But jazz and rock had a creative bite, an antagonistic edginess. Tharp avoided soft popular music—the sentimental, the hummable—until the *Nine Sinatra Songs*. And probably nothing else of hers clicked so successfully into the taste of a broad population, until the Broadway show *Movin' Out*, with its reconstructed recordings of Billy Joel.

Nine Sinatra Songs became a Tharpian trademark, even though it was virtually unique in relation to her other work. For the same reasons that it was so popular, it became a target. The newly critical field of "dance theory" attacked it as a purveyor of heterosexual gender stereotypes and a blatant bid for audience approval that didn't even have the saving grace of satire. Feminists and some critics objected to the way she portrayed women in the *Sinatra*. Music editor Michael Fleming of *The Fort Worth Star Telegram*, for example, commented that "as the dance progresses, the female member of each pair seems to become trapped in one of two obnoxious roles—either a seductress or an emotionless rag doll. . . . There was something sinister lurking in the background, something all the more frightening for the glamorous sheen that covered it."

What scholars also found alienating about Tharp's dance around this time was its use of virtuosic technique and its theatrical staging. Some early devotees were troubled by Tharp's evolving popularity. Writing in *Dance Magazine*, Joan Acocella sensed a "relaxation of concentration" in the *Sinatra* when Tharp took it to Broadway in the summer of 1984. "Most of the subtleties were removed, replaced by mugging," she thought. Fans fell away and new ones arrived, but the intellectuals' disapproval stigmatized her for a generation. The *Sinatra* may have been "something like a panorama of Middle America in middle-age" according to Arlene Croce, but it would take its place alongside *Sue's Leg, Baker's Dozen,* and *Eight Jelly Rolls* as "a masterpiece of Americana."

Before the *Nine Sinatra Songs* had seen its first New York performances, Tharp imported five of the songs to a reconditioned *Sinatra Suite.* This version, for one couple alone, went into American Ballet Theater's repertory in December 1983, and had its PBS premiere on the video collection *Baryshnikov by Tharp* in October 1984. The *Suite* preserved and even strengthened the romantic tone of the *Nine,* with the gorgeous Elaine Kudo partnered by the danseur who was every woman's heartthrob. For the video, the songs were given a Hollywood frame: a cocktail party is in progress, Baryshnikov and Kudo lock eyes across the room, and exit through a garden trellis to begin the dance.

Again the songs track the progress of an affair, and the choreography is drawn closely from the *Nine Songs.* Spread over seven couples, the dances were like variations on a theme of love. As danced by only one couple, the theme becomes more of a story. Camera close-ups draw attention to their mutual attraction and gradual divergence. When Kudo walks out, Baryshnikov dances his pain and disbelief to "One for My Baby." After Tharp's two earlier settings of the song, this solo for the first time brings to mind a much angrier dance, Fred Astaire's barroom breakdown in the 1943 movie *The Sky's the Limit.* "One for My Baby" was written for Astaire by Harold Arlen and Johnny Mercer. Distraught over his decision to jilt Joan Leslie for her own good (he's an air force hero on furlough from the war), Astaire drowns his sorrows, then smashes up the bar. Baryshnikov works up a series of ever more anguished pirouettes but eventually becomes resigned to his disappointment and leaves the party.

In one or the other of these two versions, the *Sinatra* dances became a perennial gala attraction. Baryshnikov and Kudo did the *Suite* as a tribute when Frank Sinatra received the Kennedy Center Honors in 1983. The *Nine* were performed in the East Room of the White House at a state dinner given by President Ronald Reagan for the Grand Duke of Luxembourg, in November 1984. Tharp's dancers performed them for a company fundraiser in 1982, at New York's famous Rainbow Room atop Rockefeller Center. The company rented itself out in February 1985 as part of the floor show, at a bash for three hundred guests to celebrate the opening of a high-rise condo development, a "billion dollar section of the European Riviera on Florida's Gold Coast." And Tharp succumbed to the ill-considered notion of dancing the *Suite* herself with Baryshnikov, for the closing-night benefit of the company's Brooklyn Academy season in 1984. Whatever her gifts as a dancer, they did not include playing a glamour girl. Some critics tried to ignore the embarrassing moment. Anna Kisselgoff deplored what she considered a deliberate parody, with Baryshnikov as "a beleaguered straight man grappling with a version of Carol Burnett."

Reviewing a 1982 Tharp Dance performance at Meany Hall in Seattle, critic Laura Shapiro marveled at the close coordination among dancers that made Tharp's pieces work, the intimate and the fractured ones alike. In *Short Stories,* "Suspicion, nothing better, is what sparks the choreography; but the movement remains bound by trust." None of the antisocial action in that dance could have happened "without a perfectly tuned ensemble, and that ensemble is always shaping our vision of the violence." The same performance included *Nine Sinatra Songs* and Tharp's devastating new pursuit of the violence, *Bad Smells.* During this period Tharp was in the grip of dark imaginings. She'd created the ruthless family in *The Catherine Wheel,* but atoned for their cartoonish menace with *The Golden Section.* For the less compassionate and more realistic *Short Stories* she'd depicted a "tribal bloodletting" and a "community of cannibals," according to her own clinical introduction on *Confessions of a Cornermaker.* But the characters in *Bad Smells* weren't even a dysfunctional community; perhaps they were no more than "nature's darker forces." The dancers, dressed in shredded thrift-shop underwear and wearing makeup that looked like smeared mud, had no graces to save them; if anything she boosted their heartlessness into a lurid spectacle.

In her autobiography Tharp says she started thinking about ritual sacrifice on a visit to Mexico. She visualizes priests peeling the skin off their victims and then tells how she used this horror for a dance, to work off her anger over her breakup with David Byrne. Tharp may have made the antithetical *Sinatra* and *Bad Smells* as therapy, but the self-expressive implications in both dances took second place to grander theatrical visions—in the case of *Bad Smells,* pitiless ones. Tharp says *Bad Smells* was conceived through the violent and disorienting point of view of the television camera. By the time it aired on ARTS Cable as part of the *Tharp Scrapbook* tape, in October 1982, a stage version was touring the West Coast with *Nine Sinatra Songs.*

Tharp never did things in moderation. She was capable of pushing her ideas over the brink after they'd reached perfection. Starting out as a "stark, austere minimalist . . . resentful of physicality," wrote the critic Roger Copeland in a 1982 *New York Times* Sunday piece about women and modern dance, she worked her way to a "lush, virtuosic physicality," and many other postmodern choreographers followed. "Apparently," thought Copeland, "after proving that dance could be unmistakably brainy, it then became ideologically acceptable to be 'beautiful' as well." Reviewing a Washington performance the same week, critic George Jackson called *Baker's Dozen* "a caprice for beautiful people." But after *Baker's Dozen*, what was beautiful ripened into the artificial glamour of a Hollywood escapade, in *Sinatra*. Similarly, once she broached the subject of misogyny in *When We Were Very Young*, she dug into that pit until she scraped bottom.

There was more than ritual torture in the background of *Bad Smells*. Tharp still wanted to deliver large-scale dance to a large-scale audience. The problem was how to magnify the dancers without losing the effect of their immediate presence. Film could do it, especially in close-up, as she'd already demonstrated. But filmed dance wasn't live dance, no matter how compelling you could make it. Putting the two together would risk reducing the live dancers to Lilliputian scale. She had used big effects on stages before with the graffiti writers in *Deuce Coupe* and the film-scaled scenics in *The Catherine Wheel*. She was thrilled with spectacles, like the enormous but fictional peace demonstration in the movie *Hair*, where thousands of extras had been rounded up to see her dances and a rock concert on the Washington Mall. Now, in late 1981, she was thinking about how rock concerts could be amplified to reach an almost unlimited audience, and about how rock's intense noise levels could release flamboyant and possibly lawless behavior in both performers and spectators. Around this time, live video came into use at concerts and large sports events, where the audience was too far away to see the faces and action details routinely captured on the home television screen. Tharp's plan to add a video component to *Baker's Dozen* was derailed only because she was ahead of the technology in 1979.

She commissioned one of the loudest avant-gardists of the day, Glenn Branca, to write a score for *Bad Smells*. Branca, whose concerts of massed electric guitars had been called "sonic onslaughts," wanted his music to induce a kind of mystical ecstasy. He told John Rockwell: "I always think of my own music as absolutely pure and beautiful. Sometimes it sounds distorted and disgusting, but the *idea* is for it to be beautiful."

Another important film dance, Merce Cunningham's 1979 *Locale*, preceded *Bad Smells*. *Locale* had been made for—and with—the handheld camera of Charles Atlas. At a time when film was thought of as a poor substitute for live dancing, Cunningham took a chance and programmed a film evening during his company's 1980 New York season at City Center. *Locale* was screened together with *Roamin' I*, a small documentary about *Locale* in the making. Projected in the theater, *Locale* was disorienting, a shocker. Cunningham and Atlas used a choreographed moving camera that shot the dancers from different angles, traveled among them, changed focal distances and speeds. The continuity was further disrupted with jump cuts and editing devices. *Locale* couldn't have been shown as a live dance, and Cunningham reworked it for the stage.

Bad Smells also began as a film project, with Tom Rawe wielding the camera. Three takes of the dance were superimposed and edited. "Finally no one liked it," Rawe told Minneapolis critic Mike Steele. "So maybe it was inevitable from the beginning that it would go back to being a stage work instead." In the stage version Tharp took the camera's ability to reconfigure live dance a notch further by superimposing one on the other; in fact, she put the whole process on display at once. Anticipating the motion-capture techniques of the early 2000s, she longed for a camera that would "blossom and make abstract shapes from things." She would have liked an overhead computerized camera to photograph the dance from the grid, but such a thing hadn't been invented yet either, so Tom Rawe shot the dance as it was being performed. The live video was projected simultaneously on a huge onstage screen.

Rawe's moves were as carefully choreographed and rehearsed as the organized frenzy of the dancers. Usually moving downstage of them with his back to the audience, he sliced his camera up and down their bodies and probed into their faces. The dance, seen alone in studio showings and archival tapes, was obsessive, robotic, a hellish bout of jogging and calisthenics and dance warm-ups. Branca's deafening guitars whanged and crashed, detonating sour tone clusters and pile-driver thuds. Tharp had given the dancers morbid images to work with. They chanted "Me, Me, Me, Me, Me!" and she told Barbara Hoon to imagine "dog carcasses and three-legged horses in the doorway," according to an observer of rehearsals. For one lift, where a man circled with a woman gripped horizontally in his arms, she wanted them to think of helicopter blades slicing close to the ground. There were hideous seductive gestures and halfhearted vaudeville turns, and a woman slowly somersaulting over men's rolling bodies. Mary Ann Kellogg, the victim in Part I of *Short Stories*, was once again beset and, at the end, she was throttled or murdered by Raymond Kurshals.

Despite their apparent similarities of approach, *Locale* and *Bad Smells* were very different in effect. In his anthology devoted to Merce Cunningham, Richard Kostelanetz has noted that Atlas's camera in *Locale* stands in for the audience, making it possible for the viewer to move around and look at the dance from many vantage points. Rawe's camera isn't at all detached or objective. As another moving body, Rawe becomes part of the choreography, and the camera itself enters into the dance. Stretching and tilting, bleaching and blurring the dancers' bodies, veering from amputated limbs to spasmodic laughing faces, raking over them in myopic close-ups, it creates a new dance. Like an X-ray it seems to be trying to get under the skin of the dancers, probing for their poisoned alter egos. Terrible as the dance is, the video shows us one that's even more terrible.

Cunningham's companion documentary, *Roamin' I*, revealed the complicated mechanics of *Locale*: the cameras with their cranes and dollies, the tangles of cable and the helpers who whisk the cable out of the camera's path, the dancers scurrying to get into position for the next shot. Tharp had given viewers a look at this dance of the techies in the public taping sessions for *Country Dances* (1976). *Bad Smells* was something else. The ten-minute *Scrapbook* version includes only the video footage, but the stage version, one-third longer, was a total production with three elements that could not be disentangled once they were assembled. Most viewers in the theater felt split between the dance and the video looming above it, but synthesis did occur later on, in the form of metaphor.

Bad Smells was like a news documentary, with Tom Rawe as the intermediary, the facilitator, the one who slants the news to favor his own point of view. It graphically demonstrated the dehumanizing effects of mass media. Arlene Croce thought the stage production less effective than the dance alone: "On the stage, it becomes a chunk of curiously deflected raw sensation. It's all about itself—about things of horror and how the reporting of these things keeps us from experiencing them." Burt Supree of *The Village Voice* didn't share the audience's enthusiasm for it at an early performance, but he saw enough "political, totalitarian, post-nuke resonance" to justify the feelings Tharp was exploiting. He thought such protracted violence and compression of emotions went past credibility, though. In real life they were "never so relentless, so frozen, except perhaps in some psychotic frenzy."

When the dance played New York in the 1984 BAM season, Anna Kisselgoff hit on another probable source for the production when she likened it to "clubs in which disco dancers are simultaneously reproduced on a large screen by a television camera." Mistaking Tharp's deadly design, she saw the piece as "an unintentional comic takeoff." Laura Shapiro accepted the pairing of *Bad Smells* ("deliberately repulsive") with *Nine Sinatra Songs* ("deliberately luscious"), and Tharp herself thought they made a balance between politesse and amorality. Shapiro welcomed the choreographer's radical resistance to pigeonholing. *Bad Smells* was "a dance that spans the imagery of savage chaos from primitive to punk, a dance that reduces anything human to puniness in comparison with the vivid, hungry screen, a dance that instantly, and easily, overwhelms both dancers and audience, a dance that hurts to watch."

Perhaps *Bad Smells* was Tharp's attempted exorcism of the marauding bag ladies and listless stagehands who'd haunted her Winter Garden performances, but she hadn't achieved catharsis yet. *Fait Accompli*, the company piece that immediately followed, was a dance of death, a dance about facing the onset of menopause and the end of her performing career. Tharp hadn't been dancing consistently for a couple of years; now she got herself back into shape by taking boxing lessons and a private ballet class with Rebecca Wright. She was in a fighting mood. She intended to be the first person to deal onstage with "the physical, factual entity of a dying body." She relished telling interviewers about her studies of "concentration camps, life after death, war, bombing, airplanes going down and flight recorder boxes." The dance was to be about "what the implications of dying are, and how people see fit to protect themselves," as she told dance writer Eric Taub. She also spoke about totems, and the power of the supernatural to fend off evil forces. She, in fact, was to symbolize that resistance: "The last part of the piece is a single figure against an overpowering mass . . . which can't be held back."

Fait Accompli was one of the few dances Tharp referred to publicly in such metaphorical terms. The dance itself, premiered in Austin, Texas, in November 1983, turned out to be the largest, most severely formal work she'd ever made: forty minutes of highly structured dancing for seventeen people. It didn't hold this record for long; a month after its first performances, the jumbo-sized *Bach Partita* made its debut with American Ballet Theater. In the

long run *Fait Accompli* was overshadowed by the dance it directly anticipated, *In the Upper Room*, but it was actually a more interesting work, more
unified in style and more original in concept. Admittedly reflective of
Tharp's state of mind, it gave her a platform for a late hurrah, and it earned
wild audience approval as a star turn and a company gut-buster.

The first part of the dance is another of Tharp's quartet inventions. The
dancers wore identical black tank suits, athletic socks, and sneakers. Santo
Loquasto, following Tharp's fetishistic indications, originally had wrapped
them from head to foot like mummies. She may also have had a metaphor
for birth in mind, perhaps thinking of Balanchine's Apollo being unwrapped
from swaddling cloths. This symbolic opening scene had been deleted from
the New York City Ballet production of the ballet, to intense controversy,
when it was revived for Mikhail Baryshnikov in 1979. Tharp abandoned the
idea when it proved unworkable. They also tried the dance on a Mylar
floor, which had worked for the videotape version of *Bad Smells*, but it was
discarded as too slippery and dangerous.

One by one the groups of four enter in formation. With an almost math-
ematical dexterity, Tharp brings them in and out, works them in squares and
lines, adds in new units, reorganizes the units, sets up counterpoint patterns
and canons. The aggregate pattern goes from two to sixteen dancers. Every
dancer works in tandem with at least one other dancer and every subunit is
always related spatially and rhythmically to every other unit on the stage.
On paper this sounds stupefyingly compulsive, but on the stage the patterns
evolved from one engaging design to another as the solid cadres regrouped.
Big ranks crisscrossed, creating strange effects like a camera going in and out
of focus. Tharp set a seemingly rigid but inventive vocabulary of calisthenics; fighters' sparring and feinting moves; large stiff-armed and stiff-legged
gestures; precipitous jetés, spins, and extensions; recuperative flop-overs,
stretches, and heaving breaths. The dancers were in constant motion, glued
to David Van Tieghem's propulsive techno-disco score, but varying the beat
by doubling, suspending, and syncopating their relation to it.

The movement was unforgiving. Tom Rawe remembers he would knot
his stomach at the beginning and stay clenched, just to be able to get
through it. The company worked on it in the attic studio at Brooklyn Academy during hot summer days, with the doors and windows closed, the
dancers sweating and dehydrated. Mary Ann Kellogg thought Tharp
wanted to push them to the point of exhaustion, but somehow, performing
the piece, a mysterious bonding took place. "What you were feeling inside,

that kind of total excitement and drive and push, that the audience was also getting that. . . . In a way I felt that we weren't so much dancing it for you all out there in the house as that we were dancing it for each other. . . . Being on that stage with those incredible dancers and working with each other and feeling each other and the physicality, it was orgasmic."

Jennifer Tipton supplied a fabulous environment for the dance, after Tharp complained one day that theaters weren't designed for upstage entrances and exits, only side ones. Remembering an effect created by lighting designer Jules Fisher in the Bob Fosse show *Pippin*, Tipton adapted the idea of a "curtain of light," using banks of stadium lights beamed down from behind the dancers and onto a manufactured fog, to create such a bright forestage that the background would vanish. When the dancers made upstage appearances and withdrawals, they seemed to materialize out of nowhere and then evaporate again. Tipton created the same fog-and-light-beam effects later in *In the Upper Room*, using the more economical, standard lighting instruments instead of 144 overhead PARs.

After twenty-five minutes, the whole dance shifted, from a formal group structure to an expressive, personal narrative. Tharp appeared and danced out the struggle of a lifetime. Lit by a follow spot, she summoned up the men in the company for another, more concise edition of her "phases of love" duets, while the rest crossed in the dark with faltering steps, like prospective or rejected partners. Tharp was lifted and tossed over shifting clusters of men as the light faded in and out, a star—idolized but controlled by others. She did a tight, internally focused solo dotted with trademark moves from some of her earlier dances. Then the group reprised its biggest counterpoint pattern in the brightest lights, and retreated into limbo.

Tharp faced the audience for a moment, shuddering, then turned upstage just as a row of footlights at the back flared into the eyes of the audience. With a skater's deep, lunging glide—only checked by the traction of the floor—she dissolved into the blaze as the curtain came down. Interpretations varied as to whether this symbolized Tharp's retirement from dancing or her determination to keep it up. When *Fait Accompli* entered the repertory of Hubbard Street Dance Chicago in the '90s, the whole second part of the dance was dropped, perhaps for practical reasons. Or perhaps this was one role Tharp couldn't transfer to another dancer.

Reviewing *Fait Accompli* when it premiered at BAM in early 1984, Anna Kisselgoff inferred a theme linked to some half-intelligible words in David Van Tieghem's score—an announcer reporting the recent shooting down of a Korean airliner by a Soviet plane. Neither Tharp nor Van Tieghem intended any such narrow Cold-War reference; the score's intermittent voice-overs suggested many other tense, threatening situations. Kisselgoff's interpretation cast a pall over what she acknowledged was an otherwise fine piece: "And so the end of one dancer's career is equated with the shooting down of nearly 400 civilians in an airliner. Somebody's scale of moral values is off here." Croce, who appreciated Tharp's elegant handling of the groups in Part I, thought the spectacular production was bigger than its meaning: "The fiery Wagnerian beauty of it all is so impressive that we may lose sight of how little is actually being said in the choreography or else attribute a sacerdotal meaning to its extreme asceticism."

But for theater critic James Leverett, reflecting on a dismal New York season of playgoing, *Fait Accompli* was a triumph of dance and theater, "a retrospective so energetic and incisive that it contains the future as well." Leverett discussed the physical, social, and metaphorical meanings of *Fait Accompli*, ventured that "merely by sharing the planet with Tipton and Loquasto, we live in a golden age of stage design," and interpreted the ending as an unmistakable image of "the ageless metaphorical bond between the stage and the world, theatre and life."

If *Fait Accompli* was a logical development in Tharp's stream of creative thought, it can also be seen as a pivot into a new direction. The layouts and floor patterns, the group-versus-soloist hierarchy, and the stage scoured of any clutter or peripheral information, all suggested a more balletic emphasis. *Fait Accompli* staged a Tharp company the audience had never seen before. In her previous dances, even the "abstract" ones, there was always a sense of individuals working together, often in physical or eye contact. If necessary they sacrificed visual clarity for the pleasure of their game. In *Fait Accompli* they forged designs through their adherence to the beat, their obedience to the lineup, and the uncanny ensemble radar they had developed, but there was no sign of the individual imprinting so customary in the Tharp canon. The performing style resembled the style of the first *One Hundreds*, flat, expository, and depersonalized. The movement was tough and relentless; they seemed to be doing it only to prove they could do it. But that, in a way, added to its theatrical power.

Tharp's popular success rested largely on the character and social-dance pieces, and in the '80s on her spectacular stagings. She wanted this success and she deliberately went after it. But at the core of all her dance, always, was structure and the act of dancing. *Fait Accompli*, with its expressionistic lighting effects, formal group section, and quasi-narrative conclusion, fused the two tendencies. Tharp thought of herself as a classicist, but whenever she trespassed on classical territory, she was accused of parody or viewed with distrust by some observers. "The ballet is something we all depend on," she told an interviewer for *Dance Magazine* around this time. ". . . we *use* the ballet, we don't *present* the ballet." But she was penetrating the ballet world in a big way, *her* way, and few other choreographers could equal her resources for crossing over.

In the early '80s Tharp fed the repertory from time to time with small, demanding, but disposable quasi-ballets that could be done by the chamber-sized red or blue company. Richard Colton calls them "ballet being done with interesting counterpoint and interesting textures and layers and behavior." *Third Suite*, set to the most familiar of J. S. Bach's orchestral pieces, was made at Osgood Hill in 1980. An informal showing after the residency constituted what was probably the only complete American performance. The dance made its debut at the Théâtre du Champs-Elysées in Paris in October. It didn't fare well there. For four couples, it was a fabulous but possibly overchallenging application of technique. The live orchestra proved a liability. According to Shelley Freydont the conductors' tempi were unreliable, and Tharp pulled the piece midseason. On the archival performance video that exists, the score is played at breakneck speed and the dancers hurl themselves into it quite recklessly.

The dance begins with a catalogue of subverted ballet moves: tilted balances, heel walks, upside-down supported arabesques, women flying into the men's arms, where they're less likely to open into beautiful extensions than to crumple into a ball or drop like a sandbag. These moves are threaded into a continuous spool of action. In a small duet interlude, Uchida and Whitener alternate spinning phrases, Whitener whips off immaculate pirouettes and air turns, and Uchida does ballerina steps on half-toe. When the group reenters—too quickly for the audience to applaud—the music's original fast tempo seems almost languid. After the slow, measured second-movement duet, the music suggests expansive leg swings and jumps, and dotted-rhythm chassés, skips, and hops. The whole dance takes on this buoyant idea, with jazzy dips and the partners lilting side by side like skaters.

What's noticeable even on this ghostly performance tape is how strong the dancers are technically. *Third Suite* featured fast, exacting legwork for men and women—turns, batterie, step combinations, everything except pointe work. But their technical abilities, subsumed into the articulate flow of movement, hardly looked exceptional. Few people appreciated the inventiveness with which Tharp utilized the ballet training she'd always prescribed for herself and her dancers. After the early modern dancers' severe disconnection from ballet, the generation of choreographers emerging from postmodern austerity in the 1980s were finding new fluency through increased technique training. But no other modern dancers at the time had so confidently absorbed the ballet vocabulary and embraced its musical environment.

Soon after the residency at Osgood Hill, Christine Uchida and William Whitener's *Third Suite* duet, to Bach's Air for G String, was taped for *Confessions of a Cornermaker*. As a stand-alone piece it remained for several years in repertory as the *Bach Duet*, a showpiece for these two superb Tharpians who'd started life in the Joffrey Ballet. Whitener's elegant line, his seemingly effortless turns and beats, Uchida's daring allegro and stop-on-a-dime balances, and the musical flexibility they shared, transformed the classical adagio into a suspenseful dialogue, an exploration of the ways two people, not necessarily lovers, could come together and go apart. In each of a dozen or so meetings, conventional lifts, poses, and promenades became reconfigured, gender roles got traded. The approaches and retreats were made on "everyday" walking, hurrying, or delaying steps, and created an exquisitely personal frame for the dance interactions. Without "acting" tenderness, disaffection, appeal, hesitancy, or decision, the dancers told a story that ended with an embrace and a farewell.

Tharp drastically reshaped the idea of a pas de deux here, from a series of self-important gestures to a conversational, almost casual relationship between people who might pass each other on the street every day. When she filmed it for television, she tried an alternative to zooming in and out, the usual way of keeping both dancers in the frame. As they separate and move closer, the screen splits, with one camera on each of them, then knits back together. You see what Uchida and Whitener are doing, but you lose the dance's continuity and its story, which lay in the distances between them.

Through archival videotapes it's possible to see both Bach duets Tharp did for the company, the *Third Suite* duet, in what was probably a Paris performance, and the first *Bach Duet*, danced by Rose Marie Wright and Ken Rinker outdoors at the Delacorte Theater on 7 September 1974. A lot had happened in six years. Alongside Uchida and Whitener's suave, balletic colloquy—only a shade less romantic than Baryshnikov and Kudo in *Sinatra*

Suite—fusion pioneers Wright and Rinker look spiky, a bit awkward, but easygoing. They seem younger, less comfortably attuned to each other. Their vocabulary of pivots, châiné turns, slow lunges, extensions, and swings gets disrupted by pedestrian punches, shrugs, pushes, and shoves, and arms that churn almost of their own volition. The issue between them seems to be one of dominance. Through games of leader-follower, woman-man, big person–small person, they lightly dance out a real situation in the company's history. Wright, the teacher and coach, is patient and affection-ate; Rinker, once the new kid in the group and the first man to join Tharp's enterprise, stifles his resistance and lets her show him the way.

At the beginning Rinker spits on the floor, then rubs his shoe in the spot for traction. This behind-the-scenes business caused nervous laughter when it recurred later as a dance gesture. Rinker's two-fisted temper fits and de-fensive flat-of-the-hand moves—the kind of irreverence Tharp was soon to interpolate with such success for Baryshnikov—also took the audience by surprise. The fact that this *Bach Duet* was set to a prayer probably added to the indignation of Tharp's critics. By the 1980 *Bach* she had suppressed her need to épater le bourgeois and the audience had gotten used to her free-wheeling mixture of refinement and coarseness.

Telemann made its appearance early in 1984 during the Brooklyn Acad-emy season that brought *Bad Smells*, *Fait Accompli*, *Nine Sinatra Songs*, and sev-eral older works to New York. It was very accomplished, maybe too skillful to be persuasive, as Arlene Croce believed. It starts out "a perfectly charm-ing, diverting little piece and ends up a mad game of Ping-Pong between Tharp's baroque sensibility and Telemann's." A serviceable program opener for the next year of touring, it was always overlooked in favor of the more dazzling items in the repertory. With three only slightly misbehaving cou-ples dancing to an unexceptional score, *Telemann* was an exercise in symme-try and academic variations. Revisited twenty years later it's one of the few things Tharp ever made that could be called bland.

Another little ballet for the company from that period, *Sorrow Floats*, re-volved around a solitary male character and quickly disappeared in the wake of its distant cousin, *The Little Ballet* (1983). *Sorrow Floats* premiered at the Amer-ican Dance Festival in July of 1984. Tharp had received one of four handsome commissions ($40,000) the festival made that summer for new work. She didn't exactly blow off the commission, but she was probably cruising on overload, even for her. She'd spent the spring on her important collaboration with Jerome Robbins for New York City Ballet, *Brahms/Handel*, taped the three ballets on *Baryshnikov by Tharp* with ABT in Toronto, and was in the last stages of postproduction for *Amadeus*. She had four ballets up and running at ABT. Around this time she also choreographed *The Hollywood Kiss*, then discarded it unperformed (she retrieved some of the material later on for *In the Upper Room*). Work on the movie *White Nights* was beginning in the summer. The Tharp company was coming off three months of touring. Besides the American Dance Festival, their summer schedule included a teaching residency in Lake Placid, New York, and a bonus two-week run of *Nine Sinatra Songs* and *Fait Accompli* at the Gershwin Theater on Broadway. At the ADF Tharp was not only premiering *Sorrow Floats*, which had previewed in June on a tour to Germany, she was back dancing her old role in *Eight Jelly Rolls*.

Sorrow Floats did give the impression of a sketch. John Carrafa played a Pierrot-like character, with Shelley Washington, Jennifer Way, and Katie Glasner as figments of his drooping imagination. Tharp had wanted to make a piece for Carrafa and according to local critic Linda Belans, "the success of *Sorrow Floats* depends heavily on Carrafa's gift for mime." The dance's title echoes a motif in John Irving's 1981 novel *The Hotel New Hampshire*. Disaster after disaster plagues the characters, but they keep reassuring themselves that as sorrow keeps floating to the surface, so does love.

The dance sustained a couple of mishaps at its premiere. Before the end, something in the sound system malfunctioned and the music (Georges Bizet's *Jeux d'Enfants*) abruptly ceased. Carrafa improvised to cover, until the curtain came down. Over the audience's loyal cheering everyone could hear boos from the balcony. It was Mark Morris, in residence at the festival for a Young Choreographers and Composers conference. Morris, then enjoying a reputation as the Bad Boy of modern dance, followed up his outburst at the end of the evening, yelling "No more rape!" after *Nine Sinatra Songs*. Morris apparently was reacting to the rough handling Shelley Freydont received from Tom Rawe in "That's Life." *Sorrow Floats* ran in its entirety at two subsequent Festival performances, but the dance was too insubstantial to last much longer. Tharp had persuaded American Dance Festival director Charles Reinhart not to videotape *Sorrow Floats*. Looking for a record of it ten years later, she was disappointed to learn he'd carried out her wishes.

First titled *Once Upon a Time*, *The Little Ballet* also focused on a dreamer and his muses and, like the Carrafa piece, it had a score from a chapter of musical literature Tharp had skimmed over. The waltzes by Alexander Glazunov were suggested by Baryshnikov. Tharp probably found the music congenial because it resonated with George Balanchine's multiple stagings of

Glazunov's *Raymonda*. Tharp started choreographing it late in 1981 as a duet. Three coryphées were added later for amplitude, but it ended up only a twelve-minute piece anyway. Where *Sorrow Floats* had featured the expressive acting of John Carrafa, *The Little Ballet* centered on Baryshnikov's pliability, his seemingly effortless technique, and what Dale Harris called the "vulnerability and introspectiveness behind the confidence and bravura." Baryshnikov describes it as a "nostalgia piece" about the elements of Russian classicism as seen by modern man. Young Dierdre Carberry and three other ballet women, possibly imaginary, drift in and out, wearing filmy, flowery-colored dresses of indeterminate period. He wears pants and a shirt, collar unbuttoned, sleeves rolled up, a tie casually knotted. He molds and propels Carberry as if she's just a thought. Alone, he seems wistful but never at a loss for dance ideas.

Arlene Croce contrasted Baryshnikov's persona with the one Tharp made for him in *Push Comes to Shove*. Tharp had been subtly revising *Push* ever since its premiere, with some fairly significant adaptations for the TV version. By 1983 Baryshnikov was head of ABT, not a curious interloper, and she reworked the last movement to emphasize his new relationship to the ensemble. He had adjusted his dancing too, Croce thought. "The changing imperatives . . . no longer find Baryshnikov pretending to be at their mercy. He now meets the tactical switches Tharp has devised with a nonchalance that is twice as funny as his former bafflement." In *The Little Ballet*, "he's a reflective figure steeped in the tradition of Russian ballet, pursuing its chimerical sylphs down one hopeful path after another."

Dale Harris pictured the ballet as "a succession of memorable dance images in which a thousand meanings are contained." To critic Laura Jacobs it not only evoked iconic works from "ballet's collective consciousness" but portrayed Baryshnikov "isolated within his star persona, and within the romantic classics that he's so eager to go beyond but which still reveal him to us in the most potent dosages." With a poet-and-muse pretext that suggested *Apollo*, it's not inconceivable that Tharp also wanted to pay homage to Balanchine, who died on 30 April 1983, a month before the ballet's debut, and to honor Baryshnikov's recent attempt to put himself under Balanchine's tutelage.

10

Three-Way Stretch
1983–1990

Misha Baryshnikov had always been Tharp's strongest advocate at Ballet Theater. Baryshnikov left ABT in 1978 to dance with New York City Ballet, as perhaps the one place in America where he thought Russian ballet had a future. Calling Balanchine "an incredible symbol of uncompromised creative genius," he looked forward to learning new ballets and repertory from the master. It was late for this; a heart attack had impaired Balanchine's health and initiated his long final decline. Baryshnikov learned twenty-two roles at NYCB, but the situation proved less fruitful than he'd hoped. Balanchine coached him in ballets he'd done with ABT, *Apollo* and *Prodigal Son*. He learned other Balanchine ballets, most successfully *Rubies*, but few of the extreme modern works and no new choreography. Baryshnikov found the technique hard on his body—unlike Tharp's more eccentric but less angular style.

At the end of the 1978–79 season Lucia Chase retired from ABT and Baryshnikov was offered the directorship. It was a difficult decision, but he probably realized he wasn't absorbing what he had gone to NYCB for. Robert Garis, an intense observer of the New York City Ballet, felt that, only months after showing an early aptitude for the style, "he looked like someone who had given up on a project that he had been well on the way to mastering." If the dancer had been twenty when he arrived at NYCB,

Garis thought, he might have adjusted more easily. But he was thirty, and he never quite lost his "foreign accent" in the company. He resigned from City Ballet in the middle of the 1979 fall season, and became artistic director of ABT the next year.

It took a couple of years for Baryshnikov to effect his transition from a famous dancing star to company director with authority over the repertory, the personnel, and the ever-endangered budget. Tharp was gradually reinstalled, first with a revival of *Push*, and seven months after *The Little Ballet* (May 1983), *Sinatra Suite*, and *Bach Partita* had their premieres in Washington. The company could now mount all four Tharp ballets on a single program, and this package began appearing on ABT's touring roster early in 1984. Christine Temin of *The Boston Globe* thought the program represented "Tharp's bid to become . . . the first great classical choreographer of the post-Balanchine era." She was good for business, and for company morale. When ABT put on the all-Tharp program at the Metropolitan Opera House in New York, the *Times*'s Jennifer Dunning reported that it "filled the theater with affectionate excitement." Dale Harris remarked that Baryshnikov understood "how desperately his company needs the challenge of Ms. Tharp's uncompromising originality," and after a round of internal dissension and high-level administrative shakeups, rumors were circulating that Baryshnikov might appoint her codirector. He had always hoped to bring about a permanent relationship, but her notoriously high fees were a stumbling block.

Bach Partita was audacious in several ways. Tharp seized the opportunity to employ a large ensemble; the ballet leapfrogged its immediate predecessor *Fait Accompli*, with a total of thirty-six dancers, strictly deployed according to rank—three principal couples, seven demi couples, and a corps of sixteen women. The leading women were Ballet Theater's top ballerinas, Cynthia Gregory, Martine Van Hamel, and Cynthia Harvey (alternating with Magali Messac), partnered by Fernando Bujones, Clark Tippett, and Robert LaFosse. Against this formidable array Tharp had the nerve to set a solo violin, playing the Bach Partita in D Minor, which she'd used in the studio with Baryshnikov years before during the early stages of *Push Comes to Shove*. *Bach Partita* became a shifting play of unequal forces, during which the dancers kept redistributing themselves against the violin's inexhaustible line of melody.

The *Washington Post* dance critic Alan Kriegsman thought *Bach Partita*'s "sheer density of action and intricacy of configuration are as much of a Tharp name tag as if she'd embossed her signature on the dancers' backs."

"The object is to raise allegro dancing to a speed and clarity never seen before," wrote Mindy Aloff of *The Nation*. The press took special notice of the
enlivening effect Tharp had on the company. According to Martha Duffy of
Time, Tharp provided "the role Gregory has waited a career for," and Dale
Harris thought all six principals "dance with new-found enthusiasm—like
people released from a lifetime of drudgery."

Throughout the ballet's twenty-seven minutes, the groups streamed in
and out in surprising combinations, reordering space and augmenting the
music in Balanchinian ways. Playing with scale, she began with just a few
dancers, replacing, adding and subtracting small units in quick but unpredictable relays. This suited the proportions of the music, but gave the stage
space an elasticity, a capacity to expand, shrink, and open out again. She
could then build from close-in focus on a few dancers to larger episodes: the
solo women backed by the sixteen coryphées, a supported adagio for seven
couples. But she avoided the symphonic device of assembling all the
dancers onstage at once, which might have overwhelmed the violin. Magi-
cally, she kept the tone intimate and grand at the same time.

Tharp's movement vocabulary was entirely classical, except that the
dancers were traveling most of the time. The couples resumed the super-
sonic flying double-work she'd been developing with her own dancers in
works like *The Golden Section* and the *Bach Third Suite*. Individual steps—
arabesque, attitude, brushes, leg extensions, and beats—were taken on the
run or en tournant. The landscape reeled with pirouettes and châiné turns.
Both the individual enchaînements and the counterpointed groups elaborated rhythmically on the musical line.

In a long appreciation of Tharp at the end of the '83–'84 dance season,
Arlene Croce called *Bach Partita* "an enormous, whirling, weightless ballet."
Like several other critics, Croce noted what a triumph it was for the Ballet
Theater dancers, as possibly "the hardest ballet [ABT] has ever danced," although she wondered how long the piece could remain in active repertory
without technical erosion. What Croce saw as Tharp's great distinction was
her Baroque sensibility, her talent for "seeing movement in a new light." It
was probably this quality that most invigorated dancers in her ballets. The
difference between dancing Tharp at ABT and at New York City Ballet in
Brahms/Handel, her collaboration with Jerome Robbins, was that her demands
weren't far from what the City Ballet dancers met every day: "In N.Y.C.B.
repertory, certain ballets feed certain other ballets, and the style for such a
piece as *Bach Partita* is in the dancers' bones. In A.B.T. repertory, it's anom-

alous." But neither *Bach Partita* nor *Brahms/Handel* gained a lasting purchase in its respective company.

Tharp and Jerome Robbins were friends of long standing. They'd met in 1973 through Rhoda Grauer, who at that time was working as an assistant on Robbins's "Celebration—The Art of the Pas de Deux" for the Spoleto Festival. Robbins had long wanted to collaborate, according to his biographer Deborah Jowitt. After persuading Tharp to do it, he put the project on New York City Ballet's spring 1984 schedule. The company was going through its own difficult transition, sorting out its power structure after the death of Balanchine. Robbins and Peter Martins had assumed codirectorship, and Lincoln Kirstein, no fan of Tharp's, remained a potent influence. Over the next decade Robbins gradually withdrew and Martins gained control. To date, Tharp has made only one more ballet for the company, in 2000.

Brahms/Handel was a hit, though a challenge for the ensemble, headed by Merrill Ashley, Ib Andersen, Maria Calegari, and Bart Cook, and inevitably short-lived in the NYCB's huge repertory. The collaboration gave Tharp access to a large contingent of twenty-eight excellent classical dancers. Public perception may have cast the choreographers as similar—they both flourished in many genres and applied a contemporary, eclectic sensibility to the stage. Robbins was probably the closest thing to an artistic prototype for Tharp. But their working processes and product were very different. They began the Brahms project schematically. Each of them directed half the group, with costumes color-coded, setting alternate stanzas of the Variations on a Theme of Handel orchestrated by Edmund Rubbra. But as the piece grew, they infiltrated each other's work, interconnecting and splicing material, trading dancers, breaking up and recombining the groups, and making variations on each other's variations. Their compositional process was a bit like a postmodern game with instructions by John Cage.

The ballet turned out to be an exploded version of a theme both collaborators had used before: the amiable competition. In their core behavior, the blue and green teams started out like alien tribes—Robbins's blues with smooth, elongated tendu port de bras, reminiscent of Balanchine's *Theme and Variations*, and Tharp's greens working in tandem to subvert the norms with splayed legs, flexed feet, tipped-over and rocking lifts, and displays of female bravery. As the lexicons collided and combined, references to ballet repertory flashed by, a frame or two of Balanchine, moves from old Robbins and Tharp favorites, hints of ballet classics. The teams intermingled, partners crossed over, neat floor patterns shattered into odd clumps and onslaughts. Women toppled or dove into the arms of moving masses of men. The two principal men did a challenge dance—I'll do this hard thing, see if you can copy it—an idea taken up by the principal women and then by the two couples. The whole ensemble gathered for the first time one stanza before the final fugue, with partners from the opposing side. The teams separated out again for the finale, each doing its own theme on either side of an invisible fence, and then they formed a picturesque traditional lineup behind the principals, who posed with arms linked in a quote from Balanchine's *Four Temperaments*.

Brahms/Handel, with its deliberately dualistic agenda, looked more cluttered than *Bach Partita*, more self-conscious. The color coding invited the audience to track each choreographer's contribution, and underscored the amount of information sharing they'd done. It made the ballet clearer, and perhaps cuter. But what no one disputed was how invigorating it was. Tharp hadn't made a big ballet so exhilarating and funny since *Push Comes to Shove*, and perhaps never did again.

Parenthetically amid this tremendous activity and success, in the spring of 1984 she started thinking about the twentieth anniversary of Tharp Dance, which she dated from her first choreography, *Tank Dive*, in 1965. She hatched a scheme to mount a one-day retrospective in the summer of 1985, spread across the New York venues where the works had first appeared, with buses to take the audience from place to place. *Medley* would be done in Central Park, *Torelli* in Fort Tryon Park, *Dancing in the Streets* at the Metropolitan Museum, *Eight Jelly Rolls* at the Delacorte, *Yancey Dance* and *Re-Moves* at Judson Church. The celebration would wind up with a Broadway show. It would take more dancers than just the Tharp company, and maybe they could use young nonprofessionals for the earliest works. Tharp sent Sara Rudner along with company executive director Steve Dennin to propose this extravaganza to her board of directors. According to Rudner, they weren't willing to take on the financial and logistical burden it would require.

In 1985 the cavalcade skidded to a halt. Over a period of five years Tharp had completed ten dances for her own company, four new ballets, four videos, two movies, two specialty dances, and two makeovers. She produced two big Broadway seasons of repertory, and additional engagements took place at BAM and the Gershwin Theater. The Tharp company was playing to ecstatic audiences on tour. The ballets were such big box office that ABT programmed lucrative all-Tharp evenings. But the Tharp company was beginning to feel the effects of heavy touring. The innovative two-team system and its requisite double-casting made for some resentment over the ownership of roles. Tharp wasn't touring, and the dancers felt a widening separation from a leader increasingly occupied with outside projects. Some even saw a disparity between their dancing and hers when she rejoined them in *Fait Accompli*; she was coming back to the stage in her forties after a layoff, while they were in top form as an ensemble and as individual dancers.

Rose Marie Wright left decisively in 1982, and Tharp struggled to replace her. No one knew the repertory better or could teach it more conscientiously than Wright. Rudner didn't want to take on the responsibility. Rawe and Way helped, and Rebecca Wright went along on some tours as ballet mistress, but these weren't permanent solutions. Setting the repertory pieces on new casts was always hard. As the older company members retired, new divisions appeared in the company. Arriving too late to learn the repertory from the creators, the younger dancers were aware they weren't tapping into the source. The responsibility to approximate original interpretations began to douse the excitement of learning the roles.

Tharp made no secret of how burdensome she found the company's upkeep. In a 1985 interview with Jennifer Dunning she spoke "with despair of maintaining a company in a culture she feels is not receptive to dance." While Steve Dennin struggled to convince her that the nonprofit model was a reasonable way to keep the company going, she still believed commercial enterprise was "not merely compatible with but essential to the survival and progress of art," as she told Joseph Mazo in 1984. And although she hardly lived on a grand scale, she probably saw the celebrity lifestyles and incomes of famous friends like Richard Avedon, Paul Simon, and Woody Allen as indicative not only of success but of social approbation. She thought she and her dancers deserved as much.

At that point the Broadway prize she still hadn't claimed seemed to surface within reach. A successful stage version of the beloved 1952 Gene Kelly movie *Singin' in the Rain* was running in London, produced by the Chicago team of Maurice and Lois Rosenfield and starring the English musical star Tommy Steele. After falling in love with *Nine Sinatra Songs* at BAM in early '84, the Rosenfields approached Tharp about directing and choreographing a New York edition. She went to London to see the show in June, then agreed to do it, provided her company was signed to dance "the lavish production numbers." The dancers' contracts covered the first six months of the show, which was scheduled to open at the Gershwin Theater in June 1985. After that, a hit would ensure their continuing employment. As Tharp saw it, "I would be able to park my company in the show for several seasons, providing not only an alternative to our frantic touring but also, once the show was running smoothly, the opportunity to rehearse new dances during the afternoons." Besides that, a benefit bash planned for opening night was going to wipe out the company's nagging deficit.

Tharp was apparently the only one who had no misgivings about the scheme, but the company and staff threw themselves into making it work. She assured the dancers there would be jobs for them after the show ended, although board member Lewis Lloyd told Bay Area critic Janice Ross just before their last performances, at Zellerbach Auditorium, ". . . this is a time of transition. . . . One of Twyla's great aggravations in life is that a company like hers doesn't run a surplus. In the future she wants to run [it] more like a business." No further touring was booked until January of 1986. During the period of downsizing the company's activities, longtime manager Roddy O'Connor left, along with Steve Dennin. Linda Shelton held the fort as company administrator, with a small office staff. "That worked just fine," says Shelton. "And then once the show opened . . . we were in place ready to go."

Some of the dancers were shocked when Tharp announced the plan; others had long sensed that things were beginning to unravel. They finished up their touring commitments, which stretched until February of '85, with the final runout to Berkeley in April. Those who elected to be in the show began tap and singing lessons. Fearless, they plunged into the new experience. In separate interviews with Nancy Goldner, Washington, and Rawe were excited about working in tap shoes, and all of them relished the idea of being based in New York for a decent period of time. Eleven company dancers were integrated into the show's cast of thirty-two. But a substantial segment of the company fell away. Chris Uchida had been withdrawing, and by 1983, after *Third Suite*, she had essentially left. By the time *Singin' in the Rain* rehearsals got under way, Rudner, Freydont, and Way had all become pregnant, much to Tharp's annoyance. Way stayed on to assist Tharp on the show but the women's portion of the repertory would have to be rebuilt when the company reassembled. So once again Tharp was jackknifing off the high board without much of an idea where she'd surface.

Even Tharp admitted later that *Singin' in the Rain* was a fairly unworkable idea. Not only had she had no experience directing in the legitimate theater, she would be stacking her work up against one of the icons of American cinema. Although the show seemed to release her from the dance company's dependency, it quickly snared her in another trap. In one of the only sanguine statements she released during the ordeal, she told *Playbill* writer Sheryl Flatow that she viewed the show as continuing the legacy of the movie: "It should be a part of our living theatre tradition." Her job was to translate a classic, with its affectionate plot about the early days of movies, into a medium that resisted the very premise of movies.

She decided to re-create some of the original choreography and make completely new settings for other numbers. This plan hurled her into a paradoxical situation. Preserving the original script, songs, and choreography guaranteed a nostalgic audience for the show, but her transposition of Kelly and Stanley Donen's cinematic montages to theatrical shtick invited unflattering comparisons. In her autobiography Tharp argues that the reason she left the original numbers alone and didn't do much new choreography was that the producers held the rights to the show's "original choreographic materials," and she didn't intend to relinquish ownership of her creative property to anyone else. She concocted collages of outrageous elements: eighteenth-century French peasants on roller skates, a tango, a cowboy and a stage horse that did a brush step copied from the police stallions in the movie *Hair*, a tap-dancing cavalier, and a movie-montage number with dancing dolls. If she had an overall concept for staging the movie, it was probably too brainy for Broadway. She was reported to have said she would do the show like a movie, "with the audience as the camera." She told one interviewer that the movie's chorus girls "look like they're trained dancers. In reality, those people had no training. So what you have to do is *untrain* sophisticated and technical dancers—and then get them out of unison." No Broadway critic was going to fall for this.

Besides, however brilliantly she cast it, *Singin' in the Rain* would be competing with the memorable performances of Gene Kelly, Debbie Reynolds, Jean Hagen, and Donald O'Connor. Although some big stars were considered for the Kelly role (John Travolta, Kevin Kline, Treat Williams, all unavailable), she cast Don Correia, a good dancer without a star personality, and relatively obscure actors for the other featured roles. In the few scenes from the show that have been preserved on videotape, the actors adopt a broad, overemphatic style of delivery, roughly equivalent to the hyperexpressive mode of the family in *The Catherine Wheel*.

Tharp's inexperience, plus the indulgence of her theatrically naive producers, made for a fatal combination. She called for extravagant effects and the Rosenfields acceded. The budget escalated alarmingly—topping $5 million by the time the show opened, according to a searing six-page investigation of the "turkey that refuses to lie down" in *New York* magazine three months into the run. The real rain, a must for the title song and dance, necessitated onstage plumbing and a floor with a special drainage system. One number boasted a trolley car and a replica of a classic Bugatti. Tharp ordered a life-size locomotive that never worked. A film sequence was commissioned from top cinematographer Gordon Willis, who'd worked on *Zelig*. By comparison *The Catherine Wheel* was a backyard skit.

The Rosenfields came up with extra financing when things started getting out of hand, but money wasn't the only thing that made for apprehension. Tharp brought in as many trusted collaborators as she could. There were sumptuous sets and costumes by Santo Loquasto and Ann Roth. Jennifer Tipton did the lighting. Shelley Freydont researched social dances of the 1920s. John Carrafa learned tap routines from the movie and taught them to the chorus as dance captain. But she was contemptuous of theater veterans who could have helped. The original screenwriters, Betty Comden and Adolph Green, were dispensed with when they tried to adapt the script instead of preserving the movie's scenario verbatim. Like many subsequent critics, they felt Tharp hadn't really reconceived the movie as a stage show. Two more writers worked on the show after they decamped, and were fired in turn.

Discontents sprang up all around, mostly due to Tharp's inability to establish authoritative command and her refusal to compromise. She was out of her depth. Supplying physical cues and imagery might work with her dancers, but the actors needed specific direction she didn't know how to give. As things started going wrong she clammed up and left them to work things out for themselves. Tharp's theater chums Mike Nichols, Harold Prince, and Jerome Robbins began showing up at rehearsals. If they gave her advice they weren't credited. Three successive press agents and an acting coach were called to the rescue. After previews began in May it became clear that the show needed serious doctoring. Tharp was never officially replaced but Albert Marre, who had directed *Man of La Mancha*, was hired. He refused directorial credit but he made important changes over Tharp's objections, putting most of the movie reconstructions into Act I, with the spectacular rain scene as a closer. Tharp's production numbers were stuffed anticlimactically into the second act, with almost no plot left to hold them together. The opening was put off twice, from June 13 to the 20th, then to July 2, which downgraded the long-planned Tharp company benefit from a glamorous first-night happening to a preview perk.

The reviews were devastating. The Broadway press didn't welcome this lady intruder from the art stage any more than the actors did. Frank Rich of the *Times*, the kindest of the daily critics, decided "Miss Tharp and company have turned a celestial entertainment into a mild diversion that remains resolutely earthbound." "'Singin' Down the Drain" blared the *Daily News* headline. The Rosenfields were ready to close the show immediately, but they caught the proverbial Broadway spirit. The audience had responded enthusiastically, and—assured by Shirley Herz, the last of the three publicists, that with more time it could be saved—they put up another million dollars. Expenses were shaved, the actors took a cut in pay and ballyhooed the show at the Times Square TKTS booth. They relaxed into their roles and business improved. In the end, *Singin' in the Rain* ran for almost a year, closing on 18 May 1986 after 367 performances and thirty-eight previews. "Call it an honorable mistake," wrote *Newsweek*'s Jack Kroll, almost the only major critic who had anything good to say. "Broadway needs the new blood of an artist like Twyla Tharp, but it needs her own ideas, her own energy, her own sensibility. Why hire Picasso to copy Matisse?"

Shattered, Tharp fled to California. In her autobiography she describes herself as suffering a near breakdown, but she may also have helped finish up work on *White Nights*, which premiered at the end of the year to lukewarm reviews. Eventually she pulled herself together and returned to New York and to choreographing. She started working during the day on new material with the dancers in *Singin' in the Rain*.

Tharp's huge productivity of the early '80s may have been driven partly by an effort to recoup the *Catherine Wheel* deficit, or at least stay abreast of it. *Singin' in the Rain* hadn't been a financial bonanza and she still had money worries. Issuing a call for new dancers in *The Village Voice* during the 1985 startup period, she required a $10 audition fee. She'd heard that orchestras charged a cover fee for people to audition. She paid for rental of the hall and other expenses, after all. Those who survived the audition were to become unpaid apprentices and then presumably join the company, a tryout practice Tharp had been using one way or another with new recruits for years. The dance world never got over this. The audition fee constituted "an unheard of request and a dangerous precedent for struggling young dancers," huffed *Ballet News*. People told the story, greatly inflated and with great disapproval, twenty years later. But Linda Shelton counters that Tharp's tough business practices and high fees raised the standards for the chronically downscale dance field. She had indeed set another precedent. Twenty years later a quarter of the U.S. companies listed in the *Dance Magazine* Auditions Guide were charging an audition fee.

Tharp winnowed out just two dancers from the hundreds of hopefuls who auditioned, Jamie Bishton and Liz Foldi. Bishton had danced with two of his dream choreographers, Bella Lewitzky and Lar Lubovitch, after graduating from Cal Arts in 1984. Tharp was his third ambition. In the callback sessions after the first cattle call, Bishton remembers working in small groups with company dancers on new material that later surfaced in *Bum's Rush*. "I was just in joy because here were these little pods of three people all over the studio, with Twyla choreographing on us. It was like a master class." He thought the audition fee was pretty outrageous, but the chance to work with Tharp, even for a day, was worth it. Tharp never charged for auditions again.

The reconstituted company wasn't officially announced until May of 1986, about the time the show closed, but the group had been gradually coalescing. Amy Spencer and Richard Colton had left *Singin' in the Rain* in December. Spencer joined choreographer Martha Clarke's innovative physical-theater work *Vienna Lusthaus*, and Colton stayed with Tharp. Mary Ann Kellogg had won a small speaking part in the show, and when it closed she set off to explore acting and other kinds of work for a while. Raymond Kurshals also thought it was time to move on, and instead of going back into the company he turned to an acting career. William Whitener passed up the show, returned to the reconstituted company, then left again early in 1988 to transition into a career as a choreographer and ballet company director. Once again Tharp's technical aspirations outdistanced some of the dancers' training and instincts. Katie Glasner thought she wouldn't fit into what she sensed as a more balletic company direction.

When the dust settled, only four of the former company members had returned: Colton, Washington, Whitener, and Carrafa. Tom Rawe was forty and after the show ended he reassessed his career. Performing the same material eight shows a week hadn't been his cup of tea. "I like to develop movement—to work on it together with dancers, to keep it alive, to try it different ways," he told Nancy Goldner just before the new company's debut in Philadelphia. Rawe decided to stop performing but he rejoined Tharp Dance as a teacher and coach. Uchida, Kellogg, Way, Rawe, and Spencer all came back to dance for brief periods during the next few years, but the company balance now shifted. New members Kevin O'Day and Jamie Bishton became key players, and the sixteen-member roster was filled out with ballet-trained young dancers.

Perhaps to celebrate the restart with a financial boost, or perhaps to stage another attack on a lingering deficit, the company threw a big benefit at the downtown discotheque the Palladium in May. For one thousand dollars plus a pricey ticket contribution, patrons could have their picture taken by Richard Avedon. The main event was a preview of the piece Tharp had been working on, with music by Philip Glass. *In the Upper Room* became one of Tharp's biggest hits and was eventually performed by several ballet companies as well as her own ensemble.

In the introduction to a *Dance in America* video of *In the Upper Room* made in 1996, Tharp tells one version of the dance's genesis, as a "secular mass." In her deadly-serious lecturing style she says she'd been using Glass's music in the studio for years and found it perfect for her intentions, the way it was "constantly unwinding from itself, as though scheming endlessly." The dance title came from a Mahalia Jackson gospel hymn that Tharp used while Glass was composing the new score. Jackson's melodic line "modulated relentlessly upwards." It "seemed to climb so high it pushed through the roof," and reminded Tharp of "an empty attic, a place of last resort, where one takes out one's treasures and puts them up for very special public view." This statement is packed with startling personal implications. Tharp seemed to visualize her work spiraling upward, from the idyllic days in the New Berlin attic into the glare of post-Broadway scrutiny, and beyond that to a heavenly reward. *New York Times* critic Jack Anderson supplied a New Testament reference to the Upper Room as the place where Jesus and his disciples experienced the presence of the Holy Spirit. Tharp may well have thought of dancing as an act of spiritual ascendancy, but she'd never been so explicit about it.

However literal or self-referential these clues might be, *In the Upper Room* struck most viewers as either pure composition or pure energy. Christine Uchida, who had married and moved to Vermont, returned to the newly formed company long enough to create one of the two leading roles. Sensing that Tharp would pull her back into a full-time commitment, Uchida left again, only to do the New York premiere in 1987 as a guest artist. "That to me was the ultimate," she says. "I loved that piece. I absolutely adore that piece . . . it didn't really matter if there was anybody out there. It just felt like there was so much involved. Focus and discipline, and really being aware of what was going on. Getting into the movement . . . And just to accomplish that and make it a whole piece."

Conceptually *In the Upper Room* was about contrast: men/women, modern dancers/ballet dancers, the air and the ground, high voices/low voices, foreground/background, all reflected against Glass's layered chord progressions. Two women working in tandem (Shelley Washington was the other original) began the piece with a scan of the Tharp movement lexicon—calisthenics, attitude turns, vaudeville shuffles, circular leg gestures in the air and brushes fore and aft, shoulder shimmies, punches and jabs, high extensions, baseball pitches—set on a jogging pulse (Stompers, the dancers called them), along with five others in sneakers. The twin leaders' movement served as a blueprint for variations and thematic reprises during the rest of the dance. Two women on pointe (they called themselves the Bomb Squad or the Pointers) with their partners, represented the ballet half of the contrast, contributing more and more precarious supported adagio to the mix. One woman floated between sides. The groups shared the vocabulary to some extent, but preserved their stylistic differences.

One persistent question about *In the Upper Room* is why Tharp revisited this aesthetic debate, after she'd resolved it so ingeniously in *Deuce Coupe*, *Push Comes to Shove*, and *Brahms/Handel*. For one thing, she could now do it entirely within her own company. Amy Spencer felt Tharp was trying to prove something by going back to things that had worked so well in *Fait Accompli*: "She *knew* she could make a piece that was gonna totally blow the audience away. And it seemed that she had looked at the elements she had developed and she knew exactly what she was doing. She was going after making a hit."

In the Upper Room had the audience in its grip as soon as the two Stompers emerged from Jennifer Tipton's luminous mist. As the temperature rose, from the slow, meditative opening music through successive intensifications of the vocabulary and the dynamics, the dancers shed layers of designer

Norma Kamali's costumes. Starting in black-and-white striped coveralls, the women went to red tank tops with little flared skirts for the Pointers and red unitards for the Stompers. The sneaker men ended up barechested and the danseurs wore white shirts. The music grew louder; the lights got brighter; the fog swallowed the upstage entrances and exits. Forty minutes later the music slammed to a stop and the two Stompers pulled down their fists triumphantly and jogged backwards into the void. Nancy Goldner described the tremendous effect: "what one imagines pure oxygen to be like—that's how exhilarating the dance is."

During the summer of 1986 the company worked on *Upper Room* and another new ballet, *Ballare*, to Mozart's two-piano sonata K. 448, during a seven-week residency at Skidmore College in Saratoga Springs, New York. They performed there and at the Ravinia Festival, then went off to Europe. By the time the New York public got a look at the company, in a month-long Brooklyn Academy season in February 1987, the new material and the new dancers were broken in. The generous repertory included *Baker's Dozen, Nine Sinatra Songs, The Fugue*, a revival of *As Time Goes By*, and a recondensed *Catherine Wheel*. Critical reaction to *In the Upper Room* and *Ballare* was mixed, and most longtime Tharp watchers took the opportunity to consider the company's new dimensions in terms of her whole career.

By incorporating hard-core ballet into her modern-dance sensibility Tharp had made another breakthrough. This was different from setting her eclectic dances on a ballet company or making fusion pieces for a mixed company with varying degrees of ballet training. Even before this big shift, writer Matthew Gurewitsch had put his finger on a crucial aesthetic question in a *Ballet News* essay. Tharp's determinedly nonhierarchical temperament, and her inclusive montage technique of putting the elements together, he observed, worked against organizing the material into one system, one classical framework. "She cannot assign rank and order. . . . The world as it offers itself to the mind is a jumble." This resulted, Gurewitsch thought, in a "lack of an ethical dimension in her aesthetics." Traditionalists perceived Tharp's dance as transgressive, but though it was physically complicated, spatially trackless and sometimes frenetic, it was never unprincipled. Tharp had inherited a postmodern aversion to value systems. A moralist without the certitude of doctrine, she refused to shape her imagery around given classes or classifications. To gain entry into ballet's most elite ranks she would have had to abandon her unique choreographic voice.

Arlene Croce was open to Tharp's eclecticism but the refinements of clas-

sical style still mattered. In a 1987 roundup of ballet crossovers Croce rejected Lincoln Kirstein's theoretical closure of the academy's doors to all but
the New York City Ballet's insiders. "Might it not be time for another essay,
called 'The Curse of Balanchine,' in which it would be shown how the great
choreographer created twentieth-century ballet and put it off-limits at the
same time?" Although Tharp hadn't yet mastered it, "she could be the first
[modern dancer] to acquire pointe technique and make something new of it."

Tobi Tobias went further in assessing Tharp's use of pointe work. Her
new dancers could go on pointe but they hadn't internalized the transitions
between pointe steps. "Put the performers in pointe shoes, and—instead of
growing lighter, fleeter, their range extended—they become awkward and
ponderous," said Tobias of In the Upper Room. The four-woman, three-man
Ballare, a "ballet blanc," was reminiscent of Balanchine but got Tharp into
"big trouble," wrote Tobias. She didn't mind being jolted when "obstreper-
ous Tharpisms intrude into the atmosphere of elegant decorum" but she felt
the choreographer hadn't worked out a "rhythmic continuity" between the
two idioms." Mindy Aloff assumed Tharp's contrarian pointe effects were
intentional, "to give weight to a dancer's rhythm, as an exclamation interrupting her headlong attack and, perhaps most difficult, as a brake to a
speeding phrase." Echoing Gurewitsch, though, Aloff asserted that "To use
pointe implies that one has certain philosophical positions about grace and
line. . . . Ease, authority, calm, fleetness without urgency," qualities Tharp
had yet to acquire within her own aesthetic.

Anna Kisselgoff was even more harsh about Tharp's new direction in a
Sunday piece entitled "Twyla Tharp and Ballet—An Uneasy Match." The
BAM season had been "the most successful ever in terms of popular appeal
and packed houses. Still this has been a hollow success—a case of an important talent less confident about an artistic imperative than about her ability to widen an audience." Croce saw the same opportunism more
sympathetically. In the Upper Room was crude as a ballet, Croce thought,
"where the points are only a means of advertising the newly constituted
company and what it can do." But that work was undeniably important;
"with it, Tharp reaches a new public and takes out insurance for her experiments in classicism."

Singin' in the Rain had left another coat of distemper on Tharp's grouchy
frame of mind. Around the time of the BAM season she was telling inter-

viewers New York had better shape up and support her or she would leave town. "We feel compelled-slash-obligated-slash-pleased to present the company in New York," she told Janice Berman, "but I'm seriously thinking about making this the last year, because it's just so expensive." With ABT, Eliot Feld, and Alvin Ailey about to take over the rental studio spaces at 890 Broadway, she would have nowhere to rehearse. And then there were the New York critics, who often were intentionally destructive and had "very little real imagination." She wasn't planning a fall season there because she wanted the repertory to be perfectly broken-in and foolproof before taking it to the "product-oriented" New York press. She even offered to move the company to Dallas for part of the year if someone there would come up with $2 million. She was beginning to portray herself as a businesswoman, as if she couldn't afford to get anyone else to lick stamps, do publicity, or fundraise. "It's not an easy job," she told interviewer Lois Draegin just before the BAM season. "But I do it because it's been necessary to ply these other trades in order to dance the way I wanted to, to develop my own platform."

The audience had no problem with Tharp's ambition. Immediately after the BAM season the company embarked on a touring marathon: twelve weeks in American cities in the spring of '87, South America in the summer. There was another summer workshop at Skidmore; then they spent the fall and winter crisscrossing North America from Anchorage to Boston, six weeks in Australia and New Zealand, more American cities, and a trip to Portugal in June 1988. Tharp danced in repertory on the early part of this tour, but stayed home for the Australian segment, much to the sponsors' disappointment.

Skidmore had produced more difficulties. After the South American tour, six dancers left the company. Most of them had been among the new recruits, but John Carrafa also decided to embark on his own choreographing career at that point. Once again almost half the company had to be replaced. Amy Spencer returned, and Elaine Kudo and Gil Boggs left Ballet Theater to join Tharp. Four new dancers were taken in, and the residency focused on learning the repertory. Tharp was doing two hours of weight training before each day's class and rehearsals. She was determined to dance *Sue's Leg* and *Eight Jelly Rolls* again. Jamie Bishton told a local paper that seeing Tharp coming back into the old repertory pieces "that are Twyla—the way she moves" was a phenomenal experience.

A special workshop had been planned for high school and college students, led by Tom Rawe and Jennifer Way, with Rose Marie Wright to help teach. As soon as Wright arrived, she was snatched away to bring back the style of *The Fugue* for the new company dancers; then she was pulled into more and more repertory coaching. Rawe and Way found their workshop arrangements getting shifted around to make room for the company rehearsals. By then their daughter, Hannah, had arrived, and after the planned Australian tour they decided not to go back on the road. Way realized she couldn't work administratively with Tharp, although she danced on and off during the next period and remained a faithful Tharp reconstructor and teacher for years.

Preparations for the Australian tour were complicated, and the result was outwardly a huge success. Tharp Dance was invited to visit several cities in honor of the Australian Bicentennial. The company was handsomely accommodated on the tour and paid well. Tharp received a very generous choreographic commission, with only one stipulation: the commissioned dance had to be set to music of an Australian composer. She knew nothing about Australian music and she started listening to everything she could get her hands on. Linda Shelton hired an assistant to comb through the record stores, while Tharp was working on the new piece. Rather late in the game, she discovered Bruce Smeaton, a well-known composer of Australian motion-picture and television music. Tharp thought Smeaton would know just how to make a score to fit the dance she had under way. Smeaton, on the other hand, knew Tharp's reputation as a groundbreaker and saw the commission as a chance to do some serious experimenting of his own. For once he wouldn't have to score someone else's work. They met once in New York, but their ideas never connected.

A month before the tour's February 2 opening, Tharp was still waiting for the score. She told *The New York Times* the dance material was ready. It had to do with "my frank admiration for the Marx Brothers and for that approach to the dilemmas of life." Smeaton was experimenting with "human voice. Grunts, yawns, gurgles and snorts . . . plus some snatches of unintelligible language," and he wasn't sure if Tharp would like it. When she got it, she found it unusable.

There was no good way out of this situation. Tharp had already spent most of her commission during the months of making the dance and it was too late to rethink. There were internal discussions about giving back the money, but that would probably have meant canceling the whole tour, since all the publicity had been built on Tharp's making a special Bicentennial piece. Finally Linda Shelton suggested there might be some other Tharp material suited to Smeaton's concept. *Assorted Quartets*, already a recycled product, proved adaptable again. Rawe and Way, Colton and Spencer, did most of the work to cut and splice, and to apply portions of Smeaton. The piece was retitled *Four Down Under*. The composer was understandably crushed when he discovered Tharp was only using two of the fourteen movements in his fifty-minute score. But he went to rehearsals in Melbourne and graciously threw a dinner party for the dancers on opening night.

Four Down Under wasn't presented as brand-new. Fudging tactfully, Shelley Washington told an interviewer the piece was "an ideal introduction to Tharp's work. . . . It doesn't have an Australian theme, it's simply the highlights of eight or nine years of work." Washington did identify the source after the Australian tour, when *Four Down Under* was performed briefly on the West Coast. Melbourne critic Neil Jillett described *Four Down Under* as "vigorously gymnastic fun and games accompanied by bursts of silences and part of a score (dabba-dabba-doo vocals and twangings from a Jew's harp, set to a vaguely didgeridoo beat)." As a bonus for the Australians, Tharp premiered the new piece she'd been making under the title *Untitled*, accompanied by a collage of musical selections ranging from Michael Jackson to Spike Jones. Neil Jillett called it "one of Tharp's elegantly devised choreographic grab-bags," incorporating break dancing, a classical solo to Bach by Gil Boggs, hysterical laughing, and blue jokes. Throughout the tour the company was rapturously received. *Nine Sinatra Songs* and *In the Upper Room* were the biggest hits, but *Untitled* got good reviews. A year later it morphed into *Bum's Rush* at American Ballet Theater.

The company threw one of its inimitable benefits midway through the winter-spring tour, at the Silvercup Studios in Queens, on 1 May 1988. The feature of the evening was a Tharp dance choreographed for the company and then taught to the patrons, with a few civilians assigned to each dancer. After rehearsal, the dancers stepped off the floor and let the patrons perform the dance. Longtime Tharp admirer and donor Patsy Tarr remembers having a hard time keeping up with the movement, and at one point grabbing on to Kevin O'Day's belt so she wouldn't get lost. Despite the upbeat celebrations and the months of well-received touring, the future of the company was more problematic than ever. A two-week July workshop in New York was announced, with Rudner, Rose Marie Wright, and Stacy Caddell of the New York City Ballet teaching alongside the company. At the end of June they were just back from performing in Spoleto/Charleston and Portugal when *Newsday* reported that the company had "temporarily disbanded," with the dancers on salaried vacation and no further performances scheduled. Late in the summer the public learned what was in store. As of August 22, Tharp was to become an artistic associate at American Ballet Theater. Mikhail Baryshnikov announced that "core members" of the Tharp company would join ABT with her.

Tharp had revealed the dramatic move to the whole company in a meeting, but instead of offering them a chance to come along, as she'd done in earlier rollovers, she had already decided who would go with her to ABT. "It was a harder moment," says Richard Colton. Tharp then met individually with the dancers; Amy Spencer received a check for several months of salary and returned to Martha Clarke. Rawe and Way had been edging out of the company for a while and took the opportunity to make their exit. The rest of the dancers were recent arrivals and, except for Daniel Sanchez, they were let go. Tharp took up the new post with Sanchez, Bishton, O'Day, Washington, and Colton, as well as ABT crossovers Kudo and Boggs.

Baryshnikov pushed to implement this unusual plan. The dancers were given one-year contracts. It took some intricate negotiating to install them at the highest levels possible without alienating the ABT dancers. Kudo and Boggs resumed their former soloist rankings. Longtime Tharp dancers Colton and Washington also became soloists, along with ballet-trained Kevin O'Day, who'd danced with the Joffrey II before joining Tharp in 1984. Bishton and Sanchez entered at corps de ballet level, since both of them were primarily modern dancers. Tharp's dancers were apprehensive about becoming members of a premier ballet organization, but as usual they relished a new challenge.

Total integration of the two companies didn't quite happen. ABT had a history of embracing but effectively marginalizing elements that didn't assimilate to its classical image. There were Negro and Spanish units in place at the company's inauguration in 1940, for instance, and Agnes de Mille brought in a package of outstanding African-American women for her 1965 ballet *The Four Marys*. The Tharp unit did the Tharp ballets, of course, and found slots in the rest of the repertory. The arrangement was hard for them. They weren't dancing nearly as often as they were accustomed to, but it took constant work to stay in shape for high-powered pieces like *In the Upper Room*. Although they weren't strictly classical dancers, they took character roles in the ballets. Shelley Washington mimed a memorable Madge the Witch in *La Sylphide*. Bishton and O'Day were paired as Sancho Panza and Don Quixote. O'Day danced in Paul Taylor's *Airs*, one of the modern dances Baryshnikov had acquired for ABT. Bishton remembers the sojourn as a wonderful opportunity to get a ballet education. He appeared in all the Agnes de Mille works and enjoyed playing townsmen in the big story ballets. He even danced in the corps of white-tight ballets like *Sleeping Beauty*.

Not all the ABT dancers learned the existing Tharp repertory, but she choreographed some of them into all four of her next new works. *In the Upper Room* and *The Fugue* entered the repertory right away. Then she decided to stage an evening of new ballets that would showcase what she could do with the exemplary dancer resources at her disposal. Baryshnikov gave her carte blanche. The company began phasing in *Everlast, Bum's Rush,* and *Quartet* during its winter tour, and the program made its debut at the Met in June of 1989. The effort cost a fortune and was tepidly received by the New York press. Baryshnikov enlisted his patron, the Howard Gilman Foundation, to cover the reported $575,000 cost of the venture with a loan to the company. The new program was a survey of Tharp styles from ballet to Broadway to bizarre, and the Tharpian suavity that the public loved in *Sinatra* and *The Little Ballet* was missing. *In the Upper Room* brought the evening to a heady climax.

Quartet was set to "G Song" by the important postminimalist composer Terry Riley, who was working in a more meditative vein than the stentorian Glass. The eleven-minute set of continuous variations on a G-minor scale, against a descending four-note basso ostinato, was played by the Kronos Quartet on tape. Tharp's first-cast quartet of dancers comprised ballerinas Cynthia Gregory and Cynthia Harvey partnered by the young classicists Ricardo Bustamante and Guillaume Graffin. *Quartet* made a striking counterpart to the *Upper Room*—compact and almost austere where the Glass was extravagant, quiet rather than aggressive and noisy. Like Jerome Robbins's duet *Afternoon of a Faun*, another small ballet that drew a big stage around itself, it achieved a rare feeling of intimacy. Chance encounters consolidated into brief social exchanges and tiny quadrilles. The dancers sailed through Tharp's transitionless step combinations, jumps, and leaps, completing the step with generous arm gestures that swept across the body or spiraled upward, a bit like Spanish dancing.

Quartet was downplayed by all the critics. Perhaps even Tharp thought of it as a trifle among the flamboyant attractions of the rest of the program.

With *Everlast* she was making another try at a Broadway show, perhaps to atone for *Singin' in the Rain* and cull what she had learned from that bitter experience. During the waning days of her own company she'd audited screenwriting courses at Columbia University's film school, searching for a way of putting a narrative together in dance form. The solution, which she applied again thirteen years later for her first true Broadway hit, *Movin' Out*, was to stitch together a line of existing songs that would convey the emotional tone of the story and leave the dancers unencumbered by dialogue. For *Everlast* they were Jerome Kern songs, familiar and unfamiliar, performed by an onstage trio of singers. Tharp expected that *Everlast*, as a condensed musical, would herald a future full-length popular ballet that would "be a financial godsend for the company several seasons from now."

The plot unfolded through solos and small ensemble dances marked with personal traits and narrative development, just as in a traditional story ballet. At Columbia she'd met film writer James Jones, who supplied a scenario, no flimsier than the average Broadway show or story ballet, and the plot made only enough demand on the audience to see it through forty minutes of dancing. Kevin O'Day played a famous prizefighter hooked into a betrothal of convenience with a financially embarrassed debutante (Susan Jaffe). O'Day's adoring fan (Anne Adair) masquerades as his sparring partner, knocks him out by accident, and is eventually recognized as his true love. The wedding in shambles, Jaffe pairs off with one of her many playboy suitors and everyone joins in a joyous finale.

Tharp slipped in ballet references, without making fun of them as she'd done in *Push Comes to Shove*. Just when Jaffe and O'Day are about to be married, Adair hovers around them and distracts the hero, who runs off after her like James lured by the Sylphide. O'Day discovers the cross-dressing ingenue is a girl when her cap is pulled off and her long hair tumbles down. But for the happy ending she has to exit and come back in a dress, recalling the transformation of the tomboyish heroine in de Mille's *Rodeo*. Once the plot is untangled, the whole ensemble struts downstage in lines, to the song "Who" arranged in march time, a windup worthy of *Stars and Stripes*.

Everlast worked like a show, and like a story ballet. But Tharp's dance style by now had traveled some distance from the casual resilience of her *Baker's Dozen* days. She'd worked up a vocabulary of fighting moves and tough-guy attitudes during her comeback/farewell period around *Fait Accompli*, and along the way the style had lost some of its wittiness. In absorbing pointe work the dancers' bodies had somehow grown more upright and less articulate. This didn't matter in a formal dance like the *Quartet*, or a tough, spectacular marathon like *In the Upper Room*, but it didn't suit the light, rhythmic score for *Everlast*. Arlene Croce analyzed the work in terms of the music. Jerome Kern's songs evoked the Princess shows of the jazz age, but Tharp's treatment lacked their charm.

Bum's Rush had been developing for almost five years. Even before the tryouts on tour in Australia, Tharp had taken up the subject of her family again. Jamie Bishton remembers working on phrases when he first joined the company, with himself and Kevin O'Day as the twins and Liz Foldi as Tharp's sister, Twanette. Tharp was to dance in it then too, and John Guare was on the scene to write the libretto. The sibling story was abandoned, but the material carried over into *Bum's Rush*, and resurfaced again in *Movin' Out*. "It keeps coming back, this autobiographical piece," says Bishton. Rhoda Grauer remembers the dance as "all anger, fighting, being bamboozled. All bum's rush." Tharp and the dancers gave a preview at the Guggenheim Museum as a part of the "Works and Process" series. In all seriousness and amusement, she told a crowd of connoisseurs that the Madhouse Trio (Bishton, O'Day, and Sanchez in place of Foldi) was "exactly what life in my household was like," only more disciplined.

Bum's Rush was a dance about death, about farting in the face of death. The last thing a corpse does, Tharp had learned, is to break wind. For Kudo and Boggs she made a Wind Duet. "With death just around the corner, cruelty doesn't seem so unthinkable." The cruelty she meant was found in burlesque comedy and the nasty games of children. Washington and Colton were hobo-clowns, making funny faces and bopping each other around. Ever since *When We Were Very Young* Washington had developed extreme acting skills, and she had no problem with being grotesque; she threw laughing fits and pushed Colton down while yelling the name John! for as long as she could, then the whole sequence went into retrograde: Nohhhjjj! ABT dancer Sandra Brown appeared on pointe inside a B. F. Goodrich tractor tire. Danny Sanchez did a break dance number and told dirty jokes, which were excised after the Chicago premiere. Colton and Boggs had a leaping duet. The piece was a jumble, a surrealistic cartoon. Croce thought it brought out the Katzenjammer Kid in Tharp. The audience was puzzled but entertained.

☘☘☘

As the 1980s drew to a close, values were shifting in the dance world. Baryshnikov, like Peter Martins at New York City Ballet, had taken on the leadership of a major ballet company from its founders. Reorientation was inevitable but so was resistance to change. Many critics still didn't approve of the way NYCB was evolving, and Martins was on the defensive in the late '80s as he tried to preserve the Balanchine tradition but invigorate the dancers with new choreographic energy. ABT supporters were divided about Baryshnikov's virtual elimination of the star system and his invitations to choreographic outlanders like Mark Morris, Karole Armitage, and David Gordon to do new ballets. He took a lot of criticism for his own big ballets, an expensive *Cinderella*, co-choreographed with Peter Anastos, and a new *Swan Lake*.

After nine years with ABT, Baryshnikov was restless. Now forty, he was moving out of the demanding virtuoso roles. Running a big company, with its associated administrative and fund-raising burdens, was as unappealing to him as it was to Tharp. He began withdrawing from the company's day-to-day operations, acting in a Broadway production of Kafka's *Metamorphosis*, and spending more and more time in Europe. Rumors surfaced that he was considering a post at the Berlin Opera Ballet. In another startling crossover, Mark Morris had moved his modern dance company to the Théâtre de la Monnaie in Brussels in 1988. Baryshnikov found Morris a congenial working partner. He'd made an attractive new piece for ABT, *Drink to Me Only with Thine Eyes*, with a role for Baryshnikov that suited him splendidly. In the fall of '89 Baryshnikov danced in the premiere of Morris's *Wonderland* at the Monnaie, and they soon co-founded the White Oak Dance Project under the patronage of Howard Gilman. White Oak was essentially a continuation of Baryshnikov's summer touring ensembles, oriented to contemporary and postmodern dance rather than ballet.

Right after the all-Tharp program in June 1989, Baryshnikov announced his resignation from ABT. He planned to stay another year, to see the company through its fiftieth anniversary celebrations, but internal conflicts with executive director Jane Hermann grew worse and he left suddenly, on 25 September. Tharp and fellow artistic associate Kenneth MacMillan resigned rather than keep their posts during the search for a new company head. It's pretty clear that Tharp wanted to play a bigger role at ABT than resident choreographer with an in-house stable of dancers. She pictured herself as a mighty Robin Hood of the dance world, a lone individual standing up to the big institutions and entrenched adversaries of true art making. She characterized the three new ballets, in retrospect at least, as calculated to conquer American Ballet Theater's established fiefdoms: "American" (*Everlast*), "Ballet" (*Quartet*), and "Theater" (*Bum's Rush*). She expected the company to appreciate what she was doing for it. Not only did her ballets have cachet, she assured writer Sasha Anawalt in a *New York Times* interview, they were good for the dancers. Still, even before the collapse of the shelter Baryshnikov had provided for her, in April of 1989 she had forebodings. *"Bum's Rush* stands for finality," she told the "Works and Process" audience. "We're all bums at the mercy of the history of death. Being thrown out. Forcible ejection. Abrupt dismissal."

Once she dropped off the company roster, Bishton and O'Day were left with jobs in Ballet Theater and no Tharp company as refuge. Shelley Washington had essentially stopped dancing but she remained as ballet mistress for the Tharp repertory. Her staging of *Nine Sinatra Songs* premiered in early 1990. Richard Colton and Amy Spencer, who had married during *Singin' in the Rain*, accepted an offer to teach and choreograph at Concord Academy in Massachusetts.

For the fiftieth anniversary gala, 14 January 1990, a three-hour marathon of live and filmed excerpts from Ballet Theater's history, Tharp prepared a fast-paced video survey of the eight dances she had made for the company. She also offered excerpts from her newest work, ironically titled *Brief Fling*. As a delightful bonus she made a surprise appearance substituting for the departed Baryshnikov in the last movement of *Push Comes to Shove*. Was she modeling herself as a candidate for the real-life role of artistic director?

Brief Fling began as a straightforward exposition of the building blocks of ballet. To a drumroll, small groups entered one at a time and displayed their goods: ballerina and danseur, corps de ballet, character dancers, and stompers. It was Tharp's mixed gathering again, only here the stompers were the interlopers, "these modern people that were plowing through this ballet world," Jamie Bishton thought. Fashion designer Isaac Mizrahi gave them funky outfits in color-coded imitation tartans. As soon as the introductions ended, the principal couple began a prim little variation to Percy Grainger's *Country Gardens*. From there the ballet went on to explore its own resources, with the groups interweaving and exceeding their own limits. Although it preserved its plotless formality, the ballet worked its way through dramatic and unexpected possibilities, greatly aided by composer Michel Columbier's juxtaposition of Grainger's settings of folk tunes with his own postmodernist rhythms and moods. The whole thing ended with a fugue for each of the group voices and a procession of the clans, entering across the footlights in a slow farandole reminiscent of *Deuce Coupe*.

Tharp has referred to *Brief Fling* with cold pragmatism: "It was a success but it offers no discoveries. Everything happened the way it was supposed to, just as in commercial work, because that's what the company required." But it was a great success with the audience and the critics. Arlene Croce thought it was the hit of New York's spring season and "an exhilarating statement of classicism reëngaged." Tharp had finally bowed to the power of hierarchy by sorting out the ranks in order of technical competencies, Croce thought. She had also made inspired choices of dancers, with the Argentinian prodigy Julio Bocca and the young risk-taker Cheryl Yeager as the principal couple. *Brief Fling* looked random and unpredictable at times, but the groups finally came together "in a vision of vernacular/academic parallelism as persuasive as the last act of 'Raymonda' or—the more evident source of Tharp's inspiration—[Balanchine's] 'Union Jack.'"

When the ballet premiered officially at the Met later that year, Deborah Jowitt noted: "The audience's applause amounted to a mandate to ABT's new directors. I hope they listened well." But Tharp had serious temperamental and artistic differences with Jane Hermann. The budget-minded administrator was going in a conservative direction—Croce thought it looked "as if she would rather appeal to the audience's weaknesses than to the company's strengths." Money was a big issue with Hermann, who later complained to the *Times* that Tharp's ballets could cost the company $100,000, three or four times what other choreographers charged for a work. There was no question that Tharp had enormous talent, energy, productivity, and foresight. She could make successful ballets and inspire dancers. But her brief fling had proven once again that neither she nor her ballets fared well under the severe schedules and harried personnel, the economies and box office pressures, of touring repertory life in America. After getting *Brief Fling* safely launched, she let the licenses on her ballets lapse. She didn't make another work for American Ballet Theater for five years.

II

The Anti-company

1990–1995

The long process of freeing herself from company responsibilities was now complete. It had been five years since Tharp put a hold on the touring and diverted the dancers into *Singin' in the Rain*. While the company was retrograding toward its planned extinction, she made comparatively few in-house dances—*In the Upper Room* and *Ballare*, and the four ABT ballets. In between, she was rehearsing what it would be like to have a different life, as writer, filmmaker, freelance choreographer.

Toward the end of 1985 Tharp asked the writer Laura Shapiro to work with her on an autobiographical book. She had started documenting her career at least twice before, with writers Don McDonagh and Allen Robertson, but neither effort progressed very far. Shapiro, one of Tharp's most devoted fans and an outstanding member of the new generation of dance writers, had been reviewing Tharp's work since the '70s, from Boston, then Seattle. Now based in New York, she had become the dance critic for *Newsweek*, where she also wrote about books, women's issues, and food. She had just finished her first book, *Perfection Salad—Women and Cooking at the Turn of the Century*, a sparkling contribution to cultural history. For the collaboration, Tharp would do a set of interlinear comments on a narrative by Shapiro. They worked closely together and within three years both components of the book were finished. Shapiro doesn't remember if they settled on a title, but as co-authors they held a contract with publisher Henry Holt.

Late in 1988 Tharp circulated the manuscript among some respected associates, among them Jacqueline Onassis, then an editor at Doubleday. Tharp wasn't happy with the editors at Henry Holt and began looking for another publisher. Shapiro isn't sure of the time frame, but Tharp at some point wanted to make their book less journalistic, more of a comprehensive in-depth study. Shapiro felt this ran counter to her own intentions, and Tharp terminated the deal, withdrawing the book from Henry Holt in the process. It seems to have been Onassis who encouraged Tharp to write the whole book herself. She started over from the beginning to write her life singlehanded, from a more personal standpoint. She also came to think of the story as a guidebook for women who aspired to a career in the arts. *Push Comes to Shove* was published in 1992 by Bantam Books, a division of Doubleday.

Shapiro was devastated not to see the original work come to fruition, but she understood Tharp's thinking. "I was writing a portrait of a fabulous artist in midcareer," she says now, "but it wasn't a monument to her genius." Shapiro considered herself a journalist who'd undertaken a shared project, and, with perspective, the cancelation seemed "more like losing a job than losing something I had made myself." In any case, the project had allowed her access to Tharp's rehearsals during the making of *In the Upper Room*, and that had been immensely satisfying. "I had such a crush on her work," she says. She remained friends with Tharp but vowed not to work with her again.

Push Comes to Shove turned out to be a curious but highly readable document, part memoir, part confessional, part psychoanalytic bubble wrap. The story of Tharp's choreographic trajectory is there, festooned with hyperbolic flashbacks and steamy bedroom revelations, encounters with the culturati and accolades for her dancer cohorts. It reads like an extended script for one of her videos—smart, sardonic, outspoken, entertaining, and deadly serious all the way. Margo Jefferson, who reviewed it for *The New York Times Book Review*, thought "it uncannily captures the sensibility of her dances. That teen-age girl with the flashlight [Tharp inspecting the cars at her mother's drive-in], voyeur and analyst, parsing the spectacle and longing to invade it, is the adult choreographer we've come to know so well."

Always attracted to movies and moviemakers, Tharp did a tradeoff in 1987 with Robert Redford, staging some folk dances, uncredited, for his activist film about Latino farm workers struggling against developers, *The Milagro Beanfield War*. In return, Redford lent his name as honorary chair for her company's benefit party on the opening night of their 1987 BAM season. The gossip columnists fussed over whether he would show up—he attended the performance but not the party. During a hiatus in a tour that fall, the company stayed at Redford's Sundance film colony in Utah, rehearsing for a big AIDS benefit concert at the New York State Theater. It looked as if Tharp and Redford might have some larger project in mind, but although she returned to Sundance for a while to work on her book in 1990, nothing materialized. Around that time, Tharp was also auditing classes in screenwriting at Columbia University's film school. She says this study taught her how to tell a story in dance; it may also have helped her plot the autobiography.

Shortly after moving to ABT, with the company rehearsed for *In the Upper Room* and a leg up on her three-part ballet evening, she headed for Paris, where Rudolf Nureyev, then artistic director of the Paris Opera Ballet, had invited her to make a new work. She took Richard Colton along to stage *As Time Goes By* for the French dancers. *Rules of the Game* had its premiere on 18 February 1989, alongside revivals of Léonide Massine's *Les Présages* and Balanchine's *Agon*. Once again Tharp violated the rules of ballet hierarchy by giving featured roles to young dancers as well as étoiles in her cast of four soloists with a four-man, four woman corps. She was particularly taken with Lionel Delanoé, "a young man from the lower ranks of the company," according to Dale Harris, but "a potential star." The project was not without scandal. The prodigious Sylvie Guillem, whom Tharp had made the centerpiece of the ballet, suddenly refused to participate and later left the company to join the Royal Ballet. Tharp said she had to rebuild and recast the work in a week.

Rules of the Game, like *Push Comes to Shove*, poked a little fun at the mores and mannerisms of the host company. Tharp used a Bach violin sonata, augmented with fully orchestrated variations by Michel Columbier. After an opening procession of haughty solos, the ballet proceeded to a Tharpian take on classicism. "Her phrases twist, hiccup and backtrack, bodies move in several different directions and at several speeds at once; serene classicism and utter chaos meet at every moment," wrote the London-based critic Barbara Newman. Anna Kisselgoff thought it was a "serious and fine work" despite its jokey references to the costume and design conventions at the Opéra. Kisselgoff noted perceptively that ". . . despite all her attempts to in-

tegrate herself into the world of classical ballet, Miss Tharp remains an outsider looking in—a modern dancer who does not take the classical idiom for
granted, and who cannot resist examining its parts under a microscope." The
Paris audience adored the ballet, "rhythmically slow-clapping Tharp and cast
through a long series of curtain calls," according to Allen Robertson.

Back in New York, the ABT politics were heating up to a boil. But Tharp
had something else on the fire. During this uneasy sojourn after the demise
of Tharp Dance, there was no vehicle for producing her repertory, other
than those items deemed suitable for ABT. The popular early dances like
Sue's Leg and *The Golden Section* had no current interpreters. Tharp claimed to
have no interest in maintaining the repertory herself, but perhaps she could
cultivate an existing group of dancers to perform her works credibly. That
way, she wouldn't have to support a company but the dances would be seen,
and would be producing income for her and the reconstructors she delegated to oversee them.

By now she had enlisted several dancers to help pass works on and rehearse them: Rose Marie Wright, Jennifer Way, Shelley Washington, and
Richard Colton, as well as the ballet mistresses Rebecca Wright and Susan
Jones. Through Linda Shelton's contacts, Tharp worked out an arrangement
with Hubbard Street Dance Chicago, a medium-size company of excellent
modern dancers specializing in contemporary work. The deal started with a
$300,000 three-year contract for *The Fugue* and *Sue's Leg*. Hubbard Street's
artistic director, Lou Conte, a longtime Tharp fan, became even more admiring as he saw the depth and musicality of the way she worked, and he
thought Tharp's unusually high price was well worth it. Jennifer Way and
Rose Marie Wright rehearsed the company but Tharp made six trips to
Chicago during the summer to initiate the dancers and supervise the process. The dances were shown for the first time in August 1990, at Jacob's Pillow. Eventually, under Shelley Washington's direction, Hubbard Street did
six Tharp revivals over a ten-year period, plus an original, *I Remember Clifford*
(1995).

Washington had begun to feel uncomfortable with holding down a
soloist's rank and salary in Ballet Theater. She was dancing only *Brief Fling*
and the odd character part in the ballets and Tharp works. She hadn't
thought of herself as anything but a dancer, but she was in her mid-thirties
and she realized she couldn't continue to dance as intensively as she had in
the Tharp company. With Richard Colton she had been in charge of the
Australian tour, and her acute memory and enjoyment of detail proved to be

an asset in devising rehearsal and performance schedules. She asked to be named a ballet mistress at ABT, first acting as Tharp's assistant on the revivals and new works. "She kind of just guided me," Washington says, "and then, when they decided they were gonna do *Upper Room*, I just took it and did it because I knew it. I knew what I was doing." She eased into the Hubbard Street assignment in the second phase of the project, with *Baker's Dozen*, and directing for Tharp became her full-time occupation.

A frequent winner of awards and citations, Tharp now began to collect some big ones. In 1990 the American Dance Festival gave her the $25,000 Scripps Award, an annual prize established by generous benefactor Samuel H. Scripps to recognize a choreographer who makes a significant lifetime contribution to the field. Tharp didn't have a company to do a performance, and she resisted traveling to North Carolina to accept the award at the festival, now based at Duke University. Finally she agreed to a solo residency and asked the festival to hold a square dance so that the whole community could celebrate with her. Director Charles Reinhart arranged for the invitations, music, and decorations. According to legend, Tharp gave a severe lecture to the students, which she would not allow the festival to record, danced a few sets at her square dance party, and went straight to the airport. Reinhart says Tharp's eccentricities never offended him. "She's gonna give me what she's got, at the time. But the love is always there."

A year later, after ABT had given its last all-Tharp program (a blockbuster: *Push Comes to Shove, Nine Sinatra Songs*, and *In the Upper Room*), she was named the first recipient of the $50,000 Wexner Prize. Given by the Wexner Center for the Arts at Ohio State University, the prize was set up to honor "a living artist whose career has been one of constant exploration and innovation." The prize was underwritten by Columbus businessman Leslie H. Wexner, a major donor to the spectacular modern art museum designed for the campus by Peter Eisenman and Richard Trott, which had opened in the fall of 1989. The Wexner Center took Minneapolis's Walker Art Center as a model for sponsoring creative work in the visual, media, and performing arts. Along with the Wexner Prize, Tharp received one of three first-time Residency Awards. She started assembling a company and planning for a complex, six-week assault on the campus that was to culminate in two public performances at the three thousand-seat Mershon Auditorium in the fall of 1991.

Kevin O'Day, feeling restless in ABT, had called Tharp early in 1991 to see if she wanted to get back in the studio and work. They started making duet material in a space at City Center. A new group piece, *Octet*, also got under way. By the end of the summer she had assembled a sixteen-member ensemble with a finite life span and the title Twyla Tharp and Dancers. In addition to her old associates O'Day, Bishton, Keith Young, and Shelley Washington as ballet mistress, she pulled in a stellar assortment of ballet and modern dancers. Thrilled to work with Tharp again after their experience on a 1990 revival of *Brahms/Handel*, New York City Ballet dancers Stacy Caddell, Shawn Stevens, and Allison Brown joined up. Robert La Fosse, then a principal at NYCB, took an extended leave to work with Tharp. She "borrowed" Lionel Delanoé, Stephane Elizabé, and Delphine Moussin from the Paris Opera Ballet. Jodi Melnick, a gifted protégée of Sara Rudner, and six other dancers with varied résumés completed the roster. The company was perceived as ballet oriented, perhaps because of the prestigious backgrounds of the ballet contingent, but it was in fact another fusion group. Tharp's next new dances were pointe ballets, but she also brought back some of her pre-pointe works, with the ballet dancers assimilated into them.

Officially the Ohio residency began in August, with a special workshop in the Dance Department given by Rudner and Mary Ann Kellogg, who had moved to Tucson and was heading into film and television work. In addition to repertory and video studies, a daily technique class included body-sensitive Iyengar yoga work with Kellogg. When the company arrived early in September, *Octet* was nearly completed. Washington taught repertory— the two different Mershon programs included another revision of *Deuce Coupe*, *The Little Ballet* with La Fosse in the Baryshnikov role, *The Golden Section*, and the two new works. Meanwhile Tharp continued working with O'Day and the men. She intended to dance in the men's piece herself—she hadn't really performed since the pre-ABT days of her company—and she began each day giving herself a warm-up, then improvising and dancing privately for a video camera. For several hours she worked with the men, separately and in groups, and after a late afternoon visit to the gym, she reviewed the morning's taped phrases in her hotel room to skim off the usable parts. She toyed with several titles—*Solid Men to the Front*, *The Men We Love*—called it *Untitled* in Columbus, but settled on *Men's Piece* when the dance was given in New York.

There were other activities on campus, including open rehearsals and a Wexner-sponsored Tharp film series. A performance of *The One Hundreds* almost got squeezed out of the schedule but Jamie Bishton learned the first fifty phrases and five other company members headed teams of five students each. Tharp made a highly publicized payback to the university by donating her archives to OSU's Jerome Lawrence and Robert E. Lee Theater Research Institute. At a press conference she likened the gift to a Native American potlatch, the custom of returning one's good fortune to the community. Besides her files of press clippings, choreographic notes, company records and correspondence, photographs, costumes and designs, and her personal collection of books and music, the Institute was to get her hundreds of rehearsal and performance videotapes—as soon as they were copied from their original, perishable formats.

Tharp presented the Ohio State performances of *Men's Piece/Untitled* as a work in progress, and also as a "World Premiere." By this time what started in the studio as an informal exploration of partnering had acquired several layers of performance ideas, and Tharp was not reticent about revealing them. *Men's Piece* contained three interlocking forms: a series of duets for Tharp and Kevin O'Day, a structured and rehearsed work session with Tharp as the choreographer and Bishton, Elizabé, and Young as her willing crew of dancers; and a lecture-demonstration in comedy-club style. Tharp thereby got to play all three of her roles at once: dancer, choreographer, and conceptualizer.

After improvising alone to the Gershwin song "Love Is Here to Stay," she gave a scripted running commentary on the rest of the piece. The twenty short duets she'd made, she said, centered around the question of partnering—what did it mean for a man and a woman to dance together in the '90s? Besides that, there was the matter of work and play, illustrated by a tape laid down the center of the stage floor, with the O'Day duets on one side and the three-man drills on the other. Could they be made to coexist? These questions touched off hilarious philosophizing and one-liners about the most serious issues of her life. Tharp had concocted this professorial, half-mocking tone very early, in *All About Eggs* and the open rehearsals, to entertain the audience while making sure they understood her highly serious purposes. As she danced less, she found more ways to use this talk medium.

The gist of the narrative was Tharp's pursuit of a kind of equality between men and women. She was no outspoken feminist although she'd had great success as an independent artist and entrepreneur. Somehow, in both the duets and the ensemble sections, her dance overcompensated. The three men followed her lead but ended up looking foolish. She probably wanted to send up traditional role patterns but instead she reversed them, becoming the macho boss to their submissive workers. Bishton remembers one sequence he had with Keith Young where "she wanted us to go from really strong, military, very masculine, and then drop it and come downstage in this whirlwind flurry, and just dance dance dance and go back upstage and become militarist again."

In the O'Day duets, she proposed various unworkable formulas for men and women to dance together in one another's arms, after the depredations of the Twist, "which is what tore men and women apart and put them into the disco's little *podulettes* of randomly gyrating egos." This funny line, accompanied by film clips of terribly refined, bouffant-headed twisters from the '60s, sidesteps the liberating effect that the Twist actually had on American culture, not to mention its influence on Tharp's own dance style.

In a yodeling duet, or canon, she followed O'Day's movements, but this didn't work because it was built on only one theme. She tried a "bar scene" pickup and he brushed her off. They burlesqued a role-reversal episode, she as a beer-swilling football fan, he in frat-house drag, pushing a mop. Astaire and Rogers represented only a romantic fantasy: "It would be perfection to think you could calculate every move [but] love includes an element of uncertainty." Finally, they worked out an "isometric improvisation" in which, she said, they would exert opposing but equal forces, like Romanesque vaults in buildings engineered to withstand earthquakes. She concluded with one of her greatest aphorisms: "Love is the art of constant maintenance." As the critic Tullia Limarzi noted, Tharp was a little late in her attack on sexual clichés. A younger generation of "Contact Improvisation, gay, lesbian and straight experimentalist choreographers have already come up with many more exciting and original variations on dance coupling."

Tharp had now been working on the duet form for fifteen years, since *Once More, Frank*. The culminating *Men's Piece* encounter evoked the intimate 1976 Sinatra footage on *Making Television Dance*, except that unlike the young Baryshnikov, who shared her sensuality, Kevin O'Day approached the problem in a pragmatic, objective way. Tharp now was a more cautious dancer. They might have been doing equal amounts of work, but most of the time he was hefting and hauling, while she hung on to his back and slithered round his body. Visually she was his dependent, even his incubus, despite the matching inner mechanics. Tharp's movement style by now was vastly different from what her dancers were doing, and not only because she was fifty. She was proud of the number of pounds she could bench-press, but it wasn't her muscular definition that made her a classy dancer. She moved from the center and close to the center, with innumerable small articulations and rhythmic subtleties, a dynamo of variable energy. Audiences sat spellbound during her solo, but the final duet provoked laughter.

Some of Tharp's range of small-movement possibilities carried over into the *Octet*. She now had enough ballet women of her own to develop what she'd started at ABT in *Quartet*. Dressed by Loquasto in severe black—halter tops and shorts for the women, pants and tank tops for the men—the dancers maintained a strict male-female division except when they sorted themselves into couples. They flashed reversed-gender gestures as the ballet began: the women slinking on with muscle-man arms, the men leading into a step with a shoulder or a hip, their arms akimbo. But these were mere affectations; what Tharp proposed was another exploration of partnering. She seems to have taken several Balanchinian lifts and balances as a text for elaboration.

The choreography was completely formal, but Edgar Meyer's music for electric guitar, double bass, and percussion ("The Plumed Serpent") went from funky, bluesy rhythms to misterioso tensions and agitato bow work, and created a dramatic atmosphere in which you could almost detect a story, tinted by David Finn's moody lighting. Partnered mostly from behind, the women seemed enmeshed in elaborate games of capture and escape. The dance became more and more strange, as the women wrapped their limbs around the men and were sprung into splits from behind and lifted into billowing arcs. After barely fifteen minutes, the music jittered up and up, and the women bourréed backwards, threading their way through the leaping and turning men. As the music reached its stratospheric high note, they rejoined their partners for one final supported spin, then snapped into a face-to-face embrace just before a blackout.

After a break, Tharp gathered the company together in New York for a two-week City Center season (28 January–9 February 1992) followed by a late-February tour of Japan. Then the group was scheduled to disband. At City Center they presented the same repertory as in Columbus, with the addition of *Nine Sinatra Songs*, *Ocean's Motion*, and two more new works. In exchange for the three Paris Opera dancers, Tharp had created a showpiece for étoile Isabelle Guérin and Patrick Dupond, who had succeeded Nureyev as director of the Ballet. The two stars danced *Grand Pas: Rhythm of the Saints* on opening night in New York; then Guérin stayed on for the rest of the run to dance it with Lionel Delanoé. She also appeared in the *Sinatra Songs* and Tharp's other premiere, *Sextet*.

The *Grand Pas*, a variant of ballet's showstopper format, was in some sense a miscalculation. Tharp set her duet to selections from Paul Simon's recent foray into Afro-fusion, "Rhythm of the Saints." Within what was supposed to be a high-tech display, she inserted unpredictable stops and starts that squelched applause, as the dancers put on everyday moves and over-the-top attitudes. The audience was confused. Nancy Goldner thought the false endings were intentional, that Tharp had gambled on the audience to play along with her super-campy effects, but most of the other critics passed over it lightly. "An egregiously empty bit of fluff," reported Jennifer Dunning.

Sextet was similarly lightweight, although Anna Kisselgoff thought it "an inspired piece of work, a laid-back tropical equivalent of the love dances she created in her big hit, 'Nine Sinatra Songs.'" *Sextet* was originally commissioned by a pickup group of New York City Ballet and ABT dancers who were planning a tour led by NYCB principal Damian Woetzel. The cast included Susan Jaffe partnered by Woetzel, Kelly Cass and Guillaume Graffin, Isabella Padovani and Keith Roberts, just the kind of adventurous and technically terrific dancers Tharp loved. According to Jaffe, before Tharp settled on the music, the tour was canceled, and after a studio showing—probably in the summer of 1991—the original cast never performed it. They do appear, rehearsing with Tharp, on PBS's prestigious *Dancing* series. Another of Rhoda Grauer's brainchildren, *Dancing* aimed to survey world dance in eight installments. Program Seven, "Modernizing Dance," covered the evolving notions of the twentieth-century avant-garde, from Isadora Duncan and Ruth St. Denis through Digahilev, Balanchine, Graham, Cunningham, and the postmoderns, using Tharp as a kind of throughline to articulate the unflinching individualism that seemed to define the whole century of tradition breakers.

Transferring the *Sextet* to her post-Wexner group, Tharp commissioned a carnivalesque, Latinoesque score from the eclectic composer Bob Telson, and the dance blended balleticisms with flouncy, sexy display. Robert La Fosse and Delphine Moussin held center stage, backed by Allison Brown and Lionel Delanoé, Guérin, and Elizabé. Alastair Macaulay, who was filling in while Arlene Croce took a leave of absence from *The New Yorker*, didn't see much substance in the music ("a suite of bubble-rock/Latin numbers that keep up a somewhat relentless pulse and have little fluctuation of tone") or the dance ("the piece creates its own clichés"). But Joseph Mazo compared

Tharp's Latin adaptations to the character dances in classical ballets: ". . . she takes them further from their origins and deeper into classicism than the Russians ever did."

New York was delighted to have a good look at Tharp again and the season did well. For the last four performances the City Center management opened up 568 balcony seats that usually went unsold. Anna Kisselgoff, in a year-end roundup, named *Octet* and *Sextet* as "Premieres that Restored Faith in Twyla Tharp." But some of the old loyalists had misgivings. Linda Winer, in her *Newsday* "Limelight" column, wondered about the viability of the pickup-company concept for Tharp's work. "Dancers, no matter how virtuosic, cannot learn [her style] overnight—especially if they are trained exclusively in ballet. Although some of the old pieces looked terrific, others seemed much too careful, too placed."

Tharp fell into a period of public introspection, prompted in part by her work on the autobiography. Alongside the very private individual who was most comfortable in the studio with her dancers, she constructed a more formidable, outer-directed presence who had a higher calling, a role to play in the greater scheme of American dance history. Balanchine's death had left her without a master to interrogate. She saw herself, as did many critics, as the only successor to Balanchine—with a mission, not to carry on his tradition but to carry it forward. When Martha Graham died in 1991 she felt a new responsibility to the modern dance lineage she had mostly discarded. But Tharp was always more of a dissenter than a leader. Once she broke the rules, others saw new ways to go, but she had little patience for cultivating her own sphere of influence. She spoke of the need for a school and an organization to propel her work, but she had often and openly declared her distaste for the apparatus of institution maintenance. She thought art should be marketable and competitive, and that her dance should be compensated on a par with the work of businessmen and sports stars. But she gradually priced herself out of the market. Every ballet company wanted her dances; few could afford them. Dancers got paid well for her projects, but they had no security and sometimes they worked for free. In 1992 she received a MacArthur "genius" award, with a stipend of $310,000 over five years. The grant did nothing to assuage her restlessness; if anything, she was more determined than ever to preserve the freedom of project mode.

Tharp thought of the *Men's Piece* as a definitive turn toward more dramatic work, although she didn't abandon the pure-dance idiom she was so good at. The *Men's Piece* shifted and refined the parameters she had set in the autobiographical pieces, *When We Were Very Young, The Catherine Wheel,* and *Bum's Rush.* As in *Fait Accompli,* her role in *Men's Piece* both disclosed and fictionalized her personal preoccupations about love, life, and dancing. In an analysis of the parallels between Tharp's career and that of Martha Graham, Arlene Croce compared *Men's Piece* with Graham's self-parody in the form of a rehearsal, *Acrobats of God.* By giving herself a speaking role, Tharp could make her concerns explicit. She took naturally to the role of master of ceremonies, a duty she had often performed in her videos, lectures, and open rehearsals. This funny, brazen, crankily lovable persona could convey some of her most earnest thoughts. Like the narrator of the autobiography, a theatricalized version of herself could elevate her insights and observations into lessons that would benefit everyone.

She even found a way to theatricalize the rehearsal process. In 1993 she hosted a two-week City Center season of repertory, new material, and surprises. Every night she'd invite volunteers onto the stage from the audience, to learn a new phrase along with the company dancers as she demonstrated it. Beginning in 1998, she expanded the *One Hundreds* into a pageant, a retrospective on the '60s, with the original dance concept embedded in a celebration of community. As always, recruits learned their phrases ahead of time from company dancers, but Tharp presided over an evening-long show, talking about her own history, showing videotapes, and conducting audience-participation games and costume competitions. Once the one hundred volunteers had swarmed onto the stage for their eleven-second climax, Tharp would get out in front and do the first several phrases, "teaching" them to the multitudes behind her.

During the early 1990s Tharp continued to juggle several projects at once. She was famous and successful but elusive. Her work became even more spread out. The project companies did limited repertory and new works, sometimes in provisional form. They didn't always play New York, so the critics there either had to travel to her touring venues or miss entire chunks of her development. Her ballet commissions, film, and video work received limited exposure. The public to whom dance mattered—the New York audience and critics she loudly disdained—were still the arbiters, and they were seeing more of Mark Morris and William Forsythe and Pina Bausch than Tharp.

In 1992, after the City Center season and the tour to Japan, Tharp spent some time in Boston overseeing Boston Ballet's revivals of *Brief Fling* and *In the Upper Room*. She then headed off to Hollywood with Jodi Melnick, Jamie Bishton, Shawn Stevens, Allison Brown, Stacy Caddell, Keith Young, and Michael Whaites to make a movie with writer-director James L. Brooks. *I'll Do Anything* was intended to be a groundbreaking musical. Tharp and Brooks rejected the clichéd romanticism of the 1950s MGM model, as well as the more recent Bob Fosse style of kinky pessimism. They wanted to find an upbeat but contemporary way of integrating dancing and singing into a story. None of the leading actors—Nick Nolte, Albert Brooks, Tracey Ullmann, and Julie Kavner—could dance, but the show-business story line seemed to allow for musical numbers. Jodi Melnick remembers scenes in a disco and a restaurant, and a sequence where patrons waiting on line to buy movie tickets suddenly broke into a tap dance.

Tharp looked up her old associate Sharon Kinney, who was living in Los Angeles, and asked her to assist with the staging. Kinney says Tharp was under some pressure at the time because she was already working on her next project. Kinney admired the way Tharp could hold her own among the all-male production team, often showing them how they could shoot the dance numbers effectively, and reshaping her choreography for the cameras. Tharp taught her, Kinney says, "as an artist, woman, dancer, that you go in and you try to make the situation work for you." Despite everyone's high hopes, the movie didn't gel as an integrated piece. When it was shown to preview audiences, they liked either the musical parts or the dramatic parts, but not both. Before the film was released, all the musical numbers and transitions were deleted.

I'll Do Anything was Jodi Melnick's only opportunity to work on new choreography with Tharp. In two seasons she had become another of Tharp's "finds" but after the movie Tharp wanted to work exclusively with ballet women. Melnick was called back for another season with Tharp, in 1993, but she piloted her own career back to downtown New York. She says the experience of creating new work with Tharp was amazing: "What I remember from the movie is being in the studio with her . . . and dancing behind her." Tharp still had the gift, even the appetite, for new dancers. She could walk into a studio and size them up immediately, then challenge them beyond their self-perceived limits. She kept herself in shape for dancing, because she believed her body still had unique information to transmit. She told an interviewer in 1993: "The only reason I keep dancing is because I still discover things that nobody else knows and understands about, and that I can only do them myself physically, through my own body. As long as that's the case, I'll keep working."

In 1992 Tharp began a half-year commercial project that netted a reported million dollars for herself and her costar, Mikhail Baryshnikov. With a small company (ballet dancers Stevens, Brown, Caddell, and Julie Michael; Jamie Bishton, Michael Whaites, Daniel Otevrel; and two showbiz dancers, Aaron Cash and Art Palmer) she went into rehearsal for a month at the Wexner Center prior to launching a three-month blitz tour of twenty-five cities. Booked by the prominent concert agency Columbia Artists, the tour bypassed New York. She didn't have much time to prepare, and unlike the first Wexner residency, the university didn't get a glimpse of what she was doing until *Cutting Up* was given in Mershon Auditorium at the end of November. A small tempest blew up between presenters over the fact that the University of Texas at Austin had bid to hold the official world premiere. At least two New York dailies sent their critics to Columbus a few days earlier. Although the Wexner carefully billed the show as a "first performance," Kisselgoff called it a premiere.

The ninety-minute show attracted capacity audiences at over-the-top ticket prices. At a time when other dance organizations were struggling and the Dance Boom had been declared a bust, the Twyla-Misha tour broke records. When Boston's Celebrity Series opened the box office two weeks before a weekend of performances at the 3,600-seat Wang Theater, it had the biggest sales day in its fifty-four-year history. In West Palm Beach, subscribers to the newly constructed Kravis Center bought up the whole house, and Tharp had to promise a return visit so that ordinary people could see the show. It wasn't easy for the hoi-polloi to get in. All across the country, tickets cost up to $150, not including the benefit receptions and dinners that many sponsors piggybacked onto the show's popularity.

The company traveled in a private jet with their own physical therapist, and the dancers were well paid. Although no one had any doubts about the box-office power of the two stars, the publicity was intense. A convergence of new hooks, partly fortuitous and partly calculated, began with Tharp's MacArthur and her *Dancing* segment on PBS. Prompted by the December release of her autobiography, writers combined their preview stories with book reviews. Baryshnikov gave no interviews, but Tharp made herself available, provocative as always. There was plenty to stir the public's curiosity. Both stars were pushing the age envelope, so how would Tharp (fifty-one) and Baryshnikov (forty-five) hold up in performance? More titil-lating, Tharp had described their long-ago liaison in the book, in dime-novel detail. Writers quoted the flaming parts extensively; one critic even referred readers to the spiciest page. By the time the show hit town, audi-ences were dying to see the stars together in person. Were they still an item? Would you be able to tell?

Two months before the tour opened, Tharp and Baryshnikov appeared together on PBS, in a short Annie Leibovitz film commissioned for the twentieth anniversary of *Great Performances*. Leibovitz had taken contrasting photographs of Tharp—one severe and one elfin—for an ABT fiftieth an-niversary souvenir book in 1989, when Tharp was still listed as an artistic associate. Now the photographer was interested in the early motion-picture experiments of Eadweard Muybridge and others, and she enlisted Tharp and Baryshnikov to help her make *Zoetrope*. The six-and-a-half-minute film is a modern take on the zooscope, a machine that simulated motion by affix-ing a sequence of still pictures to the inside of a drum that revolved rapidly as the viewer looked through a peephole. Tharp and Baryshnikov worked on a circular stage with the movie camera in the center. They walk, jog, do simple phrases and duologs, and end up waltzing and laughing as the cam-era accelerates. Separately but appreciatively, they comment in voiceover on each other's working abilities. Tharp says she doesn't remember much about this film, except that it was used as promotional material for the tour. Bits of *Zoetrope*'s movement also made their way into *Cutting Up*, as did mate-rial from the gutted movie musical.

Cutting Up was compared by more than one writer to a rock show and, like that sort of event, it drew attention almost exclusively to the stars. Crit-ics focused on the middle section, a duet, and no one had much to say about the ensemble choreography. Even the dancers thought of themselves as a backup group. There were precedents for the enterprise in the dance field, Baryshnikov's several summer jaunts with ABT dancers, for instance. Rudolf Nureyev scooped up the Paul Taylor Company once, and another time the entire Joffrey Ballet, for his "Nureyev and Friends" tours. But these projects invariably used existing repertory: familiar low-production dances and brief star turns.

Tharp wasn't going to rely on repertory for this venture. She devised a program of favorite ideas newly choreographed and built around an overall concept. The three sections were made of short vignettes illustrating the wide range of materials that could go into making a dance. Each section drew on a different category of resources and included special numbers featuring the stars. *Schtick* was a sort of variety show, with music that might have accompanied toe and baton classes in a neighborhood dancing school. *Bare Bones* was a duet for the two stars, presumably created from scratch with only the considerable talents at their disposal. *Food* was a social-dance survey set in four famous American night spots of the twentieth century: "Palm Court 1917," "Coconut Grove 1942," "Rainbow Room 1953," and "Morton's LA 1992."

Tharp worked hard on her profit-makers, but she invested no more art in them than necessary. She thought the axiom "something for everybody" was a good thing, she told the *Boston Globe*'s Christine Temin. "I started thinking of the show as 50 great, enjoyable moments. There's nothing criminal in that. . . . Why antagonize an audience?" But her critics called *Cutting Up* Twyla-lite. *Dance View*'s editor, Alexandra Tomalonis, dismissed it as "a colossal ripoff," but had to admit the audience at Washington's Warner Theater didn't mind at all. "A vanity production for two aging dancers," began Kisselgoff's review. Some of the material did look recycled, and only the central duet seemed choreographically substantial, but the whole show was more thoughtful and generous than it seemed at first, star-bedazzled glance.

Along with the Victorian waltzing, imitation Fosse, and rock and roll of the first act, Tharp reprised her *Men's Piece* antics—collective lifts, slow duets, and a marching drill. Baryshnikov partnered the four women in what might have been a sequel to *The Little Ballet*. Each of the restaurants in Act 3 became the pretext for a small if familiar dance portrait. In the "Palm Court," there were rags, tangos, polkas, and a rivalry on the dance floor that escalated into a silent-movie scuffle. For the '40s there were lindy hoppers and two zoot-suited singers. The "Rainbow Room" segment consisted of two solos. Tharp did her inimitable turns and high kicks and close-in undulations ("Someone to Watch over Me"). Baryshnikov danced his "One for My Baby" solo from the *Sinatra Suite*, the most recognizable item in the show, having been aired frequently on TV. She probably thought of this as the show's equivalent of *The Dying Swan*.

The evening wound up with a disco scene. During work on *I'll Do Anything*, director James Brooks had taken Tharp and Jamie Bishton, who was assisting her, on a research trip to Morton's restaurant, where they spent an evening observing the tribal behavior of the Hollywood social-climbing set. According to Bishton, there was to be a scene for Albert Brooks in the movie where, "as he was moving around through the restaurant, all this dancing was happening around him." This scene, minus Albert Brooks, turned up as the last number of *Cutting Up*.

"Bare Bones," the middle section, was a real suite of dances to the Baroque composer Giovanni Battista Pergolesi, with Tharp and Baryshnikov dancing together, then soloing. The whole thing was built on walking steps, backwards and forward, with interpolated chassés, bounces, shakes, and changes of speed and direction. She gave Baryshnikov two sequences of balletic movement that quoted gestures from his past famous roles: *Spectre de la Rose, Le Corsaire, Push Comes to Shove*. The solo suited him so well that he later acquired it, as *Pergolesi*, for his White Oak repertory.

Perhaps piqued by the purple passages in Tharp's book, critics wondered why the two never touched during the duet. Tharp at one point explained that due to Baryshnikov's past injuries, he couldn't lift her. "We dance duets in the sense of two people working in one piece." Anna Kisselgoff thought she was trying, ill-advisedly, to match her own style with the classical purity of her partner. They read, Kisselgoff thought, as "two guys doing pirouettes and other Tharp-treated ballet basics . . ." Tharp had made innumerable duets without physical contact, most recently for the Stompers of *In the Up-per Room*. The whole of "Bare Bones" is a spectacular version of her longtime investigation into choreographic doubling. Side by side, the two dancers do the same things but in their own ways; she *wanted* the audience to see them as different.

Undeniably, the relationship between Tharp and Baryshnikov frosted over during the tour. They opened the show with a life-in-the-studio evoca-tion, strolling onstage in sweats with water bottles, watching each other, try-ing steps and warm-ups accompanied by the song "I Get Along without You Very Well." "Possibly this means they hate each other," suggested Laura Shapiro. Before the tour ended, rumors circulated that they were no longer on speaking terms. When Baryshnikov arrived in Columbus shortly before the opening, he told Tharp that aside from the *Pergolesi*, he thought the show wasn't up to her standard of excellence. She didn't take kindly to his criticism. He must have been offended by Tharp's pulpy exposé of their 1975 seduction—he was just as protective of his private life as she—and he balked at promotional schemes that hinted at an ongoing liaison. Their affair was pe-ripheral, Tharp insisted when critics inevitably asked about it, but she'd felt it necessary to include certain of her romantic adventures in the book because "People have to have the information to understand the [dance] work."

Tharp's mother died during the tour. She didn't leave to go to the funeral, but, according to Stacy Caddell, "She did a very beautiful, heart-wrenching solo that night."

The tour ended in Louisville in mid-February. After a break most of the dancers joined a newly constituted sixteen-member group for a two-week season at City Center (14–25 September 1993) and another period of touring. The company prepared the season at the University of the Arts in Philadelphia in July and the Wexner in August. The new show, billed as *Twyla Tharp and Dancers: Informal Talk and Performance*, was probably the last time Tharp convened a substantial chunk of her repertory—and in New York it was scantily produced. There were no sets or lighting effects, and the dancers wore practice clothes. Tickets were priced at a modest twenty dollars.

Tharp thought of the season as a thank offering, a form of payback to the city that had given her so much. It was essentially a beefed-up lecture-demonstration. She took the opportunity to explicate the construction of specific dances. Sara Rudner made a guest appearance, reprising their old interview ploy The Talky, where she danced while answering questions Tharp threw at her. Opening the program to Buddy Guy's recording of "Fever" with a solo Arlene Croce called "wide-ranging, multifaceted, typically ambiguous," Tharp explained how the frisson of love could generate art. On the first program there were complete performances of *Octet* and *Upper Room*; the second concentrated on Tharp's social-dance style, with *Nine Sinatra Songs*, *Sextet*, and excerpts from *Baker's Dozen*. Critics and audiences seemed to like seeing the mechanics of these pieces, and despite some grumbling about the bargain-basement aspects of the show, most people found it highly entertaining.

There were, however, some signs of apprehension about the direction Tharp's career was taking. Dale Harris, a staunch supporter, didn't like the audience-friendly setup of the season, which he found self-indulgent. "Why is Twyla Tharp not devoting her energies to choreography instead of squandering them on what is in effect a high-class chat show?" he asked in *The Wall Street Journal*. Arlene Croce, on the other hand, had been worried about Tharp's apparent attempts to circumvent creative burnout—the tour, the book, the movie. She voiced misgivings about the pointe work and partnering in *Sextet* and *Octet*, a recent trend that "make[s] me wish to God Tharp had never heard of either." But with *Demeter and Persephone*, Croce thought, Tharp had gotten back on track.

The centerpiece of the City Center season was a zany preview of *Demeter and Persephone*, the dance Tharp had just made for Martha Graham's company. Graham had singled out several younger choreographers she thought could carry on her company's mission after she passed on, and Tharp was the first to be given an assignment. She donated her services. She had studied with Graham in her early days in New York, and she professed her great respect for the modern dance master. Selecting one of the major Greek myths, Tharp found "a very female story," she told Janice Berman, "a myth about women and their various ages and times, about how we go away to learn certain things and then have to be reunited with ourselves. It's a myth about living, about women as godhead, about rejuvenation, a myth about proceeding in a way that women do." She told another interviewer at the time that she saw the myth in terms of Demeter's relationships, rather than an individual's drama as Graham might have done. The Demeter character, an older woman, sees the strands of her early life separate and then reunite in a different way. At fifty-two Tharp had given considerable thought to her own menopausal changes.

At City Center she glossed the story of the fertility goddess whose daughter, Persephone, was seduced and carried off to the Underworld by Hades. Distraught, Demeter bargained for a reprieve and secured Persephone's annual return to earth, a symbol of the coming of spring. Tharp set the dance as a Passion Play enacted by pilgrims on their way to carry out the Eleusinian rites—a framework used by Graham in her 1940 dance about the Christian rituals of the Southwest Indians, *El Penitente*. For City Center and a preview performance in Ohio, Tharp dispensed a hilarious narration full of double-entendres, while dancing most of the roles herself, opposite Jamie Bishton. She described Limbo as "an infinitely repeating loop of codependent family members." According to Tharp, Demeter, the world's first kvetch, incurred the displeasure of Zeus by forming the Eleusinian cult: "Nobody likes illegal franchises."

Anna Kisselgoff, one of Graham's most ardent supporters, detected a lack of the proper veneration in Tharp's "crib-sheet version." "A full performance by the Graham company, rather than these fragments, might produce fewer giggles," she wrote. This turned out to be an accurate prediction. The Graham company's performance succeeded too, when it premiered a few weeks later in the same theater, but despite some burlesque passages, it was more festive than comic. The Graham company was beginning a difficult transition after the loss of its founder-choreographer, and Tharp came up with a work that enlivened the group, at least temporarily.

Tharp had taken up the challenge conscientiously. By this time she had evolved a process for making a coherent narrative structure in dance form. After reading extensively around the myths of Demeter and the Eleusinian Mysteries, she put together a throughline, puzzling her way through the characters, the story, the dancing, the music, the cast, and the larger mythical themes, to achieve a "lead sheet." Into this blueprint she wove clusters of movement phrases that grew into scenes. Rather than impose her own style on the dancers, she went back into the studio to recover some of the Graham technique for herself. The dance turned out to be more spacious and sculptural than anything Tharp had made for her own dancers, and also faster and more rhythmically interesting than anything in the Graham canon. She started choreographing the work to music by John Adams and Terry Riley but she made an inspired switch to klezmer music, as recorded by three popular bands. Pressed for the connections between ancient Greek and contemporary Yiddish culture, she concocted a few tenuous ones, but she told a questioner at the Columbus preview that klezmer simply had more expressive range and would give the piece life and passion.

Demeter was one of Tharp's most successful narrative dances, although it was less a narrative than a series of dramatic sketches, beginning and ending with a Tharpian farandole. It had its ambiguities, but the myth's preordained plotline restrained her questing imagination and her tendency to fall into farce whenever she confronted familial situations. She preserved the episodic and archetypal feel of a Graham dance but gave the company a new lease on movement. Declaring the dance a mutual success, Kisselgoff thought the Graham dancers "brought out a dramatic projection through movement that Ms Tharp never found anywhere else." Christine Dakin, whom Tharp had cast as Demeter, confessed to Jennifer Dunning that "In the beginning I was feeling very anxious and skeptical. Martha has been my guru for twenty years. But Twyla won me over." According to Croce, Tharp did wonders for the company: "It's an excellent opportunity for the dancers to come down from their elevated perches in the Graham repertory and get happy, and the opportunity is gratefully seized. . . . the success of the ballet doesn't derive from Tharp meeting Graham; it derives from Tharp meeting klezmer."

A few years deeper into the process of self-invention, Tharp shamelessly told a lecture-demonstration audience that her past work didn't interest her. Erasing *Deuce Coupe II, III,* and *IV, The Catherine Wheel* 2 and 3, and more modest stagings of second thoughts, she stated that she hadn't revised a dance since her populist conversion of Willie Smith into *Eight Jelly Rolls.* In 1994, while in Ohio, she reconfigured *Brahms' Paganini* for another of her extraordinary male dancers. Jamie Bishton, whom Dale Harris called "as fine a male dancer as the choreographer has ever had in her troupe," had been with Tharp through all the transmutations of the past eight years, and he was at the peak of his form—technically splendid, tough but soft, with an unconcealed appetite for movement. Tharp gave him a composite tape of William Whitener, Richard Colton, and John Carrafa dancing the original twelve-minute solo, and Jennifer Way, slipping in and out during the Book II quartet section. When Bishton had learned all the variations and their differing interpretations, Tharp came in and worked on it with him, juxtaposing material from the original solo against the quartet. Bishton thus counterpointed the quartet in much the same way Jennifer Way had done in the original, but instead of merely hinting at the solo, he conveyed it all.

The original Book I of *Brahms' Paganini* is probably the most virtuosic solo dance Tharp has ever made, not only in terms of the movement but the expressive range it encompasses. Tharp and Bishton both think most of the Book I dance material was used in the integrated version. *Brahms' Paganini Book II* isn't as oddly shaped as the original. With a more unified and concise form, it's a powerful dance of contrasting elements: Bishton's confidence and virtuosic range against the almost demonic quartet that switches from intense social-dance partnering to intricate formality. The dance wasn't shown in New York, but it was done, as a new work, on the '93–'94 tours that followed City Center. Bishton treasures a memorable performance at a Paris Opera gala, when his parents flew over to see him with ten of their friends and were seated in the presidential box.

Somehow in between the movie, City Center, *Demeter,* and the tours, Tharp made a new work for Boston Ballet, *Waterbaby Bagatelles.* It premiered on 30 April 1994 at a gala performance celebrating the company's thirtieth anniversary, and wasn't scheduled again until the following spring. Despite its title, *Waterbaby Bagatelles* is neither a trifle nor an aquatic fancy. Once again boosting a good company into a higher sphere, Tharp made a large-scale work that began mysteriously and built, like *In the Upper Room,* to an irresistible climax. With a cast of twenty-seven dancers headed by principals Jennifer Gelfand and Patrick Armand, and with featured roles for several other dancers, *Waterbabies* has the properties of a formal ballet: classical movement arranged for groups and couples, who maintain constant relationships to one another even when they aren't deployed symmetrically.

The ballet has expected Tharpian quirks. During its twenty-eight minutes there are seven short musical selections, all from the twentieth century but perversely ranging from Webern to Bang-on-a-Can percussion to an Astor Piazzolla tango to "On the Dominant Divide" from John Adams's *Grand Pianola Music*. The vocabulary shifts from Tharp's expanded classicism, to floor-bound slides, splits, crouches, and sprints, to gestures and attitudes culled from martial arts, Tarzan movies, vaudeville, and social dancing. The movement is packed, pressured. Jennifer Tipton created a dramatic, almost lurid lighting effect with four sets of neon tubes that rose and fell to change the dimensions of the stage, alternately glowing and dimming in shades of blue and mauve. With rapidly changing textures and scale, Tharp illustrated how groups of women and men can function in a ballet, for display and seduction.

In one scene, four women reclined like mermaids or sirens, as a stream of goofy men seemed to be trying to impress them with alluring tricks belonging to both genders. The mermaids seemed frightened, but they captured most of the men, and then were carried off upside down. Except for this character episode, the ballet maintained a classical abstractness. The space darkened for a sensuous duet by Gelfand and Armand; later Gelfand led the women in an airborne rush of crossing and accumulating groups.

Overriding the stylistic contradictions of the ballet is Tharp's concern with gender roles. She makes a clear distinction between air work and floor work, but she resists the conventional equation female=air=sought-after/male=ground=pursuer. The "mermaid" section contrasts the floor-bound, coy women with butch showoffs. In the adagio duet, Gelfand manipulates Armand at moments instead of always passively following his lead. By the end of the piece, as the *Grand Pianola Music* builds bombastically to its climax, the men are actually throwing the women into the highest lifts and dragging them by the arms along the floor.

Early in 1994 Tharp was gripped by a new amorous frisson of her own. She met a prominent intellectual, Leon Wieseltier, and began a serious affair that lasted almost four years. Wieseltier, based in Washington as literary editor of *The New Republic*, was a journalist-maverick attracted to brainy pundits, popular culture, and celebrities. A 1999 profile in *The New York Times Magazine* called him "Part Maimonides, Part Oscar Wilde." Like Tharp, though more overtly, he leaned toward the conservative side of politics and ethics. He was trying to write a book on his relationship with his father, which, with Tharp's help, became the widely praised *Kaddish* (1998). In 1994 Tharp dreamed up a plan to spend the summer with him in Washington and do her own work at the same time. In September *Twyla Tharp in Washington—New Works* was shown informally for three weeks in the Kennedy Center's Terrace Theater as the in-process culmination of a ten-week workshop.

Tharp issued an unusual amount of preliminary information about this project, much of it oddly blurred and sentimental. She had found a way to make new work without fund-raising, and the scheme needed some justifying. First she talked Kennedy Center director of programming Sheldon Schwartz into giving her space, facilities, and administrative support in return for a public lecture-demonstration. Then, through American University's Naima Prevots and her own personal connections, she rounded up young dancers for an audition. The setup would be similar to Tharp's old workshop/apprentice system, only bigger and more public. According to *The Washington Post*, she chose fourteen out of the sixty hopefuls. The deal was they'd work gratis. They had to pay their own transportation, room, and board, and there was no guarantee there'd be a performance at the end. In an echo of the makeshift early days on the college touring circuit, Weiseltier and other D.C. contacts helped find housing and free meals for them. Later, Tharp told Charlie Rose on a national TV interview: "It makes the participation of the artists much closer to the community." Naima Prevots told her recruits to think of it as an exceptional learning opportunity.

Halfway into the workshop period, Tharp dismissed the heroic volunteers, saying that although the dancers were terrific, she couldn't get them into shape for a performance quickly enough. She then called in seven veterans she could count on to absorb the work and bond into an ensemble quickly. They too came onboard unsalaried, but they did get a percentage of the box office take. There were, naturally, hard feelings. According to Stacy Caddell, the dance world saw Tharp setting a bad precedent, especially when she called in the professional replacement group. But Tharp took the program to BAM a few months later, and there, Caddell says, "we were paid incredibly well, so it sort of balanced itself out."

Tharp shed a glow of idealism onto this escapade. To several interviewers she invoked bygone altruistic values. ". . . in the old days, dancers just went to work for the love of it," she told Alan Kriegsman, even though she'd campaigned for decades against that practice. Executing a neat public relations cartwheel, she explained to Jean Battey Lewis of *The Washington Times*: "We've become very confused about dollars, dollars and entertainers, dollars and athletes, and pretty soon everybody is kvetching, 'My honor is involved with my paycheck.' That's not true. The honor is involved with the work you do. . . ." She told interviewers how touched she was that the dancers had chosen to work with her, but this wasn't true for either group. She had gone after them, and the risk was all theirs.

Renamed *Red, White and Blues*, the program went to Brooklyn Academy after the first of the year. It was another version of the bare-bones lecture-demonstration format, with assorted untitled bits under the general theme of patriotism. The summer in Washington had started Tharp thinking about "what it means to be an American, both as a dancer and as a citizen." Still in an unusually mellow mood, she told Jennifer Dunning before the BAM season: "This whole thing is sort of about American belief and the fact that the old American dream can still come true." Wieseltier had helped her choose the music and aroused her interest in history and current affairs, earning a program credit as Musical Advisor and General Counsel. In both Washington and Brooklyn, the program proved entertaining and fabulously danced, but uneven. More than one critic dismissed the trivia and trusted that Tharp would develop the most promising bits into major works. Some observed that her own inimitable dancing was beginning to show its age.

The one substantial segment of the program was set to about half the vignettes in Bela Bartok's *Forty-four Duets for Two Violins*. The dance, provisionally called *The Exquisite Corpse*, became *Noir a.k.a. Bartok* in Tharp's official chronologies. A dance of death with comic overtones, it set five dancers in black practice clothes against Stacy Caddell, on pointe in a red unitard, described by Washington critic Jean Battey Lewis as "an avenging or challenging angel." Caddell thought of herself as Persephone, "who had just entered the Underworld and was given control over these five souls." Caddell strode and slid through the five civilians, commanding them to stop and start according to Bartok's short musical statements. In alternating slices of action they echoed her classical movements, froze, or bobbed up and down like puppets, and mimed a shadowy plot about partner switching reminiscent of *Short Stories*. The rivalry got ugly, fighting escalated into murder, and the whole incident went into reverse, then forward, again and again, until the shooting seemed to be on an endless loop. Finally Caddell put a stop to the charade by smiting them all down, then reviving them for a macabre farandole. At the end of the dance she mounted triumphantly on their shoulders.

Noir bears a glancing relationship to *Le Jeune Homme et la Mort* by Roland Petit. That 1946 ballet, originally starring the French dancer Jean Babilée and made into a beautiful 1968 film with Rudolf Nureyev, opened the movie *White Nights*. As the film's choreographer, Tharp had probably had a hand in staging it for Baryshnikov. An artist—frustrated, blocked, and dazzlingly depressed—awaits an enigmatic woman, who teases him and drives him to suicide, then leads him off over the Parisian rooftops. In *Noir* Stacy Caddell projected a mysterious allure very much like the seductress in the Nureyev film, Zizi Jeanmaire. Tharp included some props too, a chair, a magazine, a cigarette, tokens perhaps of the Roland Petit–Jean Cocteau scenario. She even created a poet surrogate in the role for John Selya, who separated himself from the civilian group at times to confront Caddell with virtuosic acrobatics and soaring leaps.

For some time Tharp had been attracted to themes of death and its predatory companion, aging. For her, death had to be resisted with physical force, with dancing. She had done this most dramatically in the golden transfiguration of *The Catherine Wheel*, and in her marathon comeback-signoff in *Fait Accompli*. Dance itself was an affirmation in the face of death (*Bum's Rush*), a power magical enough or even ugly enough (*Bad Smells*) to confront the ultimate, like an amulet, a protective charm. Even the compositional device of retrograde could defeat death, by rewinding events so that they could start again. Emerging once a year from the grip of Hades, the mythic Persephone represented a way of cheating death, or at least wrestling it to a standoff.

12

Near Heaven

1995–2005

In the spring of 1995 Tharp returned to American Ballet Theater. Kevin McKenzie had become artistic director, ending the chilly Jane Hermann era, and the budget deficit had been subdued in the intervening years. Although not listed on the company roster, Tharp was the only choreographer featured in the handsome 1995 souvenir program book. She wrote a gracious essay, riffing on the words *American, Ballet,* and *Theater,* and expressing her optimism about making a new start. She was welcomed back with great fanfare and a gala performance of three new works (1 May 1995). Tharp now offered the company an entirely different mix of choreographic flavors from the last eclectic all-new, all-Tharp evening in 1989. Instead of a cool balletic abstraction, a farce, and a minimusical (*Quartet, Bum's Rush,* and *Everlast*), she dipped into jazz, nostalgia, and metaphysics. To a commissioned score from trumpeter Wynton Marsalis she made *Jump Start,* a lively piece remarkable only for the way it turned ballet dancers into swingers who could handle the Lindy, waltz, mambo, and rags, blues, and bebop. *Americans We,* to nineteenth-century parlor songs and instrumental showpieces, resumed her reflections on American belief and American tragedy. Neither of these was scheduled to go into the repertory that season.

The centerpiece of the program, *How Near Heaven,* drew its title from Emily Dickinson and aspired to cosmic significance. Tharp told Anna

Kisselgoff in a Sunday preview piece that the ballet was about death and the transcendence of death. "The subject matter is subjectivity and objectivity and their unification, the ending of time. . . . That would be the poem if I set out to write one. I'm interested in a poetic handling of literary content, not in a literal plot." Set to Benjamin Britten's *Variations on a Theme of Frank Bridge, How Near Heaven* was a big classical work with the forces deployed unconventionally.

A pair of women (Susan Jaffe and Kathleen Moore in the first New York cast) danced as a team but were both partnered by two men (Gil Boggs and Guillaume Graffin). The corps of twelve was divided into four men and eight women, and there was an additional featured couple (Cynthia Harvey and Charles Askegard). Dressed in silken boudoir wear by Gianni Versace, all these units seemed to play different roles in a larger scheme that consolidated around the symbolic death of the two women, a brief exalted vision, and a posthumous celebration. Leon Wieseltier had led Tharp to the music. Britten's youthful tribute to his teacher provided considerable variety, from operatic parody to classical formality, but Tharp had never worked with a score of such intense colors and neoexpressionistic imagery. Arlene Croce thought "his taffeta strings and her macramé are from separate worlds."

Tharp's catalogue of musical resources was wide-ranging but not comprehensive. She had always skirted the great architectonics and orchestrated passions of the later classics. Her approach was to embrace a musical beat, a timbre, a phrase pattern, and to construct her own frame over it. Music could establish a tone, even an idea, but her dance had to be expressive primarily on her terms. She didn't enter the music by illustrating its drama, or append the dance to the score like another musical line as Balanchine often did. Despite her admiration for *Agon*, Stravinsky wasn't a composer she found congenial for her own classical efforts. His kind of intellectual game-playing would have competed with hers. She didn't internalize the ethnic promptings of folk-derived compositions like the Bartok two-violin impressions she'd used for *Noir*. Even her jazz dances don't really imitate the styles to which their music refers, despite the insertion of period dance steps. In the Britten, she didn't feel compelled to make a melodramatic solo when the music sang its parodistic "Aria Italiana," or launch a "Wiener Walzer," or follow any other colorful suggestion made by the composer, unless it suited her own scheme, as the "Funeral March" did.

Tharp's formalistic treatment made *How Near Heaven* look abstract against Britten's textured music. "My whole career has been about counterpoint," she told Kisselgoff. Allowing dissimilar themes to blend into a whole, counterpoint "gives real energy, and it is about optimism. . . . It's a philosophical tenet. It's also, in a way, a religious tenet." She described the Harvey-Askegard couple as "intact," a reference perhaps to ideal love, but throughout the ballet she posed her large units against one another, the way she had contrasted Stacy Caddell's dominatrix with the group in *Noir a.k.a. Bartok.* Her dance counterpoint didn't always mesh with Britten's nine harmonious if dissonant variations, or even make its own convincing whole. Sometimes the groups would fall into a canon or a call-and-response pattern, but more often the soloists went their own way while the larger ensemble carried the musical momentum.

Halfway through, the ballet began to take on some drama. After the funeral section, the principal women were reunited in an unusually poignant and feminine duet. They suggested facets of one persona as they danced together, with the same movements individually shaded. Tharp had begun choreographing this duo for herself and Paloma Herrera, who danced in the ballet's first performances at the Kennedy Center with Kathleen Moore. When Susan Jaffe entered the work—she learned both parts—she thought one woman was an ingenue and one an earth mother type. For New York, Tharp assigned Jaffe the earthier role and shifted Moore into Herrera's younger persona.

It probably isn't farfetched to see this duo as a mother-daughter metaphor, given Tharp's recent immersion in the Demeter myth, and the death of her own mother shortly before that. At the end of the funeral scene, they're lifted high, horizontally, one above the other. Symbolically fused again into one body, they're carried off en cortège by the four men. This image is a more compassionate resolution of their differences than the forcible parting of *Demeter and Persephone,* who are carried off in the same positions but in opposite directions, after their temporary reunion. Tharp also told Anna Kisselgoff that she was attracted to Emily Dickinson's obsession with "the crossover point between mortality and immortality . . . because it has to do with the definition of physicality. You step across the line, and there is no longer physicality; that helps define, by its own absence, what is physical." In other words, she was translating her concerns with death and aging into the realm of thought.

How Near Heaven premiered in Washington before Tharp delivered her exegesis to Kisselgoff, and the critics there viewed it with equanimity. Tobi Tobias thought the pair of women were "guardian angels who shepherd its little society through some unnamed tribulation (war, with its handmaiden death, I assumed) to emerge serene, rather nearer to Heaven." Alan Kriegsman got the "impression of a community of dance angels in contrasting moods of joy and melancholy." In New York, despite—or because of—all Tharp's verbiage, the ballet eluded viewers on a conceptual level, and its choreographic contrasts read more like clashing idioms. Arlene Croce found it "almost totally opaque." She thought Tharp lacked the ballet dancer's built-in sense of visual coherence, which might have allowed the audience to make sense of her literary ideas. Tharp revised and tightened the work the following spring, but didn't completely extinguish what Deborah Jowitt called its "irritatingly mysterious eau de scenario."

Still under the brainy influence of Leon Wieseltier, Tharp next made an even more muddled and extravagant work for England's Royal Ballet. *Mr. Worldly Wise* premiered on 9 December 1995, a three-act spectacular with a pastiche of selections mostly drawn from the later, contemplative works of Gioachino Rossini. There were designs by David Roger and a large cast headed by RB principals Irek Mukhamedov, Darcey Bussell, and Tetsuya Kumakawa. A year after its debut, London critic Nicholas Dromgoole called it "perhaps the worst full-length ballet the Royal has ever danced," in a lengthy analysis of what he considered the sins of Anthony Dowell as RB artistic director.

The work brought out the best in the dancers, but looked frenetic. Even on paper it suffered from conceptual overload. Wieseltier's synopsis for the program book affected the archaic style of a *Pilgrim's Progress* fable, but the journey was almost untrackable on the stage. First among the ballet's many themes and scenarios there was the life of Rossini. Best known for his early theater music and operas, the composer went into a fallow period and emerged to create meditative and spiritual works. Thinking of this creative arc, which retraced her own perennial theme of salvation through art, Tharp conceived of the ballet's three acts as depicting excess, abstinence, and moderation. A musical celebrity, Rossini had inspired his own iconography, and some of the ballet's visual ideas came from amusing contemporary caricatures. Tharp was also trying to feature the RB dancers and to allegorize the company and its traditions.

The first act was a headlong divertissement of characters who might have inhabited historic operas and ballets—idealized ballerinas, demented nuns, dancing vegetables; references to the Royal's choreographic god, Frederick Ashton, and possibly to Léonide Massine's Rossini ballet *La Bou-*

tique Fantasque, with Balanchine hovering on the horizon. Mukhamedov's eponymous character was a dissolute genius with a wiser, more temperate assistant/alter ego, Master Bring-the-Bag. Nearly overwhelmed by the attractions of society, Mr. Worldly-Wise sees a vision, Mistress Truth-on-Toe, who shows him his ideal, a classical ballet in the mode of a Petipa/Ivanov second act. Reformed and purified, Mr. Worldly-Wise finds a way to balance his talents and sets off in pursuit of the ballerina. The assistant takes up his bag of tricks and prepares to become his successor.

The general scheme of *Mr. Worldly Wise* recalls that of *Push Comes to Shove.* Again Tharp was taking a fond look at the workings of a ballet company, in this case with a psychological spin: the creative artist getting in touch with his redemptive better self. But there was more clutter and slapstick than message apparent to the audience. In an appreciative essay, her old loyalist Allen Robertson deflected the naysayers and pointed out that Tharp had done "a rich, truly generous piece of dancemaking that showcases its performers as clever, sharp and dazzlingly alive. . . ." But despite its almost too-obvious icons, and the universally applauded performances by Mukhamedov, Bussell, Kumakawa, and the ensemble, the *Sunday Times*'s David Dougill spoke for the consensus in finding it "a perplexing disappointment [that] would be incomprehensible without the synopsis."

At this point Tharp was without a company. She had dissolved the *Red, White and Blues/Noir* group after BAM and spent the year freelancing at ABT, the Royal Ballet, and Hubbard Street. In the spring of 1996 ABT staged another all-Tharp gala, with revised versions of *Americans We* and *How Near Heaven,* and a new ballet, *The Elements.* For this big and compositionally dense work, set to a score by the eighteenth-century composer Jean-Fery Rebel, she revisited the order-from-chaos theme, with a few extra dance show-pieces thrown in. Despite terrific performances by the dancers, and an admiring review from Deborah Jowitt, the piece wasn't generally well received. Writing in the *Daily News,* Terry Teachout was surprised to find it "solid, respectable, and, believe it or not, dull. . . . Tharp's homegrown approach to classical choreography has long since hardened into mannerism." Clive Barnes said *The Elements* and *How Near Heaven* exhibited "the same kind of pallid expertise."

By the time *The Elements* had its premiere (3 March 1996 in New York), she and Shelley Washington were scouting around the country for a new group. After callbacks in New York on 1 April 1996, she signed on a dozen young contemporary dancers. The enterprise called Tharp! was already booked for touring two years ahead. Tharp! was to be a commercial venture—various euphemisms were applied to it: for-profit, income-earning, self-sufficient. It was conceived by the producing company IPA and booked on the basis of Tharp's audience-friendly reputation. Tharp had, for the time being, slaked her interest in ballet dancers. Explaining her return to a producing mode she had disavowed so strenuously eight years before, she spoke of getting back to some basics of her own. She wanted to create a new technique, or at least a means of training that would prepare dancers for her work.

She had experienced "the dream potential of freelancing," she told Deborah Jowitt, and now knew its limits, chiefly that the dancers of any established company came with preexisting capabilities. She could choreograph quickly when necessary, but getting dancers to the point of feeling comfortable with her movement—and then making it their own—required more rehearsal time than a freelancer could demand. Her new group, relatively inexperienced, would discover its own fundamentals. The dancers would be able to "learn their lessons together and move in the same direction." She even taught class for a while at the outset of the new company.

The dancers understood the pragmatic nature of the enterprise. A generation into the era of "crossover" dance that Tharp had so brilliantly initiated, they recognized her as a master who could enhance their careers. "I've never been the kind of dancer that gets infatuated with a choreographer," says Gabrielle Malone, who had been trained at Miami's New World School of the Arts. "I was always kind of interested in doing lots of different things. And so, whatever opportunity is available to me at the time, and I feel like it will help me extend myself, then that's where it goes." Andrew Robinson had danced with London Contemporary Dance Company and other groups. He was drawn to the concentration of choreographic energy in New York, and when Shelley Washington encouraged him to audition, he got on the plane. He felt he would be breaking new ground with Tharp.

Over the next two years Tharp made two important dances for this group and four lesser items. None of them used pointe work and all of them disappeared immediately; the best elements dissolved into subsequent dances. Later, Malone and Robinson reflected that the group might have constituted a kind of laboratory for Tharp to work out her ideas. "I guess we were sort of transitional. But it never felt that way," he says. "In a way, for

Twyla everything is transitional," Malone adds. "Every group, every piece, every project. It's just one step to the next step. No grass grows under her feet."

Sweet Fields, for the first year's Tharp! package, embodied her back-to-basics hopes for the new company, and it activated the group as a community. Inspired by the Shakers, the dance was about working together to reach the fusion of art and spirituality that Tharp called truth. *Sweet Fields* was set to eleven hymns and praise songs from the Shaker and Sacred Harp (shape-note) traditions and the eighteenth-century American composer William Billings. These a cappella choral works with their ecstatic texts and open harmonies were related to Tharp's Quaker background, and the dance they prompted was perhaps her purest and most joyful. Choreographically unencumbered by literary allusions, allegorical characters, or even the complexities of counterpoint, *Sweet Fields* shows a community of men and women dancing out their spiritual faith. In clear lines and unambiguous groupings, solemn processions and playful rituals, they acknowledge the inevitability of an afterlife, a New Jerusalem of ease and delight.

As in other utopian dances (*Mud, Baker's Dozen, Bach Partita, How Near Heaven*), Tharp signaled her intentions with white costumes. Norma Kamali layered pants for the men, shorts and peekaboo midriff tops for the women, under open organza jackets and dusters. The effect was revealing and modest at the same time. Though disconcertingly chic, the costumes allowed the dance to bypass any period associations. Belief was not some anachronism, Tharp was saying; it belonged to our times.

Choreographers have been attracted to the Shakers, an American sect of celibate Christians, because dancing was part of their worship. Doris Humphrey's 1931 modern dance classic *Shakers* used some documentary gestures of shaking and ecstatic spinning, kept its men's and women's groups strictly separated in their own halves of the stage, and had a female leader, an Eldress, according to Shaker practice. Tharp may have consulted books on Shaker traditions, but what is striking about her dance is that it doesn't copy any actual Shaker moves or look like any modern dance interpretation of them. Both her movement and floor patterns express the spare functionality of the Shaker aesthetic through the contemporary physicality of her dancers.

Sweet Fields starts with an orderly series of entrances, first for a man followed by his four companions, then a woman and four others. These groups, with a sixth man added later, begin as separate units; they don't share the stage until the fifth song. Gradually a movement vocabulary is built up from the first man's linear phrase, a walking pattern that seems to diagram the space. His arms wheel through the vertical plane; he steps to the side and behind his body, outlining a square without changing front. The women expand on the men's wheeling gestures until they're swinging both arms in big overhead circles. They bend their whole upper bodies toward the ground, they shake their hands out from the wrists. They swing their legs through the step, until they're hopping, sliding to the side, and eventually stepping into full turns. They skip out in a line behind their leader.

A slow procession of men carries a comrade lying prone above their heads—another funeral formation. While the cortege moves across the stage, the "corpse" performs acts of levitation and other magical changes, trading roles with another man almost imperceptibly. The transportee is dropped nearly to the floor and rocked by the pallbearers, tossed in the air and rotated head to foot, and finally passed through their legs and lifted overhead again before he's carried off. This horizontal image becomes part of the vocabulary during the next section, when the men begin rolling on the floor. Interrupting the sections of perfectly balanced group work, one man appears alone, gazing and leaning into one direction, then another. He seems momentarily unsure and unable to go on. Then he makes a decision and strides off after his companions.

As the movement builds up and the traveling patterns grow more intricate, the dance keeps its sense of spatial clarity and industriousness. The movement has the feeling of carpentry or kitchen work—repetitive, vigorous, finicky, or sweeping. By the end of the dance, the lexicon has proliferated into jumps, lifts, and ecstatic turning. The community spans life and death, it can accommodate believers and doubters. In the last song, the men and women interweave and work in pairs, giving each other massages between the shoulder blades with chopping gestures. The men haul the women over their backs and the women shake out their legs in a controlled but joyous outburst. Groups of men rock the prone women near the ground and lift them in high vertical exclamations. Tharp had never made a dance more organically, or expressed her beliefs with less reserve. It earned universal praise from critics and was remembered as the standout work of the Tharp! company.

Sweet Fields and a second dance on the initial program were cocommissioned by the Kennedy Center and the University of California at Berkeley. For *Heroes* Tharp teamed up with Philip Glass again, and although the work was powerful, it didn't have the impact of the monumental *In the Upper Room*. Glass composed a "symphonic ballet," a set of variations on the Heroes Symphony of David Bowie and Brian Eno. Tharp told Thea Singer of *The Boston Globe* that *Heroes* was about the ability of leaders to stand their ground in the face of adversity: "The dance has a movement base that is very aggressive. It is relatively chaotic because that's the kind of world we're building."

Heroes could have been a direct antithesis to *Sweet Fields*. Tharp even used some of the same movement tropes. The gently rocking prone bodies of the women held by three-man teams at the end of *Sweet Fields* was transformed into an assault, as one woman threw herself horizontally at a wall of men who caught her unflinching, time after time. The dance was full of aggression, both the posturing macho kind and the sexually threatening kind. Tharp may have been digging into gender stereotypes and anti-types. The dance's title seemed to ask the audience to think about who are the heroes in our society and what is demanded of them. London critic Donald Hutera saw the "ferocious precision" and "kinetic desperation" of the dancing as a message of resistance, resilience, and even redemption. For all its harshness, Hutera said, *Heroes* had none of the brutality of "Euro-crash" dance—the hybrid styles that featured casual virtuosity and abusive partnering—then gaining popularity. Tobi Tobias found the meaning of *Heroes* "almost entirely obscure," but, along with everyone else, she applauded the dancing.

Tharp has made relatively few potboilers during her long and ambitious career (she would probably not admit to any) and even the slightest of her works have invoked accolades for the dancing. The Tharp! programs included two whiffs of old success stories—*66*, a pop evocation of middle-American romance, and *Roy's Joys*, a jazz piece to music of trumpeter Roy Eldridge—and a surprising new turn, *Yemayá*, which one of the dancers described as a "pseudo-Santeria meets Buena Vista Social Club piece."

Tharp would seem the least likely choreographer to be toying with Cuban drumming and trance possession, but there was some logic to this development, aside from her unending pursuit of new musical resources. Santeria religion, like that of the Shakers, led to ecstatic dancing, and Tharp had long been interested in goddess worship. She had made dream ballets before, to disclose an alternative lifestyle or time frame behind a more palpable stage reality. Yemayá, the sea queen in several religions of the African diaspora, was Tharp's metaphor for the ideal woman according to Gabrielle Malone, who danced the role. The plot shifted from a night club to an erotic fantasy, then back to reality. Tharp wanted to show the connection between spiritual and mundane life, but the dance proved more glossy than adventurous.

The company also learned *Baker's Dozen,* but the dance was sidelined without a performance in favor of getting the new material onto the stage. It's possible that, given more time, Tharp would have deepened and clarified the Tharp! repertory. Certainly *Heroes* had more potential. But IPA's heavy touring agenda turned out to be as unsuited to her creative process as the nonprofit setups of her earlier companies. In its two-year existence, Tharp! appeared in several American cities and made three overseas trips, to dance in Paris, Edinburgh, Australia, Singapore, Italy, and London. She was productive during this time, but her ideas needed a longer gestation period to ripen fully.

While the company was on the road, she gathered up other dancers. Tharp's patron Patsy Tarr has observed: "This is her great gift, that she can make dances. . . . And I think that it must be an enormous frustration to any artist to have a gift like that and not work." She'd formed a relationship with the Australian Ballet in 1997 when it revived *In the Upper Room.* Two of the company's staff, artistic director Ross Stretton and ballet master Danilo Radojevic, had worked admiringly with Tharp at American Ballet Theater. "All her works made me a better classical dancer," Radojevic told an Australian publication. As a favor to Stretton, she said, she agreed to make a ballet for the company. Six Australian dancers flew to New York in the summer of 1997 to work with her. After performances of *The Story Teller* in late 1997 and early 1998, the Australian critics were disappointed. "Much was expected" of the piece, wrote Patricia Laughlin in *Dance Australia.* Instead it turned out to be an enjoyable lightweight.

Tharp had also accepted some lecture-demonstration dates, and she invited one of her most congenial dancers from ABT, John Selya, to work with her. They made a duet to music by the eccentric street musician Moondog. Tharp still loved informal dialogues with the public, and for these outings she and Selya would perform the dance, then she'd talk about it and they'd do it again. He remembers *Moondog* as very naive, childlike, and he felt privileged to be dancing it with her. Later Andrew Robinson partnered her in it for a few showings.

For other public-outreach opportunities on the road, Tharp brought back *The One Hundreds* in an expansive new format, casting herself as the genial host of a '60s retrospective and audience-participation evening. Now she abandoned strict authenticity in the interest of entertainment and cut the initial phrases by half. Asking a contemporary audience to sit through the whole one hundred flat-out would be like offering them *Gone With the Wind*, Malone thought. She and Robinson would do the fifty phrases sitting in chairs—the better to allow the audience to dance along with them, Tharp explained. Then they'd stand and repeat them side by side as Tharp asked the audience to notice the differences between their performing, with an applause check at the end to pick the one it liked best. In at least one of these events, on 27 Feb. 1999, at Hunter College Auditorium in New York, Sara Rudner and Rose Marie Wright joined Tharp to dance for the last time as a trio. The eleven-second volunteers paid one hundred dollars to participate, and the proceeds went to benefit Hunter College. Tharp was lecturing that year in Hunter's Dance Department on a Distinguished Visiting Professorship.

Around the middle of 1998 the Tharp! dancers' two-year contracts were coming to an end, just as they were beginning to look and feel like a company. Shelley Washington left her job as ballet mistress and Tharp recalled Jamie Bishton to replace her. The giant pure-dance work to the Beethoven 33 Variations on a waltz of Anton Diabelli, Op. 120, turned out to be Tharp's last piece for this group. Excellent concert pianists were hired to play in each of the performance venues, and Geoffrey Beene recreated the tuxedo-front, backless unisex costumes of *Eight Jelly Rolls*. The dance was hardly a jazz baby, though. To Beethoven's wide-ranging extrapolations on what she called Diabelli's ditzy little tune, Tharp released an hour-long stream of invention. She joined the tour for *Diabelli*'s premiere in Palermo, Italy, in September 1998, but the dance was never performed in New York. She had run into trouble with her producers, IPA, and when the dancers returned from Europe she told them they wouldn't be continuing as a group.

Diabelli had been created under a three-way commission, from the Barbican Center in London, the Cité de la Musique in Paris, and the Hancher Auditorium at the University of Iowa. In order to satisfy performance commitments to these sponsors, Tharp put together another unit that included four from the dissolved Tharp! group (Malone, Robinson, Sandra Stanton, and Victor Quijada); two stellar ballet dancers from Denmark, Alexander Kølpin and Thomas Lund; two newcomers, Helen Saunders and Elizabeth Zengara; and stalwarts Jamie Bishton and Stacy Caddell. For London, Paris, and Iowa City, the work constituted the entire program. In Iowa the audience was invited to a salsa party in the lobby afterward.

This project group disbanded as soon as *Diabelli* fulfilled its obligations. Lund, Caddell, Malone, and Robinson stayed with Tharp to make another Beethoven work. She had received the $100,000 Doris Duke Award from the American Dance Festival for new choreography. This time, instead of celebrating Beethoven the classicist, Tharp examined the composer's romantic side. The dance, to the Hammerklavier Sonata, was called *Grosse Sonate* for its premiere at the ADF in July of 1999. The dancers worked almost entirely in couples for the long, exhausting piece. Partnered by Lund, Caddell danced on pointe, and Malone, with Robinson, wore soft shoes. This suggested a familiar subject: the contrast between classical and contemporary dancing. But Tharp's movement was now such a stylistic mixture that the distinction didn't really apply. Caddell's pointe work was simply another ingredient in a technical panorama. Again, the work didn't get shown in New York, but Tharp expanded it into a sextet for a few more performances two years later.

These two encounters with the formidable Beethoven produced entirely different dances. *Diabelli* was like a classical ballet, with the ten dancers sorting out in seemingly infinite combinations and patterns, and moods shifting from formal to competitive to soulful. Tharp excelled at making her own theme-and-variations dances, and Beethoven's imaginative ruminations on his Diabelli motif supplied her with both psychic and dynamic energy. London critic Clement Crisp praised the piece warmly, comparing it to Jerome Robbins's *Dances at a Gathering*, "in which music and movement are no less good and responsive companions." But in its length as well as its formality, *Diabelli* could also be thought of as Tharp's *Goldberg Variations*, come to fruition a quarter century after her quixotic assertion in *The Bix Pieces*: "Today I thought of writing a dance to the *Goldberg Variations*, just because it's already been done." It had been done by Robbins in 1971.

The Hammerklavier presented a greater challenge, as one of the composer's last and most revolutionary excursions. His forty-three-minute sonata was as demanding structurally as it was virtuosic, filled with departures from traditional form, flamboyant pianism, and unexpected changes of key and tempo. Tharp's inventiveness never gave out, but the dance looks as if she simply jettisoned the density of Beethoven's work and went her own way. Balanchine saw music as the backbone of his work, she explained to critic Theodore Bale of *The Boston Herald*. "He gave a private place to music. I don't."

Stacy Caddell had become one of Tharp's indispensable lieutenants by the end of the '90s. After the demise of the *Octet* project group in 1994, Caddell had turned her formidable technique to freelance ballet jobs. For four years she guest starred in classical showpieces and danced in the ballet at the Metropolitan Opera. When the American dancer Karole Armitage was looking for a Mozart ballet by Tharp for a company she was heading in Florence, Italy, Caddell convinced the choreographer to let her direct a production of *Ballare*. She went on to stage *Noir* in Geneva, and became a trusted regisseur as well as a studio dancer when Tharp was making new work. Caddell and her dance partner at that time, Alexander Kølpin, asked Tharp to stage *Sinatra Suite* for them. She offered them a choice: *Sinatra* or a new work. Without hesitation they chose the new work. They started with music by Donald "The Junkman" Knaack, and eventually, along with New York City Ballet dancers Kelly Cass and Tom Gold, they were making the duet material that ended up in the forty-two-minute ballet *Known by Heart*. Caddell and Kølpin danced the Junkman duet in Copenhagen, and Tharp later extracted it from the larger piece for a group of her own.

Known by Heart premiered during American Ballet Theater's fall 1998 season at City Center. Tharp returned to her practice of piecing together a score to match seemingly disparate dance styles, for a couple ballet about how classicism earns its longevity. Starting out with components that might have arrived from different aesthetic planets, she gradually folded material from one dance unit into the vocabulary of another until they became compatible if not totally integrated. In fact, Tharp was careful to show from the beginning that all three styles contained impurities and inconsistencies.

In the first cast Julie Kent and Angel Corella entered to a drumroll, announcing, Tharp has said, that "the court isn't far away from the military." The music, from Mozart and two anonymous composers, pointed out an often-overlooked folk-dance ingredient in classical music. Kent and Corella began with a well-bred classical pas de deux, then, as the sound of a rollicking village band was heard, their steps became broader, less proper. They finished with a coda of unison tropes typical of early nineteenth-century ballet—side-by-side romping, call-and-response patterns, and mirroring.

Susan Jaffe and Ethan Stiefel danced the Junkman duet, to Knaack's rhythms for cowbells, hubcaps, snare drums, rasps, and buzzers. They started out as a high-classical couple with some latent discord between them. Their fast balletic stunts and furious energies soon began to punch out into distortions and disconnections. Stiefel did a pugnacious, bouncing solo that delighted the audience. Jaffe stabbed the floor with her pointes and wrenched her balances into corkscrews. They traded karate kicks and hip bumps. They confronted each other with flat "Egyptian" poses, used by Jerome Robbins in his *Glass Pieces*. They acted out a skit in which they failed to meet at appointed times and fought when they did meet. Amid the punching, rolling skirmishes, she supported two of his expansive jumps, and at another moment he fell backwards into her arms, as if they were doing a fox-trot dip.

A third couple, Keith Roberts and Griff Braun, then took over, doing a cool Tharpian dance phrase in tandem. The music for the last half of the ballet was Steve Reich's twenty-two-minute *Six Pianos*, a dazzling work of evolved minimalism in which a single phrase is manipulated, modulated, overlapped, and gradually morphed to create a succession of driving rhythms. Braun and Roberts caught the spirit of this with repeating phrases, flattened-out dynamics, and phenomenal endurance. The movement itself, a set of unrelated, continuous actions, could have been a descendant of Tharp's most minimalistic piece, the *One Hundreds*, with the simple phrase exposition shaped into a choreographic scaffold that framed the whole ballet.

Starting out with walking, their weight sinking easily into the step, their arms swinging freely, Roberts and Braun pace together forward and backward into the space. Like vaudevillian comrades, comfortably shuffling through the time step, wrangling in knockabout sketches, jogging and shadowboxing, they travel through the space and around its perimeter. They vary the pace with finely coordinated rhythms, syncopations, suspensions, and naturalistic encounters, never losing their steady internal pulse. As the other couples pass in and out, doing their signature phrases, the twinned sidemen capture and incorporate motifs, competitions, seductions, and badinage while continuing to patrol the space.

With its fast, nonstop movement and entering and leaving couples, the dance begins to blur. At some point two more men appear and replace Braun and Roberts, like relay racers. After that, the couples begin to exchange partners as well as information, until two more couples appear, the doubles of Kent-Corella and Jaffe-Stiefel. This occurs very near the end, but the music gives no indication of subsiding. Without warning, it stops. In silence the lights go down as Roberts and Braun are doing their first phrase together downstage and their male alternates jog in place in the background. Tharp's message seemed to be that there would always be more dancers, and more dance possibilities.

Steve Reich, especially during the period of *Six Pianos*, was not a composer to everyone's taste. It took some attentive listening to discern the subtle shifts and variations going on inside his insistent repetition and unchanging pulse. It was the Reich, and the male marathoners, that implemented Tharp's theme of regeneration, but some observers found the music a turnoff. *Dance Magazine*'s reviewer, Harris Green, thought the ballet worked well in spite of the "grinding monotony" of the Reich section. Both Joan Acocella, who had succeeded Arlene Croce at *The New Yorker*, and Anna Kisselgoff focused on the dancers. Kisselgoff recognized the work as "one of Ms Tharp's true classical ballets" but she found the Reich "merely repetitive" and dismissed the whole second part as overextended. She found the ballet an example of Tharp's ability to "reveal the unsuspected about virtuoso classical dancers," and "above all, a fabulous showcase for Ethan Stiefel . . ." "A Hidden Brando" proclaimed the *Times* headline. Acocella thought *Known by Heart* "the best thing that A.B.T. has commissioned in years," because Tharp was one of the few choreographers who consistently gave dancers the challenges they needed to grow.

After *Known by Heart* Tharp made two more big ballets in quick succession. Her Beethoven investigations came to a climax at New York City Ballet with *The Beethoven Seventh*, premiered on George Balanchine's birthday in January of 2000. Two months later she finished a surpassing theme-and-variations ballet for a large cast of couples at ABT, the Brahms *Variations on a Theme by Haydn*.

Tharp gave a couple of explanations for taking on the well-known Beethoven symphony. She wanted to "make a case for Beethoven in the ballet world," where Balanchine's assertion that the composer was complete without dancing had invoked a fifty-year moratorium. Continuing her *Hammerklavier* train of thought, she'd started choreographing with the composer's complex late sonatas, but when the dancers balked, she'd switched to his more approachable music. She also feared the sound of their feet would drown out the piano. She had begun to identify with the successes and tragedies of Beethoven's life; his formal structuring she'd always understood. Listening to Alfred Brendel's recordings, she told an interviewer, she learned "that on the one hand there was this extreme intelligence, which we know about; on the other hand there was this really dumb sense of humor . . . quite crude and humanistic." Tharp said she wanted to counteract a certain "bleak and barren overreaction against romanticism," and the Seventh, with its range of emotions and rhythmic sophistication, represented "real romanticism" to her.

At a lecture-demonstration for New York City Ballet patrons shortly after the *Beethoven Seventh* premiere, Tharp was asked why it had taken fifteen years for her to return to the company. She gave a curiously poignant answer. After *Brahms/Handel*, she'd turned down invitations to choreograph so as not to use rehearsal time that Jerome Robbins might have needed. She called Peter Martins after Robbins died in the summer of 1998. She had also hesitated out of a kind of reverence about the company. "You don't come here to do a ballet," she said. "You come to address Balanchine." It had taken some time before she felt she'd earned the right to bring Beethoven to the NYCB dancers.

The Seventh Symphony had its own celebrated history. Richard Wagner had famously called it the Apotheosis of the Dance; Isadora Duncan had scandalously danced it as a solo; Léonide Massine had choreographed it as an allegory on the life and death of civilization. Tharp's more immediate forerunners for the ballet were Balanchine and Robbins. Though it was rare for her to take on a large symphonic structure, Balanchine had done so frequently. Like *Symphony in C* (Bizet) or *Four Temperaments* (Hindemith), *The Beethoven Seventh* was a showpiece for dancers and dancing of different qualities, each movement a self-contained essay, with the players and themes assembling for a grand, all-inclusive finale. Robbins's 1979 *Four Seasons*, set to a suite from Verdi's opera *Les Vêpres siciliennes*, had also switched tonalities from one section to the next, and, not so incidentally, included a Bacchanalian Autumn section that Robbins made for Baryshnikov, who was then having his sabbatical year at NYCB.

Tharp selected three outstanding male dancers from the company who represented a range of possibilities suited to the music. Peter Boal was the unimaginably pure classical dancer, whose continual striving for the ideal could "leaven our difficulties with lightness." Nikolaj Hübbe would illustrate the "perfect romantic world that is tragedy." Damian Woetzel was the agile, antic incarnation of the bacchanalian scherzo, a "spirit that looks to nature," said Tharp. Each man danced with a female partner (Jenifer Ringer, Wendy Whelan, and Miranda Weese). A corps of twelve dancers, mostly working in couples, backed up all three movements. Tharp gave small solo passages to the corps dancers. Tom Gold opened the ballet in a double-entendre acknowledging his participation in the preliminary stages of choreographing. As the curtain rose he emerged from a group posed in darkness, to personify

Beethoven's preamble. A concluding Allegro con Brio enlisted the whole cast, propelled by an "optimism to weld and bind all these forces together."

Longtime NYCB supporter Robert Gottlieb, writing for *The New York Observer* later on, thought the ballet was Tharp "at her bloated worst," but the dancers once again thrilled the critics. Nikolaj Hübbe, the tragic hero of the second movement, was singled out for what Anna Kisselgoff called his "weighted passion." Acocella was disappointed that the ballet wasn't more interesting, but she thought Tharp had drawn an exceptional performance from Wendy Whelan—as Hübbe's elusive muse, she became "not just human and serious but also sexy." Most of the critics hoped that Tharp's renewed association with New York City Ballet would prove more durable than her first. The company was in chronic need of choreographers who could supply the repertory without betraying its heritage. Tharp could invigorate dancers, and she'd even conquered the classical challenge. "She walked right in and felt at home," said Kisselgoff. But the ballet's derivative form seemed tamer than what critics expected of Tharp. Perhaps she was trying too hard to be respectful. Acocella thought being in the home of Balanchine gave her the jitters.

Two months after the premiere of *The Beethoven Seventh*, the *Brahms-Haydn* made its appearance during an ABT season at the Kennedy Center. Its first New York performance took place on 9 May 2000 at the company's sixtieth anniversary gala. If Tharp had any nervousness about entering Balanchine's temple of classicism, she now felt very confident. She was back at ABT, where she'd made over a dozen ballets and where she had a cadre of dancers who loved working with her. She was also back in the room with Brahms and another theme-and-variations project, the third such score of Brahms that she'd undertaken.

Tharp told an interviewer for *USA Today* she preferred the designation "neoromantic" to "neoclassic" for her work, although neoromantic was something she was still in the process of inventing. While preparing for the ballet she'd been reading Shakespeare's sonnets, but if *Brahms-Haydn* was neoromantic, there was little romance in it. She enlisted nearly half of Ballet Theater's principal dancers for a cast that consisted of three main couples, four demisoloist couples, and a corps of eight couples. It was a massive work, tightly structured and overflowing with movement. Although the scale of the ballet shifted to allow for solos and featured duets, her real innovation here was in plotting almost all the ensemble work for pairs of dancers. Partners not only executed a virtuosic array of lifts and traveling

footwork, they created group patterns in concert with other sets of partners. It wasn't easy to detect the ballet's inner workings. Tharp explained
the scheme to Deborah Jowitt as triple counterpoint, a "support system between the foreground, the middle ground and the background." Santo Loquasto's costumes, in subtle shades of some pale but indefinite color, didn't
help the audience to differentiate among the troops streaming through.

As a compositional spectacle, the work was unique and impressive.
Tharp felt she'd finally learned how to make a big ballet, and the press
agreed. Mindy Aloff thought "*The Beethoven Seventh* is a brave work; *The
Brahms-Haydn Variations* is a mastered one." Tharp spoke about the *Brahms* as
a kind of summation: "My career has been spent preparing me to be who I
am now. I think the *Brahms* obviously shows a certain control of form. Now
it's my responsibility to move forward. . . . Right now I am where I always
intended to be." The ballet surfaced only once more in ABT's repertory, a
year later, although Stacy Caddell soon taught it in Berlin. ABT found it
cumbersome—too big for the City Center stage where the company did its
fall seasons of contemporary work, and too much strain on the available
manpower—essentially it required thirty virtuoso dancers.

Mindy Aloff offered an admiring assessment of Tharp's classical achievement in a *New Republic* essay on the new Brahms and Beethoven ballets. Acknowledging Tharp's missteps, Aloff discounted them against the bigger
picture. It was evident that

> . . . she approaches ballet very seriously, and her flaws are more interesting
> than most of her colleagues' achievements. Her choreography is vital and
> musically intelligent, her vision of the stage as an arena of forces is huge, her
> highs are thrilling, and her ballets exhibit a fierce belief in classicism as a liv-
> ing potency, something that is relevant to the accelerated, almost manic dis-
> order of contemporary life. She is also a ballet democrat: her works on point
> consist of passionate assaults on symmetry and hierarchy; and in making
> those values into issues, Tharp acknowledges that they are central to the
> very identity of classical ballet.

By the time this tribute got into print, Tharp had made another hairpin
turn. In fact, she had gone back into the dance-company business. Claiming
she needed dancers of her own and overlooking the successful Tharp! com-

pany that she'd started and dismissed within the previous four years, she un-veiled a new group, Twyla Tharp Dance, in the summer of 2000. "I need to be grounded again in my own company," she told Anna Kisselgoff. "These have been twelve years of exile." During this self-imposed exile, she hadn't exactly been on a desert island. She'd made over thirty dances, about half of them for her own groups.

For the new startup, although she didn't reveal it right away, she ex-pected to have the kind of shelter she'd always wanted—a home base and an institutional partner with connections to big-money sources. In 1999 Harvey Lichtenstein had retired as director of Brooklyn Academy and moved over to a spinoff organization, the BAM Local Development Corpo-ration. This office was ready to implement long-deferred plans for revitaliz-ing BAM's downtown Brooklyn neighborhood. Lichtenstein had helped Mark Morris acquire a five-story loft building across the street from BAM which was in the final stages of a multimillion-dollar makeover—Morris's new school and studio space was set to open in the spring of 2001. The LDC now had a visionary plan, with significant government and business support, to transform the area into a "vibrant, new cultural district—complete with museums, theaters, artist and dance studios, retail stores, restaurants, a boutique hotel and housing." As Tharp was starting her new company, she called Lichtenstein to say she was looking for a space. He knew she would be an great asset to his plan. He found a church with some vacant space and convinced her to take a look at it.

On 17 January 2001, with the company back from its inaugural perfor-mances at the American Dance Festival and the Kennedy Center, BAM Local Development Corp. staged a major press event at the 139-year-old Lafayette Avenue Presbyterian Church to announce Tharp's imminent occupancy. The story was big news for the Fort Greene section of Brooklyn. The *Times* called the deal "a coup for efforts to create a cultural district in Brooklyn." The space, a former Sunday school, was a hall above the church sanctuary, where Tharp could hold rehearsals, classes, and informal performances. With help from the LDC she would renovate the space and open the doors in the spring. Despite some vocal community concerns about gentrification and the incursion of a high-profile, high-culture dance company into an African-American church, pastor David Dyson saw the proposed residency as "a blessing." The church had launched its own campaign to repair and restore the building, and LDC's contribution to the upgrade of the dance space would be "one more thing to help in our cause with funders."

Tharp would at last get her own home, she'd be able to start a school. Suspending her nearly pathological reluctance to talk about her future plans, she laid out a grandiose three-year agenda. The company would rehearse in the space, of course, with public classes arranged around their schedule and longer workshops taking place when they were on tour. Tharp wanted to revive about forty of her early works, all the way back to *Tank Dive*, and videotape them in the space. There would be informal showings of this repertory, with the space converted to hold an audience of 200 to 250, and then regular performances, starting with a duet program, at BAM and other theatrical venues. She would double the size of the company in the next year, then double it again. By 2003 it would be called the Brooklyn Ballet and it would produce not only Tharp's dances but revivals of modernist landmarks from the twentieth century, along the lines undertaken by Robert Joffrey. As for the school, there would be classes for everyone from adults and children to professional dancers, and open rehearsals for the community. And, with teachers like Sara Rudner and Stacy Caddell, she'd consolidate her "single unified technique." All this, she acknowledged, was "totally and completely dependent on building an administrative infrastructure."

Four months later the plan was dead. Tharp had looked at the $68,000 annual rent she'd be paying to LDC—essentially to amortize their outlay for the renovations—plus the cost of running the space, and she'd backed out. She told the *Times* that she was also concerned because the church board hadn't yet signed off on the deal—she wouldn't go where she wasn't wanted—although Reverend Dyson maintained he'd thought everything was moving toward completion. Tharp said she planned to look for another space. Her thirty-year-old son, Jesse Huot, was now managing her office, and she'd acquired a new booking agency to arrange engagements for the company, but up to the pullout she still hadn't begun to erect that all-important administrative structure to support the imposing new operation.

It was hard to fathom why she panicked. She'd backed away from a similar opportunity in 1982, when BAM offered to help install the company in the Strand Theater, but now she was well established at the top of the dance field. From her account of the financial responsibilities she'd be undertaking, the venture didn't seem overwhelming. She would have been earning income through the school and saving the cost of studio rentals. The touring side of the business would go on as before. There was still the inconvenient commute to Brooklyn, and the neighborhood hadn't improved greatly, although her arrival was meant to spearhead a renewal. And then, the modest circumstances, while satisfying the side of her that approved of shoestring art, might have seemed rather too modest in comparison with Mark Morris's spiffy and expansive new space up the block.

But the most serious stumbling block seems to have been the prospect of a long-term commitment. Her initial lease at the church was to be for five years, and the whole project was loaded with implications of permanence, for both school and company. In order to take this on, she would have to bring in a professional administrator and start fund-raising. Lichtenstein had been trying to convince her that she'd need to do this early in the process, but she saw it only as another drag on the payroll. The salary of an administrator, she indignantly told reporter Anne Midgette in a *Los Angeles Times* interview, could be "three times what a principal dancer is making." She preferred to work up to an infrastructure "organically." What Tharp really wanted, she told Laura Bleiberg of *The Orange County Register*, was to be treated like a professional ball club: "We need a nice new stadium and guaranteed salaries and whatever is required to travel to other cities and perform with pride."

The cancelation of the deal, after its glowing launch, was a huge disappointment to the LDC and the church officials, an embarrassment all around. Reverend Dyson was stunned. Tharp had been "lovely and gracious with us," and he'd been convinced the difficulties would be resolved. "I was deeply saddened," Lichtenstein told the *Times*. Perhaps the January announcement had been premature, but Lichtenstein was swept away by her enthusiasm; he thought she'd stick this time.

When the scheme collapsed, Tharp stopped talking about a repertory company and a school. She had the new Tharp Dance in gear, but contrary to her statements at its inception, she wasn't necessarily planning on settling down. In the summer of 2000, as the company was getting underway, she started planning a Broadway musical to the music of Billy Joel. She visualized her new dancers "in something big and ambitious. A two-hour dance extravaganza to all the hits of a major American pop idol. . . ." John Selya remembers that "Twyla said to us at the very first rehearsal, 'My ultimate goal for this group is to get them in a big commercial project', and of course I remembered it a year later when it became a reality." Almost immediately after abandoning Brooklyn, over the summer of 2001, she started workshopping the Billy Joel material.

The new Twyla Tharp Dance consisted entirely of ballet dancers. John Selya and Keith Roberts had already left American Ballet Theater by the

time she made the *Brahms-Haydn*. Both of them had been leading interpreters of her work since the *Everlast* and *Brief Fling* period. Selya had never
risen above corps de ballet status at ABT, and partly to assuage his frustration, he'd begun making dances there. He was thinking of giving up dancing to choreograph as a freelancer, and he'd taken a job with an Internet
company when Tharp invited him to join Tharp Dance. Roberts became an
ABT principal in 1997 but segued to Broadway as the Swan in the all-male
Swan Lake by English choreographer Matthew Bourne. After the limited run
of that ballet, Roberts returned briefly to ABT but left to dance in the show
Fosse. Ashley Tuttle, also an ABT principal since 1997, arranged to divide
her time between Tharp and the ballet company. Roberts enlisted former
Joffrey Ballet dancer Elizabeth Parkinson, who was appearing with him in
Fosse. The new company was completed with Benjamin Bowman from New
York City Ballet and Alexander Brady from Miami City Ballet. Two Paul
Taylor veterans, Andrew Asnes and Francie Huber, signed on initially but
soon dropped out.

For this unit of four men and two women, Tharp immediately made two
very good dances in contrasting modalities. The Apollonian *Mozart Clarinet
Quintet K.581*, set to one of the composer's most enchanting scores, was a
sunny, carefree work, so engaging that it was sometimes mistaken for a trifle. Tharp remarked after a performance in New York that she considered
the Quintet big music on a small scale—Beethoven's Seventh Symphony
was big on a big scale. *Surfer at the River Styx*, the most defiant battle between
dancing and death that Tharp had yet staged, overcame its muddled scenario with a revved-up orgy of dancing.

Mozart Clarinet Quintet began with a male trio, each of the players taking a
solo turn, and all of them showing off a well-behaved classicism—smooth
turns and softly curving, scooping arms. Selya and Tuttle were joined by
Roberts and Parkinson for the slow second movement. Their simultaneous
but different duets featured complicated lifts in which the men hardly ever
served as stationary porteurs but continued the momentum with traveling
or turning steps while they held the women in the air. The women weren't
on pointe, but that didn't make the piece any less a classical ballet.

Having presented the group in three possible configurations—male trio,
solos, and duets—Tharp introduced another trio possibility. Selya and Bowman partnered Tuttle in tricky two-man lifts and transfers, breaking into
their teamwork with periodic dueling. Roberts and Parkinson returned during Mozart's Ländler section for a goofy waltz that romped over the coy af-

fectations of the Romantic pas de deux. During the concluding theme and variations, the groups swirled in and out. In the last few bars Roberts carried Parkinson off, Tuttle fled, and Selya hoisted Bowman for a running exit. The whole dance explored the idea of groups and individuals blending, separating, answering, and complementing one another, a little like Mozart's instrumental game-playing. *Mozart Clarinet Quintet K.581* was initially performed as a program partner with *Surfer at the River Styx*, and critics were so overcome by the Dionysian *Surfer* that the Mozart didn't get much attention. In fact, it began to disappear after the first round of touring.

Surfer at the River Styx was another of Tharp's powerful examinations of death and transfiguration. Like *The Catherine Wheel* it went abruptly from darkness to light. The dancing itself, a passionate expenditure of disciplined energy, served as a metaphor and a medium for crossing over. Selya and Roberts danced related but individual characters, one rangy and restless, one intensely classical. Selya skimmed and slid close to the ground. He used a tightly wound power to lunge and catapult into barrel turns. Roberts did compact turns and huge jumps with an airy, relaxed upper body. Separately, they encountered two other pairs of dancers—a depersonalized chorus—sometimes leading them, sometimes becoming their victims. Donald Knaack's junk band supported the dances with African and Asian-derived rhythms.

The protagonists worked up to longer solo passages of nonstop turning—Roberts spinning with smoothly changing leg positions, Selya punching out karate kicks, pirouettes, break-dance windmills. A series of jetés en tournant brought them together for a mirroring duet, then a turn-taking challenge dance. They seemed to be approaching a merger when Selya was carried out by the chorus. A minute later Roberts, seemingly at the point of exhaustion, faltered away in the other direction. Then the frenzy was suddenly spent and the mood inverted. Selya reappeared, walking meditatively as the others enacted a cathartic vision of slow lifts and regroupings, with Parkinson carried off in a split, into the light.

No one was in any doubt about the powerful performances, especially that of John Selya, but the *River Styx* baffled everyone who tried to understand it as a story or a character study. "Dithery and opaque," Joan Acocella called it. Tharp's dance was satisfyingly showy, but she was also going for depth, even secrets. She had aroused expectations by freely admitting the dance was suggested by *The Bacchae* of Euripides, a blood-and-thunder Greek drama about King Pentheus, who defied Bacchus/Dionysos by sneak-

ing into the rites presided over by his mother and was punished, then for-
given, by the Bacchantes. Tharp piled on more clues with the dance title,
but neither the idea of surfing nor the fabled boundary between earth and
the Underworld related immediately to the play. Tharp told interviewer
Robert Johnson that the dance also included "an all-purpose Chaos and explosion of the Earth," but that the ending signified "humility and compassion for human failings."

Critics went digging for connections. Some shared Anna Kisselgoff's
view of the piece as "a sketchy allegory about a hero crossing over to the
other side and toward redemption, complete with heavenly apotheosis."
Others invoked the play's antagonists to explain the presence of two featured dancers, but there was no agreement about which character either
Selya or Roberts played, or whether they were exchanging roles or playing
two sides of the same character. Selya says he and Roberts were contrasting
characters but the specifics could be left ambiguous. The four other dancers
may have stood for a Greek chorus; some writers thought they represented
water.

Surfer reads as a series of discontinuous episodes and arias rather than a
story. As usual, far too many themes were swirling around in Tharp's mind
for easy assembly. She was working like a modern dance choreographer,
layering several distantly related sources together so that the characters can
represent more than one idea and don't have to act out a plot. Martha Graham, in her Greek dramas, was a master at this kind of danced metaphor,
and Tharp had diligently pursued Graham's example with *Demeter and Persephone*. *Surfer* also followed Graham's lead; its lesson about struggle and redemption would "read" even if you didn't recognize its mythical
underpinnings.

Tharp made one more piece for these dancers, a playful Americana piece
called *Westerly Round*, with a featured role for Elizabeth Parkinson as a country girl surrounded by three male admirers. The repertory now included the
three recent pieces plus the Junkman duet from *Known by Heart*, the *Fugue*,
and the *One Hundreds/Fifties*. From the time the BAM project was scuttled, in
May of 2001, until the end of March 2002, the company played the Ah-
manson Center in Los Angeles, Jacob's Pillow, several West Coast cities, the
Holland Festival, and Lyon, France, followed by another two-month American tour. Meanwhile Tharp was working on the Billy Joel material. She

held auditions for the show in November 2001, and by spring she had la-
dled the entire Tharp Dance company into *Movin' Out*.

The show began a summer of previews at the Shubert Theater in
Chicago, with a press opening midway, on 19 July. *Movin' Out* resisted the
categories. A story ballet with popular songs and a theme out of modern
American folklore, it had no dialogue and the dancers didn't sing. The
Chicago critics disliked it, but Tharp refused to surrender. For the next
three months she worked on tightening and clarifying the plot, a story line
she'd developed by stitching together about two dozen of the Piano Man's
songs. To add a conventional Broadway opening number, she retrieved some
choreography from her 1975 Chuck Berry dance *Ocean's Motion*. When
Movin' Out arrived in New York, it still didn't fit the mold, but the score and
the dancing covered its flaws.

Pitched to a Broadway demographic, a middle-aged, suburban audience
of Billy Joel fans who remembered the Vietnam War, *Movin' Out* was the
Broadway breakthrough Tharp had been seeking for years. In a sense, there
wasn't anything in it that she hadn't done before. She'd staged parades, calisthenics, combat, psychedelic fantasies, and joggers in the park. Kids in the
'60s were surfing and dancing and fooling around with cars in *Deuce Coupe*.
They went to Vietnam and some didn't come back in *Hair*. Misfits and outlaws endured their personal hell and were redeemed in *Noir a.k.a. Bartok,
Surfer at the River Styx*, and *I Remember Clifford*, the dance she made for Hubbard
Street Dance Chicago in 1995, about the life of jazz composer Clifford
Brown, who kicked his drug addiction after a religious conversion. *Movin'
Out* was Tharp's coming-of-age mantra all over again—adaptation to the
community, order out of chaos, the story of growing up and going home. Its
upward, upbeat trajectory from innocence to trials and trauma to celebration was perfect for the Broadway audience. She had crafted not only a
tremendous choreographic throughline, she accomplished it with pacing
and emotional variety, tapping into Billy Joel's anger, his doo-wop, his ten-
der ballads, and teenage testosterone.

In Tharp's scenario for *Movin' Out*, the Long Island teens are discovered
hanging out around a '65 Mustang convertible. Seized with patriotism, they
sign up for the army and leave their girlfriends behind. They slog through
basic training. Then they're in Vietnam and the show veers into darkness—
a killing in battle, a military funeral, and a descent into guilt, drugs, desperate sex, and psychological screwups. Years pass. They heal, as Tharp wants
the audience to do, after she's pricked its conscience. Tharp has said that

the show is a tribute to the veterans who deserved more honor than they got after the Vietnam War finally ended. She wanted the show to acknowledge that Vietnam was history, "that that rift in our culture was over." But as the country sank deeper into post-9/11 politics, the dancers began getting thank-you letters from veterans, while other members of the audience were moved by what they took as an antiwar message.

Tharp had at last welded together the polar opposites of popular culture and highbrow dancing, with a concept that burrowed deep into the American psyche. If there were clichés in the plot, said *The New York Times* theater critic Ben Brantley, Tharp had demonstrated why those clichés endured. She had created "a shimmering portrait of an American generation." Both theater and dance critics recognized the extraordinary performances of singer Michael Cavanaugh and the band, and of course the dancers. Once again Tharp had given them the chance to surpass themselves, physically and dramatically, by constructing their characters out of their own qualities. John Selya was Eddie, the antihero with mercurial power and adaptability. Keith Roberts, as his pal Tony, was fast and passionate. Elizabeth Parkinson was Brenda, the party girl with the extravagant legs. Ashley Tuttle and Benjamin Bowman were the nice kids who became casualties of war. The principals were backed up by an equally committed cast of alternates and a thirteen-member dance ensemble.

Once the show was a solid success, it was going to take significant maintenance. Dancers got injured and had to be replaced. Second-cast members and swings had to be rehearsed and spaced in. People left. There were more auditions. New hires had to learn their roles. And all eight shows a week had to be kept in polished condition. It took several coaches to manage this perpetual upkeep. Stacy Caddell was hired in December 2002 as dance supervisor, and Tharp checked on the production frequently when she was in town.

No sooner had the show gotten on its feet than Tharp hired another company of eight young dancers. They began touring in January of 2003 with the *River Styx/Westerly Round/Fugue/Junkman Duet* repertory plus a new story dance, *Even the King*, to Johann Strauss waltzes orchestrated by Arnold Schönberg. Soon it became apparent that Tharp was prepping the new Tharp Dance for the rigors of *Movin' Out. Surfer at the River Styx* fell into perspective as the forerunner of the show's demonic performing style. The little company cultivated an extroverted, Broadway attitude, even when delivering the structural rigors of *The Fugue*. After only a year Tharp disbanded Tharp Dance again and drafted four of the dancers for the show's first touring company. The tour opened in Detroit in January 2004, with bookings at least two years ahead.

Ever the entrepreneur, Tharp went along on the early stages of the tour, not only to supervise the show. She combined publicizing the tour with promoting a new book. *The Creative Habit*, published in September 2003 by Simon & Schuster, was based on her 1999 Hunter College lectures. Aimed at the general public as well as artists, it was a primer of how-to-do-it exercises, quizzes, anecdotes, and advice on how to maximize one's undeveloped talents and live a livelier life.

Movin' Out received ten Tony nominations, all under the Musical category except for Lighting Designer Donald Holder. Selya and Parkinson were nominated for Best Actor and Actress; Cavanaugh, Roberts, and Tuttle for featured roles. The show was nominated as Best Musical, and Tharp as Best Director as well as Best Choreographer. When the winners were named, on 8 June 2003, Billy Joel and Stuart Malina received the Tony for their orchestrations of Joel's songs. Tharp was named Best Choreographer, although she probably was hoping for more.

Hairspray won most of the honors that year, but *Movin' Out* occupied a featured spot on the televised award ceremonies. To open the show, Billy Joel and a concert grand piano were stationed in the middle of Times Square surrounded by a small crowd. After he sang "New York State of Mind," the cameras moved inside Radio City Music Hall, where Tharp had staged a four-minute opening dance for the combined casts of *Movin' Out*. Thirty minutes later, she strode down the aisle to accept her Tony, in a black, heavily brocaded sheath dress with spaghetti straps and an indefinable hemline. She began her curt speech with a story about auditioning for the Rockettes as a youngster, and how she didn't make it because she couldn't muster a cheery face. As she went on to thank her associates, she was almost smiling.

EPILOGUE

An Audience of One

The act of watching dancing, as critics pursue it, is a selective practice. With experience you acquire certain techniques for devising flimsy barricades against the loss of the elusive and the unpredictable. You begin to watch in certain ways, to sift out and discard information efficiently. Everyone's techniques are different; every performance demands slight adjustments. But you do develop working habits. Your first goal is to track what's happening. Then you hope to imprint, consciously or unconsciously, enough information to be able to give an evocative account of something, some version of a dance that will likely be long gone by the time anyone reads what you've written.

In this intensely inquisitive process, familiar things take on the status of tropes. The way a Paul Taylor dancer moves becomes pretty much a known quantity, with portents and resonances long established. A nineteenth-century ballet's plot demands little attention. When certain dancers enter the stage in a certain way, you almost know in advance what they'll do. All of these things may continue to give you pleasure, but it's not the pleasure of discovery. The number of striking images diminishes as the years go by. The sense of seeing something original—in large part a construction of the critic herself—occurs less frequently, and the deadening sense that you've seen this before recurs more often.

All of my years as a critic I've resisted this kind of perceptual burnout. But I think it's inevitable, and unless the critic can gain some new perspectives, what was once an enviable way to spend your life will become a routine. You can learn to overcome most of the handicaps to good criticism, but boredom is fatal. I've tried many strategies to refocus my relationship to dance performance, beginning with a broad definition of the field I'm trying to cover. Every writer knows the advantages of changing formats—sprinkling long articles in among short ones, writing things other than reviews and critical essays, immersing oneself in book-length projects. Then there's looking at dance on tape or film. There's traveling to see familiar repertory on unfamiliar companies, or to look at familiar companies in unfamiliar places.

It was in the course of one of these field trips—doing a story on Twyla Tharp's 1991 residency at the Wexner Center, Ohio State University—that I ran into dancer Jamie Bishton on the stairs at a postperformance party. Excited and happy, we chatted for a minute about Tharp's spectacular month-long encampment in Columbus. We talked about what a great opportunity it had been for Tharp to make new work and gather a new company together. Then I confessed that even more than the two performances, I'd been inspired by the day I spent watching Tharp choreograph a new dance for herself and six men. "That day you were there was the best of the whole time," he said. "We were having a ball, laughing and working hard. We were dong it for an audience of one. It was special."

The implications of this remark stayed with me for a long time. What was it in that very privileged, protected, and atypical situation that was so exhilarating, for both the dancers and their singular spectator? As a critic I'd sat in theaters much of my life, always feeling an obscure gratitude toward the dancers for what they gave me. I never imagined they got anything from me in return. Not right there, anyway. Criticism's payback usually comes later, in the form of bankable reviews. The Columbus rehearsal was another kind of exchange: an immediate, spontaneous trading of energies, a mutual recognition and participation in a creative process.

Watching Tharp choreograph in Ohio brought me back to the roots, the reason I became a dance critic. It didn't really teach me anything about her talent, of which I've been convinced for ages. It put me back in touch with fundamentals. Tharp's movement can be planned or spontaneous, personal, funny, hard as hell, precise enough to look thrown-away. She doesn't so much invent or create it, she prepares for it. Crusty, driven, demanding, and admiring, she hurls challenges at the dancers. Brave, virtuosic, and cheerful, they volley back what she gives them, and more. She watches them. They watch her. It's the most subtle form of competition and cooperation, a process so intuitive, so intimate that no one can say in the end whose dance it is, and none of the parties to that dance can be removed without endangering its identity. This process is the same for all theatrical dance making, all over the world, only most of it isn't quite so inspired or obsessed.

The dance that appears on the stage no longer embodies this process. It has become a distillation of the process, a new playing out of the process that the choreographer has edited. What was being explored is learned. What was a spontaneous interchange is now a set of practiced responses. An open-ended quest has become a structure. This is the work that the critic and the audience look at, hoping for revelation. But underneath it is that other, even more ephemeral and far less presentable scenario that is part of the dance's history, whether it takes place in the humble shelter of a loft or the staid splendor of an uptown theater. I think dancers treasure this nearly secret collaboration more than any other phase of performance life. They try to carry it into the performance itself, like a rabbit's foot, and they speak of its loss most often when they're trying to recover a dance that has been out of the repertory. But only in its loss is it usually acknowledged. When a critic can capture and communicate this spark which lights the tinder of chorcographic intention, criticism unites most truly with the dance.

—Marcia B. Siegel
— reprinted from *Dance Ink*, summer 1992

NOTES

Much of the research for this book was conducted in the Twyla Tharp Archive at the Jerome Lawrence and Robert E. Lee Theatre Research Institute, The Ohio State University. Unpublished materials cited from that source are labeled with the abbreviation TTA. Other abbreviations used in the notes are as follows:

The 1995 interview of Sara Rudner by Rose Anne Thom was made for the Oral History Project of the Jerome Robbins Dance Division, New York Public Library for the Performing Arts at Lincoln Center. All quotes from that interview are used with permission of Rudner and Thom, and through the courtesy of the Dance Division.

PCTS—Twyla Tharp, *Push Comes to Shove*, 1992.
NYPL—Jerome Robbins Dance Division, New York Public Library for the Performing Arts at Lincoln Center.
NYT—*The New York Times*

I. Leotard Days 1965–1966
page
2. "sort of furry hootchy-kootchy": *PCTS*. 83.
4. "we had passed through the vale . . .": Ibid. 91.
5. "a trio in which visibility is determined . . .": Tharp Dance program book, 1981.
6. "I came out . . .": Tharp in conversation with author, April 15, 2000.

7. "The contemporary artist . . .": José Limón, "On Dance," *Seven Arts #1*, 1953.

7. "Dance form is logical . . .": Doris Humphrey, *The Art of Making Dances* (New York: Grove Press/Evergreen, 1962), 31.

8. "If nothing else is clear . . .": Ronald Sukenick, *Down and In—Life in the Underground* (New York: Collier Books, 1987), 150.

9. "simple, undistinctive activities . . .": Yvonne Rainer, "Some retrospective notes on a dance for ten people and twelve mattresses . . .", *TDR*, vol. 10 no. 2, winter 1965. 170.

9. "how to move in the spaces . . .": Ibid., 178.

9. "NO to spectacle . . .": Ibid., 178.

10. They took their timing from Rudner . . . : Sara Rudner interview with Rose Anne Thom, Feb. 19, 1995. [Oral History Project, NYPL]

11. "she was kind of a formidable . . .": Margaret Jenkins interview with author, May 30, 2000.

11. "a silent ritual": Marcia Marks, *Dance*, January 1966, 58–59.

11. Jenkins remembers: Jenkins/MBS.

12. Huot remembers: Robert Huot interview with author, June 20, 2000.

12. "a man . . . indulged in some mock . . .": Clive Barnes, *NYT*, December 4, 1965.

12. "There certainly wasn't anything . . .": Jenkins/MBS.

12. "It was very dramatic stories . . .": Rudner/Thom, NYPL.

12. "Thank *God* I'm walking . . .": Rudner interviewed by author for *Making Dances*, Blackwood Productions, 1980.

13. "I've been trained . . .": Jenkins/MBS.

13. He thought it might be possible . . . : Huot/MBS.

2. Dance Activities 1967–1969

page

15. "2 Dance Companies . . .": *NYT*, February 15, 1967.

15. football signals: Huot/MBS, June 20, 2000.

15. "classical trio . . .": chronology in *Dance Magazine*, April 1973, unpaginated.

15. Rudner remembered . . . : Rudner/Thom, NYPL.

15. When one dancer was doing her solo . . . : Rudner e-mail to author, September 6, 2000.

15. "a melodramatic trio": chronology in *Dance Magazine*, April 1973.

15. "a total rage": Rudner/Thom, NYPL.

16. "when you took a step . . .": Ibid.

16. After an advance viewing . . . : Ibid.

16–17. "I must say . . .": "Eggs Don't Bounce," *Dance and Dancers*, May 1967.

17. Jenkins also felt . . . : Jenkins/MBS.

17–18. "I had given it up a few times . . .": Theresa Dickinson interview with author, May 16, 2000.

18. "Twyla's sitting there . . .": Ibid.

18–19. a thoughtful and admiring column . . . : "Prone Sprawl," *Village Voice*, February 15, 1968.

19. Johnston's interests . . . : Jill Johnston, Preface to *Marmalade Me* (Hanover, N.H.: Wesleyan University Press, 1998), xi–xv.

19. "three and a half minute spectacular": chronology in *Dance Magazine*, April 1973.

19. "highly controlled and choreographed . . .": Rudner/Thom, NYPL.

20. "light and absence of it . . .": Daniel Webster, *Philadelphia Inquirer*, January 14, 1969.

20. "a little chaos . . .": *PCTS*, 100–102.

20. "slip phrase": Rudner/Thom, NYPL.

22. "it was incredibly invigorating . . .": Jenkins/MBS.

22. "very attracted to Twyla's . . .": Dickinson/MBS.

22. Dickinson remembers . . . : Ibid.

23. tense, historic family portrait: The picture ran on October 20, 1968. Jack Mitchell recalled years later that "The shoot was brief, not especially convivial, and no one lingered after." (*Dance Magazine*, December 2000, 16.)

23. "There was a little bit of contempt . . .": Dickinson/MBS.

23. Anna Kisselgoff seemed caught . . . : *NYT*, February 4, 1969.

24. "dealt with movement . . .": Tharp interview with Deborah Jowitt, September 1975.

24. "centered balletic movements": *NYT*, February 4, 1969.

24. "It wasn't really close enough . . .": Lord/MBS, August 31, 2000.

24–25. "Quintet in three sections . . .": chronology in *Dance Magazine*, April 1973.

25. "very very dancey . . .": Tharp/Jowitt, September 1975.

25. "logical exercises": Gerald Mast, *A Short History of the Movies* (New York: MacMillan Publishing Company, 1986), 454.

25. "performed in three adjacent squares . . .": chronology in *Dance Magazine*, April 1973.

25. "arrangement of many situations . . .": choreographic notes, TTA.

25. Tharp arrived at rehearsals . . . : Rudner/Thom, NYPL.

25–26. Laudenslager was becoming . . . : Lord/MBS.

26. Wright found her way . . . : Rose Marie Wright/MBS, December 1, 1999.

26. "enigmatic but forceful": Daniel Webster, *Philadelphia Inquirer*, January 14, 1969.

26. "organized spontaneity": James Felton, *The Evening Bulletin*, January 14, 1969.

26–27. "Double quintet . . .": chronology in *Dance Magazine*, April 1973.

27. "Watching a piece . . .": "The Avant-Garde on Broadway," *Ballet Review*, Spring 1969, vol.2 no 3.

27. "We weren't thinking about getting paid . . .": R.M. Wright/MBS, December 1, 1999.

27. "extreme moment of Nirvana": Dickinson/MBS.

27. "We knew one another's abilities . . .": *PCTS*, 104–5.

27. "The things we worked on . . .": Rudner/Thom, NYPL.

3. The End of Amazonia 1969–1971

page

29. Reinhart felt a clean sweep . . .": Charles Reinhart interview with author, September 30, 2000.

29. Doris Humphrey Choreographic Fellowship: Ibid.

30. "we would find . . .": *PCTS*, 117.

31. "a dramatic situation": choreographic notes, TTA.

31. All six company dancers . . . : *PCTS*, 120–121.

32. Actually, Rudner was dancing . . . : Rudner conversation with author, November 6, 2000.

32. Tharp spent the rest of the evening . . . : *PCTS*, 122.

32–33. For example, her notes . . . : choreographic notes, TTA.

33. For Tharp, the axiomatic pedestrianism . . . : Tharp's notes for unpublished manuscript, Laura Shapiro and Twyla Tharp, note to p. 121, Item 24.

33. "a masterly coup . . .": *NYT*, July 21, 1969.

34. "a mounting density of movement . . .": Dickinson/MBS.

34. In September of 1969 he used it . . . : Shapiro, unpublished manuscript, 130.

35. *La Prose du Transsibérien* . . . : Roger Shattuck, *The Banquet Years* (New York: Vintage, 1968), 349.

35. Historian Stephen Kern . . . : Stephen Kern, *The Culture of Time and Space 1880–1918* (Cambridge: Harvard University Press, 1983), 72–74.

35. "the last of the great '60s art spectaculars": Calvin Tomkins, *Off the Wall* (New York: Penguin Books, 1983), 291.

35. (Tharp says . . .): *PCTS*, 125–126.

35. and the auditorium passages . . . : Lincoln Kaye, *Hartford Courant*, November 16, 1969.

36. "People are more accustomed . . .": Tharp interview with author, December 13, 2000.

36. "walking around the museum . . .": program for *Dancing in the Streets*, Hartford, November 11, 1969.

36. "quietly watching a monitor . . .": Ibid.

37. Rudner was hoping . . . : Rudner/Thom, NYPL.

37. "very dancey and steppy": R.M. Wright/MBS, December 27, 2000.

37. "a spectacular solo study . . .": *Dance Magazine*, March 1970, 90–92.

38. never intended to be finished: program for *Dancing in the Streets*, Hartford, November 11, 1969.

38. "we'd just walk by . . .": Tharp/MBS, December 27, 2000.

38. At the library . . . : Rudner conversation with author, January 11, 2001.

38. Tharp created a new solo . . . : R.M. Wright/MBS, December 27, 2000.

38. "aristocratic movement . . .": Don McDonagh, *The Rise and Fall and Rise of Modern Dance* (New York: Outerbridge & Dientsfrey, 1970), 116.

38. "chewed gum and did a sort of Swedish . . .": Lincoln Kaye, *Hartford Courant*, November 11, 1969.

38. "At the count of 42 . . .": Ibid.

38. The audience and the performers . . . : program for *Dancing in the Streets*.

38–39. finding herself dancing face-to-face with one of her teachers . . . : Rosalind Newman interview with author, March 7, 2000.

39. "She'd tell us . . .": R.M. Wright/MBS, December 1, 1999.

39. "Twyla didn't come up to you . . .": Rudner/Thom, NYPL.

39. "Twyla, when she *loves* you . . .": R.M. Wright/MBS, December 7, 1999.

39–40. "She really did care . . .": Newman/MBS.

40. "We shared adversities . . .": Tharp's notes for unpublished manuscript, Laura Shapiro and Twyla Tharp, note to p. 125, Item 26.

40. Tupling confirms this: Shapiro, unpublished manuscript, 124–125.

40. costumes borrowed from choreographer-designer James Waring: Tharp/MBS, December 13, 2000.

40. Bob Huot came up with the idea . . . : Huot/MBS, June 22, 2000.

41. "Twyla never figured out . . .": Newman/MBS.

41. "I know they can't see . . .": Marcia B. Siegel, "Two Museum Pieces," *At the Vanishing Point* (New York: Saturday Review Press, 1972), 272.

41. Anna Kisselgoff of the *Times* . . . : *NYT*, January 23, 1970.

41. "wearisome": *Dance Magazine*, March 1970, 90–92.

41. Roz Newman remembers . . . : Newman/MBS.

42. "I had every intention of quitting . . .": Tharp/MBS, December 13, 2000.

42. "political declamations . . .": Ibid.

43. Tharp's hometown . . . : Robert V. Hine, *California's Utopian Colonies* (Berkeley: University of California Press, 1983), 158.

43. "go back in and do better": Tharp's notes for unpublished manuscript, Laura Shapiro and Twyla Tharp, note to p. 131, Item 2.

43. "I made more dance . . .": *PCTS*, 132.

44. "We were like people who went out . . .": Shapiro, unpublished manuscript, 142.

44. "I thought it was fabulous . . .": Isabel Garcia-Lorca interview with author, January 18, 2001.

44. According to Wright . . . : R. M. Wright/MBS, December 1, 1999.

45. Tharp's notes for this . . . : choreographic notes, TTA.

45. According to Boston critic . . . : Jane Goldberg, *Boston Globe*, September 1, 1970.

45. Perhaps prompted by a dream . . . : "Margery Tupling had a dream in which we were working on a dance with one hundred parts." Tharp's notes for *Group Activities, Ballet Review*, vol.2 no.5, 1969, 20.

45–46. All 150 could be done . . . : choreographic notes, TTA.

46. "trying to get the world . . .": Tharp quoted in email, Allen Robertson to author, January 5, 2001.

46. Tharp compared it to a man's game: Shapiro, unpublished manuscript, 135–140.

46. deliberately acknowledging Bach: Tharp's notes for unpublished manuscript, Laura Shapiro and Twyla Tharp, note to p. 136, Item 6.

47. Tharp was furious . . . : Dana Reitz interview with author, August 17, 2000, and Kenneth Rinker interview with author, January 19, 2001.

47. Dana Reitz had just graduated . . . : Reitz/MBS.

48. Tharp thought this was a bad idea . . . : Brenda Way interview with author, January 9, 2001.

50. "a leg phrase . . .": R. M. Wright/MBS, March 2, 2001.

50. At Battery Park . . . : R. M. Wright/MBS, December 1, 1999.

50. "fairly elaborate improvisations . . .": "Twyla Tharp: Questions and Answers," *Ballet Review*, vol.4, no.1, 1971, 44.

50. Rudner and Wright thought the costumes . . . : R. M. Wright/MBS, December 1, 1999.

51. Paul Epstein, an attorney . . . : Paul Epstein conversation with author, February 8, 2005.

4. The Entertainer 1971–1973

page

52. "I realized early on . . .": Huot/MBS, June 20, 2000.

52. "I think I was probably . . .": Huot/MBS, June 22, 2000.

54. "this determined little figure . . .": Kosmas/MBS, January 29, 2001.

54–55. Dana Reitz, who was rehearsing . . . : Reitz/MBS, August 17, 2000.

55–56. Tharp explained that she had not intended . . . : choreographic notes, TTA.

56. "an excruciatingly specific time score . . .": Brenda Way/MBS, January 9, 2001.

56. Tharp says she noted . . . : *PCTS*, 156.

57. 1974 broadcast of the dance: "Twyla Tharp and Eight Jelly Rolls," London Weekend Television, 1974. Derek Bailey, producer and director.

57. For Rudner's solo . . . : Rudner/Thom, NYPL.

58. "I hated that separation . . .": R. M. Wright/MBS, December 1, 1999.

59. one can't identify too closely . . . : Gerald Mast, *The Comic Mind—Comedy and The Movies* (Chicago: University of Chicago Press, 1979), 21.

59. The last Jelly Roll . . . : R. M. Wright/MBS, December 7, 1999.

60. lost interest in *The Fugue* . . . : Clive Barnes, *NYT*, September 19, 1971.

60. "two gawky, interminable essays . . .": Greer Johnson, *Cue*, September 22, 1971.

60. "Twyla Tharp's subject . . .": "Twyla Tharp's Red Hot Peppers," *Ballet Review*, winter 1971.

60. one of the hundred outstanding . . . : *The San Bernardino Sun*, June 22, 1971.

61. "You can't get to feeling safe . . .": Marcia B. Siegel, *The Boston Herald Traveler*, May 9, 1972.

61. "less bourgeois" venue . . . : Jean-Pierre Barbe, *l'Aurore*, November 4, 1971. [author's translation]

61. Tharp wanted to perform . . . : Tharp interview with Lise Brunel, *Chroniques de l'Art Vivant*, Paris, 1971.

61. Rudner only knew eighty . . . : Rudner conversation with author, February 17, 2001.

61. "We cried.": R. M. Wright/MBS, December 7, 1999.

62. nothing but pretension . . . : F. de S., *Le Figaro*, November 11, 1971. [author's translation]

62. "Poor Torelli!": Jean-Pierre Barbe, *l'Aurore*, November 4, 1971. [author's translation]

62. Claude Sarraute of *Le Monde* . . . : Sarraute, *Le Monde*, November 5, 1971.

62. John Percival came over . . . : Percival, *Dance and Dancers*, January 1972.

62. After the Festival . . . : Kosmas/MBS, January 29, 2001.

62. Tharp later acknowledged . . . : Tharp interview with Don McDonagh, May 30, 1973.

63. As recorded for television's *Camera Three* . . . : "The Bix Pieces," *Camera Three*, recorded May 18, 1973, Merrill Brockway, producer.

64. "Why They Were Made": all quotes from part two of *The Bix Pieces*, by Twyla Tharp.

65. Wright would start a phrase . . . : R. M. Wright/MBS, June 26, 2001.

67. "It's the amount of traffic . . .": William Whitener interview with author, October 15, 2001.

68. *The Raggedy Dances*: observations based on a tape made in performance at the College of St. Catherine in Minneapolis, November 1972.

68. "She dances for a long time . . .": Deborah Jowitt, "Enter the Dancers, Rippling Fastidiously," *Village Voice*, November 2, 1972.

68. "that it was somebody . . .": Garcia-Lorca/MBS, January 18, 2001.

69. Clive Barnes loved "The Bix Pieces": *NYT*, September 14, 1972.

69. "her work has a mixture . . .": Clive Barnes, *NYT*, November 5, 1972.

69. "Are modern dancers . . .": Ellen Jacobs, "Modern dance goes public," *Changes*, December/January 1973, 14.

69–70. Robert Joffrey attended the Delacorte . . . : Sasha Anawalt, *The Joffrey Ballet* (New York: Scribner, 1996), 278.

71. The rest of the songs . . . : *PCTS*, 180–181.

72. lack of condescension . . . : Greil Marcus, *Mystery Train* (New York: E.P. Dutton, 1976), 113.

72. "I was not a strong technical dancer . . .": Garcia-Lorca/MBS, January 18, 2001.

72. "I'm not a ballet dancer . . .": Rinker/MBS, January 19, 2001.

72. "I was just open . . .": Beatriz Rodriguez interview with author, July 20, 2001.

73. "Steps were being thrown out . . .": Richard Colton interview with author, June 26, 2001.

73. "I became Twyla's liaison . . .": R. M. Wright/MBS, December 7, 1999.

74. When money problems . . . : Tharp interview with DMcD, April 20, 1972.

74. "a 1950's ballet in sneakers . . .": Clive Barnes, *NYT*, March 18, 1973.

74. "choreographic squiggling": Clive Barnes, *NYT*, November 11, 1973.

74. When she heard about the mass exodus . . .": Rebecca Wright interview with author, July 19, 2001.

75. "out comes Beatriz Rodriguez . . .": Robb Baker, "Twyla Tharp's 'Deuce Coupe' or, How Alley Oop Came to Dance with the Joffrey," *Dance Magazine*, April 1973.

76. "If someone would run . . .": Colton/MBS, June 26, 2001.

76. "it felt like we were all dancing together . . .": Rinker/MBS, January 19, 2001.

76. "She was one of us . . .": Christine Uchida interview with author, April 12, 2002.

77. "An ongoing upstage mural . . .": *PCTS*, 181.

77. "I never lost sight . . .": *PCTS*, 177.

77. a cover story on graffiti: "The Graffiti 'Hit' Parade," *New York*, March 26, 1973.

78. "the marvelously zany . . .": Alan Rich, *New York*, March 26, 1973.

5. Local to Express 1973–1975

page

80. "I got on the Twyla Tharp train . . ." and subsequent quotes: Kenneth Rinker interview with author, January 19, 2001.

83. "Define classical": William Whitener interview with author, October 16, 2001.

85. "We knew exactly the direction . . .": Colton/MBS, June 26, 2001.

85. "the more feminine side . . .": Whitener/MBS, October 16, 2001.

86. Kisselgoff liked *As Time Goes By* . . . : Anna Kisselgoff, *NYT*, October 26, 1973.

86. his pleasure in it . . . : Clive Barnes, *NYT*, November 11, 1973.

86. "Miss Tharp creates for the moment . . .": Ibid.

87. "more to be censured . . .": Robert Commanday, *San Francisco Chronicle*, May 30, 1974.

87. "the Nijinska of our time.": Arlene Croce, "A Moment in Time," *The New Yorker*, November 19, 1973.

87. "a whole range of dynamics . . .": Deborah Jowitt, "Gimme a little time to play in," *Village Voice*, November 1, 1973.

87–88. She wrote rambling notes . . . : Tharp's choreographic notes, TTA.

88. "Staring success in the face . . .": Tharp interviewed by Mike Steele, *Minneapolis Tribune*, January 27, 1974.

88. "but that means traveling . . .": Tharp interview with Peter Williams, *Dance and Dancers*, May 1974.

88. In one of the three *Egg Stories* . . . : The first of the three *Egg Stories* filmed by WGBH was edited into a 1982 Tharp anthology video called the *Scrapbook*.

89. "Eggs Don't Bounce": John Percival, *Dance and Dancers*, May 1967.

89. "It involved a linear sequence . . .": Tom Rawe in email to the author, December 30, 2001.

89. She and Rinker performed . . . : R. M. Wright/MBS, December 1, 1999.

89. "taking dance into a larger context . . .": Mike Steele, *Minneapolis Tribune*, January 28, 1974.

89. introspection beneath the entertainment . . . : Peter Altman, *Minneapolis Star*, n.d.

90. "She wanted to find out . . .": Tom Rawe and Jennifer Way interview with the author, April 8, 2001.

91. "I think it was only then . . .": Ibid.

92. "When she was performing . . .": Rinker/MBS, January 19, 2001.

92. "It just makes sense . . .": Garcia-Lorca/MBS, January 18, 2001.

93. "I made it easy for her . . .": Ibid.

93. It was a risky venture . . . : Rinker/MBS, January 19, 2001.

93. two glowing reviews: Clement Crisp, "Twyla Tharp" and "The Raggedy Dances," *Financial Times*, May 1974, n.d.

93. "portentous meaning . . .": Peter Williams, "The Movable Tharp," *Dance and Dancers*, July 1974.

94. "one of my happiest evenings . . .": Mary Clarke, *Dancing Times*, May 1974.

94. "unqualified success . . .": Peter Rosenwald, *Dance News*, May 1974.

95. "With Twyla it was the intelligence . . .": Sara Rudner talking on documentary section of "Twyla Tharp and *Eight Jelly Rolls*," London Weekend Television, 1974.

95–96. Tharp came down with the flu . . . : R. M. Wright/MBS, March 2, 2001.

96. Along with *Eight Jelly Rolls* . . . : R. M. Wright/MBS, March 2, 2001, and Tharp's email to author, February 22, 2002.

97. For the finale . . . : R. M. Wright/MBS, March 2, 2001.

97. she admits to pursuing him . . . : *PCTS*, 167, 170, 186, 192.

99. She didn't have the patience . . . : William Kosmas interview with author, January 29, 2001.

99. She began a workshop . . . : Sharon Kinney interview with author, May 1, 2000.

99. "the most decisive young American . . .": *Vogue*, June 1975, 102–103.

99. "backed off . . .": Kosmas/MBS, January 29, 2001.

100. "I was out on a farm . . .": Tharp at lecture-demonstration, taped during Minneapolis-St. Paul residency, February 20, 1975.

100. "She processed information . . .": Rhoda Grauer interview with author, October 24, 2000.

100. She remembers making a deal . . . : Ibid.

101. This 1906 building . . . : *Minneapolis Star*, February 19, 1975 and Roy Close email to author, April 22, 2002.

101. Grauer saw Weil . . . : Grauer/MBS, October 24, 2000.

101. In addition to the open rehearsals . . . : press release, Walker Art Center, January 31, 1975.

101. They acquired a contingent . . . : Tom Rawe and Jennifer Way/MBS, April 8, 2001.

102. Tickets for the performances . . . : advertisement, *St. Paul Pioneer Press*, February 9, 1975.

102. "The result is like a spinning trip . . .": Allen Robertson, *Minnesota Daily*, February 28, 1975.

102. Tharp filtered the movement material . . . :" *PCTS*, 205–206.

102. she began making material . . ." : *PCTS*, 193.

102. "four desperate people . . .": *PCTS*, 194.

102. The title was a tribute . . . : Rawe and Way/MBS, April 8, 2001.

103. "really is a recapitulation . . .": R. M. Wright/MBS, June 26, 2001.

103. "The material was much more mushy . . .": Ibid.

103. the definitive Twyla Tharp style: Laura Shapiro, unpublished ms, 194.

104. a give-back piece: Rawe and Way/MBS, April 8, 2001.

104. chosen to initiate the PBS *Dance in America* series: "Sue's Leg: Remembering the '30s" first aired March 24, 1976.

104. "In my wildest imagination . . .": Rinker/MBS, January 19, 2001.

6. The Big Leagues 1975–1978

page

107. "sort of men and women on stage . . .": Mikhail Baryshnikov interview with author, July 25, 2002.

107. *The 49 Amici* . . . : *NYT*, July 13, 1975.

107. Tharp decided to dance . . . : *PCTS*, 206.

107. "how refined and delicate . . .": Baryshnikov/MBS, July 25, 2002.

107. "they were both obviously amazed . . .": Clive Barnes, *NYT*, January 11, 1976.

107. After Spoleto . . . : *PCTS*, 204.

107. "She was trying to explain to me . . .": Baryshnikov/MBS, July 25, 2002.

108. The first movement belonged to Baryshnikov . . . : These observations are based on the film *Baryshnikov by Tharp* (later called *Baryshnikov Dances Sinatra*), videotaped in 1984 and released by Kultur. I have also studied a performance taped at the Kennedy Center, April 10, 1977. The other principals in 1984 were Susan Jaffe, Elaine Kudo, Cheryl Yaeger, and Robert La Fosse. In my descriptions I have used the original cast to avoid confusion.

109–110. "She was trying to understand . . .": Baryshnikov/MBS, July 25, 2002.

110. "veneer of chaos": Laura Shapiro, *The Boston Globe*, February 1, 1976.

110. "alphabet dancing": Tharp interview with Jane Perlez, *New York Post*, January 1, 1976.

111. "We were a bit afraid . . .": Susan Jones interview with author, May 30, 2002.

113. Tharp had encouraged . . . : Tharp in studio runthrough, videotaped December 13, 1975.

113. Afterward, Gelsey Kirkland . . . : Charles France interview with author, August 1, 2002.

113. "simplistically Oedipal": John T. Elson, *Time*, January 19, 1976.

113. "It has charm, vivacity, humor . . .": Clive Barnes, *NYT*, January 11, 1976.

113. "a real work of art . . .": Arlene Croce, "More or Less Terrific," *The New Yorker*, January 26, 1976.

113. "slapstick . . .": Roger Copeland, *NYT*, February 1, 1976.

113. "rites of personality worship . . .": Dale Harris, *Atlantic Monthly*, August 1976.

114. "the hottest ticket . . .": George Gelles, *Washington Star*, February 8, 1976.

114. "a hit of such proportions . . .": Charles Payne, *American Ballet Theatre* (New York: Knopf, 1977), 251.

114. "adjusted his classic technique . . .": Ibid., 282.

114. Charles Payne relates in his company history . . . : Ibid., 243–239.

115. "lack of artistic encouragement": Dale Harris, *The Guardian*, January 20, 1976.

115. "I cannot think seriously . . .": Tharp to Alan Kriegsman, *The Washington Post*, March 28, 1976.

115. "You had to repeat it . . .": Martine Van Hamel interview with author, May 9, 2002.

115–116. "Balanchine's stage": Shapiro, unpublished ms, 244–248.

116. twenty-six photographs . . . : *Baryshnikov at Work—Mikhail Baryshnikov Discusses his Roles*, photography by Martha Swope, ed. Charles Engell France (New York: Knopf, 1976), 244–251.

116. Baryshnikov had to pull her on . . . : Baryshnikov/MBS, July 25, 2002.

116. "to experience Twyla . . .": *Baryshnikov at Work*, 245.

116. Tharp had miscalculated . . . : Ibid.

117. Tharp's real project . . . : Shapiro unpublished ms, 244–245.

117. a young television producer . . . : Don Mischer interview with author, September 18, 2002.

117. He remembers that he just couldn't . . . : Baryshnikov/MBS, July 25, 2002.

117. "I didn't make anything . . .": Tharp talking on *Making Television Dance: A Videotape by Twyla Tharp*, PBS, first aired October 4, 1977.

117. Six screens were to flank the stage . . . : Grauer/MBS, October 24, 2000.

118. "create dance with imagery . . .": Mischer/MBS, September 18, 2002.

118. Ken Rinker didn't like . . . : Rinker/MBS, January 19, 2001.

118. Rose Marie Wright was taking some time off . . . : Wright interviewed by Allen Robertson, *Minnesota Daily*, June 4, 1976.

118–119. Washington was a student . . . : Shelley Washington interview with author, May 14, 2002.

119. "All of a sudden . . .": Washington/MBS, October 28, 1991.

119. "Something about the way Twyla worked . . .": Washington/MBS, May 14, 2002.

119. Uchida, feeling stalled . . . : Christine Uchida interview with author, April 12, 2002.

119. "freezes with moves away": Mischer/MBS, September 18, 2002.

120. "skipping rope . . .": Grauer/MBS, October 24, 2000.

120. "Television can come closer . . .": Tharp talking on *Making Television Dance*.

122. Mischer notes how labor intensive . . . : Mischer/MBS, September 18, 2002.

123. she was a great fan of country music . . . : Tharp interview with author, February 24, 2003.

123. "makes an across-the-board difference . . .": Arlene Croce, "Tharp's Progress," *The New Yorker*, November 22, 1976.

123. the Joffrey Ballet was sliding . . . : Anawalt, *The Joffrey Ballet*, 314.

124. "I've always wanted to have . . .": Tharp interviewed by Amanda Smith, *womenSports*, March 1977, 22.

124. "dance, real dance, on ice . . .": Mary Grace Butler, letter to the author, May 23, 2000.

124. "I wasn't sure that I wanted to be involved . . .": Tharp/MBS, February 24, 2003.

124. Tom Rawe and Jennifer Way were able . . . : Rawe and Way/MBS, April 8, 2001.

125. The show's nearly nonexistent plot . . . : original script for *Hair*, Pocket Books, 1970.

125. Jack Kroll commented . . . : Jack Kroll, *Newsweek*, March 19, 1979.

125. "She made me realize . . .": Mischer/MBS, September 18, 2002.

125. "Milos didn't know anything about dance . . .": Rinker/MBS, January 19, 2001.

125–126. Forman managed to get the work suspended . . . : Milos Forman, *Turnaround: A Memoir* (New York: Villard Books, 1994), 241–242.

126. "a slight state of readiness": Rawe and Way/MBS, April 8, 2001.

126. On the day they finished . . . : Raymond Kurshals interview with author, February 20, 2003.

127. Tharp went on location . . . : *PCTS*, 217.

128. In an early version . . . : Tharp's choreographic notes, TTA.

129. Tharp was able to use . . . : Kurshals/MBS, February 20, 2003.

7. Hodge Podge Rummage 1975–1979

page

131. "the most inflated reputation . . .": Noel Gillespie, *Washington Times*, February 1976 (n.d.).

132. "one of the most disjointed . . .": Alan Kriegsman, *The Washington Post*, October 4, 1977.

132. "Wiggle, waggle . . .": *New York*, January 10, 1977, 54.

132. "discoveries and advances . . .": Tharp interviewed by John Rockwell, *NYT*, February 23, 1975.

132. Tom Rawe gave classes . . . : *NYT*, March 20, 1977.

133. withdrawal from dancing: Tharp interview, *The Minneapolis Star and Tribune*, 1977 (n.d.).

133. at least one newspaper preview . . . : *The Tenesseean*, October 13, 1977.

133. "Informed dance fans . . .": revised advertisement for performance of November 3, 1977.

134. "the best poems . . .": collage material, promotional flyer, Brooklyn Academy season, spring 1976.

134. One writer complained . . . : Julie Van Camp, *The HOYA*, September 30, 1977.

135. "it was such a treat . . .": Kurshals/MBS, September 2, 2003.

135. Anthony Ferro . . . : Anthony Ferro interview with author, October 8, 2003.

135. Technical problems arose . . . : Rudner/Thom, *NTPL*.

135. For the rehearsal directors . . . : Rawe and Way/MBS, April 8, 2001.

135. enjoyed seeing the alternate versions: Uchida/MBS, April 12, 2002.

135. the movement had been simple . . . : Rinker/MBS, January 19, 2001.

136. "glib and facile": Tharp interviewed by Amanda Smith, "Twyla Tharp: Dance Will Never Be the Same," *MS*, December 1976.

136. Tom Rawe and Jennifer Way discussed . . . : interview with Mike Steele, *Minneapolis Tribune*, May 30, 1977.

137. Rose Marie Wright remembers . . . : R. M. Wright/MBS, September 5, 2002.

137. "everything that I couldn't do . . .": Washington/MBS, October 28, 1991. Also discussed in Washington/MBS, May 14, 2002.

138. Washington gave a nod . . . : videotape of performance, Brooklyn Academy, March 26, 1976.

138. She felt miffed . . . : R. M. Wright/MBS, September 5, 2002.

138. After the Brooklyn performances . . . : Arlene Croce, "Twylathon," *The New Yorker*, April 12, 1976.

138. Wright injured her knee . . . : Rose Marie Wright interview with Allen Robertson, *Minnesota Daily*, June 4, 1976.

138. "As an audience piece . . .": "Twylathon," op. cit.

139. Before that show aired . . . : Tharp email to MBS, August 24, 2003.

139. participating luminaries . . . : The *Daily News*, May 8, 1977.

139. "Reviving those antics . . .": Arlene Croce, "Pure and Simple," *The New Yorker*, May 30, 1977.

140. Rudner realized how much . . . : Rudner/Thom, *NYPL*.

140. "when I first saw Ken dancing . . .": Rachel Lampert email to Kenneth Rinker, January 15, 2001.

140. "I don't think I'd ever seen . . .": Colton/MBS, June 26, 2001.

141. He felt his personal contribution . . . : Ibid.

141. Raymond Kurshals also entered the company . . . : Kurshals/MBS, February 20, 2003 and September 2, 2003.

141. Kurshals danced in the repertory . . . : David Vaughan, *Merce Cunningham—Fifty Years* (New York: Aperture Foundation, 1997), 296–297.

141. the Cage/Cunningham musical aesthetic . . . : Kurshals/MBS, February 20, 2003.

141. When Tom Rawe . . . : Kurshals/MBS, September 2, 2003.

143. an unpublished essay on *Mud* . . . : Allen Robertson, "Formalism as a State of Mind," unpublished.

143–144. Colton has commented . . . : "Making Musical Dance," *Ballet Review*, Winter 1986, 29.

144. "pensive yearnings . . .": Allen Robertson, "Formalism," op. cit.

144. "The Mozart still served . . .": "Making Musical Dance," op. cit.

145. all three performances were sold out . . . : *The Boston Globe*, September 30, 1977.

145. They got the ear . . . : Debra Cash, "The Selling of Twyla Tharp," *The Real Paper*, August 19, 1978.

145. "I had never experienced . . .": Judith Cohen interview with author, June 13, 2003.

145. "it gave real insight . . .": Ramelle Adams interview with author, June 18, 2003.

146. "learning the twenty-count base phrase . . .": Jeff Friedman interview with author, August 7, 2003.

146. turning the monitor toward a mirror . . . : Friedman/MBS, Ibid.

146. listened to the Bach B Minor Mass . . . : Colton/MBS, March 20, 2003.

146. "First and foremost . . .": Whitener/MBS, October 16, 2001.

147. Friedman had protected himself . . . : Friedman/MBS, August 7, 2003.

147. "ghosting affiliation": Katie Glasner interview with author, November 5, 2003.

148. "rebound" dances: *PCTS*, 247.

148. "she quite often needs . . .": Kimmary Williams interview with author, December 16, 2003.

148. "I had been exposed to waste . . .": Tharp commentary for *Confessions of a Cornermaker*, CBS Cable TV, first aired October 13, 1981.

149. The dancers were to enter . . . : Laura Shapiro, unpublished ms., 199.

149. "is trying to go on dancing . . .": Tharp interview with Robert J. Pierce, *Soho Weekly News*, February 1, 1979.

149. "Because of her own perceptions . . .": Santo Loquasto interview with author, November 14, 2002.

149. "this one extraordinary comic, free spirit . . .": Rudner/Thom, NYPL.

150. "She didn't really know . . .": Rudner phone conversation with author, January 3, 2004.

150. a game of jacks: *PCTS*, 246.

151. "theoretically the last passage . . .": Tharp interview with Robert J. Pierce, *Soho Weekly News*, op. cit.

8. Family Business 1979–1981

page

152. "a place where each dancer . . .": *PCTS*, 246.

152. "a society whose conventions are clear": Tharp commentary for *Confessions of a Cornermaker*.

152. Richard Colton remembers . . . : Colton/MBS, March 20, 2003.

152. "a series of small allegorical studies": Christine Temin, *The Boston Globe*, August 10, 1978.

152–153. The characters included . . . : Temin, Ibid., and Debra Cash, *The Real Paper*, August 19, 1978.

153. Tharp and the company had been listening . . . : Colton/MBS, March 20, 2003.

153. they did some of the new material . . . : *The Boston Globe*, August 3, 1978.

153. "a study in genteel cynicism": Tharp narrative for *Scrapbook Tape*, first aired on PBS, October 25, 1982.

153. "macabre figure of death . . .": Linda Small, *Other Stages*, March 8, 1979.

153. Morris auditioned more than once . . . : Joan Acocella, *Mark Morris* (New York: Farrar Straus Giroux, 1993), 45.

153. how to use big men: Colton/MBS, March 20, 2003.

154. "Three sections extracted . . .":program note, Brooklyn Academy, February 15–25, 1979.

154. the dancers had memorized . . . : Tom Rawe conversation with author, February 24, 2004.

155. Richard Colton thinks . . . : Colton/MBS, March 20, 2003.

155. Sunday overview of the season: Anna Kisselgoff, *NYT*, March 18, 1979.

155. Tharp's neutral stance . . . : Jack Anderson, *NYT*, February 15, 1979.

156. "obviously the great dance . . .": Nancy Goldner, *The Nation*, March 24, 1979.

156. "In connecting teen-agerism . . .": Nancy Goldner, *Christian Science Monitor*, February 21, 1979.

156. dramatize her own conflicts . . . : *PCTS*, 250.

156–157. Through mutual contacts . . . : *The Detroit News*, October 31, 1979 and Lewis Lloyd interview with author, April 27, 2000.

157. She had begun building . . . : Robert Coe, "Talking Legs," *Soho Weekly News*, March 19, 1980.

157. He told John Rockwell . . . : Thomas Babe interview with John Rockwell, *NYT*, March 23, 1980.

157. "it seemed to make growing up . . .": Robert Coe, op. cit.

158. "I could hear the intake . . .": Thomas Babe, program book for *When We Were Very Young*, 1981.

158. "a genuine, pleasure-seeking Broadway crowd . . .": Arlene Croce, "Murder, He Said, Said He," *The New Yorker*, April 21, 1980.

158. "I do want my work . . .": Tharp to Susan Reimer-Torn, *International Herald Tribune*, October 4–5, 1980.

159. "about the strenuousness . . .": Nancy Goldner, *Christian Science Monitor*, March 28, 1980

159. "Ironically, it is through cooperativeness . . .": Deborah Jowitt, *Village Voice*, April 7, 1980.

159. "I acknowledge the difficulty . . .": Tharp to Erica Abeel, *Cue*, February 15, 1980.

159. Tharp's foot was in a cast . . . : Colton/MBS, June 26, 2001.

159. Colton also taught . . . : Ibid.

160. "encompasses just about everything . . .": William Whitener to Josie Neal, *San Antonio Light*, February 26, 1984.

160. Deborah Jowitt contrasted . . ." *The Village Voice*, April 7, 1980.

160. "to breathe and behave": Colton/MBS, June 26, 2001.

161. "new ways to torture . . .": Tharp at preview showing, September 12, 1980, author's notes.

162. "formal movement problems . . .": Anna Kisselgoff, *NYT*, September 29, 1981.

162. she disdained being just one . . . : Steve Dennin interview with author, April 9, 2004.

162. "Brooklyn, like Berkeley . . .": Tharp to *San Francisco Chronicle*, March 5, 1981.

162. "We get the same fee . . .": Tharp to Marcia B. Siegel, "Twyla Tharp Goes Clean," *Soho Weekly News*, March 18, 1981.

162. the business became increasingly complicated: Dennin/MBS, April 9, 2004.

163. Forman called on her again: Forman, *Turnaround*, 257–279.

163. She delegated Shelley Freydont . . . : Shelley Freydont interview with author, January 12, 2004.

164. She started choreographing the scene . . . : Baryshnikov/MBS, July 25, 2002.

164. Merrill Brockway joined the venture . . . : *Dance Magazine*, August 1981.

164–165. He thinks he was offered the job . . . : Merrill Brockway interview with author, April 19, 2002.

165. Tharp got paid $50,000 . . . : *Wall Street Journal*, March 26, 1981.

165. full-page ad . . . : *Variety*, March 18, 1981.

165. But the new venture . . . : *Newsweek*, March 15, 1982.

165. within a year . . . : *Time*, September 27, 1982.

165. Five public television stations . . . : *NYT*, September 16, 1982.

165–166. According to Don Mischer . . . : Mischer/MBS, September 18, 2002.

166. In 1984 the whole American Ballet Theater cast . . . : Mischer/MBS, Ibid.

166. Arlene Croce didn't think . . . : Arlene Croce, "Murder, He Said, Said He," *The New Yorker*, April 21, 1980.

166. Thomas Babe was there too . . . : Thomas Babe, program book for *When We Were Very Young*, 1981.

166. No one remembers anything about it except . . . : Freydont/MBS, January 12, 2004.

166–167. Tharp tallied the number . . . *The Boston Globe*, June 26, 1980.

167. "Her voice was neutral . . .": *Boston Herald-American*, June 15, 1980.

167. From two retired earlier dances . . . : R. M. Wright/MBS, September 5, 2002.

167. she called the dancers . . . : *Dance Magazine*, July 1981.

167. The first Winter Garden season . . . : PCTS, 254.

168. "My company has never done . . .": Tharp to Robert Palmer, *NYT*, September 20, 1981.

168. she planned to dance this role . . . : PCTS, 264.

169–170. Byrne figured that . . . : David Byrne email to author, March 11, 2004.

170. one of 1981's ten best recordings . . . : *NYT*, December 30, 1981 and *Soho Weekly News*, December 30, 1981.

171. they quarreled bitterly . . . : Linda Shelton interview with author, June 3, 2004.

171. A complicated disposition . . . : David Byrne email, op. cit.

171. "message she has so purposefully muddled . . .": Anna Kisselgoff, *NYT*, September 23, 1981.

171. "lapses in seriousness . . .": Anna Kisselgoff, "Twyla Tharp's Growing Pains," *NYT*, October 4, 1981.

171. "a major event in our theatre . . .": Arlene Croce, "Oh, That Pineapple Rag!," *The New Yorker*, October 12, 1981.

171. Afterward Tharp claimed . . .": PCTS, 265.

172. she'd even invested . . . : Tharp/MBS, November 28, 1981.

172. the "Bumstead" narrative . . . : Anna Kisselgoff, *NYT*, September 23, 1981.

172. "sets forth the idea . . .": Janice Berman Alexander, *Newsday*, September 24, 1981.

172. "[It] begins as a grim epic . . .": Linda Winer, *New York Daily News*, September 25, 1981.

173. Tharp's story line . . . : Tharp's choreographic notes, TTA.

173. According to Tharp, Rudner's character . . . : Tharp/MBS, December 27, 1982.

173. She plotted every shot . . . : Grauer/MBS, October 24, 2000.

174. A month later she was vowing . . . : Tharp/MBS, November 28, 1981.

174. "It's quite clear . . .": *Wall Street Journal*, March 26, 1981.

175. Now, through a new BAM agency . . . : *NYT*, July 8, 1982 and *The Brooklyn Phoenix*, June 10, 1982.

9. Romance and the Opposite 1982–1983
page

177. the best *Deuce Coupe* . . . : *NYT*, August 27, 1981 and September 28, 1981.

177. "My priority has always got to be . . .": TT/MBS, November 28, 1981.

179. "world of vignettes . . .": Colton/MBS, March 20, 2003.

180. "clichéd youth culture . . .": Anna Kisselgoff, *NYT*, September 26, 1981.

180. "Its people are out of sync . . .": Tharp's narration, *Confessions of a Cornermaker*.

180. "verbs that we all know and recognize . . .": Tharp's introduction to video of *The Catherine Wheel*, first aired on the BBC, March 1, 1983 and on PBS *Dance in America*, March 28, 1983.

180. Before its stage premiere . . . : Tharp's own chronologies, in *Push Comes to Shove* and other internal documents, sometimes don't agree with premiere dates given in other sources. She often tried out works on tour, publicizing "premieres" in more than one city, then gave additional "premieres" when the company had its New York seasons.

181. Sometime after she had made the *Sinatra* . . . : PCTS, 274.

181. She worked out the early material . . . : Washington/MBS, May 14, 2002.

182. She remembers the *Sinatra* . . . : Amy Spencer interview with author, April 28, 2004.

183. She thought of it as a French nightclub dance . . . : Freydont/MBS, January 12, 2004.

183. Tharp said she'd been inspired . . . : PCTS, 271–272.

184. "the careful, faithful interdependency . . .": Burt Supree, *The Village Voice*, December 7, 1982.

184. "Older music has all its connotations . . .": Tharp to Robert Palmer, *NYT*, September 20, 1981.

185. The newly critical field of "dance theory" . . . : See Susan Leigh Foster's *Reading Dancing* (Berkeley: University of California Press, 1986), especially Chapter 4, for the initial salvo in what became a backlash against Tharp. Foster explains how she thought Tharp betrayed the postmodern agenda by making deliberately entertaining dances for the public.

185. "as the dance progresses . . .": Michael Fleming, *Fort Worth Star Telegram*, October 29, 1984.

185. "relaxation of concentration": Joan Acocella, *Dance Magazine*, November 1984.

186. "something like a panorama . . .": Arlene Croce, "Tharp's Sinatra," *The New Yorker*, February 13, 1984.

186–187. The company rented itself out . . . : *Sun Reporter*, February 14, 1985.

187. "a beleaguered straight man . . .": Anna Kisselgoff, *NYT*, February 14, 1984.

187. "Suspicion, nothing better . . .": Laura Shapiro, *Seattle Weekly*, October 27, 1982.

187. "nature's darker forces": Tharp's narration, *Scrapbook Tape*.

187. thrift-shop underwear: Santo Loquasto/MBS, November 14, 2002.

187. she started thinking about ritual sacrifice . . . PCTS, 269–270.

187. Tharp says *Bad Smells* was conceived . . . : Tharp's narration, *Scrapbook Tape*.

188. "stark, austere minimalist . . .": Roger Copeland, "Why Women Dominate Modern Dance," *NYT*, April 18, 1982.

188. "a caprice for beautiful people": George Jackson, *The Washington Post*, April 17, 1982.

188. she was thinking about how rock concerts . . . : Tharp interview with Craig Bromberg, *Theatre Crafts*, January 1984.

188. how rock's intense noise levels could release . . . : TT/MBS, November 28, 1981.

188. "I always think of my own music . . .": Glenn Branca interview with John Rockwell, *NYT*, May 2, 1982.

189. *Bad Smells* also began as a film project . . . : Tom Rawe to Mike Steele, *Minneapolis Star and Tribune*, April 6, 1984.

189. "blossom and make abstract shapes . . .": Tharp with Craig Bromberg, *Theatre Crafts*, op. cit.

189. "dog carcasses and three-legged horses . . .": Claudia Dreifus, *Mademoiselle*, July 1982.

189. she wanted them to think of helicopter blades . . . : Richard Colton conversation with author, July 14, 2004.

190. Atlas's camera in *Locale* . . . : Richard Kostelanetz, "Twenty Years of Merce Cunningham's Dance," in *Merce Cunningham: Dancing in Space and Time*, ed. Richard Kostelanetz (New York: Da Capo Press, 1998), 19.

190. "On the stage . . .": Arlene Croce, "Tharp Against Tharp," *The New Yorker*, February 27, 1984.

190. "political, totalitarian, post-nuke resonance": Burt Supree, *The Village Voice*, December 7, 1982.

191. "clubs in which disco dancers . . .": Anna Kisselgoff, *NYT*, February 19, 1984.

191. "deliberately repulsive": Laura Shapiro, *Seattle Weekly*, October 27, 1982.

191. a balance between politesse and amorality . . . : Tharp interview with Janice Berman, *Newsday*, January 22, 1984.

191. "the physical, factual entity . . .": Ibid.

191. "concentration camps, life after death . . .": Tharp interview with Eric Taub, *Ballet News*, February 1984, 19.

191. "The last part of the piece . . .": *New York Beat*, January 1984.

192. wrapped them from head to foot . . . : Loquasto/MBS, November 14, 2002.

192. Mylar floor: Freydont/MBS, January 12, 2004.

192. Tom Rawe remembers . . . : Rawe and Way/MBS, April 8, 2001.

192–193. "What you were feeling . . .": Mary Ann Kellogg interview with author, January 8, 2004.

193. Remembering an effect . . . : Jennifer Tipton interview with author, May 22, 2002.

193. perhaps for practical reasons: Washington email to author, July 28, 2004.

194. "And so the end . . .": Anna Kisselgoff, *NYT*, February 19, 1984.

194. "The fiery Wagnerian beauty . . .": Arlene Croce, "Tharp Against Tharp," *The New Yorker*, February 27, 1984.

194. "a retrospective so energetic . . .": James Leverett, *American Theatre*, April 1984.

195. "The ballet is something we all depend on . . .": Tharp interview with Michael Robertson, *Dance Magazine*, March 1980.

195. "ballets being done . . .": Colton/MBS, April 29, 2004.

195. According to Shelley Freydont . . . : Freydont/MBS, January 12, 2004.

197. "a perfectly charming, diverting little piece . . .": Arlene Croce, "Tharp Against Tharp," *The New Yorker*, February 27, 1984.

197. Tharp had received one of four . . . : *Orlando Sentinel*, July 1, 1984.

198. she retrieved some of the material . . . : Tharp email to author, August 12, 2004.

198. Work on the movie . . . : *Gannett-Westchester Newspapers*, July 8, 1984.

198. previewed in June on a tour . . . : Shelton/MBS, June 3, 2004.

198. "the success of *Sorrow Floats*": Linda Belans, *Spectator* (Raleigh, N.C.), July 25, 1984.

198. Over the audience's loyal cheering . . . : Anne Levin, *The Oak Ridger*, July 13, 1984.

198. Tharp had persuaded . . . : Charles Reinhart interview with author, September 30, 2000.

199. Tharp started choreographing it . . . : Tharp/MBS, November 28, 1981.

199. "vulnerability and introspectiveness . . .": Dale Harris, *The Guardian*, June 10, 1983.

199. "nostalgia piece": Baryshnikov/MBS, July 25, 2002.

199. Tharp had been subtly revising . . . : Susan Jones/MBS, May 30, 2002.

199. "The changing imperatives . . .": Arlene Croce, "Baryshnikov Among Sylphs," *The New Yorker*, June 20, 1983.

199. "a succession of memorable dance images . . .": Dale Harris, *The Guardian*, June 10, 1983.

199. "ballet's collective consciousness": Laura Jacobs, *Boston Phoenix*, February 14, 1984.

10. Three-Way Stretch 1983–1990

page

200. "an incredible symbol . . .": Baryshnikov quoted in Bernard Taper (*Balanchine*, Berkeley: University of California Press, 1987), 354.

200. "he looked like someone . . .": Robert Garis, *Following Balanchine* (New Haven: Yale University Press, 1995), 233.

201. "Tharp's bid to become . . .": Christine Temin, *The Boston Globe*, February 3, 1984.

201. "filled the theater . . .": Jennifer Dunning, *NYT*, June 1, 1984.

201. "how desperately his company needs . . .": Dale Harris, *Wall Street Journal*, February 14, 1984.

201. He had always hoped . . . : Baryshnikov/MBS, July 25, 2002.

201. "sheer density of action . . .": Alan Kriegsman, *The Washington Post*, December 12, 1983.

202. "The object is to raise allegro dancing . . ": Mindy Aloff, *The Nation*, December 31, 1983–January 7, 1984.

202. "the role Gregory has waited . . .": Martha Duffy, *Time*, February 11, 1984.

202. "dance with new-found enthusiasm . . .": Dale Harris, *Wall Street Journal*, February 14, 1984.

202. Throughout the ballet's twenty-seven minutes . . . : Only a low-quality archival tape was available to study this ballet, now out of the repertory. The tape provides very little movement detail and scant information as to the identities of the dancers, but it does reveal Tharp's ingenious group patterns and musicality.

202. "an enormous, whirling, weightless ballet": Arlene Croce, "Guest in the House," *The New Yorker*, July 2, 1984.

203. They'd met in 1973 through Rhoda Grauer . . . : Grauer/MBS, October 24, 2000. Many sources follow the date given by Tharp in her autobiography, 1969, but this seems inaccurate.

203. Robbins had long wanted to collaborate: Deborah Jowitt, *Jerome Robbins—His Life, His Theater, His Dance* (New York: Simon & Schuster, 2004), 472.

203. they infiltrated each other's work . . . : *PCTS*, 294.

204. She hatched a scheme . . . : Tharp to Iris Fanger, *Boston Review*, June 1984.

204. Tharp sent Sara Rudner . . . : Rudner conversation with author, August 24, 2004.

205. "with despair of maintaining a company . . .": Tharp interview with Jennifer Dunning, *NYT*, June 9, 1985.

205. While Steve Dennin struggled . . . : Dennin/MBS, April 9, 2004.

205. "not merely compatible with but essential . . .": Tharp to Joseph Mazo, *Women's Wear*, July 13, 1984.

206. the Rosenfields approached Tharp: Account of the production largely drawn from Sharon Churcher, "Still Kicking—The amazing saga of *Singin' in the Rain*, the $5.7 million turkey that refuses to lie down," *New York Magazine*, October 14, 1985, 40–47.

206. "the lavish production numbers": *New York Post*, June 19, 1984.

206. "I would be able to park my company . . .": *PCTS*, 288.

206. "this is a time of transition . . .": Lewis Lloyd to Janice Ross, *The Oakland Tribune*, April 21, 1985.

206. No further touring . . . : *San Francisco Chronicle*, April 21, 1985.

206. "That worked just fine . . .": Shelton/MBS, June 3, 2004.

206. others had long sensed . . . : Colton/MBS, April 29, 2004.

206. excited about working in tap shoes . . . : Rawe and Washington to Nancy Goldner, *The Philadelphia Inquirer*, February 2, 1985.

206. Eleven company dancers . . . : *NYT*, June 9, 1985.

207. In one of the only sanguine statements . . . : Tharp to Sheryl Flatow, *Playbill*, June 1985.

207. the reason she left the original numbers alone . . . : *PCTS*, 288–289.

207. "look like they're trained dancers . . .": *Vogue*, June 1985, 243.

207. John Carrafa learned tap routines . . . : *The Boston Globe*, March 11, 1985.

208. Tharp was never officially replaced . . . : *The New York Post*, "Page Six," June 21, 1985.

209. "Miss Tharp and company have turned a celestial entertainment . . .": *NYT*, July 3, 1985.

209. *Daily News* headline: *Daily News*, July 3, 1985.

209. "Broadway needs the new blood . . .": Jack Kroll, *Newsweek*, July 15, 1985.

209. she describes herself as suffering . . . : *PCTS*, 297.

209. an effort to recoup the *Catherine Wheel* deficit: Shapiro unpublished ms, 292–293.

210. "an unheard of request . . .": "Footnotes," *Ballet News*, December 1985.

210. People told the story . . . : Doug Rosenberg conversation with author, January 11, 2004.

210. Tharp's tough business practices . . . : Shelton/MBS, June 3, 2004.

210. Twenty years later . . . : *Dance Magazine*, February 2005.

210. "I was just in joy . . .": Jamie Bishton interview with author, September 16, 2004.

210. The reconstituted company . . . : *Dance Magazine*, May 1986.

210. Amy Spencer and Richard Colton had left . . . : Spencer/MBS, April 24, 2004.

210. Mary Ann Kellogg had won . . . : Kellogg/MBS, January 8, 2004.

210. Raymond Kurshals also thought . . . : Kurshals/MBS, September 2, 2003.

210. William Whitener passed up the show . . . : Whitener conversation with author, March 4, 2005.

210. Katie Glasner thought she wouldn't fit . . . : Glasner/MBS, November 5, 2003.

211. "I like to develop movement . . .": Tom Rawe to Nancy Goldner, *Philadelphia Inquirer*, January 4, 1987.

211. "secular mass": Tharp's narrative for *Twyla Tharp—Oppositions* videotape, directed by Derek Bailey, *Dance in America*, 1996.

211. Jack Anderson supplied a New Testament reference . . . : *NYT*, February 5, 1987.

212. Sensing that Tharp would pull her back . . . : Uchida/MBS, April 12, 2002.

212. the Bomb Squad: Jennifer Gelfand interview with author, November 4, 2004.

212. "She *knew* she could make a piece . . .": Spencer/MBS, April 28, 2004.

213. "what one imagines pure oxygen . . .": Nancy Goldner, *The Philadelphia Inquirer*, January 8, 1987.

213. a crucial aesthetic question: Matthew Gurewitsch, *Ballet News*, October 1984, 18–22.

213–214. Croce rejected Lincoln Kirstein's theoretical closure . . . : Arlene Croce, "Postmodern Ballets," *The New Yorker*, February 23, 1987.

214. "Put the performers in pointe shoes . . .": Tobi Tobias, *New York Magazine*, February 23, 1987.

214. "ballet blanc": Tobi Tobias, *New York Magazine*, March 2, 1987.

214. Mindy Aloff assumed . . . : Mindy Aloff, *The Nation*, March 28, 1987.

214. "the most successful ever . . .": Anna Kisselgoff, *NYT*, March 8, 1987.

214. Croce saw the same opportunism . . . : Arlene Croce, *The New Yorker*, February 23, 1987.

214–215. Around the time of the BAM season . . . : Tharp to Janice Berman, *Newsday*, February 1, 1987.

215. "very little real imagination": Tharp to Holly Williams, *The Dallas Morning News*, September 23, 1987.

215. She even offered to move the company . . . : *Dallas Times Herald*, October 1, 1987.

215. "It's not an easy job . . .": Tharp to Lois Draegin, *Savvy*, February, 1987.

215. After the South American tour . . . : *NYM*, June 22, 1987.

215. She was determined . . . : *Albany Times Union*, August 9, 1987.

215. Jamie Bishton told a local paper . . . : *Albany Metroland*, August 20–26, 1987.

215. A special workshop . . . : Rawe and Way/MBS, April 8, 2001.

216. Preparations for the Australian tour . . . : The Australian press recounted most of this episode, which was corroborated and amplified by Linda Shelton. Shelton/MBS, June 3, 2004.

216. the dance material was ready: *NYT*, January 3, 1988.

216. Smeaton was experimenting . . . : Smeaton quoted in *West Australian*, November 18, 1987.

217. "an ideal introduction . . .": *The Australian*, February 3, 1988.

217. Washington did identify . . . : Washington to Sasha Anawalt, *The Los Angeles Herald Examiner*, April 17, 1988.

217. "vigorously gymnastic fun and games . . .": Neil Jillett, *The Age*, February 8, 1988.

217. Patsy Tarr remembers . . . : Patsy Tarr interview with author, September 16, 2004.

218. "temporarily disbanded": *Newsday*, June 24, 1988.

218. Tharp had revealed the dramatic move . . . : Washington/MBS, May 14, 2002.

218. "It was a harder moment": Colton/MBS, April 29, 2004.

218. Amy Spencer received a check . . . : Spencer/MBS, April 28, 2004.

218. Rawe and Way had been edging out . . . : Rawe and Way/MBS, April 8, 2001.

218. Bishton and Sanchez entered . . . : Bishton/MBS, September 16, 2004.

218. There were Negro and Spanish units . . . : Nancy Reynolds and Malcolm McCormick, *No Fixed Points* (New Haven: Yale University Press, 2003), 271–272.

218. Agnes de Mille brought in a package . . . : Carol Easton, *No Intermissions* (Boston: Little, Brown & Company, 1996), 406.

219. Bishton remembers the sojourn . . . : Bishton/MBS, September 16, 2004.

219. Baryshnikov gave her carte blanche: Baryshnikov/MBS, July 25, 2002.

219. Baryshnikov enlisted his patron . . . : *NYT*, June 22, 1989.

220. she'd audited screenwriting courses . . . : Tharp/MBS, October 17, 2004.

220. Tharp expected that *Everlast* . . . : *PCTS*, 328.

221. Arlene Croce analyzed the work . . . : Arlene Croce, "The Little American Girl," *The New Yorker*, June 12, 1989.

221. Jamie Bishton remembers working . . . : Bishton/MBS, September 16, 2004.

221. "all anger, fighting, being bamboozled . . .": Grauer/MBS, October 24, 2000.

221. "With death just around the corner . . .": Tharp in lecture-demonstration, Works and Process at Guggenheim Museum, reported by the *Westsider*, April 27–May 3, 1989.

221. Washington had developed extreme acting skills . . . : Washington/MBS, May 14, 2002.

221. Danny Sanchez did a break dance number . . . : *Chicago Sun Times*, February 20, 1989.

221. the Katzenjammer Kid . . . : Croce, "Little American Girl," op. cit.

222. Rumors surfaced . . . : *The New York Post*, June 22, 1989.

222. Baryshnikov announced his resignation . . . : *NYT*, June 22, 1989.

222. Tharp and fellow artistic associate Kenneth MacMillan . . . : *Los Angeles Times*, March 14, 1990. According to *The New York Times* (May 27, 1990), in July of 1989 ABT didn't renew the contracts of Tharp and MacMillan.

223. Not only did her ballets have cachet . . . : Tharp to Sasha Anawalt, *NYT*, May 27, 1990.

223. "these modern people . . .": Bishton/MBS, September 16, 2004.

224. "It was a success . . .": *PCTS*, 331.

224. "an exhilarating statement . . .": Arlene Croce, "Classical Values," *The New Yorker*, July 2, 1990.

224. "The audience's applause . . .": Deborah Jowitt, *The Village Voice*, May 22, 1990.

224. "as if she would rather appeal . . .": Arlene Croce, "Classical Values," op. cit.

224. Tharp's ballets could cost the company $100,000 . . . : Jane Hermann to *NYT*, June 16, 1991.

II. The Anti-company 1990–1995

page

225. an autobiographical book . . . : This account draws on three conversations between author and Laura Shapiro, September 26, October 14, and November 27, 2004, and an interview between Tharp and Elizabeth Zimmer, August 9, 1992.

226. "it uncannily captures . . .": *The New York Times Book Review*, December 13, 1992.

227. he attended the performance . . . : *NYT*, February 6, 1987.

227. During a hiatus . . . : Shelton/MBS, June 3, 2004.

227. "a young man from the lower ranks . . .": Dale Harris, *Wall Street Journal*, January 31, 1989.

227. suddenly refused to participate . . . : *Pour la danse*, March 1989.

227. Tharp said she had to rebuild . . . : *PCTS*, 323–326.

227. "Her phrases twist, hiccup and backtrack . . .": Barbara Newman, *Sunday Telegraph*, March 26, 1989.

227. "serious and fine work . . .": Anna Kisselgoff, *NYT*, March 8, 1989.

228. "rhythmically slow-clapping . . .": Allen Robertson, *Los Angeles Times/Calendar*, March 5, 1989.

228. Through Linda Shelton's contacts . . . : Shelton/MBS, June 3, 2004.

228. The deal started . . . : *Chicago Tribune*, July 8, 1990.

228. Hubbard Street's artistic director . . . : Conte to Janice Berman, *Newsday*, August 23, 1990.

228. she realized she couldn't continue . . . : Washington/MBS, May 14, 2002.

229. "She kind of just guided me . . .": Ibid.

229. Finally she agreed . . . : Tharp/MBS, October 17, 2004.

229. According to legend . . . : Doug Rosenberg conversation with author, January 11, 2004.

229. Reinhart says Tharp's eccentricities . . . : Reinhart/MBS, September 30, 2000.

229. "a living artist . . .": Wexner Center Foundation press release.

230. Kevin O'Day, feeling restless . . . : Bishton/MBS, September 16, 2004.

230. She toyed with several titles . . . : author's notes, September 13, 1991.

231. Jamie Bishton learned the first fifty . . . : Vera Blaine interview with author, October 6, 1991.

231. she likened the gift . . . : tape of press conference at Ohio State, September 12, 1991.

231. rehearsal and performance videotapes . . . : Although Tharp noted at the time that she had received a National Endowment for the Arts grant to transfer the videos, most of them remained in New York more than a decade after her gift to OSU.

231. a work in progress, and also as a "World Premiere" . . . : program at Mershon Auditorium, October 4 and 5, 1991.

232. Bishton remembers one sequence . . . : Bishton/MBS, September 16, 2004.

232. "which is what tore men and women apart . . .": Tharp's narrative for *Men's Piece* in performance.

232. Tharp was a little late . . . : Tullia Limarzi, *Staten Island Advance*, January 31. 1992.

234. Nancy Goldner thought the false endings . . . : Nancy Goldner, *Philadelphia Inquirer*, January 30, 1992.

234. "An egregiously empty . . .": Jennifer Dunning, *NYT*, February 3, 1992.

234. "an inspired piece of work . . .": Anna Kisselgoff, *NYT*, February 1, 1992.

234. before Tharp settled on the music . . . : Susan Jaffe interview with author, January 21, 2004.

234. "a suite of bubble-rock/Latin numbers . . .": Alastair Macaulay, *The New Yorker*, February 12, 1992.

235. "she takes them further . . .": Joseph Mazo, *The Record*, February 5, 1992.

235. For the last four performances . . . : *New York Post*, February 6, 1992.

235. "Premieres that Restored Faith . . .": Anna Kisselgoff, *NYT*, December 27, 1992.

235. "Dancers, no matter how virtuosic . . .": Linda Winer, *Newsday*, February 7, 1992.

236. Arlene Croce compared . . . : Arlene Croce, "Someone's in the Kitchen with Demeter," *The New Yorker*, October 25, 1993.

237. Jodi Melnick remembers scenes . . .": Jodi Melnick interview with author, November 9, 2004.

237. Kinney admired the way Tharp could hold her own . . . : Sharon Kinney interview with author, May 1, 2000.

237. another of Tharp's "finds": Allen Robertson, *Dance Theatre Journal*, summer 1992, 34.

237. Melnick was called back for another season . . . : Melnick/MBS, November 9, 2004.

237–238. "The only reason I keep dancing . . .": Tharp/MBS, October 8, 1993.

238. netted a reported million dollars . . . : Laura Shapiro, *Newsweek*, December 14, 1992.

238. a small tempest . . . : Barbara Zuck, *Dance Magazine*, March 1993, 36, and Chuck Helm of Wexner Center in conversation with the author, November 16, 2004.

238. Kisselgoff called it a premiere: *NYT*, December 2, 1992.

238. the biggest sales day . . . Christine Temin, *The Boston Globe*, January 24, 1993.

238. In West Palm Beach . . . : Elizabeth Zimmer, *Dance View*, summer 1993, 15.

239. a short Annie Leibovitz film . . . : *Los Angeles Times*, September 17, 1992.

239. it was used as promotional material . . . : Tharp/MBS, October 17, 2004.

239. Bits of *Zoetrope*'s movement . . . : Stacy Caddell interview with author, October 17, 2004.

239. Even the dancers . . . : Caddell/MBS, Ibid.

240. "I started thinking of the show . . .": Tharp to Christine Temin, *The Boston Globe*, January 24, 1993.

240. "a colossal ripoff": Alexandra Tomalonis, *Dance View*, autumn 1993, 32.

240. "A vanity production . . .": Anna Kisselgoff, *NYT*, December 2, 1992.

241. "as he was moving around . . .": Bishton/MBS, December 13, 2004.

241. "We dance duets . . .": Tharp interviewed by *Toledo Blade*, November 22, 1992.

241. "Possibly this means . . .": Laura Shapiro, *Newsweek*, December 14, 1992.

241. When Baryshnikov arrived in Columbus . . . : Baryshnikov/MBS, July 25, 2002.

241. he balked at promotional schemes . . . : Bishton/MBS, December 13, 2004.

241. "People have to have the information . . .": Tharp to Barbara Zuck, *Dance Magazine*, March 1993.

242. "She did a very beautiful . . .": Caddell/MBS, October 17, 2004.

242. Tharp thought of the season . . . : TT/MBS, October 8, 1993.

242. "wide-ranging, multifaceted . . .": Arlene Croce, "Someone's in the Kitchen with Demeter," *The New Yorker*, October 25, 1993.

242. Tharp explained how the frisson . . . : Tharp in lecture-demonstration videotaped at Mershon Auditorium, August 27, 1993.

242. "Why is Twyla Tharp not devoting her energies . . .": Dale Harris, *Wall Street Journal*, September 27, 1993.

242–243. Arlene Croce, on the other hand . . . : Croce, "Someone's in the Kitchen with Demeter," op. cit.

243. She donated her services: Robert Johnson, *Dance Magazine*, October 1993.

243. "a very female story": Tharp to Janice Berman, *Newsday*, September 14, 1993.

243. she saw the myth in terms of Demeter's relationships . . . : TT/MBS, October 8, 1993.

243. "A full performance by the Graham company . . .": Anna Kisselgoff, *NYT*, September 16, 1993.

244. she had evolved a process . . . : TT/MBS, October 8, 1993.

244. klezmer simply had more expressive range . . . : Tharp in lecture-demonstration videotaped at Mershon Auditorium, August 27, 1993.

244. "brought out a dramatic projection . . .": Anna Kisselgoff, *NYT*, October 31, 1993.

244. "In the beginning I was feeling very anxious . . .": Christine Dakin to Jennifer Dunning, *NYT*, October 3, 1993.

244. "It's an excellent opportunity . . .": Croce, "Someone's in the Kitchen with Demeter," op. cit.

245. her past work didn't interest her: Tharp in lecture-demonstration videotaped at the New York State Theater, January 24, 2000.

245. "as fine a male dancer . . .": Dale Harris, *Wall Street Journal*, September 27, 1993.

245. Tharp gave him a composite tape . . . : Bishton/MBS, December 13, 2004.

245. Bishton treasures a memorable performance . . . : Bishton/MBS, Ibid.

247. A 1999 profile . . . : Sam Tanenhaus, "Wayward Intellectual," *The New York Times Magazine*, January 24, 1999, 20–23.

247. First she talked Kennedy Center director of programming . . . : Tharp to Charlie Rose, transcript of broadcast, January 13, 1995.

247. through American University's Naima Prevots and her own personal connections: Naima Prevots interview with author, April 9, 2001, and Jennifer Gelfand interview with author, November 4, 2004.

247. she chose fourteen . . . : *The Washington Post*, September 14, 1994.

247. "It makes the participation . . .": Tharp on Charlie Rose transcript, op. cit.

247. they did get a percentage . . . : George Jackson, *Dance Magazine*, December 1994.

247. "we were paid incredibly well . . .": Caddell/MBS, October 17, 2004.

248. "in the old days . . .": Tharp to Alan Kriegsman, *The Washington Post*, September 14, 1994.

248. "We've become very confused . . .": Tharp to Jean Battey Lewis, *The Washington Times*, September 11, 1994.

248. how touched she was: Tharp on Charlie Rose transcript, op. cit.

248. "what it means to be an American": Tharp to Jack Anderson, *NYT*, September 26, 1994.

248. "This whole thing . . .": Tharp to Jennifer Dunning, *NYT*, January 12, 1995.

248. her own inimitable dancing . . . : Janice Berman, *New York Newsday*, January 18, 1995.

248. "an avenging or challenging angel": Jean Battey Lewis, *The Washington Times*, September 15, 1994.

248. "who had just entered the Underworld . . .": Caddell/MBS, October 17, 2004.

12. Near Heaven 1995–2005

page

251. "The subject matter is subjectivity and objectivity . . .": Tharp to Anna Kisselgoff, *NYT*, April 30, 1995.

251. "his taffeta strings . . .": Arlene Croce, "Choreographers We," *The New Yorker*, May 22, 1995.

252. Tharp had begun choreographing this duo . . . : Janice Berman, *Newsday*, January 16, 1995.

252. When Susan Jaffe entered the work . . . : Jaffe/MBS, January 21, 2004.

252. "the crossover point . . .": Tharp to Anna Kisselgoff, *NYT*, April 30, 1995.

252–253. Tobi Tobias thought the pair of women: Tobi Tobias, *New York Magazine*, March 27, 1995.

253. "impression of a community . . .": Alan Kriegsman, *The Washington Post*, March 7, 1995.

253. "almost totally opaque": Arlene Croce, "Choreographers We," op. cit.

253. "irritatingly mysterious eau de scenario": Deborah Jowitt, *The Village Voice*, May 21, 1996.

253. "perhaps the worst . . .": Nicholas Dromgoole, *London Telegraph*, January 26, 1997.

253. Tharp conceived of the ballet's three acts . . . : Tharp interview with Allen Robertson, 1995, n.d.

253. Tharp was also trying . . . : I have never seen this dance live. The only videotape available to me lacked a soundtrack, so I am unable to discuss the way Tharp used Rossini's music.

254. "a rich, truly generous piece . . .": Allen Robertson, *Dance Now*, spring 1996.

254. "a perplexing disappointment . . .": David Dougill, *Sunday Times*, December 17, 1995.

254. an admiring review . . . : Deborah Jowitt, "In Her Elements," *The Village Voice*, May 21, 1996.

254. "solid, respectable, and, believe it or not . . .": Terry Teachout, *Daily News*, May 6, 1996.

254. "the same kind of pallid expertise": Clive Barnes, *New York Post*, May 6, 1996.

255. "the dream potential": Tharp to Deborah Jowitt, *The Village Voice*, September 30, 1997.

255. She even taught class . . . : Andrew Robinson, joint interview, Robinson and Malone, with author, January 18, 2005.

255. "I've never been the kind of dancer . . .": Robinson and Malone/MBS, January 18, 2005.

258. "a symphonic ballet": program information, I.P.A. press packet.

258. "The dance has a movement base . . .": Tharp to Thea Singer, *The Boston Globe*, March 22, 1998.

258. "ferocious precision": Donald Hutera, *Dance Now*, Winter 1996.

258. "almost entirely obscure": Tobi Tobias, *New York Magazine*, November 18, 1996.

258. "pseudo-Santeria meets Buena Vista . . .": Malone in Robinson and Malone/MBS, January 18, 2005.

259. the dance was sidelined . . . : Robinson and Malone/MBS, Ibid.

259. "This is her great gift . . .": Patsy Tarr/MBS, September 16, 2004.

259. "All her works . . .": Danilo Radojevic to *Weekend Australian*, January 10–11, 1998.

259. "Much was expected": Patricia Laughlin, *Dance Australia*, February/March 1998, 59.

259. They made a duet . . . : John Selya interview with author, January 21, 2005.

259. Later Andrew Robinson partnered her . . . : Robinson and Malone/MBS, January 18, 2005.

260. Asking a contemporary audience . . . : Gabrielle Malone in Robinson and Malone/MBS, Ibid.

260. Distinguished Visiting Professorship: *NYT*, March 2, 1999.

260. Tharp recalled Jamie Bishton . . . : Bishton/MBS, December 13, 2004.

260. Diabelli's ditzy little tune: *Des Moines Register*, September 1999.

261. Clement Crisp praised the piece: *Financial Times*, June 22, 1999.

261. "Today I thought of writing . . .": Tharp script for *The Bix Pieces*.

261. "He gave a private place . . .": Tharp to Theodore Bale, *Boston Herald*, June 22, 2001.

262. Caddell convinced the choreographer . . . : Caddell/MBS, October 17, 2004.

262. "the court isn't far away . . .": Tharp teaching class at Hunter College, November 5, 1998, author's notes.

264. "grinding monotony": Harris Green, *Dance Magazine*, January 2000, 72.

264. Acocella and Kisselgoff: *The New Yorker*, December 7, 1998 and *NYT*, November 4, 1998.

264. she'd switched to his more approachable music: Tharp during Q & A at videotaped lecture-demonstration, New York State Theater, January 24, 2000.

264. She also feared . . . : Twyla Tharp, *The Creative Habit* (New York: Simon & Schuster, 2003), 130.

264. Listening to Alfred Brendel's recordings . . . : Tharp to Astrida Weeks, *Madison*, June 1999, 57.

265. She gave a curiously poignant answer: Tharp during Q & A at videotaped lecture-demonstration, New York State Theater, January 24, 2000.

265. It had taken some time . . . : Tharp/MBS, November 10, 1999.

265. Tharp selected three . . . : Tharp at videotaped lecture-demonstration, New York State Theater, January 24, 2000.

266. "optimism to weld and bind . . .": Ibid.

266. "at her bloated worst": Robert Gottlieb, *New York Observer*, March 12, 2001.

266. "weighted passion": Anna Kisselgoff, *NYT*, January 25, 2000.

266. Acocella was disappointed . . . : Joan Acocella, *The New Yorker*, February 7, 2000.

266. she preferred the designation "neoromantic": Tharp to Cathy Lynn Grossman, *USA Today*, May 9, 2000.

267. "a support system between the foreground . . .": Tharp to Deborah Jowitt, *The Village Voice*, February 20, 2001.

267. Mindy Aloff thought . . . : Mindy Aloff, "Spitballs at Euclid," *The New Republic*, June 18, 2001.

267. "My career has been spent preparing me . . .": Tharp to Cathy Lynn Grossman, *USA Today*, op. cit.

267. "she approaches ballet very seriously . . .": Mindy Aloff, "Spitballs at Euclid," op. cit.

268. "I need to be grounded again . . .": Tharp to Anna Kisselgoff, *NYT*, July 6, 2000.

268. "vibrant, new cultural district . . .": BAM Local Development Corporation press release, January 2001.

268. As Tharp was starting her new company . . . : Tharp and Harvey Lichtenstein conversation in *NYT*, February 2001.

268. He knew she would be an asset . . . : Harvey Lichtenstein interview with author, January 17, 2001.

268. "a coup for efforts . . .": *NYT*, January 17, 2001.

268. some vocal community concerns . . . : Amy Eddings, "No Longer Slumming: A Cultural District for Downtown Brooklyn," transcript of radio piece, WNYC, air date, January 18, 2001.

268. "one more thing to help": *NYT*, January 17, 2001.

269. she laid out a grandiose three-year agenda: Tharp and Harvey Lichtenstein conversation in *NYT*, February 2001.

269. amortize their outlay . . . : Harvey Lichtenstein conversation with author, February 22, 2005.

269. the plan was dead: *NYT*. May 9, 2001.

270. Lichtenstein had been trying to convince her: Lichtenstein/MBS, February 22, 2005.

270. "three times what a principal dancer is making": Tharp to Anne Midgette, *Los Angeles Times*, June 17, 2001.

270. "We need a nice new stadium . . .": Tharp to Laura Bleiberg, *Orange County Register*, June 19, 2001.

270. Reverend Dyson was stunned: *NYT*, May 9, 2001.

270. "something big and ambitious": *The Creative Habit*, 83- 84

270. "Twyla said to us . . .": Selya/MBS, January 21, 2005.

271. Selya had never risen above corps de ballet . . . : Selya/MBS, Ibid.

271. she considered the Quintet big music . . . : Tharp in postperformance Q & A, Joyce Theater, February 21, 2001.

272. "Dithery and opaque": Joan Acocella, *The New Yorker*, March 12, 2001.

273. "an all-purpose Chaos . . .": Tharp to Robert Johnson, *Newark Star-Ledger*, February 16, 2001.

273. "a sketchy allegory . . .": Anna Kisselgoff, *NYT*, February 22, 2001.

273. Selya says he and Roberts . . . : Selya/MBS, January 21, 2005.

274. she retrieved some choreography . . . : *The Creative Habit*, 225.

274. Tharp's coming-of-age mantra . . . : TT/MBS, February 11, 2004.

274–275 . Tharp has said the show is a tribute . . . : TT/MBS, Ibid.

275. She wanted the show to acknowledge . . . : *Providence Journal*, February 22, 2004.

275. "a shimmering portrait . . .": Ben Brantley, *NYT*, October 25, 2002.

276. ten Tony nominations: *NYT*, May 13, 2003.

A NOTE ON SOURCES

I started watching and writing about Tharp dance in about 1968. With the exception of a handful of works that were not performed in New York or in touring cities accessible to me, I have seen all of her dances live at least once. Tharp was impatient with maintaining her works after they had reached what she considered their optimum form, but this determined resistance to repertory meant that a very limited sample of her phenomenal output lasted on the stage long enough to gain a wide audience. All dance is inherently vulnerable to disappearance, but history demands more. Any artwork must be able to transcend the impressions it made on first viewing in order to gain the deep appreciation that can only come with familiarity and context.

Fortunately, Tharp was ahead of the dance field in recognizing the importance of videotape and film very early in her career, and some records exist of almost everything she ever choreographed. For purposes of this book I have made every effort to revisit and study the repertory, either live or by means of videotaped records. These records vary greatly in quality, from fixed single-camera studio documentation to archival recordings of stage performances to professional television translations made for both commercial and experimental purposes. I have gleaned whatever information I could from this material, and in my viewing of it I've attempted to compensate for distortions, camera adaptations, and technical glitches. Despite their shortcomings, and in lieu of a live repertory, these videos have been essential to the writing of this book. I am grateful to Twyla Tharp and the presenting companies for having the foresight to see that they were made, and for making them available to me.

In 1991 Tharp donated her archives to The Ohio State University, where they have been scrupulously preserved and protected by curator Nena Couch and the staff of the Jerome Lawrence and Robert E. Lee Theater Research Institute. Although the public and scholars may view press clippings and design materials in this collection, Tharp hasn't permitted total access to it. I have examined it as thoroughly as her restrictions will allow. To compensate for the areas of information that were not open to me—correspondence, business records, and all "choreographic notes" except a few early ones—I have interviewed more than sixty dancers, managers, and associates during the six years of researching and writing this book. In addition, I have had access to published and unpublished materials provided by other professional dance writers. I hope that I have represented these respondents and their subject fairly.

Tharp often tried out new work on the road, announcing "world premieres" of dances in one or more locations before she considered them finished. Premiere dates as given here sometimes differ from those in Tharp's own chronologies. In the text, I have tried to indicate the circumstances of first performances discussed.

Tharp usually did not double-cast when choreographing but, especially in big ballet companies and her own touring ensembles, anything that went into repertory had more than one cast. When I've listed one set of dancers, I refer to the original cast, or to the cast on a videotape available for study.

I have adopted the practice of quoting from my interviews in the present tense, even though most of the interviews were conducted over a five-year period, in order to differentiate them from material published or recorded concurrently with the dance work. I hope that those who spoke to me can still be represented in the same terms.

The photograph of *Jam* is reprinted courtesy of the Jerome Robbins Dance Division, New York Public Library for the Performing Arts at Lincoln Center.

The photographs of *Re-Moves, Disperse, Dancing in the Streets, Deuce Coupe, Sue's Leg, Country Dances,* Carrafa and Uchida in *The Catherine Wheel, Bad Smells,* and *Fait Accompli* are used with permission from the Twyla Tharp Archive, Jerome Lawrence and Robert E. Lee Theatre Research Institute, The Ohio State University.

SELECTED BIBLIOGRAPHY

Acocella, Joan. "Twyla Tharp's Bottom Line." *The New Yorker.* Nov. 30, 1992. 166–74.

Babe, Thomas. "Twyla Tharp Dance." Program book, Twyla Tharp Dance Foundation, 1981.

Baker, Rob. "Dancing Head, Talking Feet." Interview with Twyla Tharp and David Byrne. *Soho Weekly News.* October 13, 1981. 13–15.

Brubach, Holly. "Counter to the World at Large." An interview with Twyla Tharp. *American Arts.* May 1981. 16–19.

Churcher, Sharon. "Still Kicking—The amazing saga of 'Singin' in the Rain,' the $5.7 Million turkey that refuses to lie down." *New York* magazine. Oct. 14, 1985. 39–47.

Colton, Richard et al. "Making Musical Dance." Interview-discussion, Kate Johnson, Robert Irving, Karole Armitage & Colton with John Mueller and Don McDonagh. For the Dance Critics Association and *Ballet Review. Ballet Review*, winter 1986. 23–44.

Draegin, Lois. "The World According to Tharp." *Savvy.* Feb. 1987. 30 ff.

Forman, Milos and Jan Novak, *Turnaround—a Memoir.* New York: Villard Books, 1994.

Friedman, Jeffrey Phillip. *Embodied Narrative: A Laban Movement Analysis of Dance Oral History Toward Ontological Awareness.* Ph.D. dissertation, University of California Riverside, 2003.

Guillermoprieto, Alma. "Dancing in the City." *The New Yorker*. Feb. 10, 2003. 70–79.

Johnston, Jill. *Marmalade Me* [1971], with new preface and essays by Deborah Jowitt and Sally Banes. Middletown, CT: Wesleyan University Press, 1998.

Kendall, Elizabeth. "Twyla Tharp—An unorthodox choreographer with a mind of her own." *Horizon*. April 1980. 26–33.

Kisselgoff, Anna. "Twyla Tharp and Ballet—An Uneasy Match." *The New York Times*. March 8, 1987.

———. "Twyla Tharp's Metaphysical Muse." *The New York Times*. April 30, 1995.

Kostelanetz, Richard, ed. *Merce Cunningham: Dancing in Space and Time*. [1992] New York: Da Capo Press, 1998.

Jowitt, Deborah. *Jerome Robbins: His Life, His Theater, His Dance*. New York: Simon & Schuster, 2004.

Mazo, Joseph H. "Twyla Tharp—Advance from the 1960s" in *Prime Movers—The Makers of Modern Dance in America*. New York: William Morrow & Company, 1977. 271–98.

McDonagh, Don. "Twyla Tharp / Controlled Living Space" in *The Rise and Fall and Rise of Modern Dance*. New York: Outerbridge & Dienstfrey, 1970. 105–118.

Secrest, Meryle. *Stephen Sondheim—A Life*. New York: Delta/Random House, 1998.

Shapiro, Laura, "Ain't Misbehavin': Two Decades of Twyla." *On the Edge: Challenges to American Dance*. Proceedings of the 1989 Dance Critics Association Conference. 67–73.

Siegel, Marcia B. *The Shapes of Change—Images of American Dance* (1979). Berkeley: University of California Press, 1985.

Smith, Cecil and Glenn Litton. *Musical Comedy in America*. New York: Routledge/Theatre Arts Books, 1991.

Supree, Burt. "Absolutely Twyla." *Los Angeles Times Calendar*. March 3, 1989.

Taplin, Diana Theodores. *Criticism and Choreography*. M.A. thesis. York University, Toronto. December 1978.

Tharp, Twyla. *Push Comes to Shove—An Autobiography*. New York: Bantam Books, 1992.

———. with Mark Reiter. *The Creative Habit—Learn it and use it for life*. New York: Simon & Schuster, 2003.

Throughout her long career, Tharp has been written about extensively by American and international critics. Her work seems to inspire exceptionally thoughtful writing as well as heartfelt response. In addition to works cited in the Notes, the following is a selective list of articles with informative and insightful commentary on particular dances or periods.

Company and Choreographic Style:

Albert, Steven. "Utopia Lost—and Found? A Look at Tharp's Way." *Ballet Review*. spring 1986. 17–35.

Aloff, Mindy. "Twyla Tharp Dance." (*Nine Sinatra Songs, Ballare, In the Upper Room*). *The Nation*. March 28, 1987.

————. "Spitballs at Euclid" (*The Beethoven Seventh, Brahms-Haydn*). *The New Republic*. June 18, 2001.

Brubach, Holly. "Twyla Tharp's Return." (*Ballare, In the Upper Room*). *The Atlantic*. March 1987.

Croce, Arlene. "Choreographers We." (*How Near Heaven, Americans We, Jump Start*). *The New Yorker*. May 22, 1995.

Gurewitsch, Matthew. "Kinetic Force." *Ballet News*. October 1984. 18–23.

Jacobs, Laura. "Role Model." (*Men's Piece, Octet*). *New Dance Review*. January-March 1992. 3–6.

Shapiro, Laura. "The art of Twyla Tharp." (*Nine Sinatra Songs, Bad Smells, Short Stories*). *Seattle Weekly*. October 27, 1982.

Nine Sinatra Songs:

Croce, Arlene. "Tharp's Sinatra." *Writing in the Dark, Dancing in* The New Yorker. New York: Farrar, Straus and Giroux, 2000. 463–66.

Short Stories:

Goldner, Nancy. "Twyla got her gun." *Soho Weekly News*. October 13, 1981. 47–48.

Fait Accompli:

Leverett, James. "The (Im)Pure Theatre of Twyla Tharp." *American Theatre*. April 1984. 22–23.

Push Comes to Shove (book):

Reiter, Susan. "Twyla's Way." *Dance View*. Winter 1993. 9–14.

Demeter and Persephone:

Croce, Arlene. "Someone's in the Kitchen with Demeter." *The New Yorker*. Oct. 25, 1993. 111–16.

I have not quoted from my own publications about Tharp because I wanted to look at the work with fresh eyes for this book. Several reviews and essays have been reprinted in my collections *At the Vanishing Point* (1972), *Watching the Dance Go By* (1977), and *The Tail of the Dragon* (1991). Additional pieces that may be of interest are listed below.

Features:

"The World According to Tharp" [original title: "The Saint of Cybernetics"]. (*The Catherine Wheel* on PBS). *The Dial.* March 1983.

"Home on the Residency." (Tharp at the Wexner Center, Ohio State University). *Dance Ink.* spring 1992.

Essays:

"Success Without Labels." (*Nine Sinatra Songs, Bad Smells* in San Francisco). *Hudson Review.* spring 1983.

"Couples." (*Nine Sinatra Songs, Fait Accompli*). *Hudson Review.* summer 1994.

"Tharporama." (*Bach Partita, Brahms/Handel, Sorrow Floats*). *Hudson Review.* winter 1984–85.

"Strangers in the Palace." (Tharp and company in ABT). *Hudson Review.* autumn, 1989.

"Both Doors Open." (City Center season). *Hudson Review.* summer 1992.

"Twyla's Tour." (*Cutting Up* in Boston). *Ballet Review.* spring 1993.

"Ancestral Passages." (*Demeter and Persephone*). *Hudson Review.* spring 1994.

Reviews:

"Happily On and On." (*Happily Ever After*). *Soho Weekly News.* Nov. 11, 1976.

"'In the Upper Room': Carefully crafted, constantly interesting." *Christian Science Monitor.* Feb. 10, 1987.

"Twyla Tharp hitting 'Ecstatic Highs.'" (ABT in San Francisco—*In the Upper Room, Quartet, Everlast*). *Christian Science Monitor.* Mar. 17, 1989.

"Too Brief a Fling." (*Brief Fling* at ABT gala). *Christian Science Monitor.* May 30, 1990

"Annals of mischief." (*Tharp!* in Boston—*Fugue, Heroes, Sweet Fields*). *Boston Phoenix.* Apr. 3, 1998.

"Tharpbeats." (*Known by Heart*). *Boston Phoenix.* Nov. 13, 1998.

"Tharp revels." (*Beethoven Seventh*). *Boston Phoenix.* Jan. 28, 2000.

"How choreography lives." (*Variations on a Theme by Haydn*). *Boston Phoenix*. May 19, 2000.

"Past and future." (*Mozart Clarinet Quintet K. 581, Surfer at the River Styx*). *Boston Phoenix*. Mar. 2, 2001.

"Cracking the code." (*Movin' Out*). *Boston Phoenix*. Nov. 1, 2002.

ACKNOWLEDGMENTS

T his book is not an "authorized" work. It is my own attempt to understand the immense talent of Twyla Tharp, which has always seemed bigger than anything that could be encompassed within the regular practice of criticism. To take an overview of an artist I've been watching and commenting on for the length of both our careers, I needed the help of many people, Twyla Tharp above all. The book could not have been written without her cooperation. She generously made herself available to me for interviews, responded to my quizzes and requests, and facilitated my access to primary source materials. She did this even though it was understood that she would not see or approve my manuscript before publication. I am grateful as well to Jesse Huot and Ginger Montel of Tharp Productions for answering my questions and for dubbing and sending a constant stream of videotapes.

Tharp Dance is more than a catalogue of vanished choreographic works. A continually evolving cast of extraordinary dancers and collaborators took up Tharp's challenge and carried the idea of dance into unknown territory. More than sixty individuals agreed to talk to me about their work with Tharp, and then submitted to my follow-up questions and bewildered phone calls. Getting together with old and new acquaintances to recall cherished dance experiences was a source of great pleasure to me during the course of this long, many-sided dialogue. The generosity of these respondents has added a dimension to my research that I hadn't anticipated at the start.

Rose Marie Wright dug into her phenomenal memory eight times for my tape recorder, and submitted to innumerable phone calls. Sara Rudner shared her wise and searching thoughts over the years. Shelley Washington, William Whitener, and Richard Colton supplied invaluable information and insight about the company and the work. I interviewed Twyla Tharp five times during the writing of this book.

The other friends and strangers who offered their thoughts and memories to me were: Ramelle Adams, Mikhail Baryshnikov, Jamie Bishton, Vera Blaine, Merrill Brockway, David Byrne, Stacy Caddell, Joseph Carman, Judy Cohen, Steve Dennin, Theresa Dickinson, Jeffrey Edwards, Anthony Ferro, Charles France, Shelley Freydont, Jeff Friedman, Isabel Garcia-Lorca, Jennifer Gelfand, Katie Glasner, Rhoda Grauer, Robert Huot, Susan Jaffe, Margaret Jenkins, Susan Jones, Paula Josa-Jones, Marty Kapell, Mary Ann Kellogg, Sharon Kinney, William Peter Kosmas, Elaine Kudo, Raymond Kurshals, Harvey Lichtenstein, Lewis Lloyd, Santo Loquasto, Carolyn Lord, Gabrielle Malone and Andrew Robinson, Jodi Melnick, Don Mischer, Rosalind Newman, Roddy O'Connor, Naima Prevots, Tom Rawe and Jennifer Way, Charles Reinhart, Dana Reitz, Kenneth Rinker, Beatriz Rodriguez, John Selya, Linda Shelton, Amy Spencer, Patsy Tarr, Jennifer Tipton, Christine Uchida, Martine Van Hamel, Brenda Way, Kimmary Williams, and Rebecca Wright.

The Reverend Peter Laarman, Betsy Fisher, Diane Jacobowitz, Jane Goldberg, Shelley Masar, Emma Lou Thomas, and Douglas Rosenberg talked to me informally and responded to questions.

I spent many hours examining material in the Jerome Lawrence and Robert E. Lee Theater Research Institute at The Ohio State University, Alan Woods, director, with the unfailing help of Nena Couch, curator of the Twyla Tharp Archive, and the efficient services of Val Pennington, Beth Kattleman, and the staff. In New York, at the Jerome Robbins Dance Division of the New York Public Library at Lincoln Center, Madeleine Nichols, director, I had essential help from Monica Moseley, Pat Rader, Susan Kraft, Phil Karg, and the staff of librarians and pages as I made my way through databases and archival resources.

Other individuals I turned to for information and assistance included: Charles Sens, Rosemary Hanes, and Vickie Wulff Risner at the Library of Congress; Susan Hood, Elizabeth Hoke and Eugene Gaddis at the Wadsworth Atheneum; Jennifer Williams at KUSC Los Angeles; Ben Mayer at WGBH Boston; Florence Palomo at Condé Nast Publications; Matt Hoffman of HMS Video; Christina Sterner of Baryshnikov Productions; Kelly Ryan at American Ballet Theater; Rob Daniels at New York City Ballet; Gail Kalver at Hubbard Street Dance Chicago; Cynthia Rostiac at the Stevens Estate and Conference Center at Osgood Hill; archivists Deborah Elfenbein and Greta Reisel at the American Dance Festival; and Laura Raucher at the Martha Graham Center. Charles Atlas, Steve Sheppard, Mary Waters, and Constance Old led me along the trails to sources of information.

Many dance writers responded to my call for published and unpublished documentation of their encounters with Tharp. I'm deeply grateful to longtime Tharp admirers and collaborators Laura Shapiro and Allen Robertson for their loving support. Sara Rudner and her interviewer, Rose Anne Thom, allowed me complete access to the 1995 interviews made for the Oral History Project of the Jerome Robbins Dance Division at the New York Public Library. Besides works published and collected in various archives, contributions were supplied by Joan Acocella, Sally Banes, Carl Blumenthal, Mary Grace Butler, Roy Close, Amy Eddings, Robert Greskovic, Ellen Jacobs, Elizabeth Kendall, Rachel Lampert, Katy Matheson, Selma Odom, Barbara Palfy, Susan Reiter, Elinor Rogosin, Susanna Sloat, Amanda Smith, Tobi Tobias, and Astrida Woods.

Gathering the photographs for this book afforded me the chance to revisit the dances in another way. I want to thank the photographers who made these evocative images, especially those who opened their files to me so that I could make selections. Robert Barry, Tom Brazil, Tom Caravaglia, James Elliott, Paul B. Goode, Lois Greenfield, Herb Migdoll, Tom Rawe, Tony Russell, Marty Sohl, Martha Swope, Nathaniel Tileston, Jack Vartoogian, Max Waldman, and Monroe Warshaw collectively created an extraordinary visual record. I wish I could have included more of it in these pages.

For help in the acquisition of photographs I'm also grateful to Carol Greunke of the Max Waldman Archive, Sandra Powell of London Weekend Television/Granada Films, Trudi Kammerling at REX Features, and Stephen K. Sachs at the New York Public Library.

All my visits to Ohio State were enriched by classes, performances, and collegial conversations with Dance department faculty members Candace Feck, Karen Eliot, Sheila Marion, Michael Kelly Bruce, Melanie Bales, Vera Blaine, Scott Marsh, and Dean of the College of Arts Karen Bell.

Patsy Tarr's devotion to Twyla Tharp extended to this project, much to my benefit, and I'm tremendously grateful for her encouragement, and for several research grants she provided to me through the 2wice Arts Foundation.

For their help, support, and ever-willing ears, for overnight beds and recuperative dinners, I could not have survived without my friends Deborah Jowitt and Murray Ralph, Gay Morris and Gordon Gamsu, Elizabeth Zimmer, John and Judy Mueller, and my Rockport dance companion, Jeanne Hays Beaman.

I'm grateful to my literary agent, Joe Spieler, for believing in this book before it was a book. I want to thank Katherine Tiernan and the editors and production staff at St. Martin's Press for ensuring that the book would be fastidious and beautiful. As the manuscript made its slow progress, my editor, Michael Flamini, was confident it would finally be accomplished. He has supported and encouraged me throughout the process, never losing his enthusiasm or his conviction that Tharp should be written about, and that I could do it.

INDEX